M000267694

California Criminal Law

California Criminal Law

Cases and Problems

FOURTH EDITION

Steven F. Shatz
Professor of Law, Emeritus
University of San Francisco

Scott Howe
Frank L. Williams Professor of Criminal Law
Chapman University

Amy Flynn
Assistant Professor of Law
University of San Francisco

Carolina Academic Press
Durham, North Carolina

Copyright © 2016
Carolina Academic Press, LLC
All Rights Reserved

Print ISBN 978-1-6328-4942-7
e-Book ISBN 978-1-6328-4944-1
LCCN 2016942339

Carolina Academic Press, LLC
700 Kent Street
Durham, North Carolina 27701
Telephone (919) 489-7486
Fax (919) 493-5668
www.cap-press.com

Printed in the United States of America

To Nina, Gabriel, Naomi and Julia
SFS

To Jetty, Mario and Jordan
SH

To Paul, Jesse and Margaret
AF

Contents

Table of Cases

Principal cases in bold

Preface

This fourth edition continues the approach of the first three editions, but with one significant change. Steve is excited to welcome Professors Scott Howe of the Fowler School of Law at Chapman University and Amy Flynn of the University of San Francisco School of Law as co-authors on this fourth edition. Scott and Amy bring both substantial teaching experience and a background as practicing criminal lawyers to the casebook. Users of the third edition will also note that this edition contains six new cases and a number of updated notes and problems, incorporating changes in California criminal law over the last five years.

This edition is the product of more than fifteen years of teaching with the previous editions. It reflects the philosophy that there are advantages to be gained by focusing on the law of a single jurisdiction because that focus permits the examination of the various criminal law doctrines in the larger context of the state's entire body of criminal law, allowing consideration of the relationship between doctrines—e.g., *mens rea* and insanity or "heat of passion" and self-defense—and the use of the same principle—e.g., the "reasonable person" test—for different purposes. Using a single state also facilitates the study of statutes, statutory interpretation and the interaction between the courts and the legislature. Perhaps most significantly, because criminal law tends to be relatively state-specific, the study of a single state's law—"real" law rather than general or imagined law—engages the students and leads to a more coherent understanding of the subject.

The book reflects our conviction that, while the Criminal Law course must expose students to the range of doctrines associated with substantive criminal law, the primary concern of the course, usually taught as a first year course, is to teach students how to read and understand cases and statutes and to construct legal arguments. Accordingly, the emphasis in the book is on cases and on problems. The cases are presented in relatively complete form, often including concurring and dissenting opinions, in order to give students examples of fully developed legal arguments. The 100 short problems presented in the book are all taken from real cases and ask the students to develop the appropriate legal arguments based on the cases they have read. Each chapter begins with an introduction, to give background to the cases and to outline the issues to be explored. Notes, which have been kept to a minimum, are generally used to extend the students' analysis by asking them consider theoretical or policy issues raised by the cases or alternative approaches contained in the Model Penal Code or other sources. Citations and footnotes have been eliminated from the judicial opinions without so specifying, and, where citations are included, they often are simplified, with page cites omitted. Numbered footnotes are from the original materials; lettered footnotes are ours.

Finally, Steve wants to acknowledge the generation of students at U.S.F., who, years ago, encouraged him to publish his teaching materials and the more recent students whose response to the first three editions proved an invaluable guide to us in producing this fourth edition.

Steven F. Shatz
Scott Howe
Amy Flynn

Part I

Introduction to the Course

The Criminal Law course considers how society determines and defines what conduct is deemed sufficiently undesirable that it should be subject to punishment and public condemnation and how and to what degree that punishment is imposed. Criminal law today is derived from statutes rather than from common law developed by the courts. Within limits set by the Constitution, the legislature defines the scope of the criminal law, and the courts interpret and apply the legislature's product. With the exception of United State Supreme Court cases, which set the constitutional limits for all states' criminal law, the cases and problems in this book focus on California criminal law. The current versions of the statutes discussed in the cases and problems are contained in the Appendix to the book.

The book is divided into five parts. Part I introduces certain concepts that form the background for the rest of the course: the purposes of punishment, the fundamental principles of American criminal law, and the nature of a criminal case. Part II is concerned with how culpable conduct is defined by the legislature, i.e., what has to be proved to cause someone to be punished. Part III addresses affirmative defenses available to the accused to avoid or reduce punishment on the ground that the accused's conduct was justified or should be excused. Part IV examines the issue of vicarious liability, i.e., who, beside the actual perpetrator of the crime, may also be punished. Part V concludes with a brief treatment of the death penalty, the most challenging and controversial aspect of our criminal justice system today.

Chapter 1

Introduction

The materials in this first chapter are intended to provide the necessary background for various issues to be explored in the remainder of the book. Section A considers purposes of the criminal law and the role of the courts in implementing those purposes. Section B considers three fundamental principles of American criminal law and how those principles are expressed in the Constitution. Section C provides a brief introduction to the criminal case in California by means of a clerk's and reporter's transcript of a misdemeanor case.

A. The Purposes of the Criminal Law

The first two cases are not like most criminal cases, and they are very different from each other, but they raise many of the same questions. What are the purposes of criminal punishment? What is the relationship between criminal law and morality? What role do courts play in defining crimes, and to what extent should history and precedent guide the courts' decisions? *Regina v. Dudley and Stephens* is a singular Nineteenth Century English murder case where the defendants asserted a necessity defense. The House of Lords has to decide whether "necessity" is ever a defense to murder. *Lawrence v. Texas* is a decision of the United States Supreme Court resolving a constitutional challenge to Texas's sodomy law punishing certain private sexual conduct between consenting adults. Why should the law criminalize private, "victimless" crimes, since most such conduct will not be known or prosecuted, and arguably no one is harmed by it? The final case in this section is *United States v. Bergman*, a nursing home fraud case in which the sentencing judge, in the course of sentencing the defendant to prison, examines the four commonly accepted justifications for criminal punishment.

Regina v. Dudley and Stephens

14 Q.B.D. 273 (1884)

LORD COLERIDGE, C.J.

The two prisoners were indicted for the murder of Richard Parker on the high seas on the 25th of July in the present year. They were tried before my brother Huddleston at Exeter on the 6th of November, and, under the direction of my learned brother, the jury returned a special verdict, the legal effect of which has been argued before us, and on which we are now to pronounce judgment.

The special verdict ... is as follows:

That on July 5, 1884, the prisoners, with one Brooks, all able-bodied English seamen, and the deceased also an English boy, between seventeen and eighteen years of age, the crew of an English yacht, a registered English vessel, were cast away in a storm on the high seas 1600 miles from the Cape of Good Hope, and were compelled to put into an open boat belonging to the said yacht. That in this boat they had no supply of water and no supply of food, except two 1lb. tins of turnips, and for three days they had nothing else to subsist upon. That on the fourth day they caught a small turtle, upon which they subsisted for a few days, and this was the only food they had up to the twentieth day when the act now in question was committed. That on the twelfth day the remains of the turtle were entirely consumed, and for the next eight days they had nothing to eat. That they had no fresh water, except such rain as they from time to time caught in their oilskin capes. That the boat was drifting on the ocean and was probably more than 1000 miles away from land. That on the eighteenth day, when they had been seven days without food and five without water, the prisoners spoke to Brooks as to what should be done if no succour came, and suggested that someone should be sacrificed to save the rest, but Brooks dissented, and the boy, to whom they were understood to refer, was not consulted. That on the 24th of July, the day before the act now in question, the prisoner Dudley proposed to Stephens and Brooks that lots should be cast who should be put to death to save the rest, but Brooks refused to consent, and it was not put to the boy, and in point of fact there was no drawing of lots. That on that day the prisoners spoke of their having families, and suggested it would be better to kill the boy that their lives should be saved, and Dudley proposed that if there was no vessel in sight by morrow morning the boy should be killed. That next day, the 25th of July, no vessel appearing, Dudley told Brooks that he had better go and have a sleep, and made signs to Stephens and Brooks that the boy had better be killed. The prisoner Stephens agreed to the act, but Brooks dissented from it. That the boy was then lying at the bottom of the boat quite helpless, and extremely weakened by famine and by drinking sea water, and unable to make any resistance, nor did he ever assent to being killed. The prisoner Dudley offered a prayer asking forgiveness for them all if either of them should be tempted to commit a rash act, and that their souls might be saved. That Dudley, with the assent of Stephens, went to the boy, and telling him that his time was come, put a knife into his throat and killed him then and there; that the three men fed upon the body and blood of the boy for four days; that on the fourth day after the act had been committed the boat was picked up by a passing vessel, and the prisoners were rescued, still alive, but in the lowest state of prostration. That they were carried to the port of Falmouth and committed for trial at Exeter. That if the men had not fed upon the body of the boy they would probably not have survived to be so picked up and rescued, but would have within the four days have died of famine. That the boy, being in a much weaker condition, was likely to have died before them. That at the time of the act in question there was no sail in sight, nor any reasonable prospect of relief. That under these conditions there appeared to the prisoners every probability that unless they then fed or very soon fed upon the body of one of themselves they would die of starvation. That there was no appreciable chance of saving life except by killing some one for the others to eat. That assuming any necessity to kill anybody, there was no greater necessity for killing the boy than any other of the three men. But whether upon the whole matter by the jurors found the killing of Richard Parker by Dudley and Stephens to be felony and murder the jurors are ignorant, and pray the advice of the Court thereupon, and if upon the whole matter by the jurors found the killing of Richard Parker be felony and murder, then the jurors say that Dudley and Stephens were each guilty of felony and murder as alleged in the indictment.

. . .

From these facts, stated with the cold precision of a special verdict, it appears sufficiently that the prisoners were subject to terrible temptation, to sufferings which might break down the bodily power of the strongest man, and try the conscience of the best. Other details yet more harrowing, facts still more loathsome and appalling, were presented to the jury, and are to be found recorded in my learned Brother's notes. But nevertheless, this is clear, that the prisoners put to death a weak and unoffending boy upon the chance of preserving their own lives by feeding upon his flesh and blood after he was killed, and with the certainty of depriving him of any possible chance of survival. The verdict finds in terms that "if the men had not fed upon the body of the boy they would *probably* not have survived," and that "the boy being in a much weaker condition was *likely* to have died before them." They might possibly have been picked up next day by a passing ship; they might possibly not have been picked up at all; in either case it is obvious that the killing of the boy would have been an unnecessary and profitless act. It is found by the verdict that the boy was incapable of resistance, and, in fact, made none; and it is not even suggested that his death was due to any violence on his part attempted against, or even so much as feared by, those who killed him. Under these circumstances, the jury say that they are ignorant whether those who killed him were guilty of murder, and have referred to this Court to determine what is the legal consequence which follows from the facts which they have found.

. . .

There remains to be considered the real question in this case—whether killing under the circumstances set forth in the verdict be or not be murder. The contention that it could be anything else was, to the minds of us all, both new and strange, and we stopped the Attorney General in his negative argument in order that we might hear what could be said in support of a proposition which appeared to us to be at once dangerous, immoral, and opposed to all legal principle and analogy. All, no doubt, that can be said has been urged before us, and we are now to consider and determine what it amounts to. First it is said that it follows from various definitions of murder in books of authority, which definitions imply, if they do not state, the doctrine, that in order to save your own life you may lawfully take away the life of another, when that other is neither attempting nor threatening yours, nor is guilty of any illegal act whatever towards you or nay one else. But if these definitions be looked at they will not be found to sustain this contention. The earliest point of date is the passage cited to us from Bracton, who lived in the reign of Henry III. It was at one time the fashion to discredit Bracton, as Mr. Reeve tells us, because he was supposed to mingle too much of the canonist and civilian with the common lawyer. There is now no such feeling, but the passage upon homicide, on which reliance is placed, is a remarkable example of the kind of writing which may explain it. Sin and crime are spoken of as apparently equal, and the crime of murder, is expressly declared, may be committed "*lingua vel facto*"; so that a man, like Hero "done to death by slanderous tongues", would, it seems, in the opinion of Bracton, be a person in respect of whom might be grounded a legal indictment for murder. But in the very passage as to necessity, on which reliance has been placed, it is clear that Bracton is speaking of necessity in the ordinary sense—the repelling by violence, violence justified so far as it was necessary for the object, any illegal violence used towards oneself. If, says Bracton, the necessity be "*evitablis, et evadere posset absque occisione, tunc erit reus homicidii*"—words which show clearly that he is thinking of physical danger from which escape may be possible, and that the "*inevitabilis necessitas*" of which he speaks as justifying homicide is a necessity of the same nature.

It is, if possible, yet clearer that the doctrine contended for receives no support from the great authority of Lord Hale. It is plain that in his view the necessity which justified homicide is that only which has always been and is now considered a justification. "In all these cases of homicide by necessity", says he, "as in pursuit of a felon, in killing him that assaults to rob, or comes to burn or break a house, or the like, which are in themselves no felony." (1 Hale's Pleas of the Crown.) Again, he says that "the necessity which justifies homicides is two kinds: (1) the necessity which is of a private nature; (2) the necessity which relates to the public justice and safety. The former is that necessity which obligeth a man to his own defence and safeguard, and this takes in these inquiries:—(1) What may be done for the safeguard of a man's own life;" and then follow three other heads not necessary to pursue. Then Lord Hale proceeds:—"As touching the first of these—*viz.*, homicide in defence of a man's own life, which is usually styled *se defendendo*." It is not possible to use words more clear to shew that Lord Hale regarded the private necessity which justified, and alone justified, the taking the life of another for the safeguard of one's own to be what is commonly called "self-defence".

...

But, further still, Lord Hale in the following chapter deals with the position asserted by the casuists, and sanctioned, as he says, by Grotius and Puffendorf, that in a case of extreme necessity, either of hunger or clothing; "theft is no theft, or at least not punishable as theft, as some even of our own lawyers have asserted the same". "But," says Lord Hale, "I take it that here in England, that rule, at least by the laws of England, is false; and therefore, if a person, being under necessity for want of victuals or clothes, shall upon that account clandestinely and *animo furandi* steal another man's goods, it is felony, and a crime by the laws of England punishable with death." If, therefore, Lord Hale is clear—as he is—that extreme necessity of hunger does not justify larceny, what would he have said to the doctrine that it justified murder?"

[The court considered whether there was any authority for the prisoners' position. The court found no authority in the decided cases and only Lord Bacon, among the commentators, who stated a proposition supportive of the prisoners' position: "[I]f a man steals viands to satisfy his present hunger, this is no felony or larceny. So if divers be in danger of drowning by the casting away of some boat or barge, and one of them get to some plank, or on the boat's die to keep himself above water, and another to save his life thrust him from it, whereby he is drowned, this is neither *se defendo* nor by misadventure, but justifiable." Lord Bacon, however, cited no authority for his position.]

Now, except for the purpose of testing how far the conservation of a man's own life is in all cases and under all circumstances, an absolute, unqualified, and paramount duty, we exclude from our consideration all the incidents of war. We are dealing with a case of private homicide, not one imposed upon men in the service of their Sovereign and in the defence of their county. Now it is admitted that the deliberate killing of this unoffending and unresisting boy was clearly murder, unless the killing can be justified by some well-recognized excuse admitted by the law. It is further admitted that there was in this case no such excuse, unless the killing was justified by what had been called "necessity". But the temptation to the act which existed here was not what the law has ever called necessity. Nor is this to be regretted. Though law and morality are not the same, and many things may be immoral which are not necessarily illegal, yet the absolute divorce of law from morality would be of fatal consequence; and such divorce would follow if the temptation to murder in this case were to be held by law an absolute defence of it. It is not so. To preserve one's life is generally speaking a duty, but it may be the plainest and highest duty to sacrifice it. War is full of instances in which it is a man's duty not to live, but to die. The duty, in the case of a shipwreck, of a captain to his crew, of the crew to the passengers, of soldiers to women and children, as in the noble case of the *Birkenhead*;[a] these duties impose on men the mortal necessity, not of the preservation, but of the sacrifice of their lives for others, from which in no country, least of all, it is to be hoped, in England, will men ever shrink, as indeed, they have not shrunk. It is not correct, therefore, to say that there is any absolute or unqualified necessity to preserve one's life. "*Necesse est at eam, non at vivam,*" is a saying of a Roman officer quoted by Lord Bacon himself with high eulogy in the very chapter of necessity to which so much reference has been made. It would be a very easy and cheap display of commonplace learning to quote from Greek and Latin authors, from Horace, from Juvenal, from Cicero, from Euripides, passage after passage, in which the duty of dying for others has been laid down in glowing and emphatic language as resulting from the principles of heathen ethics; it is enough in a Christian country to remind ourselves of the Great Example whom we profess to

a. The *HMS Birkenhead* was a troop ship that sank off the coast of South Africa in 1852. The ship had few serviceable lifeboats, and, as the ship was sinking, the soldiers were reported to have stood at attention on the deck while all the women and children boarded the boats. The event gave rise to the "women and children first" protocol when abandoning ship.

follow. It is not needful to point out the awful danger of admitting the principle which has been contended for. Who is to be the judge of this sort of necessity? By what measure is the comparative value of lives to be measured? Is it to be strength, or intellect, or what? It is plain that the principle leaves to him who is to profit by it to determine the necessity which will justify him in deliberately taking another's life to save his own. In this case, the weakest, the youngest, the most unresisting, was chosen. Was it more necessary to kill him than one of the grown men? The answer must be "No" ... [I]t is quite plain that such a principle once admitted might be made the legal cloak for unbridled passion and atrocious crime. There is no safe path for judges to tread but to ascertain the law to the best of their ability and to declare it according to their judgment; and if in any case the law appears to be too severe on individuals, leave it to the Sovereign to exercise that prerogative of mercy which the Constitution has intrusted to the hands fittest to dispense it.

It must not be supposed that in refusing to admit temptation to be an excuse for crime it is forgotten how terrible the temptation was; how awful the suffering; how hard in such trials to keep the judgment straight and the conduct pure. We are often compelled to set up standards we cannot reach ourselves, and to lay down rules which we could not satisfy. But a man has no right to declare temptation to be an excuse, though he might himself have yielded to it, nor allow compassion for the criminal to change or weaken in any manner the legal definition of the crime. It is therefore our duty to declare that the prisoner's act in this case was wilful murder, that the facts as stated in the verdict are no legal justification of the homicide; and to say that in our unanimous opinion the prisoners are upon this special verdict guilty of murder.[9]

[The court then proceeded to pass sentence of death upon the prisoners.][b]

Lawrence v. Texas

539 U.S. 558, 123 S.Ct. 2472 (2003)

Justice Kennedy delivered the opinion of the Court.

Liberty protects the person from unwarranted government intrusions into a dwelling or other private places. In our tradition the State is not omnipresent in the home. And there are other spheres of our lives and existence, outside the home, where the State should not be a dominant presence. Freedom extends beyond spatial

---

9. My brother Grove has furnished me with the following suggestion, too late to be embodied in the judgment but well worth preserving: "If the two accused men were justified in killing Parker, then if not rescued in time, two of the three men would be justified in killing a third, and of the two who remained the stronger would be justified in killing the weaker, so that three men might be justifiably killed to give the fourth a chance of surviving."

b. This sentence was afterwards commuted by the Crown to six months imprisonment.

bounds. Liberty presumes an autonomy of self that includes freedom of thought, belief, expression, and certain intimate conduct. The instant case involves liberty of the person both in its spatial and more transcendent dimensions.

I

The question before the Court is the validity of a Texas statute making it a crime for two persons of the same sex to engage in certain intimate sexual conduct.

In Houston, Texas, officers of the Harris County Police Department were dispatched to a private residence in response to a reported weapons disturbance. They entered an apartment where one of the petitioners, John Geddes Lawrence, resided. The right of the police to enter does not seem to have been questioned. The officers observed Lawrence and another man, Tyron Garner, engaging in a sexual act. The two petitioners were arrested, held in custody over night, and charged and convicted before a Justice of the Peace.

The complaints described their crime as "deviate sexual intercourse, namely anal sex, with a member of the same sex (man)." The applicable state law is Tex. Penal Code Ann. § 21.06(a) (2003). It provides: "A person commits an offense if he engages in deviate sexual intercourse with another individual of the same sex." The statute defines "[d]eviate sexual intercourse" as follows:

> "(A) any contact between any part of the genitals of one person and the mouth or anus of another person; or
>
> "(B) the penetration of the genitals or the anus of another person with an object." § 21.01(1).

[After their constitutional challenges to the statute were rejected, the petitioners were convicted on a plea of *nolo contendere*. The convictions were upheld on appeal, and the Supreme Court granted certiorari.]

The petitioners were adults at the time of the alleged offense. Their conduct was in private and consensual.

II

We conclude the case should be resolved by determining whether the petitioners were free as adults to engage in the private conduct in the exercise of their liberty under the Due Process Clause of the Fourteenth Amendment to the Constitution. For this inquiry we deem it necessary to reconsider the Court's holding in Bowers v. Hardwick, 478 U. S. 186 (1986).

[Justice Kennedy reviewed the Court's prior substantive due process cases, including, in particular, Griswold v. Connecticut, 381 U. S. 479 (1965) (invalidating a state law prohibiting the use of drugs or devices of contraception) and Roe v. Wade, 410 U. S. 113 (1973) (invalidating a state law prohibiting abortions).]

The facts in *Bowers* had some similarities to the instant case. A police officer, whose right to enter seems not to have been in question, observed Hardwick, in his own bedroom, engaging in intimate sexual conduct with another adult male. The conduct was in violation of a Georgia statute making it a criminal offense to engage in sodomy. One difference between the two cases is that the Georgia statute prohibited the conduct whether or not the participants were of the same sex, while the Texas statute, as we have seen, applies only to participants of the same sex. Hardwick was not prosecuted, but he brought an action in federal court to declare the state statute invalid. He alleged he was a practicing homosexual and that the criminal prohibition violated rights guaranteed to him by the Constitution. The Court, in an opinion by Justice White, sustained the Georgia law. Chief Justice Burger and Justice Powell joined the opinion of the Court and filed separate, concurring opinions. Four Justices dissented.

The Court began its substantive discussion in *Bowers* as follows: "The issue presented is whether the Federal Constitution confers a fundamental right upon homosexuals to engage in sodomy and hence invalidates the laws of the many States that still make such conduct illegal and have done so for a very long time." That statement, we now conclude, discloses the Court's own failure to appreciate the extent of the liberty at stake. To say that the issue in *Bowers* was simply the right to engage in certain sexual conduct demeans the claim the individual put forward, just as it would demean a married couple were it to be said marriage is simply about the right to have sexual intercourse. The laws involved in *Bowers* and here are, to be sure, statutes that purport to do no more than prohibit a particular sexual act. Their penalties and purposes, though, have more far-reaching consequences, touching upon the most private human conduct, sexual behavior, and in the most private of places, the home. The statutes do seek to control a personal relationship that, whether or not entitled to formal recognition in the law, is within the liberty of persons to choose without being punished as criminals.

This, as a general rule, should counsel against attempts by the State, or a court, to define the meaning of the relationship or to set its boundaries absent injury to a person or abuse of an institution the law protects. It suffices for us to acknowledge that adults may choose to enter upon this relationship in the confines of their homes and their own private lives and still retain their dignity as free persons. When sexuality finds overt expression in intimate conduct with another person, the conduct can be but one element in a personal bond that is more enduring. The liberty protected by the Constitution allows homosexual persons the right to make this choice.

Having misapprehended the claim of liberty there presented to it, and thus stating the claim to be whether there is a fundamental right to engage in consensual sodomy, the *Bowers* Court said: "Proscriptions against that conduct have ancient roots." ...

[Justice Kennedy reviewed the history of sodomy laws and concluded that the historical premises of the *Bowers* Court were "overstated." There was no longstanding history in the United States of laws directed at homosexual conduct as such. Sodomy laws were directed at heterosexual and homosexual activity and generally sought to prohibit nonprocreative sexual activity. The laws were not generally enforced against consenting adults acting in private. It was not until the 1970's that any State singled out same-sex relations for criminal prosecution, and only nine States have done so.]

It must be acknowledged, of course, that the Court in *Bowers* was making the broader point that for centuries there have been powerful voices to condemn homosexual conduct as immoral. The condemnation has been shaped by religious beliefs, conceptions of right and acceptable behavior, and respect for the traditional family. For many persons these are not trivial concerns but profound and deep convictions accepted as ethical and moral principles to which they aspire and which thus determine the course of their lives. These considerations do not answer the question before us, however. The issue is whether the majority may use the power of the State to enforce these views on the whole society through operation of the criminal law. "Our obligation is to define the liberty of all, not to mandate our own moral code." Planned Parenthood of Southeastern Pa. v. Casey, 505 U. S. 833 (1992).

Chief Justice Burger joined the opinion for the Court in *Bowers* and further explained his views as follows: "Decisions of individuals relating to homosexual conduct have been subject to state intervention throughout the history of Western civilization. Condemnation of those practices is firmly rooted in Judeao-Christian moral and ethical standards." As with Justice White's assumptions about history, scholarship casts some doubt on the sweeping nature of the statement by Chief Justice Burger as it pertains to private homosexual conduct between consenting adults. In all events we think that our laws and traditions in the past half century are of most relevance here. These references show an emerging awareness that liberty gives substantial protection to adult persons in deciding how to conduct their private lives in matters pertaining to sex. "[H]istory and tradition are the starting point but not in all cases the ending point of the substantive due process inquiry." County of Sacramento v. Lewis, 523 U. S. 833 (1998) (KENNEDY, J., concurring).

This emerging recognition should have been apparent when *Bowers* was decided. In 1955 the American Law Institute promulgated the Model Penal Code and made clear that it did not recommend or provide for "criminal penalties for consensual sexual relations conducted in private." ALI, Model Penal Code § 213.2, Comment 2, p. 372 (1980). It justified its decision on three grounds: (1) The prohibitions undermined respect for the law by penalizing conduct many people engaged in; (2) the statutes regulated private conduct not harmful to others; and (3) the laws were arbitrarily enforced and thus invited the danger of blackmail....

...

The sweeping references by Chief Justice Burger to the history of Western civilization and to Judeo-Christian moral and ethical standards did not take account of other authorities pointing in an opposite direction. A committee advising the British Parliament recommended in 1957 repeal of laws punishing homosexual conduct. Parliament enacted the substance of those recommendations 10 years later.

Of even more importance, almost five years before *Bowers* was decided the European Court of Human Rights considered a case with parallels to *Bowers* and to today's case. An adult male resident in Northern Ireland alleged he was a practicing homosexual who desired to engage in consensual homosexual conduct. The laws of Northern

Ireland forbade him that right. He alleged that he had been questioned, his home had been searched, and he feared criminal prosecution. The court held that the laws proscribing the conduct were invalid under the European Convention on Human Rights. *Dudgeon v. United Kingdom*, 45 Eur. Ct. H. R. (1981). Authoritative in all countries that are members of the Council of Europe (21 nations then, 45 nations now), the decision is at odds with the premise in *Bowers* that the claim put forward was insubstantial in our Western civilization.

In our own constitutional system the deficiencies in *Bowers* became even more apparent in the years following its announcement. The 25 States with laws prohibiting the relevant conduct referenced in the *Bowers* decision are reduced now to 13, of which 4 enforce their laws only against homosexual conduct. In those States where sodomy is still proscribed, whether for same-sex or heterosexual conduct, there is a pattern of nonenforcement with respect to consenting adults acting in private. The State of Texas admitted in 1994 that as of that date it had not prosecuted anyone under those circumstances.

. . .

The stigma this criminal statute imposes, moreover, is not trivial. The offense, to be sure, is but a class C misdemeanor, a minor offense in the Texas legal system. Still, it remains a criminal offense with all that imports for the dignity of the persons charged. The petitioners will bear on their record the history of their criminal convictions. Just this Term we rejected various challenges to state laws requiring the registration of sex offenders. Smith v. Doe, 538 U. S. 84 (2003); Connecticut Dept. of Public Safety v. Doe, 538 U. S. 1 (2003). We are advised that if Texas convicted an adult for private, consensual homosexual conduct under the statute here in question the convicted person would come within the registration laws of a least four States were he or she to be subject to their jurisdiction. This underscores the consequential nature of the punishment and the state-sponsored condemnation attendant to the criminal prohibition. Furthermore, the Texas criminal conviction carries with it the other collateral consequences always following a conviction, such as notations on job application forms, to mention but one example.

The foundations of *Bowers* have sustained serious erosion from our recent decisions in Planned Parenthood of Southeastern Pa. v. Casey, 505 U. S. 833 (1992) [upholding Roe v. Wade and confirming that the Due Process Clause protects a person's "most intimate and personal choices"] and Romer v. Evans, 517 U. S. 620 (1996) [striking down, as a violation of the Equal Protection Clause, class-based legislation aimed at homosexuals]. When our precedent has been thus weakened, criticism from other sources is of greater significance. In the United States criticism of *Bowers* has been substantial and continuing, disapproving of its reasoning in all respects, not just as to its historical assumptions. The courts of five different States have declined to follow it in interpreting provisions in their own state constitutions parallel to the Due Process Clause of the Fourteenth Amendment [citing decisions from Arkansas, Georgia, Montana, Tennessee and Kentucky].

To the extent *Bowers* relied on values we share with a wider civilization, it should be noted that the reasoning and holding in *Bowers* have been rejected elsewhere. The European Court of Human Rights has followed not *Bowers* but its own decision in *Dudgeon v. United Kingdom*. Other nations, too, have taken action consistent with an affirmation of the protected right of homosexual adults to engage in intimate, consensual conduct. The right the petitioners seek in this case has been accepted as an integral part of human freedom in many other countries. There has been no showing that in this country the governmental interest in circumscribing personal choice is somehow more legitimate or urgent.

The doctrine of *stare decisis* is essential to the respect accorded to the judgments of the Court and to the stability of the law. It is not, however, an inexorable command. In *Casey* we noted that when a Court is asked to overrule a precedent recognizing a constitutional liberty interest, individual or societal reliance on the existence of that liberty cautions with particular strength against reversing course. ("Liberty finds no refuge in a jurisprudence of doubt"). The holding in *Bowers*, however, has not induced detrimental reliance comparable to some instances where recognized individual rights are involved. Indeed, there has been no individual or societal reliance on *Bowers* of the sort that could counsel against overturning its holding once there are compelling reasons to do so. *Bowers* itself causes uncertainty, for the precedents before and after its issuance contradict its central holding.

The rationale of *Bowers* does not withstand careful analysis. In his dissenting opinion in *Bowers* Justice Stevens came to these conclusions:

> "Our prior cases make two propositions abundantly clear. First, the fact that the governing majority in a State has traditionally viewed a particular practice as immoral is not a sufficient reason for upholding a law prohibiting the practice; neither history nor tradition could save a law prohibiting miscegenation from constitutional attack. Second, individual decisions by married persons, concerning the intimacies of their physical relationship, even when not intended to produce offspring, are a form of 'liberty' protected by the Due Process Clause of the Fourteenth Amendment. Moreover, this protection extends to intimate choices by unmarried as well as married persons."

Justice Stevens' analysis, in our view, should have been controlling in *Bowers* and should control here.

Bowers was not correct when it was decided, and it is not correct today. It ought not to remain binding precedent. *Bowers v. Hardwick* should be and now is overruled.

The present case does not involve minors. It does not involve persons who might be injured or coerced or who are situated in relationships where consent might not easily be refused. It does not involve public conduct or prostitution. It does not involve whether the government must give formal recognition to any relationship that homosexual persons seek to enter. The case does involve two adults who, with full and mutual consent from each other, engaged in sexual practices common to a homosexual lifestyle. The petitioners are entitled to respect for their private lives. The State cannot demean their existence or control their destiny by making their private sexual conduct a crime. Their right to liberty under the Due Process Clause gives them the full right to engage in their conduct without intervention of the government. "It is a promise of the Constitution that there is a realm of personal liberty which the government may not enter." *Casey*, *supra*. The Texas statute furthers no legitimate state interest which can justify its intrusion into the personal and private life of the individual.

Had those who drew and ratified the Due Process Clauses of the Fifth Amendment or the Fourteenth Amendment known the components of liberty in its manifold possibilities, they might have been more specific. They did not presume to have this insight. They knew times can blind us to certain truths and later generations can see that laws once thought necessary and proper in fact serve only to oppress. As the Constitution endures, persons in every generation can invoke its principles in their own search for greater freedom.

The judgment of the Court of Appeals for the Texas Fourteenth District is reversed, and the case is remanded for further proceedings not inconsistent with this opinion.

[Justice O'Connor, concurring in the judgment, refused to join in overruling *Bowers*, and instead voted to reverse the conviction on the ground that the Texas statute was unconstitutional under the Equal Protection clause because it discriminated against homosexuals without serving a legitimate state interest.]

Justice Scalia, with whom The Chief Justice and Justice Thomas join, dissenting.

"Liberty finds no refuge in a jurisprudence of doubt." *Planned Parenthood of Southeastern Pa. v. Casey*, 505 U. S. 833 (1992). That was the Court's sententious response, barely more than a decade ago, to those seeking to overrule *Roe v. Wade*, 410 U. S. 113 (1973). The Court's response today, to those who have engaged in a 17-year crusade to overrule *Bowers v. Hardwick*, 478 U. S. 186 (1986), is very different. The need for stability and certainty presents no barrier.

Most of the rest of today's opinion has no relevance to its actual holding—that the Texas statute "furthers no legitimate state interest which can justify" its application to petitioners under rational-basis review. Though there is discussion of "fundamental proposition[s]" and "fundamental decisions" nowhere does the Court's opinion declare that homosexual sodomy is a "fundamental right" under the Due Process Clause; nor does it subject the Texas law to the standard of review that would be appropriate (strict scrutiny) if homosexual sodomy *were* a "fundamental right." Thus, while overruling the *outcome* of *Bowers*, the Court leaves strangely untouched its central legal conclusion: "[R]espondent would have us announce ... a fundamental right to engage in homosexual sodomy. This we are quite unwilling to do." Instead the Court simply describes petitioners' conduct as "an exercise of their liberty"—which it undoubtedly is—and proceeds to apply an unheard-of form of rational-basis review that will have far-reaching implications beyond this case.

I

[JUSTICE SCALIA strongly criticized the majority for its disregard of *stare decisis* principles, particularly in light of weight given to *stare decisis* in *Casey*, where the Court upheld *Roe.*]

II

Having decided that it need not adhere to *stare decisis*, the Court still must establish that *Bowers* was wrongly decided and that the Texas statute, as applied to petitioners, is unconstitutional.

Texas Penal Code Ann. § 21.06(a) (2003) undoubtedly imposes constraints on liberty. So do laws prohibiting prostitution, recreational use of heroin, and, for that matter, working more than 60 hours per week in a bakery. But there is no right to "liberty" under the Due Process Clause, though today's opinion repeatedly makes that claim. ("The liberty protected by the Constitution allows homosexual persons the right to make this choice"); ("These matters ... are central to the liberty protected by the Fourteenth Amendment"); ("Their right to liberty under the Due Process Clause gives them the full right to engage in their conduct without intervention of the government"). The Fourteenth Amendment *expressly allows* States to deprive their citizens of "liberty," *so long as "due process of law" is provided:*

> "No state shall ... deprive any person of life, liberty, or property, *without due process of law.*" Amdt. 14. (Emphasis added.)

Our opinions applying the doctrine known as "substantive due process" hold that the Due Process Clause prohibits States from infringing *fundamental* liberty interests, unless the infringement is narrowly tailored to serve a compelling state interest. We have held repeatedly, in cases the Court today does not overrule, that *only* fundamental rights qualify for this so-called "heightened scrutiny" protection—that is, rights which are "deeply rooted in this Nation's history and tradition." *Washington v. Glucksberg*, 521 U. S. 702 (1997). All other liberty interests may be abridged or abrogated pursuant to a validly enacted state law if that law is rationally related to a legitimate state interest.

Bowers held, first, that criminal prohibitions of homosexual sodomy are not subject to heightened scrutiny because they do not implicate a "fundamental right" under the Due Process Clause. Noting that "[p]roscriptions against that conduct have ancient roots," that "[s]odomy was a criminal offense at common law and was forbidden by the laws of the original 13 States when they ratified the Bill of Rights," and that many States had retained their bans on sodomy, *Bowers* concluded that a right to engage in homosexual sodomy was not "deeply rooted in this Nation's history and tradition."

The Court today does not overrule this holding. Not once does it describe homosexual sodomy as a "fundamental right" or a "fundamental liberty interest," nor does it subject the Texas statute to strict scrutiny. Instead, having failed to establish that the right to homosexual sodomy is "deeply rooted in this Nation's history and tradition," the Court concludes that the application of Texas's statute to petitioners' conduct fails the rational-basis test, and overrules *Bowers*' holding to the contrary. "The Texas statute furthers no legitimate state interest which can justify its intrusion into the personal and private life of the individual."

I shall address that rational-basis holding presently. First, however, I address some aspersions that the Court casts upon *Bowers'* conclusion that homosexual sodomy is not a "fundamental right"—even though, as I have said, the Court does not have the boldness to reverse that conclusion.

III

[JUSTICE SCALIA distinguished the due process cases relied on by the Court, or, in the case of *Roe v. Wade*, called into question its continued validity.]

After discussing the history of antisodomy laws, the Court proclaims that, "it should be noted that there is no longstanding history in this country of laws directed at homosexual conduct as a distinct matter." This observation in no way casts into doubt the "definitive [historical] conclusion," on which *Bowers* relied: that our Nation has a longstanding history of laws prohibiting *sodomy in general*—regardless of whether it was performed by same-sex or opposite-sex couples:

> "It is obvious to us that neither of these formulations would extend a fundamental right to homosexuals to engage in acts of consensual sodomy. Proscriptions against that conduct have ancient roots. *Sodomy* was a criminal offense at common law and was forbidden by the laws of the original 13 States when they ratified the Bill of Rights. In 1868, when the Fourteenth Amendment was ratified, all but 5 of the 37 States in the Union had *criminal sodomy laws*. In fact, until 1961, all 50 States outlawed *sodomy*, and today, 24 States and the District of Columbia continue to provide criminal penalties for *sodomy* performed in private and between consenting adults. Against this background, to claim that a right to engage in such conduct is 'deeply rooted in this Nation's history and tradition' or 'implicit in the concept of ordered liberty' is, at best, facetious."

It is (as *Bowers* recognized) entirely irrelevant whether the laws in our long national tradition criminalizing homosexual sodomy were "directed at homosexual conduct as a distinct matter." Whether homosexual sodomy was prohibited by a law targeted at same-sex sexual relations or by a more general law prohibiting both homosexual and heterosexual sodomy, the only relevant point is that it *was* criminalized—which suffices to establish that homosexual sodomy is not a right "deeply rooted in our Nation's history and tradition." The Court today agrees that homosexual sodomy was criminalized and thus does not dispute the facts on which *Bowers actually* relied.

Next the Court makes the claim, again unsupported by any citations, that "[l]aws prohibiting sodomy do not seem to have been enforced against consenting adults acting in private." The key qualifier here is "acting in private"—since the Court admits that sodomy laws *were* enforced against consenting adults (although the Court contends that prosecutions were "infrequent"). I do not know what "acting in private" means; surely consensual sodomy, like heterosexual intercourse, is rarely performed on stage. If all the Court means by "acting in private" is "on private premises, with the doors closed and windows covered," it is entirely unsurprising that evidence of enforcement would be hard to come by. (Imagine the circumstances that would enable a search warrant to be obtained for a residence on the ground that there was probable cause to believe that consensual sodomy was then and there occurring.) Surely that lack of evidence would not sustain the proposition that consensual sodomy on private premises with the doors closed and windows covered was regarded as a "fundamental right," even though all other consensual sodomy was criminalized. There are 203 prosecutions for consensual, adult homosexual sodomy reported in the West Reporting system and official state reporters from the years 1880–1995. There are also records of 20 sodomy prosecutions and 4 executions during the colonial period. *Bowers*' conclusion that homosexual sodomy is not a fundamental right "deeply rooted in this Nation's history and tradition" is utterly unassailable.

Realizing that fact, the Court instead says: "[W]e think that our laws and traditions in the past half century are of most relevance here. These references show *an emerging awareness* that liberty gives substantial protection to adult persons in deciding how to conduct their private lives *in matters pertaining to sex*." (Emphasis added.) Apart from the fact that such an "emerging awareness" does not establish a "fundamental right," the statement is factually false. States continue to prosecute all sorts of crimes by adults "in matters pertaining to sex": prostitution, adult incest, adultery, obscenity, and child pornography. Sodomy laws, too, have been enforced "in the past half century," in which there have been 134 reported cases involving prosecutions for consensual, adult, homosexual sodomy. In relying, for evidence of an "emerging recognition," upon the American Law Institute's 1955 recommendation not to criminalize "'consensual sexual relations conducted in private,'" the Court ignores the fact that this recommendation was "a point of resistance in most of the states that considered adopting the Model Penal Code." W. Eskridge, Gaylaw: Challenging the Apartheid of the Closet (1999).

In any event, an "emerging awareness" is by definition not "deeply rooted in this Nation's history and tradition[s]," as we have said "fundamental right" status requires. Constitutional entitlements do not spring into existence because some States choose to lessen or eliminate criminal sanctions on certain behavior. Much less do they spring into existence, as the Court seems to believe, because *foreign nations* decriminalize conduct. The *Bowers* majority opinion *never* relied on "values we share with a wider civilization," but rather rejected the claimed right to sodomy on the ground that such a right was not "deeply rooted in *this Nation's* history and tradition." (Emphasis added.) *Bowers*' rational-basis holding is likewise devoid of any reliance on the views of a "wider civilization." The Court's discussion of these foreign views (ignoring, of course, the many countries that have retained criminal prohibitions on sodomy) is therefore meaningless dicta. Dangerous dicta, however, since "this Court ... should not impose foreign moods, fads, or fashions on Americans." *Foster v. Florida*, 537 U. S. 990 (2002) (THOMAS, J., concurring in denial of certiorari).

IV

I turn now to the ground on which the Court squarely rests its holding: the contention that there is no rational basis for the law here under attack. This proposition is so out of accord with our jurisprudence—indeed, with the jurisprudence of *any* society we know—that it requires little discussion.

The Texas statute undeniably seeks to further the belief of its citizens that certain forms of sexual behavior are "immoral and unacceptable," *Bowers*, *supra*—the same interest furthered by criminal laws against fornication, bigamy, adultery, adult incest, bestiality, and obscenity. *Bowers* held that this *was* a legitimate state interest. The Court today reaches the opposite conclusion. The Texas statute, it says, "furthers *no legitimate state interest* which can justify its intrusion into the personal and private life of the individual." (Emphasis added.) The Court embraces instead Justice Stevens' declaration in his *Bowers* dissent, that "the fact that the governing majority in a State has traditionally viewed a particular practice as immoral is not a sufficient reason for upholding a law prohibiting the practice." This effectively decrees the end of all morals legislation. If, as the Court asserts, the promotion of majoritarian sexual morality is not even a *legitimate* state interest, none of the above-mentioned laws can survive rational-basis review.

...

* * *

Today's opinion is the product of a Court, which is the product of a law-profession culture, that has largely signed on to the so-called homosexual agenda, by which I mean the agenda promoted by some homosexual activists directed at eliminating the moral opprobrium that has traditionally attached to homosexual conduct. I noted in an earlier opinion the fact that the American Association of Law Schools (to which any reputable law school *must* seek to belong) excludes from membership any school that refuses to ban from its job-interview facilities a law firm (no matter how small) that does not wish to hire as a prospective partner a person who openly engages in homosexual conduct.

One of the most revealing statements in today's opinion is the Court's grim warning that the criminalization of homosexual conduct is "an invitation to subject homosexual persons to discrimination both in the public and in the private spheres." It is clear from this that the Court has taken sides in the culture war, departing from its role of assuring, as neutral observer, that the democratic rules of engagement are observed. Many Americans do not want persons who openly engage in homosexual conduct as partners in their business, as scoutmasters for their children, as teachers in their children's schools, or as boarders in their home. They view this as protecting themselves and their families from a lifestyle that they believe to be immoral and destructive. The Court views it as "discrimination" which it is the function of our judgments to deter. So imbued is the Court with the law profession's anti-anti-homosexual culture, that it is seemingly unaware that the attitudes of that culture are not obviously "mainstream"; that in most States what the Court calls "discrimination" against those who

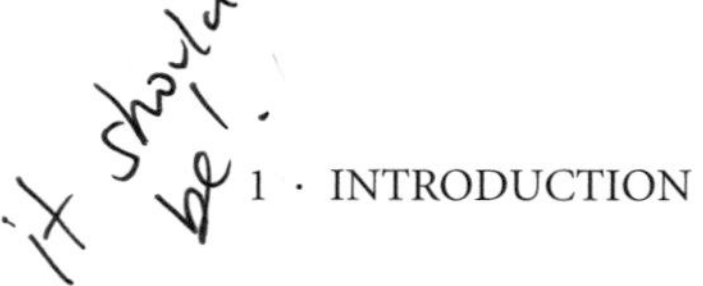

engage in homosexual acts is perfectly legal; that proposals to ban such "discrimination" under Title VII have repeatedly been rejected by Congress; that in some cases such "discrimination" is *mandated* by federal statute, see 10 U. S. C. §654(b)(1) (mandating discharge from the armed forces of any service member who engages in or intends to engage in homosexual acts); and that in some cases such "discrimination" is a constitutional right, see *BSA v. Dale*, 530 U. S. 640 (2000).

Let me be clear that I have nothing against homosexuals, or any other group, promoting their agenda through normal democratic means. Social perceptions of sexual and other morality change over time, and every group has the right to persuade its fellow citizens that its view of such matters is the best. That homosexuals have achieved some success in that enterprise is attested to by the fact that Texas is one of the few remaining States that criminalize private, consensual homosexual acts. But persuading one's fellow citizens is one thing, and imposing one's views in absence of democratic majority will is something else. I would no more *require* a State to criminalize homosexual acts—or, for that matter, display *any* moral disapprobation of them—than I would *forbid* it to do so. What Texas has chosen to do is well within the range of traditional democratic action, and its hand should not be stayed through the invention of a brand-new "constitutional right" by a Court that is impatient of democratic change. It is indeed true that "later generations can see that laws once thought necessary and proper in fact serve only to oppress"; and when that happens, later generations can repeal those laws. But it is the premise of our system that those judgments are to be made by the people, and not imposed by a governing caste that knows best.

One of the benefits of leaving regulation of this matter to the people rather than to the courts is that the people, unlike judges, need not carry things to their logical conclusion. The people may feel that their disapprobation of homosexual conduct is strong enough to disallow homosexual marriage, but not strong enough to criminalize private homosexual acts—and may legislate accordingly. The Court today pretends that it possesses a similar freedom of action, so that we need not fear judicial imposition of homosexual marriage, as has recently occurred in Canada (in a decision that the Canadian Government has chosen not to appeal). At the end of its opinion—after having laid waste the foundations of our rational-basis jurisprudence—the Court says that the present case "does not involve whether the government must give formal recognition to any relationship that homosexual persons seek to enter." Do not believe it. More illuminating than this bald, unreasoned disclaimer is the progression of thought displayed by an earlier passage in the Court's opinion, which notes the constitutional protections afforded to "personal decisions relating to *marriage*, procreation, contraception, family relationships, child rearing, and education," and then declares that "[p]ersons in a homosexual relationship may seek autonomy for these purposes, just as heterosexual persons do." (Emphasis added.) Today's opinion dismantles the structure of constitutional law that has permitted a distinction to be made between heterosexual and homosexual unions, insofar as formal recognition in marriage is concerned. If moral disapprobation of homosexual conduct is "no legitimate state interest" for purposes of proscribing that conduct; and if, as the Court coos (casting aside all pretense of neutrality), "[w]hen sexuality finds overt expression in intimate conduct with another person, the conduct can be but one element in a personal bond that is more enduring"; what justification could there possibly be for denying the benefits of marriage to homosexual couples exercising "[t]he liberty protected by the Constitution"? Surely not the encouragement of procreation, since the sterile and the elderly are allowed to marry. This case "does not involve" the issue of homosexual marriage only if one entertains the belief that principle and logic have nothing to do with the decisions of this Court. Many will hope that, as the Court comfortingly assures us, this is so.[c]

The matters appropriate for this Court's resolution are only three: Texas's prohibition of sodomy neither infringes a "fundamental right" (which the Court does not dispute), nor is unsupported by a rational relation to what the Constitution considers a legitimate state interest, nor denies the equal protection of the laws. I dissent.

[Dissenting statement of Thomas, J. omitted.]

Note

The Model Penal Code. The Court in *Lawrence* cites to provisions of the American Law Institute's Model Penal Code as demonstrating an emerging recognition that private consensual sexual relations between adults should not be criminalized. The Model Penal Code was promulgated on May 24, 1962, after a decade-long effort by eminent judges, administrators, practitioners and scholars under the direction of Herbert Wechsler, as chief reporter, to "think through the major problems of the law of crimes" and to "provide a reasoned, integrated body of material" to aid legislators contemplating a general revision of the criminal laws.[d] The promulgation of the Model Penal Code initially spurred efforts to revise California's 1872 code, but those efforts foundered, and the 1872 code remains in effect.

United States v. Bergman

416 F. Supp. 496 (S.D.N.Y. 1976)

Frankel, J.

Defendant is being sentenced upon his plea of guilty to two counts of an 11-count indictment. The sentencing proceeding is unusual in some respects. It has been the subject of more extensive submissions, written and oral, than this court has ever received upon such an occasion. The court has studied some hundreds of pages of

---

c. Twelve years later, Justice Scalia's warnings proved accurate when the Court held, in *Obergefell v. Hodges*, ___ U.S. ___, 135 S. Ct. 2584 (2015), that bans on same-sex marriage were unconstitutional.

d. H. Wechsler, *The American Law Institute: Some Observations on Its Model Penal Code*, 42 A.B.A.J. 321 (1956).

memoranda and exhibits, plus scores of volunteered letters. A broad array of issues has been addressed. Imaginative suggestions of law and penology have been tendered. A preliminary conversation with counsel, on the record, preceded the usual sentencing hearing. Having heard counsel again and the defendant speaking for himself, the court postponed the pronouncement of sentence for further reconsideration of thoughts generated during the days of studying the briefs and oral pleas. It seems fitting now to report in writing the reasons upon which the court concludes that defendant must be sentenced to a term of four months in prison.[1]

I. Defendant and His Crimes

Defendant appeared until the last couple of years to be a man of unimpeachably high character, attainments, and distinction. A doctor of divinity and an ordained rabbi, he has been acclaimed by people around the world for his works of public philanthropy, private charity, and leadership in educational enterprises. Scores of letters have come to the court from across this and other countries reporting debts of personal gratitude to him for numerous acts of extraordinary generosity. (The court has also received a kind of petition, with fifty-odd signatures, in which the signers, based upon learning acquired as newspaper readers, denounce the defendant and urge a severe sentence. Unlike the pleas for mercy, which appear to reflect unquestioned facts inviting compassion, this document should and will be disregarded.) In addition to his good works, defendant has managed to amass considerable wealth in the ownership and operation of nursing homes, in real estate ventures, and in a course of substantial investments.

Beginning about two years ago, investigations of nursing homes in this area, including questions of fraudulent claims for Medicaid funds, drew to a focus upon this defendant among several others. The results that concern us were the present indictment and two state indictments. After extensive pretrial proceedings, defendant embarked upon elaborate plea negotiations with both state and federal prosecutors. A state guilty plea and the instant plea were entered in March of this year. (Another state indictment is expected to be dismissed after defendant is sentenced on those to which he has pled guilty.) As part of the detailed plea arrangements, it is expected that the prison sentence imposed by this court will comprise the total covering the state as well as the federal convictions.[2]

For purposes of the sentence now imposed, the precise details of the charges, and of defendant's carefully phrased admissions of guilt, are not matters of prime importance. Suffice it to say that the plea on Count One (carrying a maximum of five years in prison and a $10,000 fine) confesses defendant's knowing and wilful participation in a scheme to defraud the United States in various ways, including the pres-

1. The court considered, and finally rejected, imposing a fine in addition to the prison term. Defendant seems destined to pay hundreds of thousands of dollars in restitution. The amount is being worked out in connection with a state criminal indictment. Apart from defendant's further liabilities for federal taxes, any additional money exaction is appropriately left for the state court.

2. This is not absolutely certain. Defendant has been told, however, that the imposition of any additional prison sentence by the state court will be an occasion for reconsidering today's judgment.

entation of wrongfully padded claims for payments under the Medicaid program to defendant's nursing homes. Count Three, for which the guilty plea carries a theoretical maximum of three more years in prison and another $5,000 fine, is a somewhat more "technical" charge. Here, defendant admits to having participated in the filing of a partnership return which was false and fraudulent in failing to list people who had bought partnership interests from him in one of his nursing homes, had paid for such interests, and had made certain capital withdrawals.

The conspiracy to defraud, as defendant has admitted it, is by no means the worst of its kind; it is by no means as flagrant or extensive as has been portrayed in the press; it is evidently less grave than other nursing-home wrongs for which others have been convicted or publicized. At the same time, the sentence, as defendant has acknowledged, is imposed for two federal felonies including, as the more important, a knowing and purposeful conspiracy to mislead and defraud the Federal Government.

II. The Guiding Principles of Sentencing

Proceeding through the short list of the supposed justifications for criminal sanctions, defense counsel urge that no licit purpose could be served by defendant's incarceration. Some of these arguments are plainly sound; others are not.

The court agrees that this defendant should not be sent to prison for "rehabilitation." Apart from the patent inappositeness of the concept to this individual, this court shares the growing understanding that no one should ever be sent to prison for rehabilitation. That is to say, nobody who would not otherwise be locked up should suffer that fate on the incongruous premise that it will be good for him or her. Imprisonment is punishment. Facing the simple reality should help us to be civilized. It is less agreeable to confine someone when we deem it an affliction rather than a benefaction. If someone must be imprisoned—for other, valid reasons—we should seek to make rehabilitative resources available to him or her. But the goal of rehabilitation cannot fairly serve in itself as grounds for the sentence to confinement. Equally clearly, this defendant should not be confined to incapacitate him. He is not dangerous. It is most improbable that he will commit similar, or any, offenses in the future. There is no need for "specific deterrence."

Contrary to counsel's submissions, however, two sentencing considerations demand a prison sentence in this case:

> *First*, the aim of *general deterrence*, the effort to discourage similar wrongdoing by others through a reminder that the law's warnings are real and that the grim consequence of imprisonment is likely to follow from crimes of deception for gain like those defendant has admitted.
>
> *Second*, the related, but not identical, concern that any lesser penalty would, in the words of the Model Penal Code, §7.01(1)(c), "depreciate the seriousness of the defendant's crime."

Resisting the first of these propositions, defense counsel invoke Immanuel Kant's axiom that "one man ought never to be dealt with merely as a means subservient to the purposes of another." In a more novel, but equally futile, effort, counsel urge that a sentence for general deterrence "would violate the Eighth Amendment proscription against cruel and unusual punishment." Treating the latter point first, because it is a short subject, it may be observed simply that if general deterrence as a sentencing purpose were now to be outlawed, as against a near unanimity of views among state and federal jurists, the bolt would have to come from a place higher than this.

As for Dr. Kant, it may well be that defense counsel mistake his meaning in the present context. Whether or not that is so, and without pretending to authority on that score, we take the widely accepted stance that a criminal punished in the interest of general deterrence is not being employed "merely as a means * * *." Reading Kant to mean that every man must be deemed more than the instrument of others, and must "always be treated as an end in himself," the humane principle is not offended here. Each of us is served by the enforcement of the law—not least a person like the defendant in this case, whose wealth and privileges, so long enjoyed, are so much founded upon law. More broadly, we are driven regularly in our ultimate interests as members of the community to use ourselves and each other, in war and in peace, for social ends. One who has transgressed against the criminal laws is certainly among the more fitting candidates for a role of this nature. This is no arbitrary selection. Warned in advance of the prospect, the transgressor has chosen, in the law's premises, "between keeping the law required for society's protection or paying the penalty."

But the whole business, defendant argues further, is guesswork; we are by no means certain that deterrence "works." The position is somewhat overstated; there is, in fact, some reasonably "scientific" evidence for the efficacy of criminal sanctions as deterrents, at least as against some kinds of crimes. Moreover, the time is not yet here when all we can "know" must be quantifiable and digestible by computers. The shared wisdom of generations teaches meaningfully, if somewhat amorphously, that the utilitarians have a point; we do, indeed, lapse often into rationality and act to seek pleasure and avoid pain. It would be better, to be sure, if we had more certainty and precision. Lacking these comforts, we continue to include among our working hypotheses a belief (with some concrete evidence in its support) that crimes like those in this case—deliberate, purposeful, continuing, non-impulsive, and committed for profit—are among those most likely to be generally deterrable by sanctions most shunned by those exposed to temptation.

The idea of avoiding depreciation of the seriousness of the offense implicates two or three thoughts, not always perfectly clear or universally agreed upon, beyond the idea of deterrence. It should be proclaimed by the court's judgment that the offenses are grave, not minor or purely technical. Some attention must be paid to the demand for equal justice; it will not do to leave the penalty of imprisonment a dead letter as against "privileged" violators while it is employed regularly, and with vigor, against others. There probably is in these conceptions an element of retributiveness, as counsel urge. And retribution, so denominated, is in some disfavor as a reason for punishment. It remains a factor, however, as Holmes perceived, and as is known to anyone who talks to judges, lawyers, defendants, or people generally. It may become more palatable, and probably more humanely understood, under the rubric of "deserts" or "just deserts." However the concept is formulated, we have not yet reached a state, supposing we ever should, in which the infliction of punishments for crime may be divorced generally from ideas of blame-worthiness, recompense, and proportionality.

III. An Alternative, "Behavioral Sanction"

Resisting prison above all else, defense counsel included in their thorough memorandum on sentencing two proposals for what they call a "constructive," and therefore a "preferable" form of "behavioral sanction." One is a plan for Dr. Bergman to create and run a program of Jewish vocational and religious high school training. The other is for him to take charge of a "Committee on Holocaust Studies," again concerned with education at the secondary school level.

A third suggestion was made orally at yesterday's sentencing hearing. It was proposed that Dr. Bergman might be ordered to work as a volunteer in some established agency as a visitor and aide to the sick and the otherwise incapacitated. The proposal was that he could read, provide various forms of physical assistance, and otherwise give comfort to afflicted people.

No one can doubt either the worthiness of these proposals or Dr. Bergman's ability to make successes of them. But both of the carefully formulated "sanctions" in the memorandum involve work of an honorific nature, not unlike that done in other projects to which the defendant has devoted himself in the past. It is difficult to conceive of them as "punishments" at all. The more recent proposal is somewhat more suitable in character, but it is still an insufficient penalty. The seriousness of the crimes to which Dr. Bergman has pled guilty demands something more than "requiring" him to lend his talents and efforts to further philanthropic enterprises. It remains open to him, of course, to pursue the interesting suggestions later on as a matter of unforced personal choice.

IV. "Measuring" the Sentence

In cases like this one, the decision of greatest moment is whether to imprison or not. As reflected in the eloquent submissions for defendant, the prospect of the closing prison doors is the most appalling concern; the feeling is that the length of the sojourn is a lesser question once that threshold is passed. Nevertheless, the setting of a term remains to be accomplished. And in some respects it is a subject even more perplexing, unregulated, and unprincipled.

Days and months and years are countable with a sound of exactitude. But there can be no exactitude in the deliberations from which a number emerges. Without pretending to a nonexistent precision, the court notes at least the major factors.

The criminal behavior, as has been noted, is blatant in character and unmitigated by any suggestion of necessitous circumstance or other pressures difficult to resist. However metaphysicians may conjure with issues about free will, it is a fundamental premise of our efforts to do criminal justice that competent people, possessed of their faculties, make choices and are accountable for them. In this sometimes harsh light, the case of the present defendant is among the clearest and least relieved. Viewed against the maxima Congress ordained, and against the run of sentences in other federal criminal cases, it calls for more than a token sentence.[14]

On the other side are factors that take longer to enumerate. Defendant's illustrious public life and works are in his favor, though diminished, of course, by what this case discloses. This is a first, probably a last, conviction. Defendant is 64 years old and in imperfect health, though by no means so ill, from what the court is told, that he could be expected to suffer inordinately more than many others of advanced years who go to prison.

Defendant invokes an understandable, but somewhat unworkable, notion of "disparity." He says others involved in recent nursing home fraud cases have received relatively light sentences for behavior more culpable than his. He lays special emphasis upon one defendant whose frauds appear indeed to have involved larger amounts and who was sentenced to a maximum of six months' incarceration, to be confined for that time only on week nights, not on week days or weekends. This court has examined the minutes of that sentencing proceeding and finds the case distinguishable in material respects. But even if there were a threat of such disparity as defendant warns against, it could not be a major weight on the scales.

Our sentencing system, deeply flawed, is characterized by disparity. We are to seek to "individualize" sentences, but no clear or clearly agreed standards govern the individualization. The lack of meaningful criteria does indeed leave sentencing judges far too much at large. But the result, with its nagging burdens on conscience, cannot be meaningfully alleviated by allowing any handful of sentences in a short series to fetter later judgments. The point is easy, of course, where Sentence No. 1 or Sentences 1–5 are notably harsh. It cannot be that a later judge, disposed to more leniency, should feel in any degree "bound." The converse is not identical, but it is not totally different. The net of this is that this court has considered and has given some weight to the trend of the other cited sentences (though strict logic might call for none), but without treating them as forceful "precedents" in any familiar sense.

How, then, the particular sentence adjudged in this case? As has been mentioned, the case calls for a sentence that is more than nominal. Given the other circumstances, however—including that this is a first offense, by a man no longer young and not perfectly well, where danger of recidivism is not a concern—it verges on cruelty to think of confinement for a term of years. We sit, to be sure, in a nation where prison sentences of extravagant length are more common than they are almost anywhere else. By that light, the term imposed today is not notably long. For this sentencing court, however, for a nonviolent first offense involving no direct assaults or invasions of others' security (as in bank robbery, narcotics, etc.), it is a stern sentence. For people like Dr. Bergman, who might be disposed to engage in similar wrongdoing, it should

14. Despite Biblical teachings concerning what is expected from those to whom much is given, the court has not, as his counsel feared might happen, held Dr. Bergman to a higher standard of responsibility because of his position in the community. But he has not been judged under a lower standard either.

be sufficiently frightening to serve the major end of general deterrence. For all but the profoundly vengeful, it should not depreciate the seriousness of his offenses.

. . .

Writing, as judges rarely do, about a particular sentence concentrates the mind with possibly special force upon the experience of the sentencer as well as the person sentenced. Consigning someone to prison, this defendant or any other, "is a sad necessity." There are impulses of avoidance from time to time—toward a personally gratifying leniency or toward an opposite extreme. But there is, obviously, no place for private impulse in the judgment of the court. The course of justice must be sought with such objective rationality as we can muster, tempered with mercy, but obedient to the law, which, we do well to remember, is all that empowers a judge to make other people suffer.

PUNISHMENT ALTERNATIVES

In *United States v. Bergman*, Judge Frankel saw the sentencing choice as being between prison and probation. Probation is the release of the defendant for a stated period of time on certain conditions, *e.g.*, that the defendant maintain employment, successfully complete a drug or alcohol treatment program, perform community service or consent to be searched at any time. If, during the term of the probation, the defendant violates the conditions, the court may revoke probation, in which case the defendant may then be incarcerated. In the United States today, in virtually all cases, the defendant is either sentenced to a term of incarceration or granted probation.

As a result of the "war on drugs" and the adoption of mandatory minimum sentences at the federal and state levels, incarceration (including incarceration in facilities other than prisons) is the dominant form of punishment in the United States. As of 2013, there were approximately 2.2 million people in the nation's prisons and jails, a 500% increase since 1980.[e] Although the incarceration rate has been slowly declining since 2009, the United States still incarcerates more people than any other county in the world and has a higher rate of incarceration than any other country, except the Seychelles.[f] Its rate of incarceration is more than four times the world average and 6–9 times that of such other Western nations as the United Kingdom, Canada, France, Germany and the United Kingdom.[g] In addition, there are substantial disparities in incarceration rates by race and ethnicity. For example, the incarceration rate for African-American men is almost six times that for White men, and, for Latino men, almost three times that for White men.[h]

---

e. Bureau of Justice Statistics, *Key Statistics: Total Correctional Population*, http://www.bjs.gov/index.cfm?ty=kfdetail&iid=487.

f. Institute for Criminal Policy Research, *World Prison Brief*, http://www.prisonstudies.org.

g. *Id.*

h. The Sentencing Project, *Racial Disparity*, http://www.sentencingproject.org/template/page.cfm?id=122.

The growth in the prison and jail populations in California followed the same pattern. Between 1975 and 2006, California's prison population increased eightfold, and its jail population more than tripled.[i] With California's prisons population at almost twice the stated prison capacity, prisoners brought suit alleging that the prison overcrowding violated their rights under the Eighth Amendment (forbidding cruel and unusual punishment). The three-judge District Court granted relief, ordering the state to reduce its prison population to 137.5% of capacity, and the decision was affirmed by the Supreme Court in *Brown v. Plata*, 563 U.S. 493, 131 S.Ct. 1910 (2011). Since that decision, California has taken three steps that, together, achieved the reduction ordered in *Brown*.[j] In 2012, the voters passed Proposition 36, reducing the severity of California's three-strikes law by requiring that an offender's "third strike" offense be a serious or violent felony. In 2013, the Legislature passed the Public Safety Realignment Act, which, for the first time, directed that certain low-level, non-violent felons be sentenced to county jail rather than to prison. Then, in 2014, the voters passed Proposition 47, which reclassified certain low-level drug and theft offenses as misdemeanors rather than felonies. Both the propositions applied to those already sentenced, who were now permitted to petition for resentencing. As of February, 2015, over 4,000 inmates had been released from prison as a result of resentencing.[k]

Are there alternatives to the prison/probation choice? At an earlier time, the use of the death penalty and other corporal punishments was more prevalent. At present, for all the publicity associated with the death penalty and its consequent symbolic significance, it is imposed in very few cases. In California, since the enactment of the present death penalty statute in 1978, the death penalty has been used as a penalty only in murder cases, and fewer than one in twenty convicted murderers is sentenced to death. Corporal punishments (*e.g.*, whipping) generally have been abandoned as antiquated.[l] In a society that employs the death penalty, why is there a reluctance to employ other corporal punishments?

At an earlier time, there was also a greater use of "shaming punishments," *e.g.*, the use of the stocks in colonial times. Although such punishments were generally abandoned in favor of prison or probation, some individual judges have experimented with the use of shaming punishments. Among their efforts: (1) a woman convicted of possession of drugs was ordered to take out an ad in the newspaper saying that she purchased drugs in front of her children; (2) a man convicted of shoplifting was ordered to parade in front of the store with a sign stating that he had shoplifted from the store; (3) the pictures of men convicted of soliciting prostitution were shown on local television. See Note, *Shame, Stigma, and Crime: Eval-*

---

i. Brennan Center for Justice, *California Quietly Continues to Reduce Mass Incarceration*, https://www.brennancenter.org/blog/california-quietly-continues-reduce-mass-incarceration.

j. *Id.*

k. *Id.*

l. In 1972, Delaware became the final state to abolish public whipping. See Act of July 6, 1972, ch. 497.

changes to law

uating the Efficacy of Shaming Sanctions in Criminal Law, 116 Harv. L. Rev. 2186 (2003). Are such sanctions likely to serve the purposes of punishment better than prison or probation?

Note

Additional Consequences of a Criminal Conviction. A criminal conviction, particularly a felony conviction, may have consequences beyond the sentence imposed. For example, it is estimated that nationally, more than four million Americans are denied the right to vote as a result of laws that prohibit voting by felons or ex-felons.[m] In most states, ex-felons are barred from holding certain jobs and may be denied licenses to pursue certain professions. In many states, persons convicted of drug offenses are barred from receiving welfare and food stamp benefits and are ineligible for public housing. Persons convicted of drug offenses are ineligible for federal student loans.

In 1994, Congress enacted the The Jacob Wetterling Crimes Against Children and Sexually Violent Offenders Registration Act, 42 U.S.C. § 14071, mandating that the states, at the risk of losing federal money, establish systems for sex offender registration. All the states complied. California enacted a "Megan's Law" (P.C. §§ 290, et seq.) authorizing law enforcement agencies to compile and make available to the public the names and residences of certain sex offenders. The law was amended in 2004 to require that the information be made available on a web page. Is this publicity a form of shaming punishment or is it a salutary step toward protecting communities from dangerous felons? What if it invites vigilante justice? In 1996, the legislature enacted P.C. § 645 providing for medroxyprogesterone acetate treatment, "chemical castration," of certain sex offenders upon their parole from prison. The statute gives the parolee the option of choosing surgical castration over chemical castration. The statute appears to impose corporal punishment, particularly since there is no suggestion that the "treatment" is for the benefit of the parolee. Is this cruel and unusual punishment? In 1998, the legislature imposed residency restrictions on convicted sex offenders, which were expanded by "Jessica's Law" in 2006. P.C. § 3003.5(b) provides: "Notwithstanding any other provision of law, it is unlawful for any person for whom registration is required pursuant to Section 290 to reside within 2000 feet of any public or private school, or park where children regularly gather." Does this provision serve to protect children, and what problems does it raise?

B. Three Fundamental Principles of American Criminal Law

The next five cases address three fundamental principles that structure American criminal law: *legality*, the requirement that laws clearly define crimes and set forth

---

m. In California, felons are disqualified from voting while in prison or on parole. Cal.Const. Art. 2 § 4.

punishments in advance of the conduct sought to be punished; *proportionality*, the requirement that punishment or the degree of punishment bear some relationship to the seriousness of the conduct to be punished; and *equality*, the requirement that the law accord the same treatment to all similarly situated classes of law violators. Each of these three principles finds expression in provisions of the United States Constitution and accordingly acts as a limitation on the power of Congress and the states to punish for certain conduct.[n] The first two cases concern the legality principle as it finds expression in the due process clause of the Fifth and Fourteenth Amendments. In *Papachristou v. City of Jacksonville*, the Supreme Court considers a "void for vagueness" challenge to a city's vagrancy ordinance while in *People v. Superior Court (Caswell)*, the California Supreme Court considers a similar challenge to a loitering statute. The next case, *Ewing v. California*, concerns the proportionality principle which is contained in the cruel and unusual punishment clause of the Eighth Amendment. The Supreme Court considers whether the Eighth Amendment imposes any constitutional limit on the length of prison sentences and, if so, whether the defendant's sentence of 25 years to life under California's three strikes law for the theft of three golf clubs exceeds that limit. The final two cases in this section concern the equality principle embodied in the Equal Protection Clause of the Fourteenth Amendment. In *Yick Wo v. Hopkins*, the seminal case on the Equal Protection Clause, the Supreme Court addresses a challenge to a local ordinance enforced only against Chinese. When is a state permitted to discriminate between groups in its criminal laws? The Supreme Court considers that question in *Michael M. v. Superior Court*, a challenge to a statutory rape statute punishing only males.

Papachristou v. City of Jacksonville

405 U.S. 156, 92 S.Ct. 839 (1972)

Mr. Justice Douglas delivered the opinion of the Court.

This case involves eight defendants who were convicted in a Florida municipal court of violating a Jacksonville, Florida, vagrancy ordinance.[1] ....

At issue are five consolidated cases. Margaret Papachristou, Betty Calloway, Eugene Eddie Melton, and Leonard Johnson were all arrested early on a Sunday morning,

---

n. These three constitutional principles have general application. Other constitutional principles may come into play with regard to particular crimes or defenses, *e.g.*, freedom of religion [see *Walker v. Superior Court* in Chapter 5], freedom of speech [see *People v. Rubin* in Chapter 9], freedom from unreasonable searches and seizures [see *Tennessee v. Garner* in Chapter 11].

1. Jacksonville Ordinance Code § 26-57 provided at the time of these arrests and convictions as follows:

Rogues and vagabonds, or dissolute persons who go about begging, common gamblers, persons who use juggling or unlawful games or plays, common drunkards, common night walkers, thieves, pilferers or pickpockets, traders in stolen property, lewd, wanton and lascivious persons, keepers of gambling places, common railers and brawlers, persons wandering or strolling around from place to place without any lawful purpose or object, habitual loafers, disorderly persons, persons neglecting all lawful business and habitually spending their time by frequenting houses of ill fame, gaming

and charged with vagrancy—"prowling by auto." Jimmy Lee Smith and Milton Henry were charged with vagrancy—"vagabonds." Henry Edward Heath and a codefendant were arrested for vagrancy—"loitering" and "common thief." Thomas Owen Campbell was charged with vagrancy—"common thief." Hugh Brown was charged with vagrancy—"disorderly loitering on street" and "disorderly conduct—resisting arrest with violence."

The facts are stipulated. Papachristou and Calloway are white females. Melton and Johnson are black males. Papachristou was enrolled in a job-training program sponsored by the State Employment Service at Florida Junior College in Jacksonville. Calloway was a typing and shorthand teacher at a state mental institution located near Jacksonville. She was the owner of the automobile in which the four defendants were arrested. Melton was a Vietnam war veteran who had been released from the Navy after nine months in a veterans' hospital. On the date of his arrest he was a part-time computer helper while attending college as a full-time student in Jacksonville. Johnson was a tow-motor operator in a grocery chain warehouse and was a lifelong resident of Jacksonville.

At the time of their arrest the four of them were riding in Calloway's car on the main thoroughfare in Jacksonville. They had left a restaurant owned by Johnson's uncle where they had eaten and were on their way to a nightclub. The arresting officers denied that the racial mixture in the car played any part in the decision to make the arrest. The arrest, they said, was made because the defendants had stopped near a used-car lot which had been broken into several times. There was, however, no evidence of any breaking and entering on the night in question.

Of these four charged with "prowling by auto" none had been previously arrested except Papachristou who had once been convicted of a municipal offense.

Jimmy Lee Smith and Milton Henry (who is not a petitioner) were arrested between 9 and 10 a. m. on a weekday in downtown Jacksonville, while waiting for a friend who was to lend them a car so they could apply for a job at a produce company.

---

houses, or places where alcoholic beverages are sold or served, persons able to work but habitually living upon the earnings of their wives or minor children shall be deemed vagrants and, upon conviction in the Municipal Court shall be punished as provided for Class D offenses.

Class D offenses at the time of these arrests and convictions were punishable by 90 days' imprisonment, $500 fine, or both. Jacksonville Ordinance Code § 1-8 (1965). The maximum punishment has since been reduced to 75 days or $ 450. § 304.101 (1971). We are advised that that downward revision was made to avoid federal right-to-counsel decisions. The Fifth Circuit case extending right to counsel in misdemeanors where a fine of $ 500 or 90 days' imprisonment could be imposed is *Harvey v. Mississippi*, 340 F.2d 263 (1965)....

[Florida also had a vagrancy statute, Fla. Stat. § 856.02 (1965), which read quite closely on the Jacksonville ordinance. That statute was declared unconstitutionally overbroad by a federal district court in *Lazarus v. Faircloth*, 301 F. Supp. 266 (S.D. Fla. 1969). The court said: "All loitering, loafing, or idling on the streets and highways of a city, even though habitual, is not necessarily detrimental to the public welfare nor is it under all circumstances an interference with travel upon them. It may be and often is entirely innocuous. The statute draws no distinction between conduct that is calculated to harm and that which is essentially innocent."]

Smith was a part-time produce worker and part-time organizer for a Negro political group. He had a common-law wife and three children supported by him and his wife. He had been arrested several times but convicted only once. Smith's companion, Henry, was an 18-year-old high school student with no previous record of arrest.

This morning it was cold, and Smith had no jacket, so they went briefly into a dry cleaning shop to wait, but left when requested to do so. They thereafter walked back and forth two or three times over a two-block stretch looking for their friend. The store owners, who apparently were wary of Smith and his companion, summoned two police officers who searched the men and found neither had a weapon. But they were arrested because the officers said they had no identification and because the officers did not believe their story.

Heath and a codefendant were arrested for "loitering" and for "common thief." Both were residents of Jacksonville, Heath having lived there all his life and being employed at an automobile body shop. Heath had previously been arrested but his codefendant had no arrest record. Heath and his companion were arrested when they drove up to a residence shared by Heath's girl friend and some other girls. Some police officers were already there in the process of arresting another man. When Heath and his companion started backing out of the driveway, the officers signaled to them to stop and asked them to get out of the car, which they did. Thereupon they and the automobile were searched. Although no contraband or incriminating evidence was found, they were both arrested, Heath being charged with being a "common thief" because he was reputed to be a thief. The codefendant was charged with "loitering" because he was standing in the driveway, an act which the officers admitted was done only at their command.

Campbell was arrested as he reached his home very early one morning and was charged with "common thief." He was stopped by officers because he was traveling at a high rate of speed, yet no speeding charge was placed against him.

Brown was arrested when he was observed leaving a downtown Jacksonville hotel by a police officer seated in a cruiser. The police testified he was reputed to be a thief, narcotics pusher, and generally opprobrious character. The officer called Brown over to the car, intending at that time to arrest him unless he had a good explanation for being on the street. Brown walked over to the police cruiser, as commanded, and the officer began to search him, apparently preparatory to placing him in the car. In the process of the search he came on two small packets which were later found to contain heroin. When the officer touched the pocket where the packets were, Brown began to resist. He was charged with "disorderly loitering on street" and "disorderly conduct—resisting arrest with violence." While he was also charged with a narcotics violation, that charge was nolled.[o]

Jacksonville's ordinance and Florida's statute were "derived from early English law," *Johnson v. State*, 202 So.2d 852 and employ "archaic language" in their definitions of

---

o. The reference is to *nolle prosequi*, notice by the prosecutor that a prosecution has been abandoned.

vagrants. The history is an often told tale. The breakup of feudal estates in England led to labor shortages which in turn resulted in the Statutes of Laborers,[3] designed to stabilize the labor force by prohibiting increases in wages and prohibiting the movement of workers from their home areas in search of improved conditions. Later vagrancy laws became criminal aspects of the poor laws. The series of laws passed in England on the subject became increasingly severe.[4] But "the theory of the Elizabethan poor laws no longer fits the facts," *Edwards v. California*, 314 U.S. 160. The conditions which spawned these laws may be gone, but the archaic classifications remain.

This ordinance is void for vagueness, both in the sense that it "fails to give a person of ordinary intelligence fair notice that his contemplated conduct is forbidden by the statute," *United States v. Harriss*, 347 U.S. 612, and because it encourages arbitrary and erratic arrests and convictions.

Living under a rule of law entails various suppositions, one of which is that "[all persons] are entitled to be informed as to what the State commands or forbids." *Lanzetta v. New Jersey*, 306 U.S. 451.

...

The poor among us, the minorities, the average householder are not in business and not alerted to the regulatory schemes of vagrancy laws; and we assume they would have no understanding of their meaning and impact if they read them. Nor are they protected from being caught in the vagrancy net by the necessity of having a specific intent to commit an unlawful act.

The Jacksonville ordinance makes criminal activities which by modern standards are normally innocent. "Nightwalking" is one. Florida construes the ordinance not to make criminal one night's wandering, *Johnson v. State*, *supra*, only the "habitual"

3. 23 Edw. 3, c. 1 (1349); 25 Edw. 3, c. 1 (1350).

4. See 3 J. Stephen, History of the Criminal Law of England 203–206, 266–275; 4 W. Blackstone, Commentaries 169.

Ledwith v. Roberts, [1937] 1 K. B. 232, gives the following summary:

The early Vagrancy Acts came into being under peculiar conditions utterly different to those of the present time. From the time of the Black Death in the middle of the 14th century till the middle of the 17th century, and indeed, although in diminishing degree, right down to the reform of the Poor Law in the first half of the 19th century, the roads of England were crowded with masterless men and their families, who had lost their former employment through a variety of causes, had no means of livelihood and had taken to a vagrant life. The main causes were the gradual decay of the feudal system under which the labouring classes had been anchored to the soil, the economic slackening of the legal compulsion to work for fixed wages, the break up of the monasteries in the reign of Henry VIII, and the consequent disappearance of the religious orders which had previously administered a kind of "public assistance" in the form of lodging, food and alms; and, lastly, the economic changes brought about by the Enclosure Acts. Some of these people were honest labourers who had fallen upon evil days, others were the "wild rogues," so common in Elizabethan times and literature, who had been born to a life of idleness and had no intention of following any other. It was they and their confederates who formed themselves into the notorious "brotherhood of beggars" which flourished in the 16th and 17th centuries. They were a definite and serious menace to the community and it was chiefly against them and their kind that the harsher provisions of the vagrancy laws of the period were directed.

wanderer or, as the ordinance describes it, "common night walkers." We know, however, from experience that sleepless people often walk at night, perhaps hopeful that sleep-inducing relaxation will result.

Luis Munoz-Marin, former Governor of Puerto Rico, commented once that "loafing" was a national virtue in his Commonwealth and that it should be encouraged. It is, however, a crime in Jacksonville.

"Persons able to work but habitually living upon the earnings of their wives or minor children"—like habitually living "without visible means of support"—might implicate unemployed pillars of the community who have married rich wives.

"Persons able to work but habitually living upon the earnings of their wives or minor children" may also embrace unemployed people out of the labor market, by reason of a recession or disemployed by reason of technological or so-called structural displacements.

Persons "wandering or strolling" from place to place have been extolled by Walt Whitman and Vachel Lindsay.[6] The qualification "without any lawful purpose or object" may be a trap for innocent acts. Persons "neglecting all lawful business and habitually spending their time by frequenting ... places where alcoholic beverages are sold or served" would literally embrace many members of golf clubs and city clubs.

Walkers and strollers and wanderers may be going to or coming from a burglary. Loafers or loiterers may be "casing" a place for a holdup. Letting one's wife support him is an intra-family matter, and normally of no concern to the police. Yet it may, of course, be the setting for numerous crimes.

The difficulty is that these activities are historically part of the amenities of life as we have known them. They are not mentioned in the Constitution or in the Bill of Rights. These unwritten amenities have been in part responsible for giving our people the feeling of independence and self-confidence, the feeling of creativity. These amenities have dignified the right of dissent and have honored the right to be nonconformists and the right to defy submissiveness. They have encouraged lives of high spirits rather than hushed, suffocating silence.

They are embedded in Walt Whitman's writings, especially in his "Song of the Open Road." They are reflected, too, in the spirit of Vachel Lindsay's "I Want to Go Wandering," and by Henry D. Thoreau.

This aspect of the vagrancy ordinance before us is suggested by what this Court said in 1876 about a broad criminal statute enacted by Congress: "It would certainly be dangerous if the legislature could set a net large enough to catch all possible offenders, and leave it to the courts to step inside and say who could be rightfully detained, and who should be set at large." *United States v. Reese*, 92 U.S. 214.

Reasoning

---

6. And *see* Reich, *Police Questioning of Law Abiding Citizens*, 75 Yale L.J. 1161 (1966): "If I choose to take an evening walk to see if Andromeda has come up on schedule, I think I am entitled to look for the distant light of Almach and Mirach without finding myself staring into the blinding beam of a police flashlight."

. . .

Where the list of crimes is so all-inclusive and generalized as the one in this ordinance, those convicted may be punished for no more than vindicating affronts to police authority:

> "The common ground which brings such a motley assortment of human troubles before the magistrates in vagrancy-type proceedings is the procedural laxity which permits 'conviction' for almost any kind of conduct and the existence of the House of Correction as an easy and convenient dumping-ground for problems that appear to have no other immediate solution." Foote, *Vagrancy-Type Law and Its Administration*, 104 U. Pa. L. Rev. 603.

Another aspect of the ordinance's vagueness appears when we focus, not on the lack of notice given a potential offender, but on the effect of the unfettered discretion it places in the hands of the Jacksonville police. Caleb Foote, an early student of this subject, has called the vagrancy-type law as offering "punishment by analogy." *Id.* Such crimes, though long common in Russia, are not compatible with our constitutional system. We allow our police to make arrests only on "probable cause," a Fourth and Fourteenth Amendment standard applicable to the States as well as to the Federal Government. Arresting a person on suspicion, like arresting a person for investigation, is foreign to our system, even when the arrest is for past criminality. Future criminality, however, is the common justification for the presence of vagrancy statutes. Florida has, indeed, construed her vagrancy statute "as necessary regulations," *inter alia*, "to deter vagabondage and prevent crimes." *Johnson v. State, supra.*

A direction by a legislature to the police to arrest all "suspicious" persons would not pass constitutional muster. A vagrancy prosecution may be merely the cloak for a conviction which could not be obtained on the real but undisclosed grounds for the arrest.

Those generally implicated by the imprecise terms of the ordinance—poor people, nonconformists, dissenters, idlers—may be required to comport themselves according to the lifestyle deemed appropriate by the Jacksonville police and the courts. Where, as here, there are no standards governing the exercise of the discretion granted by the ordinance, the scheme permits and encourages an arbitrary and discriminatory enforcement of the law. It furnishes a convenient tool for "harsh and discriminatory enforcement by local prosecuting officials, against particular groups deemed to merit their displeasure." *Thornhill v. Alabama*, 310 U.S. 88. It results in a regime in which the poor and the unpopular are permitted to "stand on a public sidewalk ... only at the whim of any police officer." *Shuttlesworth v. Birmingham*, 382 U.S. 87. Under this ordinance,

> "If some carefree type of fellow is satisfied to work just so much, and no more, as will pay for one square meal, some wine, and a flophouse daily, but a court thinks this kind of living subhuman, the fellow can be forced to

raise his sights or go to jail as a vagrant." Amsterdam, *Federal Constitutional Restrictions on the Punishment of Crimes of Status, Crimes of General Obnoxiousness, Crimes of Displeasing Police Officers, and the Like*, 3 Crim. L. Bull. 205 (1967).

A presumption that people who might walk or loaf or loiter or stroll or frequent houses where liquor is sold, or who are supported by their wives or who look suspicious to the police are to become future criminals is too precarious for a rule of law. The implicit presumption in these generalized vagrancy standards—that crime is being nipped in the bud—is too extravagant to deserve extended treatment. Of course, vagrancy statutes are useful to the police. Of course, they are nets making easy the roundup of so-called undesirables. But the rule of law implies equality and justice in its application. Vagrancy laws of the Jacksonville type teach that the scales of justice are so tipped that even-handed administration of the law is not possible. The rule of law, evenly applied to minorities as well as majorities, to the poor as well as the rich, is the great mucilage that holds society together.

The Jacksonville ordinance cannot be squared with our constitutional standards and is plainly unconstitutional.

MR. JUSTICE POWELL and MR. JUSTICE REHNQUIST took no part in the consideration or decision of this case.

Note

Lambert v. California. In *Lambert v. California*, 355 U.S. 225 (1957), the Supreme Court upheld a different type of fair notice challenge. An ordinance of the city of Los Angeles defined "convicted person" as a person who had been convicted of a felony, and it prohibited any convicted person from remaining in Los Angeles for more than five days or entering Los Angeles more than five times within a 30-day period unless the person had registered with the Chief of Police. The defendant, who had been a resident of Los Angeles for seven years, was convicted of forgery during that time, but had never registered under the ordinance. She was prosecuted and convicted of violating the ordinance. The Supreme Court held that the ordinance violated the Due Process clause because it punished defendant's omission without any evidence that she knew or should have known of the existence of the ordinance and her duty to register.

People v. Superior Court (Caswell)

46 Cal. 3d 381, 758 P.2d 1046 (1988)

ARGUELLES, J.

Penal Code section 647, subdivision (d) (hereafter section 647(d)) provides that any person "[who] loiters in or about any toilet open to the public for the purpose of engaging in or soliciting any lewd or lascivious or any unlawful act" is guilty of a misdemeanor. In this proceeding, petitioners Ralph Caswell, Kenneth Grassi, and 14 other persons charged with violating this provision (hereafter defendants) seek dismissal of the charges on the ground that section 647(d) is unconstitutionally vague on its face. As we explain, after a review of the governing federal and state constitutional precedents and an analysis of numerous decisions from other states which have considered comparable vagueness challenges to similar, narrowly focused loitering provisions, we have concluded that section 647(d) is sufficiently definite to withstand defendants' facial constitutional attack.

...

Discussion

That no person shall be deprived of life, liberty or property without due process of law is, of course, a cornerstone of our jurisprudence. (U.S. Const., Amends. V, XIV; Cal. Const., art. I, § 7.) "The requirement of a reasonable degree of certainty in legislation, especially in the criminal law, is a well established element of the guarantee of due process of law." (*In re Newbern* (1960) 53 Cal. 2d 786.) To withstand a facial vagueness challenge under the due process clause, a statute must satisfy two basic requirements.

First, a statute must be sufficiently definite to provide adequate notice of the conduct proscribed. "[A] statute which either forbids or requires the doing of an act in terms so vague that men of common intelligence must necessarily guess at its meaning and differ as to its application, violates the first essential of due process of law." (*Connally v. General Const. Co.* (1926) 269 U.S. 385.) "[Because] we assume that man is free to steer between lawful and unlawful conduct, we insist that laws give the person of ordinary intelligence a reasonable opportunity to know what is prohibited, so that he may act accordingly. Vague laws may trap the innocent by not providing fair warning." (*Village of Hoffman Estates v. Flipside, Hoffman Estates* (1982) 455 U.S. 489, quoting *Grayned v. City of Rockford* (1972) 408 U.S. 104.)

Second, a statute must provide sufficiently definite guidelines for the police in order to prevent arbitrary and discriminatory enforcement. "A vague law impermissibly delegates basic policy matters to policemen, judges and juries for resolution on an ad hoc and subjective basis, with the attendant dangers of arbitrary and discriminatory application." (*Grayned.*) "Where the legislature fails to provide such minimal guidelines, a criminal statute may permit 'a standardless sweep [that] allows policemen, prosecutors, and juries to pursue their personal predilections.'" (*Kolender v. Lawson* (1983) 461 U.S. 352, quoting *Smith v. Goguen* (1974) 415 U.S. 566.)

We evaluate the provisions of section 647(d) against these two due process criteria.

A. Adequate Notice

Section 647(d) provides: "Every person who commits any of the following acts is guilty of disorderly conduct, a misdemeanor: ... (d) Who loiters in or about any toilet open to the public for the purpose of engaging in or soliciting any lewd or lascivious or any unlawful act." As we shall see, particularly in light of the clarifying interpretation of the term "lewd and lascivious" in an earlier decision, it is clear that the section provides fair notice to the ordinary citizen of the act proscribed.

At the outset, we note past cases make clear that the statute is not rendered impermissibly indefinite by its use of the word "loiter." More than a quarter of a century ago, in *In re Cregler* (1961) 56 Cal. 2d 308, we sustained a different, much less specific, loitering statute against a vagueness challenge, explaining that "the word 'loiter'... in our view has a sinister or wrongful ... implication," excluding "mere waiting for any lawful purpose" but connoting "lingering in the designated places for the purpose of committing a crime as opportunity may be discovered." Section 647(d), of course, embraces such a "specific intent" requirement explicitly in its terms, providing that the statute is violated only when a person "loiters ... *for the purpose* of engaging in or soliciting any lewd or lascivious or any unlawful act." (Italics added.) Persons of ordinary intelligence need not guess at the applicability of the section; so long as they do not linger for the proscribed purpose, they have not violated the statute.

On a number of occasions, the United States Supreme Court has emphasized the value that a specific intent requirement plays in overcoming the potential vagueness of a statute. As the court noted in *Hoffman Estates*, *supra*, "a scienter requirement may mitigate a law's vagueness, especially with respect to the adequacy of notice to the complainant that his conduct is proscribed." Because section 647(d)'s prohibition on loitering is expressly limited to those who loiter with a specifically defined illicit purpose or intent, the section is considerably narrower than other loitering statutes—like the provision at issue in *Cregler*—which were historically aimed at all manner of "idlers, loafers and wanderers." (See generally *Papachristou v. City of Jacksonville* (1972) 405 U.S. 156.)

Nor do the words "in or about any toilet open to the public" appear misleading or cryptic. "It is not required that a statute, to be valid, have that degree of exactness which inheres in a mathematical theorem" (*Smith v. Peterson* (1955) 131 Cal. App. 2d 241); "no more than a reasonable degree of certainty can be demanded." It is thus clear this statutory phrase is sufficiently definite such that no reasonable person could misunderstand its meaning.

Finally, the phrase "lewd or lascivious or any unlawful act," as interpreted by prior case law, also withstands constitutional scrutiny.[3] This court was confronted with construing similar language in section 647, subdivision (a) in *Pryor v. Municipal Court* (1979) 25 Cal. 3d 238. We concluded the "terms 'lewd' and 'dissolute'... are synonymous, and refer to conduct which involves the touching of the genitals, buttocks, or female breast for the purpose of sexual arousal, gratification, annoyance or offense, if the actor knows or should know of the presence of persons who may be offended by his conduct." This limitation "serves not only to define the reach of the law but also to add a requirement of specific intent," a feature which has often served to avert

3. The phrase "or any unlawful act" has been properly construed in this context to mean a "lewd" act. "As for the 'unlawful' act prohibited by section 647, subdivision (d), the word means under the doctrine of ejusdem generis and in the context of this subdivision, a 'lewd' act." (*People v. Ledenbach* (1976) 61 Cal. App. 3d Supp. 7 [italics in original].) Thus, the dissenting opinion's concern that the term "any unlawful act" fails to provide constitutionally adequate notice is unfounded.

a determination that a statute is unconstitutionally vague. We thus conclude section 647(d) satisfies the "fair notice" prong of the void-for-vagueness test.

B. Adequate Guidelines to Permit Nonarbitrary Enforcement

Defendants' principal argument is that even if the provisions of section 647(d) are sufficiently definite to put the average citizen on notice as to the conduct which is proscribed by the statute, the statute nonetheless violates constitutional standards because it fails to set forth sufficient guidelines for law enforcement, thus creating an unconstitutional risk of arbitrary and discriminatory enforcement. In this regard, defendants rely heavily on the recent Court of Appeal opinion in *People v. Soto* (1985) 171 Cal. App. 3d 1158, which found section 647(d) unconstitutional on this very basis.

In reaching this conclusion, the *Soto* court rested its holding largely on the reasoning of the then-recent United States Supreme Court decision in *Kolender v. Lawson* (1983) 461 U.S. 352, in which the high court sustained a vagueness challenge to a different subdivision of section 647—section 647, subdivision (e) (hereafter section 647(e))—which provided that a person was guilty of a misdemeanor if he "loiters ... upon the streets ... without apparent reason or business and ... refuses to identify himself or to account for his presence when requested by an peace officer so to do...." Because of the central role *Kolender* assumed in the *Soto* court's analysis, *Kolender* is a logical starting point for our analysis of defendants' present claim.

In *Kolender*, the state defended section 647(e) against the defendant's vagueness challenge by pointing to an earlier state court decision—*People v. Solomon* (1973) 33 Cal. App. 3d 429 which, in upholding the statute against a prior constitutional challenge, had construed section 647(e) to simply require a person to present "credible and reliable" identification when stopped by the police. The *Solomon* court defined "credible and reliable" identification as that "carrying reasonable assurance that the identification is authentic and providing means for later getting in touch with the person who has identified himself."

The United States Supreme Court found even this limiting judicial gloss insufficient to save the constitutionality of the section, explaining: "Section 647(e), as presently drafted and as construed by the state courts, contains no standard for determining what a suspect has to do in order to satisfy the requirement to provide a 'credible and reliable' identification. As such, the statute vests virtually complete discretion in the hands of the police to determine whether the suspect has satisfied the statute and must be permitted to go on his way in the absence of probable cause to arrest. An individual, whom police may think is suspicious but do not have probable cause to believe has committed a crime, is entitled to continue to walk the public streets only at the whim of any police officer who happens to stop that individual under § 647(e)." Later, the high court observed: "It is clear that the full discretion accorded to the police to determine whether the suspect has provided a 'credible and reliable' identification necessarily [entrusts] lawmaking to the moment-to-moment judgment of the policeman on his beat. Section 647(e) furnishes a convenient tool for harsh and discriminatory enforcement by local prosecuting officials, against particular groups deemed to merit their displeasure, and confers on police a virtually unrestrained power to arrest and charge persons with a violation."

The *Soto* court found the high court's critical analysis of section 647(e) equally applicable to section 647(d)....

... [H]owever, we think that the *Soto* court failed to take adequate account of the significant differences between the loitering provision at issue in *Kolender* and the provisions of section 647(d), and also overlooked the significant body of out-of-state decisions which have upheld the constitutionality of loitering statutes—like section 647(d)—that narrow the discretion of enforcing officials by (1) limiting the section's reach to persons who loiter with a specified illicit purpose and (2) confining the statute's operation to defined geographical locations in which loitering for the proscribed purposes has historically been a problem.[4]

As we have seen, the key portion of the loitering provision at issue in *Kolender* was the requirement that an individual, who the police believed was loitering or wandering upon the streets without apparent reason or business, provide "credible and reliable" evidence of his or her identity; if the person failed to provide such "credible and reliable" identification, he or she was guilty of a crime. Because the statute, even with the judicial gloss, contained "no standard for determining what a suspect [had] to do to satisfy the requirement to provide a 'credible and reliable' identification," the *Kolender* court concluded that the provision effectively made the very definition of the crime subject to the personal standards of each individual law enforcement officer.

By contrast, section 647(d) vests no such discretion with law enforcement. The essence of this provision is loitering in a certain place while entertaining a specified criminal intent. One need not expressly satisfy a policeman's curiosity in order to be entitled to freely walk the streets or use public restrooms. A person is subject to arrest under the provision only if his or her conduct gives rise to probable cause to believe that he or she is loitering in or about a public restroom with the proscribed illicit intent.

The *Soto* court, while recognizing the important interests served by section 647(d), felt that the provision was unnecessary in light of the existence of other criminal provisions—for example, the provisions prohibiting the actual public solicitation of lewd or lascivious conduct or prohibiting indecent exposure. The *Soto* court reasoned that

4. I concurred in the *Soto* opinion while serving on the Court of Appeal, but I am now persuaded by the arguments supporting the constitutionality of section 647(d) and thus I have concluded that the *Soto* decision should be disapproved. Although, as Justice Jackson has noted, "it is embarrassing to confess a blunder" (*United States v. Bryan* (1950) 339 U.S. 323 (Jackson, J., conc.)), as he also noted "it may prove more embarrassing to adhere to it." And as Justice Rutledge once observed: "Wisdom too often never comes, and so one ought not to reject it merely because it comes late." (*Wolf v. Colorado* (1949) 338 U.S. 25 (Rutledge, J., dis.)).

in order to constrain section 647(d) within constitutional bounds a police officer would not have probable cause to believe an individual was loitering with the requisite illicit intent unless the individual committed such an independent criminal act. Since the commission of such an act would be separately punishable in any event, the *Soto* court concluded that section 647(d) was unnecessary and for that reason unconstitutional.

. . .

There are two problems with defendants' argument. First, we can readily envision numerous situations where noncriminal conduct may legitimately give rise to probable cause to believe an individual is in violation of section 647(d). For example, an officer may personally know an individual and may be aware that the individual has repeatedly solicited or committed lewd acts at the same location in the past. Under such circumstances, if the officer observes the individual linger suspiciously in the restroom for an inordinately long period of time, he might properly infer that the suspect did not have an innocent intent. In other cases, a police officer may have information from a reliable informant that a particular individual has disclosed his intent to frequent a particular public restroom to attempt to solicit acts in the restroom; in that situation too, the officer may well have probable cause to infer the suspect's intent even if the suspect has not yet committed indecent exposure or an actual solicitation. Similarly, complaints by citizens who have used a certain restroom that an individual was lingering inside engaging in suggestive conduct—not amounting to an actual solicitation or indecent exposure—may legitimately give rise to a reasonable inference that the individual harbors the illicit intent.

The Model Penal Code is instructive on this point. Section 251.3 of that code sets forth a loitering statute similar to section 647(d), which states: "A person is guilty of a petty misdemeanor if he loiters in or near any public place for the purpose of soliciting or being solicited to engage in deviate sexual relations." Although the commentary to this section recognizes that "the act of loitering in or near a public place [may] not itself [be] reliably confirmatory of an intent to solicit, or to be solicited for, deviate sexual relations," the commentary suggests that in applying the provision officials can assure a properly restrained enforcement by requiring "that the actor confirm the purpose that the trier of fact seeks to infer by some overt act of solicitation *or by some other firm indication that his purpose is within the objective sought to be prevented by Section 251.3.*" (Italics added.) Thus, the Model Penal Code is consistent with our view that a police officer need not observe a criminal act before he may infer a person is loitering with the requisite illicit intent.

The second flaw in both the *Soto* court's and defendants' argument that section 647(d) confers too much discretion upon police was accurately exposed by the Court of Appeal below. "The concern which the defendants expressed, and which apparently moved the *Soto* court, is that 'policemen, prosecutors, and juries' will arbitrarily disregard the definitions [of crimes] and also the rules of probable cause and proof." If this is, indeed, a constitutionally significant flaw, then it is a flaw which would invalidate not only subdivision (d) but many other criminal statutes as well. We consider such a conclusion unreasonable and unrealistic. The defendants' concerns can be adequately dealt with in the course of prosecution of individual cases on their individual facts; these concerns are not an adequate predicate for finding that the statute is invalid on its face.

...

[Dissenting opinion of MOSK, J., joined by BROUSSARD, J., omitted.]

Problem

Problem 1.

Defendant, a minor, is arrested and charged with violation of City's curfew ordinance, which reads as follows:

> No person under the age of eighteen years shall loiter about any public place ... between the hours of ten p.m. and the time of sunrise of the following day when not accompanied by his parent or legal guardian having legal custody and control of such person, or spouse of such person over twenty-one years of age.

What arguments should be made as to the constitutionality of the ordinance?

Ewing v. California

538 U.S. 11, 123 S.Ct. 1179 (2003)

JUSTICE O'CONNOR announced the judgment of the Court and delivered an opinion in which THE CHIEF JUSTICE and JUSTICE KENNEDY join.

In this case, we decide whether the Eighth Amendment prohibits the State of California from sentencing a repeat felon to a prison term of 25 years to life under the State's "Three Strikes and You're Out" law.

I

A

California's three strikes law reflects a shift in the State's sentencing policies toward incapacitating and deterring repeat offenders who threaten the public safety. The law was designed "to ensure longer prison sentences and greater punishment for those who commit a felony and have been previously convicted of serious and/or violent felony offenses." Cal.Penal Code Ann. § 667(b).[p] ...

---

p. Parallel three strikes laws were enacted by the legislature and by the voters through an initiative measure, Proposition 184. Statutory citations are to the earlier legislative version, P.C. §§ 667(b)–(i).

...

B

California's current three strikes law consists of two virtually identical statutory schemes "designed to increase the prison terms of repeat felons." *People v. Superior Court of San Diego Cty. ex rel. Romero*, 13 Cal.4th 497 (1996) (*Romero*). When a defendant is convicted of a felony, and he has previously been convicted of one or more prior felonies defined as "serious" or "violent" in §§ 667.5 and 1192.7, sentencing is conducted pursuant to the three strikes law. Prior convictions must be alleged in the charging document, and the defendant has a right to a jury determination that the prosecution has proved the prior convictions beyond a reasonable doubt.

If the defendant has one prior "serious" or "violent" felony conviction, he must be sentenced to "twice the term otherwise provided as punishment for the current felony conviction." § 667(e)(1). If the defendant has two or more prior "serious" or "violent" felony convictions, he must receive "an indeterminate term of life imprisonment." § 667(e)(2)(A). Defendants sentenced to life under the three strikes law become eligible for parole on a date calculated by reference to a "minimum term," which is the greater of (a) three times the term otherwise provided for the current conviction, (b) 25 years, or (c) the term determined by the court pursuant to § 1170 for the underlying conviction, including any enhancements. §§ 667(e)(2)(A)(i–iii).

Under California law, certain offenses may be classified as either felonies or misdemeanors. These crimes are known as "wobblers." Some crimes that would otherwise be misdemeanors become "wobblers" because of the defendant's prior record. For example, petty theft, a misdemeanor, becomes a "wobbler" when the defendant has previously served a prison term for committing specified theft-related crimes. § 490; § 666. Other crimes, such as grand theft, are "wobblers" regardless of the defendant's prior record. Both types of "wobblers" are triggering offenses under the three strikes law only when they are treated as felonies. Under California law, a "wobbler" is presumptively a felony and "remains a felony except when the discretion is actually exercised" to make the crime a misdemeanor. *People v. Williams*, 27 Cal.2d 220 (1945).

In California, prosecutors may exercise their discretion to charge a "wobbler" as either a felony or a misdemeanor. Likewise, California trial courts have discretion to reduce a "wobbler" charged as a felony to a misdemeanor either before preliminary examination or at sentencing to avoid imposing a three strikes sentence. §§ 17(b)(5), 17(b)(1). In exercising this discretion, the court may consider "those factors that direct similar sentencing decisions," such as "the nature and circumstances of the offense, the defendant's appreciation of and attitude toward the offense, ... [and] the general objectives of sentencing." *People v. Superior Court of Los Angeles Cty. ex rel. Alvarez*, 14 Cal.4th 968 (1997).

California trial courts can also vacate allegations of prior "serious" or "violent" felony convictions, either on motion by the prosecution or *sua sponte*. *Romero, supra.*

In ruling whether to vacate allegations of prior felony convictions, courts consider whether, "in light of the nature and circumstances of [the defendant's] present felonies and prior serious and/or violent felony convictions, and the particulars of his background, character, and prospects, the defendant may be deemed outside the [three strikes'] scheme's spirit, in whole or in part." *People v. Williams*, 17 Cal.4th 148 (1998). Thus, trial courts may avoid imposing a three strikes sentence in two ways: first, by reducing "wobblers" to misdemeanors (which do not qualify as triggering offenses), and second, by vacating allegations of prior "serious" or "violent" felony convictions.

C

On parole from a 9-year prison term, petitioner Gary Ewing walked into the pro shop of the El Segundo Golf Course in Los Angeles County on March 12, 2000. He walked out with three golf clubs, priced at $399 apiece, concealed in his pants leg. A shop employee, whose suspicions were aroused when he observed Ewing limp out of the pro shop, telephoned the police. The police apprehended Ewing in the parking lot.

[Ewing had previously been convicted of theft (1984), felony grand theft auto (1988), petty theft with a prior (1990), battery (1992), theft (1992), burglary (1993), possession of drug paraphernalia (1993), appropriating lost property (1993), unlawful possession of a firearm and trespassing (1993), and three burglaries and a robbery in Long Beach (1993). As a result of the last crimes, he was sentenced to prison for the first time. He was paroled in 1999.]

Only 10 months later, Ewing stole the golf clubs at issue in this case. He was charged with, and ultimately convicted of, one count of felony grand theft of personal property in excess of $400. As required by the three strikes law, the prosecutor formally alleged, and the trial court later found, that Ewing had been convicted previously of four serious or violent felonies for the three burglaries and the robbery in the Long Beach apartment complex.

At the sentencing hearing, Ewing asked the court to reduce the conviction for grand theft, a "wobbler" under California law, to a misdemeanor so as to avoid a three strikes sentence. Ewing also asked the trial court to exercise its discretion to dismiss the allegations of some or all of his prior serious or violent felony convictions, again for purposes of avoiding a three strikes sentence. Before sentencing Ewing, the trial court took note of his entire criminal history, including the fact that he was on parole when he committed his latest offense. The court also heard arguments from defense counsel and a plea from Ewing himself.

In the end, the trial judge determined that the grand theft should remain a felony. The court also ruled that the four prior strikes for the three burglaries and the robbery in Long Beach should stand. As a newly convicted felon with two or more "serious" or "violent" felony convictions in his past, Ewing was sentenced under the three strikes law to 25 years to life.

...

II

A

The Eighth Amendment, which forbids cruel and unusual punishments, contains a "narrow proportionality principle" that "applies to noncapital sentences." *Harmelin v. Michigan*, 501 U.S. 957 (1991) (KENNEDY, J., concurring in part and concurring in judgment). We have most recently addressed the proportionality principle as applied to terms of years in a series of cases beginning with *Rummel v. Estelle*, 445 U.S. 263 (1980).

In *Rummel*, we held that it did not violate the Eighth Amendment for a State to sentence a three-time offender to life in prison with the possibility of parole. Like Ewing, Rummel was sentenced to a lengthy prison term under a recidivism statute. Rummel's two prior offenses were a 1964 felony for "fraudulent use of a credit card to obtain $80 worth of goods or services," and a 1969 felony conviction for "passing a forged check in the amount of $28.36." His triggering offense was a conviction for felony theft—"obtaining $120.75 by false pretenses."

This Court ruled that "[h]aving twice imprisoned him for felonies, Texas was entitled to place upon Rummel the onus of one who is simply unable to bring his conduct within the social norms prescribed by the criminal law of the State." The recidivism statute "is nothing more than a societal decision that when such a person commits yet another felony, he should be subjected to the admittedly serious penalty of incarceration for life, subject only to the State's judgment as to whether to grant him parole." We noted that this Court "has on occasion stated that the Eighth Amendment prohibits imposition of a sentence that is grossly disproportionate to the severity of the crime." But "[o]utside the context of capital punishment, successful challenges to the proportionality of particular sentences have been exceedingly rare." Although we stated that the proportionality principle "would ... come into play in the extreme example ... if a legislature made overtime parking a felony punishable by life imprisonment," we held that "the mandatory life sentence imposed upon this petitioner does not constitute cruel and unusual punishment under the Eighth and Fourteenth Amendments."

In *Hutto v. Davis*, 454 U.S. 370 (1982) (per curiam), the defendant was sentenced to two consecutive terms of 20 years in prison for possession with intent to distribute nine ounces of marijuana and distribution of marijuana. We held that such a sentence was constitutional: "In short, *Rummel* stands for the proposition that federal courts should be reluctant to review legislatively mandated terms of imprisonment, and that successful challenges to the proportionality of particular sentences should be exceedingly rare."

Three years after *Rummel*, in *Solem v. Helm*, 463 U.S. 277 (1983), we held that the Eighth Amendment prohibited "a life sentence without possibility of parole for a seventh nonviolent felony." The triggering offense in *Solem* was "uttering a 'no account' check for $100." We specifically stated that the Eighth Amendment's ban on cruel and unusual punishments "prohibits ... sentences that are disproportionate to the crime committed," and that the "constitutional principle of proportionality has been recognized explicitly in this Court for almost a century." The *Solem* Court then explained that three factors may be relevant to a determination of whether a sentence is so disproportionate that it violates the Eighth Amendment: "(i) the gravity of the offense and the harshness of the penalty; (ii) the sentences imposed on other criminals in the same jurisdiction; and (iii) the sentences imposed for commission of the same crime in other jurisdictions."

Applying these factors in *Solem*, we struck down the defendant's sentence of life without parole. We specifically noted the contrast between that sentence and the sentence in *Rummel*, pursuant to which the defendant was eligible for parole. Indeed, we explicitly declined to overrule *Rummel*.

Eight years after *Solem*, we grappled with the proportionality issue again in *Harmelin*, *supra*. Harmelin was not a recidivism case, but rather involved a first-time offender convicted of possessing 672 grams of cocaine. He was sentenced to life in prison without possibility of parole. A majority of the Court rejected Harmelin's claim that his sentence was so grossly disproportionate that it violated the Eighth Amendment. The Court, however, could not agree on why his proportionality argument failed. Justice SCALIA, joined by THE CHIEF JUSTICE, wrote that the proportionality principle was "an aspect of our death penalty jurisprudence, rather than a generalizable aspect of Eighth Amendment law." He would thus have declined to apply gross disproportionality principles except in reviewing capital sentences.

Justice KENNEDY, joined by two other Members of the Court, concurred in part and concurred in the judgment. Justice KENNEDY specifically recognized that "[t]he Eighth Amendment proportionality principle also applies to noncapital sentences." He then identified four principles of proportionality review—"the primacy of the legislature, the variety of legitimate penological schemes, the nature of our federal system, and the requirement that proportionality review be guided by objective factors"—that "inform the final one: the Eighth Amendment does not require strict proportionality between crime and sentence. Rather, it forbids only extreme sentences that are 'grossly disproportionate' to the crime."[q]

The proportionality principles in our cases distilled in Justice KENNEDY's concurrence guide our application of the Eighth Amendment in the new context that we are called upon to consider.

B

For many years, most States have had laws providing for enhanced sentencing of repeat offenders. Yet between 1993 and 1995, three strikes laws effected a sea change

q. In *Harmelin*, Justice Kennedy described "gross disproportionality" as a "threshold" test. In the rare case where comparison of the crime committed and the sentence imposed leads to an inference of gross disproportionality, the courts should then examine the sentences imposed for other crimes in the same jurisdictions and the sentences imposed for the same crime in other jurisdictions to validate that initial judgment. 501 U.S. at 1004–05.

in criminal sentencing throughout the Nation.[1] These laws responded to widespread public concerns about crime by targeting the class of offenders who pose the greatest threat to public safety: career criminals. As one of the chief architects of California's three strikes law has explained: "Three Strikes was intended to go beyond simply making sentences tougher. It was intended to be a focused effort to create a sentencing policy that would use the judicial system to reduce serious and violent crime." Ardaiz, *California's Three Strikes Law: History, Expectations, Consequences*, 32 McGeorge L.Rev. 1 (2000) (hereinafter Ardaiz).

Throughout the States, legislatures enacting three strikes laws made a deliberate policy choice that individuals who have repeatedly engaged in serious or violent criminal behavior, and whose conduct has not been deterred by more conventional approaches to punishment, must be isolated from society in order to protect the public safety. Though three strikes laws may be relatively new, our tradition of deferring to state legislatures in making and implementing such important policy decisions is longstanding.

Our traditional deference to legislative policy choices finds a corollary in the principle that the Constitution "does not mandate adoption of any one penological theory." *Harmelin* (KENNEDY, J., concurring in part and concurring in judgment). A sentence can have a variety of justifications, such as incapacitation, deterrence, retribution, or rehabilitation. Some or all of these justifications may play a role in a State's sentencing scheme. Selecting the sentencing rationales is generally a policy choice to be made by state legislatures, not federal courts.

When the California Legislature enacted the three strikes law, it made a judgment that protecting the public safety requires incapacitating criminals who have already been convicted of at least one serious or violent crime. Nothing in the Eighth Amendment prohibits California from making that choice. To the contrary, our cases establish that "States have a valid interest in deterring and segregating habitual criminals." *Parke v. Raley*, 506 U.S. 20 (1992); *Oyler v. Boles*, 368 U.S. 448 (1962) ("[T]he constitutionality of the practice of inflicting severer criminal penalties upon habitual offenders is no longer open to serious challenge"). Recidivism has long been recognized as a legitimate basis for increased punishment.

California's justification is no pretext. Recidivism is a serious public safety concern in California and throughout the Nation. According to a recent report, approximately 67 percent of former inmates released from state prisons were charged with at least one "serious" new crime within three years of their release. In particular, released property offenders like Ewing had higher recidivism rates than those released after committing violent, drug, or public-order offenses. Approximately 73 percent of the property offenders released in 1994 were arrested again within three years, compared

1. It is hardly surprising that the statistics relied upon by Justice BREYER show that prior to the enactment of the three strikes law, "*no* one like Ewing could have served more than *10* years in prison." Profound disappointment with the perceived lenity of criminal sentencing (especially for repeat felons) led to passage of three strikes laws in the first place.

to approximately 61 percent of the violent offenders, 62 percent of the public-order offenders, and 66 percent of the drug offenders.

In 1996, when the Sacramento Bee studied 233 three strikes offenders in California, it found that they had an aggregate of 1,165 prior felony convictions, an average of 5 apiece. The prior convictions included 322 robberies and 262 burglaries. About 84 percent of the 233 three strikes offenders had been convicted of at least one violent crime. In all, they were responsible for 17 homicides, 7 attempted slayings, and 91 sexual assaults and child molestations. The Sacramento Bee concluded, based on its investigation, that "[i]n the vast majority of the cases, regardless of the third strike, the [three strikes] law is snaring [the] long-term habitual offenders with multiple felony convictions...."

The State's interest in deterring crime also lends some support to the three strikes law. We have long viewed both incapacitation and deterrence as rationales for recidivism statutes: "[A] recidivist statute['s] ... primary goals are to deter repeat offenders and, at some point in the life of one who repeatedly commits criminal offenses serious enough to be punished as felonies, to segregate that person from the rest of society for an extended period of time." *Rummel, supra.* Four years after the passage of California's three strikes law, the recidivism rate of parolees returned to prison for the commission of a new crime dropped by nearly 25 percent. California Dept. of Justice, Office of the Attorney General, "Three Strikes and You're Out"—Its Impact on the California Criminal Justice System After Four Years 10 (1998). Even more dramatically:

> "[a]n unintended but positive consequence of 'Three Strikes' has been the impact on parolees leaving the state. More California parolees are now leaving the state than parolees from other jurisdictions entering California. This striking turnaround started in 1994. It was the first time more parolees left the state than entered since 1976. This trend has continued and in 1997 more than 1,000 net parolees left California."

To be sure, California's three strikes law has sparked controversy. Critics have doubted the law's wisdom, cost-efficiency, and effectiveness in reaching its goals. This criticism is appropriately directed at the legislature, which has primary responsibility for making the difficult policy choices that underlie any criminal sentencing scheme. We do not sit as a "superlegislature" to second-guess these policy choices. It is enough that the State of California has a reasonable basis for believing that dramatically enhanced sentences for habitual felons "advance[s] the goals of [its] criminal justice system in any substantial way." See *Solem.*

III

Against this backdrop, we consider Ewing's claim that his three strikes sentence of 25 years to life is unconstitutionally disproportionate to his offense of "shoplifting three golf clubs." We first address the gravity of the offense compared to the harshness of the penalty. At the threshold, we note that Ewing incorrectly frames the issue. The gravity of his offense was not merely "shoplifting three golf clubs." Rather, Ewing was convicted of felony grand theft for stealing nearly $1,200 worth of merchandise after previously having been convicted of at least two "violent" or "serious" felonies. Even standing alone, Ewing's theft should not be taken lightly. His crime was certainly not "one of the most passive felonies a person could commit." *Solem*, *supra*.... Theft of $1,200 in property is a felony under federal law and in the vast majority of States.

That grand theft is a "wobbler" under California law is of no moment. Though California courts have discretion to reduce a felony grand theft charge to a misdemeanor, it remains a felony for all purposes "unless and until the trial court imposes a misdemeanor sentence." *In re Anderson*, 69 Cal.2d 613 (1968) (Tobriner, J., concurring). "The purpose of the trial judge's sentencing discretion" to downgrade certain felonies is to "impose a misdemeanor sentence in those cases in which the rehabilitation of the convicted defendant either does not require or would be adversely affected by, incarceration in a state prison as a felon." *Anderson*, *supra* (Tobriner, J., concurring). Under California law, the reduction is not based on the notion that a "wobbler" is "conceptually a misdemeanor." *Necochea v. Superior Court*, 23 Cal.App.3d 1012 (1972). Rather, it is "intended to extend misdemeanant treatment to a potential felon." In Ewing's case, however, the trial judge justifiably exercised her discretion not to extend such lenient treatment given Ewing's long criminal history.

In weighing the gravity of Ewing's offense, we must place on the scales not only his current felony, but also his long history of felony recidivism. Any other approach would fail to accord proper deference to the policy judgments that find expression in the legislature's choice of sanctions. In imposing a three strikes sentence, the State's interest is not merely punishing the offense of conviction, or the "triggering" offense: "[I]t is in addition the interest ... in dealing in a harsher manner with those who by repeated criminal acts have shown that they are simply incapable of conforming to the norms of society as established by its criminal law." See *Rummel*, *supra*; *Solem*, *supra*. To give full effect to the State's choice of this legitimate penological goal, our proportionality review of Ewing's sentence must take that goal into account.

Ewing's sentence is justified by the State's public-safety interest in incapacitating and deterring recidivist felons, and amply supported by his own long, serious criminal record. Ewing has been convicted of numerous misdemeanor and felony offenses, served nine separate terms of incarceration, and committed most of his crimes while on probation or parole. His prior "strikes" were serious felonies including robbery and three residential burglaries. To be sure, Ewing's sentence is a long one. But it reflects a rational legislative judgment, entitled to deference, that offenders who have committed serious or violent felonies and who continue to commit felonies must be incapacitated. The State of California "was entitled to place upon [Ewing] the onus of one who is simply unable to bring his conduct within the social norms prescribed by the criminal law of the State." *Rummel*, *supra*. Ewing's is not "the rare case in which a threshold comparison of the crime committed and the sentence imposed leads to an inference of gross disproportionality." *Harmelin* (Kennedy, J., concurring in part and concurring in judgment).

We hold that Ewing's sentence of 25 years to life in prison, imposed for the offense of felony grand theft under the three strikes law, is not grossly disproportionate and therefore does not violate the Eighth Amendment's prohibition on cruel and unusual punishments. The judgment of the California Court of Appeal is affirmed.

Justice Scalia, concurring in the judgment.

In my concurring opinion in *Harmelin v. Michigan*, 501 U.S. 957 (1991), I concluded that the Eighth Amendment's prohibition of "cruel and unusual punishments" was aimed at excluding only certain *modes* of punishment, and was not a "guarantee against disproportionate sentences." Out of respect for the principle of *stare decisis*, I might nonetheless accept the contrary holding of *Solem v. Helm*, 463 U.S. 277 (1983) that the Eighth Amendment contains a narrow proportionality principle—if I felt I could intelligently apply it. This case demonstrates why I cannot.

Proportionality—the notion that the punishment should fit the crime—is inherently a concept tied to the penological goal of retribution. "[I]t becomes difficult even to speak intelligently of 'proportionality,' once deterrence and rehabilitation are given significant weight," *Harmelin, supra* not to mention giving weight to the purpose of California's three strikes law: incapacitation. In the present case, the game is up once the plurality has acknowledged that "the Constitution does not mandate adoption of any one penological theory," and that a "sentence can have a variety of justifications, such as incapacitation, deterrence, retribution, or rehabilitation." That acknowledgment having been made, it no longer suffices merely to assess "the gravity of the offense compared to the harshness of the penalty"; that classic description of the proportionality principle (alone and in itself quite resistant to policy-free, legal analysis) now becomes merely the "first" step of the inquiry. Having completed that step (by a discussion which, in all fairness, does not convincingly establish that 25-years-to-life is a "proportionate" punishment for stealing three golf clubs), the plurality must then *add* an analysis to show that "Ewing's sentence is justified by the State's public-safety interest in incapacitating and deterring recidivist felons."

Which indeed it is—though why that has anything to do with the principle of proportionality is a mystery. Perhaps the plurality should revise its terminology, so that what it reads into the Eighth Amendment is not the unstated proposition that all punishment should be reasonably proportionate to the gravity of the offense, but rather the unstated proposition that all punishment should reasonably pursue the multiple purposes of the criminal law. That formulation would make it clearer than ever, of course, that the plurality is not applying law but evaluating policy.

Because I agree that petitioner's sentence does not violate the Eighth Amendment's prohibition against cruel and unusual punishments, I concur in the judgment.

[Concurring opinion of Thomas, J. and dissenting opinion of Stevens, J., joined by Souter, Ginsburg and Breyer, JJ., omitted.]

Justice Breyer, with whom Justice Stevens, Justice Souter, and Justice Ginsburg join, dissenting.

The constitutional question is whether the "three strikes" sentence imposed by California upon repeat-offender Gary Ewing is "grossly disproportionate" to his crime. The sentence amounts to a real prison term of at least 25 years. The sentence-triggering criminal conduct consists of the theft of three golf clubs priced at a total of $1,197. The offender has a criminal history that includes four felony convictions arising out of three separate burglaries (one armed). In *Solem v. Helm*, 463 U.S. 277 (1983), the Court found grossly disproportionate a somewhat longer sentence imposed on a recidivist offender for triggering criminal conduct that was somewhat less severe. In my view, the differences are not determinative, and the Court should reach the same ultimate conclusion here.

. . .

II

Ewing's claim crosses the gross disproportionality "threshold." First, precedent makes clear that Ewing's sentence raises a serious disproportionality question. Ewing is a recidivist. Hence the two cases most directly in point are those in which the Court considered the constitutionality of recidivist sentencing: *Rummel v. Estelle*, 445 U.S. 263 (1980) and *Solem*, *supra*. Ewing's claim falls between these two cases. It is stronger than the claim presented in *Rummel*, where the Court upheld a recidivist's sentence as constitutional. It is weaker than the claim presented in *Solem*, where the Court struck down a recidivist sentence as unconstitutional.

Three kinds of sentence-related characteristics define the relevant comparative spectrum: (a) the length of the prison term in real time, *i.e.*, the time that the offender is likely actually to spend in prison; (b) the sentence-triggering criminal conduct, *i.e.*, the offender's actual behavior or other offense-related circumstances; and (c) the offender's criminal history.

In *Rummel*, the Court held constitutional (a) a sentence of life imprisonment *with parole available within 10 to 12 years*, (b) for the offense of obtaining $120 by false pretenses, (c) committed by an offender with two prior felony convictions (involving small amounts of money). In *Solem*, the Court held unconstitutional (a) a sentence of life imprisonment *without parole*, (b) for the crime of writing a $100 check on a nonexistent bank account, (c) committed by an offender with six prior felony convictions (including three for burglary). Which of the three pertinent comparative factors made the constitutional difference?

The third factor, prior record, cannot explain the difference. The offender's prior record was *worse* in *Solem*, where the Court found the sentence too long, than in *Rummel*, where the Court upheld the sentence. The second factor, offense conduct, cannot explain the difference. The nature of the triggering offense—viewed in terms of the actual monetary loss—in the two cases was about the same. The one critical factor that explains the difference in the outcome is the length of the likely prison term measured in real time. In *Rummel*, where the Court upheld the sentence, the state sentencing statute authorized parole for the offender, Rummel, after 10 or 12 years. In *Solem*, where the Court struck down the sentence, the sentence required the offender, Helm, to spend the rest of his life in prison.

Now consider the present case. The third factor, *offender characteristics*—*i.e.*, prior record—does not differ significantly here from that in *Solem*. Ewing's prior record consists of four prior felony convictions (involving three burglaries, one with a knife) contrasted with Helm's six prior felony convictions (including three burglaries, though none with weapons). The second factor, *offense behavior*, is worse than that in *Solem*, but only to a degree. It would be difficult to say that the actual behavior itself here (shoplifting) differs significantly from that at issue in *Solem* (passing a bad check) or in *Rummel* (obtaining money through false pretenses). Rather the difference lies in the *value* of the goods obtained. That difference, measured in terms of the most relevant feature (loss to the victim, *i.e.*, wholesale value) and adjusted for the irrelevant feature of inflation, comes down (in 1979 values) to about $379 here compared with $100 in *Solem*, or (in 1973 values) to $232 here compared with $120.75 in *Rummel*. Alternatively, if one measures the inflation-adjusted value difference in terms of the golf clubs' sticker price, it comes down to $505 here compared to $100 in *Solem*, or $309 here compared to $120.75 in *Rummel*.

The difference in *length* of the real prison term—the first, and critical, factor in *Solem* and *Rummel*—is considerably more important. Ewing's sentence here amounts, in real terms, to at least 25 years without parole or good-time credits. That sentence is considerably shorter than Helm's sentence in *Solem*, which amounted, in real terms, to life in prison. Nonetheless Ewing's real prison term is more than twice as long as the term at issue in *Rummel*, which amounted, in real terms, to at least 10 or 12 years. And, Ewing's sentence, unlike Rummel's (but like Helm's sentence in *Solem*), is long enough to consume the productive remainder of almost any offender's life. (It means that Ewing himself, seriously ill when sentenced at age 38, will likely die in prison.)

The upshot is that the length of the real prison term—the factor that explains the *Solem* /*Rummel* difference in outcome—places Ewing closer to *Solem* than to *Rummel*, though the greater value of the golf clubs that Ewing stole moves Ewing's case back slightly in *Rummel*'s direction. Overall, the comparison places Ewing's sentence well within the twilight zone between *Solem* and *Rummel*—a zone where the argument for unconstitutionality is substantial, where the cases themselves cannot determine the constitutional outcome.

Second, Ewing's sentence on its face imposes one of the most severe punishments available upon a recidivist who subsequently engaged in one of the less serious forms of criminal conduct. I do not deny the seriousness of shoplifting, which an *amicus curiae* tells us costs retailers in the range of $30 billion annually. But consider that conduct in terms of the factors that this Court mentioned in *Solem*—the "harm caused or threatened to the victim or society," the "absolute magnitude of the crime," and the offender's "culpability." In respect to all three criteria, the sentence-triggering behavior here ranks well toward the bottom of the criminal conduct scale.

The Solicitor General has urged us to consider three other criteria: the "frequency" of the crime's commission, the "ease or difficulty of detection," and "the degree to which the crime may be deterred by differing amounts of punishment." When considered in terms of these criteria—or at least the latter two—the triggering conduct also ranks toward the bottom of the scale. Unlike, say, drug crimes, shoplifting often takes place in stores open to other customers whose presence, along with that of store employees or cameras, can help to detect the crime. Nor is there evidence presented here that the law enforcement community believes lengthy prison terms necessary adequately to deter shoplifting. To the contrary, well-publicized instances of shoplifting suggest that the offense is often punished without any prison sentence at all. On the other hand, shoplifting is a frequently committed crime; but "frequency," standing alone, cannot make a critical difference. Otherwise traffic offenses would warrant even more serious punishment.

This case, of course, involves shoplifting engaged in by a *recidivist*. One might argue that *any* crime committed by a recidivist is a serious crime potentially warranting a 25-year sentence. But this Court rejected that view in *Solem*, and in *Harmelin*, with the recognition that "no penalty is *per se* constitutional." Our cases make clear that, in cases involving recidivist offenders, we must focus upon "the [offense] that triggers the life sentence," with recidivism playing a "relevant," but not necessarily determinative, role. And here, as I have said, that offense is among the less serious, while the punishment is among the most serious.

Third, some objective evidence suggests that many experienced judges would consider Ewing's sentence disproportionately harsh. The United States Sentencing Commission (having based the federal Sentencing Guidelines primarily upon its review of how judges had actually sentenced offenders) does not include shoplifting (or similar theft-related offenses) among the crimes that might trigger especially long sentences for recidivists.

Taken together, these three circumstances make clear that Ewing's "gross disproportionality" argument is a strong one. That being so, his claim *must* pass the "threshold" test. If it did not, what would be the function of the test? A threshold test must permit *arguably* unconstitutional sentences, not only *actually* unconstitutional sentences, to pass the threshold—at least where the arguments for unconstitutionality are unusually strong ones. A threshold test that blocked every ultimately invalid constitutional claim—even strong ones—would not be a *threshold* test but a *determinative* test. And, it would be a *determinative* test that failed to take account of highly pertinent sentencing information, namely, comparison with other sentences. Sentencing comparisons are particularly important because they provide proportionality review with *objective* content. By way of contrast, a threshold test makes the assessment of constitutionality highly subjective. And, of course, so to transform that *threshold* test would violate this Court's earlier precedent.

III

[Justice Breyer compared Ewing's sentence, focusing on the actual time to be served, with the sentence he would have received under California law prior to the enactment of the "three strikes" law, with sentences under California law for far worse crimes, *e.g.*, first degree murder (90% of first degree murderers serve less than 20 years), arson with great bodily injury (5, 7 or 9 years), voluntary manslaughter (3, 6 or 11 years) and with the sentence he would have received under federal or other states' laws. He concluded that Ewing's sentence was "virtually unique in its harshness."

[Justice Breyer then argued that California had no "special criminal justice concerns" that might justify such a disproportionately harsh sentence. The critical line drawn by the statutes between felonies and misdemeanors was arbitrary in light of the stated purpose "to reduce serious and violent crime" and created a number of anomalies. First, since California defines a number of crimes, like Ewing's, as "wobblers," less serious crimes, *e.g.*, stealing more than $100 worth of chickens, nuts, or avocadoes, might be deemed a third strike where more serious crimes, *e.g.*, child neglect, would not. Second, the order in which the defendant committed the crimes becomes critical: if the chicken theft is the first crime and the defendant then commits two violent felonies, he is not eligible for three strikes treatment, but if the chicken theft is the third, he is. Finally, California's petty theft with a prior wobbler (which classifies a petty theft as a "felony" if, but only if, the offender has a prior record that includes at least one conviction for certain theft-related offenses) creates a situation where a petty theft may be a third strike if the defendant previously committed a theft-type crime but not if the prior crimes were all violent crimes.]

V

Justice Scalia and Justice Thomas argue that we should not review for gross disproportionality a sentence to a term of years. Otherwise, we make it too difficult for legislators and sentencing judges to determine just when their sentencing laws and practices pass constitutional muster.

I concede that a bright-line rule would give legislators and sentencing judges more guidance. But application of the Eighth Amendment to a sentence of a term of years requires a case-by-case approach. And, in my view, like that of the plurality, meaningful enforcement of the Eighth Amendment demands that application—even if only at sentencing's outer bounds.

A case-by-case approach can nonetheless offer guidance through example. Ewing's sentence is, at a minimum, 2 to 3 times the length of sentences that other jurisdictions would impose in similar circumstances. That sentence itself is sufficiently long to require a typical offender to spend virtually all the remainder of his active life in prison. These and the other factors that I have discussed, along with the questions that I have asked along the way, should help to identify "gross disproportionality" in a fairly objective way—at the outer bounds of sentencing.

In sum, even if I accept for present purposes the plurality's analytical framework, Ewing's sentence (life imprisonment with a minimum term of 25 years) is grossly disproportionate to the triggering offense conduct—stealing three golf clubs—Ewing's recidivism notwithstanding.

For these reasons, I dissent.

[Appendix to Opinion of Breyer, J. omitted.]

Note and Problem

Problem 2.

Under California's Sex Offender Registration Act, a convicted sex offender must register with the Chief of Police where he or she is living and must register any change of residence within five working days. (P.C. § 290(b)) The registrant must annually update his or her registration within five working days of his or her birthday. (P.C. § 290.012(a)) A violation of these registration requirements is a felony. Defendant previously had been convicted of possession of cocaine, lewd act with a child and attempted rape (one incident) and robbery and had served three prison terms. In May, Defendant changed his residence and registered with the police department. The following February, Defendant had a birthday, but failed to update his registration. Three months later, within a year of his prior registration, Defendant updated his registration. Defendant was convicted of a violation of P.C. § 290.012(a) for failing to update his registration in February, and he was sentenced to 28 years to life under California's Three Strikes Law (25 to life for the third strike plus a year each for his prior prison terms). Only seven states authorize a recidivist sentence of longer than 10 years, and California is the only state that mandates a life sentence with a mandatory prison term of 25 years for noncompliance with a registration requirement. What are the arguments as to whether the sentence violates the Eighth Amendment?

Sentencing for Juvenile Crimes. In contrast to the "narrow proportionality principle" the Supreme Court has applied to prison sentences, the Court has applied a more robust proportionality principle to the death penalty, holding the death penalty unconstitutional, not only as applied to particular crimes [see Chapter 15], but also as applied to particular classes of defendants. *See Atkins v. Virginia*, 536 U.S. 304 (2002) (intellectually disabled defendants); *Roper v. Simmons*, 543 U.S. 551 (2005) (juveniles). The two lines of cases came together in *Graham v. Florida*, 560 U.S. 48, 130 S.Ct. 2011 (2010). In *Graham*, the defendant was convicted of a burglary he committed when he was 16 years old, and he was sentenced to life in prison without the possibility of parole. Relying on *Roper v. Simmons*, the Court held that, because juveniles are, as a class, less culpable than adults, because a juvenile receiving a life sentence will serve more years than an adult with the same sentence and because the sentence was imposed for a nonhomicide offense, the sentence was disproportionate and violated the Eighth Amendment.

Graham was followed by *Miller v. Alabama*, ___ U.S. ___, 132 S.Ct. 2455 (2012), where the Court, relying on *Graham* and *Woodson v. North Carolina*, 428 U.S. 280 (1976) (holding unconstitutional a mandatory death penalty for particular crimes), held that mandatory life imprisonment without parole for a defendant convicted of capital murder, but under the age of 18 at the time of the crime, constitutes cruel and unusual punishment. Subsequently, in *Montgomery v. Louisiana*, ___ U.S. ___, 136 S.Ct. 718 (2016), the Court held that *Miller* announced a new rule of substantive law that had to be applied retroactively.

The California courts have wrestled with several questions about how to apply *Graham/Miller*. One question was whether *Graham* applies where cumulative sentences for a nonhomicidal crime amount to a *de facto* life without parole sentence. In *People v. Caballero*, 55 Cal.4th 262 (2012), the California Supreme Court addressed the issue in a case where the defendant received consecutive sentences plus enhancements for three counts of attempted murder committed while he was a juvenile, for a total sentence of 110 years to life. The court held that *Graham* did apply and the sentence was unconstitutional because the defendant had no "meaningful opportunity to obtain release based on demonstrated maturity and rehabilitation." Another question was whether a Penal Code section making life without the possibility of parole the "presumptive" punishment for juvenile special-circumstance murderers violated *Miller*. The California Supreme Court, in *People v. Gutierrez*, 58 Cal.4th 1354 (2014), held that, in light of *Miller*, there could be no presumption in favor of a life without parole sentence.

Yick Wo v. Hopkins

118 U.S. 356, 6 S.Ct. 1064 (1886)

Mr. Justice Matthews delivered the opinion of the court.

[The Board of Supervisors of the City and County of San Francisco passed ordinances which made it unlawful to operate a laundry without the consent of the Board of Supervisors except in a brick or stone building. Yick Wo, a Chinese subject, had operated a laundry for 22 years in a wooden building and had certificates from fire and health inspectors certifying that his laundry met all applicable standards. Nevertheless, when Yick Wo applied to the Board for permission to continue to operate his laundry, permission was denied. At the time there were about 320 laundries in the City and County of San Francisco, of which about 240 were owned and conducted by subjects of China and that of the 320, about 310 were constructed of wood. Two hundred other Chinese subjects in a similar position to Yick Wo also petitioned the Board for permission to continue their businesses, and their petitions were denied. However, all the petitions of those who were not Chinese, with one exception, were granted. Yick Wo continued to operate his laundry, and he was arrested and found guilty of violating the ordinances and sentenced to pay a fine of $10. Yick Wo sought relief by a petition for a writ of habeas corpus, and the California Supreme Court denied his petition.]

The ordinance drawn in question in the present case ... does not prescribe a rule and conditions, for the regulation of the use of property for laundry purposes, to which all similarly situated may conform. It allows, without restriction, the use for such purposes of buildings of brick or stone; but, as to wooden buildings, constituting nearly all those in previous use, it divides the owners or occupiers into two classes, not having respect to their personal character and qualifications for the business, nor the situation and nature and adaptation of the buildings themselves, but merely by an arbitrary line, on one side of which are those who are permitted to pursue their industry by the mere will and consent of the supervisors, and on the other those from whom that consent is withheld, at their mere will and pleasure. And both classes are alike only in this: that they are tenants at will, under the supervisors, of their means of living....

The rights of the petitioners, as affected by the proceedings of which they complain, are not less because they are aliens and subjects of the emperor of China.... The fourteenth amendment to the constitution is not confined to the protection of citizens. It says: "Nor shall any state deprive any person of life, liberty, or property without due process of law; nor deny to any person within its jurisdiction the equal protection of the laws." These provisions are universal in their application, to all persons within the territorial jurisdiction, without regard to any differences of race, of color, or of nationality; and the equal protection of the laws is a pledge of the protection of equal laws....

It is contended on the part of the petitioners that the ordinances for violations of which they are severally sentenced to imprisonment are void on their face, as being within the prohibitions of the fourteenth amendment, and, in the alternative, if not so, that they are void by reason of their administration, operating unequally, so as to punish in the present petitioners what is permitted to others as lawful, without any distinction of circumstances,—an unjust and illegal discrimination, it is claimed, which, though not made expressly by the ordinances, is made possible by them.

...

In the present cases, we are not obliged to reason from the probable to the actual, and pass upon the validity of the ordinances complained of, as tried merely by the opportunities which their terms afford, of unequal and unjust discrimination in their administration; for the cases present the ordinances in actual operation, and the facts shown establish an administration directed so exclusively against a particular class of persons as to warrant and require the conclusion that, whatever may have been the intent of the ordinances as adopted, they are applied by the public authorities..., with a mind so unequal and oppressive as to amount to a practical denial by the state of that equal protection of the laws which is secured to the petitioners, as to all other persons, by the broad and benign provisions of the fourteenth amendment to the constitution of the United States. Though the law itself be fair on its face, and impartial in appearance, yet, if it is applied and administered by public authority with an evil eye and an unequal hand, so as practically to make unjust and illegal discriminations between persons in similar circumstances, material to their rights, the denial of equal justice is still within the prohibition of the constitution.

The present cases are within this class. It appears that both petitioners have complied with every requisite deemed by the law, or by the public officers charged with its administration, necessary for the protection of neighboring property from fire, or as a precaution against injury to the public health. No reason whatever, except the will of the supervisors, is assigned why they should not be permitted to carry on, in the accustomed manner, their harmless and useful occupation, on which they depend for a livelihood; and while this consent of the supervisors is withheld from them, and from 200 others who have also petitioned, all of whom happen to be Chinese subjects, 80 others, not Chinese subjects, are permitted to carry on the same business under similar conditions. The fact of this discrimination is admitted. No reason for it is shown, and the conclusion cannot be resisted that no reason for it exists except hostility to the race and nationality to which the petitioners belong, and which, in the eye of the law, is not justified. The discrimination is therefore illegal, and the public administration which enforces it is a denial of the equal protection of the laws, and a violation of the fourteenth amendment of the constitution. The imprisonment of the petitioners is therefore illegal, and they must be discharged....

Reasoning

Holding

Note

Caswell Revisited. In *Baluyut v. Superior Court*, 12 Cal. 4th 826 (1996), the California Supreme Court upheld the dismissal of charges against defendants on the basis of discriminatory enforcement. Defendants, homosexual men, were charged with violation of P.C. § 647(a), soliciting or engaging in "lewd or dissolute conduct" in a public place. In support of their discriminatory enforcement claim, Defendants presented arrest reports covering ten arrests over a two-year period, all resulting from "decoy" operations at an adult bookstore frequented by homosexual men. Other evidence established that the modus operandi of the decoy officers was typical of a "cruising" pattern of homosexual men, inviting them to make contact with the decoy officer and that the operation was not directed at the bookstore because of any neutral reason (*e.g.*, complaints from neighbors). The Supreme Court rejected the prosecution's contention that Defendants were required to prove the arresting officers had the "specific intent" to punish Defendants because of their sexual orientation and found the evidence sufficient to establish discriminatory enforcement.

Michael M. v. Superior Court

450 U.S. 464, 101 S.Ct. 1200 (1981)

Supreme Court

Justice Rehnquist announced the judgment of the Court and delivered an opinion, in which The Chief Justice, Justice Stewart, and Justice Powell joined.

The question presented in this case is whether California's "statutory rape" law, § 261.5 of the Cal. Penal Code, violates the Equal Protection Clause of the Fourteenth Amendment. Section 261.5 defines unlawful sexual intercourse as "an act of sexual intercourse accomplished with a female not the wife of the perpetrator, where the female is under the age of 18 years." The statute thus makes men alone criminally liable for the act of sexual intercourse.

Issue law

Issue over CA law

facts

In July 1978, a complaint was filed in the Municipal Court of Sonoma County, Cal., alleging that petitioner, then a 17 ½-year-old male, had had unlawful sexual intercourse with a female under the age of 18, in violation of § 261.5. The evidence, adduced at a preliminary hearing showed that at approximately midnight on June 3, 1978, petitioner and two friends approached Sharon, a 16 ½-year-old female, and her sister as they waited at a bus stop. Petitioner and Sharon, who had already been drinking, moved away from the others and began to kiss. After being struck in the face for rebuffing petitioner's initial advances, Sharon submitted to sexual intercourse with petitioner. Prior to trial, petitioner sought to set aside the information on both state and federal constitutional grounds, asserting that § 261.5 unlawfully discriminated on the basis of gender. The trial court and the California Court of Appeal denied petitioner's request for relief and petitioner sought review in the Supreme Court of California.

The Supreme Court held that "section 261.5 discriminates on the basis of sex because only females may be victims, and only males may violate the section." The court then subjected the classification to "strict scrutiny," stating that it must be justified by a compelling state interest. It found that the classification was "supported not by mere social convention but by the immutable physiological fact that it is the female exclusively who can become pregnant." Canvassing "the tragic human costs of illegitimate teenage pregnancies," including the large number of teenage abortions, the increased medical risk associated with teenage pregnancies, and the social consequences of teenage childbearing, the court concluded that the State has a compelling interest in preventing such pregnancies. Because males alone can "physiologically cause the result which the law properly seeks to avoid," the court further held that the gender classification was readily justified as a means of identifying offender and victim. For the reasons stated below, we affirm the judgment of the California Supreme Court.

[The Court discussed its various decisions on the standard of review in Fourteenth Amendment sex discrimination cases.]

The justification for the statute offered by the State, and accepted by the Supreme Court of California, is that the legislature sought to prevent illegitimate teenage pregnancies. That finding, of course, is entitled to great deference. And although our cases establish that the State's asserted reason for the enactment of a statute may be rejected, if it "could not have been a goal of the legislation," *Weinberger v. Wiesenfeld*, 420 U.S. 636 (1975), this is not such a case.

We are satisfied not only that the prevention of illegitimate pregnancy is at least one of the "purposes" of the statute, but also that the State has a strong interest in preventing such pregnancy. At the risk of stating the obvious, teenage pregnancies, which have increased dramatically over the last two decades,[3] have significant social, medical, and economic consequences for both the mother and her child, and the State.[4] Of particular concern to the State is that approximately half of all teenage

3. In 1976 approximately one million 15-to-19-year-olds became pregnant, one-tenth of all women in that age group. Two-thirds of the pregnancies were illegitimate. Illegitimacy rates for teenagers (births per 1,000 unmarried females ages 14 to 19) increased 75% for 14-to-17-year-olds between 1961 and 1974 and 33% for 18-to-19-year-olds.

4. The risk of maternal death is 60% higher for a teenager under the age of 15 than for a women in her early twenties. The risk is 13% higher for 15-to-19-year-olds. The statistics further show that most teenage mothers drop out of school and face a bleak economic future.

pregnancies end in abortion.[5] And of those children who are born, their illegitimacy makes them likely candidates to become wards of the State.

We need not be medical doctors to discern that young men and young women are not similarly situated with respect to the problems and the risks of sexual intercourse. Only women may become pregnant, and they suffer disproportionately the profound physical, emotional and psychological consequences of sexual activity. The statute at issue here protects women from sexual intercourse at an age when those consequences are particularly severe.

The question thus boils down to whether a State may attack the problem of sexual intercourse and teenage pregnancy directly by prohibiting a male from having sexual intercourse with a minor female. We hold that such a statute is sufficiently related to the State's objectives to pass constitutional muster.

Because virtually all of the significant harmful and inescapably identifiable consequences of teenage pregnancy fall on the young female, a legislature acts well within its authority when it elects to punish only the participant who, by nature, suffers few of the consequences of his conduct. It is hardly unreasonable for a legislature acting to protect minor females to exclude them from punishment. Moreover, the risk of pregnancy itself constitutes a substantial deterrence to young females. No similar natural sanctions deter males. A criminal sanction imposed solely on males thus serves to roughly "equalize" the deterrents on the sexes.

We are unable to accept petitioner's contention that the statute is impermissibly underinclusive and must, in order to pass judicial scrutiny, be broadened so as to hold the female as criminally liable as the male. It is argued that this statute is not necessary to deter teenage pregnancy because a gender-neutral statute, where both male and female would be subject to prosecution, would serve that goal equally well. The relevant inquiry, however, is not whether the statute is drawn as precisely as it might have been, but whether the line chosen by the California Legislature is within constitutional limitations.

In any event, we cannot say that a gender-neutral statute would be as effective as the statute California has chosen to enact. The State persuasively contends that a gender-neutral statute would frustrate its interest in effective enforcement. Its view is that a female is surely less likely to report violations of the statute if she herself would be subject to criminal prosecution. In an area already fraught with prosecutorial difficulties, we decline to hold that the Equal Protection Clause requires a legislature to enact a statute so broad that it may well be incapable of enforcement.

. . .

In upholding the California statute we also recognize that this is not a case where a statute is being challenged on the grounds that it "invidiously discriminates" against females. To the contrary, the statute places a burden on males which is not shared

5. This is because teenagers are disproportionately likely to seek abortions. In 1978, for example, teenagers in California had approximately 54,000 abortions and 53,800 live births.

by females. But we find nothing to suggest that men, because of past discrimination or peculiar disadvantages, are in need of the special solicitude of the courts. Nor is this a case where the gender classification is made "solely for ... administrative convenience," as in *Frontiero v. Richardson*, 411 U.S. 677 (1973), or rests on "the baggage of sexual stereotypes" as in *Orr v. Orr*, 440 U.S. 268 (1979). As we have held, the statute instead reasonably reflects the fact that the consequences of sexual intercourse and pregnancy fall more heavily on the female than on the male.

JUSTICE STEWART, concurring.

Section 261.5, on its face, classifies on the basis of sex. A male who engages in sexual intercourse with an underage female who is not his wife violates the statute; a female who engages in sexual intercourse with an underage male who is not her husband does not. The petitioner contends that this state law, which punishes only males for the conduct in question, violates his Fourteenth Amendment right to the equal protection of the law. The Court today correctly rejects that contention.

A

At the outset, it should be noted that the statutory discrimination, when viewed as part of the wider scheme of California law, is not as clearcut as might at first appear. Females are not freed from criminal liability in California for engaging in sexual activity that may be harmful. It is unlawful, for example, for any person, of either sex, to molest, annoy, or contribute to the delinquency of anyone under 18 years of age. All persons are prohibited from committing "any lewd or lascivious act," including consensual intercourse, with a child under 14. And members of both sexes may be convicted for engaging in deviant sexual acts with anyone under 18. Finally, females may be brought within the proscription of § 261.5 itself, since a female may be charged with aiding and abetting its violation.[5]

Section 261.5 is thus but one part of a broad statutory scheme that protects all minors from the problems and risks attendant upon adolescent sexual activity. To be sure, § 261.5 creates an additional measure of punishment for males who engage in sexual intercourse with females between the ages of 14 and 17.[6] The question then is whether the Constitution prohibits a state legislature from imposing this additional sanction on a gender-specific basis.

...

5. See Cal. Penal Code Ann. § 31. According to statistics maintained by the California Department of Justice Bureau of Criminal Statistics, approximately 14% of the juveniles arrested for participation in acts made unlawful by § 261.5 between 1975 and 1979 were females. Moreover, an underage female who is as culpable as her male partner, or more culpable, may be prosecuted as a juvenile delinquent. Cal. Welf. & Inst. Code Ann. § 602. [N.B.—Justice Stewart is almost certainly wrong in suggesting that a girl could be prosecuted as an aider and abettor of her own statutory rape [see Chapter 13] or that she could be found to be a juvenile delinquent, since such a finding would also require proof that she committed a crime.—Ed.]

6. Males and females are equally prohibited by § 288 from sexual intercourse with minors under 14.

C

As the California Supreme Court's catalog shows, the pregnant unmarried female confronts problems more numerous and more severe than any faced by her male partner.[7] She alone endures the medical risks of pregnancy or abortion.[8] She suffers disproportionately the social, educational, and emotional consequences of pregnancy.[9] Recognizing this disproportion, California has attempted to protect teenage females by prohibiting males from participating in the act necessary for conception.

. . .

[Justice Blackmun, concurred in the judgment, but expressed distaste for the state's decision to prosecute the case at all, let alone as a felony.]

Justice Brennan, with whom Justices White and Marshall join, dissenting.

I

It is disturbing to find the Court so splintered on a case that presents such a straightforward issue: Whether the admittedly gender-based classification in Cal. Penal Code §261.5 bears a sufficient relationship to the State's asserted goal of preventing teenage pregnancies to survive the "mid-level" constitutional scrutiny mandated by *Craig v. Boren*, 429 U.S. 190 (1976). Applying the analytical framework provided by our precedents, I am convinced that there is only one proper resolution of this issue: the classification must be declared unconstitutional. I fear that the plurality opinion and Justices Stewart and Blackmun reach the opposite result by placing too much emphasis on the desirability of achieving the State's asserted statutory goal—prevention of teenage pregnancy—and not enough emphasis on the fundamental question of whether the sex-based discrimination in the California statute is substantially related to the achievement of that goal.

II

. . . [A] gender-based classification cannot withstand constitutional challenge unless the classification is substantially related to the achievement of an important governmental objective. This analysis applies whether the classification discriminates against males or against females. The burden is on the government to prove both the importance of its asserted objective and the substantial relationship between the classification and that objective. And the State cannot meet that burden without showing that a gender-neutral statute would be a less effective means of achieving that goal.

---

7. The court noted that from 1971 through 1976, 83.6% of the 4,860 children born to girls under 15 in California were illegitimate, as were 51% of those born to girls 15 to 17. The court also observed that while accounting for only 21% of California pregnancies in 1976, teenagers accounted for 34.7% of legal abortions.

8. There is also empirical evidence that sexual abuse of young females is a more serious problem than sexual abuse of young males. For example, a review of five studies found that 88% of sexually abused minors were female. Another study, involving admissions to a hospital emergency room over a 3-year period, reported that 86 of 100 children examined for sexual abuse were girls.

9. Most teenage mothers do not finish high school and are disadvantaged economically thereafter. The suicide rate for teenage mothers is seven times greater than that for teenage girls without children.

The State of California vigorously asserts that the "important governmental objective" to be served by § 261.5 is the prevention of teenage pregnancy. It claims that its statute furthers this goal by deterring sexual activity by males—the class of persons it considers more responsible for causing those pregnancies.[4] But even assuming that prevention of teenage pregnancy is an important governmental objective and that it is in fact an objective of § 261.5, California still has the burden of proving that there are fewer teenage pregnancies under its gender-based statutory rape law than there would be if the law were gender neutral. To meet this burden, the State must show that because its statutory rape law punishes only males, and not females, it more effectively deters minor females from having sexual intercourse.

The plurality assumes that a gender-neutral statute would be less effective than § 261.5 in deterring sexual activity because a gender-neutral statute would create significant enforcement problems. The plurality thus accepts the State's assertion that "a female is surely less likely to report violations of the statute if she herself would be subject to criminal prosecution. In an area already fraught with prosecutorial difficulties, we decline to hold that the Equal Protection Clause requires a legislature to enact a statute so broad that it may well be incapable of enforcement." However, a State's bare assertion that its gender-based statutory classification substantially furthers an important governmental interest is not enough to meet its burden of proof under *Craig v. Boren*. Rather, the State must produce evidence that will persuade the court that its assertion is true.

The State has not produced such evidence in this case. Moreover, there are at least two serious flaws in the State's assertion that law enforcement problems created by a gender-neutral statutory rape law would make such a statute less effective than a gender-based statute in deterring sexual activity.

First, the experience of other jurisdictions, and California itself, belies the plurality's conclusion that a gender-neutral statutory rape law "may well be incapable of enforcement." There are now at least 37 States that have enacted gender-neutral statutory rape laws. Although most of these laws protect young persons (of either sex) from the sexual exploitation of older individuals, the laws of Arizona, Florida, and Illinois permit prosecution of both minor females and minor males for engaging in mutual sexual conduct. California has introduced no evidence that those States have been handicapped by the enforcement problems the plurality finds so persuasive. Surely, if those States could provide such evidence, we might expect that California would have introduced it.

In addition, the California Legislature in recent years has revised other sections of the Penal Code to make them gender-neutral. For example, Cal. Penal Code §§ 286(b)(1) and 288a(b)(1), prohibiting sodomy and oral copulation with a "person

4. In a remarkable display of sexual stereotyping, the California Supreme Court stated: "The Legislature is well within its power in imposing criminal sanctions against males, alone, because they are the *only* persons who may physiologically cause the result which the law properly seeks to avoid." (Emphasis in original.)

who is under 18 years of age," could cause two minor homosexuals to be subjected to criminal sanctions for engaging in mutually consensual conduct. Again, the State has introduced no evidence to explain why a gender-neutral statutory rape law would be any more difficult to enforce than those statutes.

The second flaw in the State's assertion is that even assuming that a gender-neutral statute would be more difficult to enforce, the State has still not shown that those enforcement problems would make such a statute less effective than a gender-based statute in deterring minor females from engaging in sexual intercourse.[8] Common sense, however, suggests that a gender-neutral statutory rape law is potentially a greater deterrent of sexual activity than a gender-based law, for the simple reason that a gender-neutral law subjects both men and women to criminal sanctions and thus arguably has a deterrent effect on twice as many potential violators. Even if fewer persons were prosecuted under the gender-neutral law, as the State suggests, it would still be true that twice as many persons would be subject to arrest. The State's failure to prove that a gender-neutral law would be a less effective deterrent than a gender-based law, like the State's failure to prove that a gender-neutral law would be difficult to enforce, should have led this Court to invalidate § 261.5.

III

Until very recently, no California court or commentator had suggested that the purpose of California's statutory rape law was to protect young women from the risk of pregnancy. Indeed, the historical development of § 261.5 demonstrates that the law was initially enacted on the premise that young women, in contrast to young men, were to be deemed legally incapable of consenting to an act of sexual intercourse. Because their chastity was considered particularly precious, those young women were felt to be uniquely in need of the State's protection.[10] In contrast, young men were assumed to be capable of making such decisions for themselves; the law therefore did not offer them any special protection.

---

8. As it is, § 261.5 seems to be an ineffective deterrent of sexual activity. According to statistics provided by the State, an average of only 61 juvenile males and 352 adult males were arrested for statutory rape each year between 1975 and 1978. During each of those years there were approximately one million Californian girls between the ages of 13–17. Although the record in this case does not indicate the incidence of sexual intercourse involving those girls during that period, the California State Department of Health estimates that there were almost 50,000 pregnancies among 13-to-17-year-old girls during 1976. I think it is fair to speculate from this evidence that a comparison of the number of arrests for statutory rape in California with the number of acts of sexual intercourse involving minor females in that State would likely demonstrate to a male contemplating sexual activity with a minor female that his chances of being arrested are reassuringly low. I seriously question, therefore, whether § 261.5 as enforced has a substantial deterrent effect.

10. Past decisions of the California courts confirm that the law was designed to protect the State's young females from their own uninformed decisionmaking. In *People v. Verdegreen*, 106 Cal. 211 (1895), for example, the California Supreme Court stated: "The obvious purpose of [the statutory rape law] is the protection of society by protecting from violation the virtue of young and unsophisticated girls.... It is the insidious approach and vile tampering with their persons that primarily undermines the virtue of young girls, and eventually destroys it; and the prevention of this, as much as the principal act, must undoubtedly have been the intent of the legislature."...

It is perhaps because the gender classification in California's statutory rape law was initially designed to further these outmoded sexual stereotypes, rather than to reduce the incidence of teenage pregnancies, that the State has been unable to demonstrate a substantial relationship between the classification and its newly asserted goal. But whatever the reason, the State has not shown that Cal. Penal Code § 261.5 is any more effective than a gender-neutral law would be in deterring minor females from engaging in sexual intercourse. It has therefore not met its burden of proving that the statutory classification is substantially related to the achievement of its asserted goal.

I would hold that § 261.5 violates the Equal Protection Clause of the Fourteenth Amendment, and I would reverse the judgment of the California Supreme Court.

[Dissenting opinion of STEVENS, J. omitted.]

Note and Problem

The Amended § 261.5. Subsequent to the decision in *Michael M.*, the legislature amended § 261.5 to make it gender-neutral. Does that suggest that no significant state interest was being served by the previous version?

Problem 3.

Defendant is a 19-year old Marine. On an overnight pass, he and another Marine drove to Mexico. They drank beer, and, returning to their base, Defendant was driving fast and crashed into a car stopped along the side of the road, killing the occupant. Defendant had a blood alcohol concentration of 0.07. Defendant is charged with gross vehicular manslaughter while intoxicated. (P.C. § 191.5) Gross vehicular manslaughter consists of the unlawful killing of a human being in the driving of a vehicle when: (a) the driver was under the influence of alcohol; (b) the driver had a blood alcohol concentration of 0.08 or more; or (c) the driver was under the age of 21 and had a blood alcohol concentration of 0.05 or more. What arguments should be made on Defendant's equal protection challenge based on the discrimination against drivers who are under 21?

C. The Criminal Case in California

With the exception of *United States v. Bergman, supra*, and the following case, the cases in this book are all appellate cases. The majority are appeals from final trial court judgments. Since the prosecution is generally barred by double jeopardy principles from appealing a final judgment of acquittal, most cases in this book involve defense appeals from a judgment of conviction. The remaining cases involve interlocutory appeals and extraordinary writs challenging a trial court's pre-trial rulings. Such cases may be brought by either the prosecution or defense. In order to understand how a case comes to the appellate court, it is useful to examine a case in the trial court.

The following documents and transcripts are taken from the trial court record in the case of *People v. Robinson*. The case is a relatively simple case because the crime charged is a misdemeanor and there are few legal or factual issues. In reviewing the case, consider the following questions. What is the function of the complaint, and what is the relationship of the complaint to the statute cited? What does the prosecution have to prove to convict the defendant, and what is the defendant trying to prove with his witnesses? What are the respective roles of the judge and the jury in a criminal case, and, in particular, why is the motion to suppress evidence heard outside the presence of the jury? What occurs between the close of evidence and the jury's decision? What is the effect of suspending the imposition of sentence and putting the defendant on probation? On appeal, how will the issues for the appellate court differ from those decided in the trial court? (*California v. Robinson* [Chapter 2] is the Supreme Court decision on appeal of this case.) Consider also the question of what is the purpose of criminalizing the defendant's conduct and what is the relationship between this "successful" prosecution and satisfying that purpose.

The People of the State of California, *Plaintiff*, v. Lawrence Robinson, *Defendant*

in the Municipal Court of Los Angeles Judicial District
County of Los Angeles, State of California

Complaint

Personally appeared before me, the undersigned, who, first being duly sworn, complains and says: That on or about February 4, 1960, at and in Los Angeles City, in the County of Los Angeles, State of California, a misdemeanor, to wit:

Violation of Section 11721 of the Health and Safety Code was committed by Lawrence Robinson (whose true name to affiant is unknown), who at the time and place last aforesaid, was a person who did wilfully and unlawfully use, and be under the influence of, and be addicted to the use of narcotics, said narcotics not having been administered by and under the direction of a person licensed by the State of California to prescribe and administer narcotics.

All of which is contrary to the law in such cases made and provided, and against the peace and dignity of the People of the State of California. Said Complainant therefore prays that a warrant may be issued for the arrest of said defendant that he may be dealt with according to law.

Subscribed and sworn to before me on February 5, 1960.

T. M. Lundquist

George J. Barbour, Clerk of the Municipal Court of Los Angeles Judicial District, in said County and State.

By K. Hovey, *Deputy Clerk*

MUNICIPAL COURT PROCEEDINGS

Feb. 5, 1960:

Warrant Issued. Bail set at:

Bail	$1,000
Penalty Assessment	$50
Total before release:	$1,050

Feb. 6, 1960:

Defendant in Court duly arraigned, informed of charge against him and of his legal rights. Defendant gives true name as charged and enters his plea of not guilty of the offense charged.

Jury trial: Mar. 3, 1960 9:00 am, Div. 20

Bail set at:

Bail	$500
Penalty Assessment	$25
Total before release	$525

Defendant committed

Feb. 6, 1960:

$525 surety bond approved and filed.

(National Automobile & Casualty Ins. Co.)

Defendant ordered released.

...

June 6, 1960:

[The jury was selected, and both counsel waived opening argument.]

Mr.Gage [the Deputy District Attorney]: Officer Brown.

LAWRENCE E. BROWN,

called as a witness by and on behalf of the People, having been first duly sworn, was examined and testified as follows:

The Clerk: State your name, please.

The Witness: Lawrence E. Brown.

DIRECT EXAMINATION

By **Mr. Gage:**

Q. What is your occupation sir?

A. Police Officer, City of Los Angeles, assigned to Wilshire Felony Unit.

Q. Felony unit. Do you use a squad car?

A. A plain unmarked vehicle.

Q. And as such, did you have occasion to observe the defendant, Mr. Robinson?

A. Yes, sir, I did.

Q. And when you observed him, that was about February 4 of 1960?

A. Yes, sir, that is correct.

Q. Approximately what time was it that you observed the defendant?

A. Approximately 9:00 P.M.

Q. Now, just before you actually observed him—that is, recognized him as an individual, did you see him in an automobile?

A. Yes, sir, I did.

...

Q. And when you observed the defendant, approximately—when you observed this automobile, approximately how fast was it traveling?

A. I would judge it to be approximately 10 to 15 miles an hour.

Q. Do you know the speed limit in that location?

A. Yes, sir. It is 25 miles an hour.

...

Q. Now, did you notice anything unusual about the rear of the automobile itself?

A. Yes, sir. The vehicle had no rear license plate illumination. It made it impossible for us to see the license number of the car.

Q. You couldn't read the license number at that time?

A. That is correct.

Q. Did you eventually pull up to this automobile?

A. Yes, sir, we did.

...

Q. Did anybody alight from the automobile?

A. Yes, sir.

Q. Was that the defendant, or somebody else?

A. That was Charles Banks, the driver of the vehicle.

Q. Did you have occasion to observe him at the time?

A. Yes, sir, I did.

Q. And was there anything unusual about his appearance?

A. Well, he had his sleeves rolled up on his shirt above the elbow and I observed that he had, on the inside of his left and right at the crook of the elbow, what appeared to be a fresh needle mark.

Q. Did you have some conversation with him?

A. Yes, sir, I did.

Q. And after that, did you approach the automobile?

A. At this time I placed him under arrest.

Q. I don't want to go into that unless it becomes necessary, but did you eventually go to the automobile?

A. I didn't go to the automobile myself.

Q. Did your partner?

A. Yes, sir, he did.

Q. What was his name?

A. Officer Wapato.

Q. Did the persons who were in the car then get out of it?

A. Yes, sir, they did.

Q. And do you recall if the defendant was one of those persons.

A. Yes, sir, he was.

Q. Where did he come from—what part of the car?

A. As I recall it, it was from the passenger side in the front seat.

Q. Did you get close enough to the defendant to observe him?

A. Yes, sir, I did.

Q. And when you observed the defendant, did you have occasion to examine his arms?

A. Eventually, I did, yes.

Q. What did you notice about the appearance of his arms?

Mr. McMorris [the defense attorney]: At this time the defendant will object to any testimony regarding what was observed on the defendant's arms, and we request to take the officer upon voir dire as to the reasonableness and the legality of the arrest.[1]

The Court: The request is granted.

Ladies and Gentlemen of the Jury, the Court is about to grant you a 10 minute recess which I would like to have you spend outside the courtroom.

During this recess, I admonish you not to converse among yourselves nor with anyone else on any matter pertaining to this case, or express or form an opinion thereon until the matter is finally submitted to you for your decision.

(Whereupon the jury left the courtroom.)

(The following proceedings were had in open court outside the hearing of the jury.)

---

1. Under current practice, a motion to suppress evidence on the grounds of illegal search or seizure would be made prior to trial. See Pen. Code § 1538.5.

Mr. Gage: I wonder if at this time we should present the affirmative evidence on probable cause, Your Honor.

The Court: Yes, I had that in mind and I thank you for your suggestion, Mr. Gage.

The Court at this time will go into the matter of probable cause, or more correctly, perhaps, the matter of the legality of the search and seizure.

...

DIRECT EXAMINATION (RESUMED)

By **Mr. Gage:**

Q. You did not have a search warrant for this arrest, did you, sir?

A. No, sir, I did not.

Q. When you observed this automobile, ... it was in the region of Serrano traveling southbound near 12th Street?

A. Yes, sir.

Q. Was there anything that had occurred in the past that you had information on in relation to unlawful activities in this vicinity?

A. Yes, sir.

Mr. McMorris: I will object, I think, to this particular question of what happens in the vicinity. That would certainly not bind anyone just driving through there.

The Court: It will be overruled at this time. I think that goes to the weight to be afforded it, Mr. McMorris, rather than to its admissibility.

By **Mr. Gage:**

...

Q. Officer Brown, what had you information on in that connection?

A. There had been numerous purse snatchers in that vicinity and other vicinities throughout Wilshire Division.

Q. In relation to these purse snatching activities, where had you received your information?

A. I had received them via police radio, via daily occurrence sheets and through crime reports.

Q. And in the location where these purse snatching had occurred, were there any occasions where they had occurred by the use of an automobile—that is, as distinguished from somebody just walking on the street?

A. Yes, sir. There were many occasions where automobiles were used.

Q. Now, I believe you indicated the speed of the automobile was 10 or 15 miles an hour on that street?

A. That is right. I would judge it to be approximately 10 or 15 miles an hour.

Q. Now, there was no illumination of the taillight—that is, of the license on the car?

A. That is correct.

Q. When you stopped the automobile and the driver, the driver was the person who got out and came over to you?

A. Yes, sir, he was.

Q. Did you ever speak to the driver at that time?

A. Yes, sir.

Q. Do you recall his name now?

A. Charles Banks.

Q. And what did he say ?

A. He stated that he used narcotics and he had used a short time prior to the time that we stopped him. I don't recall the exact number of days that he stated.

...

CROSS EXAMINATION

By **Mr. McMorris:**

Q. Now, Officer, you mentioned something about purse snatching in this neighborhood; is that a fact?

A. Yes, sir.

Q. As a matter of fact, purse snatching goes on over the whole of the jurisdiction of your route, doesn't it?

A. Yes, sir, it does.

Q. That is right.

Q. Over the whole Wilshire District there is a certain amount of purse snatching all the time?

A. Yes.

Q. When you stopped these people, you didn't say anything to them about purse snatching, did you?

A. No, sir, I didn't.

Q. And you saw no activity on the part of anyone in the car which could actually appear to be snatching a purse from anybody?

A. No, sir.

Q. The actual reason why you stopped the car then was just to see what you might find out that might have been done by these people, wasn't it?

A. No, sir.

Q. Was the only reason why you stopped the car the slowness of the speed of the vehicle?

A. No, sir, it was not.

Q. You never said anything to them about driving too slowly, did you?

A. I don't recall if I did or not.

Q. You said nothing to them about any lack of rear view illumination, either, did you?

A. Yes, sir I did.

. . .

Q. And you state that Mr. Banks had on just a shirt with the sleeves rolled up?

A. Yes, sir, he did.

Q. With a short-sleeved shirt, or were they rolled up?

A. A long-sleeved shirt with the sleeve rolled up.

. . .

Q. Now, were you able to see these marks you say you saw on Banks' arms by the light of the street light?

A. No, sir, I was not.

Q. What did you see them with?

A. My flashlight.

Q. Were you particularly looking for marks?

A. I shined my light about his person. I look for anything. Not particularly marks, no.

Q. For anything you might find?

A. Yes.

. . .

Q. Now, after discovering the mark on his arm, you then went back to the car and you ordered the other three occupants out, didn't you?

A. No, I didn't.

Q. What happened after that?

A. I placed him under arrest.

Q. You placed Banks under arrest?

A. That is correct.

Q. And you put him in your vehicle is that right?

A. No, sir; that is not correct.

Q. What happened?

A. I took him to the sidewalk.

Q. And then what next happened?

A. In the meantime, my partner, Officer Wapato, had gotten the other three people in the vehicle outside.

Q. The next thing you observed as to Mr. Robinson, then, was that he was outside?

A. That is correct.

Q. Now, then, did you and your partner, or either, order the two females and Mr. Robinson to line up against a building, or something, there?

A. Yes. They lined up three abreast, abreast of each other across the front of the building.

Q. At that point you ordered Mr. Robinson to take off his jacket, didn't you?

A. No, sir, I didn't.

Q. He had a jacket on, of course?

A. Yes, he did.

Q. You couldn't see any marks on his arm?

A. No, sir.

Q. Did you place Mr. Robinson under arrest at that time?

A. No, sir, I didn't.

Q. When was he placed under arrest?

A. After I had questioned him.

Q. Now, before questioning him, you ran a search of him, didn't you?

A. I cursorily searched him for offensive weapons, yes.

Q. And you found no such—

A. Yes.

Q. And then you next searched him for narcotics, you or your fellow officer in your presence?

A. No. That wasn't the next occurrence. Next, I questioned him regarding his nervous condition.

Q. He appeared nervous to you?

A. He certainly did, yes.

Q. What did he say about his nervous condition?

A. He said he has been nervous all his life and he gets nervous when he talks to policemen.

Q. Then what happened in connection with Mr. Robinson?

A. I asked him if he used narcotics. He said, "Yes, I use narcotics."

Q. He told you that?

A. He stated to me that he wasn't hooked. He stated to me that he hadn't used narcotics in approximately two months. He stated then that his friends came by his house and he used their narcotics, their outfits; that he had never bought narcotics. He then stated he hadn't used narcotics in two weeks.

Q. So at that point you asked to look at his arms; is that right?

A. I did.

Q. And you ordered him to take off his coat?

A. I did.

Q. And you ordered him to roll up his sleeves of his shirt?

A. That is correct.

Q. And when he rolled up his sleeves, what did you see?

A. I saw scar tissue and discoloration on the inside of his right arm, and I saw numerous fresh needle marks on the inside of his left arm and also a fresh scab.

Q. Prior to the time you ordered Mr. Robinson out of the vehicle, or he was ordered out by your fellow officer, you had not seen Mr. Robinson in violation of any law, felony, or misdemeanor, had you?

A. No, sir, I had not.

Q. Now, how long after you first took Mr. Robinson out of the vehicle did you place him under arrest?

A. I can only guess at this one. I would say Approximately 10 minutes.

Q. May it have been 20 minutes?

A. I don't think so.

Mr. McMorris: I have no further questions of this witness.

Mr. Gage: I have a couple of questions.

I am sorry. I overlooked them previously.

REDIRECT EXAMINATION

By **Mr. Gage:**

Q. When you noticed that the defendant was nervous and perspiring, did you have occasion to examine his eyes or face, also?

A. Yes, sir, I did.

Q. Did you notice anything unusual about the appearance of his eyes?

A. His eyes were pinpointed and glassy.

Q. Did you examine them with a flashlight?

A. Yes, sir, I did, in comparison with Officer Wapato's eyes.

. . .

RECROSS EXAMINATION

By **Mr. McMorris:**

Q. At what point did you look at the defendant's eyes with a flashlight?

A. It was before I checked his arms. It was when I was interrogating and talking to him.

Q. Was this after he told you that he used narcotics; is that right?

A. Yes, sir, that is correct.

Q. And, incidentally, before testifying here today, did you refresh your recollection by use of the police report?

A. Yes, sir, I did.

Q. Calling your attention, Officer, to the arrest report that you have just read, I will ask you whether or not in that report you did not make this statement:

"Officers commanded the above suspect and passengers, Norma Banks, 873 East Vernon, and Ruth Robinson, 1043 South Kingsley, to get out of the vehicle. As above suspect got out, officers observed that he was perspiring heavily and that he appeared extremely nervous. Officers also observed that his eyes were glassy and his pupils pinpointed. In checking suspect's arms, officer discovered numerous fresh needle marks on the inside of his left arm and one scab approximately 3 inches below the crook of the elbow on the forearm. The suspect had scar tissue on his right arm.

At that time suspect made the above statements and was placed under arrest."

Q. Did you make that statement?

A. Yes, sir, I did.

[Ruth Fairlur testified that she had been in the back seat of the car with Robinson, that she had been searched, and that she had watched the officer interrogate Robinson, outside the range of her hearing. She testified that Robinson rolled up his shirt sleeve and pants leg. She stated that Officer Brown flashed the light on Robinson's legs, but, as she remembered, not his arms or face.]

LAWRENCE ROBINSON,

defendant, called to the stand in his own behalf, having been first duly sworn, was examined and testified as follows:

The Clerk: State your name, please.

The Witness: Lawrence Robinson.

...

Q. Now, what first happened between the officers and the occupant of the car?

A. Well, Mr. Banks, he got out of the car. He seen the red light. He stopped his car and got out. And I didn't pay any more attention until the officers come to the car and opened the back door where I was sitting. I was sitting in the back on the right-hand side, and he opened the door and ordered us out of the car.

Q. What did he say?

A. We got out.

Q. What did the officer say?

A. He told us to get out.

...

Q. At any time did the officers say anything to you about stopping you for purse snatching?

A. No.

Q. Or suspicion of purse snatching?

A. No.

Q. Did they say anything in your hearing about the lack of rear view illumination on the car?

A. No.

...

The Witness: Officer Wapato ... got us out of the car and over against the wall and he searched the car, and he come over and he didn't say anything to me. He was talking to Banks. And while they were talking to Banks, I seen him take his jacket off, and they placed him under arrest and put the handcuffs on him. Then they come over to where I was standing and told me to take my jacket off, so I take my jacket off. And he told me to roll my sleeves up, so I did that. Then he—this officer in the back there—he went over and he talked to his partner, and then his partner come back where I was and he looked at my arms. Then they went off again. Both of them went off and they talked again. And then they come back and both of them looked at my arms again, and they left and went back over to the car, and they talked among themselves, just the two of them, and they come back and arrested me.

By **Mr. McMorris:**

Q. How long from the time you were stopped was it before you were told you were under arrest?

A. About 30 minutes.

Q. Now, at any time did you tell the officers, during this period that we have just testified about, you used narcotics?

A. No, I didn't.

Q. Did you tell them that you used narcotics two months before?

A. No.

Q. Or two weeks before?

A. No.

Q. And was anything said about perspiration or nervousness?

A. Yes, there was.

Q. What was done and said about that?

A. He asked me why I was perspiring. And I told him I was born like that; I did it all the time every time I get the least bit upset. I don't have to be upset. I automatically perspire. He said, "Ain't you a little nervous?" And I said, "Yes, sir, I am a little nervous. I am trying to figure out what this is all about."

Q. Did you say anything about being nervous when you are stopped by policemen?

A. Not necessarily. I say when I get excited, things like this excite me.

...

Mr. McMorris: No further questions.

...

STATEMENT BY COURT OVERRULING OBJECTIONS TO SEARCH[r]

I agree with the proposition that the fact there was no light illuminating the license plate in itself would not give the officers in this case, or in any other case, in my opinion, based on that fact alone, the right to order the occupants out of the car and proceed to subject them to a minute search as an examination of arms, legs, and so forth.

We have more in this case. We have the lack of the light illuminating the license plate, which, I think, certainly is justification, and a police officer would be derelict in his duty, regardless of what detail he was attached to unless on some urgent call, if he did not at least stop the motorist and say, "Your lights are out on your license plate," and perhaps give him a ticket.

In any event, there was reasonable cause and a duty to stop the automobile, in my opinion, which was done.

Then, we have a significant factor if the officers are to be believed in this respect, and I have indicated that I do believe them, and I think it is undisputed that Mr. Robinson testified when the car stopped that Mr. Banks got out of the car and went back to the officers. That is his testimony. That is the officer's testimony. That the officers, who had a flashlight in their possession, then and there played it on Mr. Banks, saw a fresh needle mark upon the arm of Mr. Banks, which changed the entire picture then from one of a mere motor vehicle violation to one of a different significance.

It was upon that factor which I then reasoned to the conclusion that the officer had a right to make a search of the car and to order the defendant in this case, Mr. Robinson, and Miss Fairlur and the other lady, out of the car.

Now, of course, I have in mind that Mr. Robinson has denied all of this testimony; that he didn't make these statements. And I have in mind also that this is not in accord with what is set forth in the arrest report in that the arrest report, as pointed out by Mr. McMorris, points out that he was ordered to bare his arm and then he made these statements, which would seem to corroborate the defendant's statement. If he was ordered to show his arm and then made these statements, why, of course, the statements could not be used as any justification for ordering him to bare his arm.

I realize that in the preparation of these arrest reports that they cannot be always chronologically correct.

The officer has testified here. He has been cross-examined. I am disposed to believe that it is a misstatement in the arrest report, either as to composition or carelessness

r. Includes excerpts from Court's "tentative conclusion" two days earlier.

in dictation, and I believe that the officer's recollection of what occurred is more accurate than that related by Mr. Robinson as what did occur.

Of course, it is a question of credibility. You have argued the matter. I have heretofore analyzed it, and I believe that my original analysis is correct that the officer's testimony is correct.

I believe in view of Mr. Robinson's statements and the other factors in this case, there was reasonable cause to order that he bare his arm, that his person be searched in the manner which was done in this case.

For the reasons stated, the objection will be overruled.

[Jury is recalled.]

. . .

LAWRENCE E. BROWN,

was previously sworn, resumed the stand as a witness for the People, and testified as follows:

By **Mr. Gage:**

Q. Officer Brown, did you examine the defendant's arm?

A. Yes, I did.

Q. At the time you examined it, where was the defendant?

A. Standing on the sidewalk adjacent to the parked vehicle.

Q. Did you have a flashlight available to you?

A. Yes, sir, I did.

Q. Did you examine the arm, that is, after it was bared?

A. Yes, sir, I did.

Q. What did you notice about the defendant's arm, if anything?

A. On the defendant's right arm, he had scar tissue and discoloration on the inside of the right arm. On the left arm, he had what appeared to be numerous needle marks and a scab which was approximately three inches below the crook of the elbow on the inside of the arm.

. . .

THEODORE M. LUNDQUIST,

was called as a witness by the People, having been first duly sworn, testified as follow:

DIRECT EXAMINATION

By **Mr. Gage:**

Q. State your occupation and assignment.

A. Police officer for the city of Los Angeles, attached to the Narcotic Division.

Q. How long have you been attached to that particular division?

A. Going on eleven years.

...

Q. Have you seen addicts in various stages and conditions of addiction?

A. I have.

Q. Have you seen persons who have merely taken narcotics, that is, used them, who perhaps were not addicted?

A. I have.

...

Q. Is there anything distinctive about the type of injections made by addicts as opposed to injections made by a doctor, for example?

A. Yes.

Q. What differences are there, generally?

A. In general, there is an ineptness in handling the paraphernalia used, principally a hypodermic needle and a medicine dropper, in place of the medical syringe; the lack of sterility follows throughout. There is no sterilized equipment, no swabbing of the area before the injection was made with a disinfectant, such as alcohol, and it results in scabbing that remains on the arm for a period of time.

Q. Approximately how long do these scabs remain?

A. These scabs remain, depending largely upon the cleanliness habits of the individual using narcotics. If their cleanliness habits are poor, scabs remain for a longer period of time, up to 20 days. If their cleanliness habits are very good, then they may disappear within a short period of time, as much as ten days.

Q. Did you have occasion to examine the defendant in this case, Mr. Robinson?

A. I did.

Q. Approximately where and when did you examine the defendant?

A. The defendant was examined on the 5th day of February, 1960, at approximately 10:15 a.m. at the Central Jail, Felony Section.

Q. On that occasion, did you examine his arms?

A. I did.

...

Q. What, generally, did you note about his arms at that time?

A. In the area of the inner right elbow, I found two scabs. These scabs were over a vein. In the area of the inner left elbow, there was an area of discoloration and scabbing over a vein bearing five scabs. Further down the forearm, approaching the wrist and following the vein coursing toward the outer side from the inner side to the outer side of the arm, there was the presence of multi-discoloration.

. . .

Q. From your examination of these various scabs and various marks on the defendant's arm, did you form an opinion as to what caused those marks?

A. I did.

Q. What was your opinion?

A. In my opinion, these marks and the discoloration were the result of the injection of hypodermic needles into the tissue into the vein that was not sterile.

Q. From your examination of the nature of the marks and scabs of various discoloration, have you an opinion as to what was introduced into the arm by the means of the hypodermic needle?

A. I do.

Q. What is your opinion?

. . .

A. That a narcotic was injected into the vein.

. . .

Q. In connection with the examination of the defendant's arm, did you form any opinion as to the length of time or the age of these various marks that you observed on the defendant's arm?

A. I did.

Q. Relate that, please.

A. Those scabs that appear on the inner right elbow area were estimated to be approximately ten to fifteen days old. The scabbing appearing in the inner left area was estimated to be approximately three to ten days old.

Q. Three to ten?

A. Correct.

Q. And is there a difference in the appearance of these marks and scabs with age?

A. Yes.

Q. And generally, what did you notice in that connection?

A. Originally, a scab is a pinkish-orange color, and as it grows older, the blood oxidizes and ages, becoming a different color. Those scabs that were ten to fifteen days old were dark brown in appearance. They were raised from the tissue. Those scabs that appear in the inner left elbow area varied in color from a pinkish-orange to that of a lighter brown, and were adhering closely to the tissue, had not raised as yet.

Q. You indicated you had some conversation with the defendant in connection with the use of drugs. Could you relate that conversation?. . . .

A. I asked the defendant when he had first begun using narcotics, and he said it had been approximately four months ago. I then asked him if he had ever vomited upon taking an injection, and he stated yes, that he had vomited after this first fix. I then asked him if this vomiting had continued following the injection of a narcotic, and he stated that he still vomited if he had eaten beforehand. I asked him how much he was using, and he said he had started using cottons given to him about three or four times a week. I asked him if he had used anything other than cottons, and he stated he had started using powder about two months ago. I asked him how much he used, and he stated, "Two or three of us use an eight-dollar bag." I asked him when he had his last injection or fix, and he stated his last fix had been on Wednesday night. I asked him if he had split the bag, and he said, "A friend and I split the eight-dollar bag." I asked where they had been, and he said they had been in a gas station at 54th and Central Avenue. I asked him if this had been heroin, and he said that it was heroin. That was the extent of the conversation.

Q. This indication that the fix was at 54th and Central, was that indicated to be in Los Angeles?

A. Yes.

Q. The statement the defendant made in connection with the use of drugs was made voluntarily without any promise or threats made to the defendant?

A. They were.

Q. Would you describe what is meant by the use of a cotton.

A. A cotton is used to strain the impurities from the solution. A small piece of it is placed in the receptacle, generally a bottle cap or teaspoon, and the fluid is drawn through it into the medicine dropper. After the cotton dries, there are still—it has been saturated with heroin solution. After it has been dried, it can be re-saturated, and that liquid is used. If it hasn't dried, it can be squeezed, and the fluid left in the saturated cotton can be injected.

...

Q. When the defendant indicated that he had had his last fix, did he tell you whether it had been the Wednesday just previous to the day that you had examined him or a week previous to that?

A. It was the previous Wednesday.

Mr. Gage: I have no further questions.

...

CROSS-EXAMINATION

By **Mr. McMorris:**

Q. As an expert in the field of narcotics, you know the symptoms of heroin addiction, do you not?

A. Yes, sir.

Q. And among those symptoms are those termed withdrawal symptoms?

A. That is correct.

Q. And at no time did you witness any withdrawal symptoms in Mr. Robinson?

A. No, I did not.

Q. As a matter of fact, he wasn't under the influence at the time you interviewed him at all?

A. No, he wasn't.

Q. So you saw no influence and no withdrawal?

A. That is correct.

Q. You saw on his arms certain discolorations on the veins of each arm?

A. On the inner left arm, I noticed the discoloration.

Q. As a matter of fact, did you observe the whole of Mr. Robinson's body, say, above the belt?

A. You mean the nude torso?

Q. Yes.

A. No, just his arms.

Q. Then you don't—you don't know whether he has all over his body certain discolorations similar to this?

A. No, I do not.

Q. As an expert in the field, you also know there is a Nalline test that can determine conclusively the presence of narcotics?

A. Within limitations.

Q. This test wasn't given to the defendant, was it?

A. No.

Q. As to the freshest scars which you allege you saw, they were how old?

A. Approximately three days.

Q. Did you say three to five?

A. That three to five-day period was the varying period of time in which they could have been made.

Q. It might have been three to five days that there was an actual injection by your own determination?

A. Yes, sir. The freshest, three days, and the oldest being five days.

Q. And you can look at these marks and estimate three to five days or six or seven by looking at the marks on a person's arm?

A. Yes.

Q. Of a needle?

A. Yes.

Q. Can you, by looking at these marks, tell us whether or not they could have been caused by a blood test?

A. Yes. The blood test, generally, doesn't leave a scabbing for any length of time. It will have a small scab that will disappear rapidly. The needle used is larger and results in a larger scab.

Q. Such a scab might last for a day, though, a day or two?

A. Oh, yes.

Q. Simply looking at the scars on a person's arm, if such has been left by a blood test, it would be—the scab would not last as long as one made by a heroin needle, in your opinion?

A. That is correct.

...

LAWRENCE E. BROWN,

resumed the stand as a witness for the People, having been previously duly sworn, and testified further as follows:

DIRECT EXAMINATION (RESUMED)

By **Mr. Gage:**

Q. Did you have a conversation with the defendant?

A. Yes, I did.

Q. That was outside at the scene near the automobile?

A. Yes, it was.

Q. What did the defendant tell you?

...

A. The defendant stated to me that he had—that he did use narcotics, that he had not used narcotics for approximately two months prior to his arrest. He stated that he had never bought narcotics, but that he used narcotics which his friends gave him. He used the cottons. He stated that his friends would come to his house, pick him up and then they would ride around in a car, and that he would fix in the car. He then stated that he hadn't used narcotics in approximately two weeks.

Q. The first time he told you it was two months since he had last fixed?

A. Yes, sir.

Q. Later he told you he had used it about two weeks.

A. That is correct.

...

Mr. Gage: The People rest.

The Court: You may proceed.

. . .

Mr. McMorris: I would like to call the defendant to the stand.

The Court: You have been sworn, so state your name again.

The Witness: Lawrence Robinson.

LAWRENCE ROBINSON,

was previously duly sworn, resumed the stand and testified in his own behalf as follows:

DIRECT EXAMINATION (RESUMED)

By **Mr. McMorris:**

Q. You recall being arrested for the offense for which you are tried?

A. Yes, sir.

Q. On the night of that arrest, were you under the influence of narcotics?

A. No, sir.

Q. At any time prior to that arrest, had you used narcotics?

A. No, sir.

Q. Did you tell anyone at the time of the arrest, any officers, that you did use narcotics?

A. No, sir.

Q. Did you state to any officer that you used narcotics at a filling station at 54th and Central?

A. No, sir.

. . .

Q. I ask you to look at these photos of your arms. First, take this one. I will ask you to observe this and tell the jury whether or not that is, in fact, your arm as it appeared the night of the arrest?

A. Yes, that is my arm.

Q. Is there anything on that arm that was a mark made by a needle?

A. No, sir.

Q. Will you tell the jury, what, if anything, marks on this picture are?

A. Well, when I was in service, I took some overseas shots and it gave me some kind of an allergy. I don't know. I was allergic to it, I guess, and from that time on, I have had marks all over my body similar.

Q. Do you have those marks on your face?

A. Yes.

Q. I will ask you to walk before the jury and point out to them what marks you have in mind.

The Court: You may step to the jury rail, about the center of it, if you will, please, and the jurors in the back row may stand up if they wish and look over the shoulders of the jurors in the front row.

I believe your question was for Mr. Robinson to point out such marks on his face to the panel, is that correct?

(Witness goes to the jury box.)

A. If the jury will notice, I have splotches, dark spots on my face here, and a fresh one just came up, and I have them on my back and on my arms.

Q. Would you roll up your sleeves and show the jury your arms.

(Witness complied.)

A. I have them all over my body.

Q. Will you tell the jury what, if any, marks appear on your arms ?

A. Here and here.

...

Q. Will you tell what this discoloration is in the armpit?

A. That is the same as the others. They come and go. They get lighter and they get darker.

The Court: Let the record reflect the witness is indicating his right arm, and area between the shoulder and the elbow on the inside of the arm.

Mr. McMorris: We refer to a mark toward his body at the same spot about four inches from the previous mark, and I will ask you if that is the same as the other marks?

A. Yes, it is.

Mr. McMorris: The same nature.

I would like to have him reveal his back if the Court doesn't mind.

The Court: Yes, he may remove his shirt and his Tee-shirt.

(Witness complies.)

The Court: You may put your shirt and Tee-shirt on counsel table.

Q. I ask you to stand so that jury can view your back without describing it.

(Witness complied.)

The Court: Turn so the Court can see your back.

Mr. Gage: Could we allow Mr. Lundquist to make his observation of the defendant?

The Court: Yes, you may do so.

(Officer Lundquist examines the defendant.)

The Court: Officer Lundquist, do you wish to observe the back of the defendant?

Officer Lundquist: I have already done so.

The Court: Let the record indicate that Officer Lundquist has observed the arms of the defendant.

Mr. McMorris: You may put your shirt back on and resume the witness stand.

(Witness resumes the witness stand.)

Q. Those marks were occasioned from an injection of overseas shots in the arm?

A. Yes, sir.

Q. Do those marks come and go or remain static?

A. They remain that way. They get darker and they get lighter, but they stay and fresh ones will come up. When they first started, they first started on my body and now it comes up on my face. I went to the doctor and he doesn't know what to do.

. . .

Mr. McMorris: You may cross examine.

CROSS EXAMINATION

By **Mr. Gage:**

. . .

Q. It is your testimony that you never made any statement at all to any officer about the use of narcotics or answered any questions about the use of narcotics?

A. I answered a question about the use of narcotics.

Q. At the scene when they examined you, and they spoke to you, didn't you make a statement that you had had narcotics?

A. No, sir.

. . .

Q. Didn't you tell them that you hadn't fixed in about two months?

A. No, sir.

Q. Did you later make the statement that you had fixed about two weeks ago?

A. No, sir.

Q. Never had any conversation with any officer about using the cotton from your buddies' outfit when they were through?

A. No, sir.

Q. You went down to the jail after this arrest at Pico and Solano?

A. Yes, sir.

Q. Who did you go with?

A. The officers. I don't know their names. Sitting in the back there.

Q. How many of you were all together?

A. Four of us.

Q. Did you make any statement to the officers in the car about the use of narcotics?

A. No, sir.

Q. Were you interrogated at that time?

A. I was asked. The officers asked—it was a fellow and myself.

Q. You mean Mr. Banks, the driver of your car?

A. Yes.

Q. Did you make any statement at that time about the use of narcotics?

A. No, sir.

Q. The next day you were examined by Officer Lundquist, were you not?

A. I believe it was the next day, yes.

Q. And at that time did you tell him that you had had a fix about Wednesday?

A. No.

...

Q. When did you last have a needle injection into your arm?

A. The last time I had a needle injection into my arm? It was when I gave blood for a friend of mine's auntie.

Q. When was that?

A. That was in, if I am not mistaken, in '59.

Q. Was the last time you had any needle injected into your arm?

A. I have sold blood also.

Q. When was the most recent time?

A. The last time was in '59 that I had a needle stuck in my arm.

Q. What part of 1959?

A. It was just a little before Christmas, if I am not mistaken.

Q. Did that leave some scabs on your arm?

A. Yes, for a couple of days it was red.

Q. Was that in existence in February 1960?

A. No, sir.

Mr. Gage: No further questions.

(The witness left the stand.)

[Ruth Fairlur testified that she had known Robinson about three years, and that he had on his body dark spots that come and go. After the issue was introduced in cross examination, she testified to the facts surrounding the arrest in much the same vein as she had when the jury was not present. Ruby Robinson, defendant's mother, testified that he had marks on his body, that these began after his release from service in 1957, and that they changed, would get pinkish color for three weeks, and then go away leaving a dark spot.]

[Both sides rested.]

Colloquy Between Court and Counsel

The Court: Before you begin your argument would you approach the bench.

(The following was had at the bench out of the hearing of the jury.)

The Court: So we may understand a little more clearly what counsel has in mind, or perhaps the Court may have in mind, I understand, Mr. Gage, that you are not contending the defendant was under the influence of narcotics at the time of the arrest?

Mr. Gage: No, I don't think we can establish that....

The Court: I mention that because, apparently, Mr. McMorris has proceeded on some theory in that connection, and I do not intend to instruct the jury on it because I agree with Mr. Gage. The People have not made out a case, and I will instruct the jury by stating what the charge is; and failing to get forth that, therefore they will not gather that he is charged with that aspect of it.

In other words, Mr. Gage, you are proceeding on the theory that he is addicted to the use of narcotics and that he unlawfully uses narcotics.

Mr Gage: Yes, sir. However, primarily, on the question of use itself.

The Court: Then I shall instruct the jury, in effect, that the People are proceeding on the theory that the defendant is charged with unlawfully using narcotics, and that he is addicted to the use of narcotics and will instruct them accordingly.

[**Arguments of Counsel omitted.**]

INSTRUCTIONS ON USE AND ADDICTION

[**Other instructions omitted.**]

Ladies and gentlemen of the jury you are now instructed insofar as here applicable, Section 11721 of the Health and Safety Code provides that no person shall use, or be addicted to the use of narcotics, except when administered by or under the direction of a person licensed by the State of California to prescribe and administer narcotics. It shall be the burden of the defense to show that it comes within the exception. Any person convicted of violating any provision of this section is guilty of a misdemeanor.

You will note that it is a misdemeanor for a person either to use narcotics, or to be addicted to the use of narcotics, unless the use, or being addicted to narcotics, was administered or used under the direction of a person licensed by this state. In other words, the use of, or being addicted to narcotics is unlawful unless a doctor, dentist or a chiropodist of this state has prescribed such use or has administered such a narcotic. That portion of the statute referring to the "use" of narcotics is based upon the "act" of using. That portion of the statute referring to "addicted to the use" of narcotics is based upon a condition or status. They are not identical. A person may make use of narcotics once or for a short time without becoming or being addicted to the use of narcotics.

The word "addicted" means strongly disposed to some taste or practice or habituated, especially to drugs. In order to inquire as to whether a person is addicted to the use of narcotics is in effect an inquiry as to his habit in that regard. Does he use them habitually. To use them often or daily is, according to the ordinary acceptance of those words, to use them habitually.

To be addicted to the use of narcotics is said to be a status or condition and not an act. It is a continuing offense and differs from most other offenses in the fact that it is chronic rather than acute; that it continues after it is complete and subjects the offender to arrest at any time before he reforms. The existence of such a chronic condition may be ascertained from a single examination, if the characteristic reaction of that condition be found present.

. . .

Where a statute such as that which defines the crime charged in this case denounces an act and a status or condition, either of which separately as well as collectively, constitute the criminal offense charged, an accusatory pleading which accuses the defendant of having committed the act and of being of the status or condition as denounced by the statute, is deemed supported if the proof shows that the defendant is guilty of any one or more of the offenses thus specified. However, it is important for you to keep in mind that, in order to convict a defendant in such a case, it is necessary that all of you agree as to the same particular act or status or condition found to have been committed or found to exist. It is not necessary that the particular act or status or condition so agreed upon be stated in the verdict.

. . .

It is not incumbent upon the People to prove the unlawfulness of defendant's use of narcotics. All that the People must show is either that the defendant did use a narcotic in Los Angeles County, or that while in the City of Los Angeles he was addicted to the use of narcotics, and it is then up to the defendant to prove that the use of or of being addicted to the use of narcotics was administered by or under the direction of a person licensed by the State of California to prescribe and administer narcotics or at least to raise a reasonable doubt concerning the matter.

. . .

VERDICT

We, the jury in the entitled cause, find the defendant guilty of the offense charged. (viol. 11721 H.&S.)

MELVIN L. ENGLE, *Foreman* Date: June 9, 1960

June 22, 1960

Imposition of sentence suspended and defendant placed on probation for 2 years on following conditions:

1) Serve next 90 days in County Jail;

2) Take Nalline test at such time and at such places as he may be may be directed by his probation officer;

3) Remain gainfully employed;

4) Obey all laws; and

5) Comply with the directions of his probation officer and the Court

Defendant committed.

Bail ordered exonerated.

Notice of Appeal filed. Bail Appeal fixed at $500 + $25 P.A. in lieu commitment.

Part II
Defining Culpable Conduct

Except in the rare case where a constitutional provision would be violated, *e.g.*, the Due Process, Cruel and Unusual Punishment or Equal Protection clauses [see Chapter 1], the legislature is free to define crimes and apply punishments as it sees fit. As a general rule crimes are defined to require proof of both an act and a culpable mental state. The next nine chapters cover the definition of crimes. Chapters 2 and 3 develop the general rules for defining crimes. Chapter 2 deals with the act requirement, Chapter 3 with the mental state requirement. The remaining seven chapters explore the application of these general rules in the definitions of particular crimes. Chapters 4–7 concern the homicide crimes of murder and manslaughter, Chapter 8, the property crimes of theft and burglary; Chapter 9, the inchoate crimes of attempt, solicitation, and conspiracy; and Chapter 10, various crimes against the government or public authority.

Chapter 2

Act (Actus Reus)

The requirement of an act, *actus reus*, means that one cannot be criminally liable for merely having bad thoughts. The word "act" might be defined in various ways. It could be broadly defined so as to include any bodily movement, including sleepwalking, epileptic seizures, etc., or it could be more narrowly defined so as to be limited to voluntary bodily movement. Even if the narrower definition is adopted, "voluntariness" is an elusive concept. While it has long been a principle of Anglo-American law (unlike the situation in some civil law countries) that there is no general duty to act to avoid harm to others, there are some situations where an omission to act will substitute for an act and will support the imposition of criminal liability. The first two cases, *Robinson v. California* and *Powell v. Texas*, involve constitutional challenges to statutes arguably imposing liability on defendants who did no voluntary act. *Robinson* is the Supreme Court version of the trial court case examined in Chapter 1. The succeeding two cases examine when an act will be deemed to be voluntary. In *In re David W.*, the issue is whether a defendant is liable when he was "forced" to commit the criminal act by another person. In *People v. Newton*, the court considers when "unconsciousness" is a defense to a crime. Finally, in *People v. Heitzman*, the California Supreme Court, in the context of an elder abuse statute, addresses when an omission to act is punishable.

Robinson v. California

370 U.S. 660, 82 S.Ct. 1417 (1962)

Mr. Justice Stewart delivered the opinion of the Court.

A California statute makes it a criminal offense for a person to "be addicted to the use of narcotics."[1] This appeal draws into question the constitutionality of that provision of the state law, as construed by the California courts in the present case.

---

1. The statute is § 11721 of the California Health and Safety Code. It provides: "No person shall use, or be under the influence of, or be addicted to the use of narcotics, excepting when administered by or under the direction of a person licensed by the State to prescribe and administer narcotics. It shall be the burden of the defense to show that it comes within the exception. Any person convicted of violating any provision of this section is guilty of a misdemeanor and shall be sentenced to serve a term of not less than 90 days nor more than one year in the county jail...."

The broad power of a State to regulate the narcotic drugs traffic within its borders is not here in issue. More than forty years ago, in *Whipple v. Martinson*, 256 U.S. 41, this Court explicitly recognized the validity of that power: "There can be no question of the authority of the State in the exercise of its police power to regulate the administration, sale, prescription and use of dangerous and habit-forming drugs.... The right to exercise this power is so manifest in the interest of the public health and welfare, that it is unnecessary to enter upon a discussion of it beyond saying that it is too firmly established to be successfully called in question."

Such regulation, it can be assumed, could take a variety of valid forms. A State might impose criminal sanctions, for example, against the unauthorized manufacture, prescription, sale, purchase, or possession of narcotics within its borders. In the interest of discouraging the violation of such laws, or in the interest of the general health or welfare of its inhabitants, a State might establish a program of compulsory treatment for those addicted to narcotics.[7] Such a program of treatment might require periods of involuntary confinement. And penal sanctions might be imposed for failure to comply with established compulsory treatment procedures. Or a State might choose to attack the evils of narcotics traffic on broader fronts also — through public health education, for example, or by efforts to ameliorate the economic and social conditions under which those evils might be thought to flourish. In short, the range of valid choice which a State might make in this area is undoubtedly a wide one, and the wisdom of any particular choice within the allowable spectrum is not for us to decide. Upon that premise we turn to the California law in issue here.

...

This statute ... is not one which punishes a person for the use of narcotics, for their purchase, sale or possession, or for antisocial or disorderly behavior resulting from their administration. It is not a law which even purports to provide or require medical treatment. Rather, we deal with a statute which makes the "status" of narcotic addiction a criminal offense, for which the offender may be prosecuted "at any time before he reforms." California has said that a person can be continuously guilty of this offense, whether or not he has ever used or possessed any narcotics within the State, and whether or not he has been guilty of any antisocial behavior there.

It is unlikely that any State at this moment in history would attempt to make it a criminal offense for a person to be mentally ill, or a leper, or to be afflicted with a venereal disease. A State might determine that the general health and welfare require that the victims of these and other human afflictions be dealt with by compulsory treatment, involving quarantine, confinement, or sequestration. But, in the light of contemporary human knowledge, a law which made a criminal offense of such a dis-

7. California appears to have established just such a program in §§ 5350–5361 of its Welfare and Institutions Code. The record contains no explanation of why the civil procedures authorized by this legislation were not utilized in the present case.

ease would doubtless be universally thought to be an infliction of cruel and unusual punishment in violation of the Eighth and Fourteenth Amendments.[a]

We cannot but consider the statute before us as of the same category. In this Court counsel for the State recognized that narcotic addiction is an illness.[8] Indeed, it is apparently an illness which may be contracted innocently or involuntarily.[9] We hold that a state law which imprisons a person thus afflicted as a criminal, even though he has never touched any narcotic drug within the State or been guilty of any irregular behavior there, inflicts a cruel and unusual punishment in violation of the Fourteenth Amendment. To be sure, imprisonment for ninety days is not, in the abstract, a punishment which is either cruel or unusual. But the question cannot be considered in the abstract. Even one day in prison would be a cruel and unusual punishment for the "crime" of having a common cold.

We are not unmindful that the vicious evils of the narcotics traffic have occasioned the grave concern of government. There are, as we have said, countless fronts on which those evils may be legitimately attacked. We deal in this case only with an individual provision of a particularized local law as it has so far been interpreted by the California courts.

Mr. Justice Frankfurter took no part in the consideration or decision of this case.

Mr. Justice Douglas, concurring.

. . .

In Sixteenth Century England one prescription for insanity was to beat the subject "until he had regained his reason." Deutsch, The Mentally Ill in America (1937). In America "the violently insane went to the whipping post and into prison dungeons or, as sometimes happened, were burned at the stake or hanged"; and "the pauper insane often roamed the countryside as wild men and from time to time were pilloried, whipped, and jailed." Action for Mental Health (1961).

. . .

Today we have our differences over the legal definition of insanity. But however insanity is defined, it is in end effect treated as a disease. While afflicted people may be confined either for treatment or for the protection of society, they are not branded as criminals.

---

a. The Eighth Amendment's prohibition against cruel and unusual punishment by its terms applies only to the federal government, but it is made applicable to the states through the Fourteenth Amendment's due process clause.

8. In its brief the appellee stated: "Of course it is generally conceded that a narcotic addict, particularly one addicted to the use of heroin, is in a state of mental and physical illness. So is an alcoholic." Thirty-seven years ago this Court recognized that persons addicted to narcotics "are diseased and proper subjects for [medical] treatment." *Linder v. United States*, 268 U.S. 5.

9. Not only may addiction innocently result from the use of medically prescribed narcotics, but a person may even be a narcotics addict from the moment of his birth.

...

We should show the same discernment respecting drug addiction. The addict is a sick person. He may, of course, be confined for treatment or for the protection of society. Cruel and unusual punishment results not from confinement, but from convicting the addict of a crime. The purpose of § 11721 is not to cure, but to penalize. Were the purpose to cure, there would be no need for a mandatory jail term of not less than 90 days. Contrary to my Brother CLARK, I think the means must stand constitutional scrutiny, as well as the end to be achieved. A prosecution for addiction, with its resulting stigma and irreparable damage to the good name of the accused, cannot be justified as a means of protecting society, where a civil commitment would do as well. Indeed, in § 5350 of the Welfare and Institutions Code, California has expressly provided for civil proceedings for the commitment of habitual addicts. Section 11721 is, in reality, a direct attempt to punish those the State cannot commit civilly. This prosecution has no relationship to the curing of an illness. Indeed, it cannot, for the prosecution is aimed at penalizing an illness, rather than at providing medical care for it. We would forget the teachings of the Eighth Amendment if we allowed sickness to be made a crime and permitted sick people to be punished for being sick. This age of enlightenment cannot tolerate such barbarous action.[5]

MR. JUSTICE HARLAN, concurring.

I am not prepared to hold that on the present state of medical knowledge it is completely irrational and hence unconstitutional for a State to conclude that narcotics addiction is something other than an illness nor that it amounts to cruel and unusual punishment for the State to subject narcotics addicts to its criminal law. Insofar as addiction may be identified with the use or possession of narcotics within the State (or, I would suppose, without the State), in violation of local statutes prohibiting such acts, it may surely be reached by the State's criminal law. But in this case the trial court's instructions permitted the jury to find the appellant guilty on no more proof than that he was present in California while he was addicted to narcotics. Since addiction alone cannot reasonably be thought to amount to more than a compelling propensity to use narcotics, the effect of this instruction was to authorize criminal punishment for a bare desire to commit a criminal act.

...

[Dissenting opinions of CLARK, J. and WHITE, J. omitted.]

---

5. The difference between § 5350 and § 11721 is that the former aims at treatment of the addiction, whereas § 11721 does not. The latter cannot be construed to provide treatment, unless jail sentences, without more, are suddenly to become medicinal. A comparison of the lengths of confinement under the two sections is irrelevant, for it is the purpose of the confinement that must be measured against the constitutional prohibition of cruel and unusual punishments.

Powell v. Texas

392 U.S. 514, 88 S.Ct. 2145 (1968)

Mr. Justice Marshall announced the judgment of the Court and delivered an opinion in which The Chief Justice, Mr. Justice Black, and Mr. Justice Harlan join.

In late December 1966, appellant was arrested and charged with being found in a state of intoxication in a public place, in violation of Texas Penal Code, Art. 477 (1952), which reads as follows:

> Whoever shall get drunk or be found in a state of intoxication in any public place, or at any private house except his own, shall be fined not exceeding one hundred dollars.[b]

Appellant was tried in the Corporation Court of Austin, Texas, found guilty, and fined $20. He appealed to the County Court at Law No. 1 of Travis County, Texas, where a trial *de novo* was held. His counsel urged that appellant was "afflicted with the disease of chronic alcoholism," that "his appearance in public [while drunk was] ... not of his own volition," and therefore that to punish him criminally for that conduct would be cruel and unusual, in violation of the Eighth and Fourteenth Amendments to the United States Constitution.

The trial judge in the county court, sitting without a jury, made certain findings of fact, but ruled as a matter of law that chronic alcoholism was not a defense to the charge. He found appellant guilty, and fined him $50. There being no further right to appeal within the Texas judicial system, appellant appealed to this Court; we noted probable jurisdiction.

I

The principal testimony was that of Dr. David Wade, a Fellow of the American Medical Association, duly certificated in psychiatry. His testimony consumed a total of 17 pages in the trial transcript. Five of those pages were taken up with a recitation of Dr. Wade's qualifications. In the next 12 pages Dr. Wade was examined by appellant's counsel, cross-examined by the State, and re-examined by the defense, and those 12 pages contain virtually all the material developed at trial which is relevant to the constitutional issue we face here. Dr. Wade sketched the outlines of the "disease"

---

b. The comparable California statute reads as follows:

P.C. § 647— ... [E]very person who commits any of the following acts is guilty of disorderly conduct, a misdemeanor: ...

(f) Who is found in any public place under the influence of intoxicating liquor, any drug, controlled substance, toluene, or any combination of any intoxicating liquor, drug, controlled substance, or toluene, in a condition that he or she is unable to exercise care for his or her own safety or the safety of others, or by reason of his or her being under the influence of intoxicating liquor, any drug, controlled substance, toluene, or any combination of any intoxicating liquor, any drug, controlled substance, toluene, or any combination of any intoxicating liquor, drug, or toluene, interferes with or obstructs or prevents the free use of any street, sidewalk, or other public way.

concept of alcoholism; noted that there is no generally accepted definition of "alcoholism"; alluded to the ongoing debate within the medical profession over whether alcohol is actually physically "addicting" or merely psychologically "habituating"; and concluded that in either case a "chronic alcoholic" is an "involuntary drinker," who is "powerless not to drink," and who "loses his self-control over his drinking." He testified that he had examined appellant, and that appellant is a "chronic alcoholic," who "by the time he has reached [the state of intoxication] ... is not able to control his behavior, and [who] ... has reached this point because he has an uncontrollable compulsion to drink." Dr. Wade also responded in the negative to the question whether appellant has "the willpower to resist the constant excessive consumption of alcohol." He added that in his opinion jailing appellant without medical attention would operate neither to rehabilitate him nor to lessen his desire for alcohol.

On cross-examination, Dr. Wade admitted that when appellant was sober he knew the difference between right and wrong, and he responded affirmatively to the question whether appellant's act of taking the first drink in any given instance when he was sober was a "voluntary exercise of his will." Qualifying his answer, Dr. Wade stated that "these individuals have a compulsion, and this compulsion, while not completely overpowering, is a very strong influence, an exceedingly strong influence, and this compulsion coupled with the firm belief in their mind that they are going to be able to handle it from now on causes their judgment to be somewhat clouded."

Appellant testified concerning the history of his drinking problem. He reviewed his many arrests for drunkenness; testified that he was unable to stop drinking; stated that when he was intoxicated he had no control over his actions and could not remember them later, but that he did not become violent; and admitted that he did not remember his arrest on the occasion for which he was being tried. On cross-examination, appellant admitted that he had had one drink on the morning of the trial and had been able to discontinue drinking.

...

Following this abbreviated exposition of the problem before it, the trial court indicated its intention to disallow appellant's claimed defense of "chronic alcoholism." Thereupon defense counsel submitted, and the trial court entered, the following "findings of fact":

> "(1) That chronic alcoholism is a disease which destroys the afflicted person's will power to resist the constant, excessive consumption of alcohol.
>
> "(2) That a chronic alcoholic does not appear in public by his own volition but under a compulsion symptomatic of the disease of chronic alcoholism.
>
> "(3) That Leroy Powell, defendant herein, is a chronic alcoholic who is afflicted with the disease of chronic alcoholism."

Whatever else may be said of them, those are not "findings of fact" in any recognizable, traditional sense in which that term has been used in a court of law; they are the premises of a syllogism transparently designed to bring this case within the scope of this Court's opinion in *Robinson v. California*, 370 U.S. 660 (1962). Nonetheless, the dissent would have us adopt these "findings" without critical examination; it would use them as the basis for a constitutional holding that "a person may not be punished if the condition essential to constitute the defined crime is part of the pattern of his disease and is occasioned by a compulsion symptomatic of the disease."

The difficulty with that position, as we shall show, is that it goes much too far on the basis of too little knowledge. In the first place, the record in this case is utterly inadequate to permit the sort of informed and responsible adjudication which alone can support the announcement of an important and wide-ranging new constitutional principle. We know very little about the circumstances surrounding the drinking bout which resulted in this conviction, or about Leroy Powell's drinking problem, or indeed about alcoholism itself. The trial hardly reflects the sharp legal and evidentiary clash between fully prepared adversary litigants which is traditionally expected in major constitutional cases. The State put on only one witness, the arresting officer. The defense put on three—a policeman who testified to appellant's long history of arrests for public drunkenness, the psychiatrist, and appellant himself.

Furthermore, the inescapable fact is that there is no agreement among members of the medical profession about what it means to say that "alcoholism" is a "disease." One of the principal works in this field states that the major difficulty in articulating a "disease concept of alcoholism" is that "alcoholism has too many definitions and disease has practically none." [E. Jellinek, The Disease Concept of Alcoholism, (1960)] This same author concludes that "a disease is what the medical profession recognizes as such." In other words, there is widespread agreement today that "alcoholism" is a "disease," for the simple reason that the medical profession has concluded that it should attempt to treat those who have drinking problems. There the agreement stops. Debate rages within the medical profession as to whether "alcoholism" is a separate "disease" in any meaningful biochemical, physiological or psychological sense, or whether it represents one peculiar manifestation in some individuals of underlying psychiatric disorders.

. . .

It is one thing to say that if a man is deprived of alcohol his hands will begin to shake, he will suffer agonizing pains and ultimately he will have hallucinations; it is quite another to say that a man has a "compulsion" to take a drink, but that he also retains a certain amount of "free will" with which to resist. It is simply impossible, in the present state of our knowledge, to ascribe a useful meaning to the latter statement. This definitional confusion reflects, of course, not merely the undeveloped state of the psychiatric art but also the conceptual difficulties inevitably attendant upon the importation of scientific and medical models into a legal system generally predicated upon a different set of assumptions.

II

Despite the comparatively primitive state of our knowledge on the subject, it cannot be denied that the destructive use of alcoholic beverages is one of our principal social and public health problems.

...

... [F]acilities for the attempted treatment of indigent alcoholics are woefully lacking throughout the country. It would be tragic to return large numbers of helpless, sometimes dangerous and frequently unsanitary inebriates to the streets of our cities without even the opportunity to sober up adequately which a brief jail term provides. Presumably no State or city will tolerate such a state of affairs. Yet the medical profession cannot, and does not, tell us with any assurance that, even if the buildings, equipment and trained personnel were made available, it could provide anything more than slightly higher-class jails for our indigent habitual inebriates. Thus we run the grave risk that nothing will be accomplished beyond the hanging of a new sign—reading "hospital"—over one wing of the jailhouse.

One virtue of the criminal process is, at least, that the duration of penal incarceration typically has some outside statutory limit; this is universally true in the case of petty offenses, such as public drunkenness, where jail terms are quite short on the whole. "Therapeutic civil commitment" lacks this feature; one is typically committed until one is "cured." Thus, to do otherwise than affirm might subject indigent alcoholics to the risk that they may be locked up for an indefinite period of time under the same conditions as before, with no more hope than before of receiving effective treatment and no prospect of periodic "freedom."

...

Appellant ... seeks to come within the application of the Cruel and Unusual Punishment Clause announced in *Robinson v. California*, 370 U.S. 660 (1962), which involved a state statute making it a crime to "be addicted to the use of narcotics." This Court held there that "a state law which imprisons a person thus afflicted [with narcotic addiction] as a criminal, even though he has never touched any narcotic drug within the State or been guilty of any irregular behavior there, inflicts a cruel and unusual punishment...."

On its face the present case does not fall within that holding, since appellant was convicted, not for being a chronic alcoholic, but for being in public while drunk on a particular occasion. The State of Texas thus has not sought to punish a mere status, as California did in *Robinson*; nor has it attempted to regulate appellant's behavior in the privacy of his own home. Rather, it has imposed upon appellant a criminal sanction for public behavior which may create substantial health and safety hazards, both for appellant and for members of the general public, and which offends the moral and esthetic sensibilities of a large segment of the community. This seems a far cry from convicting one for being an addict, being a chronic alcoholic, being "mentally ill, or a leper...."

Robinson so viewed brings this Court but a very small way into the substantive criminal law. And unless *Robinson* is so viewed it is difficult to see any limiting principle that would serve to prevent this Court from becoming, under the aegis of the Cruel and Unusual Punishment Clause, the ultimate arbiter of the standards of criminal responsibility, in diverse areas of the criminal law, throughout the country.

It is suggested in dissent that *Robinson* stands for the "simple" but "subtle" principle that "[c]riminal penalties may not be inflicted upon a person for being in a condition he is powerless to change." In that view, appellant's "condition" of public intoxication was "occasioned by a compulsion symptomatic of the disease" of chronic alcoholism, and thus, apparently, his behavior lacked the critical element of *mens rea*. Whatever may be the merits of such a doctrine of criminal responsibility, it surely cannot be said to follow from *Robinson*. The entire thrust of *Robinson*'s interpretation of the Cruel and Unusual Punishment Clause is that criminal penalties may be inflicted only if the accused has committed some act, has engaged in some behavior, which society has an interest in preventing, or perhaps in historical common law terms, has committed some *actus reus*. It thus does not deal with the question of whether certain conduct cannot constitutionally be punished because it is, in some sense, "involuntary" or "occasioned by a compulsion."

Likewise, as the dissent acknowledges, there is a substantial definitional distinction between a "status," as in *Robinson*, and a "condition," which is said to be involved in this case. Whatever may be the merits of an attempt to distinguish between behavior and a condition, it is perfectly clear that the crucial element in this case, so far as the dissent is concerned, is whether or not appellant can legally be held responsible for his appearance in public in a state of intoxication. The only relevance of *Robinson* to this issue is that because the Court interpreted the statute there involved as making a "status" criminal, it was able to suggest that the statute would cover even a situation in which addiction had been acquired involuntarily. That this factor was not determinative in the case is shown by the fact that there was no indication of how Robinson himself had become an addict.

Ultimately, then, the most troubling aspects of this case, were *Robinson* to be extended to meet it, would be the scope and content of what could only be a constitutional doctrine of criminal responsibility. In dissent it is urged that the decision could be limited to conduct which is "a characteristic and involuntary part of the pattern of the disease as it afflicts" the particular individual, and that "[it] is not foreseeable" that it would be applied "in the case of offenses such as driving a car while intoxicated, assault, theft, or robbery." That is limitation by fiat. In the first place, nothing in the logic of the dissent would limit its application to chronic alcoholics. If Leroy Powell cannot be convicted of public intoxication, it is difficult to see how a State can convict an individual for murder, if that individual, while exhibiting normal behavior in all other respects, suffers from a "compulsion" to kill, which is an "exceedingly strong influence," but "not completely overpowering." Even if we limit our consideration to chronic alcoholics, it would seem impossible to confine the principle within the arbitrary bounds which the dissent seems to envision.

It is not difficult to imagine a case involving psychiatric testimony to the effect that an individual suffers from some aggressive neurosis which he is able to control when sober; that very little alcohol suffices to remove the inhibitions which normally contain these aggressions, with the result that the individual engages in assaultive behavior without becoming actually intoxicated; and that the individual suffers from a very strong desire to drink, which is an "exceedingly strong influence" but "not completely overpowering." Without being untrue to the rationale of this case, should the principles advanced in dissent be accepted here, the Court could not avoid holding such an individual constitutionally unaccountable for his assaultive behavior.

Traditional common-law concepts of personal accountability and essential considerations of federalism lead us to disagree with appellant. We are unable to conclude, on the state of this record or on the current state of medical knowledge, that chronic alcoholics in general, and Leroy Powell in particular, suffer from such an irresistible compulsion to drink and to get drunk in public that they are utterly unable to control their performance of either or both of these acts and thus cannot be deterred at all from public intoxication. And in any event this Court has never articulated a general constitutional doctrine of mens rea.

We cannot cast aside the centuries-long evolution of the collection of interlocking and overlapping concepts which the common law has utilized to assess the moral accountability of an individual for his antisocial deeds. The doctrines of actus reus, mens rea, insanity, mistake, justification, and duress have historically provided the tools for a constantly shifting adjustment of the tension between the evolving aims of the criminal law and changing religious, moral, philosophical, and medical views of the nature of man. This process of adjustment has always been thought to be the province of the States.

...

Mr. Justice Black, whom Mr. Justice Harlan joins, concurring.

...

I agree with Mr. Justice Marshall that the findings of fact in this case are inadequate to justify the sweeping constitutional rule urged upon us. I could not, however, consider any findings that could be made with respect to "voluntariness" or "compulsion" controlling on the question whether a specific instance of human behavior should be immune from punishment as a constitutional matter. When we say that appellant's appearance in public is caused not by "his own" volition but rather by some other force, we are clearly thinking of a force that is nevertheless "his" except in some special sense. The accused undoubtedly commits the proscribed act and the only question is whether the act can be attributed to a part of "his" personality that should not be regarded as criminally responsible. Almost all of the traditional purposes of the criminal law can be significantly served by punishing the person who in fact committed the proscribed act, without regard to whether his action was "compelled" by some elusive "irresponsible" aspect of his personality. As I have already indicated, punishment of such a defendant can clearly be justified in terms of deterrence, isolation, and treatment. On the other hand, medical decisions concerning the use of a term such as "disease" or "volition," based as they are on the clinical problems of diagnosis and treatment, bear no necessary correspondence to the legal decision whether the overall objectives of the criminal law can be furthered by imposing punishment. For these reasons, much as I think that criminal sanctions should in many situations be applied only to those whose conduct is morally blameworthy, I cannot think the States should be held constitutionally required to make the inquiry as to what part of a defendant's personality is responsible for his actions and to excuse anyone whose action was, in some complex, psychological sense, the result of a "compulsion."

III

The rule of constitutional law urged by appellant is not required by *Robinson v. California*, 370 U.S. 660 (1962). In that case we held that a person could not be punished for the mere status of being a narcotics addict. We explicitly limited our holding to the situation where no conduct of any kind is involved, stating:

> "We hold that a state law which imprisons a person thus afflicted as a criminal, *even though he has never touched any narcotic drug within the State or been guilty of any irregular behavior there*, inflicts a cruel and unusual punishment in violation of the Fourteenth Amendment." (Emphasis added.)

The argument is made that appellant comes within the terms of our holding in *Robinson* because being drunk in public is a mere status or "condition." Despite this many-faceted use of the concept of "condition," this argument would require converting *Robinson* into a case protecting actual behavior, a step we explicitly refused to take in that decision.

A different question, I admit, is whether our attempt in *Robinson* to limit our holding to pure status crimes, involving no conduct whatever, was a sound one. I believe it was. Although some of our objections to the statute in *Robinson* are equally applicable to statutes that punish conduct "symptomatic" of a disease, any attempt to explain *Robinson* as based solely on the lack of voluntariness encounters a number of logical difficulties.[3] Other problems raised by status crimes are in no way involved when the State attempts to punish for conduct, and these other problems were, in my view, the controlling aspects of our decision.

Punishment for a status is particularly obnoxious, and in many instances can reasonably be called cruel and unusual, because it involves punishment for a mere propensity, a desire to commit an offense; the mental element is not simply one part of the crime but may constitute all of it. This is a situation universally sought to be avoided in our criminal law; the fundamental requirement that some action be proved is solidly established even for offenses most heavily based on propensity, such as attempt, conspiracy, and recidivist crimes.

...

The reasons for this refusal to permit conviction without proof of an act are difficult to spell out, but they are nonetheless perceived and universally expressed in our criminal law. Evidence of propensity can be considered relatively unreliable and more dif-

3. Although we noted in *Robinson* that narcotics addiction apparently is an illness that can be contracted innocently or involuntarily, we barred punishment for addiction even when it could be proved that the defendant had voluntarily become addicted. And we compared addiction to the status of having a common cold, a condition that most people can either avoid or quickly cure when it is important enough for them to do so.

ficult for a defendant to rebut; the requirement of a specific act thus provides some protection against false charges. Perhaps more fundamental is the difficulty of distinguishing, in the absence of any conduct, between desires of the day-dream variety and fixed intentions that may pose a real threat to society; extending the criminal law to cover both types of desire would be unthinkable, since "[there] can hardly be anyone who has never thought evil. When a desire is inhibited it may find expression in fantasy; but it would be absurd to condemn this natural psychological mechanism as illegal." [citing 4 Blackstone, COMMENTARIES 2]

In contrast, crimes that require the State to prove that the defendant actually committed some proscribed act involve none of these special problems. In addition, the question whether an act is "involuntary" is, as I have already indicated, an inherently elusive question, and one which the State may, for good reasons, wish to regard as irrelevant. In light of all these considerations, our limitation of our *Robinson* holding to pure status crimes seems to me entirely proper.

IV

The rule of constitutional law urged upon us by appellant would have a revolutionary impact on the criminal law, and any possible limits proposed for the rule would be wholly illusory. If the original boundaries of *Robinson* are to be discarded, any new limits too would soon fall by the wayside and the Court would be forced to hold the States powerless to punish any conduct that could be shown to result from a "compulsion," in the complex, psychological meaning of that term. The result, to choose just one illustration, would be to require recognition of "irresistible impulse" as a complete defense to any crime; this is probably contrary to present law in most American jurisdictions.

The real reach of any such decision, however, would be broader still, for the basic premise underlying the argument is that it is cruel and unusual to punish a person who is not morally blameworthy. I state the proposition in this sympathetic way because I feel there is much to be said for avoiding the use of criminal sanctions in many such situations. But the question here is one of constitutional law. The legislatures have always been allowed wide freedom to determine the extent to which moral culpability should be a prerequisite to conviction of a crime. The criminal law is a social tool that is employed in seeking a wide variety of goals, and I cannot say the Eighth Amendment's limits on the use of criminal sanctions extend as far as this viewpoint would inevitably carry them.

But even if we were to limit any holding in this field to "compulsions" that are "symptomatic" of a "disease," in the words of the findings of the trial court, the sweep of that holding would still be startling. Such a ruling would make it clear beyond any doubt that a narcotics addict could not be punished for "being" in possession of drugs or, for that matter, for "being" guilty of using them. A wide variety of sex offenders would be immune from punishment if they could show that their conduct was not voluntary but part of the pattern of a disease. More generally speaking, a form of the insanity defense would be made a constitutional requirement throughout the Nation, should the Court now hold it cruel and unusual to punish a person afflicted with any mental disease whenever his conduct was part of the pattern of his disease and occasioned by a compulsion symptomatic of the disease.

. . .

Mr. Justice White, concurring in the result.

If it cannot be a crime to have an irresistible compulsion to use narcotics, *Robinson v. California*, 370 U.S. 660 (1962), I do not see how it can constitutionally be a crime to yield to such a compulsion. Punishing an addict for using drugs convicts for addiction under a different name. Distinguishing between the two crimes is like forbidding criminal conviction for being sick with flu or epilepsy but permitting punishment for running a fever or having a convulsion. Unless *Robinson* is to be abandoned, the use of narcotics by an addict must be beyond the reach of the criminal law. Similarly, the chronic alcoholic with an irresistible urge to consume alcohol should not be punishable for drinking or for being drunk.

Powell's conviction was for the different crime of being drunk in a public place. Thus even if Powell was compelled to drink, and so could not constitutionally be convicted for drinking, his conviction in this case can be invalidated only if there is a constitutional basis for saying that he may not be punished for being in public while drunk.

. . .

The trial court said that Powell was a chronic alcoholic with a compulsion not only to drink to excess but also to frequent public places when intoxicated. Nothing in the record before the trial court supports the latter conclusion, which is contrary to common sense and to common knowledge. The sober chronic alcoholic has no compulsion to be on the public streets; many chronic alcoholics drink at home and are never seen drunk in public. Before and after taking the first drink, and until he becomes so drunk that he loses the power to know where he is or to direct his movements, the chronic alcoholic with a home or financial resources is as capable as the nonchronic drinker of doing his drinking in private, of removing himself from public places and, since he knows or ought to know that he will become intoxicated, of making plans to avoid his being found drunk in public. For these reasons, I cannot say that the chronic alcoholic who proves his disease and a compulsion to drink is shielded from conviction when he has knowingly failed to take feasible precautions against committing a criminal act, here the act of going to or remaining in a public place. On such facts the alcoholic is like a person with smallpox, who could be convicted for being on the street but not for being ill, or, like the epileptic, who could be punished for driving a car but not for his disease.

The fact remains that some chronic alcoholics must drink and hence must drink somewhere. Although many chronics have homes, many others do not. For all practical purposes the public streets may be home for these unfortunates, not because their disease compels them to be there, but because, drunk or sober, they have no place else to go and no place else to be when they are drinking. This is more a function of economic station than of disease, although the disease may lead to destitution and perpetuate that condition. For some of these alcoholics I would think a showing could be made that resisting drunkenness is impossible and that avoiding public places when intoxicated is also impossible. As applied to them this statute is in effect a law which bans a single act for which they may not be convicted under the Eighth Amendment—the act of getting drunk.

It is also possible that the chronic alcoholic who begins drinking in private at some point becomes so drunk that he loses the power to control his movements and for that reason appears in public. The Eighth Amendment might also forbid conviction in such circumstances, but only on a record satisfactorily showing that it was not feasible for him to have made arrangements to prevent his being in public when drunk and that his extreme drunkenness sufficiently deprived him of his faculties on the occasion in issue.

These prerequisites to the possible invocation of the Eighth Amendment are not satisfied on the record before us.

...

Mr. Justice Fortas, with whom Mr. Justice Douglas, Mr. Justice Brennan, and Mr. Justice Stewart join, dissenting.

...

The sole question presented is whether a criminal penalty may be imposed upon a person suffering the disease of "chronic alcoholism" for a condition—being "in a state of intoxication" in public—which is a characteristic part of the pattern of his disease and which, the trial court found, was not the consequence of appellant's volition but of "a compulsion symptomatic of the disease of chronic alcoholism." We must consider whether the Eighth Amendment, made applicable to the States through the Fourteenth Amendment, prohibits the imposition of this penalty in these rather special circumstances as "cruel and unusual punishment." This case does not raise any question as to the right of the police to stop and detain those who are intoxicated in public, whether as a result of the disease or otherwise; or as to the State's power to commit chronic alcoholics for treatment. Nor does it concern the responsibility of an alcoholic for criminal acts. We deal here with the mere condition of being intoxicated in public.[2]

II

As I shall discuss, consideration of the Eighth Amendment issue in this case requires an understanding of "the disease of chronic alcoholism" with which, as the trial court found, appellant is afflicted, which has destroyed his "will power to resist the constant, excessive consumption of alcohol," and which leads him to "appear in public [not]

2. It is not foreseeable that findings such as those which are decisive here—namely that the appellant's being intoxicated in public was a part of the pattern of his disease and due to a compulsion symptomatic of that disease—could or would be made in the case of offenses such as driving a car while intoxicated, assault, theft, or robbery. Such offenses require independent acts or conduct and do not typically flow from and are not part of the syndrome of the disease of chronic alcoholism. If an alcoholic should be convicted for criminal conduct which is not a characteristic and involuntary part of the pattern of the disease as it afflicts him, nothing herein would prevent his punishment.

by his own volition but under a compulsion symptomatic of the disease of chronic alcoholism." It is true, of course, that there is a great deal that remains to be discovered about chronic alcoholism. Although many aspects of the disease remain obscure, there are some hard facts—medical and, especially, legal facts—that are accessible to us and that provide a context in which the instant case may be analyzed. We are similarly woefully deficient in our medical, diagnostic, and therapeutic knowledge of mental disease and the problem of insanity; but few would urge that, because of this, we should totally reject the legal significance of what we do know about these phenomena.

Alcoholism is a major problem in the United States. In 1956 the American Medical Association for the first time designated alcoholism as a major medical problem and urged that alcoholics be admitted to general hospitals for care. This significant development marked the acceptance among the medical profession of the "disease concept of alcoholism." Although there is some problem in defining the concept, its core meaning, as agreed by authorities, is that alcoholism is caused and maintained by something other than the moral fault of the alcoholic, something that, to a greater or lesser extent depending upon the physiological or psychological make-up and history of the individual, cannot be controlled by him.

. . .

Authorities have recognized that a number of factors may contribute to alcoholism. Some studies have pointed to physiological influences, such as vitamin deficiency, hormone imbalance, abnormal metabolism, and hereditary proclivity. Other researchers have found more convincing a psychological approach, emphasizing early environment and underlying conflicts and tensions. Numerous studies have indicated the influence of sociocultural factors. It has been shown, for example, that the incidence of alcoholism among certain ethnic groups is far higher than among others.

The manifestations of alcoholism are reasonably well identified. The late E. M. Jellinek, an eminent alcohologist, has described five discrete types commonly found among American alcoholics. It is well established that alcohol may be habituative and "can be physically addicting." It has been said that "the main point for the nonprofessional is that alcoholism is not within the control of the person involved. He is not willfully drinking."

. . .

Robinson stands upon a principle which, despite its subtlety, must be simply stated and respectfully applied because it is the foundation of individual liberty and the cornerstone of the relations between a civilized state and its citizens: Criminal penalties may not be inflicted upon a person for being in a condition he is powerless to change. In all probability, Robinson at some time before his conviction elected to take narcotics. But the crime as defined did not punish this conduct. The statute imposed a penalty for the offense of "addiction"—a condition which Robinson could not control. Once Robinson had become an addict, he was utterly powerless to avoid criminal guilt. He was powerless to choose not to violate the law.

In the present case, appellant is charged with a crime composed of two elements—being intoxicated and being found in a public place while in that condition. The crime, so defined, differs from that in *Robinson*. The statute covers more than a mere status. But the essential constitutional defect here is the same as in *Robinson*, for in both cases the particular defendant was accused of being in a condition which he had no capacity to change or avoid. The trial judge sitting as trier of fact found, upon the medical and other relevant testimony, that Powell is a "chronic alcoholic." He defined appellant's "chronic alcoholism" as "a disease which destroys the afflicted person's will power to resist the constant, excessive consumption of alcohol." He also found that "a chronic alcoholic does not appear in public by his own volition but under a compulsion symptomatic of the disease of chronic alcoholism." I read these findings to mean that appellant was powerless to avoid drinking; that having taken his first drink, he had "an uncontrollable compulsion to drink" to the point of intoxication; and that, once intoxicated, he could not prevent himself from appearing in public places. ...

The findings in this case, read against the background of the medical and sociological data to which I have referred, compel the conclusion that the infliction upon appellant of a criminal penalty for being intoxicated in a public place would be "cruel and inhuman punishment" within the prohibition of the Eighth Amendment. This conclusion follows because appellant is a "chronic alcoholic" who, according to the trier of fact, cannot resist the "constant excessive consumption of alcohol" and does not appear in public by his own volition but under a "compulsion" which is part of his condition.

I would reverse the judgment below.

Problem

Problem 4.

Concerned with the problems caused by the approximately 10,000 to 12,000 homeless persons living within City, the City Council enacted an ordinance which defined "camping" and otherwise read as follows:

Unlawful Camping

> It shall be unlawful for any person to camp, occupy camp facilities or use camp paraphernalia in the following areas, except as otherwise provided:
>
> (a) any street
>
> (b) any public parking lot or public area, improved or unimproved.

Storage of Personal Property in Public Places

> It shall be unlawful for any person to store personal property, including camp facilities and camp paraphernalia, in the following areas, except as otherwise provided by resolution of the City Council:

(a) any park;

(b) any street

(c) any public parking lot or public area, improved or unimproved.

Defendant is a homeless person who camps at night in a public parking structure and stores his belongings during the day in the bushes next to the parking lot. Defendant has been charged with violation of the ordinance, a misdemeanor. In light of the fact that City has no more than 975 permanent beds available for homeless persons and, even with the use of temporary shelters, cannot come close to housing City's homeless population, what arguments should be made on the constitutionality of Defendant's prosecution?

In re David W.

116 Cal. App. 3d 689, 172 Cal. Rptr. 266 (1981)

Ashby, J.

Pursuant to Welfare and Institutions Code section 602 the juvenile court found that appellant, a 15 year old, violated Penal Code section 647, subdivision (f), and placed appellant home on probation on various conditions.[1]

On February 6, 1980, Burbank Police Officers Bonnar and Stehr responded to a radio call concerning a juvenile possibly under the influence of a drug creating a disturbance. The call was initiated by appellant's mother who was concerned that appellant could not care for himself and that someone might get hurt. When the officers arrived at her home she directed them to an upstairs bedroom, stating that appellant had become very violent and was causing a disturbance. When the officers got to appellant's bedroom, they observed that appellant was being restrained by his brother and a couple of friends.

Appellant was violently attacking his brother; his speech was extremely slurred; he had trouble keeping balance when standing; his eyes were very red; and he had no aroma of alcoholic beverage about him. The officers were trained in the symptoms of persons under the influence of a drug. The officers formed the opinion that appellant was under the influence of a drug, and that he was unable to care for the safety of himself and others.

Appellant's mother said she needed help, that she could not control appellant and that she was going to call an ambulance because she was afraid appellant would be sick.

Appellant could not walk without assistance. The officers handcuffed him and assisted him downstairs by the arms. Appellant's mother had called an ambulance. One of the officers told her, "Cancel [the ambulance] and we'll take him to the hospital."

---

1. The disposition order was also based upon a finding on an unrelated petition that appellant was guilty of sale of marijuana. The appeal raises no issues with respect to that petition.

Appellant was escorted, handcuffed, to the police car, cursing the officers. He was taken to the Burbank Community Hospital. A doctor administered Ipecac to appellant. When that failed to induce vomiting, the doctor prepared to pump appellant's stomach. When the doctor ordered appellant's boots removed for this procedure, a packet containing pills appearing to be Tuinal fell to the floor. Appellant's symptoms were consistent with the influence of Tuinal, and appellant was placed under arrest for possession of a dangerous drug.

The instant petition, however, charges appellant only with violation of Penal Code section 647, subdivision (f), not with possession of any controlled substance.

Discussion

Appellant contends the record does not support the trial court's finding that appellant violated Penal Code section 647, subdivision (f). We agree.

Penal Code section 647, subdivision (f), provides in pertinent part: "Every person who commits any of the following acts is guilty of disorderly conduct, a misdemeanor: [¶] (f) Who is found in any public place under the influence of ... any drug ... in such a condition that he is unable to exercise care for his own safety or the safety of others...."

When the police found appellant, he was in a bedroom of his own home, which is manifestly not a public place within the meaning of the statute.

Appellant came to be in a public place, to wit, the sidewalk in front of his home and the police vehicle en route to the hospital, only because he was taken there by the police while handcuffed and while apparently resisting at least to the extent of cursing the officers.

While it is also clear that the police officers acted properly in taking custody of appellant and transporting him to the hospital at the request of his mother and for his own benefit by reason of urgent medical necessity, this fact should not justify appellant's prosecution for a crime he did not voluntarily commit. While he was in his home, appellant was not in violation of section 647, subdivision (f). Although the police had proper grounds and laudable motives to remove appellant for transportation to the hospital, the fact remains that he was compelled by the police officers to go to a public place.[2]

The People cite *People v. Olson* (1971) 18 Cal. App. 3d 592, and *People v. Perez* (1976) 64 Cal. App. 3d 297, both of which we find to be distinguishable. In *Olson* the intoxicated defendant rang the door bell at a home and was admitted to the home for the purpose of making a telephone call. The defendant then fell asleep

2. There is no indication the police actually arrested appellant for violation of section 647, subdivision (f). They transported him to the hospital for medical treatment and arrested him there for possession of dangerous drugs, the pills which fell from his boot during medical procedures. The prosecution, however, charged appellant only with violation of section 647, subdivision (f), not with possession. The record is unclear whether this was due to prosecutorial discretion or because the pills did not turn out to be contraband.

and the home owner requested the assistance of the police in removing the defendant from her home. After escorting the defendant outside the house and observing her symptoms, the police arrested the defendant for violation of section 647, subdivision (f), and transported the defendant to the police station, where heroin was found in her purse. The appellate court upheld the arrest and subsequent booking search, finding that the police had authority to aid a citizen in removing the defendant from her property and that once the defendant was outside, the police had reasonable cause to arrest her for violation of section 647, subdivision (f). In *Perez* the police knocked on the door of an apartment to investigate a domestic quarrel. The defendant opened the door and stepped out into the hallway, swinging an empty whisky bottle and otherwise displaying symptoms of intoxication. He was arrested for being drunk in a public place (the hallway) and was taken to the police station where heroin was discovered in his pockets. The appellate court upheld the arrest, finding that the defendant voluntarily came into the hallway. In dictum the court stated: "In any event, *People v. Olson*, indicates that whether the person under the influence of intoxicating liquor or a drug comes into a public place of his or her own volition is without legal consequence in determining whether that person has violated the subdivision."

Olson and *Perez* are qualitatively different from the instant case. In *Olson* the defendant had originally been in a public place and although she had been given temporary refuge in someone else's home, she had no business remaining there when the home owner's consent was withdrawn. Here appellant was in his own home. In *Perez* the defendant voluntarily stepped into the public hallway and the comment made by the appellate court was dictum. Neither case is good authority for the proposition that a person who is under the influence in his own home may be forcibly removed by the police and then prosecuted for being under the influence in a public place.

[The finding that appellant violated Penal Code section 647(f) was reversed.]

Problem

Problem 5.

Officer was investigating the scene of a burglary and came upon Defendant crouching in the bushes. Because Defendant was in a crouched position, his coat was open, and Officer was able to observe clearly that Defendant had a sheathed knife hanging from his belt. Officer ordered Defendant to come out of the bushes, and, when he was standing before her, his coat hung down covering his knife. Officer removed the knife and discovered that it was a dagger (a knife "capable of ready use as a stabbing weapon that may inflict great bodily injury or death"). Defendant is now charged with possession of a concealed dagger (P.C. § 21310). Knives carried in sheaths worn openly suspended from the waist are not considered to be concealed within the meaning of the statute. What arguments should be made on the charge?

People v. Newton

8 Cal. App. 3d 359, 87 Cal. Rptr. 394 (1970)

RATTIGAN, J.

Huey P. Newton[c] appeals from a judgment convicting him of voluntary manslaughter.

...

At relevant times, John Frey and Herbert Heanes were officers of the Oakland Police Department. The criminal charges against defendant arose from a street altercation in which Frey was fatally wounded by gunfire, and Heanes and defendant were shot, on October 28, 1967.

[Frey and Heanes made a traffic stop of defendant's vehicle and ordered him out.] Defendant asked "if there was any particular reason why he should." Heanes asked him "if there was any reason why he didn't want to." Frey then informed defendant that he was under arrest and ordered him out of the car.

Defendant got out of the Volkswagen and walked, "rather briskly" and in a westerly direction, to the rear of the police cars. Frey followed, three or four feet behind defendant and slightly to his (defendant's) right. Heanes followed them, but stopped at the front end of Frey's police car (the second car in line). Defendant walked to the "rear part" of Heanes's car (third in line), Frey still behind him, and turned around. He assumed a stance with his feet apart, knees flexed, both "arms down" at hip level in front of his body.

Heanes heard a gunshot and saw Officer Frey move toward defendant. As he (Heanes) drew and raised his own gun in his right hand, a bullet struck his right forearm. He grabbed his arm "momentarily" and noticed, from the corner of his eye, a man standing on the curb between the Volkswagen and Officer Frey's police car. Heanes turned and aimed his gun at the man (whom he apparently identified at the time as defendant's passenger, although he had not seen the passenger get out of the Volkswagen). The man "raised his hands and stated to me he wasn't armed, and he had no intentions of harming me." To the best of Heanes' knowledge, the man's hands were empty.

Heanes returned his attention to Officer Frey and defendant, who were "on the trunk lid of my car [the third car in line] tussling." The two were in "actual physical contact" and "seemed to be wrestling all over the trunk area of my car." He next remembered being on his knees at the front door of Frey's (the second) car, approximately "30, 35 feet" from the other two men. Defendant was then facing him; Officer Frey was "facing from the side" of defendant, toward the curb, and appeared to be "hanging onto" him. Holding his gun in his left hand, Heanes aimed at defendant

c. Huey Newton was one of the leaders of the Black Panther Party, a nationwide militant political and community service organization. Black Panthers were active in Oakland, and many were known to the Oakland police.

and fired "at his midsection." Defendant did not fall; Heanes saw no one fall at any time. He (Heanes) then heard "other gunshots ... from the area of where Officer Frey and ... [defendant] ... were tussling on the rear part of my car." Heanes did not see a gun in defendant's hand at any time.

...

Defendant, testifying in his own behalf, denied killing Officer Frey, shooting Officer Heanes, or carrying a gun on the morning of the shootings. His account of the episode was as follows: He was driving with Gene McKinney on Willow Street, and had just turned into Seventh Street when he noticed a red light through the rear window of the Volkswagen. He pulled over to the curb and stopped. Officer Frey approached the Volkswagen and said "Well, well, well, what do we have? The great, great Huey P. Newton." Frey asked for defendant's driver's license and inquired as to the ownership of the Volkswagen. Defendant handed him his (defendant's) license, and the vehicle registration, and said that the car belonged to LaVerne Williams. Officer Frey returned the license and walked back to his patrol car with the registration.

A few minutes later Officer Heanes arrived, conversed with Frey, then walked up to the Volkswagen and asked, "Mr. Williams, do you have any further identification?" Defendant said, "What do you mean, Mr. Williams? My name is Huey P. Newton ..." Heanes replied, "Yes, I know who you are." Officer Frey then ordered defendant out of the car. He got out, taking with him a criminal law book in his right hand. He asked if he was under arrest; Officer Frey said no, but ordered defendant to lean against the car. Frey then searched him, placing his hands inside defendant's trousers and touching his genitals. (Officer Heanes had testified that defendant was not searched at any time.) McKinney, who had also alighted from the Volkswagen, was then standing with Officer Heanes on the street side of the Volkswagen.

Seizing defendant's left arm with his right hand, Officer Frey told him to go back to his patrol car. Defendant walked, with the officer "kind of pushing" him, past the first police car to the back door of the second one. Defendant opened his book[4] and said, "You have no reasonable cause to arrest me." The officer said, "You can take that book and stick it up your a__, Nigger." He then struck defendant in the face, dazing him. Defendant stumbled backwards and fell to one knee. Officer Frey drew a revolver. Defendant felt a "sensation like ... boiling hot soup had been spilled on my stomach," and heard an "explosion," then a "volley of shots." He remembered "crawling ... a moving sensation," but nothing else until he found himself at the entrance of Kaiser Hospital with no knowledge of how he arrived there. He expressly testified that he was "unconscious or semiconscious" during this interval, that he was "still only semiconscious" at the hospital entrance, and that—after recalling some events at Kaiser Hospital—he later "regained consciousness" at another hospital.

The defense called Bernard Diamond, M.D., who testified that defendant's recollections were "compatible" with the gunshot wound he had received; and that "[a]

4. A criminal lawbook, with defendant's name inscribed inside, was found in a pool of blood near Officer Frey.

gunshot wound which penetrates in a body cavity, the abdominal cavity or the thoracic cavity is very likely to produce a profound reflex shock reaction, that is quite different than a gunshot wound which penetrates only skin and muscle and it is not at all uncommon for a person shot in the abdomen to lose consciousness and go into this reflex shock condition for short periods of time up to half an hour or so."

...

Although the evidence of the fatal affray is both conflicting and confused as to who shot whom and when, some of it supported the inference that defendant had been shot in the abdomen before he fired any shots himself. Given this sequence, defendant's testimony of his sensations when shot—supplemented to a degree, as it was, by Dr. Diamond's opinion based upon the nature of the abdominal wound—supported the further inference that defendant was in a state of unconsciousness when Officer Frey was shot.

Where not self-induced, as by voluntary intoxication or the equivalent, unconsciousness is a complete defense to a charge of criminal homicide. (Pen. Code, § 26, subd. Five.) "Unconsciousness," as the term is used in the rule just cited, need not reach the physical dimensions commonly associated with the term (coma, inertia, incapability of locomotion or manual action, and so on); it can exist—and the above-stated rule can apply—where the subject physically acts in fact but is not, at the time, conscious of acting. The statute underlying the rule makes this clear,[11] as does one of the unconsciousness instructions originally requested by defendant.[12] Thus, the rule has been invoked in many cases where the actor fired multiple gunshots while inferably in a state of such "unconsciousness," including some in which the only evidence of "unconsciousness" was the actor's own testimony that he did not recall the shooting.

Where evidence of involuntary unconsciousness has been produced in a homicide prosecution, the refusal of a requested instruction on the subject, and its effect as a complete defense if found to have existed, is prejudicial error. The fact, if it appears, that such evidence does not inspire belief does not authorize the failure to instruct: "However incredible the testimony of a defendant may be he is entitled to an instruction based upon the hypothesis that it is entirely true." *People v. Modesto*, (1963) 59 Cal.2d 722. It follows that the evidence of defendant's unconsciousness in the present case was "deserving of consideration" upon a material issue.

Defendant did not request instructions upon unconsciousness; as we have seen, his original request therefor was "withdrawn." But a trial court is under a duty to instruct upon diminished capacity, in the absence of a request and upon its own motion,

---

11. Penal Code section 26 provides in pertinent part that "All persons are capable of committing crimes except those belonging to the following classes: ... Five-Persons who *committed the act charged without being conscious thereof*." (Italics added.)

12. CALJIC 71-C, which read in pertinent part as follows: "Where a person commits *an act without being conscious thereof*, such act is not criminal even though, if committed by a person who was conscious, it would be a crime...." (Italics added.)

where the evidence so indicates. The difference between the two states—of diminished capacity and unconsciousness—is one of degree only: where the former provides a "partial defense" by negating a specific mental state essential to a particular crime, the latter is a "complete defense" because it negates capacity to commit any crime at all. Moreover, evidence of both states is not antithetical; jury instructions on the effect of both will be required where the evidence supports a finding of either. We hold, therefore, that the trial court should have given appropriate unconsciousness instructions upon its own motion in the present case, and that its omission to do so was prejudicial error.

...

Problems

Problem 6.

The facts are taken from *People v. Wu* [Chapter 4]. Defendant, a Chinese woman, was lured to the United States by Father and had a tumultuous and irregular relationship with him, during which she bore a child, Son. On the night of the homicide, Defendant was with Son, who was ten years old. Son reported being abused by Father and told Defendant that Father was living with another woman. Defendant began experiencing heart palpitations and breathing problems. She told Son she wanted to die and asked him if he would go too. She went to another room, returned with a cord cut from a window blind, strangled Son and attempted suicide.

Defendant testified that she did not remember strangling Son. One of Defendant's experts, a psychiatrist, testified:

Q. Did Defendant tell you what were the details of the strangulation of Son?

A. No. She did not remember the act afterward.

Q. Did you find that to be unusual?

A. Not unusual. When somebody has such a heat of passion or emotional state, under such a strong stress, it is not uncommon to have that kind of memory loss. But sometimes we call that a fugue state or dissociation or dissociated disorder.

Q. What does that really mean in laymen's terms?

A. A fugue state is kind of a mental state occurring when somebody cannot understand the reality that they are facing and there's a kind of automatic mechanism that changes the mentality into a different state. To give you an example, if a child is killed in front of the mother by a truck, I have seen the mother, who was in deep shock or grief, suddenly start laughing like nothing had happened. Laughing is a kind of counter mechanism to the grief, shock or sadness that she cannot accept.... Obviously [defendant] was under a kind of heat of emotion and was in a dreamy state. She remembered picking up the scissors to cut the cord, but she did not remember exactly how she

> picked them up or cut the rope. She remembered thinking after the strangulation that she was surprised how quickly a boy could die.

What arguments should be made as to whether Defendant is entitled to an instruction on unconsciousness?

Problem 7.

Defendant was charged with driving under the influence of drugs (Veh. Code § 23152(a)), with three prior driving under the influence convictions. The charge was based on the fact that Defendant was seen driving erratically on an interstate highway at 1:00 a.m., and a blood test after Defendant's arrest, revealed that he had .13 mg/liter of Ambien (trade name for zolpidem), a prescription sleep aid drug, in his system. The peak concentration after taking the maximum recommended dose would generally be no more than .12 mg/liter. When prescribed, Ambien comes with a warning that it may cause "drowsiness, dizziness, confusion, poor motor coordination, and erratic and impulsive behavior." The user is further advised not to drive or operate heavy machinery. In rare cases, Ambien has caused users to engage in complex behaviors a person does not typically engage in while asleep, including sleep walking, preparing food, eating, making phone calls and engaging in conversations, and sleep driving. Defendant testified as follows: that he was prescribed Ambien as a sleep aid seven years earlier and took it regularly; that he knew of the possible effects of Ambien and, on a few occasions, had made calls and had conversations while asleep, but that he had never engaged in sleep driving; and that, on the night he was arrested, he had no intent to drive and no knowledge that he had driven. Defendant has raised the defense of unconsciousness, and the trial judge intends to instruct the jury on the effect of intoxication on that defense as follows:

> A person is involuntarily intoxicated if he voluntarily ingested a legally prescribed drug that caused him to act unconsciously. In determining whether intoxication by prescription drug is involuntary, consider whether the defendant knew or had reason to anticipate that his use of the prescription drug could cause such intoxicating effects.

What are the arguments regarding whether the instruction is correct and whether, under the instruction, the defendant should be found not guilty because he was unconscious?

People v. Heitzman

9 Cal. 4th 189, 886 P.2d 1229 (1994)

Lucas, Chief Justice.

Penal Code section 368, subdivision (a), is one component of a multi-faceted legislative response to the problem of elder abuse. The statute imposes felony criminal liability on "[a]ny person who, under circumstances or conditions likely to produce great bodily harm or death, willfully causes or permits any elder or dependent adult, with knowledge that he or she is an elder or dependent adult, to suffer, or inflicts thereon unjustifiable physical pain or mental suffering, or having the care or custody of any elder or dependent adult, willfully causes or permits the person or health of the elder or dependent adult to be injured, or willfully causes or permits the elder or dependent adult to be placed in a situation such that his or her person or health is endangered...."[2]

In this case, we must decide whether the statute meets constitutional standards of certainty. As we shall explain, we conclude initially that, on its face, the broad statutory language at issue here fails to provide fair notice to those who may be subjected to criminal liability for "willfully ... permit[ting]" an elder or dependent adult to suffer pain, and similarly fails to set forth a uniform standard under which police and prosecutors can consistently enforce the proscription against "willfully ... permit[ting]" such suffering. Under these circumstances, section 368(a) would be unconstitutionally vague absent some judicial construction clarifying its uncertainties.

We conclude that the statute may properly be upheld by interpreting its imposition of criminal liability upon "[a]ny person who ... permits ... any elder or dependent adult ... to suffer ... unjustifiable pain or mental suffering" to apply only to a person who, under existing tort principles, has a duty to control the conduct of the individual who is directly causing or inflicting abuse on the elder or dependent adult. Because the evidence in this case does not indicate that defendant had the kind of "special relationship" with the individuals alleged to have directly abused the elder victim that would give rise to a duty on her part to control their conduct, she was improperly charged with a violation of section 368(a). We therefore reverse the judgment of the Court of Appeal.

I. Facts

The egregious facts of this case paint a profoundly disturbing family portrait in which continued neglect of and apparent indifference to the basic needs of the family's most vulnerable member, an elderly dependent parent, led to a result of tragic proportion. Sixty-seven-year-old Robert Heitzman resided in the Huntington Beach home of his grown son, Richard Heitzman, Sr., along with another grown son, Jerry Heitzman, and Richard's three sons. On December 3, 1990, police were summoned to the house, where they discovered Robert dead in his bedroom. His body lay on a mattress that was rotted through from constant wetness, exposing the metal springs. The stench of urine and feces filled not only decedent's bedroom, but the entire house as well. His bathroom was filthy, and the bathtub contained fetid, green-colored water that appeared to have been there for some time.

[Robert Heitzman had suffered a series of strokes twenty years earlier that had left him unable to care for himself. At the time of his death, Richard Heitzman, Sr. was

---

2. "Elder" is defined as "any person who is 65 years of age or older." (§ 368, subd. (d).) Section 368, subdivision (e), defines "dependent adult" as any person between 18 and 64 years of age "who has physical or mental limitations which restrict his or her ability to carry out normal activities or to protect his or her rights...."

working two jobs to support the household and also collecting his father's Social Security and pension checks, and Jerry Heitzman was primarily responsible for his father's care and was rendering caretaking services in exchange for room and board. Defendant Susan Valerie Heitzman, the victim's daughter, had previously lived in the home and had been her father's primary caregiver at that time, but she moved away more than a year prior to the death. She visited the household on a regular basis (primarily to see Richard, Jr., her boyfriend/nephew) and was aware that the house had become filthy and that her father was being neglected. She suggested to Jerry that he take the victim to the doctor, but she took no action herself. During the last two weeks of the victim's life, Susan had twice stayed overnight at the house, although she did not go into her father's room.][3]

...

II. Discussion

A. *Criminal Liability for a Failure to Act*

Section 368(a) purportedly reaches two categories of offenders: (1) any person who willfully causes or permits an elder to suffer, or who directly inflicts, unjustifiable pain or mental suffering on any elder, and (2) the elder's caretaker or custodian who willfully causes or permits injury to his or her charge, or who willfully causes or permits the elder to be placed in a dangerous situation. The statute may be applied to a wide range of abusive situations, including within its scope both active, assaultive conduct, as well as passive forms of abuse such as extreme neglect. (Cf. *People v. Smith* (1984) 35 Cal. 3d 798 [construing identical language in felony child abuse statute].)

Defendant here was charged under section 368(a) with willfully permitting her elder father to suffer the infliction of unjustifiable pain and mental suffering. It was thus her failure to act, *i.e.*, her failure to prevent the infliction of abuse on her father, that created the potential for her criminal liability under the statute.[6] Unlike the imposition of criminal penalties for certain positive acts, which is based on the statutory proscription of such conduct, when an individual's criminal liability is based on the failure to act, it is well established that he or she must first be under an existing legal duty to take positive action.

A legal duty to act is often imposed by the express provisions of a criminal statute itself ...

When a criminal statute does not set forth a legal duty to act by its express terms, liability for a failure to act must be premised on the existence of a duty found elsewhere. A criminal statute may thus incorporate a duty imposed by another criminal or civil statute....

---

3. The prosecution of Jerry and Richard, Sr., for their role in their father's death was clearly proper, and is not being challenged here.

6. There was no claim that defendant willfully caused the infliction of pain on her father, and we do not address that portion of the statute here.

A criminal statute may also embody a common law duty based on the legal relationship between the defendant and the victim, such as that imposed on parents to care for and protect their minor children. ([S]ee, e.g., *People v. Burden* (1977) 72 Cal. App. 3d 603 [murder defendant father under common law duty to care for young son].) Similarly, other special relationships may give rise to a duty to act....

Accordingly, in order for criminal liability to attach under section 368(a) for willfully permitting the infliction of physical pain or mental suffering on an elder, a defendant must first be under a legal duty to act. Whether the statute adequately denotes the class of persons who owe such a duty is the focus of the constitutional question presented here.

[The court determined that, as written, the statute did not define the offense "with sufficient definiteness that ordinary people can understand what conduct is prohibited and in a manner that does not encourage arbitrary and discriminatory enforcement" because it appeared to apply to any person—"for example, a delivery person who, having entered a private home, notices an elder in a disheveled or disoriented state and purposefully fails to intervene"—regardless of the person's relationship to the elder.[8] However, the court concluded that the statute would be constitutional if given a limiting construction]

In the law of torts, as a general principle, one is under no legal duty to control another's conduct. An exception exists, however, if the defendant stands in a special relationship to the actor whose conduct needs controlling. Such a relationship, if established, may support an affirmative duty for the benefit of third persons.

The Restatement Second of Torts provides guidance as to both the nature and the scope of the special relationships that would give rise to a duty to prevent an individual from inflicting pain or suffering on an elder, pursuant to section 368(a). These special relationships are defined as those between (1) parent and minor child, (2) employer and employee, (3) landowner and licensee, and (4) "[o]ne who takes charge of a third person whom he knows or should know to be likely to cause bodily harm to others if not controlled...." (Rest.2d Torts, §§ 316–319.) Case law applying and refining the "duty to control" principles serves as a further guide to determining when, under section 368(a), an individual may be held criminally liable for the failure to control the conduct of an individual who inflicts pain or suffering on an elder.

For example, as to the individual who takes charge of a third person whom he or she knows or should know is likely to cause bodily harm to others if not controlled, under existing principles of tort law, in order for one to "take charge" of a person

---

8. According to one treatise [Perkins & Boyce], the failure of the law to impose a broad legal duty to render assistance to one in need "has probably been due to the difficulty of definition coupled with a rather pronounced mind-your-own-business philosophy." As Professor Jerome Hall has suggested, "the reason the stranger who refuses food to a hungry child escapes any liability while the latter's father might be guilty of a criminal homicide is that, despite avowals, we have not reached the point of really believing that everyone is morally obliged to be his brother's keeper; or, at least, that is not believed sufficiently to be given implementation by the criminal law." Hall, *General Principles of Criminal Law* (2d Ed. 1960) Criminal Conduct, p. 210.

such that a legal duty to control his or her conduct is created, one must possess the ability to control. When such ability does not exist, no duty arises, rendering inactionable a civil claim against a defendant for the failure to control the conduct of another. From this it follows that one will be criminally liable for the abusive conduct of another only if he or she has the ability to control such conduct.

To construe section 368(a) as set forth above is reasonable in that it gives meaning to the specific statutory language at issue here, while at the same time it refrains from extending the reach of the statute in a manner that is unlikely to have been intended by the Legislature. Although, as so interpreted, the class of potential offenders may indeed be relatively small, it is one that is clearly not covered by that portion of the statute imposing a duty on caretakers and custodians to prevent injury or endangerment to their charge, no matter how broadly the terms "care" or "custody" are defined. For example, the parent found to be under a legal duty to supervise and control his or her child who, with criminal negligence, fails to prevent the child from inflicting pain on an elder, is subject to criminal liability under section 368(a). Criminal liability in such a case is properly based not on the relationship between the defendant and the elder, but rather, on that between the defendant and the abuser.

The reasonableness of our construction of the statutory language is further supported by the structure of the statute itself. We previously noted that section 368(a) imposes felony criminal liability on any person who affirmatively causes or inflicts unjustifiable pain or suffering on an elder, as well as on anyone who permits the infliction of such abuse on an elder. Under this statutory language, the class of potential defendants includes both those who directly inflict the abuse as well as those who passively fail to act. It is appropriate, therefore, that the duty imposed on an individual to prevent abuse be of sufficient stature and seriousness to warrant the same potential for felony liability as that faced by the individual who directly inflicts or causes an elder to suffer unjustifiable pain or mental suffering.

Moreover, as noted earlier, the statutory scheme also provides that a caretaker or custodian who causes or permits injury or physical endangerment will incur criminal liability with a lesser degree of harm or potential harm to the victim. By limiting potential criminal liability for the failure to prevent abuse of an elder to those under an existing legal duty to control the conduct of the person inflicting the abuse, the apparent relationship of culpability to harm inherent in the statutory structure is both recognized and maintained.

. . .

Kennard, Arabian and George, JJ., concur.

[Dissenting opinion of Baxter, J., joined by Mosk and Werdegar, JJ. omitted.]

Note and Problems

Punishment for Omissions. Most crimes are committed by affirmative action rather than by omission. There are, however, a number of crimes that are specifically defined in terms of omissions, *e.g.*, failure to file an income tax return. Other crimes, often defined in terms of achieving or causing a certain result, *e.g.*, permitting an elder or dependent adult to suffer, might in theory be committed either by an act or an omission. The former situation presents no particular difficulty—the legal duty is clear since it is written into the statute. In the latter situation, however, the courts have struggled to define when an omission to act should be treated the same as an act and have generally concluded, as did the court in *Heitzman*, that an omission is punishable only when the law otherwise establishes a duty to act. In *Jones v. United States*, 308 F.2d 307 (D.C. Cir. 1962), a decision that has come to be thought of as stating the general rule in this country, the court described four situations in which the failure to act might constitute breach of a legal duty: first, where a statute imposes a duty to care for another; second, where one stands in a certain status relationship to another (*e.g.*, parent to child, husband to wife, master to apprentice, ship's master to crew and passengers); third, where one has assumed a contractual duty to care for another; and fourth, where one has voluntarily assumed the care of another and so secluded the helpless person as to prevent others from rendering aid. The Model Penal Code adopts a similar approach:

> **§ 2.01(3)** Liability for the commission of an offense may not be based on an omission unaccompanied by action unless:
>
> (a) the omission is expressly made sufficient by the law defining the offense; or
>
> (b) a duty to perform the omitted act is otherwise imposed by law.

Problem 8.

Defendant, a married man, and Victim were lovers from time to time. On the weekend in question, Defendant's wife was out of town, and he and Victim engaged in a weekend-long debauch at his apartment. Clerk, a young employee of Defendant, was called on during the weekend to bring liquor to the apartment. On Monday, Clerk came to the apartment, and Defendant said that the rooms had to be straightened up because his wife was due back at any time. Defendant and Clerk then saw Victim begin to take some morphine tablets from a box. Defendant knocked the box out of her hand; some tablets fell on the floor; and Defendant crushed them. Clerk went away and was called by Defendant an hour later to come to the apartment and take Victim, who was in a stupor, to another apartment, where Friend lived. Defendant was too drunk to help, but requested Friend to look after Victim until she woke up. Several hours later she died in Friend's room. Had Victim been provided medical care during the first two hours after she took the morphine, she would have survived. What arguments should be made as to whether Defendant is guilty of homicide?

Problem 9.

Defendant and her boyfriend met Victim in a bar, and the three drank together for some time. When Defendant left to go home, Victim, who was extremely drunk, accompanied her. At Defendant's house, Victim asked for a spoon and to use the bathroom. Defendant was aware that Victim wanted the spoon to use to inject heroin in the bathroom. Victim came out of the bathroom and collapsed on the floor, and, when Defendant was unable to rouse him, she left the house. A short time later, Daughter (Defendant's daughter) arrived home, and, finding Victim unconscious and snoring on the floor, she called Defendant. Defendant told Daughter that Victim had shot up with heroin and instructed her to drag Victim outside in case he was violent when he woke up. Daughter dragged Victim outside and left him behind a shed, where he would not be seen by neighbors. Daughter later checked on Victim and found him with a pulse and still snoring. During the night, Victim died of a heroin overdose. Prompt medical attention shortly after Victim's collapse would have saved his life. What arguments should be made on whether Defendant or Daughter is guilty of homicide?

Defense Prosecution

Chapter 3

Mental State (Mens Rea)

Most crimes are defined to require proof, not only of a prohibited act (or omission), but also of "fault" (a culpable mental state) on the part of the actor. The culpable mental state is variously referred to as *mens rea* ("guilty mind"), scienter, or criminal intent. Criminal law recognizes two species of fault: (1) subjective fault, requiring proof of the particular actor's actual state of mind with regard to his/her actions or the surrounding circumstances; and (2) objective or imputed fault determined according to a reasonable person standard. Although one or the other form of *mens rea* is an element of most crimes, some crimes or elements of crimes are defined without regard to fault *i.e.*, the defendant is held strictly liable for the act alone. The mental state element(s) of any crime necessarily will fall into one of these three categories. The difficulty for the courts is that the California Penal Code (unlike, for example, the Model Penal Code) has no general provision defining the terms used in the various Penal Code sections. As a result, a variety of "mental state" terms are used in the statutes, and sometimes no term at all is used. For example, consider the following statutory language:

> **Resisting public officers** (P.C. § 148)—Every person who *wilfully* resists, delays, or obstructs....
>
> **Mayhem** (P.C. § 203)—Every person who *unlawfully* and *maliciously* deprives a human being of a member of his body....
>
> **Robbery** (P.C. § 211)—Robbery is the *felonious* taking of personal property in the possession of another....
>
> **Rape** (P.C. § 261)—Rape is an act of sexual intercourse accomplished with a person ... against a person's will by means of force, violence, duress, menace....
>
> **Burglary** (P.C. § 459)—Every person who enters any house, ... with the *intent* to commit grand or petit larceny or any felony....
>
> **Receiving stolen property** (P.C. § 496)—Every person who buys or receives any property that has been stolen..., *knowing* the property to be so stolen....

The difficulty in categorizing crimes according to whether a culpable mental state element is either subjective or objective has been compounded in California because of the California Supreme Court's failure to address the issue in those terms. Instead, the court has drawn a distinction between "specific intent" and "general intent" crimes. A specific intent crime is one requiring, in addition to proof of the defendant's intent to do the proscribed act, his/her "intent to do some further act or achieve some additional consequence." Since there are some subjective mental state elements of crimes which do not fall within the definition of specific intent (*e.g.* malice, knowledge), the category of general intent crimes includes some subjective fault crimes in addition to all objective fault crimes. Section A addresses the general principals of *mens rea.* The cases in Section B deal with a defendant's claimed mistake of fact in the context of sex crimes. The cases in Section C involve defendants who made a mistake as to the law.

A. General Principles of *Mens Rea*

The cases in this section involve the courts' categorization of the mental state element for the particular crime charged. The issue of whether a given crime requires proof of a subjective mental state, objective mental state or no mental state at all can be raised in two contexts, by a challenge to the jury instructions as to the mental state element or by a challenge to exclusion of evidence relevant to the defendant's mental state.[a] The first two cases concern the *mens rea* of the crime of assault. In *People v. Hood*, the California Supreme Court considers whether the crime of assault with a deadly weapon is a specific intent or general intent crime in order to determine whether the defendant is entitled to present evidence of voluntary intoxication. The decision in *Hood* did not finally resolve the issue of the *mens rea* for assault, and thirty years later, the issue is reprised in *People v. Williams*, with a somewhat different result. In *People v. Reyes*, the question is whether voluntary intoxication evidence is admissible in a prosecution for receiving stolen property, a crime requiring proof of knowledge, but not specific intent. *People v. Scott*, concerns a defendant charged with the specific intent crime of joyriding who claimed that he was *involuntarily* intoxicated, and the court has to decide whether his intoxication disproves the mental element of the crime or establishes an affirmative defense of necessity. In the last case, *In re Jorge M.*, the Supreme Court must determine the *mens rea* of possession of an assault weapon, and, in particular, whether possession of an assault weapon is a strict liability crime.

People v. Hood

1 Cal. 3d 444, 462 P.2d 370 (1969)

TRAYNOR, C. J.

An indictment charged defendant in count I with assault with a deadly weapon upon a peace officer, Alfred Elia (Pen. Code, § 245, subd. (b)), in count II with battery upon a peace officer, Donald Kemper (Pen. Code, §§ 242, 243), and in count III with

---

a. In the process of determining what evidence is admissible on the issue of the defendant's mental state, the courts often refer to the defense of intoxication or the defense of mistake. Such "defenses" should be distinguished from the "affirmative defenses" considered in Chapters 11 and 12. The cases in this section deal with evidence that may *disprove the existence of an element of the crime.* An affirmative defense, *e.g.*, self-defense, does not negate an element of the crime charged, but constitutes a justification or excuse for committing what would otherwise be a crime.

assault with intent to murder Officer Elia. (Pen. Code, § 217.) A jury found him guilty on counts I and III and not guilty on count II, and the trial court entered judgment on the verdicts.

...

On September 11, 1967, at about 2 a.m., defendant, his brother Donald, and a friend, Leo Chilton, all of whom had been drinking for several hours, knocked on the door of the house of Susan Bueno, defendant's former girlfriend, and asked if they could use the bathroom. Susan said no, but defendant forced his way in and started to hit her. He knocked her to the floor and kicked her. Donald Hood then took Susan aside, and defendant, Chilton, and Gene Saunders, a friend of Susan's who was staying at the house, went to the kitchen and sat down.

Gilbert A. Nielsen, Susan's next-door neighbor, was awakened by the sound of Susan's screams and called the police. Officers Elia and Kemper responded to his call. After talking to Nielsen, they went to Susan's house, knocked on the door, which was opened by Stella Gonzales, Susan's cousin, and asked if "Susie" was there. Miss Gonzales said, "Yes, just a minute," and in a few seconds Susan came running to the door crying. Officer Elia asked Susan if she had been beaten and who did it. She pointed to the kitchen and said, "They're in there right now." The two officers walked through the living room, where Susan, Susan's seven-year-old son Ronnie, and Stella remained, and went into the kitchen. There they observed defendant on the right-hand side of the room leaning against a door. On the left side of the kitchen, the three other men were seated at a table. Officer Elia walked to the middle of the room and questioned the men at the table. Defendant interrupted the questioning and asked Officer Elia if he had a search warrant. Officer Elia replied that he did not need one since the person who rented the house had given him permission to enter. Defendant then directed a stream of obscenities at Officer Elia, who turned and, according to his testimony, started to place defendant under arrest for a violation of Penal Code section 415 (using vulgar, profane, or indecent language within the presence or hearing of women or children). He got no further than to say, "Okay fella, you are...," when defendant swung at him with his fist. When Officer Kemper attempted to go to Officer Elia's assistance, Donald Hood jumped on him from behind. During the ensuing struggle, Officer Elia fell with defendant on top of him in a corner of a pantry adjoining the kitchen at the rear. While struggling on the floor, Officer Elia felt a tug at his gun belt and then heard two shots fired.

A third officer, Laurence Crocker, who had arrived at the house shortly after the other two officers, came into the kitchen as the scuffle between Officer Elia and defendant was beginning. After he had control of Donald Hood, he looked across the kitchen and saw defendant with a gun in his right hand. He testified that defendant pointed the gun towards Officer Elia's midsection and pulled the trigger twice.

Both Officers Crocker and Kemper testified that after the shots, defendant's arm came up over his head with the revolver in his hand. The struggle continued into the bathroom. Defendant was finally subdued when Officer Elia regained possession of the gun and held it against the side of defendant's neck. Officer Elia then noticed that defendant had shot him once in each leg.

[The court reversed the conviction because the jury had been improperly instructed.]

To guide the trial court on retrial, we consider the question of the effect of intoxication on the crime of assault with a deadly weapon.

...

The distinction between specific and general intent crimes evolved as a judicial response to the problem of the intoxicated offender. That problem is to reconcile two competing theories of what is just in the treatment of those who commit crimes while intoxicated. On the one hand, the moral culpability of a drunken criminal is frequently less than that of a sober person effecting a like injury. On the other hand, it is commonly felt that a person who voluntarily gets drunk and while in that state commits a crime should not escape the consequences.

Before the nineteenth century, the common law refused to give any effect to the fact that an accused committed a crime while intoxicated. The judges were apparently troubled by this rigid traditional rule, however, for there were a number of attempts during the early part of the nineteenth century to arrive at a more humane, yet workable, doctrine. The theory that these judges explored was that evidence of intoxication could be considered to negate intent, whenever intent was an element of the crime charged. As Professor Hall notes, however, such an exculpatory doctrine could eventually have undermined the traditional rule entirely, since some form of *mens rea* is a requisite of all but strict liability offenses. (Hall, *Intoxication and Criminal Responsibility*, 57 Harv. L. Rev. 1045.) To limit the operation of the doctrine and achieve a compromise between the conflicting feelings of sympathy and reprobation for the intoxicated offender, later courts both in England and this country drew a distinction between so-called specific intent and general intent crimes.

Specific and general intent have been notoriously difficult terms to define and apply, and a number of text writers recommend that they be abandoned altogether. (Hall, General Principles of Criminal Law, *supra*; Williams, Criminal Law—The General Part (2d ed. 1961) § 21.) Too often the characterization of a particular crime as one of specific or general intent is determined solely by the presence or absence of words describing psychological phenomena—"intent" or "malice," for example—in the statutory language defining the crime. When the definition of a crime consists of only the description of a particular act, without reference to intent to do a further act or achieve a future consequence, we ask whether the defendant intended to do the proscribed act. This intention is deemed to be a general criminal intent. When the definition refers to defendant's intent to do some further act or achieve some additional consequence, the crime is deemed to be one of specific intent. There is no real difference, however, only a linguistic one, between an intent to do an act already performed and an intent to do that same act in the future.

The language of Penal Code section 22, drafted in 1872 when "specific" and "general" intent were not yet terms of art, is somewhat broader than those terms: "No act committed by a person while in a state of voluntary intoxication is less criminal by reason of his having been in such condition. But whenever the actual existence of any particular purpose, motive, or intent is a necessary element to constitute any particular species or degree of crime, the jury may take into consideration the fact that the accused was intoxicated at the time, in determining the purpose, motive, or intent with which he committed the act." Even this statement of the relevant policy is no easier to apply to particular crimes. We are still confronted with the difficulty of characterizing the mental element of a given crime as a particular purpose, motive, or intent necessary to constitute the offense, or as something less than that to which evidence of intoxication is not pertinent.

Even if we assume that the presence or absence of words clearly denoting mental activity is a valid criterion for determining the significance of intoxication, our present problem is not resolved. The difficulty with applying such a test to the crime of assault or assault with a deadly weapon is that no word in the relevant code provisions unambiguously denotes a particular mental element, yet the word "attempt" in Penal Code section 240 strongly suggests goal-directed, intentional behavior.[6] This uncertainty accounts for the conflict over whether assault is a crime only of intention or also of recklessness.

We need not reconsider our position in *Carmen* that an assault cannot be predicated merely on reckless conduct. Even if assault requires an intent to commit a battery on the victim, it does not follow that the crime is one in which evidence in intoxication ought to be considered in determining whether the defendant had that intent. It is true that in most cases specific intent has come to mean an intention to do a future act or achieve a particular result, and that assault is appropriately characterized as a specific intent crime under this definition. An assault, however, is equally well characterized as a general intent crime under the definition of general intent as an intent merely to do a violent act. Therefore, whatever reality the distinction between specific and general intent may have in other contexts, the difference is chimerical in the case of assault with a deadly weapon or simple assault. Since the definitions of both specific intent and general intent cover the requisite intent to commit a battery, the decision whether or not to give effect to evidence of intoxication must rest on other considerations.

A compelling consideration is the effect of alcohol on human behavior. A significant effect of alcohol is to distort judgment and relax the controls on aggressive and antisocial impulses. Alcohol apparently has less effect on the ability to engage in simple goal-directed behavior, although it may impair the efficiency of that behavior. In other words, a drunk man is capable of forming an intent to do something simple, such as strike another, unless he is so drunk that he has reached the stage of unconsciousness.

6. Penal Code, section 240 provides: "An assault is an unlawful attempt, coupled with a present ability, to commit a violent injury on the person of another." It was the strong suggestion of intent in the ordinary usage of the word "attempt" that was at the basis of this court's remark in *People v. Carmen*, (1951) 36 Cal. 2d 768, that "[one] could not very well 'attempt' or try to 'commit' an injury on the person of another if he had no intent to cause any injury to such other person."

What he is not as capable as a sober man of doing is exercising judgment about the social consequences of his acts or controlling his impulses toward anti-social acts. He is more likely to act rashly and impulsively and to be susceptible to passion and anger. It would therefore be anomalous to allow evidence of intoxication to relieve a man of responsibility for the crimes of assault with a deadly weapon or simple assault, which are so frequently committed in just such a manner. As the court said in *Parker v. United States* (D.C. Cir. 1966) 359 F.2d 1009, "Whatever ambiguities there may be in distinguishing between specific and general intent to determine whether drunkenness constitutes a defense, an offense of this nature is not one which requires an intent that is susceptible to negation through a showing of voluntary intoxication."

Those crimes that have traditionally been characterized as crimes of specific intent are not affected by our holding here. The difference in mental activity between formulating an intent to commit a battery and formulating an intent to commit a battery for the purpose of raping or killing may be slight, but it is sufficient to justify drawing a line between them and considering evidence of intoxication in the one case and disregarding it in the other.[7] Accordingly, on retrial the court should not instruct the jury to consider evidence of defendant's intoxication in determining whether he committed assault with a deadly weapon on a peace officer or any of the lesser assaults included therein.

. . .

Notes

The Model Penal Code and Mens Rea. In place of specific intent and general intent as used in California law, the Model Penal Code defines four culpable mental states, as follows:

> **§2.02(2):** Kinds of Culpability Defined.
>
> (a) **Purposely.**
>
> A person acts purposely with respect to a material element of an offense when:
>
> (i) if the element involves the nature of his conduct or a result thereof, it is his conscious object to engage in conduct of that nature or to cause such a result; and
>
> (ii) if the element involves the attendant circumstances, he is aware of the existence of such circumstances or he believes or hopes that they exist.

---

7. It should be pointed out that the fact that intent may be inferred from the defendant's conduct does not affect the nature of the requisite intent. Whether the intent be merely to do that which was done or to do a further act or achieve a particular consequence, the jury may infer from defendant's acts that defendant acted with the requisite intent, if such an inference is warranted by the evidence.... In the crimes of simple assault and assault with a deadly weapon, the jury may infer from defendant's conduct that he entertained the necessary intent to commit an injury. Such an inference does not affect the nature of that intent or determine what significance should be accorded to evidence of intoxication.

(b) **Knowingly.**

A person acts knowingly with respect to a material element of an offense when:

(i) if the element involves the nature of his conduct or the attendant circumstances, he is aware that his conduct is of that nature or that such circumstances exist; and

(ii) if the element involves a result of his conduct, he is aware that it is practically certain that his conduct will cause such a result.

(c) **Recklessly.**

A person acts recklessly with respect to a material element of an offense when he consciously disregards a substantial and unjustifiable risk that the material element exists or will result from his conduct. The risk must be of such a nature and degree that, considering the nature and purpose of the actor's conduct and the circumstances known to him, its disregard involves a gross deviation from the standard of conduct that a law-abiding person would observe in the actor's situation.

(d) **Negligently.**

A person acts negligently with respect to a material element of an offense when he should be aware of a substantial and unjustifiable risk that the material element exists or will result from his conduct. The risk must be of such a nature and degree that the actor's failure to perceive it, considering the nature and purpose of his conduct and the circumstances known to him, involves a gross deviation from the standard of care that a reasonable person would observe in the actor's situation.

How does this scheme compare to the California approach? To the extent it differs, is it preferable?

The Model Penal Code and Intoxication. The Model Penal Code's approach to intoxication is as follows:

§ 2.08: Intoxication

(1) Except as provided in Subsection (4) of this Section, intoxication of the actor is not a defense unless it negatives an element of the offense.

(2) When recklessness establishes an element of the offense, if the actor, due to self-induced intoxication, is unaware of a risk of which he would have been aware had he been sober, such unawareness is immaterial.

(3) Intoxication does not, in itself, constitute mental disease within the meaning of Section 4.01 [defining insanity].

(4) Intoxication which (a) is not self-induced or (b) is pathological [where the intoxication is grossly excessive given the amount of the intoxicant and the actor did not know of his/her susceptibility], is an affirmative defense if by reason of such intoxication the actor at the time of his conduct lacks sub-

> stantial capacity either to appreciate its criminality [wrongfulness] or to conform his conduct to the requirements of law.

How does this approach compare to the California approach? To the extent it differs, is it preferable?

The Court Reconsiders the Mens Rea of Assault. The *Hood* case generated considerable confusion in the lower courts concerning the *mens rea* of assault, and, in *People v. Rocha*, 3 Cal.3d 893 (1971), the court revisited the issue in an attempt to eliminate the confusion. In *Rocha*, as in *Hood*, the defendant, who was charged with assault with a deadly weapon, argued that the crime was one of specific intent and that his voluntary intoxication constituted a defense. The court held that the *mens rea* of assault was "the general intent to wilfully commit an act the direct, natural and probable consequences of which if successfully completed would be the injury to another" and that, consequently, intoxication was no defense. *Rocha* did not eliminate the confusion, and the court again returned to the issue in *People v. Colantuono*, 7 Cal.4th 206 (1994). In *Colantuono*, the defendant was charged with assault with a deadly weapon in a shooting incident. Unlike the defendants in *Hood* and *Rocha*, the defendant did not claim that he was intoxicated, but rather that the shooting was an accident. The trial court gave seemingly inconsistent instructions on the mens rea of assault. On the one hand, the court instructed that the crime was one of general intent and that, to convict, the jury had only to find (in language taken from *Rocha*) that the defendant "intended to commit an act the direct, natural and probable consequences of which if successfully completed would be the injury to another." On the other hand the court also instructed that, "Reckless conduct alone, does not constitute a sufficient basis for assault ... However, when an act inherently dangerous to others is committed with a conscious disregard of human life and safety, the act transcends recklessness, and the intent to commit a battery is presumed." The supreme court affirmed the conviction on the basis of *Rocha*, holding that assault was a general intent crime and that the prosecution need only prove that the defendant performed a "willful act that by its nature [would] directly and immediately cause the least touching." *Colantuono* proved no more successful than *Rocha* in clearing up the confusion, so the court tried again in the following case.

People v. Williams

26 Cal.4th 779, 29 P.3d 197 (2001)

Brown, J.

Thirty years ago, we examined the mental state for assault and concluded assault requires only a general criminal intent and not a specific intent to cause injury. (*People v. Rocha* (1971) 3 Cal.3d 893 (*Rocha*).) Seven years ago, we reaffirmed *Rocha* and reiterated that assault was a general intent crime. (*People v. Colantuono* (1994) 7 Cal.4th 206 (*Colantuono*).) We further explained that the "mens rea [for assault] is established upon proof the defendant willfully committed an act that by its nature will probably and directly result in injury to another, i.e., a battery." Today, we once again clarify the mental state for assault and hold that assault requires actual knowledge of the facts sufficient to establish that the defendant's act by its nature will probably and directly result in injury to another. In light of this clarification, any technical error in the instructions given was harmless.

Holding

Facts

Gregory King and Deborah Nicholson married in 1989. Their marriage lasted only about two weeks, but they continued to have sexual relations. In 1992, Nicholson became romantically involved with defendant Lebarron Keith Williams. Nicholson had a son in November 1994, but did not know which of the two men had fathered the child. After the child's birth, defendant and King continued to compete for Nicholson's affections. Their rivalry resulted in several confrontations culminating in this case.

Prior to the confrontation at issue here, King repeatedly telephoned Nicholson, trying to persuade her to accompany him and his two teenage sons on an outing. When Nicholson disconnected her phone, King drove to Nicholson's home with his sons and parked his compact pickup truck at the front curb. Defendant's pickup truck was in the driveway. King walked up to Nicholson's front door and put a note on the door. He then knocked and returned to his truck, hoping Nicholson would come out and talk to him.

Defendant opened the door and told King to stay away from Nicholson. Defendant then walked to his own truck and removed a shotgun, which he loaded with two 12 gauge shotgun rounds. Defendant walked back toward the house and fired, in his words, a "warning shot" directly into the rear passenger side wheel well of King's truck. Defendant testified that, at the time he fired the shot, King's truck was parked between him and King, and that he saw King crouched approximately a foot and a half away from the rear fender well of the truck. Defendant further testified that he never saw King's sons before he fired and only noticed them afterwards standing on a curb outside the immediate vicinity of King's truck. King, however, testified that both of his sons were getting into the truck when defendant fired.

Although defendant did not hit King or King's sons, he did hit the rear tire of King's truck. The shotgun pellets also left marks on the truck's rear wheel well, its undercarriage, and its gas tank.

Defendant was charged with one count of shooting at an occupied motor vehicle (Pen. Code, § 246), and three counts of assault with a firearm (§ 245, subd. (a)(2)), one count each for King and his two sons.... The trial court gave the standard jury instruction on assault. That instruction provides in pertinent part that the crime of assault requires proof of these elements: "1. A person willfully and unlawfully committed an act that by its nature would probably and directly result in the application of physical force on another person; and [¶] 2. At the time the act was committed, such person had the present ability to apply physical force to the person of another." The jury convicted defendant of assaulting King with a firearm, but deadlocked on the remaining counts. The trial court later dismissed the deadlocked counts in the interests of justice.

On appeal, the Court of Appeal found the assault instruction erroneous because the instruction incorrectly stated the mental state required for the offense. After finding the instructional error prejudicial, the court reversed defendant's assault conviction.

We granted review to clarify the mental state for assault.

Discussion

I

The trial court instructed the jury that defendant was guilty of assault only if he "willfully and unlawfully committed an act that by its nature would probably and directly result in the application of physical force being applied to the person of another." The Court of Appeal found this instruction erroneous because it described a mental state of negligence and allowed the jury to find defendant guilty if "under an objective view of the facts ... an application of physical force on another person was reasonably foreseeable." Concluding that the instruction misstated the mental state for assault, the court held that assault requires either a desire to cause an application of physical force or substantial certainty that such an application would result.

The People urge us to reverse. They contend assault only requires general criminal intent, and the Court of Appeal improperly transformed assault into a specific intent crime by injecting the concepts of purpose and knowledge. As explained below, we agree that the Court of Appeal's description of the mental state for assault is erroneous and that assault is a general intent crime. We further conclude that assault requires actual knowledge of those facts sufficient to establish that the offending act by its nature would probably and directly result in physical force being applied to another.

[The court reviewed its decisions in *Hood*, *Rocha* and *Colantuono*.]

Although we conclusively classified assault as a general intent crime in *Colantuono*, we have recently recognized that such a classification, by itself, may not fully describe the requisite mental state for every criminal offense. Thus, in *People v. Hering* (1999) 20 Cal.4th 440, we cautioned against the rote application of the general/specific intent framework. We have also suggested that "[s]uch classification of offenses is necessary only when the court must determine whether a defense of voluntary intoxication or mental disease, defect, or disorder is available." (*People v. Rathert* (2000) 24 Cal.4th 200.) The apparent confusion engendered by *Colantuono* suggests that assault may be such a case.

With this in mind, we revisit the mental state for assault. As always, we begin with the statute and seek to ascertain the Legislature's intent at the date of enactment. Assault is "an unlawful *attempt*, coupled with a present ability, to commit a violent injury on the person of another." (§ 240, italics added.) Because section 240 was enacted in 1872 and has not been amended, we must construe the Legislature's intent as of 1872.

To ascertain the mental state for assault, we must first determine the meaning of the term "attempt." In 1872, attempt apparently had three possible definitions: (1) "[a]n endeavor to accomplish a crime carried beyond mere preparation, but falling short of execution of the ultimate design in any part of it" (1 Bouvier's Law Dict. (1872)); (2) "[a]n intent to do a thing combined with an act which falls short of the thing intended" (*ibid.*); and (3) "an intent to commit some act which would be indictable, if done, either from its own character or that of its natural and probable consequences" (*ibid.*) With respect to mental states, the third definition requires only an intent to commit the act—and not a specific intent to obtain some further objective—and focuses on the objective nature of that act. The first definition is ambiguous. It focuses on the nature of the act but may or may not require an intent to "accomplish a crime." The second definition appears to describe the traditional formulation of criminal attempt later codified in section 21a, which requires a specific intent.

In determining which meaning of "attempt" the Legislature intended to use in section 240, we must look to the historical "common law definition" of assault. " 'The original concept of criminal assault developed at an earlier day than the doctrine of criminal attempt in general.' " (*Colantuono*, quoting Perkins on Criminal Law (2d ed. 1969) ch. 2, § 2.) Assault "is not simply an adjunct of some underlying offense [like criminal attempt], but an independent crime statutorily delineated in terms of certain unlawful conduct immediately antecedent to battery." (*Colantuono*.) Unlike criminal attempt where the "act constituting an attempt to commit a felony may be more remote, [a]n assault is an act done toward the commission of a battery" and must "immediately" precede the battery. (Perkins & Boyce, Criminal Law (3d ed. 1982).) Indeed, our criminal code has long recognized this fundamental distinction between criminal attempt and assault by treating these offenses as *separate and independent* crimes. (Compare § 240 with §§ 663, 664.)

Consequently, criminal attempt and assault require different mental states. Because the act constituting a criminal attempt "need not be the last proximate or ultimate step toward commission of the substantive crime," criminal attempt has always required "a specific intent to commit the crime." (*People v. Kipp* (1998) 18 Cal.4th 349.) In contrast, the crime of assault has always focused on the nature of the act and not on the perpetrator's specific intent. An assault occurs whenever "[t]he next movement would, *at least to all appearance*, complete the battery." (Perkins, italics added.) Thus, assault "lies on a definitional ... *continuum of conduct* that describes its essential relation to battery: An assault is an incipient or inchoate battery; a battery is a consummated assault." (*Colantuono*, italics added.) As a result, a specific intent to injure is not an element of assault because the assaultive act, by its nature, subsumes such an intent.

The term "attempt" as used in the 1872 assault statute therefore does not refer to a definition of attempt that requires a specific intent, such as the definition later codified in section 21a.[2] Rather, the Legislature, consistent with the historical under-

2. In reaching this conclusion, we acknowledge that parts of the code commissioners comment to section 240 suggest that assault requires a specific intent to injure. We do not, however, find these parts of the comment compelling in light of the historic conception of assault and the Legislature's decision to make assault a statutorily distinct crime from criminal attempt. Indeed, the Legislature

standing of assault, presumably intended to adopt the third 1872 definition of attempt: "an intent to commit some act which would be indictable, if done, either from its own character or that of its natural and probable consequences ..." Thus, we explained in *Colantuono* that "the mental state for assault ... is established upon proof the defendant willfully committed an act that *by its nature will probably and directly result* in injury to another, i.e., a battery." (*Colantuono*, italics added.)

Although *Colantuono*'s description of the mental state for assault reflects the meaning of "attempt" intended by the Legislature in 1872, its exclusive reliance on the concept of general intent has resulted in some confusion. We may attribute much of this confusion to the fact that "[t]he gravamen [of assault] ... is the *likelihood* that the force applied or attempted to be applied will result in great bodily injury." (*People v. McCaffrey* (1953) 118 Cal.App.2d 611.) Because assault criminalizes conduct based on what *might* have happened—and not what *actually* happened—the mental state for assault incorporates the language of probability, i.e., direct, natural and probable consequences. This language, however, arguably implies an objective mental state consistent with a negligence standard.

Recognizing that *Colantuono*'s language may have been confusing, we now clarify the mental state for assault. Based on the 1872 definition of attempt, a defendant is only guilty of assault if he intends to commit an act "which would be indictable [as a battery], if done, either from its own character or that of its natural and probable consequences." (1 Bouvier's Law Dict.) Logically, a defendant cannot have such an intent unless he actually knows those facts sufficient to establish that his act by its nature will probably and directly result in physical force being applied to another, i.e., a battery. In other words, a defendant guilty of assault must be aware of the facts that would lead a reasonable person to realize that a battery would directly, naturally and probably result from his conduct. He may not be convicted based on facts he did not know but should have known. He, however, need not be subjectively aware of the risk that a battery might occur.[3]

In adopting this knowledge requirement, we do not disturb our previous holdings. Assault is still a general intent crime, and juries should not "consider evidence of defendant's intoxication in determining whether he committed assault." (*Hood*.) Likewise, mere recklessness or criminal negligence is still not enough, because a jury cannot find a defendant guilty of assault based on facts he should have known but did not know.

We also reaffirm that assault does not require a specific intent to injure the victim. As explained above, our rejection of a specific intent requirement is consistent with the statutory language and the historic conception of criminal assault. In any event, even if we erred 30 years ago in *Rocha* and compounded this error seven years ago

---

could have omitted assault from the Penal Code and allowed prosecutors to charge defendants with "attempted battery," if it wished to make assault a specific intent crime.

3. For example, a defendant who honestly believes that his act was not likely to result in a battery is still guilty of assault if a reasonable person, viewing the facts known to defendant, would find that the act would directly, naturally and probably result in a battery.

in *Colantuono*, the Legislature's subsequent conduct strongly militates against any belated correction of this "error" today.

[The legislature's 1982 amendment of P.C. § 22 "to make clear that voluntary intoxication could only negate specific intent and not general criminal intent" was meant to preserve existing law (including *Hood*). In addition, the legislature's 1986 enactment of P.C. § 21a—which codified the elements of criminal attempt for the first time—strongly suggested that the Legislature approved of *Rocha* because legislative history indicated that the section was meant to codify the attempt definition then used in jury instructions. Finally, the Legislature's failure to overturn *Rocha* in the thirty years since it was decided indicates its acquiescence in the court's interpretation.]

Accordingly, we hold that assault does not require a specific intent to cause injury or a subjective awareness of the risk that an injury might occur. Rather, assault only requires an intentional act and actual knowledge of those facts sufficient to establish that the act by its nature will probably and directly result in the application of physical force against another.

...

Dissenting Opinion by Kennard, J.

I dissent.

This court last tried to define the mental state required for the crime of assault in *People v. Colantuono* (1994) 7 Cal.4th 206. There, a majority of this court held that assault, as defined in Penal Code section 240, is *not* a specific intent crime and does *not* require proof that the defendant intended to injure another person. I disagreed with that holding. Based on the plain meaning of the statutory definition of assault—"an unlawful attempt, coupled with a present ability, to commit a violent injury on the person of another" (Pen. Code, § 240)—and on the 1872 code commissioners' note to Penal Code section 240 (stating that "[i]f there is no present purpose to do an injury, there is no assault"), I concluded that assault requires proof of an intent to injure another and that, for this reason, assault is a specific intent crime.

Because the *Colantuono* majority never clearly explained what the required mental state for assault *is*, but only what it *is not*, this court is again faced with the task of defining the mental state required for assault. Reexamining the issue, the majority now compounds the error in *Colantuono* by holding that a defendant, to be guilty of assault, need only be aware of facts that would lead a reasonable person to realize that a battery would directly, naturally, and probably result from the defendant's conduct, even though the defendant honestly but mistakenly believes that no battery is likely to result.

I

...

To ascertain the Legislature's intent in 1872 when it enacted the statutory definition of assault as part of the original Penal Code, the majority relies on *the third of three definitions* of "attempt" in the 1872 edition of Bouvier's Law Dictionary as "'an intent to commit some act which would be indictable, if done, either from its own character or that of its natural and probable consequences ....'" The majority asserts that this definition of "attempt" supports its conclusion that in 1872 the Legislature intended to require, as the mental state for assault, an intent to commit an act that would, if successfully completed, result in the injury of another as a direct, natural and probable consequence.

The majority quickly dismisses the first and second definitions of "attempt" appearing in the 1872 edition of Bouvier's Law Dictionary, because these definitions inconveniently do nothing to support its position. Indeed, as applied to the crime of assault, both of these definitions of "attempt" lead to the conclusion that assault requires an intent to inflict a battery—that is, an intent to injure.[1] The majority has chosen Bouvier's third definition of attempt to construe Penal Code section 240 because that definition appears on quick reading to support this court's mistaken holding in *Colantuono*. Whether it actually supports it, however, is questionable. If an "attempt" requires an "intent" to commit an act that "would be indictable if done," and if an assault is an "attempt" to commit a battery, then an assault must require an intent to commit an act that would be punishable as a battery—that is, an intent to apply force unlawfully to another or, in other words, an intent to injure the other.

Tellingly, the majority fails to cite one appellate decision or one text writer from the 1872 period applying Bouvier's third definition of attempt to the crime of assault, or any other evidence that any member of the 1872 Legislature was aware of or relied upon this definition of attempt as explaining that term's meaning in Penal Code section 240. The majority also must acknowledge that the meaning it gives to the term "attempt" in Penal Code section 240 cannot be given to the same word in other sections of the original 1872 Penal Code, such as sections 663 and 664. In those sections, which apply to the crime of criminal attempt, the word "attempt" requires a specific intent or purpose to commit the target crime. (See Pen. Code, § 21a.) The majority thus acknowledges its failure to apply a normal rule of statutory construction: "[I]dentical words used in different parts of the same act are intended to have the same meaning." (*Department of Revenue of Ore. v. ACF Industries, Inc.* (1994) 510 U.S. 332.) The majority asks us to believe, contrary to this rule, that the 1872 Legislature, when it adopted the original Penal Code by a single legislative act, intended that "attempt" would mean one thing in sections 663 and 664, and something quite different in section 240.

The majority dismisses as mistaken the code commissioners' comment to Penal Code section 240. In so doing, it flouts another rule of statutory construction: "When a statute proposed by the California Code Commission for inclusion in the Penal Code of 1872 has been enacted by the Legislature without substantial change, the report of the commission is entitled to great weight in construing the statute and in determining the intent of the Legislature." (*People v. Wiley* (1976) 18 Cal.3d 162.)

When they submitted their draft of the Penal Code to the Legislature, the code commissioners provided an extensive comment describing the crime of assault. Be-

1. In the context of assault and battery, the term "injure" does not require bodily harm and includes any "least touching" that is wrongful or offensive to the person who receives it.

cause the Legislature adopted without change the recommendation of the code commissioners, their comment deserves this court's attention and consideration. Their note to Penal Code section 240 states in relevant part: "INTENT TO STRIKE.—An assault has also been said to be an intentional attempt, by violence, to do an injury to the person of another. It must be *intentional.* If there is no present purpose to do an injury, there is no assault. There must also be an *attempt.* A purpose not accompanied by an effort to carry into immediate execution falls short of an assault. Thus no words can amount to an assault. But rushing towards another with menacing gestures, and with a *purpose to strike,* is an assault, though the accused is prevented from striking before he comes near enough to do so.... So, where an Embassador exhibited a painting in the window of his house which gave offense to the crowd without, and defendant, among the crowd, fired a pistol at the painting at the very time when the Embassador and his servants were in the window to remove it, but did not intend to hurt any of them, and in fact did not. *Held,* that there being no intent to injure the person there could be no conviction for an assault." Thus, the code commissioners have unambiguously declared their understanding that the crime of assault as codified in Penal Code section 240 requires the mental state of a *purpose to injure.*

The majority mentions the code commissioners' comment only as evidence that the Legislature sought to codify "the historical 'common law definition' of assault." The majority ultimately rests its argument about the intent of the 1872 Legislature on its assertion that the common law definition of assault did not require an intent to injure. But the majority is mistaken. As the commissioners' comment accurately indicates, at common law the crime of assault "was an attempt to commit a battery and nothing else" and therefore "the need for an intent to inflict such harm has been emphasized." (Perkins & Boyce, Criminal Law (3d ed. 1982).) The authors of another criminal law treatise make the same point: "An attempt to commit any crime requires a specific intent to commit that crime; and so assault of the attempted-battery sort requires an intent to commit a battery, i.e., an intent to cause physical injury to the victim." (LaFave & Scott, Criminal Law (2d ed. 1986).)

Turning to the majority opinion in *Colantuono,* the majority here correctly observes that it "has resulted in some confusion." Seeking to end the confusion, the majority states that the mental state required for assault is knowledge of "those facts sufficient to establish that [the defendant's] act by its nature will probably and directly result in physical force being applied to another, i.e., a battery." Acknowledging that the *Colantuono* majority stated that merely reckless conduct cannot constitute an assault, the majority here assures us that under the standard it adopts "mere recklessness or criminal negligence is still not enough," and this is because "a jury cannot find a defendant guilty of assault based on facts he should have known but did not know." I do not agree that the majority's formulation requires a mental state more culpable than criminal negligence or recklessness.

Criminal negligence is determined by an objective standard based on whether a reasonable person *in the defendant's position* would have been aware of the risk of harm to another. To be "in the defendant's position" means, among other things, to be aware of the facts that the defendant knew. Thus, criminal negligence requires actual knowledge of facts that would lead a reasonable person to conclude that the conduct in question involved a high risk of injury to another. Recklessness, a mental state more culpable than criminal negligence, requires not only knowledge of the facts making the conduct excessively dangerous, but also a subjective appreciation of the risk of harm to another.

Thus, the *Colantuono* majority, in requiring *more than* criminal negligence or recklessness, must have intended to require not only knowledge of facts making the conduct dangerous and a subjective appreciation of the risk of injury to another, but also an awareness of a *higher degree of risk* than that required for ordinary criminal negligence or recklessness. The majority here, in holding that a subjective appreciation of the risk of harm is *not* required, is not faithful to *Colantuono*, much less to the plain meaning of the statutory definition of assault or the intent of the 1872 Legislature that enacted that definition, as reflected in the code commissioners' comment to Penal Code section 240.

As its last line of defense, the majority asserts that the Legislature has twice signaled its approval of this court's muddled decision in *Rocha*, holding that assault with a deadly weapon was not a specific intent crime and stating that the intent required for assault is "the intent to attempt to commit a battery." The majority declares that the Legislature implicitly approved *Rocha* in 1982 when it amended Penal Code section 22 to clarify that voluntary intoxication is admissible only on "whether or not the defendant actually formed a required specific intent," and again in 1986 when it adopted Penal Code section 21a, defining the elements of criminal attempt.

But the definition of attempt in Penal Code section 21a—as requiring "a specific intent to commit the crime"—is entirely inconsistent with the majority's construction of the same word in Penal Code section 240 defining assault. How the Legislature's adoption of this inconsistent definition of a key term in Penal Code section 240 constitutes an approval of *Rocha* or of what the majority does here today escapes me entirely. Nor do I see anything in Penal Code section 22 that supports the majority's decision here or suggests that the Legislature was thinking of the definition of assault in 1982 when it amended that section.

Finally, and unlike the majority, I attach no significance to the Legislature's failure to amend Penal Code section 240 after this court's decisions in *Rocha* and *Colantuono*. Legislative inaction is normally a poor indicator of legislative intent. This is especially true in this instance. Since it first defined the crime in 1850, using language that passed unchanged into the 1872 Penal Code, the Legislature has never amended its definition of assault. It did not do so after this court defined assault to require a purpose to injure (*People v. Bird* (1881) 60 Cal. 7), and it has not done so since this court has held assault does not require a purpose to injure. Throughout this contradictory course of judicial construction, the Legislature has allowed the statutory definition of assault to remain an attempt to commit a violent injury. In 1850, "attempt" meant what it meant at common law, namely that one "commits an attempt when, with intent to commit a particular crime, he performs an act which tends toward but falls short of the consummation of such crime." (4 Wharton's Criminal Law (15th ed.1996) § 693.)[2]

How far this court has strayed from the Legislature's definition of assault as "an unlawful attempt, coupled with a present ability, to commit a violent injury on the person of another"! Under the definition of assault that the majority approves today, as the Attorney General was forced to acknowledge at oral argument in this case, a trial court instructing a jury in the exact words of this statute would not accurately define the crime of assault.

...

WERDEGAR, J., concurs.

Note and Problems

The Model Penal Code and Assault. The Model Penal Code provision on assault is as follows:

> § 211.1 — Assault
>
> (1) Simple Assault. A person is guilty of assault if he:
>
> (a) attempts to cause or purposely, knowingly or recklessly causes bodily injury to another; or
>
> (b) negligently causes bodily injury to another with a deadly weapon; or
>
> (c) attempts by physical menace to put another in fear of imminent serious bodily injury....

"Attempt" in the Model Penal Code is defined as: purposely engaging in conduct which would constitute the crime or a substantial step in commission of the crime if the attendant circumstances were as the actor believes them to be or, where the crime is defined in terms of result, engaging in conduct which the actor believes will cause the result. MPC § 5.01. How does assault in the Model Penal Code differ from assault in California?

Problem 10.

Defendant has a long history of mental illness dating from his war-time service in the military. He has been hospitalized ten times, suffering from psychoses. Shortly after his last release, Defendant, who was homeless, came to believe that he "owned" a certain apartment, and, when he tried the door and it opened, he was convinced

---

2. I do not mean to suggest that the Legislature should not reexamine its definition of the crime of assault. Given developments in other jurisdictions, and this court's own difficulties with the existing definition, such an examination may be overdue. As the authors of a treatise on criminal law in this country have observed, the common law definition of assault, as codified in Penal Code section 240, was once very common but now "is rarely found in the modern codes." (LaFave & Scott, Criminal Law, *supra*, at p. 691.)

the apartment was his. The actual owner, Renter, was away for the weekend. Defendant entered the apartment and lived there for the next two days, wearing Renter's clothes, eating his food and destroying some posters he felt were inappropriate. When Renter returned home, Defendant was shocked and embarrassed. Defendant was arrested and charged with burglary (P.C. § 459), which is defined as follows:

> Every person who enters any house, room, apartment, tenement, shop, warehouse, store, mill, barn, stable, outhouse or other building, tent, vessel, ... floating home, ... railroad car, locked or sealed cargo container, whether or not mounted on a vehicle, trailer coach, ... any house car, ... inhabited camper, ... vehicle..., when the doors are locked, aircraft..., or mine or any underground portion thereof, with intent to commit grand or petit larceny or any felony is guilty of burglary ...

What arguments should be made regarding whether Defendant is guilty?

Problem 11.

Defendant and Victim, a prostitute, agreed that Defendant would pay Victim $20 for a sex act. After Victim entered Defendant's car, Defendant showed her a badge and handcuffs and threatened to arrest her unless a deal could be worked out. (Defendant was not in fact a police officer.) Defendant then asked whether Victim could afford to post $2500 bail, and, when she said she could not, he said he might be able to get bail reduced. Victim believed Defendant wanted money, so she took $50 from her pocket and gave it to him. Defendant then forced Victim to engage in a sex act. Defendant is charged, *inter alia*, with extortion, which is defined in Penal Code section 518 as follows:

> Extortion is the obtaining of property from another, with his consent, or the obtaining of an official act of a public officer, induced by a wrongful use of force or fear, or under color of official right.

Is Defendant entitled to an instruction that extortion is a specific intent crime? How would such an instruction help Defendant?

Problem 12.

Defendant was charged with violating Penal Code § 647(b) (solicitation of an act of prostitution). Solicitation is a specific intent crime requiring that the defendant have the specific intent to commit the proposed crime. The court instructed the jury that the specific intent required was to "communicate to another an offer of sex for money or other considerations." What is wrong with the instruction?

Problem 13.

Defendant, Victim and Friend, a friend of Victim's, are all students at High School. One day Victim and Friend were standing near their lockers when Defendant approached. Defendant had been harassing Victim for some time. Defendant had a belt wrapped around his fist with the buckle exposed. Defendant pushed Victim against a locker and swung at him. Victim swung back, knocking Defendant to the ground. Defendant called Friend the following day on the phone and told her he was angry about the fight. When Friend asked what he was going to do, Defendant told her to listen. She heard a metallic clicking sound. Friend asked what made the sound and Defendant replied, "It's a gun, stupid." Defendant told Friend that he was going to shoot Victim. The next day, Friend told Victim of the threat. Defendant is charged with violating Penal Code § 422 which provides in relevant part:

> Any person who willfully threatens to commit a crime which will result in death or great bodily injury to another person, with the specific intent that the statement is to be taken as a threat, even if there is no intent of actually carrying it out, which, on its face and under the circumstances in which it is made, is so unequivocal, unconditional, immediate, and specific as to convey to the person threatened a gravity of purpose and an immediate prospect of execution of the threat, and thereby causes that person reasonably to be in sustained fear for his or her own safety or for his or her immediate family's safety, shall be punished by imprisonment in the county jail not to exceed one year, or by imprisonment in the state prison.

What arguments should be made regarding Defendant's guilt?

People v. Reyes

52 Cal. App. 4th 975, 61 Cal.Rptr.2d 39 (1997)

HUFFMAN, ACTING PRESIDING JUSTICE.

After a jury found Ramiro Jaime Reyes guilty of receiving stolen property, he was sentenced to 25 years to life in prison. The pivotal issue is whether, under Penal Code §§ 22 and 28, evidence of Reyes's voluntary intoxication and mental disorders is admissible to refute an essential element of the crime—that he knew the property was stolen. For the reasons discussed below, we hold such evidence is admissible, and the trial court committed prejudicial error in disallowing it. Accordingly, we reverse the judgment.

Factual and Procedural Background

Reyes was charged in an information with vehicular burglary (§ 459) and receiving stolen property. (§ 496, subd. (a).) The evidence adduced at trial was as follows.

Michael Conlon and Bertha Whitford were next door neighbors. Conlon customarily parked his work truck beside his driveway, approximately 20 to 25 feet from Whitford's bedroom window. The truck was brightly illuminated by Conlon's garage light. One day shortly before 2 a.m., Whitford looked out her bedroom window and saw a man leaning into the driver's side window of Conlon's truck. The man was slightly built, had long curly black hair and wore a white tank top and long white shorts. Whitford was not alarmed because she assumed he was Conlon's friend. Fifteen to twenty minutes later, Whitford saw the man at Conlon's truck again, after which he left in a white car idling nearby....

Within an hour, Brett Rhoades, a police officer for the City of Chula Vista, stopped Reyes for speeding. When he searched the light-colored automobile, Rhoades found a red metal toolbox, a cellular phone and several identification badges bearing the name "Michael Conlon." Rhoades went to Conlon's home, and Conlon advised the articles had been taken from his work truck. The driver's side window was rolled down; Conlon did not recall having left it down, but agreed he might have.

...

Before trial, Reyes successfully moved to strike the vehicular burglary count because there was no evidence Conlon's truck was locked when the items were stolen. Instead of amending the information to allege theft, the People proceeded to trial solely on the receiving stolen property count.

In his defense, Reyes testified he had used controlled substances since 1978, including marijuana, cocaine, methamphetamine, LSD and heroin; he began smoking methamphetamine and cocaine a few days before the incident, and during the day before the incident he smoked two grams of methamphetamine and one gram of cocaine. Late in the evening, Reyes wanted to get cigarettes and beer; however, because he "had done too [many] chemicals, he didn't trust [himself] to drive alone ..." Consequently, he took along his girlfriend; however, he drove the car. Reyes could not recall where they stopped to get the items, stating, "I have trouble when I use a lot of drugs remembering things of that nature." On the way home, Reyes stopped to pick up a red toolbox and other items he spotted on a street curb. When asked why he did so, Reyes stated:

> [B]ecause I have a problem. When I use drugs, I—well, in laymen's terms, people that use drugs, they call it tweaking. They just go dipster-dumpster diving. In my case, I have a problem with that. I just have a compulsion, you know, just to pick, ... on trash cans. I've had that compulsion since I was a child....
>
> [¶] In my state of mind, I think I'm treasure hunting.

Reyes also sought to introduce the testimony of a psychologist, Raymond Murphy, Ph.D., to show he lacked knowledge the property was stolen, an essential element of the crime of receiving stolen property. During the offer of proof, Dr. Murphy testified Reyes had a variety of mental disorders, including schizophrenia and "a paranoid, antisocial, and borderline style of personality disorder." Further, Reyes was "seriously disturbed emotionally in terms of his basic functioning," "showed deficits in his cognitive realm that might be identified as dementia or difficulty in basic cognitive functioning," and had a "serious, enduring history of polysubstance dependence." According to Dr. Murphy, such a person "could be functioning in a manner that was highly disorganized, distracted from reality, could be manifesting issues of delusion or hallucination, and at times severe disruption in the manner in which [he] ... [made] decisions about how [he] did things." It would be possible for such a person to lack knowledge of his acts. The trial court, however, disallowed the testimony, finding it went to "diminished capacity," an abolished defense.

. . .

Discussion
I. Expert Testimony Re Voluntary Intoxication and Mental Disorders

The diminished capacity defense, which addressed an accused's "general capacity or ability to form a specific intent or harbor a mental element of an offense," was abolished in 1982....

[Evidence of voluntary intoxication or mental disorders] is admissible, however, solely to negate an element of the crime which must be proven by the prosecution. At the time of trial, section 22, subdivision (b), provided: "Evidence of voluntary intoxication is admissible solely on the issue of whether or not the defendant *actually formed a required specific intent*, premeditated, deliberated, or harbored malice aforethought, *when a specific intent crime is charged*." (Italics added.)[5] Likewise, section 28, subdivision (a) makes evidence of mental disorders admissible solely on the issue of whether defendant *"actually formed a required specific intent ... when a specific intent crime is charged."* (Italics added.) Here, the People successfully argued the proffered testimony of Dr. Murphy was inadmissible because receiving stolen property has been characterized as a general intent crime as opposed to a specific intent crime.

. . .

"A general intent crime may also involve a specific mental state, such as knowledge." (*People v. Cleaves* (1991) 229 Cal. App. 3d 367.) "Among the several definitions of 'knowledge' are the following: 'the fact or condition of being cognizant, conscious, or aware of something'; 'the scope of one's awareness'; 'extent of one's understanding'; 'the fact or condition of apprehending truth, fact, or reality immediately with the mind or senses.'" (*People v. Foster* (1971) 19 Cal. App. 3d 649.) In *People v. Foster*, where unlawful possession of narcotics was charged, the court held, "[i]t is apparent that to convict the accused of the crime..., the People must, in addition to proving general intent to possess the substance constituting the contraband, prove that the accused had knowledge that the material in his possession was a narcotic." In determining the latter, "[i]ntoxication has obvious relevance to the question of awareness, familiarity, understanding and the ability to recognize and comprehend."

In *People v. Whitfield* (1994) 7 Cal. 4th 437, the court held that evidence of voluntary intoxication was admissible, notwithstanding classification of the crime—murder in the second degree based on implied malice—as one of general intent. "Malice is implied when a person does an act, the natural consequences of which are dangerous to life, which act was deliberately performed by a person who knows that his conduct endangers the life of another and who acts with conscious disregard for life ..." The court reasoned, "Although it can be argued that implied malice does not constitute

5. Section 22, subdivision (b) was amended in 1995, effective January 1, 1996, and now permits the admission of evidence of voluntary intoxication on the issue of whether or not the defendant actually formed a required specific intent, without regard to whether the charged crime is a specific intent crime or a general intent crime.

a specific intent as described in *People v. Hood* (1969) 1 Cal. 3d 444, because it does not involve an 'intent to do some further act or achieve some additional consequence,' it is quite clear that implied malice does not fit *Hood*'s description of general intent, which is 'an intent merely to do a violent act.' Although implied malice may not fall literally within the *Hood* formulation of specific intent, the element of implied malice that requires that the defendant act with knowledge of the danger to, and in conscious disregard of, human life, is closely akin to *Hood*'s definition of specific intent, which requires proof that the defendant acted with a specific and particularly culpable mental state. Thus, read in context, the phrase 'when a specific intent crime is charged' in section 22 includes murder, even where the prosecution relies exclusively upon the theory that malice is implied, rather than express." Under *Hood* and *Whitfield*, "the criteria of specific intent for [the purpose of section 22] are not necessarily the same as the criteria of specific intent as a measure of the scienter required for an offense."

Applying the above principles to this case, we conclude Dr. Murphy's testimony was admissible. "[P]roof of the crime of receiving stolen property requires establishing that the property in question was stolen, that the defendant was in possession of it, and that the defendant knew the property to be stolen." (*People v. Anderson* (1989) 210 Cal. App. 3d 414.) Conscious possession of recently stolen property alone is insufficient to permit the inference defendant knew the property was stolen, however, "the attributes of the possession—time, place, and manner—may furnish the additional quantum of evidence needed." (*People v. Hallman* (1973) 35 Cal. App. 3d 638.) "[P]roof of knowing possession by a defendant of recently stolen property raises a strong inference of the other element of the crime: the defendant's knowledge of the tainted nature of the property. This inference is so substantial that only 'slight' additional corroborating evidence need be adduced in order to permit a finding of guilt." (*People v. Anderson, supra.*)

...

Thus, here, as in *Whitfield*, the classification of the crime as one of general intent has nothing to do with the required element of knowledge, a specific mental state. "[I]f a crime requires a particular mental state, the Legislature cannot deny a defendant the opportunity to prove he did not entertain that state." (*People v. Bobo* (1990) 229 Cal. App. 3d 1417.) "[T]he defendant's evidence of intoxication can no longer be proffered as a defense to a crime but rather is proffered in an attempt to raise a doubt on an element of a crime which the prosecution must prove beyond a reasonable doubt. In such a case the defendant is attempting to relate his evidence of intoxication to an element of the crime." (*People v. Saille* (1991) 54 Cal. 3d 1103.) Accordingly, we hold that with regard to the element of knowledge, receiving stolen property is a "specific intent crime," as that term is used in section 22, subdivision (b), and section 28, subdivision (a).

While Reyes testified he was intoxicated with drugs when found with Conlon's property, the court instructed the jury that receiving stolen property was solely a general intent crime, to which voluntary intoxication was no defense; correspondingly, the court refused Reyes's request for instructions that "there must exist a union or joint operation of act or conduct and a certain mental state in the mind of the perpetrator," and that the "mental state with which an act is done may be shown by the circumstances surrounding the commission of the act." We conclude the total preclusion of evidence regarding Reyes's myriad of mental disorders, and their exacerbation by drug abuse, unfairly denied him the opportunity to prove he lacked the requisite knowledge. That, in conjunction with instructional errors resulting from the court's misapplication of sections 22 and 28, prejudiced Reyes and requires reversal of the judgment.

...

Note

From "Diminished Capacity" to "Diminished Actuality." As the court in *Reyes* explains, prior to 1982, a defendant could assert a "diminished capacity" defense, *i.e.*, that because of intoxication or mental illness, the defendant lacked the *capacity* to harbor a subjective mental state that was an element of the crime. That defense came under political attack as a result of the double murder prosecution of Dan White. White was a member of the San Francisco Board of Supervisors. He resigned this position, but then changed his mind and asked Mayor George Moscone to appoint him to the vacant position. Moscone refused, and White became enraged and went to City Hall with a loaded pistol and killed the mayor. He then reloaded his pistol and went across the hall and shot Harvey Milk, another member of the Board of Supervisors, a leader in the gay community in San Francisco, and a political adversary of White's.[b] At his trial, White presented expert psychiatric evidence that he was a manic/depressive and that his actions resulted from the combination of his political and financial problems and his mental disorder. His psychiatrist testified that one symptom of White's manic/depressive disorder was his consumption of large amounts of junk food, including "Twinkies." The jury failed to convict White of murder, finding him guilty of two counts of voluntary manslaughter instead. The public widely interpreted the verdict as establishing a "Twinkie defense" and as being symptomatic of the California courts' receptiveness to even the most far-fetched psychiatric defenses.

As a result, in 1982, the legislature amended the Penal Code, and the voters passed an initiative, eliminating the diminished capacity defense. Although a defendant may not introduce evidence going to his capacity to harbor a mental state, Penal Code §§ 28(a) and 29.4(b) permit the defendant to introduce evidence of mental illness or intoxication to prove he/she did not have a particular subjective mental state. Penal Code § 28(a) provides:

> [M]ental disease, mental defect, or mental disorder is admissible solely on the issue of whether or not the accused actually formed a required specific

b. These events were the subject of the 2008 film, *Milk*, which earned Sean Penn an Oscar for his portrayal of Harvey Milk.

> intent, premeditated, deliberated, or harbored malice aforethought, when a specific intent crime is charged.

Penal Code § 29.4(b) is to the same effect regarding intoxication:

> Evidence of voluntary intoxication is admissible solely on the issue of whether or not the defendant actually formed a required specific intent, or, when charged with murder, whether the defendant premeditated, deliberated, or harbored express malice aforethought.

The California Supreme Court has characterized a defense based on these sections as one of "diminished actuality." See *People v. Steele*, 27 Cal.4th 1230, 1253 (2002).

People v. Scott

146 Cal. App. 3d 823, 194 Cal. Rptr. 633 (1983)

Kaufman, J.

Defendant Walter Stephen Scott appeals from a judgment of conviction of two counts of attempted unlawful driving or taking of a vehicle (Pen. Code, § 664, Veh. Code, § 10851).

...

Testimony presented at the preliminary hearing and at trial revealed the following facts.

On the evening of August 1, 1981, defendant, accompanied by his brother Charles Scott, attended a family reunion-type party. The brother noticed a large punch bowl filled with red punch and saw the punch bowl refilled several times during the course of the party. He also observed defendant drinking some of the punch.

At some point in the evening the supply of ice ran low and the brother volunteered to go to the store to get more. When he left, everyone, including defendant, appeared to be behaving normally. However, when he returned the brother noticed that the behavior of the party guests had changed dramatically. He began looking for defendant and while doing so he noticed a number of guests holding cups of punch behaving strangely and in some cases bizarrely. One man, pointing to the floor, stated there was a dog in the room. Several people holding glasses of punch in their hands were vomiting. When the brother finally located defendant, he noticed that defendant's eyes were unusually large and dilated, and that defendant appeared uncoordinated. Defendant also appeared not to recognize his brother. Feeling that something was wrong, the brother took defendant by the hand and led him out of the house and into his car.

On the way home defendant told his brother he could see a big fireball in the sky and that he could see the brother and his in-laws in the flames. Defendant described it as "Hell" and he stated either that they were trying to pull him in there or he was trying to pull them out. At some point during the ride home, defendant stuck his head out of the car window and stated that he felt "good enough to fly home." The brother, who had received some instruction on drug intoxication and had also previously seen people who were on PCP (phencyclidine), believed defendant might be on PCP.

...

Defendant ... told [the forensic psychiatrist] that the next day he felt a little more hyperactive than usual but attended church with his family and proceeded through the day without incident. However, when he awakened on Monday morning, August 3, 1981, he felt queasy and decided not to go to work. After taking his children to school, defendant took his mother-in-law, Frances Nichols, with him to purchase some glass to replace broken windows at his house. While inside the store, defendant began to feel the same feelings he had at the party. The clerk "spooked" him because he (the clerk) "looked like he was from Mars." Defendant ran out of the store and into his car, and then imagined he observed a long funeral go by in which he sensed that he was the deceased. Defendant began to drive on the freeway at a high speed.

Defendant made similar statements to two other psychiatrists, Dr. Flanagan and Dr. Oshrin.

In testifying as to the basis for his opinion Dr. Summerour reported that Ms. Nichols related to him that on the return glass-purchase trip defendant drove past her house without stopping, stating that he was driving to Bakersfield to talk with his mother. Ms. Nichols observed defendant looking over his shoulder frequently, driving fast and making rapid lane changes. While on the freeway defendant stated to Ms. Nichols the CIA was after him and was following him in an airplane because he was a secret agent. He said he had to get to the police for help. He started calling Ms. Nichols "Baby," an affectionate term that he usually addressed to his wife. Defendant was sweating profusely and repeatedly stated that he was thirsty. Ms. Nichols observed that defendant's eyes were "glassy and weird," that he was talking fast and that he did not seem to be making sense. Finally, when the car overheated and stopped running, defendant jumped out of the car and ran up the offramp. Ms. Nichols eventually lost sight of him.

About this time, 13-year-old Robert Briggs was sitting on his motor bike in the driveway of a gas station in Riverside County. Defendant approached him, stated he was a secret agent and demanded the boy give him the motor bike. When Robert refused, defendant hit him on the helmet, knocking him off the bike, and then proceeded to mount the bike. Defendant attempted to kick-start the cycle, but was unsuccessful.

Douglas Bushlen was driving his pickup truck toward the highway 91 onramp when he observed a man knock a kid off a motor bike at a Shell service station. He then observed other people trying to get the man off the bike and decided to drive into the service station and offer assistance. The man, defendant, then ran toward Bushlen's stopped truck and jumped on the back of it. Defendant told Bushlen to drive on, that he was from the FBI and the CIA. Bushlen then drove to and parked at the Magnolia Lumber Yard; a few minutes later defendant got off the truck.

Bushlen testified that defendant seemed "kind of crazy" and appeared restless and hyperactive. He also appeared frightened and stated in a loud voice that the President of the United States and he had fallen out of an airplane. He appeared to be under the influence of something and did not seem to know who or where he was.

Christopher Bell was operating a forklift at the Magnolia Lumber Yard when defendant arrived in the back of Bushlen's pickup truck. Bell observed defendant banging on the side of the truck stating that he was with the secret police and that he wanted to get inside the truck. At some point defendant got off the truck, walked toward Bell and pointed toward the freeway, stating that the President was going by. Bell stopped the forklift and got off. Defendant then jumped on top of the forklift and tried to start it, declaring that he needed the forklift for police business. Bell removed the key from the ignition and told defendant he could use the telephone inside the store to call the police. According to Bell defendant was speaking in a loud voice and was perspiring profusely.

Once inside the building, defendant called Information in an attempt to get in touch with Washington, D.C., stating that he was "John Shaft" and that he was from the CIA. When the call failed to go through, defendant hung up and re-dialed the operator. This time he asked for the police and stated that "they" were trying to "kill the President." He stated either that he or the President had fallen out of an airplane.

Defendant then hung up the phone, ran out of the building, jumped into a nearby truck and tried to start it. The truck's owner, Cecil Endeman, followed close behind. Endeman's stepson was sitting in the passenger seat when defendant jumped inside, closed the door and asked, "How do you start this vehicle?" Defendant then announced in a loud voice, "I'm with the CIA and I need to use the car." Endeman demanded that defendant get out of the car, at which point defendant ran back inside the building.

Defendant then telephoned his mother, stating: "I don't know where I'm at but tell somebody to come get me." He then asked the owner of the lumber yard to call the police. Defendant asked for everyone's names and addresses, indicating that he needed them for his "report." He appeared restless and frightened to those who were present.

After delivering defendant to the lumber yard, Douglas Bushlen had returned to the Shell service station and contacted police. Police Officer Dennis Wensel followed Bushlen back to Magnolia Lumber where Bushlen pointed defendant out. Wensel handcuffed defendant and placed him in the squad car. While in the squad car, defendant screamed that he was innocent, that he was a CIA agent and had credentials. At some point defendant began thrusting his feet against the car door. Wensel eventually placed additional restraints on him. Defendant repeatedly demanded that he be released immediately. He continued to scream for about 45 minutes; however, he later appeared quite calm at the booking interview.

Discussion

Defendant contends the trial court erred in finding he had the specific intent to deprive the victims of their vehicles. He argues the court's finding of specific intent was based on a misconception of the law of diminished capacity and that the evidence is insufficient to support a finding of specific intent.

Section 10851 of the Vehicle Code provides in part: "Any person who drives or takes a vehicle not his own, without the consent of the owner thereof, and with intent either permanently or temporarily to deprive the owner thereof of his title to or possession of the vehicle, whether with or without intent to steal the same, ... is guilty of a public offense ..." Conviction under this section requires a finding that the accused had the specific intent to deprive the owner of title to or possession of his vehicle.

At trial, to negate the specific intent requirement of section 10851, defendant asserted a defense of diminished capacity resulting from involuntary intoxication. He presented the testimony of several witnesses who stated in essence that at the time of the commission of the alleged offenses defendant was acting irrationally and in a bizarre manner and appeared to be under the influence of something. Defendant also introduced the testimony of three psychiatrists who all stated that, in their opinions, at the time of the incident defendant did not have the mental capacity to form the specific intent to deprive the owners of their vehicles....

...

[T]he evidence establishes that defendant unknowingly and therefore involuntarily ingested some kind of hallucinogen which caused him to act in a bizarre and irrational manner and that, acting under the delusion that he was a secret agent and that he was acting to save his own life or possibly that of the President, defendant attempted to "take" vehicles belonging to others without their consent. The only question is whether or not a crime has been committed. Under the circumstances we believe not.

Subdivision Three (formerly subd. Four) of Penal Code section 26 includes among persons incapable of committing a crime, "Persons who committed the act or made the omission charged under an ignorance or mistake of fact, which disproves any criminal intent." It is clear that in attempting to commandeer the vehicles defendant acted under a mistake of fact: he thought he was a secret government agent acting to protect his own life or possibly that of the President. When a person commits an act based on a mistake of fact, his guilt or innocence is determined as if the facts were as he perceived them. If in fact defendant were a government agent and either his life or the life of the President were in danger and defendant attempted to commandeer the vehicles for the purpose of saving his own life or that of the President, his actions would have been legally justified under the doctrine of necessity.[c]

Penal Code section 26 does not expressly require that the vitiating mistake be reasonable, but we may assume for purposes of this decision that it must. Although defendant's mistake of fact was undoubtedly irrational, it was also undoubtedly

---

c. The affirmative defense of necessity is discussed in Chapter 12. In brief, the defense requires a showing by the defendant that he or she committed a criminal act because of a reasonable belief that the act was necessary to prevent or avoid a greater harm.

reasonable under the circumstances, because the circumstances include that the mistake emanated from a delusion caused by defendant's involuntary intoxication resulting from unknowingly ingesting some unspecified hallucinogenic substance.[4]

We conclude therefore that even if the evidence is sufficient to support the trial court's finding that defendant intended to temporarily deprive the owners of possession of their vehicles, defendant's actions clearly fall within the purview of Penal Code section 26, subdivision Three, and were therefore not criminal.[5]

Problem

Problem 14.

Defendant, a teenager, built a wooden cross, which he originally intended to set on fire at the beach with his friends. One night, after getting drunk, Defendant changed his mind, and he and Friend burned the cross at the house of Victims, a Jewish family, in order to show their "white power beliefs." Defendant is charged with violating P.C. § 11411(d), which punishes:

> Any person who burns or desecrates a cross or other religious symbol, knowing it to be a religious symbol, on the private property of another without authorization for the purpose of terrorizing the owner or occupant of that private property or in reckless disregard of the risk of terrorizing the owner or occupant of that private property.

What are the arguments as to whether Defendant can defend on the basis of his intoxication?

In re Jorge M.

23 Cal.4th 866, 4 P.3d 297 (2000)

WERDEGAR, J.

Jorge M., a minor, was adjudicated a ward of the juvenile court and ordered into a juvenile camp program, in part because he was found to have been in possession of an assault weapon, in violation of Penal Code section 12280, subdivision (b) (here-

---

4. Had defendant's delusions resulted from voluntary intoxication, his mistake of fact could not be considered reasonable. (Cf. Pen. Code, § 22 [which provides in part: "No act committed by a person while in a state of voluntary intoxication is less criminal by reason of his having been in such condition...."].)

5. It is quite possible that subdivision Five of Penal Code section 26 would also be applicable, rendering defendant's conduct noncriminal. Subdivision Five, formerly subdivision Six, of Penal Code section 26, includes among those persons incapable of committing a crime, "Persons who committed the act or made the omission charged through misfortune or accident, when it appears that there was no evil design, intention, or culpable negligence." In view of defendant's involuntary intoxication and resulting delusions it might fairly be said Defendant's Attempts to commandeer vehicles resulted from "misfortune or accident."

after section 12280(b)). The Court of Appeal reversed that finding on the ground the record contained insufficient evidence the minor knew the firearm had the characteristics bringing it within the definition of an assault weapon under the Assault Weapons Control Act (hereafter the AWCA)), a mental element the Court of Appeal found implicit in section 12280(b) despite the absence of any express scienter language in the statute itself.

We agree with the Court of Appeal that section 12280(b), an alternative felony/misdemeanor punishable by up to three years in state prison was not intended to define a strict liability offense. We disagree, however, that actual knowledge regarding the firearm's prohibited characteristics is required. Such a requirement would be inconsistent with the public safety goals of the AWCA. Effective enforcement of that law demands, instead, that a conviction be obtainable upon *proof of negligent failure to know*, as well as actual knowledge of, the weapon's salient characteristics; the People must prove, that is, that a defendant charged with possessing an unregistered assault weapon *knew or reasonably should have known* the characteristics of the weapon bringing it within the registration requirements of the AWCA. Because the record of this case contains sufficient evidence to prove the requisite mens rea, we reverse the judgment of the Court of Appeal.

Factual and Procedural Background

On December 5, 1996, while the 16-year-old minor was on in-home probation for possession of a controlled substance, law enforcement officers conducted a probation investigation at the minor's home. The main room of the house had bunk beds in one corner; a door led off this main room to the minor's parents' bedroom. Probation Officer Brian Tsubokawa asked the minor where he kept his personal possessions. The minor pointed to the bunk bed area in the main room. Los Angeles Police Department Officer Manuel Ramirez went to the bunk bed and found three rifles on the top bunk, which the minor told Officer Ramirez was his bed. On a clothes cabinet three feet or less from the minor's bed, Officer Ramirez also found an unregistered SKS-45 semiautomatic rifle with a detachable "banana clip" magazine.

The present petition was then filed against the minor under Welfare and Institutions Code section 602, charging him with possession of an assault weapon (§ 12280(b)) and with firearm possession in violation of the terms and conditions of his probation (§ 12021, subd. (d)).

At the adjudication hearing, the officers testified as described above. The minor testified he slept on the floor of his sisters' bedroom and that the weapons belonged to his father. He denied ever "playing" with the weapons. The minor's brother testified that all the rifles belonged to him and his father, not to the minor. He said that he slept on the top bunk bed and that the minor slept in a bedroom used by their sisters. The minor's mother corroborated the brother's account.

The juvenile court found the allegations of the petition true....

The Court of Appeal reversed the section 12280(b) finding for insufficient evidence. Relying heavily on the persuasive authority of *Staples v. United States* (1994) 511 U.S.

600, in which the United States Supreme Court held conviction under a federal firearms possession law required proof the defendant knew the features of the gun that brought it within the criminal prohibition, and *People v. Simon* (1995) 9 Cal.4th 493, in which this court held conviction under a law proscribing the sale or purchase of securities by misrepresentation required proof the defendant knew or should have known the false or misleading nature of the representation, the Court of Appeal held that conviction under section 12280(b) requires proof the defendant "knew that the weapon possessed characteristics which brought it within the statutory definition of an assault weapon." The Court of Appeal, without elaborating the point, further asserted there was "no evidence" of such knowledge in this case.

We granted the Attorney General's petition for review.

Discussion

The AWCA, inter alia, requires registration of assault weapons, sets time periods for such registration, prohibits the possession of unregistered assault weapons, restricts the circumstances under which even registered assault weapons may be possessed (including a prohibition on their possession by minors) and allows exceptions to these restrictions by permit on good cause shown. At the time of the minor's charged offense, the restricted firearms included only those defined as assault weapons in section 12276 and those declared to be assault weapons pursuant to section 12276.5. The definition in section 12276, subdivisions (a) through (c), consists of a list, one item of which is "SKS with detachable magazine." The question on review, therefore, is whether the Court of Appeal correctly held that the finding the minor possessed an unregistered assault weapon, in violation of section 12280(b), required proof the minor knew the weapon was an SKS with a detachable magazine. To answer that question we must decide whether knowledge of the characteristics bringing a firearm within the AWCA is an element of section 12280(b)'s bar on possession.

Section 12280(b) provides in pertinent part: "[A]ny person who, within this state, possesses any assault weapon, except as provided in this chapter, is guilty of a public offense and upon conviction shall be punished by imprisonment in the state prison, or in a county jail, not exceeding one year."

That the statute contains no reference to knowledge or other language of mens rea is not itself dispositive. As we recently explained, the requirement that, for a criminal conviction, the prosecution prove some form of guilty intent, knowledge, or criminal negligence is of such long standing and so fundamental to our criminal law that penal statutes will often be construed to contain such an element despite their failure expressly to state it. "Generally, the existence of a mens rea is the rule of, rather than the exception to, the principles of Anglo-American criminal jurisprudence. In other words, there must be a union of act and wrongful intent, or criminal negligence. (Pen.Code, §20.) So basic is this requirement that it is an invariable element of every crime unless excluded expressly or by necessary implication." (*People v. Coria* (1999) 21 Cal.4th 868.)

Equally well recognized, however, is that for certain types of penal laws, often referred to as public welfare offenses, the Legislature does not intend that any proof of scienter or wrongful intent be necessary for conviction. "Such offenses generally are based upon the violation of statutes which are purely regulatory in nature and involve widespread injury to the public. Under many statutes enacted for the protection of the public health and safety, e.g., traffic and food and drug regulations, criminal sanctions are relied upon even if there is no wrongful intent. These offenses usually involve light penalties and no moral obloquy or damage to reputation. Although criminal sanctions are relied upon, the primary purpose of the statutes is regulation rather than punishment or correction. The offenses are not crimes in the orthodox sense, and wrongful intent is not required in the interest of enforcement." (*People v. Coria, supra.*)

Whether section 12280(b) can properly be categorized as a public welfare offense, for which the Legislature intended guilt without proof of any scienter, is a question of first impression to which the answer is not obvious....

A leading criminal law treatise (1 LaFave & Scott, Substantive Criminal Law (1986)) lists several considerations courts have commonly taken into account in deciding whether a statute should be construed as a public welfare offense: (1) the legislative history and context; (2) any general provision on mens rea or strict liability crimes; (3) the severity of the punishment provided for the crime ("Other things being equal, the greater the possible punishment, the more likely some fault is required"); (4) the seriousness of harm to the public that may be expected to follow from the forbidden conduct; (5) the defendant's opportunity to ascertain the true facts ("The harder to find out the truth, the more likely the legislature meant to require fault in not knowing"); (6) the difficulty prosecutors would have in proving a mental state for the crime ("The greater the difficulty, the more likely it is that the legislature intended to relieve the prosecution of that burden so that the law could be effectively enforced"); (7) the number of prosecutions to be expected under the statute ("The fewer the expected prosecutions, the more likely the legislature meant to require the prosecuting officials to go into the issue of fault"). Finding this framework useful here, where the legislative intent is not readily discerned from the text itself, we consider each factor in turn.

1. The Statute's History and Context

The AWCA's origins and legislative history are reviewed in detail in *Kasler v. Lockyer* (2000) 23 Cal.4th 472. Suffice it to say here the legislation, enacted in 1989, was prompted by the belief that assault weapons posed a real, severe and growing threat to public safety, urgently requiring regulation and restriction to reduce the number of such weapons finding their way into the hands of street gangs, drug dealers and the mentally ill....

The law's origins as a legislative response to a serious public safety problem, reflected in this history and in the statutory findings and statement of purpose (§ 12275.5), tend to place the AWCA, including section 12280(b), in the category of public welfare offenses, of which the primary goal is regulation for the public welfare or safety rather than punishment of individual offenders. Moreover, from the fact that the list in section 12276 apparently was intended to provide "a more exact definition" (*Kasler*) of assault weapons than the original bill, one might infer the Legislature viewed the provisions of the law, as finally enacted, as providing a definition sufficiently certain and detailed that ordinary gun owners would have little difficulty determining if their firearms had to be registered. In this sense, the statute's history suggests, if only weakly, that the Legislature intended to place on the owners or possessors of semiautomatic weapons the onus of determining whether their firearms had the characteristics bringing them within the new law.

On the other hand, the legislative statement of purpose in section 12275.5 includes, as its last sentence, the following: "It is not, however, the intent of the Legislature by this chapter to place restrictions on the use of those weapons which are primarily designed and intended for hunting, target practice, or other legitimate sports or recreational activities." As the AWCA restricts only certain semiautomatic weapons, one could infer the Legislature believed those it left unrestricted did have significant sporting or recreational uses. In this sense, as the minor argues, the AWCA was clearly not premised on the view that "all semiautomatic firearms were henceforth suspect and to be possessed only at the risk of subjecting oneself to criminal liability."

Beyond these conflicting and somewhat attenuated inferences, the legislative history reveals no specific evidence of an intent to include or exclude any particular scienter in the elements of section 12280(b). Nor does the language of any of the AWCA's other substantive provisions clearly indicate a legislative intent to eliminate any mens rea element for a section 12280(b) violation.

...

2. General Provision on Mens Rea

California law contains a generally applicable rule on mens rea: section 20, which provides, "In every crime or public offense there must exist a union, or joint operation of act and intent, or criminal negligence." The interpretive rule embodied in this statute is by no means inflexible, public welfare offenses being the chief recognized exception. Nonetheless, at least where the penalties imposed are substantial, section 20 can fairly be said to establish a presumption against criminal liability without mental fault or negligence, rebuttable only by compelling evidence of legislative intent to dispense with mens rea entirely.

3. Severity of Punishment

As already noted, possession of an unregistered assault weapon under section 12280(b) is an alternative felony/misdemeanor, also known as a wobbler; that is, the offense is a felony unless charged as a misdemeanor or reduced to a misdemeanor by the sentencing court (§ 17, subd. (b)). Because the felony punishment specified is simply "imprisonment in the state prison," the prison sentence for a felony violation of section 12280(b) may be 16 months, two years, or three years, in the guided discretion of the sentencing court. If qualifying prior felony convictions are pleaded and proven, a person convicted of a felony violation of section 12280 (b) could face even greater punishment, including an indeterminate sentence of 25 years to life.

In *Staples*, the United States Supreme Court observed that its own early cases "might suggest that punishing a violation as a felony is simply incompatible with the theory of the public welfare offense." The high court ultimately found it unnecessary to embrace that view as a definitive rule, but did conclude the harsh potential penalties—up to 10 years' imprisonment—imposed under the federal law at issue for possession of an unregistered machine gun militated strongly against a construction dispensing with mens rea. This court agreed with *Staples*'s skepticism about felony punishment for putative public welfare offenses in *People v. Coria*, observing that manufacturing methamphetamine "is a felony, which is as bad a word as you can give to man or thing." Such an offense, we concluded, is difficult to characterize as "a mere regulatory statute which imposes light penalties with no damage to reputation."

Like the high court in *Staples*, we refrain from stating any inflexible rule regarding punishment for public welfare offenses. The Legislature's choice of potential felony punishment for violation of section 12280(b), however, reinforces the presumption expressed by section 20 and suggests that correspondingly strong evidence of legislative intent is required to exclude mens rea from the offense.

4. Seriousness of Harm to the Public

As already discussed, the Legislature in 1989 regarded the use of assault weapons by criminals and the mentally ill as a grave public safety threat. The information reflected in the AWCA's legislative history, and that collected since in connection with federal regulatory efforts directed at the same problem, give this court no cause to question or qualify the legislative assessment of the harm caused by the proliferation of such firearms in civilian society.

The AWCA is a remedial law aimed at protecting the public against a highly serious danger to life and safety. The Legislature presumably intended that the law be effectively enforceable, i.e., that its enforcement would actually result in restricting the number of assault weapons in the hands of criminals and the mentally ill. In interpreting the law to further the legislative intent, therefore, we should strive to avoid any construction that would significantly undermine its enforceability. This is not to suggest this court would or should read any element out of a criminal statute simply to ease the People's burden of proof. But, when a crime's statutory definition does not expressly include any scienter element, the fact the Legislature intended the law to remedy a serious and widespread public safety threat militates against the conclusion it also intended impliedly to include in the definition a scienter element especially burdensome to prove.

5. Difficulty of Ascertaining Facts

Courts have been justifiably reluctant to construe offenses carrying substantial penalties as containing no mens rea element "where ... dispensing with *mens rea* would require the defendant to have knowledge only of traditionally lawful conduct." (*Staples*.) This interpretive guideline holds with particular strength when the characteristics that bring the defendant's conduct within the criminal prohibition may not be obvious to the offender. In *Staples*, for example, the federal statute at issue criminalized possession only of fully automatic firearms, but the briefing and record before the court indicated that many or most semiautomatic firearms may be converted by internal modification to fire automatically. Observing that, certain military arms and notoriously criminal weapons aside, firearms, including semiautomatic firearms, enjoy "a long tradition of widespread lawful ... ownership by private individuals in this country" and, despite their destructive potential, "have been widely accepted as lawful possessions," the high court found it "unthinkable to us that Congress intended to subject such law-abiding, well-intentioned citizens to a possible ten-year term of imprisonment if ... what they genuinely and reasonably believed was a conventional semi-automatic [weapon] turns out to have worn down into or been secretly modified to be a fully automatic weapon."

...

The parties debate the application of these principles to construction of section 12280(b). The Attorney General maintains the weapons listed in section 12276 are "highly dangerous offensive weapons which are unambiguously hazardous. Assault weapons are typically used by soldiers in a war.... The assault weapons listed in section 12276, like the SKS with detachable magazine, are not ambiguous substances such that a person would not be aware of the dangerous character of the weapon after looking at one." The minor, in contrast, again stresses that the AWCA restricts only a subset of semiautomatic firearms, leaving the remainder available for lawful uses such as hunting and target shooting, and that even those semiautomatic firearms classified as assault weapons may, if registered, be lawfully possessed and used for these purposes.

On this point the minor has the better argument. The Attorney General may be correct that anyone who knew the firearm he or she possessed was an "assault weapon" would be likely to know it was potentially regulated or contraband. But this begs the question, for the issue is precisely whether a person violates section 12280(b) if he or she does *not* know the gun has the characteristics making it an assault weapon.

As to whether the possessor of a weapon listed in section 12276 would, in all or most cases, "be aware of the dangerous character of the weapon after looking at one," the Attorney General does not demonstrate, or even attempt to demonstrate, that the listed weapons are universally distinguishable by their appearance from firearms not listed in section 12276. Comparison of the photographs of listed rifles in the California Attorney General's Assault Weapons Identification Guide (1993) (hereafter Identification Guide) with photographs of unlisted rifles in a general reference work fails to bear out the assumption....

Nor can it be said that all semiautomatic rifles, or even all assault rifles, lack all lawful use, so that anyone in possession of one is overwhelmingly likely to be aware they are restricted or banned firearms. [In a recent federal government survey, a large number of professional hunting guides reported that their clients used semiautomatic rifles in hunting, and thirty-one competitive shooting groups responded that they conducted events using high-power semiautomatic rifles, all but one reporting that they permitted the use of the assault rifles under review.]

As the Legislature recognized (see § 12275.5), many semiautomatic weapons, including some of the listed assault weapons, have lawful uses; moreover, that a particular semiautomatic weapon is likely to be specially regulated as an assault weapon may not be readily apparent to all those who possess it. Thus, a construction of section 12280(b) that dispenses completely with scienter may result in the severe punishment of innocent possessors, a result we do not believe the Legislature intended.

6. Difficulty of Proving Mental State

We previously noted the seriousness of the public safety threat the Legislature perceived and sought to alleviate by the AWCA and the corresponding unsuitability, to the legislative intent, of any statutory construction that would likely impair the law's effective enforcement. It follows we should not read section 12280(b) as containing any mental state requirement that the prosecution would foreseeably and routinely have special difficulty proving.

An actual knowledge element has significant potential to impair effective enforcement. Although knowledge may be proven circumstantially, in many instances a defendant's direct testimony or prior statement that he or she was actually ignorant of the weapon's salient characteristics will be sufficient to create reasonable doubt. Although the People could rebut a claim of actual ignorance by evidence of the defendant's long and close acquaintance with the particular weapon or familiarity with firearms in general, production of such evidence would predictably constitute a heavy burden for the prosecution.

A scienter requirement satisfied by proof the defendant *should* have known the characteristics of the weapon bringing it within the AWCA, however, would have little or no potential to impede effective enforcement. In most instances the fact a firearm is of a make and model listed in section 12276, or added pursuant to section 12276.5, can be expected to be sufficiently plain on examination of the weapon so that evidence of the markings, together with evidence the accused possessor had sufficient opportunity to examine the firearm, will satisfy a knew-or-should-have-known requirement.

The Attorney General suggests that if section 12280(b) is construed to require some mens rea, it should be "knowledge simply of possession" of the firearm. We agree section 12280(b), like criminal possession laws generally, requires knowledge of the object's existence and of one's control over it. But we believe the Legislature intended section 12280(b) to require, as well, a degree of scienter regarding the *character* of the firearm; without such a scienter element, the possibility of severely punishing innocent possession is too great.

A group of amici curiae argues for a required mens rea even greater than knowledge of the weapon's characteristics: "actual knowledge by defendants that a firearm they possessed is one that is covered by the Act." According to their brief, such an extraordinary level of scienter is needed here because "the ordinary citizenry does not have the esoteric firearms knowledge necessary to follow what this complex and confusing Act allows, and what it prohibits." Amici curiae's prime concrete example of this complexity and confusion consists of the fact that the Attorney General's office has inconsistently interpreted section 12276, subdivision (a)(11), listing "SKS with detachable magazine," as to whether that designation includes certain SKS models originally manufactured with a fixed magazine but adapted to accept a detachable magazine.

... In cases where the information reasonably available to a gun possessor is too scant to prove he or she should have known the firearm had the characteristics making it a defined assault weapon, the possessor will not be subject to section 12280(b) as construed here. This is sufficient to protect against any significant possibility of punishing innocent possession. To require more—especially to require knowledge of the law as the amici curiae propose—would seriously impede effective enforcement of the AWCA, contrary to the legislative intent. Nothing in the language or history of the AWCA suggests the Legislature intended to create, in section 12280, an exception to the fundamental principle that all persons are obligated to learn of and comply with applicable laws.

7. Number of Expected Prosecutions

As previously discussed here and in *Kasler*, the Legislature enacted the AWCA in response to what it viewed as a statewide problem of increasing gravity, the rapidly growing use of assault weapons in incidents of criminal violence. Attacking what it perceived to be a widespread threat, the Legislature presumably anticipated a significant number of prosecutions would ensue under the law. Again, our construction should not impose a scienter requirement that would unduly impede the ability to prosecute substantial numbers of violators.

Conclusion

Although the AWCA can be characterized as a remedial law aimed at protecting public welfare, its text, history and surrounding statutory context provide no compelling evidence of legislative intent to exclude all scienter from the offense defined in section 12280(b). Section 20's generally applicable presumption that a penal law requires criminal intent or negligence, the severity of the felony punishment imposed for violation of section 12280(b), and the significant possibility innocent possessors would become subject to that weighty sanction were the statute construed as dispensing entirely with mens rea, convince us section 12280(b) was not intended to be a strict liability offense. The gravity of the public safety threat addressed in the AWCA, however, together with the substantial number of prosecutions to be expected under it and the potential difficulty of routinely proving actual knowledge on the part of defendants, convince us section 12280(b) was not intended to contain such an actual knowledge element. Consequently, we construe section 12280(b) as requiring knowledge of, or negligence in regard to, the facts making possession criminal. In a prosecution under section 12280(b), that is to say, the People bear the burden of proving the defendant *knew or reasonably should have known* the firearm possessed the characteristics bringing it within the AWCA.[11]

...

11. Our "reasonably should have known" formulation departs somewhat from the usual description of criminal negligence. (See, e.g., *People v. Peabody* (1975) 46 Cal.App.3d 43 ["[T]o constitute a

[JUSTICE KENNARD, dissenting in an opinion joined by JUSTICE BAXTER, would have held that "an element of the offense of possessing an unregistered assault weapon is actual knowledge by the accused that the firearm has the characteristics that make it an assault weapon."]

Note and Problem

The Model Penal Code and Strict Liability. The Model Penal Code prohibits the creation of strict liability *crimes*, although it allows the creation of strict liability *violations* with punishments limited to a fine, fine and forfeiture or other civil penalties. MPC § 2.05. The commentators, too, have been hostile to strict liability crimes:

> The consensus can be summarily stated: to punish conduct without reference to the actor's state of mind is both inefficacious and unjust. It is inefficacious because conduct unaccompanied by an awareness of the factors making it criminal does not mark the actor as one who needs to be subjected to punishment in order to deter him or others from behaving similarly in the future, nor does it single him out as a socially dangerous individual who needs to be incapacitated or reformed. It is unjust because the actor is subjected to the stigma of a criminal conviction without being morally blameworthy. Consequently, on either a preventive or retributive theory of criminal punishment, the criminal sanction is inappropriate in the absence of *mens rea.*

Herbert Packer, Mens Rea *and the Supreme Court*, 1962 S. CT. REV. 107, 109.

Problem 15.

Defendant and Juvenile (who was 20 years old) worked together. Defendant purchased beer for Juvenile, who, after drinking the beer, drove away from Defendant's house and collided with another car injuring its occupants and himself. Defendant is charged with violating Business and Professions Code § 25658, which provides as follows:

> (a) Except as otherwise provided in subdivision (c), every person who sells, furnishes, gives, or causes to be sold, furnished, or given away, any alcoholic beverage to any person under the age of 21 years is guilty of a misdemeanor.
>
> . . .
>
> (c) Any person who violates subdivision (a) by purchasing an alcoholic beverage for a person under the age of 21 years and the person under the age of 21 years thereafter consumes the alcohol and thereby proximately causes

---

criminal act the defendant's conduct must go beyond that required for civil liability and must amount to a 'gross' or 'culpable' departure from the required standard of care. The conduct must be aggravated or reckless . . ."].) At issue here, however, is defendant's awareness of the characteristics of a possessed item rather than his awareness of the harmful consequences of an action. Moreover, as we have explained, the AWCA has some of the key characteristics of a public welfare offense, justifying the inference the Legislature intended guilt to be established by proof of a mental state slightly lower than ordinarily required for criminal liability.

> great bodily injury or death to himself, herself, or any other person, is guilty of a misdemeanor [and is punishable "by imprisonment in a county jail for a minimum term of six months not to exceed one year, by a fine not exceeding one thousand dollars ($1,000), or by both imprisonment and fine."].

What arguments should be made as to whether Defendant can defend on the ground that he honestly and reasonably believed that Juvenile was an adult?

B. Mistake of Fact: Sex Crimes

Claims of reasonable mistake of fact often have arisen in the context of "sex" crimes, and the four cases in this section explore the law in this area. In each case, the defendant contends that his mistake was reasonable and therefore negated an objective mental state element of the crime charged, *i.e.*, that, since a reasonable person would have made the same mistake, the defendant had no culpable mental state. The defendant's contention raises two potential questions: (1) does the crime require proof of a culpable mental state at all, or does it impose strict liability; and (2) was the defendant's mistake reasonable? In *People v. Hernandez*, the defendant, convicted of statutory rape, contends he should have been allowed to defend on the ground that he made a reasonable mistake as to the victim's age. In *People v. Olsen*, the issue is again one of mistake as to age, this time in the context of a prosecution for lewd and lascivious acts on a child. Why does the California Supreme Court come to different conclusions in the two cases? In *People v. Mayberry*, the defendant, convicted of kidnapping and rape, argues that he should have been allowed to defend on the ground that he made a reasonable mistake as to whether the victim had consented. *People v. Barnes* concerns the issue of what evidence is sufficient to establish lack of consent or lack of reasonable belief in consent in a "date rape" situation.

People v. Hernandez

61 Cal. 2d 529, 393 P.2d 673 (1964)

PEEK, J.

By information defendant was charged with statutory rape. (Pen. Code, § 261, subd. 1.) Following his plea of not guilty he was convicted as charged by the court sitting without a jury and the offense determined to be a misdemeanor.

Section 261 of the Penal Code provides in part as follows: "Rape is an act of sexual intercourse, accomplished with a female not the wife of the perpetrator, under either of the following circumstances: 1. Where the female is under the age of eighteen years; ...."

The sole contention raised on appeal is that the trial court erred in refusing to permit defendant to present evidence going to his guilt for the purpose of showing that he had in good faith a reasonable belief that the prosecutrix was 18 years or more of age.

The undisputed facts show that the defendant and the prosecuting witness were not married and had been companions for several months prior to January 3, 1961—the date of the commission of the alleged offense. Upon that date the prosecutrix was 17 years and 9 months of age and voluntarily engaged in an act of sexual intercourse with defendant.

In support of his contention defendant relies upon Penal Code, section 20, which provides that "there must exist a union, or joint operation of act and intent, or criminal negligence" to constitute the commission of a crime. He further relies upon section 26 of that code which provides that one is not capable of committing a crime who commits an act under an ignorance or mistake of fact which disproves any criminal intent.

Thus the sole issue relates to the question of intent and knowledge entertained by the defendant at the time of the commission of the crime charged.

Consent of the female is often an unrealistic and unfortunate standard for branding sexual intercourse a crime as serious as forcible rape. Yet the consent standard has been deemed to be required by important policy goals. We are dealing here, of course, with statutory rape where, in one sense, the lack of consent of the female is not an element of the offense. In a broader sense, however, the lack of consent is deemed to remain an element but the law makes a conclusive presumption of the lack thereof because she is presumed too innocent and naive to understand the implications and nature of her act. The law's concern with her capacity or lack thereof to so understand is explained in part by a popular conception of the social, moral and personal values which are preserved by the abstinence from sexual indulgence on the part of a young woman. An unwise disposition of her sexual favor is deemed to do harm both to herself and the social mores by which the community's conduct patterns are established. Hence the law of statutory rape intervenes in an effort to avoid such a disposition. This goal, moreover, is not accomplished by penalizing the naive female but by imposing criminal sanctions against the male, who is conclusively presumed to be responsible for the occurrence.

The assumption that age alone will bring an understanding of the sexual act to a young woman is of doubtful validity. Both learning from the cultural group to which she is a member and her actual sexual experiences will determine her level of comprehension. The sexually experienced 15-year-old may be far more acutely aware of the implications of sexual intercourse than her sheltered cousin who is beyond the age of consent. A girl who belongs to a group whose members indulge in sexual intercourse at an early age is likely to rapidly acquire an insight into the rewards and penalties of sexual indulgence. Nevertheless, even in circumstances where a girl's actual comprehension contradicts the law's presumption, the male is deemed criminally responsible for the act, although himself young and naive and responding to advances which may have been made to him.[1]

---

1. The inequitable consequences to which we may be led are graphically illustrated by the following excerpt from *State v. Snow* (Mo. 1923) 252 S.W. 629: "We have in this case a condition and not a theory. This wretched girl was young in years but old in sin and shame. A number of callow youths,

The law as presently constituted does not concern itself with the relative culpability of the male and female participants in the prohibited sexual act. Even where the young woman is knowledgeable it does not impose sanctions upon her. The knowledgeable young man, on the other hand, is penalized and there are none who would claim that under any construction of the law this should be otherwise. However, the issue raised by the rejected offer of proof in the instant case goes to the culpability of the young man who acts without knowledge that an essential factual element exists and has, on the other hand, a positive, reasonable belief that it does not exist.

The primordial concept of *mens rea*, the guilty mind, expresses the principle that it is not conduct alone but conduct accompanied by certain specific mental states which concerns, or should concern, the law. In a broad sense the concept may be said to relate to such important doctrines as justification, excuse, mistake, necessity and mental capacity, but in the final analysis it means simply that there must be a "joint operation of act and intent," as expressed in section 20 of the Penal Code, to constitute the commission of a criminal offense. The statutory law, however, furnishes no assistance to the courts beyond that, and the casebooks are filled to overflowing with the courts' struggles to determine just what state of mind should be considered relevant in particular contexts. In numerous instances culpability has been completely eliminated as a necessary element of criminal conduct in spite of the admonition of section 20 to the contrary.

...

Statutory rape has long furnished a fertile battleground upon which to argue that the lack of knowledgeable conduct is a proper defense. The law in this state now rests, as it did in 1896, with this court's decision in *People v. Ratz* (1896) 115 Cal. 132, where it is stated: "The claim here made is not a new one. It has frequently been pressed upon the attention of courts, but in no case, so far as our examination goes, has it met with favor. The object and purpose of the law are too plain to need comment, the crime too infamous to bear discussion. The protection of society, of the family, and of the infant, demand that one who has carnal intercourse under such circumstances shall do so in peril of the fact, and he will not be heard against the evidence to urge his belief that the victim of his outrage had passed the period which would make his act a crime." The age of consent at the time of the *Ratz* decision was 14 years, and it is noteworthy that the purpose of the rule, as there announced, was to afford protection to young females therein described as "infants." The decision on which the court in *Ratz* relied was The *Queen v. Prince*, L.R. 1 Crown Cas. 154. However England has now, by statute, departed from the strict rule, and excludes as a crime an act of sexual intercourse with a female between the ages of 13 and 16 years

---

of otherwise blameless lives ... fell under her seductive influence. They flocked about her, ... like moths about the flame of a lighted candle and probably with the same result. The girl was a common prostitute.... The boys were immature and doubtless more sinned against than sinning. They did not defile the girl. She was a mere 'cistern for foul toads to knot and gender in.' Why should the boys, misled by her, be sacrificed? What sound public policy can be subserved by branding them as felons? Might it not be wise to ingraft an exception in the statute?"

if the perpetrator is under the age of 24 years, has not previously been charged with a like offense, and believes the female "to be of the age of sixteen or over and has reasonable cause for the belief."[2]

The rationale of the *Ratz* decision, rather than purporting to eliminate intent as an element of the crime, holds that the wrongdoer must assume the risk; that, subjectively, when the act is committed, he consciously intends to proceed regardless of the age of the female and the consequences of his act, and that the circumstances involving the female, whether she be a day or a decade less than the statutory age, are irrelevant.[3] There can be no dispute that a criminal intent exists when the perpetrator proceeds with utter disregard of, or in the lack of grounds for, a belief that the female has reached the age of consent. But if he participates in a mutual act of sexual intercourse, believing his partner to be beyond the age of consent, with reasonable grounds for such belief, where is his criminal intent? In such circumstances he has not consciously taken any risk. Instead he has subjectively eliminated the risk by satisfying himself on reasonable evidence that the crime cannot be committed. If it occurs that he has been misled, we cannot realistically conclude that for such reason alone the intent with which he undertook the act suddenly becomes more heinous.

While the specific contentions herein made have been dealt with and rejected both within and without this state, the courts have uniformly failed to satisfactorily explain the nature of the criminal intent present in the mind of one who in good faith believes he has obtained a lawful consent before engaging in the prohibited act. As in the *Ratz* case the courts often justify convictions on policy reasons which, in effect, eliminate the element of intent. The Legislature, of course, by making intent an element of the crime, has established the prevailing policy from which it alone can properly advise us to depart.

---

2. The American Law Institute in its Model Penal Code (1962) provides in part as follows at pages 149 and 150:

> "Section 213.6. Provisions Generally Applicable (Article 213 [Sexual Offenses].)
>
> "(1) Mistake as to Age. Whenever in this Article the criminality of conduct depends upon a child's being below the age of 10, it is no defense that the actor did not know the child's age, or reasonably believed the child to be older than 10. When criminality depends upon the child's being below a critical age other than 10, it is a defense for the actor to prove that he reasonably believed the child to be above the critical age."

3. "When the law declares that sexual intercourse with a girl under the age of ten years is rape, it is not illogical to refuse to give any credence to the defense, 'I thought she was older, and I therefore did not believe that I was committing a crime when I had sexual intercourse with her.'... But when age limits are raised to sixteen, eighteen, and twenty-one, when the young girl becomes a young woman, when adolescent boys as well as young men are attracted to her, the sexual act begins to lose its quality of abnormality and physical danger to the victim. Bona fide mistakes in the age of girls can be made by men and boys who are no more dangerous than others of their social, economic and educational level.... Even if the girl looks to be much older than the age of consent fixed by the statute, even if she lies to the man concerning her age, if she is a day below the statutory age sexual intercourse with her is rape. The man or boy who has intercourse with such girl still acts at his peril. *The statute is interpreted as if it were protecting children under the age of ten*" (Italics added.) (Plascowe, Sex and Law (1951)).

We have recently given recognition to the legislative declarations in sections 20 and 26 of the Penal Code, and departed from prior decisional law which had failed to accord full effect to those sections as applied to charges of bigamy. (*People v. Vogel* (1956) 46 Cal. 2d 798.) We held there that a good faith belief that a former wife had obtained a divorce was a valid defense to a charge of bigamy arising out of a second marriage when the first marriage had not in fact been terminated.

...

We are persuaded that the reluctance to accord to a charge of statutory rape the defense of a lack of criminal intent has no greater justification than in the case of other statutory crimes, where the Legislature has made identical provision with respect to intent. "At common law an honest and reasonable belief in the existence of circumstances, which, if true, would make the act for which the person is indicted an innocent act, has always been held to be a good defense.... So far as I am aware it has never been suggested that these exceptions do not equally apply to the case of statutory offenses unless they are excluded expressly or by necessary implication." (*Matter of Application of Ahart* (1916) 172 Cal. 762.) Our departure from the views expressed in *Ratz* is in no manner indicative of a withdrawal from the sound policy that it is in the public interest to protect the sexually naive female from exploitation. No responsible person would hesitate to condemn as untenable a claimed good faith belief in the age of consent of an "infant" female whose obviously tender years preclude the existence of reasonable grounds for that belief. However, the prosecutrix in the instant case was but three months short of 18 years of age and there is nothing in the record to indicate that the purposes of the law as stated in *Ratz* can be better served by foreclosing the defense of a lack of intent. This is not to say that the granting of consent by even a sexually sophisticated girl known to be less than the statutory age is a defense. We hold only that, in the absence of a legislative direction otherwise, a charge of statutory rape is defensible wherein a criminal intent is lacking.

...

People v. Olsen

36 Cal. 3d 638, 685 P.2d 52 (1984)

Opinion by Bird, C. J.

Is a reasonable mistake as to the victim's age a defense to a charge of lewd or lascivious conduct with a child under the age of 14 years (Pen. Code, § 288, subd.(a)?[1]

I

In early June 1981, Shawn M. was 13 years and 10 months old. At that time, her parents were entertaining out-of-town guests. Since one of the visitors was using

1. Section 288, subdivision (a) provides in relevant part:

Any person who shall willfully and lewdly commit any lewd or lascivious act ... upon or with the body, or any part or member thereof, of a child under the age of 14 years, with

Shawn's bedroom, Shawn suggested that she sleep in her family's camper trailer which was parked in the driveway in front of the house. Shawn's parents agreed to this arrangement on the condition that she keep the windows shut and the door locked.

On the night of June 3rd, Shawn's father, who is partially blind, was awakened by the barking of the family's three dogs. He went out the front door and heard male voices coming from the trailer. Mr. M. opened the door of the trailer and heard somebody remark about his presence. He then heard a male voice say, "Let's get the hell out of here."

Mr. M. could see three persons on the bed. One of the males, appellant Edward Olsen, jumped off the bed and tried to get out the door. Mr. M. wrestled with him and held him around the throat. Appellant called for help. The other male, James Garcia, stabbed Mr. M. in the right shoulder. Both appellant and Garcia then ran away.

At trial, Shawn testified to the following events. On her third night in the trailer, she locked the door as instructed by her parents. She then fell asleep, but was awakened by appellant Olsen who was knocking on the window and asking to be let in. Shawn said nothing and appellant left. Approximately a half-hour later, Garcia came up to the window and asked if he could enter. Shawn did not respond so he left. Shortly thereafter, appellant returned and again asked to be allowed in. Shawn did not answer. After both appellant and Garcia left, Shawn went to sleep.

Shawn was then awakened by the sound of barking dogs and by Garcia, who had a knife by her side and his hand over her mouth.[2] Garcia called to appellant to come in, and appellant entered the trailer.

Garcia told Shawn to let appellant "make love" to her, or he—Garcia—would stab her. Garcia gave the knife to appellant who held it to Shawn's neck and then gave it back to Garcia. Shawn asked Garcia to put the knife away and he complied.

Appellant and Garcia then removed Shawn's nightgown and underpants. Garcia told her again to let appellant "make love" to her. Shawn refused. Garcia then took out his knife. Appellant proceeded to have sexual intercourse with Shawn for about 15 minutes. During this time, Garcia knelt on the bed and said nothing. While appellant was still having intercourse with Shawn, her father entered the trailer. Mr. M. grabbed appellant as he was trying to leave, and Garcia stabbed Mr. M. in order to free appellant.

Shawn testified that she knew Garcia "pretty well" and had known him for approximately one year. She had last seen him about four days before the incident. She also testified that she was very good friends "off and on" with appellant and that during one three-month period she spent almost every day at appellant's house. At the time

---

the intent of arousing, appealing to, or gratifying the lust or passions or sexual desires of such person or of such child, shall be guilty of a felony and shall be imprisoned in the state prison for a term of three, six, or eight years.

2. Although Shawn testified she locked the trailer door, she failed to explain how Garcia entered the trailer. A subsequent examination of the trailer revealed that there were no signs of a forced entry.

of the incident, however, Shawn considered Garcia her boyfriend.[3] Finally, Shawn admitted that she told both Garcia and appellant that she was over 16 years old. She also conceded that she looked as if she were over 16.[4]

Garcia testified to quite a different set of events. He first met Shawn in the summer of 1980 when she introduced herself to him. On the afternoon of June 2, 1981—the day before the offense—Shawn invited him to spend the night in the trailer with her so that they could have sex. He and Shawn engaged in sexual intercourse about four times that evening. Shawn invited Garcia to come back the following night at midnight.

The next night, after two unsuccessful attempts to enter the trailer, Garcia and appellant were told by Shawn to return at midnight. Garcia knocked on the trailer door. Shawn, wearing only a pair of panties, opened the door and invited them in. She told them she wanted to "take both [of them] on." She then told Garcia that she wanted "to make love" with appellant first. When Mr. M. entered the trailer, appellant was on top of Shawn. Garcia denied threatening Shawn with a knife, taking her nightgown off, breaking into the trailer or forcing her to have sex with them.[5]

At the conclusion of the trial, the court found[6] Garcia and appellant guilty of violating section 288, subdivision (a).[7] In reaching its decision, the court rejected defense counsel's argument that a good faith belief as to the age of the victim was a defense to the section 288 charge. Appellant was sentenced to the lower term of three years in state prison. This appeal followed.

Appellant's sole contention on appeal is that a good faith, reasonable mistake of age is a defense to a section 288 charge.

---

3. Shawn admitted that she had engaged in intercourse before the night of June 3rd, but denied having any such prior experience with either Garcia or appellant. However, she did admit having had sexual relations, short of intercourse, with both of them in the past.

4. Patricia Alvarez, a police officer, testified that appellant told her that he thought Shawn was 17.

5. Appellant's sister corroborated Shawn's testimony that Shawn made daily visits to the Olsen home during a three-month period. She testified that during these visits Shawn and appellant would go into the latter's bedroom and close the door. On one occasion, appellant's sister saw the two in bed together. On several occasions, his sister entered the bedroom after Shawn had left and noticed the bedcovers "messed up" and an odor which she associated with sex. Appellant's next-door neighbor testified that he often encountered appellant and Shawn emerging from appellant's bedroom in the morning. Joseph W., Garcia's 16-year-old friend who also knew Shawn, testified that he and Chuck A., a 15-year-old neighbor, had simultaneously gone to bed with Shawn on two occasions. On one of the occasions, Chuck's father caught them in bed and ordered Shawn out of the house. Both Chuck and his father corroborated Joseph's testimony.

6. Appellant had waived jury trial on the condition that if convicted, he would be sentenced to no more than five years in state prison.

7. Garcia was also found guilty of assault with a deadly weapon (§ 245, subd. (a)) with infliction of great bodily injury. (§ 12022.7.) Both Garcia and appellant were found not guilty of burglary (§ 459), forcible rape (§ 261, subd. (2)), and lewd or lascivious acts upon a child under the age of 14 by use of force (§ 288, subd. (b)). Appellant was also found not guilty of assault with a deadly weapon. (§ 245, subd. (a).)

II

The language of section 288 is silent as to whether a good faith, reasonable mistake as to the victim's age constitutes a defense to a charge under that statute. Resort is thus made to judicial decisions discussing the defense. Although this court has not considered the question, it has recognized a mistake of age defense in other contexts.

[The court reviewed the *Hernandez* case.]

The *Hernandez* court, however, cautioned that its holding was not "indicative of a withdrawal from the sound policy that it is in the public interest to protect the sexually naive female from exploitation. No responsible person would hesitate to condemn as untenable a claimed good faith belief in the age of consent of an 'infant' female whose obviously tender years preclude the existence of reasonable grounds for that belief." The court then concluded that there was nothing to indicate that "the purposes of the law [could] be better served by foreclosing the defense of a lack of intent."

One Court of Appeal has declined to apply *Hernandez* in an analogous context. In *People v. Lopez* (1969) 271 Cal. App. 2d 754, the court refused to recognize a reasonable mistake of age defense to a charge of offering or furnishing marijuana to a minor. The court noted that the act of furnishing marijuana is criminal regardless of the age of the recipient and that furnishing marijuana to a minor simply yields a greater punishment than when the substance is furnished to an adult. "[A] mistake of fact relating only to the gravity of an offense will not shield a deliberate offender from the full consequences of the wrong actually committed."[14]

In deciding whether to apply the philosophy of *Hernandez* to the offense of lewd or lascivious conduct with a child under the age of 14, this court is guided by decisions of the Courts of Appeal. The three post-*Hernandez* Court of Appeal decisions which have considered the issue have refused to apply *Hernandez*.

[In *People v. Tober* (1966) 241 Cal. App. 2d 66, the court upheld the conviction of a defendant convicted of lewd or lascivious acts on a 10-year-old child. In *People v. Toliver* (1969) 270 Cal. App. 2d 492, the court also rejected a reasonable mistake of age defense, noting that "[under] the Roman and common laws, childhood was considered to exist until puberty, which was determined to be at age 14 ..." and holding that the same distinction should continue to be applied. In *People v. Gutierrez* (1978) 80 Cal. App. 3d 829, the court relied on *Tober* and *Toliver* to reach the same result.]

---

14. On the other hand, *Hernandez* has been extended to some offenses involving children. For example, in *People v. Atchison* (1978) 22 Cal. 3d 181, this court apparently concluded that a reasonable mistake as to the victim's age was a defense to the charges of annoying or molesting a child under the age of 18 (§ 647a) and contributing to the delinquency of a child under the age of 18. (§ 272.) In *People v. Peterson* (1981) 126 Cal. App. 3d 396, the Court of Appeal held the defense applicable to a charge of oral copulation with a person under 18. (§ 288a, subd. (b)(1).) Most recently, a mistake of age defense was recognized in a case involving the inducement of a minor to use a narcotic drug (Health & Saf. Code, § 11353) and marijuana (Health & Saf. Code, § 11361). (*People v. Goldstein* (1982) 130 Cal. App. 3d 1024.) It is significant for our purposes that none of these offenses involved children under the age of 14.

The reasoning of the *Tober*, *Toliver* and *Gutierrez* courts is persuasive. There exists a strong public policy to protect children of tender years. As *Gutierrez* indicates, section 288 was enacted for that very purpose. Furthermore, even the *Hernandez* court recognized this important policy when it made clear that it did not contemplate applying the mistake of age defense in cases where the victim is of "tender years."

Moreover, other language in *Hernandez* strongly suggests that a reasonable mistake as to age would not be a defense to a section 288 charge. As *Hernandez* noted, when *People v. Ratz* (1896) 115 Cal. 132 was decided, an accused could be convicted of statutory rape only if the victim were under 14. *Hernandez* also found it "noteworthy that the purpose of the rule [announced in *Ratz*] was to afford protection to young females therein described as 'infants.'" Thus, an "infant" at the time of *Ratz* was any child under 14. The *Hernandez* court's use of that term, therefore, evidenced a belief that a mistake of age defense would be untenable when the offense involved a child that young.

The language in *Hernandez*, together with the reasoning in *Tober*, *Toliver* and *Gutierrez*, compel the conclusion that a reasonable mistake as to the victim's age is not a defense to a section 288 charge.

This conclusion is supported by the Legislature's enactment of section 1203.066. Subdivision (a)(3) of that statute renders certain individuals convicted of lewd or lascivious conduct who "honestly and reasonably believed the victim was 14 years old or older" eligible for probation. The Legislature's enactment of section 1203.066, subdivision (a)(3), in the face of a corresponding failure to amend section 288 to provide for a reasonable mistake of age defense, strongly indicates that the Legislature did not intend such a defense to a section 288 charge. To recognize such a defense would render section 1203.066, subdivision (a)(3) a nullity, since the question of probation for individuals who had entertained an honest and reasonable belief in the victim's age would never arise. It is well established that courts are "exceedingly reluctant to attach an interpretation to a particular statute which renders other existing provisions unnecessary." (*Bowland v. Municipal Court* (1976) 18 Cal. 3d 479.)

Other legislative provisions also support the holding that a reasonable mistake of age is not a defense to a section 288 charge. Time and again, the Legislature has recognized that persons under 14 years of age are in need of special protection. This is particularly evident from the provisions of section 26. That statute creates a rebuttable presumption that children under the age of 14 are incapable of knowing the wrongfulness of their actions and, therefore, are incapable of committing a crime. A fortiori, when the child is a victim, rather than an accused, similar "special protection," not given to older teenagers, should be afforded. By its very terms, section 288 furthers that goal.

...

It is significant that a violation of section 288 carries a much harsher penalty than does unlawful sexual intercourse (§ 261.5), the crime involved in *Hernandez*. Section 261.5 carries a maximum punishment of one year in the county jail or three years in state prison (§ 264), while section 288 carries a maximum penalty of eight years in state prison. The different penalties for these two offenses further supports the view that there exists a strong public policy to protect children under 14.

In recent years, the Legislature has increased the state prison sentence for violations of section 288 without increasing the punishment for unlawful sexual intercourse. In 1978, the penalty for section 288 was increased from three, four or five years to three, five or seven years. In 1981, the punishment was increased to the present three-, six- or eight-year term. During this same period, the penalty for a violation of section 261.5 has remained constant.

It is true that at common law "an honest and reasonable belief in the existence of circumstances, which, if true, would make the act for which the person is indicted an innocent act, has always been held to be a good defense." (*Hernandez.*) However, it is evident that the public policy considerations in protecting children under the age of 14 from lewd or lascivious conduct are substantial—far more so than those associated with unlawful sexual intercourse. These strong public policies are reflected in several Penal Code statutes, and they compel a different rule as to section 288.

The legislative purpose of section 288 would not be served by recognizing a defense of reasonable mistake of age. Thus, one who commits lewd or lascivious acts with a child, even with a good faith belief that the child is 14 years of age or older, does so at his or her peril.

III

The trial court properly rejected appellant's claim that his good faith, reasonable mistake as to the victim's age was a defense to a lewd or lascivious conduct charge with a child under 14 years of age. Accordingly, the judgment of conviction is affirmed.

GRODIN, J., concurring and dissenting.

I agree that the enactment of Penal Code section 1203.066, which renders eligible for probation persons convicted of lewd or lascivious conduct who "honestly and reasonably believed the victim was 14 years old or older" is persuasive evidence that in the eyes of the Legislature such a belief is not a defense to the crime.[1] What troubles me is the notion that a person who acted with such belief, and is not otherwise shown to be guilty of any criminal conduct,[2] may not only be convicted but be sentenced to

1. I do not agree that legislative intent to eliminate good faith mistake of fact as a defense can be inferred from the imposition of relatively higher penalties for that crime. On the contrary, as this court has stated in connection with the crime of bigamy: "The severe penalty imposed … the serious loss of reputation conviction entails, the infrequency of the offense, and the fact that it has been regarded … as a crime involving moral turpitude, make it extremely unlikely that the Legislature meant to include the morally innocent to make sure the guilty did not escape." (*People v. Vogel* (1956) 46 Cal. 2d 798.)

2. The People suggest that defendant was at least guilty of "sexual intercourse accomplished with a female not the wife of the perpetrator, where the female is under the age of 18 years." Defendant was neither charged nor convicted of that offense, however, and it is by no means clear from the record that he had sexual intercourse with the victim.

prison notwithstanding his eligibility for probation when it appears that his belief did not accord with reality. To me, that smacks of cruel or unusual punishment.[3]

I fully accept that "fault" even for purposes of the criminal law, may at times be predicated upon conduct, short of "intentional," which exposes others to substantial and unjustified risks. I recognize also that our legal system includes certain "strict liability" crimes, but generally these are confined to the so-called "regulatory" or "public welfare" offenses, which "do not fit neatly into any of such accepted classifications of common-law offenses, such as those against the state, the person, property, or public morals.... Many violations of such regulations result in no direct or immediate injury to person or property but merely create the danger or probability of it which the law seeks to minimize." (*Morissette v. United States* (1952) 342 U.S. 246.) Moreover, with respect to such crimes, *"The accused, if he does not will the violation, usually is in a position to prevent it with no more care than society might reasonably expect ... from one who assumed his responsibilities. Also, penalties commonly are relatively small, and conviction does no grave damage to an offender's reputation."* (*Id.*, italics added.)

Even in the regulatory context, "judicial and academic acceptance of liability without fault has not been enthusiastic." (Jeffries & Stephan, *Defenses, Presumptions, and Burden of Proof in the Criminal Law* (1979) 88 Yale L.J. 1325.) And "with respect to traditional crimes, it is a widely accepted normative principle that conviction should not be had without proof of fault. At least when the offense carries serious sanctions and the stigma of official condemnation, liability should be reserved for persons whose blameworthiness has been established." (*Id.*)

...

Problem

Problem 16.

Father learned that, against his orders, his 13-year-old daughter, Teen, maintained a MySpace page. Father viewed the page and discovered that she used a false name and falsely stated she was 18 years old. While Father was viewing the page, Teen received an e-mail from Defendant asking if she wanted to have oral sex. Pretending to be Teen, Father answered, "I'm 13," is that "okay with you?" The conversation continued, with Father pretending to be a very sexually experienced teenage girl, who had been with older men in the past and had been pregnant. In the end, Defendant agreed to meet "Teen" at a convenience store for the purpose of engaging in sexual activity. When Defendant showed up at the convenience store, Father took his picture and that of his truck, and Defendant was subsequently arrested. Defendant is charged with attempted lewd or lascivious conduct with a child under 14. (P.C. §§ 288(a); 664) "An attempt to commit a crime consists of two elements: a specific intent to

---

3. Defendant has not made this argument; thus, I do not fault my colleagues for failing to consider it.

commit the crime, and a direct but ineffectual act done toward its commission." (P.C.§ 21a) What are the arguments regarding whether Defendant can raise a mistake-of-age defense?

People v. Mayberry

15 Cal. 3d 143, 542 P.2d 1337 (1975)

Richardson, J.

An information was filed charging Franklin Mayberry and his brother Booker T. Mayberry with various offenses against the prosecutrix (Miss Nancy B.). Booker was charged with assault with intent to commit rape (Pen. Code, § 220). Franklin was charged with kidnapping (Pen. Code, § 207), rape by means of force and threat (Pen. Code, § 261, subds. 2 & 3), assault by means of force likely to produce great bodily injury (Pen. Code, § 245), and oral copulation (Pen. Code, § 288a). Following a joint trial, a jury found defendants guilty as charged on all counts, except that the jury found Franklin guilty of assault (Pen. Code, § 240), a lesser included offense in the alleged violation of section 245. Franklin received a jail term for the assault, and he and Booker received prison terms for the other offenses.

Defendants appeal from the judgments, contending that the prosecutrix' testimony is inherently improbable and that inadequate instructions, an improper charge, and certain other matters also require reversal of the judgments. We have concluded that the court erred in refusing to give instructions concerning mistake of fact and that the error requires reversal of the rape and kidnapping convictions. In all other respects the judgments will be affirmed.

Miss B., the prosecutrix, testified to the following effect:

About 4 p.m. on July 8, 1971, she left her apartment in Oakland to walk to a nearby grocery store. As she passed a liquor store, she heard "catcalls" from some men, and Franklin, whom she had never seen before, grabbed her arm. She dug her fingernails into his wrist, and he released her. After she turned to leave, he kicked her, threw a bottle which struck her, and shouted obscenities at her. She remonstrated and continued on her way.

After she entered the grocery store, Franklin suddenly appeared beside her and said something to the effect that she was going to go outside with him and if she did not cooperate she would "pay for it." She replied she did not want to accompany him and looked for a store security guard but saw none. The only store personnel she observed were busy with customers and were too far away for her to gain their attention. Because of her own confusion and fear of Franklin, she accompanied him outside the store, where they remained for approximately 20 minutes. During this time Miss B. observed no one available to assist her although two women left the store in her vicinity.

Franklin, in a threatening manner, mentioned to Miss B. having sex. She rejected this, but Franklin told her she "was going to have to go with him," and, when she refused, struck her in the chest with his fist, knocking her down. Franklin directed obscenities at her, held his fist up to her face, and told her "you are going to come with me" and added that if she did not do so he would "knock every tooth out of [her] mouth." She asked him to leave her alone, but Franklin seized her wrist and said "come on." In an attempt "to buy time," she told Franklin she wanted to purchase some cigarettes, and he agreed. Placing his hand beneath her elbow, he accompanied her to a store, approximately 100 feet away, where she purchased cigarettes for herself and Franklin. She did not explain to the clerk her predicament because she was feeling "completely beaten" and did not think the clerk would help her.

After completing the purchase, she sat on a curb, attempted to engage Franklin in conversation and smoked a cigarette. During this period, in her words, she "put on an act" and tried "to fool" Franklin, thinking that she might be able to escape. He eventually said, "we are leaving." She "tried to talk him out of it," and he became angry and, uttering an obscenity, ordered her to "get up." She complied, and he again seized her elbow and started to guide her. While walking several blocks, they passed some business establishments, but Miss B. noticed no one on the street. She did not want to accompany him but, because of fear, did not resist.

Franklin led her to an apartment house and entered ahead of her. After they entered his apartment, he barricaded the door behind them. She did not attempt to flee because, having a leg that was stiff from an arthritic condition, she could not run fast. Approximately 15 minutes of further conversation ensued during which she unsuccessfully attempted to persuade Franklin "to change his mind." Without her consent, he then engaged in several acts of sexual intercourse and oral copulation with her. During the sexual assault he struck her, and because of fear she did not physically resist his advances.

[According to Miss B., Booker then entered the apartment and assaulted and attempted to rape her. When she resisted, he attempted to strangle her. Franklin intervened and permitted her to escape. Booker testified that when he entered the apartment, he found the other two in bed together and that he laughed and Miss B. became embarrassed and fled. He denied assaulting her.]

At trial a police officer testified that around 10:40 p.m. on July 8, 1971, he went to Miss B's address in response to a kidnap-rape call and observed much bruising and swelling on her face, left arm and leg.

Franklin took the stand in his own behalf and testified as follows: he saw Miss B. about 4 p.m. on July 8, 1971, and engaged her in conversation, after which he accompanied her to the grocery and the store where she purchased cigarettes. They then walked to his home. He did not threaten her, nor did she protest but accompanied him willingly and agreed to, and did engage in, intercourse. He denied seeing Booker hit her, but recalled that Booker entered the apartment while she was there and began laughing. She looked upset, said, "I'll fix you," and left.

In rebuttal the prosecution presented two witnesses. One described bruises on Miss B's face and arms on the night of July 8, 1971; the other testified that she noticed nothing unusual about Miss B's face on July 7, 1971, but that when the witness observed Miss B. on July 9, 1971, her face was bruised and swollen, one eye was almost shut, and her arm was bruised.

...

Franklin's Claim that Court Erred in Refusing to Give Requested Instructions
A. Mistake of Fact Instructions

The court refused to give requested instructions that directed the jury to acquit Franklin of the rape and kidnapping if the jury had a reasonable doubt as to whether Franklin reasonably and genuinely believed that Miss B. freely consented to her movement from the grocery store to his apartment and to sexual intercourse with him. Franklin contends that the court thereby erred. The Attorney General argues that the court properly refused to give the instructions because "mistake of fact [instructions] as to consent should be rejected as against the law and public policy."

Penal Code section 207 provides, "Every person who forcibly ... takes ... any person in this state, and carries him into ... another part of the same county, ... is guilty of kidnapping." Penal Code section 261 provides, "Rape is an act of sexual intercourse, accomplished with a female not the wife of the perpetrator, under either of the following circumstances: ...; 2. Where she resists, but her resistance is overcome by force or violence; 3. Where she is prevented from resisting by threats of great and immediate bodily harm, accompanied by apparent power of execution ..." There is, of course, no kidnapping when one, ... with knowledge of what is taking place ... voluntarily ... consents to accompany another ... and similarly there is no rape if a female of sufficient capacity consents to sexual intercourse.

Penal Code section 26 recites, generally, that one is incapable of committing a crime who commits an act under a mistake of fact disproving any criminal intent. Penal Code section 20 provides, "In every crime ... there must exist a union, or joint operation of act and intent, or criminal negligence." The word "intent" in section 20 means "wrongful intent." "So basic is this requirement [of a union of act and wrongful intent] that it is an invariable element of every crime unless excluded expressly or by necessary implication." *People v. Vogel*, 46 Cal.2d 798.

[The Court reviewed the *Hernandez* case]

Although *Hernandez* dealt solely with statutory rape, its rationale applies equally to rape by means of force or threat and kidnapping. Those statutory provisions, like that involved in *Hernandez*, neither expressly nor by necessary implication negate the continuing requirement that there be a union of act and wrongful intent. The severe penalties imposed for those offenses [kidnapping: 1 to 25 years in prison; rape: 3 years to life] and the serious loss of reputation following conviction make it extremely unlikely that the Legislature intended to exclude as to those offenses the element of wrongful intent. If a defendant entertains a reasonable and bona fide belief that a prosecutrix voluntarily consented to accompany him and to engage in sexual intercourse, it is apparent he does not possess the wrongful intent that is a prerequisite under Penal Code section 20 to a conviction of either kidnapping or rape by means of force or threat.

. . .

The Attorney General urges that the Legislature did not make "the state of mind or belief on the part of the perpetrator of rape relevant as a defense to that crime except as to the circumstances set forth in subdivisions 4 and 5 of section 261." Those subdivisions do require specified mental states on the part of the accused. However, it is implicit in *Hernandez* that the absence of such a requirement in other subdivisions of section 261 does not warrant the conclusion that the Legislature intended the accused's state of mind to become irrelevant in prosecutions under the other subdivisions.

The Attorney General further argues that a defense based on mistake of fact as to the prosecutrix' consent in prosecutions for kidnapping or rape should not be permitted because it will promote greater resistance by the victim to assure there is no misunderstanding as to consent and that such resistance could result in harm to the victim. The Attorney General notes that utmost resistance by the female to establish lack of consent to intercourse is not required. Such an argument, in our view, invokes a policy consideration for the Legislature—adoption of the argument would result in effective nullification of Penal Code sections 20 and 26 when applied to cases of kidnapping and rape.

The Attorney General next argues that, even if instructions regarding mistake of fact as to consent are appropriate in some cases of kidnapping and rape, here the court properly determined that the evidence did not warrant such instructions. However, Franklin's testimony summarized above could be viewed as indicating that he reasonably and in good faith believed that Miss B. consented to accompany him to the apartment and to the subsequent sexual intercourse. In addition, part of Miss B's testimony furnishes support for the requested instructions. It appears from her testimony that her behavior was equivocal. Although she did not want Franklin to think she was consenting, her "act" and admitted failure physically to resist him after the initial encounter or to attempt to escape or obtain help might have misled him as to whether she was consenting. We by no means intimate that such is the only reasonable interpretation of her conduct, but we do conclude that there was some evidence "deserving of ... consideration" which supported his contention that he acted under a mistake of fact as to her consent both to the movement and to intercourse. It follows, accordingly, that the requested instructions, if correctly worded, should have been given.

The People's final argument on the point is that the instructions are erroneous on the theory that the burden resting on the defendant to prove mistake of fact as to consent is not satisfied by merely raising a reasonable doubt as to that issue. The People err in this regard. In *People v. Vogel*, we concluded that the burden was on the defendant to prove as a defense to a bigamy charge that he had a bona fide and reasonable belief that facts existed which left him free to remarry. Similarly here the burden was on Franklin to prove that he had a bona fide and reasonable belief that the prosecutrix consented to the movement and to sexual intercourse. As to that issue, he was only required to raise a reasonable doubt as to whether he had such a belief. The requested instructions so providing are thus correct, and the court erred in refusing to give them.

. . .

Note and Problems

The Model Penal Code and Rape. The Model Penal Code defines rape and related offenses as follows:

> **§ 213.1** Rape and related offenses.
>
> (1) Rape. A male who has sexual intercourse with a female not his wife is guilty of rape if:
>
> (a) he compels her to submit by force or by threat of imminent death, serious bodily injury, extreme pain or kidnapping, to be inflicted on anyone; or
>
> (b) he has substantially impaired her power to appraise or control her conduct by administering or employing without her knowledge drugs, intoxicants or other means for the purpose of preventing resistance; or
>
> (c) the female is unconscious; or
>
> (d) the female is less than 10 years old.
>
> Rape is a felony of the second degree unless (i) in the course thereof the actor inflicts serious bodily injury upon anyone, or (ii) the victim was not a voluntary social companion of the actor upon the occasion of the crime and had not previously permitted him sexual liberties, in which cases the offense is a felony of the first degree.
>
> (2) Gross Sexual Imposition. A male who has sexual intercourse with a female not his wife commits a felony of the third degree if:
>
> (a) he compels her to submit by any threat that would prevent resistance by a woman of ordinary resolution; or
>
> (b) he knows that she suffers from a mental disease or defect which renders her incapable of appraising the nature of her conduct; or
>
> (c) he knows that she is unaware that a sexual act is being committed upon her or that she submits because she mistakenly supposes that he is her husband.

How does the Model Penal Code definition of rape differ from California's? A particular innovation of the Code was the creation, in effect, of three degrees of rape in place of the single crime at the common law. What arguments can be made for and against such a scheme?

Problem 17.

Defendant is charged with rape (P.C. § 261). At trial, Victim testified as follows. She was a homeless person. She met Defendant, and the two walked and talked for awhile. Defendant invited Victim to watch T.V. and took her to a transient hotel where he rented a room for $20 and was given a bedsheet. Victim entered the room and noticed there was no T.V. When she attempted to leave, Defendant blocked her way, yelled at her, punched her in the eye and ordered her to take off her pants and get on the bed. Victim was scared and gave in to Defendant's demands. Over her screams and protests, Defendant had intercourse with Victim. Afterward, he offered her $50, and she refused the money.

In his defense, Defendant testified as follows. Prior to entering the hotel room, he had no thought of engaging in sex. Once in the room, Victim initiated sexual activity, and Defendant responded. Afterward, Victim requested that Defendant give her $50, but Defendant refused. Victim then became angry and threatened to "fix" him by telling everyone she was raped. Clerk, the hotel clerk, testified that, during the hour that Defendant and Victim were inside the room, he did not hear any screams or other sounds indicating physical violence.

What arguments should be made as to whether the court should give the jury a *Mayberry* instruction on reasonable mistake of fact?

Problem 18.

Defendant and Girlfriend (his Girlfriend) were alcoholics. On the day in question both consumed a substantial amount of hard liquor while sitting on the curb of a street, and both were very intoxicated. Defendant and Girlfriend then went behind some bushes, and each took off some of their clothes. A passerby saw the two and called the police. When the police arrived, Girlfriend was naked and in a semiconscious condition, and Defendant was lying beside her with his pants off. Subsequently, tests showed that Defendant had engaged in intercourse with Girlfriend. Her blood alcohol level was .53 %, more than six times the amount necessary to convict someone of driving under the influence. Defendant is charged with rape (P.C. § 261(a)(3)) on the theory that sexual intercourse was accomplished under circumstances "[w]here a person is prevented from resisting by any intoxicating or anesthetic substance, or any controlled substance, and this condition was known, or reasonably should have been known by the accused." What arguments should be made on the validity of the statute and whether Defendant is guilty of violating it?

People v. Barnes

42 Cal. 3d 284, 721 P.2d 110 (1986)

Bird, C.J.

Was the Court of Appeal correct in relying on a rape complainant's lack of "measurable resistance" to overturn convictions of rape and false imprisonment as unsupported by sufficient evidence?

I

Since the sufficiency of evidence to support the convictions is in issue, it is necessary to present a somewhat detailed statement of the factual circumstances of this case.

Marsha M. had known appellant about four years as of May of 1982. They were neighbors and acquaintances. She had been to his house briefly once before to buy some marijuana. A couple of weeks before the present incident, they had drunk wine together at her house.

Around 10 p.m. on May 27, 1982, appellant called Marsha and invited her over for some drinks to celebrate his parents' having come into a sum of money. Marsha was undecided and told appellant to call back or she would call him.

Over the next two hours, appellant called twice to see what Marsha had decided to do. She finally told him she would come over and that she wanted to buy a little marijuana from him. She asked him to meet her outside his house.

Marsha arrived at appellant's house around 1 a.m. Appellant was waiting for her outside the front gate. It was cold. Appellant suggested they go inside and smoke some marijuana. At first Marsha refused. She told appellant she had to get up early and wanted to buy the marijuana and go home. However, after a couple of minutes, appellant persuaded her to come inside.

Marsha followed appellant through the house to a room off the garage. At first, they carried on a conversation which Marsha described as "normal chatter." Appellant provided some marijuana and they both smoked it. Appellant offered some cocaine, but she refused. She kept telling appellant she wanted to hurry up and leave.

After 10 or 15 minutes, appellant began to hug Marsha. She pushed him away and told him to stop. She did not take him seriously as he was "just coming on."

Appellant continued his advances despite Marsha's insistence that she only wanted to buy marijuana and leave. When appellant asked her why she was in such a hurry, she reiterated she just wanted him to give her the marijuana and let her go since she had to get up early in the morning. Appellant told her he did not want her to leave. Marsha finally said good-bye and walked out of the room. Until this point, things between them had been "decent and friendly."

As Marsha approached the front gate, appellant, who was behind her and appeared angry, stated, "No, you don't go leaving. You don't just jump up and leave my goddamn house." He began "ranting and raving" and arguing with her. He wanted to know why she was "trying to leave." He told her that she made him feel as if she had stolen something; that she was acting like he was "a rapist or something." Marsha characterized appellant's behavior as "psychotic."

When she reached the front gate, Marsha did not try to open it because she did not know how. She asked appellant to open it, but he just stood looking at her. This behavior made her nervous. When she asked appellant what was wrong, he "reared back" as if he were going to hit her.

They argued at the gate for about 20 minutes.[3] Marsha told appellant she did not understand what he was arguing with her about and that he seemed to be trying to

3. During this argument, Marsha asked appellant several times to open the gate.

find a reason to be angry with her. She told him, "I came to your house to get some grass. Now, I want to leave. You won't let me leave."

Appellant replied that he was going to let her leave but needed to put his shoes on first. He then returned to the room and Marsha followed. She said she returned to the room because she felt she could not get out the front gate by herself.

[After they entered the room, Appellant began acting strangely, looking at her "funny," telling her he was a man and displaying the muscles in his arms and talking of past sexual exploits. At one point he said, "I can make you do anything I want. You understand me?" At another point, he said, "You're so used to see [*sic*] the good side of me. Now you get to see the bad."]

Appellant continued talking but then suddenly turned and started hugging Marsha "affectionately." He told her he did not mean to "fuss" at her. By now, Marsha felt she was in the room with a "psychotic person" who had again changed personalities. Approximately 40 minutes had elapsed since they entered the room a second time. It was at this juncture that Marsha began to "play along" and feign compliance with appellant's desires.

In an effort to get out of appellant's house, Marsha suggested they go to her house where they could be alone. Appellant told her not to worry about his parents coming home. He continued to hug and talk to her. After a few minutes, appellant stated, "I have to have some of this right now," and told Marsha to remove her clothes. Marsha refused. Appellant reacted by telling her she was going to upset him and by making some type of gesture. In response, Marsha removed her clothes. An act of sexual intercourse ensued which lasted about one hour and included the exchange of kisses. Afterward, both appellant and Marsha fell asleep.

Marsha testified she engaged in sexual intercourse with appellant because she felt if she refused, he would become physically violent. She based this assessment on appellant's actions and words, including his statements that she was about to "see the bad side" of him and that he could throw her out if he wanted.

Marsha awoke around 4 a.m. She cajoled appellant into walking her to the front gate and opening it so she could leave. She returned home and immediately called Kaiser Hospital to request an examination.

The defense was consent. Appellant's testimony was substantially similar to Marsha's regarding the events prior to her arrival at his house. However, the versions differed markedly as to the subsequent events.

Appellant testified that the first time they were in the room together he gave Marsha some marijuana and refused payment for it. They smoked some marijuana. Appellant told Marsha he had "feelings for her," he was sexually attracted to her and did not want her to leave so quickly. According to appellant, they did not argue over anything. He was surprised that she was in such a rush to leave.

At the front gate, they continued to talk. He again expressed feelings of sexual attraction for her. According to appellant, it was Marsha who first returned to the room. There, she told him she would stay a little while longer. Then, without being asked, she started removing her clothes. Consensual sexual intercourse ensued during which Marsha returned appellant's hugs and kisses. Appellant testified he did not threaten Marsha in any way, make gestures toward her, display his muscles or force her to stay....

Appellant was convicted after a jury trial of one count each of rape and false imprisonment (Pen. Code, §§ 261, subd. (2), 236) as to Marsha M. The Court of Appeal reversed these convictions as unsupported by substantial evidence. This court granted the Attorney General's petition for review in order to clarify the requirements for conviction under section 261, subdivision (2) as amended by the Legislature in 1980.

II

Until its amendment in 1980, former section 261, subdivisions 2 and 3 defined rape as an act of sexual intercourse under circumstances where the person resists, but where "resistance is overcome by force or violence" or where "a person is prevented from resisting by threats of great and immediate bodily harm, accompanied by apparent power of execution...."

The Legislature amended section 261 in 1980 to delete most references to resistance.[7] In pertinent part, the statute now defines rape as "an act of sexual intercourse accomplished with a person not the spouse of the perpetrator, under any of the following circumstances: ... [¶] (2) Where it is accomplished against a person's will by means of force or fear of immediate and unlawful bodily injury on the person or another."

[The court concluded that the legislature intended to make a material change with its amendment.]

At common law, the crime of rape was defined as "the carnal knowledge of a woman forcibly and against her will." (4 Blackstone, Commentaries 201.) Historically, it was considered inconceivable that a woman[14] who truly did not consent to sexual intercourse would not meet force with force.[15] The law originally demanded "utmost resistance" from the woman to ensure she had submitted rather than consented. Not only must she have resisted to the "utmost" of her physical capacity, the resistance must not have ceased throughout the assault.

California long ago rejected this "primitive rule" of utmost resistance. "A woman who is assaulted need not resist to the point of risking being beaten into insensibility. If she resists to the point where further resistance would be useless or, ... until her resistance is overcome by force or violence, submission thereafter is not consent." (*People v. McIlvain* (1942) 55 Cal. App. 2d 322.) In our state, it had long been the

---

7. Subdivision (3) of the amended statute retains a reference to the prevention of resistance through the administering of certain substances.

14. Although the balance of this opinion frequently refers to the rape complainant as female, the discussion applies equally to male rape complainants.

15. Thus, for example, in passing on a claim of rape, the court in *People v. Dohring* (1874) 59 N.Y. 374 was prompted to query: "Can the mind conceive of a woman ... revoltingly unwilling that this deed should be done upon her, who would not resist so hard and so long as she was able?"

rule that the resistance required by former section 261, subdivision 2, was only that which would reasonably manifest refusal to consent to the act of sexual intercourse.

Nevertheless, courts refused to uphold a conviction of rape by force where the complainant had exhibited little or no resistance. The law demanded some measure of resistance, for it remained a tenet that a virtuous woman would by nature resist a sexual attack.

The requirement that a woman resist her attacker appears to have been grounded in the basic distrust with which courts and commentators traditionally viewed a woman's testimony regarding sexual assault. According to the 17th century writings of Lord Matthew Hale, in order to be deemed a credible witness, a woman had to be of good fame, disclose the injury immediately, suffer signs of injury and cry out for help. (1 Hale, History of the Pleas of the Crown (1st Am. ed. 1847).)

This distrust was formalized in the law in several areas. For example, juries were traditionally advised to be suspect and cautious in evaluating a rape complainant's testimony, particularly where she was "unchaste."

In most jurisdictions, corroboration of the complaining witness was necessary for a conviction of rape. Skeptical of female accusers, the majority of courts and commentators considered it appropriate that the "prosecutrix" in all sexual assault cases undergo psychiatric examination before trial.

Such wariness of the complainant's credibility created "an exaggerated insistence on evidence of resistance." As an objective indicator of nonconsent, the requirement of resistance insured against wrongful conviction based solely on testimony the law considered to be inherently suspect. In our state, it supplied a type of intrinsic corroboration of the prosecuting witness's testimony, a collateral demanded even when extrinsic corroboration was not required. Thus did the resistance requirement continue even in its modified form, to nurture and reflect the perspective, still held by some modern commentators, that "human nature will impel an unwilling woman to resist unlawful sexual intercourse with great effort."

Recently, however, the entire concept of resistance to sexual assault has been called into question. It has been suggested that while the presence of resistance may well be probative on the issue of force or nonconsent, its absence may not.

For example, some studies have demonstrated that while some women respond to sexual assault with active resistance, others "freeze." One researcher found that many women demonstrate "psychological infantilism"—a frozen fright response—in the face of sexual assault. (Symonds, *The Rape Victim: Psychological Patterns*, 26 Am. J. Psychoanalysis 27.) The "frozen fright" response resembles cooperative behavior. Indeed, as Symonds notes, the "victim may smile, even initiate acts, and may appear relaxed and calm." Subjectively, however, she may be in a state of terror.[16] Symonds

16. Symonds writes: "In light of the traumatic psychological infantilism ... that most victims of violent crime undergo, it is surprising we see any resisting patterns at all."

also reports that the victim may make submissive signs to her assailant and engage in propitiating behavior in an effort to inhibit further aggression. These findings belie the traditional notion that a woman who does not resist has consented. They suggest that lack of physical resistance may reflect a "profound primal terror" rather than consent.

Additionally, a growing body of authority holds that to resist in the face of sexual assault is to risk further injury.

In a 1976 study of rape victims and offenders, the Queen's Bench Foundation found that over half of the sexual assault offenders studied reported becoming more violent in response to victim resistance. Injury as reported by victims correlated with some form of resistance, including verbal stalling, struggling and slapping. Those victims who resisted during coitus suffered increased violence as the assailant forced compliance. Victim resistance, whether passive or active, tended to precede an increase or intensification of the assailant's violence.

On the other hand, other findings indicate that resistance has a direct correlation with deterring sexual assault. Of the 75 convicted rapists the Queen's Bench Foundation questioned, half believed that their sexual assaults could have been deterred by active victim resistance. Brownmiller argues that submissive behavior is not necessarily helpful to a rape victim and suggests that strong resistance on the part of women can thwart rape. (Brownmiller, Against Our Will, Men, Women and Rape (1975).) She suggests it would be well for women to undergo systematic training in self-defense in order to fight back against their attackers.

Reflecting the foregoing uncertainties about the advisability of resistance, the Queen's Bench Foundation concluded: "Overall, the research findings suggest that rape prevention is more possible through vigorous resistance[;] however, resistance incurs greater risk of injury. When confronted with attack, each woman must make a choice which is highly personal and may be affected by situational factors beyond her control." These conclusions are also contained in a pamphlet for distribution to the general public in which the reader is advised that physical resistance may increase the danger or may thwart the attack; the woman must therefore evaluate the threat she faces and decide how to react based on the kind of person she is.

In sum, it is not altogether clear what the absence of resistance indicates in relation to the issue of consent. Nor is it necessarily advisable for one who is assaulted to resist the attack. It is at least arguable that if it fails to deter, resistance may well increase the risk of bodily injury to the victim. This possibility, as well as the evolution in societal expectations as to the level of danger a woman should risk when faced with sexual assault, are reflected in the Legislature's elimination of the resistance requirement. In so amending section 261, subdivision (2), the Legislature has demonstrated its unwillingness to dictate a prescribed response to sexual assault. For the first time, the Legislature has assigned the decision as to whether a sexual assault should be resisted to the realm of personal choice.

...

By removing resistance as a prerequisite to a rape conviction, the Legislature has brought the law of rape into conformity with other crimes such as robbery, kidnapping and assault, which require force, fear, and nonconsent to convict. In these crimes, the law does not expect falsity from the complainant who alleges their commission and thus demand resistance as a corroboration and predicate to conviction. Nor does the law expect that in defending oneself or one's property from these crimes, a person must risk injury or death by displaying resistance in the face of attack. The amendment of section 261, subdivision (2), acknowledges that previous expectational disparities, which singled out the credibility of rape complainants as suspect, have no place in a modern system of jurisprudence.

This court therefore concludes that the Legislature's purposes in amending section 261 were (1) to relieve the state of the need to establish resistance as a prerequisite to a rape conviction, and (2) to release rape complainants from the potentially dangerous burden of resisting an assailant in order to substantiate allegations of forcible rape.

As noted, it is no longer proper to instruct the jury that it must find the complainant resisted before it may return a verdict of guilt. Nor may lack of resistance be employed by courts—like the Court of Appeal here—to support a finding of insufficient evidence of rape under section 261, subdivision (2).[19]

For these reasons, the Court of Appeal's reliance upon any absence of resistance by Marsha was improper.

III

The question remains whether proper application of amended section 261 to the instant facts compels reversal of appellant's convictions of rape by means of force or fear of unlawful bodily injury and false imprisonment.

...

Under prior law, forcible rape required that the accused employ that degree of force necessary under the circumstances to overcome the victim's resistance. Although resistance is no longer the touchstone of the element of force, the reviewing court still looks to the circumstances of the case, including the presence of verbal or non-verbal threats, or the kind of force that might reasonably induce fear in the mind of the victim, to ascertain sufficiency of the evidence of a conviction under section 261, subdivision (2). Additionally, the complainant's conduct must be measured against the degree of force manifested or in light of whether her fears were genuine and reasonably grounded.[20] In the words of one commentator, the trier of fact "should be permitted to measure consent by weighing both the acts of the alleged attacker and

19. The statutory change does not mean that when resistance does exist, it is irrelevant to nonconsent. Absence of resistance may also continue to be probative of whether the accused honestly and reasonably believed he was engaging in consensual sex. (See *People v. Mayberry* (1975) 15 Cal. 3d 143.)

20. In some circumstances, even a complainant's unreasonable fear of immediate and unlawful bodily injury may suffice to sustain a conviction under section 261, subdivision (2), if the accused knowingly takes advantage of that fear in order to accomplish sexual intercourse.

the response of the alleged victim, rather than being required to focus on one or the other." (Com. *Towards a Consent Standard in the Law of Rape* (1976) 43 U. Chi. L. Rev. 613.)

[The court held that Marsha's testimony constituted substantial evidence of rape by means of force or fear. Marsha consistently communicated that she only wanted to purchase marijuana and did not want to stay. Nevertheless, the defendant engaged in a variety of conduct apparently aimed at intimidating her—cursing and berating her, "rearing back" as if to hit her, boasting of his physical and sexual prowess and warning her of his anger.]

In light of the totality of these circumstances, the jury, having observed the witnesses and their demeanor, could reasonably have concluded that Marsha's fear of physical violence from appellant if she did not submit to sexual intercourse was genuine and reasonable. Under these facts, a reasonable juror could have found that Marsha's subsequent compliance with appellant's urgent insistence on coitus was induced either by force, fear, or both, and, in any case, fell short of a consensual act.

Additionally, Marsha several times communicated her unwillingness to stay and have sexual intercourse with appellant. Appellant should have realized that his threatening conduct, combined with Marsha's rejection of his sexual advances and repeated requests to leave, created a situation where he was able to overcome rather than respect her will. That appellant may have deluded himself into believing her eventual submission represented a consensual act could have been rejected by a rational trier of fact as an unreasonable response to Marsha's conduct. Therefore, the jury's rejection of appellant's defense that he reasonably believed she consented was proper given the totality of these circumstances. (See *People v. Mayberry*.)

...

Note and Problems

Gender-neutral statutes. As was true at the common law, rape, under the Model Penal Code, is a gender specific crime: only males can be guilty of rape, and only females can be victims of rape. Although, by the time of the *Barnes* case, the California statute had been amended to make it gender neutral, the Court's analysis and the studies it cited concerned the situation of men raping women. Should rape statutes be framed in gender-neutral terms?

Problem 19.

Victim was staying overnight at the apartment of Friend, whom Victim had known for 12 years and considered to be like an aunt. Defendant (Friend's boyfriend) arrived at the apartment in a somewhat "tipsy" condition, and Defendant, Friend and Victim had dinner together and drank some wine. At about 11:30 p.m., Victim went to sleep in the living room, sleeping in pants and a shirt on top of her sleeping bag. Several hours later, Victim awoke and, lying on her stomach, she saw Defendant, who was naked, approach her from behind. Defendant outweighed Victim by 100 pounds. Without saying anything, Defendant pulled down Victim's pants, fondled her and achieved penetration. Victim was afraid, so she did not say or do anything. After a minute, Defendant returned to Friend's room, and Victim called a friend to pick her up and fled the apartment. Defendant is charged with rape (P.C. § 261). What arguments should be made as to whether he is guilty?

Problem 20.

Defendant, a teenage boy, and Victim, a 17-year-old girl, were visiting at the house of Friend, also a teenage boy. Victim engaged in consensual sexual activity with both boys, but balked when, after Defendant left the room, Friend tried to engage in sexual intercourse with her. Subsequently Friend left the room, and Defendant returned, unclothed. He lay down beside Victim, and they began kissing. Although Defendant at no time asked for Victim's consent, he achieved penetration, and they engaged in intercourse for several minutes. At that point, Victim said she needed to go home, but Defendant said, "Just give me a minute," and did not stop. Victim insisted that she needed to go, but defendant again ignored her. Finally Victim said, "No, I have to go home." Defendant finally stopped, about a minute to a minute and a half after Victim first said she needed to go. Defendant is charged with forcible rape (P.C. § 261). What arguments should be made regarding whether he is guilty?

Problem 21.

Defendant had sexual intercourse with Woman under the following circumstances. Defendant called Woman one morning and, without identifying himself, whispered that he was under arrest for hit and run driving after striking a pedestrian. Woman believed the caller was her husband. Defendant told Woman she should speak to his lawyer. Using a different voice and playing the role of the lawyer, Defendant said that "his client" was facing a mandatory jail sentence unless Woman could meet with the accident victim and persuade him to drop charges or decline to testify. Defendant suggested that Woman might have to pay off the victim. He also asked Woman to rate her looks on a scale of one to ten and told her that it was important to make the victim like her. To that end, he suggested that she should "dress sexily, wear a short skirt and play her femininity." Woman agreed to meet with the accident victim, and, at the prearranged meeting spot, Defendant identified himself as the victim and got into Woman's car. Initially she offered him money to drop the charges, but Defendant rejected the offer and, at various points in the conversation, said he thought it was his duty to cooperate with the police. At one point, Defendant started to leave, and, when Woman tried to convince him to stay, he let her know he wanted some kind of sexual contact. After getting Defendant's assurances that he would not press charges, Woman agreed to accompany him to a motel, where they had sexual intercourse. In the following three months, Defendant successfully used the same scheme (with minor variations) on three other women. Defendant is now charged with four counts of rape (P.C. §261(2)). What arguments should be made as to whether he is guilty of the crimes?

Problem 22.

Defendant makes sadomasochistic movies. Defendant met Victim in a North Beach bar, and the two made a movie together in which, among other things, Defendant whips Victim, who is tied to a light fixture. The film fell into the hands of the local prosecutor, who has charged Defendant with violating P.C. §§242, 243 (battery). Could Defendant raise a defense of consent?

C. Mistake of Law

The last three cases on *mens rea* involve claimed mistakes of law. It has long been the rule that "ignorance of the law is no excuse," so a defendant's mistake of law, no matter how reasonable, is generally no defense. What accounts for this different treatment of factual and legal mistakes? Despite the general rule, there are two narrow circumstances in which a mistake of law might be a defense, and these are considered in the three cases. In *People v. Goodin*, the defendant contends that mistake of law is a defense because the crime in issue is defined to require proof of the defendant's knowledge of the law. In *People v. Snyder*, the court considers several challenges to the defendant's conviction for being an ex-felon in possession of a firearm, particularly her claim that she had been misled by others into thinking she was not an ex-felon and her conduct was therefore legal. In *People v. Stark*, the defendant, a county auditor-controller charged with engaging in "unauthorized" financial transactions on behalf of the county, claims that he did not know the transactions were "unauthorized," and the court has to determine the *mens rea* of the crime.

People v. Goodin

136 Cal. 455, 69 P. 85 (1902)

HAYNES, C.

The information charged that the defendant on May 17, 1901, did willfully, maliciously, and feloniously injure a public highway..., by digging up, displacing, and removing the earth from the roadbed thereof. He was tried and found guilty, and sentenced to imprisonment in the county jail for the period of four months; and he appeals from the judgment, and from an order denying a new trial.

... His defense, briefly stated, is that he believed in good faith that he had a right to fence it up for his own benefit and convenience; and whether such belief constitutes a defense in this criminal action is the principal question, and is presented in the following instructions given to the jury at the request of the prosecution ...: "(12) If the jury find from the evidence that the road referred to in the information is a public highway or road, and has been used as such for fifteen years or more, and if you further find from the evidence that the defendant, B. F. Goodin, maliciously dug up, removed, displaced, broke, or otherwise injured or destroyed, said public road, and you further find from the evidence that the defendant believed he had a legal right to injure or destroy the same, when he had no legal grounds for such belief, and when he had in fact no such right, the fact of such belief does not justify the said acts of the defendant. (13) It is no defense for the defendant to claim that he thought, or had an honest belief, that he had a right to dig up or injure said public highway."

The road upon which the alleged injury was done is described in the information as "a public highway leading from the Mountain House to the town of Leesville, commonly known as the 'Old Leesville Grade.'" It was regularly laid out and established in 1879, and had been improved and used as a public highway down to the date of the alleged injury committed by the defendant. Defendant's son owned 320 acres of land through which said road ran, which land was occupied by the defendant under a lease. Prior to the date of the act charged, the board of supervisors laid out a new road, called the "New Leesville Grade," between the termini of the old grade above stated. It was completed and accepted by the board in the fall of 1900.... Mr. Rathbun, one of the supervisors, called by the prosecution, testified that he was interested in a stage line that went over this road; that "his driver went up the old grade most of the time"; that he thought most of the people traveled the old grade at that time; that the new grade had just been repaired, and the people were afraid of it.... It was testified by Mr. Perdue, through whose land it also ran, that the new grade was constructed to take the place of the old one, and this fact was not controverted. The statute authorizes the board of supervisors to "alter" an existing road, but to say that a road may be altered, and the old road continue to exist in the altered part as it was before, is an absurdity. If the new road was constructed to take the place of the old one, it is implied that the old one is abandoned and ceases to exist as a highway. Whether it would be so held in an action of trespass, the whole record being before the court, we need not decide; but, upon the uncontradicted facts before us, it is clear beyond question that the defendant had ample grounds for his belief that the old road was abandoned, and that he had a right to fence it up with his other lands for his own convenience and benefit, and, so believing, he could have had no intent to commit the crime of which malice is a necessary ingredient.

Counsel for respondent cites section 294 of Bishop's New Criminal Law, where the maxim, "*Ignorantia juris non excusat*," is quoted as "a rule in our jurisprudence." The same author, however, ... further says: "There are crimes which cannot be committed of general malevolence, but they require a particular evil condition of the mind, existing in actual fact. And ignorance of the law, the same as any other cause, if it renders the special state of mind impossible, takes away the offense. Thus larceny exists only where there is an intent to steal, and an indispensable element in this intent is the knowledge that the property taken does not belong to the taker. Therefore if all the facts concerning the title are known to him, and so the question is simply of law,—whether or not the property is his,—still he may show, and it will be adequate in defense, that he honestly believed it his, through misapprehending the law." In this connection the author applies the same principle to cases of malicious mischief, perjury, official corruption, and some other offenses....

The court erred not only in the instructions hereinbefore quoted, but in striking out defendant's testimony stating the grounds of his belief that he had a right to fence up the road, ...

People v. Snyder

32 Cal. 3d 590, 652 P.2d 42 (1982)

Opinion by Richardson, J.

Defendant Neva Snyder appeals from a judgment convicting her of possession of a concealable firearm by a convicted felon (Pen. Code, § 12021), based upon her 1973 conviction for sale of marijuana, a felony (former Health & Saf. Code, § 11531). Defendant contends that the trial court erred in excluding evidence of her mistaken belief that her prior conviction was only a misdemeanor. We will conclude that defendant's asserted mistake regarding her legal status as a convicted felon did not constitute a defense to the firearm possession charge. Accordingly, we will affirm the judgment.

At trial, defendant offered to prove the following facts supporting her theory of mistake: The marijuana possession charge resulted from a plea bargain not involving a jail or prison sentence. At the time the bargain was struck, defendant's attorney advised her that she was pleading guilty to a misdemeanor. Believing that she was not a felon, defendant thereafter had registered to vote, and had voted. On one prior occasion, police officers found a gun in her home but, after determining that it was registered to her husband, the officers filed no charges against defendant.

The trial court refused to admit any evidence of defendant's mistaken belief that her prior conviction was a misdemeanor and that she was not a felon. The court also rejected proposed instructions requiring proof of defendant's prior knowledge of her felony conviction as an element of the offense charged.

Penal Code section 12021, subdivision (a), provides: "Any person who has been convicted of a felony under the laws of the ... State of California ... who owns or has in his possession or under his custody or control any pistol, revolver, or other firearm capable of being concealed upon the person is guilty of a public offense, ..."

The elements of the offense proscribed by section 12021 are conviction of a felony and ownership, possession, custody or control of a firearm capable of being concealed on the person. No specific criminal intent is required, and a general intent to commit the proscribed act is sufficient to sustain a conviction. With respect to the elements of possession or custody, it has been held that knowledge is an element of the offense.

Does section 12021 also require knowledge of one's legal status as a convicted felon? No case has so held. Penal Code section 26 provides that a person is incapable of committing a crime if he acted under a "mistake of fact" which disproves criminal intent. In this regard, the cases have distinguished between mistakes of fact and mistakes of law. As we stated in an early case: "It is an emphatic postulate of both civil and penal law that ignorance of a law is no excuse for a violation thereof. Of course it is based on a fiction, because no man can know all the law, but it is a maxim which the law itself does not permit any one to gainsay ... The rule rests on public necessity; the welfare of society and the safety of the state depend upon its enforcement. If a person accused of a crime could shield himself behind the defense that he was ignorant of the law which he violated, immunity from punishment would in most cases result." (*People v. O'Brien* (1892) 96 Cal. 171.) Accordingly, lack of actual knowledge of the provisions of Penal Code section 12021 is irrelevant; the crucial question is whether the defendant was aware that he was engaging in the conduct proscribed by that section.

In the present case, defendant was presumed to know that it is unlawful for a convicted felon to possess a concealable firearm. She was also charged with knowledge that the offense of which she was convicted ... was, as a matter of law, a felony. That section had prescribed a state prison term of from five years to life, and the express statutory definition of a "felony" is "a crime which is punishable with death or by imprisonment in the state prison." (Pen. Code § 17(a).)

Thus, regardless of what she reasonably believed, or what her attorney may have told her, defendant was deemed to know under the law that she was a convicted felon forbidden to possess concealable firearms. Her asserted mistake regarding her correct legal status was a mistake of law, not fact. It does not constitute a defense to section 12021.

None of the California cases relied on by defendant is apposite here. *People v. Hernandez* (1964) 61 Cal. 2d 529, and *People v. Mayberry* (1975) 15 Cal. 3d 143, each involved mistakes of fact, not law. In *Hernandez*, the mistake concerned the age of the alleged victim of a statutory rape. In *Mayberry*, defendant erred in assuming that the adult victim of forcible rape consented to his acts. *People v. Vogel* (1956) 46 Cal. 2d 798, involved the good faith belief of a defendant charged with bigamy that he is free to remarry. We were careful to explain that defendant's mistake was a factual one: "We have concluded that defendant is not guilty of bigamy, if he had a bona fide and reasonable belief that *facts* existed that left him free to remarry." (Italics added.) Moreover, *Vogel* characterized bigamy as a crime which "has been regarded for centuries as ... involving moral turpitude ..." Obviously a bona fide belief that one is free to remarry nullifies the moral opprobrium attached to the charge. On the other hand, being an ex-felon in possession of a concealable firearm, while illegal, hardly stamps the person charged as a moral leper. His belief that he is not a felon thus does not affect the criminality of his conduct.

Our conclusion is confirmed by federal cases interpreting a similar federal statute forbidding possession of a firearm by one convicted of a felony. The only element of the federal offense which is not found in section 12021 of the Penal Code is an effect upon "commerce." The federal statute has been uniformly interpreted as requiring only that the defendant was in fact a convicted felon, and not that he actually knew he was a felon. As stated in *United States v. Locke* (9th Cir. 1976) 542 F.2d 800, "Because the crimes here charged do not require a specific intent, the fact that appellant may have been advised by a public defender that he was not a convicted felon, has no relevance."

Defendant relies primarily upon *People v. Bray* (1975) 52 Cal. App. 3d 494, but that case is distinguishable. There defendant pleaded guilty in Kansas to being an accessory before the fact and was placed on two years' summary probation, which he successfully completed. When he subsequently sought to register to vote, he filled out an explanatory form referring to a Kansas offense, and indicating that he was uncertain whether he had been convicted of a felony. He was permitted to vote. Seeking employment as a security guard, he stated that he had not been convicted of a felony but described the circumstances of his arrest and probation. The Bureau of Collection and Investigative Services registered him as a guard. On several other job applications he indicated his uncertainty as to his status while fully setting forth the circumstances of his arrest and probation.

In *Bray*, the court concluded that under these unusual circumstances the trial court erred in refusing to instruct on mistake or ignorance of fact and knowledge of the facts which make the act unlawful. The court cautioned, however, that its decision "should not be interpreted to mean instructions on mistake or ignorance of fact and knowledge of the facts are required every time a defendant claims he did not know he was a felon ... It is only in very unusual circumstances such as these that the giving of these instructions is necessary."

In the present case, unlike *Bray*, defendant made no attempt to inform government officials of the circumstances of her conviction or to seek their advice regarding her correct legal status. (Some authorities have suggested that reliance upon the erroneous advice of governmental authorities might constitute an exception to the general rule that a mistake of law is no defense.)

We conclude that the trial court properly excluded evidence of defendant's asserted mistake regarding her status as a convicted felon.

Broussard, J., dissenting.

I dissent.

The two elements of a violation of Penal Code section 12021 are felony status and possession of a concealable firearm. While no specific criminal intent is required, a general criminal intent should be required as to both elements in accordance with long-settled rules of statutory interpretation, and an honest and reasonable mistake as to either element of the offense, however induced, should negate the requisite general criminal intent. Defendant's testimony if believed would have established an honest and reasonable mistaken belief that her prior offense was not a felony but a misdemeanor, and it was prejudicial error to refuse to admit the evidence and to refuse instructions on the mistake doctrine.

The majority have adopted a special strict liability rule as to section 12021, holding that a felon is charged with knowledge of his status and that an honest and reasonable mistaken belief as to the nature of the conviction is not a defense unless apparently it is induced or corroborated in whole or in part by governmental conduct. The traditional and longstanding defense of mistake negating criminal intent should not be limited to situations where the mistake is induced or corroborated by government officials. Irrebuttable presumptions of knowledge are not favored in the criminal law, and because the source of an honest and reasonable mistake does not affect the question of the existence of criminal intent, we should not accept the government source limitation.

. . .

Penal Code section 26 provides generally that a person is incapable of committing a crime when the act was committed under a mistake of fact disproving any criminal intent. Section 20 of that code provides: "In every crime or public offense there must exist a union, or joint operation of act and intent, or criminal negligence."

"The word 'intent' in section 20 means 'wrongful intent.' (See *People v. Vogel* (1956) 46 Cal. 2d 798.) 'So basic is this requirement [of a union of act and wrongful intent] that it is an invariable element of every crime unless excluded expressly or by necessary implication'" (*People v. Mayberry* (1975) 15 Cal. 3d 143).

At common law an honest and reasonable belief in circumstances which, if true, would make the defendant's conduct innocent was held to be a good defense. (*People v. Hernandez* (1964) 61 Cal. 2d 529.) The concept of mens rea, the guilty mind, expresses the principle that it is not conduct alone but conduct accompanied by certain mental states which concerns, or should concern the law. While in some cases, culpability had been completely eliminated as a necessary element of criminal conduct, the court has moved away from imposition of criminal liability in the absence of culpability where the governing statute, by implication or otherwise, expresses no legislative intent or policy to be served by strict liability.

The elements of the offense proscribed by section 12021 are conviction of a felony and ownership, possession, custody or control of a firearm capable of being concealed on the person. While no specific criminal intent is required, a general intent to commit the proscribed act is necessary. As to the element of possession or custody, it has been held that knowledge is an element of the offense.

There does not appear to be any provision in section 12021 by implication or otherwise indicating legislative intent or policy to be served by refusing to apply the general criminal intent requirement to both of the elements of the offense. The Attorney General argues that, because knowledge of possession or custody of the gun are essential to conviction, strict liability would not result from holding that knowledge of a felony conviction is irrelevant. While under such construction the offense would not involve strict liability as to those who were unaware that they possessed a handgun, it would impose strict liability upon those who were unaware of their felony convictions and could legally possess handguns in the absence of conviction. The language of section 12021 sets forth both elements of the offense in parallel construction, and there is no basis in the language or grammatical construction of the statute warranting a distinction between the two elements with respect to the mens rea requirement. In the absence of any provision reflecting legislative intent or policy to establish strict liability, the mens rea requirement is applicable to the felony conviction element of the offense as well as the possession and custody element.

To hold otherwise is contrary to the settled California rule that a mens rea requirement is an "invariable" element of every crime unless excluded expressly or by necessary implication. (*People v. Mayberry*, *supra*; *People v. Vogel*, *supra*.) Having established the rule, we must assume the Legislature is aware of it and acting in accordance with it, and the absence of any provision to establish strict liability must be read as reflecting legislative intent to require wrongful intent.

The majority rely upon federal cases interpreting a federal statute forbidding possession of a firearm by one convicted of a felony or certain misdemeanors.

None of the federal cases cite or discuss statutes comparable to Penal Code sections 20 and 26. Concluding that there is no scienter or mens rea requirement, the courts reason that the crime is a statutory offense rather than a common law offense and that as to statutory offenses there ordinarily is no scienter requirement in the absence of express provision therefor. Penal Code sections 20 and 26 are part of our statutory law, and there is no basis for a conclusion that they apply only to common law offenses and not to statutory offenses. Because of those statutes, we have adopted a rule of construction directly contrary to the federal rule, *i.e.*, wrongful intent "is an invariable element of every crime unless excluded expressly or by necessary implication." (*People v. Vogel*.) Just as the federal courts adhere to their rules as to the effect of congressional silence, we should adhere to the legislative direction in sections 20 and 26 and our rules as to legislative silence. Having established the ground rules for statutory interpretation, we may not abrogate them on the basis of federal cases applying contrary ground rules.

In determining whether a defendant's mistaken belief disproves criminal intent pursuant to Penal Code section 26, the courts have drawn a distinction between mistakes of fact and mistakes of law. Criminal intent is the intent to do the prohibited act, not the intent to violate the law. "It is an emphatic postulate of both civil and penal law that ignorance of a law is no excuse for a violation thereof. Of course it is based on a fiction, because no man can know all the law, but it is a maxim which the law itself does not permit any one to gainsay ... The rule rests on public necessity; the welfare of society and the safety of the state depend upon its enforcement. If a person accused of a crime could shield himself behind the defense that he was ignorant of the law which he violated, immunity from punishment would in most cases result." (*People v. O'Brien*, (1892) 96 Cal. 171.) Accordingly, lack of knowledge of the provisions of Penal Code section 12021 is irrelevant; the crucial question is whether the defendant was aware that he was engaging in the conduct proscribed by that section.

While mistake as to whether the conduct is violative of a statute is not a defense, a mistaken impression as to the legal effect of a collateral matter may mean that a defendant does not understand the significance of his conduct and may negate criminal intent. When the victim's status is an element of the crime, a mistaken belief as to the status has been held a defense in several decisions by this court. In *People v. Hernandez*, it was held that a reasonable and honest belief that the prosecutrix was 18 years or more of age would be a defense to a charge of statutory rape, negating the requisite mental intent. Similarly, in *People v. Atchison* (1978) 22 Cal. 3d 181, it was held that a reasonable and honest belief that the victim was 19 years of age was a defense to charges of annoying or molesting a child under age 18 and of contributing to the delinquency of a minor. And in *People v. Mayberry*, it was held that a mistaken belief that the prosecutrix had consented would be a defense to a charge of forcible rape and kidnapping.

This court has also held that criminal intent may be negated by defendant's reasonable and bona fide but erroneous belief as to his status. In *People v. Vogel*, the defendant was prosecuted for bigamy, and it was held that the defendant's bona fide and reasonable belief that his first wife had divorced him and remarried would be a good defense. The court reasoned in part that it would not be reasonable to hold "that a person is guilty of bigamy who remarries in good faith in reliance on a judgment of divorce or annulment that is subsequently found not to be the 'judgment of a competent court,' particularly when such a judgment is obtained by the former husband or wife of such person in any one of the numerous jurisdictions in which such judgments can be obtained. Since it is often difficult for laymen to know when a judgment is not that of a competent court, we cannot reasonably expect them always to have such knowledge and make them criminals if their bona fide belief proves to be erroneous." The court also pointed out that at common law an honest and reasonable belief in circumstances which, if true, would make the act for which the person is indicted an innocent act, has always been held to be a good defense.

People v. Flumerfelt (1939) 35 Cal. App. 2d 495 also illustrates the distinction between mistake of fact and mistake of law. In that case, the defendant was charged with selling corporate securities without a permit. The defendant claimed that before she sold the securities, her attorney told her that a permit to sell had been obtained, and it was held that her honest but mistaken belief that a permit to sell had been issued constituted a defense. However, the court distinguished the situation where counsel erroneously advises that the instrument to be sold is not a security, pointing out that a mistake as to the legal consequences of the act which constitutes a violation of the statute would not be a defense.

The *O'Brien*, *Hernandez*, *Atchison*, *Mayberry*, *Vogel* and *Flumerfelt* cases, read together, make clear that a mistake of law is one premised on ignorance of the terms of the statute which the defendant is charged with violating. However, when the defendant reasonably and honestly believes that the statute is not applicable to him or that he has complied with it, there is a mistake of fact. There is a mistake of fact even though the matter as to which the defendant is mistaken is a question of law. The questions of age in *Hernandez* and *Atchison* were matters resolved as a matter of law as was marital status in *Vogel* and the nonissuance of a permit in *Flumerfelt*.

The Court of Appeal has held that a mistaken belief that a conviction was not a felony conviction could negate criminal intent in a prosecution for violation of Penal

Code section 12021. [Justice Broussard reviewed the decision in *People v. Bray* (1975) 52 Cal. App. 3d 494.]

The Court of Appeal stated that its decision should not be interpreted to mean instructions on mistake or ignorance of fact or knowledge of the facts are required every time a defendant claims he did not know he was a felon. Relying on that statement, the majority concludes that *Bray* should be limited to situations where a state agency has misled the defendant. The statement relied upon merely reflects that only in rare cases will there be a basis for a reasonable belief that a felony conviction was a misdemeanor conviction. The reasoning in *Bray* applies to any case where there is a reasonable and good faith mistake and is in accord with the common law and our statutory rule. The source of the reasonable and good faith mistake does not affect the existence of criminal intent.[2]

Had the trial court in the instant case admitted the offered evidence and given the requested instruction, the jury could properly have concluded that defendant had a reasonable and good faith belief that her conviction was not a felony conviction. She was granted probation without jail or prison sentence. Her attorney had advised her that the offense was a misdemeanor,[3] and there were additional circumstances reflecting a good faith belief.

The errors in excluding the offered evidence and refusing the offered instructions denied defendant the right to have the jury determine substantial issues material to her guilt and require reversal of the conviction.

I would reverse the judgment.

Notes and Problem

The Model Penal Code and Mistake of Law Induced by the Government. The defense recognized in the *Bray* case and discussed in *Snyder*—that the defendant attempted to ascertain the law and was misled as to the law by a government official—is defined in the Model Penal Code § 2.04(3) as follows:

> "A belief that conduct does not legally constitute an offense is a defense to a prosecution for that offense based upon such conduct when:
>
> . . .
>
> (b) he acts in reasonable reliance upon an official statement of the law, afterward determined to be invalid or erroneous, contained in (i) a statute or other enactment; (ii) a judicial decision, opinion or judgment; (iii) an ad-

---

2. I am perplexed by the majority's apparent limitation of the mistake doctrine to would-be "moral [lepers]." The more heinous the crime the more reason to limit defenses, and the majority's suggested limitation appears to turn the usual relationship between law and morality upside down.

3. It has been held that advice of counsel that prohibited conduct is lawful is not a defense because it would place the advice of counsel above the law. Counsel's advice in the instant case is relevant to establish good faith; it does not in and of itself establish a defense.

> ministrative order or grant of permission; or (iv) an official interpretation of the public officer or body charged by law with responsibility for the interpretation, administration or enforcement of the law defining the offense."

"***Entrapment by Estoppel.***" The defense of mistake of law induced by the government has a constitutional dimension. In *Raley v. Ohio*, 360 U.S. 423 (1959), the defendant, after being advised by the chairperson of a state commission that he had a state privilege not to answer certain questions, refused to answer the questions and was prosecuted and convicted of contempt. The Supreme Court held that the defendant's due process rights were violated by the "indefensible sort of entrapment by the State." *Id.* at 426. The defense has been recognized in a number of cases in the lower courts. According to the Sixth Circuit the Due Process defense of "entrapment by estoppel" has the following elements:

> (1) a government must have announced that the charged criminal act was legal; (2) the defendant relied on the government announcement; (3) the defendant's reliance was reasonable; and, (4) given the defendant's reliance, the prosecution would be unfair.

United States v. Levin, 973 F.2d 463, 468 (6th Cir. 1992).

Problem 23.

Defendant was a member of City's city council, and she desired to be appointed to the vacant position of city manager. However, City had an ordinance requiring that any council member was ineligible for city employment while on the council and for one year after leaving the council. Defendant notified the other members of the council of her interest in the job and of her proposed salary and terms, and she consulted with City Attorney regarding whether the ordinance could be repealed or whether it was required by state law and whether it would be legal for a council member to become city manager. City Attorney advised Defendant and the council that the ordinance could be repealed and that it would be legal to employ Defendant. The council (without defendant being present) voted to repeal the ordinance and directed City Attorney to meet with Mayor and Defendant about her terms. City Attorney reported back to the council about Defendant's terms, and the council, altering some of the terms, authorized her hiring. City Attorney drafted the employment contract, which Defendant signed. Defendant is now charged with violating Government Code § 1090 (prohibiting members of legislative bodies having a financial interest in any contract made by the body). What arguments should be made on Defendant's defense of entrapment by estoppel?

Stark v. Superior Court

52 Cal.4th 368, 257 P.3d 41 (2011)

Corrigan, J.

This case involves serious allegations against Robert E. Stark, the auditor-controller of Sutter County. In that position, Stark made decisions about allocations and expenditures of public money.... A grand jury ultimately indicted Stark on 13 counts of violating Penal Code section 424 for acts and omissions involving public funds between 2003 and 2005.... We granted review to resolve the following question[s]:

1. Does a violation of section 424 require intentional violation of a known legal duty or is it a general intent crime?[d]

We resolve [this question] as follows:

1. At issue here are [the] provisions of section 424, ... which proscribe general intent offenses. Three of those provisions criminalize acting without authority or failing to act as required by law or legal duty. We conclude those offenses additionally require that the defendant knew, or was criminally negligent in failing to know, the legal requirements that governed the act or omission.

...

I. FACTUAL AND PROCEDURAL BACKGROUND

[The indictment was based on a report from Larry Combs, the county administrative officer (CAO) criticizing Stark for various actions, including, *inter alia*, that: Stark filed the final budget for fiscal year 2003–2004 six and one-half months late; Stark acted unilaterally in amending the county budget even though state law reserves that authority to the Board; Stark claimed he had the authority to approve the rates some county departments were charging other county departments for services provided; Stark withheld overtime pay from the county's firefighters in January 2003; and Stark unilaterally transferred money from the county's general fund reserve to Sutter County Waterworks District No. 1. Stark moved to set aside the indictment, and the superior court set aside one count. On Stark's petition for a writ of mandate or prohibition to review the trial court's order, the Court of Appeal ordered six counts set aside, but concluded the trial correct did not err in denying Stark's motion to set aside the remaining counts.]

As to the issues for which we granted review, the Court of Appeal ruled that, as to certain provisions of section 424, a defendant must know that his actions or omissions regarding public funds are without legal authority. As to the remaining counts for which that mental state is required, the Court of Appeal concluded that grand jurors "could reasonably entertain a strong suspicion" that Stark had such knowledge.

...

II. DISCUSSION

A. Penal Code Section 424—Mental State

Section 424 was enacted in 1872 as part of the original Penal Code. More than 80 years ago, this court explained in *People v. Dillon* (1926) 199 Cal. 1 that section 424 "has to do solely with the protection and safekeeping of public moneys as defined by section 426 of the Penal Code, and with the duties of the public officer charged with its custody or control...."

d. Discussion of the remaining questions omitted.

The current statute contains seven subparts, all of which were part of the statute as originally enacted, although renumbered by amendment in 1905. The remaining counts of the indictment allege violations of four of those provisions:

"(a) Each officer of this state, or of any county, city, town, or district of this state, and every other person charged with the receipt, safekeeping, transfer, or disbursement of public moneys, who either:

> "1. Without authority of law, appropriates the same, or any portion thereof, to his or her own use, or to the use of another ...[e]

"Is punishable by imprisonment in the state prison for two, three, or four years, and is disqualified from holding any office in this state."

1. The Indictment

We begin with a review of the evidence presented to the grand jury as to the counts of the indictment remaining on appeal.

a. Third Count (Section 424(a)1)

The People claim that Stark misappropriated public money in violation of section 424(a)1 when, without authorization by the Board, he transferred money in the 2003–2004 final budget from the county's general fund to the Waterworks District.

...

Various county funds maintain reserves. Within the county general fund there are several different reserves, such as those for capital expenditures and vehicle replacement. At issue in this count of the indictment is the general fund's general reserve (hereafter general reserve). The general reserve is subject to unique restrictions. The Board is legally authorized to reduce or increase the amount of the general reserve during the budget process. Once the final budget is adopted, however, that reserve can be accessed only in an emergency declared by a four-fifths vote of the Board.

One of the special districts governed by the Board is the Waterworks District, an enterprise fund that provides sewer and water services to the community of Robbins. Under an enterprise fund operation, people in the area pay for the cost of services. No money from the county general fund is required to operate the Waterworks District. The Waterworks District's sewer system was installed and purchased by a grant obtained by the county on behalf of the residents of Robbins. The Board had decided not to fund the depreciation of the sewer system because those expenses would have had to be financed by user fees, which the Board considered too burdensome for the area residents.

...

When the final budget for the fiscal year 2003–2004 was released on June 14, 2004, the CAO discovered that the Waterworks District budget included a contribution

e. Discussion of the counts charging violations of the other sections of § 424 and raising similar *mens rea* issues is omitted.

from the county general fund of $336,485. Assistant county administrator Coad explained that Stark, through a series of transactions, took general reserve money, placed it into the general fund, and then transferred that money to the Waterworks District fund. As Coad explained, "Bottom line, he used general fund reserve money to balance the [Waterworks District] fund. And, no, we did not sign off on that."

Coad told the grand jury that nothing in the final budget resolution authorized Stark to transfer money from the general reserve, "which belonged to all the People of Sutter County," and give it to the Waterworks District serving the community of Robbins alone. Such a transfer from the general reserve required a vote of four-fifths of the Board and "special findings of general public benefit." The Board ordered Stark to return the money to the county's general fund. Stark complied.

...

2. Analysis

As to the counts at issue, we first consider the mental state required for those crimes defined in the provisions of section 424 that refer to authorization of law or legal requirements. Section 424(a)1 applies to a defendant who appropriates public money to his own use or the use of another without authority of law....

The People claimed in the trial court and the Court of Appeal that section 424 requires only a general intent to do the act or make the omission, without a further mental state. The Court of Appeal rejected this argument. It held that a defendant must have appropriated public money, knowing that his action was unauthorized ... Here, the People now agree that a defendant must act or fail to act with knowledge of the unlawfulness of his actions, but urge that the mental state can be satisfied by either actual knowledge or criminal negligence.

Applying long-standing principles of criminal intent, we reaffirm that the violations of section 424 at issue are general intent crimes. Further, settled authority teaches that even general intent crimes often require some kind of knowledge. We first resolve whether the applicable provisions of section 424 require any additional mental state beyond a general intent to do the act.

a. What Is the Required Mental State?

More than 80 years ago in *Dillon, supra*, this court first examined the mental state required for a violation of section 424. *Dillon* concerned unlawful purchases made by Fresno's commissioner of finance, who was also the city's purchasing agent. Purchases made for the city's benefit were granted substantial discounts. Dillon made a number of purchases for private parties using city money and receiving the discounted price. The private beneficiaries then reimbursed the city for those expenditures. Dillon was convicted of violations of section 424(a) 1 and 2.

Dillon argued the Legislature did not intend that section 424 should apply to the facts of his case. He asserted that he should have been prosecuted for embezzlement under section 504, which requires a specific intent to defraud. The *Dillon* court rejected this claim, observing that while embezzlement requires "the specific intent to appropriate [another's property] to one's self with a fraudulent intent," the framers of section

424 did not intend "to incorporate or adopt, by implication or otherwise, the elements essential to constitute embezzlement as defined by section 504." Rather, "the subject matter and the language of section 424 clearly indicate that the legislative mind was intently concerned with the single, specific subject of the safekeeping and protection of public moneys and the duties of public officers in charge of the same." To this end, a violation of section 424 "is committed by a public officer when he uses public funds in a manner forbidden by law even though he may have no fraudulent intent when he does so.... It is sufficient that he intentionally committed the forbidden act."

There was no question that Dillon knew he acted without lawful authority. He did not claim otherwise. Instead, he argued that even though he knew the act was unauthorized, he had no specific intent to defraud, and that the city was reimbursed. The *Dillon* decision was limited to clarifying that violations of section 424(a) 1 and 2 are general intent crimes....

In reaching its general intent conclusion, the *Dillon* court relied on section 20, which provides: "In every crime or public offense there must exist a union, or joint operation of act and intent, or criminal negligence." The *Dillon* court stated: "The only construction that may be placed upon [section 20] is that there must be an intent to do the forbidden thing or commit the interdicted act. It furnishes no basis for the claim that there must exist in the mind of the transgressor a specific purpose or intent to violate law."

The *Dillon* court had no occasion to consider what knowledge, if any, is required for a violation of the statute because the issue was not before it. In the years since *Dillon,* this court has not further addressed the mental state required for a violation of section 424. We do so now, in light of more recent jurisprudence.

Thirty years after *Dillon,* this court clarified that the "intent" referred to in section 20 means *wrongful* intent. (*People v. Vogel* (1956) 46 Cal.2d 798.) Vogel was charged with bigamy, and the case turned on the question of knowledge. The evidence showed Vogel married a second time without having divorced his first wife. By way of affirmative defense, Vogel wanted to introduce evidence that he had a reasonable, good faith belief that his first wife had divorced him. The trial court rejected his proffers, ruling that his good faith belief that he had been divorced was immaterial.

Vogel held the ruling was error. It emphasized that the "intent" provided in section 20 is *wrongful* intent, and thus for bigamy, as in other crimes, there must be a union of act and *wrongful* intent. Under section 26, those incapable of committing a crime include persons who commit the act "under an ignorance or mistake of fact, which disproves any criminal intent."

...

Thus, the *Vogel* court recognized that wrongful intent requires that a defendant know the material facts. This clarification of section 20 was significant in view of the expanded creation of strict liability statutes. The traditional rule is that some form of mens rea is required in "all but strict liability offenses." (*People v. Hood* (1969) 1 Cal.3d 444.) Strict liability statutes often involve public health and safety concerns and "criminal sanctions are relied upon even if there is no wrongful intent. These offenses usually involve light penalties and no moral obloquy or damage to reputation.... The offenses are not crimes in the orthodox sense, and wrongful intent is not required in the interest of enforcement." (*Vogel, supra.*)

[The court reviewed additional cases, including: *Staples v. United States* (1994) 511 U.S. 600 (generally knowledge of the facts is necessary to prove *mens rea*); *People v. Simon* (1995) 9 Cal.4th 493 (statute prohibiting the sale of securities by means of materially false statements requires proof of knowledge of, or criminal negligence with regard to, the falsity of the statement); *People v. Coria* (1999) 21 Cal.4th 868 (crime of manufacturing methamphetamine requires proof that a defendant knows the character of the substance being produced); *In re Jorge M.* (2000) 23 Cal.4th 866 (statute outlawing possession of assault weapons requires proof of knowledge of, or negligence in regard to, the facts making possession criminal); *People v. King* (2006) 38 Cal.4th 617 (conviction of possession of a short-barreled firearm requires proof of the possessor's knowledge of the weapon's illegal characteristics.)]

...

As the statutory language provides, it is not simply appropriation of public money ... that is criminalized. Criminal liability attaches when those particular actions or omissions are contrary to laws governing the handling of public money. Unlike many statutory provisions, these provisions make the presence or absence of legal authority part of the definition of the offense. The People must prove that legal authority was present or absent.

Without a mental state as to legal authorization, a defendant could be convicted of violating the section 424 provisions by simply acting or failing to act, even if he was unaware of the facts, as defined by statute, that made his intent wrongful. Such an interpretation is inconsistent with *Vogel* and the common law upon which *Vogel* relied. Section 424 has never been construed as a strict liability offense. The purpose of section 424 is punishment, rather than regulation. The penalties for its violation are severe, including a prison sentence and the disqualification from public office.

The plain language of the statute and our own recent jurisprudence compel the conclusion that section 424(a) 1 ... must be construed to include a mental element as to the presence or absence of legal authorization or obligation.

Our holding is not inconsistent with *Dillon, supra.* In *Dillon,* there was no question that the defendant knew the nature of the act he was doing. He knew he was making purchases at a discounted price for persons who did not work for the City of Fresno, and so knew "the facts that [made] his conduct fit the definition of the offense." (*Staples v. United States, supra.*) Because Dillon acted with general intent to do the proscribed act while aware of the material facts, he acted with wrongful intent. *Dillon* does not stand for the proposition that section 424 requires no knowledge of the facts or that section 424 is a strict liability crime.

As we have noted, Stark and the People disagree as to the nature of the required mental state. Before we address that issue, we clarify what must be "known." We use the term "knowledge" here for ease of discussion, mindful of the People's position that criminal negligence is sufficient to satisfy the mental state.

b. What Must Be Known?

In considering what must be known by a defendant in order to prove wrongful intent, the law has long distinguished between ignorance of fact and ignorance of law. The ancient maxim, stated partially in *Staples v. United States, supra*, is "*ignorantia facti excusat, ignorantia juris non excusat.*" Ignorance of facts excuses, ignorance of the law does not excuse. "It is an emphatic postulate of both civil and penal law that ignorance of a law is no excuse for a violation thereof." (*People v. Snyder* (1982) 32 Cal.3d 590.) This principle is reflected in our Penal Code: "The word 'knowingly' imports only a knowledge that the facts exist which bring the act or omission within the provisions of this code. It does not require any knowledge of the unlawfulness of such act or omission." (§7, subd. 5.)

A defendant must know the facts that affect the material nature of his conduct, that is, the facts that must be proven to show his act is the kind of conduct proscribed by the statute. He need not know that his behavior in light of those facts is regulated by a statute. In a prosecution for bigamy, for example, the defendant must know that he is marrying and that he is already married to another. Both those material facts taken together make his action bigamy. They change the nature of his act of marrying from legitimate behavior to illegal conduct. The defendant need not know his conduct is illegal, but he must know the fact (i.e., he is already married) that affects the material nature of his conduct.

A defendant does not have to know that his conduct is a crime.... A defendant may not escape criminal liability by asserting that he did not know the criminal law.

Section 424, however, is an unusual statute, in which the definition of some of the offenses incorporates a legal element derived from other *noncriminal* legal provisions. Each of the three provisions at issue refers to "law" or "legal duty." These references are "shorthand," used to encompass the wide variety of requirements relating to the official's duties.

The "law" applicable to the acts and omissions in these provisions of section 424 is the *authorizing* law, which is extraneous to the penal statute. Liability under section 424 arises when the officer or custodian, bound by these authorizing laws, acts without authority[9] ... For the sake of clarity, we will refer to these authorizing laws as "nonpenal laws," to distinguish them from the crimes defined in section 424. In Stark's circumstances, for example, the nonpenal law relied on by the People includes the Government Code and the Board resolutions.

---

9. As section 424(a) 1 is worded, "[r]ather than prohibiting specifically enumerated behavior, it prohibits any behavior which has not been previously approved by statute or ordinance." (*People v. Battin* (1978) 77 Cal.App.3d 635.) Depending on the circumstances, it may be that no lawful authority sanctioned the defendant's actions, or that the defendant's action was expressly prohibited by particular lawful authority.

As we have explained, presence or absence of legal authorization is an essential element of each of the offenses at issue. It also [is] a "fact" about which the defendant must have knowledge in order to act with wrongful intent. Thus, the People must prove, as a matter of fact, *both* that legal authority was present or absent, *and* that the defendant knew of its presence or absence.

The People do not have to prove that defendant knew chapter and verse of the nonpenal law. It is sufficient that the defendant knew generally that a nonpenal law required or prohibited his conduct. As with any mental state, the People may prove this knowledge by reference to the facts and circumstances of the case.

c. What Is the Required Scienter?

. . .

Stark maintains that the prosecution must prove a defendant's actual knowledge of the legal requirements underlying the section 424(a) 1 charge[]. The People argue that it is sufficient for the prosecution to prove that a defendant knew, or was criminally negligent in failing to know, those legal requirements.

. . .

We agree with the People ... Strong public policy supports a rule requiring either actual knowledge or criminal negligence in failing to know the legal requirements underlying the section 424 charges. "Criminal negligence refers to "a higher degree of negligence than is required to establish negligent default on a mere civil issue. The negligence must be aggravated, culpable, gross, or reckless." (*People v. Penny* (1955) 44 Cal.2d 861.)

. . .

A mental state limited solely to actual knowledge is too rigid a formulation in light of the purpose of section 424. The statute applies to public officers and others charged with "the receipt, safekeeping, transfer, or disbursement" of public funds. Because the Legislature intended that such persons fulfill their obligations "in strict compliance with the law" (*Dillon, supra*), we expect them to be aware of and indeed embrace the duties the law imposes upon them. It would be antithetical to the intent of the Legislature that those entrusted with control of public funds could evade an actual knowledge requirement by failing to conduct the research that would inform them of their duties, or by failing to seek the advice of persons who could provide that information. Limiting the requirement to actual knowledge would operate to shield those whose efforts at determining their duties does not comport with the significant public responsibility these individuals bear.

Given that "[t]he safekeeping of public moneys has, from the first, been safeguarded and hedged in by legislation most strict and severe in its exactitudes" (*Dillon, supra*), a strict actual knowledge standard would impair effective enforcement. It would defy the exacting nature of the statute if one could escape criminal liability by claiming lack of subjective knowledge in circumstances that are objectively unreasonable. Consequently, we agree with the People that we should construe the applicable subdivisions of section 424 to require actual knowledge *or* criminal negligence.

A criminal negligence standard protects both the public and the accused. If public officials and others entrusted with control of public funds subjectively believe their actions or omissions are authorized by law, they are protected from criminal liability unless that belief is objectively unreasonable, i.e., is the product of criminal negligence in ascertaining legal obligations. Public officials and others should not be criminally liable for a reasonable, good faith mistake regarding their legal responsibilities. Nor is section 424 intended to criminalize ordinary negligence or good faith errors in judgment.

...

Finally, Stark opposes a criminal negligence standard because he urges there is a civil remedy against those public officials who make unauthorized expenditures by acting without due care. He relies on *Stanson v. Mott* (1976) 17 Cal.3d 206, in which we held that a public official who, in good faith, authorizes the improper expenditure of public funds may be personally liable to repay such funds. We stated that "public officials must use 'due care,' i.e., reasonable diligence, in authorizing the expenditure of public funds, and may be subject to personal liability ... in the absence of such due care." But the availability of a civil remedy against public officials for unauthorized expenditures does not deprive the Legislature of authority to impose criminal sanctions as well.

Stark argues that the conduct underlying the charges here is better resolved in a civil forum. It is not for this court to question the wisdom of the Sutter County District Attorney's Office in employing section 424 to address Stark's conduct as county auditor-controller. The Legislature enacted a statute that imposes criminal liability for the acts and omissions it describes. It is for the prosecution to decide whether to bring charges and for a jury to decide if those charges can be proven.

...

Problem

Problem 24.

Defendant was arrested on narcotics charges. Officer visited Defendant in jail, and Defendant offered to become an informant in exchange for leniency on the charges facing him. Officer told Defendant that he wanted information leading to narcotics arrests and that the general police policy was to require evidence leading to three arrests in exchange for leniency. During the ensuing weeks Defendant provided Officer with information resulting in two arrests and convictions. Defendant then arranged with Social Worker to smuggle marijuana to him in jail in return for some marijuana for herself. Defendant called Friend and asked him to supply Social Worker with some marijuana, but Friend revealed the plan to the police. Acting on behalf of the police, Friend delivered the marijuana to Social Worker, and police arrested Social Worker and Defendant and charged them with conspiracy to smuggle narcotics into a county jail (P.C. §§ 182, 4573).

Health and Safety Code § 11367 provides:

> All duly authorized peace officers, while investigating violations of this division in performance of their official duties, and any person working under their immediate direction, supervision or instruction, are immune from prosecution under this division.

If, as Defendant now contends, he set up the smuggling plan in order to provide the information to Officer and had been attempting to inform Officer of the plan, is Defendant entitled to a defense based on his good faith belief that he was acting with immunity?

Defense	Prosecution
- Mistake of fact	- Mistake of law

Introduction to Homicide

The following four chapters deal with unlawful homicide, the crimes of murder and manslaughter.

At common law, murder was the unlawful killing of another human being with "malice aforethought." The traditional definition of murder was given by Sir Edward Coke in the seventeenth century: "When a man of sound memory and of the age of discretion unlawfully kills any reasonable creature in being, and under the King's peace, with malice aforethought, either express or implied by the law, the death taking place within a year and a day." Quoted in MPC Commentaries, Pt II, Vol. 1, p. 14. Although, in its early form, malice aforethought appears to have suggested a premeditated killing, especially one committed by lying in wait, the term eventually came to encompass four types of unlawful homicides: (1) intentional homicides; (2) homicides committed by an actor attempting to do grievous bodily harm; (3) "depraved heart" homicides, *i.e.*, where an actor exhibited extreme recklessness regarding the homicidal risk; and (4) homicides committed during the perpetration of another felony. The crime of manslaughter was developed by statute in the early 1500s to differentiate some unlawful killings from the more heinous killings with malice aforethought. Manslaughter then encompassed all homicides done without malice aforethought, but also without justification or excuse. Eventually, there came to be two versions of manslaughter: (1) homicides committed upon a sudden quarrel or in the heat of passion upon adequate provocation and (2) homicides resulting from acts which were unduly dangerous or were otherwise unlawful.

The common law definitions of murder and manslaughter were generally adopted in the United States. The most significant modification of the common law was initiated by a 1794 Pennsylvania statute, adopted in order to limit the application of the death penalty. The statute provided that "all murder, which shall be perpetrated by means of poison, or by lying in wait, or by another kind of willful, deliberate or premeditated killing, or which shall be committed in the perpetration, or attempt to perpetrate any arson, rape, robbery or burglary shall be deemed murder in the first degree; and all other kinds of murder shall be deemed murder in the second degree." Pa. Laws of 1794, ch. 257, §§ 1, 2. The death penalty was applicable only to first degree murders.

In its first penal legislation in 1850, California adopted the common law definitions of murder and manslaughter. The 1872 Penal Code, which is still in effect, defined four homicide offenses: two degrees of murder, first degree and second degree, and two forms of manslaughter, voluntary and involuntary. *See* Penal Code §§ 187–189 and 192. California today is one of a minority of states still to adhere to the common law definitions of these crimes. The act requirement for the four homicide offenses is the same—causing the death of another human being or, in the case of the two murder offenses, a fetus.[1] The offenses are distinguished principally by the mental state element. In theory, the difference in punishments for the four offenses reflects a societal understanding that some unlawful killings are more culpable than others.[2]

Each of the four homicide offenses encompasses more than one type of unlawful killing. Consequently, homicide is better analyzed, not according to the offense categories, but according to the three theories under which the prosecution can prove an unlawful homicide. Chapters 4–6 each address one of the three theories. Chapter 4 involves cases where the homicide was intentional. Chapter 5 deals with the situation where the homicide was unintentional (or the prosecution cannot prove that it was intentional), but the prosecution can prove the accused had another culpable mental state. Chapter 6 considers the rules—the felony-murder and misdemeanor-manslaughter rules—permitting the prosecution (in lieu of proving the accused's mental state with regard to the homicide) to prove an unlawful homicide through proof that the killing occurred while the accused was committing another crime. Chapter 7 considers cases at the intersection of the three theories, cases in which the accused may be liable for a killing done by someone other than the accused or an accomplice, *e.g.*, the victim of the felony, a police officer or a bystander.

1. A fetus is the subject of the murder statutes if it has progressed beyond the embryonic stage (about seven or eight weeks after conception) and if the killing was not solicited, aided, abetted, or consented to by the mother of the fetus. *People v. Davis*, 7 Cal. 4th 797 (1994).

2. For a thorough review and critical appraisal of the California murder statutes generally, and their treatment of malice aforethought in particular, see S. Mounts, *Malice Aforethought in California: A History of Legislative Abdication and Judicial Vacillation*, 33 U.S.F. L. Rev. 313 (1999).

Chapter 4

Homicide: Intentional Killings

An intentional homicide, if not justified or excused [see Chapters 11 and 12], is either murder or voluntary manslaughter. It is murder if the defendant killed with malice aforethought. (P.C. § 187) Penal Code § 188 describes two types of malice, and it is express malice, "a deliberate intention unlawfully to take away the life of a fellow creature," which is at issue in the case of an intentional killing. Section A explores the dividing line between murder and voluntary manslaughter. Penal Code § 189 defines three categories of murder as first degree murder, and Section B considers the most significant of the three in the context of intentional killings, premeditation and deliberation.[a]

A. Murder or Voluntary Manslaughter?

Although Penal Code § 188 purports to define malice, in fact, the interpretation of the term derives less from the statutory language than from a century and a half of common law development by the California Supreme Court. Prior to 1981, the court had recognized three forms of voluntary manslaughter. One form was the traditional "sudden quarrel or heat of passion" killing described in Penal Code § 192(a). The first two cases in the section consider this form of voluntary manslaughter. In *People v. Berry*, the Supreme Court reviews the meaning of "heat of passion" and "adequate provocation." *People v. Wu* also concerns the heat of passion defense, and the Court of Appeal considers whether the defendant's cultural background could be considered in applying the reasonable person standard.

The other two forms of voluntary manslaughter had no express statutory basis. However, the California Supreme Court held that § 192 was not to be considered to contain an exhaustive list of nonmalicious criminal homicides, so the court might identify other forms of voluntary manslaughter. One form of non-statutory voluntary manslaughter evolved from the concept of "diminished capacity." The leading case on the issue was *People v. Conley*, 64 Cal. 2d 310 (1966), where an intoxicated defendant shot and killed his former lover and her husband. The court reversed the de-

a. The second category—killings by certain means (which, according to § 189, are types of premeditated and deliberate killings)—accounts for only a small portion of first degree murders, and some examples of such killings are noted at the end of the chapter. The third category—killings occurring during the commission of, or attempt to commit, certain felonies—is discussed in Chapter 6.

fendant's two first degree murder convictions on the ground that the jury should have been instructed to consider the effect of his intoxication on the issue of malice. The Court held that an intentional killing, even one done with premeditation, would be voluntary manslaughter rather than murder if, because of the defendant's diminished mental condition, the defendant lacked "an awareness of the obligation to act within the general body of laws regulating society." In 1981, the Legislature overturned *Conley* by amending P.C. § 188 to state:

> When it is shown that the killing resulted from the intentional doing of an act with express or implied malice as defined above, no other mental state need be shown to establish the mental state of malice aforethought. Neither an awareness of the obligation to act within the general body of laws regulating society nor acting despite such awareness is included within the definition of malice.

See *People v. Saille*, 54 Cal. 1103 (1991).

The other form of non-statutory voluntary manslaughter was based on "imperfect self-defense." In *People v. Flannel*, 25 Cal. 3d 668 (1979), the Court held, that when a defendant claims the killing was in self-defense, the defendant is entitled to an instruction that an honest (but unreasonable) belief in the need for self-defense negates malice. The court reasoned that a person who believes in a state of facts which would make his/her conduct lawful, cannot be acting with malice. The last two cases in the section concern this form of voluntary manslaughter. In *In re Christian S.*, the court has to decide whether the 1981 amendment to P.C. § 188 eliminated "unreasonable defense" voluntary manslaughter. In *People v. Elmore*, the court addresses whether a defendant who intentionally kills on the basis of a "purely delusional belief in the need to act in self-defense" can assert imperfect self-defense.

People v. Berry

18 Cal. 3d 509, 556 P.2d 777 (1976)

SULLIVAN, J.

Defendant Albert Joseph Berry was charged by indictment with one count of murder (Pen. Code, § 187) and one count of assault by means of force likely to produce great bodily injury (Pen. Code, § 245, subd. (a)). The indictment was amended to allege one prior felony conviction which defendant admitted. The assault was allegedly committed on July 23, 1974, and the murder on July 26, 1974. In each count, the alleged victim was defendant's wife, Rachel Pessah Berry. A jury found defendant guilty as charged and determined that the murder was of the first degree.

...

Defendant, a cook, 46 years old, and Rachel Pessah, a 20-year-old girl from Israel, were married on May 27, 1974....

...

After their marriage, Rachel lived with defendant for only three days and then left for Israel. Immediately upon her return to San Francisco she told defendant about her relationship with and love for Yako [a man she met in Israel]. This brought about further argument and a brawl that evening in which defendant choked Rachel and she responded by scratching him deeply many times. Nonetheless they continued to live together. Rachel kept taunting defendant with Yako and demanding a divorce. She claimed she thought she might be pregnant by Yako. She showed defendant pictures of herself with Yako. Nevertheless, during a return trip from Santa Rosa, Rachel demanded immediate sexual intercourse with defendant in the car, which was achieved; however upon reaching their apartment, she again stated that she loved Yako and that she would not have intercourse with defendant in the future.

On the evening of July 22nd defendant and Rachel went to a movie where they engaged in heavy petting. When they returned home and got into bed, Rachel announced that she had intended to make love with defendant, "But I am saving myself for this man Yako, so I don't think I will." Defendant got out of bed and prepared to leave the apartment whereupon Rachel screamed and yelled at him. Defendant choked her into unconsciousness.

Two hours later defendant called a taxi for his wife to take her to the hospital. He put his clothes in the Greyhound bus station and went to the home of his friend Mrs. Berk for the night. The next day he went to Reno and returned the day after. Rachel informed him by telephone that there was a warrant for his arrest as a result of her report to the police about the choking incident. On July 25th defendant returned to the apartment to talk to Rachel, but she was out. He slept there overnight. Rachel returned around 11 a.m. the next day. Upon seeing defendant there, she said, "I suppose you have come here to kill me." Defendant responded, "yes," changed his response to "no," and then again to "yes," and finally stated "I have really come to talk to you." Rachel began screaming. Defendant grabbed her by the shoulder and tried to stop her screaming. She continued. They struggled and finally defendant strangled her with a telephone cord.

Dr. Martin Blinder, a physician and psychiatrist, called by the defense, testified that Rachel was a depressed, suicidally inclined girl and that this suicidal impulse led her to involve herself ever more deeply in a dangerous situation with defendant. She did this by sexually arousing him and taunting him into jealous rages in an unconscious desire to provoke him into killing her and thus consummating her desire for suicide. Throughout the period commencing with her return from Israel until her death, that is from July 13 to July 26, Rachel continually provoked defendant with sexual taunts and incitements, alternating acceptance and rejection of him. This conduct was accompanied by repeated references to her involvement with another man; it led defendant to choke her on two occasions, until finally she achieved her unconscious desire and was strangled. Dr. Blinder testified that as a result of this cumulative series of provocations, defendant at the time he fatally strangled Rachel, was in a state of uncontrollable rage, completely under the sway of passion.

We first take up defendant's claim that on the basis of the foregoing evidence he was entitled to an instruction on voluntary manslaughter as defined by statute which is "the unlawful killing of a human being, without malice ... upon a sudden quarrel or heat of passion." (Pen. Code, § 192.) In *People v. Valentine* (1946) 28 Cal. 2d 121, this court, in an extensive review of the law of manslaughter, specifically approved the following as a correct statement of the law: "In the present condition of our law *it is left to the jurors* to say whether or not the facts and circumstances in evidence are sufficient to lead them to believe that the defendant did, or to create a reasonable doubt in their minds as to whether or not he did, commit his offense under a heat of passion. The jury is further to be admonished and advised by the court that this heat of passion must be such a passion as would naturally be aroused in the mind of an ordinarily reasonable person under the given facts and circumstances, and that, consequently, no defendant may set up his own standard of conduct and justify or excuse himself because in fact his passions were aroused, unless further the jury believe that the facts and circumstances were sufficient to arouse the passions of the ordinarily reasonable man.... For the fundamental of the inquiry is whether or not the defendant's reason was, at the time of his act, so disturbed or obscured by some passion—not necessarily fear and never, of course, the passion for revenge—to such an extent as would render ordinary men of average disposition liable to act rashly or without due deliberation and reflection, and from this passion rather than from judgment." (Italics in original.)

We further held in *Valentine* that there is no specific type of provocation required by section 192 and that verbal provocation may be sufficient. In *People v. Borchers* (1958) 50 Cal. 2d 321 in the course of explaining the phrase "heat of passion" used in the statute defining manslaughter we pointed out that "passion" need not mean "rage" or "anger" but may be any "[violent], intense, high-wrought or enthusiastic emotion" and concluded there "that defendant was aroused to a heat of 'passion' by a series of events over a considerable period of time...." Accordingly we there declared that evidence of admissions of infidelity by the defendant's paramour, taunts directed to him and other conduct, "supports a finding that defendant killed in wild desperation induced by [the woman's] long continued provocatory conduct." We find this reasoning persuasive in the case now before us. Defendant's testimony chronicles a two-week period of provocatory conduct by his wife Rachel that could arouse a passion of jealousy, pain and sexual rage in an ordinary man of average disposition such as to cause him to act rashly from this passion. It is significant that both defendant and Dr. Blinder testified that the former was in the heat of passion under an uncontrollable rage when he killed Rachel.

The Attorney General contends that the killing could not have been done in the heat of passion because there was a cooling period, defendant having waited in the apartment for 20 hours. However, the long course of provocatory conduct, which had resulted in intermittent outbreaks of rage under specific provocation in the past, reached its final culmination in the apartment when Rachel began screaming. Both defendant and Dr. Blinder testified that defendant killed in a state of uncontrollable rage, of passion, and there is ample evidence in the record to support the conclusion that this passion was the result of the long course of provocatory conduct by Rachel, just as the killing emerged from such conduct in *Borchers*.

...

... Since this theory of provocation constituted defendant's entire defense to the first count, we have no difficulty concluding that the failure to give such instruction was prejudicial error and requires us to reverse the conviction of murder of the first degree.

...

Notes and Problems

The Nature of the Provocation. In the past, only certain categories of provocation were legally adequate to support a heat of passion defense. Unless the defendant could establish that the provocation he/she encountered fell within one of the recognized categories, the issue of the effect of the provocation would not be submitted to the jury. The categories generally recognized were (1) serious physical injury or assault, (2) mutual combat, (3) illegal arrest, and (4) witnessing one's spouse in the act of adultery. The cases were in general agreement that "mere words," no matter how insulting or abusive, could not constitute adequate provocation. This is still the law in many jurisdictions. See, *e.g., Girouard v. State*, 583 A.2d 718 (Md. 1991). There was also generally a requirement that the provocation be "sudden," as suggested by the language of Section 192, requiring a "sudden quarrel or heat of passion." How does California's approach, as set forth in *Berry*, differ from the traditional rule?

The state argued in *Berry* that, even if the conduct of the victim had constituted adequate provocation, Berry could not take advantage of that mitigation because he should have "cooled off" by the time of the killing. This argument reflects an accepted principle that the time between the provoking acts and the killing must be sufficiently short that it can be safely assumed the killing was the direct result of the provocation. How should the law assess whether one who has been provoked has, or should have, "cooled off"?

Problem 25.

Defendant arrived at the scene of the murder of his brother in a very excited and upset state and began running around asking various of the onlookers gathered there who had killed his brother. Prior to Defendant's arrival, police had placed Victim in a patrol car for questioning and to protect him from members of the crowd who suspected him of the killing. Approximately an hour after his arrival, Defendant was permitted to speak to Victim, and Victim told Defendant that "Silk" had killed his brother. Defendant then left, apparently to determine Silk's identity and to find him, but returned shortly thereafter and pulled open the door to the police car and began struggling with Victim. After Defendant and Victim were separated, Defendant left the scene. Victim was released by the police, and an hour after he had departed, Defendant returned and shot and killed Victim.

Defendant is charged with first degree murder (P.C. §§ 187–189) and has raised a "heat of passion" defense. What arguments should be made to the jury on whether Defendant is guilty of murder or voluntary manslaughter?

Problem 26.

Victim, who had previously been convicted of molestation charges, allegedly molested Defendant's son (who was six years old at the time) and three other boys. In the ensuing four years, Defendant said, on several occasions, that she would kill Victim. On the date of Victim's preliminary hearing on the molestation charges, Defendant's son could not stop vomiting as he prepared to testify. When Victim walked into the courtroom prior to the hearing, he smirked at Defendant and her son. Later, outside the courtroom, another mother who had testified against Victim told Defendant that Victim "was going to walk." At that point, Defendant retrieved a gun—apparently from her sister's purse (although on one occasion Defendant told the police she had brought the gun to the courtroom in her car). She walked into the courtroom, and fired five shots at Victim, who sat handcuffed at the defense table. Victim was killed, and Defendant has been charged with first degree murder (P.C. §§ 187–189). What are the arguments on whether she is guilty of this charge or the lesser included offense of voluntary manslaughter?

The Model Penal Code and the Murder/manslaughter Distinction in Intentional Killings. Under the Model Penal Code, a criminal homicide constitutes murder if "it is committed purposely or knowingly." (§ 210.2) However, a homicide that would otherwise be murder is manslaughter if it is "committed under the influence of extreme mental or emotional disturbance for which there is reasonable explanation or excuse. The reasonableness of such explanation or excuse shall be determined from the viewpoint of a person in the actor's situation under the circumstances as he believes them to be." (§ 210.3) Exactly what constitutes the defendant's "situation" is deliberately left vague in the Code, thus giving the jury complete discretion to determine what factors should be taken into account. The Commentaries define only the outer limits of this discretion: "personal handicaps" and "some external circumstances" must be taken into account, and the defendant's "idiosyncratic moral values" may not be. MPC Commentaries, Pt. II, V. 1, p. 62. How does manslaughter under the Code compare with "heat of passion" manslaughter in California?

People v. Wu

286 Cal. Rptr. 868 (1991)[b]

Timlin, Acting Presiding Justice.

I
Introduction

Helen Wu ... was convicted of the second degree murder of her son, Sidney Wu (Sidney), following trial by jury. Her motion for a new trial was denied and she was sentenced to a prison term of 15 years to life. She filed timely notice of appeal, and contends that the court committed reversible error by (1) refusing to instruct the jury on the defense of unconsciousness, and (2) refusing to instruct the jury on her theory of the case.

Initially, we note that the facts presented at trial, while not in conflict as to certain specific events, did vary considerably as to whether defendant had "motherly" feelings toward the victim, her son, whether she was a "traditional" Chinese woman, and, based on the above-noted factors, whether the motive for his death was a desire for revenge against Sidney's father or guilt over having not taken good care of the child and fear that he would be ill-treated in the future.

The prosecution's theory seems to have been that defendant killed Sidney because of anger at Sidney's father, and to get revenge. The defense's theory was that defendant believed that Sidney, who lived with his father in the United States, was looked down upon and was ill-treated by everyone except his paternal grandmother because he had been borne out of wedlock, and that when she learned that the grandmother was dying of cancer, she felt trapped and, in an intense emotional upheaval, strangled Sidney and then attempted to kill herself so that she could take care of Sidney in the afterlife.

The only issues on appeal are whether the trial court committed prejudicial error by refusing to give two instructions requested by defendant, one related to the defense of unconsciousness, and one related to the effect her cultural background might have had on her state of mind when she killed Sidney.

When the issue is whether it was error to give an improper instruction, on appeal "we must assume that the jury might have believed the evidence upon which the instruction favorable to the losing party was predicated, and that if the correct instruction had been given upon that subject the jury might have rendered a verdict in favor of the losing party." *Henderson v. Harnischfeger Corp.* (1974) 12 Cal.3d 663.

Therefore, for purposes of this appeal, we shall set forth the evidence, which the jury might have found credible and upon which defendant's requested instructions were predicated.

---

b. In denying review, the Supreme Court ordered that the opinion be not officially published (See Cal. Rules of Court, Rule 976). While all opinions of the Supreme Court are officially published, only about 10% of the Court of Appeal decisions in criminal cases are officially published. An opinion which is not officially published may not be cited as precedent in another case (*Id.*, Rule 977).

II
Facts

[Defendant was born in China, and, at the age of 19 she moved to Macau, where she first met Gary Wu ("Wu"). During the next fifteen years they did not see each other. Defendant married, had a daughter and then divorced, and Wu moved to the United States and also married. In 1978 or 1979, defendant was contacted by Wu, who told her his marriage was unsatisfactory because his wife could not have children. According to defendant, Wu told her he planned to divorce his wife. They discussed the possibility that defendant could come to the United States and conceive a child for Wu and that Wu would marry her after he divorced his wife. Defendant came to the United States, lived with Wu's mother ("Gramma") and conceived a child with Wu. Sydney Wu was born in November, 1980. However, although Wu's divorce had become final, he did not inform defendant of the fact and did not offer to marry her. Depressed, defendant returned to China in early 1981. She did not take the baby because no one knew she had a baby out of wedlock, and she and Sidney would have been humiliated in China. During the next seven years, defendant did not see Sydney. In early 1988, Wu was apparently lured by defendant's promise to loan him money for his business, and he brought Sydney to Hong Kong to visit defendant. During the visit, defendant became so distressed at Wu's apparent disregard for her that she attempted suicide. A year and a half later, defendant learned that Gramma was dying, so she went to California to visit her. Gramma told defendant that, when she died, defendant should take Sidney because Wu would not take good care of him. Two weeks later, Wu proposed marriage to defendant, and they were married on September 1. However, shortly thereafter they had a fight, and defendant told Wu "he would be sorry," later explaining that she meant "that she was thinking about returning to Macau and killing herself."]

On September 9, the evening of the killing, defendant was playing with Sidney. Earlier that day defendant had interceded on Sidney's behalf when Wu hit Sidney when Sidney would not get out of the family car. Wu had gone to the restaurant to put on two birthday parties, apparently for his friend Rosemary. Defendant and Sidney played and talked, and defendant told Sidney that she knew what he liked because of the mother-child bond between them.

Sidney told defendant that Wu said she was "psychotic" and "very troublesome." He then told defendant that Rosemary was Wu's girlfriend, and that the house they lived in belonged to Rosemary. He also told her that Wu made him get up early so Wu could take Rosemary's daughters to school in the morning and if he did not get up, Wu would scold and beat him. He said Wu loved Rosemary more than him. Defendant began to think about what she had been told by Sidney's grandmother … concerning her taking care of Sidney. She began to experience heart palpitations and to have trouble breathing. She told Sidney she wanted to die, and asked him if he would go too. He clung to her neck and cried. She then left the bedroom, and obtained a rope by cutting the cord off a window blind. She returned to the bedroom and strangled Sidney. According to defendant, she did not remember the strangling itself.

She stopped breathing, and when she started breathing again, she was surprised at how quickly Sidney had died. She then wrote a note to Wu to the effect that he had bullied her too much and "now this air is vented. I can die with no regret," but did not mention Sidney's killing in the note. She then attempted to strangle herself, failed, went to the kitchen and slashed her left wrist with a knife, and then returned to the bedroom and lay down next to Sidney on the bed, having first placed a waste-paper basket under her bleeding wrist to catch the blood so that the floor would not be dirtied.

[Sydney died, and defendant was found alive but with a "decreased level of consciousness." Although she had only cut the veins in her wrist (not the arteries) and venous bleeding does not normally lead to death, there was testimony by the medical experts that defendant's action appeared to be a serious attempt to commit suicide. Defendant was charged with murder (Pen. Code, § 187) and, following a trial by jury, was convicted of second degree murder. The Court reversed the conviction because the trial court had failed to instruct the jury on the defense of unconsciousness.]

B. Upon Retrial, the Trial Court Should, if so Requested, Instruct the Jury on How Evidence of Defendant's Cultural Background Relates to Defendant's Theory of the Case

Defendant contends that the trial court erred by refusing to give an instruction which pinpointed a significant aspect of her theory of the case, i.e., an instruction which told the jury it could choose to consider the evidence of defendant's cultural background in determining the presence or absence of the various mental states which were elements of the crimes with which she was charged. Because we have already determined that the judgment must be reversed because of the failure to give an instruction on unconsciousness, we will address the issue of the propriety of an instruction pinpointing the cultural background theory of defendant's case for purposes of guiding the trial court on retrial.[c]

...

The essential mental states at issue here were (1) premeditation and deliberation, (2) malice aforethought, and (3) specific intent to kill. Generally speaking, all relevant evidence is admissible, and the trier of fact may consider any admitted evidence. Here, the admission of evidence of defendant's cultural background was never objected to by the People; there is no argument that the evidence was relevant. The question then is, on what issues was such evidence relevant? As discussed below, this evidence clearly related to certain mental states, which are elements of the charged offense.

[The court held that the evidence of defendant's cultural background was clearly relevant on the issue of premeditation and deliberation.]

Second, the evidence of defendant's cultural background was also relevant on the issue of malice aforethought and the existence of heat of passion at the time of the

c. Elsewhere, the court noted that, in refusing defendant's instruction concerning cultural background, the trial court had commented that it did not want to put the "stamp of approval on actions in the United States, which would have been acceptable in China."

killing, which eliminates malice and reduces an intentional killing to voluntary manslaughter. The court recognized that "heat of passion" was an issue in this case because it instructed the jury regarding heat of passion negating malice and further instructed the jury regarding the lesser included offense of manslaughter.

...

To satisfy the objective or "reasonable person" element of this form of voluntary manslaughter, the accused's heat of passion must be due to "sufficient provocation." However, as this court stated in *People v. Berry* (1976) 18 Cal. 3d 50, "there is no specific type of provocation required by [Penal Code] section 192 [defining manslaughter] and ... verbal provocation may be sufficient."

The subjective element requires that the actor be under the actual influence of a strong passion at the time of the homicide.... [T]hat "passion" need not mean "rage" or "anger" but may be any "[v]iolent, intense, high-wrought or enthusiastic emotion." (*People v. Berry.*)[4] However, if sufficient time has elapsed between the provocation and the fatal blow for passion to subside and reason to return, the killing is not voluntary manslaughter—"the assailant must act under the smart of that sudden quarrel or heat of passion." (*People v. Wickersham* (1982) 32 Cal. 3d 307.)

Here, there was evidence that defendant had experienced a series of events for a 10-year period before and during her stay in late August and early September 1989 with Wu in California, from which the jury could have concluded that defendant was suffering from "pre-existing stress" at the time that Sidney told her things which confirmed her fear that Sidney, because he was not legitimate and because he had no mother to care for him, was not well-treated, and that things were going to get worse for him upon the death of his Gramma. The testimony related to defendant's cultural background was relevant to explain the source of such stress, as well to explain how Sidney's statements could have constituted "sufficient provocation" to cause defendant to kill Sidney in a "heat of passion."

The experts on transcultural psychology specifically testified that, in their opinion, defendant was acting while in an emotional crisis during the time that she obtained the knife and cord, strangled Sidney and then slashed her own wrist, and that her emotional state was intertwined with, and explainable by reference to, her cultural background. Specifically, the following testimony was given:

Dr. Chien testified:

"So when all of this thought came up to her mind, all of a sudden she said she couldn't breathe. She almost got into some kind of state that she did not know what she was doing other than thinking that, 'There's no way out other than bringing the son together with her to the other life.'"

After then describing the Chinese belief in an afterlife, he testified that:

4. The effect of "a series of events over a period of time" may be that the defendant, just before the provoking incident, is under "pre-existing stress."

"She told me wondering that is a heaven, paradise. She thought the only way to find out a way out is to bring this Sidney to go together so the mother and son can finally live together in the other heaven, other world if that cannot be done in this realistic earth."

Dr. Chien further testified: "And at that time, she said during the strangulation or that kind of emotional heat—obviously, she was under the heat of passion when she realized that her son was unwanted son, uncared by Gary, passed around from one woman to the other woman, and now the grandmother is dying and she was planning to leave, 'What will happen to Sidney?'

"And all this information came up to her mind to stimulate all her guilt feeling which was probably more than ordinary guilt feeling that some depressive person would feel."

...

Dr. Chien was asked about the significance of the "depression in [defendant's] thought processes" on her decision to strangle Sidney and he testified:

"It was very—in my expertise as a transcultural psychiatry, in my familiarity, with my familiarity with the Chinese culture translate and from the information interview I obtain from Helen, she thought she was doing that out from the mother's love, mother's responsibility to bring a child together with her when she realized that there was no hope for her or a way for her to survive in this country or in this earth.

"Q Well, are you telling us that the death of Sidney was her act of love?

"A Yes. It's a mother's altruism. This may be very difficult for the Westerner to understand....

"But in the Asian culture when the mother commits suicide and leave the children alone, usually they'll be considered to be a totally irresponsible behavior, and the mother will usually worry what would happen if she died, 'Who is going to take care of the children? Anybody [sic—nobody?] can supply the real love that mother could provide,' so and so."

...

Dr. Terry Gock, a clinical psychologist who interviewed defendant for a total of nine and a half hours in three interview sessions and a witness for the defense, testified on direct examination that on the day Sidney was killed, defendant was experiencing a very high level of emotional turmoil, i.e., an emotional crisis, which he described as "when our, when our feelings are so conflicting, so confused and so, so distressful that we, that we don't perhaps know exactly how to plan a course of action, plan a solution in the most rational way." He testified that in his opinion, defendant's cultural background was very intertwined with her emotional state on the evening of the killing. Specifically, Dr. Gock testified:

"Is very difficult to divorce ourselves from our culture and act in a totally culturally different way. And so, you know, she in many ways is a product of her past experiences, including her culture. And also when she experience certain things, like some of the information that she, that she got from her son that evening, it was, it was very distressful for her. And in some sense the kind of alternatives that she, if you would perhaps, you know, it's not as rational as an alternative that the only way she saw out was perhaps—you know, maybe that's the best word is the way she saw how to get out of that situation was quite culturally determined.

...

"And then in terms of what are some of the alternatives then for her. In—perhaps in this country, even with a traditional woman may, may see other options. But in her culture, in her own mind, there are no other options but to, for her at that time, but to kill herself and take the son along with her so that they could sort of step over to the next world where she could devote herself, all of herself to the caring of the son, caring of Sidney.

"Q Was that the motive for killing him?

"A Motive, if you will, yes.

"Q What was her purpose?

"A Her purpose is to, is that she, is, in many ways is, is a benevolent one. It's a positive one where she believed—and this, this sounds sort of implausible to some, some of us whose, who are raised in another culture. That what she believed was that she was not exactly killing but, through death, both of them would be reunited in the next world where she could provide the kind of caring that Sidney did not get in this world."

...

Because the requested instruction was ... applicable to the evidence and one of defendant's two basic defenses in this case, upon retrial defendant is entitled to have the jury instructed that it may consider evidence of defendant's cultural background in determining the existence or nonexistence of the relevant mental states.

...

Notes and Problems

The "Cultural Defense." The *Wu* case parallels an earlier trial court case, *People v. Kimura*, No. A-091133 (Los Angeles Sup. Ct., filed Apr. 24, 1985), which attracted nation-wide attention. In that case, the defendant, a traditional Japanese woman, learned that her husband had been keeping a mistress for three years, and, to escape the shame and humiliation, she attempted to commit suicide by drowning herself and her two children in the ocean. They died, and she survived. In Japan, parent/child suicide, or *oyako-shinju*, is apparently common, and in Japan, as Wu argued was true in China, a mother who kills herself and leaves her children behind is criticized more harshly than the mother who also takes the lives of her children. In Japan, the crime is apparently punishable as involuntary manslaughter rather than murder. Here, Kimura faced the death penalty because she was charged with multiple murder. The case was resolved on the basis of a plea bargain whereby Kimura pled guilty to two counts of voluntary manslaughter and was granted probation on the condition she spend a year in jail. Did the *Wu* court reach the right result in allowing consideration of Wu's cultural defense? If not, should the prosecutor in *Kimura* nevertheless have taken culture into account in deciding to offer Kimura a plea bargain? Whether cultural defenses should be permitted has been the subject of substantial debate. See A. Renteln, The Cultural Defense (2004) (collecting and discussing cases, including *Wu* and *Kimura*).

Problem 27.

Defendant is an Italian immigrant from Sicily who is a house painter by trade. Victim, an Italian immigrant from Rome, hired Defendant to paint an apartment he had bought. The two agreed on a price of $1,000, and Victim paid $500 in advance. While the work was in progress, Victim decided he wanted to finish the job himself, and he paid Defendant $300 and promised the other $200 in a day or two. Defendant left his materials for Victim to use in the work. Some time passed and Victim failed to pay the balance or to return Defendant's materials. The two had several encounters, which turned into quarrels, during one of which Victim said, "If you don't go, I'll shoot you through the head." Victim later apologized, but, at their next meeting at Victim's shop, they quarreled again, and Victim said, "Remember that I am a Roman and to Sicilians like you, I make their a___ like this." He also called Defendant a "cornuto," which is Italian for cuckold. Defendant was in a rage and went home, armed himself, returned to Victim's shop and shot and killed him.

Defendant is charged with first degree murder (P.C. §§ 187–189). In support of his heat of passion defense, he wishes to introduce expert testimony on Sicilian history and culture to explain the significance of Victim's insults, including the following proof: (1) Sicilians have always been subjugated by Northern Italians, who consider themselves racially superior; (2) the word "cornuto" is highly offensive to a Sicilian, meaning not only a cuckold but also the passive partner in homosexual sodomy; (3) passive homosexuality is considered by Sicilian men to be extremely debasing; and (4) the tools of one's trade are of utmost importance to a male Sicilian. He also has requested the following instruction:

> "You may consider the cultural context in which this conflict arose in determining whether there was sufficient provocation to arouse such passion as would be aroused in the mind of an ordinarily reasonable person in the same circumstances."

What arguments should be made as to whether Defendant is entitled to introduce the above evidence and to have the court give the requested instruction?

More on the Reasonable Person. As the Court said in *Berry*, to make out a heat of passion defense, the defendant not only must have been in a passion at the time of the killing, but the "facts and circumstances" must have been sufficient to arouse the passions of "the ordinarily reasonable man" to the point where he would be "liable to act rashly or without due deliberation." *Wu* and the problem case concern whether certain class-based characteristics should be considered part of the defendant's "circumstances" for purposes of the reasonableness test. What about individual, rather than class-based, characteristics? Consider, for example, the fact situation in *Bedder v. Director of Public Prosecutions*, 2 All E.R. 801 (1954), where the defendant was convicted of murder. The defendant, who was 18 years old, was impotent and had allowed that fact to "prey on his mind." On the night of the killing, he approached a prostitute who agreed to have intercourse with him. When defendant was unsuccessful in his attempts at intercourse, the prostitute jeered at him and attempted to get away. He tried to hold her, and she slapped him in the face, punched him in the stomach, and kicked him in the groin. Defendant then pulled out a knife and killed her. At defendant's trial, the court instructed the jury that in order to find the provocation sufficient to warrant a conviction for manslaughter rather than murder, the jury would have to find that the provocation would cause a "reasonable person ... to lose his self-control" and that "an unusually excitable or pugnacious individual, or a drunken one or a man who is sexually impotent is not entitled to rely on provocation which would not have led an ordinary person to have acted in the way which was in fact carried out." The House of Lords found the instruction proper and affirmed the conviction. But see *Director of Public Prosecutions v. Camplin*, 2 All E.R. 168 (1978), where, in reviewing the murder conviction of a 15-year old, the House of Lords held the accused was entitled to an instruction that the jury should consider his age in judging reasonableness, *i.e.*, that the reasonable person with whom the accused was to be compared was a person of the same age.

Problem 28.

Defendant and Buddy, Defendant's best friend since childhood, were present at a well-attended party. While Defendant was in the kitchen, Roxie, a woman at the party, attacked Buddy in the living room and severely slashed his face with a beer bottle. Buddy tried to retaliate against Roxie, but she fled. At about the same time Victor left the party with his girlfriend, Victoria, who was similar in appearance to Roxie. When Defendant returned to the living room, he became enraged at what had been done to Buddy. He muttered that he would "get that b___" and ran to his car. Two minutes later, Defendant caught up with Victor's car, and, thinking Victoria was the one who had attacked Buddy, Defendant signaled Victor to pull over. Defendant approached Victor's car with a shotgun and ordered Victor and Victoria to get out. As they left the car, Defendant was screaming at Victoria and threatening to kill her. Victor attempted to intervene to defend Victoria, and Defendant pushed him aside. Victor then rushed at Defendant, and Defendant shot and killed both Victor and Victoria. Defendant is charged with two counts of first degree murder (P.C. §§ 187–189) and has asked for a heat of passion instruction on both counts. What arguments should be made as to his entitlement to such an instruction?

In re Christian S.

7 Cal. 4th 768, 872 P.2d 574 (1994)

Baxter, J.

Under the doctrine of imperfect self-defense, when the trier of fact finds that a defendant killed another person because the defendant *actually* but unreasonably believed he was in imminent danger of death or great bodily injury, the defendant is deemed to have acted without malice and thus can be convicted of no crime greater than voluntary manslaughter. The question is whether the Legislature abrogated this doctrine in 1981 by amending the Penal Code to eliminate the diminished capacity defense. We hold the doctrine of imperfect self-defense was not abolished.

The 1981 amendments to Penal Code sections 28, 29, and 188 do not manifest the Legislature's intention to mandate a murder conviction for a person who actually but unreasonably believes he must use lethal force to defend himself against imminent death or great bodily injury. Those amendments were a direct response to the public outcry against the diminished capacity defense successfully used in the infamous trial of a San Francisco City and County supervisor who had killed the city's mayor and another supervisor. That case raised no question of self-defense. Nothing in the language, history, or context of the amendments compels the conclusion that the Legislature intended to abrogate the well-established doctrine of imperfect self-defense—a doctrine that differs significantly from the doctrine of diminished capacity.

Facts

Christian S., a minor, seeks review of a judgment making him a ward of the juvenile court after sustaining a petition charging him with the second degree murder of Robert Elliott (Elliott). Because we shall determine only a question of law and remand for further proceedings, extended factual recitation is unnecessary.

Briefly stated, the evidence shows that Elliott was a so-called skinhead and a possible gang member. After being physically and verbally harassed and threatened by Elliott's friends for about a year, Christian (hereafter, defendant) began to carry a handgun. Elliott, who blamed defendant for damaging Elliott's truck, chased defendant down the beach one day, repeatedly threatening "to get him" and challenging him to fire his weapon. Elliott halted his advance each time defendant pointed his gun at Elliott. Finally, after some additional taunting by Elliott, defendant shot and killed Elliott from a range of at least 20 feet.

Challenging the ensuing murder charge, defendant raised claims of self-defense (Pen. Code, § 197) and heat of passion or provocation (Pen. Code, § 192, subd. (a)), and contended the doctrine of imperfect self-defense negated malice, thereby reducing his offense to voluntary manslaughter. The trial court rejected all the defenses, concluding defendant had committed a killing that, if committed by an adult, would have constituted second degree murder. The court made no formal findings at the time of its ruling, but it implicitly found inadequate provocation or heat of passion for a voluntary manslaughter finding. And, although the court also rejected the claims of self-defense and imperfect self-defense, we cannot determine from the record whether the court rejected imperfect self-defense on the ground that the doctrine was no longer a tenable legal doctrine in any case or on the fact-based ground that defendant had no actual belief in the need for self-defense so that the doctrine did not apply in this case.

The Court of Appeal reversed. It ruled that the record "unequivocally established" that when defendant fired the gun, he feared that Elliott was about to "seriously" harm him. The court also interpreted the record as reflecting that the trial court had found that defendant had acted with an "honest belief" in the need to defend himself. The Court of Appeal held the Legislature had not abrogated the doctrine of imperfect self-defense and that, applying the doctrine, defendant's state of mind—that is, his honest belief—negated any finding that defendant acted with malice....

Discussion

1. *Status of imperfect self-defense and diminished capacity doctrines in 1981*

"Murder is the unlawful killing of a human being, or a fetus, with malice aforethought." (Pen. Code, § 187, subd. (a).) By contrast, "Manslaughter is the unlawful killing of a human being without malice." (Pen. Code, § 192.) "The vice is the element of malice; in its absence the level of guilt must decline." (*People v. Flannel* (1979) 25 Cal. 3d 668 [*Flannel*].) The doctrines of imperfect self-defense and diminished capacity arose from this principle.

We explained imperfect self-defense in *Flannel.* "It is the honest belief of imminent peril that negates malice in a case of complete self-defense; the reasonableness of the belief simply goes to the justification for the killing." We concluded that "An *honest but unreasonable* belief that it is necessary to defend oneself from imminent peril to life or great bodily injury negates malice aforethought, the mental element necessary for murder, so that the chargeable offense is reduced to manslaughter." (Although *Flannel* and other opinions referred to an "honest belief" we shall use the more precise term "*actual belief*" because it avoids the confusing suggestion inherent in the phrase "honest belief" that a person could have a "dishonest belief," i.e., that a person could believe something he does not believe.)[1]

This principle had common law antecedents but was not a purely common law defense. Rather, because malice is a *statutory* requirement for a murder conviction (Pen. Code, § 187, subd. (a)), the statute required courts to determine whether an actual but unreasonable belief in the imminent need for self-defense rose to the level

1. It is well established that the ordinary self-defense doctrine—applicable when a defendant *reasonably* believes that his safety is endangered—may not be invoked by a defendant who, through his own wrongful conduct (e.g., the initiation of a physical assault or the commission of a felony), has created circumstances under which his adversary's attack or pursuit is legally justified. It follows, a fortiori, that the imperfect self-defense doctrine cannot be invoked in such circumstances. For example, the imperfect self-defense doctrine would not permit a fleeing felon who shoots a pursuing police officer to escape a murder conviction if the felon killed his pursuer with an actual belief in the need for self-defense.

of malice within the statutory definition. The doctrine thus had statutory as well as common law roots.

We observed in *Flannel* that the doctrine had been "obfuscated by infrequent reference and inadequate elucidation" and thus, before the trial in that case, had not become a general principle of law requiring a sua sponte instruction. More important for our present purpose, though, is *Flannel*'s conclusion that in future cases imperfect self-defense would be deemed to be so well-established a doctrine that it "should be considered a general principle for purposes of jury instruction." Thus, by 1981 imperfect self-defense was demonstrably and firmly established.

Diminished capacity was also well established by that time. "[M]alice aforethought could be negated by showing that a person who intentionally killed was incapable of harboring malice aforethought because of a mental disease or defect or intoxication. To explain how diminished capacity negated malice, we redefined and expanded the mental component of malice aforethought beyond that stated in [Penal Code] section 188 to include a requirement that the defendant was able to comprehend the duty society places on all persons to act within the law, i.e., that he had an 'awareness of the obligation to act within the general body of laws regulating society.'" (*People v. Saille* (1991) 54 Cal. 3d 1103, quoting *People v. Conley* (1966) 64 Cal. 2d 310.) Absent this awareness by the defendant, a court could not find malice.

Because imperfect self-defense and diminished capacity were firmly established by 1981, we assume the Legislature was aware of both doctrines and would have made clear any intent to abolish either doctrine.

2. *The statutory amendments*

The language and history of the 1981 Penal Code amendments leave no question that the Legislature intended to abolish the diminished-capacity defense. The Legislature explicitly and repeatedly stated that it was doing so. Conspicuously absent, however, is any similarly clear indication the Legislature also intended to eliminate imperfect self-defense.

A. The language

"We begin with the fundamental rule that our primary task in construing a statute is to determine the Legislature's intent." (*Brown v. Kelly Broadcasting Co.* (1989) 48 Cal. 3d 711.) We must begin with the words of the statute. Several amendments were enacted together as part of Senate Bill No. 54. Those amendments included the addition to the Penal Code of section 28, which eliminated the diminished-capacity defense, and section 29, which limited psychiatric testimony regarding a defendant's mental state. The Legislature also changed Penal Code section 189's definition of premeditation and deliberation and amended section 22 to restrict a defendant's use of evidence of voluntary intoxication to negate mental capacity.

None of these amendments contains a single reference to imperfect self-defense. Rather, they show that the Legislature referred specifically to the defenses and types of evidence that were being eliminated or restricted. For example, Penal Code section 28, subdivision (b) states, "As a matter of public policy there shall be no defense of *diminished capacity, diminished responsibility, or irresistible impulse* in a criminal action or juvenile adjudication hearing." (Italics added.) The most reasonable inference to be drawn from the absence in these amendments of any reference to imperfect self-defense is that the Legislature intended no change in that doctrine, much less its abrogation.

Penal Code section 188, the statute on which respondent primarily relies, is likewise devoid of any reference to imperfect self-defense. Before the 1981 amendments, section 188 stated: "Such malice may be express or implied. It is express when there is manifested a deliberate intention unlawfully to take away the life of a fellow creature. It is implied, when no considerable provocation appears, or when the circumstances attending the killing show an abandoned and malignant heart." The 1981 amendments did not change this language. Rather, the amendments added the following language: "When it is shown that the killing resulted from the intentional doing of an act with express or implied malice as defined above, no other mental state need be shown to establish the mental state of malice aforethought. *An awareness of the obligation to act within the general body of laws regulating society* is not included within the definition of malice." (Italics added.) This new language clearly refers to the diminished-capacity defense. The amendment uses the same language we used before 1981 in explaining the premise that malice required an "... *awareness of the obligation to act within the general body of laws regulating society....*" (*People v. Conley, supra*, italics added.) The Legislature made absolutely clear its intent to abrogate the diminished-capacity defense.

There is no similar reference to imperfect self-defense in the 1981 amendment to Penal Code section 188. We decline to insert into the statute what the Legislature omitted. That is not our function.

Respondent seems to suggest, however, that the doctrines of diminished capacity and imperfect self-defense were so closely related that, when the Legislature abrogated the former in 1981, it must have acted, albeit silently and perhaps inadvertently, to eliminate imperfect self-defense as well. We disagree.

First, we are aware of no authority that supports the notion of legislation by accident. If respondent means the Legislature abrogated imperfect self-defense by implication, we reject that view as well.

Second, respondent reads too much into the discussion in *Flannel* of mental capacity, as it had been construed and applied in *People v. Conley, supra.* Although "*Flannel* relied upon the expanded mental component of malice in formulating its imperfect self-defense doctrine, its reliance was only partial. Independent of this expanded mental component and independent of diminished capacity, *Flannel* regarded imperfect self-defense as a factor which—just like 'the statutorily suggested "sudden quarrel or heat of passion"—can negate malice aforethought....'" (*People v. De Leon* (1992) 10 Cal. App. 4th 815.) The *De Leon* court's observation was well taken.... Indeed, 30 years before the diminished-capacity defense was allowed, a California court approved the imperfect self-defense doctrine: "'[I]f the act is committed under the influence of an uncontrollable fear of death or great bodily harm, caused by the circumstances, but without the presence of all the ingredients necessary to excuse the act on the ground of self-defense, the killing is manslaughter.'" (*People v. Best* (1936) 13 Cal. App. 2d 606.) ...

Put simply, ... *Flannel* had two independent premises: (1) the notion of mental capacity set forth in *Conley* and (2) a grounding in both well-developed common law and in the statutory requirement of malice. The 1981 amendments make clear the Legislature intended to eliminate the notion of diminished capacity. Thus, that part of the reasoning in *Flannel* is no longer valid. But, *Flannel*'s other premise was not affected by the amendments.

...

Fourth, even if we had not emphasized the difference between the two doctrines, that difference would have been patent, and we assume the Legislature would have understood this. The two doctrines relate to the concept of malice, but the similarity ends there. Unlike diminished capacity, imperfect self-defense is not rooted in any notion of mental capacity or awareness of the need to act lawfully. To the contrary, a person may be entirely free of any mental disease, defect, or intoxication and may be fully aware of the need to act lawfully—and thus not have a diminished capacity—but actually, although unreasonably, believe in the need for self-defense. Put simply, an awareness of the need to act lawfully does not—in fact or logic—depend on whether the putative victim's belief in the need for self-defense is correct. A person who actually believes in the need for self-defense necessarily believes he is acting lawfully. He is thus aware of the obligation to act lawfully. A defendant could assert one doctrine even though the facts did not support the other. The diminished-capacity defense could be—and often has been—asserted when self-defense was not an issue; and, conversely, imperfect self-defense could be raised when there was no claim of diminished capacity.

In short, respondent fails to persuade us that the doctrines of diminished capacity and imperfect self-defense were so closely related that the Legislature believed its elimination of diminished capacity also would abrogate, silently but necessarily, the doctrine of imperfect self-defense. The Legislature did not refer to imperfect self-defense. The language added to Penal Code section 188 by the 1981 amendments did not eliminate imperfect self-defense.

The question then is whether Penal Code section 188's pre-1981 definition of malice mandates a finding of malice (and thus murder) when a person kills with an actual but unreasonable belief in the need for self-defense against imminent death or great bodily injury. Section 188 states, "It [malice] is express when there is manifested a deliberate *intention unlawfully to take away the life* of a fellow creature. It is implied, when no considerable provocation appears, or when the circumstances attending the killing show an abandoned and malignant heart." (Italics added.)

This inartful language leads to two conflicting views of Penal Code section 188's definition of express malice. Defendant contends the word "unlawfully" modifies the word "intend" so that the statute requires an intent to act unlawfully or, put in everyday language, the defendant must have a wrongful intent. Taking a different view, respondent construes the definition of express malice to mean that "unlawful" refers not to the defendant's intent, but only to whether the act is later found to be unlawful. That is, the defendant need not have intended to act unlawfully. Rather, he need only to have intended to kill. Even if he intended to act lawfully, he had express malice and thus committed murder if the killing is later found to be unlawful.

We believe defendant's construction of the statute is the more reasonable. Respondent's approach substitutes an unlawful consequence for an unlawful intent. This view also reverses the normal way in which malice and murder are understood. As respondent would have it, if a person kills someone lawfully, the killer has no malice, but if he kills someone unlawfully, he has malice. Of course, whether the killing is unlawful is the ultimate question and can be determined only with hindsight. Thus, under respondent's view, the defendant's mental state at the time of the killing will depend on whether the killing is later determined to be unlawful. The defendant's intent would become—not a fact to be determined—but the result of a determination of whether he acted unlawfully.[3]

...

Perhaps most important, even though we are not persuaded by respondent's view of Penal Code section 188, we acknowledge the inherent ambiguity in the statute's definition of express malice. "When language which is reasonably susceptible of two constructions is used in a penal law ordinarily that construction which is more favorable to the offender will be adopted." (*People v. Stuart* (1956) 47 Cal. 2d 167.) Because the language of section 188's definition of express malice is, at the very least, reasonably susceptible to the construction asserted by defendant, we adopt that construction.

...

[Concurring opinion of Mosk, J. omitted.]

Lucas, C.J., dissenting.

I respectfully dissent.

Impressed, or possibly blinded, by what it perceives to be sound public policy, the majority resurrects a legal doctrine long ago abrogated by the Legislature. Ironically, the resurrection occurs in the midst of a fierce legislative/political debate on the very question whether or not to restore the doctrine, and if so, to what extent.

---

3. We emphasize that our discussion of this point is limited to the context of a claim of imperfect self-defense, which is based on a defendant's assertion that he lacked malice under Penal Code section 188 because he acted under an unreasonable mistake of fact—that is, the need to defend himself against imminent peril of death or great bodily harm. We do not suggest that an unreasonable mistake of fact would be a defense under Penal Code section 26. Nor do we suggest that malice would be negated by a mistake of law, for example, if a defendant killed with the mistaken belief that he could properly use deadly force to protect his parked automobile against a vandal.

In a nutshell, when the Legislature redefined the legal concept of "malice" in 1981 by amendment to Penal Code section 188, it completely uprooted the doctrinal framework for the "imperfect self-defense" doctrine and left nothing in its place to support it. If, as confirmed by this court in *People v. Flannel* (1979) 25 Cal. 3d 668 (hereafter *Flannel*), the sole statutory underpinning for the doctrine was a broad, now abrogated, definition of malice as including an awareness of one's proper legal obligations to society, then there remains no statutory basis for the doctrine. No court, not even a supreme one, may create new defenses or revive abrogated ones simply as a matter of policy or preference. Nor may a court create a new, nonstatutory offense (see Pen. Code, §6), yet the majority's revival of imperfect self-defense does just that, creating a type of "imperfect" voluntary manslaughter not requiring heat of passion or provocation, and thus not provided by statute.

...

... [T]he doctrine of imperfect self-defense, like diminished capacity/voluntary manslaughter, was derived from an expansive definition of malice that included an awareness of one's legal and societal obligations. Yet as *People v. Saille*, 54 Cal.3d 1103 (1991) observes, that broadened definition of malice has now been abrogated, and no mental state need be shown to establish malice other than "an intent unlawfully to kill." Under *Saille*, it would appear to follow that imperfect self-defense is no longer available to negate the element of malice arising from an unlawful intentional killing, and thereby to reduce a murder to voluntary manslaughter.

The majority stresses that the legislative history that accompanied the 1981 amendments indicates no express intent to abrogate imperfect self-defense. First, I am not convinced of the validity of that premise, for the materials provided to the Legislature at the time it was considering these amendments included an analysis by the Assembly Committee on Criminal Justice stating as follows: "The purpose of this bill [including the 1981 amendments] is to eliminate the use of diminished capacity defenses; to eliminate psychiatric opinions on the ultimate issue of intent; *and to reverse Supreme Court decisions that require certain cognitive requirements for first and second degree murder.*" The underscored language indicates a broader reach than merely abrogating the diminished capacity defense and could include reliance on *Flannel*'s imperfect self-defense doctrine to rebut malice.

But whether or not the Legislature intended to abrogate *Flannel*, the fact remains that it did amend Penal Code section 188 to exclude the only statutory support for the imperfect self-defense doctrine. I find no authority for the majority's apparent assumption that a statutory amendment can have no unanticipated consequences.

...

The 1981 amendments rewrote the law of malice. *Conley* was discredited and *Flannel*'s statutory justification for the doctrine vanished. Unless we wish to exercise unprecedented judicial power and create the doctrine afresh based on our personal views of suitable public policy, we must forthrightly acknowledge the problem and allow the Legislature to deal with it as it deems appropriate.

I would reverse the judgment of the Court of Appeal with directions to resolve the minor's remaining appellate issues.

PUGLIA, J., concurs.

Note

Imperfect Defense of Another. In light of the fact that defense of another, like self-defense, is an affirmative defense [see Chapter 11], is unreasonable defense of another a partial defense? The California Supreme Court seemed to assume so in *People v. Michaels*, 28 Cal.4th 486, 530 (2002) and then so held in *People v. Randle* [Chapter 11]. Are there reasons to distinguish the two situations and to reject imperfect defense of another?

People v. Elmore

59 Cal.4th 121, 325 P.3d 951 (2014)

CORRIGAN, J.

A killing committed because of an unreasonable belief in the need for self-defense is voluntary manslaughter, not murder. "Unreasonable self-defense, also called imperfect self-defense, "obviates malice because that most culpable of mental states 'cannot coexist' with an actual belief that the lethal act was necessary to avoid one's own death or serious injury at the victim's hand." (*People v. Rios* (2000) 23 Cal.4th 450.) The question here is whether the doctrine of unreasonable self-defense is available when belief in the need to defend oneself is entirely delusional. We conclude it is not. No state, it appears, recognizes "delusional self-defense" as a theory of manslaughter. We have noted that unreasonable self-defense involves a mistake of *fact.* (*In re Christian S.* (1994) 7 Cal.4th 768.) A purely delusional belief in the need to act in self-defense may be raised as a defense, but that defense is insanity. Under our statutory scheme, a claim of insanity is reserved for a separate phase of trial. At a trial on the question of guilt, the defendant may not claim unreasonable self-defense based on insane delusion.

I. BACKGROUND

The relevant facts are undisputed. Defendant was, by all accounts, mentally ill. He had repeatedly been institutionalized and diagnosed as psychotic. On the day of the killing, he was living in a rehabilitation center. While visiting his grandmother's house that morning, he became fidgety and anxious. At one point, he began to crawl under cars as his family and a friend tried to speak with him. He left his grandmother's home around 12:30 p.m. Meanwhile, 53-year-old Ella Suggs was doing her weekend shopping. She wore a necklace with a charm in the shape of a turtle, which had a magnifying glass in place of the shell. She also wore reading glasses on a chain around her neck. About 1:00 p.m., Brandon Wilson looked out a restaurant window and noticed Suggs sitting at a bus stop across the street. He saw defendant walk past Suggs, stop, look in both directions, and return to confront her. Defendant did not seem to be talking to himself.

Defendant grabbed Suggs and appeared to pull on something around her neck. Suggs raised her hands defensively, stood, and tried to walk away. Defendant pushed her back to a seated position, brought his hands together over his head, and plunged them toward Suggs's chest. Then he fled, looking around as he ran. Suggs stood for a moment before falling. She had been stabbed with a paintbrush handle sharpened to a point. The weapon penetrated six or seven inches, through a lung and into her heart. Neither the turtle necklace nor the reading glasses were found at the scene or among Suggs's possessions.

Within half an hour, Wilson saw defendant return and approach the bus stop. He appeared to be puzzled, and fled. After Wilson alerted a security officer, police apprehended defendant. It took four officers to subdue him. His behavior was sufficiently bizarre that he was referred for psychiatric evaluation.

Charged with murder, defendant pleaded both not guilty and not guilty by reason of insanity. At the guilt phase, forensic psychiatrists were called by both prosecution and defense. They agreed that defendant suffered from schizophrenia, but disputed whether he was actively psychotic when he stabbed Suggs.

Defendant testified, and gave a confused account of the killing. On direct examination, he repeatedly said, "something went wrong out there in the street." When asked for detail, he said, "Somebody was saying something violent to me, and I didn't really—it was something violent happening while I was out there." Defense counsel pursued the question of who was violent. Defendant said, "Some person out there," but could not say whether the person was a man or a woman. He claimed to have blacked out. Counsel asked, "Did you pick that paint brush off the ground?" Defendant said, "Yeah, I made an object." "What was it?" counsel asked. "I made an object after I was out on the ground dazed somewhere. After I was on the ground or whatever. However it happened." Defendant admitted using the object but refused to say how. Asked if he stabbed someone with it, he responded, "I suppose." When asked why he stabbed Suggs, defendant answered, "Person said something and did something to me, I didn't just go do it to be doing it." Defendant refused to say what had been done to him, and denied taking anything from Suggs.

The prosecutor was no more successful at eliciting a coherent version of the events. Defendant said that when he was at the bus stop, "They said something to me." He denied asking Suggs for money or being angry that she would not give him any. He admitted making the paintbrush into a weapon "after I got up. I was mad and scared." He then said he did not know if he had made it and thought he picked it up in that condition. He admitted stabbing Suggs, but claimed the act was unintentional. He denied trying to steal anything.

The prosecutor argued for first degree murder, relying on both malice aforethought and felony murder theories. The defense requested jury instructions on unreasonable self-defense, mistake of fact, and the effect of hallucination on the degree of murder. The court refused those requests, but did tell the jury to consider the evidence of defendant's mental illness in deciding whether he had acted with malice or the intent to rob Suggs.

The jury returned a first degree murder conviction. After the guilt phase, against the advice of counsel, defendant withdrew his plea of not guilty by reason of insanity and was sentenced to 25 years to life in prison. On appeal, he challenged the court's refusal to instruct on unreasonable self-defense and hallucination. The Court of Appeal summarily rejected his argument on unreasonable self-defense, relying on *People v. Mejia-Lenares* (2006) 135 Cal.App.4th 1437 for the rule that the doctrine does not apply when belief in the need for self-defense arises solely from the defendant's delusional mental state. However, the court held that the refusal to instruct on hallucination was prejudicial error. It remanded with directions for retrial or a conviction of second degree murder, at the prosecutor's election.[2]

In this court, defendant contends he was entitled to an instruction on unreasonable self-defense. He does not claim there was any factual basis for him to believe he had to defend himself. His argument is that unreasonable self-defense may be based solely on a defendant's delusional mental state.... We granted defendant's petition for review in order to settle the question.

II. DISCUSSION

A. *The Law of Homicide and Unreasonable Self-defense*

Homicide, the killing of one human being by another, is not always criminal. In certain circumstances, a killing may be excusable or justifiable. Murder and manslaughter are the forms of criminal homicide. "Murder is the unlawful killing of a human being ... with malice aforethought." (§ 187, subd. (a).) Malice aforethought may be express or implied. (§ 188.)

The Penal Code defines express malice as "a deliberate intention unlawfully to take away the life of a fellow creature." (§ 188.) In *Christian S.*, we explained that this "inartful language" means the defendant must intend to act unlawfully, or in other words, have a "wrongful intent." We rejected the argument that malice turns on whether the *killing* is deemed lawful, without regard to the defendant's intent. However, the defendant need not intend to break the law or commit a crime. Rather, malice requires an *intent to kill* that is "unlawful" because the law deems it so....

Malice is implied when an unlawful killing results from a willful act, the natural and probable consequences of which are dangerous to human life, performed with conscious disregard for that danger. (§ 188; *People v. Knoller* (2007) 41 Cal.4th 139.)

"A killing with express malice formed willfully, deliberately, and with premeditation constitutes first degree murder." (*People v. Beltran* (2013), 56 Cal.4th 935.) "Second degree murder is the unlawful killing of a human being with malice aforethought but

2. The Attorney General has not sought review. Thus, we have no occasion to consider this aspect of the Court of Appeal's judgment.

without the additional elements, such as willfulness, premeditation, and deliberation, that would support a conviction of first degree murder." (*People v. Knoller, supra.*) Thus, the mens rea required for murder is malice, express or implied.

Manslaughter, a lesser included offense of murder, is an unlawful killing without malice. (§ 192.) Section 192 establishes three kinds of manslaughter: voluntary, involuntary, and vehicular. Only voluntary manslaughter is at issue here. Punishment is mitigated for this offense, which the law deems less blameworthy than murder because of the attendant circumstances and their impact on the defendant's mental state. Two factors may preclude the formation of malice and reduce murder to voluntary manslaughter: heat of passion and unreasonable self-defense. Heat of passion is recognized by statute as a mitigating factor. (§ 192, subd. (a).) Unreasonable self-defense is founded on both statute and the common law.

Self-defense, when based on a *reasonable* belief that killing is necessary to avert an imminent threat of death or great bodily injury, is a complete justification, and such a killing is not a crime. A killing committed when that belief is *unreasonable* is not justifiable. Nevertheless, "one who holds an honest but unreasonable belief in the necessity to defend against imminent peril to life or great bodily injury does not harbor malice and commits no greater offense than manslaughter." (*People v. Flannel* (1979) 25 Cal.3d 668.) We have also described this mental state as an "unreasonable but good faith belief" in the need for self-defense. (E.g., *People v. Barton* (1995) 12 Cal.4th 186.) However, it is most accurately characterized as an *actual* but unreasonable belief.[4]

A person who actually believes in the need for self-defense necessarily believes he is acting lawfully. Because express malice requires an intent to kill unlawfully, a killing in the belief that one is acting lawfully is not malicious. The statutory definition of implied malice does not contain similar language, but we have extended the imperfect self-defense rationale to any killing that would otherwise have malice, whether express or implied." (*People v. Anderson* (2002) 28 Cal.4th 767.) "A defendant who acts with the requisite actual belief in the necessity for self-defense does not act with the base motive required for implied malice ..." (*Christian S., supra.*).[6] Unreasonable self-defense is "not a true defense; rather, it is a shorthand description of one form of voluntary manslaughter." (*Barton, supra.*) Whenever there is substantial evidence that the defendant killed in unreasonable self-defense, the trial court must instruct on this theory of manslaughter.

Here, defendant claims his request for an instruction on unreasonable self-defense should have been granted, even though his perception of a threat was entirely delusional. The claim fails, under both case law and statute. California cases reflect the

---

4. As noted in *Christian S., supra*, the "*actual belief*" formulation "avoids the confusing suggestion inherent in the phrase 'honest belief' that a person could have a 'dishonest belief,' i.e., that a person could believe something he does not believe."

6. Malice is imputed in cases of felony murder, and unreasonable self-defense has no application in such cases.

understanding that unreasonable self-defense involves a misperception of objective circumstances, not a reaction produced by mental disturbance alone. And the statutory scheme, though it permits evidence of mental illness to show that the defendant did not harbor malice, reserves the issue of legal insanity for a separate phase of trial. As shall be seen, a belief in the need for self-defense that is purely delusional is a paradigmatic example of legal insanity.

B. *Case Law*

The difference between unreasonable self-defense and a claim that mental deficiency prevented the formation of malice was made clear in *Christian S., supra.* There we considered whether the Legislature intended to do away with unreasonable self-defense when it abolished the defense of diminished capacity, in 1981. Diminished capacity was a judicially created concept. It allowed defendants to argue that because of mental infirmity, they lacked "awareness of the obligation to act within the general body of laws regulating society," and therefore were incapable of acting with malice. (*People v. Conley* (1966) 64 Cal.2d 310.) In *Christian S.*, we concluded that the Legislature did not mean to abrogate unreasonable self-defense along with diminished capacity. In reaching that conclusion, we firmly distinguished the two theories. "The doctrine of imperfect self-defense had a lineage independent of the notion of mental capacity set forth in *Conley, supra.* In *Flannel*, we traced the long development of the doctrine in California courts. Indeed, 30 years before the diminished-capacity defense was allowed, a California court approved the imperfect self-defense doctrine: "[I]f the act is committed under the influence of an uncontrollable fear of death or great bodily harm, caused by the circumstances, but without the presence of all the ingredients necessary to excuse the act on the ground of self-defense, the killing is manslaughter." (*People v. Best* (1936) 13 Cal.App.2d 606.)

Flannel, we noted, had rejected the idea that "the doctrine of unreasonable belief is necessarily bound up with or limited by the concepts of either heat of passion *or diminished capacity.*" (*Christian S., supra.*) "The two doctrines relate to the concept of malice, but the similarity ends there. Unlike diminished capacity, imperfect self-defense is not rooted in any notion of mental capacity or awareness of the need to act lawfully." (*Christian S., supra.*)

Thus, unreasonable self-defense is not premised on considerations of mental disorder. From its earliest appearance in California law, unreasonable self-defense has been deemed to apply when the defendant's act was "*caused by the circumstances,*" rather than by cognitive defects alone. As we said in *Christian S.*, unreasonable self-defense "is based on a defendant's assertion that he lacked malice ... because he acted under an unreasonable *mistake of fact*—that is, the need to defend himself against imminent peril of death or great bodily harm." (*Christian S., supra*, italics added.)

...

... [U]nreasonable self-defense, as a form of mistake of fact, has no application when the defendant's actions are entirely delusional. A defendant who makes a factual mistake misperceives the objective circumstances. A delusional defendant holds a belief that is divorced from the circumstances. The line between mere misperception and delusion is drawn at the absence of an objective correlate. A person who sees a stick and thinks it is a snake is mistaken, but that misinterpretation is not delusional. One who sees a snake where there is nothing snakelike, however, is deluded. Unreasonable self-defense was never intended to encompass reactions to threats that exist only in the defendant's mind.

...

Defendant ... places great weight on this statement in *Flannel*: "*No matter how the mistaken assessment is made,* an individual cannot genuinely perceive the need to repel imminent peril or bodily injury and simultaneously be aware that society expects conformity to a different standard." Defendant contends delusions are necessarily included in *Flannel's* expansive characterization of the misperceptions that may motivate an act of unreasonable self-defense. However, the comment on which he relies was predicated on a concept of malice that was central to the diminished capacity defense. The Legislature has specifically repudiated that concept. Section 188, as amended in 1981 and revised in 1982, declares that "[n]either an awareness of the obligation to act within the general body of laws regulating society nor acting despite such awareness is included within the definition of malice."

In *Christian S.,* we observed that *Flannel's* discussion of unreasonable self-defense "had two *independent* premises: (1) the notion of mental capacity set forth in *Conley, supra* [i.e., diminished capacity], and (2) a grounding in both well-developed common law and in the statutory requirement of malice (... § 187). The 1981 amendments make clear the Legislature intended to eliminate the notion of diminished capacity. Thus, that part of the reasoning in *Flannel* ... is no longer valid. But, *Flannel's* other premise was not affected by the amendments." (*Christian S., supra.*) Defendant seeks support from the part of *Flannel's* discussion that is now invalid. In the surviving aspect of its analysis, based on the common-law and statutory roots of unreasonable self-defense, *Flannel* incorporated the observation made in *People v. Best, supra,* that unreasonable self-defense entails a reaction that is "caused by the circumstances."

The phrase "caused by the circumstances" denotes a motivation arising from objective facts, not delusions. Accordingly, *Flannel* comports with our view that purely delusional perceptions of threats to personal safety cannot be relied upon to claim unreasonable self-defense. This understanding of the doctrine is consistently reflected in the decisions of other state courts.

C. *Statute*

Defendant asserts a statutory basis for his claim in section 28, subdivision (a). This provision states that evidence of mental disorders is admissible "on the issue of whether or not the accused actually formed a required specific intent, premeditated, deliberated, or harbored malice aforethought, when a specific intent crime is charged," a theory sometimes referred to as "diminished actuality." Section 28(a) bars evidence of the defendant's *capacity* to form a required mental state, consistent with the abolition of the diminished capacity defense.

Defendant contends the plain language of section 28(a) permits him to introduce evidence of the mental disorder that gave rise to his belief in the need for self-defense, and precluded him from actually harboring malice. If section 28(a) is viewed in isolation, this construction is logically defensible. However, it is unsustainable when the provision is considered in light of the statutory scheme governing evidence of mental illness, and the legislative history of section 28.

...

A claim of unreasonable self-defense based solely on delusion is quintessentially a claim of insanity under the *M'Naghten* standard of inability to distinguish right from wrong. Its rationale is that mental illness caused the defendant to perceive an illusory threat, form an actual belief in the need to kill in self-defense, and act on that belief without wrongful intent. In *M'Naghten's Case* (1843) 8 Eng. Rep. 718, itself, the judges observed: "[I]f under the influence of [a] delusion [the defendant] supposes another man to be in the act of attempting to take away his life, and he kills that man, as he supposes, in self-defence, he would be exempt from punishment." We noted in *People v. Skinner* (1985) 39 Cal.3d 765 that this example "applies the right/wrong prong of the M'Naghten test to an insane delusion in the same manner as it is applied to other forms of insanity. The delusion ... results in an inability to appreciate that the act is wrong. The defendant believes he is defending himself."

Thus, what defendant attempted here was to assert a claim of legal insanity at the guilt phase of his trial. That is not allowed under our statutes. Section 1026 sets out the applicable procedure when, as in this case, the defendant pleads both not guilty and not guilty by reason of insanity. The trial is bifurcated, with the question of guilt tried first. The defendant is presumed innocent, of course, but in order to preserve the issue of sanity for the second phase of trial the defendant is also conclusively presumed to have been legally sane at the time of the offense. Evidence of the defendant's mental state may not be admitted at the guilt phase to prove insanity. If the defendant is found guilty, the trial proceeds to the sanity phase, where the defendant bears the burden of proof by a preponderance of the evidence.

...

Section 28(a) allows defendants to introduce evidence of mental disorder to show they did not actually form a mental state required for guilt of a charged crime. But the scope of the diminished actuality defense is necessarily limited by the presumption of sanity, which operates at a trial on the question of guilt to bar the defendant from claiming he is not guilty *because he is legally insane.* This limitation was explored in *People v. Wells* (1949) 33 Cal.2d 330. Although *Wells* predated the enactment of section 28, its analysis established the distinction between *actual* formation of a mental state and *capacity* to form a mental state that is now found in section 28(a).

...

Wells explained that evidence challenging the defendant's actual formation of a mental state is admissible, but only so long as it does not go toward a claim of legal insanity: "As a general rule, on the not guilty plea, evidence ... tending to show that the defendant, who at this stage is conclusively presumed sane, either *did* or *did not,* in committing the overt act, possess the specific essential mental state, is admissible, but evidence tending to show legal sanity or legal insanity is not admissible. Thus, if the proffered evidence tends to show not merely that he *did* or *did not,* but rather that because of legal insanity he *could* not, entertain the ... essential mental state, then that evidence is inadmissible under the not guilty plea and is admissible only on the trial on the plea of not guilty by reason of insanity.... Evidence which tends to show legal insanity (likewise, sanity) is not admissible at the first stage of the trial because it is not pertinent to any issue then being litigated; but competent evidence, other than proof of sanity or insanity, which tends to show that a (then presumed) legally sane defendant either did or did not in fact possess the required specific intent or motive is admissible." (*Wells, supra.*)

...

"As a result of these developments, the current state of California law on the insanity defense and proof of the defendant's mental state is generally consistent with the principles set out in *Wells.*" (*People v. Mills* (2012) 55 Cal.4th 663.) Accordingly, the provisions of section 28(a) allowing evidence of diminished actuality are "qualified" by the caveat that at a trial on the question of guilt, "evidence tending to show lack of mental capacity to commit the crime because of legal insanity is barred...." (*Wells, supra.*) The *Wells* court squarely rejected the idea that defendants have the right to present evidence of insanity at the guilt phase to persuade the jury they did not entertain a required mental state.

...

Our construction of section 28(a) has no effect on evidence of mental disorders that do not amount to legal insanity. As noted in *People v. Mills, supra,* "a defendant may suffer from a diagnosable mental illness without being legally insane under the *M'Naghten* standard." All relevant evidence of mental states short of insanity is admissible at the guilt phase under section 28(a), including evidence bearing on unreasonable self-defense, as in *Mills* and *Wells.* The *M'Naghten* test is a narrow one. It is only when "mental illness is manifested in delusions which render the individual incapable either of knowing the nature and character of his act, or of understanding that it is wrong, [that] he is legally insane under the California formulation of the M'Naghten test." (*Skinner, supra.*)

Furthermore, our holding does not prevent the defense from presenting evidence of mental disease, defect, or disorder to support a claim of unreasonable self-defense based on a mistake of fact. A defendant who misjudges the external circumstances may show that mental disturbance contributed to the mistaken perception of a threat, without presenting the jury with the same question it would confront at a sanity trial.

The jury must find there was an actual, unreasonable belief in the necessity of self-defense based on the circumstances, and it should be so instructed. An insanity defense, on the other hand, requires no showing that the defendant responded to objective circumstances. At a sanity trial, and only at a sanity trial, the defense can maintain that purely delusional perceptions caused the defendant to believe in the necessity of self-defense.

In sum, defendants who mistakenly believed that actual circumstances required their defensive act may argue they are guilty only of voluntary manslaughter, even if their reaction was distorted by mental illness. But defendants who contend they killed in self-defense because of a purely delusional perception of threat must make that claim at a sanity trial. Unreasonable self-defense and legal insanity are distinct theories, and must be adjudicated separately.

Here, defendant's claim of unreasonable self-defense was based entirely on a delusional mental state that amounted to legal insanity. The trial court properly denied his request for an instruction on unreasonable self-defense.

Kennard, J., concurring and dissenting.

...

II

"Murder is the unlawful killing of a human being ... with malice aforethought." (§ 187, subd. (a).) A defendant who kills with the "deliberate intention unlawfully to take away the life of a fellow creature" (§ 188) acts with express malice; implied malice occurs when "no considerable provocation appears, or when the circumstances attending the killing show an abandoned and malignant heart." A person who kills in the belief that the killing is necessary to avert an imminent threat of death or great bodily injury lacks malice, an element of the crime of murder. If that belief is *reasonable*, the killing is justified and therefore not a crime. (§ 197, subd. (3).) But if that belief is *unreasonable*, the crime is voluntary manslaughter (an unlawful killing without malice) under the doctrine of imperfect self-defense. This court has observed: "*Imperfect self-defense* obviates malice because that most culpable of mental states cannot coexist with an actual belief that the lethal act was necessary to avoid one's own death or serious injury at the victim's hand." (*People v. Rios* (2000) 23 Cal.4th 450.) The unreasonable belief in the need for self-defense may stem from mental illness, negligence, subaverage intelligence, or a variety of other causes. To negate malice, it should not matter *why* the killer perceived a need for self-defense. *Any* genuine belief in the need for self-defense precludes a murder conviction, because such a belief "cannot coexist" with the mental state of malice, an essential component of the crime of murder. It follows, therefore, that imperfect self-defense can arise from a delusion caused entirely by mental illness.

California's statutory criminal law expressly allows criminal defendants to introduce evidence of mental illness to show they lack the requisite mental state of malice, a statutory element of murder. Pertinent here is section 28's subdivision (a), which states: "*Evidence of mental disease, mental defect, or mental disorder is admissible solely on the issue of whether or not the accused actually* formed a required specific intent, premeditated, deliberated, or *harbored malice aforethought,* when a specific intent crime is charged." (Italics added.) It follows from section 28's plain language that someone who kills in the belief that the killing is necessary to avert death or great bodily injury may introduce evidence that the unreasonable belief arose as the result of a delusion that was caused by mental illness.

Disregarding this statutory directive, the majority instead adopts the analysis of the Court of Appeal in *People v. Mejia-Lenares* (2006) 135 Cal.App.4th 1437. That court seized on this court's fleeting reference to the affirmative defense of mistake of fact contained in footnote three in *Christian S., supra*. Echoing the Court of Appeal's explanation in *Mejia-Lenares,* the majority here concludes: (1) Imperfect self-defense "is a species of mistake of fact"; (2) a killer whose unreasonable belief in the necessity of self-protection stems entirely from a delusion is not acting under a mistake of fact; and (3) therefore, the doctrine of imperfect self-defense can play no role in a killing caused entirely by the killer's delusional belief in the need for self-defense. I disagree, for two reasons.

First, the majority is wrong, as was the Court of Appeal in *Mejia-Lenares*, in describing this court's 1994 decision in *Christian S.* as holding that imperfect self-defense is a "species of mistake of fact." What *Christian S.* does hold is that the Legislature did not abrogate imperfect self-defense when, in 1981, it abolished the "diminished capacity" defense to murder. As I noted in the preceding paragraph, that decision's only mention of mistake of fact appears in a brief footnote. That footnote states in passing that the defendant in *Christian S.,* who claimed he killed in imperfect self-defense, asserted that "he acted under an unreasonable mistake of fact." The footnote then *distinguishes* the affirmative defense of "ignorance or mistake of fact" (§ 26, subd. (Three)) from imperfect self-defense. Thus, this court's decision in *Christian S.* does not hold that imperfect self-defense is a form of mistake of fact. Rather, that decision explains that imperfect self-defense is rooted in the notion that someone who kills in the belief that the killing is necessary to avert an imminent threat of death or great bodily injury does not have a "wrongful intent" (*Christian S., supra*), and therefore lacks malice, an essential element of the crime of murder. This absence of malice, in my view, also pertains to a person whose genuine but unreasonable belief in the need for self-defense stems entirely from a delusion caused by a mental disorder. As a Court of Appeal decision explained, "A defendant's mental state is the same when he kills in the honest-but-mistaken belief that the victim was reaching for a gun whether such belief is the product of a delusion or a mistaken interpretation of the victim's reaching for his car keys." (*People v. Uriarte* (1990) 223 Cal.App.3d 192.)

Second, even if mistake of fact *were* a critical part of imperfect self-defense, a person whose genuine belief in the need for self-defense is based entirely on a delusion does act under a mistake of fact. The person's mistaken belief that an attack is occurring or is about to occur is a mistake of fact, even if that belief is entirely delusional.

The majority perceives its holding—that a person who kills based on an entirely delusional belief in the need for self-protection is not acting in imperfect self-defense—as necessary so that questions pertaining to the sanity of a possibly delusional defendant are resolved at the sanity phase, rather than the guilt phase. But the majority's reasoning presents two problems. First, the majority's holding cannot be reconciled with the plain language of section 28's subdivision (a). The majority essentially concedes this when it says that, in construing that section, it must look beyond "the letter of the law." Second, as explained below, the majority's holding does not accomplish its stated goal of relegating sanity issues to the sanity phase.

Because a killer's genuine belief in the need for self-defense negates malice, under my approach the jury at the guilt phase need not decide whether that belief was delusional, but only decides whether that belief was genuine, and if so, whether it was reasonable. Under the majority's approach, by contrast, the jury at the guilt phase must decide whether the killer's belief in the need for self-defense was based at least partially on fact (in which case the defendant lacked malice and committed voluntary manslaughter) or based entirely on a delusion caused by mental illness (in which case the defendant acted with malice and committed murder). Notwithstanding the majority's claim that it is removing the question of the defendant's sanity from the guilt phase and confining it to the sanity phase, it is doing the opposite.

The majority limits its holding to a defendant whose belief in the need for self-defense is "entirely" or "purely" delusional. According to the majority, a belief is entirely or purely delusional if it is "divorced from the circumstances," meaning that there is an "absence of objective correlate." Under the majority's definition, someone who "sees a snake where there is nothing snakelike" is delusional, but one who thinks a stick is a snake is not delusional, even if the mistaken belief persists in the face of irrefutable evidence. Thus, it would appear that, under the majority's view, Don Quixote was not delusional because each of his famous misperceptions, including his belief that windmills were "monstrous giants" had, in the majority's words, an "objective correlate." Under the majority's decision, defendants may continue to present Don Quixote-style delusional beliefs to support claims of imperfect self-defense based on mistakes of fact. The unenviable task of distinguishing such partly delusional beliefs having some objective basis from those that are "purely" or "entirely" delusional will be left to trial courts and juries.

III

[Justice KENNARD concurred in the judgment because defendant's testimony—that he was sitting at a bus stop when someone said "something violent" and "did something" to him and he then stabbed Suggs—did not support the giving of instructions on imperfect self-defense for three reasons: (1) there was no evidence that he perceived an *imminent* threat of death or great bodily injury; (2) there was no evidence that he thought Suggs was the source of any threat; and (3) there was no evidence that he thought deadly force was necessary to protect himself.]

WERDEGAR and LIU, JJ concur.

Note

Malice and Mental Illness. As the court itself acknowledges, Elmore was mentally ill. Even if the court is correct that his killing did not fit within "imperfect self-defense," was the killing "malicious," and, therefore, murder (subject to a possible finding that he was insane)? Consider the facts in *People v. Molina*, 202 Cal. App. 3d 1168 (1988):

> The prosecution's evidence established that on June 7, 1986, appellant killed her son by stabbing him repeatedly in the heart. She then inflicted life-threatening wounds to her own chest, set fire to her house, and resisted efforts to remove her from the house. A garbled suicide note was found.
>
> The defense evidence showed that after the crime, appellant spent six days in a hospital's intensive care unit and then transferred to the psychiatric ward for four or five weeks. A hospital psychiatrist (Dr. Hayes) diagnosed her as having a major depression with psychotic features, including auditory hallucinations which gave her commands. She also suffered from delusions that her husband and mother were going to kill her and that people were out to get her and her son.
>
> In Dr. Hayes's opinion, appellant became psychotic about two days before the homicide. Tests for drugs were negative. There was no evidence that her illness was feigned.
>
> Appellant testified that in the months after the baby was born she became increasingly depressed and anxious and had trouble eating, sleeping, and leaving the house. She began hearing voices, and thought her mother was going to kill her and the baby.
>
> Appellant further testified that on the day before the killing she drove off to visit friends nearby and next found herself in San Diego. That evening she thought that her husband wanted her dead. The voices told her that she had to die. Her husband, a medical doctor, gave her some medicine so she could sleep. The next morning, after her husband left for work, the voices told her that she had to die and take her son with her. She put her son in his crib and strangled him. Then she got a knife from the kitchen and stabbed herself. When she saw her son lying very pale in the crib, she stabbed him. At some point she talked briefly on the telephone to a friend who called her. She then started several fires in the house.
>
> Appellant's husband, mother and best friend all testified that she had been a warm, happy, extroverted person who underwent a major personality change following the birth of her son. She became dejected, overwhelmed by routine household tasks, and obsessed with the fact that a planned family move to her parents' home in Arizona did not occur because her brother moved there instead. She told nobody that she was hearing voices. When her friend called her on the day of the homicide, appellant had spoken in a

> monotone, sounded ill, and had not recognized the friend's voice. The homicide had come as a complete surprise to everyone.

The defendant was found guilty of second degree murder. Is that outcome justified?

B. First or Second Degree Murder?

In the two cases in this section, *People v. Anderson* and *People v. Wharton*, the Supreme Court discusses the standards for determining whether the evidence is sufficient to support a finding of first degree murder on the basis of premeditation and deliberation.[d]

People v. Anderson

70 Cal. 2d 15, 447 P.2d 942 (1968)

TOBRINER, J.

Defendant was indicted for the murder of Victoria Hammond, a 10-year-old girl, in 1962. The jury found defendant guilty of first degree murder, found that he was sane, and fixed the penalty at death.

...

The Facts

Defendant, a San Jose cab driver, had been living for about eight months with a Mrs. Hammond and her three children, Cynthia, aged 17, Kenneth, aged 13, and the victim, Victoria, aged 10. On the morning of the day of the murder, December 7, 1962, Mrs. Hammond left for work at 7:30 a.m., leaving only Victoria at home with the defendant. Defendant was still in bed. He had been home from work for the previous two days, during which time he had been drinking heavily, and apparently he did not go to work on the day of the murder.

The owner of a nearby liquor store testified that defendant purchased a quart of whiskey from him sometime between 1 and 2 p.m. on December 7, 1962. The only other witness who testified as to defendant's whereabouts that day prior to the discovery of the murder was the victim's 13-year-old brother Kenneth.

Kenneth testified that he arrived home from school at 3:30 p.m. on December 7. He found the front door locked, which was not unusual, so he went around to the back of the house and down to the basement. Kenneth stayed there awhile working with his microscope. In a short time he heard noise coming from upstairs in the house which sounded like boxes and other things being moved around, like someone was cleaning up. He then heard the shower water running. A police officer later

---

d. For a critical review of the Court's decisions in this area, see S. Mounts, *Premeditation and Deliberation in California: Returning to a Distinction Without a Difference*, 36 U.S.F. L. Rev. 261 (2002).

verified that a person in the basement could hear water running in the shower and movement in Victoria's bedroom.

Kenneth testified further that he then came up from the basement and went to the back porch screen door. The screen door was locked, which also was not unusual, so Kenneth jerked on it so the hook would pop out. Kenneth then went from the back porch directly into his bedroom to change his clothes. He then returned through the back porch to the kitchen door which was also locked. Kenneth knocked on the door and the defendant opened it. Kenneth testified that the defendant was wearing slacks only. Kenneth went into the kitchen and asked defendant for $1.00 for a teen club dance he intended to attend that evening. Defendant obtained a dollar for him out of the pocket of another pair of slacks hanging on the knob of a bedroom door. When Kenneth noticed the blood on the kitchen floor and asked defendant about it, the defendant told Kenneth that he had cut himself. This explanation apparently satisfied Kenneth, as he finished dressing and left the house sometime before 4 p.m.

Kenneth testified that no one else was at his house when he was there between 3:30 and 4 p.m. He further testified that about 6:30 he realized that he had forgotten his wallet and returned home. As he approached the front door, his mother came out and asked to see the cut on his arm, and Kenneth explained that he had no cut. His mother then asked defendant about the blood she had noticed and defendant told her that Victoria had cut herself, but that the mother should not worry, as the cut was not serious. After defendant told her that Victoria was at a friend's for dinner, the mother wanted to take Kenneth with her to get Victoria. Kenneth went back to his room to get a jacket. Because he had a "weird" feeling, he looked into Victoria's room. He found her nude, bloody body under some boxes and blankets on the floor near her bed. Kenneth ran out of the room screaming that defendant had killed her. Mrs. Hammond, after seeing Victoria's body, went next door to phone the police.

...

A classmate of Victoria, who was the last person to see Victoria alive, testified that she left Victoria in front of the Hammond house about 3:45 p.m. after the two of them had walked home from school.

When the police arrived at 7 p.m. the shades were down on all the windows and the doors were locked. Defendant finally opened the front door for one of the officers who arrested and handcuffed defendant. The arresting officer testified that defendant was wearing slacks, no shirt or shoes, and that there was no blood on him.

The arresting officer found Victoria's body on the floor near her bed. He found defendant's blood-spotted shorts on a chair in the living room, and a knife and defendant's socks, with blood encrusted on the soles, in the master bedroom. The evidence established that the victim's torn and bloodstained dress had been ripped from her, that her clothes, including her panties out of which the crotch had been ripped, were found in various rooms of the house, that there were bloody footprints matching the size of the victim's leading from the master bedroom to Victoria's room, and that there was blood in almost every room including the kitchen, the floor of which appeared to have been mopped.

The TV cameraman who covered the murder story for channel 11, the officer who drove defendant to the police station, and the officer who "observed" defendant for four hours at the station the night of December 7, 1962, all testified that defendant did not appear intoxicated. The officers who talked to defendant testified, however, that they smelled alcohol on his breath; a blood test taken at 7:45 p.m. indicated that the alcohol content in defendant's blood was .34 percent, which was more than necessary for an automobile driver to be classified as "under the influence."

Over 60 wounds, both severe and superficial, were found on Victoria's body.... Several of the wounds, including the vaginal lacerations, were post mortem. No evidence of spermatozoa was found in the victim, on her panties, or on the bed next to which she was found.

...

2. The evidence is insufficient to support a verdict of first degree murder.

We must, in the absence of substantial evidence to support the verdict of first degree murder, reduce the conviction to second degree murder.

...

Recognizing the need to clarify the difference between the two degrees of murder and the bases upon which a reviewing court may find that the evidence is sufficient to support a verdict of first degree murder, we set forth standards, derived from the nature of premeditation and deliberation as employed by the Legislature and interpreted by this court, for the kind of evidence which is sufficient to sustain a finding of premeditation and deliberation.

...

... [W]e have held that in order for a killing with malice aforethought to be first rather than second degree murder, "[the] intent to kill must be ... formed upon a *pre-existing reflection*, ... [and have] been the subject of actual deliberation or *forethought*." (*People v. Thomas* (1945) 25 Cal. 2d 880, italics added.) We have therefore held that "[a] verdict of murder in the first degree ... [on a theory of a wilful, deliberate, and premeditated killing] is proper only if the slayer killed as a result of careful thought and weighing of considerations; as a deliberate judgment or plan; carried on coolly and steadily, [especially] according to a preconceived design." (*People v. Bender* (1945) 27 Cal. 2d 164.)

The type of evidence which this court has found sufficient to sustain a finding of premeditation and deliberation falls into three basic categories: (1) facts about how and what defendant did prior to the actual killing which show that the defendant was engaged in activity directed toward, and explicable as intended to result in, the killing—what may be characterized as "planning" activity; (2) facts about the defendant's prior relationship and/or conduct with the victim from which the jury could reasonably infer a "motive" to kill the victim, which inference of motive, together with facts of type (1) or (3), would in turn support an inference that the killing was the result of "a pre-existing reflection" and "careful thought and weighing of considerations" rather than "mere unconsidered or rash impulse hastily executed"; (3) facts about the nature of the killing from which the jury could infer that the manner of killing was so particular and exacting that the defendant must have intentionally killed according to a "preconceived design" to take his victim's life in a particular way for a "reason" which the jury can reasonably infer from facts of type (1) or (2).

Analysis of the cases will show that this court sustains verdicts of first degree murder typically when there is evidence of all three types and otherwise requires at least extremely strong evidence of (1) or evidence of (2) in conjunction with either (1) or (3). As will become clear from the following analysis of representative cases, the present case lacks evidence of any of the three types.

In *People v. Hillery* (1965) 62 Cal. 2d 692, the jury could reasonably infer that the defendant engaged in the following "extended course of conduct": defendant parked his car near the victim's (a 15-year-old girl's) house, entered the house surreptitiously, seized the victim while she was sewing and covered her head with a towel and slip to prevent outcry or identification, cut a length of cord in another room to secure her hands behind her, took the victim's scissors, dragged her to a nearby irrigation ditch where her body was subsequently found, engaged in a struggle with the victim, and then plunged the scissors directly into her chest.

Hillery represents a case of very strong type (1) evidence: the defendant's surreptitious conduct, subjection of his victim to his complete control, and carrying off of his victim to a place where others were unlikely to intrude, can be described as "planning" activity directly related to the killing. Moreover, there is also strong evidence of type (3): directly plunging a lethal weapon into the chest evidences a deliberate intention to kill as opposed to the type of "indiscriminate" multiple attack of both severe and superficial wounds which defendant engaged in in the instant case.

...

In *People v. Kemp* (1961) 55 Cal. 2d 458, the defendant entered his victim's apartment through a window after removing the screen, found the victim alone in bed, tied stockings around her neck and hands, gagged her with a washcloth, and then raped and strangled her. In *Kemp*, as in *Hillery*, defendant's surreptitious coming upon the victim and calculated efforts to prevent her from identifying her assailant or crying out for help, together with the deliberate manner of killing—evidence of types (1) and (3)—point to a killing which is the result of "preconceived design" as opposed to "an explosion of violence."

...

People v. Cole (1956) 47 Cal. 2d 99, involved a defendant living with an impecunious woman (his victim) and desirous of marrying a well-to-do woman. The evidence established that the defendant secretly took the latter's gun from her dresser the week before the killing, that he was carrying it on the evening of the killing, and that he used it to kill his victim. Moreover, the evidence also tended to show that defendant planned to implicate the wealthier woman so as to secure her assistance in concealing his guilt and that he killed the victim to remove her as an obstacle to his marital plans. As the court pointed out, "a showing of motive indicating that the killing was planned" tends to support an inference of premeditation and deliberation. *Cole* thus represents a case of primarily type (2) evidence supported by type (1) evidence.

...

The present case is strikingly similar to *People v. Granados* (1957) 49 Cal. 2d 490, in which this court reduced a verdict of first degree murder to second degree murder on the ground that the evidence was insufficient to show either premeditation and deliberation or that the killing occurred in the course of an attempted violation of section 288 of the Penal Code. The evidence of premeditation and deliberation in *Granados*, while clearly insufficient to sustain the verdict of first degree murder on that theory, was stronger than in the present case in which we find no evidence from which the jury could reasonably infer that defendant acted "with a deliberate and clear intent to take life."

In *Granados*, defendant lived in a common law relationship with the mother of his victim, a 13-year-old girl. After taking the deceased and her brother to a real estate office, defendant gave the brother a note requesting money to take to his mother who worked nearby. When the brother returned home with the requested money he saw defendant at the rear of the house. As he started to enter the house, defendant came running to him and asked him to get some alcohol for his sister (decedent) who had fainted. The brother noticed blood on one of defendant's hands and that defendant had the other hand behind his back.

The brother unsuccessfully looked for some alcohol. Defendant then suggested they get a doctor and an ambulance. The brother then noticed that defendant's hand had been washed. Defendant then drove the brother to a drugstore, gave him 50 cents for some alcohol, and told him he would wait for him. The defendant drove away and did not return for the brother.

Defendant then called the mother and told her the victim had poisoned herself. The mother returned to the house with a friend who found the victim's body in the bedroom lying on the floor. Her skirt was pulled up exposing her private parts, there were bloodstains on the wall, floor, and decedent's head, and a machete covered with blood was lying in a corner of the living room behind a small heater.

Defendant testified that on the day of the killing the girl was helping him clean the house and that he asked her if she was a virgin, to which she replied that it was none of his business. Defendant said that she had never answered him in that way and that he therefore struck her with his hand, but did not remember striking her with the machete.

Decedent's mother testified that she had warned defendant that the next time he bothered her daughter, she would tell the police, and that defendant in reply threatened to kill her and both her children if she did.

The prosecution argued that the murder was sexually motivated. This court, per Justice McComb, held that the evidence was insufficient as a matter of law to support a verdict of first degree murder.

Applying the standards developed above to *Granados*, we find that the only evidence of (1) defendant's behavior prior to the killing which could be described as "planning" activity related to a killing purpose was defendant's sending the victim's brother on an errand and apparently returning home alone with the decedent. Such evidence is highly ambiguous in terms of the various inferences it could support as to defendant's purpose in so behaving. The evidence of (2) defendant's prior behavior with the victim (alleged sexual molestation and his question as to her virginity) is insufficient to support a reasonable inference that defendant had a "motive" to kill the girl, which could in turn support an inference that the striking with the machete was the result of a "preconceived design" and "forethought." Finally, the evidence of (3) the manner of killing (brutal hacking) does not support a reasonable inference of deliberately placed blows, which could in turn support an inference that the act of killing was premeditated rather than "hasty and impetuous."

Justice Carter dissented in *Granados* on the ground that the following evidence was sufficient to sustain a finding of premeditation and deliberation: the nature of the instrument, the condition of the body, defendant's sending the brother on an errand immediately prior to the time of the killing, and defendant's prior threats against the girl and her family. Justice Carter's dissent demonstrates that there was some evidence of premeditation and deliberation in *Granados*, albeit insufficient. Here, on the other hand, we do not have any evidence of either (1) any conduct by defendant prior to the killing which would indicate that he was planning anything, felonious or otherwise, or (2) any behavior towards Victoria from which the jury could reasonably infer that defendant had a "motive" or desire to sexually attack and/or kill her. The evidence of (3), the manner of killing and the condition of the body, is the same in both cases: the only inference which the evidence reasonably supports in either case is that the killing resulted from a "random," violent, indiscriminate attack rather than from deliberately placed wounds inflicted according to a preconceived design.

...

We conclude that a finding of premeditation and deliberation cannot be sustained in the absence of any evidence of (1) defendant's actions prior to the killing, (2) a "motive" or "reason" from which the jury could reasonably infer that defendant intended to kill Victoria, or (3) a manner of killing from which the jury could reasonably infer that the wounds were deliberately calculated to result in death.

...

[Dissenting opinion of Burke, J., joined by McComb, J. and dissenting opinion of Sullivan, J., omitted.]

Notes

"Deliberation". In *People v. Wolff*, 61 Cal. 2d 795 (1964), a case decided prior to *Anderson*, the Supreme Court had attempted to give meaning to term "deliberation" and to differentiate it from "premeditation." The facts of the case were as follows. The defendant was a 15-year old boy at the time of the killing. In the year preceding the killing the defendant "spent a lot of time thinking about sex." He made a list of the names and addresses of seven girls in his community whom he did not know personally but whom he planned to anesthetize by ether and then either rape or photograph nude. One night about three weeks before the murder he took a container of ether and attempted to enter the home of one of these girls through the chimney, but he became wedged in and had to be rescued. Thereafter, the defendant deliberated and decided that, to accomplish his purposes, he would have to bring the girls to his house and, to do so, he would have to get rid of his mother. Several days before the killing, he took an axe handle from the garage and hid it under his mattress. After one abortive attempt, the defendant attacked his mother with the axe handle and, in the ensuing struggle, strangled her to death. He was found guilty of first degree murder and found to be sane.

The court began its analysis by reasoning that the division of murder into two degrees was meant to recognize differences in "the quantum of personal turpitude of the offenders." The court then held that, even if a defendant planned a killing, if the defendant lacked the capacity to "maturely and appreciatively reflect upon his contemplated act," the defendant had not demonstrated sufficient personal turpitude to be found guilty of first degree murder.

In 1981 the California Legislature amended Penal Code section 189 to add the following paragraph:

> To prove the killing was "deliberate and premeditated," it shall not be necessary to prove the defendant maturely and meaningfully reflected upon the gravity of his or her act.

In *People v. Stress*, 205 Cal. App. 3d 1259 (1988), the court held that the amendment to Penal Code section 189 had overruled *Wolff*. As the court explained:

> [A] finding of deliberation and premeditation is not negated by evidence a defendant's mental condition was abnormal or his perception of reality delusional unless those conditions resulted in the failure to plan or weigh considerations for and against the proposed course of action. The mental process necessary for a finding of deliberation and premeditation is not dependent on the motivation for the act.... Nor is the necessary mental process lacking when the considerations reflected on by the defendant were the product of mental disease or defect. *Id.* at 1270–71.

The Model Penal Code and Murder. The Model Penal Code does not divide murder into degrees. MPC § 210.1. As was noted earlier, the division of murder into degrees was begun in 1794 by the Pennsylvania legislature in order to limit capital punishment to the more egregious murderers. Since the Model Penal Code separately defines and limits death-eligibility (§ 210.6), the drafters concluded that there was no longer any need to maintain degrees of murder. MPC Part II Commentaries vol. 1, p. 8. California limits death-eligibility to first degree murderers who meet at least one of a list of "special circumstances" set out in Penal Code § 190.2. Since it is the special circumstances that limit the application of the death penalty, should California abandon the distinction between first and second degree murder?

People v. Wharton

53 Cal. 3d 522, 809 P.2d 290 (1991)

Lucas, C. J.

[Officers found the body of Linda Smith inside a barrel in her home.]

... A search of the apartment uncovered, among other things, several empty prescription drug bottles and a note pad with a note that began "Dear Dr. Hamilton." While most of the bottles bore the victim's name, one bore defendant's name. In addition, police found a toolbox in the garage.

An autopsy revealed the victim had been struck three times on the head with a blunt instrument, probably a hammer. The victim received one direct blow and two glancing blows. Any of the blows would have caused instant unconsciousness. Although the victim had no other broken bones or lacerations, the presence or absence of defensive wounds such as bruises could not be determined because of the advanced state of decomposition of the body. Dr. Failing, the pathologist in charge of the autopsy, testified that in his opinion, the victim died of asphyxia rather than the cerebral contusions. Because of the condition of the body, Dr. Failing could not pinpoint the time of death but opined it was probably 10 to 14 days earlier.

Police located defendant that morning in a restaurant, but he fled when police arrived. After a brief search, police found him hiding under a truck and took him into custody.

Defendant waived his *Miranda* rights (*Miranda v. Arizona* (1966) 384 U.S. 436) and agreed to speak with Officer Tonello. Defendant stated that he lived with Smith and that he spent the night of February 26th with her in their home. He affirmed that Smith was alive that night. He eventually admitted, however, that they argued and that he killed her. He explained that they had been drinking heavily that night and began to argue.[1] She threw a book at him and he hit her twice in the head. She may have hit her head on a table, but he was not sure. He admitted he was mentally aware he was hitting her but stated that he was in a rage. He eventually realized she was dead. He began writing a letter to his psychotherapist, Dr. Hamilton, and then took several pills and lay down beside Smith. He tried to kill himself by inhaling gas from the oven. He did not know what he intended to do with the body, moving it from room to room. He also stated he lit a fire in the fireplace and brought Smith's body into the room to keep her "warm." At one point, he held Smith's body to his

1. There was evidence that both defendant and the victim regularly abused alcohol, marijuana, and cocaine.

own. He eventually wrapped Smith's body in blankets and plastic bags and placed it in the barrel, where it was found by police.

Leighton Smith, the victim's ex-husband, was sorting through the victim's belongings after defendant was taken into custody. Although police had already searched the house, Leighton Smith contacted police when he discovered a hammer lying under a day bed. He also noticed many of the victim's possessions were missing, including coins, furs, jewelry, china, a television, a camera, a microwave oven, and a stereo.

There was evidence that, in order to buy cocaine, defendant sold the victim's property after, and possibly before, her death. He bartered away her car to Albert and Americo Perez for a quarter gram of cocaine plus a promise of more cocaine in the future. The Perez brothers sold the car in Mexico but agreed to retrieve it and testify against defendant in exchange for a grant of immunity. Sandra Barney testified that she helped defendant cash some of the victim's checks; on at least two occasions, she saw him write the victim's name on a check. She also testified that they used the money from the checks to buy drugs and alcohol and that defendant tried to sell the victim's jewelry. Jackie Dennis testified that defendant gave her some women's clothes and jewelry to sell and asked if she knew anyone who wanted to buy some dishes.

In addition, defendant's two psychotherapists testified and related various inculpatory statements defendant made in therapy. Defendant did not present an affirmative defense.

. . .

Discussion
Guilt Phase

1. Sufficiency of Evidence of Premeditation and Deliberation

Defendant contends there is insufficient evidence of premeditation and deliberation to support the jury's first degree murder verdict. Although defendant relies heavily on the circumstances of the crime as he described them in his confession to Officer Tonello to conclude there was insufficient evidence of premeditation, there was other evidence from which a rational trier of fact could have concluded defendant premeditated before killing. This latter evidence was admittedly not overwhelming, but "we need not be convinced beyond a reasonable doubt that defendant premeditated the murder[ ]. The relevant inquiry on appeal is whether *any* rational trier of fact could have been so persuaded." (*People v. Lucero* (1988) 44 Cal. 3d 1006.)

As in past cases, we rely on the tripartite test first set forth in *People v. Anderson* (1968) 70 Cal. 2d 15. Accordingly, we determine whether there was evidence of (1) defendant's planning activity prior to the homicide; (2) his motive to kill, as gleaned from his prior relationship or conduct with the victim; and (3) the manner of killing, from which may be inferred that defendant had a preconceived design to kill. "[T]his court sustains verdicts of first degree murder typically when there is evidence of all three types and otherwise requires at least extremely strong evidence of (1) or evidence of (2) in conjunction with either (1) or (3)."

In asserting there was no evidence of planning activity, defendant points to his confession, which tends to paint a picture of a killing during a spontaneous and uncontrolled explosion of anger, frustration, and rage. As the prosecutor argued in his closing summation, however, the fact that the hammer the likely murder weapon was not found in the toolbox suggests defendant may have removed it ahead of time and placed it nearby, "planning to be in a rage." This possibility was given some support by the testimony of defendant's psychotherapists that he was seeing them because he was afraid he would strike Smith.

Another possible scenario raised by the prosecutor in closing argument is that defendant and Smith quarreled, he became angry, went to the garage to obtain the hammer with the intent to kill Smith with it, came back and struck her as she slept. (There was evidence she was not standing when struck.) As the prosecutor properly informed the jury, "premeditation can occur in a very short period of time." Under this version, defendant's act of retrieving the hammer would constitute planning activity.

Either version of the actual crime is indicative of planning activity and reasonably inferable from the evidence. Although both are inconsistent with the circumstances of the crime as related by defendant to Officer Tonello, the jury was entitled to disbelieve defendant's self-serving statements, especially in light of the fact that he was less than forthcoming during that critical interview, at one point sarcastically directing Tonello to "do some detective work. That's what you're there for, you know." Defendant was also somewhat inconsistent in his description of the killing, at one point saying he might have strangled Smith in addition to striking her on the head, but that he was not sure. Under these circumstances, the jury's decision to disbelieve his story was not unreasonable.

The prosecutor also identified a plausible motive for the slaying. The evidence clearly showed that defendant sold some of Smith's belongings after her death and there was evidence from which the jury could have reasonably inferred that defendant was also stealing from Smith before her demise. Sometime before Smith's death, defendant told his psychotherapist that their house was apparently burglarized and some of Smith's coins and jewelry were missing. Defendant and Smith placed the remaining valuables in the car, intending to take them to the bank for safekeeping, but the car was also burglarized and the remaining items lost. Later, however, Smith found in the house property allegedly taken in the burglaries. The clear implication was that defendant took the property himself, intending to sell it, and blamed the loss on a bogus burglary.

This possibility was consistent with other evidence. Shortly before her murder, Linda Smith, defendant, and one Lewis Smith (no apparent relation) had dinner together. Defendant and Lewis Smith took Linda Smith's car to buy some liquor. She called the police and reported her car as stolen when defendant was gone for more than 45 minutes. The prosecutor invited the jury to conclude that she must have known about the prior thefts of her property because she was so quick to conclude defendant had stolen her car.

We admit that these inferences are by no means the only ones that may be drawn from the evidence and that the evidence of premeditation and deliberation is not strong. Nevertheless, the inferences urged by the prosecutor were permissible ones in that they are reasonably deducible from the evidence. Viewing the evidence in a light most favorable to the People and presuming all reasonable facts in support of the judgment, we conclude a "rational trier of fact" could have been persuaded that there was evidence of (1) planning activity, and (2) motive. Although the manner of killing was not indicative of a preconceived design to kill, appellate courts sustain verdicts of first degree murder where there is evidence of motive in conjunction with planning activity. (*Anderson, supra.*) We thus conclude there was sufficient evidence to support the jury's verdict that defendant premeditated and deliberated the killing.

. . .

Mosk, J.

I dissent.

Plainly, the evidence is insufficient to support the jury's verdict finding defendant guilty of first degree murder on the sole theory presented by the prosecution willful, deliberate, and premeditated murder. Specifically, it is insufficient as to premeditation and deliberation.

When a court assesses the sufficiency of the evidence, its "task is to determine whether a reasonable trier of fact could have found that the prosecution sustained its burden of proving the defendant guilty beyond a reasonable doubt. The judgment must be supported by substantial evidence, which has been defined as evidence that reasonably inspires confidence and is of solid value." (*People v. Morris* (1988) 46 Cal. 3d 1.) The term "substantial evidence," of course, means solid *evidence* and not mere speculation. In any given case, a court "may *speculate* about any number of scenarios that may have occurred ... A reasonable inference, however, may not be based on suspicion alone, or on imagination, speculation, supposition, surmise, conjecture, or guess work.... A finding of fact must be an inference drawn from evidence rather than ... a mere speculation as to probabilities without evidence." (*Id.*; italics in the original.)

. . .

It is plain that a rational trier of fact could not have found defendant guilty beyond a reasonable doubt of willful, deliberate, and premeditated murder: premeditation and deliberation were not proved beyond a reasonable doubt. Indeed, the evidence of these two elements is practically nonexistent, and is certainly far too insubstantial to support a finding *beyond a reasonable doubt.* At most, the record supports an inference that the killing resulted from an explosion of violence without significant forethought or reflection on the part of defendant.

Specifically, there is no substantial evidence that defendant planned his attack. In support of their opposite conclusion, the majority present what they label "possible scenario[s]" assertedly indicative of planning. Those "scenarios" rest on a crucial factual assumption, to wit, that a hammer, which was the likely murder weapon, was missing from a toolbox in a garage and was taken from that location not long before the fatal attack. That assumption, however, is unsupported. *There is simply no evidence whatever that the hammer BELONGED in the toolbox. Nor is there any evidence whatever that it had been removed RECENTLY.* The majority derive their "scenarios" from an unconventional source: argument made by the prosecutor and not from evidence adduced by the parties. The prosecutor's argument may have encouraged jury speculation that defendant planned the killing. But neither a prosecutor's argument nor "speculation" is "evidence," less still "*substantial* evidence."

Next, there is no substantial evidence that defendant had a motive to kill. In support of their opposite conclusion, the majority again turn not to evidence but to the prosecutor's argument. It is possible to indulge in speculation that defendant had a motive but it is elementary that "speculation" is not "evidence."

Finally, there is no substantial evidence that defendant employed a manner of killing that indicates a preconceived design to kill in a certain way. The majority expressly concede as much. In this they do only what necessity demands: it is pellucid that substantial evidence on the point is lacking.

Therefore, the evidence is insufficient to support the jury's verdict finding defendant guilty of willful, deliberate, and premeditated murder. The conviction must accordingly be reversed.

...

[Dissenting opinion of Broussard, J., joined by Kennard, J., omitted.]

Notes and Problem

Problem 29.

On December 22, Defendant admitted Father (his father) to the hospital. Father, who had previously been hospitalized, was suffering from numerous serious ailments, and, by the morning of December 23, his medical condition was determined to be untreatable and terminal. On December 24, Defendant visited Father. Defendant was very upset and sniffling, and kept repeating to the nurses that Father was dying. While alone in the room with Father, Defendant began to cry and to tell Father how much he loved him. Father began to cough, emitting a gurgling and rattling noise, and Defendant became very upset. Defendant then pulled a small pistol from his pants pocket, put it to Father's temple and fired four shots, killing Father. Defendant made the following statements to the police: "You can't do anything to him now. He's out of his suffering." "I promised my dad I wouldn't let him suffer."

Defendant is charged with first degree murder (P.C. §§ 187–189). What arguments should be made on whether he is guilty of that offense or of any lesser degree of homicide?

First Degree Murder by "Atrocious Means"

Although almost all first degree murders in California are such because the defendant killed with premeditation and deliberation or during the commission of, or attempt to commit, one of the listed felonies [see Chapter 6], the California Supreme Court has had occasion to discuss the elements of two of the atrocious means—lying in wait and torture.

The Court has described the elements of lying in wait as follows:

> To prove lying in wait, the prosecution must prove there was a concealment of purpose, a substantial period of watching and waiting for a favorable or opportune time to act, and that immediately thereafter the defendant launched a surprise attack on an unsuspecting victim from a position of advantage.

People v. Gurule, 28 Cal.4th 557, 630 (2002). The concealment does not have to be physical concealment—it is sufficient if the defendant concealed his purpose and intent. *People v. Ceja*, 4 Cal.4th 1134, 1140 (1993). The watching and waiting need not continue for any particular period of time, "provided that its duration is such as to show a state of mind equivalent to premeditation or deliberation." *People v. Ruiz*, 44 Cal.3d 589, 614 (1988).

In order to establish a first degree murder by torture, the prosecution must prove that the defendant caused the victim's death by means of acts involving a high probability of death and the defendant must have committed such acts with the intent to cause "cruel pain and suffering for the purpose of revenge, extortion, persuasion or for any sadistic purpose." *People v. Mincey*, 2 Cal. 4th 408, 432 (1992). The prosecution does not have to prove that the defendant intended to kill the victim, nor that the victim experienced any pain from the torturous acts. *People v. Wiley*, 18 Cal. 3d 162, 168–69 (1976).

Transferred Intent. All the cases and problems in this chapter involve defendants who killed the person they intended to kill. What is the consequence if a defendant, intending to kill one person, kills another instead? The California Supreme Court has explained why the killing is still viewed as an intentional killing:

> "[U]nder the common law doctrine of transferred intent, if *A* shoots at *B* with malice aforethought but instead kills *C*, who is standing nearby, *A* is deemed liable for murder notwithstanding lack of intent to kill *C*."

People v. Roberts, 2 Cal.4th 271, 317 (1992). Transferred intent is a legal fiction used to reach a result commensurate with the defendant's culpability, *i.e.*, a person who has intended a killing and executed his/her plans should not be punished any less because the person killed was not the intended victim.

Chapter 5

Homicide: Unintentional Killings

An unintentional killing is murder if the defendant acted with implied malice, *i.e.*, "when the circumstances attending the killing show an abandoned and malignant heart." (P.C. § 188) If malice is established, Penal Code § 189 again comes into play to determine the degree of the murder, but *the fact that a killing was unintentional precludes a finding that it was done with premeditation and deliberation.* Thus an unintentional murder can only be a first degree murder if done through the agency of one of the listed means or in the perpetration of one of the enumerated felonies. If the prosecution cannot prove malice, the defendant will be guilty of involuntary manslaughter (or vehicular manslaughter if the killing resulted from the defendant's driving) if the prosecution can prove the defendant acted with criminal negligence. Section A addresses the problem of proof of *mens rea* in the case of unintentional killings. In the case of unintentional killings, the defendant may also challenge proof of the *actus reus*, causing the death of another. Section B addresses the issue of causation.

A. The Mens Rea of Unintentional Homicides

The first three cases concern what evidence will support a finding of implied malice. In *People v. Watson*, the defendant committed a drunk driving homicide, and the Supreme Court has to decide whether, and upon what evidence, the defendant could be prosecuted for murder rather than vehicular manslaughter. *People v. Taylor* concerns a defendant convicted of murder of a fetus based on his deadly attack on a pregnant woman, and the issue is whether he can be said to have acted with implied malice even though he did not know of the fetus's existence. In *People v. Knoller*, the defendant was convicted of murder when her dogs mauled the victim, and the Supreme Court sets out the standard for the subjective component of implied malice. In the last case in the section, *Walker v. Superior Court*, the defendant is charged with involuntary manslaughter as the result of the death of the defendant's child from meningitis. The Supreme Court has to determine whether the defendant's decision not to seek medical care for her child, but to treat her child according to religious teachings, can constitute criminal negligence and, if so, whether the defendant's conduct was constitutionally protected.

People v. Watson

30 Cal. 3d 290, 637 P.2d 279 (1981)

Richardson, J.

Defendant was charged with both second degree murder (see Pen. Code, §§ 187–189) and vehicular manslaughter (§ 192, subd. 3(a)). In this pretrial proceeding, he contends that the facts underlying the alleged offense disclose, at most, gross negligence punishable under the manslaughter statute. We have concluded, however, that the facts also support a finding of implied malice (§ 188) justifying the murder charge as well.

The circumstances of the offense, as elicited at the preliminary examination, are as follows: In the late night and early morning hours of January 2 and 3, 1979, defendant Robert Watson consumed large quantities of beer in a Redding bar. Approximately an hour and a half after leaving the bar, defendant drove through a red light on a Redding street and avoided a collision with another car only by skidding to a halt in the middle of the intersection. After this near collision, defendant drove away at high speed, approached another intersection and, although he again applied his brakes, struck a Toyota sedan. Three passengers in the Toyota were ejected from the vehicle and the driver and her six-year-old daughter were killed. Defendant left 112 feet of skid marks prior to impact, and another 180 feet of skid marks to the vehicle's point of rest.

The applicable speed limit at the accident scene was 35 miles per hour. Expert testimony based on the skid marks and other physical evidence estimated defendant's speed immediately prior to applying his brakes at 84 miles per hour. At point of impact, the experts concluded that defendant's speed was approximately 70 miles per hour. Eyewitness Henke testified that defendant's car passed him "real fast" (estimated by Henke at 50 to 60 miles per hour) shortly before the collision. According to Henke, defendant swerved from the slow lane into the fast lane, suddenly braked and skidded into the intersection, and thereupon struck the other vehicle. Henke believed that the traffic light was green when defendant entered the intersection.

Defendant's blood alcohol content one-half hour after the collision was .23 percent, more than twice the percentage necessary to support a finding that he was legally intoxicated.

The complaint herein charged defendant with two counts each of second degree murder and vehicular manslaughter. At the preliminary examination, the magistrate found probable cause to charge defendant with vehicular manslaughter, but refused to hold him to answer the second degree murder counts, concluding that the facts elicited at the preliminary examination were insufficient to demonstrate the essential element of implied malice. Despite the magistrate's ruling, the People included in the information the two counts of second degree murder which were rejected by the magistrate. Defendant's section 995 motion to dismiss the murder counts was granted by the superior court, and the People appeal from the order of dismissal.

Based upon his review of the legislative history of the vehicular manslaughter statute (§ 192, subd. 3(a)), defendant claims that a murder charge is precluded. He asserts that the Legislature intended separately to classify and punish all vehicular homicide as manslaughter. We hold otherwise, concluding that nothing in the legislative history of this section suggests such an intent. Rather, we conclude that if the facts surrounding the offense support a finding of "implied malice," second degree murder may be charged; if the facts demonstrate only "gross negligence," a vehicular manslaughter charge may be sustained. Although the terms "gross negligence" and "implied malice" are similar in requiring an awareness of a risk of harm, the degrees of awareness differ. Because of that fact, the more specific vehicular manslaughter statute does not preclude application of the more general murder statute.

Finally, because the conduct of defendant in this case, reasonably viewed, exhibited wantonness and a conscious disregard for life which would support a finding of implied malice, we conclude that the order of dismissal must be reversed.

1. Application of murder statutes to vehicular homicides

Section 187, subdivision (a), provides that "Murder is the unlawful killing of a human being, or a fetus, with malice aforethought." Under section 188, malice may be express or implied, and implied malice is present "when no considerable provocation appears, or when the circumstances attending the killing show an abandoned and malignant heart." Section 189 defines first degree murder as all murder committed by specified lethal means "or by any other kind of willful, deliberate, and premeditated killing," or a killing which is committed in the perpetration of enumerated felonies; all other kinds of murder are of the second degree.

Under section 192, manslaughter is "the unlawful killing of a human being, without malice." One kind of manslaughter is defined in subdivision 3 of that section: "In the driving of a vehicle — [¶] (a) In the commission of an unlawful act, not amounting to felony, with gross negligence; or in the commission of a lawful act which might produce death, in an unlawful manner, and with gross negligence."

Defendant reasons that the general murder statutes (§§ 187–189) are preempted by the more specific provisions applicable to vehicular homicides (§ 192, subd. 3(a)). In *In re Williamson* (1954) 43 Cal. 2d 651, we said that: "[Where] the general statute standing alone would include the same matter as the special act, and thus conflict with it, the special act will be considered as an exception to the general statute whether it was passed before or after such general enactment." Defendant observes that the murder statutes deal generally with the unlawful killing of a human being, whereas the vehicular manslaughter provision deals specifically with such killing while driving a vehicle. He therefore contends that the latter statute bars the application of the former under the *Williamson* rule.

The argument contains a flaw. We have held that the *Williamson* preemption rule is applicable (1) when each element of the general statute corresponds to an element on the face of the special statute, or (2) when it appears from the statutory context that a violation of the special statute will necessarily or commonly result in a violation of the general statute. Neither of these two categories applies here. A prosecution for murder under section 187 requires a finding of malice, while section 192 specifically defines manslaughter as a killing without malice. Moreover, in light of the malice requirement, a violation of the vehicular manslaughter statute would not necessarily or commonly result in a violation of the general murder statute. Thus, the *Williamson* rule is inapplicable.

Nonetheless, defendant asserts that by charging him with second degree murder based upon implied malice, the prosecution has charged him with an unintentional killing. He argues that because vehicular manslaughter also is an unintentional killing, the two crimes are coterminous, and that the more specific statute excludes the more general one.

This argument is not persuasive. The requisite culpability for the vehicular manslaughter charged here is gross negligence, which has been defined as the exercise of so slight a degree of care as to raise a presumption of conscious indifference to the consequences. On the other hand, malice may be implied when a person, knowing that his conduct endangers the life of another, nonetheless acts deliberately with conscious disregard for life. Though these definitions bear a general similarity, they are not identical. Implied malice contemplates a subjective awareness of a higher degree of risk than does gross negligence, and involves an element of wantonness which is absent in gross negligence.

Furthermore, we have applied different tests in determining the required mental states of gross negligence or malice. A finding of gross negligence is made by applying an objective test: if a reasonable person in defendant's position would have been aware of the risk involved, then defendant is presumed to have had such an awareness. However, a finding of implied malice depends upon a determination that the defendant actually appreciated the risk involved, *i.e.*, a subjective standard.

In the present case, the prosecution will be required to show a higher degree of culpability in support of the second degree murder charge than it will to establish vehicular manslaughter. Accordingly, because section 187 and section 192, subdivision 3(a), contemplate different kinds of culpability or criminal activity, the *Williamson* rule would not preclude a second degree murder charge.

. . .

2. Probable cause to charge second degree murder

Having determined that a defendant may be charged with second degree murder upon facts which also would support a charge of vehicular manslaughter, we inquire whether the facts in the present case imply malice and therefore justify charging the greater offense, that is, whether there was probable cause to hold defendant to answer the second degree murder charge.

The magistrate and superior court concluded that no probable cause existed to support a charge of second degree murder. This determination, based upon undisputed facts, constituted a legal conclusion which is subject to independent review on appeal. In such a case, our function is to determine whether a person of ordinary caution or prudence would be led to believe and conscientiously entertain a strong suspicion that defendant committed the crime charged.

We have said that second degree murder based on implied malice has been committed when a person does "an act, the natural consequences of which are dangerous to life, which act was deliberately performed by a person who knows that his conduct endangers the life of another and who acts with conscious disregard for life." (*People v. Sedeno* (1974) 10 Cal. 3d 703.) Phrased in a different way, malice may be implied when defendant does an act with a high probability that it will result in death and does it with a base antisocial motive and with a wanton disregard for human life. (*People v. Washington* (1965) 62 Cal. 2d 777.)

Based upon our independent review of the record, we believe that there exists a rational ground for concluding that defendant's conduct was sufficiently wanton to hold him on a second degree murder charge. The facts upon which we base this conclusion are as follows: Defendant had consumed enough alcohol to raise his blood alcohol content to a level which would support a finding that he was legally intoxicated. He had driven his car to the establishment where he had been drinking, and he must have known that he would have to drive it later. It also may be presumed that defendant was aware of the hazards of driving while intoxicated. As we stated in *Taylor v. Superior Court* (1979) 24 Cal. 3d 890: "One who wilfully consumes alcoholic beverages to the point of intoxication, knowing that he thereafter must operate a motor vehicle, thereby combining sharply impaired physical and mental faculties with a vehicle capable of great force and speed, reasonably may be held to exhibit a conscious disregard of the safety of others." Defendant drove at highly excessive speeds through city streets, an act presenting a great risk of harm or death. Defendant nearly collided with a vehicle after running a red light; he avoided the accident only by skidding to a stop. He thereafter resumed his excessive speed before colliding with the victims' car, and then belatedly again attempted to brake his car before the collision (as evidenced by the extensive skid marks before and after impact) suggesting an actual awareness of the great risk of harm which he had created. In combination, these facts reasonably and readily support a conclusion that defendant acted wantonly and with a conscious disregard for human life.

We do not suggest that the foregoing facts conclusively demonstrate implied malice, or that the evidence necessarily is sufficient to convict defendant of second degree murder. On the contrary, it may be difficult for the prosecution to carry its burden of establishing implied malice to the moral certainty necessary for a conviction. Moreover, we neither contemplate nor encourage the routine charging of second degree murder in vehicular homicide cases. We merely determine that the evidence before us is sufficient to uphold the second degree murder counts in the information, and to permit the prosecution to prove, if it can, the elements of second degree murder.

We need not consider defendant's contention that the degree of his intoxication rendered him incapable of entertaining malice. Such an argument would relate to a diminished capacity defense which properly should be raised and considered at trial.

The judgment of dismissal is reversed.

Bird, C. J., dissenting.

Today, this court not only rewrites the law of implied malice but makes it a virtual certainty that any individual who knowingly drives to a social outing, takes a few drinks, and while driving home is involved in an accident in which a death occurs, may be charged with murder in the second degree. In order to achieve this unusual result, the majority ignore facts and apply an improper legal standard to reverse the magistrate's refusal to hold respondent to answer and the superior court's grant of respondent's motion to dismiss the charge of murder under Penal Code section 995.

...

At the preliminary hearing, the prosecution was required to present evidence of each element of a murder based on an implied-malice theory. As the majority recognize, those elements are that the accused, "knowing that his conduct [endangered] the life of another, nonetheless [acted] deliberately with conscious disregard for life." In other words, the accused must have (1) intended to commit an act likely to kill with (2) conscious disregard for life. (*People v. Washington* (1965) 62 Cal. 2d 777.) The majority fail to demonstrate that the existence of either element can reasonably be inferred from the facts presented below.

Given Henke's testimony, it cannot be found that respondent committed an act likely to kill. The act of speeding through a green light at 55 or 60 miles per hour in a 35-mile-per-hour zone was dangerous, but was not an act likely to result in the death of another. It was 1 o'clock in the morning. The person whose car respondent nearly collided with testified that he saw no other cars around.

...

The fact that respondent was under the influence of alcohol made his driving more dangerous. A high percentage of accidents is caused by such drivers. No one holds a brief for this type of activity. However, a rule should not be promulgated by this court that driving while under the influence of alcohol is sufficient to establish an act "likely to kill." Death or injury is not the probable result of driving while under the influence of alcohol. "Thousands, perhaps hundreds of thousands, of Californians each week reach home without accident despite their driving intoxicated." (*Taylor v. Superior Court* (1979) 24 Cal. 3d 890 (Clark, J. dis.).)

The majority also fail to demonstrate that it is reasonable to infer that respondent had a conscious disregard for life. Can a conscious disregard for life be established by the fact that several hours before the accident respondent drove his car to a bar? The majority hold as a matter of law that he "must have known" he would have to drive his car later and that he wilfully drank alcohol until he was under its influence.

How does respondent's state of mind at the time he drove to the bar and began drinking justify an inference that he had a reckless state of mind at the time of the accident? This meager evidence does not justify the inference that by drinking alcohol he harbored a conscious disregard for life when he later drove his car! I submit that the majority's reasoning that such an inference may be drawn to support a finding of implied malice will be used to establish second degree murder in every case in which a person drives a car to a bar, a friend's home, or a party, drinks alcohol so that he is under its influence, drives away and is involved in a fatal accident. Moreover, newly enacted legislation will make it easier than ever to establish implied malice. Under a bill recently signed by the Governor, the rebuttable presumption that a person is under the influence of alcohol if his blood alcohol content is 0.10 percent or more has been eliminated. Instead, the new statute makes it a crime to drive with a blood alcohol content of 0.10 percent or more. In effect, it creates a conclusive presumption that the driver is under the influence of alcohol. Under this conclusive presumption and the majority's erroneous expansion of the concept of implied malice, a person who had only a few drinks could readily find himself charged with and convicted of second degree murder.

The majority's reasoning also perpetuates the fiction that when a person drinks socially, he wilfully drinks to come under the influence of alcohol and with this knowledge drives home at a later time. This unfounded conclusion ignores social reality. "[Typically] [a person] sets out to drink without becoming intoxicated, and because alcohol distorts judgment, he overrates his capacity, and misjudges his driving ability after drinking too much." (*Taylor, supra* (Clark, J. dis.).)

Clearly, evidence regarding respondent's drinking earlier in the evening bears little relevance to his state of mind at the time of the accident. The majority's reliance on evidence of respondent's presumed state of mind before he began driving violates the basic principle that a crime cannot be committed unless there is unity of act and intent. (Pen. Code, § 20.)

The majority's errors are compounded by the fact that they improperly presume that respondent harbored a conscious disregard for life. Thus, they state that respondent "must have known" he would drive after drinking, and that it "may be presumed that [he] was aware of the hazards of driving while intoxicated." These presumptions improperly dilute the requirement that the prosecution must prove the accused's intent to commit an act likely to kill with conscious disregard for life.

The majority point to respondent's drinking as evidence of the implied-malice element that he committed an act likely to kill. However, they ignore the fact that driving while under the influence may also show lack of a conscious appreciation of the risk of harm presented to others. The majority err in deeming this evidence relevant only at trial when and if a diminished capacity defense is raised.

Finally, the majority distort the evidence and draw the wrong inference from the testimony presented at the preliminary examination that respondent put on his brakes just before the fatal accident. They infer that this shows that respondent knew of the risk he created to the lives of others. However, the majority fail to draw the obvious inference that respondent consciously sought to avoid the risk of injuring or killing anyone. The latter inference tends to disprove the element required for implied malice that the act evidenced a conscious disregard for life.

The elements of implied malice have not been established. Speeding through a green light is not an act likely to kill. Nor was this act done intentionally with conscious disregard for life. The fact that respondent earlier that evening drove to a bar is of little probative value in determining his state of mind sometime later.

The only evidence bearing significantly on respondent's state of mind was the fact that he was driving at a time when he was under the influence of alcohol. This fact tends to disprove the element of conscious disregard for life. To rule otherwise is to establish with one stroke of the pen a new crime of second degree murder for anyone who is involved in an accident when driving a vehicle while under the influence of alcohol, where the accidents results in the death of another person.

The fact that the Legislature adopted a vehicular manslaughter statute (Pen. Code. § 192, subd. 3), indicates that the Legislature intended to cover these situations. I am certain the Legislature never foresaw that this court would expand the concept of implied malice so as to rewrite the law in this area. I cannot so lightly rewrite the Legislature's statutes nor so blithely ignore the pertinent facts to achieve a judicial result. I respectfully dissent.

[Dissenting opinion of IBAÑEZ, J. omitted.]

Problem

Problem 30.

Prior to 1995, Penal Code § 22(b) had provided in part that "[e]vidence of voluntary intoxication is admissible solely on the issue of whether or not the defendant actually formed a specific intent, premeditated, deliberated, *or harbored malice* ..." In 1995, the Legislature amended the section to provide instead that such evidence "is admissible solely on the issue of whether or not the defendant actually formed a required specific intent, or, when charged with murder, whether the defendant premeditated, deliberated, or harbored *express malice aforethought* ..." What is the effect of the change? What arguments should be made as to whether the present section is constitutional?

People v. Taylor

32 Cal.4th 863, 86 P.3d 881 (2004)

BROWN, J.

A defendant shoots a woman, killing her. As a result, her fetus also dies. In the absence of evidence the defendant knew the woman was pregnant, may the defendant be held liable for the second degree implied malice murder of the fetus? We conclude he may....

[Defendant and the victim, Patty Fansler, dated and then lived together along with Fansler's three children. After a time, Fansler moved out, and defendant was upset by the breakup. In the succeeding months, defendant threatened and harassed Fansler, and, nine months after the breakup, he broke into her apartment and fired two shots, one of which killed her. At the time of her death, Fansler was not visibly pregnant, but an autopsy revealed that she was carrying a fetus between 11 and 13 weeks old. Defendant was convicted of two counts of second degree murder on a theory of implied malice.]

II. DISCUSSION

"Murder is the unlawful killing of a human being, or a fetus, with malice aforethought." (*People v. Hansen* (1994) 9 Cal.4th 300 (*Hansen*); § 187, subd. (a).) "[V]iability is not an element of fetal homicide under section 187, subdivision (a)," but the state must demonstrate "that the fetus has progressed beyond the embryonic stage of seven to eight weeks." (*People v. Davis* (1994) 7 Cal.4th 797.)

"Malice may be either express or implied. It is express when the defendant manifests 'a deliberate intention unlawfully to take away the life of a fellow creature.' (§ 188.) It is implied ... when the killing results from an intentional act, the natural consequences of which are dangerous to life, which act was deliberately performed by a person who knows that his conduct endangers the life of another and who acts with conscious disregard for life. For convenience, we shall refer to this mental state as 'conscious disregard for life.'" (*People v. Lasko* (2000) 23 Cal.4th 101.) "[I]mplied malice has both a physical and a mental component, the physical component being the performance of an act, the natural consequences of which are dangerous to life, and the mental component being the requirement that the defendant knows that his conduct endangers the life of another and ... acts with a conscious disregard for life." (*Hansen, supra.*)

"It is plain that *implied* malice aforethought does not exist in the perpetrator only in relation to an intended victim. Recklessness need not be cognizant of the identity of a victim or even of his existence." (*People v. Scott* (1996) 14 Cal.4th 544 (conc. opn. of Mosk, J.) When a defendant commits an act, the natural consequences of which are dangerous to human life, with a conscious disregard for life in general, he acts with implied malice towards those he ends up killing. There is no requirement the defendant specifically know of the existence of each victim.

To illustrate, in *People v. Watson* (1981) 30 Cal.3d 290, the defendant killed a mother and her six-year-old daughter while driving under the influence of alcohol. We found the evidence supported a conclusion that the defendant's conduct was sufficiently wanton to hold him to answer on two charges of second degree murder. Nowhere in our discussion did we indicate the defendant was required to have a subjective awareness of his particular victims, i.e., the mother and daughter killed, for an implied malice murder charge to proceed. Nothing in the language of section 187, subdivision (a), allows for a different analysis for a fetus. Indeed, had the mother in *Watson* been pregnant, it is difficult to see any logical basis on which to argue the defendant could not have been held to answer for three charges of second degree murder.

Here, as the Attorney General notes, defendant "knowingly put human life at grave risk when he fired his gun twice in an occupied apartment building." As the Attorney General observed during oral argument, if a gunman simply walked down the hall of an apartment building and fired through the closed doors, he would be liable for the murder of all the victims struck by his bullets—including a fetus of one of his anonymous victims who happened to be pregnant. Likewise, defense counsel conceded at oral argument that defendant would be guilty of implied malice murder if one of his bullets had struck an infant concealed by the bed covers. On this point, both counsel are right. Had one of Fansler's other children died during defendant's assault, there would be no inquiry into whether defendant knew the child was present for implied malice murder liability to attach. Similarly, there is no principled basis on which to require defendant to know Fansler was pregnant to justify an implied malice murder conviction as to her fetus.

In battering and shooting Fansler, defendant acted with knowledge of the danger to and conscious disregard for life in general. That is all that is required for implied malice murder. He did not need to be specifically aware how many potential victims his conscious disregard for life endangered.

...

[Dissenting opinion of Kennard, J. omitted.]

Problem

Problem 31.

Defendant shot and killed Victim, unaware that Victim was pregnant. Defendant was charged with first degree murder of Victim and second degree murder of the fetus (P.C. §§ 187–189) and with a multiple murder special circumstance (P.C. § 190.2(a)(3)). At trial, Defendant had sought, unsuccessfully, to present medical evidence to the effect that the fetus would not have survived past the second trimester because of a fatal medical condition. Defendant was convicted and the special circumstance found true, and he was sentenced to life imprisonment without possibility of parole. On appeal, what arguments might Defendant make to challenge the conviction and sentence?

People v. Knoller

41 Cal.4th 139, 158 P.3d 731 (2007)

Kennard, J.

On January 26, 2001, two dogs owned by defendant Marjorie Knoller and her husband, codefendant Robert Noel, attacked and killed Diane Whipple in the hallway of an apartment building in San Francisco. Defendant Knoller was charged with second degree murder (Pen. Code, § 189) and involuntary manslaughter (§ 192, subd. (B)); codefendant Noel, who was not present at the time of the attack on Whipple, was charged with involuntary manslaughter but not murder. Both were also charged with owning a mischievous animal that caused the death of a human being, in violation of § 399.

After a change of venue to Los Angeles County, a jury convicted defendants on all counts. Both moved for a new trial (see § 1181, subd. 6 [a trial court may grant a new trial when "the verdict or finding is contrary to law or evidence"]). The trial court denied Noel's motion. It granted Knoller's motion in part, giving her a new trial on the second degree murder charge, but denying her motion for a new trial on the other two crimes of which she was convicted (involuntary manslaughter and possession of a mischievous animal that causes death).

With respect to Knoller, whose conviction of second degree murder was based on a theory of implied malice, the trial court took the position that, to be guilty of that crime, Knoller must have known that her conduct involved *a high probability of resulting in the death of another.* Finding such awareness lacking, the trial court granted Knoller's motion for a new trial on the second degree murder conviction.

...

The Court of Appeal reversed the trial court's order granting Knoller a new trial on the second degree murder charge. It remanded the case to the trial court for reconsideration of the new trial motion in light of the Court of Appeal's holding that implied malice can be based simply on a defendant's conscious disregard of the risk of *serious bodily injury to another.* In all other respects, the Court of Appeal affirmed the convictions of both defendants.

Both defendants petitioned this court for review. We granted only Knoller's petition, limiting review to two questions: "(1) Whether the mental state required for implied malice includes only conscious disregard for human life or can it be satisfied by an awareness that the act is likely to result in great bodily injury," and "(2) Whether the trial court abused its discretion in granting Knoller's motion for new trial under Penal Code section 1181[, subdivision 6]."

With respect to the first issue, we reaffirm the test of implied malice we set out in *People v. Phillips* (1966) 64 Cal.2d 574 and reiterated in many later cases: Malice is implied when the killing is proximately caused by "an act, the natural consequences of which are dangerous to life, which act was deliberately performed by a person who knows that his conduct endangers the life of another and who acts with conscious disregard for life." In short, implied malice requires a defendant's awareness of engaging in conduct that endangers the life of another—no more, and no less.

Measured against that test, it becomes apparent that the Court of Appeal set the bar too low, permitting a conviction of second degree murder, based on a theory of implied malice, if the defendant knew his or her conduct risked causing death *or serious bodily injury.* But the trial court set the bar too high, ruling that implied malice requires a defendant's awareness that his or her conduct had a *high probability* of resulting in death, and that granting defendant Knoller a new trial was justified because the prosecution did not charge codefendant Noel with murder....

I. FACTS AND PROCEEDINGS

[In 1998, Pelican Bay State Prison inmates, Schneider and Bretches, members of the Aryan Brotherhood prison gang, set up a business with two women outside the prison to buy, raise and breed Presa Canario dogs. This breed tends to be very large, and it is "a gripping dog," used and bred for combat and guarding. The defendants are attorneys who represented one of the two women in a lawsuit over the dogs, and in the resolution of the lawsuit, the defendants acquired two of the Presa Canario dogs, Hera and Bane. Noel took the dogs to a veterinarian for examination and vaccinations and was subsequently warned by him that the dogs were huge and untrained and undisciplined and were therefore dangerous. In April, 2000, the defendants brought Hera to their sixth-floor apartment in San Francisco, and in September, 2000, they brought Bane.

[Between the time Noel and Knoller brought the dogs to their apartment and the date of the mauling of Whipple, there were about 30 incidents of the two dogs being out of control, threatening humans and other dogs. One neighbor was bitten, and several people, including a postal worker, had the dogs snarl and lunge at them. The dogs attacked other dogs, and Noel was seriously injured, requiring surgery and the insertion of steel pins in his hand, when he was bitten by one of the dogs while breaking up a dogfight. Noel and Knoller had trouble controlling the dogs, Knoller admitting in a letter to Schneider that she did not have the upper body strength to handle Bane and was having trouble with Hera. Noel and Knoller ignored all advice they received regarding handling the dogs, including advice from a dog trainer to have the dogs trained and to use a choke collar.]

Mauling victim Diane Whipple and her partner Sharon Smith lived in a sixth-floor apartment across a lobby from defendants. Smith encountered defendants' two dogs as often as once a week. In early December 2000, Whipple called Smith at work to say, with some panic in her voice, that one of the dogs had bitten her. Whipple had come upon codefendant Noel in the lobby with one of the dogs, which lunged at her and bit her in the hand. Whipple did not seek medical treatment for three deep, red indentations on one hand. Whipple made every effort to avoid defendants' dogs, checking the hallway before she went out and becoming anxious while waiting for the elevator for fear the dogs would be inside. She and Smith did not complain to apartment management because they wanted nothing to do with defendants Knoller and Noel.

On January 26, 2001, Whipple telephoned Smith to say she was going home early. At 4:00 p.m., Esther Birkmaier, a neighbor who lived across the hall from Whipple, heard dogs barking and a woman's "panic-stricken" voice calling, "Help me, help me." Looking through the peephole in her front door, Birkmaier saw Whipple lying facedown on the floor just over the threshold of her apartment with what appeared to be a dog on top of her. Birkmaier saw no one else in the hallway. Afraid to open the door, Birkmaier called 911, the emergency telephone number, and at the same time heard a voice yelling, "No, no, no" and "Get off." When Birkmaier again approached her door, she could hear barking and growling directly outside and a banging against a door. She heard a voice yell, "Get off, get off, no, no, stop, stop." She chained her door and again looked through the peephole. Whipple's body was gone and groceries were strewn about the hallway. Birkmaier called 911 a second time.

At 4:12 p.m., San Francisco Police Officers Sidney Laws and Leslie Forrestal arrived in response to Birkmaier's telephone calls. They saw Whipple's body in the hallway;

her clothing had been completely ripped off, her entire body was covered with wounds, and she was bleeding profusely. Defendant Knoller and the two dogs were not in sight.

The officers called for an ambulance. Shortly thereafter, defendant Knoller emerged from her apartment. She did not ask about Whipple's condition but merely told the officers she was looking for her keys, which she found just inside the door to Whipple's apartment.

[Whipple died, having suffered over 77 discrete injuries to her body. The medical examiner stated that, although earlier medical attention would have increased Whipple's chances of survival, she might have died anyway because she had lost one-third or more of her blood at the scene.]

[At trial,] Codefendant Noel did not testify, but he presented evidence of positive encounters between the two dogs and veterinarians, friends, and neighbors. Defendant Knoller did testify in her own defense. She referred to herself, her husband, and Pelican Bay prisoner Schneider as the "triad," and she spoke of Schneider as her "son." The two dogs had become a focal point in the relationship. She denied reading literature in the apartment referring to the vicious nature of the dogs. She thought the dogs had no personality problems requiring a professional trainer. She denied receiving or otherwise discounted any warnings about the two dogs' behavior and she maintained that virtually all the witnesses testifying to incidents with the dogs were lying. She said she never walked both dogs together. Ordinarily, she would walk Hera and codefendant Noel would walk Bane, because she had insufficient body strength to control Bane. But after Noel was injured while breaking up a fight between Bane and another dog, Knoller would sometimes walk Bane, always on a leash. She said she had just returned from walking Bane on the roof of the apartment building, and had opened the door to her apartment while holding Bane's leash, when Bane dragged her back across the lobby toward Whipple, who had just opened the door to her own apartment. The other dog, Hera, left defendants' apartment and joined Bane, who attacked Whipple. Knoller said she threw herself on Whipple to save her. She denied that Hera participated in the attack. She acknowledged not calling 911 to get help for Whipple.

Asked whether she denied responsibility for the attack on Whipple, Knoller gave this reply: "I said in an interview that I wasn't responsible but it wasn't for the—it wasn't in regard to what Bane had done, it was in regard to knowing whether he would do that or not. And I had no idea that he would ever do anything like that to anybody. How can you anticipate something like that? It's a totally bizarre event. I mean how could you anticipate that a dog that you know that is gentle and loving and affectionate would do something so horrible and brutal and disgusting and gruesome to anybody? How could you imagine that happening?"

In rebuttal, the prosecution presented evidence that the minor character of defendant Knoller's injuries—principally bruising to the hands—indicated that she had not been as involved in trying to protect mauling victim Whipple as she had claimed. Dr. Randall Lockwood, the prosecution's expert on dog behavior, testified that good behavior by a dog on some occasions does not preclude aggressive and violent behavior on other occasions, and he mentioned the importance of training dogs such as Bane and Hera *not* to fight.

The jury found Knoller guilty of second degree murder; it also found both Knoller and Noel guilty of involuntary manslaughter and owning a mischievous animal that caused the death of a human being. Both defendants moved for a new trial. The trial court denied Noel's motion. We quote below the pertinent statements by the trial court in granting Knoller's motion for a new trial on the second degree murder count.

The trial court observed: "The law requires that there be a subjective understanding on the part of the person that on the day in question—and I do not read that as being January 26th, 2001 because by this time, with all of the information that had come out dealing with the dogs, the defendants were fully on notice that they had a couple of wild, uncontrollable and dangerous dogs that were likely going to do something bad. [¶] Is the 'something bad' death? That is the ultimate question in the case. There is no question but that the something bad was going to be that somebody was going to be badly hurt. I defy either defendant to stand up and tell me they had no idea that those dogs were going to hurt somebody one day. *But can they stand up and say that they knew subjectively—not objectively and that's an important distinction—that these dogs were going to stand up and kill somebody?*" (Italics added.)

The trial court continued: "I am guided by a variety of principles. One of them is that public emotion, public outcry, feeling, passion, sympathy do not play a role in the application of the law. The other is that I am required to review all of the evidence and determine independently rather than as a jury what the evidence showed. I have laid out most of the evidence as it harms the defendants in this case. Their conduct from the time that they got the dogs to the time—to the weeks after Diane Whipple's death was despicable."

...

The trial court went on: "... When you take everything as a totality, *the question is whether or not as a subjective matter and as a matter of law Ms. Knoller knew that there was a high probability that day, or on the day before on the day after,*—I reject totally the argument of the defendants that she had to know when she walked out the door—*she was going to kill somebody that morning. The Court finds that the evidence does not support it.*" (Italics added.)

The trial court concluded it had "no choice, ... taking the Legislature's scheme, the evidence that was received, as despicable as it is, but to determine not that [defendant Knoller] is acquitted of second degree murder but to find that on the state of the evidence, *I cannot say as a matter of law that she subjectively knew on January 26th that her conduct was such that a human being was likely to die.*" (Italics added.)

The trial court mentioned another consideration: "The Court also notes a great troubling feature of this case that Mr. Noel was never charged [with murder] as Ms. Knoller was. In the Court's view, given the evidence, Mr. Noel is more culpable than she. Mr. Noel personally knew that she could not control those dogs. He could not control those dogs. Mr. Noel was substantially haughtier than she was. In brushing off all of the incidents that happened out in the street, Mr. Noel knew as a theological certainty that that dog, which had recently been operated on, was taking medication that had given it diarrhea, was going to go out into the hallway or out into the street possibly, at the hands of Ms. Knoller. He ... left her there to do that. [¶] ... And yet Mr. Noel was not charged [with murder]. Equality of sentencing and the equal administration of justice is an important feature in any criminal court. That played a role as well." The trial court then granted defendant Knoller's motion for a new trial on the second degree murder count.

...

II. THE ELEMENTS OF IMPLIED MALICE

Murder is the unlawful killing of a human being, or a fetus, with malice aforethought (§ 187, subd. (a)). Malice may be express or implied (§ 188). At issue here is the definition of "implied malice."

Defendant Knoller was convicted of second degree murder as a result of the killing of Diane Whipple by defendant's dog, Bane. Second degree murder is the unlawful killing of a human being with malice aforethought but without the additional elements, such as willfulness, premeditation, and deliberation, that would support a conviction of first degree murder. Section 188 provides: "[M]alice may be either express or implied. It is express when there is manifested a deliberate intention to take away the life of a fellow creature. It is implied, when no considerable provocation appears, or when the circumstances attending the killing show an abandoned and malignant heart."

The statutory definition of implied malice, a killing by one with an "abandoned and malignant heart" (§ 188), is far from clear in its meaning. Indeed, an instruction in the statutory language could be misleading, for it "could lead the jury to equate the malignant heart with an evil disposition or a despicable character" (*People v. Phillips*) instead of focusing on a defendant's awareness of the risk created by his or her behavior. "Two lines of decisions developed, reflecting judicial attempts 'to translate this amorphous anatomical characterization of implied malice into a tangible standard a jury can apply.'" (*People v. Nieto Benitez* (1992) 4 Cal.4th 91, quoting *People v. Protopappas* (1988) 201 Cal.App.3d 152.) Under both lines of decisions, implied malice requires a defendant's awareness of the risk of death to another.

The earlier of these two lines of decisions, as this court observed in *Nieto Benitez*, originated in Justice Traynor's concurring opinion in *People v. Thomas* (1953) 41 Cal.2d 470, which stated that malice is implied when "the defendant for a base, antisocial motive and with wanton disregard for human life, does an act that involves a high degree of probability that it will result in death." (We here refer to this as the *Thomas* test.) The later line dates from this court's 1966 decision in *People v. Phillips*: Malice is implied when the killing is proximately caused by "an act, the natural consequences of which are dangerous to life, which act was deliberately performed by a person who knows that his conduct endangers the life of another and who acts with conscious disregard for life." (The *Phillips* test.)

In *People v. Watson* (1981) 30 Cal.3d 290, we held that these two definitions of implied malice in essence articulated the same standard. Concerned, however, that juries might have difficulty understanding the *Thomas* test's concept of "wanton disregard for human life," we later emphasized that the "better practice in the future is to charge juries solely in the straightforward language of the 'conscious disregard for human life' definition of implied malice," the definition articulated in the *Phillips* test. (*People v. Dellinger* (1989) 49 Cal.3d 1212.) The standard jury instructions thereafter did so....

III. THE COURT OF APPEAL'S TEST FOR IMPLIED MALICE

As discussed in the preceding part, the great majority of this court's decisions establish that a killer acts with implied malice only when acting with an awareness of *endangering human life*. This principle has been well settled for many years, and it is embodied in the standard jury instruction given in murder cases, including this one. The Court of Appeal here, however, held that a second degree murder conviction, based on a theory of implied malice, can be based simply on a defendant's awareness of the risk of causing *serious bodily injury* to another.

[The court distinguished three cases relied on by the Court of Appeal, concluding that neither *People v. Conley* (1966) 64 Cal.2d 310, nor *People v. Poddar* (1974) 10 Cal.3d 750 addressed the issue presented in the instant case and that any language in *People v. Coddington* (2000) 23 Cal.4th 529 suggesting that knowledge of the likelihood of serious bodily injury permits an inference of implied malice, was inconsistent, not only with the holding in that case, but also with the court's views expressed in other decisions.]

... We conclude that a conviction for second degree murder, based on a theory of implied malice, requires proof that a defendant acted with conscious disregard of the danger to human life. In holding that a defendant's conscious disregard of the risk of serious bodily injury suffices to sustain such a conviction, the Court of Appeal erred.

IV. THE TRIAL COURT'S GRANT OF A NEW TRIAL ON THE SECOND DEGREE MURDER CHARGE

We now turn to the second issue raised by the petition for review—whether the trial court abused its discretion in granting defendant Knoller a new trial on the second degree murder charge. Such an abuse of discretion arises if the trial court based its decision on impermissible factors or on an incorrect legal standard.

In granting Knoller a new trial, the trial court properly viewed implied malice as requiring a defendant's awareness of the danger that his or her conduct will result in another's *death* and not merely in serious bodily injury. But the court's ruling was legally flawed in other respects. As we explain below, the trial court based its ruling on an inaccurate definition of implied malice, and it inappropriately relied on the prosecutor's failure to charge codefendant Noel with murder.

As discussed earlier in part II, this court before its decision in *People v. Dellinger*, had defined implied malice in two similar but somewhat different ways....

Here, the trial court properly instructed the jury in accordance with the *Phillips* test. But when the court evaluated defendant Knoller's new trial motion, it relied on language from the *Thomas* test, and as explained below, its description of that test was inaccurate. The court stated that a killer acts with implied malice when the killer "*subjectively knows*, based on everything, that the conduct that he or she is about to engage in has a *high probability of death* to another human being" and thus the issue in this case was "whether or not as a *subjective* matter and as a matter of law Ms. Knoller *knew* that there was a *high probability*" that her conduct would result in someone's death. (Italics added.) But "high probability of death" is the *objective*, not the *subjective*, component of the *Thomas* test, which asks whether the defendant's act or conduct "involves a high probability that it will result in death." The *subjective* component of the *Thomas* test is whether the defendant acted with "a base, antisocial motive and with wanton disregard for human life." Nor does the *Phillips* test require a defendant's awareness that his or her conduct has a *high probability* of causing death. Rather, it requires only that a defendant acted with a "conscious disregard for human life."

As just shown, in treating the objective component of the *Thomas* test as the subjective component of that test, the trial court applied an erroneous definition of implied malice in granting defendant Knoller a new trial on the second degree murder charge.

[The court also was troubled by the fact that the trial judge seemed to base his grant of a new trial at least in part on the different treatment received by the co-defendant Noel. Without deciding whether such consideration was ever appropriate, the court held that it was not appropriate in this case because the differential charging was justified because the defendant was present and nominally in control of the dogs at the time of the killing and Noel was not.]

V. CONCLUSION AND DISPOSITION

In sum, the trial court abused its discretion in granting defendant Knoller a new trial on the second degree murder charge. That court erroneously concluded both that Knoller could not be guilty of murder, based on a theory of implied malice, unless she appreciated that her conduct created a high probability of someone's death, and that a new trial was justified because the prosecution did not charge codefendant Noel with murder. It is uncertain whether the trial court would have reached the same result using correct legal standards. Moreover, the Court of Appeal, in reversing the trial court's order, also erred, mistakenly reasoning that implied malice required only a showing that the defendant appreciated the risk of serious bodily injury. Under these circumstances, we conclude that the matter should be returned to the trial court to reconsider its new trial order in light of the views set out in this opinion.

Note and Problems

Problem 32.

Although it is a misdemeanor to keep a fighting dog (P.C. § 597.5), Defendant raised dogs for fighting purposes and bought "Willy," a pit bull, from a breeder of fighting dogs. The breeder told Defendant that Willy was a good fighter and had an exceptionally hard bite, and he said, "[A] dog won't go an hour with Willy and live." Defendant kept Willy on a conditioning program to increase his endurance and fought him in matches around the country. Willy was tethered in Defendant's backyard, where he blocked access to Defendant's marijuana plants, but there was no obstacle to reaching Willy. Willy had never attacked a human being, but, even pit bulls with no prior history of aggression have been known to become highly aggressive "when at large, in a pack, when confronted by any aggressive dog or under other unpredictable situations." Victim was 2 1/2 years old, and his family lived next door to Defendant. Defendant had warned Victim's mother that Willy was a dangerous dog but assured her that she should not be concerned because the dog was behind a fence. One afternoon, when Victim's mother left him for a minute, he wandered into Defendant's yard and was attacked and killed by Willy. Defendant is charged with second degree murder (P.C. §§ 187–189). What arguments should be made as to his guilt?

Problem 33.

Defendant lived in a house with her boyfriend, Boyfriend, and her four children. Defendant had a long history of drug addiction, and she sold drugs from the house and regularly smoked methamphetamine. One of her children was Baby, who was three months old. She normally fed Baby from a bottle, but she also breast-fed him. On one occasion when Defendant was breast-feeding Baby, Boyfriend saw her and demanded to know what she was doing and warned her that she better not be breast-feeding the baby. Defendant told him to mind his own business. Baby subsequently died of methamphetamine poisoning as a result of ingesting substantial amounts of methamphetamine through breast-feeding. Defendant is now charged with second degree murder (P.C. §§ 187–189). What are the arguments as to her guilt of the charge?

Heat of Passion and Imperfect Self-Defense in Unintentional Killings. Do the heat of passion and imperfect self-defense defenses to malice [see Chapter 4] apply to unintentional killings, and, if so, what crime has the defendant who kills under such circumstances committed? The California Supreme Court answered the question in *People v. Lasko*, 23 Cal.4th 101 (2000) (heat of passion) and *People v. Blakeley*, 23 Cal.4th 82 (2000) (imperfect self-defense), holding that these partial defenses do apply to unintentional killings and that a defendant successfully asserting the defense is guilty of voluntary manslaughter. The court overruled lower court cases which had held that intent to kill was an element of voluntary manslaughter.

Walker v. Superior Court

47 Cal. 3d 112, 763 P.2d 852 (1988)

Mosk, J.

We consider in this case whether a prosecution for involuntary manslaughter (Pen. Code, § 192, subd. (b)) … can be maintained against the mother of a child who died of meningitis after receiving treatment by prayer in lieu of medical attention. We conclude that the prosecution is permitted by statute as well as the free exercise and due process clauses of the state and federal Constitutions.

Defendant Laurie Grouard Walker is a member of the Church of Christ, Scientist (hereafter the Church). Her four-year-old daughter, Shauntay, fell ill with flu-like symptoms on February 21, 1984, and four days later developed a stiff neck. Consistent with the tenets of her religion, defendant chose to treat the child's illness with prayer rather than medical care.[1] Defendant contacted an accredited Christian Science prayer practitioner who thereafter prayed for Shauntay and visited the child on two occasions. Defendant also engaged a Christian Science nurse who attended Shauntay on February 27 and again on March 6 and 8.[2] Shauntay nevertheless lost weight, grew disoriented and irritable during the last week of her illness, and died on March 9 of acute purulent meningitis after a period of heavy and irregular breathing. During the 17 days she lay ill, the child received no medical treatment.

[The court first addressed and rejected defendant's claim that the exemption for treatment by spiritual means provided for in P.C. § 270[3] constituted, under *In re Williamson* 43 Cal.2d 651, 276 P.2d 593 (1954), an exemption for purposes of Pen. Code § 192 (b). The court also held that other statutes recognizing prayer healing did not create exemptions for purposes of the manslaughter statute.]

C. Defendant's Conduct and the Standard for Criminal Culpability

Taking a wholly different tack, defendant next contends that she cannot be convicted ... regardless of the availability of a religious exemption. She rests this contention on a claim that the People will be unable to prove the degree of culpability necessary to convict her [criminal negligence] ... We have defined criminal negligence

1. Members of the Church "believe that disease is a physical manifestation of errors of the mind." The use of medicine is believed to perpetuate such error and is therefore discouraged. Nonetheless, "the Church sets up no abstract criteria for determining what diseases or injuries should be treated by prayer or other methods but, rather, leaves such questions to individual decision in concrete instances.... If some turn in what they think is an urgent time of need to medical treatment for themselves or their children, they are *not*—contrary to some recent charges—stigmatized by their church."

2. The Church describes in an amicus curiae brief the role of Christian Science practitioners and nurses: "[Christian Science practitioners are] individuals who devote their full time to healing through prayer, or spiritual treatment. These individuals are approved for listing by the Church in The Christian Science Journal, after having given evidence of moral character and healing ability. Practitioners determine their own charges, usually from seven to fifteen dollars per day of treatment, and are paid by their patients.... The practitioner's work, however, is a religious vocation, a ministry of spiritual healing in its broadest sense. [¶] Christian Scientists may also call upon the services of a Christian Science nurse, who provides such practical care as dressing of wounds for those having spiritual treatment."

3. The statute reads in pertinent part: "If a parent of a minor child willfully omits, without lawful excuse, to furnish necessary clothing, food, shelter or medical attendance, or other remedial care for his or her child, he or she is guilty of a misdemeanor.... [¶] If a parent provides a minor with treatment by spiritual means through prayer alone in accordance with the tenets and practices of a recognized church or religious denomination, by a duly accredited practitioner thereof, such treatment shall constitute 'other remedial care', as used in this section."

as "aggravated, culpable, gross, or reckless, that is, the conduct of the accused must be such a departure from what would be the conduct of an ordinarily prudent or careful man under the same circumstances as to be incompatible with a proper regard for human life, or, in other words, a disregard of human life or an indifference to consequences.... [Such negligence] is ordinarily to be determined pursuant to the general principles of negligence, the fundamental of which is knowledge, actual or imputed, that the act of the slayer tended to endanger life." (*People v. Penny* (1955) 44 Cal. 2d 861.) Defendant makes two arguments for the claim that her conduct cannot, as a matter of law, constitute such negligence.

She first contends that the defenses recognized at English common law are available to her under Civil Code section 22.2, which reads: "The common law of England, so far as it is not repugnant to or inconsistent with the Constitution of the United States, or the Constitution or laws of this State, is the rule of decision in all the courts of this State." She cites two English cases from the 19th century in support of the proposition that the common law recognized treatment by prayer in lieu of medicine as legally insufficient to constitute criminal negligence. While we note that common law defenses, with limited exceptions, are unavailable in California, we need look no further than the cases themselves to dispose of defendant's contention.

The opinion of the court in *Regina v. Wagstaffe* (Cen. Crim. Ct. 1868) 10 Cox. Crim. Cas. 530, consists of a vaguely worded jury charge. The court instructed the jury that criminal negligence "was a very wide question.... At different times people had come to different conclusions as to what might be done with a sick person.... [A] man might be convicted of manslaughter because he lived in a place where all the community was of a contrary opinion, and in another he might be acquitted because they were all of his opinion...." The court asked rhetorically whether it was "intended by God Almighty that persons should content themselves by praying for His assistance, without helping themselves, or resorting to such means as were within their reach for that purpose?" and concluded with the observation that the defendants appeared sincere and affectionate. Although the defendants were subsequently acquitted, the fact that the jury itself resolved the question of criminal negligence negates the claim that the court in *Wagstaffe* recognized a legal defense to the charge. Furthermore, its jury instructions merely restated the principle that criminal negligence is a question of fact to be determined in light of contemporary community standards, which at the time made the particular question a close one.

The second case cited by defendant makes this point quite clearly. In *Regina v. Hines* (1874) 80 Cent. Crim. Ct. 309, the court dismissed an indictment for manslaughter against a parent who had exclusively prayed for an ill child. Although the court ruled that the conduct was not criminally negligent as a matter of law, to state the holding is to refute its application 114 years later: the court considered and rejected the proposition that a parent who treated a child by spiritual care "instead of calling in a doctor to apply blisters, leeches, and calomel," was guilty of criminal negligence. Were blisters, leeches and calomel the medical alternative to prayer today, quite likely defendant's reliance on *Hines* would more fully resonate with this court. Medical science has advanced dramatically, however, and we may fairly presume that the community standard for criminal negligence has changed accordingly. Nineteenth-century English common law thus fails to establish a defense, as a matter of law, to charges arising today for criminal negligence in the death of a child treated by prayer alone.

Defendant next contends that her actions are legally insufficient to constitute criminal negligence under the definition of that conduct established in the decisions of this court. Emphasizing her sincere concern and good faith in treating Shauntay with prayer, she claims that her conduct is incompatible with the required degree of culpability. Defendant does not dispute, however, that criminal negligence must be evaluated objectively (*People v. Watson* (1981) 30 Cal. 3d 290; *People v. Penny* (1955) 44 Cal. 2d 861). The question is whether "a reasonable person in defendant's position would have been aware of the risk involved ..." If so, "defendant is presumed to have had such an awareness."

The significance of this principle was well illustrated in *People v. Burroughs* (1984) 35 Cal. 3d 824, a case involving a "self-styled 'healer'" who provided "'deep' abdominal massages" to a leukemic who thereafter died of a massive abdominal hemorrhage. We observed that "There is no allegation made, nor was there any evidence adduced at trial, that [the defendant] at any time harbored any intent even to harm [the victim] in the slightest fashion." "Indeed, nowhere is it claimed that defendant attempted to perform any action with respect to [the victim] other than to heal him...." Nonetheless, we determined that the defendant could be charged with criminally negligent involuntary manslaughter. The relevant inquiry, then, turns not on defendant's subjective intent to heal her daughter but on the objective reasonableness of her course of conduct.[17]

In view of this standard, we must reject defendant's assertion that no reasonable jury could characterize her conduct as criminally negligent for purposes of sections 192(b) and 273a(1) [felony child endangerment]. As the court in *People v. Atkins* (1975) 53 Cal. App. 3d 348, observed in affirming the involuntary manslaughter and felony child-endangerment conviction of a parent whose child died for want of medical care, criminal negligence "could have been found to have consisted of the [mother's] failure to seek prompt medical attention for [her son], rather than waiting several days. There is evidence she knew, or should have known, that [her son] was seriously injured.... Viewing [the evidence] in the light most favorable to the prosecution, there is substantial evidence here of involuntary manslaughter based on the lack of due caution and circumspection in omitting to take the child to a doctor." When divorced of her subjective intent, the alleged conduct of defendant here is essentially indistinguishable.

...

17. Compare LaFave and Scott's comment that "an honest belief that prayer is a better cure than medicine, that Providence can heal better than doctors, might serve to negative the awareness of risk which is required for manslaughter in those states which use a *subjective* test of criminal negligence" (LaFave & Scott, Criminal Law (1972) p. 590, fn. 23, italics added).

In sum, we reject the proposition that the provision of prayer alone to a seriously ill child cannot constitute criminal negligence as a matter of law. Whether this defendant's particular conduct was sufficiently culpable to justify conviction of involuntary manslaughter and felony child endangerment remains a question in the exclusive province of the jury.

II.
Constitutional Defenses

A. Free Exercise Under the First Amendment

In the absence of a statutory basis to bar defendant's prosecution, we necessarily reach her constitutional claims. Defendant and the Church first contend that her conduct is absolutely protected from criminal liability by the First Amendment to the United States Constitution and article I, section 4, of the California Constitution. We do not agree.

The First Amendment bars government from "prohibiting the free exercise" of religion. Although the clause absolutely protects religious belief, religiously motivated conduct "remains subject to regulation for the protection of society." *Cantwell v. Connecticut* (1940) 310 U.S. 296. To determine whether governmental regulation of religious conduct is violative of the First Amendment, the gravity of the state's interest must be balanced against the severity of the religious imposition. If the regulation is justified in view of the balanced interests at stake, the free exercise clause requires that the policy additionally represent the least restrictive alternative available to adequately advance the state's objectives.

Defendant does not dispute the gravity of the governmental interest involved in this case, as well she should not. Imposition of felony liability for endangering or killing an ill child by failing to provide medical care furthers an interest of unparalleled significance: the protection of the very lives of California's children, upon whose "healthy, well-rounded growth … into full maturity as citizens" our "democratic society rests, for its continuance …" *Prince v. Massachusetts* (1944) 321 U.S. 158. Balanced against this interest is a religious infringement of significant dimensions. Defendant unquestionably relied on prayer treatment as an article of genuine faith, the restriction of which would seriously impinge on the practice of her religion. We note, however, that resort to medicine does not constitute "sin" for a Christian Scientist, does not subject a church member to stigmatization, does not result in divine retribution, and, according to the Church's amicus curiae brief, is not a matter of church compulsion.

Regardless of the severity of the religious imposition, the governmental interest is plainly adequate to justify its restrictive effect. As the United States Supreme Court stated in *Prince*, "Parents may be free to become martyrs themselves. But it does not follow they are free, in identical circumstances, to make martyrs of their children before they have reached the age of full legal discretion when they can make that choice for themselves." The court in *Prince* considered a free-exercise claim asserted by parents whose religious beliefs required that their children sell religious tracts in violation of child labor laws. If parents are not at liberty to "martyr" children by taking their labor, it follows a fortiori that they are not at liberty to martyr children by taking their very lives. As the court explained, "The right to practice religion freely does not include liberty to expose the community or child to communicable disease or the latter to ill health or death."

In an attempt to avoid this inexorable conclusion, the Church argues at length over the purportedly pivotal distinction between the governmental compulsion of a religiously objectionable act and the governmental prohibition of a religiously motivated act. Accepting arguendo the force of the distinction, we find that it has no relevance in a case involving an interest of this magnitude. As the court in *Prince* recognized, parents have *no* right to free exercise of religion at the price of a child's life, regardless of the prohibitive or compulsive nature of the governmental infringement. Furthermore, the United States Supreme Court has specifically sustained the compulsion of religiously prohibited conduct for interests no more compelling than here implicated. In *Jacobson v. Massachusetts* (1905) 197 U.S. 11, the court upheld a law compelling the vaccination of children for communicable diseases in the face of parental religious objections. In *United States v. Lee* (1982) 455 U.S. 252, the court upheld a law requiring that the Amish violate the tenets of their faith by participating in the Social Security system. And in *Gillette v. United States* (1971) 401 U.S. 437, the court upheld the government's right to compel certain conscientious objectors to make war despite the religious character of their objections. We see no basis in these precedents for the conclusion that parents may constitutionally insulate themselves from state compulsion so long as their life-threatening religious conduct takes the form of an omission rather than an act.

The imposition of felony liability for failure to seek medical care for a seriously ill child is thus justified by a compelling state interest. To survive a First Amendment challenge, however, the policy must also represent the least restrictive alternative available to the state. Defendant and the Church argue that civil dependency proceedings advance the governmental interest in a far less intrusive manner. This is not evident. First, we have already observed the profoundly intrusive nature of such proceedings; it is not clear that parents would prefer to lose custody of their children pursuant to a disruptive and invasive judicial inquiry than to face privately the prospect of criminal liability. Second, child dependency proceedings advance the governmental interest only when the state learns of a child's illness in time to take protective measures, which quite likely will be the exception rather than the rule: "Under ordinary circumstances, ... the case of a true believer in faith healing will not even come to the attention of the authorities, unless and until someone dies." (Comment, *Religious Beliefs and the Criminal Justice System: Some Problems of the Faith Healer* (1975) 8 Loy. L.A. L. Rev. 396.) Finally, the imposition of criminal liability is reserved for the actual loss or endangerment of a child's life and thus is narrowly tailored to those instances when governmental intrusion is absolutely compelled.

We conclude that an adequately effective and less restrictive alternative is not available to further the state's compelling interest in assuring the provision of medical care to gravely ill children whose parents refuse such treatment on religious grounds.

Accordingly, the First Amendment and its California equivalent do not bar defendant's criminal prosecution.

B. Due Process Right to Fair Notice of Illegal Conduct

[Defendant argued that to convict her would violate due process because Penal Code § 270 authorized treatment by prayer, and the manslaughter statute gave no fair notice regarding the point at which lawful prayer treatment becomes unlawful.] Justice Holmes correctly answers: "[The] law is full of instances where a man's fate depends on his estimating rightly, that is, as the jury subsequently estimates it, some matter of degree.... An act causing death may be murder, manslaughter, or misadventure, according to the degree of danger attending it by common experience in the circumstances known to the actor." (*Nash v. United States* (1913) 229 U.S. 373.) The "matter of degree" that persons relying on prayer treatment must estimate rightly is the point at which their course of conduct becomes criminally negligent. In terms of notice, due process requires no more.

...

Note

Criminal Negligence. In general, reference to negligence in criminal law means "gross negligence" or "criminal negligence." Courts have been inconsistent in defining precisely what is meant by these terms, but there is general agreement that something more than simple tort negligence is involved. Notice the definition given in *Walker*:

> We have defined criminal negligence as "aggravated, culpable, gross, or reckless, that is, the conduct of the accused must be such a departure from what would be the conduct of an ordinarily prudent or careful man under the same circumstances as to be incompatible with a proper regard for human life, or, in other words, a disregard of human life or an indifference to consequences ..."

Though this definition refers to "recklessness," criminal negligence is an objective mental state, *i.e.*, the prosecution need not prove that the accused foresaw the risk, only that a reasonable person would have.

B. Causation

In the last two cases in the chapter, the issue is causation. Unlike the situation in torts, the issue of causation arises relatively infrequently in criminal law, in large part because most crimes (other than homicides) are defined in terms of particular *acts* rather than particular *results*. The traditional rule is that a defendant will be guilty of homicide if his/her actions are a cause-in-fact of the death and if there is no intervening cause that is so overwhelming as to be superseding. Thus, the analysis of causation involves two steps. The first step is determining whether the defendant's actions were the cause-in-fact of a death.[a] If the defendant was not, then there was no causation. Even if the defendant was a cause-in-fact, he/she may nonetheless not be liable if the death actually resulted from an intervening cause and was unforeseeable. Both of the cases address this issue of proximate causation. In *People v. Roberts*, the issue arose because the defendant had taken no action toward the ultimate victim, who was killed by the man the defendant did attack. In *People v. Armitage*, the issue arose because the defendant and the victim were joint participants in a course of reckless behavior, and the victim's own actions were the immediate cause of his death.

People v. Roberts

2 Cal. 4th 271, 826 P.2d 274 (1992)

Mosk, J.

[Defendant Roberts, an inmate in a state prison, participated with others in a knife attack on Gardner, another prisoner. Gardner received 11 stab wounds which were ultimately fatal. In a daze after the attack, Gardner picked up a knife dropped by one of the assailants and staggered up a flight of stairs in pursuit of Menefield, an accomplice of defendant. Officer Patch, a guard in the prison, attempted to stop Gardner, and Gardner, in a "purely reflexive" response, stabbed Patch who died as a result of the wound. Defendant was convicted of the murder of Patch.]

. . .

C. *Liability for the Killing of Officer Patch*

At trial, defendant moved for a judgment of acquittal on the charge of the murder of Officer Patch, on the ground there was insufficient evidence of his criminal liability for that death. The court denied the motion. Defendant now contends there was insufficient evidence to find him liable for the first degree murder of Patch. He also contends the jury was incorrectly instructed on the issue.

As will appear, we conclude there was sufficient evidence for the jury to find that defendant's act was the proximate cause of the murder of Patch. But the instruction removed the element of proximate cause from the jury's consideration, an error of constitutional magnitude that requires reversal under United States Supreme Court precedent. We therefore reverse defendant's conviction for that murder.

. . . [T]he prosecution persuaded the court that if defendant caused Gardner to lose his faculties and stab Patch impulsively or unreasoningly, Gardner's blow was a dependent intervening act for which foreseeability was not required. The court read the following instruction: "A defendant is the proximate cause of the death of another

---

a. Generally, it is relatively easy to resolve whether the defendant was the cause-in-fact of a death. The question is whether the result would have occurred "but for" the accused's conduct. Even if the victim was suffering from a preexisting condition, if the defendant's actions made a substantial contribution to the death, he/she is the cause-in-fact. See *People v. Stamp*, 2 Cal. App. 3d 203 (1969) (defendants guilty of murder when robbery precipitated victim's heart attack).

even though the immediate cause of the death is the act of a third person, if the third person is no longer a free moral agent as the direct result of the defendant's unlawful act. [¶] A defendant who, in conscious and reckless disregard for human life, intentionally and unlawfully inflicts an injury upon a third person is criminally responsible for the acts of that person while in delirium or a similar state of unconsciousness where such condition is the direct result of the defendant's unlawful act. [¶] It is immaterial that the defendant could not reasonably have foreseen the harmful result.... [¶] If the evidence establishes that, at the time of the assault upon Albert Patch, Charles Gardner was unconscious due to hypovolemic shock caused by the unlawful act of a defendant, he was not a free moral agent and the defendant is responsible for his act."[9]

The precise causation question may be posed as follows: what is the liability of A for an assault on B that deprives B of his reason and causes him to attack C, who lies some distance away? ...

The object of the criminal law is to deter the individual from committing acts that injure society by harming others, their property, or the public welfare, and to express society's condemnation of such acts by punishing them. "The purpose of the criminal law is to define socially intolerable conduct, and to hold conduct within ... limits ... reasonably acceptable from the social point of view" (Perkins & Boyce, Criminal Law (3d ed. 1982)). "Modern penal law is founded on moral culpability. The law punishes a person for a criminal act only if he is morally responsible for it. To do otherwise would be both inhumane and unenlightened" (*United States v. Fielding* (D.D.C. 1957) 148 F. Supp. 46).

Of course, moral culpability is found in homicide cases when, despite the lack of any intent to kill, the consequences of the evil act are so natural or probable that liability is established as a matter of policy. Thus, for example, the Legislature has chosen to designate certain felonies as so inherently dangerous that death in the course of their commission or completion constitutes first degree murder (§ 189). Or, under the common law doctrine of transferred intent, if A shoots at B with malice aforethought but instead kills C, who is standing nearby, A is deemed liable for murder notwithstanding lack of intent to kill C. And liability for second degree murder will attach if the circumstances of an act show express or implied malice, which latter mental state may be found "when the circumstances attending the killing show an abandoned and malignant heart" (§ 188).

In other words, implied malice may be found when a defendant, knowing that his or her conduct endangers life and acting with conscious disregard of the danger, commits an act the natural consequences of which are dangerous to life. Thus, to invoke a classic example, a person who fires a bullet through a window, not knowing or caring whether anyone is behind it, may be liable for homicide regardless of any intent to kill.

---

9. The jury was told that only if Gardner was a free moral agent should it undertake a foreseeability analysis. The jury found that "Gardner was unconscious due to hypovolemic shock or similar cause" and rejected the option that he was a free moral agent.

Likewise, principles of proximate cause may sometimes assign homicide liability when, foreseeable or not, the consequences of a dangerous act directed at a second person cause an impulsive reaction that so naturally leads to a third person's death that the evil actor is deemed worthy of punishment. The few cases on point find their foundation in the famous intentional tort case of *Scott v. Shepherd* (1773) 96 Eng. Rep. 525. Young Shepherd threw a lighted gunpowder squib into a crowded marketplace. The recipient threw it to another, who threw it to another, who threw it to Scott, another minor. Scott was partially blinded when the device exploded. The jury awarded Scott £ 100 and the court affirmed, holding that the chain of causation was not broken.

Our research discloses a few cases in the annals of American law that, following *Scott v. Shepherd*, have found criminal liability for the death of a third party from the second party's impulsive reaction to the dangerous act. In those cases, physical proximity allowed the trier of fact to find the victim's death to be the natural and probable consequence of the defendant's violence and hence proximately caused by the defendant's act.

Letner v. State (Tenn. 1927) 299 S.W. 1049 is prototypical. The defendant was angry about a theft and a burglary and decided to sink the boat that the miscreants, Walter and Alfred, were using to cross the Emory River. The defendant fired two shots at the boat; neither found its mark, but both landed within six feet. To save himself, Walter dove out, causing the boat to capsize. Both he and Alfred drowned. Defendant was indicted for Alfred's murder; the jury found him guilty of involuntary manslaughter.

The Tennessee Supreme Court upheld the conviction. Citing, inter alia, *Scott v. Shepherd*, the court concluded, "By firing the gun the defendant caused Walter ... to take to the water, resulting in the overturning of the boat and the drowning of Alfred." "We are of the opinion that the wrongful act of the defendant ... was the primary proximate cause of their death; that the act of Walter ... in capsizing the boat was the natural result of the wrongful act of defendant, and renders the latter liable for their consequential death."

As alluded to above, the key fact in *Letner v. State*, as in *Scott v. Shepherd*, was that the eventual victim was physically close enough that the court could hold his death to be the natural and probable consequence of the defendant's act. The same circumstance accompanied another early case considering analogous facts. In *Belk v. The People* (Ill. 1888) 17 N.E. 744, the defendants were alleged to have negligently allowed their team of horses to break loose on a narrow country lane. The team collided with a wagon in plain sight just ahead, causing that wagon's team of horses to panic and run away and thereby throwing the victim, a passenger, to her death. The court reversed the resulting manslaughter convictions on other grounds, but noted, "Between the acts of omission or commission of the defendants, by which it is alleged the collision occurred, and the injury of the deceased, there was not an interposition of a human will acting independently ... or any extraordinary natural phenomena, to break the causal connection. It may be fairly said that what followed the colliding of the defendants' team with the wagon in which the deceased was riding, was the natural and probable effect of the collision ..."

...

Here, following an instruction that foreseeability was not to be considered, the jury found defendant guilty of murder in the first degree for Gardner's killing of Patch. The questions are threefold: was there sufficient evidence to confer liability for first degree murder; was there sufficient evidence of proximate cause for any criminal liability to attach to defendant for Patch's death; and does the instruction regarding foreseeability require reversal of defendant's conviction?

The first question need not long detain us. Liability for first degree murder cannot attach absent evidence of premeditation and deliberation or of other acts irrelevant to this discussion. There is no evidence whatever that defendant contemplated the murder of Patch, much less premeditated and deliberated it. On that ground, the first degree murder conviction cannot stand, for we discern no other doctrine, such as felony murder or transferred intent, that would suffice to confer liability for that degree of murder in this case.[b]

The next question is whether the evidence permitted the jury to determine that defendant's acts were the proximate cause of Patch's death. We hold there was sufficient evidence of proximate cause for the jury to decide that liability attached for defendant's acts.

We have consumed much space explaining that if the eventual victim's death is not the natural and probable consequence of a defendant's act, then liability cannot attach. Shots that cause a driver to accelerate impulsively and run over a nearby pedestrian suffice to confer liability; but if the driver, still upset, had proceeded for several miles before killing a pedestrian, at some point the required causal nexus would have become too attenuated for the initial bad actor to be liable even for manslaughter, much less for first degree murder. It is a natural consequence that shots fired at a boat may cause a passenger to leap out and thereby cause another in the boat to drown; but if the boat had capsized, floated some miles down the river and over a waterfall, and fallen on the head of another boater, the shooter probably would not be criminally liable for that boater's death.

After considerable reflection, however, we conclude that the evidence sufficed to permit the jury to conclude that Patch's death was the natural and probable consequence of defendant's act. This is so because Patch was in the area in which harm could foreseeably occur as a result of a prison stabbing. Defendant mortally wounded Gardner, but the latter nevertheless was able to seize a knife that an assailant had left on the floor. As the jury found, the attack left Gardner in a daze, without the ability to reason or calculate. In that condition he staggered up a flight of stairs to the second

b. This aspect of the holding has been overruled by *People v. Concha* [Chapter 7].

floor in pursuit of defendant's accomplice Menefield. There he engaged in a purely reflexive struggle with Patch and plunged the knife into him. It is foreseeable that a wounded inmate might try to arm himself with a weapon abandoned at the scene of a prison melee and pursue his attackers a short distance. The jury was entitled to find that the distance Gardner pursued Menefield was not so great as to break the chain of causation.

As stated above, however, our inquiry does not end here. Because the jurors found that Gardner was unconscious when he attacked Patch, the instruction directed them not to consider whether the attack on Patch was foreseeable. Under that instruction, whether Patch was standing next to Gardner or half a mile away was not to be taken into account, as long as Patch's killing was the "direct result" of defendant's act.

As we have explained, the instruction incorrectly stated the law of proximate cause. A result cannot be the natural and probable cause of an act if the act was unforeseeable. An instruction that told the jury to disregard foreseeability would inevitably lead it to ignore the nature of Gardner's response to defendant's attack, and hence would substantially distract the jury from considering the causation element of the offense—an element that was very much at issue in the case. The instructional error thus cannot be said to have been harmless beyond a reasonable doubt and defendant's conviction of the murder of Patch must be reversed.

…

Note and Problems

The Model Penal Code and Causation. Model Penal Code § 203 sets out the rules governing causation:

> (1) Conduct is the cause of a result when:
>
> (a) it is an antecedent but for which the result in question would not have occurred; and
>
> (b) the relationship between the conduct and result satisfies any additional causal requirements imposed by the Code or by the law defining the offense.
>
> (2) When purposely or knowingly causing a particular result is an element of an offense, the element is not established if the actual result is not within the purpose or the contemplation of the actor unless:
>
> (a) the actual result differs from that designed or contemplated, as the case may be, only in the respect that a different person or different property is injured or affected or that the injury or harm designed or contemplated would have been more serious or more extensive than that caused; or
>
> (b) the actual result involves the same kind of injury or harm as that designed or contemplated and is not too remote or accidental in its occurrence to have a [just] bearing on the actor's liability or on the gravity of his offense.

(3) When recklessly or negligently causing a particular result is an element of an offense, the element is not established if the actual result is not within the risk of which the actor is aware or, in the case of negligence, of which he should be aware unless:

(a) the actual result differs from the probable result only in the respect that a different person or different property is injured or affected or that the probable injury or harm would have been more serious or more extensive than that caused; or

(b) the actual result involves the same kind of injury or harm as the probable result and is not too remote or accidental in its occurrence to have a [just] bearing on the actor's liability or on the gravity of his offense.

(4) When causing a particular result is a material element of an offense for which absolute liability is imposed by law, the element is not established unless the actual result is a probable consequence of the actor's conduct.

How does this approach differ from California's? Is it preferable?

Problem 34.

At about 10:00 p.m., Defendant was stopped by the police because he was driving a stolen vehicle. He fled the scene and led police on a 48-mile chase covering both surface streets and freeways. During the chase, he drove at speeds between 60 and 90 miles an hour, ran stop signs and red lights, and drove on the wrong side of streets, causing oncoming traffic to scatter or swerve to avoid colliding with him. Throughout the pursuit, Defendant weaved in and out of traffic, cutting in front of other cars and causing them to brake suddenly. At one point on the freeway, he crossed three lanes of traffic, struck another car, jumped the divider between the freeway and a transition lane, and passed a tanker truck, forcing it to swerve suddenly to avoid a collision. Near the end of the chase, one of the car's front tires blew out, but Defendant continued to drive at 55 to 60 mph, crossing freeway traffic lanes.

Police helicopters from two different jurisdictions assisted in the chase by tracking Defendant. When Defendant, who had been driving in A County, neared the county line of B County, the pilot of the B County helicopter suggested that he change places with the A County helicopter, which had been in the lead position. The normal procedure for such a maneuver is for the lead helicopter to move to the right and swing around clockwise behind the other helicopter while climbing to an altitude of 1,000 feet. At the same time, the trailing helicopter descends to 500 feet while maintaining a straight course. While attempting this maneuver, the helicopters crashed into each other, and the three occupants of the A County helicopter were killed.

Defendant is charged, *inter alia*, with three counts of second degree murder (P.C. §§ 187–189). At trial, Expert testified as to his conclusion that the accident occurred because the A County helicopter made a 360-degree turn and closed too rapidly on the B County helicopter. In Expert's opinion, the A County pilot violated an FAA regulation prohibiting careless and reckless operation of an aircraft by failing to properly clear the area, not maintaining communication with the B County helicopter, failing to keep other aircraft in view at all times, and not changing his altitude. Expert also testified that the A County pilot violated another FAA regulation prohibiting operation of one aircraft so close to another as to create a collision hazard. He added that the maneuver was not a difficult one and was not affected by the ground activity at the time. He also testified that he could think of no reason for the pilots' actions and had never heard of a midair collision between two police helicopters involved in tracking a ground pursuit.

What arguments should be made regarding whether Defendant caused the deaths? If Defendant caused the deaths, did he act with malice aforethought?

Problem 35.

Defendant was stopped in his car at a stop sign in a residential neighborhood when Racer pulled alongside of him on his right. Both drivers raced their engines and then accelerated rapidly. As they approached the next intersection, they were abreast of each other traveling at a speed of over 50 m.p.h. At that moment, Victim's car entered the intersection from the cross street. Defendant swerved sharply to his left and avoided a collision. Racer swerved sharply to his right but hit Victim's car killing Victim. Defendant is charged with second degree murder (P.C. §§ 187–189). What arguments should be made on whether he is guilty of murder or the lesser included offense of involuntary manslaughter? Would the outcome be different if Racer had been killed instead of Victim?

People v. Armitage

194 Cal. App. 3d 405, 239 Cal. Rptr. 515 (1987)

Sparks, J.

On a drunken escapade on the Sacramento River in the middle of a spring night, defendant David James Armitage flipped his boat over and caused his companion to drown. As a result of this accident, defendant was convicted of the felony of drunk boating causing death in violation of former Harbors and Navigation Code section 655, subdivision (c).[1]

...

1. At the time of defendant's crime Harbors and Navigation Code, section 655, subdivision (c) provided: "No person shall operate any boat or vessel or manipulate any water skis, aquaplane, or similar device while under the influence of intoxicating liquor, any drug, or under the combined influence of intoxicating liquor and any drug, and while so operating, do any act forbidden by law, or neglect any duty imposed by law, in the use of the boat, vessel, water skis, aquaplane, or similar device, which act or neglect proximately causes death or serious bodily injury to any person other than himself."....

Facts

On the evening of May 18, 1985, defendant and his friend, Peter Maskovich, were drinking in a bar in the riverside community of Freeport.[2] They were observed leaving the bar around midnight. In the early morning hours defendant and Maskovich wound up racing defendant's boat on the Sacramento River while both of them were intoxicated.[3] The boat did not contain any personal flotation devices. About 3 a.m. Gary Bingham, who lived in a house boat in a speed zone (five miles per hour, no wake), was disturbed by a large wake. He went out to yell at the boaters and observed a small aluminum boat with two persons in it at the bend in the river. The boaters had the motor wide open, were zig-zagging, and had no running lights on at the time. About the same time, Rodney and Susan Logan were fishing on the river near the Freeport Bridge when they observed an aluminum boat with two men in it coming up the river without running lights. The occupants were using loud and vulgar language, and were operating the boat very fast and erratically.

James Snook lives near the Sacramento River in Clarksburg. Some time around 3 a.m. defendant came to his door. Defendant was soaking wet and appeared quite intoxicated. He reported that he had flipped his boat over in the river and had lost his buddy. He said that at first he and his buddy had been hanging on to the overturned boat, but that his buddy swam for shore and he did not know whether he had made it. As it turned out, Maskovich did not make it; he drowned in the river.

Mr. Snook notified the authorities of the accident. Deputy Beddingfield arrived and spent some time with defendant in attempting to locate the scene of the accident or the victim. Eventually Deputy Beddingfield took defendant to the sheriff's boat shed to meet with officers who normally work on the river. At the shed they were met by Deputy Snyder. Deputy Snyder attempted to question defendant about the accident and defendant stated that he had been operating the boat at a high rate of speed and zig-zagging until it capsized. Defendant also stated that he told the victim to hang on to the boat but his friend ignored his warning and started swimming for the shore. As he talked to defendant, the officer formed the opinion that he was intoxicated. Deputy Snyder then arrested defendant and informed him of his rights. Defendant waived his right to remain silent and repeated his statement.

---

2. Defendant was originally charged with one count of involuntary manslaughter (Pen. Code, § 192, subd. (b)), as well as felony drunk boating (Harb. & Nav. Code, § 655, subd. (c)). Pursuant to a bargain the People dismissed the involuntary manslaughter charge, and agreed that if found guilty defendant would not be sentenced to more than the middle base term (two years) for the felony drunk-boating charge. Defendant agreed to submit the issue of his guilt to the trial court on the preliminary hearing transcript and the evidence taken on his motion to suppress the evidence. Our recitation of the facts is derived from these sources.

3. An autopsy revealed that at the time of his death Maskovich had a blood alcohol level of .25 percent. A blood sample taken from defendant at approximately 7 a.m. revealed a blood alcohol level at that time of .14 percent. Defendant does not dispute that he was intoxicated at the time of the accident.

Discussion

. . .

II

Defendant next contends his actions were not the proximate cause of the death of the victim. In order to be guilty of felony drunk boating the defendant's act or omission must be the proximate cause of the ensuing injury or death. Defendant asserts that after his boat flipped over he and the victim were holding on to it and the victim, against his advice, decided to abandon the boat and try to swim to shore. According to defendant the victim's fatally reckless decision should exonerate him from criminal responsibility for his death.

We reject defendant's contention. The question whether defendant's acts or omissions criminally caused the victim's death is to be determined according to the ordinary principles governing proximate causation. Proximate cause of a death has traditionally been defined in criminal cases as "a cause which, in natural and continuous sequence, produces the death, and without which the death would not have occurred." (CALJIC nos. 8.55, 8.93.) Thus, as Witkin notes, "[proximate] cause is clearly established where the act is directly connected with the resulting injury, with no intervening force operating." (1 Witkin, Cal. Crimes (1963) § 79.)

Defendant claims that the victim's attempt to swim ashore, whether characterized as an intervening or a superseding cause, constituted a break in the natural and continuous sequence arising from the unlawful operation of the boat. The claim cannot hold water. It has long been the rule in criminal prosecutions that the contributory negligence of the victim is not a defense. In order to exonerate a defendant the victim's conduct must not only be a cause of his injury, it must be a superseding cause. "A defendant may be criminally liable for a result directly caused by his act even if there is another contributing cause. If an intervening cause is a normal and reasonably foreseeable result of defendant's original act the intervening act is 'dependent' and not a superseding cause, and will not relieve defendant of liability." (*People v. Harris* (1975) 52 Cal. App. 3d 419.) As Witkin further notes, "[an] obvious illustration of a dependent cause is the victim's attempt to escape from a deadly attack or other danger in which he is placed by the defendant's wrongful act." Thus, it is only an unforeseeable intervening cause, an extraordinary and abnormal occurrence, which rises to the level of an exonerating, superseding cause. Consequently, in criminal law a victim's predictable effort to escape a peril created by the defendant is not considered a superseding cause of the ensuing injury or death. As leading commentators have explained it, an unreflective act in response to a peril created by defendant will not break a causal connection. In such a case, the actor has a choice, but his act is nonetheless unconsidered. "When defendant's conduct causes panic an act done under the influence of panic or extreme fear will not negative causal connection unless the reaction is wholly abnormal." (Hart & Honore, Causation in the Law (2d ed. 1985) p. 149.)

Here defendant, through his misconduct, placed the intoxicated victim in the middle of a dangerous river in the early morning hours clinging to an overturned boat.

The fact that the panic-stricken victim recklessly abandoned the boat and tried to swim ashore was not a wholly abnormal reaction to the perceived peril of drowning. Just as "[detached] reflection cannot be demanded in the presence of an uplifted knife" (*Brown v. United States* (1921) 256 U.S. 335, Holmes, J.), neither can caution be required of a drowning man. Having placed the inebriated victim in peril, defendant cannot obtain exoneration by claiming the victim should have reacted differently or more prudently. In sum, the evidence establishes that defendant's acts and omissions were the proximate cause of the victim's death.

...

Problems

Problem 36.

Defendant stabbed Victim in the course of attempting to rape her. Victim was a Jehovah's Witness, and she died when she would not agree to a blood transfusion, which would have saved her life. Defendant is charged with first degree murder (P.C. §§ 187–189). What arguments should be made as to whether Defendant caused Victim's death?

Problem 37.

On several occasions, Boyfriend and Mother had abused Victim, Mother's 2-year-old son. A week prior to Victim's death, Boyfriend struck Victim hard in the stomach. Victim told Mother he had been struck, and he complained of pain and vomited several times. The next day, Victim complained of pain, and his stomach was hard, but Mother failed to seek medical help until shortly before his death. His death resulted from peritonitis caused by traumatic perforation of the small bowel. Are Boyfriend and/or Mother guilty of homicide, and, if so, in what degree?

Problem 38.

Defendant and several associates abducted Victim, a woman he had known socially for several months, and, in the ensuing two days he subjected her to various forms of sexual abuse, including rape and the infliction of extensive and severe bite wounds. At one point, Victim was permitted to leave Defendant's hotel room in the company of one of the associates to "buy a hat." However, in a drug store, she secretly purchased bichloride of mercury tablets and, returning to the hotel room, took them in an effort to commit suicide. Victim became violently ill. Defendant had her drink a bottle of milk and suggested that he take her to the hospital, but she refused.

Defendant then proceeded to drive her to her home, several hours away. On the way, Victim's pain grew worse, and she screamed for a doctor, but Defendant did not stop driving until he reached her house. Victim's parents summoned a doctor, who treated her for poisoning. In the next ten days, all her wounds healed but one which became infected. She grew worse and died, although the infected wound had healed at the time of her death. The medical cause of death was apparently a combination of shock, loss of food and rest, action of the poison and the infection, and lack of early treatment, probably none of which, taken singly, would have been sufficient to result in death. Defendant was convicted of second degree murder.

On appeal, Defendant argues that his actions were not the cause of death. The court will consider the following four common law cases in reaching its decision;

> **Case #1**—The defendant fought with his wife at night, and she left to go to her father's house nearby. When she was about 200 yards from her father's house, she decided not to go until morning, and she lay down in a bedcover she had with her. The night was cold, and, by the morning, she was suffering from exposure, from which she ultimately died. The defendant was found not guilty of homicide.
>
> **Case #2**—The defendant wounded the victim, who was taken to the hospital, where she caught scarlet fever from the doctor and died. The defendant was found not guilty of homicide.
>
> **Case #3**—The defendant and others went to the victim's house, tied him up and said they were going to kill him. As they were transporting the victim to the woods in a wagon, he jumped from the wagon into the river and, as they stood by and watched, he drowned. The defendant was found guilty of murder.
>
> **Case #4**—The defendant induced a young teenage girl to go with him to his apartment where he had sex with her, following which she jumped from a window to get away from him and was killed in the fall. The defendant was found guilty of murder.

What arguments should be made as to whether Defendant's conviction should be affirmed?

Chapter 6

Homicide: Killings in the Commission of Another Crime

At the common law, the felony-murder rule defined one species of malice aforethought, providing that any killing done in the commission or attempted commission of a felony was murder. Similarly, the misdemeanor-manslaughter rule provided that any killing during the commission or attempted commission of a misdemeanor was involuntary manslaughter, substituting proof of the commission of a misdemeanor for proof of criminal negligence. Note how these rules constitute a departure from the general rule in criminal law that the intent to do one crime does not "transfer" to establish the mental state of another crime. Since these rules apply even in the case of unintended or even unforeseeable killings, their effect is to introduce strict liability concepts into the law of homicide. The felony-murder rule and its limitations are discussed in Section A. Misdemeanor-manslaughter is addressed in Section B.

A. Felony-Murder

The six cases in this section deal with the felony-murder rule. As the California Supreme Court has regularly stated, the felony-murder rule is a "disfavored doctrine" because "in almost all cases in which it is applied it is unnecessary and it erodes the relation between criminal liability and moral culpability." *People v. Washington*, 62 Cal.2d 777, 783 (1965). Accordingly, the court has sought to give the rule the "narrowest possible application consistent with its ostensible purpose," which is to deter felons from killing negligently or accidentally during a felony. *People v. Satchell*, 6 Cal.3d 28, 34 (1971).

In the first case, *People v. Dillon*, the court explains the legal basis for the felony-murder rule in California and then limits the application of the rule in light of the California Constitution's "cruel or unusual punishment" provision (art. 1 § 17). In *People v. Chun (Part 1)*, the court again reconsiders the legal basis for the felony-murder rule and adopts an interpretation at odds with its interpretation in *Dillon*. The remaining cases address four qualifications on the felony-murder rule. *People v. Fields* and *People v. Washington* concern the requirement that the killing be committed in the "perpetration" of the felony. In *Fields*, the issue is raised in a robbery felony-murder case because the killing occurred several hours after the defendant obtained the money which was the object of the robbery and at a time when he was not in flight from the crime. In *Washington*, another robbery felony-murder case, the issue is raised because the killing was not done by one of the felons, but by the robbery victim resisting the robbery. In *People v. Sears*, the court develops a second qualification on the rule, *i.e.*, that the prosecution must prove the felon had the specific intent to commit the underlying felony. The remaining two qualifications apply only to the second degree felony-murder rule. In *People v. Patterson*, the court explains the requirement that the underlying felony has to be "inherently dangerous to life" to support a second degree felony-murder conviction. Finally, *People v. Chun (Part 2)* explains and applies the "merger rule," which bars use of the felony-murder rule as to certain felonies deemed too closely connected to the death itself.

People v. Dillon

34 Cal. 3d 441, 668 P.2d 697 (1983)

Mosk, J.

Defendant appeals from a judgment convicting him of first degree felony murder and attempted robbery....

At the time of these events defendant was a 17-year-old high school student living in the Santa Cruz Mountains not far from a small, secluded farm on which Dennis Johnson and his brother illegally grew marijuana. Told by a friend about the farm, defendant set out with two schoolmates to investigate it and to take some of the marijuana if possible. After crossing posted barricades and evading a primitive tin-can alarm system, the three boys reached the farm, a quarter-acre plot enclosed by a six-foot wire fence. In an effort to avoid being seen by Johnson, who was guarding the property, the boys tried several different approaches, then hid in a hollow tree stump. Johnson appeared with a shotgun, cocked the weapon, and ordered them out; defendant remained in hiding, but his companions complied. Johnson demanded to know what they were doing there; disbelieving their story that they were hunting rabbits, he told them to get off the property. He warned them that his brother would have shot them if he had met them, adding that the next time the youths came on his property he might shoot them himself. Defendant overheard these threats.

The two boys departed promptly, but defendant stayed inside the tree trunk until it grew dark. Finally emerging, he went to take another look at the plantation. Again Johnson confronted him with a shotgun, pointed the weapon at him, and ordered him to go. He left without further ado.

Some weeks later defendant returned to the farm to show it to his brother. As the latter was looking over the scene, however, a shotgun blast was heard and once more the boys beat a hasty retreat.

After the school term began, defendant and a friend discussed the matter further and decided to attempt a "rip-off" of the marijuana with the aid of reinforcements. Various plans were considered for dealing with Johnson; defendant assertedly suggested that they "just hold him up. Hit him over the head or something. Tie him to a tree." They recruited six other classmates, and on the morning of October 17, 1978, the boys all gathered for the venture. Defendant had prepared a rough map of the farm and the surrounding area. Several of the boys brought shotguns, and defendant carried a .22 caliber semi-automatic rifle. They also equipped themselves with a baseball bat, sticks, a knife, wirecutters, tools for harvesting the marijuana, paper bags to be used as masks or for carrying plants, and rope for bundling plants or for restraining the guards if necessary. Along the way, they found some old sheets and tore them into strips to use as additional masks or bindings to tie up the guards. Two or three of the boys thereafter fashioned masks and put them on.

The boys climbed a hill towards the farm, crossed the barricades, split into four pairs, and spread out around the field. There they saw one of the Johnson brothers tending the plants; discretion became much the better part of valor, and they made little or no progress for almost two hours. Although the testimony of the various participants was not wholly consistent, it appears that two of the boys abandoned the effort altogether, two others were chased away by dogs but began climbing the hill by another route, and defendant and his companion, with the remaining pair, watched cautiously just outside the field of marijuana.

One of the boys returning to the farm then accidentally discharged his shotgun, and the two ran back down the hill. While the boys near the field reconnoitered and discussed their next move, their hapless friend once more fired his weapon by mistake. In the meantime Dennis Johnson had circled behind defendant and the others, and was approaching up the trail. They first heard him coming through the bushes, then saw that he was carrying a shotgun. When Johnson drew near, defendant began rapidly firing his rifle at him. After Johnson fell, defendant fled with his companions without taking any marijuana. Johnson suffered nine bullet wounds and died a few days later.

[The court rejected defendant's contentions that standing crops could not be the subject of robbery or attempted robbery and that greater proof of "attempt" was required in felony-murder cases than in attempt crimes generally.]

III

On the murder charge the court gave the jury the standard CALJIC instructions defining murder, malice aforethought, wilful, deliberate and premeditated first degree murder, first degree felony murder, second degree murder, manslaughter, and self-defense. The felony-murder instruction (CALJIC No. 8.21) informed the jury that an unlawful killing, whether intentional, negligent, or accidental, is murder in the first degree if it occurs during an attempt to commit robbery. Defendant mounts a two-fold attack on the first degree felony-murder rule in this state: he contends (1) it is an uncodified common law rule that this court should abolish, and (2) if on the contrary it is embodied in a statute, the statute is unconstitutional.

Defendant first asks us in effect to adopt the position taken by the Michigan Supreme Court in *People v. Aaron* (Mich. 1980) 299 N.W.2d 304 and to abolish the felony-murder rule in a further exercise of the power we invoke in part II of this opinion, *i.e.*, our power to conform the common law of this state to contemporary conditions and enlightened notions of justice. Defendant emphasizes the dubious origins of the felony-murder doctrine, the many strictures levelled against it over the years by courts and scholars, and the legislative and judicial limitations that have increasingly circumscribed its operation. We do not disagree with these criticisms; indeed, our opinions make it clear we hold no brief for the felony-murder rule. We have repeatedly stated that felony murder is a "highly artificial concept" which "deserves no extension beyond its required application." *People v. Phillips*, 64 Cal.2d 574 (1966). And we have recognized that the rule is much censured "because it anachronistically resurrects from a bygone age a 'barbaric' concept that has been discarded in the place of its origin" (*Phillips, supra*) and because "in almost all cases in which it is applied it is unnecessary" and "it erodes the relation between criminal liability and moral culpability." *People v. Washington*, 62 Cal.2d 777 (1965).

Nevertheless, a thorough review of legislative history convinces us that in California—in distinction to Michigan—the first degree felony-murder rule is a creature of statute. However much we may agree with the reasoning of *Aaron*, therefore, we cannot duplicate its solution to the problem: this court does not sit as a super-legislature with the power to judicially abrogate a statute merely because it is unwise or outdated.

[In its initial session, on April 16, 1850, the California Legislature adopted "An Act concerning Crimes and Punishments," the first statute regulating the criminal law of California. As at common law, murder was defined as the unlawful killing of a human being with malice aforethought (§ 19). Also as at common law, an involuntary killing occurring during the commission of a felony was defined as murder (§ 25). There was only one degree, and it was punishable by death (§ 21). In 1856, the Legislature amended § 21 to divide the crime of murder into two degrees: first degree murder was defined as that committed by certain listed means or in the perpetration of certain listed felonies, while all other murders were of the second degree. The amendment was modeled on the 1794 Pennsylvania statute and was designed to limit the use of the death penalty to only the most aggravated murders.]

Thus on the eve of the enactment of the Penal Code of 1872, two relevant statutes were in force in California: (1) section 25 of the 1850 act, which codified the felony-murder rule; and (2) amended section 21 of the same act, which divided the crime of murder into degrees and tailored the punishment accordingly. The two statutes were not only consistent but complementary. When a killing occurred in the commission of a felony, section 25 declared it to be murder; thereupon section 21 prescribed the degree of that murder according to the particular felony involved—first degree if the felony was arson, rape, robbery, or burglary, second degree if it was any other felony....

What was plainly evident before 1872, however, was much less so after the adoption of the Penal Code. The enactment of that code operated to repeal the Act of 1850, including therefore sections 21 and 25 (Pen. Code, § 6). But of those two provisions only section 21 reappeared in the Penal Code, as section 189 thereof; by contrast, the felony-murder provision of section 25 was not reenacted in the new code, and hence "ceased to be the law." From the drawing of such a deliberate distinction between the two provisions, and from the wording of section 189 itself, certain inferences arise which point to a conclusion that the Legislature meant the section to operate, like its predecessor, solely as a degree-fixing measure.

First, "It is ordinarily to be presumed that the Legislature by deleting an express provision of a statute intended a substantial change in the law." *People v. Valentine* (1946) 28 Cal.2d 121. Under this principle, the Legislature's decision not to reenact the felony-murder provision of section 25 in the 1872 codification implied an intent to abrogate the common law felony-murder rule that the section had embodied since 1850.

Second, aside from a few grammatical changes the wording of section 189 was identical to that of section 21. Indeed, its draftsmen acknowledged this obvious fact: "This section is founded upon Sec. 21 of the Crimes and Punishment Act, as amended by the Act of 1856.—Stats. 1856, p. 219. The Commission made no material change in the language." In these circumstances, the code itself decreed the proper construction of section 189: "The provisions of this Code, so far as they are substantially the same as existing statutes, must be construed as continuations thereof, and not as new enactments." (Pen. Code, § 5.)

Third, when a statute defines the meaning to be given to one of its terms, that meaning is ordinarily binding on the courts. It is presumed the word was used in the sense specified by the Legislature, and the statute will be construed accordingly. In the 1872 Penal Code the Legislature simultaneously enacted section 187, defining the crime of "murder" as "the unlawful killing of a human being, with malice aforethought," and section 189, providing that "murder" committed in certain ways constituted murder in the first degree. Under this principle, the word "murder" in section 189 would have had the meaning prescribed for it in section 187, *i.e.*, an unlawful killing "with malice aforethought."

Fourth, it is generally presumed that when a word is used in a particular sense in one part of a statute, it is intended to have the same meaning if it appears in another part of the same statute. This rule would seem to apply a fortiori to section 189, where in a single compound sentence the Legislature used the word "murder" only once but with two referents: the section defined first degree murder as all "murder" (1) which is committed by certain listed methods or (2) which is committed during certain listed felonies. As noted above, in the first half of this sentence the word "murder" means an unlawful killing committed with malice aforethought; under the foregoing rule, the same word would have had the same meaning in the second half of the same sentence (*i.e.*, murder during the listed felonies).

[The Court found no contrary evidence in the history of the murder statutes. The Court stated that the text of the manslaughter statute (P.C. § 192), describing one form of manslaughter as a killing during an unlawful act "not amounting to a felony" reasonably might imply that killings during felonies were dealt with elsewhere, but the question remained, "which other statute was believed by the commission to codify the felony-murder rule?"]

For the answer, the Attorney General turns to his third and last piece of evidence, to wit, the legislative history not of homicide but of the crime of arson. The arson statute in force before adoption of the Penal Code contained a specialized felony-murder rule applicable to that felony alone.[18] In 1872 the commission rewrote the prior law of arson into sections 447 to 455 of the Penal Code, but omitted the specialized felony-murder rule from the new statutory scheme. Its official comment to section 455 read in its entirety: "This chapter is founded upon Secs. 4, 5, and 6, of Act concerning crimes and punishments of 1856.—Stats. 1856, p. 132. The text omits the clause in Sec. 4 [sic] which provides that 'should the lives of any persons be lost in consequence of such burning the offender shall be deemed guilty of murder, and shall be indicted and punished accordingly.' *This provision is surplusage, for the killing in that case is in the perpetration of arson, and falls within the definition of murder in the first degree.—See Sec. 189, ante.*" (Italics added.)

From the emphasized language the Attorney General asks us to infer that the commission intended its proposed version of section 189 to incorporate a statutory first degree felony-murder rule, i.e., that as to any killing occurring during the commission of one of the listed felonies (including therefore arson) the section served both (1) the felony-murder function of making such killing the crime of murder and (2) the degree-fixing function of making that crime murder in the first degree. Again the inference is not unreasonable, although it may be doubted that the commission thought the matter through as carefully as the Attorney General would have us conclude. Rather, it appears the commission simply assumed it was making no change in the law: its heavy reliance on the 1864 *Sanchez* opinion [*People v. Sanchez* (1864) 24 Cal. 17] in its note to section 189 suggests the commission read that opinion to mean that the predecessor to section 189—i.e., amended section 21 of the 1850 act—had itself codified the felony-murder rule.... [T]hat reading of either *Sanchez* or section 21 would have been mistaken.

Nevertheless, for present purposes any such error by the commission is immaterial. It no longer matters that the commission may have misread pre-1872 law on this point; what matters is (1) the commission apparently believed that its version of section 189 codified the felony-murder rule as to the listed felonies, and (2) the Legislature adopted section 189 in the form proposed by the commission. "When a statute proposed by the California Code Commission for inclusion in the Penal Code of 1872 has been enacted by the Legislature without substantial change, the report of the commission is entitled to great weight in construing the statute and in determining the intent of the Legislature." (*People v. Wiley* (1976) 18 Cal. 3d 162.) If we assume the 1872 Legislature drew the inferences that the Attorney General now asks us to draw regarding the intent of the commission, the quoted rule compels us to conclude that the Legislature acted with the same intent when it adopted section 189.

18. After prescribing a term of imprisonment for arson, the statute declared in section 5: "and should the life or lives of any person or persons be lost in consequence of such burning as aforesaid, such offender shall be deemed guilty of murder, and shall be indicted and punished accordingly." By another quirk of draftsmanship the statute purported to apply this proviso to second degree arson (§5) but not to first degree arson (§4), and again a literal reading of the statute would have been absurd. The proviso had been taken verbatim from our first arson statute, which recognized only one degree of that crime. The discrepancy arose in 1856 when the Legislature divided arson into two degrees but did not make the proviso plainly applicable to both.

Nothing in the ensuing history of section 189 suggests that the Legislature acted with any different intent when it subsequently amended the statute in various respects, most recently in 1981. We infer that the Legislature still believes, as the code commission apparently did in 1872, that section 189 codifies the first degree felony-murder rule. That belief is controlling, regardless of how shaky its historical foundation may be.

Accordingly, although the balance remains close, we hold that the evidence of present legislative intent thus identified by the Attorney General is sufficient to outweigh the contrary implications of the language of section 189 and its predecessors. We are therefore required to construe section 189 as a statutory enactment of the first degree felony-murder rule in California.[19]

IV

[Defendant argued that if section 189 was read to create a felony-murder rule, it was unconstitutional under the Due Process Clause. In *In re Winship*, 397 U.S. 358 (1970), the Supreme Court had held that "the Due Process Clause protects the accused against conviction except upon proof beyond a reasonable doubt of every fact necessary to constitute the crime with which he is charged." Defendant reasoned that, since malice is an element of murder (P.C. § 187), and since the prosecution, if permitted to invoke the felony-murder rule, is relieved of the obligation of proving malice and can instead rely on a "conclusive presumption" of malice, *Winship* is violated.] In every case of murder other than felony murder the prosecution undoubtedly has the burden of proving malice as an element of the crime. (Pen. Code, §§ 187, 188.) Yet to say that (1) the prosecution must also prove malice in felony-murder cases, but that (2) the existence of such malice is "conclusively presumed" upon proof of the defendant's intent to commit the underlying felony, is merely a circuitous way of saying that in such cases the prosecution need prove only the latter intent. In Wigmore's words, the issue of malice is therefore "wholly immaterial for the purpose of the proponent's case" when the charge is felony murder. In that event the "conclusive presumption" is no more than a procedural fiction that masks a substantive reality, to wit, that as a matter of law malice is not an element of felony murder.

... This is "a rule of substantive law in California and not merely an evidentiary shortcut to finding malice as it withdraws from the jury the requirement that they find either express malice or ... implied malice." *People v. Stamp* (1969) 2 Cal.App.3d 203.) In short, "malice aforethought is not an element of murder under the felony-murder doctrine." (People v. Avalos (1979) 98 Cal.App.3d 701.)[a] ... Because the felony-murder

---

19. We recognize that from the standpoint of consistency the outcome of this analysis leaves much to be desired. Although the misdemeanor-manslaughter rule is plainly a creature of statute (Pen. Code, § 192, par. 2), we reach the same conclusion as to the first degree felony-murder rule only by piling inference on inference; and the second degree felony-murder rule remains, as it has been since 1872, a judge-made doctrine without any express basis in the Penal Code. A thorough legislative reconsideration of the whole subject would seem to be in order.

a. This statement is directly contrary to statements by the Court in earlier felony-murder cases. *E.g., People v. Washington*, 62 Cal. 2d 777, 780 (1965) ("The felony-murder doctrine ascribes malice aforethought to the felon who kills in the perpetration of an inherently dangerous felony."); *People v.*

rule thus does not in fact raise a "presumption" of the existence of an element of the crime, it does not violate the due process clause....

V

It follows from the foregoing analysis that the two kinds of first degree murder in this state differ in a fundamental respect: in the case of deliberate and premeditated murder with malice aforethought, the defendant's state of mind with respect to the homicide is all-important and must be proved beyond a reasonable doubt; in the case of first degree felony murder it is entirely irrelevant and need not be proved at all. From this profound legal difference flows an equally significant factual distinction, to wit, that first degree felony murder encompasses a far wider range of individual culpability than deliberate and premeditated murder. It includes not only the latter, but also a variety of unintended homicides resulting from reckless behavior, or ordinary negligence, or pure accident; it embraces both calculated conduct and acts committed in panic or rage, or under the dominion of mental illness, drugs, or alcohol; and it condemns alike consequences that are highly probable, conceivably possible, or wholly unforeseeable.

A

Despite this broad factual spectrum, the Legislature has provided only one punishment scheme for all homicides occurring during the commission of or attempt to commit an offense listed in section 189: regardless of the defendant's individual culpability with respect to that homicide, he must be adjudged a first degree murderer and sentenced to death or life imprisonment with or without possibility of parole—the identical punishment inflicted for deliberate and premeditated murder with malice aforethought. (Pen. Code, § 190 *et seq.*) As the record before us illustrates, however, in some first degree felony-murder cases this Procrustean penalty may violate the prohibition of the California Constitution against cruel or unusual punishments. (Cal. Const., art. I, § 17.)

[In a series of cases beginning with *In re Lynch* (1972) 8 Cal. 3d 410, the court had held that, although "[t]he Legislature is ... accorded the broadest discretion possible in enacting penal statutes," a statute might violate the constitutional provision, "not only if it is inflicted by a cruel or unusual method, but also if it is grossly disproportionate to the offense for which it is imposed."]

We proceed to a similar analysis of the record in the case at bar. As noted at the outset, when he committed the offenses herein defendant was a 17-year-old high school student.[28] At trial he took the stand in his own behalf and told the jury his side of the story. From that testimony a plausible picture emerged of the evolution of defendant's state of mind during these events—from youthful bravado, to un-

---

Satchell, 6 Cal. 3d 28, 43 (1971) (commission of an inherently dangerous felony "renders logical an imputation of malice on the part of all who commit it.").

28. In the rural setting in which he lived, it was apparently common for youths of his age to have .22 caliber rifles. Defendant also held a hunting license.

easiness, to fear for his life, to panic. Although such an explanation is often discounted as self-serving, in this case the record repeatedly demonstrates that the judge and jury in fact gave defendant's testimony large credence and substantial weight.

Thus defendant stated that when he heard the first shotgun blast accidentally set off by his hapless colleague, he became concerned that one of his friends might have been shot. Next he watched as a man guarding the marijuana plantation walked towards the sound while carrying a shotgun, and five or ten minutes later he heard a second shotgun blast from the same direction. At that point anxiety turned to alarm, and he testified that "we just wanted to get the hell out of there, because there were shotgun blasts going off and we thought our friends were being blown away."

One of defendant's companions then told him he had overheard a guard say, "These kids mean business." Shortly afterwards the boys heard a man stealthily coming up the trail behind them; they believed at first it was one of their friends, but soon saw it was Dennis Johnson, carrying a shotgun at port arms. The boys could neither retreat nor hide, and defendant was sure that Johnson had seen them. According to defendant, as Johnson drew near he shifted the position of his shotgun and "he was pointing it outwards and I thought he was getting ready to shoot me ... I just didn't know what to do ... I just saw him swing the gun behind the trees, and that's when I started firing." Defendant raised his rifle to his waist and "pointed it somewhere in his direction." He testified that "I just pressed the trigger, I was so scared ... I just kept squeezing it, and shots just went off. I don't know how many ..." He denied having any ill-will towards Johnson, whom he did not personally know, and reiterated that he began shooting only because "I was afraid he was going to shoot me ... He knew where I was at. I couldn't do anything. I just shot him. I didn't even think about it. I never thought of shooting anybody." Defendant stopped firing when Johnson fell.

On cross-examination defendant testified that when Johnson pointed the shotgun in his direction, "Nobody told me what to do and I had no support, and I just pulled the trigger so many times because I was so scared ..." When asked why he had fired nine times, defendant replied, "I never thought between pulling the trigger the first time or the ninth time. I just kept pulling because he was going to shoot me and I had to do something. I didn't have it aimed at him. I didn't know whether it would hit him or not. I just had it pointed. I just pulled the trigger so many times because I was so frightened."

Called as an expert witness, a clinical psychologist testified that after conducting a series of tests and examinations he concluded that defendant was immature in a number of ways: intellectually, he showed poor judgment and planning; socially, he functioned "like a much younger child"; emotionally, he reacted "again, much like a younger child" by denying the reality of stressful events and living rather in a world of make-believe. In particular, the psychologist gave as his opinion that when confronted by the figure of Dennis Johnson armed with a shotgun in the circumstances of this case, defendant probably "blocked out" the reality of the situation and reacted reflexively, without thinking at all. There was no expert testimony to the contrary.

...

Against this showing of defendant's attenuated individual culpability we weigh the punishment actually inflicted on him. That punishment, we first observe, turned out to be far more severe than all parties expected. After the trial court committed defendant to the Youth Authority and he took this appeal, the People collaterally attacked the commitment order on the ground of excess of jurisdiction. The Court of Appeal held that at the time of the offense herein a minor convicted of first degree murder was ineligible as a matter of law for commitment to the Youth Authority. It therefore issued a writ of mandate directing the trial court to vacate the order of commitment, and that court was left with no alternative but to sentence defendant to life imprisonment in state prison. Defendant's punishment is thus the massive loss of liberty entailed in such a sentence, coupled with the disgrace of being stigmatized as a first degree murderer.[37]

Because of his minority no greater punishment could have been inflicted on defendant if he had committed the most aggravated form of homicide known to our law—a carefully planned murder executed in cold blood after a calm and mature deliberation. Yet despite the prosecutor's earnest endeavor throughout the trial to prove a case of premeditated first degree murder, the triers of fact squarely rejected that view of the evidence: as the jurors' communications to the judge made plain, if it had not been for the felony-murder rule they would have returned a verdict of a lesser degree of homicide than first degree murder. Moreover, after hearing all the testimony and diligently evaluating defendant's history and character, both the judge and the jury manifestly believed that a sentence of life imprisonment as a first degree murderer was excessive in relation to defendant's true culpability: as we have seen, they made strenuous but vain efforts to avoid imposing that punishment.

The record fully supports the triers' conclusion. It shows that at the time of the events herein defendant was an unusually immature youth. He had had no prior trouble with the law, and ... was not the prototype of a hardened criminal who poses a grave threat to society. The shooting in this case was a response to a suddenly developing situation that defendant perceived as putting his life in immediate danger. To be sure, he largely brought the situation on himself, and with hindsight his response might appear unreasonable; but there is ample evidence that because of his immaturity he neither foresaw the risk he was creating nor was able to extricate himself without panicking when that risk seemed to eventuate.

Finally, the excessiveness of defendant's punishment is underscored by the petty chastisements handed out to the six other youths who participated with him in the same offenses.[40] It is true that it was only defendant who actually pulled the trigger

---

37. We are aware that defendant will eventually be eligible for release on parole. Because of the circumstances of the killing, however, his potential parole date lies many years in the future: under Board of Prison Terms regulations, defendant faces a base term of 14, 16, or 18 years, plus 2 additional years for use of a firearm.

40. The remaining member of the group was granted immunity for giving evidence against all the others.

of his gun; but several of his companions armed themselves with shotguns, and the remainder carried such weapons as a knife and a baseball bat. Because their raid on the marijuana plantation was an elaborately prepared and concerted attempt evidenced by numerous overt acts, it appears they were all coconspirators in the venture. At the very least they were aiders and abettors and hence principals in the commission of both the attempted robbery and the killing of Johnson. (Pen. Code, § 31.) Yet none was convicted of any degree of homicide whatever, and none was sentenced to state prison for any crime. Instead, the one member of the group who was an adult was allowed to plead no contest to charges of conspiracy to commit robbery and being an accessory (*i.e.*, after the fact) to a felony, and was put on three years' probation with one year in county jail. Five of defendant's fellow minors were simply made wards of the court; of these, only one was detained—in a juvenile education and training project—while the other four were put on probation and sent home. In short, defendant received the heaviest penalty provided by law while those jointly responsible with him received the lightest—the proverbial slap on the wrist.

...

For the reasons stated we hold that in the circumstances of this case the punishment of this defendant by a sentence of life imprisonment as a first degree murderer violates article I, section 17, of the Constitution. Nevertheless, because he intentionally killed the victim without legally adequate provocation, defendant may and ought to be punished as a second degree murderer.

The judgment is affirmed as to the conviction of attempted robbery. As to the conviction of murder, the judgment is modified by reducing the degree of the crime to murder in the second degree and, as so modified, is affirmed. The cause is remanded to the trial court with directions to arraign and pronounce judgment on defendant accordingly, and to determine whether to recommit him to the Youth Authority.

Bird, C.J. and Kingsley, J., concur.

Bird, C. J., concurring.

I join in Justice Mosk's opinion for the court. However, I write separately to emphasize that today's decision still leaves unresolved some important challenges to the felony-murder rule.

...

... As the majority opinion notes, the rule encompasses a wide range of individual culpability. With regard to those felons who come within its ambit—i.e., those who kill deliberately and with premeditation and malice in the course of the enumerated felonies—the first degree felony-murder rule is superfluous. These individuals would be convicted of first degree murder by the traditional malice-plus-premeditation route, regardless of the existence or nonexistence of the felony-murder rule.

The elimination of the element of malice for felony murder is also unnecessary to obtain the conviction of those felons who, in the course of the enumerated felonies, (1) kill intentionally but without premeditation or (2) cause a death through "an intentional act involving a high degree of probability that it will result in death, which act is done for a base, anti-social purpose and with a wanton disregard for human life." Such persons act with malice.

Thus, the only actual consequence of this first degree felony-murder rule is to mete out to certain persons who cause a death unintentionally or accidentally the punishment which society prescribes for premeditated murder. Serious questions remain as to whether the state and federal Constitutions permit the government to exact such extreme punishment in the absence of proof that an accused deliberated or harbored malice.

...

[Separate concurring opinions of Reynoso, J., Kaus, J. and Kingsley, J. omitted.]

Richardson, J., concurring and dissenting.

I fully concur with the majority insofar as it (1) affirms defendant's conviction of attempted robbery, and (2) sustains the constitutionality of the first degree felony-murder rule.

I respectfully dissent, however, from the majority's conclusions that, as applied to defendant, the penalty of life imprisonment with possibility of parole constitutes cruel or unusual punishment under the California Constitution (art. I, § 17), and that accordingly the judgment must be modified to reduce the offense to second degree murder. In my view, modification of the judgment in reliance on the cruel or unusual punishment clause constitutes an unwarranted invasion both of the powers of the Legislature to define crimes and prescribe punishments, and of the Governor to exercise clemency and commute sentences.

...

The majority stresses defendant's youth, his immaturity, his lack of a prior criminal record, and the asserted fact that "The shooting in this case was a response to a suddenly developing situation ..." Each of these factors properly may be considered by the Board of Prison Terms in determining defendant's parole date. They do not, however, assist us one whit in measuring the constitutional propriety of a "life" sentence for first degree murder.

The majority's mild characterization of the killing as a mere benign "response to a suddenly developing situation" finds little support in the record. This is the way I read this record: Defendant had previously attempted to invade the marijuana plantation for the purpose of seizing some of the contraband. He met armed resistance by the owners and was forced to retreat. He thereupon carefully planned his second foray. He was going to "get even." He and a friend each planned to recruit three other friends. They chose the month of October because the marijuana would be ready for harvesting. Defendant told the gang to arm themselves, saying that he would bring his .410 and .22 rifles but that he needed ammunition. He rejected one proposal to start a diversionary fire, telling one companion that they should "just go up there. If the guy came out, we would just hold him up, hit him over the head or something. Tie him to a tree."

The time of the departure and place and time of assembly of the crew were agreed upon. Defendant prepared a map. Six of the persons, one of them armed with a shotgun, rendezvoused and obtained shotgun shells, paper bags to be used as masks or containers, and diagonal pliers for nipping the marijuana buds. Then, by prearrangement, they met defendant and still another person, making a party of eight. Defendant had a .22 rifle and was handed some ammunition. Two of the others carried shotguns, another grabbed a baseball bat, still another had brought wire cutters and a pocket knife. Defendant also carried some rope to be used either in tying up the marijuana or one of their intended victims. The young men tore up some old sheets and fashioned them into masks, obtained sticks to fight off the dogs, and then, with the use of the map, reviewed final plans for the raid. At this point defendant loaded his rifle. He was not hunting rabbits!

The men split into either three or four separate groups for their final approach to the marijuana field from different directions. Defendant and three other companions heard someone coming up a trail. Two of the party hid. Defendant either remained standing or, having crouched, then stood, and as the victim emerged from the bushes, defendant fired at him point blank at a distance of 10 to 30 feet. The victim did not point his gun at defendant and no words were exchanged. Defendant's rifle required that its trigger be pressed separately each time a bullet was fired. A subsequent autopsy of the victim's body revealed that nine bullets had found their mark. Defendant knew exactly what he was doing. He had carefully prepared for this ultimate culmination of his lethal plans.

There was nothing unplanned about this killing; indeed, under the circumstances recited above, an armed confrontation with tragic consequences appeared almost inevitable. The felony-murder rule, specifying that any homicide occurring during the perpetration or attempted perpetration of a robbery is first degree murder, clearly was designed to foreclose any argument regarding the actor's lack of premeditation or planning. Yet it is precisely such an argument that the majority accepts when it agrees to reduce defendant's sentence to second degree murder.

...

... Defendant was personally responsible for, and morally guilty of, a homicide committed in the attempted perpetration of a robbery. Although defendant, had he been a year older, could have been sentenced to death or life imprisonment without parole, by reason of his youth he received a far less severe sentence. A probable 7- to 20-year "life" sentence is very modest penal treatment for a deliberate killing. Any further clemency should rest with the Governor.

I would affirm the judgment in its entirety.

Broussard, J., concurring and dissenting.

I concur in part I of the majority opinion, which holds that the trial court properly instructed the jury on the crime of attempted robbery. I join also in part II, which overturns the common law doctrine that a standing crop cannot be the subject of larceny or robbery. Finally, I agree in principle with part IV of the majority opinion;

a statute codifying the common law felony-murder rule would not violate the state or federal Constitutions by conclusively presuming malice.

In part III of their opinion, however, the majority pile "inference on inference" to reach the conclusion that Penal Code section 189 codifies the common law rule that a killing during the commission of a felony is considered to be murder without requiring proof of malice. The majority's account of the history of section 189, however, persuades me to a contrary conclusion.

As the majority explain, as of 1872 California had two felony-murder statutes: former section 25, which codified the common law felony-murder rule; and former section 21, which fixed the degree of the murder. The 1872 Penal Code reenacted section 21 (now renumbered as § 189) but omitted section 25.

We do not know why the Legislature failed to reenact section 25. (It seems fanciful to attempt to trace that failure to a mistaken comment by the Code Commissioners in their discussion of an arson statute.) It is possible that the Legislature intended to reenact the common law felony-murder rule and failed through inadvertence or oversight. But the fact remains that the Legislature did not reenact that rule, but retained only the statute which fixed the degree of the murder.

I do not believe the language of section 189, the degree-fixing statute, can reasonably be construed to encompass the common law felony-murder rule. As the majority carefully explain, the language of section 189 derives from former section 21 and similar enactments in other states—enactments clearly intended to serve solely the function of distinguishing between first and second degree murder. The current wording of section 189 reflects this limited purpose. It does not refer to a killing to perpetrate a felony—the subject of the common law rule—but to a "murder" to perpetrate six specific felonies. In fixing the degree of the murder, moreover, section 189 includes not only murders in perpetration of the listed felonies, but also those committed by explosive, poison, lying in wait, or torture. A killing committed by such means, however, is not murder without proof of malice. There is no reasonable way to read the language of section 189 to make killings in perpetration of the six listed felonies murder without proof of malice, but to require malice for all other killings described in that section.

I conclude that the felony-murder rule remains judge-created and judge-preserved common law. It is therefore within the power of this court to overturn that rule. If we were to consider that matter, we would have to recognize that numerous decisions of this court have upheld and applied that rule. (Some, written without the guidance of the majority's historical analysis, have mistakenly assumed the rule was statutory.) The Legislature has undoubtedly relied on those decisions in considering and enacting other penal legislation. This long-continued pattern of judicial precedent and legislative reliance would weigh heavily against repudiation of the felony-murder rule, serving to offset the logical weakness of that rule and the occasional inequities it brings about. But the majority's conclusion that the felony-murder rule is statutory moots that issue.

[Justice Broussard also dissented from the decision to reduce the conviction to second degree murder.]

Notes and Problem

Criticism of the Felony-murder Rule. The Michigan Supreme Court, in *People v. Aaron*, 299 N.W.2d 304, 316–17 (1980) (distinguished by the Court in *Dillon*) had the following to say about the felony-murder rule:

> "If one had to choose the most basic principle of the criminal law in general ... it would be that criminal liability for causing a particular result is not justified in the absence of some culpable mental state in respect to that result ..." [quoting B. Gegan, *Criminal Homicide in the Revised New York Penal Law*, 12 N.Y. L. Forum 565, 586 (1966).]
>
> The most fundamental characteristic of the felony-murder rule violates this basic principle in that it punishes all homicides, committed in the perpetration or attempted perpetration of proscribed felonies whether intentional, unintentional or accidental, without the necessity of proving the relation between the homicide and the perpetrator's state of mind. This is most evident when a killing is done by one of a group of co-felons. The felony-murder rule completely ignores the concept of determination of guilt on the basis of individual misconduct. The felony-murder rule thus "erodes the relation between criminal liability and moral culpability." [quoting *People v. Washington*, *infra*]
>
> The felony-murder rule's most egregious violation of basic rules of culpability occurs where felony murder is categorized as first-degree murder. All other murders carrying equal punishment require a showing of premeditation, deliberation and willfulness while felony murder only requires a showing of intent to do the underlying felony. Although the purpose of our degree statutes is to punish more severely the more culpable forms of murder, an accidental killing occurring during the perpetration of a felony would be punished more severely than a second-degree murder requiring intent to kill, intent to cause great bodily harm or wantonness and willfulness....

Is there anything to be said in favor of the rule? *See* David Crump & Susan Waite Crump, *In Defense of the Felony Murder Doctrine*, 8 Harv. J. of Law & Soc. Pol'y 359 (1985) (arguing that the felony-murder rule comports with the idea of "just desserts" by taking account of the harm caused, that it deters felonies and that it simplifies the processing of murder cases and limits the incidence of perjury). In a later article, Professor Crump reiterated his defense of the felony-murder rule, but refined his argument to distinguish between "well-drafted" and "clumsier" versions of the rule. See David Crump, *Reconsidering the Felony Murder Rule in Light of Modern Criticisms: Doesn't the Conclusion Depend Upon the Particular Rule at Issue?* 32 Harv. J.L. & Pub. Pol'y 1155 (2009). He put California in the "clumsier" category, describing the California rule as "poorly designed" with "arbitrary" and "odd" distinctions. *Id.* at 1161.

The Constitutionality of the Felony-murder Rule. In *Dillon*, the court rejected the defendant's constitutional challenge to the felony-murder rule by holding that the rule created, not a presumption of malice, but rather a species of murder without malice. Did the court thereby invite a different constitutional challenge to the rule? It has been argued that such a rule—imposing strict liability on the defendant for a homicide solely because it occurred in the course of a felony—violates the Eighth Amendment's prohibition against disproportionate punishments and a requirement, argued to be derived from the due process clause, that, except in the case of regulatory crimes, *mens rea* must be proved as to each element of a crime. See N. Roth & S. Sundby, *The Felony-murder Rule: A Doctrine at Constitutional Crossroads*, 70 Cornell L. Rev. 446 (1985).

The Model Penal Code and Felony-murder. The Model Penal Code abandons the felony-murder rule as a separate basis for liability for murder. MPC § 210.2. Under the Code, murder is established only by proof that the defendant killed purposely or knowingly or acted with recklessness manifesting extreme indifference to the value of human life. Proof that the defendant killed during the commission, or attempt to commit, or the flight from commission of, one of seven listed felonies creates a presumption of such recklessness and extreme indifference, but it is not a conclusive presumption and may be rebutted by the defendant or ignored by the jury. MPC Part II Commentaries vol. 1, p. 30.

Problem 39.

Defendant stole an armful of expensive clothes from a department store. He threw the clothes into his car, which had been illegally parked with its engine running and its driver's door open, and drove off. Citizen observed Defendant throw the clothes into the car and gave chase, following Defendant for approximately two and a half miles. Eventually, Defendant ran a red light and collided with another car, killing a passenger in that car. Defendant was convicted of first degree murder on a felony-murder theory because he committed a burglary (entering the department store with the intent to commit a theft) and his attempted escape is considered part of the burglary for felony-murder purposes (see *People v. Fields, infra*). In light of the fact that Defendant has never been convicted of a crime of violence, although he has a twenty-five year history of criminal activity, what arguments should be made on whether Defendant's conviction should be reduced to second degree murder?

People v. Chun (Part 1)

45 Cal.4th 1172, 203 P.3d 425 (2009)

CHIN, J.

In this murder case, the trial court instructed the jury on second degree felony murder with shooting at an occupied vehicle under Penal Code section 246 the underlying felony.[1] We granted review to consider various issues concerning the validity and scope of the second degree felony-murder rule.

We first discuss the rule's constitutional basis. Although the rule has long been part of our law, some members of this court have questioned its constitutional validity. We conclude that the rule is based on statute, specifically section 188's definition of implied malice, and hence is constitutionally valid.

...

I. FACTS AND PROCEDURAL HISTORY

We take our facts primarily from the Court of Appeal's opinion.

Judy Onesavanh and Sophal Ouch were planning a party for their son's birthday. Around 9:00 p.m. on September 13, 2003, they and a friend, Bounthavy Onethavong, were driving to the store in Stockton in a blue Mitsubishi that Onesavanh's father owned. Onesavanh's brother, George, also drives the car. The police consider George to be highly ranked in the Asian Boys street gang (Asian Boys).

That evening Ouch was driving, with Onesavanh in the front passenger seat and Onethavong behind Ouch. While they were stopped in the left turn lane at a traffic light, a blue Honda with tinted windows pulled up beside them. When the light changed, gunfire erupted from the Honda, hitting all three occupants of the Mitsubishi. Onethavong was killed, having received two bullet wounds in the head. Onesavanh was hit in the back and seriously wounded. Ouch was shot in the cheek and suffered a fractured jaw.

Ouch and Onesavanh identified the Honda's driver as "T-Bird," known to the police to be Rathana Chan, a member of the Tiny Rascals Gangsters (Tiny Rascals), a criminal street gang. The Tiny Rascals do not get along with the Asian Boys. Chan was never found. The forensic evidence showed that three different guns were used in the shooting, a .22, a .38, and a .44, and at least six bullets were fired. Both the .38 and the .44 struck Onethavong; both shots were lethal. Only the .44 was recovered. It was found at the residence of Sokha and Mao Bun, brothers believed to be members of a gang.

Two months after the shooting, the police stopped a van while investigating another suspected gang shooting. Defendant was a passenger in the van. He was arrested and subsequently made two statements regarding the shooting in this case. He admitted he was in the backseat of the Honda at the time; T-Bird was the driver and there were two other passengers. Later, he also admitted he fired a .38-caliber firearm. He said he did not point the gun at anyone; he just wanted to scare them.

Defendant, who was 16 years old at the time of the shooting, was tried as an adult for his role in the shooting. He was charged with murder, with driveby and gang special circumstances, and with two counts of attempted murder, discharging a firearm from a vehicle, and shooting into an occupied vehicle, all with gang and firearm-use

1. All further statutory citations are to the Penal Code unless otherwise indicated.

allegations, and with street terrorism. At trial, the prosecution presented evidence that defendant was a member of the Tiny Rascals, and that the shooting was for the benefit of a gang. Defendant testified, denying being a member of the Tiny Rascals or being involved in the shooting.

The prosecution sought a first degree murder conviction. The court also instructed the jury on second degree felony murder based on shooting at an occupied motor vehicle (§ 246) either directly or as an aider and abettor. The jury found defendant guilty of second degree murder. It found the personal-firearm-use allegation not true, but found that a principal intentionally used a firearm and the shooting was committed for the benefit of a criminal street gang. The jury acquitted defendant of both counts of attempted murder, shooting from a motor vehicle, and shooting at an occupied motor vehicle. It convicted defendant of being an active participant in a criminal street gang.

...

II. DISCUSSION

A. The Constitutionality of the Second Degree Felony-murder Rule

Defendant contends California's second degree felony-murder rule is unconstitutional on separation of power grounds as a judicially created doctrine with no statutory basis. To explain the issue, we first describe how the doctrine fits in with the law of murder. Then we discuss defendant's contention. We will ultimately conclude that the doctrine is valid as an interpretation of broad statutory language.

Section 187, subdivision (a), defines murder as "the unlawful killing of a human being, or a fetus, with malice aforethought." Except for the phrase "or a fetus," which was added in 1970..., this definition has been unchanged since it was first enacted as part of the Penal Code of 1872. Murder is divided into first and second degree murder. (§ 189.) "Second degree murder is the unlawful killing of a human being with malice, but without the additional elements (i.e., willfulness, premeditation, and deliberation) that would support a conviction of first degree murder. (§§ 187, subd. (a), 189)." (*People v. Hansen* (1994) 9 Cal.4th 300.)

Critical for our purposes is that the crime of murder, as defined in section 187, includes, as an element, malice. Section 188 defines malice. It may be either express or implied. It is express "when there is manifested a deliberate intention unlawfully to take away the life of a fellow creature." (§ 188.) It is implied "when no considerable provocation appears, or when the circumstances attending the killing show an abandoned and malignant heart." (*Ibid.*) This definition of implied malice is quite vague. Trial courts do not instruct the jury in the statutory language of an abandoned and malignant heart. Doing so would provide the jury with little guidance. "The statutory definition of implied malice has never proved of much assistance in defining the concept in concrete terms." (*People v. Dellinger* (1989) 49 Cal.3d 1212.) Accordingly, the statutory definition permits, even requires, judicial interpretation. We have interpreted implied malice as having "both a physical and a mental component. The physical component is satisfied by the performance of an act, the natural consequences of which are dangerous to life. The mental component is the requirement that the defendant knows that his conduct endangers the life of another and ... acts with a conscious disregard for life." (*People v. Patterson* (1989) 49 Cal.3d 615 (lead opn. of Kennard, J.) (*Patterson*).)[2]

A defendant may also be found guilty of murder under the felony-murder rule. The felony-murder rule makes a killing while committing certain felonies murder without the necessity of further examining the defendant's mental state. The rule has two applications: first degree felony murder and second degree felony murder. We have said that first degree felony murder is a "creation of statute" (i.e., § 189) but, because no statute specifically describes it, that second degree felony murder is a "common law doctrine." (*People v. Robertson* (2004) 34 Cal.4th 156 (*Robertson*).) First degree felony murder is a killing during the course of a felony specified in section 189, such as rape, burglary, or robbery. Second degree felony murder is "an unlawful killing in the course of the commission of a felony that is inherently dangerous to human life but is not included among the felonies enumerated in section 189." (*Robertson, supra.*)

In *Patterson*, Justice Kennard explained the reasoning behind and the justification for the second degree felony-murder rule: "The second degree felony-murder rule eliminates the need for the prosecution to establish the *mental* component [of conscious-disregard-for-life malice]. The justification therefor is that, when society has declared certain inherently dangerous conduct to be felonious, a defendant should not be allowed to excuse himself by saying he was unaware of the danger to life because, by declaring the conduct to be felonious, society has warned him of the risk involved. The *physical* requirement, however, remains the same; by committing a felony inherently dangerous to life, the defendant has committed an act, the natural consequences of which are dangerous to life, thus satisfying the physical component of implied malice." (*Patterson, supra.*)

The second degree felony-murder rule is venerable. It "has been a part of California's criminal law for many decades. Because of this, we declined to reconsider the rule in *Patterson*....

But some former and current members of this court have questioned the rule's validity because no statute specifically addresses it. [Citing: Chief Justice Bird, concurring in *People v. Burroughs* (1984) 35 Cal.3d 824; Justice Brown, dissenting in *Robertson* and concurring and dissenting in *People v. Howard* (2005) 34 Cal.4th 1129; Justices Werdegar, dissenting, and Moreno, concurring, in *Robertson*; Justice Panelli, concurring and dissenting in *Patterson*.]

In line with these concerns, defendant argues that the second degree felony-murder rule is invalid on separation of powers grounds. As he points out, we have repeatedly said that "the power to define crimes and fix penalties is vested exclusively in the legislative branch." (*People v. Superior Court (Romero)* (1996) 13 Cal.4th 497.) Defendant

2. For ease of discussion, we will sometimes refer to this form of malice by the shorthand term, "conscious-disregard-for-life malice." *Patterson, supra,* had no majority opinion. Unless otherwise indicated, all further citations to that case are to Justice Kennard's lead opinion.

asks rhetorically, "How, then, in light of the statutory abrogation of common law crimes and the constitutional principle of separation of powers, does second degree felony murder continue to exist when this court has repeatedly acknowledged that the crime is a judicial creation?"

This court has never directly addressed these concerns and this argument, or explained the statutory basis of the second degree felony-murder rule. We do so now. We agree with Justice Panelli that there are no nonstatutory crimes in this state. Some statutory or regulatory provision must describe conduct as criminal in order for the courts to treat that conduct as criminal. (§6.) But, as we explain, the second degree felony-murder rule, although derived from the common law, is based on statute; it is simply another interpretation of section 188's abandoned and malignant heart language.

Many provisions of the Penal Code were enacted using common law terms that must be interpreted in light of the common law. For example, section 484 defines theft as "feloniously" taking the property of another. The term "feloniously"—which has little meaning by itself—incorporates the common law requirement that the perpetrator must intend to permanently deprive the owner of possession of the property. Accordingly, we have looked to the common law to determine the exact contours of that requirement. Thus, the intent-to-permanently-deprive requirement, although nonstatutory in the limited sense that no California statute uses those words, is based on statute. The murder statutes are similarly derived from the common law. "It will be presumed ... that in enacting a statute the Legislature was familiar with the relevant rules of the common law, and, when it couches its enactments in common law language, that its intent was to continue those rules in statutory form." (*Keeler v. Superior Court* (1970) 2 Cal.3d 619 [looking to the common law to determine the exact meaning of "human being" under section 187].)

Even conscious-disregard-for-life malice is nonstatutory in the limited sense that no California statute specifically uses those words. But that form of implied malice is firmly based on statute; it is an interpretation of section 188's abandoned and malignant heart language. Similarly, the second degree felony-murder rule is nonstatutory in the sense that no statute specifically spells it out, but it is also statutory as another interpretation of the same "abandoned and malignant heart" language. We have said that the "felony-murder rule eliminates the need for proof of malice in connection with a charge of murder, thereby rendering irrelevant the presence or absence of actual malice, both with regard to first degree felony murder and second degree felony murder." (*Robertson, supra.*) But analytically, this is not precisely correct. The felony-murder rule renders irrelevant *conscious-disregard-for-life* malice, but it does not render malice itself irrelevant. Instead, the felony-murder rule "acts as a substitute" for conscious-disregard-for-life malice. (*Patterson, supra.*) It simply describes a different form of malice under section 188. "The felony-murder rule imputes the requisite malice for a murder conviction to those who commit a homicide during the perpetration of a felony inherently dangerous to life." (*Hansen, supra.*)

[Justice Chin reviewed the history of the murder statutes leading up to the adoption of the 1872 Penal Code, as had the court in *People v. Dillon*. However, Justice Chin concluded that the court's analysis in *Dillon* was not entirely correct and that its statement, "the Legislature's decision not to reenact the felony-murder provision of section 25 in the 1872 codification implied an intent to abrogate the common law felony-murder rule that the section had embodied since 1850," was dicta and was incorrect. Rather, he read the history to show that the Legislature had understood the common law felony-murder rule to be continued under the new code. This view is supported by the fact that the Code Commissioners' notes accompanying the 1872 adoption of the Penal Code "provide no hint of an intent to abrogate the felony-murder rule." Further, no contemporaneous case, or indeed any case prior to *Dillon*, suggested that the failure to reenact section 25 had repealed the felony-murder rule.]

People v. Fields

35 Cal.3d 329, 673 P.2d 680 (1983)

Broussard, Justice.

This case arises on an automatic appeal from a death sentence imposed under the 1977 death penalty statute....

I. Summary of proceedings.

On September 13, 1978, defendant was paroled from prison after serving a sentence for manslaughter. In the next three weeks, he became a one-man crime wave. He was eventually convicted in this proceeding of the following offenses: the robbery murder of Rosemary C., with the special circumstance of willful, deliberate, and premeditated murder during the commission of a robbery [and twelve additional felonies committed against four other victims].

The jury determined that defendant was sane, and fixed the punishment at death. The trial court denied defendant's motion for new trial and for modification of the verdict. The case comes to us on automatic appeal.

II. Summary of the evidence.

(a) *The murder and robbery of Rosemary C.*

Rosemary C.... worked as a student librarian at the University of Southern California. On September 27, Gail Fields, defendant's sister, saw Rosemary and defendant at the Fields residence. The next morning Gail entered defendant's bedroom; defendant was standing by the door and Rosemary was naked in the bed. Defendant handed Gail a check signed by Rosemary C. for $185. Defendant then examined Rosemary's checkbook and said that she probably had more money. Defendant called Rosemary a "bitch" and told her to write another check for $222 and some cents. He then told Rosemary he would "bump her off" because "she run a game on him," by writing a check for less than the balance of her account. Gail took the $222 check, cashed it at a bank, and gave the money to defendant, who returned $22 to her.

About 1 p.m. on September 28, Debbie M., a 16-year-old girl who was the former girlfriend of defendant's brother, went to the Fields residence. Debbie saw Rosemary and defendant go into defendant's bedroom.... A short while later Debbie saw defendant enter the bedroom with a gun, tell Rosemary that he would kill her if she did not give him money, and say that he was going to take her on a long trip "and she wasn't never going to come back."

Later in the afternoon Gail borrowed a car from Clifton B., Debbie's godfather. Debbie saw defendant, Gail, and Rosemary leave the house; Rosemary was dressed and carrying her purse. Gail testified that defendant and Rosemary got in the back seat of B.'s car. Defendant told Gail to drive them toward the Santa Monica freeway. As the car entered the on-ramp, Gail heard a shot. Rosemary cried out, "Oh, God." Defendant told Gail to keep on driving. Gail heard more shots. Defendant then said that Rosemary was not dead and he had to make sure she was dead. Gail then heard the noise of a blow. Rosemary died of five gunshot wounds and a blunt injury to the head.

Gail drove to an alley near the Fields residence. Defendant removed the body from the car and left it in the alley while Gail covered the car's license plates. They drove to a car wash and cleaned the blood from the car. Debbie saw defendant and Gail return without Rosemary. When she heard police sirens, Debbie went to the alley and saw the body. She walked back to the house and asked defendant if the body was the girl who had been at the house. He laughed and said, "She was going on a long trip and was never coming back."

[The prosecution introduced additional evidence which corroborated the testimony of Gail and Debbie.]

(c) ***Jury instructions and evidence on felony murder.***

Former Penal Code section 190.2 provided that a defendant found guilty of first degree murder may be sentenced to death if he "was personally present during the commission of the act or acts causing death, and with intent to cause death physically aided or committed such act or acts causing death and any of the following additional circumstances exists: [¶] (3) The murder was willful, deliberate, and premeditated and was committed *during the commission* or attempted commission *of* any of the following crimes: [¶] (i) *Robbery*, in violation of Section 211...." (Italics added.)

In *People v. Green* (1980) 27 Cal.3d 1, we explained the basis of the felony murder special circumstance under the 1977 law. "At the very least," we said, "the Legislature must have intended that each special circumstance provide a rational basis for distinguishing between those murderers who deserve to be considered for the death penalty and those who do not. The Legislature declared that such a distinction could be drawn, inter alia, when the defendant committed a 'willful, deliberate and premeditated' murder 'during the commission' of a robbery or other listed felony. [Citation.] The provision thus expressed a legislative belief that it was not unconstitutionally arbitrary to expose to the death penalty those defendants who killed in cold blood in order to advance an independent felonious purpose...."

In other words, while either premeditation or a killing during the commission of a felony will raise the crime to first degree murder, neither standing alone rendered a defendant liable to the death penalty. Both elements were essential to a felony murder special circumstance. By this requirement, the 1977 death penalty law limited the number of those persons who would face special circumstance proceedings and avoided arbitrary infliction of the death penalty upon defendants of lesser culpability.

The jury in the present case, instructed on both premeditated and felony murder, found defendant guilty of the first degree murder of Rosemary C. It also found him guilty of robbery of Rosemary. Finally, it found true the special circumstance allegation of premeditated murder "during the commission of a robbery." Defendant contends that no substantial evidence supports this finding, and that the jury was improperly instructed on this subject.

We briefly recapitulate the undisputed evidence bearing on the felony murder issue. Defendant robbed Rosemary C. by compelling her to write a check to Gail Fields, who cashed the check and turned over most of the money to defendant. Several hours later defendant, Gail, and the victim entered a car. While Gail drove, defendant shot and struck Rosemary, killing her. He then dumped the body in an alley near his house. The testimony suggests two possible motives for the killing: (1) revenge because Rosemary tried to frustrate the robbery—in defendant's words, to "run a game" on him—by writing a check for less than the maximum possible; or (2) to eliminate her as a witness against him.

After hearing this evidence, the court instructed the jury that: "A robbery is still in progress after the original taking of physical possession of the stolen property while the perpetrator is in hot flight, that is, while in possession of the stolen property he is fleeing in an attempt to escape.... [¶] A robbery is complete when the perpetrator ... has reached a place of temporary safety and is in unchallenged possession of the stolen property after having effected an escape with such property." (CALJIC No. 9.15 as modified by the court.)

[The reference to "hot flight" in the jury instructions was inappropriate but, because it favored the defendant, could not have been prejudicial.]

We turn therefore to the question whether substantial evidence supports the jury's finding that Rosemary C. was murdered "during the commission of the robbery."[15] A sizeable body of California decisions have discussed the duration of the crime of robbery and the relationship of that crime to some other offense which occurs after

15. The Attorney General emphasizes the evidence that Rosemary took her purse with her when she went with defendant and Gail, and that the purse was later discovered in the Fields house. He argues that the robbery of the purse, contemporaneous with the murder, alone is sufficient to support the special circumstance finding. In *People v. Green, supra,* we explained that a robbery which is merely incidental to a murder will not support a felony murder special circumstance finding. Whenever a defendant kills a clothed victim and takes possession of the body to dispose of it, he acquires possession of the victim's clothes and any personal effects the victim may have been carrying. Unless, however, the killer has an independent felonious purpose to acquire those items, this possession, wholly incidental to the killing, will not support a felony murder finding. In the present case, we find no evidence that defendant killed Rosemary with the independent felonious purpose of robbing her of her purse.

the exact moment when the property changed hands. Although some of these cases arise under statutes whose wording differs from the statute at issue here, they address a problem common to this case—whether the relationship between a robbery and another crime is sufficiently close to justify an enhanced punishment. We therefore look to these cases for guidance in our analysis of the felony murder issue in the present case.

In *People v. Carroll* (1970) 1 Cal.3d 581 defendant robbed Gulsvig in a restroom, pursued him into a bar and shot him. He was convicted of inflicting great bodily injury on Gulsvig "in the course of the commission of the robbery." We said that "[t]he fact that defendant was not engaged in the asportation of any loot at the time he shot Gulsvig is immaterial. He became angry after discovering no money in the wallet and having the rest room door slammed in his face. His purpose in running into the bar appears to have been to exact his revenge from Gulsvig. Under the circumstances, the robbery and shooting of Gulsvig constituted one indivisible transaction...."

In *People v. Laursen* (1972) 8 Cal.3d 192, fleeing robbers kidnaped a motorist and compelled him to drive them from the scene of the robbery. We held defendant could be found guilty of kidnaping "to commit robbery"; "[t]he assault of the victim, the seizure of his property and the robber's escape to a location of temporary safety are all phases in the commission of the crime of robbery linked not only by a proximity of time and distance, but a single-mindedness of the culprit's purpose as well."

In *People v. Green, supra*, when we explained the basis for the felony murder special circumstance, we illustrated that special circumstance by describing a killing resembling the present case, e.g., a murder by a defendant "who carried out an execution-style slaying of the victim of or witness to a holdup, a kidnaping, or a rape."

Finally, in the recent case of *People v. Ramos* (1982) 30 Cal.3d 553, defendant and his partner compelled two workers at a restaurant to go into the walk-in refrigerator. When the robbers had finished taking money from the safe, defendant reentered the refrigerator and shot both workers, killing one of them. We upheld the jury's finding that the murder occurred during the commission of the robbery under section 190.2, stating that "[i]n the instant case, the killing occurred at the same location as the robbery and within a short time after the money was taken from the safe. Moreover, the jury could well have concluded that the purpose of the killing was to eliminate a witness to the robbery."

Two decisions of the Court of Appeal present an even closer analogy to the present case. The first, *People v. Powell* (1974) 40 Cal.App.3d 107, was described in the book The Onion Field. Defendants in *Powell* kidnaped two police officers in Los Angeles, took their guns and money, and drove them to Kern County where defendant Powell shot and killed one officer. The court held the felony murder rule (based on the robbery of the guns and money) applicable because as long as the defendants were accompanied by and saddled with the officers they had not reached a place of temporary safety.

The second case is *People v. Sirignano* (1974) 42 Cal.App.3d 794. Defendant lured the victim to a hotel room, struck him, and robbed him. "Long after it was apparent that no additional money would be forthcoming from the victim, the persons involved, including defendant, continued to assault him; when he was dead, the group took steps to avoid apprehension for the robbery and death." Defendant contended that the robbery was completed before the killing, and that she had reached a place of temporary safety. The court, noting the inference that defendant planned to kill the victim so he would not be able to testify, held that "[t]here was substantial evidence to support the conclusion that the events of the evening formed one 'continuous transaction,' and such a finding clearly results in felony-murder, in the first degree."

Defendant, on the other hand, calls our attention to *People v. Ford* (1966) 65 Cal.2d 41, but we find that decision distinguishable. Explaining why we could not uphold a conviction of first degree murder under the felony-murder rule, we said that "[i]n the present case…, many hours elapsed between the time of the robbery and the shooting of Officer Stahl. [T]here was here no direct evidence that defendant was endeavoring to escape the robbery when he shot the deputy; on the contrary, there is strong evidence that he was not…. Additionally, it should be pointed out that defendant had the opportunity to and did spend some of his loot prior to the shooting; that during the period of approximately four hours between the robbery and the killing he drove aimlessly over a great distance; and that, with respect at least to the robbery, he had won his way to places of temporary safety before he committed the homicide. Considering the facts as a whole, it must be held that the robbery and escape therefrom did not motivate defendant's subsequent conduct, but were merely incidental to his primary objectives. Thus, it cannot be held that the homicide can be promoted to murder of the first degree on the theory that the homicide was committed in the perpetration of a robbery."

On the basis of the cases discussed, we conclude that the jury finding of special circumstances in the present case should be sustained. We recognize that when Gail Fields returned with the proceeds of Rosemary's check and gave them to defendant, he had control of the robbery proceeds in his own residence. That residence, however, was not a place of safety so long as Rosemary was held prisoner. In an unguarded moment, she might escape, notify the police, and render the Fields residence quite unsafe for defendant. In order to complete a successful escape with the robbery proceeds, defendant either had to dispose of her, which he did, or flee to some other place which she could not identify for the police. Thus, the trier of fact could reasonably find that defendant's murder was a continuation of the robbery, done because until the robbery victim was killed, Fields' home was not a place of even temporary safety.[18]

Moreover, despite the span in space and time between the taking and the murder, defendant's purpose in killing his victim serves to link the two crimes. As we noted, the record suggests two motives: to prevent her from reporting the crime (compare *People v. Ramos, supra*; *People v. Sirignano, supra*); and to punish her for attempting

18. The fact that defendant took Rosemary away from the residence to kill her is also suggestive. Defendant may have wanted to prevent other persons, such as Debbie M., from witnessing the killing, or avoid having evidence of the killing in the house, because the existence of such witnesses or evidence would also render the house an unsafe refuge.

to frustrate the robbery (compare *People v. Carroll, supra*). Such motives would not enable a court to find a killing occurred during the commission of a robbery if it took place days later and in a far distant locale. But here the murder occurred within a few hours of the robbery, and at a site only a few miles distant, and the events are linked not only by defendant's motives but by his continued control over the victim, forcing her to remain at his house and then transporting her to the murder site. We conclude that the evidence supports the verdict finding the special circumstance of murder during the commission of robbery.

...

[Opinion of KAUS, J., concurring and opinions of BIRD, C.J. and REYNOSO, J., dissenting on other grounds omitted.]

Problems

Problem 40.

Defendant held up the manager of a market in City at closing time and left the manager tied up in the back room. Defendant fled in his car. About 25 minutes after leaving the market, Defendant was on a freeway 30 miles from City. He was speeding at 70–75 miles per hour, when he was pulled over by Officer. When Officer approached Defendant's car with his citation book, Defendant shot and killed him. Defendant mistakenly thought Officer had learned of the robbery and was going to arrest him. Defendant is now charged, *inter alia*, with first degree murder (P.C. §§ 187–189). What are the arguments on whether he can be convicted on a felony-murder theory?

Problem 41.

Defendant and two others agreed to hold up a card game which they understood to be taking place at Victim's apartment. They knocked on the door, and, when it was opened, defendant and another pushed their way into the apartment. Victim became enraged and pushed the holdup men out of the apartment and shut the door. She then grabbed a bottle and reopened the door, cursing at the men outside. An argument ensued, and, when Victim raised the bottle to strike one of the men, Defendant shot and killed her. What arguments should be made as to whether Defendant can be prosecuted for first degree murder (P.C. §§ 187–189) on a felony-murder theory?

Problem 42.

Each week, Farmer paid his workers at a certain time in a building on his farm. Defendant was the leader of a group which decided to rob Farmer one payday. Victim was stationed outside as a lookout, and Defendant and other members of the group entered the building and held up Farmer at gunpoint. The group inside the building seized Farmer's money, and they were leaving the building when they heard two gunshots. Coming out of the building, Defendant realized that Victim had fired the shots at some passersby. Shouting, "Damn you, what did you shoot for," Defendant shot and killed Victim. Defendant is charged with first degree murder (P.C. §§ 187–189). What arguments should be made as to whether Defendant is guilty of felony-murder?

People v. Washington

62 Cal. 2d 777, 402 P.2d 130 (1965)

TRAYNOR, C.J.

Defendant appeals from a judgment of conviction entered upon jury verdicts finding him guilty of first degree robbery (Pen. Code, §§ 211, 211a) and first degree murder and fixing the murder penalty at life imprisonment. (Pen. Code, §§ 187, 189, 190, 190.1.) He was convicted of murder for participating in a robbery in which his accomplice was killed by the victim of the robbery.

Shortly before 10 p.m., October 2, 1962, Johnnie Carpenter prepared to close his gasoline station. He was in his office computing the receipts and disbursements of the day while an attendant in an adjacent storage room deposited money in a vault. Upon hearing someone yell "robbery," Carpenter opened his desk and took out a revolver. A few moments later, James Ball entered the office and pointed a revolver directly at Carpenter, who fired immediately, mortally wounding Ball. Carpenter then hurried to the door and saw an unarmed man he later identified as defendant running from the vault with a moneybag in his right hand. He shouted "Stop." When his warning was not heeded, he fired and hit defendant who fell wounded in front of the station.

The Attorney General, relying on *People v. Harrison* (1959) 176 Cal. App. 2d 330, contends that defendant was properly convicted of first degree murder. In that case defendants initiated a gun battle with an employee in an attempt to rob a cleaning business. In the crossfire, the employee accidentally killed the owner of the business. The court affirmed the judgment convicting defendants of first degree murder, invoking *Commonwealth v. Almeida* (Pa. 1949) 68 A.2d 595 and *People v. Podolski* (Mich. 1952) 52 N.W.2d 201, which held that robbers who provoked gunfire were guilty of first degree murder even though the lethal bullet was fired by a policeman.

Defendant would distinguish the *Harrison*, *Almeida*, and *Podolski* cases on the ground that in each instance the person killed was an innocent victim, not one of the felons. He suggests that we limit the rule of the *Harrison* case just as the Supreme Courts of Pennsylvania and Michigan have limited the *Almeida* and *Podolski* cases by holding that surviving felons are not guilty of murder when their accomplices are killed by persons resisting the felony. (*Commonwealth v. Redline* (Pa. 1958) 137 A.2d 472; *People v. Austin* (Mich. 1963) 120 N.W.2d 766.) A distinction based on the person killed, however, would make the defendant's criminal liability turn upon the marksmanship of victims and policemen. A rule of law cannot reasonably be based on such a fortuitous circumstance. The basic issue therefore is whether a robber can be convicted of murder for the killing of any person by another who is resisting the robbery.

"Murder is the unlawful killing of a human being, with malice aforethought." Except when the common-law-felony-murder doctrine is applicable, an essential element of murder is an intent to kill or an intent with conscious disregard for life to commit acts likely to kill. The felony-murder doctrine ascribes malice aforethought to the felon who kills in the perpetration of an inherently dangerous felony. That doctrine is incorporated in section 189 of the Penal Code, which provides in part: "All murder ... committed in the perpetration or attempt to perpetrate ... robbery ... is murder of the first degree." Thus, even though section 189 speaks only of degrees of "murder," inadvertent or accidental killings are first degree murders when committed by felons in the perpetration of robbery.

When a killing is not committed by a robber or by his accomplice but by his victim, malice aforethought is not attributable to the robber, for the killing is not committed by him in the perpetration or attempt to perpetrate robbery. It is not enough that the killing was a risk reasonably to be foreseen and that the robbery might therefore be regarded as a proximate cause of the killing. Section 189 requires that the felon or his accomplice commit the killing, for if he does not, the killing is not committed to perpetrate the felony. Indeed, in the present case the killing was committed to thwart a felony. To include such killings within section 189 would expand the meaning of the words "murder ... which is committed in the perpetration ... [of] robbery ..." beyond common understanding.

The purpose of the felony-murder rule is to deter felons from killing negligently or accidentally by holding them strictly responsible for killings they commit. This purpose is not served by punishing them for killings committed by their victims.

It is contended, however, that another purpose of the felony-murder rule is to prevent the commission of robberies. Neither the common-law rationale of the rule nor the Penal Code supports this contention. In every robbery there is a possibility that the victim will resist and kill. The robber has little control over such a killing once the robbery is undertaken as this case demonstrates. To impose an additional penalty for the killing would discriminate between robbers, not on the basis of any difference in their own conduct, but solely on the basis of the response by others that the robber's conduct happened to induce. An additional penalty for a homicide committed by the victim would deter robbery haphazardly at best. To "prevent stealing, [the law] would do better to hang one thief in every thousand by lot" (Holmes, The Common Law, p. 58).

A defendant need not do the killing himself, however, to be guilty of murder. He may be vicariously responsible under the rules defining principals and criminal conspiracies. All persons aiding and abetting the commission of a robbery are guilty of first degree murder when one of them kills while acting in furtherance of the common design. Moreover, when the defendant intends to kill or intentionally commits acts that are likely to kill with a conscious disregard for life, he is guilty of murder even though he uses another person to accomplish his objective.

Defendants who initiate gun battles may also be found guilty of murder if their victims resist and kill. Under such circumstances, "the defendant for a base, antisocial motive and with wanton disregard for human life, does an act that involves a high degree of probability that it will result in death," and it is unnecessary to imply malice by invoking the felony-murder doctrine. To invoke the felony-murder doctrine to imply malice in such a case is unnecessary and overlooks the principles of criminal liability that should govern the responsibility of one person for a killing committed by another.

To invoke the felony-murder doctrine when the killing is not committed by the defendant or by his accomplice could lead to absurd results. Thus, two men rob a grocery store and flee in opposite directions. The owner of the store follows one of the robbers and kills him. Neither robber may have fired a shot. Neither robber may have been armed with a deadly weapon. If the felony-murder doctrine applied, however, the surviving robber could be convicted of first degree murder, even though he was captured by a policeman and placed under arrest at the time his accomplice was killed.

. . .

Burke, J., dissenting, joined by McComb, J.

I dissent. The unfortunate effect of the decision of the majority in this case is to advise felons:

"Henceforth in committing certain crimes, including robbery, rape and burglary, you are free to arm yourselves with a gun and brandish it in the faces of your victims without fear of a murder conviction unless you or your accomplice pulls the trigger. If the menacing effect of your gun causes a victim or policeman to fire and kill an innocent person or a cofelon, you are absolved of responsibility for such killing unless you shoot first."

Obviously this advance judicial absolution removes one of the most meaningful deterrents to the commission of armed felonies.

In the present case defendant's accomplice was killed when the robbery victim fired after the accomplice had pointed a revolver at him. In *People v. Harrison* (1959) 176 Cal. App. 2d 330 (hearing in Supreme Court denied without a dissenting vote), the rationale of which the majority now disapprove, the robbery victim was himself accidentally killed by a shot fired by his employee after defendant robbers had opened fire, and the robbers were held guilty of murder for the killing. The majority now attempt to distinguish Harrison on the ground that there the robbers "initiated" the gun battle; in the present case the victim fired the first shot. As will appear, any such purported distinction is an invitation to further armed crimes of violence. There is no room in the law for sporting considerations and distinctions as to who fired first when dealing with killings which are caused by the actions of felons in deliberately arming themselves to commit any of the heinous crimes listed in Penal Code section 189. If a victim—or someone defending the victim—seizes an opportunity to shoot first when confronted by robbers with a deadly weapon (real or simulated), any "gun battle" is initiated by the armed robbers. In such a situation application of the felony-murder rule of section 189 of the Penal Code supports, if not compels, the conclusion that the surviving robbers committed murder even if the lethal bullet did not come from one of their guns, and whether it is an innocent person or an accomplice who dies.

...

Despite these declared principles—long established and effective in their deterrence of crimes of violence—the majority now announce that "When a killing is not committed by a robber or by his accomplice but by his victim, malice aforethought is not attributable to the robber, for the killing is not committed by him in the perpetration or attempt to perpetrate robbery. It is not enough that the killing was a risk reasonably to be foreseen.... Section 189 requires that the felon or his accomplice commit the killing, for if he does not, the killing is not committed *to* perpetrate the felony.... To include such killings within section 189 would expand the meaning of the words 'murder ... which is committed in the perpetration ... [of] robbery ...' beyond common understanding." (Italics added.)

But section 189 carries not the least suggestion of a requirement that the killing must take place *to* perpetrate the felony. If that requirement now be read into the section by the majority, then what becomes of the rule—which they purport to recognize—that an accidental and unintentional killing falls within the section? How can it be said that such a killing takes place *to* perpetrate a robbery?

Moreover, as already noted, the malice aforethought of the abandoned and malignant heart is shown from the very nature of the crime, here armed robbery, the defendant is attempting to commit. This truism was confirmed in *People v. Bostic* (1914) 167 Cal. 754, wherein the court pointed out that the argument that to be first degree murder a killing during robbery must be planned as a part of the scheme, carries its own refutation, "for it must be apparent that without reference to the robbery such a murder would be a 'wilful, deliberate and premeditated killing,'" and hence, first degree murder; further, said the court, "The moment [defendant] entered that [train] car with a deadly weapon in his hand, with the purpose of committing robbery, the law fixed upon him the intent which would make any killing in the perpetration of the robbery or in the attempt ... a murder of the first degree. In such cases the law does not measure the delicate scruples of the robber with reference to shooting his victim." ...

A homicide which arises out of an attempt at armed robbery is a direct causal result of the chain of events set in motion by the robbers when they undertook their felony. When a victim fires the lethal bullet, whether or not he fires first, the killing is caused by the act of the felon and the felon is as responsible therefor as when the firing is by his accomplice or when it is accidental or unintentional. The majority suggest, "it is unnecessary to imply malice by invoking the felony-murder doctrine" where the robber "initiates" a gun battle by shooting first. This suggestion by the majority, I respectfully submit, emphasizes the inconsistency of their opinion. First they declare that "When a killing is *not committed by* a robber ... *but by* his victim, *malice* aforethought is *not attributable* to the *robber*, for the killing is not committed by him in ... robbery." (Italics added.) Later they state that "*Defendants* who initiate gun battles *may also be found guilty of murder* if their *victims* resist and *kill* ... and it is unnecessary to imply malice by invoking the felony-murder doctrine." (Italics added.)

But malice aforethought is an essential element of murder. If it is not attributable to the robber when a killing is "committed by" his victim rather than by himself in a gun battle initiated by the robber, is the essential malice express—or is it to be implied under some doctrine other than the felony-murder rule? Do the majority imply the malice of the abandoned and malignant heart (Pen. Code, § 188) only if the robber shoots first, but not if he merely creates the foreseeable risk that "the victim will resist and kill"? And this despite the fact that, as the majority further affirm, "the robbery might therefore be regarded as a proximate cause of the killing"?

...

Note and Problem

The Purpose of the Felony-murder Rule. In *Washington*, the majority and dissent disagree over the purpose of the felony-murder rule. The majority adopts an "agency" theory based on its understanding that the purpose of the rule is to "deter felons from killing negligently or accidentally." The dissent adopts a "proximate cause" theory based on its understanding that the purpose of the rule is to deter the underlying felonies. Which rationale for the rule makes the most sense?

Problem 43.

Defendant, Accomplice and Victim conspired to commit arson of Defendant's truck for purposes of insurance fraud. Defendant and Victim drove the truck to an isolated road, with Accomplice following in his car. The three set the truck on fire after dousing it with diesel fuel. However, Victim had spilled some of the fuel on himself, and he caught fire and was killed. Defendant is charged with first degree felony-murder (P.C. §§ 187–189) on the ground that the killing occurred during the commission of arson (P.C. § 451). What arguments should be made as to whether Defendant is guilty of felony-murder?

People v. Sears

62 Cal. 2d 737, 401 P.2d 938 (1965)

TOBRINER, J.

The jury found defendant guilty of the first degree murder of his stepdaughter Elizabeth Olives, the attempted murder of his estranged wife Clara Sears and the attempted murder of his mother-in-law Frances Montijo. As to the first degree murder conviction, the jury fixed the penalty at death.

...

Defendant married Clara Sears in 1960. Mrs. Sears had three children from previous marriages, the youngest being Elizabeth Olives, the murder victim. Approximately three weeks prior to May 16, 1963, the defendant moved from the family residence in Monte Vista to a hotel in San Jose.

After leaving his place of employment on the afternoon of May 16, 1963, defendant went to a neighborhood tavern where he remained until 7:30 p.m. drinking beer with friends. After returning to his hotel, defendant met Robert Kjaerbye, and the two men had dinner in a nearby restaurant. They then went to a bar but left after 20 minutes because defendant wanted to drive to the house in Monte Vista to pick up his mail.

The two men entered the house through the unlocked front door. Defendant had a piece of reinforced steel pipe under his shirt. Clara and Elizabeth were already in bed. Defendant told Clara that he wanted to talk with her. Although she complained about the lateness of the hour, Clara joined defendant in the kitchen while Kjaerbye stayed in the living room. Noticing that the floor was cold, Clara returned to the bedroom to put on her robe and slippers. As she reentered the kitchen, defendant grabbed the collar of her robe and said, "You don't want me to come back to you." He pulled out the steel pipe and struck her about the head and face. Elizabeth came into the living room and shouted at defendant to let her mother alone. Clara tried to place herself between defendant and Elizabeth, but defendant grabbed the little girl and struck Clara several times, rendering her unconscious.

Frances Montijo, who lived next door, heard the noise from her daughter's home and decided to investigate. As she approached the Sears' residence she encountered Kjaerbye leaving the house and asked him what was happening inside. He responded that he did not know.

As Frances entered, she saw the defendant struggling with Elizabeth on the floor. When defendant saw Frances, he attacked her with a knife, cutting her face and neck, and threw her into a chair, pressing the steel pipe against her chest and throat. Frances cut her hand in a struggle for possession of the knife. She then effected her escape and ran to the nearby home of her son-in-law Patrick to get help.

When Patrick entered he saw defendant standing over the prone body of Clara with a barbecue fork in his upraised hand. Patrick also observed that Elizabeth was lying on the floor in a pool of blood. When Patrick asked defendant what he was doing, defendant lunged at him with the fork. Patrick wrestled with defendant, chasing him out of the house and down the driveway. Defendant then ran to his car and drove away.

Elizabeth died as a result of a knife wound which punctured her jugular vein. She also suffered a scalp wound and several lacerations to her face. Clara Sears suffered a fractured jaw and arm. Frances Montijo received several cuts and wounds to her face and hands.

...

Turning to defendant's second contention, his objection to the instruction as to felony murder mayhem, we hold that in the absence of a showing that the defendant specifically intended to commit mayhem, the court should not have instructed on felony murder mayhem. Penal Code section 203 provides: "Every person who unlawfully and maliciously deprives a human being of a member of his body, or disables, disfigures, or renders it useless, or cuts or disables the tongue, or puts out an eye, or slits the nose, ear, or lip, is guilty of mayhem." Penal Code section 189 states, "All murder … committed in the *perpetration* or *attempt to perpetrate* arson, rape, robbery, burglary, *mayhem* … is murder of the first degree…." (Italics added.)

The Legislature has decreed that any person who undertakes to commit any of the enumerated felonies will be guilty of first degree murder if such undertaking results in the loss of a human life. This dictate emanates from the extreme risk of harm inherent in the felonious conduct involved. Yet, in order to establish a defendant's guilt of first degree murder on the theory that he committed the killing during the perpetration of one of the enumerated felonies, the prosecution must prove that he harbored the specific intent to commit one of such enumerated felonies.

We recognize that some decisions have held that a specific intent to inflict the injuries proscribed in Penal Code section 203 does not constitute a requisite for a conviction of mayhem. In *People v. Nunes* (1920) 47 Cal. App. 346, the defendant slugged the victim in the eye. The blow shattered the glasses that the victim wore at the time; a fragment pierced the eye causing a loss of sight. In *People v. Crooms* (1944) 66 Cal. App. 2d 491, the defendant threw lye on the victim. In neither case did the court require proof of a specific intent to maim; a malicious and unlawful commission of an aggressive act which resulted in an injury enumerated in section 203 sufficed….

Even assuming the propriety of the above holdings, a distinction may be drawn between the showing of intent necessary to support a conviction of felony murder mayhem and the showing of intent necessary to uphold a conviction of mayhem. Under the felony murder doctrine, the intent required for a conviction of murder is imported from the specific intent to commit the concomitant felony. In the above cases the courts, in order to sustain the convictions of mayhem, presumed the intent from the acts or types of injuries sustained. But to presume an intent to maim from the act or type of injury inflicted, and then to transfer such "presumed intent" to support a felony murder conviction is artificially to extend the fiction. We cannot compound such fictions. The doctrine of felony murder, therefore, must be limited to those cases in which an intent to commit the felony can be shown from the evidence.

In the instant case the evidence discloses that defendant struck Elizabeth several times with a steel pipe; one of the blows resulted in a laceration of the lip; another, a laceration of the nose. But such evidence does no more than indicate an indiscriminate attack; it does not support the premise that defendant specifically intended to maim his victim. In the absence of such a showing of specific intent to commit mayhem, the court should not give the jury an instruction on felony murder mayhem.

…

[Concurring opinion of Dooling, J. and dissenting opinion of Schauer, J., joined by McComb, J., omitted.]

People v. Patterson

49 Cal. 3d 615, 778 P.2d 549 (1989)

KENNARD, J.

The issue before us is whether the second degree felony-murder doctrine applies to a defendant who, in violation of Health and Safety Code section 11352, furnishes cocaine to a person who dies as a result of ingesting it. We reaffirm the rule that, in determining whether a felony is inherently dangerous to human life under the second degree felony-murder doctrine, we must consider "the elements of the felony in the abstract, not the particular 'facts' of the case." *People v. Williams* (1965) 63 Cal.2d 452. While Health and Safety Code section 11352 includes drug offenses other than the crime of furnishing cocaine, which formed the basis for the prosecution's theory of second degree felony murder here, we conclude that the inquiry into inherent dangerousness must focus on the felony of furnishing cocaine, and not on section 11352 as a whole. We further hold that—consistent with the established definition of the term "inherently dangerous to life" in the context of implied malice as an element of second degree murder—a felony is inherently dangerous to life when there is a high probability that its commission will result in death.

...

Factual and Procedural Background

According to the testimony at the preliminary hearing, victim Jennie Licerio and her friend Carmen Lopez had been using cocaine on a daily basis in the months preceding Licerio's death. On the night of November 25, 1985, the two women were with defendant in his motel room. There, all three drank "wine coolers," inhaled "lines" of cocaine, and smoked "cocopuffs" (hand-rolled cigarettes containing a mixture of tobacco and cocaine). Defendant furnished the cocaine. When Licerio became ill, Lopez called an ambulance. Defendant stayed with the two women until the paramedics and the police arrived. The paramedics were unable to revive Licerio, who died of acute cocaine intoxication.

The People filed an information charging defendant with one count each of murder (Pen. Code, § 187), possession of cocaine (Health & Saf. Code, § 11350), and possession of cocaine for sale (Health & Saf. Code, § 11351). Defendant was also charged with three counts of violating Health and Safety Code section 11352, in that he "did willfully, unlawfully and feloniously transport, import into the State of California, sell, furnish, administer, and give away, and attempt to import into the State of California and transport a controlled substance, to wit: cocaine."

Defendant moved under Penal Code section 995 to set aside that portion of the information charging him with murder, contending the evidence presented at the preliminary hearing did not establish probable cause to believe he had committed murder. In opposing the motion, the People did not suggest the murder charge was based on a theory of implied malice. Instead, they relied solely on the second degree felony-murder doctrine. They argued that by furnishing cocaine defendant committed an inherently dangerous felony, thus justifying application of the rule. The trial court denied the motion. However, when the case was reassigned for trial, the court dismissed the murder charge under Penal Code section 1385.

...

Discussion

1. Second degree felony-murder doctrine

There is no precise statutory definition for the second degree felony-murder rule. In *People v. Ford* (1964) 60 Cal. 2d 772, we defined the doctrine as follows: "A homicide that is a direct causal result of the commission of a felony inherently dangerous to human life (other than the ... felonies enumerated in Pen. Code, § 189) constitutes at least second degree murder." In determining whether the felony is inherently dangerous, "we look to the elements of the felony in the abstract, not the particular 'facts' of the case."

The Court of Appeal's opinion in this case criticized the second degree felony-murder rule in its present form, suggesting the doctrine should either be completely eliminated or considerably "reformed." In response, defendant and *amici curiae* on his behalf have urged us to abolish the rule. The People and their *amici curiae*, on the other hand, have asked that we "reform" the doctrine by looking solely to the actual conduct of a defendant, thereby dispensing with the requirement that the elements of the offense be viewed in the abstract. We decline both invitations for the reasons discussed below.

The second degree felony-murder doctrine has been a part of California's criminal law for many decades. In recent years, we have characterized the rule as "anachronistic" and "disfavored," based on the view of many legal scholars that the doctrine incorporates an artificial concept of strict criminal liability that "erodes the relationship between criminal liability and moral culpability." The Legislature, however, has taken no action to alter this judicially created rule, and has declined our more recent suggestion in *People v. Dillon* (1983) 34 Cal. 3d 441 that it reconsider the rules on first and second degree felony murder and misdemeanor manslaughter. In this case, our limited purpose in granting the People's petition for review was to determine the applicability of the second degree felony-murder doctrine to the crime of furnishing cocaine. We decline defendant's invitation that we determine the continued vitality of the rule.

We also turn down the People's invitation that we expand the second degree felony-murder doctrine by eliminating the requirement that the elements of the offense be viewed "in the abstract," and by adopting a new standard focusing instead on the actual conduct of a defendant in determining whether the felony is inherently dangerous.

...

2. Determining "inherent dangerousness" of the felony of furnishing cocaine

As discussed earlier, in determining whether defendant committed an inherently dangerous felony, we must consider the elements of the felony "in the abstract." Because Health and Safety Code section 11352 also proscribes conduct other than that involved here (furnishing cocaine), the issue still to be resolved is whether we must consider only the specific offense of furnishing cocaine or the entire scope of conduct prohibited by the statute.

The Court of Appeal examined Health and Safety Code section 11352 in its entirety. It felt compelled to do so because of a series of recent cases where we held that, to determine a felony's inherent dangerousness, the statute as a whole had to be examined. However, unlike the situation here, each of those cases involved a statute that proscribed an essentially single form of conduct.

[In *People v. Lopez*, 6 Cal. 3d 45 (1971), a case involving a fatal assault in the course of what was initially a non-violent escape from custody, the court held that the crime of escape (Pen. Code, §4532) was not an inherently dangerous felony. In *People v. Henderson*, 19 Cal. 3d 86 (1977), the court held that aggravated false imprisonment—imprisonment "effected by violence, menace, fraud, or deceit" (Pen. Code, §§236, 237)—was also not an inherently dangerous felony. In *People v. Burroughs*, 35 Cal. 3d 824 (1984), the court held that a violation of Business and Professions Code section 2053, which prohibits the practice of medicine without a license "under circumstances or conditions which cause or create a risk of great bodily harm, serious physical or mental illness, or death," was not a felony inherently dangerous to human life.]

In both *Henderson* and *Burroughs*, we observed that the offense in question had a "primary element." In *Henderson*, the primary element was "the unlawful restraint of another's liberty," while in *Burroughs* it was "the practice of medicine without a license." *Lopez*, too, involved an offense with a primary element, namely, escape. In contrast, Health and Safety Code section 11352, the statute at issue here, has no primary element. For instance, the elements of the crime of transporting a controlled substance bear no resemblance to those underlying the offense of administering such a substance; yet these two offenses are included in the same statute.

The fact that the Legislature has included a variety of offenses in Health and Safety Code section 11352 does not require that we treat them as a unitary entity. Rather, we must decide whether in "[r]eading and considering the statute as a whole in order to determine the true legislative intent ... we find [a] basis for severing" the various types of conduct it forbids. There are more than 100 different controlled substances that fall within the confines of Health and Safety Code section 11352. To create statutes separately proscribing the importation, sale, furnishing, administration, etc., of each of these drugs, would require the enactment of hundreds of individual statutes. It thus appears that for the sake of convenience the Legislature has included the various offenses in one statute.

The determination whether a defendant who furnishes cocaine commits an inherently dangerous felony should not turn on the dangerousness of other drugs included in the same statute, such as heroin and peyote; nor should it turn on the danger to life, if any, inherent in the transportation or administering of cocaine. Rather, each offense set forth in the statute should be examined separately to determine its inherent dangerousness.

For the reasons discussed above, we hold the Court of Appeal and the trial court erred in concluding that Health and Safety Code section 11352 should be analyzed in its entirety to determine whether, in furnishing cocaine, defendant committed an inherently dangerous felony. Defendant, however, argues that even the more narrow offense of furnishing cocaine is not an inherently dangerous felony and therefore the trial court acted correctly in dismissing the murder charge, despite its faulty analysis....

The task of evaluating the evidence on this issue is most appropriately entrusted to the trial court, subject, of course, to appellate review. We therefore direct the Court of Appeal to remand the matter to the trial court for further proceedings in light of this opinion....

3. Meaning of the term "inherently dangerous to human life"

For the guidance of the trial court on remand, we shall elaborate on the meaning of the term "inherently dangerous to life" for purposes of the second degree felony-murder doctrine.

The felony-murder rule generally acts as a substitute for the mental state ordinarily required for the offense of murder....

Implied malice, for which the second degree felony-murder doctrine acts as a substitute,[8] has both a physical and a mental component. The physical component is satisfied by the performance of "an act, the natural consequences of which are dangerous to life." (*People v. Watson* (1981) 30 Cal. 3d 290.) The mental component is the requirement that the defendant "knows that his conduct endangers the life of another and ... acts with a conscious disregard for life." (*Id.*)

The second degree felony-murder rule eliminates the need for the prosecution to establish the mental component. The justification therefor is that, when society has declared certain inherently dangerous conduct to be felonious, a defendant should not be allowed to excuse himself by saying he was unaware of the danger to life because, by declaring the conduct to be felonious, society has warned him of the risk involved. The physical requirement, however, remains the same; by committing a felony inherently dangerous to life, the defendant has committed "an act, the natural consequences of which are dangerous to life," thus satisfying the physical component of implied malice.

The definition of "inherently dangerous to life" in the context of the implied malice element of second degree murder is well established. An act is inherently dangerous

8. Although the second degree felony-murder doctrine operates as a substitute for implied malice, this does not mean that the doctrine results in a "conclusive presumption" of malice. Nevertheless, in determining the proper scope of the second degree felony-murder doctrine, it is appropriate for the courts, in recognition of the Legislature's authority to define criminal offenses, to attempt to minimize the disparity between the legislatively created and the judicially recognized categories of second degree murder.

to human life when there is "a high probability that it will result in death." (*People v. Watson.*)

We therefore conclude—by analogy to the established definition of the term "dangerous to life" in the context of the implied malice element of second degree murder (see *People v. Watson*)—that, for purposes of the second degree felony-murder doctrine, an "inherently dangerous felony" is an offense carrying "a high probability" that death will result. A less stringent standard would inappropriately expand the scope of the second degree felony-murder rule reducing the seriousness of the act which a defendant must commit in order to be charged with murder.

We share the concern Chief Justice Lucas has expressed in his dissent regarding the tragic effects that the abuse of illegal drugs, particularly "crack" cocaine, has on our society. However, it is the Legislature, rather than this court, that should determine whether expansion of the second degree felony-murder rule is an appropriate method by which to address this problem. In the absence of specific legislative action, we must determine the scope of the rule by applying the established definition of inherent dangerousness.

We reverse the decision of the Court of Appeal, and direct that court to remand the matter to the trial court for further proceedings consistent with this opinion.

Lucas, C.J., concurring and dissenting:

I concur in the judgment. As several prior cases have indicated, the second degree felony-murder doctrine performs a valuable function in deterring the commission of crimes which, though involving no express or implied malice, are nonetheless so inherently dangerous as to justify a murder charge when a death occurs during their commission. Accordingly, the majority quite properly refuses to accept defendant's invitations (1) to abrogate the doctrine entirely, or (2) to permit consideration of other felonies not involved in the case in determining the inherent dangerousness of the defendant's own offense.

I dissent, however, to the majority's unrealistic, unwise and unprecedented definition of inherent dangerousness as involving "a high probability of death." With that one broad, gratuitous stroke, the majority has precluded application of the second degree felony-murder doctrine to most, if not all, drug furnishing offenses (as well as many nondrug offenses)....

...

The majority indicates that its "high probability of death" standard was borrowed from second degree murder cases requiring proof of implied malice. Such a standard may be appropriate for measuring whether defendant's general course of conduct should warrant a murder charge based on implied malice, but it is singularly inappropriate for determining whether felonious conduct should lead to such a charge. Notions of implied malice have never before been imported into felony murder, where the commission of the felony itself acts as a substitute for malice.

The anomalous and inconsistent nature of the majority's holding is confirmed by the fact that a defendant can be charged with first degree felony murder by committing such offenses as burglary, robbery, rape or child molestation (see Pen. Code, § 189), none of which offenses, viewed in the abstract, involves a high probability of death, although each of which may present substantial risks of death. If a first degree murder charge can be based on an offense not involving a high probability of death, surely the lesser charge of second degree murder can be based on similar offenses, so long as the requisite substantial risk of death can be demonstrated.

For all the foregoing reasons, I dissent to the majority's improper new formulation of the standard for determining inherent dangerousness.

Mosk, J., concurring and dissenting.

I dissent.

In determining whether the death in this case resulted from a felony inherently dangerous to human life, the majority attempt to draw a distinction between (1) a statute that proscribes a single course of criminal conduct that can be committed in different ways, and (2) a statute that groups together, for legislative convenience, a number of related but distinct crimes. The majority then put Health and Safety Code section 11352 (hereafter section 11352) into the latter category, carve out of its provisions the assertedly distinct felony of "furnishing cocaine," and ask the trial court to decide whether "furnishing cocaine" is a felony inherently dangerous to human life.

In my view, however, the correct question is whether *a violation of section 11352*—not merely "furnishing cocaine"—is a felony inherently dangerous to human life. And the trial court has already answered that question: after reviewing our decisions on the topic, the trial court ruled that "*violating section [11352] of the Health and Safety Code* [is] not so inherently dangerous that, by its very nature, it cannot be committed without creating a substantial risk that someone will be killed. And, while the felonies [charged in the case at bar] may, in many circumstances, pose a threat to human life, *the commission of the crime as defined by the statute* does not inevitably pose a danger to human life." (Italics added.) The court therefore dismissed the murder count at the invitation of the prosecutor and in the interest of justice. As will appear, our precedents amply support the court's ruling.

[Justice Mosk reviewed *People v. Phillips*, 64 Cal. 2d 574 (1966) where the Court had said: "once the Legislature's own definition is discarded, the number or nature of the contextual elements which could be incorporated into an expanded felony terminology would be limitless. We have been, and remain, unwilling to embark on such an uncharted sea of felony murder." He then discussed *Lopez*, *Henderson*, and *Burroughs* (cases distinguished by Justice Kennard) and found them supportive of his position.]

Equally unpersuasive is the majority's conclusion that the Legislature chose the present wording of section 11352 simply "for the sake of convenience." This is sheer speculation, easily outweighed by rational inferences that we can and should draw under settled rules of statutory construction. Those rules are primarily two: section 11352 must be viewed in the light of both its history and its context. When so viewed, it will be seen as a deliberately crafted response by the Legislature to a single evil: trafficking in illegal narcotics.

...

"A statute must be construed in the context of the entire statutory system of which it is a part, in order to achieve harmony among the parts." (*People v. Woodhead* (1987) 43 Cal. 3d 1002.) When section 11352 is thus construed in the context of the Uniform Controlled Substances Act, it is apparent that the Legislature intended by this section to prohibit all forms of trafficking in illegal narcotics, just as other sections of the law prohibited all forms of possession, or possession for sale, or sales involving minors, etc.... Although section 11352 lists a number of prohibited acts, they all relate to a single legislative goal—the goal of stopping the flow of illegal narcotics in our society. By means of this list the Legislature seeks to reach the principal ways in which illegal narcotics enter and move through the community: i.e., it recognizes that narcotics can be *imported* into our state or can be *transported* within the state, and they can be sold by one person to another or can be given (or furnished or administered) by one person to another. What is true of the transportation component of section 11352 is thus true of the entire statute: it attempts "to prevent or deter the movement of drugs from one location to another, thereby *inhibiting trafficking in narcotics* and their proliferation in our society." (*People v. Cortez* (1985) 166 Cal. App. 3d 994, italics added.)

...

... It follows that under the rule of *Henderson* and the related cases discussed above, the dispositive issue here is whether a violation of section 11352 as a whole is a felony inherently dangerous to human life.

That issue is not difficult to decide. As both the trial court and the Court of Appeal correctly observed, section 11352 can be violated in various ways that do not create a substantial risk of death. For example, it is violated by one who simply carries a small amount of cocaine home in his pocket for his personal use, or by a motorist who simply offers a ride in his car to a friend who he knows is carrying a similar amount of cocaine for his own use; no other act or intent need be proved for a conviction. Accordingly, as the trial court ruled, a violation of section 11352 is not "inherently so dangerous that by its very nature, it cannot be committed without creating a substantial risk that someone will be killed." Because section 11352 is not a felony inherently dangerous to human life, it cannot serve as a predicate for the second degree felony-murder rule; and because the prosecutor indicated to the court that felony murder was his sole theory on the homicide count, the court correctly dismissed that count in the interest of justice.

On a different issue, I agree that for purposes of the second degree felony-murder rule a felony inherently dangerous to human life should be defined as a felony carrying a high probability that it will result in death. In future cases that standard will contribute to greater fairness and proportion in the application of the second degree felony-murder rule. But even if the court had used that definition in the case at bar, its ruling would have been correct. The court found that a violation of section 11352 is not an inherently dangerous felony under the "substantial risk that someone will be killed." Because that test is less stringent than the "high probability" standard we now adopt, it is obvious that the court would have made the same ruling under our new standard.

I would affirm the judgment of the Court of Appeal.

[Concurring and dissenting opinion of PANELLI, J., omitted.]

Notes and Problems

Narcotics Crimes as Dangerous to Life. The courts have yet to decide whether furnishing cocaine is dangerous to life in the abstract, although the Court of Appeal has held that manufacturing methamphetamine is dangerous to life (*People v. James*, 62 Cal. App. 4th 244 (1998)) and furnishing PCP is not (*People v. Taylor*, 6 Cal. App. 4th 1084 (1992)).

Killings During Non-dangerous Felonies. What if the trial court determines that furnishing cocaine is not inherently dangerous to life? Involuntary manslaughter is described in Penal Code § 192 as a killing, without malice "in the commission of an unlawful act, not amounting to a felony; or in the commission of a lawful act which might produce death in an unlawful manner, or without due caution or circumspection." Thus, a killing in the course of a non-inherently dangerous felony does not appear to come within the definition of involuntary manslaughter. The court in *People v. Burroughs*, 35 Cal. 3d 824 (1984), held that "the only logically permissible construction of section 192 is that an unintentional homicide committed in the course of a non-inherently dangerous felony may properly support a conviction of involuntary manslaughter if that felony is committed without due caution and circumspection." In a footnote the court indicated that "due caution and circumspection" within the meaning of section 192 is equivalent to criminal negligence which is conduct that is "such a departure from what would be the conduct of an ordinarily prudent or careful man under the same circumstances as to be incompatible with a proper regard for human life, or, in other words, a disregard of human life or indifference to consequences."

Problem 44.

Defendant is an ex-felon who, in the course of a sidewalk dispute with Victim, retrieved a sawed-off shotgun from his car and shot and killed Victim. It is a felony for an ex-felon to possess such a weapon (P.C. § 29800(a)). What arguments should be made as to whether Defendant can be convicted of second degree felony-murder using his violation of § 29800(a) as the underlying felony?

Problem 45.

In the process of stealing a pickup, Defendant was spotted by police officers. The officers attempted to stop Defendant, but Defendant fled in the pickup. Defendant entered a freeway and began driving the wrong direction at 60 miles per hour with the officers in pursuit. He eventually drove head-on into an oncoming car killing the car's driver. Defendant is charged with a violation of Veh. Code § 2800.2 and second degree murder (P.C. §§ 187–189). V.C. § 2800.2 provides in relevant part:

> (a) If a person flees or attempts to elude a pursuing peace officer … and the pursued vehicle is driven in a willful or wanton disregard for the safety of persons or property, the person driving the vehicle, upon conviction, shall be punished by imprisonment in the state prison, by imprisonment in the county jail … or by a fine. …
>
> (b) For purposes of this section, a willful or wanton disregard for the safety of persons or property includes, but is not limited to, driving while fleeing or attempting to elude a pursuing peace officer during which time either three or more violations that are assigned a traffic violation point count … occur, or damage to property occurs.

What arguments should be made as to whether Defendant can be prosecuted for murder on a felony-murder theory?

Problem 46.

Defendant was 17 years old and lived with her boyfriend and her two sons, Toddler (who was a year old) and Baby (who was a month old). While caring for Toddler and Baby, she struck Baby several times to stop him from crying, and the blows broke his ribs and collapsed his lungs, resulting in his death. Defendant was charged with violating P.C. § 273ab, which provides:

> Any person who, having the care or custody of a child who is under eight years of age, assaults the child by means of force that to a reasonable person would be likely to produce great bodily injury, resulting in the child's death, shall be punished by imprisonment in the state prison for 25 years to life.

At trial, Defendant presented evidence to the effect that: Defendant was a good mother to Toddler, but suffered from post-partum depression after the birth of Baby; Baby was a fussy baby who cried inconsolably; and Defendant had been up all night with Baby the night before his death and was depressed and exhausted when she hit Baby. Defendant was convicted and sentenced to 25 years to life in prison. On appeal what are the arguments as to the constitutionality of the sentence?

People v. Chun (Part 2)

45 Cal.4th 1172, 203 P.3d 425 (2009)

CHIN, J.

In this murder case, the trial court instructed the jury on second degree felony murder with shooting at an occupied vehicle under Penal Code section 246 the underlying felony.[1] ...

...

... [W]e reconsider the contours of the so-called merger doctrine this court adopted in *People v. Ireland* (1969) 70 Cal.2d 522 (*Ireland*). After reviewing recent developments, primarily some of our own decisions, we conclude the current state of the law in this regard is untenable. We will overrule some of our decisions and hold that all assaultive-type crimes, such as a violation of section 246, merge with the charged homicide and cannot be the basis for a second degree felony-murder instruction. Accordingly, the trial court erred in instructing on felony murder in this case....

Holding

[The facts are set forth in *People v. Chun (Part 1)*, *supra*.]

B. The Merger Rule and Second Degree Felony Murder

Although today we reaffirm the constitutional validity of the long-standing second degree felony-murder rule, we also recognize that the rule has often been criticized and, indeed, described as disfavored. For these reasons, although the second degree felony-murder rule originally applied to all felonies, this court has subsequently restricted its scope in at least two respects to ameliorate its perceived harshness.

First, "[i]n *People v. Ford* (1964) 60 Cal.2d 772, the court restricted the felonies that could support a conviction of second degree murder, based upon a felony-murder theory, to those felonies that are 'inherently dangerous to human life." (*People v. Hansen* (1994) 9 Cal.4th 300.) Whether a felony is inherently dangerous is determined from the elements of the felony in the abstract, not the particular facts. This restriction is not at issue here. Section 246 makes it a felony to "maliciously and willfully discharge a firearm at an ... occupied motor vehicle...."[5] In *Hansen, supra*, we held that shooting at an "inhabited dwelling house" under section 246 is inherently dangerous even

Restriction #1

1. All further statutory citations are to the Penal Code unless otherwise indicated.

5. In its entirety, section 246 provides: "Any person who shall maliciously and willfully discharge a firearm at an inhabited dwelling house, occupied building, occupied motor vehicle, occupied aircraft, inhabited housecar, as defined in Section 362 of the Vehicle Code, or inhabited camper, as defined in Section 243 of the Vehicle Code, is guilty of a felony, and upon conviction shall be punished by imprisonment in the state prison for three, five, or seven years, or by imprisonment in the county jail for a term of not less than six months and not exceeding one year. "As used in this section, 'inhabited' means currently being used for dwelling purposes, whether occupied or not."

though the inhabited dwelling house does not have to be actually occupied at the time of the shooting. That being the case, shooting at a vehicle that is actually occupied clearly is inherently dangerous.

But the second restriction—the "merger doctrine"—is very much at issue. The merger doctrine developed due to the understanding that the underlying felony must be an independent crime and not merely the killing itself. Thus, certain underlying felonies "merge" with the homicide and cannot be used for purposes of felony murder. The specific question before us is how to apply the merger doctrine in this case. In this case, the Court of Appeal divided on the question and on how to apply our precedents. But the majority and dissent agreed on one thing—that the current state of the law regarding merger is "muddled." We agree that the scope and application of the merger doctrine as applied to second degree murder needs to be reconsidered. To explain this, we will first review the doctrine's historical development. Then we will discuss what to do with the merger doctrine and, ultimately, conclude that the trial court should not have instructed on felony murder.

1. Historical Review

[Justice Chin reviewed the court's "muddled" history with regard to second degree felony-murder and the merger rule. The seminal case was *Ireland*, where the court found that the underlying felony—assault with a deadly weapon—merged. The court held that a felony would merge when the felony was an "integral part" of the homicide. In *People v. Mattison* (1971) 4 Cal.3d 177, the defendant, who was a prison inmate, was charged with murder because he sold methyl alcohol to another inmate who died from methyl alcohol poisoning. The court found that the underlying felony—mixing poison with food, drink or medicine with the intent that it be taken—did not merge because the court found that the felony was committed with a "collateral and independent felonious design." In *People v. Smith* (1984) 35 Cal.3d 798, the defendant was convicted of the murder of her daughter, with the underlying felony being felony child abuse. The court applied the merger doctrine because, as to felony child abuse of the assaultive variety, the court could "conceive of no independent purpose" for the felony. In *Hansen, supra*, the underlying felony was shooting into an inhabited dwelling house. The court, rejecting both *Ireland*'s "integral part of the homicide" test, and *Mattison*'s "collateral and independent felonious design" test, held that the felony did not merge, using language seeming to restrict the merger doctrine to assaultive felonies. In *People v. Robertson*, (2004) 34 Cal.4th 156, the underlying felony was discharging a firearm in a grossly negligent manner. The defendant claimed he fired into the air in order to frighten away several men who were burglarizing his car. The court stating that the *Mattison*, "collateral purpose" test provided the "most appropriate framework" for deciding the merger issue, held that the felony did not merge. Finally, in *People v. Randle* (2005) 35 Cal.4th 987, the underlying felony again was discharging a firearm in a grossly negligent manner. However, the defendant in *Randle* admitted that he shot at the victim, allegedly to rescue a third person who was being attacked. The court found that the fact that the defendant intended to shoot the victim distinguished the case from *Robertson* and required application of the merger doctrine because the shooting lacked an independent felonious purpose.]

2. Analysis

The current state of the law regarding the *Ireland* merger doctrine is problematic in at least two respects.

First, two different approaches currently exist in determining whether a felony merges. *Hansen, supra,* which we have never expressly overruled, held that a violation of section 246, at least when predicated on shooting at an inhabited dwelling house, *never* merges. *Robertson, supra* and *Randle, supra,* held that a violation of section 246.3 *does* merge unless it is done with a purpose collateral to the resulting homicide. If *Hansen,* on the one hand, and *Robertson* and *Randle* on the other hand, are all still valid authority, the question arises which approach applies here. This court has never explained whether *Hansen* retains any viability after *Robertson* and *Randle* and, if so, how a court is to go about determining which approach to apply to a given underlying felony.

Second, *Randle,* when juxtaposed with *Robertson,* brings into sharp focus the anomaly that we noted in *Robertson* and accepted as inherent in the second degree felony-murder rule, and that we noted in *Hansen* and avoided by concluding that the merger rule never applies to shooting at an inhabited dwelling house. In combination, *Robertson* and *Randle* hold that, when the *Hansen* test does not apply (i.e., at least when the underlying felony is a violation of 246.3), the underlying felony merges, and the felony-murder rule does *not* apply, if the defendant intended to shoot *at* the victim (*Randle*), but the underlying felony does not merge, and the felony-murder rule *does* apply, if the defendant merely intended to frighten, perhaps because he believed the victim was burglarizing his car (*Robertson*). This result is questionable for the reasons discussed in the separate opinions in *Robertson.* Moreover, as we discuss further below, the *Robertson* and *Randle* approach injected a factual component into the merger question that did not previously exist.

In light of these problems, we believe we need to reconsider our merger doctrine jurisprudence. As Justice Werdegar observed in her dissenting opinion in *Robertson,* "sometimes consistency must yield to a better understanding of the developing law." In considering this question, we must also keep in mind the purposes of the second degree felony-murder rule. We have identified two. The purpose we have most often identified "is to deter felons from killing negligently or accidentally by holding them strictly responsible for killings they commit." (*People v. Washington* (1965) 62 Cal.2d 777.) Another purpose is to deter commission of the inherently dangerous felony itself. (*Robertson, supra* ["the second degree felony-murder rule is intended to deter both carelessness in the commission of a crime and the commission of the inherently dangerous crime itself"].)

We first consider whether *Hansen* has any continuing vitality after *Robertson,* and *Randle, supra.* In *Robertson* and *Randle,* we unanimously rejected the *Hansen* test, at least when the underlying felony is a violation of section 246.3. Although *Hansen* avoided the problems inherent in the *Robertson* approach by simply stating the felony at issue will never merge, we see no basis today to resurrect the *Hansen* approach for a violation of section 246.3. Indeed, doing so would arguably be inconsistent with *Hansen*'s reasoning. *Hansen* explained that most homicides do not involve violations of section 246, and thus holding that such homicides do not merge would not "subvert the legislative intent." But most fatal shootings, and certainly those charged as murder, do involve discharging a firearm in at least a grossly negligent manner. Fatal shootings, in turn, are a high percentage of all homicides. Thus, holding that a violation of section 246.3 never merges would greatly expand the range of homicides subject to the second degree felony-murder rule. We adhere to *Robertson* and *Randle* to the extent they declined to extend the *Hansen* approach to a violation of section 246.3.

But if, as we conclude, the *Hansen* test does not apply to a violation of section 246.3, we must decide whether it still applies to *any* underlying felonies. The tests stated in *Hansen* and in *Robertson* and *Randle* cannot both apply at the same time. If *Hansen* governs, the underlying felony will *never* merge. If *Robertson* and *Randle* governs, the underlying felony will *always* merge unless the court can discern some independent felonious purpose. But we see no principled basis by which to hold that a violation of section 246 never merges, but a violation of section 246.3 does merge unless done with an independent purpose. We also see no principled test that another court could use to determine which approach applies to other possible underlying felonies.... The *Robertson* and *Randle* test and the *Hansen* test cannot coexist. Our analysis in *Robertson* and *Randle* implicitly overruled the *Hansen* test. We now expressly overrule *Hansen* to the extent it stated a test different than the one of *Robertson* and *Randle.*

But the test of *Robertson* and *Randle* has its own problems that were avoided in *Hansen* but resurfaced when we abandoned the *Hansen* test. Our holding in *Randle* made stark the anomalies that Justices Kennard and Werdegar identified in *Robertson.* On reflection, we do not believe that a person who claims he merely wanted to frighten the victim should be subject to the felony-murder rule (*Robertson*), but a person who says he intended to shoot at the victim is not subject to that rule (*Randle*). Additionally, *Robertson* said that the intent to frighten is a collateral *purpose*, but *Randle* said the intent to rescue another person is not an independent purpose but merely a *motive.* It is not clear how a future court should decide whether a given intent is a purpose or merely a motive.

The *Robertson* and *Randle* test presents yet another problem. In the past, we have treated the merger doctrine as a legal question with little or no factual content. Generally, we have held that an underlying felony either never or always merges (e.g., *People v. Smith, supra* [identifying certain underlying felonies that do not merge]), not that the question turns on the specific facts. Viewed as a legal question, the trial court properly decides whether to instruct the jury on the felony-murder rule, but if it does so instruct, it does not also instruct the jury on the merger doctrine. The *Robertson* and *Randle* test, however, turns on potentially disputed facts specific to the case. In *Robertson*, the defendant claimed he merely intended to frighten the victim, which caused this court to conclude the underlying felony did not merge. But the jury would not necessarily have to believe the defendant. Whether a defendant shot *at* someone intending to injure, or merely tried to frighten that someone, may often be a disputed factual question.

Defendant argues that the factual question whether the defendant had a collateral felonious purpose—and thus whether the felony-murder rule applies—involves an element of the crime and, accordingly, that the *jury* must decide that factual question. When the merger issue turns on potentially disputed factual questions, there is no obvious answer to this argument. Justice Kennard alluded to the problem in her dissent in *Robertson* when she observed that "the jury never decided whether he had that intent [to frighten]." Because this factual question determines whether the felony-murder rule applies under *Robertson* and *Randle*, and thus whether the prosecution would have to prove some other form of malice, it is not clear why the jury should not have to decide the factual question.

To avoid the anomaly of putting a person who merely intends to frighten the victim in a worse legal position than the person who actually intended to shoot at the victim, and the difficult question of whether and how the jury should decide questions of merger, we need to reconsider our holdings in *Robertson* and *Randle*. When the underlying felony is assaultive in nature, such as a violation of section 246 or 246.3, we now conclude that the felony merges with the homicide and cannot be the basis of a felony-murder instruction. An "assaultive" felony is one that involves a threat of immediate violent injury. In determining whether a crime merges, the court looks to its elements and not the facts of the case. Accordingly, if the elements of the crime have an assaultive aspect, the crime merges with the underlying homicide even if the elements also include conduct that is not assaultive. For example, in *People v. Smith, supra*, the court noted that child abuse under section 273a "includes both active and passive conduct, i.e., child abuse by direct assault and child endangering by extreme neglect." Looking to the facts before it, the court decided the offense was "of the assaultive variety," and therefore merged. It reserved the question whether the nonassaultive variety would merge. Under the approach we now adopt, both varieties would merge. This approach both avoids the necessity of consulting facts that might be disputed and extends the protection of the merger doctrine to the potentially less culpable defendant whose conduct is not assaultive.

This conclusion is also consistent with our repeatedly stated view that the felony-murder rule should not be extended beyond its required application. We do not have to decide at this point exactly what felonies are assaultive in nature, and hence may not form the basis of a felony-murder instruction, and which are inherently collateral to the resulting homicide and do not merge. But shooting at an occupied vehicle under section 246 is assaultive in nature and hence cannot serve as the underlying felony for purposes of the felony-murder rule.

[The court went on to find that the instructional error was harmless.]

Baxter, J., concurring and dissenting.

...

Although the majority reaffirms the constitutional validity of the second degree felony-murder rule, they go on to render it useless in this and future cases out of strict adherence to the so-called "merger rule" announced in *People v. Ireland* (1969) 70 Cal.2d 522 (*Ireland*). Under the merger rule, no assaultive-type felony can be used as a basis for a second degree felony-murder conviction. The single rationale given in *Ireland* for the merger rule was that to allow assaultive-type felonies to serve as a basis for a second degree felony-murder conviction "would effectively preclude the jury from considering the issue of malice aforethought in all cases wherein homicide has been committed as a result of a felonious assault ... a category which includes the great majority of all homicides. This kind of bootstrapping finds support neither in logic nor in law."

In the 40 years since the *Ireland* court announced its sweeping "merger rule," this court has struggled mightily with its fallout in an attempt to redefine the contours of the venerable second degree felony-murder rule. The history of our "muddled" case law on the subject is accurately recounted in painstaking detail in the majority opinion.

...

In the end, this case presented us with a clear opportunity to finally get this complex and difficult issue right. The majority's recognition and unequivocal pronouncement, in part II.A of its opinion—that the second degree felony-murder rule is simply a rule for imputing malice under section 188—furnishes the missing piece to this complex and confusing legal jigsaw puzzle. With that clear pronouncement of the second degree felony-murder rule's true nature and function firmly in hand, I would go on to reach the following logical conclusions with regard to the long-standing tension between that rule and *Ireland*'s merger doctrine.

First, when a homicide has occurred during the perpetration of a felony inherently dangerous to human life, a jury's finding that the perpetrator satisfied all the elements necessary for conviction of that offense, without legal justification or defense, *is* a finding that he or she acted with an "abandoned and malignant heart" (i.e., acted with malice) within the meaning of section 188. Put in terms of the modern definition of implied malice, where one commits a felony inherently dangerous to human life without legal justification or defense, then under operation of the second degree felony-murder rule, a homicide resulting therefrom *is* a killing "proximately result[ing] from an act, the natural consequences of which are dangerous to life, which act was deliberately performed by a person who knows that his conduct endangers the life of another and who acts with conscious disregard for life." (*People v. Dellinger* (1989) 49 Cal.3d 1212.)

Once it is understood and accepted that the second degree felony-murder rule is simply *a rule for imputing malice* from the circumstances attending the commission of an inherently dangerous felony during which a homicide occurs, no grounds remain to support the sole rationale offered by the *Ireland* court for the merger doctrine—that use of an assaultive-type felony as the basis for a second degree felony-murder instruction "effectively preclude[s] the jury from considering the issue of malice aforethought in all cases wherein homicide has been committed as a result of a felonious assault." (*Ireland, supra.*) The majority's holding in part II.A of its opinion makes clear it understands and accepts that the second degree felony-murder rule is but a means by which juries impute malice under the Legislature's statutory definition of second degree implied malice murder. The majority's holding in part II.B of its opinion nonetheless fails to follow through and reach the logical conclusions to be drawn from the first premise, and instead simply rubberstamps the *Ireland* court's misguided belief that the second degree felony-murder rule improperly removes consideration of malice from the jury's purview.

Second, when a jury convicts of second degree murder under the second degree felony-murder rule, it *has* found the statutory element of malice necessary for conviction of murder. (§§ 187, 188.) Hence, there are no constitutional concerns with regard to whether the jury is finding all the elements of the charged murder, or is not finding all the "facts" that can increase punishment where the defendant is convicted of second degree murder in addition to conviction of the underlying inherently dangerous felony.

Third, our recognition today that the second degree felony-murder rule is simply a rule under which the jury may impute malice from the defendant's commission of inherently dangerous criminal acts, thereby undercutting the very rationale given by the *Ireland* court for the merger rule, should logically *eliminate* any impediment to the use of inherently dangerous felonies—such as the violation of section 246 (maliciously and willfully shooting at an occupied vehicle) at issue in this case—as the basis for an instruction on second degree felony murder.

The majority's holding, in contrast, works just the opposite result. Prior to this court's decision in *Ireland*, this court had already restricted the felonies that could support a second degree felony-murder conviction to those "inherently dangerous to human life." (*People v. Ford* (1964) 60 Cal.2d 772.) The justification for the imputation of implied malice under these circumstances is that, "when society has declared certain inherently dangerous conduct to be felonious, a defendant should not be allowed to excuse himself by saying he was unaware of the danger to life." (*People v. Patterson* (1989) 49 Cal.3d 615.) Hence, whatever felonies may remain available for use in connection with the second degree felony-murder rule after today's holding will both have to qualify as inherently dangerous felonies, and not be "assaultive in nature" or contain any elements that have "an assaultive aspect." I fail to see how the second degree felony-murder rule, thus emasculated, will continue to serve its intended purposes of "deter[ring] felons from killing negligently or accidentally" while "deter[ring] commission of the inherently dangerous felony itself."

In sum, the majority has turned the second degree felony-murder rule on its head by excluding *all felonies* that are "assaultive in nature," including a violation of section 246, in whatever form, from future use as a basis for second degree felony-murder treatment. In reaching its holding, the majority has rejected decades of sound felony-murder jurisprudence in deference to *Ireland*'s merger rule, a doctrine grounded on a single false premise, that use of the second degree felony-murder rule improperly insulates juries from the requirement of finding malice and thereby constitutes unfair "bootstrapping."

...

[Justice Moreno, in his concurring and dissenting opinion, argued that, although the majority's reformulation of the merger rule was an "improvement," the second degree felony-murder rule was "deeply flawed" and should be abolished.]

Problem

Problem 47.

Defendant had, hidden in his locked garage, two bombs wired together with a safety device on. The bombs were wrapped in bungee cords designed to attach the bombs to a car or some other object. The bombs were not time bombs, but relied on the movement of human victims to detonate them. Police searched defendant's home pursuant to a warrant and found the bombs. Defendant was placed under arrest and transported to the station. The house was evacuated and the bomb squad was called. Two officers of the bomb squad were dismantling a bomb when it exploded and both were killed. Defendant is charged with two counts of first degree murder. The prosecution has requested a felony-murder instruction based on Penal Code § 18715 which provides:

> (a) Every person who recklessly or maliciously has in possession any destructive device or any explosive in any of the following places is guilty of a felony:
>
> (1) On a public street or highway.
>
> (2) In or near any theater, hall, school, college, church, hotel, or other public building.
>
> (3) In or near any private habitation.
>
> (4) In, on, or near any aircraft, railway passenger train, car, cable road, cable car, or vessel engaged in carrying passengers for hire.
>
> (5) In, on, or near any other public place ordinarily passed by human beings.

What arguments should be made as to: (1) whether Defendant is guilty of felony-murder, and (2) if he is guilty of murder, whether he is guilty of first degree murder?

B. Misdemeanor-Manslaughter

The two cases in this section concern the scope of the misdemeanor-manslaughter rule. Should the court limit the application of the misdemeanor-manslaughter rule as it has limited the felony-murder rule? In *People v. Cox*, the court examines whether the underlying misdemeanor must be "dangerous to human life or safety" in order to support a misdemeanor-manslaughter conviction. In *People v. Nieto-Benitez*, the court clarifies the relationship between the misdemeanor-manslaughter rule and proof of malice.

People v. Cox

23 Cal.4th 665, 2 P.3d 1189 (2000)

BAXTER, J.

We granted review in this case to determine whether conviction of involuntary manslaughter based on "an unlawful act, not amounting to felony" (Pen. Code, § 192, subd. (b)), i.e., a killing resulting from the commission of a misdemeanor offense committed with general criminal intent, requires a further showing that the predicate misdemeanor was dangerous under the circumstances of its commission....

FACTS AND PROCEDURAL BACKGROUND

Defendant was tried by a jury for involuntary manslaughter by an unlawful act not amounting to felony, to wit, misdemeanor battery. (§§ 192, subd. b), 242.) During the early morning hours of August 22, 1996, after drinking alcohol and smoking crack cocaine, Evelonia Hunter and the deceased, Duane Spann, ran into defendant and Steve Vickers in front of the motel where Hunter was renting a room in Pomona. Hunter and Vickers, her former boyfriend, began arguing. Vickers spit in Hunter's face and slapped Spann with his open left hand. About a minute later defendant punched Spann with a "solid blow" on the right side of his head, using his fist. Spann had not hit defendant or Vickers. Spann fell to the pavement and appeared to have been knocked unconscious. Defendant and Vickers left the scene.

Hunter tried to arouse Spann by touching his face and calling his name. After two or three minutes, Spann regained consciousness and Hunter managed to assist him to his feet. He was still off-balance and unable to walk by himself. Hunter helped Spann move about 20 feet to a brick ledge where he sat for two to three minutes. Hunter then helped Spann walk the remaining 35 feet to her motel room.

Once inside the room, Hunter and Spann sat on the bed and talked for a while. Spann was unable to speak clearly; his speech, which had previously been normal, was slow and slurred. Spann was still off-balance but able to help Hunter prepare the bed for sleep. Hunter asked Spann if he was all right or if he wanted to call 911. Spann replied that he did not want to call 911. Spann and Hunter went to sleep between 3:00 and 4:00 a.m.

[Spann died later that day, and an autopsy revealed an extensive skull fracture and internal head injuries that had resulted in hemorrhaging of the blood vessels. The defendant was prosecuted for involuntary manslaughter, and the jury was instructed, as a matter of law, battery is an inherently dangerous offense and therefore a predicate for involuntary manslaughter without any further proof regarding the circumstances surrounding commission of the battery. He was convicted of involuntary manslaughter as charged, and the Court of Appeal affirmed the conviction.]

We granted review to determine whether our holding in *People v. Wells* (1996) 12 Cal.4th 979, requiring that the underlying unlawful act on which a charge of involuntary manslaughter is based must be shown to be dangerous under the circumstances of its commission, applies equally to all misdemeanors committed with general criminal intent on which a charge of involuntary manslaughter is predicated.

Discussion

Instruction on Involuntary Manslaughter

In *Wells*, this court resolved the issue of whether an unlawful act on which a charge of involuntary manslaughter is predicated must be inherently dangerous, that is, dangerous in the abstract, or dangerous under the circumstances of its commission. We held that "the offense must be dangerous under the circumstances of its commission. The inherent or abstract nature of a misdemeanor which underlies an involuntary manslaughter charge is not dispositive."

Wells involved a prosecution for vehicular manslaughter under section 192, subdivision (c)(1). The evidence established that the defendant had been speeding on a curving, hilly road when his out-of-control car struck another vehicle, injuring the driver and killing a passenger. Section 192, subdivision (c)(1) defines one of the three kinds of vehicular manslaughter described in section 192 as "driving a vehicle in the commission of an unlawful act, not amounting to felony, and with gross negligence; or driving a vehicle in the commission of a lawful act which might produce death, in an unlawful manner, and with gross negligence." In *Wells* we were asked to decide "if the 'unlawful act' to which the statute refers must be an offense that is inherently dangerous to human life or safety, and if so, whether exceeding the maximum speed limit [constitutes] such an unlawful act."

Although the precise issue in *Wells* was one of statutory construction of section 192, subdivision (c)(1) (defining vehicular manslaughter), we agreed with the Court of Appeal in that case that "the use of the term 'in the commission of an unlawful act, not amounting to felony' in both section 192(b) and section 192(c)(1) reflects legislative intent that the same meaning be accorded the term in each subdivision." Accordingly, our analysis and holding in *Wells* informs our construction of the term "unlawful act, not amounting to felony" found in section 192, subdivision (b) (section 192(b)) and directly at issue in this case.

We explained in *Wells* that the Court of Appeal in that case, as well as several previously reported appellate decisions, had misinterpreted this court's earlier decision in *People v. Stuart* (1956) 47 Cal.2d 167 as requiring that the predicate misdemeanor offense underlying a conviction of involuntary manslaughter be "inherently dangerous in the abstract." The term "unlawful act, not amounting to felony" as used in section 192(b) codifies the traditional common law form of involuntary manslaughter as the predicate for finding that a homicide committed without malice was involuntary manslaughter. "When that phrase was construed in *Stuart*, this court had stated that to support an involuntary manslaughter conviction under section 192(b) the 'unlawful act' must be dangerous to human life and safety and committed with criminal intent or criminal negligence pursuant to section 20. Although *Stuart* had said only that the unlawful act must be dangerous to human life and safety, the Court of Appeal [in *Wells*] understood the holding of *Stuart* to be that the underlying misdemeanor offense must be one that is inherently dangerous in the abstract."

Section 20 provides that "In every crime or public offense there must exist a union, or joint operation of act and intent, or criminal negligence." In *Stuart*, a pharmacist violated a Health and Safety Code provision by unwittingly preparing and selling an adulterated and misbranded drug. He was convicted of the crime of involuntary manslaughter. This court reversed his conviction, concluding the requirements of section 20 had not been met.

The defendant in *Stuart* had filled a prescription for sodium citrate from a bottle so labeled which actually contained some sodium nitrite. The defendant was unaware that the bottle was mislabeled, and the two substances, virtually identical in appearance, could not be distinguished absent a chemical analysis. The patient died from the effects of sodium nitrite after ingesting the prescribed medication. However, there was no evidence "that would justify an inference that [the] defendant knew or should have known that the bottle labeled sodium citrate contained sodium nitrite."

We concluded in *Stuart* that the "act" underlying the offense of involuntary manslaughter "must be committed with criminal intent or criminal negligence to be an unlawful act within the meaning of section 192." Although the pharmacist's conduct in *Stuart* constituted a malum prohibitum or strict liability violation of the applicable Health and Safety Code provision, because he neither intentionally nor through criminal negligence prepared or sold an adulterated or misbranded drug, a requisite to criminal liability was absent and the manslaughter conviction could not stand. We summarized our analysis and holding in *Stuart* as follows: "To be an unlawful act within the meaning of section 192, therefore, the act in question must be dangerous to human life or safety and meet the conditions of section 20."

...

... [I]n *Wells*, [we] ... explained: "In stating that 'the act in question must be dangerous to human life or safety and meet the conditions of section 20,' we did not in *Stuart* require that 'the unlawful act, not amounting to felony,' constitute an 'inherently dangerous act,' or be malum in se [i.e., commonly requiring general or specific intent]. Instead, we required that commission of the unlawful act involve criminal culpability, i.e., have been done in a dangerous manner." "Thus, *Stuart* does not require an act 'inherently dangerous in the abstract' for any form of manslaughter. It merely requires that the unlawful act causing death be committed 'through criminal negligence.'" (*Wells*.) "We are satisfied therefore that the offense must be dangerous under the circumstances of its commission. The inherent or abstract nature of a misdemeanor which underlies an involuntary manslaughter charge is not dispositive."

...

As has been shown, over 40 years ago, this court rejected a misdemeanor-manslaughter rule that elevates any killing resulting from the commission of a misdemeanor to involuntary manslaughter, when we construed the "unlawful act, not amounting to felony" language of section 192(b) as requiring a showing that the predicate unlawful act or misdemeanor offense is dangerous to human life or safety. (*Stuart.*) *Wells* reaffirmed this principle, clarifying that the test is not whether the predicate misdemeanor is inherently dangerous in the abstract, but whether it is dangerous under the circumstances of its commission.

[The case was remanded to the Court of Appeal for a determination whether the erroneous instruction was prejudicial.]

Note

The Model Penal Code and Misdemeanor-manslaughter. The misdemeanor-manslaughter rule is abolished in the Model Penal Code. MPC § 210.3. Unlike the case with the felony-murder rule, most states that have revised their penal codes have followed the Code's lead and abolished the rule.

People v. Nieto-Benitez

4 Cal. 4th 91, 840 P.2d 969 (1992)

George, J.

This case presents the question whether the act of brandishing a firearm may constitute an act sufficiently dangerous to life to support a conviction of second degree murder on an implied malice theory....

I.
Facts

On July 8, 1989, in the early evening, defendant was at the intersection of Jeffrey Drive and Lynne Avenue in Anaheim, eating his dinner near a catering truck. Defendant was seated on a milk crate, while directly behind him, the victim, known as Guero,[2] and another man, identified only as Caballo, were engaged in horseplay. Guero reached around Caballo and attempted to tip over Caballo's plate. In response, Caballo spun around and threw the entire plate of food at Guero. When Guero ducked, the plate of food struck defendant on the back of his head, the food falling down defendant's back and staining his shirt.

Defendant threw away his plate and took off his shirt. Holding the shirt in his hand, he walked over to where Guero and Caballo stood, and asked, "Who is going to wash my shirt?"

---

2. No witness knew Guero by any other name. To avoid confusion, we shall refer to him by that name. His true name was Lorenzo Lopez Mena.

Guero and Caballo feigned ignorance, and Guero then replied, "We're not going to wash your shirt." Defendant insisted that one of them wash his shirt. Guero, who was holding a broomstick, responded, "[N]o way, it was an accident."

An argument ensued. Guero said, "What are you going to do about it? You going to bring a gun or knife or what?" He added, "It was an accident, anyway, so why don't you go ahead and leave?"

Defendant replied, "It's going to be an accident if a bullet goes off and hits one of you, too."

Guero, becoming angry, responded, "Okay, go ahead and bring it. Bring what you want, a knife or a gun." Guero, holding the broomstick, turned and walked away.

Defendant, who lived nearby, went home and told his roommate, Carlos Arreola, that some persons had been playing around near the catering truck, and that one of them had thrown food on his shirt. Defendant's shirt was stained, and he was angry. He told Arreola that he was going to go back and make those "cabrones" wash his shirt. Defendant went to his room, obtained a clean shirt, and then left his apartment, repeating that he was going to make those "cabrones" wash his shirt. The evidence suggested that defendant concealed on his person a handgun and extra ammunition before leaving the apartment.

Defendant returned to the catering truck a few minutes later. Appearing frightened and angry, he walked to within three feet of Guero. Broomstick in hand, Guero stepped closer to defendant. When Guero asked defendant what he wanted, defendant inquired who was going to wash his shirt. Guero replied that no one was. In response, defendant said, "Well, then one of you two is going to leave."

After defendant and Guero argued for two or three minutes, Guero said either "Let's get it on," or "Take out your knife or whatever you have." Guero, dropping the broomstick, lunged toward defendant as if to grab or punch him.

Guero never reached defendant. As Guero lunged forward, defendant drew a firearm from his waistband, his finger on the trigger. The evidence was in conflict as to whether defendant pointed the gun horizontally (toward Guero) or vertically (toward the sky)....

The weapon fired as it was drawn. Guero slumped to the ground, having suffered a mortal bullet wound to the neck. Defendant ran to his apartment, chased by a bottle-throwing crowd of Guero's friends. At his apartment, defendant told his roommate, Carlos Arreola, "I think I killed the 'cabron,' a 'marijuano.'"[5] ...

Guero died at the hospital approximately one hour after the shooting. The cause of death was blood loss from a single gunshot wound to the neck. The path of the bullet was slightly upward (about 10 degrees), perforating the jugular vein. There

5. "Marijuano" was defined at trial by Arreola as a derogatory term signifying someone "who is out in the streets," or a drug addict. Guero had traces of cocaine in his system, as well as a blood-alcohol level of .09 percent measured after Guero had received transfusions at the hospital.

was stippling around the entrance wound, indicating the bullet was fired from a short distance, probably six inches or less.

Defendant did not testify at trial. Rather, he sought to demonstrate through the testimony of others that he had not pointed the firearm toward Guero, and therefore could not have intended to kill him. Defense witnesses also testified that defendant's actions were taken in response to Guero's aggressive and combative behavior, and that Guero had a reputation in the neighborhood as a short-tempered fighter.

II.
Procedural History
A. The trial court's instructions to the jury

Following the parties' presentation of evidence, the prosecutor, in making his closing argument, asked the jury to return a verdict of first degree murder. Defense counsel, in closing, argued that defendant was, at most, guilty of manslaughter. The trial court instructed the jury consistent with the parties' respective theories. Additionally, and of particular relevance to the present discussion, is the trial court's instruction of the jury pursuant to CALJIC No. 8.31, which provides: "Murder of the second degree is [also] the unlawful killing of a human being when: 1. The killing resulted from an intentional act, 2. The natural consequences of the act are dangerous to human life, and 3. The act was deliberately performed with knowledge of the danger to, and with conscious disregard for, human life. When the killing is the direct result of such an act, it is not necessary to establish that the defendant intended that his act would result in the death of a human being."

During its deliberations, the jury asked the court to explain the term, "intentional act," as used in CALJIC No. 8.31. The prosecutor requested that the court answer the jury's question by referring specifically to the "pulling of a handgun in the manner described" as one example of an "intentional act" as that term is used in CALJIC No. 8.31. Defense counsel objected to the prosecutor's request, contending that "the pulling of the handgun ... is an act precedent to death resulting, but it is not itself the intentional act that is referred to in [CALJIC No.] 8.31."

The trial court rejected defense counsel's argument, adopting instead the prosecutor's proposed answer to the jury's inquiry. The court thus informed the jury: "The word 'intentional' as it is used in CALJIC [No.] 8.31 has no special or unique legal meaning and should be construed as it would be in everyday language. The word 'act' as it is used in CALJIC [No.] 8.31 refers to an act from which death in fact results. In the instant case the pulling of a handgun in the manner described and/or the shooting of the handgun in the manner described are possible acts for your consideration. There may be others. Whether any such act occurred and whether any such act otherwise meets the requirements of CALJIC [No.] 8.31 is a matter solely for your determination based on the evidence. Please do not construe this proposed explanation of an intentional act to be a comment by the Court on the evidence or a suggestion by the Court on what you should find to be the facts. Please remember that you are the exclusive judges of the facts and you may disregard any or all of my comments if they do not coincide with your views of the evidence." (The final two sentences were added by the court to the response suggested by the prosecutor.)

Twenty-five minutes after receiving the court's response to its question, the jury returned its verdict finding defendant guilty of second degree murder. The verdict form signed by the foreperson stated: "We the Jury find the Defendant, MARTIN NIETO-BENITEZ, GUILTY of the crime of felony, to wit: Violation of Section 187 of the Penal Code of the State of California (Murder), in the Second Degree ..." The jury annotated the verdict form, immediately following the word, "Degree," to include the words, "WITH IMPLIED (NOT EXPRESS) MALICE." ...

...

III.
Discussion

[The Court reviewed its prior cases defining implied malice and concluded that CALJIC 8.31, given in this case, adequately conveyed the elements of implied malice to the jury.]

The issue presented in defendant's case ... does not turn on that portion of the implied-malice definition relevant to defendant's state of mind. Rather, the present controversy relates to the nature of the act (as the term is used in CALJIC No. 8.31) that can give rise to a conviction on a theory of implied malice.

As noted above, the jury in the present case asked the trial court to define the term "intentional act" as used in CALJIC No. 8.31. The court responded by informing the jury that "the pulling of a handgun in the manner described and/or the shooting of the handgun in the manner described are possible acts for your consideration...."

The People contend the trial court properly instructed the jury, and assert that brandishing a loaded firearm in a threatening manner, when viewed in context, may constitute a sufficiently dangerous act to support a finding that defendant acted with implied malice.

In reply, defendant contends that the trial court's response permitted the jury to imply malice from defendant's act of "pulling a handgun," an offense punishable as a misdemeanor under section 417, subdivision (a)(2).[b] Defendant's contention rests on parallel assertions: (1) because the act of brandishing a firearm is not "inherently dangerous," it was insufficient to support a finding that defendant acted with implied malice; and (2) because (as noted by the Court of Appeal majority) the killing was "involuntary" and occurred in the commission of an unlawful act, not amounting to a felony (*i.e.*, while defendant brandished a firearm), the death that resulted from defendant's act involved, at most, a manslaughter pursuant to section 192, subdivision (b), and not a murder....

---

b. Section 417, subdivision (a)(2), provides in pertinent part: "Every person who, except in self-defense, in the presence of any other person, draws or exhibits any firearm, whether loaded or unloaded, in a rude, angry, or threatening manner, or who in any manner, unlawfully uses the same in any fight or quarrel is guilty of a misdemeanor...."

We agree with the People that the trial court properly instructed the jury and, for the reasons set forth below, conclude that defendant's assertions are without merit.

In determining whether implied malice was shown, the jury was not required to consider "in the abstract" the offense of brandishing a firearm.

Defendant contends his act of brandishing a firearm cannot supply the implied malice necessary to support a murder conviction. In advancing this argument, defendant seeks to focus attention on the nature of the underlying act "in the abstract," rather than on defendant's specific course of conduct in the present case. As we shall explain, however, defendant's argument is based upon a distinct body of law that interprets the felony-murder rule and is thus inapplicable in the present context.

Where the felony-murder rule is applicable, a court looks to the underlying felony in the abstract in order to determine whether the underlying felony was so inherently dangerous that malice can be ascribed to the defendant without reference to the particular facts of the case. "The purpose of the felony-murder rule is to deter felons from killing negligently or accidentally, by holding them strictly responsible for killings they commit" (*People v. Mattison* (1971) 4 Cal. 3d 177) during the course of enumerated felonies. For certain felonies deemed inherently dangerous to human life, the rule operates to render irrelevant any evidence of actual malice or of the lack thereof.

In contrast, a murder committed with implied malice requires that the prosecution demonstrate the defendant in fact acted with malice. The concept of implied malice has both a physical and a mental component. The physical component is satisfied by the performance of "an act, the natural consequences of which are dangerous to life." (*People v. Patterson* (1989) 49 Cal. 3d 615.) The mental component, as set forth earlier, involves an act "deliberately performed by a person who knows that his conduct endangers the life of another and who acts with conscious disregard for life." (*People v. Dellinger* (1989) 49 Cal. 3d 1212.) Whether a defendant's underlying acts are inherently dangerous in the abstract is not dispositive in the jury's determination as to whether a defendant acted with malice.

Thus, the analytical approach applicable to murder committed with implied malice differs significantly from that applicable to felony murder. Nevertheless, by arguing that misdemeanor brandishing of a firearm is not inherently dangerous, defendant attempts to borrow from the analysis applicable to felony murder in order to escape the applicability of the principles involved in the concept of implied malice. Defendant's contention lacks support. Numerous cases have held that even where the felony-murder rule is inapplicable because the underlying felony is not inherently dangerous, the defendant still may be tried on a theory of implied malice.

...

2. Death resulting from the commission of a misdemeanor can support a murder conviction if malice is shown.

Defendant contends the jury's finding that he acted with implied malice suggests that the shooting was accidental. Defendant further contends that an unlawful killing resulting from the accidental discharge of a firearm, even one brandished in violation of section 417, is, at most, manslaughter. In support of this argument, defendant relies on the provisions of section 192, subdivision (b), which define manslaughter to include an "unlawful killing of a human being without malice ... in the commission of an unlawful act, not amounting to a felony...."

Defendant's argument rests on a misinterpretation of section 192, subdivision (b). The statute does not classify all killings resulting from the commission of a misdemeanor as manslaughter. Rather, the statute's threshold provision—ignored by defendant—is that only those unlawful killings committed without malice are defined as manslaughter. (§ 192.) It is well established that a defendant who commits an unlawful killing with malice, but whose underlying offense is classified as a misdemeanor, is not insulated by that classification from liability for murder.

...

Thus, the classification of the underlying offense as a misdemeanor does not in itself preclude a resulting death from constituting murder. The circumstance that an act may be punishable as a misdemeanor does not render it incapable of being performed in a manner that, under the circumstances, is sufficiently dangerous to human life to support a jury's finding of implied malice. Even if the act results in a death that is accidental, as defendant contends was the case here, the circumstances surrounding the act may evince implied malice.

...

[Concurring opinion of Mosk, J. joined by Kennard, J. omitted.]

Chapter 7

Homicide: Third Party Killings

The four cases in this chapter all involve the prosecution of a defendant for murder, even though neither the defendant, nor an accomplice of the defendant, fired the fatal shot. Although in the first three cases, the killing occurs while the defendant is in the process of committing a felony, as the court indicated in *People v. Washington*, the defendant cannot be guilty of murder on a felony-murder theory. Instead, the defendants in those cases are prosecuted on a conscious disregard implied malice theory.

These cases raise the questions of what conduct demonstrates the requisite malice, and what circumstances establish causation in fact and proximate cause. In *Taylor v. Superior Court*, the issue is what conduct beyond the commission of the felony is sufficient to establish malice. In *Pizano v. Superior Court*, the issue is whether the defendants can be liable when the killing is not in response to any provocative acts by the defendants. *In re Joe R.* raises both issues: what acts are sufficiently provocative to invite lethal resistance, and when can it be said that the acts caused the killing. In *People v. Concha*, the court has to decide whether the defendant can be prosecuted on an express malice theory when the killing is done by a third party.

Taylor v. Superior Court

3 Cal. 3d 578, 477 P.2d 131 (1970)

BURKE, J.

Petitioner and his codefendant Daniels were charged by information with the murder of John H. Smith, robbery, assault with a deadly weapon against Linda West, and assault with a deadly weapon against Jack West. The superior court denied petitioner's motion to set aside the information as to the murder count (Pen. Code, § 995), and we issued an alternative writ of prohibition.

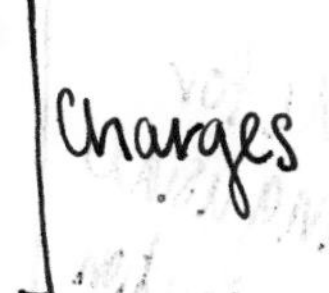

At the preliminary hearing, the following facts were adduced regarding the murder count: On the evening of January 12, 1969, two men attempted to rob Jax Liquor Store which was operated by Mrs. Linda Lee West and her husband Jack. Mrs. West testified that James Daniels entered the store first and asked Mr. West, who was behind the counter, for a package of cigarettes. While Mr. West was getting the cigarettes, John Smith entered the store and approached the counter. Mrs. West, who was on a ladder at the time the two men entered the store, then heard her husband say something about money. Turning her attention to the counter, she heard Daniels repeatedly saying, "Put the money in the bag," and observed her husband complying with the order.

While Mr. West was putting the money from the register in the bag, Daniels repeatedly referred to the fact that he and Smith were armed. According to Mrs. West, Daniels "chattered insanely" during this time, telling Mr. West "Put the money in the bag. Put the money in the bag. Put the money in the bag. Don't move or I'll blow your head off. He's got a gun. He's got a gun. Don't move or we'll have an execution right here. Get down on the floor. I said on your stomach, on your stomach." Throughout this period, Smith's gun was pointed at Mr. West. Mrs. West testified that Smith looked "intent" and "apprehensive" as if "waiting for something big to happen." She indicated that Smith's apparent apprehension and nervousness was manifested by the way he was staring at Mr. West.

While Daniels was forcing Mr. West to the floor, Mrs. West drew a pistol from under her clothing and fired at Smith, who was standing closest to her. Smith was struck on the right side of the chest. Mrs. West fired four more shots in rapid succession, and observed "sparks" coming from Smith's gun, which was pointed in her direction. A bullet hole was subsequently discovered in the wall behind the place Mrs. West had been standing, approximately eight or nine feet above the floor. During this period, Mr. West had seized a pistol and fired two shots at Smith. Mrs. West's last shot was fired at Daniels as he was going out of the door. He "lurched violently and almost went down, [but] picked himself up and kept going." Smith died as the result of multiple gunshot wounds.

The evidence at the preliminary examination indicated that petitioner was waiting outside the liquor store in a getaway car. He was apprehended later and connected with the crime through bills in his possession and through the automobile which was seen by a witness leaving the scene of the robbery.

Under Penal Code section 995, an information must be set aside if the defendant has been committed without "reasonable or probable cause." Of course, the probable cause test is not identical with the test which controls a jury in a murder case. The jury must be convinced to a moral certainty and beyond a reasonable doubt of the existence of the crime charged in the information and of every essential element of that crime. But a magistrate conducting a preliminary examination must be convinced of only such a state of facts as would lead a man of ordinary caution or prudence to believe, and conscientiously entertain a strong suspicion of the guilt of the accused. In other words, "Evidence that will justify a prosecution need not be sufficient to support a conviction.... An information will not be set aside or a prosecution thereon prohibited if there is some rational ground for assuming the possibility that an offense has been committed and the accused is guilty of it."

The information herein charged petitioner with the crime of murder. "'Murder is the unlawful killing of a human being, with malice aforethought.' (Pen. Code, § 187.) Except when the common-law-felony-murder doctrine is applicable, an essential element of murder is an intent to kill or an intent with conscious disregard for life to commit acts likely to kill" (*People v. Washington* (1965) 62 Cal. 2d 777). Petitioner correctly contends that he cannot be convicted under the felony-murder doctrine, since "When a killing is not committed by a robber or by his accomplice but by his victim, malice aforethought is not attributable to the robber, for the killing is not committed by him in the perpetration or attempt to perpetrate robbery" (*Id.*) However, apart from the felony-murder doctrine, petitioner could be found guilty of murder on a theory of vicarious liability.

As stated in *People v. Gilbert* (1965) 63 Cal. 2d 690, "When the defendant or his accomplice, with a conscious disregard for life, intentionally commits an act that is likely to cause death, and his victim or a police officer kills in reasonable response to such act, the defendant is guilty of murder. In such a case, the killing is attributable, not merely to the commission of a felony, but to the intentional act of the defendant or his accomplice committed with conscious disregard for life. [¶] Thus, the victim's self-defensive killing or the police officer's killing in the performance of his duty cannot be considered an independent intervening cause for which the defendant is not liable, for it is a reasonable response to the dilemma thrust upon the victim or the policeman by the intentional act of the defendant or his accomplice."

Therefore, if petitioner were an accomplice to the robbery, he would be vicariously responsible[1] for any killing attributable to the intentional acts of his associates committed with conscious disregard for life, and likely to result in death. We must determine whether the committing magistrate had any rational ground for believing that Smith's death was attributable to intentional acts of Smith and Daniels meeting those criteria.

Petitioner relies upon the following language in *Washington*, wherein defendant's accomplice merely pointed a gun at the robbery victim who, without further provocation, shot and killed him: "In every robbery there is a possibility that the victim will resist and kill. The robber has little control over such a killing once the robbery is undertaken as this case demonstrates. To impose an additional penalty for the killing would discriminate between robbers, *not on the basis of any difference in their own conduct*, but solely on the basis of the response by others that the robber's conduct happened to induce." (Italics added.)

As indicated by the italicized words in the foregoing quotation, the central inquiry in determining criminal liability for a killing committed by a resisting victim or police officer is whether the conduct of a defendant or his accomplices was sufficiently provocative of lethal resistance to support a finding of implied malice. If the trier of fact concludes that under the particular circumstances of the instant case Smith's death proximately resulted from acts of petitioner's accomplices done with conscious

1. "Under the rules defining principals and criminal conspiracies, the defendant may be guilty of murder for a killing attributable to the act of his accomplice. To be so guilty, however, the accomplice must cause the death of another human being by an act committed in furtherance of the common design." Petitioner does not dispute that the conduct of his confederates set forth above was in furtherance of the robbery.

disregard for human life, the natural consequences of which were dangerous to life, then petitioner may by convicted of first degree murder.[2]

For example, we pointed out in *Washington* that "Defendants who initiate gun battles may also be found guilty of murder if their victims resist and kill. Under such circumstances, 'the defendant, for a base, antisocial motive and with wanton disregard for human life, does an act that involves a high degree of probability that it will result in death,' and it is unnecessary to imply malice by invoking the felony-murder doctrine."

Petitioner contends that since neither Daniels nor Smith fired the first shot, they did not "initiate" the gun battle which led to Smith's death. However, depending upon the circumstances, a gun battle can be initiated by acts of provocation falling short of firing the first shot. Thus, in *People v. Reed* (1969) 270 Cal. App. 2d 37, defendant resisted the officers' commands to "put up your hands," and pointed his gun toward the officers and toward the kidnap-robbery victim. The officers commenced firing, wounding defendant and killing the victim. Although defendant did not fire a single shot, his murder conviction was upheld on the theory that his "aggressive actions" were sufficient evidence of implied malice, and that "[under] these circumstances it may be said that defendant initiated the gunplay ..."

Similarly, in *Brooks v. Superior Court* (1966) 239 Cal. App. 2d 538, petitioner had directed "opprobrious language" to the arresting officer and had grasped the officer's shotgun. The officer, being startled and thinking that petitioner was trying to disarm him, yanked backwards and fired the gun, mortally wounding a fellow officer. In upholding an indictment for murder, the court concluded that under the circumstances, the petitioner's act of reaching for and grasping the officer's shotgun was "fraught with grave and inherent danger to human life," and therefore sufficient to raise an inference of malice.

In the instant case, the evidence at the preliminary hearing set forth above discloses acts of provocation on the part of Daniels and Smith from which the trier of facts could infer malice, including Daniels' coercive conduct toward Mr. West and his repeated threats of "execution," and Smith's intent and nervous apprehension as he held Mr. West at gunpoint. The foregoing conduct was sufficiently provocative of lethal resistance to lead a man of ordinary caution and prudence to conclude that Daniels and Smith "initiated" the gun battle, or that such conduct was done with conscious disregard for human life and with natural consequences dangerous of life.[3] Accordingly,

2. When murder has been established pursuant to the foregoing principles, Penal Code section 189 may be invoked to determine its degree (*People v. Gilbert*).

3. Petitioner contends that we should ignore evidence regarding Smith's conduct, on the theory that Smith could not have been held responsible for his own death. We rejected a similar contention in *Washington*, stating that "A distinction based on the person killed, however, would make the defendant's criminal liability turn upon the marksmanship of victims and policemen. A rule of law cannot reasonably be based on such a fortuitous circumstance. The basic issue therefore is whether a robber can be convicted of murder for the killing of *any* person by another who is resisting the robbery." (Italics added.) Therefore, the trier of fact may find that Smith set into motion, through the intentional commission of acts constituting implied malice and in furtherance of the robbery, a gun battle resulting in his own death. Since petitioner may be held vicariously responsible for any killing

we conclude that the evidence supported the magistrate's finding that reasonable and probable cause existed to charge petitioner with first degree murder. The alternative writ heretofore issued is discharged and the peremptory writ is denied.

Peters, J.

I dissent.

In holding that petitioner can be convicted of murder of John H. Smith, the majority repudiate this court's holdings in *People v. Washington* (1965) 62 Cal. 2d 777, and *People v. Gilbert* (1965) 63 Cal. 2d 690, that robbers cannot be convicted of murder for a killing by a victim unless the robbers commit malicious acts, in addition to the acts constituting the underlying felony, which demonstrate culpability beyond that of other robbers. The majority conveniently ignore the facts of *Gilbert* and its entire discussion concerning implied malice. They purport to distinguish *Washington* from the instant case, resulting in the absurd distinction that robbers who point guns at their victims without articulating the obvious threat inherent in such action cannot be convicted of murder for a killing committed by the victims, whereas robbers who point guns at their victims and articulate their threat can be convicted of murder in the same situation. To hold, as do the majority, that petitioner can be convicted of murder for acts which constitute a first degree robbery solely because the victims killed one of the robbers is in effect to reinstate the felony-murder rule in cases where the victim resists and kills.

...

In *Washington*, a gun was pointed at the victim by a robber appearing suddenly in the victim's office; in the instant case, a gun was pointed at one of the victims and threatening language was used. The majority are making the incredible statement that because the robber in *Washington* did not articulate his obvious threat—because, in the majority's words, he "merely" pointed a gun at the victim—it cannot be said that he committed an act with conscious disregard for life and likely to result in death, whereas if he articulated his threat—as did the robbers in the instant case—his act could be found to have met such criteria.

To me, it is too obvious to dispute that inherent in the brandishing of a gun in a robbery is the conditional threat of the robber that he will use the gun if his demands are not complied with. The fact that the robber makes his threat express does not serve to distinguish *Washington*. It is unreasonable to assume that, just because the robber in *Washington* did not articulate his threat, the victim in that case had less reason to fear for his safety or, as the majority assert, less "provocation" for shooting the robber than did the victims in the instant case. It is absurd to suggest that the robber's acts in *Washington* were, as a matter of law, not "sufficiently provocative of lethal resistance to support a finding of implied malice," whereas the robbers' acts in the instant case could be so considered.

---

legally attributable to his accomplices, he may be charged with Smith's death. [**N.B.** This aspect of the holding was overruled in *People v. Antick*, 15 Cal. 3d 79 (1975).—Ed.]

In sum, the articulation of threats does not without more show that the robber's acts were done "with wanton disregard for human life," involving "a high degree of probability that it will result in death" from which malice can be implied. The difference between an implied and an express threat furnishes no significant basis for discrimination between robbers.

...

Not only is the majority's holding contrary to the holdings and language of *Washington* and *Gilbert*, it is also contrary to the fundamental rationale of those cases—that the culpability of criminal defendants should be determined by their own acts, not by the fortuitous acts of their victims which are beyond the defendants' control and this logically irrelevant to the defendants' culpability. In rejecting the contention that a purpose of the felony-murder rule is to prevent the commission of robberies, this court in *Washington* reasoned that whether robbers can be convicted of murder should not depend on the uncontrollable responses of their victims....

In the instant case as in *Washington*, the robbers committed acts constituting a first degree robbery; they committed no additional acts—such as initiating a gun battle—that would reflect a culpability beyond that of any other first degree robbers and that would justify the additional charge of murder. As *Washington* stated, "[in] every robbery there is a possibility that the victim will resist and kill," and robbers cannot be charged with murder for a killing by a victim unless they commit acts in addition to those constituting a robbery upon which additional acts a murder charge can be based. Any murder instruction in the instant case would be based solely on acts constituting first degree robbery. To convert such acts—i.e., to convert a first degree robbery—into murder solely because the victim killed one of the robbers is in effect to reinstitute the felony-murder doctrine in such a situation—contrary to the basic *Washington* holding that a defendant cannot be convicted of murder simply because he and his accomplices committed a felony in which a death resulted. In the instant case as in *Washington*, to impose an additional penalty on the defendant, not because of any independently malicious act (such as initiating a gun battle) by him or his accomplices, but because of the uncontrollable act of the victim who resists and kills is to "deter robbery haphazardly at best."

In conclusion, the majority have rejected the *Washington* holding that robbers can be convicted of murder for a killing by a victim only if the robbers commit malicious acts, in addition to the acts which constitute the underlying felony, which demonstrate culpability beyond that of other robbers. By purporting to distinguish *Washington* from the instant case, the majority have set forth a new, wholly irrational, rule: if robbers point guns at the victims without articulating the obvious threat inherent in such action they cannot be convicted of murder for a killing committed by the victims, whereas if they articulate their threat they can be convicted of murder in the same situation. As we have seen, the majority's purported distinction of *Washington* makes absolutely no sense. In my opinion, it simply demonstrates a desire on the part of the majority to overrule *Washington sub silentio*.

...

[Tobriner, J. concurs in the dissent. Dissenting opinion of Mosk, J. omitted.]

Problem

Problem 48.

Defendant is a member of a criminal gang, the Avenue Gang. Several days earlier, the Cypress Gang had shot an Avenue Gang member. Defendant and four other members of the Avenue Gang decided to drive to the territory of the Cypress Gang to seek revenge by shooting a member of the Cypress Gang. Defendant was driving the Avenue Gang car, and several of the others were armed. They drove down the main street of the Cypress Gang territory firing at a house and at a car occupied by Cypress Gang members, who returned the fire. The Avenue Gang car then turned around and made another pass down the street with the passengers again firing their weapons. Cypress Gang members again returned the fire, killing Victim, a passenger in the Avenue Gang car. Defendant is charged with second degree murder (P.C. §§ 187–189). What arguments should be made as to Defendant's guilt in light of the fact that the gang did no provocative acts beyond their intended felony, attempted murder?

Pizano v. Superior Court

21 Cal. 3d 128, 577 P.2d 659 (1978)

Clark, J.

The question presented is whether an armed robber—using his victim as a shield to effect escape—is guilty of murder under an implied malice theory when a third party—unaware of the victim's presence—accidentally kills the victim while trying to prevent the robber's escape.

Statements made by this court in *People v. Gilbert* (1965) 63 Cal. 2d 690 suggest that the robber is not guilty of murder because the third party, not even realizing that the victim is present, is not responding to the robber's malicious conduct in using the victim as a shield. He is reacting, instead, to the robbery itself, trying to foil it by preventing the escape.

We conclude that the *Gilbert* test—whether the killing was in response to malicious conduct additional to the underlying felony—is inapplicable to shield cases. As we explain below, the function of the *Gilbert* test is to provide the trier of fact with a guideline for determining whether the malicious conduct, rather than the underlying felony, proximately caused the victim's death. In a shield case this determination may be made without employing that test. The third party in this case did not fire the fatal shot in response to the robber's malicious conduct in using the victim as a shield. Nevertheless, there is ample evidence from which the trier of fact may conclude that the victim's death was proximately caused by that malicious conduct rather than by the robbery itself.

The factual context in which this question arises was developed at petitioner's preliminary hearing.

Two men, one carrying a pistol, forced their way into a house shared by Mr. Vaca and Miss Coverdell, robbing them of 13 cents. Coverdell identified the robber with the pistol as codefendant Esquivel and testified petitioner resembled the second robber.

Mrs. Fernandez, her children and Mr. Cuna lived next door to Vaca. The children informed Fernandez and Cuna that two masked men had entered Vaca's house. Fernandez ran next door, peered through a window, and observed a masked man; she returned home and called the police. Arming himself with a rifle, Cuna went to Vaca's house, kicked the door partially open, and saw two men, one carrying a pistol. Cuna returned home and waited on his porch.

Mistaking Cuna for a policeman, petitioner told Esquivel the police were outside. Esquivel responded by grabbing Vaca, twisting his arm behind his back, pointing the pistol at him, and stating he would shoot Vaca if the police intervened. Petitioner opened the door and ran out of the house, followed by Vaca and Esquivel.

Not realizing Vaca was present, Cuna shot at Esquivel as they came out of the house. He fired "because they were robbing" and "because the police didn't arrive." Esquivel was not pointing the pistol at Cuna when Cuna fired. When he recognized Vaca, Cuna did not fire again.

As Vaca fell mortally wounded by Cuna's shot, petitioner and Esquivel fled.

...

... [I]t is clear, first, that the felony-murder doctrine is inapplicable here because the fatal shot was fired by someone other than the felons. [citing *Washington*, *Gilbert* and *Taylor*]

However, contrary to petitioner's contention, the principles announced in *Gilbert* and its progeny are not limited to cases in which the person actually committing the homicide is either a victim of the felony or a police officer. Although *Gilbert* and subsequent cases refer only to victims and police officers, none states that the vicarious liability/implied malice doctrine is limited to such persons, and no logical basis exists for such a limitation.

The magistrate erred in concluding that the People failed to prove implied malice. Initiating a gun battle is not the only means of manifesting malice. The malicious acts of Esquivel *in addition to the robbery* are abundantly evidenced. Taking Vaca as a hostage, pointing a pistol at him, stating he would be shot if the police intervened, and then using him as a shield provided a more than sufficient basis for an inference of malice. Indeed, it has been argued that malice is express in such cases on the ground that using the victim as a shield is a "direct and deliberate creation of immediate lethal danger to the deceased and to him alone." (Morris, *The Felon's Responsibility for the Lethal Acts of Others* (1956) 105 U. Pa. L. Rev. 50.)

We now reach the question which began our discussion. Petitioner contends that the People failed to satisfy the second *Gilbert* principle—that "[the] killing must be attributable to the act of the defendant or his accomplice." His argument rests on two passages in *Gilbert*. First, in explaining the foregoing principle, this court stated that a defendant is guilty of murder "[when] the defendant or his accomplice, with a conscious disregard for life, intentionally commits an act that is likely to cause death, and his victim or a police officer kills *in reasonable response to such act* ..." (Italics added.) Second, applying the foregoing principle as explained to the facts of that case, the *Gilbert* court stated that the instruction given there was erroneous insofar as it "withdrew from the jury the crucial issue of whether the shooting of [a cofelon] was in response to the shooting of [a policeman] or solely to prevent the robbery."

If Cuna had realized that Vaca was being used as a shield and had fired "in reasonable response" to this malicious act, then Esquivel and, as his accomplice, petitioner would clearly be liable for murder under *Gilbert*. However, as petitioner points out, Cuna did *not* fire in response, whether reasonable or unreasonable, to Vaca's being used as a shield; he was not even aware of Vaca's presence. Instead, Cuna fired because the police had not arrived and the robbers were about to escape. In short, petitioner concludes, Cuna fired "solely to prevent the robbery" which *Gilbert* states to be insufficient to create liability for murder on the part of either Esquivel or petitioner.

The People respond that culpability should not rest on the state of mind of the person firing the fatal shot but on the conduct of the defendant or his accomplice. They point to this court's statement in *Washington* that: "In every robbery there is a possibility that the victim will resist and kill. The robber has little control over such a killing once the robbery is undertaken as this case demonstrates. To impose an additional penalty for the killing would discriminate between robbers, not on the basis of any difference in their own conduct, but solely on the basis of the response by others that the robber's conduct happened to induce." Adopting petitioner's position would, the People argue, impose an additional penalty for a killing solely on the basis of the state of mind in others that the felon's additional malicious conduct happened to induce.

The People contend that the question whether a killing was "in reasonable response" to the malicious conduct should be treated as "an objective proximate cause determination, and not a subjective response determination." They argue that the use of the term "independent intervening cause" in the same passage indicates that the *Gilbert* court had proximate cause in mind.

The use of that term does appear to so indicate for this court subsequently stated in *Taylor v. Superior Court* (1970) 3 Cal. 3d 578, that "[if] the trier of fact concludes that ... [the] death [of one of the robbers] *proximately resulted* from acts of petitioner's accomplices done with conscious disregard for human life, the natural consequences of which were dangerous to life, then petitioner may be convicted of ... murder." (Italics added.)

We need not overrule *Gilbert* in order to conclude there is probable cause to believe that Esquivel proximately caused Vaca's death by using him as a shield. *Gilbert* does not state that the only circumstance in which a killing is attributable to the malicious act of the defendant or his accomplice is when the third person's action is a reasonable response to that act. Proximate cause problems in criminal cases cannot be solved by applying a simple rule-of-thumb applicable to every conceivable fact situation.

The police officer in *Gilbert* may well have fired because he and his brother officer were fired upon. Returning the felon's fire would certainly have been a reasonable response under the circumstances. Therefore, the question of liability in such a case becomes, to use the People's term, a "subjective" one: Did the officer fire in response to the felon's additional malicious conduct or simply in response to the felony itself?

However, the reasonable response test is clearly inappropriate in shield cases. A police officer would not ordinarily shoot at a felon because the felon was using a hostage as a cover. The reasonable response in such a situation would ordinarily be to withhold fire lest the hostage be further endangered. The felon foresees this, of course. One of the primary purposes of using a hostage as a shield is to deter the police from countering force with force.

However, if for example the officer is a sharpshooter who has a good angle for a shot, he may fire at the felon in spite of the hostage's being used for cover. Or the officer may accidentally hit the hostage while firing at the felon's accomplice. Or, as was true of Cuna, the officer may simply be unaware of the hostage's presence. The felon foresees these possibilities as well for, if one of the purposes of using a hostage as a shield is to deter hostile fire, the other is to absorb it.

As we stated earlier, the function of the reasonable response test in a *Gilbert* situation is to provide the trier of fact with a guideline for determining whether the malicious conduct rather than the underlying felony proximately caused the victim's death. In a shield case this determination may be made without employing that test. Cuna did not fire the fatal shot in response to Esquivel's malicious conduct in using Vaca as a shield. Nevertheless, there is ample evidence from which the trier of fact may conclude that Vaca's death was proximately caused by that malicious conduct rather than by the robbery itself.

...

Bird, C.J.

I respectfully dissent. In permitting petitioner to be tried for murder in the first degree, the majority's opinion directly conflicts with the specific language of Penal Code section 189 and carves out an impermissible exception which the Legislature never intended.

...

In the present case, the majority concedes that neither petitioner nor his accomplice fired the shot which killed Vaca and, therefore, petitioner may not be found guilty of murder—of any degree—on the basis of the felony-murder rule, since "[s]ection

189 requires that the felon or his accomplice commit the killing, for if he does not, the killing is not committed to perpetrate the felony. Indeed, in the present case the killing was committed to thwart a felony. *To include such killings within section 189 would expand the meaning of the words 'murder ... which is committed in the perpetration ... [of] robbery ...' beyond common understanding.*" (Italics added.) (*People v. Washington* (1965) 62 Cal. 2d 777.)

Although the majority opinion holds that petitioner cannot be tried on a felony-murder theory, it finds there is sufficient evidence in the record to justify a trial of petitioner for murder on a vicarious liability/implied malice theory. The majority reasons that there is probable cause to believe that the death of Vaca was attributable to an act of implied malice by petitioner's accomplice and that petitioner may be held vicariously liable for this act.

Relying on *People v. Gilbert* (1965) 63 Cal. 2d 690, the majority holds that the killing here would be murder of the first degree, if it had been committed in the perpetration of one of the felonies enumerated in section 189. However, this proposition, concerning the degree of implied-malice murder, contradicts the *express* language of section 189, which specifies the two "kinds" of murder which may be first degree. One "kind" of first degree murder is a murder "perpetrated by means of a destructive device or explosive, poison, lying in wait, torture, or by any other kind of willful, deliberate, and premeditated killing ..." None of these enumerated "means" was employed in petitioner's case. Therefore, the only other basis for a first degree murder finding is the felony-murder rule, *i.e.*, a killing "committed in the perpetration of, or attempt to perpetrate, ... robbery ..." However, as this court has repeatedly held and as the majority expressly concedes, a killing is not "committed in the perpetration of ... robbery ..." (§ 189) where, as here, the fatal shot is not fired by a principal in the robbery.

Since the killing in the present case does not fall within either of these two categories, it obviously must be some other "kind" of murder. Section 189 unambiguously states that "*all* other kinds of murders are of the second degree." (Italics added.) The majority's conclusion that petitioner's "implied malice" murder would be first degree murder squarely contradicts this statutory law.

Since it is axiomatic that this court should not create a rule that directly conflicts with a valid legislative enactment, this holding in the majority opinion and in *Gilbert* should not stand.

Problem

Problem 49.

Defendant, Friend (Defendant's companion) and Victim were drug dealers. Defendant and Friend approached Victim on the street to rob him. Victim fled, and Defendant fired at Victim, without hitting him. Bystander, another armed drug dealer in the area, heard the shots and thought someone was shooting at him. He began firing his weapon in the general direction of the shots, and one of his shots hit and killed Victim. Defendant is charged with first degree murder (P.C. §§187–189). What arguments should be made as to whether Defendant is guilty?

In re Joe R.

27 Cal. 3d 496, 612 P.2d 927 (1980)

NEWMAN, J.

A juvenile court petition filed against Joe R., a minor, charged him with two robberies (Pen. Code, §211) and a murder (Pen. Code, §187). After hearing, the court found all charges true, declared him a ward of the court, and committed him to the California Youth Authority.

He appeals, contending that (1) the murder allegation is not supported by the evidence....

On June 1, 1976, Renard Murray was working as night manager of the Taco Bell food stand at 60th and Crenshaw in Los Angeles. About 20 minutes after midnight the minor and another young male, Michael Ryles, approached the service window. As they approached, Murray saw each was pointing a pistol at him. Ryles ordered him to take money from the cash register and put it in a Taco Bell bag. The pair took approximately $140 in various denominations, including a large number of one dollar bills, and about $50 in change wrapped in rolls. Murray also was forced to surrender cash on his person.

The robbers fled in the car of the minor's mother, parked nearby. While driving they saw Wayne Anderson sitting on a bus bench at the corner of Century and Vermont, and they decided to rob him. They parked the car and approached him at about 45 minutes past midnight. Ryles asked Anderson questions and then, pointing his gun at Anderson's head, announced it was a robbery.

Ryles ordered Anderson to walk behind nearby buildings—a gas station and a weight-control center. As they walked, Ryles repeatedly asked for money; and Anderson said he had no money. Both robbers made threats on his life. On direct examination he testified that the minor said, "If you don't do what he says I'll kill you" and "If you don't do what he says he'll kill you." On cross-examination, however, Anderson agreed that the minor never said he (the minor) would do anything to Anderson. Anderson never saw the minor display a gun.

The group stopped behind the buildings, and Ryles ordered Anderson to give his coat and watch to the minor. Anderson complied and repeated he had no money. Ryles gestured with his gun toward an alley and said, "Let's go back there." At that moment Anderson grabbed for the gun, and the two struggled for about 10 seconds. During the struggle Anderson was hit on the back of the head with a fist. The blow caused his glasses to be shaken loose. He did not see who hit him but knew that it was not Ryles and that the only other person present was the minor, who was in back of Anderson.

Anderson got possession of Ryles' gun and, as he did so, saw the minor running away. Ryles yelled, "Shoot him man; he's got my gun." Anderson then shot Ryles twice, within five seconds after being hit in the back of the head. Ryles died from the wounds.

...

Murder?

The murder allegation (Paragraph III) was based on the premise that the minor is liable for the death of his accomplice, Ryles, at the hands of the robbery victim, Anderson, under the doctrine pronounced in *People v. Washington* (1965) 62 Cal. 2d 777 and *People v. Gilbert* (1965) 63 Cal. 2d 690. The minor argues that the evidence is insufficient to sustain a *Washington-Gilbert* murder finding, since it shows no life-threatening acts on his part other than those implicit in the crime of armed robbery. We agree.

...

[The court reviewed the *Washington-Gilbert* doctrine and described *Taylor v. Superior Court*, explaining how the majority concluded that the conduct of Daniels and Smith could be viewed as initiating a gun battle[5] and how the dissenters contended that the majority had "obliterated the additional conduct limitation established in *Washington* and *Gilbert*."[6]]

Here the People argue that the minor's conduct in the Anderson robbery was as "provocative of lethal resistance" as that found sufficient for murder liability in *Taylor*. They rely in particular on (1) his part in moving Anderson away from relative safety at the lighted bus stop into the shadows of nearby buildings, (2) his repeated threats and references to Ryles' pistol, and (3) his interference in the struggle between Ryles and Anderson. All these acts, the People urge, went beyond the underlying felony and were calculated to make Anderson fear for his safety and offer lethal resistance.

First, we reject the minor's blow to the back of Anderson's head during the struggle as a basis of his responsibility for Ryles' death. Anderson testified he had feared for

---

5. This court held more recently that *Washington-Gilbert* murder liability cannot be imposed for the "provocative conduct" of the accomplice who was killed. *People v. Antick* (1975) 15 Cal.3d 79 reasoned that, since a deceased felon cannot be held liable for his own murder, his conduct causing the killing similarly cannot be the basis for vicarious liability of another person. Thus, a burglary suspect was not liable for murder when his sole accomplice fired at arresting officers and was shot down by the police. *Antick* was deemed consistent with *Taylor* because the provocative conduct there relied on was primarily that of the surviving accomplice, Daniels. The People concede here that the minor cannot be held vicariously liable for the conduct of his deceased accomplice, Ryles.

6. We recently reemphasized that conduct *beyond* the original felony is required for "malicious conduct" murder liability. In *Pizano v. Superior Court* (1978) 21 Cal.3d 128, a "shield" was killed by one attempting to prevent robbers' escape but unaware of the hostage's presence. We upheld murder charges against the robbers. We stated that *Gilbert* established "a guideline for determining whether the malicious conduct, *rather than the underlying felony, proximately caused* the victim's death." When such "malicious conduct" produces death, we said, murder liability is not confined by *Gilbert*'s suggestion that the death must occur as a "reasonable response" to the life-threatening acts. Thus, when a third party shoots and kills a robber's hostage, the robber is guilty of murder regardless of the motive behind the bullet.

his life from the moment the robbers displayed a gun and announced their intention. He decided to fight for the weapon and shoot Ryles when, after robbing him, Ryles suggested they move from the building shadows to an alley even darker. It was then, Anderson declared, that he knew he would be "executed" unless he fought for the gun. He stated that when he grabbed for the pistol he anticipated having to use it. Indeed, though the minor's subsequent blow dislodged his glasses, Anderson said it was not severe enough for him to "notice it."

That "rabbit punch" was certainly a malicious act taken in conscious disregard for life, since foreseeably it could have allowed Ryles to prevail and shoot Anderson, or at least caused the gun to discharge accidentally. However, it fails to meet the second requirement of *Washington-Gilbert-Pizano* murder liability since it did not provoke Anderson's lethal resistance and was not the proximate cause of Ryles' death.

...

We thus must decide whether, prior to commencement of the struggle between Ryles and Anderson, the minor committed intentional and malicious acts, in addition to the underlying robbery, that proximately caused Ryles' death. We conclude he did not. Before the struggle began he had done no more than participate actively in an armed robbery. His repeated admonitions to do what Ryles said or "he'll kill you" were directed toward safe completion of the underlying felony. The warnings and commands were conditional and explicitly aimed at obtaining Anderson's property. Nothing he said or did suggested that Anderson was going to be killed whether he cooperated or not.[7] The minor simply voiced the threats already inherent in the dangerous felony. That alone is insufficient for a finding of *Washington-Gilbert* murder even when it helped provoke the victim's lethal response.

Nor did the minor's participation in moving Anderson from the bus stop into the shadows, a distance of less than 20 yards, constitute life-threatening conduct in addition to the underlying felony. All evidence indicates that this first movement was effected solely to lessen the risk that the robbery would be observed. Robbers do not become strictly liable for a killing by their victim simply because they encounter him at a spot too visible for their purposes and therefore move him a small distance in order to complete their robbery safely. To assess murder liability on this basis would cause guilt to depend arbitrarily on the fortuitous circumstances in which the robbery occurs.

We recognize that Ryles' desire to move Anderson further into isolation, after the robbery had occurred, might suggest that Ryles had an unconditional intent to kill. However, no statements or conduct of the minor indicated assent to that decision. It therefore does not form a basis for the minor's liability for Ryles' death.

Our conclusion can be reconciled with *Taylor, supra.* There the majority correctly stated that provocative conduct beyond that inhering in an armed robbery is necessary

---

7. Even if the minor's statements are placed in context of the entire situation the conclusion is the same. Ryles had threatened no unconditional killing at this time to which the minor, by his own remarks or conduct, could be deemed to have agreed.

for *Washington-Gilbert* murder liability. It concluded that the particular facts there proved would support a finding of additional conduct because the robbers' demeanor suggested peculiar instability and a propensity for gratuitous violence. The record here yields no similar indication that the minor was prepared to kill whether or not Anderson complied with the robbers' demands. We therefore hold that the allegations of Paragraph III of the complaint cannot be sustained.

. . .

Clark, J., dissenting.

I dissent from the majority opinion insofar as it absolves defendant of vicarious responsibility for the murder of his accomplice....

Defendant struck Mr. Anderson on the back of the head as Anderson struggled with Ryles for the pistol. This malicious conduct, I conclude, was a proximate cause of Ryles' death. The majority reject this conclusion on the ground Anderson had already decided, before defendant struck him, to use the gun if he gained control of it. This is a fair reading of the record. However, it ignores certain obvious, if unspoken, facts.

Anderson disarmed Ryles and shot him with his own pistol. Had Anderson believed defendant was no threat to him, that defendant would not come to Ryles' assistance, Anderson might well have not shot Ryles but rather simply held him at gunpoint until the police arrived. However, defendant had come to Ryles' assistance seconds before when Anderson was struggling with him for the pistol. Even if the minor's statements are placed in context of the entire situation the conclusion is the same. Ryles had threatened no unconditional killing at this time to which the minor, by his own remarks or conduct, could be deemed to have agreed. Therefore, when Ryles shouted to defendant, "Shoot him, man; he's got my gun," Anderson could reasonably conclude defendant would do so and that he (Anderson) had to shoot Ryles to protect himself from the two assailants.[2]

Admittedly, Anderson did not testify that he engaged in the analysis suggested. However, he was required to react instantaneously to a complex situation of which defendant's malicious conduct was a significant element. That Anderson may not have consciously assessed the significance of defendant's conduct or may not recall having done so does not mean it did not play a crucial role in his shooting of Ryles. In situations of this sort we should not focus exclusively on the victim's recall of his subjective response to the defendant's malicious conduct. Rather, we should also consider whether a reasonable man, given the opportunity and presence of mind to assess the significance of the defendant's conduct, would have been provoked to lethal resistance by it. Applying this standard I conclude defendant was vicariously responsible for the murder of his accomplice.

2. Although defendant had personally used a pistol in robbing the fast food stand minutes earlier, he did not brandish a weapon during the Anderson robbery. Nevertheless, Anderson could reasonably conclude that, unless defendant were armed, Ryles would not have shouted to him, "Shoot him, man; he's got my gun."

The orders declaring defendant a ward of the juvenile court and committing him to the Youth Authority should be affirmed without modification.

[Dissenting statement of Manuel, J., omitted.]

Problems

Problem 50.

Driver, Passenger and Victim held up a fast-food outlet. As they were making their getaway in a car driven by Driver, sheriff's deputies arrived, and a high speed chase, ultimately involving four patrol cars and covering 5–10 miles, ensued. When the robbers were finally cornered and their car stopped, Passenger pointed a shotgun out the window at Officer #1's car, and Officer #1 then rammed the robbers' car, causing the shotgun to discharge and fly out of Passenger's hands. The officers then took cover with their guns drawn, and Driver and Passenger crouched behind their doors, while Victim pointed a revolver out the window. Officers ordered the robbers to "freeze" and "drop the gun." When Victim failed to respond and instead pointed the gun at Officers they opened fire at all the robbers and Officer #2's bullet killed Victim.

What are the arguments as to whether Driver and Passenger are guilty of first degree murder (P.C. §§ 187–189)?

Are the arguments different if there was the following testimony:

(1) the testimony of all officers that the Victim's pointing of his gun constituted some or all of the reason they opened fire?

(2) the testimony of Officer #2 that, when his bullet hit Victim, he was firing at Driver because he thought (mistakenly) that Driver had a gun pointed at Officer #1?

Problem 51.

Defendant is a member of the Highland gang, and he and other gang members attended a large party thrown by members of the Alley gang. Defendant attempted to pick up a woman associated with the Alley gang, and a dispute occurred leading to angry words and the brandishing of guns by an Alley gang member and Defendant. Alley gang member Cool stepped between the disputants attempting to diffuse the situation and put his hands on their shoulders to push them back. Defendant stated, "nobody touches me," and he shot Cool through the arm and chest. At that, witnesses shouted that the Highland gang had attacked the Alley gang. A melee erupted, and gang challenges were exchanged. A minute or so later, when five Alley gang members spotted Victim, a Highland gang member getting into a car to drive away, all five fired at him, and he was killed. Defendant is charged, *inter alia*, with second-degree murder in the killing of Victim. What are the arguments as to whether he is guilty of the crime?

People v. Concha

47 Cal.4th 653, 218 P.3d 660 (2009)

CHIN, J.

Reyas Concha, Julio Hernandez, and Max Sanchez attempted to murder Jimmy Lee Harris. During the attempt, Harris responded in self-defense by stabbing Max Sanchez to death. Relying on the so-called provocative act murder doctrine, the jury convicted defendants Concha and Hernandez of first degree murder for the death of Sanchez. We granted review to determine whether a defendant may be liable for first degree murder when his accomplice is killed by the intended victim in the course of an attempted murder. We hold that a defendant may be convicted of first degree murder under these circumstances if the defendant personally acted willfully, deliberately, and with premeditation during the attempted murder.

I. FACTS AND PROCEDURAL HISTORY

On July 14, 2005, Reyas Concha, Julio Hernandez, Max Sanchez, and a fourth unidentified man threatened to kill Jimmy Lee Harris during an apparent attempted robbery. Harris fled from the assailants and ran down the middle of a street in Los Angeles. The four men pursued Harris for over a quarter of a mile before cornering him against a fence. Harris attempted to scale the fence and one or more of the assailants began stabbing him. The stabbing continued for several seconds. Harris, realizing that his life was in danger, turned around and attempted to fight the four men off. Harris pulled a pocket knife from his pocket and "began to stab as many of them as [he] could." Harris then fled and found someone who called the police. Harris suffered severe injuries, but he survived. Sanchez died from the stab wounds that Harris inflicted during the attack.

The jury convicted defendants of attempted first degree murder of Harris. (Pen. Code, §§ 187, 664(a).) Relying on the provocative act murder doctrine, the jury also convicted defendants of the first degree murder of Sanchez. (§ 187(a).) ... The jury deadlocked as to each defendant on an attempted second degree robbery charge and the trial court granted the prosecution's motion to dismiss the attempted robbery charges.

...

We granted review limited to the following issue: "Did the trial court err in allowing the jury to return verdicts of first degree murder when the case was tried on a theory of provocative-act murder?"

II. DISCUSSION

Defendants contend the provocative act murder doctrine limits a defendant's liability to second degree murder when the defendant's accomplice is killed by the victim during a willful, deliberate, and premeditated attempt to commit murder. We disagree.

Murder is the unlawful killing of a person with malice aforethought (§ 187). Murder includes both actus reus and mens rea elements. To satisfy the actus reus element of murder, an act of either the defendant *or an accomplice* must be the proximate cause of death. (*People v. Roberts* (1992) 2 Cal.4th 271 (*Roberts*); *People v. McCoy* (2001) 25 Cal.4th 1111 (*McCoy*).) For the crime of murder, as for any crime other than strict liability offenses, "there must exist a union, or joint operation of act and intent, or criminal negligence" (§ 20). To satisfy the mens rea element of murder, the defendant must personally act with malice aforethought. (*McCoy, supra.*)

A defendant can be liable for the unlawful killings of both the intended victims and any unintended victims. "[T]here is no requirement of an unlawful intent to kill *an intended victim.* The law speaks in terms of an unlawful intent to kill *a* person, not *the* person *intended to be killed.*" (*People v. Bland* (2002) 28 Cal.4th 313 (*Bland*).)

For example, a defendant is liable for both murder and attempted murder if he or an accomplice attempts to kill a specific person and instead kills a bystander. Similarly, a defendant is liable for two murders if, in the course of killing his intended victim, he or an accomplice also kills a bystander. In short, a defendant may be liable for murder when he possesses the appropriate mens rea and either the defendant or an accomplice causes an unlawful death. As we explained in *Bland*, "[a] *mens rea* ... is an elastic thing of unlimited supply.... It may combine with a single actus reus to make a single crime. It may as readily combine with a hundred *acti rei*, intended and unintended, to make a hundred crimes.... Unforeseen circumstances may multiply the criminal acts for which the criminal agent is responsible. A single state of mind, however, will control the fact of guilt and the level of guilt of them all."

However, the defendant is liable only for those unlawful killings proximately caused by the acts of the defendant or his accomplice. "In all homicide cases in which the conduct of an intermediary is the actual cause of death, the defendant's liability will depend on whether it can be demonstrated that his own conduct *proximately caused* the victim's death." (*People v. Cervantes* (2001) 26 Cal.4th 860.) "[I]f the eventual victim's death is not the natural and probable consequence of a defendant's act, then liability cannot attach." (*Roberts, supra.*) Our prior decisions make clear that, where the defendant perpetrates an inherently dangerous felony, the victim's self-defensive killing is a natural and probable response.

In the present case, although it is apparent that defendants Concha and Hernandez did not intend to kill their accomplice, they had the intent to kill *a* person when they attacked their intended victim, and therefore are guilty of murder as to any killing either of them proximately caused while acting together pursuant to their intent to kill.

Once liability for murder "is otherwise established, section 189 may be invoked to determine its degree." (*People v. Gilbert*, 63 Cal.2d 690.) Section 189 states that if an unlawful killing is "willful, deliberate, and premeditated," or is perpetrated by means of "poison, lying in wait, torture..., discharging a firearm from a motor vehicle, intentionally at another person outside of the vehicle with the intent to inflict death," specific types of weapons, destructive devices, explosives, or ammunition, or in the perpetration of certain enumerated felonies,[2] it is murder of the first degree (§ 189).

2. We note that the felony-murder rule cannot support liability for first degree murder under the facts presented here for two reasons. First, the felony-murder rule can be invoked only when the de-

"All other kinds of murders are of the second degree." (*Ibid.*) Therefore, "assuming legal causation, a person maliciously intending to kill is guilty of the murder of all persons actually killed. If the intent is premeditated, the murder or murders are first degree." (*Bland, supra.*) ...

Therefore, "[i]f a jury finds that a defendant proximately caused a death, either solely through his own conduct or through the actions of others where his conduct is shown to be a substantial concurrent cause of the death, and the defendant did so with a premeditated intent to kill, then the defendant is guilty of *first degree* murder." (*People v. Sanchez* (2001) 26 Cal.4th 834 (*Sanchez*).)

Defendants contend provocative act murder is limited to "second degree as a matter of law," impliedly arguing that provocative act murder is an independent crime with a fixed level of liability. However, that is not the case. While each of our prior decisions dealing with provocative act murder found the defendant liable for second degree murder, a statement that provocative act murder *is* second degree murder is not universally correct. In our prior cases, malice was *implied* from the provocative act. However, as here, when malice is *express* because the defendant possessed a specific intent to kill, first degree murder liability may be proper if the charged defendant personally acted willfully, deliberately, and with premeditation.

...

We note that the doctrine of transferred intent occasionally has been used to explain defendant's liability in provocative act murder cases. Under the "classic formulation" of the transferred intent doctrine, where a defendant intends to kill a victim but misses and instead kills a bystander, the intent to kill the intended victim is imputed to the resulting death of the bystander and the defendant is liable for murder. However, under the transferred intent doctrine, the defendant's intent is not actually transferred from the intended victim to the unintended victim. "Rather, as applied here, [the transferred intent doctrine] connotes a *policy*—that a defendant who shoots at an intended victim with intent to kill but misses and hits a bystander instead should be subject to the same criminal liability that would have been imposed had he hit his intended mark." (*People v. Scott*, 14 Cal.4th 544.) "For purposes of applying the rule of transferred intent, it does not matter whether defendant himself fired the fatal shot or instead induced or provoked another to do so; in either situation, defendant's culpable mental state is determined as if the person harmed were the person defendant meant to harm." (*Sanchez, supra* (conc. opn. of Kennard, J.).)

While the transferred intent doctrine would reach the same result as the proximate cause analysis adopted above if the defendant proximately caused the death of someone other than his intended victim and the jury found that the defendant personally acted during an attempted murder willfully, deliberately, and with premeditation, we choose not to rely on the transferred intent doctrine in our analysis of provocative act murder. We have recognized that the transferred intent doctrine has the potential to cause

---

fendant or an accomplice actually commits the killing (*People v. Washington* (1965) 62 Cal.2d 777). Second, attempted murder is not one of the enumerated felonies in section 189.

"conceptual difficulties"... Here, although the traditional transferred intent formulation and a proximate causation analysis reach the same result, we shall rely on a proximate cause analysis to explain the general basis for criminal liability and, in a provocative act murder case, the available degrees of murder.

[Relying on *People v. McCoy* [see Chapter 13], the court held that the jury had not been properly instructed that, for a defendant to be found guilty of *first degree murder*, he *personally* has to have acted willfully, deliberately, and with premeditation when he committed the attempted murder. The court remanded the case to the Court of Appeal to consider whether this instructional error was prejudicial.]

Problem

Problem 52.

Defendant and Co-defendant were members of rival gangs that had shot at one another in the past. Defendant was the passenger in a car driven by a fellow gang member, and the two drove to a street in the rival gang's territory where Co-defendant lived. Co-defendant was standing in front of his house with another member of his gang when Defendant's car came slowly up the street. As the car passed Co-defendant's house, Defendant and Co-defendant shouted their gang affiliations and threw gang hand signs at one another. At the end of the block, Defendant's car turned around and again passed slowly by Co-defendant's house with more shouts and hand signs. At the end of the block, the car turned for a third pass at the house, and, on this pass, both Defendant and Co-defendant opened fire on each other. A bullet from one of their guns—although there is no evidence indicating from which gun—struck and killed Neighbor, who was sitting on his porch several houses away from the shooters. Defendant and Co-defendant are charged with first degree murder (P.C. §§ 187–189). What are the arguments on whether each of them is guilty of the charge?

Chapter 8

Property Crimes

This chapter considers the two most important crimes against property: theft and burglary. Section A deals with theft. Theft is actually not a single crime, but a class of crimes concerning the involuntary transfer of personal property. The crimes are differentiated from each other by the circumstances of the wrongdoer's acquisition or retention of the property. The cases and problems in this chapter discuss the following eight theft crimes, which are briefly defined:

> **Embezzlement**—the fraudulent appropriation of property by a person to whom it has been intrusted. (P.C. § 503)
>
> **Extortion**—the obtaining of property (or official favors) from another, with consent, induced by the wrongful use of force or fear, or under color of official right. (P.C. § 518)
>
> **False pretenses**—the fraudulent appropriation of title to another's property. (P.C. § 532)
>
> **Forgery**—the fraudulent creation of a false document with apparent legal significance. (P.C. §§ 470, *et seq.*)
>
> **Larceny**—the felonious taking (*i.e.*, taking with the intent to permanently deprive the owner of the property) and carrying away of the property of another. (P.C. § 484)
>
> **Misappropriation**—the appropriation of found property without reasonable and just efforts to find the owner and restore the property. (P.C. § 485)
>
> **Receiving stolen property**—the receipt or concealment of property knowing the property to have been stolen. (P.C. § 496)
>
> **Robbery**—the felonious taking of the personal property of another, from his person or immediate presence, against his will accomplished by force or fear. (P.C. § 211)

Section B deals with burglary. At the common law, burglary was a crime against real property, punishing entry into another's home with the intent to commit a felony. Today, however, burglary has been expanded to cover, not only entry into various structures associated with real property, but also entries into some forms of personal property, *e.g.*, automobiles, tents.

A. Theft

The first four cases in this section concern the mental state or *mens rea* element common to the various theft crimes. In the early case of *People v. Brown*, the California Supreme Court defines the mental state element of larceny. In *People v. Davis*, decided more than 100 years after *Brown*, the court again considers what it means to intend to *permanently* deprive the owner of property. In *People v. Tufunga*, the issue is whether the defendant can assert a "claim of right" defense to the mental state element of robbery. Finally, in *People v. Anderson*, a case where the defendant claimed he had hit the theft victim by accident, the court has to determine the appropriate *mens rea* for the "force or fear" element of robbery.

The remaining six cases concern the act elements of the various theft crimes. In *People v. Ashley*, the Supreme Court defines "fraud" for purposes of the crime of obtaining property under false pretenses and, in the process, explains the difference between that crime and other theft crimes. *People v. Moses* explores the crimes of receiving stolen property and theft by misappropriation. *People v. Hays*, *People v. Webster* and *People v. Mungia* all concern the act elements of robbery. In *Hays*, the defendant challenged the sufficiency of the evidence that he obtained the property (1) by means of force or fear, and (2) from the "immediate presence" of the victim. *Webster* is the supreme court's latest word on the meaning of the "immediate presence" element of robbery. In *Mungia*, the issue is what constitutes sufficient force to turn a theft into a robbery. The last case in the section, *People v. Beggs* concerns the act element of extortion, specifically what constitutes a wrongful threat.

People v. Brown

105 Cal. 66, 38 P. 518 (1894)

Garoutte, J.

The appellant was convicted of the crime of burglary, alleged by the information to have been committed in entering a certain house with intent to commit grand larceny. The entry is conceded, and also it is conceded that appellant took therefrom a certain bicycle, the property of the party named in the information, and of such a value as to constitute grand larceny.

The appellant is a boy of seventeen years of age, and, for a few days immediately prior to the taking of the bicycle, was staying at the place from which the machine was taken, working for his board. He took the stand as a witness, and testified:

"I took the wheel to get even with the boy, and of course I didn't intend to keep it. I just wanted to get even with him. The boy was throwing oranges at me in the evening, and he would not stop when I told him to, and it made me mad, and I left Yount's house Saturday morning. I thought I would go back and take the boy's wheel. He had a wheel, the one I had the fuss with. Instead of getting hold of his, I got Frank's, but I intended to take it back Sunday night; but before I got back they caught me. I took it down by the grove, and put it on the ground, and covered it with brush, and crawled in, and Frank came and hauled off the brush and said: 'What are you doing here'? Then I told him ... I covered myself up in the brush so that they could not find me until evening, until I could take it back. I did not want them to find me. I expected to remain there during the day, and not go back until evening."

Upon the foregoing state of facts the court gave the jury the following instruction: "I think it is not necessary to say very much to you in this case. I may say, generally, that I think counsel for the defense here stated to you in this argument very fairly the principles of law governing this case, except in one particular. In defining to you the crime of grand larceny he says it is essential that the taking of it must be felonious. That is true; the taking with the intent to deprive the owner of it; but he adds the conclusion that you must find that the taker intended to deprive him of it permanently. I do not think that is the law. I think in this case, for example, if the defendant took this bicycle, we will say for the purpose of riding twenty-five miles, for the purpose of enabling him to get away, and then left it for another to get it, and intended to do nothing else except to help himself away for a certain distance, it would be larceny, just as much as though he intended to take it all the while. A man may take a horse, for instance, not with the intent to convert it wholly and permanently to his own use, but to ride it to a certain distance, for a certain purpose he may have, and then leave it. He converts it to that extent to his own use and purpose feloniously."

This instruction is erroneous, and demands a reversal of the judgment. If the boy's story be true he is not guilty of larceny in taking the machine; yet, under the instruction of the court, the words from his own mouth convicted him. The court told the jury that larceny may be committed, even though it was only the intent of the party taking the property to deprive the owner of it temporarily. We think the authorities form an unbroken line to the effect that the felonious intent must be to deprive the owner of the property permanently. The illustration contained in the instruction as to the man taking the horse is too broad in its terms as stating a correct principle of law. Under the circumstances depicted by the illustration the man might, and again he might not, be guilty of larceny. It would be a pure question of fact for the jury, and dependent for its true solution upon all the circumstances surrounding the transaction. But the test of law to be applied to these circumstances for the purpose of determining the ultimate fact as to the man's guilt or innocence is, Did he intend to permanently deprive the owner of his property? If he did not intend so to do, there is no felonious intent, and his acts constitute but a trespass. While the felonious intent of the party taking need not necessarily be an intention to convert the property to his own use, still it must in all cases be an intent to wholly and permanently deprive the owner thereof.

For the foregoing reasons it is ordered that the judgment and order be reversed and the cause remanded for a new trial.

Note

The Model Penal Code and Theft. The Model Penal Code makes "purpose to deprive" the *mens rea* of theft (MPC § 223.2) and defines "deprive" to mean "(a) to withhold property of another permanently or for so extended a period as to appropriate a major portion of its economic value, or with intent to restore only upon payment of reward or other compensation; or (b) to dispose of the property so as to make it unlikely that the owner will recover it." MPC § 223.0(1). The Code also requires proof that the defendant *knew* the property belonged to another and that the defendant had no right to deal with it as he or she did. MPC Part II Commentaries vol. 2, p. 177.

People v. Davis

19 Cal. 4th 301, 965 P.2d 1165 (1998)

Mosk, Justice.

. . .

Facts

Defendant entered a Mervyn's department store carrying a Mervyn's shopping bag. As he entered he was placed under camera surveillance by store security agent Carol German. While German both watched and filmed, defendant went to the men's department and took a shirt displayed for sale from its hanger; he then carried the shirt through the shoe department and into the women's department on the other side of the store. There he placed the shirt on a sales counter and told cashier Heather Smith that he had "bought it for his father" but it didn't fit and he wanted to "return" it. Smith asked him if he had the receipt, but he said he did not because "it was a gift." Smith informed him that if the value of a returned item is more than $20 and there is no receipt, the store policy is not to make a cash refund but to issue a Mervyn's credit voucher. At that point Smith was interrupted by a telephone call from German; German asked her if defendant was trying to "return" the shirt, and directed her to issue a credit voucher. Smith prepared the voucher and asked defendant to sign it; he did so, but used a false name. German detained him as he walked away from the counter with the voucher. . . .

Count 1 of the information charged defendant with the crime of petty theft with a prior theft-related conviction, a felony-misdemeanor. . . .

The only theories of theft submitted to the jury in the instructions were theft by larceny and theft by trick and device. The jury found defendant guilty of petty theft as charged in the information. [Defendant was sentenced to prison.]

I

. . .

The elements of theft by larceny are well settled: the offense is committed by every person who (1) takes possession (2) of personal property (3) owned or possessed by another, (4) by means of trespass and (5) with intent to steal the property, and (6) carries the property away. The act of taking personal property from the possession of another is always a trespass[2] unless the owner consents to the taking freely and unconditionally[3] or the taker has a legal right to take the property. The intent to steal or *animus furandi* is the intent, without a good faith claim of right, to permanently deprive the owner of possession. And if the taking has begun, the slightest movement of the property constitutes a carrying away or asportation.

Applying these rules to the facts of the case at bar, we have no doubt that defendant (1) took possession (2) of personal property—the shirt—(3) owned by Mervyn's and (4) moved it sufficiently to satisfy the asportation requirement. Defendant does not contend otherwise.

Defendant does contend, however, that the elements of trespass and intent to steal are lacking. He predicates his argument on a distinction that he draws by dividing his course of conduct into two distinct "acts." According to defendant, his first "act" was to take the shirt from the display rack and carry it to Smith's cash register. He contends that act lacked the element of intent to steal because he had no intent to permanently deprive Mervyn's *of the shirt*; he intended to have the shirt in his possession only long enough to exchange it for a "refund." His second "act," also according to defendant, was to misrepresent to Smith that he had bought the shirt at Mervyn's and to accept the credit voucher she issued. He contends that act lacked the element of trespass because the store, acting through its agent German, consented to the issuance of the voucher with full knowledge of how he came into possession of the shirt.

Defendant's argument misses the mark on two grounds: it focuses on the wrong issue of consent, and it views that issue in artificial isolation from the intertwined issue of intent to steal.

...

As noted earlier, the general rule is that the intent to steal required for conviction of larceny is an intent to deprive the owner *permanently* of possession of the property. For example, we have said it would not be larceny for a youth to take and hide another's bicycle to "get even" for being teased, if he intends to return it the following day. (*People v. Brown* (1894) 105 Cal. 66.) But the general rule is not inflexible ... Our research discloses three relevant categories of cases holding that the requisite intent to steal may be found even though the defendant's primary purpose in taking the property is not to deprive the owner permanently of possession: i.e., (1) when the defendant intends to "sell" the property back to its owner, (2) when the defendant intends to claim a reward for "finding" the property, and (3) when, as here, the defendant intends to return the property to its owner for a "refund." There is thus ample

2. This is not traditional trespass onto real property, of course, but trespass *de bonis asportatis* or trespass "for goods carried away."

3. When the consent is procured by fraud it is invalid and the resulting offense is commonly called larceny by trick and device.

authority for the *result* reached in the case at bar; the difficulty is in finding a rationale for so holding that is consistent with basic principles of the law of larceny. . . .[4]

A. *The "sale" cases*

The classic case of the first category is *Regina v. Hall* (1848) 169 Eng. Rep. 291. The defendant, an employee of a man named Atkin who made candles from tallow, took a quantity of tallow owned by Atkin and put it on Atkin's own scales, claiming it belonged to a butcher who was offering to sell it to Atkin. The jury were instructed that if they found the defendant took Atkin's property with the intent to sell it back to him as if it belonged to another and appropriate the proceeds, he was guilty of larceny. The jury so found, and the conviction was upheld on further review.

The defendant contended that his assertion of temporary ownership of the property for a particular purpose was not enough to constitute the required intent to permanently deprive. The justices expressed two rationales for holding to the contrary. First, one justice stressed that the deprivation would in fact have been permanent unless the owner had agreed to the condition imposed by the defendant, i.e., to "buy" the property. . . .

The second rationale was that the defendant's claim of the right to sell the property was an assertion of a right of ownership and therefore evidence of an intent to permanently deprive: Chief Justice Denman reasoned, "The only question attempted to be raised here is as to the *animus furandi*, the intent to deprive the owner of his property. What better proof can there be of such intent, than the assertion of such a right of ownership by the prisoner as to entitle him to sell it."

. . .

B. *The "reward" cases*

The cases in the second category hold that a defendant who takes property for the purpose of claiming a reward for "finding" it has the requisite intent to permanently deprive. Again the courts invoke differing rationales for this holding. One line of these cases is exemplified by *Commonwealth v. Mason* (1870) 105 Mass. 163. The defendant took possession of a horse that had strayed onto his property, with the intent to conceal it until the owner offered a reward and then to return it and claim the reward, or until the owner was induced to sell it to him for less than its worth. The court affirmed a conviction of larceny on the theory that the requisite felonious intent was shown because the defendant intended to deprive the owner of "a portion of the value of the property." The court did not explain this theory further, but later cases suggested that the "portion of the value" in question was the right to claim a reward—ordinarily less than the property's full value—for its return.

---

4. Other categories of cases of temporary taking amounting to larceny have also been recognized. Thus the commentators agree there is an intent to steal when the nature of the property is such that even a temporary taking will deprive the owner of its primary economic value, *e.g.*, when the property is dated material or perishable in nature or good for only seasonal use. Another such category is composed of cases in which the defendant takes property with intent to use it temporarily and then to abandon it in circumstances making it unlikely the owner will recover it.

. . .

Another line of cases in this category also noted the taker's intent to appropriate "part of the value" of the property, but went on to emphasize a different rationale, i.e., that the taker had made the return of the property contingent on the offer of a satisfactory reward, and if the contingency did not materialize the taker would keep the property. . . .

. . .

C. *The "refund" cases*

The third category comprises a substantial number of recent cases from our sister states affirming larceny convictions on facts identical or closely similar to those of the case at bar: in each, the defendant took an item of merchandise from a store display, carried it to a sales counter, claimed to own it, and asked for a "refund" of cash or credit. Although the cases are thus factually in point, the reasoning of their opinions is, ironically, of less assistance than the "sale" or "reward" cases in our search for a satisfactory rationale on the issue of the intent to permanently deprive.

[The court found the reported "refund" cases fell into three categories. In the first category were cases where the opinion offered no rationale at all for the finding of intent. In the second category were cases apparently decided on the basis that the defendant committed theft of the cash obtained as a refund, rather than theft of the property used to obtain the refund. In the third category were cases which were statute-specific, i.e., where the decision turned on the wording of the larceny statute in force in that particular jurisdiction.]

II

Several of the rationales articulated in the "sale" and "reward" cases, however, are also applicable to the "refund" cases. On close analysis, moreover, the relevant rationales may be reduced to a single line of reasoning that rests on both a principled and a practical basis.

First, as a matter of principle, a claim of the right to "return" an item taken from a store display is no less an assertion of a right of ownership than the claim of a right to "sell" stolen property back to its owner. And an intent to return such an item to the store only if the store pays a satisfactory "refund" is no less conditional than an intent to return stolen property to its owner only if the owner pays a satisfactory "reward." . . . It follows that a defendant who takes an item from a store display with the intent to claim its ownership and restore it only on condition that the store pays him a "refund" must be deemed to intend to permanently deprive the store of the item within the meaning of the law of larceny.

Second, as a practical matter, the risk that such a taking will be permanent is not a mere theoretical possibility; rather, by taking an item from a store display with the intent to demand a refund a defendant creates a substantial risk of permanent loss. This is so because if the defendant's attempt to obtain a refund for the item fails for any reason, he has a powerful incentive to keep the item in order to avoid drawing attention to the theft. A person who has taken an item from a store display and has claimed the right to "return" it at a sales counter, but has been rebuffed because, for example, he has no receipt, will not be inclined to run the risk of confirming the suspicions of the sales clerk or store security personnel by putting the item back in the display. Instead, just as in the case of a failed attempt to "sell" property back to its owner, "the trespasser would take away the property in order to conceal his own wrongdoing." (Perkins & Boyce, Criminal Law (3rd Ed.) (1982).)

...

III

Applying the foregoing reasoning to the facts of the case at bar, we conclude that defendant's intent to claim ownership of the shirt and to return it to Mervyn's only on condition that the store pay him a "refund" constitutes an intent to permanently deprive Mervyn's of the shirt within the meaning of the law of larceny, and hence an intent to "feloniously steal" that property within the meaning of Penal Code section 484, subdivision (a). Because Mervyn's cannot be deemed to have consented to defendant's taking possession of the shirt with the intent to steal it, defendant's conduct also constituted a trespassory taking within the meaning of the law of larceny. It follows that the evidence supports the final two elements of the offense of theft by larceny, and the Court of Appeal was correct to affirm the judgment of conviction.

...

People v. Tufunga

21 Cal.4th 935, 987 P.2d 168 (1999)

Baxter, J.

The claim-of-right defense provides that a defendant's good faith belief, even if mistakenly held, that he has a right or claim to property he takes from another negates the felonious intent necessary for conviction of theft or robbery. At common law, a claim of right was recognized as a defense to larceny because it was deemed to negate the *animus furandi*, or intent to steal, of that offense. Since robbery was viewed as an aggravated form of larceny, it was likewise subject to the same claim-of-right defense.

In *People v. Butler* (1967) 65 Cal.2d 569, we reaffirmed that a claim-of-right defense can negate the requisite felonious intent of robbery as codified in Penal Code section 211 and extended the availability of the defense to forcible takings perpetrated to satisfy, settle or otherwise collect on a debt, liquidated or unliquidated.

In light of the strong public policy considerations disfavoring self-help through force or violence, including the forcible recapture of property, we granted review in this case to consider whether claim of right should continue to be recognized as a defense to robbery in California. Since *Butler* was decided over 30 years ago, courts around the nation have severely restricted, and in some cases eliminated altogether, the availability of the defense in prosecutions for robbery. As will be explained, however, the "felonious taking" required for robbery under section 211, as well as that for theft under section 484, is a taking accomplished with felonious intent, that is, the intent to steal, a state of mind that California courts for over 150 years have recognized as inconsistent with a good faith belief that the specific property taken is one's own. When our Legislature incorporated this mental state element into the definition of robbery upon codifying the offense in 1872, it effectively recognized claim of right as a defense to that crime. This court is therefore not free to expand the statutorily defined mens rea of robbery by eliminating claim of right as a defense altogether on policy grounds.

Since the Legislature incorporated the claim-of-right doctrine into the statutory definition of robbery over a century ago, the question whether it continues to reflect sound public policy as we enter the 21st century must be addressed to that body and not to this court. Nonetheless, as will further be explained, we find nothing in the language of section 211 to suggest the Legislature intended to incorporate into the robbery statute *Butler*'s broad extension of the claim-of-right defense to forcible takings perpetrated to satisfy, settle or otherwise collect on a debt, liquidated or unliquidated. To the extent *Butler*'s expansion of the claim-of-right defense in that regard is unsupported by the language of the robbery statute and contrary to sound public policy, it is overruled.

[The defendant was charged, *inter alia*, with robbery (P.C. § 211) as a result of an incident at the home of Shelly Tufunga (Shelly), his former wife. The facts of the incident were in dispute. According to the prosecution witnesses, the defendant, who arrived with another former wife and his daughter from that marriage, pushed his way into the house and attacked Shelly, stabbing at her with a scissors. Shelly's mother arrived at the house, and gave Shelly $200 to purchase vitamins and medicine for her. When the mother realized that Shelly had been beaten, she attempted to call the police, at which point the defendant assaulted both the women and took the money and fled. According to the defendant and his witnesses, the defendant stayed from time to time at Shelly's. On the day in question, the defendant was paid $200 by his employer and brought the money to give to Shelly to help with a bill she had. They argued, and Shelly put the money in her bra. When Shelly's mother arrived and threatened to call the police on the defendant because he had an outstanding warrant, he became convinced that Shelly was going to give the money to her mother rather than use it to pay the bill, so he forcibly wrestled the money away from Shelly and left.]

II. DISCUSSION

At trial, the defense requested instruction on a claim-of-right defense to the charge of robbery. The trial court concluded the facts would not support the defense and refused to instruct on it. On appeal, defendant urged that even if he had used force to take back his $200, that fact is immaterial to the existence of his bona fide belief in his right to take back the money he conditionally gave to Shelly, once he concluded in good faith that she was not going to use it to pay bills and would instead turn it over to her mother. The People responded that defendant furnished no substantial evidence of a bona fide belief in his right to reclaim the money. Although the source of the money present in the apartment during the incident was therefore disputed at trial—Shelly claiming her mother brought over the money, which defendant then stole from them; defendant claiming he had brought over the $200 to give to Shelly to pay bills, then took it back upon concluding she would not use it for the purpose for which it was offered—it was not disputed that the same $200 in currency was at the heart of the controversy. In other words, if defendant's version of the incident was believed, there was no further evidence or claim by the People that Shelly had commingled the specific currency he gave her with her own funds before he grabbed it back and fled from the apartment.

We recently summarized the nature and scope of a claim-of-right defense to robbery after this court's decision in *Butler*, as follows: "In [*Butler*], the defendant was accused of felony murder based on the underlying crime of robbery. At trial, the defendant testified he had been employed by the victim, who had not paid him for some work. The defendant, armed with a gun, went to the victim's home one evening to collect payment. Although the victim had at one point agreed to pay the defendant, he subsequently changed his mind and approached the defendant with a pistol. During the ensuing scuffle, the defendant shot and killed the victim, and also shot another person present in the victim's home. After quickly searching the home for money and finding none, the defendant grabbed a wallet and ran from the house. In recounting the events, the defendant claimed he did not intend to commit robbery when he went to the house, but intended only to recover the money he was owed. Over the defendant's objection, the prosecutor was permitted to argue to the jury that a robbery had been committed even if the defendant honestly believed the victim owed him money. The jury convicted the defendant of first degree felony murder and fixed the penalty at death.

"A majority of this court reversed, concluding: 'Although an intent to steal may ordinarily be inferred when one person takes the property of another, particularly if he takes it by force, proof of the existence of a state of mind incompatible with an intent to steal precludes a finding of either theft or robbery. It has long been the rule in this state and generally throughout the country that a bona fide belief, even though mistakenly held, that one has a right or claim to the property negates felonious intent. A belief that the property taken belongs to the taker, or that he had a right to retake goods sold is sufficient to preclude felonious intent. Felonious intent exists only if the actor intends to take the property of another without believing in good faith that he has a right or claim to it.'" (*People v. Barnett* (1998) 17 Cal.4th 1044.)

a. ***Sufficient evidence supported the giving of a claim-of-right instruction***

[Although "[a] party is not entitled to an instruction on a theory for which there is no supporting evidence" (*People v. Memro* (1995) 11 Cal.4th 786), in the present case, there was sufficient evidence to support an inference that the defendant believed he had a lawful claim to the $200.]

In *Butler* we observed that a forcible taking of property from another "ordinarily" allows an inference of an intent to steal, as opposed to a claim of right. Here, however, if defendant's version of the events was believed, even his self-admitted use of force did not preclude his raising a claim-of-right defense to the robbery charge, given his further testimony that he brought $200 into the victim's home and took back the same currency upon fleeing. Although defendant's and the victim's respective versions of the events differed considerably, defendant's testimony, together with that of the other defense witnesses, constituted sufficient evidence to warrant the giving of a claim-of-right instruction.

b. ***A good faith claim of right to title or ownership of specific property taken from another can negate the element of felonious taking (a taking accomplished with intent to steal) necessary to establish theft (§ 484) or robbery (§ 211)***

At common law, claim of right was recognized as a defense to the crime of larceny because it was deemed to negate the *animus furandi*—or felonious intent to steal—of that offense. Because robbery was viewed as simply an aggravated form of larceny, it was likewise subject to the same claim-of-right defense.

When the Legislature created the first statutory scheme codifying this state's criminal law in 1850, it incorporated portions of the then-existing common law into the new statutes. Thus, the 1850 robbery statute closely tracked the definition of robbery set out in Blackstone's Commentaries. From this historical perspective alone, it can be inferred that the Legislature intended to incorporate the common law recognition of the defense of claim of right as negating the felonious taking or *animus furandi* element common to theft and robbery when it first codified those offenses in the 1850 statutes.

Moreover, the fact that the Legislature used the same terminology, i.e., "felonious taking," in both the larceny and robbery statutes of 1850 most reasonably indicates an intent to ascribe the same meaning to that element which is common to both offenses, that is, recognition of the common law claim-of-right defense as applying to both theft and robbery. Put differently, by adopting the identical phrase "felonious taking" as used in the common law with regard to both offenses, the Legislature in all likelihood intended to incorporate the same meanings attached to those phrases at common law.

Thirteen years later, in *People v. Vice* (1863) 21 Cal. 344, this court held that property feloniously taken must belong to someone other than the defendant in order to constitute robbery: "The owner of property is not guilty of robbery in taking it from the person of the possessor, though he may be guilty of another public offense." *Vice* held that an indictment charging robbery was deficient for failing to affirmatively allege that the property did not belong to the defendant. In so holding, the *Vice* court looked to the actual title or ownership of the property taken and essentially read into the 1850 robbery statute an affirmative requirement, derived from the common law rule of larceny, that the thief (or robber) must take property belonging to someone other than himself ("another") in order to be guilty of robbery. Similarly, this court found the same common law rule applicable to the 1850 theft statutes (see *People v. Stone* (1860) 16 Cal. 369 ["It is not every trespass that is a larceny. The felony is in the intent to appropriate another's property, *the taker knowing that he had no right or claim to it.*" (Italics added.)].)

In 1872, nine years after *Vice* was decided, the Legislature enacted the first comprehensive Penal Code establishing a finite list of crimes punishable under California law. As part of this complete codification, the Legislature enacted section 211, the current robbery provision which has remained unchanged since first enacted 127 years ago. Section 211 provides: "Robbery is the *felonious taking* of personal property in the possession of another, from his person or immediate presence, and against his will, accomplished by means of force or fear." (Italics added.) As with the 1850 robbery statute, the most logical inference is that by use of the identical term "felonious taking" in section 211, the Legislature was yet again incorporating into the 1872 robbery statute the affirmative requirement, derived from the common law rule applicable to larceny and robbery, that the thief or robber has to intend to take property belonging to someone other than himself in order to be guilty of theft or robbery, that is to say, the common law recognition of the defense of claim of right.

Decisions, including those of this court, postdating the 1872 codification of the crime of robbery in section 211, continued to follow the 1863 holding in *Vice*, to wit, that the earlier robbery statute had incorporated the common law rule that a felonious taking does not occur when the defendant has a good faith claim of right to the specific property taken.

Also significant is a note accompanying section 211 in the first annotated edition of the 1872 Penal Code that plainly reflects the Legislature's intent to incorporate the common law claim-of-right defense as part and parcel of the *animus furandi* element found in the current robbery statute. The note cites this court's decision in *Vice*, for the proposition that "the owner of property is not guilty of robbery in taking it from the possession of the possessor."

As recently as last year, in *People v. Davis* (1998) 19 Cal.4th 301, in the course of discussing the elements of larceny, we cited Perkins and Boyce, Criminal Law (3d ed. 1982), for the well-settled principle that "The intent to steal or *animus furandi* is the intent, *without a good faith claim of right*, to permanently deprive the owner of possession." (Second italics added.)

Lastly, it has long been recognized that "[t]heft is a lesser included offense of robbery, which includes the additional element of force or fear," (*People v. Ortega* (1998) 19 Cal.4th 686) and that robbery "is a species of aggravated larceny." (*Ibid.*) A conclusion here that a claim of right, for policy reasons, should no longer be recognized as a defense to robbery—even where the defendant can establish that he is taking back specific property to which he has lawful title or a bona fide claim of ownership—would mean such a defendant could be convicted of robbery *based on theft of his own property*, a proposition that would stand in patent conflict with both the commonsense notion that someone cannot steal his own property, and the corollary rule that "theft," the taking of "the personal property of *another*," is a lesser included offense at the core of every robbery. Wholesale elimination of the claim-of-right defense in such cases would stand in sharp conflict with these basic legal principles, principles that have their roots in the early common law, have recently been affirmed by this court, and have never seriously been questioned as a matter of California law.

[Recognition of a claim-of-right defense is unlikely to affect any large number of cases, and, even in cases where the defendant can make out a successful claim-of-right defense, in all likelihood the defendant will be found guilty of other charges, e.g., assault.].

In sum, we find that the Legislature over 100 years ago codified in the current robbery statute the common law recognition that a claim-of-right defense can negate the *animus furandi* element of robbery where the defendant is seeking to regain specific property in which he in good faith believes he has a bona fide claim of ownership or title. Whatever be our views on the wisdom of the Legislature's chosen delineation of the mental state necessary for robbery, the separation of powers clause prohibits this court from abolishing the claim-of-right defense altogether on policy grounds, as such would effectively alter a statutorily defined element of that offense by judicial fiat. The Legislature of course remains free to amend section 211 to preclude a claim-of-right defense in robbery prosecutions. The question whether such amendment would better reflect sound public policy is one properly addressed to that body rather than to this court.

c. *Expansion of the claim-of-right defense to robberies perpetrated to satisfy, settle or collect on a debt*

As noted above, *Butler* broadly held that "a bona fide belief, even though mistakenly held, that one has a right or claim to the property [taken in a robbery] negates felonious intent." ...

In *Barnett*, we confronted claims of instructional error, ineffective assistance of counsel and prosecutorial misconduct stemming from the trial court's failure to instruct on a claim-of-right defense as to one of two robbery victims in a capital case in which a robbery-murder special circumstance was alleged. After reviewing the rationale and holding of *Butler*, we made the following observations regarding the policy implications of permitting a claim-of-right defense to robbery:

"In his dissent in *Butler*, Justice Mosk took a dim view of the majority's apparent authorization of armed robbery as a self-help measure. Pointing out that the statutory provision defining robbery (§ 211) raised no issue of ownership of property forcibly taken, but only its possession, Justice Mosk saw no statutory basis for the defense. Moreover, noting that the leading cases permitting forcible recapture of property were all decided before the turn of the century, Justice Mosk concluded that a six-shooter was no longer 'an acceptable device for do-it-yourself debt collection' and that the 'might-makes-right' doctrine of the previous century was of 'dubious adaptability' to modern times. [¶] Since *Butler* was decided, a number of other jurisdictions have rejected the claim-of-right defense for public policy reasons in cases where force, violence, or weapons are used for self-help debt collection. As several courts have observed, the proposition that a claim of right negates the felonious intent in robbery 'not only is lacking in sound reason and logic, but it is utterly incompatible with and has no place in an ordered and orderly society such as ours, which eschews self-help through violence. Adoption of the proposition would be but one step short of accepting lawless reprisal as an appropriate means of redressing grievances, real or fancied.'"

In *Barnett* we were not asked by the People "to revisit *Butler*'s increasingly anachronistic authorization of the claim-of-right defense in the context of armed robbery." However, noting "the obvious public policy reasons for strictly circumscribing the circumstances under which persons should be permitted *to enforce their debt demands* at gunpoint], we conclude[d] the defense is not available *where the claimed debt* is uncertain and subject to dispute."

The People in this case urge that "[t]he rationale for declining to permit a defendant to assert a claim of right defense in a robbery case is quite simple: An ordered society founded on the rule of law does not countenance self-help when it is accomplished by the use of fear, intimidation, or violence."

...

The legitimacy of the need for our laws to discourage forcible or violent self-help as a remedy seems beyond question. Defendant himself acknowledges the strong public policy considerations militating against retention of the claim-of-right defense for robbery.... [H]owever, we have concluded that California's Legislature incorporated the common law claim-of-right doctrine into the statutorily defined mens rea element of robbery when it codified that offense over 100 years ago, and that consequently, we are not free to judicially abolish it and thereby effectively expand the statutory definition of the crime.[4]

We nonetheless conclude that *Butler* went well beyond the basic underlying notion that a thief or robber must intend to steal *another*'s property when, on the facts before it, the court extended the availability of a claim-of-right defense to perpetrators who rob their victims assertedly to settle, satisfy, or otherwise collect on a debt. Specifically, we find nothing in the language of section 211 to suggest the Legislature intended to incorporate such a broad and expansive extension of the claim-of-right doctrine into the robbery statute.

Many of the out-of-state decisions that have rejected *Butler*'s expansive extension of the claim-of-right defense to so-called "debt collection" robbery cases have retained it as a viable defense where the defendant takes *specific property* in which he has a bona fide claim of ownership or title.

---

4. It should be noted that many of the out-of-state decisions rejecting claim of right as a defense to robbery in its entirety were interpreting statutory provisions and legislative history very different from that which we face in this case.

We note further that both this court and the intermediate appellate courts of this state have already placed significant policy limitations on the claim-of-right defense to robbery. The courts have indicated that the defense may not be raised when the defendant is attempting to collect on an *unliquidated* debt or damages claim. This court has also held that the defense is not available where the claim of right to the property is founded in a "notoriously illegal" transaction. [*e.g.*, fee collection for prostitution services, distribution of proceeds from forgery ring, payment for a drug deal]. The rationale and holdings of these decisions do not contravene our conclusion in this case that the availability of the claim-of-right defense to robbery was envisioned by the Legislature and incorporated into the statutory definition of that offense, for robberies in which the defendant sought to recover specific property for which he believed in good faith he had a bona fide claim of ownership or title, that is, a recognition that one cannot feloniously intend to steal one's own property.

The Wisconsin Supreme Court in *Edwards v. State* (Wis. 1970) 181 N.W.2d 383, cogently set forth the rationale for rejecting a claim-of-right defense to robberies involving forcible debt collection: "The distinction between specific personal property and money in general is important. A debtor can owe another $150 but the $150 in the debtor's pocket is not the specific property of the creditor. One has the intention to steal when he takes money from another's possession against the possessor's consent even though he also intends to apply the stolen money to a debt. The efficacy of self-help by force to enforce a bona fide claim for money does not negate the intent to commit robbery. Can one break into a bank and take money so long as he does not take more than the balance in his savings or checking account? Under the majority rule [as it then existed, allowing a claim of right defense to any robbery] the accused must make change to be sure he collects no more than the amount he believes is due him on the debt. A debt is a relationship and in respect to money seldom finds itself embedded in specific coins and currency of the realm. Consequently, taking money from a debtor by force to pay a debt is robbery. The creditor has no such right of appropriation and allocation."

We agree with the rationale of *Edwards v. State, supra*, and similar decisions drawing a distinction for debt collection cases....

...

We therefore hold that to the extent *Butler*, extended the claim-of-right defense to robberies perpetrated to satisfy, settle or otherwise collect on a debt, liquidated or unliquidated—as opposed to forcible takings intended to recover specific personal property in which the defendant in good faith believes he has a bona fide claim of ownership or title—it is unsupported by the statutory language, further contrary to sound public policy, and in that regard is overruled.

...

Problems

Problem 53.

Defendant tried to pay for a purchase at Store by using a forged check. Clerk became suspicious and took the check to the office to talk with Supervisor. After a few minutes, Defendant entered the office, seized the check from Clerk and left. Defendant is now charged, *inter alia*, with grand theft from the person (P.C. §§ 484, 487) for taking the check back. What are the arguments as to whether Defendant is guilty of the charge or any lesser included offense?

Problem 54.

Owner, the owner of a jewelry store, agreed with Defendants on a plan whereby they would break into the store, hold up the employees and loot the store and Owner would then file an insurance claim for the "losses." With Owner's connivance, Defendants, on a Sunday night, drilled into the store from a vacant store next to the jewelry store safe room and hid in the safe room. When the store's three employees arrived the next morning, Defendants were waiting with guns drawn. They forced the employees to open the safes, then bound the employees with handcuffs and duct tape, took jewels worth approximately $4.5 million dollars and fled out the hole in the wall. Defendants are now charged with robbery (P.C. § 211). What are the arguments as to their guilt?

Problem 55.

Defendant, who was engaged in various criminal activities, received information that his recently estranged wife, Victim, had informed the police of his activities. He also learned that she was seeing another man. Defendant conceived of a plan to punish Victim. He convinced her to come for a drive with him, then drove her to a secluded location and ordered her out of the car. She complied, leaving her purse in the car. Outside the car, Defendant pointed a gun at Victim and told her to take off her clothes, which he then placed in the car. Defendant had sexual intercourse with Victim and then killed her. He removed her wedding ring and shot the body multiple times to make it unidentifiable. When he arrived home, he buried the clothes, purse and ring in his backyard. Defendant is now charged, *inter alia*, with robbery (P.C. § 211) and robbery felony-murder (P.C. §§ 187–189). What arguments should be made regarding whether Defendant is guilty of robbery?

People v. Anderson

51 Cal.4th 989, 252 P.3d 968 (2011)

WERDEGAR, J.

We hold here that the intent element of robbery does not include an intent to apply force against the victim or to cause the victim to feel fear. It is robbery if the defendant committed a forcible act against the victim motivated by the intent to steal, even if the defendant did not also intend for the victim to experience force or fear. We also hold a trial court has no obligation to provide a sua sponte instruction on accident where, as here, the defendant's theory of accident is an attempt to negate the intent element of the charged crime.

BACKGROUND

Defendant Paul D. Anderson is a longtime methamphetamine addict. As of the time of the crimes at issue here, he had been out of work for a year, was separated from his wife, had neither a job nor a car, and was living on the streets or spending nights in the homes of other methamphetamine users. He obtained money by breaking into cars, sometimes by means of a shaved key, and stealing things. He used stolen credit cards and sometimes tried to pass forged checks. He had once stolen a car. Defendant's criminal history does not appear to have involved any act of force or violence directed against his victims. Defendant spent the morning and afternoon of November 7, 2003, at the home of Ginger Lyle, a drug dealer, where he smoked methamphetamine and socialized with Lyle and several other users. After leaving Lyle's home, he went to an apartment complex a few blocks away, later stating he went with the intention of finding a car to steal so he could visit his wife and children.

On November 7, 19-year-old Pamela Thompson came home from work around 9:00 p.m. She parked her car in the apartment complex's carport and went to her apartment to change her clothing before going out, leaving her purse in the car. In the meantime, defendant entered the complex looking for a car he could enter with his key. After failing to break into several cars, defendant successfully opened the door to Pamela's car, started it, and attempted to drive out of the complex. After discovering the gate to the complex did not open automatically, defendant backed the car into a parking space to wait for someone else to open the gate. By this time, Pamela had discovered her car was gone. She telephoned her stepfather, Joe Deitz, asking if he had taken it. When he said he had not, she told him the car had been stolen. Pamela also called her mother, Barbara Thompson, telling her the car had been stolen and she was looking for it. After they spoke for a few minutes, Barbara heard Pamela say, loudly, "Oh, my God. Here comes my car real fast." The phone went silent....

Defendant had run over Pamela. He did not deny hitting her, but claimed it was an accident. He stated he saw the gate to the complex open to admit a car. After the car passed, he drove toward the gate, which began to close. He drove quickly around the gate, estimating his speed at 25–30 miles per hour. He claimed he had not heard anyone shout, explaining the car's windows were closed. He stated he had kept his head down as he was driving, theorizing that for that reason, and because it was night and the gate obscured his vision, he had not seen anything until he looked up and saw Pamela standing just outside the gate, approximately 10–12 feet from him, with her hand up. He swerved, explaining he did not think he could stop in time. Defendant admitted feeling an impact, stating he thought he might have struck the girl, but he also thought it was possible she had hit the side of the car or he had gone up over the curb. He was frightened, did not stop to see if he had injured anyone, and drove away without looking back. Defendant maintained he had not intended to run over, injure, or frighten anyone. He had been thinking about getting away and had not contemplated the possibility that someone might be on the other side of the gate.

...

Defendant was convicted, following a jury trial, of first degree felony murder with the special circumstance of killing during the course of a robbery, robbery, and receipt of stolen property. He appealed, arguing that the trial court erred by failing to provide a sua sponte instruction on accident as a defense to the crime of robbery, thus requiring reversal not only of his robbery conviction, but also of his conviction of first degree felony murder and the special circumstance.[1] The Court of Appeal agreed. We reverse the judgment of the Court of Appeal.

---

1. The only intent required for felony murder is the specific intent to commit the underlying felony. Thus, for purposes of first degree felony murder, it is irrelevant that Pamela's death might have been the accidental result of a robbery, if the robbery was intentional.

DISCUSSION

I. Robbery

Robbery is defined as "the felonious taking of personal property in the possession of another, from his person or immediate presence, and against his will, accomplished by means of force or fear." (Pen.Code, § 211.) Robbery is larceny with the aggravating circumstances that "the property is taken from the person or presence of another" and "is accomplished by the use of force or by putting the victim in fear of injury." (*People v. Gomez* (2008) 43 Cal.4th 249.) In California, "[t]he crime of robbery is a continuing offense that begins from the time of the original taking until the robber reaches a place of relative safety." (*People v. Estes* (1983) 147 Cal.App.3d 23.) It thus is robbery when the property was peacefully acquired, but force or fear was used to carry it away. (*Gomez, supra.*) … The intent required for robbery has been described as the specific intent to deprive the victim of the property permanently. (*People v. Huggins* (2006) 38 Cal.4th 175.) Thus, "the act of force or intimidation by which the taking is accomplished in robbery must be motivated by the intent to steal…." (*People v. Green* (1980) 27 Cal.3d 1.)

Defendant concedes he committed a forcible act against Pamela, killing her, and that the act was motivated by his intent to steal Pamela's property. But he argues the forcible taking was not robbery unless he applied the force with the intent to strike or frighten Pamela. He cites *People v. Bolden* (2002) 29 Cal.4th 515, where we recognized that the standard jury instructions adequately explain that "for the crime of robbery the defendant must form the intent to steal before or during rather than after the application of force to the victim, and *that the defendant must apply the force for the purpose of accomplishing the taking.*" (Italics added.) But we were not there concerned with whether the defendant intended to harm the victim, and our explanation that it is not robbery if the intent to steal is formed only after the forcible act was committed cannot reasonably be read to hold that the act by which the taking is accomplished must be motivated by the intent to apply force against the victim or cause the victim to feel fear.

Other cases cited by defendant also are not on point, explaining instead that the requisite forcible act may be an act committed after the initial taking if it is motivated by the intent to retain the property….

In sum, no authority cited to us provides positive support for defendant's argument. Nor do we find anything in the law, or the facts of this case, to convince us robbery contains a heretofore unidentified element of intent to cause the victim to experience force or fear. The law does require that the perpetrator exert some quantum of force in excess of that "necessary to accomplish the mere seizing of the property." (*People v. Morales* (1975) 49 Cal.App.3d 134.) But even under his version of the facts, defendant drove Pamela's car with more force than necessary to move it to a place of safety. And his motive for exerting the additional force was to retain the property and facilitate his escape. In short, he committed the requisite forcible act with the requisite intent.

It was robbery even if, as he claims, he did not intend to strike Pamela, but did so accidentally.[2]

...

[Justice KENNARD concurred on the ground that the trial court was not required to instruct the jury on "accident" as a defense absent a request by the defendant. She would not have reached the question whether, as the Court of Appeal held, robbery requires proof of a general intent to use force or fear against the victim because "ascertaining the 1872 Legislature's intent could well have been daunting."]

Note

Intended Object of Taking. Theft has traditionally involved tangible property. There are, of course, many ways to inflict financial loss on another without taking his or her tangible property. One can obtain the services of another by false promises that the person will be paid. One can use materials in violation of copyright laws. One can appropriate technical information which is obtained in confidence in an employment situation and later use it to unfairly compete with one's former employer. Because it is not clear that the traditional theft statutes cover these situations, they are often dealt with in special statutes. See, *e.g.*, Penal Code Section 499c covering theft of trade secrets. But see *People v. Kwok, infra.*

People v. Ashley

42 Cal. 2d 246, 267 P.2d 271 (1954)

TRAYNOR, J.

Defendant was convicted of four counts of grand theft under section 484 of the Penal Code. He "appeals from the verdicts and judgments as to each count," and from the order denying his motion for a new trial.

The first two counts charged that defendant feloniously took $13,590 from Mrs. Maude Neal on June 19, 1948, and $4,470 from her on August 3, 1948. The remaining two counts charged that he feloniously took $3,000 from Mrs. Mattie Russ on November 19, 1948, and $4,200 from her on December 4, 1948.

[Defendant was the business manager of a corporation chartered for the purpose of "introducing people." The evidence revealed that defendant obtained a loan of

---

2. In a supplemental brief, defendant argues that because robbery is sometimes described as an assaultive crime, it must be concluded it not only requires an intent to steal, but also has an intent element comparable to the intent required for assault.... That an offense has assaultive aspects does not mean it *is* an assault. In any event, even under defendant's version of the facts, the evidence defendant drove blindly through the gates of the apartment complex at a speed of 25–30 miles per hour and made no effort to brake when he saw Pamela established the requisite willful commission of an act that by its nature was likely to result in injury to another. (See *People v. Williams* (2001) 26 Cal.4th 779.)

$7,200 from a Mrs. Russ, a woman of 70 years of age, by promising that the loan would be secured by a first mortgage on certain improved property of the corporation and that the money would be used to build a theater on other property owned by the corporation. In fact the corporation leased but did not own the improved property and no theater was ever built, the money having been used to meet the corporation's operating expenses. After defendant received the money, Mrs. Russ frequently quarreled with him over his failure to deliver the promised first mortgage. She finally received a note of the corporation secured by a second trust deed on some unimproved property owned by the corporation. She testified that she accepted this security because defendant told her to "take that or nothing." She subsequently received four post-dated checks in payment of the loan. After it became apparent that these checks would not be paid, defendant requested an extension. Mrs. Russ granted the extension after defendant had threatened to destroy himself if she refused so that she might be paid from the proceeds of his life insurance policies.

Defendant obtained $13,590 from a Mrs. Neal representing that the corporation intended to use the money to buy the El Patio Theater. She was initially told that the loan would be secured by a trust deed on the theater building and that she would have good security for her loan because the corporation was worth a half million dollars. However, after obtaining the money, defendant issued Mrs. Neal a note of the corporation for $13,500. Subsequently, she loaned the corporation an additional $4,470 receiving a note for $17,500 in exchange for the previous note. Mrs. Neal testified that when she hesitated in making the loan, defendant placed a gun on his desk and said: "Now look here, Mrs. Neal, I don't want no monkey business out of you. Do you understand that?" The corporation did not buy the theater; Mrs. Neal never received the trust deed; and the money was deposited to the corporation's account.

Evidence was introduced indicating that the corporation was in a strained financial condition and was worth nothing like a half million dollars. There was also evidence that the defendant received no salary from the corporation, but that he drove an expensive automobile paid for by the corporation and that he had drawn numerous checks on corporation funds for the payment of expenses.]

Although the crimes of larceny by trick and device and obtaining property by false pretenses are much alike, they are aimed at different criminal acquisitive techniques. Larceny by trick and device is the appropriation of property, the possession of which was fraudulently acquired; obtaining property by false pretenses is the fraudulent or deceitful acquisition of both title and possession.

In this state, these two offenses, with other larcenous crimes, have been consolidated into the single crime of theft (Pen. Code, § 484), but their elements have not been changed thereby.

The purpose of the consolidation was to remove the technicalities that existed in the pleading and proof of these crimes at common law. Indictments and informations charging the crime of "theft" can now simply allege an "unlawful taking." Juries need no longer be concerned with the technical differences between the several types of theft, and can return a general verdict of guilty if they find that an "unlawful taking" has been proved.

The elements of the several types of theft included within section 484 have not been changed, however, and a judgment of conviction of theft, based on a general verdict of guilty, can be sustained only if the evidence discloses the elements of one of the consolidated offenses.

In the present case, it is clear from the record that each of the prosecuting witnesses intended to pass both title and possession, and that the type of theft, if any, in each case, was that of obtaining property by false pretenses.

Defendant was not prejudiced by the instruction to the jury relating to larceny by trick and device. Indeed, he requested instructions relating to both larceny by trick and device and obtaining property by false pretenses. Moreover, his defense was not based on distinctions between title and possession, but rather he contends that there was no unlawful taking of any sort.

To support a conviction of theft for obtaining property by false pretenses, it must be shown that the defendant made a false pretense or representation with intent to defraud the owner of his property, and that the owner was in fact defrauded. It is unnecessary to prove that the defendant benefitted personally from the fraudulent acquisition. The false pretense or representation must have materially influenced the owner to part with his property, but the false pretense need not be the sole inducing cause....

[The court reviewed the history of the crime of obtaining property by false pretenses, which was not a crime at common law, but was made a crime under an Eighteenth Century English statute. According to the court, that statute was misinterpreted in cases both in England and the United States, leading Wharton to state the general American rule as follows: "... the false pretense to be within the statute, must relate to a state of things averred to be at the time existing, and not to a state of things thereafter to exist." (Wharton, American Criminal Law 542 [1st ed., 1846].)

...

The Court of Appeals for the District of Columbia has ... advanced the following reasons in defense of the majority rule: "It is of course true that then [at the time of the early English cases cited by Wharton, *supra*] as now, the intention to commit certain crimes was ascertained by looking backward from the act and finding that the accused intended to do what he did do. However, where, as here, the act complained of—namely, failure to repay money or use it as specified at the time of borrowing it—is as consonant with ordinary commercial default as with criminal conduct, the danger of applying the technique to prove the crime is quite apparent. Business affairs would be materially incumbered by the ever present threat that a debtor might be subjected to criminal penalties if the prosecutor and jury were of the view that at the time of borrowing he was mentally a cheat. The risk of prosecuting one who is guilty of nothing more than a failure or inability to pay his debts is a very real consideration....

"If we were to accept the government's position the way would be open for every victim of a bad bargain to resort to criminal proceedings to even the score with a judgment proof adversary. No doubt in the development of our criminal law the zeal with which the innocent are protected has provided a measure of shelter for the guilty. However, we do not think it wise to increase the possibility of conviction by broadening the accepted theory of the weight to be attached to the mental attitude of the accused." We do not find this reasoning persuasive.

In this state, and in the majority of American states as well as in England, false promises can provide the foundation of a civil action for deceit. In such actions something more than nonperformance is required to prove the defendant's intent not to perform his promise.

Nor is proof of nonperformance alone sufficient in criminal prosecutions based on false promises.

In such prosecutions the People must, as in all criminal prosecutions, prove their case beyond a reasonable doubt. Any danger, through the instigation of criminal proceedings by disgruntled creditors, to those who have blamelessly encountered "commercial defaults" must, therefore, be predicated upon the idea that trial juries are incapable of weighing the evidence and understanding the instruction that they must be convinced of the defendant's fraudulent intent beyond a reasonable doubt, or that appellate courts will be derelict in discharging their duty to ascertain that there is sufficient evidence to support a conviction.

The problem of proving intent when the false pretense is a false promise is no more difficult than when the false pretense is a misrepresentation of existing fact, and the intent not to perform a promise is regularly proved in civil actions for deceit. Specific intent is also an essential element of many crimes.[4]

Moreover, in cases of obtaining property by false pretenses, it must be proved that any misrepresentations of fact alleged by the People were made knowingly and with intent to deceive. If such misrepresentations are made innocently or inadvertently, they can no more form the basis for a prosecution for obtaining property by false pretenses than can an innocent breach of contract.

Whether the pretense is a false promise or a misrepresentation of fact, the defendant's intent must be proved in both instances by something more than mere proof of nonperformance or actual falsity, and the defendant is entitled to have the jury instructed to that effect. "[The] accepted theory of the weight to be attached to the mental attitude of the accused" is, therefore, not "broadened," but remains substantially the same.

...

If false promises were not false pretenses, the legally sophisticated, without fear of punishment, could perpetrate on the unwary fraudulent schemes like that divulged

4. For example, arson, burglary, larceny, malicious mischief, and robbery. In prosecutions for attempted crimes, or for assault with intent to commit murder, robbery, rape, etc., the specific intent must also be proved.

by the record in this case. To hold that false promises are not false pretenses would sanction such schemes without any corresponding benefit to the public order. The inclusion of false promises within sections 484 and 532 of the Penal Code will not "materially encumber" business affairs. "Ordinary commercial defaults" will not be the subject of criminal prosecution, for the essence of the offense of obtaining property by false pretenses is (as it has always been) the fraudulent intent of the defendant. This intent must be proved by the prosecution; a showing of nonperformance of a promise or falsity of a representation will not suffice.

. . .

Schauer, J., concurring and dissenting.

I concur in the judgment solely on the ground that the evidence establishes, with ample corroboration, the making by the defendant of false representations as to existing facts. On that evidence the convictions should be sustained pursuant to long accepted theories of law.

It is unnecessary on the record to make of this rather simple case a vehicle for the revolutionary holding, contrary to the weight of authority in this state and elsewhere, that a promise to pay or perform at a future date, if unfulfilled, can become the basis for a criminal prosecution on the theory that it was a promise made without a present intention to perform it and that, therefore, whatever of value was received for the promise was property procured by a false representation. Accordingly, I dissent from all that portion of the opinion which discusses and pronounces upon the theories which in my view are extraneous to the proper disposition of any issue actually before us.

The majority opinion strikes down a rule of law, relating to the character and competence of proof of crime, which has been almost universally respected for 200 years—and the reasoning which has been advanced for the innovation is that creditors, grand jurors, and prosecutors must not be expected to institute any criminal charges against innocent people, and that even if they do the intelligence of trial jurors and the wisdom of appellate judges can be depended upon to right the wrong, hence the time honored rule may be scrapped. The unreality of this reasoning and the wisdom of the old rule become obvious on reflection.

In a prosecution for obtaining property by the making of a false promise, knowingly and with intent to deceive, the matter to be proved, as to its criminality, is purely subjective. It is not, like the specific intent in such a crime as burglary, a mere element of the crime; it is, in any significant sense, all of the crime. The proof will necessarily be of objective acts, entirely legal in themselves, from which inferences as to the ultimate illegal subjective fact will be drawn. But, whereas in burglary the proof of the subjective element is normally as strong and reliable as the proof of any objective element, in this type of activity the proof of such vital element can almost never be reliable; it must inevitably (in the absence of confession or something tantamount thereto) depend on inferences drawn by creditors, prosecutors, jurors, and judges from facts and circumstances which by reason of their nature cannot possibly exclude innocence with any certainty, and which can point to guilt only when construed and interpreted by the creditor, prosecutor or trier of fact adversely to the person charged. Such inferences as proof of the alleged crime have long been recognized as so unreliable that they have been excluded from the category of acceptable proof.

As a basis for overturning the rule that proof of the mere making of a promise to perform in the future and of subsequent failure to perform is not proof of a false pretense, the majority opinion first purportedly adheres to the rule by stating that "proof of nonperformance alone [is not] sufficient in criminal prosecutions based on false promises," then argues that "Any danger, through the instigation of criminal proceedings by disgruntled creditors, to those who have blamelessly encountered 'commercial defaults' must, therefore, be predicated upon the idea that trial juries are incapable of weighing the evidence and understanding the instruction that they must be convinced of the defendant's fraudulent intent beyond a reasonable doubt, or that appellate courts will be derelict in discharging their duty to ascertain that there is sufficient evidence to support a conviction." This doctrine, if universally applied, would eliminate all rules governing the quality and sufficiency of proof. The credence to be placed in the testimony of accomplices, or other complaining witnesses, would be left entirely to the sagacity of jurors and the presumed omniscience of appellate judges. I am unwilling to accept as a premise the scholastic redaction of the majority that rules of proof may be set aside because appellate judges will always know when a jury has been misled and the proof is not sufficient. The most important function which courts have to perform in respect to criminal law is not to make easier the conviction of alleged miscreants; it is the protection of the innocent against false conviction. The highest duty which this court has to perform in the cause of justice is to protect the individual person against the power of the state; the most grievous injury it can do to the people is to assist in building a superstate by countenancing encroachments on the rights of individuals and whittling away at the rules which protect them.

The suggestion in the majority opinion that it is inconceivable "that trial juries are incapable of weighing the evidence [impliedly, with omniscient accuracy however inconclusive it be] and understanding the instruction that they must be convinced of the defendant's fraudulent intent beyond a reasonable doubt, or that appellate courts will be derelict [less than omniscient] in discharging their duty" affords no substantial basis for striking down a rule of proof. The opinion naively continues: "If ... misrepresentations are made innocently or inadvertently, they can no more form the basis for a prosecution for obtaining property by false pretenses than can an innocent breach of contract"!

The tragic part of the above quoted philosophy is that the very declaration of it as a rule of law makes it false in fact. It becomes false in fact because when published as a rule of law it cuts the heart out of a pertinent safeguard which the accumulated wisdom of at least two centuries has found to be necessary to prevent the conviction of the innocent who have met with commercial misfortune.

With the rule that the majority opinion now enunciates, no man, no matter how innocent his intention, can sign a promise to pay in the future, or to perform an act at a future date, without subjecting himself to the risk that at some later date others, in the light of differing perspectives, philosophies and subsequent events, may conclude that, after all, the accused should have known that at the future date he could not perform as he promised and if he—as a "reasonable" man from the point of view of the creditor, district attorney and a grand or trial jury—should have known, then, it may be inferred, he did know. And if it can be inferred that he knew, then this court and other appellate courts will be bound to affirm a conviction.

A trial by jury, under circumstances easily to be foreseen, would offer but hazardous protection in such a case. I have faith—great faith—in our jury system as now constituted. But I have developed that faith through seeing it operate under wise and time-tested regulations and limitations as to the essential characteristics of proof which do not unrealistically assume that any human—whether a district attorney or a grand juror or a trial juror or a judge or justice of a court—is beyond error.

...

Problem

Problem 56.

Defendant and Victim had known each other and had business dealings for about ten years. One day, Defendant called Victim from Reno, Nevada and told Victim that he could obtain certain transmissions for Victim in Reno, if Victim would wire him $300. Victim wired $300 to Defendant the same day. When Victim next encountered Defendant and asked him where the transmissions were, Defendant said his truck had broken down in Nevada and he was returning that weekend to get the transmissions. Defendant never delivered the transmissions. What form of theft has Defendant committed?

People v. Moses

217 Cal. App. 3d 1245, 266 Cal.Rptr. 538 (1990)

DAVIS, J.

Defendant Susan Charlene Moses, appeals from a conviction of one count of receiving stolen property in violation of Penal Code section 496.[1] (Further undesignated statutory citations refer to the Penal Code.) A jury convicted defendant of

1. Section 496 states in part: "Every person who buys or receives any property which has been stolen or which has been obtained in any manner constituting theft or extortion, knowing the property to be so stolen or obtained, or who conceals, sells, withholds or aids in concealing, selling, or withholding any such property from the owner, knowing the property to be so stolen or obtained, [is guilty of a crime]."

receiving or concealing a 14-month-old heifer belonging to Cecilia Murray.[2] On appeal, defendant makes numerous challenges to the proceedings below. We need only address her claim that the record lacks substantial evidence that anyone stole the heifer.

The prosecution charged and tried the case on a theory of a larcenous taking and requested instructions only on theft by larceny. We agree with defendant that the record contains no evidence of theft by larceny. On appeal, the People now argue that the heifer became stolen once defendants misappropriated it under section 485.[3] We hold that defendants cannot be convicted on a theory neither advanced at trial nor factually determined by the jury. Moreover, we conclude that the acts of alleged misappropriation under section 485 formed one uninterrupted course of conduct with the acts alleged as concealment under section 496. As such, as a matter of law, defendants cannot be convicted of concealing or withholding property misappropriated by the same acts. Accordingly, we shall reverse.

Background

[In April 1987, Cecilia Murray sold all of her cattle, with the exception of a 14-month-old heifer, to Jim White, a neighbor who lived about a mile from Murray. On several occasions thereafter, Murray's heifer strayed from its pen. The first time, the heifer returned to Murray's; the second, time other neighbors, the Shields, put the heifer in a pen on their property. Before Murray retrieved the heifer, it again got loose. Murray did not immediately look for the heifer, assuming that it had merely walked from the Shields's property to White's property to rejoin its former herd. Two to two and a half weeks later, White phoned Murray and told her that defendants, who were White's neighbors, possessed a heifer about the same amount of time that Murray's heifer had been missing. Murray and her daughter, Deborah Garman, drove to the defendants' house. Murray saw a heifer which looked like hers and confronted Susan Moses about it, but Moses insisted that the heifer was hers. A short time later, Garman learned that defendants were moving the heifer, and she summoned Deputy Sheriff Hiebert, who stopped defendants with the disputed heifer in their trailer.]

Hiebert arrested both defendants for grand theft. On September 16, 1987, the People filed separate informations against each defendant. Each defendant was charged with one count of grand theft by larceny and one count of receiving stolen property "... knowing that said property had been *stolen*." (Italics added.)

Prior to trial, the court consolidated the two cases. At trial, the defendants presented a misidentification defense. In essence, they claimed that the heifer Murray lost was

---

2. The jury also convicted defendant's husband, Thomas Reed Moses, of the same offense.... For convenience, ... we refer to Thomas and Susan Moses as "defendant" or "defendants" as the context requires.

3. Section 485 states: "One who finds lost property under circumstances which give him knowledge of or means of inquiry as to the true owner, and who appropriates such property to his own use, or to the use of another person not entitled thereto, without first making reasonable and just efforts to find the owner and to restore the property to him, is guilty of *theft*." (Italics added.)

not the heifer they had penned in their yard. The evidence over the heifer's identity conflicted greatly.

Following closing argument, the court instructed the jury on the elements of theft by larceny and receiving stolen property. The court told the jury that the two charges were "made in the alternative" and that it could only convict the defendants, if at all, on one of the two counts. After less than a day of deliberation, the jury acquitted defendants of grand theft but found them guilty of receiving stolen property.

...

Discussion

On appeal, we need only address defendants' claim that the record lacks substantial evidence to support conviction of receipt of stolen property in violation of section 496. In order to establish the commission of the crime of receiving stolen property on a theory of a larcenous taking, it must be established by substantial evidence (1) that the particular property was stolen, (2) that the accused received, concealed or withheld it from the owner thereof, and (3) that the accused knew that the property was stolen.

"In reviewing a judgment of conviction, an appellate court, of course, must view the evidence in the light most favorable to the People and presume in support of that judgment the existence of every fact the trier could reasonably deduce from the evidence...." *People v. Vann*, 12 Cal.3d 220 (1974) "[T]he relevant question is whether, after viewing the evidence in the light most favorable to the prosecution, *any* rational trier of fact could have found the essential elements of the crime beyond a reasonable doubt." (*People v. Johnson* (1980) 26 Cal.3d 557, italics in original.) "The test on appeal is whether substantial evidence supports the conclusion of the trier of fact, not whether the evidence proves guilt beyond a reasonable doubt." (*Ibid.*) Substantial evidence must be "reasonable in nature, credible, and of solid value...." (*Estate of Teed* (1952) 112 Cal.App.2d 638.)

As noted above, in this case the prosecution attempted to establish the heifer's "stolen" character by arguing and instructing only on theft by larceny. In many cases involving receipt or concealment of stolen property, the theft itself is uncontroverted. Such cases turn frequently on the defendant's knowledge of the theft. Since direct evidence of defendant's knowledge rarely exists, circumstantial evidence often comes from "possession of stolen property accompanied by no explanation or unsatisfactory explanation, or by suspicious circumstances...." *People v. Myles* (1975) 50 Cal.App.3d 423.

The usual case, however, involves inanimate property. Since jewelry, televisions, and automobiles rarely disappear on their own volition, the circumstances can usually suggest that someone took them without permission. The People need not prove who stole the property; they only need show that someone stole it.

Here, however, the missing property had a mind of its own. The heifer had wandered off twice from Murray's pen in the week before her disappearance from the Shields's pen. No evidence of any type suggests that anyone stole the heifer from the

Shields's pen prior to this last disappearance. No one saw anyone enter the Shields's premises and leave with the heifer. No one reported strange noises, footprints, tire marks, clipped fence wires, or jimmied locks on the Shields's property. No suspicious circumstances of any kind suggest any human involvement in the heifer's departure from the Shields's pen. Indeed, Murray herself suspected no wrongdoing initially. In sum, absolutely nothing suggests that anyone stole the heifer out of her pen. (See fn. 7.) On this record, we can only infer that the heifer strayed again before ending up on defendants' property.[7]

Thus, under the theory of theft expressly charged in the information, and the only theory of theft presented to the jury, no evidence supports a finding that anyone, much less the defendants before us, stole the heifer by larceny. Accordingly, absent such evidence, defendants could only be found to have concealed or withheld a stray heifer.

On appeal, the People now argue that the property became "stolen" by the defendants' misappropriation of the heifer. The People argue that, under section 485, "[m]isappropriation of the heifer, even if initially an 'estray,' did constitute the offense of receiving stolen property." The prosecution, however, cannot now change its theory on appeal and argue that the heifer had not been stolen but instead had been obtained by misappropriation under section 485. "It is elementary that a new theory cannot be raised on appeal where, as here, the theory contemplates factual situations the consequences of which are open to controversy and were not put in issue in the lower court" (*People v. Smith* (1977) 67 Cal. App.3d 638). Section 485 requires that the lost property be found under circumstances which give the finder "knowledge of or the means of inquiry as to the true owner." That factual question was not litigated and was subject to controversy. Consequently, that theory cannot be used to save the conviction. And since the only theory buttressing the conviction lacks evidentiary support, the judgment must be reversed for lack of evidence.

Moreover, the People's argument ignores the well established rules governing the interaction of the laws of theft and receipt of stolen property. In particular, it fails

7. In his closing argument below, the prosecutor admitted that "it hasn't been proven that [the defendants] actually went over to ... the victim's house and took the cow and put it in their pen. It could have strayed over there or it could have strayed somewhere else and they physically took control over it. But in any event, they took the calf and put it in their pen. Therefore, we have a taking. And we do not have to prove that they actually took it from the victim's pen."

To constitute a taking, however, the defendants must remove it from the owner's actual or constructive possession. The record lacks any evidence suggesting that the defendants took the heifer from the victim's actual possession. Rather, it merely appears to have strayed.

Of course, the owner of lost property may retain constructive possession of the property. Nevertheless, absent notice to the finder of the owner's identity, a finder who retains lost property commits no theft. Thus, a taking from the true owner's "constructive possession" arises only if the finder has the requisite notice. The record here shows the defendants had no notice of Murray's claims until her arrival at their ranch and her talk with Susan Moses.

to distinguish the acts forming misappropriation under section 485 from the acts forming concealment or withholding under section 496.

"It has been held a thief may not be convicted under section 496 for 'concealing' or 'withholding' stolen property as these acts are part and parcel of the theft." *People v. Tabarez* (1988) 206 Cal.App.3d 551. In *People v. Tatum* (1962) 209 Cal. App. 2d 179, the court discussed at length the problems of convicting a thief of concealing the stolen property. The court initially reiterated the longstanding rule that "a thief may not be convicted under [section 496] of 'buying' or 'receiving' the goods which he has previously stolen, with the possible exception of the situation where the thief has disposed of the property and subsequently received it back in a transaction separate from the original theft." The court then found two reasons why the same rule generally applies to attempts to convict the thief of concealing or withholding the stolen property.

First, the court discussed the legislative intent behind section 496. According to the court, the Legislature directed the statute "at the traditional 'fence' and at those who lurk in the background of criminal ways in order to provide the thieves with a market or depository for their loot. Such offenses are essentially different from the actual theft of property prohibited by [the theft statutes.] *Every theft, every wrongful misappropriation, of necessity, contemplates and involves a permanent withholding from the owner. To conceal and withhold is the thief's purpose from the very moment that he gains possession of the property. It is part and parcel of the theft. But such concealment and withholding is not that envisaged by section 496.* If the Legislature had intended in that section to embrace concealment of stolen property by the thief, it would have been a simple matter to say 'every thief or any other person … who conceals, etc.'" (Italics added.)

Second, the court noted that the statutory scheme governing theft and concealment of stolen property frequently imposes harsher punishment on the fence than on the thief. The court noted: "These conflicts and untoward results are avoided, leaving the underlying purposes unimpaired, by construing section 496 as a statute directed primarily at persons who do not physically participate in the actual theft of the property."

Finally, the court summarized its conclusions: "in the absence of facts indicating a complete divorcement of the concealing activities from the course of conduct of the thief in the initial concealing of the property stolen by him, a thief may not be found guilty of concealment in violation of [section 496.]" It then applied its rule to the case before it: "there was no evidence of concealment independent of that involved in the theft. In the absence of such evidence it was error to instruct the jury that they could find defendant guilty of concealment even though they believed he had stolen [the property.] [¶] *Had there been evidence of acts of concealment entirely separate and apart from the theft and sufficiently removed therefrom to constitute an independent course of conduct, then an instruction which clearly spelled out such distinction could properly have been given.*" (Italics added.)

…

Here, … the evidence shows that the earliest defendants had notice of the true owner's identity was upon Murray's visit to their ranch and her talk with Susan Moses.

Shortly after Murray left the defendants' ranch and returned to her home, she learned that they had taken the heifer away in their van. As a matter of law, we find that the defendants' acts upon Murray's visit and departure formed a single, undivorced course of concealment. As such, defendants cannot be liable for concealing the property they misappropriated, since the acts of concealment were part and parcel of the acts of misappropriation itself.

Accordingly, defendant's conviction for violation of section 496 cannot stand.

Note

Theft and Receiving Stolen Property. In 1992, Penal Code § 496(a) was amended to provide as follows:

> A principal in the actual theft of the property may be convicted pursuant to this section. However, no person may be convicted both pursuant to this section and of the theft of the same property.

Section 2 of the amending statute (which was not codified) declared the legislative intent:

> It is the intent of the Legislature to provide for the prosecution of principals in the actual theft of the property who continue to possess that property after the statute of limitations has run on the theft of the property.

In *People v. Ceja*, 49 Cal.4th 1 (2010), the California Supreme Court held that, in a case where the defendant is charged with both theft and receiving stolen property, the factfinder should first decide on the theft charge and should only consider the receiving charge if it found the defendant not guilty of theft.

People v. Hays

147 Cal. App. 3d 534, 195 Cal.Rptr. 252 (1983)

Stanforth, J.

Upon a second trial (the first ended in mistrial) the jury convicted defendant Charles Lee Hays, Sr., of robbery (Pen. Code, § 211) and assault with a deadly weapon (§ 245, subd. (a)).

...

Facts

At about 8 a.m. Marsha Pederson, bookkeeper of the Sav-On drug store in Escondido, was in her office on the second story of a commercial building. Her office contained two safes which were set by a time clock to open shortly after 8 a.m. Her manager, Virgil Naveau, had just left when Pederson heard the ceiling above her giving way. She saw a person come crashing through the acoustical ceiling of her office. Before the man dropped out of the ceiling she heard no sounds on the roof. A rifle was slung across the man's chest. Pederson described the invader as a male with his face covered with mask or facial hair. He was wearing a green sweater-like garment with cream colored pants and dark stocking knit cap. This sweater was a similar shade of green to the sweatshirt later found in the Builder's Emporium (next door) where Hays was captured. Pederson testified the rifle on the man's chest was similar to a sawed-off M1 carbine wrapped inside the green sweatshirt. The man did not point a gun at her, yet Pederson felt she was threatened and was afraid. She screamed and ran out of her office and quickly down the stairs. She thought a robbery was taking place and did not want to participate.

...

Discussion

I

Hays contends his robbery conviction should be reversed upon the ground of insufficiency of the evidence a larceny was accompanied by an assault. Hays misunderstands the legal prerequisites to the crime of robbery. Section 211 defines robbery as the felonious taking of personal property in the possession of another from his or her person or immediate presence and against his or her will accomplished by means of force or fear. There is no need to prove both force and fear. The Supreme Court recently said in *People v. Green* (1980) 27 Cal. 3d 1, robbery is but larceny aggravated by the use of force or fear to accomplish the taking of the property from the person or presence of the possessor. Evidence of the victim's fear for her own safety or that of her company's is sufficient to sustain a conviction.

Hays next argues his conviction for robbery of Pederson must be reversed because he did not take property "from [her] person or immediate presence." The violent appearance of the armed robber forced Pederson to flee in fear for her safety, abandoning immediate bodily presence and control over her employer's personal property. She remained near enough to hear a second body arrive via the ceiling hole in the office. Thus, Hays' argument rests on the happenstance of a fear induced flight.

The term "immediate presence" is to be liberally construed. Any and all the sensory perceptions are included in determining "presence." The actual corporeal presence of the victim is not required. In *People v. Lavender* (1934) 137 Cal. App. 582, the court held the robbery occurred in the victim's presence because the victim perceived, through hearing, the commission of the robbery. Important factors in the victim's perception were his or her ability to hear, see or smell "things that clearly indicate the commission of a robbery...."[2] Here, Pederson was as near as was safe to be with at least constructive control over the money in the safe. The fact the robber(s) forced her to flee does not breathe life into a claim the money in the safe was not taken from her immediate presence. Pederson was "constructively" present during the taking.

---

2. "If a large herd of cattle that was scattered for a mile or more on a plain was in charge of a cowboy, who was located on a hill or knoll where he might watch the cattle, was the subject of a felonious asportation by thieves, who preparatory to their nefarious work, had 'held up' the cowboy, would it be contended that the crime was not committed in the 'immediate presence' of the cowboy, and consequently that it did not constitute a robbery?" (*People v. Lavender* (1934) 137 Cal. App. 582.)

Here there is more than substantial evidence (direct and circumstantial) to convince a reasonable trier of fact beyond any reasonable doubt the person who descended through the roof into Pederson's immediate presence was Hays; he was armed with a rifle; his purpose was robbery and his presence was menacing. This show of force was sufficient to cause the intended victim to flee in fear. Personal property was carried away, possessed by the robbers, until retaken by the police from the captured Mark Hays. Beyond any reasonable doubt, the evidence proves personal property was taken pursuant to the robbers' (father and son) plan for breaking in through the roof, robbing and then departing either over the roof, escaping through to the nearby Builders Emporium or by the rear exit of Sav-On.

This plethora of evidence more than satisfies the statutory elements for robbery as well as the burden of proof requirements. To say the robbery was not accomplished by means of force or fear is to simply ignore the web of convicting facts.

. . .

Note and Problem

"Constructive Possession" of Property. The court in *Hayes* assumed that Pederson, as the bookkeeper for the company, was in possession of the company's property. The California Supreme Court has since held that every employee on duty at the time of a robbery of the employer's business is in "constructive possession" of the employer's property and therefore is a victim of the robbery. See *People v. Scott*, 45 Cal.4th 743 (2009). As a result a defendant may be convicted of as many counts of robbery as there are employees on duty.

Problem 57.

Owner and Friend were driving a backhoe down the street in the course of their work when they saw Defendant burglarizing Owner's pickup truck. Owner stopped the backhoe, and the two jumped down and approached the truck on opposite sides. Defendant emerged, carrying Owner's speakers, on Friend's side of the truck. Friend told him to stop and hit him, but Defendant ran off chased by Friend. Some distance away, Defendant stopped, pulled out a gun and pointed it at Friend. Friend stopped, and Defendant ran off. Defendant is charged, *inter alia*, with robbery (P.C. § 211). What arguments should be made on the robbery charge?

People v. Webster

54 Cal. 3d 411, 814 P.2d 1273 (1991)

BAXTER, J.

Defendant Larry Junior Webster and three other men were jointly tried on charges arising from the death of William Burke. A jury convicted defendant of first degree murder ... robbery [and other crimes]. Under the 1978 death penalty law, the jury found as special circumstances of the murder that defendant intentionally committed it while lying in wait (§ 190.2, subd. (a)(15)) and while engaged in the commission or attempted commission of a robbery (id., subd. (a)(17)(i)). After a penalty trial, the jury fixed defendant's punishment at death. His motion for modification of the death verdict was denied. Defendant's appeal is automatic.

We find no prejudicial error affecting either the guilt or penalty judgments. We will therefore affirm them in full.

GUILT TRIAL

1. *Prosecution evidence.*

The principal prosecution witnesses were Bruce Smith and Michelle Cram. As the jury knew, Smith had already pled guilty to second degree murder in connection with the homicide, and Cram had been granted immunity in return for her testimony.

Smith and Cram provided the following account, differing only in minor details: In late August 1981, defendant, Joseph Madrigal, Carl Williams, Robert Coville, Smith, and the 17-year-old Cram were living at a riverbank encampment in Sacramento. Defendant was the group leader. On the night of August 29, Smith, Madrigal, and Coville robbed a nearby convenience store. Quick response by the police forced the trio to hide for several hours before returning to camp.

The next day, August 30, defendant and Williams made one of several trips to buy beer, which the camp residents were consuming at a steady pace. When the men returned in early afternoon, defendant said they had met two "outlaws" ("street persons" or "survivors") at the Shell station near the convenience store. Defendant reported there was still intense police activity in the area because of the robbery, and he suggested the group needed to leave town. Defendant said he had arranged to use the "outlaws'" car for joint drug purchases or robberies that evening. The opportunity arose, he suggested, to lure one of the "outlaws" back to the camp, kill him, and steal the car.

Madrigal, Coville, and Williams expressed enthusiasm for the plan. According to Cram, defendant said he personally would kill and dismember the victim; according to Smith, Coville said he "hadn't killed somebody in quite a while" and would "take care of it." When Cram expressed skepticism about defendant's boasts, he insisted he was serious. Defendant said this would be Cram's first criminal lesson and would help her become more independent from Williams, with whom she was living.

It was decided that because the "outlaws" knew Williams, he would walk back to the Shell station with defendant to meet them. Madrigal would go along. Once the three returned to camp with the intended victim, either defendant (according to Cram) or Coville (according to Smith) would kill him. Defendant showed Smith where to dig a grave and told Cram to clean up the campsite and pack in preparation for the group's departure. Defendant, Williams, and Madrigal then left for a 7:30 p.m. meeting with the "outlaws." Defendant had drunk beer all day and may have taken amphetamines. As usual, defendant was wearing glasses; Williams wore a cowboy hat.

While the three men were gone, Smith and Cram worked at their assignments; Coville sat and drank beer. After half an hour's absence, defendant called out from the top of a levee that his group had returned. Four men walked single file down the trail to the camp. Williams was in the lead, followed in order by Madrigal, the victim Burke, and defendant. When the four were about halfway down the trail, defendant suddenly grabbed Burke and pulled a knife. According to Smith, defendant moved around to the front of Burke and stabbed him; Cram saw defendant reach from behind to stab Burke in the chest. Burke protested, and a struggle ensued. Madrigal turned back to assist defendant. Burke began to make gurgling sounds.

Cram became hysterical, so defendant and Williams told Smith to take her to "Fag Beach" and wait.[2] Ten minutes later, defendant, Madrigal, Williams, and Coville arrived at the "Fag Beach" parking lot with the group's belongings. Defendant gave Coville a car key, which Coville used to unlock the trunk of a car parked in the lot. The group loaded their possessions in the car, proceeded to Interstate 5, and drove all night toward Southern California. Defendant indicated that they should eventually turn east, toward Missouri.

...

About 3:30 p.m. the next day, as defendant was driving, an officer of the California Highway Patrol (CHP) stopped the group's car for speeding on Interstate 15 near Barstow. Investigation stemming from the traffic stop eventually led to the arrest of all six passengers, and to statements by Smith and Cram concerning the Burke homicide.

[Defendant testified in his own behalf, denying any plan to kill the victim and steal his car. He said that his remarks to the group were just bluster. Burke handed him the car keys at the "Fag Beach" parking lot. As they walked back to the camp Burke and Defendant got into an argument. Burke pulled a knife and slashed Defendant, and Defendant and Madrigal killed Burke in self-defense.]

...

6. *Sufficiency of robbery evidence.*

Defendant claims the robbery evidence is insufficient, because there was no proof that property was taken from Burke's "person or immediate presence" against his will, and by means of force or fear. (§ 211.) If the robbery conviction is based on theft of the car key, defendant suggests, there is no evidence the key left Burke's "person or immediate presence" without his consent or by force. If Glover's auto was the property

2. "Fag Beach" is the name by which Smith referred to the riverbank area at the foot of North 10th Street, directly below the parking lot where Burke's auto had been left. The record discloses no official name for the beach. The informal name is used by the parties to this appeal, and we employ it, in quotation marks, for convenience only.

taken, defendant asserts, it also was not obtained from Burke's "immediate presence" by force; the vehicle was a significant distance from where Burke was assaulted, and it was appropriated only after his death.

Courts of Appeal have held that the "immediate presence" element is satisfied, even when the actual taking of property is far from the scene of the assault, "so long as [the victim] perceives any overt act in the commission of the robbery and is subjected to the requisite force or fear." (*People v. Martinez* (1984) 150 Cal. App. 3d 579.) Under these cases, it would be enough that defendant and his companions killed Burke for the purpose of taking or retaining property entrusted to Burke's possession and control.

However, in *People v. Hayes* (1990) 52 Cal. 3d 577, we disapproved such an expansive interpretation of "immediate presence" for purposes of robbery. As we explained, to ignore the distance between the act of taking and the application of "force or fear" would deny meaning to the separate requirement of robbery that the property be "tak[en]" from the victim's person or "immediate presence."

Adopting the prevailing American rule, we held that "[a] thing is in the [immediate] presence of a person, in respect to robbery, which is so within his reach, inspection, observation, or control, that he could, if not overcome by violence or prevented by fear, retain his possession of it." The zone of immediate presence includes the area "within which the victim could reasonably be expected to exercise some physical control over his property."

The distance between Burke's auto and the murder scene was not so great as to violate these standards as a matter of law. Defendant, Madrigal, Williams, and Burke had brought the car from a remote location to the "Fag Beach" lot, which apparently was a common and convenient public parking spot for persons using the nearby riverbank. Burke and the three other men then walked the relatively short distance to the riverbank campsite a mere quarter of a mile by defendant's own calculation. Like Burke, the robbers were on foot, and they were no closer to the car at the moment they assaulted Burke than was Burke himself. There was no evidence that Burke was too far away to perceive and resist an attempt to seize the vehicle.

The jury could thus reasonably infer that but for defendant's attack, Burke's relative proximity to the car would have allowed him to take effective physical steps to retain control of the vehicle, and to prevent defendant and his companions from stealing it. The jury could also conclude that the theft was "by means of" force, in that defendant attacked Burke to eliminate his resistance to the taking.

Moreover, nothing in *Hayes* suggests that criminals may escape robbery convictions simply by luring their victim far enough away from the property to make his control more difficult or the application of force or fear more convenient. *Hayes* disapproved several decisions holding that "immediate presence" is satisfied by the victim's perception of any overt act committed in aid of the taking, but our opinion expressly excepted a long-standing decision, *People v. Lavender* (1934) 137 Cal. App. 582.

In *Lavender*, robbers induced a hotel clerk to show them a room; once there, they tied up the clerk, extorted the combination to the office cash register, returned to the adjacent office, and rifled the register. The Court of Appeal reviewed decisions suggesting that "immediate presence" is satisfied if the victim is close enough to perceive the taking, but the court also observed that "[a]t least as early as the time when the clerk was induced to leave the hotel office ... the crime of robbery was commenced; ... The trick or device by which the physical presence of the clerk was detached from the property under his protection and control should not avail defendant in his claim that the property was not taken from the 'immediate presence' of the victim."

Similar principles have traditionally applied to the requirement that the taking be both from the victim's person or immediate presence and by force or fear. Cases untouched by *Hayes*, hold that even if the perpetrator used peaceful means, such as a pretext, to separate the property from the victim, "what would have been a mere theft is transformed into robbery if the perpetrator ... [later] uses force to retain or escape with [the property]" (*People v. Winkler* (1986) 178 Cal. App. 3d 750).

We affirm these principles. One commits robbery when, with intent to rob, he uses peaceful means to move the victim away from a place where the victim could physically protect the property, then employs force or fear upon the victim in order to make good the theft or escape. The act of "taking" begins when the separation of the victim from his property occurs, and it continues through the forcible consummation. Hence, the defendant may be found guilty of a "taking" which is both from the victim's "person or immediate presence" and "by means of force or fear" (§ 211). At oral argument, defendant's counsel conceded as much. Here, the prosecution evidence indicated that defendant and his companions, acting by prearrangement, induced victim Burke to leave his car in the "Fag Beach" parking lot, then to walk with them to a more secluded place where their attack would be safer and his ability to protect the vehicle from seizure would be reduced. The jury could therefore conclude they robbed Burke of the car.

Furthermore, the evidence supports a conclusion that the key to the car was taken from Burke's "person or immediate presence" by force or fear. Even under defendant's version of events, he obtained the key from Burke's "person"; defendant said Burke handed him the key at the "Fag Beach" parking lot. If the jury believed this, it could still conclude that defendant later used force to prevent Burke from retrieving the key.

Finally, the jury could determine that defendant did use force in the first instance to gain possession of the key from Burke's "person." Burke's body was found with his pants pocket turned out, but his wallet was not missing. A reasonable inference arises that the key was obtained by killing Burke, then rifling his body. The evidence of robbery was sufficient.[16]

16. Evidence that the *key* may have been taken from Burke's person or presence by force or fear does not spare us from deciding whether there was similar evidence with respect to the *car*. The instructions did not specify the object or objects of the robbery, nor was the jury required to do so in its verdicts and findings. In his closing argument, the prosecutor focused entirely on the plan to steal the car; he never mentioned the key or the evidence that it was taken from Burke's "immediate pres-

. . .

[Opinions of Mosk, J. and Broussard, J., concurring and dissenting, omitted.]

Kennard, J., concurring and dissenting.

I concur in the judgment. I cannot agree, however, with the majority's treatment of the "immediate presence" element of robbery, and therefore write separately.

Penal Code section 211, defining the crime of robbery, requires that property be taken from the person or immediate presence of the victim through the use of force or fear. In *People v. Hayes* (1990) 52 Cal. 3d 577, we held that "immediate presence" means "an area over which the victim, at the time force or fear was employed, could be said to exercise some physical control."

In this case the evidence, viewed in the light most favorable to the prosecution, showed that at the time of the attack the victim was approximately one-quarter mile from his car, and was walking down a narrow trail single file with defendant and two others. The majority sets forth two reasons why, in its view, the immediate presence requirement of robbery was met in this case. Neither is convincing.

First, the majority reasons that "[t]he jury could ... reasonably infer that but for defendant's attack, [the victim's] relative proximity would have allowed him to take effective physical steps to retain control of the vehicle...." This reasoning is unpersuasive.

In effect, the majority substitutes a concept of relative proximity to the stolen property for the statutory element of immediate presence. The defect in the majority's reasoning can be best understood by hypothesizing that at the time of the attack the victim and his attackers were not one-quarter mile but two miles from the car. The majority's reasoning would be equally applicable to that situation, since one could reasonably infer that but for the attack the victim's "relative proximity" would have enabled him to take effective physical steps to retain control of the vehicle. Yet it cannot be rationally argued that a car two miles from its driver is within the driver's "immediate presence," that is, in an area in which the driver could exercise physical control over the vehicle.

Still another example reveals the defects of the majority's approach. Let us assume that the victim and defendant had merely decided to go for a walk, and that a third party stole the car from the lot where it was parked when the victim was a quarter-mile away. The victim, who was walking away from the car and down a narrow trail with defendant at the time of the theft, would not have known the car was gone until

---

ence." Defense counsel exploited the omission. He accused the prosecutor of "glossing over" the object of the robbery, argued that the auto was not within Burke's "immediate presence," pointed to evidence that the key might simply have remained in the car, and disputed inferences that the key was taken from Burke's pocket after his death. Defense counsel also urged there was no robbery of the key if Burke handed it over voluntarily, as defendant testified. Under these circumstances, we cannot be certain the jury based its robbery findings on the premise that the key was taken separately from the car. Hence, we may not uphold the robbery findings unless we conclude there was substantial evidence to support all the robbery theories before the jury. (E.g., *People v. Green* (1980) 27 Cal.3d 1.) For this reason, we must confront the issue of the auto's "immediate presence."

he returned. In other words, in all probability the car would not have been within the victim's sensory perception at the time it was taken. If the "immediate presence" requirement of the robbery statute is not tested by sensory perception, however, then it is difficult to see what it means. For instance, defendant and his companions could have walked with the victim not a quarter-mile, but a mile, or three miles, or five, and apparently the immediate presence requirement would still be met under the majority's approach. The majority's "relative proximity" theory thus nullifies the statutory requirement of immediate presence.

Second, the majority finds the immediate presence requirement of the robbery statute satisfied on a "luring away" theory. Under the majority's approach, robbery is committed when the defendant "uses peaceful means to move the victim away from a place where the victim could physically protect the property, then employs force or fear upon the victim in order to make good the theft or escape."

This approach presumes that the elements of robbery can occur over a theoretically limitless time span. But less than 10 months ago, the members of this court unanimously agreed that the term immediate presence means "an area over which the victim, *at the time force or fear was employed*, could be said to exercise some physical control." (*People v. Hayes*, italics added.) The majority's conclusion in this case that a defendant who lures the victim away from the immediate presence of the property, then employs force or fear, can be guilty of robbery directly conflicts with this unambiguous language from our recent decision in *Hayes*.

The majority correctly finds that the evidence supports a conclusion that the key to the victim's car was taken from his person by means of force or fear. But because, as the majority observes, we cannot be certain under the circumstances of this case that the jury based its robbery finding on the taking of the key and not the car, this rationale alone cannot support the robbery special circumstance (see *People v. Green* (1980) 27 Cal. 3d 1). Accordingly, I would strike the robbery special circumstance, and affirm the death verdict in this case based solely on the lying-in-wait special circumstance.

Problem

Problem 58.

Owner saw Defendant in the back seat of Owner's car removing objects through an opening into the trunk. As Owner approached the car, Defendant got out of the car carrying a black bag and started to flee. Owner gave chase and quickly caught Defendant by his shirt. Defendant dropped the bag and started slugging Owner in the head. Friend, who had been with Owner, caught up to the two men and grabbed Defendant. Defendant continued to struggle, kicking, punching, biting and kneeing both Owner and Friend. They eventually subdued and held Defendant until the police arrived and arrested him. Inside the bag the police found granola bars belonging to Owner, money and a watch belonging to Friend, and burglar tools. Defendant is charged with two counts of robbery (PC §211), of Owner and Friend. What arguments should be made as to his guilt?

People v. Mungia

234 Cal. App. 3d 1703, 286 Cal.Rptr. 394 (1991)

TIMLIN, ACTING P. J.

[Defendant was charged with, and convicted of, robbery (P.C. §211).]

Facts

On December 16, 1989, Margret Hogeland, accompanied by her five year-old daughter, went to a K-mart store in Riverside shortly after 5 o'clock in the evening. After returning a game her child had received, she left the store and walked toward her parked car, carrying her purse on a strap over her right shoulder, and holding her daughter's hand with her right hand.

Just as she passed one end of her car, and let go of the child's hand, "someone came up behind me and shoved me enough to get my purse off my shoulder." Ms. Hogeland specified that she had been shoved on her right shoulder. She testified that the shove was a separate motion from the motion used to remove the purse from her shoulder. Before the purse was removed from her shoulder, she did not see or hear the person who seized it, nor did he say anything to her.

Ms. Hogeland screamed, realized there was no one else around, and gave chase. Although she was unable to retrieve her purse before the perpetrator reached a getaway car, she did manage to note his clothing and physical appearance and the description of the car. She also memorized the license number of the car and later wrote it down.

Using the license plate number, the police quickly apprehended defendant and also the driver of the car. Approximately one and a half hours after the commission of the crime, Ms. Hogeland made an in-field identification of defendant as the perpetrator based on his clothing and physical appearance. At the same time, she also identified the getaway car.

At trial, the prosecuting attorney asked Ms. Hogeland if she had been eight months pregnant at the time of the crime. Defendant's attorney objected on the ground of irrelevancy, and the prosecuting attorney argued that her physical condition was relevant on the issue of the force needed to establish robbery. The objection was overruled and she then stated that she had been eight months' pregnant. On cross-examination, when asked if she had fallen forward because of the push, Ms. Hogeland replied, "No, it's a good thing I didn't because I was eight months pregnant and had toxemia." On redirect, she explained that toxemia is a condition "you get when you are pregnant, causes you to retain water and you have high blood pressure and it's dangerous for you and the baby." She also testified that she was 5 feet 4 inches tall and had weighed 180 pounds at the time of the crime.

Discussion

1. *There Is Sufficient Evidence That Defendant Used the Required Force to Sustain His Conviction of Robbery*

Defendant contends that there is insufficient evidence of force or fear to establish that the crime alleged in count 1 of the information was robbery (§ 211) rather than a necessarily included lesser offense of grand theft from the person (§ 487, subd. 2).

Robbery is "the felonious taking of personal property in the possession of another, from his person or immediate presence, and against his will, accomplished by means of force or fear" (§ 211). It is the use of force or fear which distinguishes robbery from grand theft from the person.

Defendant acknowledges that whether there is force or fear is a factual question for the jury, but contends that there must be evidence of something more than the amount of force necessary to accomplish the mere taking of the property itself.

As examples, defendant cites (1) *People v. Roberts* (1976) 57 Cal. App. 3d 782, in which evidence that the victim's purse was snatched from her arm with enough force to break its handle, was sufficient evidence of force to support a robbery conviction, (2) *People v. Lescallett* (1981) 123 Cal. App. 3d 487, in which evidence that the victim's purse was snatched from her hand after she first observed the defendant running toward her, and she was frightened, was sufficient evidence of fear to support a robbery conviction, and (3) *People v. Church* (1897) 116 Cal. 300, in which there was evidence that defendant grabbed a watch and chain from the victim's vest. One witness testified that there was some "difficulty" between the victim and defendant, and that the victim began to fall backwards. Other witnesses' testimony indicated nothing more than that defendant had quickly snatched the watch from the victim's person. In spite of the apparently conflicting testimony, it was held that there was sufficient evidence to require that the trial court instruct the jury on *both* robbery and larceny.

After discussing the above noted cases, defendant contends that in this case, "it is clear that the amount of force used was no more than that necessary to remove the property. There was no additional force, no resistance, and no threats necessary to make the offense a robbery."

...

"Force" is a relative concept. An able-bodied and/or large person may experience a given physical act applied to her body as less forceful than would a feeble, handicapped or small person. The concept that some persons are more vulnerable, i.e., more "defenseless, unguarded, unprotected, accessible, assailable, [or] ... susceptible to the defendant's criminal act" has been recognized by the courts and Legislature. Although we have not found any cases which explicitly hold that the victim's physical characteristics may be taken into account by the jury in determining whether the physical act applied to the victim constituted "force" within the meaning of section 211, the fact that "force" is a factual question to be determined by the jury using its own common sense leads us to conclude that the jury may properly consider such characteristics.

Furthermore, the defendant's physical characteristics in comparison to those of the victim may also be particularly relevant in determining whether the physical act applied by the defendant to the victim constituted "force." A shove by a defendant who is larger or stronger than his victim may lead a jury to find that the shove amounted to the necessary "force."

Here, given Ms. Hogeland's testimony that defendant shoved her, separate and apart from snatching her purse, as well as the jury's ability to view the relative size and apparent strength of defendant and Ms. Hogeland, and her further testimony that at the time of the crime she was eight months pregnant, and thus inferably more susceptible to being shoved off-balance and less able to recover her equilibrium quickly, we cannot say that there was insufficient evidence to support the jury's implied finding, when it returned a verdict of guilty of robbery rather than grand theft from the person, that defendant used more force than necessary to accomplish the snatching of Ms. Hogeland's purse and to overcome any resistance by her.[1]

Problem

Problem 59.

Defendants, transients living in an abandoned building in an area where there were a large number of sailors, agreed on a plan to find a sailor, take him back to their place, get him drunk, and take his money. Later, Defendants encountered Sailor and asked if he wanted to come with them and have some beer. Sailor agreed, and Defendants bought several six-packs of beer. They went back to the building and played a game called "Quarters," which is played by flipping a quarter into a cup of beer, and, if the quarter lands in the cup, then the person who flipped the quarter can require another person to drink the whole cup. Sailor eventually passed out, and defendants took $200 out of his wallet and left. Defendants are charged with robbery (P.C. § 211). What arguments might be made as to whether they can be convicted of

---

1. The People also argued that there was sufficient evidence of fear to support defendant's conviction of robbery. We disagree.

Although the victim need not explicitly testify that he or she was afraid in order to show the use of fear to facilitate the taking, there must be evidence from which it can be inferred that the victim was in fact afraid, and that such fear allowed the crime to be accomplished.

The evidence showed that Ms. Hogeland was not aware of defendant's approach or planned purse snatch until he had actually snatched her purse from behind. After realizing that her purse was gone and that no one was nearby, she pursued him on foot, and, failing to catch him, nonetheless bent over behind his getaway car long enough to repeat its license number to herself three times in her successful attempt to memorize it.

Although the People attempt to characterize the K-mart parking lot as being deserted, thus adding to the frightening aspect of the crime, a fair reading of the testimony does not indicate that the lot was deserted, but only that there was no one close enough that Ms. Hogeland could call him or her to stop defendant. There is nothing in the record which indicates, or from which it can be inferred, that Ms. Hogeland's purse was taken from her through the use of fear.

this charge or any lesser charge? Would the situation be different if it could be shown that Defendants placed drugs in the beer that Sailor drank?

People v. Beggs

178 Cal. 79, 172 P. 152 (1918)

Victor E. Shaw, Judge ***pro tem.***

Defendant, who is an attorney at law, appeals from the judgment pronounced upon the verdict of a jury finding him guilty of the crime of extortion, as defined in section 518 of the Penal Code. The verdict was based upon facts which the evidence tended to establish, as follows:

Joseph Steining was the proprietor of a store from which goods had from time to time been stolen. Acting upon information which pointed to Joseph N. Da Rosa, an employe of the store, as the one guilty of the thefts, Steining caused him to be arrested by a detective and taken to the police station, where, in the absence of a complaint filed, he was "booked" as charged with the crime of petit larceny. At the time of his arrest Da Rosa admitted that he was guilty of purloining certain articles, including two suits of clothes, the value of all of which did not exceed $50, which sum he then offered to pay Steining. On the following morning Mr. and Mrs. Steining, accompanied by defendant, who meanwhile had been employed by them as an attorney in the matter, went to the police station, where, in response to a request made by defendant, he was permitted to see Da Rosa, who was brought into a private office, and, in the interview had, defendant learned that Da Rosa had about $2,500 on deposit in two banks. Accompanied by a police officer, Da Rosa was taken by defendant to the house of his sister, where he said he kept the bank books, and after a prolonged search one of them was found, and either taken by or turned over to defendant, who, with the officer, accompanied by Da Rosa, went to the office of defendant, where, leaving the officer in an outer room, he took Da Rosa alone into his private office, where he impressed upon him the gravity of his offense, stating that he could be sent to San Quentin, and that unless he immediately paid defendant $2,000, for the purpose of settling with Steining, he would be sent to prison for 7 or 10 years. As a result of what defendant said, and by reason of the fear induced by such threats, Da Rosa went with defendant to the banks where his money was deposited, and, as directed by Beggs, signed receipts upon which $2,000 was drawn and delivered to defendant in payment of what he claimed to be due Steining on account of the thefts committed by Da Rosa, $900 of which sum defendant paid to Steining. It is unnecessary for our purpose to quote further from the testimony. Suffice it to say that it appears therefrom that Da Rosa stole certain articles from Steining, who, after having him lodged in jail upon a charge of petit larceny, and without at any time filing a complaint against him, employed defendant as his attorney, who, by means of threats that he would send him to state prison for 7 to 10 years, induced him to pay $2,000, the purpose of which payment, as claimed by defendant, was to compensate Steining for loss due to thefts committed by Da Rosa.

Several alleged errors in the trial are asserted as grounds for reversal, chief of which in importance is the claim that the court erred in refusing, at defendant's request, to give certain instructions to the jury, among which were the following:

> The effort on the part of a creditor to collect a debt by threat to accuse the debtor of the crime out of which the debt arose does not constitute extortion, nor does it cover the case of an owner who demands from an employe compensation for property which he has stolen or embezzled. The threat of one to prosecute for the theft of his property unless settlement is made does not constitute extortion. In order to constitute extortion, there must exist in the person making the threats an intent to gain unlawfully.

Other instructions of like import were requested and refused. While refusing the instruction so requested, the court instructed the jury that:

> The law does not permit the collection of money by the use of fear induced by means of threats to accuse the debtor of crime. It makes no difference whether Da Rosa stole any goods from Steining, nor how much he stole

—and that:

> It is your duty to convict the defendant, even though you should also find that he believed that Da Rosa was guilty of the theft of Steining's goods in an amount either less than, equal to, or greater than any sum of money obtained from Da Rosa.

Other like instructions were given, the effect of which was to withdraw from the consideration of the jury all questions as to the good faith with which defendant acted in thus enforcing payment of the money alleged to be due to Steining.

Section 518 of the Penal Code provides that: "Extortion is the obtaining of property from another with his consent, induced by a wrongful use of force or fear, or under color of official right."

The consent of the injured party in surrendering his property must, in the language of the statute, be "induced by the wrongful use of fear." This implies there may be a rightful use of fear. What meaning is to be ascribed to the word "wrongful"? Is it wrongful for A., from whom B. has stolen goods, to threaten the latter with prosecution unless he pay the value thereof, and thus, by means of the fear induced by such threat, obtain from B. that which is justly due to A.? In our opinion, the answer is found in provisions of the Code other than section 518, which, read in connection with section 518, clearly show that the use of fear induced by such threats, as a means of collecting a debt, is wrongful. Thus section 519 of the Penal Code provides:

> Fear, such as will constitute extortion, may be induced by a threat either: 1. To do an unlawful injury to the person … of the individual threatened.… 2. To accuse him … of any crime.

And section 523, Penal Code, provides that one who, with intent to extort money from another by means of a letter containing—"any threat such as is specified in section 519, is punishable in the same manner as if such money ... was actually obtained by means of such threat."

Section 650, Penal Code, makes it a misdemeanor for one by letter to threaten another with the accusation of a crime. These provisions, all adopted at the same time and relating to the same subject-matter, clearly indicate that the Legislature, in denouncing the wrongful use of fear as a means of obtaining property from another, had in mind threats to do the acts specified in section 519, the making of which for the purpose stated is declared to be a wrongful use of fear induced thereby. The first subdivision of section 519 provides that fear, such as will constitute extortion, may be induced by a threat to do an unlawful injury, thus excluding fear induced by threat to do a lawful injury. No such qualifying words are used in other subdivisions of the section. Subdivision 2 thereof, under which the prosecution in the instant case was had, in effect declares that fear as a means of extortion may be induced by a threat to accuse one of crime. The absence of any qualifying words, such as are found in subdivision 1 of the section, is significant. In reading section 518 with sections 519, 523, and 650, we cannot escape the conclusion that, assuming Da Rosa had in fact stolen goods of the value of $2,000 from Steining, the threats made by defendant to prosecute Da Rosa therefor unless he paid the value of said goods, which sum of $2,000 the latter, by reason of fear induced by such threat, paid, constitutes the crime of extortion....

Notes and Problem

Extortion and Robbery. While the crime in *Beggs* was clearly extortion and not robbery, in other cases it is not obvious which of the two crimes has been committed. Because both crimes have their roots in the common law crime of larceny and address the acquisition of property by means of force or fear, the courts have had difficulty distinguishing between the two. See *People v. Kozlowski* 96 Cal.App.4th 853, 866 (2002); *People v. Torres*, 33 Cal.App.4th 37, 50 (1995). As a result, some defendants convicted of robbery or extortion have argued that their convictions should be reversed because they were really guilty of the other crime. *E.g.*, *People v. Torres*, *supra* (defendant convicted of robbery claiming he committed extortion); *People v. Peck*, 43 Cal.App. 638 (1919) (defendant convicted of extortion claiming he committed robbery). The usual distinction made by the courts is that robbery covers situations where the taking is against the will of the victim, while extortion applies if the taking is with the victim's consent. *People v. Torres*, *supra*, at 50. However, since extortion requires that the taking be with "force or fear," it would seem that the victim's relinquishment of his or her property is no more "consensual" than in the case of robbery. Perhaps the distinction may be traced to the nature of the threat—a threat of immediate bodily harm being sufficient to overcome the victim's will, while any other threat (which at least leaves the victim with a choice, albeit unpleasant) results in a taking by consent. There are, of course, some other differences between the two crimes. Robbery requires that the property be taken from the person or immediate presence of the victim. Extortion covers the "obtaining of an official act," in addition to the taking of property. Finally, as *Beggs* points out, "claim of right," although a defense to robbery, is not a defense to extortion.

Problem 60.

Victim is a recent immigrant to this country and speaks little English. He was drunk and had passed out at the counter in a restaurant waiting for his food. Defendants, who had just finished their meal, woke Victim up, told him he had to leave the restaurant because it wasn't a lodging place and steered him out the door. Outside, they told Victim they were officers and he was under arrest. They took him to a bar and told him he had to be searched, and, when he took out his wallet, they took all his money and then turned him loose. Victim believed Defendants were officers and believed they would beat him up if he refused to cooperate. Defendants are charged with robbery (P.C. §211). What arguments should be made as to the charge? If Defendants are not guilty of robbery, what are they guilty of?

Asportation. At the common law, to be guilty of theft, the defendant had, not only to "take," but also to "carry away," the property, and, as the court indicated in *People v. Davis, supra*, this element—asportation—remains an element of theft crimes in California today. Asportation is not an element difficult to prove: "[I]f the taking has begun, the slightest movement of the property constitutes a carrying away or asportation." *Davis* at 305. As *Davis* indicates, the property does not have to be removed from the premises of the owner to constitute asportation—it is enough that the defendant took possession of it and moved it from the place where it was kept by the owner. *People v. Khoury*, 108 Cal.App.3d Supp. 1, 4 (1980). *People v. Meyer* 75 Cal. 383 (1888) appears to be the only published case reversing a theft conviction for failure to prove asportation. The evidence was that the defendant had attempted to steal an overcoat from off a dummy standing on the sidewalk outside a clothing store. The defendant had unbuttoned the coat and removed it from the dummy, but could not carry away the coat because it was chained to the dummy through the sleeve of the coat and the dummy was tied to the building.

B. Burglary

Burglary is a crime unique to Anglo-American law. At the common law, burglary was a felony which consisted of the breaking and entering of the dwelling of another in the nighttime with the intent to commit a felony therein. The common law felonies which would support a burglary conviction were: murder, manslaughter, rape, robbery, mayhem, arson and larceny. The crime was punishable by death, and an officer or private person was authorized to use deadly force to prevent a burglary or to capture a fleeing burglar.

In California, Penal Code § 459 has expanded the crime of burglary in at least four respects. *First*, burglary is not limited to entry of a "dwelling house," but may be committed by entry into virtually any building or vehicle. *Second*, burglary is not limited to an entry "in the nighttime." *Third*, burglary is not limited to entries accomplished by a "breaking," but may be committed by an entry without the use of any force whatsoever ("constructive breaking"). *Fourth*, burglary is not limited to cases where the intent is to commit the object crime within the structure. Despite the broad sweep of the current burglary statute, the penalties for burglary remain substantial, and, if a death occurs during the perpetration, or attempt to perpetrate, a burglary, the burglar will be guilty of first degree murder and eligible for the death penalty. Consider whether the common law definition of burglary or the present penalties for burglary ought to affect the courts' interpretation of the statute.

In *People v. Gauze*, the court explains the purpose of the burglary statute and then considers whether, in light of that purpose, a person can be guilty of burglarizing his/her own residence. In *People v. Davis*, the issue for the court is whether submission of a forged check through a walk-up window of a check-cashing business or insertion of a stolen ATM card into an ATM machine constitutes an "entry" for purposes of burglary. *People v. Sparks* concerns when entry of a "room," rather than a building, falls within the statute. *People v. Kwok* addresses the question whether, to constitute a burglary, the object crime must be part of a continuous course of action with the entry. Finally, *People v. Salemme* considers what object crimes will support a burglary conviction.

People v. Gauze

15 Cal. 3d 709, 542 P.2d 1365 (1975)

Mosk, J.

Can a person burglarize his own home? That is the quandary which emerges in the case of James Matthew Gauze, who appeals from a judgment of conviction of assault with a deadly weapon (Pen. Code, § 245, subd. (a)) and burglary (Pen. Code, § 459).

Defendant shared an apartment with Richard Miller and a third person and thus had the right to enter the premises at all times. While visiting a friend one afternoon, defendant and Miller engaged in a furious quarrel. Defendant directed Miller to "Get your gun because I am going to get mine." While Miller went to their mutual home, defendant borrowed a shotgun from a neighbor. He returned to his apartment, walked into the living room, pointed the gun at Miller and fired, hitting him in the side and arm. Defendant was convicted of assault with a deadly weapon and burglary; the latter charge was predicated on his entry into his own apartment with the intent to commit the assault.

Common law burglary was generally defined as "the breaking and entering of the dwelling *of another* in the nighttime with intent to commit a felony." (Italics added.)

(Perkins on Criminal Law (2d ed. 1969) p. 192.) The present burglary statute, Penal Code section 459, provides in relevant part that "Every person who enters *any* house, room, apartment ... with intent to commit grand or petit larceny or any felony is guilty of burglary." (Italics added.)

Facially the statute is susceptible of two rational interpretations. On the one hand, it could be argued that the Legislature deliberately revoked the common law rule that burglary requires entry into the building of another.[1] On the other hand, the Legislature may have impliedly incorporated the common law requirement by failing to enumerate one's own home as a possible object of burglary. No cases directly on point have been found. Therefore, in determining which statutory interpretation should be adopted it is necessary to examine the purposes underlying common law burglary and how they may have been affected by the enactment of the Penal Code.

Common law burglary was essentially an offense "against habitation and occupancy." (Perkins, *supra.*) By proscribing felonious nighttime entry into a dwelling house, the common law clearly sought to protect the right to peacefully enjoy one's own home free of invasion. In the law of burglary, in short, a person's home was truly his castle (2 Blackstone, COMMENTARIES (Jones ed. 1916) § 258, p. 2430). It was clear under common law that one could not be convicted of burglary for entering his own home with felonious intent. This rule applied not only to sole owners of homes, but also to joint occupants. The important factor was occupancy, rather than ownership.

California codified the law of burglary in 1850 (Stats. 1850, ch. 99, § 58, p. 235). That statute and subsequent revisions and amendments preserved the spirit of the common law, while making two major changes. First, the statute greatly expanded the type of buildings protected by burglary sanctions. Not only is a person's home his castle under the statute, but so, inter alia, are his shop, tent, airplane, and outhouse (see fn. 1, *ante*). This evolution, combined with elimination of the requirement that the crime be committed at night, signifies that the law is no longer limited to safeguarding occupancy rights. However, by carefully delineating the type of structures encompassed under section 459, the Legislature has preserved the concept that burglary law is designed to protect a possessory right in property, rather than broadly to preserve any place from all crime.

The second major change effected by codification of the burglary law was the elimination of the requirement of a "breaking": under that statute, every person who enters with felonious intent is a burglar. This means, at a minimum, that it no longer matters whether a person entering a house with larcenous or felonious intent does so through a closed door, an open door or a window. The entry with the requisite intent constitutes the burglary.

The elimination of the breaking requirement was further interpreted in *People v. Barry* (1892) 94 Cal. 481, to mean that trespassory entry was no longer a necessary element of burglary. In *Barry*, this court held a person could be convicted of burglary

1. The term "building" is used throughout this opinion for literary convenience; section 459 actually encompasses entry into a variety of structures, not all of them buildings.

of a store even though he entered during regular business hours. A long line of cases has followed the *Barry* holding.

Barry and its progeny should not be read, however, to hold that a defendant's right to enter the premises is irrelevant. Indeed, the court in *Barry*, by negative implication, substantiated the importance of determining the right of an accused to enter premises. When the defendant thief in *Barry* argued he had a right to be in the store, the court could have replied that his right to enter the store was immaterial. Instead the court declared, "To this line of reasoning we can only say, a party who enters with the intention to commit a felony enters without an invitation. He is not one of the public invited, nor is he entitled to enter. Such a party could be refused admission at the threshold, or ejected from the premises after the entry was accomplished." Thus, the underlying principle of the *Barry* case is that a person has an implied invitation to enter a store during business hours for legal purposes only. The cases have preserved the common law principle that in order for burglary to occur, "The entry must be *without consent*. If the possessor actually invites the defendant, or actively assists in the entrance, e.g., by opening a door, there is no burglary." (1 Witkin, Cal. Crimes (1963) Crimes Against Property, §457) (Italics in original.)

Thus, section 459, while substantially changing common law burglary, has retained two important aspects of that crime. A burglary remains an entry which invades a possessory right in a building. And it still must be committed by a person who has no right to be in the building.

Applying the foregoing reasoning, we conclude that defendant cannot be guilty of burglarizing his own home. His entry into the apartment, even for a felonious purpose, invaded no possessory right of habitation; only the entry of an intruder could have done so. More importantly, defendant had an absolute right to enter the apartment. This right, unlike that of the store thief in *Barry*, did not derive from an implied invitation to the public to enter for legal purposes. It was a personal right that could not be conditioned on the consent of defendant's roommates. Defendant could not be "refused admission at the threshold" of his apartment, or be "ejected from the premises after the entry was accomplished." (*People v. Barry*.) He could not, accordingly, commit a burglary in his own home.

The People argue, however, that a contrary conclusion is compelled by a dictum in *People v. Sears* (1965) 62 Cal. 2d 737. In *Sears*, defendant was convicted of felony murder. For three years prior to the murder, defendant had slept in a garage nearby the cottage occupied by his wife. Then the spouses separated and defendant moved to a hotel. Three weeks later, he returned to the cottage, looking for his wife and hiding a reinforced steel pipe under his shirt. In an ensuing struggle, he killed his wife's daughter. This court reversed his conviction because a confession was improperly admitted, but for guidance upon retrial we declared valid a felony-murder instruction based on burglary—entering the cottage with intent to assault his wife—as the felony. In answer to defendant's argument that he could not be guilty of burglary because he had a right to enter the house, the court replied, "One who enters a room or building with the intent to commit a felony is guilty of burglary even though permission to enter has been extended to him personally or as a member of the public. The entry need not constitute a trespass. Moreover, since defendant had moved out of the family home three weeks prior to the crime, he could claim no right to enter the residence of another without permission. Even if we assume that defendant could properly enter the house for a lawful purpose, such an entry still constitutes burglary if accomplished with the intent to commit a felonious assault within it."

As the above quotation indicates, our opinion that Sears could be convicted of burglary was based on two separate considerations. First, Sears had no right to enter his wife's house; that fact alone supported the conviction. Second, even if he had a right to enter, the right was based on former section 157 of the Civil Code, which gave a person the right to enter the separate property of his or her spouse, subject to certain conditions. Thus Sears' "right" to enter his wife's house, like the "right" of the felon to enter the store in *Barry*, was at best conditional. An entry for anything but a legal purpose was a breach of his wife's possessory rights, in marked contrast to the entry in the present case.[4]

Only if the *Sears* dictum is read in an expansive manner can it be used to support the prosecution theory that a person can burglarize his own home. Such a reading would be entirely inconsistent with the purposes of section 459. As aptly articulated by the Court of Appeal in *People v. Lewis* (1969) 274 Cal. App. 2d 912, "Burglary laws are based primarily upon a recognition of the dangers to personal safety created by the usual burglary situation—the danger that the intruder will harm the occupants in attempting to perpetrate the intended crime or to escape and the danger that the occupants will in anger or panic react violently to the invasion, thereby inviting more violence. The laws are primarily designed, then, not to deter the trespass and the intended crime, which are prohibited by other laws, so much as to forestall the germination of a situation dangerous to personal safety." Section 459, in short, is aimed at the danger caused by the unauthorized entry itself.

In contrast to the usual burglary situation, no danger arises from the mere entry of a person into his own home, no matter what his intent is. He may cause a great deal of mischief once inside. But no emotional distress is suffered, no panic is engendered, and no violence necessarily erupts merely because he walks into his house. To impose sanctions for burglary would in effect punish him twice for the crime he committed while in the house. In such circumstances it serves no purpose to apply section 459.[5]

---

4. The dictum in *Sears* proved not to be controlling even for Sears himself. This court subsequently reversed a second conviction on the ground that felony murder must be based on a felony independent of the homicide. (*People v. Sears* (1970) 2 Cal.3d 180.) The burglary was predicated on Sears' intent to commit assault with a deadly weapon, a crime not independent of the homicide. We did not reconsider the issue whether Sears could be convicted of burglary.

5. Thus the People's argument that we should examine the purposes of the burglary laws from the victim Miller's perspective misses the mark. Miller, in contrast to the usual burglary victim, was not endangered by defendant's entry into the apartment. He was in jeopardy because defendant borrowed a shotgun and chose to use it for an assault. Miller's safety would not have been enhanced if the two roommates had never left the premises, had quarreled inside the apartment and defendant

It has been urged that the purpose of burglary laws is to protect persons inside buildings because indoor crime is more dangerous than outdoor crime. It is true that in *People v. Wilson* (1969) 1 Cal. 3d 431, we said, "We have often recognized that persons within dwellings are in greater peril from *intruders* bent on stealing or engaging in other felonious conduct." (Italics added.) However, we have never categorized all indoor crimes to be more dangerous than all outdoor crimes. Nor would such a conclusion be relevant to the purposes of section 459. The statute protects against *intruders* into indoor areas, not persons committing crimes in their own homes.

To hold otherwise could lead to potentially absurd results. If a person can be convicted for burglarizing his own home, he could violate section 459 by calmly entering his house with intent to forge a check. A narcotics addict could be convicted of burglary for walking into his home with intent to administer a dose of heroin to himself. Since a burglary is committed upon entry, both could be convicted even if they changed their minds and did not commit the intended crimes.

In positing such hypotheticals, we indulge in no idle academic exercise. The differing consequences are significant, for the punishment for burglary is severe. First degree burglary is punishable by imprisonment for five years to life,[6] while a second degree burglar is subject to imprisonment in the county jail for a one-year maximum or in state prison for one to fifteen years. In contrast, the punishment for assault with a deadly weapon, the underlying crime committed in this case, is less severe: imprisonment in state prison for six months to life or in county jail for a maximum of one year, or a fine (Pen. Code, § 245, subd. (a)).[7]

For the foregoing reasons, we conclude defendant cannot be guilty of burglarizing his own home, and the judgment of conviction for burglary must therefore be reversed.

...

Notes and Problems

Problem 61.

Defendant and Wife were having marital problems, and one morning, Wife kicked Defendant out of their house. Later in the morning, Wife gave Neighbor a suitcase, $50 and a note to deliver to Defendant and asked him to collect a set of house keys from Defendant. The note told Defendant to "get a job, be accountable, and talk to me." Neighbor delivered the items to Defendant, collected the keys and returned the keys to Wife. That night, Defendant broke into the house, sexually assaulted Wife

---

there produced a gun. In either case, the crime committed is assault with a deadly weapon, and application of the burglary statute adds nothing to the victim's protection.

6. First degree burglary, the crime charged in the present case, includes nighttime burglaries of dwellings and armed burglaries (Pen. Code, § 460).

7. The penalties for both burglary and assault with a deadly weapon are substantially increased when a firearm is used in commission of the crime (Pen. Code, § 12022.5).

and kidnapped her. Defendant is charged with various crimes, including burglary (P.C. § 459). What arguments should be made on the burglary charge?

The Model Penal Code and Burglary. The Model Penal Code definition of burglary is substantially narrower than that in Penal Code § 459:

> A person is guilty of burglary if he enters a building or occupied structure, or separately secured or occupied portion thereof, with purpose to commit a crime therein, unless the premises are at the time open to the public or the actor is licensed or privileged to enter. It is an affirmative defense to prosecution for burglary that the building or structure was abandoned.

MPC § 221.1(1). The drafters of the Model Penal Code gave serious consideration to eliminating the crime of burglary but decided to retain it because of its long history and acceptance by the public and because it might be the only provable offense as to an intruder whose criminal intentions are sufficiently unclear as to prevent conviction of a particular attempt crime. MPC Part II Commentaries vol. 2, pp. 67–68.

Entry Consented to by the Owner. In *People v. Superior Court (Granillo)*, 205 Cal. App. 3d 1478 (1988), the Court of Appeal extended the reasoning of *Gauze*. There, the defendant entered an undercover officer's apartment upon invitation of the officer who knew the accused was in possession of stolen property he wanted to sell. The invitation and entry were orchestrated by the police in a "sting" operation, in order to recover stolen property. The court held there was no burglary because, when the officer invited the defendant in, he knew the defendant intended to commit a felony and expected he would commit a felony once inside, so there was no violation of the officer's possessory right in his apartment.

Problem 62.

Defendant, an adult man, met Victim, a 13-year old girl (whose "profile" showed her to be 14) in an internet chat room. Victim's parents were divorced, and Victim stayed every other week at each parent's house. When she was at her mother's house, with her mother and grandmother, she had a bedroom which she occupied alone. Without her mother's knowledge, Victim began seeing Defendant. On their fourth "date," at Victim's invitation, Defendant entered her bedroom through the bedroom window, and the two engaged in sex. Defendant made four more similar visits. The two were found out, and Defendant was arrested and charged with multiple counts of molesting a minor (P.C. § 288(a)) and with five counts of burglary (P.C. § 459). What arguments should be made regarding whether Defendant is guilty of burglary?

People v. Davis

18 Cal. 4th 712, 958 P.2d 1083 (1998)

GEORGE, CHIEF JUSTICE.

Defendant was convicted of forgery, receiving stolen property, and burglary, based upon evidence that he presented a stolen and forged check to the teller at a check-cashing business by placing the check in a chute in a walk-up window. Defendant maintains that the burglary conviction must be reversed because he did not enter the check-cashing facility. For the reasons that follow, we agree.

I

On May 27, 1995, defendant approached the walk-up window of a check-cashing business named the Cash Box and presented a check to the teller by placing the check in a chute in the window. The teller later described the chute as follows: "It has a handle, and it opens out like a flap. It opens out, and they put the check in. They pass the check through." The check was drawn on the account of Robert and Joan Tallman, whose names were imprinted on the check, and was payable in the amount of $274 to Mike Woody, a name defendant sometimes used. The check was signed with the name Robert Tallman.

The teller placed a small, white, oval sticker on the back of the check, passed the check back to defendant, and asked him to place his thumbprint on the sticker and endorse the check. Defendant placed his thumbprint on the sticker, signed the back of the check with the name Michael D. Woody, and passed the check back to the teller, using the chute.

The teller telephoned Robert Tallman, who denied having written the check. Tallman later discovered that a group of checks, including this one, had been stolen from his automobile. The teller placed Tallman on hold and telephoned the police. An officer arrived within minutes and arrested defendant, who still was waiting at the window. At the police station, the police directed defendant to give several examples of his handwriting by repeatedly signing the name "Robert Tallman."

At trial, Tallman testified that neither the signature nor any of the other writing on the check was his.

Defendant was convicted of forgery (Pen. Code, § 470), burglary (§ 459), and receiving stolen property (§ 496, subd. (c)).... The Court of Appeal affirmed the judgment. We granted review to determine whether there was sufficient evidence to support the conviction for burglary.

II

Under section 459, a person is guilty of burglary if he or she enters any building (or other listed structure) with the intent to commit larceny or any felony. We must determine whether the Legislature intended the term "enter," as used in the burglary statute, to encompass passing a forged check through a chute in a walk-up window of a check-cashing or similar facility.

The burglary statutes do not define the term "enter." In the present case, the Attorney General conceded at oral argument that no part of defendant's body entered the building, but it long has been established that a burglary also can be committed by using an instrument to enter a building.

In his Commentaries on the Laws of England, Sir William Blackstone stated regarding the elements of burglary: "As for the entry, any the least degree of it, with any part of the body, or with an instrument held in the hand, is sufficient; as to step over the threshold, to put a hand or a hook in at a window to draw out goods, or a pistol to demand one's money, are all of them burglarious entries" (4 Blackstone's Commentaries 227). But the common law drew a puzzling distinction. An entry by instrument was sufficient for burglary only if the instrument was used to commit the target larceny or felony. Insertion of an instrument for the sole purpose of gaining entry to the building did not constitute burglary.

The common law drew no such distinction if any part of the defendant's body entered the building. As Rollin Perkins observes in his textbook on Criminal Law: "Where it is a part of the body itself, its insertion into the building is an entry, within the rules of burglary, whether the purpose was to complete the felonious design or merely to effect a breaking. Thus, if the miscreant should open a window too small to admit his body, and should insert his hand through this opening merely for the purpose of unlocking a door, through which he intends to gain entrance to the building, he has already made an 'entry' even if he should get no farther. But where a tool or other instrument is intruded, without any part of the person being within the house, it is an entry if the insertion was for the purpose of completing the felony but not if it was merely to accomplish a breaking. If the instrument is inserted in such a manner that it is calculated not only to make a breach but also to accomplish the completion of the felonious design, this constitutes both a breach and an entry." (Perkins, Criminal Law (3d ed.1982) ch. 3, pp. 253–254.) ...

Although many jurisdictions adhere to the rule that entry by means of an instrument is sufficient for burglary only if the instrument was used to commit the intended larceny or felony, the reason for this rule is not clear, and California courts have declined to adopt it.

...

In *People v. Osegueda* (1984) 163 Cal. App. 3d Supp. 25, burglars were apprehended after they had succeeded in creating a small hole in the wall of an electronics store. It reasonably could be inferred that, in creating the hole in the wall, some portion of the tools had entered the building, but that the entry of these implements was not for the purpose of completing the intended larceny. The Appellate Department of the Los Angeles Superior Court found this was a sufficient entry for purposes of burglary: "We reject the decisions of out-of-state jurisdictions which differentiate between an entry by body and by instrument. We find no plausible reason for holding that an entry by instrument must be for the purpose of removing property. We find no California authority for contrary reasoning."

The Court of Appeal followed *Osegueda* in *People v. Moore* (1994) 31 Cal. App. 4th 489 in holding there was sufficient entry for burglary where the defendant had attempted to pry open the front door of an apartment using a tire iron, and an occupant of the apartment had seen the tip of the tire iron protrude into the apartment.

We agree that a burglary may be committed by using an instrument to enter a building—whether that instrument is used solely to effect entry, or to accomplish the intended larceny or felony as well. Thus, using a tire iron to pry open a door, using a tool to create a hole in a store wall, or using an auger to bore a hole in a corn crib are sufficient entries to support a conviction of burglary. But it does not necessarily follow that the placement of a forged check in the chute of a walk-up window constitutes entering the building within the meaning of the burglary statute, although that conclusion would be compelled were we to follow the decision in *People v. Ravenscroft* (1988) 198 Cal. App. 3d 639, the only California authority to address an analogous question. As we shall explain, we do not find the reasoning in *Ravenscroft* persuasive.

The defendant in that case was convicted of two counts of burglary based upon his conduct of "surreptitiously stealing and inserting the automatic teller machine (ATM) card of his traveling companion, Barbara Ann Lewis, in two ATMs and punching in her personal identification number, which he had previously noted, on the ATM keypads in order to withdraw funds from her account." The Court of Appeal first concluded that an ATM is a structure protected by the burglary statute. The court then turned to the question whether insertion of the ATM card constituted an entry into that structure. The court rejected the defendant's arguments that insertion of the card did not violate the air space of the ATM, and that insertion of the card did not constitute an entry, because the defendant lost control of the card once it entered the ATM: "The insertion of an ATM card to effectuate larcenous intent is no less an entry into the air space of a bank as would be the use of any other tool or instrument. Although the California Penal Code does not define 'entry' for the purpose of burglary, the California courts have found that a burglary is complete upon the slightest partial entry of any kind, with the requisite intent, even if the intended larceny is neither committed nor even attempted. By pushing Lewis's card into an ATM's slot, the defendant completed the crime. Further control of the card is unnecessary."

...

The appellate court in *Ravenscroft* properly rejected various arguments presented by the defendant, correctly concluding that the card was inserted into the air space of the ATM, that the circumstance that the defendant lost control of the card is not dispositive, and that the rule governing entry by means of an instrument is not limited to traditional burglar tools. Instruments other than traditional burglar tools certainly can be used to commit the offense of burglary. A laser could be used to cut an opening in a wall, a robot could be used to enter a building, or an ATM card could be used to "jimmy" a lock. But it does not necessarily follow from these conclusions that insertion of a stolen card into an ATM constitutes burglary.

The Court of Appeal in *Ravenscroft* appeared to reason that because an entry by means of an instrument is not limited to the use of traditional burglar's tools, there are no limitations within the meaning of the burglary statute on what constitutes entry by means of an instrument. It certainly is within the scope of the burglary statute to recognize that using a cutting tool to breach the walls, doors, or windows of a building constitutes an entry, whether the burglar uses traditional burglar tools or a laser, and that using an instrument to reach into a building and remove property constitutes burglary whether that instrument is a hook or a robot. These are the traditional types of entry prohibited by the burglary statute, even though the entry may be accomplished in new ways.

Inserting a stolen ATM card into the designated opening in an ATM is markedly different from the types of entry traditionally covered by the burglary statute, as is passing a forged check through a chute in a walk-up window. In each situation the defendant causes an object to enter the air space of a building, but it is not apparent that the burglary statute was meant to encompass such conduct. It is important to establish reasonable limits as to what constitutes an entry by means of an instrument for purposes of the burglary statute. Otherwise the scope of the burglary statute could be expanded to absurd proportions. For example, the Attorney General asserted at oral argument that mailing a forged check from New York to a bank in California, or sliding a ransom note under a door, would constitute burglary. A person who mails a forged check to a bank or slides a ransom note under a door causes that forged check or ransom note to enter the building, but it cannot reasonably be argued that these acts constitute burglary. Under the expansive approach to the burglary statute taken by the Attorney General and reflected in the *Ravenscroft* decision, it is difficult to imagine what reasonable limit would be placed upon the scope of the burglary statute. It could be argued similarly that a defendant who, for a fraudulent purpose, accesses a bank's computer from his or her home computer via a modem has electronically entered the bank building and committed burglary.

The crucial issue, not considered by the court in *Ravenscroft*, is whether insertion of the ATM card was the type of entry the burglary statute was intended to prevent. In answering this question, we look to the interest sought to be protected by the burglary statute in general, and the requirement of an entry in particular.

The interest sought to be protected by the common law crime of burglary was clear. At common law, burglary was the breaking and entering of a dwelling in the nighttime. The law was intended to protect the sanctity of a person's home during the night hours when the resident was most vulnerable. As one commentator observed: "The predominant factor underlying common law burglary was the desire to protect the security of the home, and the person within his home. Burglary was not an offense against property, real or personal, but an offense against the habitation, for it could only be committed against the dwelling of another.... The dwelling was sacred, but a duty was imposed on the owner to protect himself as well as looking to the law for protection. The intruder had to break and enter; if the owner left the door open, his carelessness would allow the intruder to go unpunished. The offense had to occur at night; in the daytime home-owners were not asleep, and could detect the intruder and protect their homes." (Note, *Statutory Burglary—The Magic of Four Walls and a Roof* (1951) 100 U. Pa. L. Rev. 411.) The drafters of the Model Penal Code observed: "The notable severity of burglary penalties is accounted for by the fact that the offense was originally confined to violent nighttime assault on a dwelling. The dwelling was and remains each man's castle, the final refuge from which he need not flee even if the alternative is to take the life of an assailant. It is the place of security for his family, as well as his most cherished possessions. Thus it is perhaps understandable that the offense should have been a capital felony at common law." (Model Pen. Code & Commentaries (1980) com. to § 221.1.)

. . .

More than a century ago, in *People v. Barry* (1892) 94 Cal. 481, this court addressed the subject of what constitutes an entry for purposes of burglary. The defendant in Barry entered a grocery store during business hours and attempted to commit larceny. This court, rejecting the contention that a burglary had not occurred because the defendant had entered lawfully as part of the public invited to enter the store, stated: "[A] party who enters with the intention to commit a felony enters without an invitation. He is not one of the public invited, nor is he entitled to enter."

In *People v. Gauze* (1975) 15 Cal. 3d 709, we clarified our holding in *Barry* and held that a person cannot burglarize his or her own home. We observed that "[a] burglary remains an entry which invades a possessory right in a building." We then discussed the interest protected by the burglary statute: "Burglary laws are based primarily upon a recognition of the dangers to personal safety created by the usual burglary situation—the danger that the intruder will harm the occupants in attempting to perpetrate the intended crime or to escape and the danger that the occupants will in anger or panic react violently to the invasion, thereby inviting more violence. The laws are primarily designed, then, not to deter the trespass and the intended crime, which are prohibited by others laws, so much as to forestall the germination of a situation dangerous to personal safety. Section 459, in short, is aimed at the danger caused by the unauthorized entry itself."

We repeated that sentiment in *People v. Montoya* (1994) 7 Cal. 4th 1027, in which we held that, "for the purpose of assessing the liability of an aider and abettor, a burglary is considered ongoing during the time the perpetrator remains inside the structure." We stated: "The crime of burglary consists of an act—unlawful entry—accompanied by the 'intent to commit grand or petit larceny or any felony.'" We noted that the "underlying basis for the criminal sanction" of burglary is "the danger caused by the unauthorized entry itself." The Model Penal Code echoes this theme by noting that the crime of burglary "reflects a considered judgment that especially severe sanctions are appropriate for criminal invasion of premises under circumstances likely to terrorize occupants." (Model Pen. Code & Commentaries, supra, com. to art. 221, p. 59.)

Inserting a stolen ATM card into an ATM, or placing a forged check in a chute in the window of a check-cashing facility, is not using an instrument to effect an entry within the meaning of the burglary statute. Neither act violates the occupant's possessory interest in the building as does using a tool to reach into a building and remove property. It is true that the intended result in each instance is larceny. But the use of a tool to enter a building, whether as a prelude to a physical entry or to remove property or commit a felony, breaches the occupant's possessory interest in the building. Inserting an ATM card or presenting a forged check do not. Such acts are no different, for purposes of the burglary statute, from mailing a forged check to a bank or check-cashing facility.

By analogy, a person who returns books to a library by depositing them in a book drop, causing the books to slide down a chute into the library, has not entered the library. It would be unreasonable to characterize the books as "instruments" used to enter the library. But if a person reaches his or her hand into the book drop, or uses a tool, in an attempt to steal books, such an act would constitute burglary.[6]

Our conclusion that the limits of the burglary statute should not be stretched beyond recognition does not leave the public without reasonable protection from criminal conduct, for the Legislature has enacted a variety of penal statutes that apply to the criminal activity involved in cases such as *Ravenscroft* or the present case. The use of an ATM card with intent to defraud, for example, specifically is penalized by section 484g and the Legislature, of course, could enact a similar statute pertaining to check-cashing facilities. Unauthorized entry into a computer system is addressed by sections 502 and 502.01. And in the present case, our reversal of defendant's conviction of burglary does not affect his convictions for forgery and receiving stolen property, or his resulting sentence of four years in prison.

For the reasons discussed above, we conclude that defendant's placement of a forged check in the chute of the walk-up window of the check-cashing facility at issue cannot reasonably be termed an entry into the building for purposes of the burglary statute. Accordingly, the judgment of the Court of Appeal is reversed to the extent it affirms defendant's conviction for burglary, and affirmed in all other respects.

Mosk, Kennard and Werdegar, JJ., concur.

[Dissenting opinion of Baxter, J., joined by Chin and Brown, JJ., omitted.]

Note and Problem

A New Shoplifting Statute. The *Barry* case, discussed in both *Gauze* and *Davis*, was superseded by the Safe Neighborhoods and Schools Act Initiative in 2014. The initiative included a new section, P.C. § 459.5, which provided:

> (a) Notwithstanding Section 459, shoplifting is defined as entering a commercial establishment with intent to commit larceny while that establishment is open during regular business hours, where the value of the property that is taken or intended to be taken does not exceed nine hundred fifty dollars ($950). Any other entry into a commercial establishment with intent to commit larceny is burglary. Shoplifting shall be punished as a misdemeanor [ex-

---

6. The record in the present case does not disclose whether, or to what extent, defendant reached into the chute of the walk-up window as he passed the check into the facility. As noted above, the Attorney General conceded at oral argument that no part of defendant's body entered the check-cashing facility. We need not, and therefore do not, consider whether a slight entry of a portion of defendant's body into the chute of the walk-up window would be a sufficient entry under the statute defining the offense of burglary.

cept if the defendant had previously been convicted of certain enumerated crimes].

(b) Any act of shoplifting as defined in subdivision (a) shall be charged as shoplifting. No person who is charged with shoplifting may also be charged with burglary or theft of the same property.

Problem 63.

Defendant entered the Easy Money Check Cashing business to cash a check for $148. The Easy Money employee contacted the owner of the check, who reported that his checkbook had been stolen and that he had not written the check in question. Defendant was arrested and charged, *inter alia*, with burglary (P.C. § 459). In light of the shoplifting statute, what arguments should be made regarding whether Defendant is guilty of burglary?

People v. Sparks

28 Cal.4th 71, 47 P.3d 289 (2002)

George, C.J.

Section 459 of the Penal Code provides, in part, that one who "enters *any* house, *room*, apartment, ... store, ... or other building ... with intent to commit ... larceny or any felony is guilty of burglary." (Italics added.) We granted review to address a conflict in Court of Appeal decisions concerning whether a defendant's entry into a bedroom within a single-family house with the requisite intent can support a burglary conviction if that intent was formed only after the defendant's entry into the house. We conclude that such an entry can support a burglary conviction under section 459, and hence reverse the judgment of the Court of Appeal, which reached a contrary conclusion.

I.

[At approximately noon, 22-year-old Ana I. answered defendant's knock at the door of her single-family home. Defendant, then 25 years of age, attempted to sell Ana some magazines, but she stated she was not interested. Defendant asked Ana for a glass of water, which she provided to him as he remained outside the house. Defendant eventually asked Ana whether he could enter the house, and he did so. (Ana could not recall at trial whether she invited defendant to enter.) The two conversed at the kitchen table for about 15 minutes. Eventually Ana asked defendant to leave, telling him that she had to pick up her niece, but defendant ignored her request. When defendant made no move to comply with several further requests to leave, Ana walked down the hall to the bedroom to find outdoor shoes to wear upon leaving the house. Although Ana did not ask defendant to go with her into the bedroom, he followed her into the room blocked her from exiting and forcibly raped her.]

The trial court instructed the jury on the offense of burglary ... as follows: "The defendant is accused in count one of having committed the crime of burglary, a violation of section 459 of the Penal Code. [¶] Every person who enters a building or *any room within a building* with the specific intent to commit rape, a felony, is guilty of the crime of burglary in violation of Penal Code section 459." (Italics added.) Based upon these and related instructions, the prosecution argued to the jury that defendant could be found guilty of burglary if he formed the intent to rape either (i) prior to entering the house, or (ii) after entering the house, but prior to entering the bedroom in which the sexual assault occurred.

The jury convicted defendant of first degree burglary (§§459, 460) and forcible rape (§261, subd. (a)(2)) ...

The Court of Appeal upheld defendant's conviction for forcible rape, but in a split decision reversed the burglary conviction for instructional error ... We granted the Attorney General's petition for review.

II.

The Attorney General asserts that the plain words of section 459 (defining as burglary the entry of "any ... room ... with intent to commit ... larceny or any felony") establish that the court's instructions were correct and that the elements of the offense of burglary were established in this case.

Defendant contends, as the Court of Appeal majority held below, that the Legislature could not have intended for the circumstances presented here to constitute a burglary. He maintains that the word "room" in section 459 applies only to those rooms as to which there is an expectation of protection from intrusion—from room to room—that is comparable to the expectation of protection from intrusion into a house from outside the house. In other words, defendant argues that the term "any ... room" as used in section 459 was intended to encompass only certain types of rooms—for example, a locked room within a single-family house or a separate dwelling unit within a boarding house, entry into which is generally unauthorized even for other legal occupants of the house.

If we were to view the issue before us from the perspective of how the offense of burglary currently is defined in other jurisdictions in the nation, defendant's proposed interpretation of that offense would have substantial support. During the past few decades, the legislatures of many of our sister states have been quite active in amending their respective burglary statutes in ways that either clarify or limit the meaning of the term "room," or otherwise narrow the circumstances in which entry of a room can constitute burglary. At the present time, statutes in most jurisdictions, consistent with the recommendation of the Model Penal Code,[6] make clear that the burglary

6. Model Penal Code, section 221.1(1), first adopted in 1962, reads in relevant part: "A person is guilty of burglary if he enters a building or occupied structure, *or separately secured or occupied portion thereof*, with purpose to commit a crime therein ..." (Italics added.) As explained in the comment to this section, "[t]he provision in Subsection (1) as to separately secured or occupied portions of buildings and occupied structures takes care of the situation of apartment houses, office buildings, hotels, steamships with a series of private cabins, etc., where occupancy is by unit. It is the individual unit as well as the overall structure that must be safeguarded. Thus, while it would violate this section for a person to make an unprivileged entry into an apartment house for the purpose of stealing money

statutes in these jurisdictions apply only to entry of a "room" that constitutes a "separate unit" or a "separately secured" or "separately occupied" portion of a building or structure.

As noted, the interpretation proposed by defendant would focus upon the nature of the room entered and would inquire whether an occupant's reasonable expectation of protection from intrusion into that room *from the other rooms* is comparable to the expectation of protection from intrusion *into a house from outside the house.* As the dissenting justice in the Court of Appeal observed, under this view no burglary occurs "unless the nature of the room is such that it is considered as secure from entry from the interior of the structure as from the exterior, e.g., it is a *separate dwelling place or is kept locked.*" (Italics added.) In other words, the limiting gloss proposed by defendant essentially would embrace the "separately secured or occupied" standard endorsed by the Model Penal Code and adopted, in one form or another, in most (but not all) other jurisdictions.

Although the interpretation of the statute proposed by defendant (and endorsed by the majority in the Court of Appeal below) is not unreasonable, as explained below we do not write on a clean slate. In view of the history and prior interpretation of the California statute, we are not free to adopt by judicial construction a limitation on the term "room" that has been explicitly established in other jurisdictions only by explicit legislative action. Instead, in light of governing California precedent, we conclude that section 459 reasonably must be interpreted in the manner urged by the Attorney General.

III.

...

A.

This court directly ruled upon the meaning of the word "room," as used in section 459, for the first time in *People v. Young* (1884) 65 Cal. 225. In that case, the defendant entered a public railway station and thereafter entered a ticket office (which apparently had walls that were eight to nine feet high but did not reach the ceiling) located within the station. We rejected the theory that section 459 required the defendant to have formed the required intent prior to entering the railway station, so long as he formed that intent prior to entering a room within that structure—the ticket office. Accordingly, we held that the trial court did not err in refusing a requested defense instruction that if the defendant conceived his intent to steal after he entered the railway station building, the jury should find the defendant not guilty. We stated: "One who enters, with burglarious intent, a room of a house enters the house with such intent ..." In this regard, *Young* reflected the prevailing common law understanding that entry from inside a structure into a room within that structure could constitute a burglary.

---

or other valuables from a common safe, it also would violate the burglary provision if an intrusion is made into a single unit, even by an occupant of another unit of the same structure" (Model Pen.Code & Commentaries, com. 3(b) to § 221.1, p. 73).

Subsequent to *Young*, a number of California appellate court decisions have held that entry into various types of rooms can constitute burglary.

...

Of all the cases applying section 459, only one, *People v. McCormack* (1991) 234 Cal.App.3d 253, concerns the precise type of entry we face here—entry, by an ostensible guest in the home, from inside the living quarters of a single-family home, into the unsecured bedroom of a member of a family living in the home. Most of the other recent decisions described above—specifically, *People v. Elsey* (2000) 81 Cal.App.4th 948, *People v. Thomas* (1991) 235 Cal.App.3d 899, and People v. OKeefe (1990) 222 Cal.App.3d 517 have made a point of distinguishing *McCormack* and the normal single-family-home setting. We first discuss *McCormack*, and then the three other cited appellate decisions.

B.

The defendant in *McCormack*, entered a single-family home through an unlocked door, assertedly at the occupant's invitation. The occupant—the brother of the homeowner—observed the defendant in the kitchen and asked him to leave the house, but the defendant refused to do so. Instead, the defendant asked the occupant whether he wanted a beer and requested permission to use the telephone. The occupant departed and telephoned the police from a neighbor's residence. When the police arrived, they found the defendant (in a hallway of the home) holding items taken from bedrooms. The defendant was charged with a single count of burglary. The trial court instructed that the "intent [to steal the personal property of another] need not be in the mind of the person at the time of the initial entry into the structure, if he subsequently forms the intent and enters a room within the structure." Consistent with this instruction, the prosecutor argued to the jury that the defendant committed burglary even if he formed the intent to steal after entering the house, so long as he did so before he entered one of the bedrooms. The defendant was convicted of burglary and appealed.

The Court of Appeal in *McCormack* found the trial court's instruction "consistent with the literal language of the controlling code section. In its current form this code section states: 'Every person who enters any ... room ... with intent to commit grand or petit larceny or any felony is guilty of burglary' (§ 459). We have found no published decisions by a court of this state holding, on facts similar to those present here, that burglary is not committed when the intent to steal is formed after entry to a building but before entering a room therein from which the defendant intends to steal property" (*McCormack*). Relying upon our decision in *Young*, and some of the Court of Appeal decisions, the court held that because "the plain language of the code includes entry into a room within the definition of burglary," the instruction was proper.

The court in *McCormack* also found that the basic policy underlying the burglary statute supported its view: "Just as the initial entry into a home carries with it a certain degree of danger [to personal safety], subsequent entries into successive rooms of the home raise the level of risk that the burglar will come into contact with the home's occupants with the resultant threat of violence and harm. Applying the plain language of the statute therefore serves rather than frustrates the policy of the law."[15]

[One year prior to *McCormack*, the Court of Appeal, in *O'Keefe*, upheld convictions on separate burglary counts based on the defendant's entries into separate rooms in a college dormitory. Rejecting the defendant's attempt to analogize the situation to that of separate entries into rooms of a single-family home, the court found the dormitory to be more akin to a hotel or apartment complex since each student, unlike a family member living in a single-family home, enjoyed "separate privacy." Shortly after the decision in *McCormack*, the Court of Appeal, in *Thomas*, upheld the defendant's burglary conviction based on his entry into a locked residence from the attached garage, finding that the defendant's entry was precisely the evil that the burglary statute was designed to prevent. In dictum, however, the court added: "[W]here a burglar enters several rooms in a single structure, each with felonious intent, and steals something from each, ordinarily he or she cannot be charged with multiple burglaries and punished separately for each room burgled *unless* each room constituted a separate, individual dwelling place within the meaning of sections 459 and 460." In *Elsey*, the Court of Appeal upheld six burglary convictions based on the defendant's entry into six classrooms, some of them located in the same building, on a single school campus. The court distinguished "entry into multiple rooms of a single-family house [from] the entries into multiple secured classrooms."]

IV.

Defendant asserts that the interpretation of section 459 set out in *McCormack*, will produce bizarre results. He echoes the Court of Appeal majority below, which observed that the defendant in *McCormack* entered the kitchen in the home without the intent necessary for burglary, and that if the defendant had formed the requisite intent while in the kitchen and yet thereafter did not enter any other room, he would not have been guilty of burglary[17]—but if the defendant had gone into another room and then reentered the kitchen, this time with the requisite intent, he would have been guilty of burglary. The Court of Appeal majority also asserted that allowing a conviction of burglary on the present facts improperly would subject defendants to conviction of multiple counts of burglary for every room in the house entered with the requisite intent.

---

15. The court in *McCormack* also observed: "The statute specifically prohibits entry into a 'room.' If this wording did not serve the policy intended by the Legislature it need not have been included in the statute and it could have been removed or modified at any time in the more than 100 years since this code section was first adopted."

17. The statutes in some jurisdictions provide otherwise and include in their definition of burglary the situation where one enters *or remains* with the requisite intent. Section 459, by contrast, requires an *entry* with requisite intent. Accordingly, in the present case, defendant would not have committed burglary if, after entering the home as a guest, he formed the requisite intent in the dining room or in the living room, but thereafter did not enter another room within the home with that intent.

Justice Benke, dissenting in the Court of Appeal below, conceded that under *McCormack's* interpretation of the statute, whether a particular entry into a room constitutes burglary will depend upon "the location of an actor when the requisite intent is formed," but further observed that this consequence "is not the result of the *McCormack* rule but of the nature of the crime of burglary itself as defined in section 459." Moreover, Justice Benke noted that even if the interpretation of the statute set out in *McCormack*, may "allow[ ] the creative mind to formulate disconcerting hypotheticals about the application of the law of burglary," the rule proposed by defendant would do so as well: "For example, a person may enter a residence without the intent to commit a theft. He walks down a hall off of which there are two indistinguishable bedrooms. The first is the bedroom of a family member, the second the bedroom rented by a family friend. Under the [rule proposed by defendant and the majority below], if the person enters the first with the intent to commit a theft, he commits no burglary [because he has not invaded a separate possessory interest]. If he enters the second [with the intent to commit a theft], he commits a first degree burglary. This distinction makes no sense ... and does not serve the policy basis of the crime." Accordingly, Justice Benke concluded that the rule proposed by defendant "simply exchanges one set of potential anomalies ... for another," and she asserted that "[i]f I must choose my anomalies..., then I believe I am duty bound to choose those created by the Legislature."

V.

As noted above, California decisions applying section 459 have upheld burglary convictions based upon entry into diverse types of rooms—among them ticket offices, liquor cages, business offices, enclosed counter areas, school classrooms, hotel rooms, apartments, a kitchen in a single-family home, and, in *McCormack*, a bedroom within a single-family home. These decisions—and *McCormack* in particular—are consistent with common law cases from other jurisdictions, recognizing as burglary the entry (with requisite intent), from within a home, into a bedroom inside the home. Although the burglary statute historically has been the subject of frequent amendments, our Legislature has not revised section 459 to disapprove any of these decisions. Furthermore, although in recent years the legislatures of many of our sister states have enacted statutes that have narrowed and confined the type of room that will qualify as the subject of a burglary, the California Legislature, when presented with legislation that proposed similar amendments, did not adopt any similar amendment to our burglary statute.[20]

---

20. In the 1970's, a period during which many other jurisdictions amended their burglary statutes consistent with the Model Penal Code to limit the subject of burglary to certain categories of rooms (for example, those that are "separately occupied or secured"), omnibus legislative proposals that would have incorporated that *same* limitation in section 459 were introduced in the California Legislature on four occasions but were not enacted.

To be sure, it is important that we be careful not to place undue significance on these unsuccessful legislative proposals. Each of the bills referred to in the prior paragraph proposed omnibus legislation that would have substantially overhauled the entire Penal Code. As we have noted, "unpassed bills,

As the court observed in *McCormack*, treating the entry at issue here as an entry for burglary is consistent with the personal security concerns of the burglary statute, because entry, from inside a home, into a bedroom of the home "raise[s] the level of risk that the burglar will come into contact with the home's occupants with the resultant threat of violence and harm." Here, the 22-year-old victim, living in her family's home, reasonably could expect significant additional privacy and security when she retreated into her own bedroom. Accordingly, consistent with California decisions construing section 459, reaching back to *People v. Young*, and consistent with the common law and the history of section 459, we conclude that the unadorned word "room" in section 459 reasonably must be given its ordinary meaning. It follows that the trial court did not err in this case by instructing the jury that entry into Ana's bedroom with the specific intent to commit rape constitutes a burglary in violation of section 459.

...

Problem

Problem 64.

Victim, an elderly woman, answered a knock on her apartment door and saw Defendant standing there with a paper shopping bag. Defendant said something, and Victim thought he was a salesman of some sort, so she said she had no money and attempted to shut the door. Defendant forced open the door and shoved Victim backward onto a sofa. Victim screamed, at which point another man entered and Victim's roommate appeared and began screaming. Defendant and the other man fled. Defendant is now charged with burglary (P.C. § 459). What arguments should be made as to whether he is guilty?

People v. Kwok

63 Cal. App. 4th 1236, 75 Cal.Rptr.2d 40 (1998)

Phelan, Presiding Justice.

Elliot Kwok appeals from a final judgment of conviction following jury trial. He claims he could not be found guilty of residential burglary for an entry into the victim's residence where he removed a lock mechanism, took it to a locksmith who made a key which appellant retained, and then returned the lock to its original position. He argues that no burglary was committed because he did not take the lock

---

as evidences of legislative intent, have little value" (*Dyna-Med, Inc. v. Fair Employment & Housing Com.* (1987) 43 Cal.3d 1379, and cases cited), and provisions contained within unpassed *omnibus* bills are, if anything, even less reliable indicants of legislative intent. Nonetheless, this history does reveal that although there have been some relatively recent attempts to limit the term "room" in section 459, to date no such proposal has been adopted.

with the intent permanently to deprive the victim of it. Rather, his intent at time of entry was to commit a felony assault on the victim on a future date.

We reject his arguments and affirm.

Factual and Procedural Background

1. *Procedural History*

A grand jury indictment was filed in Contra Costa County accusing appellant of the attempted murder of Desli L. on March 6, 1995, in violation of sections 187 and 664 (count 1). The indictment also included two counts of first degree burglary of her Walnut Creek residence (count 2 and count 3) in violation of sections 459 and 460, subdivision (a). Count 2 accused him of entering her residence on or about March 6, 1995, with intent to commit false imprisonment, assault with intent to commit rape, and intent to commit murder. Count 3 accused appellant of entering Desli's home on February 24, 1995, with intent to commit theft, false imprisonment, assault with intent to commit rape, and intent to commit murder.

A jury found appellant not guilty of attempted murder, but guilty of the lesser included offense of assault by means of force likely to produce great bodily injury (§ 245, subd. (a)(1)). The jury also found him guilty of both first degree burglaries.

2. *Facts*

[Appellant and Desli first met two and a half years earlier when she was a nursing student and he was her instructor. In the nine months before the incident, they saw each other two or three times a month for dinner or walks.]

In January 1995, while appellant was dining at Desli's home, he mentioned that he was very handy and that if she required any household repairs he might be able to help her. She asked him to look at the door between her garage and her kitchen because it was hard to lock; she believed the strike plate needed to be adjusted so it would line up with the deadbolt. After tinkering with the strike plate, appellant asked if he could remove the whole lock. She told him that was not necessary because, as far as she knew, there was nothing wrong with the lock itself; only the strike plate needed to be adjusted. She told appellant she would have it fixed by a friend who was already doing some repairs around her home.

Desli did not have a key to the door between the garage and the kitchen, so it remained unlocked whenever she left her home through the garage. When she was home, however, she always deadbolted the door from the inside. Appellant knew there was no key for this door because once, when he and Desli were leaving the residence through the garage, he pointed out that she had forgotten to lock the door between the garage and the kitchen. She responded that she did not have a key for that door and that it did not need to be locked because the garage door would be closed.

Desli testified that she never asked appellant to make a key for the kitchen door. Although he admitted she had never asked him to have a key made, he claimed that he volunteered to do so and that she did not object. He also claimed that, in late January, she allowed him to copy the code from her garage door opener so he could program one of his old openers, which would allow him to enter her garage to fix the kitchen door when she was not at home. Desli denied she ever gave appellant permission to enter her home when she was not there, either to repair the kitchen door or for any other purpose. She also denied ever giving him permission to have a garage door opener programmed with her code. She did, however, describe an occasion in early February 1995 when appellant had access to her garage door opener outside her presence and thus an opportunity to copy the code.

On February 24, 1995, appellant came to Desli's house when he knew she would be at work and used the garage door opener programmed with her code to enter. He then removed the lock from the kitchen door and took it to a nearby locksmith to have a key made. The locksmith was able to make the key within an hour by using a code machine and information obtained from the lock assembly itself. Appellant then returned to the house and reinstalled the lock. He claimed that the day before he removed the lock he left a message on Desli's answering machine informing her that he was going to have a key made the following day, and that the day after the key was made, he left another message telling her it had been done. Desli denied receiving any such messages. Appellant did not leave the key when he reinstalled the lock. Desli testified that when she came home from work on February 24th, she saw nothing unusual about the door.

Appellant and Desli planned to have dinner together on Monday, March 6, 1995, when he was going to help her with a laptop computer she borrowed from him. On Sunday, March 5, however, she left him a telephone message, asking if they could reschedule their dinner to a date later in the week. She told him she had been asked to work that evening—Sunday—until 11 p.m., and because he would probably be in bed by the time she got home, he could call her Monday morning, presumably to discuss their revised dinner plans.

Since early February, before he had the key made, appellant had been planning what he characterized as a "surprise" for Desli. He testified that he planned this "surprise" because she told him he was "always shy" and that he "needed to be more outgoing[,] outrageous." He thought that after the "surprise," which he said would involve hiding in her house and acting like a "ghost" or a "robber," he and Desli would "laugh about it" and "have fun," which might possibly lead to sexual intercourse. He got the idea for the "surprise" when watching the movie *True Lies*, in which a husband breaks into his wife's hotel room while wearing a disguise and plays some sort of tape to her. Inspired by the movie, in early February he made an audio tape of a character in the movie *Beverly Hills Cop II*, saying "Shut up. I'm going to kill you," which he thought he might use as part of the "surprise."

When appellant received Desli's telephone message on Sunday, March 5, he thought this would be an opportune time to go forward with his plan. Shortly before he expected her to arrive home from work, he went to her house and entered it using the garage door opener programmed with her code. Apparently he did not need to use the key to get into the kitchen because Desli was not yet inside with the deadbolt locked behind her. He brought with him a duffel bag containing a video camera, a

Polaroid camera, a bottle of whiskey, a piece of wire cut from a coat hanger, a flashlight, a can of topical anesthetic spray, the taped dialog from *Beverly Hills Cop II*, and a condom. Appellant also took considerable pains to prevent his identity from being discovered and to insure that his surreptitious entry would not be detected before he could spring his "surprise." He wore dark clothing, gloves, and a ski mask and drove a car which Desli had never before seen him drive. He parked the car around the corner from her house, and covered the license plate with an old plate he had in his garage. Because appellant knew that Desli had a part-time housemate, he also rang the door bell before entering the garage to make sure no one was home. After entering the house, he gathered a number of additional items to use in playing out the "surprise," including a pillow, which he stuffed in his sweatshirt to make himself look fat; a large kitchen knife; and a martingale, which is a bridle-like piece of equestrian equipment Desli kept in her garage. In addition, he had a roll of duct tape, a pair of Desli's panty hose, and a pair of her panties.

Although Desli had told appellant she would be working until 11 p.m. Sunday night, in fact, she unexpectedly had to work until 2 a.m. Monday morning. Appellant testified that when she failed to arrive as expected, he fell asleep in a spare room and did not wake up until after 3 a.m. By that time she was already asleep. He then proceeded with the "surprise," the details of which need not be recounted here because they are not relevant to the issues on appeal. Suffice it to say that Desli was, indeed, surprised when appellant climbed onto her bed, put his hands around her neck, and played the tape that said, "Shut up. I'm going to kill you." She woke up, and after a fierce struggle, managed to escape after smashing appellant in the face with her clock radio. She ran to the home of a neighbor, who took her in and called 911. When Contra Costa County sheriff deputies arrived, they apprehended appellant, who was still lying on the floor in her bedroom.

Discussion

I. *There is Substantial Evidence of the Requisite Intent to Support the Conviction of the February 1995 Burglary.*

...

Appellant's argument that the February entry into Desli's residence was not a burglary is two-fold: first, he asserts that there is no evidence that he "intended to permanently deprive [Desli] of any property when he entered her home on February 24th," and, second, he asserts that, even if he entered with the intent to commit a felony at a later time, that does not constitute "the requisite intent to commit a theft or a felony at the time of the entry ..." We address the second argument first.

A. Entry with Intent to Facilitate Commission of Theft or a Felony on a Later Occasion Satisfies the Intent Requirement of Section 459.

Appellant now concedes that, "The evidence in this case is clear the February 24th entry was made with the intent to facilitate the later entry," and that the later entry was made "for purposes of committing the assault on [Desli.]" He contends, however, that entry into her residence with the intent to facilitate commission of crimes on a future occasion does not constitute the requisite intent for burglary. In other words, he argues that the February 24th entry was not a burglary because there was no evidence he intended to commit theft or any felony on the same occasion as the entry. Appellant interprets the phrase "enters ... with intent to commit grand or petit larceny or any felony" in section 459 as if it pertains to the time when the target or predicate crime must be committed, rather than to the time when the intent must exist. Appellant cites no authority for his reading of the statute, and, indeed, the phrase "enters ... with intent" has been uniformly construed to mean that the intent to commit the theft or felony must exist at the time of entry, not that the target crime must be committed then and there. As a practical matter, if the defendant commits, or gives some indication of intending to commit, theft or a felony in a building shortly after entering it, no great inferential leap is necessary to conclude that the intent to commit the supporting offense existed at the time of entry. Thus, temporal or spatial proximity between the entry and the target or predicate crime are factors that may reasonably be considered by the jury when determining whether the requisite intent existed at the moment of entry, but they are not elements of the crime of burglary.

In *People v. Wright* (1962) 206 Cal. App. 2d 184, a case that focused on the issue of spatial proximity, the defendant argued that his entry into a building to gain access to an adjoining bin-like shed (which was not subject to the burglary statute) in order to steal tires was not burglary because he did not intend to steal property from the building itself. The court rejected this argument, observing that the defendant was attempting to read the word "therein" into the statute. The court held that, for purposes of section 459, the requisite intent is not limited to an intent to commit the target crime within the building entered. The *Wright* court explained, a burglary is committed "if the intent at the time of entry is to commit the offense in the immediate vicinity of the place entered by defendant; if the entry is made as a means of facilitating the commission of the theft or felony; and if the two places are so closely connected that intent and consummation of the crime would constitute a single and practically continuous transaction." The *Wright* test was also applied in *People v. Nance* (1972) 25 Cal. App. 3d 925, where the court held that defendant committed burglary when he entered a gas station in order to flip a switch to enable him to steal gasoline from pumps located outside the structure and in *People v. Nunley* (1985) 168 Cal. App. 3d 225, where the court held that defendant committed burglary when he entered the lobby of an apartment building with the intent to burglarize one of the units.

Like the defendant in *Wright* who attempted to read the word "therein" into section 459, appellant here attempts to read the phrase "on the same occasion" into the statute. He concedes, however, that what he refers to as the "requirements of temporal and physical proximity" were relaxed in *People v. Ortega* (1992) 11 Cal. App. 4th 691, in which the court held that one who enters a home to commit extortion is guilty of burglary even though the extortion will not be completed until sometime in the future and at a location other than where the entry took place. He attempts to distinguish *Ortega* by asserting "extortion is unique," and argues that, "Under the facts of this case, there is no reason to further relax the 'immediate vicinity' or 'continuous transaction' tests set forth in *People v. Wright*." We agree, as the *Ortega* court noted, that extortion differs from "the typical theft committed in a burglary" because "in extortion, there is usually a passage of time between the threat and the completed extortion." However, there is no principled way to distinguish extortion from other felonies or from larceny, if the facts and circumstances of the case permit a reasonable inference that the entry was made in order to facilitate commission of the subsequent crime, even though the entry and the subsequent crime "may not share the attributes of proximity in time and place."

As respondent persuasively argues, the "continuous transaction test" and the "immediate vicinity test" invoked by appellant are artifacts of the particular factual contexts of *Wright*, *Nance*, and *Nunley*. The fact that the entry and the intended felony were part of a continuous transaction or that the defendant intended to commit the supporting felony in the immediate vicinity of the building entered describe the crimes in those cases, but not the law as generally applicable when some felony other than a theft from an adjacent area is intended. Even *Ortega*, which purported to rely on the "continuous transaction" factor of *Wright*, rested principally on the "facilitation" factor, because the burglary conviction was based on the fact that the defendant entered the victim's room in order to obtain the means of committing extortion, not only at a different place, but also at a later time. Thus, the entry and the planned extortion were not truly a "continuous transaction," if that phrase is taken to mean a temporally seamless event or sequence of events that occurs within a very short period of time. Rather, the entry and the extortion were separate but causally or transactionally related events, the entry having been made to secure the means of committing the later crime.

Here, a jury could reasonably infer from the circumstances of this case that appellant entered Desli's residence with the intent to take steps that would facilitate commission of the subsequent crimes. Given the nature of the "surprise" he planned, it is reasonable to infer that he intended to assault Desli while she was sleeping. Obtaining a key to the kitchen door facilitated the attack, not in the sense that using the key was an integral part of the assault or that it provided the direct means by which the assault was committed, but in the sense that it made appellant's scheme more convenient and less risky for him.

If the jury can reasonably infer from a defendant's conduct and other circumstances of a case that he or she entered a building in order to facilitate commission of theft or a felony, we conclude the defendant need not intend to commit the target crime in the same building or on the same occasion as the entry in order to be guilty of burglary. Here, the burglary conviction is supported by substantial evidence because the jury could reasonably infer from the nature of the "surprise" and the steps appellant took to carry it out that he entered Desli's residence on February 24 with the intent to obtain a key to facilitate the commission of the assault nine days later.

[The court also upheld the conviction for the February 24 burglary on the alternate ground that the entry with the intent to acquire a key to Desli's house was an entry to commit theft. Although acknowledging that there was no California authority on the issue, the court reasoned that "property is something that one has the exclusive right to possess and use" and that, by making an unauthorized copy of Desli's key, defendant had effectively stolen her exclusive right to control access to her house just as thoroughly as if he had stolen an existing key to the house.]

Problem

Problem 65.

Defendant and Victim had been dating for four months. On the night in question, Defendant had decided that, one way or another, he was going to have sex with Victim that night. When they returned to Victim's apartment, Defendant tried to seduce Victim, but she refused him. Defendant then attempted to force himself upon Victim, but she fought back, and he gave up and left. Defendant is now charged with burglary (P.C. § 459). What arguments should be made as to his guilt?

People v. Salemme

2 Cal. App. 4th 775, 3 Cal.Rptr.2d 398 (1992)

SCOTLAND, J.

This case poses the question whether defendant's alleged entry into the home of an intended victim for the purpose of selling fraudulent securities constituted burglary. Defendant contends it did not because the purpose of our state's burglary statutes is "to protect against dangers inherent in intrusion" and, on the facts of this case, "there could be no danger from the mere entry of [the victim's] residence [for the purpose of selling fraudulent securities]." The People retort that defendant committed burglary when he entered the victim's residence to commit a felony, sale of fraudulent securities, whether or not the entry presented an imminent threat of physical harm to the victim. In the People's view, California's burglary statutes (Pen. Code, §§ 459, 460) encompass an entry into a structure with the intent to commit any felony, not just "felonies of violence or felonies which may induce a violent response from the victim."

...

Facts

At the preliminary examination in this action, the People introduced evidence that, on two occasions, defendant entered the home of William Zimmerman with the intent to sell him fraudulent securities and that defendant twice succeeded in convincing Zimmerman to purchase the securities. The victim initially invested $9,900. He later spent an additional $1,100.

By amended information, defendant was charged with two counts of burglary (Pen. Code, §§ 459, 460) ... Pursuant to Penal Code section 995, defendant moved to set aside the burglary counts. He argued the evidence elicited at the preliminary hearing was insufficient to support the charges because "the purpose of the burglary laws are [sic] to protect against dangers inherent in intrusion; no such situation arises on the facts of this case." The trial court agreed and granted the motion. The People appeal.

Discussion

Penal Code section 459 provides in pertinent part: "Every person who enters any house ... or other building ... with intent to commit grand or petit larceny or *any* felony is guilty of burglary...." (Italics added.)

A century ago, our Supreme Court held that an entry into a store with the intent to commit larceny constituted burglary under section 459 (*People v. Barry* (1892) 94 Cal. 481). Noting that "common law burglary and the statutory burglary of this state have but few elements in common," the court concluded: "the language [of section 459] is so plain and simple that rules of statutory construction are not required to be consulted; the meaning is patent upon the face of the statute. No words are found in the statute qualifying the character, kind, time, or manner of the entry, save that such entry must be accompanied with a certain intent; and it would be judicial legislation for this court to interpolate other conditions into the section of the code."

For 83 years, this plain meaning applied: any entry with the intent to commit a felony into any structure enumerated in section 459 constituted burglary regardless of the circumstances of the entry.

In 1975, the Supreme Court revisited the issue of statutory interpretation of section 459 when the court was presented with the question whether a person can burglarize his or her own home (*People v. Gauze* (1975) 15 Cal. 3d 709). Examining "the purposes underlying common law burglary and how they may have been affected by the enactment of the Penal Code," the court concluded that the plain meaning of the statute is inconsistent with its purpose when applied to one accused of burglarizing his or her own home....

[The court reviewed the precedent cases.]

We learn from these cases that, since burglary is a breach of the occupant's possessory rights, a person who enters a structure enumerated in section 459 with the intent to commit a felony is guilty of burglary except when he or she (1) has an unconditional possessory right to enter as the occupant of that structure or (2) is invited in by the occupant who knows of and endorses the felonious intent.

Neither condition was satisfied in this case. Nevertheless, defendant argues his alleged entry did not constitute burglary because the act posed no physical danger to the victim who had invited defendant in to negotiate the sale of securities.

It is true that dicta in *Gauze* and *People v. Superior Court (Granillo)* (1988) 205 Cal.App.3d 1478 indicate one of the purposes of California's burglary laws is to protect against the dangers to personal safety created by the "usual burglary situation." However, as noted above, the primary purpose is to protect a possessory right in property.

Thus, if there is an invasion of the occupant's possessory rights, the entry constitutes burglary regardless of whether actual or potential danger exists.

For example, the shoplifter who surreptitiously enters a store with the intent to steal commits burglary even though his or her clandestine effort to slip merchandise into a jacket does not necessarily threaten anyone's personal safety. Defendant has not distinguished the shoplifting scenario from this case and, in our view, there is no logical way to do so. As in the shoplifting cases, defendant did not have an unconditional possessory right to enter the victim's residence. Rather, he allegedly did so with the victim's uninformed consent, i.e. his lack of knowledge of defendant's felonious intent. Had the victim known thereof, he could have refused admission at the threshold or ejected defendant after entry was accomplished. Consequently, defendant's alleged entry constituted burglary regardless of whether his intent "to swindle the victim out of money by misleading him into buying unqualified securities" posed a physical danger to the victim.

In effect, defendant would write into section 459 the requirement that the perpetrator must intend to commit a felony which poses a physical danger to the victim, rather than "any felony" as specified by the Legislature. This interpretation is not compelled by the purpose of the burglary statutes as discussed above and would constitute impermissible judicial legislation. Moreover, it creates an unworkable test. Whether a felonious entry poses a physical danger to the victim is fact specific; it depends not on the particular felony, but on the sophistication of the perpetrator, the potential for detection, and the reactions of the victim and perpetrator if the felonious purpose is detected. It is not unreasonable to envision a fraudulent securities transaction where, upon probing questioning about the purchase, the victim discovers the illegality, attempts to call the police, and is attacked by the perpetrator. Other than speculation, how is one to determine whether such a potential threat existed in this case? On the other hand, there are residential burglaries which pose no physical danger to the victim, as where the perpetrator breaks into a house knowing the occupants are away on vacation. Would defendant argue this is not a burglary simply because it poses no physical threat to the victims?

For the reasons we have stated, the trial court erred in setting aside the burglary counts.

[Concurring opinion of Blease, Acting P.J. omitted.]

Chapter 9

Inchoate Crimes

The crimes covered in this chapter—attempt (Section A), solicitation (Section B) and conspiracy (Section C)—have in common the fact that they deal with conduct that is intended to culminate in the commission of another offense but that falls short of achieving that result. Because, by definition, the ultimate harm to society has not occurred, in each of these crimes, the mental element assumes a greater role than in other crimes. As to each of the crimes, consider what the justification is for punishing a defendant who has not caused harm to society or whether it can be said that, merely by taking steps toward criminal activity, the defendant has in fact harmed society. Section D addresses an issue common to all three crimes: when does the fact that completion of the object crime was, under the circumstances, impossible, constitute a defense?

A. Attempt

The following four cases deal with attempt crimes. Under Penal Code § 664, attempt crimes are generally punished with half the penalty of the completed crime. *People v. Collie* discusses the mental state element of attempt crimes, in particular, the issue of whether one can attempt an unintentional crime. In *People v. Smith*, the court divides over the question whether the defendant, who fired a single shot in the direction of two people, can be guilty of attempted murder as to both. *People v. Staples* concerns what conduct is sufficient to constitute an attempt, as opposed to "mere preparation." The court in *Staples* also discusses the significance of a defendant's abandonment of criminal activity prior to the completion of the crime. In *People v. Decker*, the court explores the difference between attempt and the lesser crime of solicitation.

People v. Collie

30 Cal. 3d 43, 634 P.2d 534 (1981)

Mosk, J.

...

I

On the evening of July 6, 1978, defendant Bertram Collie visited his estranged wife at her residence, as he had often done before. She and her daughter were in the bedroom watching television and, as defendant entered, the daughter retired to her own room, where she remained for the evening.

Defendant invited his wife to drink and to have sexual intercourse with him, but she refused. He subsequently bound her feet and hands and forcibly sodomized her. He then taped her mouth, ransacked the bedroom, left the room, and locked the door behind him. His wife heard him leave the house at about midnight.

Mrs. Collie then detected the odor of gas. She managed to free herself and unlock the door, and found that the stove burners were turned on, unlit. She turned them off. In the dining room she discovered and extinguished a lighted candle surrounded by combustible material. She then awakened her daughter, who was safe in her own bedroom and oblivious to all that had occurred.

[Defendant asserted an alibi defense.]

The jury found defendant guilty of attempted first degree murder of his wife, attempted second degree murder of his daughter, and forcible sodomy.

. . .

III

Defendant correctly contends that the trial court erred in instructing the jury that it could convict of attempted second degree murder despite the absence of a specific intent to kill. The court instructed the jury in the language of CALJIC No. 8.31 (1974 rev.) which, as modified by the court in the language we have italicized, reads as follows: "Murder of the second degree is [also] the unlawful killing of a human being as the direct causal result of an act involving a high degree of probability that it will result in death, which act is done for a base, antisocial purpose and with wanton disregard for human life by which is meant an awareness of a duty imposed by law not to commit such acts followed by the commission of the forbidden act despite that awareness. When the killing, *or the attempted killing in this case*, is the direct result of such an act, it is not necessary to establish that the defendant intended that his act would result in the death of a human being."

In *People v. Murtishaw* (1981) 29 Cal. 3d 733, we held that an assault with intent to commit murder required express malice, and could not be founded on the malice implied from reckless conduct with wanton disregard for human life. Relying on a line of authority originating in *People v. Mize* (1889) 80 Cal. 41, we observed, "once a defendant intends to kill, any malice he may harbor is necessarily express malice. Implied malice, as defined in CALJIC No. 8.11 [and CALJIC No. 8.31], cannot coexist with a specific intent to kill. To instruct on implied malice in that setting, therefore, may confuse the jury by suggesting that they can convict without finding a specific intent to kill."

The same reasoning applies to attempted murder. "Specific intent to kill is a necessary element of attempted murder. It must be proved, and it cannot be inferred merely from the commission of another dangerous crime" (*People v. Belton* (1980) 105 Cal. App. 3d 376). Hence the trial court erred in instructing the jury that it need not find a specific intent to kill in order to convict of attempted murder.

The instructional error was harmless regarding the conviction for the attempted first degree murder of Mrs. Collie, because the jury was properly instructed that the verdict required findings of premeditation and deliberation, which entail a specific intent to kill. But the verdict of guilt on the attempted second degree murder charge was not insulated from error. Although the jury was properly instructed that a specific intent to kill would satisfy the intent requirement of an attempted second degree murder charge, it is impossible to determine whether the verdict rested on that ground, for which there was little evidence, or on the impermissible basis of defendant's wanton conduct, which was more clearly supported by the record. Because we cannot know on which instruction the jury relied, the conviction for attempted second degree murder of defendant's daughter must be reversed.

...

People v. Smith

37 Cal.4th 733, 124 P.3d 730 (2005)

Baxter, J.

The defendant in this case challenges the sufficiency of the evidence to support his conviction of two counts of attempted murder where he fired a single bullet into a slowly moving vehicle, narrowly missing a mother and her infant son. The evidence showed that the mother, who was known to defendant and was driving, and her baby, who was secured in a car seat directly behind her, were each in defendant's line of fire when he fired a single .38-caliber round at them from behind the car as it pulled away from the curb. The bullet shattered the rear windshield, narrowly missed both the mother and baby, passed through the mother's headrest, and lodged in the driver's side door.

On appeal, defendant contends his conviction of the attempted murder of the baby must be reversed for lack of substantial evidence that he harbored the requisite specific intent to kill the child. We disagree. Under the applicable deferential standard of review, we conclude the evidence is sufficient to support the jury's verdict finding defendant acted with intent to kill the baby as well as the mother. The fact that only a single bullet was fired into the vehicle does not, as a matter of law, compel a different conclusion. Accordingly, the judgment of the Court of Appeal shall be affirmed.

FACTS AND PROCEDURAL BACKGROUND

On the afternoon of February 18, 2000, Karen A. drove her boyfriend, Renell T., Sr. (Renell), to a friend's house on Greenholme Lane in Sacramento. She was driving her four-door Chevy Lumina, with Renell seated in the front passenger seat and their three-month-old baby, Renell T., Jr., secured in a rear-facing infant car seat in the backseat directly behind her. She parked alongside the curb on the street in front of the house, and Renell got out of the car. As Karen waited in the car to make sure Renell's friend was home, she saw defendant approaching from behind. Karen recognized defendant as a former friend. She had last spoken to him during a telephone conversation eight to nine months earlier during which he had told her the next time he saw her he would "slap the s___ out of [her]."

Defendant walked up to the open front passenger window of Karen's car, looked inside and said, "Don't I know you, bitch?" Overhearing the statement, Renell turned around from the walkway leading to the house and said, "Well, you don't know me." As Renell walked back toward the car, defendant lifted his shirt to display a handgun tucked in his waistband. Renell said, "It is cool," and backed away from defendant. According to Karen, a group of men on the street corner began approaching the car, and as Renell was entering the vehicle through the front passenger door, defendant and the other men began hitting him.

As soon as Renell was securely inside the car, Karen started to pull away from the curb. After driving about one car length, she looked in her rearview mirror and saw defendant standing "[s]traight behind" her holding a gun. She heard a single gunshot, and although she did not see defendant pull the trigger, he was the only person she had seen with a gun. The bullet shattered the rear windshield, narrowly missed both Karen and the baby, passed through the driver's headrest, and lodged in the driver's side door. As soon as Karen reached a place of safety, she stopped to check the baby for injuries. He was screaming, his face covered with pieces of broken glass.

...

[Defendant's testimony—that it was Renell, not he, who had the gun and that Defendant did not fire at the car—was evidently disbelieved by the jury which found him guilty of attempted murder of Karen A., attempted murder of the baby, shooting at an occupied vehicle, child endangerment and assault with a firearm.]

DISCUSSION

Defendant does not challenge his conviction of the attempted murder of Karen. A. But he argues his conviction of the attempted murder of the baby must be reversed because, as stated in his opening brief, "only a single attempted murder conviction was possible on the facts here." Specifically, defendant asserts that the fact that he fired only one bullet into the vehicle reflects his intent to kill only one victim—Karen A. He urges that "there was no proof of animus toward the baby," and argues his conviction of the attempted murder of that victim must be reversed for lack of substantial evidence that he harbored specific intent to kill the child.

In reviewing a sufficiency of evidence claim, the reviewing court's role is a limited one. "The proper test for determining a claim of insufficiency of evidence in a criminal case is whether, on the entire record, a rational trier of fact could find the defendant guilty beyond a reasonable doubt. On appeal, we must view the evidence in the light most favorable to the People and must presume in support of the judgment the existence of every fact the trier could reasonably deduce from the evidence" (*People v. Ochoa* (1993) 6 Cal.4th 1199).

"Although we must ensure the evidence is reasonable, credible, and of solid value, nonetheless it is the exclusive province of the trial judge or jury to determine the credibility of a witness and the truth or falsity of the facts on which that determination depends. Thus, if the verdict is supported by substantial evidence, we must accord due deference to the trier of fact and not substitute our evaluation of a witness's credibility for that of the fact finder." (*Id.*)

We first consider the mental state required for conviction of attempted murder. "The mental state required for attempted murder has long differed from that required for murder itself. Murder does not require the intent to kill. Implied malice—a conscious disregard for life—suffices." (*People v. Bland* (2002) 28 Cal.4th 313 (*Bland.*)) In contrast, "[a]ttempted murder requires the specific intent to kill and the commission of a direct but ineffectual act toward accomplishing the intended killing." (*People v. Lee* (2003) 31 Cal.4th 613.) Hence, in order for defendant to be convicted of the attempted murder of the baby, the prosecution had to prove he acted with specific intent to kill that victim. (*Bland, supra.*)

Intent to unlawfully kill and express malice are, in essence, "one and the same." (*People v. Saille* (1991) 54 Cal.3d 1103.) To be guilty of attempted murder of the baby, defendant had to harbor express malice toward that victim. Express malice requires a showing that the assailant "either desires the result, i.e., death, or knows, to a substantial certainty, that the result will occur." (*People v. Davenport* (1985) 41 Cal.3d 247.)

The mental state required for *attempted* murder is further distinguished from the mental state required for murder in that the doctrine of "transferred intent" applies to murder but not attempted murder. (*Bland, supra.*) "In its classic form, the doctrine of transferred intent applies when the defendant intends to kill one person but mistakenly kills another. The intent to kill the intended target is deemed to transfer to the unintended victim so that the defendant is guilty of murder." (*Id.*) In contrast, the doctrine of transferred intent does not apply to attempted murder: "To be guilty of attempted murder, the defendant must intend to kill the alleged victim, not someone else." (*Bland, supra.*) Whether the defendant acted with specific intent to kill "must be judged separately as to each alleged victim." (*Id.*)

...

Applying these principles to the facts at hand, and viewing the evidence in the light most favorable to the People, presuming the existence of every fact the jury could reasonably deduce from the evidence in support of the judgment, we conclude the evidence is sufficient to support defendant's conviction of the attempted murder of the baby.

...

.... [W]e conclude a rational jury could find beyond a reasonable doubt that defendant intended to kill the baby as well as the mother. Defendant suggests in his brief on the merits that "there was no proof of [his] animus toward the baby." But his very act of discharging a firearm into the car from close range and narrowly missing both mother and baby could itself support such an inference. Indeed, given defendant's claim at trial that Karen was his ex-girlfriend, and given the circumstance that she had just arrived on the scene with a new boyfriend and their baby, the jury could well have inferred that defendant felt "animus" toward both the mother and her baby when he started shooting. In any event, even if defendant subjectively believed he had a particular reason or cause to shoot at the mother, that does not preclude a finding that he also harbored express malice toward the baby when he fired into the vehicle with both victims directly in his line of fire. Defendant's assertion on appeal—that his motive to kill Karen but not the baby establishes his intent to kill her but precludes a finding that he also harbored express malice toward the baby—is without support in the facts or the law.

Defendant further argues that "[he] fired from a point very near the car, and thus a 'high potential for accuracy' existed." He asks this court to infer from that circumstance that "the fact that the baby was *not* hit, under such conditions of accuracy, tends to prove the baby was *not* a target." In light of the deferential standard of review that applies to this sufficiency of evidence claim, we must reject his interpretation of the evidence.

...

In urging the Court of Appeal to reverse his conviction of the attempted murder of the baby on grounds of insufficient evidence, defendant asserted that this court's opinion in *Bland, supra*, "provide[s] the essential key for analysis of the sufficiency of the evidence issue here." He argued to the court that *Bland* "makes it perfectly clear that only one count of attempted murder can stand on these facts" because, according to defendant, here there was "no evidence whatsoever that [defendant] had any motive or intent to kill the baby, himself," and *Bland*'s kill zone exception does not apply because "[t]his is not a bomb-on-the-airplane case or a rocket-propelled-grenade case or a hail-of-bullets case; this is a single-shot case."

Defendant misreads this court's decision in *Bland*. *Bland*'s "kill zone" theory does not preclude a conclusion that defendant's act of firing a single bullet at Karen and her baby, both of whom were in his direct line of fire, can support two convictions of attempted murder under the totality of the circumstances shown by the evidence. *Bland* simply recognizes that a shooter may be convicted of multiple counts of attempted murder on a "kill zone" theory where the evidence establishes that the shooter used lethal force designed and intended to kill everyone in an area around the targeted victim (i.e., the "kill zone") as the means of accomplishing the killing of that victim. Under such circumstances, a rational jury could conclude beyond a reasonable doubt that the shooter intended to kill not only his targeted victim, but also all others he knew were in the zone of fatal harm. As we explained in *Bland*, "This concurrent intent [i.e., 'kill zone'] theory is not a legal doctrine requiring special jury instructions.... Rather, it is simply a reasonable inference the jury may draw in a given case: a primary intent to kill a specific target does not rule out a concurrent intent to kill others."

...

Defendant's display of hostility toward Karen A. surely constituted some evidence that he had a motive to shoot at her, which in turn was probative of whether he intended to kill her. But the fact that defendant displayed "overt hostility" toward Karen A. moments before the shooting was not the *only* evidence that he shot at her with intent to kill. Defendant's very act of discharging a lethal firearm at her from close range "in a manner that could have inflicted a mortal wound" (*People v. Chinchilla* (1997) 52 Cal.App.4th 683) is itself evidence sufficient to support an inference of intent to kill.

The question whether the evidence was sufficient to support defendant's conviction of the attempted murder of the baby must be analyzed in the same way. The physical evidence showed both Karen A. and her baby were directly in defendant's line of fire; the testimonial evidence established defendant had looked into the open passenger window of the vehicle moments before the shooting and knew the baby was positioned in the backseat directly behind her. The bullet missed both the mother *and* the baby by inches. Although there was evidence that defendant exhibited overt animosity toward Karen A., which is probative of whether he acted with intent to kill her, the facts also support an inference that defendant intended to kill the baby as well. The infant was the offspring of Karen A. and her current boyfriend, the baby's father, all three of whom had just arrived on the scene only moments before defendant's hostile verbal exchange with the mother, his physical altercation with the father, and his determination to shoot at the mother and child as the vehicle pulled away from the curb. The jury could have concluded that because defendant viewed Karen A. as his former girlfriend, he harbored animosity toward the child she had with her current boyfriend.

Viewing the record in the light most favorable to the conviction obtained by the prosecution below, we conclude the evidence is sufficient to support defendant's conviction of the attempted murder of the baby. The fact that only a single bullet was fired into the vehicle, or that defendant exhibited overt animosity toward the mother but not the baby moments before the shooting, does not, as a matter of law, compel a different result.

CONCLUSION

The judgment of the Court of Appeal is affirmed, and the matter remanded to that court for further proceedings consistent with the views expressed herein.

Werdegar, J., dissenting, joined by Moreno, J.

I respectfully dissent. In my view, defendant's conviction for the attempted murder of Renell T., Jr., is unsupported by substantial evidence.

Defendant fired a single bullet into a moving car, narrowly missing the driver and her infant son, after quarreling with the driver and the driver's boyfriend. There was ample evidence to support the jury's finding defendant was trying to kill the driver. The evidence was ample also that he acted recklessly, or even with conscious disregard for life, as to the baby. The evidence was insufficient, however, to permit the jury to infer beyond a reasonable doubt that defendant *intended to kill the baby*, with whom, as far as the evidence showed, defendant had no quarrel at all. The majority struggles to articulate grounds for upholding the second attempted murder conviction. In the course of that struggle, the majority loses sight of the crucial difference between implied malice, or conscious disregard for life, and express malice, which is the specific intent to kill a person.

The majority reasons that because both Karen and her son were in the line of defendant's fire, and therefore defendant's single shot could have killed either, the jury could infer he intended to kill both. That defendant had displayed overt hostility toward Karen and none at all toward the baby is, in the majority's view, immaterial because conviction of attempted murder does not require proof of a motive for killing. The majority is of course correct that intent may ordinarily be inferred from action. But to support the inference that defendant intended to kill the infant, the majority points to no aspect of defendant's action other than that he placed the infant's life in danger by shooting in his direction. The majority thus permits knowing endangerment, which establishes at most *implied* malice, to serve, by itself, as proof beyond a reasonable doubt of intent to kill. This result is contrary to fundamental concepts of California homicide law recognized in the majority opinion and discussed further below, in particular the distinction between implied and express malice and the requirement that the latter be proven as an element of attempted murder.

...

DISCUSSION

The only question before the court is the sufficiency of evidence to prove defendant attempted to kill Renell T., Jr., Karen and Renell's three-month-old infant....

"Attempted murder requires the specific intent to kill and the commission of a direct but ineffectual act toward accomplishing the intended killing." (*People v. Lee* (2003) 31 Cal.4th 613.) "The mental state required for attempted murder has long differed from that required for murder itself." (*People v. Bland* (2002) 28 Cal.4th 313.) For murder, malice may be express or implied. "Malice is *express* when the killer harbors a deliberate intent to unlawfully take away a human life. Malice is *implied* when the killer lacks an intent to kill but acts with conscious disregard for life, knowing such conduct endangers the life of another." (*People v. Lasko* (2000) 23 Cal.4th 101; § 188.) To be guilty of attempted murder, the defendant must harbor express malice; implied malice will not suffice. Express malice, or intent to kill, requires more than knowingly placing the victim's life in danger: it requires at the least that the assailant either "desire the result," i.e., death, or "know, to a substantial certainty, that the result will occur." (*People v. Davenport* (1985) 41 Cal.3d 247.)

We also "distinguish between a completed murder and attempted murder regarding transferred intent." (*Bland, supra.*) "In its classic form, the doctrine of transferred intent applies when the defendant intends to kill one person but mistakenly kills another. The intent to kill the intended target is deemed to transfer to the unintended victim so that the defendant is guilty of murder." (*Id.*) Transferred intent, however, does not apply to attempted murder: "To be guilty of attempted murder, the defendant must instead intend to kill the alleged victim, not someone else." (*Id.*) Thus the defendant's mental state "must be judged separately as to each alleged victim." (*Id.*) Thus defendant's specific intent to kill Karen, which was adequately proven by the evidence, does not "transfer" to provide the specific intent to kill her baby; the prosecution was required to prove defendant's mental state as to the baby individually.

In determining whether the prosecution met its burden, the test is whether a rational jury could have found beyond a reasonable doubt that defendant harbored the requisite specific intent to kill the baby. In his briefing, the Attorney General posited two factual theories to support the conviction: (1) that defendant actually targeted and thus intended to kill the baby, and (2) that defendant had the concurrent intent to kill the baby's mother, his primary target, and the baby, a nontargeted person.

Actual Targeting

The Attorney General contends the evidence is sufficient to support the conviction for the attempted murder of the baby on a theory of actual targeting because defendant knew the baby was seated directly behind Karen when he fired a bullet into the vehicle. The majority agrees.

. . .

The majority's argument reduces to this claim: from defendant's knowledge of the baby's location and his shooting in the direction of both Karen and the baby, the jury could reasonably infer defendant intended to kill them both. In so reasoning, the majority stretches the meaning of intent to kill so far as to make it indistinguishable from the conscious disregard for life that constitutes implied malice. If conscious disregard of a risk of death—shown here by defendant's act of firing in the baby's direction—suffices to support an inference of intent to kill, no difference is discernable between the two types of malice.

As we held in *Bland, supra,* intent to kill does not "transfer" from victim to victim for purposes of attempted murder; to prove defendant attempted to kill the baby, the prosecution had to prove he intended to kill *the baby.* Intent to kill Karen is insufficient for this charge. Defendant's evident lack of motive for killing the baby, in contrast to his marked animosity toward Karen, is critical not because motive is an element of the crime, but because his lack of motive as to the baby points to the only rational answer to the question, whom did defendant in firing his single shot actually target and intend to kill?

The majority reasons that defendant's act of firing in the child's direction, thereby placing the child's life at serious risk, shows defendant harbored animus toward the child, from which the jury could find he desired the child's death. But if, as the majority argues, the act of placing a person's life at risk, in itself, shows the intent to kill that person, nothing differentiates the two types of malice, a conclusion contrary to the fundamental California law of homicide embodied in section 188. The suggestion that endangerment also shows animus adds nothing to the analysis, for the inference of intent to kill is still being drawn from the act of endangerment.

In short, the majority would sanction an inference of intent to kill solely from an act knowingly endangering the victim. But, as noted earlier, intent to kill requires that the assailant either "desire" the victim's death or "know, to a substantial certainty, that the result will occur." (*Davenport, supra.*) Here there was no evidence, other than his act endangering the baby, that defendant *desired* the baby dead. Nor was defendant's means of attack so powerful that it made *substantially certain* the death of both Karen and her infant son. If, as the majority would have it, proof of knowing endangerment suffices to support a finding of intent to kill—without any evidence the assailant either wanted to kill the victim or acted so as to make the victim's death substantially certain—then the distinction between implied and express malice has been effectively obliterated.

The majority's reasoning potentially opens the door to an unlimited number of attempted murder convictions based on a single act intended to kill a single person—without proof the defendant used means intended to create a kill zone around the target. How, one must ask, is the number of attempted murder convictions arising from a single shot limited under the majority's reasoning? If assailant D shoots a handgun once at close range in the direction of a targeted victim, V1, who is standing in a close crowd of strangers, V2 through V10, could a jury find D intended to kill all 10 victims, even in the absence of evidence D had any reason to want V2 through V10 dead? To the suggestion D bore no animus against anyone but V1, the majority would presumably respond that "his very act of discharging a firearm into the [crowd] from close range and narrowly missing [V2 through V10] could itself support such an inference." The majority's reasoning cannot be correct, for it results in the absurd conclusion that an assailant has tried to murder everyone his act endangers.

...

Despite claiming evidence of motive is unnecessary in these circumstances, the majority repeatedly suggests defendant might have wanted to kill Karen and Renell's baby because, according to him, Karen was his former girlfriend (rather than just a friend as she testified). The jury, however, obviously did not believe defendant's version of events; if they had, they would not have convicted him at all. Even defendant's testimony, moreover, fails to support the inference the majority puts forward; defendant testified his argument with Karen the day before the confrontation with Renell arose because Karen was reluctant to give him a ride in her car, as she sometimes did. His testimony indicates he was angry at *Karen* for her reluctance and for the language she used toward him in the ensuing argument. Nothing suggests he was angry with or about the baby she had recently had with Renell.

The inference the majority would draw as to why defendant might wish to harm the infant is thus entirely speculative. It *could* be true (if one disbelieves Karen and believes defendant as to their prior relationship), but no evidence to that effect appears in the record. Speculation does not constitute substantial evidence.

Finally, even indulging this speculation and assuming defendant wanted to kill Renell T., Jr., because he was another man's son, in order to find defendant intended to kill both Karen and the baby one would also have to infer he intended somehow to hit and kill both with his single shot. Though the majority does not fully articulate its factual theory, its repeated invocation of the "large-caliber" bullet used here is presumably intended to suggest defendant intended to shoot Karen *through* her baby.

Of course, a single bullet *can* hit and even kill two people, but here (where the baby presented a notably small target and the bullet would, in addition, have had to traverse the infant car seat and the driver's seat without deflection) there was no evidence defendant was capable, or believed himself capable, of such a feat of marksmanship. Again, an appellate court's speculation cannot substitute for evidence at trial.

Concurrent Intent to Kill

Although the majority purports not to rely on this point, the Attorney General alternatively contends the evidence is sufficient to support defendant's conviction for the attempted murder of the baby on a concurrent intent theory because defendant intentionally created a "kill zone," from which the jury could reasonably infer he concurrently intended to kill both Karen, his intended target, and her baby.

We have explained that multiple attempted murder convictions may be sustained on a "kill zone," or "concurrent intent," theory when the evidence shows the defendant used lethal force of a type and extent calculated to kill everyone in an area, including but not limited to the victim shown to be the defendant's primary target, as a means of accomplishing the killing of the primary target. Under these circumstances, the fact finder could rationally infer the defendant intended to kill not only his or her primary target, but also concurrently intended to kill all those in the zone of fatal harm. (*Bland, supra.*) A kill zone, or concurrent intent, analysis, therefore, focuses on (1) whether the fact finder can rationally infer from the type and extent of force employed in the defendant's attack on the primary target that the defendant intentionally created a zone of fatal harm, and (2) whether the nontargeted alleged attempted murder victim inhabited that zone of harm.

In *Bland*, we illustrated the operation of the kill zone, or concurrent intent, theory of attempted murder with several examples: "[A]n assailant who places a bomb on a commercial airplane intending to harm a primary target on board ensures by this method of attack that all passengers will be killed. Similarly, consider a defendant who intends to kill A and, in order to ensure A's death, drives by a group consisting of A, B, and C, and attacks the group with automatic weapon fire or an explosive device devastating enough to kill everyone in the group. The defendant has intentionally created a 'kill zone' to ensure the death of his primary victim, and the trier of fact may reasonably infer from the method employed an intent to kill others concurrent with the intent to kill the primary victim." In *Bland* itself, we explained, the evidence strongly supported an inference of concurrent intent to kill: the defendant and a fellow gang member intentionally created a zone of fatal harm when they fired a "flurry of bullets" into a fleeing car, justifying convictions for attempted murder of the passengers.

Here, defendant did not fire multiple shots at Karen; he fired one bullet in Karen's direction at a distance of about a car's length from the rear of the moving vehicle. By firing a single shot, defendant did not use a type or degree of force reasonably calculated to kill everyone in the vehicle. Defendant's method of attack was not comparable to the "kill zone" examples and decisions we cited in *Bland:* detonating a bomb on a commercial airplane, using an explosive device or automatic weapon fire against a group of people, spraying wall-piercing bullets at occupied houses or mailing poisoned candy to a household. Nor was defendant's method of attack comparable to the firing of multiple gunshots into a fleeing car by the defendant in *Bland* itself. That the bullet came close to hitting Karen *and* her baby does not, without more, establish that by firing a single shot in the direction of Karen, his intended target, defendant intentionally created a zone of fatal harm around Karen such that he may be deemed to have intended to ensure her death by killing the baby as well.

The Attorney General, nevertheless, insists defendant intentionally created a zone of fatal harm by firing one bullet into the car because "[t]he baby and Karen were positioned in the car in such a way that [defendant], firing from the rear, could not have killed Karen without shooting through the baby first." This argument finds no support in the record; the evidence shows neither that the bullet necessarily had to pass through the baby to kill Karen, nor that the ammunition defendant used was of a kind likely to kill two persons in the manner the Attorney General suggests.

Although the majority disavows any reliance on the kill zone theory, the import of the majority opinion is that an act aimed at killing one person creates a kill zone that includes everyone who *could* have been killed by the act, regardless of whether the assailant used means actually calculated to kill everyone in the target's vicinity. If a single shot with a handgun constitutes not only an attempt on the life of a person at whom the jury could find the shot was actually aimed, but also an attempt on the life of anyone else nearby, the careful analysis in *Bland* was unnecessary: the limited concurrent intent theory of *Bland* would be obviated, subsumed in a much broader endangerment theory.

The majority's expansion of attempted murder liability to cover mere endangerment is unnecessary in order to ensure assailants are appropriately punished for acts that place victims' lives in danger. Unjustified shooting in other people's direction, even when not intended to kill them, will ordinarily subject the shooter to liability for assault or a related offense. Here, as noted, defendant was convicted of assault with a firearm, child endangerment and shooting at an occupied vehicle in addition to the attempted murder counts …

…

People v. Staples

6 Cal. App. 3d 61, 85 Cal. Rptr. 589 (1970)

Reppy, J.

Defendant was charged in an information with attempted burglary (Pen. Code, §§664, 459). Trial by jury was waived, and the matter submitted on the testimony contained in the transcript of the preliminary hearing together with exhibits. Defendant was found guilty. Proceedings were suspended before pronouncement of sentence, and an order was made granting defendant probation. The appeal is from the order which is deemed a final judgment.

I. The Facts

In October 1967, while his wife was away on a trip, defendant, a mathematician, under an assumed name, rented an office on the second floor of a building in Hollywood which was over the mezzanine of a bank. Directly below the mezzanine was the vault of the bank. Defendant was aware of the layout of the building, specifically of the relation of the office he rented to the bank vault. Defendant paid rent for the period from October 23 to November 23. The landlord had 10 days before commencement of the rental period within which to finish some interior repairs and painting. During this prerental period defendant brought into the office certain equipment. This included drilling tools, two acetylene gas tanks, a blow torch, a blanket, and a linoleum rug. The landlord observed these items when he came in from time to time to see how the repair work was progressing. Defendant learned from a custodian that no one was in the building on Saturdays. On Saturday, October 14, defendant drilled two groups of holes into the floor of the office above the mezzanine room. He stopped drilling before the holes went through the floor. He came back to the office several times thinking he might slowly drill down, covering the holes with the linoleum rug. At some point in time he installed a hasp lock on a closet, and planned to, or did, place his tools in it. However, he left the closet keys on the premises. Around the end of November, apparently after November 23, the landlord notified the police and turned the tools and equipment over to them. Defendant did not pay any more rent. It is not clear when he last entered the office, but it could have been after November 23, and even after the landlord had removed the equipment. On February 22, 1968, the police arrested defendant. After receiving advice as to his constitutional rights, defendant voluntarily made an oral statement which he reduced to writing.

Among other things which defendant wrote down were these:

> Saturday, the 14th ... I drilled some small holes in the floor of the room. Because of tiredness, fear, and the implications of what I was doing, I stopped and went to sleep.
>
> At this point I think my motives began to change. The actutal [sic] commencement of my plan made me begin to realize that even if I were to succeed a fugitive life of living off of stolen money would not give the enjoyment of the life of a mathematician however humble a job I might have.
>
> I still had not given up my plan however. I felt I had made a certain investment of time, money, effort and a certain pschological [sic] commitment to the concept.
>
> I came back several times thinking I might store the tools in the closet and slowly drill down (covering the hole with a rug of linoleum square). As time went on (after two weeks or so). My wife came back and my life as bank robber seemed more and more absurd.

II. Discussion of Defendant's Contentions

Defendant's position in this appeal is that, as a matter of law, there was insufficient evidence upon which to convict him of a criminal attempt under Penal Code section 664. Defendant claims that his actions were all preparatory in nature and never reached a stage of advancement in relation to the substantive crime which he concededly intended to commit (burglary of the bank vault) so that criminal responsibility might attach.

In order for the prosecution to prove that defendant committed an attempt to burglarize as proscribed by Penal Code section 664, it was required to establish that he had the specific intent to commit a burglary of the bank and that his acts toward that goal went beyond mere preparation.

The required specific intent was clearly established in the instant case. Defendant admitted in his written confession that he rented the office fully intending to burglarize the bank, that he brought in tools and equipment to accomplish this purpose, and that he began drilling into the floor with the intent of making an entry into the bank.

The question of whether defendant's conduct went beyond "mere preparation" raises some provocative problems. The briefs and the oral argument of counsel in this case point up a degree of ambiguity and uncertainty that permeates the law of attempts in this state. Each side has cited us to a different so-called "test" to determine whether this defendant's conduct went beyond the preparatory stage. Predictably each respective test in the eyes of its proponents yielded an opposite result.

Defendant relies heavily on the following language: "Preparation alone is not enough [to convict for an attempt], there must be some appreciable fragment of the crime committed, *it must be in such progress that it will be consummated unless interrupted by circumstances independent of the will of the attempter,* and the act must not be equivocal in nature." (Italics added.) (*People v. Buffum* (1953) 40 Cal. 2d 709.) Defendant argues that while the facts show that he did do a series of acts directed at the commission of a burglary—renting the office, bringing in elaborate equipment and actually starting drilling—the facts do not show that he was interrupted by any outside circumstances. Without such interruption and a voluntary desistence on his part, defendant concludes that under the above stated test, he has not legally committed an attempt....

... [T]he Attorney General suggests that another test, as set out in *People v. Anderson* (1934) 1 Cal. 2d 687, is more appropriate: "Whenever the design of a person to commit crime is clearly shown, slight acts in furtherance of the design will constitute an attempt." (Note absence of reference to interruption.) The People argue that defendant's felonious intent was clearly set out in his written confession; that the proven overt acts in furtherance of the design, although only needing to be slight, were, in fact, substantial; that this combination warrants the affirmance of the attempt conviction.

We suggest that the confusion in this area is a result of the broad statutory language of section 664, which reads in part: "Any person who attempts to commit any crime, but fails, or is prevented or intercepted in the perpetration thereof, is punishable ..." This is a very general proscription against all attempts not specifically made a crime. The statute does not differentiate between the various types of attempts which may be considered culpable. Reference must be made to case law in order to determine precisely what conduct constitutes an attempt. However, the statute does point out by the words "fails," "prevented," and "intercepted," those *conditions* which separate an attempt from the substantive crime.

An examination of the decisional law reveals at least two general categories of attempts, both of which have been held to fall within the ambit of the statute.

In the first category are those situations where the actor does all acts necessary (including the last proximate act) to commit the substantive crime, but nonetheless he somehow is unsuccessful. This lack of success is either a "failure" or a "prevention" brought about because of some extraneous circumstances, e.g., a malfunction of equipment, a miscalculation of operations by the actor or a situation wherein circumstances were at variance with what the actor believe them to be.[2] Certain convictions for attempted murder illustrate the first category. Some turn on situations wherein the actor fires a weapon at a person but misses; takes aim at an intended victim and pulls the trigger, but the firing mechanism malfunctions; plants on an aircraft a homemade bomb which sputters but does not explode. Another first category example is highlighted in *People v. Fulton* (1961) 188 Cal. App. 2d 105. The factual setting and legal reasoning in *Fulton* is well characterized by Justice Kingsley in *People v. Orndorff* (1968) 261 Cal. App. 2d 212: "*Fulton* … involved an alleged Jamaica Switch, practiced on two alleged intended victims. The schemes failed, in one instance because a bank officer told the intended victim that it was a bunco scheme … [The] court unanimously held that … [this] instance was a punishable attempt … All three judges lay stress on the element of the procuring cause of failure, saying that it must be 'by extraneous circumstances,' or 'by circumstances independent of any actions of their [defendants'] part.'" The defendants in *Fulton* did every act in their preconceived plan. It was only the extraneous circumstance of the intended victim acquiring knowledge that the defendants' proposal to him was a bunco scheme which resulted in the defendants not obtaining the money.

In the above situations application of the rule stated in *People v. Buffum*, which defendant herein seeks to have applied, would appear to be quite appropriate. After a defendant has done all acts necessary under normal conditions to commit crime, he is culpable for an attempt if he is unsuccessful because of an extraneous or fortuitous circumstance.

However, it is quite clear that under California law an overt act, which, when added to the requisite intent, is sufficient to bring about a criminal attempt, need not be the last proximate or ultimate step towards commission of the substantive crime. "It is not necessary that the overt act proved should have been the ultimate step toward the consummation of the design. It is sufficient if it was the first or some subsequent step in a direct movement towards the commission of the offense after the preparations are made." (*People v. Gibson* (1949) 94 Cal. App. 2d 468.) Police officers need not wait until a suspect, who aims a gun at his intended victim, actually

2. The "classic" case, often used as a law school hypothetical example, occurs when the pickpocket thrusts his hand into an empty pocket.

pulls the trigger before they arrest him; nor do these officers need to wait until a suspect, who is forcing the lock of a bank door, actually breaks in before they arrest him for attempted burglary.

This rule makes for a second category of "attempts." The recognition of this separate category is well articulated by Mr. Chief Judge Learned Hand in *United States v. Coplon* (2d Cir. 1950) 185 F.2d 629, as follows: "A neat doctrine by which to test when a person, intending to commit a crime which he fails to carry out, has 'attempted' to commit it, would be that he has done all that it is within his power to do, but has been prevented by intervention from outside; in short that he has passed beyond any *locus poenitentiae.* Apparently that was the original notion, and may still be law in England; but it is certainly not now generally the law in the United States, for there are many decisions which hold that the accused has passed beyond 'preparation,' although he has been interrupted before he has taken the last of his intended steps."

Applying criminal culpability to acts directly moving toward commission of crime (but short of the last proximate act necessary to consummate the criminal design) under section 664 is an obvious safeguard to society because it makes it unnecessary for police to wait before intervening until the actor has done the substantive evil sought to be prevented. It allows such criminal conduct to be stopped or intercepted when it becomes clear what the actor's intention is and when the acts done show that the perpetrator is actually putting his plan into action. *Discovering precisely what conduct falls within this latter category, however, often becomes a difficult problem.* Because of the lack of specificity of section 664, police, trial judges, jurors, and in the last analysis, appellate courts, face the dilemma of trying to identify that point beyond which conduct passes from innocent to criminal absent a specific event such as the commission of a prohibited substantive crime.

Our courts have come up with a variety of "tests" which try to distinguish acts of preparation from completed attempts. "The preparation consists in devising or arranging the means or measures necessary for the commission of the offense; the attempt is the direct movement toward the commission after the preparations are made." (*People v. Murray* (1859) 14 Cal. 159.) "[The] act must reach far enough towards the accomplishment of the desired result to amount to the commencement of the consummation." (*People v. Miller* (1935) 2 Cal. 2d 527.) "[Where] the intent to commit the substantive offense is ... clearly established ... [,] acts done toward the commission of the crime may constitute an attempt, where the same acts would be held insufficient to constitute an attempt if the intent with which they were done is equivocal and not clearly proved." (*People v. Berger* (1955) 131 Cal. App. 2d 127.)

None of the above statements of the law applicable to this category of attempts provide a litmus-like test, and perhaps no such test is achievable. Such precision is not required in this case, however. There was definitely substantial evidence entitling the trial judge to find that defendant's acts had gone beyond the preparation stage. Without specifically deciding where defendant's preparations left off and where his activities became a completed criminal attempt, we can say that his "drilling" activity clearly was an unequivocal and direct step toward the completion of the burglary. It was a fragment of the substantive crime contemplated *i.e.*, the beginning of the "breaking" element. Further, defendant himself characterized his activity as the *actual commencement of his plan*. The drilling by defendant was obviously one of a series of acts which logic and ordinary experience indicate would result in the proscribed act of burglary. (see *People v. Berger*.)

The instant case provides an out-of-the-ordinary factual situation within the second category. Usually the actors in cases falling within that category of attempts are intercepted or caught in the act. Here, there was no direct proof of any actual interception. But it was clearly inferable by the trial judge that defendant became aware that the landlord had resumed control over the office and had turned defendant's equipment and tools over to the police. This was the equivalent of interception.

The inference of this nonvoluntary character of defendant's abandonment was a proper one for the trial judge to draw. However, it would seem that the character of the abandonment in situations of this type, whether it be voluntary (prompted by pangs of conscience or a change of heart) or nonvoluntary (established by inference in the instant case), is not controlling. The relevant factor is the determination of whether the acts of the perpetrator have reached such a stage of advancement that they can be classified as an attempt. Once that attempt is found there can be no exculpatory abandonment. "One of the purposes of the criminal law is to protect society from those who intend to injure it. When it is established that the defendant intended to commit a specific crime and that in carrying out this intention he committed an act that caused harm or sufficient danger of harm, it is immaterial that for some collateral reason he could not complete the intended crime." (*People v. Camodeca* (1959) 52 Cal. 2d 142.)

The order is affirmed.

Note and Problems

Problem 66.

Late at night, someone accessed an ATM machine to withdraw $20 and then left the money in the machine, causing a bill trap and alerting ATM technicians to come out and fix the machine. An hour later, Defendants were found in a car near the bank. A search of the immediate area resulted in the discovery of two handguns in the bushes nearby. A search of the car disclosed duct tape, a stun gun, gloves, ammunition suitable for the handguns and the card which had activated the ATM machine. Defendants are charged with attempted robbery (P.C. §§ 211, 664). What arguments should be made as to their guilt?

Problem 67.

After Defendant crashed his car, he hid it and reported to the police that it had been stolen. He then wrote a letter to his insurance company asking how he could make a claim on his theft policy. Before any claim was filed, however, the car was found by the police. What are the arguments on whether Defendant is guilty of attempted obtaining money under false pretenses? (P.C. §§ 532, 664).

The Model Penal Code and Attempt and Abandonment. Unlike California, the Model Penal Code would recognize a defense of abandonment in some circumstances. The Code creates an affirmative defense for a defendant who abandoned his or her criminal efforts or otherwise prevented the crime "under circumstances manifesting a complete and voluntary renunciation of his criminal purpose." MPC § 5.01(4). Renunciation is not effective if motivated by the defendant's discovery of circumstances making the crime harder or detection more likely or if motivated by the intent merely to postpone the criminal efforts. *Id.*

People v. Superior Court (Decker)

41 Cal.4th 1, 157 P.3d 1017 (2007)

BAXTER, J.

Defendant and real party in interest Ronald Decker has been charged with the attempted willful, deliberate, and premeditated murder of his sister, Donna Decker, and her friend, Hermine Riley Bafiera. According to the evidence offered at the preliminary hearing, Decker did not want to kill these women himself—as he explained, "he would be the prime suspect" and "would probably make a mistake somehow or another"—so he sought the services of a hired assassin.

Decker located such a person (or thought he did). He furnished the hired assassin with a description of his sister, her home, her car, and her workplace, as well as specific information concerning her daily habits. He also advised the assassin to kill Hermine if necessary to avoid leaving a witness behind. Decker and the hired assassin agreed on the means to commit the murder, the method of payment, and the price. The parties also agreed that Decker would pay $5,000 in cash as a downpayment. Before Decker handed over the money, the assassin asked whether Decker was "sure" he wanted to go through with the murders. Decker replied, "I am absolutely, positively, 100 percent sure, that I want to go through with it. I've never been so sure of anything in my entire life." All of these conversations were recorded and videotaped because, unknown to Decker, he was talking with an undercover police detective posing as a hired assassin.[a]

Decker does not dispute that the foregoing evidence was sufficient to hold him to answer to the charge of solicitation of the murder of Donna and Hermine but argues

---

a. [Decker had contacted Russell Wafer, a gunsmith, and informed Wafer that he was looking for someone to kill a certain victim and would pay $35,000 for the job, along with a $3,000 "finder's fee" to Wafer. After telling Decker that he thought he could find someone, Wafer called the Sheriff's Department and spoke with Detective Wayne Holston. The two agreed to set up a "sting" operation with Holston posing as the "assassin."]

that this evidence was insufficient to support a charge of their attempted murder. The magistrate and the trial court, believing themselves bound by *People v. Adami* (1973) 36 Cal.App.3d 452 (*Adami*), reluctantly agreed with Decker and dismissed the attempted murder charges. The Court of Appeal disagreed with *Adami* and issued a writ of mandate directing the respondent court to reinstate the dismissed counts. We granted review to address the conflict and now affirm.

...

Discussion

...

Attempted murder requires the specific intent to kill and the commission of a direct but ineffectual act toward accomplishing the intended killing. The uncontradicted evidence that Decker harbored the specific intent to kill his sister (and, if necessary, her friend Hermine) was overwhelming. Decker expressed to both Wafer and Holston his desire to have Donna killed. He researched how to find a hired assassin. He spent months accumulating cash in small denominations to provide the hired assassin with a downpayment and had also worked out a method by which to pay the balance. He knew the layout of his sister's condominium and how one might enter it surreptitiously. He had tested the level of surveillance in the vicinity of her home and determined it was "not really that sharp." He chronicled his sister's daily routine at both her home and her office. He offered Holston recommendations on how his sister should be killed and what materials would be necessary. And, at both meetings with Holston, he insisted that Hermine, if she were present, be killed as well, so as to prevent her from being a witness.

The controversy in this case, as the parties readily concede, is whether there was also a direct but ineffectual act toward accomplishing the intended killings. For an attempt, the overt act must go beyond mere preparation and show that the killer is putting his or her plan into action; it need not be the last proximate or ultimate step toward commission of the crime or crimes, nor need it satisfy any element of the crime. However, as we have explained, "[b]etween preparation for the attempt and the attempt itself, there is a wide difference. The preparation consists in devising or arranging the means or measures necessary for the commission of the offense; the attempt is the direct movement toward the commission after the preparations are made." (*People v. Murray* (1859) 14 Cal. 159.) "[I]t is sufficient if it is the first or some subsequent act directed towards that end after the preparations are made." (*People v. Memro* (1985) 38 Cal.3d 658.)

As simple as it is to state the terminology for the law of attempt, it is not always clear in practice how to apply it. As other courts have observed, "[m]uch ink has been spilt in an attempt to arrive at a satisfactory standard for telling where preparation ends and attempt begins. Both as fascinating and as fruitless as the alchemists' quest for the philosopher's stone has been the search, by judges and writers, for a valid, single statement of doctrine to express when, under the law of guilt, preparation to commit a crime becomes a criminal attempt." (*Minshew v. State* (Ala. Crim. App. 1991) 594 So.2d 703.) Indeed, we have ourselves observed that "none of the various 'tests' used by the courts can possibly distinguish all preparations from all attempts." (*People v. Memro, supra.*)

Although a definitive test has proved elusive, we have long recognized that "[w]henever the design of a person to commit crime is clearly shown, slight acts in furtherance of the design will constitute an attempt." (*People v. Anderson* (1934) 1 Cal.2d 687 [attempted robbery].) Viewing the entirety of Decker's conduct in light of his clearly expressed intent, we find sufficient evidence under the slight-acts rule to hold him to answer to the charges of attempted murder.

....

.... [A]t the time Decker handed Holston the downpayment on the murder, Decker's intention was clear. It was equally clear that he was "actually putting his plan into action." (*People v. Dillon* (1983) 34 Cal.3d 441.) Decker had secured an agreement with Holston to murder Donna (and, if necessary, her friend Hermine); had provided Holston with all the information necessary to commit the crimes; had given Holston the $5,000 downpayment; and had understood that "it's done" once Holston left with the money. These facts would lead a reasonable person to "believe a crime is about to be consummated absent an intervening force"—and thus that "the attempt is underway." Indeed, as Justice Epstein noted for the Court of Appeal, "[t]here was nothing more for Decker to do to bring about the murder of his sister." Although Decker did not himself point a gun at his sister, he did aim at her an armed professional who had agreed to commit the murder.[1]

As contrary authority, Decker relies on *Adami*, which affirmed the dismissal of an attempted murder charge on similar facts, and relies also on the small number of out-of-state majority and minority opinions that have followed *Adami*. In *Adami*, the defendant sought to have his wife killed because she had stolen money from him. He agreed on a price with an undercover police agent posing as an assassin and supplied the agent with a photograph of the victim, a description of the victim and her residence and vehicles, and other pertinent information. The defendant gave the police agent $500 as a downpayment and announced he was not going to change his mind. *Adami* declared that these acts "consisted solely of solicitation or mere preparation" and concluded, in accordance with the "weight of authority," that "solicitation alone is not an attempt."

We perceive several flaws in *Adami's* analysis.

First, the opinion makes no mention of the slight-acts rule, which has long been the rule for attempted crimes in California. Indeed, *Adami*'s progeny make no pretense of reconciling their analysis with the slight-acts rule and instead explicitly reject it.

Decker argues that the slight-acts rule should not be applied to the crime of attempted murder, but his argument lacks legal or logical support. Our adoption of the slight-acts rule in *People v. Anderson, supra*, was supported by a citation to *Stokes*

1. Decker does not argue here that the attempted murder charges must be dismissed because, notwithstanding Decker's own conduct, Detective Holston never intended to commit the murders.

v. State (Miss. 1908) 46 So. 627, which is "[o]ne of the leading cases in the United States on attempt to commit a crime" (*Duke v. State* (Miss. 1976) 340 So.2d 727) and which (like the present case) involved a defendant who hired another to perform a murder. The cases on which Decker relies thus conflict not only with California law, but also with the "fairly general agreement ... that slight acts are enough when the intent to murder is clearly shown." (Annot., What Constitutes Attempted Murder (1974) 54 A.L.R.3d 612.) Indeed, where (as here) the crime involves concerted action—and hence a greater likelihood that the criminal objective will be accomplished—there is a *greater* urgency for intervention by the state at an *earlier* stage in the course of that conduct. Had Decker struck an agreement with and paid earnest money to a real hired killer, he could have been prosecuted for conspiracy to commit murder, which is punishable to the same extent as the completed crime of first degree murder. Because of the fortuity that Decker's hired killer was actually an undercover detective, Decker faces the much less serious charge of attempted murder. Neither Decker nor the dissent has offered any reason for us create an exception to the slight-acts rule for attempted murder, especially in *Stokes*'s classic formulation where the attempt involves concerted action with others, merely so that Decker's maximum potential punishment may be further reduced.

Second, *Adami* has misconceived the issue under these circumstances to be "whether the solicitation itself was sufficient to establish probable cause to believe that defendant attempted the murder." Decker similarly expends considerable effort to convince us that "solicitation of another to commit a crime is an attempt to commit that crime if, but only if, it takes the form of urging the other to join with the solicitor in perpetrating that offense, not at some future time or distant place, but here and now, and the crime is such that it cannot be committed by one without the cooperation and submission of another." But a solicitation requires only that a person invite another to commit or join in an enumerated crime (including murder) with the intent that the crime be committed (Pen. Code, §653f). The solicitation is complete once the request is made and is punishable "irrespective of the reaction of the person solicited." (*In re Ryan N.* (2001) 92 Cal.App.4th 1359.) In this case, the solicitation was complete early in Decker's first conversation with Holston, when he asked Holston to kill Donna. But the People do not contend that this request was sufficient to prosecute Decker for attempted murder. They argue instead that the solicitation, in combination with Decker's subsequent conduct, revealed his plan to have Holston murder Donna (and, if necessary, her friend Hermine) and that Decker put this plan into operation no later than the point at which he completed the agreement with Holston, finalized the details surrounding the murders, and paid Holston $5,000 in earnest money.

The issue, then, is not whether "solicitation alone" is sufficient to establish an attempt, but whether a solicitation to commit murder, combined with a completed agreement to hire a professional killer and the making of a downpayment under that agreement, can establish probable cause to believe Decker attempted to murder these victims. A substantial number of our sister states have held that it can. [citing cases from Arizona, Georgia, Louisiana, Nebraska, New Hampshire, New York, Virginia,

Washington and West Virginia]. Additional jurisdictions have held that a solicitation to murder, in combination with a completed agreement to hire a professional killer and further conduct implementing the agreement, can similarly constitute an attempted murder. We find these authorities persuasive.

Third, *Adami* mistakenly assumes that there can be no overlap between the evidence that would tend to prove solicitation to murder and that which would tend to prove attempted murder. Indeed, Decker asserts that these are "mutually exclusive crimes." But it could not be plainer, as Chief Justice Holmes put it, that while "preparation is not an attempt," nonetheless "*some* preparations may amount to an attempt." (*Commonwealth v. Peaslee* (Mass. 1901) 59 N.E. 55, italics added.) Conduct that qualifies as mere preparation and conduct that qualifies as a direct but ineffectual act toward commission of the crime exist on a continuum, "since all acts leading up to the ultimate consummation of a crime are by their very nature preparatory." (*State v. Sunzar* (N.J. Super. 1999) 751 A.2d 627.) The difference between them "is a question of degree." (*Commonwealth v. Peaslee, supra.*) There is thus no error in resting a finding of attempted murder in part on evidence that *also* tends to establish solicitation to commit murder and vice versa. After all, even under Decker's analysis, evidence of a solicitation to commit murder can tend to support a finding of attempted murder if the defendant then "provides the hit man the instrument or other means to procure the death." Decker offers no principled basis for a different result when the hit man already has a weapon and the defendant instead begins payment under the contract to kill.

Fourth, we reject the contention, endorsed by Decker and by *Adami*'s progeny, that there is "no persuasive reason" why a solicitation to commit murder "should be treated differently under the law merely because part of the agreed upon fee has passed hands. There is no greater proximity, no significantly greater likelihood of consummation, and no act of a nature other than incitement or preparation inherent in the solicitation itself." As the People point out, though, a downpayment on a contract to murder serves the same purpose as a downpayment on any other type of contract. It evidences the solicitor's "seriousness of purpose" and makes the object of the contract "closer to fruition." It blinks reality to equate the threat posed by an individual who has merely invited another, perhaps unsuccessfully, to commit murder with the threat posed by an individual who has already reached an agreement with a hired killer to commit murder, finalized the plans, and made the downpayment under the contract to kill. But for Holston's status as an undercover detective, it is likely that Decker's conduct would have resulted in the murder of these victims. Where, as here, the defendant's intent is unmistakable, "the courts should not destroy the practical and common-sense administration of the law with subtleties as to what constitutes preparation and what constitutes an act done toward the commission of a crime." (*People v. Memro, supra.*)

The purpose of requiring an overt act is that until such act occurs, one is uncertain whether the intended design will be carried out. When, by reason of the defendant's conduct, the situation is "without any equivocality," and it appears the design will be carried out if not interrupted, the defendant's conduct satisfies the test for an overt act. Here, the record supported at least a strong suspicion that Decker's intent to have his sister (and, if necessary, her friend) murdered was unambiguous and that he had commenced the commission of the crime by doing all that he needed to do to accomplish the murders.

In finding the record sufficient to hold Decker to answer to the charges of attempted murder here, we do not decide whether an agreement to kill followed by a downpayment is *always* sufficient to support a charge of attempted murder. Whether acts done in contemplation of the commission of a crime are merely preparatory or whether they are instead sufficiently close to the consummation of the crime is a question of degree and depends upon the facts and circumstances of a particular case. A different situation may exist, for example, when the assassin has been hired and paid but the victims have not yet been identified. In this case, however, Decker had effectively done all that he needed to do to ensure that Donna and her friend were executed. Accordingly, he should have been held to answer to the charges of attempted murder. We disapprove *People v. Adami* to the extent it is inconsistent with this opinion.

Dissenting Opinion by Werdegar, J.

My colleagues hold that defendant's conduct in soliciting the murder of his sister, reaching an agreement with a hired assassin to do the killing, and making a downpayment under the agreement establishes probable cause to believe defendant himself attempted the murder. I respectfully dissent. "An attempt to commit a crime consists of two elements: a specific intent to commit the crime, and a direct but ineffectual act done toward its commission." (Pen.Code, § 21a.) Defendant's conduct in this case does not include "a direct but ineffectual act" done toward the murder's commission. Accordingly, he cannot be guilty of attempted murder.

As we have long recognized, the required act for an attempt under California law must be "directed towards immediate consummation" (*People v. Dillon* (1983) 34 Cal.3d 441) of the crime attempted. As the majority details, defendant's conduct included numerous *indirect* acts toward accomplishing the murder of his sister: he sought the services of a hired assassin; he located a person (actually an undercover police detective) he thought would act as such; he furnished the supposed assassin with a description of his sister, her home, her car and her workplace, as well as specific information concerning her daily habits; he discussed how the murder would be done and how and when he would pay for the work, agreeing to furnish $5,000 in cash as a downpayment; and, finally, just before he was arrested, he stated he was "absolutely, positively, 100 percent sure, that I want to go through with it" and urged the supposed assassin to do it "as fast as you can."

I agree with the majority that as evidence defendant harbored the specific intent to kill his sister, these facts are overwhelming. None of them, however, constitutes a *direct* but ineffectual act done toward the murder's commission. (Pen.Code, § 21a.) As the majority states, defendant "did not himself point a gun at his sister"; neither did he otherwise directly menace her. Instead, he relied on the person he thought had agreed to commit the murder to do the actual deed.[1] The direct preparatory acts was the person he sought to engage as his agent-not the ultimate, intended victim of the scheme.

We previously have stated that for attempt, it must be "clear from a suspect's acts what *he* intends to do." (*People v. Dillon, supra*, italics added.) In this case, what defendant intended to do was have his sister killed *by someone else.* Defendant's own conduct did not include even "slight" acts toward actual commission of the murder. That he hired another, supplied him with information, and paid him a downpayment only highlights his intention not to perform the act himself.

The California cases the majority purports to rely on generally involve single actors, i.e., defendants who acted directly on their victims. These cases simply confirm that for attempt a defendant must have committed a direct act toward commission of the crime. Defendant here committed no direct act toward commission of the murder, since his scheme interposed a third party between himself and his intended victim, and the third party never acted. The majority goes astray in applying to this solicitation-of-murder case, where action by another person was required to effectuate (or attempt) the intended killing, principles applicable when an offense is intended and attempted by a single individual.

Although defendant's conduct went beyond the minimum required for solicitation, for purposes of attempt law his arrangements constitute mere preparation. Reprehensible as they were, his acts "did not amount to any more than the mere arrangement of the proposed measures for [the] accomplishment" of the crime. (*People v. Adami* (1973) 36 Cal.App.3d 452.) This is because, as a logical matter, they did no more than "leave the intended assailant only in the condition to commence the first direct act toward consummation of the defendant's design." To do all one can to motivate and encourage another to accomplish a killing—even to make a downpayment on a contract to kill—while blameworthy and punishable, is neither logically nor legally equivalent to attempting the killing oneself. In concluding to the contrary, the majority blurs the distinction between preparation and perpetration the Legislature intended by requiring that an attempt include a direct act. (Pen.Code, § 21a.) The majority's supportive reasoning likewise conflates the two separate elements of attempt, specific intent and direct act: "Viewing the entirety of [defendant's] conduct *in light of his clearly expressed intent*, we find sufficient evidence under the slight-acts rule to hold him to answer to the charges of attempted murder." As a court, we are not authorized to ignore the statutory requirements.

---

1. Although the majority asserts defendant "did aim at [his sister] an armed professional who had agreed to commit the murder," the armed professional referred to (i.e., the detective) only *pretended* to agree so that in fact there was no agreement, though defendant thought there was. This absence of actual agreement presumably is why the case was not prosecuted as a conspiracy. (See *People v. Jurado* (2006) 38 Cal.4th 72 ["A conviction of conspiracy requires proof that the defendant and another person had the specific intent to agree or conspire to commit an offense, as well as the specific intent to commit the elements of that offense, together with proof of the commission of an overt act 'by one or more of the parties to such agreement' in furtherance of the conspiracy"].)

The majority's criticisms of *Adami* are unpersuasive. The majority faults *Adami* for not mentioning the slight acts rule, but since the *Adami* court concluded no "appreciable fragment of the crime charged was accomplished," the rule had no application. Nor, contrary to the majority's account, did *Adami* assume that evidence of solicitation cannot also be evidence of attempt. *Adami* simply held that hiring a murderer, planning the murder, and making a downpayment logically constitute "solicitation or mere preparation," not attempted murder.

Confronted with statutory language and judicial precedent contrary to its conclusion, the majority relies on out-of-state cases. Several of these interpret attempt statutes distinguishable from our own. Others involve more than a completed agreement with a hired killer, including a direct act *toward the victim*. The remaining cases are in my view mistaken for the same reason the majority is mistaken: they implicitly allow that a defendant may be guilty of attempt when no direct act toward the commission of the crime has been done. Courts in some other jurisdictions have, as the majority fails to acknowledge, maintained the distinction between preparation and attempt in cases similar to this.

Had the supposed assassin hired to kill defendant's sister actually attempted to kill her, defendant would be punishable under Penal Code section 31 as a principal in the offense, either as an aider and abettor or as a coconspirator. But in this case, neither defendant nor the supposed assassin took a direct act toward commission of the offense. Defendant's conduct was confined to encouraging and enabling his intended agent to kill (or attempt to kill), but the detective with whom he dealt took no such action. There was no attempt.

For the foregoing reasons, I dissent.

...

Problem

Problem 68.

Defendant, a 53-year-old plumber, invited Victim, a 14-year-old girl, to work for him for $5.00 per hour. When Victim accompanied Defendant into his office, he talked to her about sex, offered her methamphetamine ("speed") and said that he was a criminal and was dangerous. The following is Victim's testimony about Defendant's solicitations of sexual activity:

Q. Did he ask you if you wanted to have sex with him?

A. Not at that time but he asked me if I would.

Q. Tell us when he did it and what he said.

A. It was like towards the end of the interview, he says he would be willing to pay me to do it.

Q. Did he tell you how much money he would give you to have sex with him?

A. He never told me.

Q. He just said he would pay you?

A. Yes.

Q. What did you say to him about that?

A. I just told him I wouldn't do it.

...

Q. He asked you at that time if you would have sex with him?

A. ... [H]e said like would I be willing to, not at that point in time ... He said sometime in the future if I like would.

Q. Did he indicate to you any particular time in the future?

A. No, he didn't.

After this conversation, Defendant drove Victim home. Several days later Defendant made a similar offer to two other girls Victim's age. The two girls accepted the offer, smoked amphetamine and then submitted to sexual activity with Defendant. In addition to being charged with two counts of lewd and lascivious conduct with a minor (P.C. § 288(c)) based on his activities with the other girls, Defendant is charged with attempted lewd and lascivious conduct with a minor (P.C. §§ 664, 288(c)) based on his conduct with Victim. What arguments should be made as to whether Defendant's conduct with Victim constituted attempt or only solicitation?

B. Solicitation

The next two cases deal with solicitation crimes. *People v. Gordon* concerns what conduct is sufficient to constitute solicitation, in this case, solicitation of a bribe. *People v. Rubin* is a more complicated case concerning solicitation of murder. Not only is there an issue as to whether the elements of solicitation can be proved, but, because the alleged solicitation occurred in the context of a public statement, there is an issue as to whether the defendant's speech was protected by the First Amendment.

People v. Gordon

47 Cal. App. 3d 465, 120 Cal. Rptr. 840 (1975)

Compton, J.

Defendant was indicted by the Grand Jury of Los Angeles County for one count of violation of Penal Code section 653f (solicitation of a bribe). Prior to trial defendant moved under Penal Code section 995 to set aside the indictment. That motion was denied and in the jury trial which followed defendant was found guilty as charged. She appeals the judgment of conviction and among other things contends that her motion under section 995 should have been granted.

The indictment alleged that on or about the 3d of January 1973, the defendant did "willfully and unlawfully and feloniously solicit another to offer, accept and join in the offer acceptance of a bribe." According to the evidence the person alleged to have been solicited was Officer Joseph Stanley of the Los Angeles Police Department who was at the time in question assigned to the narcotic detail.

. . .

Defendant was an attorney at law and shared office space with another practitioner Mr. Bane. Mr. Bane had formerly been a member of the staff of the City Attorney of the City of Los Angeles. During that tenure he had become acquainted with Officer Stanley.

At some point late in the year 1972, defendant contacted Mr. Bane and stated that she knew where there was a two- or three-pound quantity of cocaine to be seized. She inquired whether Mr. Bane believed Officer Stanley would be interested and whether he could be trusted. Mr. Bane replied in the affirmative. Defendant asked Mr. Bane to contact Officer Stanley.

Mr. Bane mentioned the matter to Officer Stanley and the officer expressed an interest in seizing the cocaine. Mr. Bane advised the defendant of Officer Stanley's interest.

In late December of 1972, the defendant called Officer Stanley at the Administrative Narcotics Division of the Los Angeles Police Department and inquired if he had discussed with Mr. Bane the two or three pounds of cocaine and whether he was interested in seizing the cocaine and making an arrest. Officer Stanley stated that he was and arrangements were made for the defendant and Officer Stanley to meet. Defendant gave the officer her business and home telephone numbers.

On January 3, Officer Stanley called defendant at her office and a meeting was arranged at the building of the Los Angeles Community College Board of Trustees. That same afternoon Officer Stanley went to the agreed location. He saw the defendant sitting in the gallery observing a meeting of the board. Defendant nodded to Officer Stanley and the two went to a coffee shop located in the building.

In the conversation that followed defendant told the officer that she had a client who "wanted someone taken care of." The officer asked her if she meant "killed" and she replied "no" that she meant "discredited." She identified the person whom her client wanted discredited as Monroe Richman, a member of the Los Angeles Community College Board of Trustees. She stated that her client was highly politically oriented and that he, the client, had inquired of her if it could be arranged to have Mr. Richman "planted" with a quantity of narcotics and then arrested. Defendant also stated in that conversation that "she wouldn't even consider a situation like this unless it was worth money for everybody concerned." Defendant suggested that narcotics be planted either on Mr. Richman's person or in his car. Defendant offered to provide Officer Stanley with information upon which to effect the arrest of a person in possession of two or three pounds of cocaine and then asked if it would be possible to take a portion of that seized cocaine and plant it on Mr. Richman. Officer Stanley replied that it was possible. Defendant indicated that "it might be worth around

$10,000." There were subsequent conversations between the two concerning the acquisition of the cocaine. On January 10, 1973, Officer Stanley called the defendant at her home and surreptitiously recorded the conversation which in part went as follows:

> Stanley: I wanna talk about the original 2 to 3 pounds.
>
> Gordon: Um-hum.
>
> Stanley: All right. We gotta have that for our supply.
>
> Gordon: I don't know if I'm gonna be able to get that.
>
> Stanley: You don't think—you don't think you're gonna be able to get that?
>
> Gordon: I'm not sure about that. Assuming I can't get that, can we still do this other thing?
>
> Stanley: Well, assuming you can't get the 2–3 pounds of coke, I don't know how we can come up with any other cocaine.
>
> Gordon: Maybe the price will just raise a little bit on the whole deal.
>
> Stanley: Well, can your man bear the traffic?
>
> Gordon: I don't know what the traffic is.
>
> Stanley: Well, I don't either. What do you think?
>
> Gordon: Well, I'm thinking in terms of 10 grand.
>
> Stanley: For the whole—For the whole thing 10 grand?
>
> Gordon: Um-hum. That too little?
>
> Stanley: Well, then what do you and I do with it?
>
> Gordon: *I don't care. I'll take a third, you can take three-quarters. You can take—give me a quarter. I don't care. Whatever you think is fair.*
>
> Stanley: All right.
>
> Gordon: Uh—You know I'm not out to—to take 50. I'm not out to take very much at all. It depends.
>
> Stanley: Okay, well—
>
> Gordon: I'd like—I'd like—uh—you know—a couple—$2500.
>
> Stanley: All right. But I—
>
> Gordon: I didn't—matter of fact I would like to—if you think that's not enough we may have to go out and make a purchase and let's up it.
>
> Stanley: Well, I don't know. You're right. We may have to make a purchase. (Italics added.)

The following day the officer called defendant at her office. In that conversation defendant told the officer that she had decided not to be a party to this scheme, that she felt she had a political career ahead of her and she did not want to take a chance on ruining that career. Subsequently the officer made several more contacts with the defendant in an effort to get her to introduce him to her client who originally proposed the scheme. Such meeting, however, was never consummated.

Contentions On Appeal

Defendant contends that there was insufficient evidence to sustain the conviction because there was no evidence that on January 3 she actually solicited the officer to accept the bribe, the argument being that she was "merely feeling out" the officer.

Solicitation consists of the asking of another to commit one of the specified crimes with intent that the crime be committed. The intent may be inferred from the circumstances of the asking.

"The solicitation of a bribe need not be stated in any particular language; such a solicitation may be in the form of words which carry the import of a bribe and were evidently intended to be so understood." (*People v. King* (1968) 218 Cal. App. 2d 602.)

The jury by its verdict found the defendant did in fact, and with the requisite intent, ask the officer to accept a bribe. On appeal from the judgment of conviction we view the evidence in the light most favorable to supporting the jury's determination and indulge in all reasonable inferences—which the evidence will support.

Officer Stanley testified to statements by the defendant from which it could be reasonably inferred that the defendant was asking the officer, in return for the lion's share of $10,000 to arrange to falsely arrest Monroe Richman for possession of narcotics. The jury's verdict is well supported by substantial evidence. The jury could consider defendant's statements subsequent to January 3, in determining her intent on that earlier date. In fact, since the indictment alleged that the crime was committed "on or about January 3," the jury could have based its verdict on the aggregate of the conversations between defendant and Officer Stanley.

...

These later conversations, though they show to defendant's credit, that she gradually and finally lost her ardor for participating in such a nefarious and despicable venture, leave no doubt that as of January 3, 1973, and continuing to at least January 10, 1973, she was intentionally trying to enlist Officer Stanley's assistance in the scheme.

Since the crime was fully committed on January 3, it is no defense that the defendant later withdrew or failed to consummate the crime which was the object of the solicitation. The offense of solicitation "is complete when the solicitation is made, and it is immaterial that the object of the solicitation is never consummated, or that no steps are taken toward its consummation." (*People v. Burt* (1955) 45 Cal. 2d 311.)

...

People v. Rubin

96 Cal. App. 3d 968, 158 Cal. Rptr. 488 (1979)

FLEMING, J.

[The following facts are taken from the dissenting opinion:

On March 16, 1978, respondent, a national director of the Jewish Defense League, held a press conference wherein he stated inter alia:

> R: We wish to announce two events. On April twentieth,[b] a number of Neo-Nazis perhaps, a hundred fifty, perhaps two hundred, will march into the Jewish area in Skokie, Illinois. We the Jewish Defense League of the West Coast and East Coast will a mass [sic] at least five thousand to six thousand people in that area, to literally stop the Neo-Nazi movement. We're not going there under the intention to be pacifists. They like to have a nice non-violent quiet protest. We're going there to take names and bury them if we have to. We're not going to allow Neo-Nazis to come into Skokie and advocate the Judacide of the Jewish people there. We're not going to allow them, with stench of the crematoria still existing in that city, with seven thousand survivors with numbers on their arms. We're not gonna allow them to be insulted, intimidated again by Nazis. We believe if we would have done it thirty years ago there might have been a different story. Many more Jews would have been alive today. And we're going there and we're sponsoring the way of people. If they don't have the money, we're providing them a round-trip ticket from Chicago, Los Angeles, it'll cost us—we now have a travel agent who is going to eliminate his commission, and it'll cost us between a hundred and sixty, a hundred seventy dollars per person. If the individual cannot afford his way, we the Jewish Defense League will be sponsoring him, providing he meets our qualifications. The qualifications [sic] is: that he is of sound mind and he is of sound body. And I mean that he is able-willing, ready, and able to handle himself or herself in the streets.
>
> [Questioner:] Are you really ...
>
> R: And that means. We also have an added feature. We are offering five hundred dollars, that I have in my hand, to any member of the community, be he Gentile or Jewish, who kills, maims, or seriously injures a member of the American Nazi Party. This offer is being made on the East Coast, on the West Coat. [sic] And if they bring us the ears, we'll make it a thousand dollars. The fact of the matter is, that we're deadly serious. This is not said in jest, we are deadly serious. In the defense of the Jewish community, should any Nazi even dream of attacking a Jew like they did.
>
> R: This is a nationwide offer. We absolutely feel desperate in the sense that, as I've said before, in the last nine months the Nazis have gained a tremendous amount of notoriety. They are building a national movement. They've got money behind them, and we're fearful if we allow it to grow. We begged the Jewish community many years ago, that if we don't stop the Nazis now, in several years they'll be marching through our community. And the Jewish community didn't listen and so we were right. And this is the, this is the end result ... [we] sincerely mean what we say, that we're going after the Nazis.

---

b. This was Adolph Hitler's birthday.

> We're not going to relax, we're not going to let up, we're going to declare all out war on people who want to advocate our destruction....
>
> R: April 20. And the Nazis plan to march through Skokie, Illinois, which is 70% Jewish, 7,000 survivors of the holocaust. They plan to bring big shields with gigantic swastikas on them: they plan to state that, we missed you 30 years ago, and we're going to try it again. As I said before, it will cause a tremendous grief to the people who are living there, specifically, the survivors of the holocaust. And we feel it's a desecration of our God, and we feel it's a desecration of the Jewish people to allow it to happen in the name of freedom of speech ... [we're] deadly serious, that we'll even go to jail, that we'll risk spending time in jail, if we have to, in order to stop the Nazis, because we think we've learned from history....
>
> R: This was announced the other day in Chicago, when our national director stated that we're there, and we're coming there, and we're going to stop the Nazi march at all cost. And it's a nationwide thing, and we're bringing people as far away as Montreal, Canada. And you can expect a major turnout of Jewish activists, of Jewish militants who are willing to go into the streets and fight Nazis....
>
> [Questioner:] I need to get one thing clarified before I go off here, ah the $500 reward ...
>
> R: Right.
>
> [Questioner:] Ah that is not just blanket for any Jew or Gentile who maims or seriously injures any member of the Nazi party. Is that for anybody who does this in defense of the Jewish ...
>
> R: That's in defense of the Jewish or Gentile community.
>
> [Questioner:] So it would be incorrect to say just a blanket offer.
>
> R: You could say it's a blanket offer, providing that they could prove that it was in the defense of the community.
>
> [Questioner:] Don't you think that you're really opening the door?
>
> R: No. No. It doesn't enter my mind at all. I want people to know, that if they go out there and they take the consequences of being arrested, in either the attack of an American Nazi or whatever, that there are people who are grateful. That there are people who are right behind them 100%; and if money is a motivating factor, which it seems to be in America, that seems to be the bottom line, yeah. That's where we're at....]

... [A] complaint was issued on April 3, 1978 charging respondent with violation of Penal Code section 653f and he was held to answer at a preliminary hearing conducted June 9, 1978.

On June 26, an information alleging in one count that appellant had, on or about March 26, solicited "another to commit and join in the commission of the crime of murder...."

...

Two issues are presented. First, whether the information should have been dismissed for lack of evidence of intent to solicit murder. Second, whether defendant's advocacy of crime is constitutionally protected speech and thus immune from prosecution as criminal solicitation.

I. Probable Cause Supports the Information

Both the examining magistrate and the superior court found probable cause to believe Rubin had committed a public offense, and the trial court, apart from First Amendment grounds, denied the motion to set aside the information. Such a motion does not tender the issue of the guilt or innocence of the accused or the quantum of evidence necessary to sustain a conviction. Rather it presents the question whether the magistrate could entertain a reasonable suspicion that defendant had committed a crime.... Defendant argues there was no substantial evidence of his specific intent to solicit the crime of murder, that his only specific intent had been to stimulate action in defense of the Jewish community, that by reason of the lack of evidence of specific intent to solicit murder, probable cause to support the accusation did not exist as a matter of law. The trial court rejected this argument, concluding that Rubin's intent was susceptible to several interpretations, one of which was intent to solicit murder. Solicitation of murder to prevent a march through Skokie, said the judge, would constitute a crime.

We agree with this conclusion of the trial judge, in that under the standard of probable cause defendant's statements could be interpreted as a solicitation of murder. "Solicitation consists of the asking of another to commit one of the specified crimes with intent that the crime be committed." (*People v. Gordon* (1975) 47 Cal. App. 3d 465.) Defendant's true state of mind, his intent in offering a $500 reward to anyone "who kills, maims, or seriously injures a member of the American Nazi Party," presents a question of fact to be determined by the trier of fact on the basis of evidence produced at a trial. Neither the superior court nor this court is entitled to resolve that question as a matter of law. Accordingly, apart from First Amendment grounds, the information charging the crime of solicitation of murder is valid and is supported by probable cause.

II. Solicitation of Crime as Protected Advocacy

...

The paradoxical issue before us is the extent to which a summons to crime is protectable as free speech. All tests for protected speech purport to distinguish abstract advocacy of indeterminate measures from concrete solicitation of specific and determinate acts. In a given case the issue is whether the summons is constitutionally protected advocacy of resort to crime in general or whether it is incitement to specific crime prosecutable as criminal solicitation. In past years free speech cases have presented two contrasting images—one, the classroom professor lecturing his students on the need to resort to terrorism to overthrow an oppressive government (constitutionally protected speech; *cf. Sweezy v. New Hampshire* (1957) 354 U.S. 234); the other, the street demonstrator in the town square urging a mob to burn down city hall and lynch the chief of police (unprotected criminal incitement to violence; *cf.*

Feiner v. New York (1951) 340 U.S. 315). But in these days of the global village and the big trumpet the line between advocacy and solicitation has become blurred; and when advocacy of crime is combined with the staging of a media event, the prototype images tend to merge. The classroom becomes a broadcasting studio, the mob in the town square becomes a myriad of unknown viewers and listeners throughout the broadcast area, and the critical distinction between abstract advocacy of crime in general and concrete solicitation of crime in particular breaks down. When, as here, political assassination is urged upon a greatly enlarged audience, the incitement to crime may possess a far greater capacity for civil disruption than the oral harangue of a mob in the town square, for the unseen audience of unknown listeners may contain another Oswald, or Ruby, or Sirhan, or Ray, or Bremer, or Moore, or Fromm, who may respond literally to the invitation of the speaker, regardless of the speaker's true intent. The threat to civil order presented by advocacy of assassination must be realistically evaluated in the light of its potential for deadly mischief.

...

The facts and circumstances which differentiate advocacy of crime from solicitation of crime are those which differentiate advocacy of abstract doctrine from advocacy of incitement to unlawful action. Their application may be seen in *Brandenburg v. Ohio* (1969) 395 U.S. 444, a conviction under Ohio's criminal syndicalism law of a leader of the Ku Klux Klan for advocating the general propriety of crime at a rally held for media reporters during which a cross had been burned and statements made derogatory to Negroes and Jews. In reversing the conviction the court declared that "the constitutional guarantees of free speech and free press do not permit a State to forbid or proscribe advocacy of the use of force or of law violation except where such advocacy is directed to inciting or producing imminent lawless action and is likely to incite or produce such action." Mere abstract teaching of the moral propriety of resort to force and violence, said the court, is not the same as preparing and steeling a group for violent action. A similar case is *Watts v. United States* (1969) 394 U.S. 705, a prosecution for threat against the President by a participant in a public discussion group who had said that if inducted into the Army and made to carry a rifle, "the first man I want to get in my sights is L.B.J." In reversing the conviction the court declared that threat must be distinguished from constitutionally protected speech, that the prosecution must prove a true threat rather than the kind of political hyperbole that occurred here. A recent informative case dealing with threat is *United States v. Kelner* (2 Cir. 1976) 534 F.2d 1020, where defendant, a member of the Jewish Defense League, was convicted of transmitting over television a threat to assassinate Yasser Arafat. On appeal, the court rejected the claim of freedom of expression, declined to identify the assassination threat as political hyperbole, and declared it the function of the jury to evaluate the intent behind the threat.

Although these cases deal primarily with threats to assassinate rather than solicitation of assassination they delineate the factors that differentiate advocacy of crime as abstract doctrine from advocacy of crime as incitement to concrete action. In *Brandenberg v. Ohio*, the Supreme Court suggested evaluation of the language of advocacy in the light of two considerations: (1) its incitement to imminent lawless action; (2)

its likelihood of producing such action. This particular formula parallels the test delineated by Justice Holmes on behalf of the Supreme Court in *Schenck v. United States* (1919) 249 U.S. 47, in which, after saying that the most stringent protection of free speech would not protect a man in falsely shouting fire in a theatre and causing a panic, he refers to the test of clear and present danger and declares that protection of free speech is a question of proximity and degree. We consider the application of these factors to the cause at bench.

Proximity: Incitement to Imminent Lawless Action. Since murder is lawless action and an offer of reward for murder is, assuredly, an incitement, imminence is the critical element here in the factor of proximity. Imminence, a function of time, refers to an event which threatens to happen momentarily, is about to happen, or is at the point of happening. But time is a relative dimension and imminence a relative term, and the imminence of an event is related to its nature. A total eclipse of the sun next year is said to be imminent. An April shower 30 minutes away is not. The event which concerns us here was the scheduled Nazi Party demonstration and march to be held in Skokie in five weeks, an event which had already attracted national attention. We think that in terms of political assassination the demonstration could be said to have been proximate and imminent, just as a Papal visit to Belfast, a Soviet chief of state's visit to Rome, a presidential campaign trip to Dallas, and a presidential inauguration in Washington, can each be said to be proximate and imminent, even though occurrence may be some weeks away.

...

We think solicitation of murder in connection with a public event of this notoriety, even though five weeks away, can qualify as incitement to imminent lawless action.

Degree: Likelihood of Producing Action. Here we are concerned with the practicality and feasibility of the solicitation—was it likely to incite or produce violence? We cannot, of course, answer this question with assurance, for the effect of emotional appeals for political violence on the actions of inherently unstable personalities remains obscure. But we think it a reasonable inference that serious reportage by respectable news media of a reward for murder tends in some degree to give respectability to what otherwise would remain an underground solicitation of limited credibility addressed to a limited audience, and thereby tends to increase the risk and likelihood of violence. Undoubtedly, the prosecution's case would be stronger if a specific Nazi Party member had been named as the target for assassination and if the demonstration had been one scheduled to take place in Los Angeles rather than in Skokie. Yet murder remains a crime, whether or not a specified victim is identified as the target, and solicitation in California of murder in Illinois is nonetheless solicitation of murder.

The solicitation to murder here was not made in a jesting or conditional manner, nor was it the outcome of an improvised piece of braggadocio (*Cf. Watts v. United States*; *United States v. Kelner*). Its words and circumstances suggest the possibility it might incite or produce the violence sought. Rubin himself referred to earlier bloodshed in St. Louis, and he predicted bloodshed in Skokie unless the permit for the demonstration were revoked. Some of the comments of the court in *United States v. Kelner*, are germane. "... we believe that important national interest similar to those in *Watts* exist here, more specifically, the governmental interest of reducing the climate of violence to which true threats of injury necessarily contribute. As a part of the Government's constitutional responsibility to insure domestic tranquility, it is properly concerned—in an era of ever-increasing acts of violence and terrorism, coupled with technological opportunities to carry out threats of injury—with prohibiting as criminal conduct specific threats of physical injury to others, whether directed toward our own or another nation's leaders or members of the public."

From the words and circumstances of Rubin's offer we conclude there was sufficient likelihood of his solicitation being interpreted as a call to arms, as a preparation and steelment of his group to violent action, as a systematic promotion of future bloodshed in the streets, rather than as a communication of ideas through reasoned public discussion, to remove it from the category of protected speech and require Rubin to answer the charges against him.

The order setting aside the information is reversed.

[Dissenting opinion of Roth, P. J., omitted.]

C. Conspiracy

Conspiracy is a crime with two aspects. First, it is an inchoate crime. A conspiracy is complete and punishable when two or more parties agree to commit a crime (or a lawful act by criminal or unlawful means) and one of them then commits an overt act toward the agreed-upon crime. Second, conspiracy is a means by which vicarious liability is established. This latter aspect of conspiracy is discussed in Chapter 14. In *People v. Johnson*, the California Supreme Court reviews the elements of conspiracy in the course of deciding whether conspiracy to actively participate in a criminal street gang is a punishable crime or rather, as the Court of Appeal described it, "the People essentially charged defendants with conspiracy to actively participate in a conspiracy."[c] In *People v. Swain*, the Supreme Court must decide whether there is such a crime as conspiracy to commit second degree murder. In *People v. Lauria*, the court sets out the factors to be considered in evaluating the sufficiency of the proof of *mens rea*, the specific intent to see the object crime committed. *Lorenson v. Superior Court* concerns the sufficiency of the proof of the act element, the agreement to see the object crime committed. *People v. Mayers* discusses two possible limitations on the use of the conspiracy doctrine when the object crime itself necessarily involves two or more actors.

---

c. *People v. Johnson*, 140 Cal.Rptr.3d 711, 719 (Cal. App. 2012).

People v. Johnson

57 Cal.4th 250, 303 P.3d 379 (2013)

CORRIGAN, J.

We granted review to decide whether one may conspire to actively participate in a criminal street gang.[1] One can. When an active gang participant possessing the required knowledge and intent agrees with fellow gang members to commit a felony, he has also agreed to commit the gang participation offense. That agreement constitutes conspiracy to commit the offense of active gang participation, and may be separately charged once a conspirator has committed an overt act.

I. BACKGROUND

Defendants Corey Ray Johnson, Joseph Kevin Dixon, and David Lee, Jr., were part of a 200-member Bakersfield gang called the Country Boy Crips (CBC). CBC's rival gangs included the Eastside Crips and the Bloods. Dupree Jackson, a CBC member, testified for the prosecution under a grant of immunity. He was defendant Johnson's cousin and sold drugs for the gang. He described the gang's structure and the different roles members filled. Some sold drugs. Some patrolled the boundaries of the gang's territory to keep out enemies and outsiders. Some would "hang out," and some were "pretty boys" who brought women into the gang. Others would "ride with the guns" to seek out and kill enemies. Defendant Johnson sold drugs and was also a shooter for the gang with the moniker "Little Rifleman." Defendant Dixon was considered a gang leader because he had been to prison and had family ties to the gang. Defendant Lee would sell drugs, obtain cars, and drive for and "ride" with other gang members.

Testimony of several witnesses established that between March and August 2007, defendants were involved in various retaliatory shootings against perceived rivals....

The jury convicted all defendants of three counts of first degree murder with multiple-murder and gang-murder special circumstances, two counts of attempted murder, shooting at an occupied vehicle, active gang participation, and conspiracy, as well as various enhancements. Conspiracy was charged as a single count against each defendant. That count alleged each had engaged in conspiracy to commit felony assault, robbery, murder, and gang participation. The jury found each defendant guilty of conspiracy as charged. All defendants received three terms of life without the possibility of parole for the murder counts [as well as multiple additional prison sentences].

As relevant here, the Court of Appeal held that conspiracy to actively participate in a criminal street gang did not qualify as a crime. It affirmed the conspiracy con-

1. Penal Code sections 182, 186.22, subdivision (a) (the gang participation offense, or active gang participation).

victions, however, because each was also based on the valid theory of conspiracy to commit murder. We granted the Attorney General's petition for review.

II. DISCUSSION

A. The Law of Conspiracy

Section 182 prohibits a conspiracy by two or more people to "commit any crime." "A conviction of conspiracy requires proof that the defendant and another person had the specific intent to agree or conspire to commit an offense, as well as the specific intent to commit the elements of that offense, together with proof of the commission of an overt act 'by one or more of the parties to such agreement' in furtherance of the conspiracy." (*People v. Morante* (1999) 20 Cal.4th 403.) "[T]he law of attempt and conspiracy covers inchoate crimes and allows intervention before" the underlying crime has been completed. (*People v. Perez* (2005) 35 Cal.4th 1219.)

Criminal activity exists along a continuum. At its conclusion is the commission of a completed crime, like murder. The principle of attempt recognizes that some measure of criminal culpability may attach before a defendant actually completes the intended crime. Thus, a person who tries to commit a crime but who fails, or is foiled, may still be convicted of an attempt to commit that crime. Yet, attempt still involves both mens rea and actus reus. "An attempt to commit a crime consists of ... a specific intent to commit the crime, and a direct but ineffectual act done toward its commission." (§ 21a.) To ensure that attempt principles do not punish a guilty mental state alone, an act toward the completion of the crime is required before an attempt will be recognized. "When a defendant acts with the requisite specific intent, that is, with the intent to engage in the conduct and/or bring about the consequences proscribed by the attempted crime, and performs an act that goes beyond mere preparation ... and ... shows that the perpetrator is putting his or her plan into action, the defendant may be convicted of criminal attempt." (*People v. Toledo* (2001) 26 Cal.4th 221.) For example, if a person decides to commit murder but does nothing more, he has committed no crime. If he buys a gun and plans the shooting, but does no more, he will not be guilty of attempt. But if he goes beyond preparation and planning and does an act sufficiently close to completing the crime, like rushing up to his intended victim with the gun drawn, that act may constitute an attempt to commit murder.

Conspiracy law attaches culpability at an earlier point along the continuum than attempt. "Conspiracy is an inchoate offense, the essence of which is an agreement to commit an unlawful act." (*Iannelli v. United States* (1975) 420 U.S. 770.) Conspiracy separately punishes not the completed crime, or even its attempt. The crime of conspiracy punishes the agreement itself and "does not require the commission of the substantive offense that is the object of the conspiracy." (*People v. Swain* (1996) 12 Cal.4th 593.) "Traditionally the law has considered conspiracy and the completed substantive offense to be separate crimes." (*Iannelli, supra.*)

Under our statute, an agreement to commit a crime, by itself, does not complete the crime of conspiracy. The commission of an overt act in furtherance of the agreement is also required. "No agreement amounts to a conspiracy, unless some act, beside such agreement, be done within this state to effect the object thereof, by one or more of the parties to such agreement...." (§ 184.) "[A]n overt act is an outward act done in pursuance of the crime and in manifestation of an intent or design, looking toward the accomplishment of the crime." (*People v. Zamora* (1976) 18 Cal.3d 538.) One purpose of the overt act requirement "is to show that an indictable conspiracy exists because evil thoughts alone cannot constitute a criminal offense." (*People v. Russo* (2001) 25 Cal.4th 1124.) The overt act requirement also "provide[s] a *locus penitentiae*—an opportunity for the conspirators to reconsider, terminate the agreement, and thereby avoid punishment for the conspiracy." (*Zamora, supra.*) Once one of the conspirators has performed an overt act in furtherance of the agreement, "the association becomes an active force, it is the agreement, not the overt act, which is punishable. Hence the overt act need not amount to a criminal attempt and it need not be criminal in itself." (*People v. George* (1968) 257 Cal.App.2d 805.)

B. Conspiracy to Commit Active Gang Participation a Valid Offense

"The elements of the gang participation offense in section 186.22(a) are: First, active participation in a criminal street gang, in the sense of participation that is more than nominal or passive; second, knowledge that the gang's members engage in or have engaged in a pattern of criminal gang activity; and third, the willful promotion, furtherance, or assistance in any felonious criminal conduct by members of that gang. A person who is not a member of a gang, but who actively participates in the gang, can be guilty of violating section 186.22(a). A criminal street gang is defined as "any ongoing organization, association, or group of three or more persons, whether formal or informal, having as one of its primary activities the commission of [enumerated offenses], having a common name or common identifying sign or symbol, and whose members individually or collectively engage in or have engaged in a pattern of criminal gang activity." (§ 186.22, subd. (f).) A pattern of criminal gang activity is "the commission of, attempted commission of, conspiracy to commit, or solicitation of, sustained juvenile petition for, or conviction of two or more [enumerated offenses]." (§ 186.22, subd. (e).)

The Attorney General argues conspiracy to commit active gang participation comes within the plain language of sections 182 and 186.22(a). Recognizing such an offense would be neither contrary to legislative intent nor violative of due process. In evaluating this claim, "[w]e begin with the familiar canon that, when construing statutes, our goal is to ascertain the intent of the enacting legislative body so that we may adopt the construction that best effectuates the purpose of the law." (*People v. Albillar* (2010) 51 Cal.4th 47.) "When interpreting statutes, we begin with the plain, commonsense meaning of the language used by the Legislature. If the language is unambiguous, the plain meaning controls." (*People v. Rodriguez* (2012) 55 Cal.4th 1125.)

Nothing in the plain language of either section 182 or 186.22(a) supports the Court of Appeal's holding. The offense of conspiracy to "commit any crime" was included in the original 1872 Penal Code. When the Legislature added section 186.22 in 1989, it expressed no intention to preclude a conviction for a conspiracy to commit the crime of active gang participation. Entering its 15th decade since enactment, section 182 continues to prohibit a conspiracy to commit "any crime."

Concluding that one can conspire to actively participate in a gang is fully consistent with the underlying purposes of section 186.22(a). That provision is part of the California Street Terrorism Enforcement and Prevention Act (STEP Act). "Underlying the STEP Act was the Legislature's recognition that California is in a state of crisis which has been caused by violent street gangs whose members threaten, terrorize, and commit a multitude of crimes against the peaceful citizens of their neighborhoods. The act's express purpose was to seek the eradication of criminal activity by street gangs." (*People v. Gardeley* (1996) 14 Cal.4th 605.) In concluding the felonious conduct underlying the gang participation offense need not be gang related, we observed in *Albillar:* "Gang members tend to protect and avenge their associates. Crimes committed by gang members, whether or not they are gang related or committed for the benefit of the gang, thus pose dangers to the public and difficulties for law enforcement not generally present when a crime is committed by someone with no gang affiliation. These activities, both individually and collectively, present a clear and present danger to public order and safety ..." Recognizing conspiracy to commit active gang participation as a valid offense furthers these purposes by affording prosecutors additional charging options in gang cases, and making additional punishment available.

The Court of Appeal found a contrary intent expressed in section 182.5, a different statute enacted by voters as part of Proposition 21. Section 182.5 defines the following conduct as a type of conspiracy: "Notwithstanding subdivisions (a) or (b) of Section 182, any person who actively participates in any criminal street gang, as defined in subdivision (f) of Section 186.22, with knowledge that its members engage in or have engaged in a pattern of criminal gang activity, as defined in subdivision (e) of Section 186.22, and who willfully promotes, furthers, assists, or benefits from any felonious criminal conduct by members of that gang is guilty of conspiracy to commit that felony and may be punished as specified in subdivision (a) of Section 182." The Legislative Analyst's comments appeared in the ballot pamphlet, and stated that the measure would "*expand* [ ] the law on conspiracy *to include gang-related activities.*" The Court of Appeal concluded that "this is an implicit recognition that the general conspiracy statute could not be applied to section 186.22, subdivision (a) because a criminal street gang was itself a species of conspiracy." In this the court erred. Its interpretation would rely on the language of the ballot statement to *limit* existing law when the intended effect of the measure was to *expand* the law to encompass gang-related activities more broadly.

Section 182.5 created a new form of conspiracy that is distinct from the traditional understanding of the crime in five significant ways. First, under traditional conspiracy principles, when two or more defendants conspire to commit a substantive offense, they need not have previously known each other, have any ongoing association, or plan to associate in any way beyond the commission of the substantive offense. Traditional conspiracy, then, encompasses a stand-alone agreement by former strangers to commit a single crime. In order to violate section 182.5 and, thus, commit a "182.5 conspiracy," a defendant cannot be a complete stranger to the gang. He or she must be an active gang participant with knowledge of other members' pattern of criminal gang activity.

Second, a traditional conspiracy encompasses an agreement to commit "any crime." Therefore, it is possible to conspire to commit a misdemeanor. A 182.5 conspiracy relates only to the commission of a felony.

Third, traditional conspiracy requires both the specific intent to agree, and specific intent to commit a target crime. A 182.5 conspiracy does not require any prior agreement among the conspirators to promote, further, or assist in the commission of a particular target crime. Even without a prior agreement, an active and knowing gang participant who acts with the required intent to promote, further, or assist in the commission of a felony by other gang members can violate section 182.5. That act of assistance or promotion replaces the required prior agreement to commit a crime that is ordinarily at the heart of a traditional conspiracy.

Fourth, traditional conspiracy liability attaches once an overt act is committed. A 182.5 conspiracy requires the actual commission of felonious criminal conduct as either an attempt or a completed crime.

Fifth, section 182.5 brings within its ambit not only a gang member who promotes, furthers, or assists in the commission of a felony. It also embraces an active and knowing participant who merely *benefits* from the crime's commission, even if he or she did not promote, further, or assist in the commission of that particular substantive offense. This constitutes a substantial expansion of a traditional conspiracy application. The "one who benefits" provision recognizes that gang activities both individually and collectively endanger the public and contribute to the perpetuation of the gang members' continued association for criminal purposes. Due to the organized nature of gangs, active gang participants may benefit from crimes committed by other gang members. When such benefits are proven along with the other elements of the statute, section 182.5 permits those benefitting gang participants to be convicted of conspiracy to commit the specific offense from which they benefitted.

The creation of a new basis for conspiracy liability under section 182.5 does not reflect a legislative intent to *preclude* the use of section 186.22(a) as an object of a traditional conspiracy under section 182. Indeed, sections 182 and 182.5 are quite different provisions covering different kinds of conduct. If evidence reflects that an active and knowing gang participant, acting with the required intent, agrees with other gang members to commit a felony, and an overt act in furtherance of the plan has been committed, a prosecutor may charge a traditional conspiracy to commit the gang participation offense under section 182, even if the target offense is not ultimately committed. Rather than expressing an intent to limit the scope of section 182, the enactment of section 182.5 provided prosecutors additional flexibility in charging a different kind of conspiracy, consistent with the Legislative Analyst's statement that the new provision "expand[ed] the law on conspiracy to include gang-related activities."

The Court of Appeal suggested in a footnote that its decision would be the same whether a conspiracy to commit the gang participation offense was viewed as "an absurd redundancy that results in unconstitutional vagueness" or a "conclusive legal falsehood." Recognizing such an offense would result in neither. The Attorney General points to analogous federal statutes, such as the Racketeer Influenced and Corrupt Organizations Act (RICO) (18 U.S.C. § 1961 et seq.), which criminalizes the maintenance of a group engaging in racketeering activity, including the commission of various felonies such as murder, robbery, and extortion. Likewise, the Smith Act (18 U.S.C. § 2385) criminalizes the organization of a group advocating the violent overthrow of the government. Both criminalize conduct involving multiple participants and may involve predicate conspiracies. Both recognize, as a separate offense, a conspiracy to violate its provisions.

...

Defendants' analogy to *People v. Iniguez* (2002) 96 Cal.App.4th 75 is inapt. The court there held that one could not conspire to commit *attempted* murder "because the crime of attempted murder requires a specific intent to actually commit the murder, while the agreement underlying the conspiracy pleaded to contemplated no more than an ineffectual act." Stated another way, under a traditional conspiracy approach, one cannot conspire to *try* to commit a crime. An agreement to commit a crime is required, even if nothing more than an overt act is ultimately done. By contrast, the conspiracy to commit the gang participation offense does not contemplate an agreement to commit an ineffectual act. Under the traditional application of section 182, a conspiracy to violate section 186.22(a) requires that a defendant be an active and knowing gang participant and agree to willfully promote, further, or assist gang members in the commission of an intended target felony. Unlike *Iniguez,* there is no logical impossibility or absurdity in recognizing the crime of conspiracy to actively participate in a gang.

Defendants argue the so-called Wharton's Rule should preclude recognition of conspiracy to commit gang participation. The rule "owes its name to Francis Wharton, whose treatise on criminal law identified the doctrine and its fundamental rationale...." (*Iannelli, supra.*) The rule states "Where the cooperation of two or more persons is necessary to the commission of the substantive crime, and there is no ingredient of an alleged conspiracy that is not present in the substantive crime, then the persons necessarily involved cannot be charged with conspiracy to commit the substantive offense and also with the substantive crime itself." (*People v. Mayers* (1980) 110 Cal.App.3d 809.) Classically, Wharton's Rule applies to crimes that an individual could not commit acting alone. Wharton's Rule "has current vitality only as a judicial presumption, to be applied in the absence of legislative intent to the contrary." (*Iannelli, supra.*) "[T]he Rule is essentially an aid to the determination of legislative intent [and] must defer to a discernible legislative judgment."

The presumption of Wharton's Rule has no application here. "The classic Wharton's Rule offenses—adultery, incest, bigamy, dueling—are crimes that are characterized by the general congruence of the agreement and the completed substantive offense. The parties to the agreement are the only persons who participate in commission of the substantive offense, and the immediate consequences of the crime rest on the parties themselves rather than on society at large. Finally, the agreement that attends the substantive offense does not appear likely to pose the distinct kinds of threats to society that the law of conspiracy seeks to avert. It cannot, for example, readily be assumed that an agreement to commit an offense of this nature will produce agreements to engage in a more general pattern of criminal conduct." (*Iannelli, supra.*) *Iannelli* concluded Wharton's Rule had no application to the federal gambling statute at issue there ...

Similar reasoning applies here. The immediate harm flowing from the gang participation offense is not limited to its participants. Indeed, an integral component of a *criminal* street gang is to commit felonies against others. Like the large-scale gambling operation at issue in *Iannelli,* a criminal street gang also involves a network of participants with different roles and varying kinds of involvement. The gang at issue here had over 200 members who performed diverse functions. Further, it cannot be said that active gang participation is not likely to generate additional criminal agreements. To the contrary, the gang structure makes such agreements much easier and more likely. These circumstances provide no justification for applying the presumption of Wharton's Rule.

...

D. Conclusion

The plain language of both sections 182 and 186.22(a) reflects no legislative intent to preclude a conviction for a traditional conspiracy to commit the gang participation offense. Defendants were active gang members, well aware of each other's active status and the gang's pattern of criminal gang activity. Their agreement to commit the various shootings here constituted an agreement to commit the gang participation offense and, once an overt act was performed, all the elements of conspiracy to violate section 186.22(a) were satisfied.

...

Note

The STEP Act. The STEP Act, like the federal Racketeer Influenced and Corrupt Organizations Act ("RICO"), 18 U.S.C. §§ 1961, *et seq.*, on which it was modeled, punishes membership in a criminal enterprise, giving prosecutors an alternative to a traditional conspiracy prosecution for group crimes. How does prosecution under this statute differ from a conspiracy prosecution?

In addition to directly criminalizing membership in a street gang, California's STEP statute embodies three other approaches to dealing with street gangs. First, the statute imposes enhanced penalties on anyone convicted of committing a felony "for the benefit of, at the direction of, or in association with any criminal street gang." P.C. § 186.22(b). Second, the statute amends P.C. § 272 (contributing to the delinquency of a minor) by adding the following language: "For purposes of this section, a parent or legal guardian to any person under the age of 18 years shall have the duty to exercise reasonable care, supervision, protection, and control over their minor child." Thus the section makes parents and guardians guilty of a misdemeanor if they are criminally negligent and breach this duty. *Williams v. Garcetti*, 5 Cal. 4th 561, 573 (1993). Third, the statute declares that any building or place used for specified illegal activities by a street gang is a nuisance which may be enjoined and for which damages may be recovered in a public or private nuisance action. P.C. § 186.22a.

The STEP remedies supplemented the already-existing remedy of a public nuisance action against the gang itself. *People ex rel. Gallo v. Acuna*, 14 Cal. 4th 1090 (1997). In nuisance actions, municipalities have obtained broad injunctions against gang members. For example, in *People v. Gonzalez*, 12 Cal. 4th 804, 808–09 (1996), the court described the injunction in that case as follows:

> The City of Los Angeles ... secured a preliminary injunction limiting the activities of members of the Blythe Street Gang within a certain geographical area of Los Angeles. Among other things, the injunction prohibited gang members from using or possessing deadly weapons, including such items as glass bottles, large metal belt buckles and ball bearings. It prohibited gang members from using or possessing numerous other items, including pagers and cellular phones, whistles and car parts. No gang member was to "annoy, harass, or intimidate any person," or contact any person who "will complain about the defendants' activities," or be present on private property in the absence of the owner without the written consent of the owner. In addition, gang members were enjoined from climbing any tree, wall or fence, and from being on the roof of any building except in an emergency, from obstructing traffic, or if underage, from violating a specified curfew. Adults, too, were enjoined from being present in a specified area between 8 p.m. and 6 a.m., without proper identification and proof of legal residence in the area.

Which, if any, of these remedies is likely to prove effective in dealing with street gangs?

People v. Swain

12 Cal. 4th 593, 909 P.2d 994 (1996)

Baxter, Associate Justice.

Defendants Jamal K. Swain and David Chatman were each convicted of conspiracy to commit murder and other crimes, stemming from the drive-by shooting death of a 15-year-old boy. As we shall explain, we hold that intent to kill is a required element of the crime of conspiracy to commit murder. In light of the jury instructions given, and general verdicts returned, we cannot determine beyond a reasonable doubt whether the jury found that the defendants conspired with an intent to kill. That conclusion requires us to reverse defendants' conspiracy convictions.

Facts and Procedural Background

The question before us is one of law; the facts found by the Court of Appeal, summarized below, are not disputed.

Prosecution evidence established that a brown van passed through the Hunter's Point neighborhood of San Francisco about 2:00 a.m. on January 13, 1991. It slowed down near the spot where the young victim, who was of Samoan descent, and his friends were listening to music on the street.

A young Black male who appeared to have no hair was driving the van. Suddenly several shots were fired from the front of the van. Defendant Chatman and another young man also fired guns from the rear of the van. One of the intended victims had yelled out "drive-by" as a warning of the impending shooting, so most of the people on the street ducked down. The 15-year-old victim, Hagbom Saileele, who was holding the radio from which music was playing, was shot twice from behind. He later died in surgery.

Afterward, defendant Swain was in jail and boasted to jailmates about what good aim he had with a gun: "He was talking about what a good shot he was.

[¶] ...

[¶] He was saying he had shot that Samoan kid when they were in the van going about 30 miles an hour up a hill." The area where the shooting occurred is hilly; the van would have had to have been traveling uphill as it passed by the scene of the shooting.

[Several other items of evidence pointed to Swain and Chatman as being the shooters.]

At trial, Chatman admitted he had been in the van, which was driven to Hunter's Point to retaliate for a car theft attributed to a neighborhood youth who was not the victim of the shooting. The original plan was allegedly to steal the car of the thief. Chatman admitted he had fired shots, but claimed he fired wildly and only in self-defense. In support of this self-defense theory, he testified he heard an initial shot and thought it was fired by someone outside the van shooting at him, so he returned the fire. As noted, Chatman claimed Swain was not in the van.

Swain testified he was not in the van during the shooting and did not do any shooting. He claimed he had entered the van earlier in the evening, but had left because "the smell of marijuana bothered him." He claimed he took BART (Bay Area Rapid Transit) to Berkeley, where he spent the evening at a relative's home. He denied boasting about shooting the victim and denied having threatened any witnesses.

The jury first returned a verdict finding defendant Chatman guilty of second degree murder and conspiracy. As instructed, the jury also made a finding that the target offense of the conspiracy was murder in the second degree. Several days later, the jury returned verdicts against defendant Swain, finding him not guilty of murder or its lesser included offenses, but guilty of conspiracy and of attempting to dissuade a witness from testifying by threats. Once again, the jury made a finding under the conspiracy count that the target offense of the conspiracy was murder in the second degree.

...

Discussion

I

Defendants contend the jury should have been instructed that proof of intent to kill is required to support a conviction of conspiracy to commit murder, whether the target offense of the conspiracy—murder—is determined to be in the first or second degree. More particularly, defendants assert it was error to instruct the jury on the principles of implied malice second degree murder in connection with the determination of whether they could be found guilty of conspiracy to commit murder, since implied malice does not require a finding of intent to kill. As we shall explain, we agree.

...

We have noted that conspiracy is a specific intent crime requiring an intent to agree or conspire, and a further intent to commit the target crime, here murder, the object of the conspiracy. Since murder committed with intent to kill is the functional equivalent of *express malice* murder, conceptually speaking, no conflict arises between the specific intent element of conspiracy and the specific intent requirement for such category of murders. Simply put, where the conspirators agree or conspire with specific intent to kill and commit an overt act in furtherance of such agreement, they are guilty of conspiracy to commit express malice murder. The conceptual difficulty arises when the target offense of murder is founded on a theory of implied malice, which requires no intent to kill.

Implied malice murder, in contrast to express malice, requires instead an intent to do some act, the natural consequences of which are dangerous to human life. "*When the killing is the direct result of such an act,*" the requisite mental state for murder—malice aforethought—is implied. (CALJIC No. 8.31, italics added.) In such circumstances, "... it is not necessary to establish that the defendant intended that his act would result in the death of a human being." (*Ibid.*) Hence, under an *implied malice* theory of second degree murder, the requisite mental state for murder—malice aforethought—is by definition "implied," as a matter of law, from the specific intent to do some act dangerous to human life *together with the circumstance that a killing has resulted from the doing of such act.*

Stated otherwise, all murders require, at the core of the corpus delicti of the offense, a "killing." "Murder is the unlawful killing of a human being ... with malice aforethought." (Pen. Code, § 187, subd. (a).) But only in the case of *implied malice* murder is the requisite mental state—malice aforethought—implied from the specific intent to do some act other than an intentional killing and the resulting circumstance: a killing that has in fact occurred as "the direct result of such an act."

The element of malice aforethought in implied malice murder cases is therefore derived or "implied," in part through hindsight so to speak, from (i) proof of the specific intent to do some act dangerous to human life *and* (ii) the circumstance that a killing has resulted therefrom. It is precisely due to this nature of *implied malice* murder that it would be *illogical* to conclude one can be found guilty of conspiring to commit murder where the requisite element of malice is implied. Such a construction would be at odds with the very nature of the crime of conspiracy—an "inchoate" crime that "fixes the point of legal intervention at [the time of] agreement to commit a crime," and indeed "reaches further back into preparatory conduct than [the crime of] attempt" (Model Pen. Code & Commentaries, *supra*, com. 1 to § 5.03)—precisely because commission of the crime could never be established, or deemed complete, unless and until a killing actually occurred.

[The court found support for its holding in *People v. Collie* (1981) 30 Cal. 3d 43, where the court had held that there was no such crime as *attempted* implied malice murder. "To constitute an attempt, there must be (i) proof of specific intent to commit the target crime and (ii) a direct, ineffectual act done towards its commission. Concluding in *Collie* that the trial court erred in instructing the jury it could convict the defendant of attempted murder on the basis of implied malice and without a finding of intent to kill, we explained: 'Specific intent to kill is a necessary element of attempted murder. It must be proved, and it cannot be inferred merely from the commission of another dangerous crime.' "]

We conclude that a conviction of conspiracy to commit murder requires a finding of intent to kill, and cannot be based on a theory of implied malice.

. . .

[Concurring opinions of Mosk and Kennard, JJ., omitted.][d]

Note

Problems with the Crime of Conspiracy. The crime of conspiracy (along with its various supporting doctrines) has been frequently criticized by judges and academics. Perhaps the most oft-cited critique is that of Justice Jackson in his concurring opinion in *Krulewitch v. United States*, 336 U.S. 440 (1949). His catalogue of the numerous problems with conspiracy doctrine follows:

> The modern crime of conspiracy is so vague that it almost defies definition. Despite certain elementary and essential elements, it also, chameleon-like, takes on a special coloration from each of the many independent offenses on which it may be overlaid. It is always "predominantly mental in composition" because it consists primarily of a meeting of minds and an intent.
>
> The crime comes down to us wrapped in vague but unpleasant connotations. It sounds historical undertones of treachery, secret plotting and violence on

---

d. In *People v. Cortez*, 18 Cal.4th 1223 (1998), the Supreme Court went on to hold that there is no such crime as conspiracy to commit even express malice second degree murder.

> "[W]here two or more persons conspire to commit murder—i.e., intend to agree to conspire, further intend to commit the target offense of murder, and perform one or more overt acts in furtherance of the planned murder—each has acted with a state of mind functionally indistinguishable from the mental state of premeditating the target offense of murder."

Id. at 1232.

a scale that menaces social stability and the security of the state itself. "Privy conspiracy" ranks with sedition and rebellion in the Litany's prayer for deliverance. Conspiratorial movements do indeed lie back of the political assassination, the coup d'etat, the putsch, the revolution, and seizures of power in modern times, as they have in all history.

But the conspiracy concept also is superimposed upon many concerted crimes having no political motivation. It is not intended to question that the basic conspiracy principle has some place in modern criminal law, because to unite, back of a criminal purpose, the strength, opportunities and resources of many is obviously more dangerous and more difficult to police than the efforts of a lone wrongdoer. It also may be trivialized, as here, where the conspiracy consists of the concert of a loathsome panderer and a prostitute to go from New York to Florida to ply their trade and it would appear that a simple Mann Act prosecution [for transporting a woman across state lines for the purpose of prostitution, debauchery or other immoral practices] would vindicate the majesty of federal law. However, even when appropriately invoked, the looseness and pliability of the doctrine present inherent dangers which should be in the background of judicial thought wherever it is sought to extend the doctrine to meet the exigencies of a particular case.

Conspiracy in federal law aggravates the degree of crime over that of unconcerted offending. The act of confederating to commit a misdemeanor, followed by even an innocent overt act in its execution, is a felony and is such even if the misdemeanor is never consummated. The more radical proposition also is well-established that at common law and under some statutes a combination may be a criminal conspiracy even if it contemplates only acts which are not crimes at all when perpetrated by an individual or by many acting severally.

Thus the conspiracy doctrine will incriminate persons on the fringe of offending who would not be guilty of aiding and abetting or of becoming an accessory, for those charges only lie when an act which is a crime has actually been committed.

Attribution of criminality to a confederation which contemplates no act that would be criminal if carried out by any one of the conspirators is a practice peculiar to Anglo-American law. "There can be little doubt that this wide definition of the crime of conspiracy originates in the criminal equity administered in the Star Chamber." (8 Holdsworth, History of English Law, 382) In fact, we are advised that "The modern crime of conspiracy is almost entirely the result of the manner in which conspiracy was treated by the court of Star Chamber." (*Id.* at 379) The doctrine does not commend itself to jurists of civil-law countries, despite universal recognition that an organized society must have legal weapons for combatting organized criminality. Most other countries have devised what they consider more discriminating principles upon which to prosecute criminal gangs, secret associations and subversive syndicates.

A recent tendency has appeared in this Court to expand this elastic offense and to facilitate its proof. In *Pinkerton v. United States*, 328 U.S. 640 (1946),[e] it sustained a conviction of a substantive crime where there was no proof of participation in or knowledge of it, upon the novel and dubious theory that conspiracy is equivalent in law to aiding and abetting.

Doctrines of conspiracy are not only invoked for criminal prosecution, but also in civil proceedings for damages or for injunction, and in administrative proceedings to apply regulatory statutes. They have been resorted to by military commissions and on at least one notable occasion when civil courts were open at the time and place to punish the offense. This conspiracy concept was employed to prosecute laborers for combining to raise their wages and formed the basis for abuse of the labor injunction. The National Labor Relations Act found it necessary to provide that concerted labor activities otherwise lawful were not rendered unlawful by mere concert. But in other fields concert may still be a crime though it contemplates only acts which each could do lawfully on his own.

The interchangeable use of conspiracy doctrine in civil as well as penal proceedings opens it to the danger, absent in the case of many crimes, that a court having in mind only the civil sanctions will approve lax practices which later are imported into criminal proceedings. In civil proceedings this Court frankly has made the end a test of the means, saying, "To require a greater showing would cripple the Act," in dispensing with the necessity for specific intent to produce a result violative of the statute. Further, the Court has dispensed with even the necessity to infer any definite agreement, although that is the gist of the offense. "It is elementary that an unlawful conspiracy may be and often is formed without simultaneous action or agreement on the part of the conspirators ..." One might go on from the reports of this and lower courts and put together their decisions condoning absence of proof to demonstrate that the minimum of proof required to establish conspiracy is extremely low, and we may expect our pronouncements in civil cases to be followed in criminal ones also.

---

e. In *Pinkerton*, two brothers, Walter and Daniel, were convicted of a number of substantive counts of manufacturing and distributing whiskey without paying federal taxes ("moonshining"), and they were also convicted of conspiracy to engage in moonshining. The evidence showed that, while Walter and Daniel had jointly engaged in moonshining previously, all of the substantive offenses proved in the instant case were committed by Walter alone. In fact, Daniel was in prison when some of the substantive offenses were committed. The majority upheld Daniel's convictions for the substantive crimes committed by Walter, finding that there was a continuous conspiracy and that Daniel was liable for all Walter's crimes in furtherance of the conspiracy until he withdrew. Justice Rutledge dissented, arguing that Daniel could not be convicted of substantive crimes absent some evidence that he aided and abetted the crimes. Justice Jackson did not participate in the case because he was in Nuremburg as one of the prosecutors in the war crimes trials.

Of course, it is for prosecutors rather than courts to determine when to use a scatter-gun to bring down the defendant, but there are procedural advantages from using it which add to the danger of unguarded extension of the concept.

An accused, under the Sixth Amendment, has the right to trial "by an impartial jury of the State and district wherein the crime shall have been committed." The leverage of a conspiracy charge lifts this limitation from the prosecution and reduces its protection to a phantom, for the crime is considered so vagrant as to have been committed in any district where any one of the conspirators did any one of the acts, however innocent, intended to accomplish its object. The Government may, and often does, compel one to defend at a great distance from any place he ever did any act because some accused confederate did some trivial and by itself innocent act in the chosen district. Circumstances may even enable the prosecution to fix the place of trial in Washington, D. C., where a defendant may lawfully be put to trial before a jury partly or even wholly made up of employees of the Government that accuses him.

When the trial starts, the accused feels the full impact of the conspiracy strategy. Strictly, the prosecution should first establish *prima facie* the conspiracy and identify the conspirators, after which evidence of acts and declarations of each in the course of its execution are admissible against all. But the order of proof of so sprawling a charge is difficult for a judge to control. As a practical matter, the accused often is confronted with a hodgepodge of acts and statements by others which he may never have authorized or intended or even known about, but which help to persuade the jury of existence of the conspiracy itself. In other words, a conspiracy often is proved by evidence that is admissible only upon assumption that conspiracy existed. The naive assumption that prejudicial effects can be overcome by instructions to the jury all practicing lawyers know to be unmitigated fiction.

The trial of a conspiracy charge doubtless imposes a heavy burden on the prosecution, but it is an especially difficult situation for the defendant. The hazard from loose application of rules of evidence is aggravated where the Government institutes mass trials. Moreover, in federal practice there is no rule preventing conviction on uncorroborated testimony of accomplices, as there are in many jurisdictions, and the most comfort a defendant can expect is that the court can be induced to follow the "better practice" and caution the jury against "too much reliance upon the testimony of accomplices."

A co-defendant in a conspiracy trial occupies an uneasy seat. There generally will be evidence of wrongdoing by somebody. It is difficult for the individual to make his own case stand on its own merits in the minds of jurors who are ready to believe that birds of a feather are flocked together. If he is silent, he is taken to admit it and if, as often happens, codefendants can be prodded into accusing or contradicting each other, they convict each other. There are many practical difficulties in defending against a charge of conspiracy which I will not enumerate.

People v. Lauria

251 Cal. App. 2d 471, 59 Cal. Rptr. 628 (1967)

FLEMING, J.

In an investigation of call-girl activity the police focused their attention on three prostitutes actively plying their trade on call, each of whom was using Lauria's telephone answering service, presumably for business purposes.

On January 8, 1965, Stella Weeks, a policewoman, signed up for telephone service with Lauria's answering service. Mrs. Weeks, in the course of her conversation with Lauria's office manager, hinted broadly that she was a prostitute concerned with the secrecy of her activities and their concealment from the police. She was assured that the operation of the service was discreet and "about as safe as you can get." It was arranged that Mrs. Weeks need not leave her address with the answering service, but could pick up her calls and pay her bills in person.

On February 11, Mrs. Weeks talked to Lauria on the telephone and told him her business was modelling and she had been referred to the answering service by Terry, one of the three prostitutes under investigation. She complained that because of the operation of the service she had lost two valuable customers, referred to as tricks. Lauria defended his service and said that her friends had probably lied to her about having left calls for her. But he did not respond to Mrs. Weeks' hints that she needed customers in order to make money, other than to invite her to his house for a personal visit in order to get better acquainted. In the course of his talk he said "his business was taking messages."

On February 15, Mrs. Weeks talked on the telephone to Lauria's office manager and again complained of two lost calls, which she described as a $50 and a $100 trick. On investigation the office manager could find nothing wrong, but she said she would alert the switchboard operators about slip-ups on calls.

On April 1 Lauria and the three prostitutes were arrested. Lauria complained to the police that this attention was undeserved, stating that Hollywood Call Board had 60 to 70 prostitutes on its board while his own service had only 9 or 10, that he kept separate records for known or suspected prostitutes for the convenience of himself and the police. When asked if his records were available to police who might come to the office to investigate call girls, Lauria replied that they were whenever the police had a specific name. However, his service didn't "arbitrarily tell the police about prostitutes on our board. As long as they pay their bills we tolerate them." In a subsequent voluntary appearance before the grand jury Lauria testified he had always cooperated with the police. But he admitted he knew some of his customers were prostitutes, and he knew Terry was a prostitute because he had personally used her services, and he knew she was paying for 500 calls a month.

Lauria and the three prostitutes were indicted for conspiracy to commit prostitution, and nine overt acts were specified. Subsequently the trial court set aside the indictment as having been brought without reasonable or probable cause. The People have appealed, claiming that a sufficient showing of an unlawful agreement to further prostitution was made.

To establish agreement, the People need show no more than a tacit, mutual understanding between coconspirators to accomplish an unlawful act. Here the People attempted to establish a conspiracy by showing that Lauria, well aware that his codefendants were prostitutes who received business calls from customers through his telephone answering service, continued to furnish them with such service. This approach attempts to equate knowledge of another's criminal activity with conspiracy to further such criminal activity, and poses the question of the criminal responsibility of a furnisher of goods or services who knows his product is being used to assist the operation of an illegal business. Under what circumstances does a supplier become a part of a conspiracy to further an illegal enterprise by furnishing goods or services which he knows are to be used by the buyer for criminal purposes?

The two leading cases on this point face in opposite directions. In *United States v. Falcone* (1940) 311 U.S. 205, the sellers of large quantities of sugar, yeast, and cans were absolved from participation in a moonshining conspiracy among distillers who bought from them, while in *Direct Sales Co. v. United States* (1943) 319 U.S. 703, a wholesaler of drugs was convicted of conspiracy to violate the federal narcotic laws by selling drugs in quantity to a codefendant physician who was supplying them to addicts. The distinction between these two cases appears primarily based on the proposition that distributors of such dangerous products as drugs are required to exercise greater discrimination in the conduct of their business than are distributors of innocuous substances like sugar and yeast.

In the earlier case, *Falcone*, the sellers' knowledge of the illegal use of the goods was insufficient by itself to make the sellers participants in a conspiracy with the distillers who bought from them. Such knowledge fell short of proof of a conspiracy, and evidence on the volume of sales was too vague to support a jury finding that respondents knew of the conspiracy from the size of the sales alone.

In the later case of *Direct Sales*, the conviction of a drug wholesaler for conspiracy to violate federal narcotic laws was affirmed on a showing that it had actively promoted the sale of morphine sulphate in quantity and had sold codefendant physician, who practiced in a small town in South Carolina, more than 300 times his normal requirements of the drug, even though it had been repeatedly warned of the dangers of unrestricted sales of the drug. The court contrasted the restricted goods involved in *Direct Sales* with the articles of free commerce involved in *Falcone*: "All articles of commerce may be put to illegal ends," said the court. "But all do not have inherently the same susceptibility to harmful and illegal use.... This difference is important for two purposes. One is for making certain that the seller knows the buyer's intended illegal use. The other is to show that by the sale he intends to further, promote, and cooperate in it. This intent, when given effect by overt act, is the gist of conspiracy. While it is not identical with mere knowledge that another purposes unlawful action it is not unrelated to such knowledge.... The step from knowledge to intent and agreement may be taken. There is more than suspicion, more than knowledge, acquiescence, carelessness, indifference, lack of concern. There is informed and interested cooperation, stimulation, instigation. And there is also a 'stake in the venture' which, even if it may not be essential, is not irrelevant to the question of conspiracy."

While *Falcone* and *Direct Sales* may not be entirely consistent with each other in their full implications, they do provide us with a framework for the criminal liability of a supplier of lawful goods or services put to unlawful use. Both the element of knowledge of the illegal use of the goods are services and the element of intent to further that use must be present in order to make the supplier a participant in a criminal conspiracy.

Proof of *knowledge* is ordinarily a question of fact and requires no extended discussion in the present case. The knowledge of the supplier was sufficiently established when Lauria admitted he knew some of his customers were prostitutes and admitted he knew that Terry, an active subscriber to his service, was a prostitute. In the face of these admissions he could scarcely claim to have relied on the normal assumption an operator of a business or service is entitled to make, that his customers are behaving themselves in the eyes of the law. Because Lauria knew in fact that some of his customers were prostitutes, it is a legitimate inference he knew they were subscribing to his answering service for illegal business purposes and were using his service to make assignations for prostitution. On this record we think the prosecution is entitled to claim positive knowledge by Lauria of the use of his service to facilitate the business of prostitution.

The more perplexing issue in the case is the sufficiency of proof of intent to further the criminal enterprise. The element of intent may be proved either by direct evidence, or by evidence of circumstances from which an intent to further a criminal enterprise by supplying lawful goods or services may be inferred. Direct evidence of participation, such as advice from the supplier of legal goods or services to the user of those goods or services on their use for illegal purposes provides the simplest case. When the intent to further and promote the criminal enterprise comes from the lips of the supplier himself, ambiguities of inference from circumstance need not trouble us. But in cases where direct proof of complicity is lacking, intent to further the conspiracy must be derived from the sale itself and its surrounding circumstances in order to establish the supplier's express or tacit agreement to join the conspiracy.

In the case at bench the prosecution argues that since Lauria knew his customers were using his service for illegal purposes but nevertheless continued to furnish it to them, he must have intended to assist them in carrying out their illegal activities. Thus through a union of knowledge and intent he became a participant in a criminal conspiracy. Essentially, the People argue that knowledge alone of the continuing use of his telephone facilities for criminal purposes provided a sufficient basis from which his intent to participate in those criminal activities could be inferred.

In examining precedents in this field we find that sometimes, but not always, the criminal intent of the supplier may be inferred from his knowledge of the unlawful use made of the product he supplies. Some consideration of characteristic patterns may be helpful.

1. Intent may be inferred from knowledge, when the purveyor of legal goods for illegal use has acquired a stake in the venture. (*United States v. Falcone*, 109 F.2d 579.) For example, in *Regina v. Thomas*, [1957] 2 All Eng. 181, a prosecution for living off the earnings of prostitution, the evidence showed that the accused, knowing the woman to be a convicted prostitute, agreed to let her have the use of his room between the hours of 9 p.m. and 2 a.m. for a charge of 3 pounds a night. The Court of Criminal Appeal refused an appeal from the conviction, holding that when the accused rented a room at a grossly inflated rent to a prostitute for the purpose of carrying on her trade, a jury could find he was living on the earnings of prostitution.

In the present case, no proof was offered of inflated charges for the telephone answering services furnished the codefendants.

2. Intent may be inferred from knowledge, when no legitimate use for the goods or services exists. The leading California case is *People v. McLaughlin* (1952) 111 Cal. App. 2d 781, in which the court upheld a conviction of the suppliers of horse-racing information by wire for conspiracy to promote bookmaking, when it had been established that wire-service information had no other use than to supply information needed by bookmakers to conduct illegal gambling operations.

In *Rex v. Delaval* (1763) 3 Burr. 1434, 97 Eng. Rep. 913, the charge was unlawful conspiracy to remove a girl from the control of Bates, a musician to whom she was bound as an apprentice, and place her in the hands of Sir Francis Delaval for the purpose of prostitution. Lord Mansfield not only upheld the charges against Bates and Sir Francis, but also against Fraine, the attorney who drew up the indentures of apprenticeship transferring custody of the girl from Bates to Sir Francis. Fraine, said Lord Mansfield, must have known that Sir Francis had no facilities for teaching music to apprentices so that it was impossible for him to have been ignorant of the real intent of the transaction.

In *Shaw v. Director of Public Prosecutions*, [1962] A.C. 220, the defendant was convicted of conspiracy to corrupt public morals and of living on the earnings of prostitution, when he published a directory consisting almost entirely of advertisements of the names, addresses, and specialized talents of prostitutes. Publication of such a directory, said the court, could have no legitimate use and serve no other purpose than to advertise the professional services of the prostitutes whose advertisements appeared in the directory. The publisher could be deemed a participant in the profits from the business activities of his principal advertisers.

Other services of a comparable nature come to mind: the manufacturer of crooked dice and marked cards who sells his product to gambling casinos; the tipster who furnishes information on the movement of law enforcement officers to known lawbreakers. (*Cf. Jackson v. State of Texas* (Tex. 1957) 298 S.W.2d 837, where the furnisher of signaling equipment used to warn gamblers of the police was convicted of aiding the equipping of a gambling place.) In such cases the supplier must necessarily have an intent to further the illegal enterprise since there is no known honest use for his goods.

However, there is nothing in the furnishing of telephone answering service which would necessarily imply assistance in the performance of illegal activities. Nor is any inference to be derived from the use of an answering service by women, either in any particular volume of calls, or outside normal working hours. Night-club entertainers, registered nurses, faith healers, public stenographers, photographic models, and free lance substitute employees, provide examples of women in legitimate occupations whose employment might cause them to receive a volume of telephone calls at irregular hours.

3. Intent may be inferred from knowledge, when the volume of business with the buyer is grossly disproportionate to any legitimate demand, or when sales for illegal use amount to a high proportion of the seller's total business. In such cases an intent to participate in the illegal enterprise may be inferred from the quantity of the business done. For example, in *Direct Sales*, the sale of narcotics to a rural physician in quantities 300 times greater than he would have normal use for provided potent evidence of an intent to further the illegal activity. In the same case the court also found significant the fact that the wholesaler had attracted as customers a disproportionately large group of physicians who had been convicted of violating the Harrison Act. In *Shaw v. Director of Public Prosecutions*, [1962] A.C. 220, almost the entire business of the directory came from prostitutes.

No evidence of any unusual volume of business with prostitutes was presented by the prosecution against Lauria.

Inflated charges, the sale of goods with no legitimate use, sales in inflated amounts, each may provide a fact of sufficient moment from which the intent of the seller to participate in the criminal enterprise may be inferred. In such instances participation by the supplier of legal goods to the illegal enterprise may be inferred because in one way or another the supplier has acquired a special interest in the operation of the illegal enterprise. His intent to participate in the crime of which he had knowledge may be inferred from the existence of his special interest.

Yet there are cases in which it cannot reasonably be said that the supplier has a stake in the venture or has acquired a special interest in the enterprise, but in which he has been held liable as a participant on the basis of knowledge alone. Some suggestion of this appears in *Direct Sales*, supra, where both the knowledge of the illegal use of the drugs and the intent of the supplier to aid that use were inferred. In *Regina v. Bainbridge* (1959) 3 Week. L. 656 [(C.C.A. 6) [3 All Eng. 200]], a supplier of oxygen cutting equipment to one known to intend to use it to break into a bank was convicted as an accessory to the crime. In *Sykes v. Director of Public Prosecutions* [1962] A.C. 528, one having knowledge of the theft of 100 pistols, 4 submachine guns, and 1,960 rounds of ammunition was convicted of misprision of felony for failure to disclose the theft to the public authorities. It seems apparent from these cases that a supplier who furnishes equipment which he knows will be used to commit a serious crime may be deemed from that knowledge alone to have intended to produce the result. Such proof may justify an inference that the furnisher intended to aid the execution of the crime and that he thereby became a participant. For instance, we think the operator of a telephone answering service with positive knowledge that his service was being used to facilitate the extortion of ransom, the distribution of heroin, or the passing of counterfeit money who continued to furnish the service with knowledge of its use, might be chargeable on knowledge alone with participation in a scheme to extort money, to distribute narcotics, or to pass counterfeit money. The same result would follow the seller of gasoline who knew the buyer was using his product to make Molotov cocktails for terroristic use.

Logically, the same reasoning could be extended to crimes of every description. Yet we do not believe an inference of intent drawn from knowledge of criminal use properly applies to the less serious crimes classified as misdemeanors. The duty to take positive action to dissociate oneself from activities helpful to violations of the criminal law is far stronger and more compelling for felonies than it is for misdemeanors or petty offenses. In this respect, as in others, the distinction between felonies and misdemeanors, between more serious and less serious crime, retains continuing vitality. In historically the most serious felony, treason, an individual with knowledge of the treason can be prosecuted for concealing and failing to disclose it. (Pen. Code, § 38; 18 U.S.C. § 2382.) In other felonies, both at common law and under the criminal laws of the United States, an individual knowing of the commission of a felony is criminally liable for concealing it and failing to make it known to proper authority. But this crime, known as misprision of felony, has always been limited to knowledge and concealment of felony and has never extended to misdemeanor. A similar limitation is found in the criminal liability of an accessory, which is restricted to aid in the escape of a principal who has committed or been charged with a felony. (Pen. Code, § 32.) We believe the distinction between the obligations arising from knowledge of a felony and those arising from knowledge of a misdemeanor continues to reflect basic human feelings about the duties owed by individuals to society. Heinous crime must be stamped out, and its suppression is the responsibility of all. Venial crime and crime not evil in itself present less of a danger to society, and perhaps the benefits of their suppression through the modern equivalent of the posse, the hue and cry, the informant, and the citizen's arrest, are outweighed by the disruption to everyday life brought about by amateur law enforcement and private officiousness in relatively inconsequential delicts which do not threaten our basic security.

...

With respect to misdemeanors, we conclude that positive knowledge of the supplier that his products or services are being used for criminal purposes does not, without more, establish an intent of the supplier to participate in the misdemeanors. With respect to felonies, we do not decide the converse, *viz.*, that in all cases of felony knowledge of criminal use alone may justify an inference of the supplier's intent to participate in the crime. The implications of *Falcone* make the matter uncertain with respect to those felonies which are merely prohibited wrongs. But decision on this point is not compelled, and we leave the matter open.

From this analysis of precedent we deduce the following rule: the intent of a supplier who knows of the criminal use to which his supplies are put to participate in the criminal activity connected with the use of his supplies may be established by (1) direct evidence that he intends to participate, or (2) through an inference that he intends to participate based on, (a) his special interest in the activity, or (b) the aggravated nature of the crime itself.

When we review Lauria's activities in the light of this analysis, we find no proof that Lauria took any direct action to further, encourage, or direct the call-girl activities of his codefendants and we find an absence of circumstance from which his special interest in their activities could be inferred. Neither excessive charges for standardized services, nor the furnishing of services without a legitimate use, nor an unusual quantity of business with call girls, are present. The offense which he is charged with furthering is a misdemeanor, a category of crime which has never been made a required subject of positive disclosure to public authority. Under these circumstances, although proof of Lauria's knowledge of the criminal activities of his patrons was sufficient to charge him with that fact, there was insufficient evidence that he intended to further their criminal activities, and hence insufficient proof of his participation in a criminal conspiracy with his codefendants to further prostitution. Since the conspiracy centered around the activities of Lauria's telephone answering service, the charges against his codefendants likewise fail for want of proof.

In absolving Lauria of complicity in a criminal conspiracy we do not wish to imply that the public authorities are without remedies to combat modern manifestations of the world's oldest profession. Licensing of telephone answering services under the police power, together with the revocation of licenses for the toleration of prostitution, is a possible civil remedy. The furnishing of telephone answering service in aid of prostitution could be made a crime. (Cf. Pen. Code, § 316, which makes it a misdemeanor to let an apartment with knowledge of its use for prostitution.) Other solutions will doubtless occur to vigilant public authorities if the problem of call-girl activity needs further suppression.

The order is affirmed.

Lorenson v. Superior Court

35 Cal. 2d 49, 216 P.2d 859 (1950)

Edmonds, Justice.

Harry M. Lorenson and twelve other persons were indicted for conspiracy to commit robbery, to commit assault with a deadly weapon and to pervert or obstruct justice or the due administration of the laws. The present proceeding to restrain the Superior Court, by writ of prohibition, from proceeding with the trial of the action, is prosecuted chiefly upon the ground that there was insufficient evidence before the grand jury to show that Lorenson committed any crime.

From the testimony presented to the grand jury, it appears that Alfred Pearson was the principal employee of the Sky Pilot Radio Shop located in a residential district of Los Angeles. His general reputation as an unreliable business man was not bettered by newspaper publicity to the effect that he had obtained title to the home of a Mrs. Phillips by legal proceedings arising out of a controversy over a repair bill of less than $10. The accounts of his dealings with Mrs. Phillips, coupled with stories of his assertedly unfair business practices in other transactions, had brought about a general wave of indignation in the neighborhood.

For some time prior to Pearson's difficulties with Mrs. Phillips, Lorenson, a captain in the Police Department of Los Angeles, had been assigned to duty with the Police Commission. He had directed the arrest and prosecution of Pearson on several criminal charges. Pearson was acquitted in each of these cases with the exception of one in which he was fined $500 for a violation of the federal law administered by the Office of Price Administration.

Each man intensely disliked the other. At one time Pearson sued Lorenson and several other persons, claiming damages because of an asserted conspiracy to ruin his business. Lorenson made no effort to conceal his ill will toward Pearson and repeatedly voiced his hatred and enmity toward the radio man.

"Mickey" Cohen is a shadowy character in this picture of the situation at the time of the events which are the basis for the challenged indictment. According to testimony presented to the grand jury, Cohen is a well known hoodlum of Los Angeles and a generally nefarious character. The indictment is based upon evidence tending to show that Lorenson interested himself in Mrs. Phillips' difficulties with Pearson and enlisted as aids in his purpose to help her, and punish Pearson, a lawyer and seven of "Mickey's" henchmen.

The overt acts of Lorenson and those indicted with him took place within about 24 hours before a severe beating of Pearson on a Saturday afternoon. The story commences with a conversation between Lorenson and Jerome Weber, an attorney, which took place the previous morning. At that time, Lorenson asked Weber whether he would represent Mrs. Phillips in a suit to set aside the sale of her home to Pearson. When Weber agreed to act as her attorney, Lorenson stated that he would talk with Mrs. Phillips and make an investigation for the purpose of obtaining facts to be used in the prosecution of the action.

Lorenson then went to the Wilshire Police Station and discussed Mrs. Phillips' case with Acting Captain Swan. While commenting upon Pearson, Swan remarked that if Pearson came to the Wilshire Station he would be thrown down the stairs. Lorenson then called upon Mrs. Phillips, telling her he was sure her home could be recovered and that Jerome Weber would do the legal work without charge. Lorenson then saw Weber, who said he would take the case without fee.

In the afternoon, Lorenson received a telephone call from an unknown person who told him that there would be pickets in front of Pearson's store the next day carrying banners stating in substance: "Don't patronize Mr. Pearson. He took a widow's home away for this repair bill, eight (or) nine dollars." Lorenson made no official report of this conversation.

[The next morning, Cohen's associates had signs made up for the pickets. Then two of them, James Rist and David Ogul, went to Pearson's store looking for him. He was out, but the two returned in the afternoon, and, after a short conversation, Pearson threw them out and informed them he had recorded the conversation. Later in the afternoon, the two returned with two others and attacked Pearson, beating him with a gun, clubs, iron rods and other heavy objects. Pearson's arm was broken and his head cut in five places. They tore telephones from the wall and took Pearson's recording machine. They escaped in a waiting car.]

Because of a minor traffic violation, officers in a passing patrol car gave chase. Tire irons, a gun, and a riding crop were thrown from the speeding car. In response to a radio call for assistance, four police cars responded. When the automobile was overtaken, the officers found that it had seven occupants, [including the four who had beaten Pearson], all associates of Cohen. After the men were arrested and while they were being searched, an amateur photographer took pictures of the party. The officers with their prisoners arrived at the Wilshire Station about 4:25 p.m.

At approximately 4:10 p.m., which places the conversation just at the time of the beating of Pearson and the pursuit of the men who had attacked him, Jerome Weber called the Wilshire Station and asked if anyone had been arrested in connection with a disturbance at Pearson's place of business. Upon being informed by Officer Barkley that no such person had been brought in, Weber requested that the booking of any one arrested on that charge be delayed until he had arrived at the station. Burton Mold interrupted Weber's conversation and asked Barkley, to whom he was known, if Dave Ogul and two others, whom he named, had been arrested because of a disturbance of the peace or a fight. When he was told that they were not at the station, Mold asked Barkley to extend every courtesy to Weber, as he and Weber were very good friends.

Just before Weber and Mold were talking with Barkley, Lorenson received a telephone call at his home from a man who identified himself as a newspaper reporter. Lorenson stated that he thought that his caller gave the name of Beacon or Bacon, but no reporter having either name was ever located. The alleged reporter asked Lorenson, "Have you heard about any trouble out at Pearson's, the Sky Pilot radio repair man?" Lorenson replied that he had not, and the supposed reporter said, "I understand he got beat up and they took him to the station." According to the testimony of Lorenson fixing the time of this conversation, it occurred before the seven arrested men reached the station. No report of the incident had then been made by the arresting officers. Lorenson then called the Wilshire Station and spoke to the Desk Sergeant and Officer Shea of the Detective Bureau. After asking Shea if any arrests had been made of pickets at Pearson's radio shop, Lorenson said, "It would be too bad if some pickets got in trouble by being pushed around or getting pushed around at Pearson's place."

[A few minutes after the arrested men arrived at the Wilshire Station, Acting Captain Swan called from his home concerning the arrests. When he was told the names of the arrestees and had confirmed their connection with the Sky Pilot Radio Shop, he ordered them released immediately, before Pearson could arrive to identify any of them. He also ordered the tire irons, guns, recording device, and other objects returned to the arrestees, and he ordered Officer Wolfe to caution the arresting officers not to talk about the incident. Wolfe told those officers that they should destroy their notes concerning the arrest, say nothing about the incident and, if questioned, deny that an arrest had been made. Swan subsequently told the press that no arrests had been made as a result of the Pearson beating, adding that he knew nothing of the affair. He later stated that some legitimate business men, all of whom had permits to carry guns, had been arrested by mistake but had been released.]

Some hours later, Swan telephoned to Lorenson and told him of Pearson's claim that he had been attacked as the result of Lorenson's activities. He also stated that the arrested men had been released. At no time during this conversation did Lorenson inquire as to why the men were released without being booked.

Despite Swan's instructions to the arresting officers to deny the arrest, and Cohen's attempts to purchase the pictures taken on the street at the time the seven men were being searched, photographs of the group were published in a newspaper with a story concerning the Pearson affray. Shortly afterward, the district attorney presented all of this testimony, with Pearson's account of the attack upon him, to the grand jury, which returned an indictment against Lorenson, Swan, Wolfe, Weber and Mold. Cohen and the seven men arrested when the automobile in which they endeavored to escape was overtaken were also named as defendants.

Lorenson attacks this indictment principally upon the ground that there was no evidence presented to the grand jury which connects him with the conspiracy in which he is asserted to have been a participant. He declares that the evidence shows no conduct by him which constitutes a crime, and that he should not be required to stand trial upon the charge against him.

...

From the facts upon which the indictment of Lorenson is based, certain inferences reasonably may be drawn. The grand jury could infer from the events which transpired that an understanding or agreement had been entered into among Lorenson, Cohen and his associates, Weber, Mold, Swan and other members of the Police Department, to assault and rob Pearson and also to obstruct the administration of justice in the litigation between him and Mrs. Phillips. Certainly the evidence justifies the conclusion that the recording machine was stolen from Pearson in order to protect those persons who took part in the conversations which were recorded. Also, the inference reasonably may be drawn that Lorenson and police officers of the Wilshire Station were to furnish protection to the participants in the conspiracy by refusing to disclose the identity of Pearson's attackers, if they were arrested, and to effect their release from custody. The conduct of Lorenson, Weber and Mold subsequent to the arrest may well have been in furtherance of the conspiracy and to carry out its unlawful object, as well as to protect the parties to it from detection.

The telephone conversations, considered in their relation to the time when the beating was administered to Pearson, fit into a common scheme or plan by Lorenson, Weber, Mold and the arrested men....

Direct proof of a formal understanding between parties to the conspiracy is not required as the basis of an indictment or information. "[I]t was not necessary for the state to prove that the parties actually came together, mutually discussed their common design, and after reaching a formal agreement set out upon their previously agreed course of conduct. The extent of the assent of minds which are involved in a conspiracy may be, and from the secrecy of the crime usually must be, inferred by the jury from the proofs of the facts and circumstances which, when taken together, apparently indicate that they are parts to the same complete whole."

According to Lorenson, the grand jury should have concluded that the seemingly related events were unconnected and occurred by mere happenstance. But assuming that the facts are consistent with such a construction of them, the conduct shown by the record does not, as a matter of law, require it. Certainly it cannot be said that there is no basis for a strong suspicion of guilt. Such a conclusion is not unreasonable nor one which could not be held by a man of ordinary caution or prudence. The testimony as to the events shown by the record provide the basis for an inference that there was a broad plan in which Lorenson was an active participant....

The petitioner relies upon the [principle] that mere association does not make a conspiracy; there must be evidence of some participation or interest in the commission of the offense....

In the present case, Lorenson's acts may well have been in furtherance of a common plan to accomplish an unlawful purpose. A conclusion that the conversations and the arrangements made by him were not merely a series of strange coincidences, but a part of that plan, has much more foundation than mere suspicion. Indeed, it is a logical inference which reasonably may be drawn from the testimony regarding his conduct in connection with that of the other persons named as conspirators....

Lorenson attacks the statute making criminal conspiracy an offense upon the ground that it is so vague and uncertain as to be violative of the constitutional requirements of due process. He also contends that the indictment is equally vague and indefinite.

Section 182 defines as criminal conspiracy acts committed with the purpose "... to pervert or obstruct justice, or the due administration of the laws." Generally speaking, conduct which constitutes an offense against public justice, or the administration of law includes both malfeasance and nonfeasance by an officer in connection with the administration of his public duties, and also anything done by a person in hindering or obstructing an officer in the performance of his official obligations. Such an offense was recognized at common law and generally punishable as a misdemeanor.

Now, quite generally, it has been made a statutory crime and, under some circumstances, a felony.

In California, the statutes relating to "Crimes Against Public Justice" are found in Part I, Title VII, of the Penal Code. Bribery, escapes, rescues, perjury, falsifying evidence, and other acts which would have been considered offenses against the administration of justice at common law are made criminal by legislative enactment. Section 182, subdivision 5, is a more general section making punishable a conspiracy to commit any offense against public justice. The meaning of the words "to pervert or obstruct justice, or the due administration of the laws" is easily ascertained by reference either to the common law or to the more specific crimes enumerated in Part I, Title VII. A conspiracy with or among public officials not to perform their official duty to enforce criminal laws is an obstruction of justice and an indictable offense at common law.

...

Considering the well-settled meaning at common law of the words "to pervert or obstruct justice, or the due administration of the laws," the other and more specific provisions in the Penal Code concerning "Crimes Against Public Justice," and the relative certainty of words employed in statutes which have been held valid, it cannot be said that subsection 5 of section 182 of the Penal Code is unconstitutional. For substantially the same reasons, the indictment against Lorenson is not vague, indefinite, or uncertain and it complies with the statutory requirement for such an accusation....

The petition for the peremptory writ of prohibition is denied, and the alternative writ is discharged.

Shenk, Schauer and Spence, JJ., concur.

Carter, Justice.

I dissent.

...

We should not lose sight of the fact that this indictment was based on an alleged conspiracy. The only evidence that will support such an indictment is evidence that will connect the petitioner with the "promotion of the venture" that is the basis of the indictment. Without such evidence, acts done by other persons, with whom there is evidence of petitioner's lawful association, cannot be permitted to support an indictment....

Viewing the evidence most favorable to the prosecution, it can only be said that wrongdoing by someone was established and that petitioner was in some insubstantial way generally associated with some of the wrongdoers and placed on the periphery of the events that constituted the wrongdoing. Petitioner disliked Pearson because of the latter's alleged unfair practices; he engaged Weber to represent a plaintiff (Mrs. Phillips) in a case against Pearson based upon those practices. There is evidence that he was informed that Pearson's shop was going to be picketed by irate housewives. There is no evidence that he knew that the picketing would not be peaceful or that it would not be conducted by housewives. There is evidence that he subsequently learned that the picketing had resulted in injury to someone and the arrest of the pickets, but there is no evidence that he was then aware of their identity or that he took any action to obtain their release as charged in the indictment. None of these acts were unlawful or unusual. They do not constitute even "some" evidence of a conspiracy. The evidence falls short of showing any agreement between petitioner and others to engage in the perpetration of a crime. It does no more than establish that he, among many others besides the conspirators, disliked a person against whom a conspiracy was brewing and that he had some foreknowledge and knew some of the conspirators.

...

As there is no evidence whatever connecting petitioner with the crime charged in the indictment in this case, I would grant the writ of prohibition prayed for.

Gibson, C. J., and Traynor, J., concur.

Notes and Problem

Conspiracies Against the Public Health or Public Morals. In *Lorenson*, the court rejected the defendant's vagueness challenge because the meaning of "to pervert or obstruct justice, or the due administration of the laws" was well understood at the common law and, in any event, could be ascertained from other sections of the Penal Code. Penal Code § 182(5) also punishes an agreement to commit any act injurious "to the public health," or "to public morals." Would a prosecution under either of these standards be constitutional? The California Court of Appeal has upheld such a prosecution. See *People v. Rehman*, 253 Cal. App. 2d 119 (1967). On the other hand, at least two other state courts have held such provisions unconstitutional. See *State v. Musser*, 223 P.2d 193 (Utah 1950); *State v. Bowling*, 427 P.2d 928 (Ariz. Ct. App. 1967). The Model Penal Code limits conspiracy to an agreement to commit a crime. *See* MPC § 5.03.

Bilateral v. Unilateral Conspiracies. Since Penal Code § 182 punishes an agreement between "two or more persons," the prosecution must prove a *bilateral* agreement, *i.e.*, an agreement between at least two real conspirators. Thus, if a person agrees with an undercover officer or other feigned accomplice to commit crimes, there is no conspiracy. By contrast, the Model Penal Code would punish the *unilateral* agreement by one person to commit a crime whether or not the other party or parties to the agreement were themselves conspirators. See MPC § 5.03.

Problem 69.

Defendants were students at College. One of the streets bordering College was heavily traveled and had no lights or stop signs where it passed the entrance to College. As a result, a number of accidents involving pedestrians occurred. In order to protest the city's failure to install traffic lights, defendants and others decided to conduct a traffic "slowdown" in the street by crossing the street back and forth in crowds and in a leisurely fashion and by occasionally feigning injury and falling down. Interfering with the free flow of traffic is an infraction under the Vehicle Code. Defendants were arrested and charged with conspiracy to interfere with traffic. What are the arguments on whether they can be convicted of conspiracy? (P.C. § 182)

People v. Mayers

110 Cal. App. 3d 809, 168 Cal. Rptr. 252 (1980)

STANIFORTH, ASSOCIATE JUSTICE.

The jury convicted Thomas Eugene Mayers of participating and operating a game of three card monte (Pen. Code, § 332) and conspiracy to cheat and defraud another in a three card monte game (Pen. Code § 182, subd. (4))....

Facts

Mayers and Charles Jackson were observed by vice officer Victor E. Schuman as they conducted a game of three card monte aboard a bus. Schuman testified that three card monte originated in the 1800's as a variation of the "pea in the thimble" game. The game uses a combination of two black cards and one red, or the reverse. The cards are bent into tent fashion for easy handling, and each card is manipulated with a different finger by the dealer in order to give a false appearance as to where the winning (odd) card has been placed after the shuffle. In addition to the dealer, there are minimally two other participants in the game, a shill associated with the dealer and a mark or chump. According to Schuman's expertise, the card scheme cannot be perpetrated without the collaboration of the dealer and shill.

A shill's function includes verbally encouraging onlookers to participate, placing enticing bets, as well as distracting the crowd from the dealer's sleight of hand. Mayers acted in classic capacity as shill, picked up one of the two black cards and tossed it over Jackson's shoulder. As Jackson turned around to retrieve it, Mayers bent up the corner of the red card in full view of the onlookers. Onlooker Hart, the mark, believed he now knew the correct card but was unable to detect the dealer's sleight of hand. He bet and lost—was defrauded of—$80. When the bus stopped, Mayers was arrested for participating as the shill in this confidence scheme. Jackson slipped away into the crowd and was not caught until much later. The action against Jackson was ultimately dismissed for want of prosecution.

Mayers appeals the judgment.

Discussion

I

Mayers contends the specific provision of Penal Code section 332 proscribing "three card monte" must prevail over the general sanction against conspiracy to defraud embodied in section 182, subdivision (4).

Section 332 in pertinent part provides: "Every person who by the game of 'three card monte' so-called, or any other game, device, sleight of hand, ... fraudulently obtains from another person money or property of any description, shall be punished as in the case of larceny of property of like value." Under the plain explicit language of this section, the law governing larceny (Pen. Code, §§ 486, 487) determines whether a particular "three card monte" scam constitutes a misdemeanor or a felony. Therefore, if the value of the property taken was $200 or less, the offense is classified as petty theft—a misdemeanor. (§§ 486, 487.)

The substantive act (a three card monte scam) charged against Mayers was for an amount less than $200, a misdemeanor punishable by maximum of six months in the county jail and/or a $1,000 fine.

Section 182 provides in pertinent part: "If two or more persons conspire:....

"4. To cheat and defraud any person of any property, by any means which are in themselves criminal, or to obtain money or property by false pretenses or by false promises with fraudulent intent not to perform such promises....

"They are punishable as follows: ...

"When they conspire to do an act described in subdivision 4 of this section, they shall be punishable by imprisonment in the state prison, or by imprisonment in the county jail for not more than one year, or by a fine not exceeding five thousand dollars ($5,000), or both."

It is a firmly established principle where specific conduct is prohibited by a special statute, a defendant cannot be prosecuted under a general statute.

It was explained in *In re Williamson* (1954) 43 Cal. 2d 651: "It is the general rule that where the general statute standing alone would include the same matter as the special act, and thus conflict with it, the special act will be considered as an exception to the general statute whether it was passed before or after such general enactment...."

...

The foregoing rule is necessary to prevent a general statute from swallowing up the exceptions contained in specific enactments. Section 332 makes Mayers' offense a misdemeanor. By simple logic, if section 182 is applicable under these narrow facts, any section 332 misdemeanor violation would be automatically elevated to a felony by applying the general law of section 182, subd. (4).[2] Noteworthy was the Legislature's revision in the year 1880 of section 332 from a pure felony statute to one which provided for "punish[ment] as in the case of *larceny* of property of *like value*" (§ 332; italics added). Punishment here as a section 182, subdivision (4), felony would render this legislative amendment void.

...

---

2. Transformation of misdemeanor offenses to felonies by application of the law of conspiracy has been criticized as obsolete. Dispelling the "group danger" rationale that all persons combining to commit even a petty offense are more dangerous than individual offenders, one commentator observes conspiracy law is an inexcusably clumsy way to provide increased punishment against organized crime. "Conspiracy makes the individual ... bettor just as much as felon as the professional manager." (Johnson, *The Unnecessary Crime of Conspiracy* (1973) 61 Cal. L. Rev. 1137.)

II

A separate legal doctrine supports dismissal of the conspiracy charge. Where the cooperation of two or more persons is necessary to the commission of the substantive crime, and there is no ingredient of an alleged conspiracy that is not present in the substantive crime, then the persons necessarily involved cannot be charged with conspiracy to commit the substantive offense and also with the substantive crime itself. This is the "concert of action rule" or Wharton's Rule. (1 Anderson, Wharton's Criminal Law & Procedure 191 (1957).) The classic Wharton's Rule has been applied to crimes characterized by a general congruence of the agreement and the completed offenses. The rule is considered in modern legal thinking as an aid in construction of statutes, a presumption that the Legislature intended the general conspiracy section be merged with the more specific substantive offense. Thus Wharton's Rule further substantiates our earlier conclusion that the specific conduct prohibited, made a misdemeanor by a special statute, cannot be prosecuted under a general statute punishing the identical conduct as a felony.

...

Problem

Problem 70.

Woman and Man, who are not married, traveled from San Francisco to Reno to spend the weekend and have sexual intercourse. They are now charged with conspiracy to violate the federal Mann Act, which provides:

> Any person who shall knowingly transport or cause to be transported, or aid or assist in obtaining transportation for, or in transporting, in interstate or foreign commerce, or in any Territory or in the District of Columbia, any woman or girl for the purpose of prostitution or debauchery, or for any other immoral purpose, or with the intent and purpose to induce, entice, or compel such woman or girl to become a prostitute or to give herself up to debauchery, or to engage in any other immoral practice ... shall be deemed guilty of a felony ...

What arguments should be made as to whether Woman or Man is guilty of conspiracy?

D. The Defense of "Impossibility"

Common to all three crimes discussed in this chapter is the issue of the effect of attendant circumstances on a defendant's culpability. If a defendant intended to commit the object crime and took sufficient steps to commit an attempt, solicitation or conspiracy, will the fact that, unbeknownst to the defendant, the object crime was impossible, warrant an acquittal? The courts have attempted to analyze this problem by distinguishing between "legal impossibility," which is held to be a defense, and "factual impossibility," which is not. In cases of true legal impossibility, the defendant has simply misunderstood the law, as in the following examples: (1) defendant and others agree to import a rare animal, believing it is on the endangered species list and importation is forbidden, but the animal was recently taken off the list; (2) defendant alters a check by adding another zero to the amount and believes he has committed forgery, but adding the zero has no legal significance since the written amount is controlling. In cases of true factual impossibility, the defendant has made a factual miscalculation which prevents the defendant from achieving his/her purpose, as in the following examples: (1) defendant and others plan to blow up the bank safe with explosives in their possession, but the explosives are wholly inadequate for the job; (2) defendant puts her hand into victim's pocket to steal his wallet, but the pocket is empty. *People v. Rojas*, in the context of an attempt crime, and *People v. Peppars*, in the context of conspiracy, both involve fact situations not clearly falling within either one of the above categories.

People v. Rojas

55 Cal. 2d 252, 358 P.2d 921 (1961)

SCHAUER, J.

In a trial by the court, after proper waiver of jury, defendants Rojas and Hidalgo were found guilty of a charge of receiving stolen property. Defendants' motions for new trial were denied. Rojas was granted probation without imposition of sentence and Hidalgo was sentenced to state prison. They appeal, respectively, from the order granting probation, the judgment, and the orders denying the motions for new trial.

Defendants urge that they were guilty of no crime (or, at most, of an attempt to receive stolen property) because when they received the property it had been recovered by the police and was no longer in a stolen condition. The attorney general argues that because the thief stole the property pursuant to prearrangement with defendants he took it as their agent, and the crime of receiving stolen property was complete when the thief began its asportation toward defendants and before the police intercepted him and recovered the property.[1] We have concluded that defendants are guilty of attempting to receive stolen goods; that other matters of which they complain do not require a new trial; and that the appeal should be disposed of by modifying the finding that defendants are guilty as charged to a determination that they are guilty of attempting to receive stolen property, and by reversing with directions to the trial court to enter such judgments or probation orders as it deems appropriate based upon the modified finding.

---

1. Whether under the established circumstances the defendants might be guilty of theft (under Pen. Code, §31) is not discussed because the defendants were not charged with that crime either specifically or as an included offense.

During the night of March 3, 1959, electrical conduit worth about $4,500 was stolen from John Taft in Ventura. On the day of March 4 Officer Lovold of the Los Angeles Police Department, who was investigating the Ventura offense, saw William Hall sitting in an automobile on a Los Angeles street opposite a truck which contained Taft's conduit. Hall was arrested and he and the truck were taken to a police station. Hall said that "he had an understanding with Mr. Hidalgo [one of the defendants] that he would buy any and all electrical appliances or electrical materials that he could get and that he had several transactions with him in the past."

[With Officer Lovold listening in, Hall made several calls to arrange delivery of the conduit to Hidalgo.]

On the night of March 4, Hall, accompanied by Police Officer Saville in plain clothes, drove the truck of conduit to about two blocks from Hidalgo's electrical shop. They walked to the shop. Hall introduced Officer Saville to Hidalgo as "Rudy" (the name of Hall's cousin). Hidalgo said that he did not want the truck brought to his shop because "his place was 'hot' and was being watched by the police." At Hidalgo's request Hall and Saville returned to the truck and drove it, following Hidalgo in his car, to Mott Street, where they parked. There Hidalgo left for about 30 minutes, returned and told Hall and Saville to leave the keys in the truck, and drove them to still another location in Hidalgo's car. Hidalgo referred to the "last time I got stuff from you guys," and said that "I know you guys will let me make money"; that he would pay $700 for the present load; that "in the future he would prefer ... doing business with Hall alone. Who Hall split with was his business but for his protection, Hall's protection, to come alone." Hidalgo paid Hall $200 and "instructed Hall to call him the following day at noon and he would tell him where to get the truck and ... the balance of the money which was $500.00."

Officers Lovold and Bischonden, meanwhile, had followed the truck from the police station. On Mott Street, after Hall and Hidalgo left the truck, defendant Rojas arrived and drove it to a lot by Rojas' place of business (a shop and warehouse). The officers "staked out" the truck and later on the night of March 4 saw the two defendants examine its contents and then leave.

At 8 o'clock the following morning Rojas opened his shop and began to unload the conduit from the truck. Rojas was then placed under arrest.

Lieutenant Lauritzen, one of the arresting officers, said, "You know that this property was stolen." Rojas replied, "I know that it was stolen but I'm not making any money out of it myself ... I'm not kidding and it's no use trying to kid you. You know it's stolen and I know it's stolen."

The offense with which defendants were charged and of which they were convicted was receiving "property which has been *stolen ..., knowing the same to be so stolen.*" (Pen. Code, § 496, subd. 1; italics added.) Defendants, relying particularly upon *People v. Jaffe* (N.Y. 1906) 78 N.E. 169, urge that they neither received stolen goods nor criminally attempted to do so because the conduit, when defendants received it, was not in a stolen condition but had been recovered by the police. In the *Jaffe* case the stolen property was recovered by the owner while it was en route to the would-be receiver and, by arrangement with the police, was delivered to such receiver as a decoy, not as property in a stolen condition. The New York Court of Appeals held that there was no attempt to receive stolen goods "because neither [defendant] nor anyone else in the world could know that the property was stolen property inasmuch as it was not in fact stolen property.... If all which an accused person intends to do would if done constitute no crime it cannot be a crime to attempt to do with the same purpose a part of the thing intended."

...

In the case at bench the criminality of the attempt is not destroyed by the fact that the goods, having been recovered by the commendably alert and efficient action of the Los Angeles police, had, unknown to defendants, lost their "stolen" status, any more than the criminality of the attempt in the case of *In re Magidson* (1917), 32 Cal. App. 566, was destroyed by impossibility caused by the fact that the police had recovered the goods and taken them from the place where the would-be receiver went to get them. In our opinion the consequences of intent and acts such as those of defendants here should be more serious than pleased amazement that because of the timeliness of the police the projected criminality was not merely detected but also wiped out. (*Cf. People v. Jelke* (1956), 152 N.Y.S.2d 479, explaining the *Jaffe* decision as a case "like selling oil stock and being surprised to discover that oil was actually in the ground where the accused vendor had represented but not believed it to be"—conduct which the New York Court of Appeals apparently feels is not criminal.)

...

The People would have us go farther and hold that the evidence here supports the finding that defendants are guilty of the consummated offense of receiving stolen property. In this regard the People advance two theories. The first is that the goods, when they came into the hands of defendants, had not lost their stolen character because Officer Saville, the "undercover man," was acting as "agent" of the city and not of the true owner. We believe that both the owner and the police would take unkindly to the suggestion that property which has been the subject of larceny and has then been recovered by law enforcement officers remains "stolen" while it is under the surveillance of the police. It seems obvious that stolen property, recaptured by the police, no longer has the status of stolen goods but, rather, is held by the police in trust for, or for the account of, the owner....

The People's second theory that the evidence supports the finding that the crime of receiving stolen property was consummated proceeds as follows: The thief, Hall, stole pursuant to a prearranged "understanding with Mr. Hidalgo that he [defendant Hidalgo] would buy any and all electrical appliances or electrical materials that he [Hall] could get." Therefore, they were accomplices; both Hall and defendants, as members of the conspiracy, were liable to prosecution as principals either in the crime of theft or in the crime of receiving stolen property. Upon this view of the situation, the People say, the crime of receiving stolen goods was completed by Hall, as "agent" for defendants, when he put the goods in his truck in Ventura and started driving to Los Angeles.

The People's attempt to apply rules of the law of agency to the law of crimes in this situation is inappropriate. The thief, even when he steals pursuant to a conspiracy with a prospective receiver, cannot receive the stolen goods from himself.

...

Note And Problem

Problem 71.

Defendant met with Cop, an undercover police officer, in a bar, and he told Cop that he would buy any stolen watches Cop could come up with. The next day, Cop bought a watch from a department store and later offered to sell it to Defendant, telling Defendant that the watch was stolen. Defendant bought the watch. What are the arguments on whether Defendant is guilty of attempted receiving stolen property? (P.C. § 496.)

The Model Penal Code and "Non-stolen" Property. The Model Penal Code solves the problem of the *Rojas* case with a broader definition of receiving stolen property, encompassing property which the defendant *believes* has probably been stolen. MPC § 223.6. Under the Code, then, Rojas would have been guilty of receiving (rather than attempted receiving) stolen property.

People v. Peppars

140 Cal. App. 3d 677, 189 Cal. Rptr. 879 (1983)

Poche, J.

Byron Martin Peppars appeals from a judgment of conviction entered upon a jury verdict finding him guilty of conspiracy to commit second degree burglary. (Pen. Code, §§ 182, 459.) The judgment is affirmed.

Facts

Appellant and his brother, Damon Elliott Peppars, were charged by a two count amended information: conspiracy to commit burglary (count I); and attempted burglary (count II). Also charged in count II, and tried with appellant and Damon, was Darryl Demingos Lee. The jury returned a guilty verdict as to appellant on the conspiracy charge, and a not guilty verdict with respect to Lee on the attempted burglary charge. The jury was unable to reach a verdict as to Damon on both counts and as to appellant on the attempted burglary count; accordingly, the trial court declared a mistrial on those charges.

This appeal is directed only to appellant's conviction of conspiracy to commit second degree burglary.

Prosecution's Case

In May of 1981, Sonoma County Sheriff's Deputy Roger Rude was assigned to work in an undercover capacity. On May 21, Rude met with Paul Johnson and appellant on Bellevue Avenue in Santa Rosa. Although Rude was wearing a transmitting device, no recording of this conversation was made. Rude testified that at this meeting the three men discussed a wedding ring which Rude was going to sell for appellant. At some point the subject changed: appellant asked Rude if he knew of a warehouse to "rip off."

Rude met with appellant and Johnson again at the same location on May 29, at about 9 a.m. This conversation was recorded and can be summarized as follows:

Rude informed appellant and Johnson that he had learned of a warehouse that he could get them into: "[It'll] just be a matter of walkin in, loadin up and walkin out. No break in, no alarms or nothin." Rude asked appellant, "remember the last time we got together you were, uh, talked to me that you said you, uh, you might have some folks who could do somethin?" Appellant responded, "Yeah, yeah, I talked to em about, what kinda place is it?" Rude explained that he knew of a former employee who had keys to a warehouse "full of ... stereo equipment, ... t.v.s and video recorders ... what happened was he got canned, they didn't know he made a set of duplicate keys, ... and, uh, if I purchase the keys, they should get us into the building ..." Appellant asked if there was an alarm on the building system. Rude replied that he did not have all the facts, but he understood that if there were an alarm system that he could get the key to that also. Appellant responded, "O.K." Appellant asked where it was, Rude responded, "Santa Rosa." Appellant responded, "sortova good." Rude stated that he had not yet seen the warehouse and had not yet purchased the keys, but that he wanted to "make sure that I had you on this end to deal this with and then I could go ahead and do it." Appellant responded, "You know, well all I need now is just, you know, just to know all the information about it." Rude replied that he would get the information and the keys to the building. Johnson asked him to find out whether there was a security guard, and Rude said that he would.

[Peppars and Deputy Rude had five subsequent conversations during which they worked out plans for the theft.]

Rude and other deputy sheriffs had arranged that day for storage unit 20 of the warehouse to be stocked with six or eight televisions in boxes, some empty television boxes, and a stereo, which had been loaned from a local businessman and secured by a padlock, also donated. Thereafter, the unit was placed under surveillance.

At about 8:30 p.m., a U-Haul arrived at the storage unit. The truck was driven by Damon Peppars, and accompanying him was Lee. Damon unlocked the padlock and began to hand the merchandise to Lee who was in the back of the truck. Both were arrested while in the process of loading the truck, and the key and padlock were found in Damon Peppars' pocket. Inside the truck, the officers found a rental agreement executed by appellant.

Appellant was arrested on June 3. After being advised of his rights, he agreed to waive them and to speak to the officers. That conversation was tape recorded and played to the jury.

Appellant told the officers that what "actually happened" was that Paul Johnson's friend Roger had hired him to move furniture: "I wasn't aware that this was a burglary being set up or was in progress. I said I was gonna make a few extra dollars just by ... just by moving ... moving some furniture." Appellant denied giving Rude a ring to sell for him and when shown a picture of it, he stated that he had never seen it before.

Defense Case

The sole defense witness was Darryl Lee. He testified that on June 2 he was helping appellant move his furniture. Appellant did not tell him what he was to move or to where he was to move it, but appellant did promise to pay him for his help. Lee was unaware any crime had been planned or that one was in progress at the warehouse.

Discussion

[Defendant's entrapment defense was rejected.]

The superior court did not err in denying the motion to set aside the information on the ground that the evidence was insufficient to hold appellant to answer on the charge of conspiracy to commit burglary.

Appellant contends that the superior court erred in denying his motion to set aside the information on the ground that the evidence was insufficient to hold him to answer to conspiracy to commit burglary. In his view, it was factually impossible for appellant to commit a burglary because the police had given their consent to the entry into the warehouse. Appellant therefore posits that the only chargeable crime was conspiracy to commit attempted burglary.

Federal courts have routinely upheld a conviction of conspiracy to commit a substantive crime although completion of the substantive crime is impossible.[5]

The reasons for adopting such a rule in California are quite obvious. Completion of the crime of conspiracy does not require that the object of the conspiracy be accomplished. It is a crime separate and distinct from the substantive offense. As the court explained in *People v. Williams* (1980) 101 Cal. App. 3d 711: "[The] basic conspiracy principle has some place in modern criminal law, because to unite, back of a criminal purpose, the strength, opportunities and resources of many is obviously more dangerous and more difficult to police than the efforts of a lone wrongdoer. Collaboration magnifies the risk to society both by increasing the likelihood that a given quantum of harm will be successfully produced and by increasing the amount of harm that can be inflicted."

5. "Legal impossibility" denotes conduct where the goal of the actor is not criminal, although he believes it to be. "Factual impossibility" denotes conduct where the objective is proscribed by the criminal law, but a circumstance unknown to the actor prevents him from bringing it about.

For such reasons, it is well settled in California that a conspiracy conviction will stand even though the defendant is acquitted of the substantive crime. It is a short step from that principle to join the federal courts in holding that factual impossibility is not a defense to the charge of conspiracy to commit the substantive crime. Such a conclusion is in harmony with the law of attempt in California: factual impossibility is not a defense to a charge of attempt. (*People v. Rojas* (1961) 55 Cal. 2d 252.)

For these reasons we conclude that factual impossibility is not a defense to conspiracy. Therefore, the trial court properly denied the motion to set aside the information.

The judgment is affirmed.

Note and Problem

The Model Penal Code's and the Federal Courts' Treatment of "Impossibility." The Model Penal Code follows the approach of the *Rojas* case and does not recognize a defense of impossibility based on misapprehension of the facts by the defendant. MPC Part I Commentaries vol. 2, pp. 307–20. Federal courts have reached different results in addressing this issue. For example, in *United States v. Berrigan*, 482 F.2d 171 (3rd Cir. 1973), the defendant was a federal prison inmate convicted of violating a federal regulation forbidding,

> the introduction or attempt to introduce into or upon the grounds of any federal penal or correctional institution or the taking or attempt to take or send therefrom anything whatsoever without the knowledge and consent of the warden or superintendent of such federal penal or correctional institution.

The defendant had attempted to smuggle letters out to a friend, but the warden knew of the plan and permitted the letters to be taken out so that he could charge Defendant with violating the regulation. The court found legal impossibility and reversed the conviction. By contrast, in *United States v. Everett*, 692 F.2d 596 (9th Cir. 1982), the court rejected an impossibility defense in the following situation. The defendants were charged with conspiracy to obstruct the collection of tax revenues for selling phony tax shelters. An IRS agent, purporting to represent a taxpayer client, had answered the defendants' ad and, over the course of numerous conversations, had worked out with the defendants, and paid for, backdated documents creating a phony tax shelter. The court rejected the defendants' argument that there could be no crime of attempted defrauding the government when the government had knowledge of the scheme and there was no actual taxpayer in any event.

Problem 72.

Defendant was an inmate in the county jail. He had tested positive for HIV, and he had, on several occasions, threatened to kill the guards by spitting on them or biting them. The apparent medical consensus is that there has never been a controlled study of a sufficiently large number of cases to establish to any scientific certainty that transmission of HIV is even possible by biting and, if it is, how likely transmission is from a single bite. Defendant bit one of the guards and is now charged with attempted murder. (P.C. §§ 187–189, 664.) What arguments should be made on his defense of impossibility?

Chapter 10

Crimes against the Government

Although in theory all crimes are crimes against the government and, in California, are prosecuted in the name of "The People of the State of California," the crimes addressed in previous chapters generally also have individual victims. The crimes in this chapter—bribery, compounding a felony, perjury and threatening and interfering with officers—have no individual victims. Rather, they punish conduct tending to disrupt the functioning of the government. The cases raise, in various guises, the following questions: When should conduct be punished in the absence of any harm to the government from the conduct? When may the state criminalize speech which is an affront to governmental authority? The first case, *People v. Pic'l*, involves the prosecution of an attorney for his conduct in trying to "settle" a case with a theft victim and thereby prevent prosecution of his client. The court has to decide if his conduct constituted bribery of the victim not to testify or offering the victim a reward to conceal a felony. The next two cases, *Cabe v. Superior Court* and *People v. Darcy*, concern the elements of perjury. In *Cabe*, the issue is what constitutes a false statement, and, in *Darcy*, the issue is when is a false statement material. The last two cases involve interfering with officers in the performance of their duties. In *In re Manual G.*, the juvenile was prosecuted for threatening an officer who was questioning him, and in *People v. Robles*, the defendant was prosecuted for identifying an undercover officer attempting to make a narcotics buy. Both cases concern the dividing line between free speech and criminal conduct.

People v. Pic'l

31 Cal. 3d 731, 646 P.2d 847 (1982)

Mosk, Justice.

The People appeal an order setting aside three counts of an indictment returned against defendant Dean Richard Pic'l, an attorney, in connection with the alleged bribery of a prospective complaining witness in a criminal prosecution. For the reasons that follow, we hold that the court erred in ruling there was no reasonable cause to charge defendant with the offenses. We therefore reverse the order, reinstating all three counts.

Defendant was charged with six felonies: count I, conspiracy (Pen. Code, § 182); count II, extortion (id., § 520); count III, bribing a witness not to attend trial (id., § 136 ½); count IV, bribing a witness to withhold testimony (id., § 137); count V, compounding a felony (id., § 153); count VI, receiving stolen property (id., § 496). Defendant moved to set aside the indictment under Penal Code section 995. The motion was granted as to counts III, IV, and V, but denied as to the others. A jury found defendant guilty of the remaining counts, and the judgment of conviction was affirmed on appeal.

Evidence was presented to the grand jury that a racing car and related equipment worth $120,000 were stolen from Douglas Kerhulas, a professional drag racer, on July 30, 1978. Since racing provided a significant portion of Kerhulas' income, he placed a $2,000 reward notice in a dragster magazine for information about the theft. On August 3, Randall Martin approached the owner of an auto parts shop in Pasadena and offered to sell a racing car differential, worth $1,000, for $150. The owner became suspicious and notified Kerhulas and the police. When they arrived at the shop, Kerhulas identified the differential as part of his stolen property. Martin was arrested.

Kerhulas contacted Martin after his release on bail and offered to give Martin $3,000 if the remainder of the property was returned. Martin agreed. On August 6, an anonymous caller telephoned Kerhulas and stated that he, together with Martin and others, had stolen Kerhulas' car and equipment. He confirmed the agreement that Kerhulas had made with Martin, but demanded that Kerhulas also sign a pledge not to prosecute. The following day the man called again to tell Kerhulas that he would soon receive final instructions for retrieving his property. Kerhulas then informed sheriff's deputies of the calls, and they attached a tape recorder to his telephone. That evening defendant Pic'l called and reiterated the planned exchange of the stolen property for Kerhulas' cash and promise of nonprosecution, with the exception that the price had been lowered to $2,500. Pic'l and Kerhulas subsequently met at a restaurant, with the police surreptitiously monitoring the conversation by means of a transmitter on Kerhulas' leg. Kerhulas paid defendant the $2,500 and signed the nonprosecution agreement.

The agreement, prepared by defendant, consisted of the following terms:

"I, DOUG KERHULAS, owner of a certain 1977 Chevrolet pickup, bearing California License Number 1E43451, and a special contruction [sic] trailer bearing California license number UB7406, as well as a top fuel dragster and miscellaneous parts, all of which were recently taken from my possession, for the purpose of reobtaining their possession, do hereby agree as follows:

> A. I accept from Dean R. Pic'l, Attorney-at-law, that portion of the aforesaid property that he was able to recover.
>
> B. I hereby release the said Dean R. Pic'l from any and all liabilities which may arise by virtue of his participation in this matter and acknowledge that he has acted solely as an intermediatery [sic] for the purpose of resolving this matter.
>
> C. I agree to seek the dismissal of all criminal charges which may have been filed relative to this matter and to do everything within my power to prevent the filing of any additional charges against any person. I hereby acknowledge

> full restitution and request the dismissal of all criminal charges pursuant to Penal Code Sections 1377 and 1378. As consideration for the restoration to me of my property, I shall refuse to prosecute criminal charges against anyone, or, in the alternative, shall be fully responsible for damages."

Defendant then led Kerhulas to a house in which the stolen items were stored. The police arrested defendant as he left the premises; he surrendered the nonprosecution pledge to the arresting officer, and the $2,500 in cash was removed from his pocket. When interviewed by the police, he stated that he would not have released Kerhulas' property had Kerhulas not signed the document and paid the $2,500.

When asked to explain to the grand jury the meaning of the phrase "I shall refuse to prosecute" in the agreement he had drafted, defendant testified that in nonmisdemeanor criminal cases the only way a witness can prevent prosecution is to "refuse to testify."

...

The Charge of Bribing a Prospective Witness Not to Attend Trial

Count III of the indictment charged defendant with violating section 136 ½ of the Penal Code, which provides: "Every person who gives or offers or promises to give to any witness or person about to be called as a witness, any bribe upon any understanding or agreement that such person shall not attend upon any trial or other judicial proceeding, or every person who attempts by means of any offer of a bribe to dissuade any such person from attending upon any trial or other judicial proceeding, is guilty of a felony."

The first ground announced by the court for setting aside count III was that because Kerhulas was a "feigned cooperator" there could be no "understanding or agreement" that he would not attend trial if called as a witness. In other words, in order for a briber to violate section 136 ½, there has to be a so-called "meeting of the minds" between the briber and the witness, in which both parties intend to enter into a corrupt bargain. Such an element of the offense could not have been shown by the evidence in the present case because Kerhulas, the prospective witness, never intended to carry out the pledge he signed. As will appear, however, in requiring such a "meeting of the minds" the court erroneously assumed the existence of an element of the offense of bribery that has never been established by decisional law in California.

The Court of Appeal in *People v. Gliksman* (1978) 78 Cal. App. 3d 343, made a thorough survey of cases in this state and other jurisdictions interpreting the statutes that forbid bribery "upon any understanding or agreement" resulting in the corruption of governmental processes. As here, *Gliksman* involved an act of bribery of a witness in which one party secretly cooperated with the police. The court was called upon to construe Penal Code section 138, which makes it a felony for a witness to seek a bribe "upon any understanding" that he will alter his testimony.

Gliksman initially observed that the courts in California have almost uniformly rejected the contention that a statutory requirement of a bribe "upon any agreement or understanding" refers to formation of a bilateral agreement. Rather, the language means that bribery must be proposed by the person offering to give or to receive the bribe, as the case may be, with the criminal intent that a corrupt act will be committed by the one accepting the bribe; if the offender has that intent, the fact that the other party does not subjectively intend to perform is irrelevant.

Agreeing with the rule of these cases, *Gliksman* reasoned that the intent of the Legislature in specifying a bribe sought "upon any understanding" (Pen. Code, § 138) was to punish bribery in which one party proposes a corrupt act by the other. "If the Legislature had intended that a mutual understanding is essential, it could have reasonably provided that the essence of the crime be 'entering into an agreement' or 'agreeing' with another to be bribed."

...

We approve of the reasoning of *Gliksman* and the authority cited therein, and believe it is equally applicable to the language of section 136 ½, the statute at issue here. An additional reason supports our conclusion. The purpose of the laws against bribery is to prevent corrupt interference with the administration of justice. To hold that section 136 ½ requires a "meeting of the minds" would make it exceedingly difficult to enforce the provision. First, those who offer to bribe witnesses would escape punishment in cases in which "others might feign to be their accomplices and in which no evidence against the defendants exists except that to come from those feigned accomplices." (*People v. Montgomery* (1976) 61 Cal. App. 3d 718.) A person knowledgeable in the law could bribe with impunity, knowing that the one individual with evidence of his misdeed would save him from punishment by the very act of informing the police at the time the bribe is offered. Without clear wording to that effect, we cannot assume that the Legislature meant to predicate criminal liability of a defendant on the criminal intent of another. And we are especially hesitant to make such an assumption when the integrity of our system of justice is at stake.

We therefore hold that a bilateral agreement is not a necessary element of the crime of offering a bribe to a witness to prevent his attendance at trial. It is sufficient if the defendant offers the bribe with the intent of persuading the witness to "agree" not to testify....

The court's second ground for setting aside count III was that the pledge signed by the victim of the theft, Kerhulas, did not expressly state that he would "not attend ... trial" (Pen. Code, § 136 ½). The court was apparently persuaded by defendant's argument that the document was at most a promise to "drop the case." Defendant relied on *Lichens v. Superior Court* (1960) 181 Cal. App. 2d 573, which held that a bribe offered to convince a witness to drop the case was not an effort to prevent attendance at trial within the meaning of section 136 ½.

The document drafted by defendant provided that Kerhulas would agree to "seek the dismissal of all criminal charges which may have been filed ... and to do everything within my power to prevent the filing of any additional charges against any person."

Kerhulas would also promise to "refuse to prosecute criminal charges against anyone." The People are correct in maintaining that a reasonable grand juror would have probable cause to believe that such language was a promise not to attend "trial or other judicial proceeding." Nonattendance is clearly within the scope of Kerhulas' pledge to "do everything within my power." With regard to the agreement that Kerhulas would "refuse to prosecute," defendant himself testified that the only act a witness can perform to prevent prosecution in nonmisdemeanor cases is to "refuse to testify." The grand jury could reasonably conclude that defendant had that meaning in mind when he drafted the agreement and presented it to Kerhulas.

...

Defendant's reliance on *Lichens v. Superior Court* is misplaced. The case concerned a defendant charged with rape who offered a bribe to the prosecutrix in return for her pledge to "drop the case." The court held that the evidence failed to show an agreement not to attend trial within the meaning of former section 136 ½, since the only way to drop the case would be to request the district attorney to give his necessary consent; thus the promise did not imply nonattendance at trial. But Kerhulas' burden in the present case was much greater, since under the agreement he had to "refuse to prosecute" and "do everything" to prevent further charges. Absenting himself from trial would have been an obvious means of keeping the bargain.

...

The Charge of Bribery to Influence Testimony

Count IV of the indictment charged defendant with a violation of Penal Code section 137, which at the time provided in pertinent part: "(a) Every person who gives, or offers, or promises to give, to any witness, or person about to be called as a witness, any bribe, upon any understanding or agreement that the testimony of such witness shall be thereby influenced is guilty of a felony."

The court relied on the same ground in setting aside count IV as it did in dismissing count III: *i.e.*, because the agreement drafted by defendant did not expressly refer to the withholding or adulteration of Kerhulas' "testimony," it could not represent an effort to influence testimony within the terms of section 137, subdivision (a).

Because our reasoning with respect to section 136 ½ applies to section 137 as well, we need not repeat it here. The court was incorrect in requiring a literal reference to "testimony" as an element of section 137. The grand jury had probable cause to believe that defendant intended to influence Kerhulas' testimony by way of persuading him to withhold it altogether, in exchange for the return of his property.

The Charge of Compounding a Felony

The final count set aside by the trial court—count V—charged defendant with compounding a felony. The pertinent part of Penal Code section 153 makes punishable "Every person who, having knowledge of the actual commission of a crime, takes money or property of another, or any gratuity or reward, or any engagement, or promise thereof, upon any agreement or understanding to compound or conceal such crime, or to abstain from any prosecution thereof, or to withhold any evidence thereof...."

The court justified its dismissal of count V by a two-step evaluation of the evidence. First, as it was Kerhulas rather than defendant who was to "abstain from prosecution," Kerhulas would be the compounder and defendant could at most be an aider and abettor. Secondly, because Kerhulas was only pretending to ratify the nonprosecution agreement, there was no crime for defendant to aid and abet.

We are persuaded by the People's contention that the court read section 153 in a manner not supported by its text. The statute encompasses conduct by "every person" who takes money or other "reward ... or promise thereof ... upon any agreement or understanding to compound" a crime. The court, without discussion, limited the meaning of "every person" to the victim of a crime who is paid not to prosecute. No dispositive authority in California confirms that restrictive interpretation.

...

[The elements of compounding are:] (1) knowledge of the crime; (2) an agreement not to prosecute that crime; (3) receipt of consideration. We have already noted that defendant prepared the nonprosecution agreement and was promised payment for the task; he also obviously had knowledge of the theft and whereabouts of Kerhulas' property. A factfinder could thus conclude that his actions supplied all the elements of compounding ...

...

Richardson, Newman and Reynoso, JJ., concur.

[Justice Kaus, in an opinion joined by the Chief Justice, and Justice Broussard, concurred as to Counts III and IV, but dissented as to Count V (compounding a felony).]

Note and Problems

Hoines v. Barney's Club, Inc. In the full opinion in *Pic'l,* the supreme court distinguished its decision in *Hoines v. Barney's Club, Inc.*, 28 Cal. 3d 603 (1980). *Hoines* involved the not uncommon situation where the prosecutor offers to dismiss charges against a defendant in return for the defendant's "stipulation to probable cause" or waiver of the defendant's right to bring a civil suit against the parties responsible for the defendant's arrest. Hoines entered into such an agreement in return for dismissal of a pending criminal charge, but, after dismissal of the charge, he filed a civil suit for damages occasioned by his arrest. The Supreme Court, in a 4–3 decision, upheld a judgment for the defendants based on the agreement, in the process deciding that the prosecutor had not been guilty of compounding a crime for making the agreement. The court said:

> No claim is made that the prosecutor in the instant case personally received any consideration for moving to dismiss charges pending against plaintiff. So far as research discloses the crime may be committed only by a person—

> including accomplices—receiving consideration pursuant to agreement to frustrate prosecution for criminal conduct.

Id. at 610. Is this argument persuasive?

Problem 73.

Defendant allowed Husband and Wife to move in with him. One day, Defendant and Husband were drinking, and when Husband went out to the liquor store, Defendant raped Wife. Husband returned and called the police, and Defendant was arrested. The next day Defendant called Wife from jail. He apologized for what he had done and blamed it on his drinking, and he begged her to drop the charges. She asked him for money, and he said he would get some money for her as soon as he got out of jail. Meanwhile, Defendant had told the members of his family, including Brother, that he was innocent and that Husband and Wife were just out to extort money from him. As a result, Brother (unaware of Defendant's conversation with Wife) also approached Wife in an effort to resolve the case. He offered her $500 if she would withdraw the charges and suggested that she and Husband say that they were both so drunk that they really don't remember what happened. Defendant and Brother are both charged with bribing a witness (P.C. § 137). What are the arguments as to their guilt?

Problem 74.

Defendant, a police officer, accepted a payment from Gambler on the understanding that Defendant would not make any arrests for gambling violations that might occur in his jurisdiction. Defendant is charged with a violation of P.C. § 68, which provides:

> Every executive or ministerial officer, employee or appointee of the State of California, county or city therein ... who asks, receives, or agrees to receive any bribe, upon any agreement or understanding that his vote, opinion, or action upon any matter then pending, or which may be brought before him in his official capacity, shall be influenced thereby, is punishable by imprisonment ...

May Defendant defend on the ground that there is no evidence that he was, or ever would be, aware of any gambling activity in his jurisdiction?

Cabe v. Superior Court

63 Cal. App. 4th 732, 74 Cal.Rptr.2d 331 (1998)

Boren, Presiding Justice.

I.
Factual and Procedural Background

Petitioner, while undergoing voir dire by a judge, was asked the following question: "Anybody in your immediate family or yourself been arrested?" Petitioner answered: "One of my boys was arrested." It was true that one of petitioner's sons had been arrested. However, petitioner failed to reveal that he, too, had at one time been arrested. Later, the judge asked a "catchall" question which asked the potential jurors to disclose whether they knew anything which would cause them to be biased. Petitioner did not respond.

Petitioner was charged by information with perjury. (Pen. Code, § 118.) Later, petitioner filed a section 995 motion to set aside the information. Relying on *Bronston v. United States* (1973) 409 U.S. 352 (*Bronston*) and *In re Rosoto* (1974) 10 Cal.3d 939 (*Rosoto*), petitioner asserted that a charge for perjury cannot be based on a statement which is literally true, even if the statement is misleading, unresponsive or leaves a false impression. The prosecution, citing *People v. Meza* (1987) 188 Cal. App. 3d 1631 (*Meza*), argued that prospective jurors may be prosecuted for perjury based on an "omission" to the court during voir dire. When the trial court denied petitioner's motion to dismiss, this petition for writ of mandate followed.

II.
Contentions

Petitioner contends the trial court erred in denying his motion to dismiss the perjury charge because, while his answer to the court's question during voir dire may have been misleading, it was literally true.

The People contend that petitioner may be prosecuted for perjury based on his "misleading response" to the court during voir dire since "jury selection is not an adversarial proceeding."

III.
Discussion
A. Elements of Perjury

In order to lawfully hold a person to answer on the charge of perjury under section 118, evidence must exist of a "willful statement, under oath, of any material matter which the witness knows to be false." (*People v. Howard* (1993) 17 Cal. App. 4th 999.)[4]

B. The Law of Perjury
1. Perjury During Adversarial Hearings

In *Bronston* the United States Supreme Court held that a witness may not be "convicted of perjury for an answer, under oath, that is literally true but not responsive to the question asked and arguably misleading by negative implication."

The defendant, Samuel Bronston, was the president and sole owner of Samuel Bronston Productions, Inc., a movie production company. He had personal as well as company bank accounts in various European countries. The company petitioned for bankruptcy. At a bankruptcy examination, the following colloquy occurred between the lawyer for a creditor and Bronston:

---

4. Petitioner concedes for purposes of this petition that the "matter" at issue is material.

"Q. Do you have any bank accounts in Swiss banks, Mr. Bronston?

"A. No, sir.

"Q. Have you ever?

"A. The company had an account there for about six months, in Zurich.

"Q. Have you any nominees who have bank accounts in Swiss banks?

"A. No, sir.

"Q. Have you ever?

"A. No, sir."

In actuality, Bronston had once had a large personal bank account in Switzerland for about five years. However, Bronston's answers were literally truthful. Bronston did not at the time of questioning have a Swiss bank account. Bronston Productions, Inc., did have the account in Zurich described by Bronston. Neither at the time of questioning nor before did Bronston have nominees who had Swiss accounts.

Bronston was tried for perjury. The government's theory at trial was that in order to mislead his questioner, Bronston answered the second question with literal truthfulness but unresponsively addressed his answer to the company's assets and not to his own—thereby implying that he had no personal Swiss bank account at the relevant time.

The trial court concluded that Bronston's answer could form the basis of a perjury charge, and instructed the jury that Bronston could be convicted if he gave an answer "not literally false but when considered in the context in which it was given, nevertheless constitute[d] a false statement." Bronston was convicted, and the appellate court affirmed.

The United States Supreme Court reversed. It found that Bronston had answered the second question nonresponsively, and also found that a negative implication arose from the answer that Bronston himself did not have any Swiss accounts. Nonetheless, the court held this was not perjury. "Beyond question [Bronston's] answer to the crucial question was not responsive if we assume, as we do, that the first question was directed at personal bank accounts. There is, indeed, an implication in the answer to the second question that there was never a personal bank account; in casual conversation this interpretation might reasonably be drawn. But we are not dealing with casual conversation and the statute does not make it a criminal act for a witness to willfully state any material matter that *implies* any material matter that he does not believe to be true."(Italics added.)

The *Bronston* court could "perceive no reason why Congress would intend the drastic sanction of a perjury prosecution to cure a testimonial mishap that could readily have been reached with a single additional question by counsel alert—as every examiner ought to be—to the incongruity of petitioner's unresponsive answer." The court noted that "testimonial interrogation, and cross-examination in particular, is a probing, prying, pressing form of inquiry. If a witness evades, it is the lawyer's responsibility to recognize the evasion and to bring the witness back to the mark, to flush out the whole truth with the tools of adversary examination." And, the court noted, "[i]t does not matter that the unresponsive answer is stated in the affirmative, thereby implying the negative of the question actually posed; for again, by hypothesis, the examiner's awareness of unresponsiveness should lead him to press another question or reframe his initial question with greater precision. Precise questioning is imperative as a predicate for the offense of perjury. [¶] It may well be that [Bronston]'s answers were not guileless but were shrewdly calculated to evade. Nevertheless, ... any special problems arising from the literally true but unresponsive answer are to be remedied through the 'questioner's acuity' and not by a federal perjury prosecution."

The *Bronston* holding was applied by the California Supreme Court in *Rosoto.* There, a hearing was held on a habeas corpus petition wherein an investigator for the prosecution (Frank Oxandaboure) was asked questions under oath concerning a key prosecution witness, Michael Rosoto. Oxandaboure stated that he had not given Rosoto immunity if he testified at an upcoming trial, and had not given a guarantee that Rosoto would not be prosecuted for unrelated crimes. The truth of the matter was that Oxandaboure had given Rosoto conditional guarantees that he would receive immunity and not face further prosecution if he told the truth when he testified at trial.

In a subsequent habeas corpus case the petitioners claimed Oxandaboure had lied during the previous habeas corpus hearing. The California Supreme Court held that although Oxandaboure had testified in a manner that left the impression that no guarantees of any kind had been given to Rosoto, Oxandaboure did not commit perjury. "Insofar as appears from the record before us Oxandaboure's denials at the hearing on the prior reference of guarantees or assurances of immunity were literally true. The questions put to him asked whether he had guaranteed or assured Michael [Rosoto] immunity if he testified. The guarantee conversation occurred during investigation before charges were brought against petitioners, and the guarantee of immunity was conditioned not on merely testifying but on telling the truth. Oxandaboure was not required to volunteer testimony as to a guarantee other than the one of which he was asked, and although his answers to the questions asked may have left a misleading impression that not even a conditional guarantee was made, he was never asked whether a conditional guarantee of any kind was made."

The court, citing *Bronston,* concluded that "when, as here, a witness' answers are literally true he may not be faulted for failing to volunteer more explicit information. Although such testimony may cause a misleading impression due to the failure of counsel to ask more specific questions, the witness' failure to volunteer testimony to avoid the misleading impression does not constitute perjury because the crucial element of falsity is not present in his testimony."

...

2. Perjury in a Nonadversarial Setting

Although the United States Supreme Court implied in *Bronston* that silence can never constitute perjury, California rejected this proposition in *Meza.*

Meza was a prospective juror in a burglary trial. Before voir dire commenced the court clerk administered an oath to all the potential jurors. The court then introduced the defendant and asked whether any of the potential jurors knew him. One raised his hand and another orally responded. The court inquired if there was anyone else. Meza remained silent and did not raise his hand. The court then asked a further series of questions, specifically directing jurors to raise their hands to indicate an affirmative response. One of the questions was whether there was any reason a juror could not be fair and impartial. Meza did not speak or raise his hand, and was selected as a juror. The trial court subsequently learned that Meza was the defendant's brother-in-law, and discharged him.

The district attorney's office brought a perjury charge against Meza for his failure to inform the judge that he was related to the defendant. Meza, arguing that failure to respond to questions could not constitute perjury, moved to set aside the information. The motion was granted.

On appeal, the order dismissing the perjury charge was reversed. The court noted that the collective questioning of prospective jurors is a proper voir dire method, and held that a juror's silence under those conditions is tantamount to a negative answer. In reaching its conclusion that silence can be construed as a statement, the court referred to Evidence Code section 125, which defines "conduct" as, inter alia, passive and nonverbal behavior, and Evidence Code section 225, which defines "statement" as nonverbal conduct. The *Meza* court concluded, "When the trial judge asked if anyone on the jury panel knew the defendant ... did Meza intend his silence to mean 'No'? We think this is a question for the trier of fact." Thus, if the trier of fact found Meza's silence meant "No," then Meza committed perjury.

C. Petitioner's Perjury Charge Must be Dismissed

1. Petitioner's Response was Unresponsive, but Literally True

Petitioner was asked the following imprecise, compound question: "Anybody in your immediate family *or* yourself been arrested?" (Italics added.) His answer—that one of his sons had been arrested—was partially unresponsive, but literally true. We conclude, therefore, that *Bronston* and *Rosoto* apply, and that no perjury charge is permissible.

The People argue, in essence, that *Bronston* and *Rosoto* are inapplicable because petitioner did not give a "true and complete" answer to the second part of a two-part question. According to the People, the court asked petitioner whether anyone is his immediate family had been arrested, and whether petitioner had ever been arrested. The People claim that petitioner answered the first question fully and completely by stating that his son had been arrested, but failed to answer the second question. According to the People, only one conclusion is possible, *i.e.*, that petitioner intended by his silence to convey the message that he had never been arrested. This being so, the People argue, *Meza* is applicable, and petitioner can be prosecuted for intentionally communicating a specific message through silence.

Meza stands for the proposition that in some cases perjury convictions may be based on silence. Because it is consistent with the rule set forth in *Bronston* and *Rosoto*, we fully concur with the *Meza* holding. *Meza* cannot, however, be applied to the facts of this case. In *Meza* the judge, during collective questioning, told the potential jurors that failure to raise a hand in response to a question would constitute a negative answer. *Meza*'s inaction was, therefore, reasonably understood to signal a negative response to the questions posed by the judge. Petitioner's prosecution for perjury is not based on the lack of an answer during collective questioning. Petitioner gave a literally true answer to a compound question which implied a negative implication.

...

The People claim that if we adopt petitioner's view of jury selection, "the court would be required to cross-examine potential jurors and ferret out evasive answers," and that "[j]ury service would become an ordeal to be feared." In our opinion, if we adopt the People's view, we may cause jurors to avoid jury service for fear of being prosecuted for the criminal offense of perjury because of a failure to volunteer information, or because of a failure to fully and completely answer a poorly crafted question which invites a misleading and/or incomplete answer.

We conclude that the *Bronston/Rosoto* rule applies during the questioning of potential jurors because, in our view, a judge must be an "alert questioner" who can bring a potential juror "back to the mark" when necessary. This is especially true since both the prosecutor and defense counsel are available to suggest follow-up questions should they believe the answer given was misleading or nonresponsive.

...

People v. Darcy

59 Cal. App. 2d 342, 139 P.2d 118 (1943)

WARD, J.

Appellant was indicted, tried by a jury and convicted of perjury. The indictment contains one count which alleges in substance that on March 27, 1934, in an affidavit of registration as an elector he stated under oath before a deputy registrar of voters authorized to administer oaths in the department of elections at San Francisco that his name was "Sam Darcy" and his place of birth "New York," whereas his true name is Samuel Dardeck or Samuel Adams Dardeck and his place of birth Ukraine, Russia.

[The evidence at trial established that defendant's given name was Srool Adam Dardeck and he was born in Orinion, Russia. Subsequently, he immigrated to the United States with his family and secured citizenship when his father was naturalized. When he applied for a passport in 1927 and again in 1935, he gave his name as Samuel Adams Dardeck and his birthplace as Russia. On the other hand, at various other times—including an interview with the police in 1932, in voter affidavits in 1931, 1932 and 1934 and in his 1934 declaration of candidacy for governor—he gave his name as Samuel Adams Darcy and his birthplace as New York. As a journalist and political writer, advocating the principles of the Communist Party, he was known as Sam Darcy, and there was no evidence that he used that name for any fraudulent purpose.]

...

A false statement must be material to the matter at issue and must be made willfully. (Penal Code, sec. 118.) By this section defining perjury, the word "willfully" is used in the sense of knowingly or intentionally and should be differentiated from the same word when used in an indictment charging a fraudulent purpose. To sustain a perjury charge it is not necessary that the false statement be made for the purpose of injuring another. From the evidence as recounted the jury could easily conclude, to a moral certainty and beyond reasonable doubt, that the statements in the affidavit of registration were made "willfully." Whether a false statement has been made willfully or as the result of an honest mistake is a question of fact solely for the jury to decide.

Contrary to the contention of appellant that he was an elector, entitled to vote irrespective of whether he was born in Russia or New York, the statements assigned as perjurious were material as a matter of law. The words "elector" and "voter" are often used interchangeably but there is a difference in meaning. An elector is one who has the qualifications to vote but may not have complied with the legal requirements, that is, the conditions precedent to the exercise of his right to vote. An elector possessed of the necessary constitutional and statutory qualifications is entitled to hold office though his name is not on the great register of voters. (*Bergevin v. Curtz* (1899) 127 Cal. 86.) Appellant argues that if the holding in the *Bergevin* case is correct, it is immaterial whether he made false statements as to his name and place of birth since he could have accomplished the same result by registering under his real name and giving his correct place of birth.

Under appellant's analysis, if the person who makes the affidavit actually has the qualifications to vote, it is immaterial whether or not his answers under oath be truthful. Following his theory a person could register under an assumed name and give a false place of birth, and not be subject to a charge of perjury. Information required in registration is material, its purpose being to make sure that only qualified persons register and vote. It is to effect this purpose that such information is required to be given under oath, and it serves as a basis for an investigation of qualifications of a person who registers. Citizenship is a material factor in the right to register, and subsequently to vote. If registrants were permitted to make false statements of the type herein with impunity, election frauds would be furthered. One person could register several times giving different names and places of birth, or varying statements of the basis of his right to vote. The test in a perjury charge is not that injury actually occurred as a result of the false statements, but that the falsehoods could have influenced or changed the status of the subject of the statement to the benefit of the falsifier or the detriment of others. It is sufficiently material if it might have affected the proceeding in or for which it was made. In the present instance the Registrar of the City and County of San Francisco was prevented from examining the father's naturalization papers for the purpose of verifying appellant's citizenship, and appellant was benefitted at least to the extent of eliminating delay in the determination of that question, or trouble and possible embarrassment in explaining the names given or assumed by him.

The law views with abhorrence the use of falsehoods to such an extent that it is no defense to a prosecution for perjury that the oath was administered in an irregular manner. A person who, being required by law to make a statement under oath, willfully and knowingly falsifies such statement, purportedly made under oath, in any particular, is guilty of perjury as a matter of law whether or not the oath was in fact taken, and regardless of whether the maker knew the materiality of the falsehood, and the offense is complete upon delivery of the affidavit to another person, with the intent that it be uttered or published as true.

[The court rejected defendant's contention that he was prosecuted for the sole reason that he was a Communist and that he was therefore denied equal protection of the laws. The court distinguished *Yick Wo v. Hopkins* [Chapter 1.]]

The facts and the law are not analogous. If appellant herein, otherwise legally entitled to register, had been refused such privilege solely upon the ground that he was a member of a designated political party, or that he professed a certain creed, or that he was of another than the white race, and subsequently appellant voted or attempted to vote and was prosecuted and convicted therefor, the *Yick Wo* case might be of some assistance to him. If *Yick Wo* had made false statements in his application for a license to operate a laundry, and had been charged with perjury in connection therewith instead of with operating such business without a license, a holding that he could make such statements with impunity is inconceivable....

...

Knight, J., concurred.

Peters, P. J.

I dissent.

This appellant has been found guilty of perjury. The alleged perjury consists in the charge that in his affidavit of registration he gave his name as Sam Darcy when his true name is alleged to be Samuel Dardeck, and that he gave his place of birth as New York, when, in fact, it was Russia. This, the lower court held to be perjury, although the evidence admittedly shows that appellant possessed all of the requirements of an elector, and was legally entitled to register as a voter. In other words, the statements found to have been false in no way impaired the purity of the ballot, in no way qualified an otherwise incompetent elector, and in no way gave the franchise to a person not entitled to it. For this offense appellant has been found guilty of perjury for which he could have been subjected to imprisonment for a maximum period of fourteen years. (Pen. Code, sec. 126.) It is my opinion that the evidence, as a matter of law, is insufficient to support the conviction.

...

It seems to be the theory of the majority opinion that the use of other than a birth name in registering, unless a change in name is confirmed by court decree, as a matter of law, constitutes the crime of perjury. That is not the law. Under the common law rule, where it is not done for a fraudulent purpose, a person may lawfully change his name without resort to legal proceedings. A statute such as exists in this state providing a statutory proceeding for securing court approval of a change of name, as long as the statute does not provide that the statutory method is exclusive (and the statute of this state does not so provide), in no way affects this rule. Such statute is in aid of the common law rule. As long as it is not done for a fraudulent purpose, a man may change his name without resort to the courts, and the name so assumed becomes his legal name.

In the instant case there was neither charge nor evidence that appellant used the name Darcy for any false, fraudulent or criminal purpose. This is admitted by respondent. The evidence is uncontradicted that in this state he had never been known by any other name. The fact that he occasionally used his birth name of Dardeck in his passport applications in no way detracts from the fact that he was generally known as Darcy. In view of the fact that his citizenship was dependent upon the naturalization of his father, it is obvious he had to use such name in such applications, because, otherwise, there would have been no record of his citizenship. In this state appellant's name was legally Darcy, and no crime was committed by registering under that name.

The second charge is that appellant falsely averred he was born in New York, when, in fact, he was born in Russia. It may be conceded that the evidence supports the finding that this statement was wilfully false. This, however, does not make it perjurious. In order to be perjury the false statement must be material. The material issue in an affidavit of registration is whether the registrant has the right to vote. Under the Constitution and laws of this state, citizenship, age and residence are the three main requisites for an elector. Electors possessing those qualifications may lawfully register, and, if registered, may vote. The object of registration laws is to prevent unqualified persons from voting. Such laws are aimed at preserving the purity of the ballot box and are not aimed at preventing a qualified elector from voting. They are for the purpose of preventing fraudulent voting. The registration laws are not intended to act as a trap for a qualified elector, so that for minor discrepancies he is either to be deprived of the right to vote or subjected to a trial for perjury. Neither in the majority opinion nor in the brief of the attorney general is one case cited (and I have found none) where a conviction for perjury has been sustained for a misstatement in an affidavit of registration where, in fact, the registrant was qualified to vote. Darcy was admittedly a qualified elector. He was lawfully entitled to register. He was a citizen. At most, his registration was a faulty one that could have been canceled or corrected. The election law provides sufficient penalties for faulty registration. Under section 300 of the Elections Code any person may proceed by action to cancel an illegal registration, while under section 139 of that code every person who allows himself to be registered "knowing himself ... not to be entitled to registration" is subject to imprisonment for a maximum of three years. It is inconceivable that the Legislature intended that a faulty registration of a qualified person should constitute perjury with a maximum punishment of fourteen years when a deliberate illegal registration by an unqualified person should only be punished by three years maximum. It was never the purpose of the perjury statute to permit prosecutions on matters not material to the purpose of the affidavit. The affidavit signed by appellant required him, among other things, to answer as to his occupation and his height. If he had incorrectly designated his occupation, or his height, being qualified to register, could he be subjected to the penalties of perjury? Obviously, it was never the intent or purpose of the perjury statute to include such immaterial misstatements. The only material misstatements that could constitute perjury are those in relation to the qualifications set forth for a qualified elector in section 1, article II of the Constitution. That section requires that the registrant be twenty-one years of age, a citizen for at least ninety days, a resident of the state for one year and of the county for ninety days, and of the precinct forty days. There was no false statement as to any of these matters....

The attorney general argues that false statements as to place of birth could be used for a fraudulent purpose by an unqualified person to qualify himself as a voter. That is not the test. The test is whether this false statement was material to the matter then in issue—i.e., the legal right of Sam Darcy to register. We are not interested in what might be done by some fraudulent person. If a fraudulent act is committed, so that an unqualified person apparently qualifies as a voter by means of a fraudulent affidavit, he may be punished for perjury or for the offense defined in section 139 of the Elections Code. Because someone might be guilty because of fraud is weak ground indeed to justify a conviction of Darcy where fraud was admittedly not present.

...

In re Manuel G.

16 Cal. 4th 805, 941 P.2d 880 (1997)

George, Chief Justice.

The juvenile court declared minor Manuel G. a ward of the court after finding that he had violated Penal Code section 69 by attempting by means of threats to deter a deputy sheriff from performing his duties. The Court of Appeal stated that one element of an offense under section 69 is that the officer must have been engaged in the lawful performance of his or her duties at the time the offense was committed. After determining that the deputy illegally had detained the minor before the minor threatened the deputy, the Court of Appeal reversed the juvenile court's finding that the minor had violated section 69.

As we shall explain, we disagree with the Court of Appeal's determination on two separate grounds. First, whether or not the deputy unlawfully had detained the minor at the time the minor threatened the deputy, the juvenile court's finding that the minor violated section 69 may be upheld on the ground that the minor's threat reasonably could be interpreted as intended to deter the deputy and other law enforcement officers from lawfully performing, in the future, a duty imposed upon them by law with regard to the investigation of the minor and his fellow gang members; as we shall see, such a threat—attempting to deter an officer from the lawful performance of his or her duties in the future—constitutes a violation of section 69 without regard to whether the officer is engaged in the lawful performance of his or her duties at the time the threat is made ... Accordingly, we conclude that the judgment of the Court of Appeal must be reversed.

I

The Orange County District Attorney filed a petition to declare the minor a ward of the court (Welf. & Inst. Code, § 602), charging him with attempting by means of threats to deter and prevent an executive officer from performing a duty imposed by law, in violation of section 69. At the jurisdictional hearing on the petition, Deputies Brian Sims and Dominick Montalbano of the Orange County Sheriff's Department testified concerning the events that gave rise to the charge against the minor.

Deputy Sims testified that in the course of investigating a gang-related shooting, he attempted to locate active gang members in order to obtain additional information concerning the case. While patrolling on the evening of April 19, 1994 (three days after the shooting), he saw the minor walking on the street. Sims recognized the minor as a gang member and broadcast over the police radio that he was making a gang-related "pedestrian check." After Sims got out of his patrol car, the minor continued walking toward him. The deputy asked something like, "Hey, can I talk to you?," and indicated he wanted to speak with the minor about the shooting. The minor stated he had no information. Sims continued to speak to the minor and asked him whether he knew of the circumstances involving the case. Sims did not draw his gun or deter or stop the minor from continuing what he was doing. In response to Sims's questioning, the minor stated that he was going to contact "Internal Affairs," presumably to complain about the deputy's conduct. The minor said he was tired of the Orange County Sheriff's Department contacting him.

Sims testified that immediately following the minor's statement about contacting internal affairs, the minor said, "Me and my home boys are going to start killing you and your friends." Sims informed the minor that making any kind of threat against him was against the law. The minor continued making threats, such as: "Hey, you better be watching your back. And we're going to start knocking you guys off. You guys aren't so bad. I'm not afraid of dying. You guys are the ones that should be afraid of dying."

Deputy Montalbano testified that he heard Sims's radio broadcast that he was "doing a pedestrian stop." Montalbano arrived at the scene two to five minutes later. He encountered the minor sitting on the curb and Sims standing nearby, talking to the minor. The minor seemed agitated and said to Sims, "I'm tired of you guys f___ with us, and you better watch out, we're going to start knocking you guys off." At that point, Sims arrested the minor and seated him in the back of the patrol car. Montalbano then asked the minor why he was so angry with Sims. The minor again remarked, "We're tired of being f___ with. We're going to start knocking you guys off."

The minor did not make a motion to suppress evidence (§ 1538.5), nor did he present any evidence of his own, at the jurisdictional hearing. At the conclusion of the hearing, the juvenile court sustained the allegations of the petition. At the dispositional hearing, the court continued the minor's wardship and placed him on probation, ordering that he serve 180 days in a juvenile facility.

...

II

Section 69 provides: "Every person who attempts, by means of any threat or violence, to deter or prevent an executive officer from performing any duty imposed upon such officer by law, or who knowingly resists, by the use of force or violence, such officer, in the performance of his duty, is punishable by a fine not exceeding ten thousand dollars ($10,000), or by imprisonment in the state prison, or in a county jail not exceeding one year, or by both such fine and imprisonment."

The statute sets forth two separate ways in which an offense can be committed. The first is attempting by threats or violence to deter or prevent an officer from performing a duty imposed by law; the second is resisting by force or violence an officer in the performance of his or her duty. Because the minor is accused only of attempting by threats to deter or prevent an officer from performing a duty imposed by law, we are concerned here only with the first type of offense under section 69.

A threat, unaccompanied by any physical force, may support a conviction for the first type of offense under section 69. To avoid the risk of punishing protected First Amendment speech, however, the term "threat" has been limited to mean a threat of unlawful violence used in an attempt to deter the officer. The central requirement of the first type of offense under section 69 is an attempt to deter an executive officer from performing his or her duties imposed by law; unlawful violence, or a threat of unlawful violence, is merely the means by which the attempt is made.

...

The first type of offense under section 69 ... prohibits the use of threats of violence to attempt to deter or prevent an officer from performing any duty imposed by law. Although the statute applies only when the conduct that the threat is intended to deter is a "duty imposed upon such officer by law"—i.e., only when the conduct that the defendant attempts to deter is lawful conduct to be performed by the officer in connection with his or her duties as an officer—the statutory language does not require that the officer be engaged in the performance of his or her duties at the time the threat is made. Instead, the plain language of the statute encompasses attempts to deter either an officer's immediate performance of a duty imposed by law or the officer's performance of such a duty at some time in the future. Thus, for example, a person who telephones an off-duty officer at his or her home and threatens to kill the officer if he or she continues to pursue a lawful investigation the following day or week may be convicted of the first type of offense under section 69, even though the officer was not engaged in the performance of his or her duties at the time the threat was made.

Of course, when a defendant threatens an on-duty officer in an attempt to deter or prevent the officer from continuing to perform the specific conduct in which the officer is then currently engaged, and the officer's conduct is unlawful, the defendant would not violate the statute, because he or she would not have attempted to deter the officer's performance of lawful conduct. When a defendant threatens an officer in an attempt to deter the officer from performing a duty at some later time, however, only the future performance of such duty must be lawful, and the circumstance that the officer may not have been acting in the lawful performance of his or her duties—or may not have been engaged in his or her official duties at all—at the time the threat is made, would not preclude a finding that the defendant violated section 69. In sum, under the first type of offense prohibited by section 69, the relevant factor is simply the lawfulness of the official conduct that the defendant (through threat or violence) has attempted to deter, and not the lawfulness (or official nature) of the conduct in which the officer is engaged at the time the threat is made.

...

The minor ... contends that the first type of offense under section 69 is limited to an attempt to deter an officer from lawfully executing process or performing similar duties such as making an arrest. The minor observes that the "duty" requirements in the two types of offenses set forth in section 69 are phrased differently from one another. The first offense involves attempting to deter performance of "any duty imposed upon such officer by law," whereas the second offense concerns obstructing or resisting an officer "in the performance of his duty." The minor maintains that the Legislature would not have used different language in setting forth the two duty requirements if it did not intend different meanings. To ascertain such meaning, the minor looks to certain of section 69's predecessor statutes that prohibited interference with an officer's lawful execution of some process or order of the court. According to the minor, the phrase "any duty imposed ... by law" in the initial portion of section 69 is limited to such narrowly defined duties, while the "duty" referenced in the second portion of section 69 refers to any and all lawful conduct in which an officer might be engaged during the course of his or her employment.

Again, because the language of the statute is clear, we need not resort to legislative history to interpret it. The phrase "any duty imposed upon such officer by law" reasonably cannot be limited solely to execution of process and similar duties, because the law requires and authorizes officers to perform numerous other duties. Indeed, the term "executive officer" as used in section 69 is not limited to peace officers such as police officers or deputy sheriffs, but extends to other executive officers who would have no occasion to engage in the execution of court process or similar duties described by the minor. If we were to accept the minor's interpretation, we would be writing the term "executive officer" out of the statute. Contrary to the minor's argument, we discern no legislative intent to distinguish among different types of duties simply because the statute uses the phrase "performing any duty imposed ... by law" in the first portion of section 69, and the phrase "in the performance of his duty" in the second portion.

The interpretation of section 69 that we have set forth above furthers the statute's purpose of prohibiting the use of threats or violence as a tool for attempting to interfere with executive action. As the Court of Appeal stated in *People v. Superior Court (Anderson)* (1984) 151 Cal. App. 3d 893, "[T]he act is not excused by the fact that the actor does not presently have the executive officer in the sights of his gun."

Executive officers, including peace officers investigating criminal activity, must feel free to pursue their lawful duties without fear of violent retaliation.

We proceed to apply this interpretation of section 69 to the facts of this case. The record indicates that the minor's threats to kill Sims and his fellow officers reasonably could be construed as an attempt to deter the Orange County Sheriff's Department's future investigation of gang-related activities. In response to Sims's questions concerning the shooting, the minor said he was tired of the department contacting him. The minor's threats were not directed solely at Sims, but also toward others in the department. Thus, he stated: "Me and my home boys are going to start killing you and your friends." "I'm tired of you guys f___ with us, and you better watch out, we're going to start knocking you guys off." Taken in context, these statements suggest that the minor felt frustrated at being contacted in the course of the department's investigations, and that his threats constituted an attempt to deter deputies from initiating further contacts with him or other gang members. The minor does not contend, and there is nothing in the record to suggest, that any future investigation of, or contact with, gang members by the department would be unlawful.

Therefore, even assuming for the sake of argument that the record establishes (as the Court of Appeal determined) that the minor was unlawfully detained by Sims before the minor uttered these threats, the juvenile court still properly could find that the minor violated section 69. Accordingly, we conclude that the Court of Appeal erred in reversing the juvenile court's finding on the ground that section 69 necessarily required Sims to have been engaged in the lawful performance of his duties at the time the minor made the threats in question.[8]

...

Problem

Problem 75.

Defendant was an inmate in the county jail awaiting trial on murder charges, and, as a result of various statements, he was charged with one count each of threat-

---

8. As noted, the Court of Appeal's disposition of the appeal rendered it unnecessary for that court to address the minor's argument that there is insufficient evidence to support his conviction under section 69 because the prosecution evidence fails to establish that he acted with the intent to prevent or deter, rather than simply to express his displeasure with, the deputy's actions. The appellate court briefly stated in a footnote that "had [Deputy] Sims been acting in the lawful performance of his duties, Manuel's threats would have supported a finding of a violation of section 69." Contrary to the Attorney General's argument, we do not believe this brief statement may be considered to be a discussion or resolution of the minor's argument that he lacked the specific intent necessary to establish a violation of section 69. The Court of Appeal neither analyzed the minor's argument nor mentioned the authority upon which the minor relied. Under these circumstances, we believe it is appropriate for the Court of Appeal to consider that issue in the first instance on remand, and we therefore express no opinion as to whether the evidence is sufficient to establish that the minor made threats constituting an attempt to deter present or future duties imposed by law.

ening Officer 1 and threatening Officer 2 (P.C. § 69). At trial Officer 1 testified that, on the day after Defendant's arrest, Defendant had used profanity, threatened to throw soap bars at Officer 1 and to kick him in the face. Later that day, Defendant said to Officer 1, "I am going to kill you. This is a threat. You're dead." Officer 2 testified that he and defendant had engaged in several "verbal altercations" while Defendant was in custody, and Witness (another officer) testified that he heard Defendant say of Officer 2 (while Officer 2 was not present) that Defendant would "beat his behind" and that "his days are short." Both Officer 1 and Officer 2 testified they were not afraid as a result of Defendant's threats. What arguments should be made as to Defendant's guilt on each count?

People v. Robles

48 Cal. App. 4th Supp. 1, 56 Cal.Rptr.2d 369 (1996)

Johnson, Acting Presiding Judge.

Luis Martin Robles (appellant) appeals from his conviction for obstructing an officer in the discharge of his duties in violation of Penal Code section 148, subdivision (a) [willfully resisting, delaying or obstructing any public officer, peace officer or emergency medical technician in the discharge of his or her duty] ...

...

II.

The evidence presented in the People's case was as follows: Officer Samuel Huizar testified that he is a police officer for the City of Los Angeles, assigned to West Bureau narcotics. On March 17, 1995, at approximately 5:30 p.m., he was working undercover, attempting to buy narcotics in the area of Braddock and Slauson, an area with heavy narcotic and gang activity. The undercover investigation involved approximately four uniformed officers, eight to ten detectives, six undercover officers and three supervisors. Officer Huizar was dressed in civilian clothing and was wearing a "wire" on his body in order to communicate with his supervisors. He was driving a white Beretta with no lights.

Officer Huizar observed a male Hispanic about 17 years old (the suspect) on a bicycle in the middle of the street. Officer Huizar stopped his vehicle next to the suspect and asked him if he had "rock," the street term for rock cocaine. The suspect asked Officer Huizar how much he wanted, and Officer Huizar told him he wanted a "dime," the street term for $10 worth of narcotics.[1] The suspect then asked the officer, "You only want a dime?" The officer responded, "Yes," and reached into his right front pants pocket and removed two precoded $5 bills. Then Officer Huizar heard someone yell, "Get away from that guy! The guy's a cop!" The suspect looked at Officer Huizar and asked, "Are you a cop?" Officer Huizar responded, "No, I'm not."

---

1. Officer Huizar testified he knew he had a "buy" because the suspect asked him how much he wanted and did not walk away.

Appellant then walked up to the suspect and said, "I told you to get away from that guy. The guy's a cop." The suspect told Officer Huizar he was not going to sell him anything because he was a cop and rode away on his bicycle. Officer Huizar then contacted his supervisors, who detained appellant.

Officer Huizar testified that getting "burned," *i.e.*, being identified as a police officer, compromises an officer's safety and prevents him from doing his duty. Since a suspect will not deal with an individual who has been identified as a police officer, once an officer has been so identified, the officer must be replaced by another undercover officer.

...

IV.

Appellant ... contends his conviction violated his right to free speech under the First and Fourteenth Amendments to the United States Constitution and article I, section 2 of the California Constitution.

...

Penal Code section 148 does not apply solely to nonverbal conduct involving flight or forcible interference with an officer's activities. "No decision has interpreted the statute to apply only to physical acts, and the statutory language does not suggest such a limitation." (*People v. Quiroga* (1993) 16 Cal. App. 4th 961.) Nevertheless, we recognize that "the First Amendment protects a significant amount of verbal criticism and challenge directed at police officers." (*Houston v. Hill* (1987) 482 U.S. 451.) We further recognize that Penal Code section 148 must be applied with great caution to speech.

Appellant claims his conduct was constitutionally protected because he did not utter "fighting words," breach the peace or engage in disorderly conduct. He argues he should not be punished merely for discouraging the suspect from committing a crime. However, the record contains substantial evidence that appellant willfully obstructed the officer in the performance of his undercover duties.

Appellant does not dispute the fact that he knew Officer Huizar was a police officer. It may be inferred from the content of appellant's warning and the nature of the area in question that appellant knew the officer was conducting an undercover investigation. Appellant not only alerted the suspect to the officer's identity but directed the suspect to "get away from [the officer]." When the suspect failed to heed appellant's initial warning, appellant approached the suspect and stated, "I told you to get away from that guy. That guy's a cop." As a result of appellant's warning the suspect fled, preventing the officer from obtaining evidence of a crime he might otherwise have obtained.

"[S]peech is generally protected by the First Amendment, even if it is intended to interfere with the performance of an officer's duty, *provided no physical interference results*." (*Long v. Valentino* (1989) 216 Cal. App. 3d 1287, italics added.) In this case, appellant's speech did not constitute mere verbal criticism and challenge directed at the officer. Appellant's speech accomplished a physical event, *i.e.*, the flight of the suspect, which interfered with the officer's ability to complete his investigation.

As the Court of Appeal explained in *Long v. Valentino*: "[W]e do not literally punish a bandit for mere use of the words, 'Stick 'em up, you moron.' We punish him for the act of attempting to take the property of another by force and fear. It is of no moment that language was the vehicle to the goal in this ... hypothetical case. Physical force alone could have been employed ... and the words, while they may have contained a kernel of expression ... (e.g., 'you moron'), amount to conduct designed to accomplish a direct violation of the law and not primarily a means of conveying an idea or point of view." Based on the reasoning in *Long*, we are persuaded that appellant's speech was not constitutionally protected under the federal and state Constitutions.

The judgment is affirmed.

Kakita, J., concurs.

Todd, J., dissenting:

I concur in the majority's conclusion that Officer Huizar was discharging a duty of his office in conducting the undercover operation. I am of the view, however, that appellant's verbal warning to a third party before any obvious illegal activity had taken place was protected speech and therefore cannot constitute a violation of Penal Code section 148, subdivision (a).

...

As there appears to be no California case directly on point, a review of decisions from other jurisdictions may be helpful in determining whether one can obstruct an undercover officer by giving a verbal warning to a third party. In *State v. CLR* (Wash. 1985) 700 P.2d 1195, CLR was convicted by a juvenile court of obstructing a police officer. In that case, a police officer on undercover duty approached a woman standing on the street. After talking to the officer through the open window of the officer's truck, the woman agreed to engage in an act of prostitution. CLR, who recognized the officer as a member of the vice squad, observed but could not hear the exchange. The woman walked around the truck and opened the passenger door, at which point CLR yelled, " 'he's vice.' " At that point the woman closed the door and started to walk away from the truck.

The reviewing court held there was insufficient evidence that the defendant knew "that a public servant [was] engaged in a discharge of official duties ..." The officer was working undercover, and the defendant "could not have known that a crime had been committed and that the officer would be proceeding to make an arrest ..." The reviewing court also held there was insufficient evidence of "hindering, delaying, or obstructing ..." Finally, the court there noted: "Courts have found that similar obstruction statutes do not apply where there was no obvious, contemporaneous, illegal activity when the warning was given."

Likewise, in *State v. Jelliffe* (Ohio Mun.Ct.1982) 449 N.E.2d 810, the defendant was attending a rock concert and recognized an individual in plainclothes as a police officer. "Defendant then told at least one other individual, evidently in the hearing of the officer, that the large person was 'a cop.' " The court found the defendant not guilty, based in part on the following reasoning: "[T]here is no allegation that defendant's conduct actually prevented the arrest of any persons who were then violating the law. While it may have made detection of violations more difficult, it is equally possible that it may have inhibited the commission of crimes in the first place. Surely that is one goal of law enforcement."

...

In the present case, the warning occurred before any obvious illegal activity had taken place. In addition, as in *State v. Jelliffe*, appellant's warning may have prevented a crime from being committed. Furthermore, appellant's speech was nonthreatening, was not accompanied by physical force, was not so loud or intense that it interfered with Officer Huizar's duty, and did not incite an unlawful resistance by the suspect. As appellant notes, the suspect had no duty to continue to talk to the undercover officer.

Although appellant's disclosure of the officer's identity might make it more difficult for Officer Huizar to continue to perform plainclothes duty in that area, it is clear that at least one person in the area, appellant, already knew or suspected that Huizar was a police officer. An officer working undercover places himself in danger, and an inherent risk of this kind of duty is that the officer's identity may be known or may become known.

...

I am persuaded by the reasoning set forth above that the imposition of criminal sanctions for the words spoken here would violate appellant's constitutional rights under the First Amendment of the federal Constitution as well as article I, section 2, subdivision (a) of the California Constitution. I would therefore reverse the conviction.

Problem

Problem 76.

In each of the following cases, what are the arguments as to whether Defendant has violated P.C. § 148?

a. Officer was working as an undercover narcotics agent. She learned that Defendant, a bartender, might be involved with drugs, and, as a result, she made several unsuccessful attempts to trade him drugs. In part because Defendant twice saw Officer in the company of a police sergeant, Defendant decided that Officer was an undercover officer. Officer learned of Defendant's suspicions, so she stopped approaching him. Late one night, Defendant was standing on the street just outside his bar, in an area populated with drug users, drug sellers and biker gangs, and Officer and another undercover officer were walking down the street intending to meet with two "targets." When they were 10 feet from them, Defendant said to a friend, in a loud voice, that the two were "narcs" or "undercover detectives." Concerned for their safety, the two officers left. Defendant was later arrested and charged.

b. Late at night, officers responded to a burglary alarm, and a citizen they encountered told them that three teenagers had run away after breaking a store window and he thought one had gone into Defendant's apartment. The officers went to the apartment and saw, through the partially opened door, that several people were asleep in the studio apartment. They knocked on the door. Defendant woke up and came to the door, and the officers explained the situation and requested permission to search the apartment for the teenager. Defendant said, "Get the hell out of here if you don't have a damn warrant." The officers said they did not need a warrant because they were pursuing a suspect, and they again asked permission to enter. Defendant refused and continued to stand in the doorway. Defendant was arrested.

c. Defendant was part of a student sit-in protest at the university. He refused to leave when the protest was declared an illegal assembly. When police came to arrest him, he went limp and had to be carried to the police car.

Part III
Affirmative Defenses

The defenses considered in *Part II* (*e.g.*, unconsciousness, mental impairment, mistake) are defenses to the prosecution's proof of one or more elements of the charged crime. The defenses considered in the next two chapters are affirmative defenses and differ from the defenses considered earlier in that they do not challenge the prosecution's proof but instead rely on new matter which justifies or excuses conduct that would otherwise be criminal. The two chapters consider six affirmative defenses: (1) self-defense and defense of others; (2) use of force to prevent crime or apprehend criminals; (3) duress; (4) necessity; (5) entrapment and the related due process defense ("outrageous police conduct"); and (6) insanity. With regard to all affirmative defenses, the defendant bears the "burden of production," *i.e.*, the defendant must present some evidence in support of the defense in order to raise the issue. However, the defenses differ in terms of who has the ultimate burden of proof. Chapter 11 addresses the first three defenses, those as to which the prosecution has the burden of proof and must disprove the defense beyond a reasonable doubt. Chapter 12 addresses the last three defenses, where the defendant bears the burden of proving the defense by a preponderance of the evidence.

Chapter 11

Affirmative Defenses—Part I

This chapter examines three affirmative defenses where the prosecution bears the burden of disproving the defense once it is raised: (1) self-defense and defense of others; (2) use of force to prevent crime or apprehend criminals; and (3) duress. With regard to the first two categories, although the Penal Code does identify certain circumstances where the use of force is justifiable (*e.g.*, §§ 196–198 [justifiable homicide], §§ 692–694 [resistance to the commission of crimes]), the California Supreme Court has paid little attention to statutory law in defining the defenses. As a result, the court has sometimes recognized a defense in circumstances not provided for by statute and sometimes refused to recognize a defense despite its statutory basis. With regard to duress, Penal Code § 26 codifies a limited duress defense (for "[p]ersons (unless the crime be punishable with death) who committed the act or made the omission charged under threats or menaces sufficient to show that they had reasonable cause to and did believe their lives would be endangered if they refused"), but the courts have at times recognized a broader duress defense.

A. Self-Defense and Defense of Others

In *People v. Hecker*, an Old West shootout, the supreme court sets out the basic law of self-defense in California and describes its application in a variety of fact situations. In *People v. Humphrey*, a case in which a battered woman killed her husband, the court again addresses an issue from *Part II*—what circumstances are to be considered in determining the reasonableness of a defendant's perceptions or conduct. The court has to decide whether, and how, the fact that the defendant suffered from battered women's syndrome is relevant to her claim of self-defense. In *People v. Randle*, the court considers to what extent self-defense principles apply when deadly force is used to defend others. *People v. Curtis* concerns the defendant's use of force to resist arrest, and the court has to decide whether the use of force is justifiable to resist an illegal arrest and/or an arrest effected by excessive force.

People v. Hecker

109 Cal. 451, 42 P. 307 (1895)

HENSHAW, J.

The appellant, Hecker, was tried for the murder of one Patrick Riley, and by the jury found guilty of murder in the second degree. The killing was admitted, but it was claimed to have been done in self-defense.

It appeared by the evidence that Riley peddled wares through the country, using for the purpose a two-horse team and wagon. He had camped near the farm house of one Briceland and turned his horses into Briceland's enclosure. From this they strayed and were lost in the hills. They had been gone for several days when Riley, who had been in vain pursuit of them, met Hecker and offered to give him ten dollars if he would find and return them.

Hecker was an old resident of the vicinity, and owned a sheep range which was contiguous to the land of Briceland. He searched for the horses that day and found them upon his land, put them in his corral over night, and the next morning proceeded with them to Briceland's.

Riley was away at the time of his arrival, and Hecker either made a voluntary surrender of the horses to Mrs. Riley, who put them in Briceland's barn, as was claimed by the people, or, as was contended by the defense, they were put there by Mrs. Riley for Hecker, who thus still retained constructive possession of and a lien upon them for the promised reward of ten dollars. The point is one in dispute.

Hecker rode on to the little town of Briceland, and passed the day in waiting for Riley. He did not see him and went home. The next day he returned to town and met Riley about 11 o'clock in the morning. Riley called him to one side and the finding of the horses was discussed. There having been no one else present at that interview the only account of it is Hecker's. But it appears from other evidence that Riley suspected that his horses had been taken and secreted in the hills in expectation of a reward, and the promptness with which Hecker found and returned them seems to have confirmed him in his suspicion, and created the conviction that Hecker had purloined them. There was no question but that Riley's suspicions were unfounded and unjust. It was in evidence that Riley said he would kill the man who stole his horses.

Hecker testified that Riley accused him of stealing the horses, and refused to pay him any money for their recovery. The men parted, Hecker returned to the store and saloon, and, after thinking and talking the matter over, as he says, concluded he would take the horses from Briceland's barn and put them elsewhere until he was paid.

Hecker was a cripple, Riley a powerful man. Hecker armed himself, thinking that Riley would be at Briceland's, and knowing that "he would be trying to get a row."

Arriving at Briceland's a little after noon Hecker found but one horse, the other having been ridden off by Sam Pollock, who had gone to find Riley and tell him the search was at an end. Hecker took possession of the animal, and led it from the stable.

Riley saw him and came forward, calling to him and forbidding the act. Hecker half drew his pistol from the bosom of his shirt, and in turn told Riley to advance no further. Riley answered that he was unarmed, and turned out his pockets in proof, and a second time the two men parted, Hecker leading away the horse.

He returned with it to the town where he spent the afternoon discussing his grievance. As was shown, he used some loose talk and indulged in some threats; he would not let Riley beat him out of his money; he would have the money or would have Riley's blood; while, to add to the bitterness of his feeling, he was informed that Riley had gone off to procure his arrest for stealing the horses. This information was brought to him by men whom he had sent to see Riley to fix up the matter, telling them that he wanted no fuss and to take what they could get and settle it for him.

So the time passed until about half past six of this July afternoon when Hecker espied Pollock riding by on the other horse. Hecker, who was himself then mounted, hailed him and demanded the horse, believing, as he testified, that he "had to have both horses in order to make the lien good." Pollock declined to surrender the animal, saying he would put it where he got it; and so Hecker rode on once more to Briceland's, and to the fatal meeting with Riley.

As the two men rode up to the stable Riley came forward to take his horse. Pollock dismounted. Riley started to remove the saddle. Hecker leaned forward to seize the bridle. There was a struggle for possession, and then, by the evidence for the people, Hecker drew his pistol and with it struck Riley over the head, and as he staggered back fired at him. Hecker's account is that he spurred his horse that he might seize the other's bridle; that as his horse sprang forward her fore shoulder struck Riley and staggered him: "When I broke his hold he ran right back and had his hand twisted to pull his pistol, and at last he pulled his pistol out and pointed at me, and I saw him shut his eye to pull the trigger, and just as he was about to pull the trigger I threw myself out of the saddle like that [shows] over the side of my horse and grabbed my pistol at the same time, and as I raised mine up he had his pistol up and we both shot about the same time. If anything he shot a little before I did."

The defendant was riding a nervous two-year-old colt, using a "hackamore" in lieu of bridle, and, at the shooting, she either bolted or, as Hecker says, he started her to go around Briceland's house, and get out of the way. Riley fired again at him as he went. At some beehives Hecker reined up, and the two men exchanged shots. Hecker then rode on in another direction to a place in the yard where there were four stumps, having abandoned, as he says, his first intention to pass around Briceland's house, and endeavoring to get away by another route, or, as the people claim, coming back to engage Riley at closer quarters. Riley ran toward a granary, calling upon one of the bystanders, of whom there were several, to lend him his pistol, and to his wife and daughter to go to the wagon and bring him more cartridges. Whether Riley ran to the granary to escape further combat, or whether he designed to use it as a shield that he might fire with more security upon Hecker, is disputed. Near the granary, and, as Riley was about to pass a corner of it, there was shooting, and Riley, struck through the heart, ran a few yards and fell dead.

Nothing of the foregoing narrative is to be taken as expressing the views of this court upon the weight of the evidence. That consideration is not before us. The account is designed to throw into prominence the claims made by prosecution and defense for the better understanding of the propositions of law which we are called upon to consider.

. . .

. . . There is no fixed rule applicable to every case, though certain general principles, well established, stand forth as guides for the action of men and measures for the jury's determination of their deportment.

1. Self-defense is not available as a plea to a defendant who has sought a quarrel with the design to force a deadly issue and thus, through his fraud, contrivance, or fault, to create a real or apparent necessity for killing.

2. It is not available as a plea to one who by prearranged deal, or by consent, has entered into a deadly mutual combat in which he slays his adversary. In both of these cases the same rule applies. A man may not wickedly or willfully invite or create the appearances of necessity or the actual necessity which, if present to one without blame, would justify the homicide.

3. Where one without fault is placed under circumstances sufficient to excite the fears of a reasonable person that another designs to commit a felony or some great bodily injury upon him, and to afford grounds for reasonable belief that there is imminent danger of the accomplishment of this design, he may, acting under these fears alone, slay his assailant and be justified by the appearances. And, as where the attack is sudden and the danger imminent, he may increase his peril by retreat, so situated he may stand his ground, that becoming his "wall," and slay his aggressor even if it be proved that he might more easily have gained his safety by flight. So, too, under such circumstances, he may pursue and slay his adversary. But the pursuit must not be in revenge, nor after the necessity for defense has ceased, but must be prosecuted in good faith to the sole end of winning his safety and securing his life.

4. Where one is making a felonious assault upon another, or has created appearances justifying that other in making a deadly counter attack in self-defense, the original assailant cannot slay his adversary and avail himself of the plea unless he has first and in good faith declined further combat, and has fairly notified him that he has abandoned the contest. And if the circumstances are such, arising either from the condition of his adversary, caused by the aggressor's acts during the affray or from the suddenness of the counter attack, that he cannot so notify him, it is the first assailant's fault and he must take the consequences. For, as the deceased, acting upon the appearances created by the wrongful acts of the aggressor, would have been justified in killing him, he whose fault created these appearances cannot make the natural and legal acts of the deceased looking to his own defense a justification for the homicide. Before doing so he must have destroyed these appearances and removed, to the other's knowledge, his necessity, actual or apparent, for self-preservation.

5. Where one is the first wrongdoer, but his unlawful act is not felonious, as a simple assault upon the person of another, or a mere trespass upon his property, even though forcible, and this unlawful act is met by a counter assault of a deadly character, the right of self-defense to the first wrongdoer is not lost. For, as his acts did not justify upon the part of the other the use of deadly means for their prevention, his killing by the other would be criminal, and one may always defend himself against a criminal attempt to take his life. But in contemplation of the weakness and passions of men, and of the provocation, which, though inadequate, was wrongfully put upon the other, it is the duty of the first wrongdoer before he can avail himself of the plea to have retreated to the wall, to have declined the strife and withdrawn from the difficulty, and to have killed his adversary, under necessity, actual or apparent, only after so doing. If, however, the counter assault be so sudden and perilous that no opportunity be given to decline or to make known to his adversary his willingness to decline the strife, if he cannot retreat with safety, then as the greater wrong of the deadly assault is upon his opponent, he would be justified in slaying, forthwith, in self-defense.

The distinction between this principle and the one preceding it consists in this: In the former case the provocation for making a deadly counter attack in self-defense is adequate, and therefore the first aggressor must remove the necessity for it and make that fact known before his own right of self-defense can exist; in the latter case the provocation is inadequate, and if the other by his own unlawful act deprives the first wrongdoer of the opportunity to decline a deadly strife, that fault lies not at the door of the slayer but of the slain.

So much it has seemed necessary to say in view of the varying theories upon the facts attending this homicide and in contemplation of a new trial.

If at the time of the affray Hecker was a trespasser and no more in his endeavor to take the horse, and Riley met his endeavor by a deadly assault upon him with a pistol, it was Hecker's first duty to decline the strife, and if the suddenness of the assault precluded this, he was justified, so long as the imminence of his danger continued, or apparently continued, in meeting it by a deadly return.

If, however, Hecker was not a wrongdoer in seeking to take the horse, and Riley met his attempt by a felonious assault with a pistol, Hecker, if the assault was sudden and the danger great or apparently great, would have been justified in standing his ground, or even, as above set forth, in pursuing and slaying his adversary to win his safety.

If, on the other hand, Hecker made the first deadly assault, his right to slay Riley in self-defense did not exist, even though willing thereafter to decline further combat, until he had in good faith declined and fairly made known to Riley his willingness to do so. And if he did not do this, even though he failed because of his own imminent danger, and under these circumstances killed Riley, his act was criminal.

And lastly, if, upon the other hand, he made the first felonious assault, and thereafter and before firing the fatal shot did in good faith withdraw and decline further combat, and this was fairly made known to Riley by his conduct, and thereafter Riley pursued him and forced a new combat upon him, and under these circumstances Riley was killed, the killing was justifiable.

...

Note and Problems

The Model Penal Code and Defensive Use of Force. The Model Penal Code provision on the use of force in self-defense differs from California law in two significant respects:

> (1) The Code does not require that the defendant's belief in the need for self-defense be reasonable. The defendant may assert the defense of self-defense even if the defendant's determination to use force and determination how much force to use was negligent or reckless. In that case the defendant might still be prosecuted for any crime for which negligence or recklessness was a sufficient *mens rea.*
>
> (2) The Code does not recognize a defense to the use of deadly force if the defendant could have avoided the use of such force "by retreating [except from the defendant's own house or, in some circumstances, place of work] or by surrendering possession of a thing to a person asserting a claim of right thereto or by complying with a demand that he abstain from any action that he has no duty to take...."

See MPC § 3.04.

Problem 77.

Defendant is a 5' 4" Native American woman, who, at the time of the incident, had a broken leg. Several months prior to the day of the homicide, Friend's 7-year-old daughter ("Daughter") had been sexually molested, but had refused to identify the molester. On the day of the homicide, Defendant's son ("Son") was visiting at the home of Friend and entered the house saying that a man had tried to pull him off his bicycle and drag him into a house. Shortly thereafter, Victim arrived and said through the door, "I didn't touch the kid." At that point, Daughter identified Victim as the one who had molested her. Friend's landlord saw Victim leave and told Friend that Victim had tried to molest another young boy who had previously lived in the house and Victim had been committed to a state hospital for the mentally ill. Earlier in the week, there had been a prowler at Friend's house, and she suspected Victim. Friend called the police but was told that nothing could be done until after the weekend.

That evening Friend asked Defendant to spend the night with her. Defendant arrived with a pistol in her handbag. Because they were afraid to stay alone, Defendant and Friend asked Defendant's sister and brother-in-law to spend the night with them. Ultimately, there were four adults and eight children staying in Friend's home. The adults stayed up talking and watching for possible prowlers. Without telling the others, Defendant's brother-in-law went to Victim's house and accused Victim of molesting the children. Victim then suggested that they go over to Friend's and get things straightened out. Victim, a large man who was visibly intoxicated, entered the home and refused to leave when asked. There was considerable shouting and a child who had been sleeping on the couch awoke crying. Victim approached the child, saying, "My what a cute little boy," or words to that effect. Defendant's sister, the mother of the child, stepped between Victim and the child, and Friend was screaming at Victim to get out of the house. Defendant went to the door to call her brother-in-law. When she turned around and found Victim standing directly behind her, she was very startled and shot Victim.

Defendant is charged with voluntary manslaughter (P.C. § 192(a)). The judge proposes instructing the jury as follows:

> To justify killing in self-defense, there need be no actual or real danger to the life or person of the party killing, but there must be, or reasonably appear to be, at or immediately before the killing, some overt act or some circumstances which would reasonably indicate to the party killing that the person slain is, at the time, endeavoring to kill him or inflict upon him great bodily harm.
>
> However, when there is no reasonable ground for the person attacked to believe that his person is in imminent danger of death or great bodily harm, and it appears to him that only an ordinary battery is all that is intended, and all that he has reasonable grounds to fear from his assailant, he has a right to stand his ground and repel such threatened assault, yet he has no right to repel a threatened assault with naked hands, by the use of a deadly weapon in a deadly manner, unless he believes, and has reasonable grounds to believe that he is in imminent danger of death or great bodily harm.

What objections might Defendant make, or what modifications might defendant offer, to the proposed instructions?

Problem 78.

Defendant went to the home of Daughter (his wife's daughter by a former marriage) in search of Wife. Victim, the ex-husband of Wife and father of Daughter, was also present. After talking to Wife, Defendant made various hostile remarks to Victim, and Victim jumped out of bed threatening to kill Defendant if he did not get out of the house. Defendant had a pocket knife in his hand. He rushed at Victim and, in the course of wrestling with him, cut his own hand. Defendant then put his knife in his pocket and attempted to run out of the house. Victim pursued and cornered Defendant in the kitchen where they again began to wrestle. When Victim began choking Defendant, Defendant pulled out his knife and killed Victim. What are the arguments on whether Defendant has available the defense of self-defense?

People v. Humphrey

13 Cal. 4th 1073, 921 P.2d 1 (1996)

CHIN, JUSTICE.

The Legislature has decreed that, when relevant, expert testimony regarding "battered women's syndrome" is generally admissible in a criminal action. (Evid. Code, § 1107.) We must determine the purposes for which a jury may consider this evidence when offered to support a claim of self-defense to a murder charge.

The trial court instructed that the jury could consider the evidence in deciding whether the defendant actually believed it was necessary to kill in self-defense, but not in deciding whether that belief was reasonable. The instruction was erroneous. Because evidence of battered women's syndrome may help the jury understand the circumstances in which the defendant found herself at the time of the killing, it is relevant to the reasonableness of her belief. Moreover, because defendant testified, the evidence was relevant to her credibility. The trial court should have allowed the jury to consider this testimony in deciding the reasonableness as well as the existence of defendant's belief that killing was necessary.

Finding the error prejudicial, we reverse the judgment of the Court of Appeal.

I. The Facts

A. *Prosecution Evidence*

During the evening of March 28, 1992, defendant shot and killed Albert Hampton in their Fresno home. Officer Reagan was the first on the scene. A neighbor told Reagan that the couple in the house had been arguing all day. Defendant soon came outside appearing upset and with her hands raised as if surrendering. She told Officer Reagan, "I shot him. That's right, I shot him. I just couldn't take him beating on me no more." She led the officer into the house, showed him a .357 magnum revolver on a table, and said, "There's the gun." Hampton was on the kitchen floor, wounded but alive.

A short time later, defendant told Officer Reagan, "He deserved it. I just couldn't take it anymore. I told him to stop beating on me." "He was beating on me, so I shot him. I told him I'd shoot him if he ever beat on me again." A paramedic heard her say that she wanted to teach Hampton "a lesson." Defendant told another officer at the scene, Officer Terry, "I'm fed up. Yeah, I shot him. I'm just tired of him hitting me. He said, 'You're not going to do nothing about it.' I showed him, didn't I? I shot him good. He won't hit anybody else again. Hit me again; I shoot him again. I don't care if I go to jail. Push come to shove, I guess people gave it to him, and, kept hitting me. I warned him. I warned him not to hit me. He wouldn't listen."

Officer Terry took defendant to the police station, where she told the following story. The day before the shooting, Hampton had been drinking. He hit defendant while they were driving home in their truck and continued hitting her when they arrived. He told her, "I'll kill you," and shot at her. The bullet went through a bedroom window and struck a tree outside. The day of the shooting, Hampton "got drunk," swore at her, and started hitting her again. He walked into the kitchen. Defendant saw the gun in the living room and picked it up. Her jaw hurt, and she was in pain. She pointed the gun at Hampton and said, "You're not going to hit me anymore." Hampton said, "What are you doing?" Believing that Hampton was about to pick something up to hit her with, she shot him. She then put the gun down and went outside to wait for the police.

Hampton later died of a gunshot wound to his chest. The neighbor who spoke with Officer Reagan testified that shortly before the shooting, she heard defendant, but not Hampton, shouting. The evening before, the neighbor had heard a gunshot. Defendant's blood contained no drugs but had a blood-alcohol level of .17 percent. Hampton's blood contained no drugs or alcohol.

B. *Defense Evidence*

Defendant claimed she shot Hampton in self-defense. To support the claim, the defense presented first expert testimony and then nonexpert testimony, including that of defendant herself.

1. *Expert Testimony*

Dr. Lee Bowker testified as an expert on battered women's syndrome. The syndrome, he testified, "is not just a psychological construction, but it's a term for a wide variety of controlling mechanisms that the man or it can be a woman, but in general for this syndrome it's a man, uses against the woman, and for the effect that those control mechanisms have."

Dr. Bowker had studied about 1,000 battered women and found them often inaccurately portrayed "as cardboard figures, paper-thin punching bags who merely absorb the violence but didn't do anything about it." He found that battered women often employ strategies to stop the beatings, including hiding, running away, counter-violence, seeking the help of friends and family, going to a shelter, and contacting police. Nevertheless, many battered women remain in the relationship because of lack of money, social isolation, lack of self-confidence, inadequate police response, and a fear (often justified) of reprisals by the batterer. "The battering man will make the battered woman depend on him and generally succeed at least for a time." A battered woman often feels responsible for the abusive relationship, and "she just can't figure out a way to please him better so he'll stop beating her." In sum, "It really is the physical control of the woman through economics and through relative social isolation combined with the psychological techniques that make her so dependent."

Many battered women go from one abusive relationship to another and seek a strong man to protect them from the previous abuser. "[W]ith each successful victimization, the person becomes less able to avoid the next one." The violence can gradually escalate, as the batterer keeps control using ever more severe actions, including rape, torture, violence against the woman's loved ones or pets, and death threats. Battered women sense this escalation. In Dr. Bowker's "experience with battered women who kill in self-defense their abusers, it's always related to their perceived change of what's going on in a relationship. They become very sensitive to what sets off batterers.

They watch for this stuff very carefully. [¶] … Anybody who is abused over a period of time becomes sensitive to the abuser's behavior and when she sees a change acceleration begin in that behavior, it tells them something is going to happen …"

Dr. Bowker interviewed defendant for a full day. He believed she suffered not only from battered women's syndrome, but also from being the child of an alcoholic and an incest victim. He testified that all three of defendant's partners before Hampton were abusive and significantly older than she.

Dr. Bowker described defendant's relationship with Hampton. Hampton was a 49-year-old man who weighed almost twice as much as defendant. The two had a battering relationship that Dr. Bowker characterized as a "traditional cycle of violence." The cycle included phases of tension building, violence, and then forgiveness-seeking in which Hampton would promise not to batter defendant any more and she would believe him. During this period, there would be occasional good times. For example, defendant told Dr. Bowker that Hampton would give her a rose. "That's one of the things that hooks people in. Intermittent reinforcement is the key." But after a while, the violence would begin again. The violence would recur because "basically … the woman doesn't perfectly obey. That's the bottom line." For example, defendant would talk to another man, or fail to clean house "just so."

The situation worsened over time, especially when Hampton got off parole shortly before his death. He became more physically and emotionally abusive, repeatedly threatened defendant's life, and even shot at her the night before his death. Hampton often allowed defendant to go out, but she was afraid to flee because she felt he would find her as he had in the past. "He enforced her belief that she can never escape him." Dr. Bowker testified that unless her injuries were so severe that "something absolutely had to be treated," he would not expect her to seek medical treatment. "That's the pattern of her life…."

Dr. Bowker believed defendant's description of her experiences. In his opinion, she suffered from battered women's syndrome in "about as extreme a pattern as you could find."

2. *Nonexpert Testimony*

Defendant confirmed many of the details of her life and relationship with Hampton underlying Dr. Bowker's opinion. She testified that her father forcefully molested her from the time she was seven years old until she was fifteen. She described her relationship with another abusive man as being like "Nightmare on Elm Street." Regarding Hampton, she testified that they often argued and that he beat her regularly. Both were heavy drinkers. Hampton once threw a can of beer at her face, breaking her nose. Her dental plates hurt because Hampton hit her so often. He often kicked her, but usually hit her in the back of the head because, he told her, it "won't leave bruises." Hampton sometimes threatened to kill her, and often said she "would live to regret it." Matters got worse towards the end.

The evening before the shooting, March 27, 1992, Hampton arrived home "very drunk." He yelled at her and called her names. At one point when she was standing by the bedroom window, he fired his .357 revolver at her. She testified, "He didn't miss me by much either." She was "real scared."

The next day, the two drove into the mountains. They argued, and Hampton continually hit her. While returning, he said that their location would be a good place to kill her because "they wouldn't find [her] for a while." She took it as a joke, although she feared him. When they returned, the arguing continued. He hit her again, then entered the kitchen. He threatened, "This time, bitch, when I shoot at you, I won't miss." He came from the kitchen and reached for the gun on the living room table. She grabbed it first, pointed it at him, and told him "that he wasn't going to hit [her]." She backed Hampton into the kitchen. He was saying something, but she did not know what. He reached for her hand and she shot him. She believed he was reaching for the gun and was going to shoot her.

Several other witnesses testified about defendant's relationship with Hampton, his abusive conduct in general, and his physical abuse of, and threats to, defendant in particular. This testimony generally corroborated defendant's. A neighbor testified that the night before the shooting, she heard a gunshot. The next morning, defendant told the neighbor that Hampton had shot at her, and that she was afraid of him. After the shooting, investigators found a bullet hole through the frame of the bedroom window and a bullet embedded in a tree in line with the window. Another neighbor testified that shortly before hearing the shot that killed Hampton, she heard defendant say, "Stop it, Albert. Stop it."

C. *Procedural History*

Defendant was charged with murder with personal use of a firearm. At the end of the prosecution's case-in-chief, the court granted defendant's motion under Penal Code section 1118.1 for acquittal of first degree murder.

The court instructed the jury on second degree murder and both voluntary and involuntary manslaughter. It also instructed on self-defense, explaining that an actual and reasonable belief that the killing was necessary was a complete defense; an actual but unreasonable belief was a defense to murder, but not to voluntary manslaughter. In determining reasonableness, the jury was to consider what "would appear to be necessary to a reasonable person in a similar situation and with similar knowledge."

The court also instructed: "Evidence regarding Battered Women's Syndrome has been introduced in this case. Such evidence, if believed, may be considered by you only for the purpose of determining whether or not the defendant held the necessary subjective honest [belief] which is a requirement for both perfect and imperfect self-defense. However, that same evidence regarding Battered Women's Syndrome may not be considered or used by you in evaluating the objective reasonableness requirement for perfect self-defense....

"Battered Women's Syndrome seeks to describe and explain common reactions of women to that experience. Thus, you may consider the evidence concerning the syndrome and its effects only for the limited purpose of showing, if it does show, that the defendant's reactions, as demonstrated by the evidence, are not inconsistent with her having been physically abused or the beliefs, perceptions, or behavior of victims of domestic violence."

During deliberations, the jury asked for and received clarification of the terms "subjectively honest and objectively unreasonable." It found defendant guilty of voluntary manslaughter with personal use of a firearm. The court sentenced defendant to prison for eight years, consisting of the lower term of three years for manslaughter, plus the upper term of five years for firearm use. The Court of Appeal remanded for resentencing on the use enhancement, but otherwise affirmed the judgment.

We granted defendant's petition for review.

II. Discussion

A. *Background*

With an exception not relevant here, Evidence Code section 1107, subdivision (a), makes admissible in a criminal action expert testimony regarding "battered women's syndrome, including the physical, emotional, or mental effects upon the beliefs, perceptions, or behavior of victims of domestic violence...." Under subdivision (b) of that section, the foundation for admission is sufficient "if the proponent of the evidence establishes its relevancy and the proper qualifications of the expert witness." Defendant presented the evidence to support her claim of self-defense. It is undisputed that she established the proper qualifications of the expert witness. The only issue is to what extent defendant established its "relevancy." To resolve this question we must examine California law regarding self-defense.

For killing to be in self-defense, the defendant must actually and reasonably believe in the need to defend (*People v. Flannel* (1979) 25 Cal. 3d 668). If the belief subjectively exists but is objectively unreasonable, there is "imperfect self-defense," i.e., "the defendant is deemed to have acted without malice and cannot be convicted of murder," but can be convicted of manslaughter. (*In re Christian S.* (1994) 7 Cal. 4th 768.) To constitute "perfect self-defense," i.e., to exonerate the person completely, the belief must also be objectively reasonable. As the Legislature has stated, "[T]he circumstances must be sufficient to excite the fears of a reasonable person...." Moreover, for either perfect or imperfect self-defense, the fear must be of imminent harm. "Fear of future harm—no matter how great the fear and no matter how great the likelihood of the harm—will not suffice. The defendant's fear must be of imminent danger to life or great bodily injury." (*In re Christian S., supra.*)

Although the belief in the need to defend must be objectively reasonable, a jury must consider what "would appear to be necessary to a reasonable person in a similar situation and with similar knowledge...." It judges reasonableness "from the point of view of a reasonable person in the position of defendant." (*People v. McGee* (1947) 31 Cal. 2d 229.) To do this, it must consider all the "facts and circumstances ... in determining whether the defendant acted in a manner in which a reasonable man would act in protecting his own life or bodily safety." (*People v. Moore* (1954) 43 Cal. 2d 517.) As we stated long ago, "... a defendant is entitled to have a jury take into consideration all the elements in the case which might be expected to operate on his mind." (*People v. Smith* (1907) 151 Cal. 619.)

...

With these principles in mind, we now consider the relevance of evidence of battered women's syndrome to the elements of self-defense.

B. *Battered Women's Syndrome*[3]

Battered women's syndrome "has been defined as 'a series of common characteristics that appear in women who are abused physically and psychologically over an extended period of time by the dominant male figure in their lives.'" (*State v. Kelly* (N.J. 1984) 478 A.2d 364.)

The trial court allowed the jury to consider the battered women's syndrome evidence in deciding whether defendant actually believed she needed to kill in self-defense. The question here is whether the evidence was also relevant on the reasonableness of that belief. Two Court of Appeal decisions have considered the relevance of battered women's syndrome evidence to a claim of self-defense.

[In *People v. Aris*, 215 Cal. App. 3d 1178 (1989), a case where "a battered woman kill[ed] the batterer while he slept after beating her and threatened serious bodily injury and death when he awoke," the Court of Appeal upheld the exclusion of expert testimony on BWS on the issue of "perfect" self-defense. In *People v. Day*, 2 Cal. App. 4th 405 (1992), a case where the battered woman killed the batterer in the course of an evening of intermittent fighting, the Court of Appeal held that BWS evidence was admissible on the issue of whether the defendant actually believed in the need for self-defense and on the issue of the defendant's credibility (which was attacked by the prosecution) but was not admissible on the issue of the reasonableness of her belief or her response.]

The Attorney General argues that *People v. Aris* and *People v. Day* were correct that evidence of battered women's syndrome is irrelevant to reasonableness. We disagree. Those cases too narrowly interpreted the reasonableness element. *Aris* and *Day* failed to consider that the jury, in determining objective reasonableness, must view the situation from the *defendant's perspective*. Here, for example, Dr. Bowker testified that the violence can escalate and that a battered woman can become increasingly sensitive to the abuser's behavior, testimony relevant to determining whether defendant reasonably believed when she fired the gun that this time the threat to her life was im-

3. We use the term "battered women's syndrome" because Evidence Code section 1107 and the cases use that term. We note, however, that according to amici curiae California Alliance Against Domestic Violence et al., "... the preferred term among many experts today is 'expert testimony on battering and its effects' or 'expert testimony on battered women's experiences.' Domestic violence experts have critiqued the phrase 'battered women's syndrome' because (1) it implies that there is one syndrome which all battered women develop, (2) it has pathological connotations which suggest that battered women suffer from some sort of sickness, (3) expert testimony on domestic violence refers to more than women's psychological reactions to violence, (4) it focuses attention on the battered woman rather than on the batterer's coercive and controlling behavior and (5) it creates an image of battered women as suffering victims rather than as active survivors."

minent. Indeed, the prosecutor argued that, "from an objective, reasonable man's standard, there was no reason for her to go get that gun. This threat that she says he made was like so many threats before. There was no reason for her to react that way." Dr. Bowker's testimony supplied a response that the jury might not otherwise receive. As violence increases over time, and threats gain credibility, a battered person might become sensitized and thus able reasonably to discern when danger is real and when it is not. "[T]he expert's testimony might also enable the jury to find that the battered [woman] … is particularly able to predict accurately the likely extent of violence in any attack on her. That conclusion could significantly affect the jury's evaluation of the *reasonableness* of defendant's fear for her life." (*State v. Kelly, supra* (italics added).)

The Attorney General concedes that Hampton's behavior towards defendant, including prior threats and violence, was relevant to reasonableness, but distinguishes between evidence of this *behavior*—which the trial court fully admitted—and *expert testimony* about its effects on defendant. The distinction is untenable. "To effectively present the situation as perceived by the defendant, and the reasonableness of her fear, the defense has the option to explain her feelings to enable the jury to overcome stereotyped impressions about women who remain in abusive relationships. It is appropriate that the jury be given a professional explanation of the battering syndrome and its effects on the woman through the use of expert testimony." (*State v. Allery* (Wash. 1984) 682 P.2d 312.)

The Attorney General also argues that allowing consideration of this testimony would result in an undesirable "battle of the experts" and raises the specter of other battles of experts regarding other syndromes. The Legislature, however, has decided that, if relevant, expert evidence on battered women's syndrome is admissible. (Evid. Code, § 1107.) We have found it relevant; it is therefore admissible. We express no opinion on the admissibility of expert testimony regarding other possible syndromes in support of a claim of self-defense, but we rest today's holding on Evidence Code section 1107.

Contrary to the Attorney General's argument, we are not changing the standard from objective to subjective, or replacing the reasonable "person" standard with a reasonable "battered woman" standard. Our decision would not, in another context, compel adoption of a "'reasonable gang member' standard." Evidence Code section 1107 states "a rule of evidence only" and makes "no substantive change." The jury must consider defendant's situation and knowledge, which makes the evidence relevant, but the ultimate question is whether a reasonable *person*, not a reasonable battered woman, would believe in the need to kill to prevent imminent harm. Moreover, it is the *jury*, not the expert, that determines whether defendant's belief and, ultimately, her actions, were objectively reasonable.

Battered women's syndrome evidence was also relevant to defendant's credibility. It "would have assisted the jury in objectively analyzing [defendant's] claim of self-defense by dispelling many of the commonly held misconceptions about battered women" (*People v. Day, supra*). For example, in urging the jury not to believe defendant's testimony that Hampton shot at her the night before the killing, the prosecutor argued that "if this defendant truly believed that [Hampton] had shot at her, on that night, I mean she would have left.... [¶] If she really believed that he had tried to shoot her, she would not have stayed." Dr. Bowker's testimony "would help dispel the ordinary lay person's perception that a woman in a battering relationship is free to leave at any time. The expert evidence would counter any 'common sense' conclusions by the jury that if the beatings were really that bad the woman would have left her husband much earlier. Popular misconceptions about battered women would be put to rest" (*Day*). "[I]f the jury had understood [defendant's] conduct in light of [battered women's syndrome] evidence, then the jury may well have concluded her version of the events was sufficiently credible to warrant an acquittal on the facts as she related them." (*Day*.)

...

We do not hold that Dr. Bowker's entire testimony was relevant to both prongs of perfect self-defense. Just as many types of evidence may be relevant to some disputed issues but not all, some of the expert evidence was no doubt relevant only to the subjective existence of defendant's belief. Evidence merely showing that a person's use of deadly force is scientifically explainable or empirically common does not, in itself, show it was objectively reasonable. To dispel any possible confusion, it might be appropriate for the court, on request, to clarify that, in assessing reasonableness, the question is whether a reasonable person in the defendant's circumstances would have perceived a threat of imminent injury or death, and not whether killing the abuser was reasonable in the sense of being an understandable response to ongoing abuse; and that, therefore, in making that assessment, the jury may not consider evidence merely showing that an abused person's use of force against the abuser is understandable.

We also emphasize that, as with any evidence, the jury may give this testimony whatever weight it deems appropriate in light of the evidence as a whole. The ultimate judgment of reasonableness is solely for the jury. We simply hold that evidence of battered women's syndrome is generally *relevant* to the reasonableness, as well as the subjective existence, of defendant's belief in the need to defend, and, to the extent it is relevant, the jury may *consider* it in deciding both questions. The court's contrary instruction was erroneous.

[The Court found the error to be prejudicial because it appeared that the jury's voluntary manslaughter verdict was based on a finding that the defendant had an honest, but unreasonable belief in the need for self-defense.]

George, C.J., and Mosk, Kennard and Werdegar, JJ., concur.

[Concurring opinions of Baxter, J. and Werdegar, J., omitted.]

Brown, Justice, concurring.

For years the lower courts, poised precariously upon the slippery slope of personalized defenses, have tried valiantly not to ski down it. Early cases focused on the general admissibility of evidence of battered woman's syndrome (BWS) to support claims of self-defense. By 1991, with that question answered by legislative fiat, concern shifted to a more nuanced discussion of relevance. Courts found expert testimony admissible to rehabilitate the defendant's credibility and to explain her subjective state of mind, but not relevant to the jury's determination of the objective reasonableness of her actions.

Today we hold that "evidence of battered women's syndrome is generally relevant to the reasonableness, as well as the subjective existence, of defendant's belief in the need to defend and, to the extent it is relevant, the jury may consider it in deciding both questions." But, this conclusion only begins, rather than ends, the discussion. As always, the devil is in the details.

...

... We must identify those aspects of BWS not only sufficiently beyond the ken of the average juror to warrant expert testimony but also specifically relevant to the jury's determination whether the defendant had "a reasonable belief that [she would] lose [her] life or suffer serious bodily injury unless [she] immediately defend[ed] [herself] against the attack of the adversary." (*People v. Scoggins* (1869) 37 Cal. 676.)

Despite the extensive and vivid, even lurid, details of battering relationships, the literature and published opinions contain relatively limited discussion, even on an anecdotal basis, of BWS directly relating to objective reasonableness. The single most pertinent aspect, which defendant here invokes, is the hypervigilance generated by the cycles of abuse that mark these relationships. As the commentators explain: "[T]he battered woman's familiarity with her husband's violence may enable her to recognize the subtle signs that usually precede a severe beating.... Moreover, even if the woman kills her husband when he is only threatening her, rather than actually beating her, she knows from past experience that he is not merely making idle comments but is fully capable of carrying out his threats. Thus, the battered woman may reasonably fear imminent danger from her husband when others unfamiliar with the history of abuse would not." (Kinports, *Defending Battered Women's Self-Defense Claims* (1988) 67 Or. L. Rev. 393.) "[E]xperts testify that, because a battered woman is attuned to her abuser's pattern of attacks, she learns to recognize subtle gestures or threats that distinguish the severity of attacks and that lead her to believe a particular attack will seriously threaten her survival." (*Developments in the Law—Legal Responses to Domestic Violence* (1993) 106 Harv. L. Rev. 1498.)

In a related vein, researchers also note that "[w]hen a woman kills her batterer, the abuse almost always will have escalated both in frequency and intensity in the period immediately preceding the killing." (Rosen, *On Self-Defense, Imminence, and Women Who Kill Their Batterers* (1993) 71 N.C.L. Rev. 371.) "Expert testimony [shows] that among battered women who kill, the final incident that precipitates the killing is viewed by the battered woman as 'more severe and more life-threatening than prior incidents.'" (*Commonwealth v. Stonehouse* (Pa. 1989) 555 A.2d 772.) On the basis of her experience, a battered woman may thus be "better able to predict the likely degree of violence in any particular battering incident" (Ewing, Battered Women Who Kill (1987)) and in turn may more precisely assess the measure and speed of force necessary to resist.

...

[In other than "classic" self-defense circumstances], the situation may be confrontational but lack such overt or obvious potential for serious harm. Nevertheless, in light of her history of battering by the victim, the defendant may anticipate imminent bodily injury or death. Or, following an initial struggle in which she gained a temporary advantage, she may continue to fear the victim because she knows he reacts violently to loss of control or she senses an escalating severity to his violence. "The cyclical nature of an intimate battering relationship enables a battered spouse to become expert at recognizing the warning signs of an impending assault from her partner—signs frequently imperceptible to outsiders. For some victims, the sign may be 'that look in his eye'; for others, it is the advent of heavy drinking, or heightened irrational jealousy." (*Banks v. State* (Md. App. 1992) 608 A.2d 1249.)

Although a jury might not find the *appearances* sufficient to provoke a reasonable person's fear, they might conclude otherwise as to a reasonable person's perception of the *reality* when enlightened by expert testimony on the concept of hypervigilance. The expert evidence thus "is aimed at an area where the purported common knowledge of the jury may be very much mistaken, an area where jurors' logic, drawn from their own experience, may lead to a wholly incorrect conclusion, an area where expert knowledge would enable the jurors to disregard their prior conclusions as being common myths rather than common knowledge." (*State v. Kelly*, *supra*.)

Nevertheless, the expert must not usurp the function of the jury and reach the ultimate question of reasonableness. The concept of hypervigilance is not the evidentiary equivalent of, or substitute for, an actual perception of impending danger, only a possible explanation for the defendant's reaction to a perceived threat. "Either the jury accepts or rejects that explanation.... No expert is needed, ... once the jury has made up its mind on those issues, to tell the jury the logical conclusion, namely, that a person who has in fact been severely and continuously beaten might very well reasonably fear that the imminent beating she was about to suffer could be either life-threatening or pose a risk of serious injury." (*Kelly*.) The determination must remain objective even though the inquiry may be individualized by consideration of BWS.

Finally, since BWS is admissible only narrowly on the issue of objective reasonableness, a limiting instruction is appropriate upon request to "restrict the evidence to its proper scope...." In assessing a claim of self-defense the jury must not confuse the question whether a reasonable person in the defendant's circumstances would have perceived a threat of imminent injury or death with the notion that killing the abuser would be a "reasonable," *i.e.*, understandable, response to ongoing physical and psychological abuse....

...

George, C.J., and Baxter, J., concur.

Notes and Problem

The Scientific Basis for "Battered Women's Syndrome." The scientific basis for "battered women's syndrome," as described in Evidence Code § 1107 and by experts such as Dr. Bowker, has been examined and called into question in a number of studies. The results of those studies have been summed up as follows:

> Neither Walker's data[a] nor the later studies sufficiently support the battered woman syndrome as a pattern regularly produced by battering relationships. Some evidence supports the contention that battered women suffer from depression and anxiety. Moreover, less evidence supports the contention that they experience lower self-esteem, and have difficulty with certain types of problem-solving tasks.... The data provide no support for the contentions that battered women have traditional attitudes toward the female role in society nor that they demonstrate external locus of control.... Taken collectively, the currently available data do not justify the claim that the battered woman syndrome, as usually formulated, provides a general portrait of those who have suffered battering relationships.
>
> The data provide substantial support for the contention that battered women suffer significant depression and anxiety. This elevated level of distress may resemble the pattern of distress suffered by others who experience various types of trauma or ongoing stress. The argument for expert testimony regarding the battered woman syndrome does not rest, however, on the claim that battered women suffer distress. Rather, it requires that battered women typically suffer a particular syndrome, specific to battered women, that carries special significance for self-defense. The presence of depression, anxiety, or a general distress syndrome does not substantiate this claim.
>
> Perhaps most importantly from the perspective of the criminal courts, learned helplessness has been the aspect of the battered woman syndrome most frequently cited as central to cases of self-defense by battered women, yet it draws very little support from the available data. The complete body of work provides neither any clear conception of learned helplessness nor any good reason to believe that it regularly occurs in battered women.... Collectively, the data reviewed supports the proposition that battered women do not suffer learned helplessness, at least as well as it supports the claim that they do. Finally, it would be more consistent with the theoretical and empirical foundations of learned helplessness to contend that battered women who kill their batterers differ from those who remain in the battering relationships without killing their batterers precisely because those who kill do not manifest learned helplessness.

---

a. The reference is to Lenore Walker's two books, Battered Woman (1979) and The Battered Woman Syndrome (1984), the seminal works on the battered women's syndrome.

R. Schopp, B. Sturgis & M. Sullivan, *Battered Woman Syndrome, Expert Testimony, and the Distinction Between Justification and Excuse*, 1994 U. Ill. Law Rev. 45, 63–64. See also D. Faigman & A. Wright, *The Battered Woman Syndrome in the Age of Science*, 39 Ariz. L. Rev. 67 (1997) (arguing that the "battered woman syndrome" was a product of political ideology and that the claimed scientific basis for the syndrome "would provide an excellent case study for psychology graduate students on how *not* to conduct empirical research."). Given the existence of Evidence Code § 1107, would a court be free to agree with the critics and find that there is no battered women's syndrome?

Problem 79.

What arguments should be made as to whether the court should admit the "syndrome" evidence in the following cases?

a. Defendants Elder and Younger, two brothers 21 and 18 years old, are charged with two counts of first degree murder (P.C. §§ 187–189) on evidence that, on the day of the killings, they purchased shotguns, entered their own home and fired 16 rounds, killing both their parents, Father and Mother, who had been sitting watching television. In support of their self-defense claim, the defendants propose to introduce the following evidence tending to establish that they suffered from "battered child syndrome": the defendants had each suffered from years of sexual abuse by Father, assisted by Mother; days before the killing, Younger revealed to Elder that Younger had been sodomized by Father for 12 years; when Elder confronted Father and insisted that the abuse stop or he would make it public, Father threatened to kill the defendants.

b. Defendant, Brother (Defendant's younger brother) and several others (all of whom are Hispanic) had been drinking and were crossing the street on the way to a party. Victim came driving up at a high rate of speed and had to brake hard to avoid hitting the group. Defendant and others in the group yelled at Victim as they crossed in front of him, and Defendant yelled again as Victim pulled away. Victim then parked his car, and the group approached shouting at Victim. Victim got out of his car, and Defendant and Victim swore at each other and challenged each other to fight. One of the group hit Victim, and he, in turn, tried to kick Defendant and Brother, at which point Defendant stabbed and killed Victim. Defendant is charged with second degree murder (P.C. §§ 187–189), and, in support of his self-defense claim, he proposes to call an expert to testify to the following: (1) street fighters have a special understanding of what is expected of them; (2) for a street fighter in Hispanic culture, there is no retreat; (3) the Hispanic culture is based on honor, and honor defines a person; and (4) in this culture a person in Defendant's situation would have a strong motivation to protect his younger brother.

The "Abuse Excuse." Evidence of "battered women's syndrome" and "battered child syndrome" has been introduced to support a claim of self-defense, to *justify* the killing of the batterer. In recent years, defendants have been permitted to introduce a wide variety of "syndrome" evidence in an attempt to wholly or partially *excuse* killings of persons other than batterers. For example, among the syndromes which have made their way into murder trials are the "black rage" syndrome, the "post-partum" syndrome and the "Vietnam veterans" syndrome. The proliferation of such syndrome evidence in criminal cases has been decried by some scholars who have charged that such syndrome evidence is based on "junk science," that it focuses the criminal trial away from the defendant's conduct and onto the defendant's history or environment or the conduct of the victim and that it sanctions and thereby encourages a willful lack of self-control. See generally A. Dershowitz, The Abuse Excuse and Other Cop-outs, Sob Stories and Evasions of Responsibility (1994); J. Wilson, Moral Judgment: Does the Abuse Excuse Threaten Our Legal System? (1997). Should the criminal justice system consider syndrome evidence in determining whether otherwise criminal conduct is justified or excused?

People v. Randle

35 Cal.4th 987, 111 P.3d 987 (2005)

Brown, J.

The central question presented by this case is whether one who kills in the actual but unreasonable belief he must protect another person from imminent danger of death or great bodily injury is guilty of voluntary manslaughter, and not murder, because he lacks the malice required for murder. In other words, should California recognize the doctrine of *imperfect defense of others?* We conclude the answer is, yes.

I. FACTUAL AND PROCEDURAL BACKGROUND

The homicide victim Brian Robinson lived with his parents and his cousin, Charles Lambert. Late one evening, as Robinson drove up to their home, he saw defendant getting out of Lambert's car, holding a large stereo speaker he had just stolen from it.

Robinson confronted defendant, saying he was going to "beat your ass." Defendant pulled a .25-caliber pistol from his pocket and fired it several times. Defendant and his cousin Byron W., who had helped him break into Lambert's car, then fled on foot. Byron retained a backpack full of Lambert's stereo equipment.

Defendant claimed he fired after Robinson "reached for his hip." However, he did not claim he thought Robinson was reaching for a gun or other deadly weapon. Moreover, Byron testified Robinson approached them with a cup or bottle in his hand. Defendant and Byron agreed it was some sort of object made of glass that Robinson threw at them after defendant fired the pistol.

Defendant gave conflicting accounts as to his aim. On the one hand, he claimed he "fired the gun in the air." On the other hand, he earlier testified, "I shot at him."

Defendant testified he heard Robinson say something about getting a gun himself, and that he heard two loud bangs behind them as they fled. Byron testified he also heard gunshots as they ran. There was no evidence to corroborate these claims.

Robinson went into his house and roused Lambert. The two men got into a truck and pursued defendant and Byron. Defendant eluded them, but they caught Byron.

According to Lambert's testimony, he and Robinson took turns beating Byron with their fists. After Byron fell to the ground, Robinson kicked him. Lambert pulled Robinson off Byron. Having recovered the stolen stereo equipment, they returned to the truck. However, Robinson jumped out of the truck and began beating Byron again. As he did, Robinson yelled at Lambert to "get pops," meaning Robinson's father; Lambert drove off to do so. While Lambert was present, the beating of Byron lasted "[p]robably five, ten minutes."

Byron testified his assailants hit and kicked him. One of them stomped on his chest, stepped on his head, and kicked him in the mouth. The beating continued for five minutes. One of the men spoke of putting Byron in the truck and taking him into the hills. Byron was bleeding from the mouth; his nose was broken. He was hollering his lungs out. He thought he was going to die. He was being beaten when defendant cried out, "Get off my cousin." Byron's assailant continued beating him, and then defendant opened fire. Defendant, Byron believed, saved his life.

Defendant testified he ran away, but then backtracked in search of Byron. He heard someone yelling for help and someone else saying, "I'm going to kill this little nigger." Coming closer, defendant saw someone beating Byron. Defendant shouted, "Stop. Get off my cousin." Byron's assailant glanced at defendant, but then resumed beating Byron. Defendant testified he fired his gun to make the man stop beating Byron.

Two prior statements defendant had made, one to the police and the other to a deputy district attorney, were played for the jury. According to defendant's statement to the police, Robinson was beating Byron when defendant first shot at him. Defendant was, he said, "mainly thinking about getting him off my little cousin." However, defendant admitted shooting at Robinson after Robinson started running away. In his statement to the deputy district attorney, defendant said he warned Robinson to get off Byron, shot once in the air, and then when Robinson did not respond, shot at him. Again, defendant admitted shooting at Robinson while he was running away. Defendant added he ceased firing because he ran out of ammunition.

Sharalyn Lawrence and Jennifer Wellington witnessed the beating from Lawrence's upstairs window. They could see that Byron was "being really hurt." Still, for a couple of minutes they were undecided what they should do. "I am like, this is Oakland," Wellington testified; "what do you do [?]" Finally, hearing Byron cry out, "Somebody help me," Lawrence telephoned 911, reporting a man "getting his ass beat." She said an ambulance should be dispatched. Defendant shot Robinson after Lawrence called 911 to report Byron was being badly beaten.

As previously stated, although defendant and Byron testified Robinson was still beating Byron when defendant fired the shots, defendant, in his statements to the police and the deputy district attorney, said he fired one shot at Robinson while Robinson was running away. The testimony of Wellington and Lawrence tends to support the view that defendant shot at Robinson after Robinson stopped beating

Byron and while he was running away. Wellington so testified, and Lawrence's testimony, while not very clear on this point, suggested that at least some of the shots were fired as Robinson was running away.

The cause of Robinson's death was a bullet wound in the abdomen. The bullet was a .25 caliber. It entered Robinson's lower right chest or upper abdomen and lodged in the left side of his abdomen. Robinson was not wounded in the back.

At trial, defendant asked for an instruction on imperfect defense of another. The trial court denied the request. After deliberating five days, the jury convicted defendant of second degree murder (Pen. Code, §§ 187, 189) and automobile burglary (§ 459)....

...

II. DISCUSSION
A. Imperfect Defense of Others

Again, the central question presented by this case is whether one who kills in the actual but unreasonable belief he must protect another person from imminent danger of death or great bodily injury is guilty of voluntary manslaughter, and not murder, because he lacks the malice required for murder.

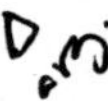

Defendant contends such a person is guilty, under the doctrine of imperfect defense of others, of only voluntary manslaughter, and that the trial court prejudicially erred in refusing his request to instruct the jury on the doctrine.

The Attorney General contends (1) California has not recognized the doctrine of imperfect defense of others; (2) even assuming California does recognize the doctrine, defendant was not entitled to invoke it because he created the circumstances leading to the killing; and (3) in any event, any error in refusing to give the requested instruction was harmless here.

1. Whether California recognizes the doctrine

[The Court reviewed the development and rationale of the law of imperfect self-defense. See *In re Christian S.* [Chapter 4].]

Defendant contends that the defense of others, like self-defense, has an imperfect form. That is, defendant contends, if a killing is committed by someone who actually but unreasonably believes he is acting under the necessity of defending another person from imminent danger of death or great bodily injury, then the killing is voluntary manslaughter, not murder, because the killer is not acting with malice.

[Defendant relied on dicta in the court's decision in *People v. Michaels* (2002) 28 Cal.4th 486, where the court addressed a claim that an instruction on imperfect defense of others should have been given *sua sponte*, *i.e.*, even though not requested by the defendant, but found the doctrine not well-established at the time of the trial and of "doubtful" applicability on the facts.]

Again, as we said in *Michaels*, the doctrine of imperfect defense of others "follows logically from the interplay between statutory and decisional law." The doctrine is based on statute in that (1) malice is required for murder (§ 187) and (2) perfect self-defense and perfect defense of others are complete defenses to charges of murder (§ 197). One who kills in imperfect self-defense—in the actual but unreasonable belief he must defend himself from imminent death or great bodily injury—is guilty of manslaughter, not murder, *because he lacks the malice required for murder.* For the same reason, one who kills in imperfect defense of others—in the actual but unreasonable belief he must defend another from imminent danger of death or great bodily injury—is guilty only of manslaughter.

The Attorney General contends that, contrary to *Michaels,* California has rejected the doctrine of imperfect defense of others. California has done so, the Attorney General argues, by treating the reasonableness requirement differently for self-defense than for defense of others. In self-defense, the Attorney General notes, reasonableness is determined from the point of view of a reasonable person in the defendant's position. The jury must consider all the facts and circumstances it might expect to operate on the defendant's mind. In defense of others, the Attorney General asserts, reasonableness is determined, not from the point of view of the defendant, but rather from the point of view of the person the defendant was seeking to defend. That is, the California rule for defense of others, the Attorney General argues, is the alter ego rule, under which one who attempts to defend another person steps into the shoes of the other person, and so acts at his peril if that person was in the wrong.

The Attorney General bases his argument on his construction of section 197, on his interpretation of the case law, and on his reading of public policy. He is, we conclude, mistaken in every respect.

a. *Section 197*

Section 197 provides in pertinent part: "Homicide is also justifiable when committed by any person in any of the following cases: 1. When resisting any attempt to murder any person, or to commit a felony, or to do some great bodily injury upon any person; [ ] ... [ ] 3. When committed in the lawful defense of such person, or of a wife or husband, parent, child, master, mistress, or servant of such person, when there is reasonable ground to apprehend a design to commit a felony or to do some great bodily injury, and imminent danger of such design being accomplished; but such person, or the person in whose behalf the defense was made, if he was the assailant or engaged in mutual combat, must really and in good faith have endeavored to decline any further struggle before the homicide was committed."

Section 197, the Attorney General argues, impliedly rejects the doctrine of imperfect defense of others. His argument runs as follows: The statutory basis of the doctrine of self-defense is subdivision 3, while the statutory basis of the doctrine of defense of others is subdivision 1. Section 197, subdivision 3 expressly incorporates a reasonable person standard: "when there is *reasonable ground to apprehend* a design to commit a felony or to do some great bodily injury, and imminent danger of such design being accomplished..." (Italics added.) Since subdivision 1 does not expressly incorporate such a reasonableness standard, the Attorney General argues, the Legislature must have intended, with regard to defense of others, to adopt the alter ego rule.

A problem with the Attorney General's argument is that section 197 does not compartmentalize the doctrines of self-defense and defense of others as neatly as that. Subdivision 1, which the Attorney General characterizes as the defense-of-others provision, may also be read as including self-defense. No reason appears why the phrase "any person," which occurs both in the stem of section 197 and in subdivision 1, would not cover oneself as well as others. Under section 197, subdivision 1, a homicide is justifiable when committed by "any person" "resisting any attempt to murder *any person*, or to commit a felony, or to do some great bodily injury upon *any person*." (Italics added.)

On the other hand, subdivision 3, which the Attorney General characterizes as the self-defense provision, also expressly covers the defense of others, albeit others in specified relationships with the person who comes to their defense. Under this provision, a homicide is justifiable when committed by any person "in the lawful defense of such person, *or of a wife or husband, parent, child, master, mistress, or servant of such person*, when there is reasonable ground to apprehend a design to commit a felony or to do some great bodily injury, and imminent danger of such design being accomplished." (§ 197, subd. 3, italics added.)

Moreover, the Attorney General's argument—that the Legislature must have intended to adopt the alter ego rule for defense of others because it did not expressly incorporate a reasonable person standard in subdivision 1—finds no support in the legislative history of section 197.

Section 197, enacted in 1872, was based on the Crimes and Punishment Act of 1850. Under the Crimes and Punishment Act, a reasonable person standard governed defense of others as well as self-defense. Both of the defenses were covered by section 29. "Justifiable homicide is the killing of a human being *in necessary self-defence, or in defence of habitation, property, or person*, against one who manifestly intends or endeavors, by violence or surprise, to commit a felony ..." The applicability of the reasonable person standard to section 29 was made clear in the next section. "A bare fear of any of these offences, to prevent which the homicide is alleged to have been committed, shall not be sufficient to justify the killing. It must appear that the circumstances were sufficient to excite the fears of *a reasonable person*, and that the party killing really acted under the influence of those fears, and not in a spirit of revenge." There is no reason to believe the Legislature, by enacting section 197, intended to substitute the alter ego standard for the reasonable person standard with regard to defense of others. To the contrary, the code commissioners noted: "The commission have modified the language [of specified sections of the Crimes and Punishment Act of 1850], making it accord, in many respects, with that of the New York Penal Code [Field's Draft] 260, 261, and 262. *The legal effect, however, has not been changed.*" (Italics added.)

b. ***Case law***

The Attorney General also misreads our cases. He asserts: "Early California cases observe that one who kills in the defense of another steps into the shoes of the person defended for purposes of evaluating a claim that homicide was justified. 'A person interfering in a difficulty in behalf of another simply steps in the latter's shoes; he may lawfully do in another's defense what such other might lawfully do in his own defense but no more ...' (*People v. Will* (1926) 79 Cal. App. 101) [(*Will*)], citing *People v. Travis* (1880) 56 Cal. 251 [(*Travis*)]...."

By calling to our attention the fact that *Will* cites *Travis*, the Attorney General implies that our decision in *Travis* supports the passage he quotes from the Court of Appeal's opinion in *Will*. However, it does not. In *Travis*, Wirt Travis was convicted of manslaughter for killing A.G. Hill. Wirt, along with his sister Georgia and their brother John, attended a social function also attended by Hill. Georgia walked out, explaining to Wirt that she could not remain in the hall with Hill because he had impugned her virtue. Wirt so informed his brother John. The two of them went back into the hall and took seats apart from one another but near Hill. John hit Hill. Hill drew a pistol on John. Wirt then shot Hill in the back, killing him.

Wirt claimed he acted in defense of John, believing Hill was about to shoot John. His claimed fear had some basis. A witness testified that Hill had previously told him, "the first thing he was going to do with them boys [the Travis brothers], he would commence killing them, if he got in a row with them." While the witness did not tell the Travises of Hills threat against them, they may well have heard of it because the witness had told "fifty or sixty [other] people," and word like that presumably traveled fast in Forestville in 1878.

Contrary to the Attorney General's argument, *Travis* does *not* stand for the proposition that the reasonableness of a claim of defense of others is tested from the point of view of the person the defendant was seeking to defend. Indeed, in *Travis*, we upheld a jury instruction to the effect that Wirt's killing of Hill would have been justifiable if the jury had found that Wirt shot Hill in order to prevent Hill from shooting John, "if that was necessary to prevent [Hill] from executing his design; provided there was, *or appeared to the defendant to be*, imminent danger to the life or limb of his brother from the hostile and threatening attitude of Hill." John was closely related to Wirt. However, their relationship as brothers was not one of the relationships specified in subdivision 3 of section 197, in that John was not Wirt's "wife or husband, parent, child, master, mistress, or servant."[4] Nevertheless, we upheld a jury instruction that

4. Perkins explains the origins and evolution of such catalogues of relationships in statutory provisions covering self-defense and defense of others. "The privilege of using force in defense of others, as a separate privilege, developed partly by accident. It had its roots in the law of property. The privilege of one to protect what was 'his' was extended to include the protection of his wife, his children and his servants. In the course of time this privilege outgrew the property analogy and came to be regarded as a 'mutual and reciprocal defence.' The household was regarded as a group, any member of which had a privilege to defend any other member. 'A man may defend his family, his servants or his master, whenever he may defend himself.' Even this concept of the privilege was outgrown and it came to include the members of one's immediate family or household and any other 'whom he is under a legal or socially recognized duty to protect.' Thus a conductor was privileged to defend his passenger, and a man privileged to defend a lady friend whom he was escorting at the moment. The present position, which represents a merging of the privilege of crime prevention with the privilege

focused on Wirt's point of view, and not upon the point of view of the brother he was seeking to defend.

People v. Will, supra, 79 Cal. App. 101, is disapproved insofar as it is inconsistent with the views expressed herein.

c. *Public policy*

The Attorney General's public policy argument is that the doctrine of imperfect self-defense is "an open invitation to assaults, not just upon undercover officers effectuating arrests, but upon innocent bystanders in many situations not the least of them being mob violence and gang warfare." However, the controlling public policy decision here was made by the Legislature when it decided the unlawful killing of a human being without malice is manslaughter, not murder (§ 192).

2. Whether defendant may invoke the doctrine

The Attorney General, relying on *In re Christian S.* (1994) 7 Cal.4th 768, contends defendant is not entitled to invoke the doctrine of imperfect defense of others because he created the circumstances leading to the killing. In *Christian S.*, we observed, "It is well established that the ordinary self-defense doctrine—applicable when a defendant *reasonably* believes that his safety is endangered—may not be invoked by a defendant who, through his own wrongful conduct (e.g., the initiation of a physical assault or the commission of a felony), has created the circumstances under which his adversary's attack or pursuit is legally justified. It follows, a fortiori, that the imperfect self-defense doctrine cannot be invoked in such circumstances. For example, the imperfect self-defense doctrine would not permit a fleeing felon who shoots a pursuing police officer to escape a murder conviction even if the felon killed his pursuer with an actual belief in the need for self-defense."

...

The Attorney General's argument fails because although defendant's criminal conduct certainly set in motion the series of events that led to the fatal shooting of Robinson, the retreat of defendant and Byron and the subsequent recovery of the stolen equipment from Byron extinguished the *legal justification* for Robinson's attack on Byron.

The record supports the conclusion that Robinson was taking the law into his own hands, meting out the punishment he thought Byron deserved, and not making a citizen's arrest as the Attorney General claims.[5] While Robinson may well have had a

---

of defending others, is that one may go to the defense of a stranger if that person is the innocent victim of an unlawful attack." (Perkins & Boyce, Criminal Law (3d ed. 1982) Self-Defense, § 5.) While acknowledging some courts had adopted the alter ego rule, Perkins states the "sound" view was that one coming to the defense of others "is protected by the usual mistake-of-fact doctrine and may act upon the situation as it reasonably seems to be." He adds: "Most of the codes that deal separately with the defense of another seem to leave no trace of the view that one who goes to the aid of another 'acts at his peril' with reference to the right of that person to receive such aid ..."

5. Had Robinson and Lambert been attempting to effect a citizen's arrest, the use of reasonable force may have been permitted. (§§ 835, 837.) However, none of the witnesses, not even Lambert, suggested the beating was incidental to a citizen's arrest. Indeed, Lambert testified that Robinson, in renewing the beating, yelled at him to "get pops," not "get the police." According to Byron, one of his

right to pursue Byron for the purpose of recovering Lambert's stolen property, and to use reasonable force to retrieve it, the beating of Byron by Robinson and Lambert went well beyond any force they were entitled to use. Moreover, after they recovered the stolen stereo equipment and returned to their truck, Robinson jumped out of the truck and began beating Byron again. At that point Robinson's use of force was completely unjustified, and it was at that point, or shortly thereafter, that defendant shot Robinson.

While we hold defendant's conduct did not create circumstances legally justifying Robinson's attack on Byron, we should not be understood as condoning it in any respect. By making two fateful choices defendant triggered an escalating series of events that transformed the most mundane of property crimes into a fatal shooting. When he set out to burglarize cars, defendant chose to arm himself. When he was surprised in the act of burglary, defendant chose to use the weapon. Whether, during that initial confrontation, he fired the pistol at Robinson, or fired in the air, as he variously testified, he raised the stakes enormously.

[The court found that the failure to instruct on the doctrine was prejudicial, *i.e.*, that it is reasonably probable a result more favorable to defendant would have been reached had the jury been properly instructed.]

[Concurring opinion of Baxter, J. omitted.]

People v. Curtis

70 Cal. 2d 347, 450 P.2d 33 (1969)

Mosk, J.

Defendant Albert Allen Curtis appeals from a conviction of battery upon a peace officer, a felony. (Pen. Code, § 243.) He challenges both the construction and the constitutionality of Penal Code section 834a and the second sentence of Penal Code section 243, as applied to an allegedly unlawful arrest. We conclude that the proper construction of these sections requires a reversal of defendant's conviction.

Defendant was arrested on the night of July 9, 1966, by Lt. Riley of the Stockton Police Department. Riley was investigating a report of a prowler and had received a cursory description of the suspect as a male Negro, about six feet tall, wearing a white shirt and tan trousers. While cruising the neighborhood in his patrol car, the officer observed defendant, who matched the foregoing general description, walking along the street. Riley pulled up next to defendant and called to him to stop; defendant complied. The officer then emerged from his patrol car in full uniform and told defendant he was under arrest and would have to come along with him. Riley reached for the arm of defendant, and the latter attempted to back away. A violent struggle

---

assailants spoke of taking him, not to a police station, but into the hills. According to defendant, someone said, "I'm going to kill this little nigger."

ensued, during which both men were injured, and defendant was finally subdued and taken into custody by several officers.

Defendant was subsequently acquitted of a charge of burglary, but was convicted of battery upon a peace officer. He challenges this conviction on several grounds.

I

Defendant initially contends that his arrest was unlawful due to a lack of probable cause and that it was accomplished by the use of excessive force, and therefore his resistance was justified. Under the general common law rule prevailing in most states, an unlawful arrest may be resisted reasonably, and excessive force used by an officer in effecting an arrest may be countered lawfully. Until 1957, this rule prevailed in California. However, as we shall first discuss, Penal Code section 834a, enacted in 1957, revised the first aspect of that rule.

Section 834a provides: "If a person has knowledge, or by the exercise of reasonable care, should have knowledge, that he is being arrested by a peace officer, it is the duty of such person to refrain from using force or any weapon to resist such arrest."

...

We hold, therefore, that section 834a prohibits forceful resistance to unlawful as well as lawful arrests. Immediately, however, we are met with a challenge to the constitutionality of that construction; it is said to violate the Fourth Amendment's prohibition against unreasonable seizures and the due process clause of the Fourteenth Amendment.

An arrest is a "seizure" and an arrest without a warrant or probable cause is "unreasonable" within the purview of the Fourth Amendment. If section 834a, by eliminating the remedy of self-help, facilitates or sanctions arrests which are by definition unlawful, it could be urged with considerable persuasion that defendant's constitutional rights would be violated by the statute.

While defendant's rights are no doubt violated when he is arrested and detained a matter of days or hours without probable cause, we conclude the state in removing the right to resist does not contribute to or effectuate this deprivation of liberty. In a day when police are armed with lethal and chemical weapons, and possess scientific communication and detection devices readily available for use, it has become highly unlikely that a suspect, using reasonable force, can escape from or effectively deter an arrest, whether lawful or unlawful. His accomplishment is generally limited to temporary evasion, merely rendering the officer's task more difficult or prolonged. Thus self-help as a practical remedy is anachronistic, whatever may have been its original justification or efficacy in an era when the common law doctrine permitting resistance evolved. Indeed, self-help not infrequently causes far graver consequences for both the officer and the suspect than does the unlawful arrest itself. Accordingly, the state, in deleting the right to resist, has not actually altered or diminished the remedies available against the illegality of an arrest without probable cause; it has merely required a person to submit peacefully to the inevitable and to pursue his available remedies through the orderly judicial process.

We are not unmindful that under present conditions the available remedies for unlawful arrest—release followed by civil or criminal action against the offending officer—may be deemed inadequate. However, this circumstance does not elevate physical resistance to anything other than the least effective and desirable of all possible remedies; as such its rejection, particularly when balanced against the state's interest in discouraging violence, cannot realistically be considered an affirmative "seizure" or deprivation of liberty.

Thus there is no denial of due process because the deprivation of liberty which an individual suffers upon an unlawful arrest is in no substantial or practical way effectuated, sanctioned or increased by section 834a. There is no constitutional impediment to the state's policy of removing controversies over the legality of an arrest from the streets to the courtroom.

II

Our task, however, is by no means completed with the foregoing construction of section 834a. Defendant was charged not with simply battery, a misdemeanor, but with battery upon a peace officer "engaged in the performance of his duties," a felony under Penal Code section 243. Unlike section 834a, which had no predecessor when enacted in 1957, the language of section 243, speaking in terms of the officer's "duty," has been incorporated in section 148 of the Penal Code since 1872. The latter section makes it a misdemeanor to resist, delay or obstruct an officer in the discharge of "any duty of his office." Section 148 has long been construed by the courts as applying only to lawful arrests, because "An officer is under no duty to make an unlawful arrest." (Jackson v. Superior Court (1950) 98 Cal.App.2d 183). Even if section 834a now makes it a citizen's duty not to resist an unlawful arrest, this change in the law in no way purports to include an unlawful arrest within the performance of an *officer's* duty.

Moreover, simply as a matter of statutory construction, it is clear that section 834a was meant at most to eliminate the common law defense of resistance to unlawful arrest, and not to make such resistance a new substantive crime. This interpretation is borne out by reference to legislative hearings at which there were discussions on the purpose of section 834a. Significantly, both the Uniform Arrest Act, from which the language of section 834a was drawn, and the Model Penal Code take the approach of eliminating the defense but declining to make resistance a separate and additional crime. When section 834a was enacted in 1957, the Legislature amended the penalty provisions but did not change the "duty" language of section 148, thereby impliedly adopting the prior judicial interpretation of "duty." In 1961 the Legislature chose to use the same key language in amending section 243, the statute with which we are here concerned. "[The] rule of law is well established that where the legislature uses terms already judicially construed, the presumption is almost irresistible that it used them in the precise and technical sense which had been placed upon them by the courts." (*City of Long Beach v. Marshall* (1938) 11 Cal. 2d 609.) Therefore we must construe section 243, like section 148, as excluding unlawful arrests from its definition of "duty." This in no way thwarts the legislative purpose to consign to the courtroom all controversies over legality. We confirm that a resisting defendant commits a public offense; but if the arrest is ultimately determined factually to be unlawful, the defendant can be validly convicted only of simple assault or battery. Cases holding or implying the contrary are disapproved.[6]

III

Defendant contends that his arrest was not only lacking in probable cause and thus unlawful, but also was accomplished with excessive force and hence he was justified in employing counterforce in self-defense. Some courts appear to have incorrectly treated these two problems unitarily, as if a technically unlawful arrest were identical with an overly forceful arrest.

There are, however, two distinct and separate rights at stake. The common law rule allowing resistance to technically unlawful arrests protects a person's freedom from unreasonable seizure and confinement; the rule allowing resistance to excessive force, which applies during a technically lawful or unlawful arrest, protects a person's right to bodily integrity and permits resort to self-defense. Liberty can be restored through legal processes, but life and limb cannot be repaired in a courtroom. Therefore any rationale, pragmatic or constitutional, for outlawing resistance to unlawful arrests and resolving the dispute over legality in the courts has no determinative application to the right to resist excessive force. The commentators are unanimous on this point, and the Model Penal Code states it explicitly.[7] ...

To summarize, then, construing sections 834a and 243, it is now the law of California that a person may not use force to resist any arrest, lawful or unlawful, except that he may use reasonable force to defend life and limb against excessive force; but if it should be determined that resistance was not thus justified, the felony provisions of section 243 apply when the arrest is lawful, and if the arrest is determined to be unlawful the defendant may be convicted only of a misdemeanor.

IV

[The court determined that the officer had arrested the defendant without probable cause.]

The question of the exercise of reasonable force and the right to self-defense, which we emphasize is distinct from that of the lawfulness of the arrest, is for the trier of

---

6. ... The above construction of sections 148 and 243 as not applying to unlawful arrests makes it unnecessary to reach a potentially difficult constitutional question. Unlike section 834a, which applies only to forceful resistance, section 148 penalizes even passive delay or obstruction of an arrest, such as refusal to cooperate. The United States Supreme Court has made it clear that "one cannot be punished for failing to obey the command of an officer if that command is itself violative of the Constitution." (*Wright v. Georgia* (1963) 373 U.S. 284.) Yet this would be the result if "duty" were construed to include unlawful arrests, since, as we have seen, an arrest without probable cause is by definition an "unreasonable seizure" within the Fourth Amendment.

7. Model Penal Code (Tent. Draft No. 8, 1958) section 3.04. The comments thereto state, at page 19: "The paragraph, it should be noted, forbids the use of force for the purpose of preventing an arrest; it has *no application when the actor apprehends bodily injury*, as when the arresting officer unlawfully employs or threatens deadly force, unless the actor knows that he is in no peril greater than arrest if he submits to the assertion of authority." (Italics added.)

fact to determine. Here the jury had before it evidence which could justify a finding either way, depending upon the credibility of witnesses and the weight of the evidence. The court's instructions merely quoted or paraphrased the Penal Code sections regarding the privilege of self-defense, the duty not to resist an arrest, and an officer's privilege to use reasonable force in effecting an arrest. In view of our conclusions on the law, we must hold that the jury was not adequately instructed as to the rights and duties of the respective parties.

...

The judgment is reversed.

B. Use of Force to Prevent Crime or Apprehend Criminals

The general rule, and the rule in California, is that anyone may use reasonable, non-deadly force to prevent a crime or to apprehend a criminal. The more difficult question, and the question addressed in the next two cases, is when deadly force may be used for either purpose. In *People v. Ceballos*, the defendant used a "spring" gun to shoot a would-be burglar, and the California Supreme Court has to decide when a person can use deadly force to resist a felony and whether that force can be applied by means of a mechanical device. *Tennessee v. Garner* is a civil case concerning the use of deadly force to apprehend a criminal. The Supreme Court sets out the standard for evaluating whether use of deadly force by the police is prohibited by the Fourth Amendment as amounting to an "unreasonable seizure."

People v. Ceballos

12 Cal. 3d 470, 526 P.2d 241 (1974)

Burke, J.

Don Ceballos was found guilty by a jury of assault with a deadly weapon (Pen. Code, § 245). Imposition of sentence was suspended and he was placed on probation. He appeals from the judgment, contending primarily that his conduct was not unlawful because the alleged victim was attempting to commit burglary when hit by a trap gun mounted in the garage of defendant's dwelling and that the court erred in instructing the jury. We have concluded that the former argument lacks merit, that the court did not commit prejudicial error in instructing the jury, and that the judgment should be affirmed.

Defendant lived alone in a home in San Anselmo. The regular living quarters were above the garage, but defendant sometimes slept in the garage and had about $2,500 worth of property there.

In March 1970 some tools were stolen from defendant's home. On May 12, 1970, he noticed the lock on his garage doors was bent and pry marks were on one of the doors. The next day he mounted a loaded .22 caliber pistol in the garage. The pistol was aimed at the center of the garage doors and was connected by a wire to one of the doors so that the pistol would discharge if the door was opened several inches.

The damage to defendant's lock had been done by a 16-year-old boy named Stephen and a 15-year-old boy named Robert. On the afternoon of May 15, 1970, the boys returned to defendant's house while he was away. Neither boy was armed with a gun or knife. After looking in the windows and seeing no one, Stephen succeeded in removing the lock on the garage doors with a crowbar, and, as he pulled the door outward, he was hit in the face with a bullet from the pistol.

Stephen testified: He intended to go into the garage "[for] musical equipment" because he had a debt to pay to a friend. His "way of paying that debt would be to take [defendant's] property and sell it" and use the proceeds to pay the debt. He "wasn't going to do it [i.e., steal] for sure, necessarily." He was there "to look around," and "getting in, I don't know if I would have actually stolen."

Defendant, testifying in his own behalf, admitted having set up the trap gun. He stated that after noticing the pry marks on his garage door on May 12, he felt he should "set up some kind of a trap, something to keep the burglar out of my home." When asked why he was trying to keep the burglar out, he replied, "... Because somebody was trying to steal my property ... and I don't want to come home some night and have the thief in there ... usually a thief is pretty desperate ... and ... they just pick up a weapon ... if they don't have one ... and do the best they can."

When asked by the police shortly after the shooting why he assembled the trap gun, defendant stated that "he didn't have much and he wanted to protect what he did have."

As heretofore appears, the jury found defendant guilty of assault with a deadly weapon. (Pen. Code, § 245.) An assault is "an unlawful attempt, coupled with a present ability, to commit a violent injury on the person of another." (Pen. Code, § 240.)

Defendant contends that had he been present he would have been justified in shooting Stephen since Stephen was attempting to commit burglary (Pen. Code, § 459), that under cases such as *United States v. Gilliam* (D.C. 1882) 25 F. Cas. 1319, defendant had a right to do indirectly what he could have done directly, and that therefore any attempt by him to commit a violent injury upon Stephen was not "unlawful" and hence not an assault. The People argue that the rule in *Gilliam* is unsound, that as a matter of law a trap gun constitutes excessive force, and that in any event the circumstances were not in fact such as to warrant the use of deadly force.

The issue of criminal liability under statutes such as Penal Code section 245 where the instrument employed is a trap gun or other deadly mechanical device appears to be one of first impression in this state, but in other jurisdictions courts have considered the question of criminal and civil liability for death or injuries inflicted by such a device.

At common law in England it was held that a trespasser, having knowledge that there are spring guns in a wood, cannot maintain an action for an injury received in consequence of his accidentally stepping on the wire of such gun. That case aroused such a protest in England that it was abrogated seven years later by a statute, which made it a misdemeanor to set spring guns with intent to inflict grievous bodily injury but excluded from its operation a spring gun set between sunset and sunrise in a dwelling house for the protection thereof.

In the United States, courts have concluded that a person may be held criminally liable under statutes proscribing homicides and shooting with intent to injure, or civilly liable, if he sets upon his premises a deadly mechanical device and that device kills or injures another. However, an exception to the rule that there may be criminal and civil liability for death or injuries caused by such a device has been recognized where the intrusion is, in fact, such that the person, were he present, would be justified in taking the life or inflicting the bodily harm with his own hands. The phrase "were he present" does not hypothesize the actual presence of the person, but is used in setting forth in an indirect manner the principle that a person may do indirectly that which he is privileged to do directly.

Allowing persons, at their own risk, to employ deadly mechanical devices imperils the lives of children, firemen and policemen acting within the scope of their employment, and others. Where the actor is present, there is always the possibility he will realize that deadly force is not necessary, but deadly mechanical devices are without mercy or discretion. Such devices "are silent instrumentalities of death. They deal death and destruction to the innocent as well as the criminal intruder without the slightest warning. The taking of human life [or infliction of great bodily injury] by such means is brutally savage and inhuman." (See *State v. Plumlee* (La. 1933) 149 So. 425.)

It seems clear that the use of such devices should not be encouraged. Moreover, whatever may be thought in torts, the foregoing rule setting forth an exception to liability for death or injuries inflicted by such devices "is inappropriate in penal law for it is obvious that it does not prescribe a workable standard of conduct; liability depends upon fortuitous results." (See Model Penal Code (Tent. Draft No. 8), § 3.06, com. 15.) We therefore decline to adopt that rule in criminal cases.

Furthermore, even if that rule were applied here, as we shall see, defendant was not justified in shooting Stephen. Penal Code section 197 provides: "Homicide is ... justifiable ... 1. When resisting any attempt to murder any person, or to commit a felony, or to do some great bodily injury upon any person; or, 2. When committed in defense of habitation, property, or person, against one who manifestly intends or endeavors, by violence or surprise, to commit a felony...." Since a homicide is justifiable under the circumstances specified in section 197, a fortiori an attempt to commit a violent injury upon another under those circumstances is justifiable.

By its terms subdivision 1 of Penal Code section 197 appears to permit killing to prevent any "felony," but in view of the large number of felonies today and the inclusion of many that do not involve a danger of serious bodily harm, a literal reading of the section is undesirable. *People v. Jones* (1961) 191 Cal. App. 2d 478, in rejecting the defendant's theory that her husband was about to commit the felony of beating her (Pen. Code, § 273d) and that therefore her killing him to prevent him from doing so was justifiable, stated that Penal Code section 197 "does no more than codify the common law and should be read in the light of it." *Jones* read into section 197, subdivision 1, the limitation that the felony be "some atrocious crime attempted to be committed by force." *Jones* further stated, "The punishment provided by a statute is not necessarily an adequate test as to whether life may be taken for in some situations it is too artificial and unrealistic. We must look further into the character of the crime, and the manner of its perpetration. *When these do not reasonably create a fear of great bodily harm*, as they could not if defendant apprehended only a misdemeanor assault, *there is no cause for the exaction of a human life*." (Italics added.)

Jones involved subdivision 1 of Penal Code section 197, but subdivision 2 of that section is likewise so limited. The term "violence or surprise" in subdivision 2 is found in common law authorities, and, whatever may have been the very early common law, the rule developed at common law that killing or use of deadly force to prevent a felony was justified only if the offense was a forcible and atrocious crime. "Surprise" means an unexpected attack—which includes force and violence, and the word thus appears redundant.

Examples of forcible and atrocious crimes are murder, mayhem, rape and robbery. In such crimes "from their atrocity and violence human life [or personal safety from great harm] either is, or is presumed to be, in peril." (*See United States v. Gilliam.*)

Burglary has been included in the list of such crimes. However, in view of the wide scope of burglary under Penal Code section 459, as compared with the common law definition of that offense, in our opinion it cannot be said that under all circumstances burglary under section 459 constitutes a forcible and atrocious crime.[2]

Where the character and manner of the burglary do not reasonably create a fear of great bodily harm, there is no cause for exaction of human life, or for the use of deadly force. The character and manner of the burglary could not reasonably create such a fear unless the burglary threatened, or was reasonably believed to threaten, death or serious bodily harm.

In the instant case the asserted burglary did not threaten death or serious bodily harm, since no one but Stephen and Robert was then on the premises. A defendant is not protected from liability merely by the fact that the intruder's conduct is such as would justify the defendant, were he present, in believing that the intrusion threatened death or serious bodily injury. There is ordinarily the possibility that the de-

2. At common law burglary was the breaking and entering of a mansion house in the night with the intent to commit a felony. Burglary under Penal Code section 459 differs from common law burglary in that the entry may be in the daytime and of numerous places other than a mansion house, and breaking is not required. For example, under section 459 a person who enters a store with the intent of committing theft is guilty of burglary. It would seem absurd to hold that a store detective could kill that person if necessary to prevent him from committing that offense.

fendant, were he present, would realize the true state of affairs and recognize the intruder as one whom he would not be justified in killing or wounding.

We thus conclude that defendant was not justified under Penal Code section 197, subdivisions 1 or 2, in shooting Stephen to prevent him from committing burglary.

...

We recognize that our position regarding justification for killing under Penal Code section 197, subdivisions 1 and 2, differs from the position of section 143, subdivision (2), of the Restatement Second of Torts, regarding the use of deadly force to prevent a "felony ... of a type ... involving the breaking and entry of a dwelling place"[5] but in view of the supreme value of human life, we do not believe bodily force can be justified to prevent all felonies of the foregoing type, including ones in which no person is, or is reasonably believed to be, on the premises except the would-be burglar.

Defendant also argues that had he been present he would have been justified in shooting Stephen under subdivision 4 of Penal Code section 197, which provides, "Homicide is ... justifiable ... 4. When necessarily committed in *attempting*, by lawful ways and means, *to apprehend* any person for any felony committed...." (Italics added.) The argument cannot be upheld. The words "attempting ... to apprehend" contain the idea of acting for the purpose of apprehending. An attempt to commit a crime includes, inter alia, the specific intent to commit a particular crime. Here no showing was made that defendant's intent in shooting was to apprehend a felon. Rather it appears from his testimony and extrajudicial statement heretofore recited that his intent was to prevent a burglary, to protect his property, and to avoid the possibility that a thief might get into defendant's house and injure him upon his return.

...

We conclude that as a matter of law the exception to the rule of liability for injuries inflicted by a deadly mechanical device does not apply under the circumstances here appearing.

...

Note

Penal Code § 198.5. After the *Ceballos* decision, the California Legislature added Penal Code § 198.5:

5. Section 143, subdivision (2), of Restatement Second of Torts, reads, "The use of force ... intended or likely to cause death or serious bodily harm is privileged if the actor reasonably believes that the commission or consummation of the felony cannot otherwise be prevented and the felony for the prevention of which the actor is intervening is of a type threatening death or serious bodily harm or *involving the breaking and entry of a dwelling place.*" (Italics added.) The comment to that subsection states: "The Statement in this Subsection permits the use of means intended or likely to cause death or serious bodily harm for the purpose of preventing such crimes as murder, voluntary manslaughter, mayhem, robbery, common law rape, kidnapping, and *burglary.*" (Italics added.)

> Any person using force intended or likely to cause death or great bodily injury within his or her residence shall be presumed to have held a reasonable fear of imminent peril of death or great bodily injury to self, family, or a member of the household when that force is used against another person, not a member of the family or household, who unlawfully and forcibly enters or has unlawfully and forcibly entered the residence and the person using the force knew or had reason to believe that an unlawful and forcible entry occurred.
>
> As used in this section, great bodily injury means a significant or substantial physical injury.

How does this section affect the law as explained in *People v. Ceballos*?

Tennessee v. Garner

471 U.S. 1, 105 S. Ct. 1694 (1985)

Justice White delivered the opinion of the Court.

This case requires us to determine the constitutionality of the use of deadly force to prevent the escape of an apparently unarmed suspected felon. We conclude that such force may not be used unless it is necessary to prevent the escape and the officer has probable cause to believe that the suspect poses a significant threat of death or serious physical injury to the officer or others.

I.

At about 10:45 p. m. on October 3, 1974, Memphis Police Officers Elton Hymon and Leslie Wright were dispatched to answer a "prowler inside call." Upon arriving at the scene they saw a woman standing on her porch and gesturing toward the adjacent house.[1] She told them she had heard glass breaking and that "they" or "someone" was breaking in next door. While Wright radioed the dispatcher to say that they were on the scene, Hymon went behind the house. He heard a door slam and saw someone run across the backyard. The fleeing suspect, who was appellee-respondent's decedent, Edward Garner, stopped at a 6-feet-high chain link fence at the edge of the yard. With the aid of a flashlight, Hymon was able to see Garner's face and hands. He saw no sign of a weapon, and, though not certain, was "reasonably sure" and "figured" that Garner was unarmed. He thought Garner was 17 or 18 years old and about 5'5" or 5'7" tall.[2] While Garner was crouched at the base of the fence, Hymon called out "police, halt" and took a few steps toward him. Garner then began to climb over the fence. Convinced that if Garner made it over the fence he would elude capture,[3]

---

1. The owner of the house testified that no lights were on in the house, but that a back door light was on. Officer Hymon, though uncertain, stated in his deposition that there were lights on in the house.

2. In fact, Garner, an eighth-grader, was 15. He was 5'4" tall and weighed somewhere around 100 or 110 pounds.

3. When asked at trial why he fired, Hymon stated:

> Well, first of all it was apparent to me from the little bit that I knew about the area at the

Hymon shot him. The bullet hit Garner in the back of the head. Garner was taken by ambulance to a hospital, where he died on the operating table. Ten dollars and a purse taken from the house were found on his body.

In using deadly force to prevent the escape, Hymon was acting under the authority of a Tennessee statute and pursuant to Police Department policy. The statute provides that "[if], after notice of the intention to arrest the defendant, he either flee or forcibly resist, the officer may use all the necessary means to effect the arrest." Tenn. Code Ann. §40-7-108 (1982). The Department policy was slightly more restrictive than the statute, but still allowed the use of deadly force in cases of burglary. The incident was reviewed by the Memphis Police Firearm's Review Board and presented to a grand jury. Neither took any action.

...

II

Whenever an officer restrains the freedom of a person to walk away, he has seized that person. *United States v. Brignoni-Ponce*, 422 U.S. 873 (1975). While it is not always clear just when minimal police interference becomes a seizure, there can be no question that apprehension by the use of deadly force is a seizure subject to the reasonableness requirement of the Fourth Amendment.

A

A police officer may arrest a person if he has probable cause to believe that person committed a crime. Petitioners and appellant argue that if this requirement is satisfied the Fourth Amendment has nothing to say about how that seizure is made. This submission ignores the many cases in which this Court, by balancing the extent of the intrusion against the need for it, has examined the reasonableness of the manner in which a search or seizure is conducted. To determine the constitutionality of a seizure "[we] must balance the nature and quality of the intrusion on the individual's Fourth Amendment interests against the importance of the governmental interests alleged to justify the intrusion." *United States v. Place*, 462 U.S. 696 (1983). We have described "the balancing of competing interests" as "the key principle of the Fourth Amendment." *Michigan v. Summers*, 452 U.S. 692 (1981). Because one of the factors is the extent of the intrusion, it is plain that reasonableness depends on not only when a seizure is made, but also how it is carried out. *United States v. Ortiz*, 422 U.S. 891 (1975); *Terry v. Ohio*, 392 U.S. 1 (1968).

> time that he was going to get away because, number 1, I couldn't get to him. My partner then couldn't find where he was because, you know, he was late coming around. He didn't know where I was talking about. I couldn't get to him because of the fence here, I couldn't have jumped this fence and come up, consequently jumped this fence and caught him before he got away because he was already up on the fence, just one leap and he was already over the fence, and so there is no way that I could have caught him.

He also stated that the area beyond the fence was dark, that he could not have gotten over the fence easily because he was carrying a lot of equipment and wearing heavy boots, and that Garner, being younger and more energetic, could have outrun him.

Applying these principles to particular facts, the Court has held that governmental interests did not support a lengthy detention of luggage, *United States v. Place*, an airport seizure not "carefully tailored to its underlying justification," *Florida v. Royer*, 460 U.S. 491 (1983) (plurality opinion), surgery under general anesthesia to obtain evidence, *Winston v. Lee*, 470 U.S. 753 (1985), or detention for fingerprinting without probable cause, *Davis v. Mississippi*, 394 U.S. 721 (1969); *Hayes v. Florida*, 470 U.S. 811 (1985). On the other hand, under the same approach it has upheld the taking of fingernail scrapings from a suspect, *Cupp v. Murphy*, 412 U.S. 291 (1973), an unannounced entry into a home to prevent the destruction of evidence, *Ker v. California*, 374 U.S. 23 (1963), administrative housing inspections without probable cause to believe that a code violation will be found, *Camara v. Municipal Court*, 387 U.S. 523 (1967), and a blood test of a drunken-driving suspect, *Schmerber v. California*, 384 U.S. 757 (1966). In each of these cases, the question was whether the totality of the circumstances justified a particular sort of search or seizure.

B

The same balancing process applied in the cases cited above demonstrates that, notwithstanding probable cause to seize a suspect, an officer may not always do so by killing him. The intrusiveness of a seizure by means of deadly force is unmatched. The suspect's fundamental interest in his own life need not be elaborated upon. The use of deadly force also frustrates the interest of the individual, and of society, in judicial determination of guilt and punishment. Against these interests are ranged governmental interests in effective law enforcement.[8] It is argued that overall violence will be reduced by encouraging the peaceful submission of suspects who know that they may be shot if they flee. Effectiveness in making arrests requires the resort to deadly force, or at least the meaningful threat thereof. "Being able to arrest such individuals is a condition precedent to the state's entire system of law enforcement."

Without in any way disparaging the importance of these goals, we are not convinced that the use of deadly force is a sufficiently productive means of accomplishing them to justify the killing of nonviolent suspects. The use of deadly force is a self-defeating way of apprehending a suspect and so setting the criminal justice mechanism in motion. If successful, it guarantees that that mechanism will not be set in motion. And while the meaningful threat of deadly force might be thought to lead to the arrest of more live suspects by discouraging escape attempts,[9] the presently available evidence

8. The dissent emphasizes that subsequent investigation cannot replace immediate apprehension. We recognize that this is so; indeed, that is the reason why there is any dispute. If subsequent arrest were assured, no one would argue that use of deadly force was justified. Thus, we proceed on the assumption that subsequent arrest is not likely. Nonetheless, it should be remembered that failure to apprehend at the scene does not necessarily mean that the suspect will never be caught....

9. We note that the usual manner of deterring illegal conduct—through punishment—has been largely ignored in connection with flight from arrest.... In the few States that do outlaw flight from an arresting officer, the crime is only a misdemeanor. Even forceful resistance, though generally a separate offense, is classified as a misdemeanor.

This lenient approach does avoid the anomaly of automatically transforming every fleeing misdemeanant into a fleeing felon—subject, under the common-law rule, to apprehension by deadly

does not support this thesis. The fact is that a majority of police departments in this country have forbidden the use of deadly force against nonviolent suspects. If those charged with the enforcement of the criminal law have abjured the use of deadly force in arresting nondangerous felons, there is a substantial basis for doubting that the use of such force is an essential attribute of the arrest power in all felony cases. Petitioners and appellant have not persuaded us that shooting nondangerous fleeing suspects is so vital as to outweigh the suspect's interest in his own life.

The use of deadly force to prevent the escape of all felony suspects, whatever the circumstances, is constitutionally unreasonable. It is not better that all felony suspects die than that they escape. Where the suspect poses no immediate threat to the officer and no threat to others, the harm resulting from failing to apprehend him does not justify the use of deadly force to do so. It is no doubt unfortunate when a suspect who is in sight escapes, but the fact that the police arrive a little late or are a little slower afoot does not always justify killing the suspect. A police officer may not seize an unarmed, nondangerous suspect by shooting him dead. The Tennessee statute is unconstitutional insofar as it authorizes the use of deadly force against such fleeing suspects.

It is not, however, unconstitutional on its face. Where the officer has probable cause to believe that the suspect poses a threat of serious physical harm, either to the officer or to others, it is not constitutionally unreasonable to prevent escape by using deadly force. Thus, if the suspect threatens the officer with a weapon or there is probable cause to believe that he has committed a crime involving the infliction or threatened infliction of serious physical harm, deadly force may be used if necessary to prevent escape, and if, where feasible, some warning has been given. As applied in such circumstances, the Tennessee statute would pass constitutional muster.

III

A

It is insisted that the Fourth Amendment must be construed in light of the common-law rule, which allowed the use of whatever force was necessary to effect the arrest of a fleeing felon, though not a misdemeanant. As stated in Hale's posthumously published Pleas of the Crown:

> "[If] persons that are pursued by these officers for felony or the just suspicion thereof ... shall not yield themselves to these officers, but shall either resist or fly before they are apprehended or being apprehended shall rescue themselves and resist or fly, so that they cannot be otherwise apprehended, and are upon necessity slain therein, because they cannot be otherwise taken, it is no felony." 2 M. Hale, Historia Placitorum Coronae 85 (1736).

---

force—solely by virtue of his flight. However, it is in real tension with the harsh consequences of flight in cases where deadly force is employed. For example, Tennessee does not outlaw fleeing from arrest. The Memphis City Code does, § 22-34.1 (Supp. 17, 1971), subjecting the offender to a maximum fine of $50, § 1-8 (1967). Thus, Garner's attempted escape subjected him to (a) a $50 fine, and (b) being shot.

Most American jurisdictions also imposed a flat prohibition against the use of deadly force to stop a fleeing misdemeanant, coupled with a general privilege to use such force to stop a fleeing felon.

The State and city argue that because this was the prevailing rule at the time of the adoption of the Fourth Amendment and for some time thereafter, and is still in force in some States, use of deadly force against a fleeing felon must be "reasonable." It is true that this Court has often looked to the common law in evaluating the reasonableness, for Fourth Amendment purposes, of police activity. On the other hand, it "has not simply frozen into constitutional law those law enforcement practices that existed at the time of the Fourth Amendment's passage." *Payton v. New York* 445 U.S. 573 (1980). Because of sweeping change in the legal and technological context, reliance on the common-law rule in this case would be a mistaken literalism that ignores the purposes of a historical inquiry.

B

It has been pointed out many times that the common-law rule is best understood in light of the fact that it arose at a time when virtually all felonies were punishable by death.[11] "Though effected without the protections and formalities of an orderly trial and conviction, the killing of a resisting or fleeing felon resulted in no greater consequences than those authorized for punishment of the felony of which the individual was charged or suspected." American Law Institute, Model Penal Code § 3.07, Comment 3, p. 56 (Tentative Draft No. 8, 1958). Courts have also justified the common-law rule by emphasizing the relative dangerousness of felons.

Neither of these justifications makes sense today. Almost all crimes formerly punishable by death no longer are or can be. And while in earlier times "the gulf between the felonies and the minor offenses was broad and deep" 2 F. Pollock & F. Maitland, The History of English Law (2d ed. 1909), today the distinction is minor and often arbitrary. Many crimes classified as misdemeanors, or nonexistent, at common law are now felonies. These changes have undermined the concept, which was questionable to begin with, that use of deadly force against a fleeing felon is merely a speedier execution of someone who has already forfeited his life. They have also made the assumption that a "felon" is more dangerous than a misdemeanant untenable. Indeed, numerous misdemeanors involve conduct more dangerous than many felonies.[12]

There is an additional reason why the common-law rule cannot be directly translated to the present day. The common-law rule developed at a time when weapons were rudimentary. Deadly force could be inflicted almost solely in a hand-to-hand struggle during which, necessarily, the safety of the arresting officer was at risk. Hand-

11. The roots of the concept of a "felony" lie not in capital punishment but in forfeiture. Not all felonies were always punishable by death. Nonetheless, the link was profound. Blackstone was able to write: "The idea of felony is indeed so generally connected with that of capital punishment, that we find it hard to separate them; and to this usage the interpretations of the law do now conform. And therefore if a statute makes any new offence felony, the law implies that is shall be punished with death, *viz.* by hanging, as well as with forfeiture...." 4 W. Blackstone, COMMENTARIES.

12. White-collar crime, for example, poses a less significant physical threat than, say, drunken driving.

guns were not carried by police officers until the latter half of the last century. Only then did it become possible to use deadly force from a distance as a means of apprehension. As a practical matter, the use of deadly force under the standard articulation of the common-law rule has an altogether different meaning—and harsher consequences—now than in past centuries.[13]

One other aspect of the common-law rule bears emphasis. It forbids the use of deadly force to apprehend a misdemeanant, condemning such action as disproportionately severe.

In short, though the common-law pedigree of Tennessee's rule is pure on its face, changes in the legal and technological context mean the rule is distorted almost beyond recognition when literally applied.

[The court examined the laws of other jurisdictions and concluded that there was a long-term trend away from the common-law rule and that police departments themselves were adopting policies more restrictive than the common-law rule. The court also found no evidence that abandonment of the common-law rule had hampered enforcement agencies.]

The dissent argues that the shooting was justified by the fact that Officer Hymon had probable cause to believe that Garner had committed a nighttime burglary. While we agree that burglary is a serious crime, we cannot agree that it is so dangerous as automatically to justify the use of deadly force. The FBI classifies burglary as a "property" rather than a "violent" crime. Although the armed burglar would present a different situation, the fact that an unarmed suspect has broken into a dwelling at night does not automatically mean he is physically dangerous. This case demonstrates as much. In fact, the available statistics demonstrate that burglaries only rarely involve physical violence. During the 10-year period from 1973–1982, only 3.8% of all burglaries involved violent crime.[14]

. . .

[Dissenting opinion of O'Connor, J., joined by Burger, C.J., and Rehnquist, J., omitted.]

---

13. It has been argued that sophisticated techniques of apprehension and increased communication between the police in different jurisdictions have made it more likely that an escapee will be caught than was once the case, and that this change has also reduced the "reasonableness" of the use of deadly force to prevent escape. We are unaware of any data that would permit sensible evaluation of this claim. Current arrest rates are sufficiently low, however, that we have some doubt whether in past centuries the failure to arrest at the scene meant that the police had missed their only chance in a way that is not presently the case. In 1983, 21% of the offenses in the Federal Bureau of Investigation crime index were cleared by arrest. The clearance rate for burglary was 15%.

14. The dissent points out that three-fifths of all rapes in the home, three-fifths of all home robberies, and about a third of home assaults are committed by burglars. These figures mean only that if one knows that a suspect committed a rape in the home, there is a good chance that the suspect is also a burglar. That has nothing to do with the question here, which is whether the fact that someone has committed a burglary indicates that he has committed, or might commit, a violent crime. The dissent also points out that this 3.8% adds up to 2.8 million violent crimes over a 10-year period, as

Problem

Problem 80.

Defendant was asleep in his second floor apartment, above the business office of his construction company. At about 2:00 a.m. Defendant awoke to the noise of scraping outside his apartment. He went to his open living room window and opened the curtains. There he encountered Burglar standing on an extension ladder approximately 18 inches from Defendant. Burglar was trying to open the window screen. Defendant rushed to his bedroom and obtained a loaded handgun. He ran down the stairs and out the front door. Burglar was still on the ladder and Defendant pulled it out from under him, knocking him to the ground. Burglar leapt to his feet, facing Defendant. Defendant screamed, "freeze" two or three times as Burglar backed away. Defendant then fired twice into the ground in front of Burglar, and Burglar ran away on a zig-zag course. Defendant fired four bullets in the direction of Burglar, each of which struck the asphalt pavement behind Burglar. The bullet from the last shot ricocheted off the asphalt and a fragment of it struck Burglar in the back of the neck, killing him instantly. Defendant has been charged with involuntary manslaughter (PC § 192). What arguments should be made as to his defenses to this charge?

C. Duress

The duress defense excuses the commission of a crime when the defendant acted in response to the order of another person and under the reasonable belief that the defendant would suffer great bodily injury or death if he refused the order. The California Supreme Court, in *People v. Anderson*, the single case in this section, sets out the theory and history of the duress defense in the course of deciding whether duress can ever be a defense to murder.

People v. Anderson

28 Cal.4th 767, 50 P.3d 368 (2002)

CHIN, J.

Over two centuries ago, William Blackstone, the great commentator on the common law, said that duress is no excuse for killing an innocent person: "And, therefore, though a man be violently assaulted, and hath no other possible means of escaping death, but by killing an innocent person, this fear and force shall not acquit him of murder; for he ought rather to die himself than escape by the murder of an innocent." (2 Jones's Blackstone (1916).)

We granted review to decide whether these words apply in California. We conclude that, as in Blackstone's England, so today in California: fear for one's own life does

---

if to imply that today's holding will let loose 2.8 million violent burglars. The relevant universe is, of course, far smaller. At issue is only that tiny fraction of cases where violence has taken place and an officer who has no other means of apprehending the suspect is unaware of its occurrence.

not justify killing an innocent person. Duress is not a defense to murder. We also conclude that duress cannot reduce murder to manslaughter. Although one may debate whether a killing under duress should be manslaughter rather than murder, if a new form of manslaughter is to be created, the Legislature, not this court, should do it.

I. THE FACTS AND PROCEDURAL HISTORY

Defendant was charged with kidnapping and murdering Margaret Armstrong in a camp area near Eureka called the South Jetty. Defendant and others apparently suspected the victim of molesting two girls who resided in the camp. Ron Kiern, the father of one of the girls, pleaded guilty to Armstrong's second degree murder and testified at defendant's trial.

The prosecution evidence showed that a group of people, including defendant and Kiern, confronted Armstrong at the camp. Members of the group dragged Armstrong to a nearby field, beat her, put duct tape over her mouth, tied her naked to a bush, and abandoned her. Later, defendant and Kiern, in Kiern's car, saw Armstrong going naked down the street away from the jetty. The two grabbed Armstrong, forced her into the car, and drove away. [Subsequently, defendant and Kiern placed Armstrong in the trunk of the car, and Kiern bludgeoned her with a large rock handed to him by defendant. One witness testified that Kiern admitted that he had later stepped on Armstrong's neck to make sure she was dead. Defendant testified that he had tried to convince Kiern to take Armstrong to the hospital after she had been beaten and that he had only retrieved the rock for Kiern because Kiern had said, "Give me the rock or I'll beat the s___ out of you." Defendant gave him the rock because Kiern was bigger than he and he was "not in shape" to fight, and he thought Kiern would "[p]unch me out, break my back, break my neck. Who knows." According to defendant, after driving for awhile, Kiern stopped the car, and went back to the trunk where Armstrong was still alive and moaning. When Kiern reentered the car, he said, "She's dead now. I stomped on her neck and broke it."]

A jury convicted defendant of first degree murder and kidnapping. Based primarily on his testimony that Kiern threatened to "beat the s___ out of" him, defendant contended on appeal that the trial court erred in refusing to instruct the jury on duress as a defense to the murder charge. The Court of Appeal concluded that duress is not a defense to first degree murder and affirmed the judgment. We granted defendant's petition for review to decide to what extent, if any, duress is a defense to a homicide-related crime, and, if it is a defense, whether the trial court prejudicially erred in refusing a duress instruction.

II. DISCUSSION

A. Whether Duress Is a Defense to Murder

At common law, the general rule was, and still is today, what Blackstone stated: duress is no defense to killing an innocent person.[1] "Stemming from antiquity, the

1. By "innocent," we mean merely that the person did not cause the duress, not that the person has never committed a crime.

nearly unbroken tradition of Anglo-American common law is that duress never excuses murder, that the person threatened with his own demise ought rather to die himself, than escape by the murder of an innocent." (Dressler, *Exegesis of the Law of Duress: Justifying the Excuse and Searching for Its Proper Limits* (1989) 62 So. Cal. L. Rev. 1331.)

The basic rationale behind allowing the defense of duress for other crimes "is that, for reasons of social policy, it is better that the defendant, faced with a choice of evils, choose to do the lesser evil (violate the criminal law) in order to avoid the greater evil threatened by the other person." (LaFave, Criminal Law (3d ed. 2000) § 5.3.) This rationale, however, "is strained when a defendant is confronted with taking the life of an innocent third person in the face of a threat on his own life.... When the defendant commits murder under duress, the resulting harm—i.e. the death of an innocent person—is at least as great as the threatened harm—i.e. the death of the defendant." (*U.S. v. LaFleur* (9th Cir. 1991) 971 F.2d 200.) We might add that, when confronted with an apparent kill-an-innocent-person-or-be-killed situation, a person can always choose to resist. As a practical matter, death will rarely, if ever, inevitably result from a choice not to kill. The law should require people to choose to resist rather than kill an innocent person.

A state may, of course, modify the common law rule by statute. The Model Penal Code, for example, does not exclude murder from the duress defense. Defendant contends the California Legislature modified the rule in the 19th century and made duress a defense to some murders.

Since its adoption in 1872, Penal Code section 26 has provided: "All persons are capable of committing crimes except those belonging to the following classes: ... Persons (unless the crime be punishable with death) who committed the act or made the omission charged under threats of menaces sufficient to show that they had reasonable cause to and did believe their lives would be endangered if they refused." Defendant contends the reference to a "crime ... punishable with death" means that the crimes to which duress is not a defense include only those forms of murder that are punishable with death, and that these forms change with changes in death penalty law. In 1872, when the current Penal Code was adopted, all first degree murder was punishable with death. Today only first degree murder with special circumstances is so punishable. Accordingly, defendant contends that today, duress is a defense to all murder except first degree murder with special circumstances. In effect, he argues that a killing under duress is either first degree murder with special circumstances or no crime at all. Because the prosecution did not allege special circumstances in this case, he continues, duress provides a full defense.

The sparse relevant California case law is inconclusive....

In this case, the Court of Appeal concluded that, because all first degree murders were punishable with death in 1872, when section 26 was enacted, duress is not a defense to any first degree murder. In effect, the court concluded that section 26's exception for a "crime ... punishable with death" includes any crime punishable with death as of 1872 unaffected by later changes in death penalty law. As we explain, we agree, except that the Court of Appeal did not go back far enough in time. The exception for a crime punishable with death refers to a crime punishable with death as of *1850,* not 1872. Section 26 derives from section 10 of the original 1850 Act Concerning Crimes and Punishments, which similarly excepted a crime "punishable with death" from the duress defense.[4] Section 5, enacted as part of the original Penal Code in 1872 and unchanged since, provides: "The provisions of this Code, so far as they are substantially the same as existing statutes, must be construed as continuations thereof, and not as new enactments." As relevant, section 26 was merely a continuation of the then existing 1850 statute. For this reason, we must "begin ... by inquiring into the intent of the Legislature in 1850. . . ." (*Keeler v. Superior Court* (1970) 2 Cal.3d 619.)

In 1850, all murder was punishable with death. Not until 1856 was murder divided into degrees, with death the punishment for first degree but not second degree murder. This means that in 1850, duress was no defense to any murder. Thus, like many of California's early penal statutes, section 26 effectively adopted the common law, although the Legislature used a problematic method in which to do so. The question before us is whether the exception for a crime punishable with death changes with every change in death penalty law, which would mean that by 1872, the exception included only first degree murder and today it includes only first degree murder with special circumstances. We think not, for several reasons.

We see no suggestion that the 1850, or any, Legislature intended the substantive law of duress to fluctuate with every change in death penalty law. That interpretation would create strange anomalies. For example, special circumstances were added to the murder laws in the 1970's to conform California's death penalty law to the requirements of the United States Constitution. Defendant's position would mean that constitutional death penalty jurisprudence would control the substantive law of duress, something we doubt the Legislature intended. Even more anomalously, defendant's position would mean that when the Legislature created special circumstances to give California a valid death penalty law, it simultaneously *expanded* the circumstances in which someone may kill an innocent person.

The presence or absence of special circumstances has no relationship to whether duress should be a defense to killing an innocent person. For example, because a prior murder conviction is a special circumstance (§ 190.2, subd. (a)(2)), defendant's position would mean that a person with a prior murder conviction who intentionally kills an innocent person under duress without premeditating commits no crime, but if the person premeditates, the killing is a capital crime. A person without the prior conviction committing the same premeditated killing would commit no crime

4. The original 1850 statute provided: "A person committing a crime not punishable with death, under threats or menaces which sufficiently show that his or her life was in danger, or that he or she had reasonable cause to believe and did believe that his or her life was in danger, shall not be found guilty, and such threats or menaces being proved and established, the person or persons compelling by such threats or menaces the commission of the offence, shall be considered as principal or principals, and suffer the same punishment as if he or she had perpetrated the offence."

unless some other special circumstance happened to attach, in which case the killing would be a capital crime. The Legislature can hardly have intended such random results.

Defendant's interpretation would also force prosecutors to charge special circumstances to prevent duress from becoming a defense. As the Court of Appeal said in this case, "a rule making the availability of the duress defense turn on the manner in which prosecutorial discretion is exercised is potentially pernicious, and may do an unnecessary disservice to criminal defendants. The decision of whether to seek the death penalty... should not be encumbered by tactical considerations, such as blocking anticipated defenses. The charging decision must be governed by more sagacious considerations than whether the punishment charged will deprive a defendant of a defense to the crime."

...

Moreover, no reason appears for the Legislature to have silently abrogated the common law rule. The reasons for the rule applied as well to 19th-century California as to Blackstone's England. They apply, if anything, with greater force in California today. A person can always choose to resist rather than kill an innocent person. The law must encourage, even require, everyone to seek an alternative to killing. Crimes are often committed by more than one person; the criminal law must also, perhaps especially, deter those crimes. California today is tormented by gang violence. If duress is recognized as a defense to the killing of innocents, then a street or prison gang need only create an internal reign of terror and murder can be justified, at least by the actual killer. Persons who know they can claim duress will be more likely to follow a gang order to kill instead of resisting than would those who know they must face the consequences of their acts. Accepting the duress defense for any form of murder would thus encourage killing. Absent a stronger indication than the language of section 26, we do not believe the Legislature intended to remove the sanctions of the criminal law from the killing of an innocent even under duress.

...

Defendant and the concurring and dissenting opinion cite the principle of statutory construction that where a reference to another law is specific, the reference is to that law as it then existed and not as subsequently modified, but where the reference is general, "such as ... to a system or body of laws or to the general law relating to the subject in hand," the reference is to the law as it may be changed from time to time. (*Palermo v. Stockton Theatres, Inc.* (1948) 32 Cal.2d 53.) They argue that section 26's reference to a "crime ... punishable with death" is general rather than specific. The question is not so clear. Section 26 does not cite specific statutes, but the subject of crimes punishable with death is quite specific. It is, for example, far narrower than the reference that the *Palermo* court found to be *specific* for this purpose: "any treaty now existing between the government of the United States and the nation or country of which such alien is a citizen or subject." In any event, when the statutory words themselves "do not make clear whether [the statute] contemplates only a time-specific incorporation, the determining factor will be ... legislative intent...." (*In re Jovan B.*

6 Cal.4th 801.) Here, for the reasons stated, we believe the Legislature intended to refer to crimes punishable with death as they existed in 1850.

The concurring and dissenting opinion also argues that duress especially should be a defense to implied malice second degree murder. It evokes the image of an innocent person who is forced at gunpoint by fleeing armed robbers to drive recklessly, and who is then charged with murder when a fatal accident ensues. In reality, the situation is not so grim. Although duress is not an affirmative defense to murder, the circumstances of duress would certainly be relevant to whether the evidence establishes the elements of implied malice murder. The reasons a person acted in a certain way, including threats of death, are highly relevant to whether the person acted with a conscious or wanton disregard for human life. (*People v. Watson* (1981) 30 Cal.3d 290.) This is not due to a special doctrine of duress but to the requirements of implied malice murder.

Defendant argues that the rule of lenity compels a different result. We disagree. As explained in *People v. Avery* (2002) 27 Cal.4th 49, the rule of lenity compels courts to resolve true statutory ambiguities in a defendant's favor, but this rule applies only if two reasonable interpretations of the statute stand in relative equipoise. Courts should not strain to interpret a penal statute in a defendant's favor if they can fairly discern a contrary legislative intent. Here, for the reasons stated, the possible interpretations of section 26 do not stand in relative equipoise. Reasonably construed, section 26 preserves the common law rule that duress is not a defense to murder.

...

B. Whether Duress Can Reduce Murder to a Lesser Crime

Defendant also argues that even if duress is not a complete defense to murder, at least it reduces the crime to manslaughter by negating malice.

Manslaughter is the unlawful killing of a human being without malice. A defendant lacks malice and is guilty of voluntary manslaughter in limited, explicitly defined circumstances: either when the defendant acts in a "sudden quarrel or heat of passion" (§ 192(a)), or when the defendant kills in "unreasonable self-defense"—the unreasonable but good faith belief in having to act in self-defense. Neither of these two circumstances describes the killing of an innocent person under duress. Nevertheless, defendant argues that we should make duress a third way in which a defendant lacks malice.

...

This court has never decided the question. The problem with making a killing under duress a form of manslaughter is that no statute so provides. The difference between murder and manslaughter "is that murder includes, but manslaughter lacks, the element of malice." (*People v. Rios* (2000) 23 Cal.4th 450.) Both forms of voluntary manslaughter currently recognized—provocation and imperfect self-defense—are grounded in statutory language. The provocation form of manslaughter is obviously based on statute. Section 192 "specif[ies] that an unlawful killing that lacks malice because committed 'upon a sudden quarrel or heat of passion' is voluntary manslaughter." (*People v. Rios, supra.*)

Although less obvious, the imperfect self-defense form of manslaughter is also based on statute. Express malice exists "when there is manifested a deliberate intention *unlawfully* to take away the life of a fellow creature." (§ 188, italics added.) A killing in self-defense is *lawful.* Hence, a person who actually, albeit unreasonably, believes it is necessary to kill in self-defense intends to kill lawfully, not unlawfully. "A person who actually believes in the need for self-defense necessarily believes he is acting lawfully." (*In re Christian S.* (1994) 7 Cal.4th 768.) Because express malice requires an intent to kill unlawfully, a killing in the belief that one is acting lawfully is not malicious. The statutory definition of implied malice does not contain similar language, but we have extended the imperfect self-defense rationale to any killing that would otherwise have malice, whether express or implied. "[T]here is no valid reason to distinguish between those killings that, absent unreasonable self-defense, would be murder with express malice, and those killings that, absent unreasonable self-defense, would be murder with implied malice." (*People v. Blakeley* (2000) 23 Cal.4th 82.)

...

We recognize that policy arguments can be made that a killing out of fear for one's own life, although not justified, should be a crime less than the same killing without such fear. On the other hand, because duress can often arise in a criminal gang context, the Legislature might be reluctant to do anything to reduce the current law's deterrent effect on gang violence. These policy questions are for the Legislature, not a court, to decide. Accordingly, we reject defendant's argument that we should create a new form of voluntary manslaughter. His arguments are better directed to the Legislature.

Defendant also argues that, at least, duress can negate premeditation and deliberation, thus resulting in second degree and not first degree murder. We agree that a killing under duress, like any killing, may or may not be premeditated, depending on the circumstances. If a person obeys an order to kill without reflection, the jury might find no premeditation and thus convict of second degree murder. As with implied malice murder, this circumstance is not due to a special doctrine of duress but to the legal requirements of first degree murder. The trial court instructed the jury on the requirements for first degree murder. It specifically instructed that a killing "upon a sudden heat of passion or *other condition precluding the idea of deliberation*" would not be premeditated first degree murder. (Italics added.) Here, the jury found premeditation. In some other case, it might not. It is for the jury to decide. But, unless and until the Legislature decides otherwise, a malicious, premeditated killing, even under duress, is first degree murder.

On a final point, we note, contrary to the Attorney General's argument, that duress can, in effect, provide a defense to murder on a felony-murder theory by negating the underlying felony. If one is not guilty of the underlying felony due to duress, one cannot be guilty of felony murder based on that felony. Here, for example, the court instructed the jury that duress could be a defense to the kidnapping charge. It also instructed on felony murder with kidnapping as the underlying felony. If the jury had found defendant not guilty of kidnapping due to duress (it did not), it could not have found that he killed during the commission of that kidnapping. Defendant could not have killed during the perpetration of a crime of which he was innocent.

Our conclusion that duress is no defense to murder makes it unnecessary to decide whether the evidence would have warranted duress instructions in this case.

...

Concurring and Dissenting Opinion by KENNARD, J.

Under California law, the death penalty may be imposed for the crime of murder only if the murder is of the first degree and committed with one or more of the statutorily defined special circumstances. California law allows a person accused of crime to defend against any criminal charge on the ground that the defendant acted under duress "unless the crime be punishable with death." Here, defendant contends that, because the death penalty may not be imposed for second degree murder, the trial court erred in not instructing the jury that duress, if proven, was a complete defense to second degree murder.

The majority concludes that the trial court did not err because, under California law, duress is not a defense to second degree murder, or to any form of murder, whether or not the particular form of murder is punishable by death. I disagree. Applying established rules of statutory construction, I would hold that duress is unavailable as a defense only when the offense is capital murder—that is, first degree murder with a special circumstance—and that duress is available as a defense to all noncapital forms of murder, including murder in the second degree. Because no substantial evidence of duress was presented here, however, I agree with the majority that defendant was not entitled to have the trial court instruct the jury on that defense.

I

When deciding what a statute means, courts seek to determine what effect the legislative body that enacted it intended to achieve. To make this determination, courts begin with the text of the statute, because the words used are the best evidence of legislative intent. Unless there is reason to believe that a special or technical meaning was intended, courts give the words of the statute their usual, ordinary meaning. If the statutory text, viewed in light of the ordinary meaning of its words, is not ambiguous, courts usually accept this meaning as the proper construction of the statute without further inquiry. If the statutory text is ambiguous, however, courts examine the context of the statute and consider its legislative history and the historical circumstances of its enactment to arrive at the interpretation that is most likely to reflect legislative intent.

Here, the provision to be construed, subdivision Six of Penal Code section 26 (section 26), includes among the persons who are incapable of committing crimes "[p]ersons (*unless the crime be punishable with death*) who committed the act or made the omission charged under threats or menaces sufficient to show that they had reasonable cause to and did believe their lives would be endangered if they refused." (Italics added.) As applied to the crime of murder, the italicized phrase is ambiguous because some but not all forms of murder are punishable by death.

...

This ambiguity is resolved by applying two well-established rules of statutory construction. The first of these rules is used to determine whether a statutory provision mentioned in another provision is incorporated only in its contemporary form or instead as it might later be changed from time to time. The rule is this: If the reference to the other law is specific, as to a particular code provision by section number, then the referenced provision is incorporated only as it then existed, but if instead the reference is general, "such as ... to a system or body of laws or to the general law relating to the subject in hand, the referring statute takes the law or laws referred to not only in their contemporary form, but also as they may be changed from time to time...." (*Palermo v. Stockton Theatres, Inc.* (1948) 32 Cal.2d 53.)

Section 26, making duress a defense "unless the crime be punishable with death," implicitly incorporates by reference other statutory provisions defining crimes and prescribing their punishments. Section 26's reference to other statutory provisions is general rather than specific. A specific reference would identify by name or by the Penal Code section the crimes to which duress is not a defense. By instead referring generally to "a crime not punishable with death," the Legislature expressed an intention to incorporate the general body of law relating to capital punishment as it might change from time to time.

The question remains, however, whether, as applied to the crime of murder, the phrase "crime ... punishable with death" in section 26 means murder in all its forms or only capital murder.

This question is best answered by applying another settled rule of statutory construction, long accepted by both this court and the United States Supreme Court: "A term appearing in several places in a statutory text is generally read the same way each time it appears." (*Ratzlaf v. U.S.* (1994) 510 U.S. 135.) Here, the Legislature adopted the original Penal Code of 1872 as a single statutory text, and references to crimes "punishable by death" appear in several places in that text. Until now, this court has consistently interpreted this phrase as excluding all noncapital forms of murder.

...

Thus, two established rules of statutory construction resolve the ambiguity in section 26 concerning the availability of duress as a defense to murder. In making duress unavailable for a "crime ... punishable with death," the Legislature intended to bar the defense only as to those murders for which capital punishment was authorized as punishment when the murder was committed. Under current law, the category includes only first degree murders with special circumstances. This conclusion is consistent with every published decision that has in any way spoken to the issue. (See *Tapia v. Roe* (9th Cir.1999) 189 F.3d 1052 [stating that "[a]s defined by California law, duress can excuse crimes, including murder without special circumstances ..."]; *People v. Petro* (1936) 13 Cal.App.2d 245 [stating that duress is unavailable "where the crime charged may be punished with death, and the evidence clearly shows that the death penalty may be imposed"]; see also *People v. Beardslee* (1991) 53 Cal.3d 68 [quoting with apparent approval a standard jury instruction stating that duress is unavailable "[w]here a person commits first degree murder with a special circumstance"].)

II

[Justice Kennard argued that the majority was wrong to treat the 1872 Code on duress as a continuation of the 1850 Act, which, in turn was a continuation of the common law. The 1850 Act was not simply a continuation of the common law because the common law permitted duress as a defense to treason, but the 1850 Act did not. "A code section is presumed to be a continuation of the common law only when it and the common law are *substantially* the same." (*People v. Valentine* (1946) 28 Cal.2d 121, italics added.) Because the duress provision of the 1850 Act was not substantially the same, there is no basis for presuming that it was a continuation of the common law.]

Nor do I agree with the majority that the 1850 Legislature intended duress to remain unavailable as a defense to all those crimes, and only those crimes, that in 1850 were punishable with death, regardless of any later changes in laws relating to capital punishment. Had the 1850 Legislature wanted to exclude the effects of later changes in the scope of capital punishment, it need only have referred by name to the three crimes that the 1850 act made punishable by death—murder, treason, and perjury procuring an innocent person's execution—or to the sections of the 1850 Act defining those crimes.

. . .

III

The majority appears to argue that this court *must* construe section 26 as not permitting the defense of duress to any form of murder because sound considerations of public policy require that no amount of threats or menaces can justify the taking of innocent human life. In my view, such public policy considerations have a very limited role to play in the process of statutory construction. In general, this court may not substitute its public policy views for those of the Legislature under the guise of statutory construction. When the language of a statute is ambiguous, however, this court may prefer a resolution of the ambiguity that avoids absurd consequences or that no reasonable legislative body could have intended.

Here, a construction of section 26 that makes the defense of duress unavailable as to capital murder but available as to noncapital murder does not produce results that are absurd or that no reasonable legislative body could have intended. On the contrary, the question of the proper boundaries or limits on the defense of duress is one on which reasonable minds can differ and have differed, and the construction of section 26 that I have arrived at by applying well-established rules of statutory construction represents a moderate approach in line with mainstream legal thinking.

For example, the Model Penal Code allows the defense of duress to be asserted against *all* criminal charges, including murder. Under the Model Penal Code's formulation of the defense, duress is a defense whenever "a person of reasonable firmness in [the defendant's] situation would have been unable to resist." In the official comment to this provision, the American Law Institute explains that "persons of reasonable firmness surely break at different points depending on the stakes that are involved"; it further observes "that even homicide may sometimes be the product of coercion that is truly irresistible, that danger to a loved one may have greater impact on a person of reasonable firmness than a danger to himself, and, finally, that long and wasting pressure may break down resistance more effectively than a threat of immediate destruction."

The states of Connecticut, New York, North Dakota, Tennessee, Texas, and Utah have adopted statutes similar to the Model Penal Code allowing duress as a defense to homicide. Also, the laws of most civil law countries—including Belgium, Greece, the Netherlands, Germany, Switzerland and Sweden—recognize duress as a defense to any crime, including murder.

As a leading commentator on the law of duress has stated, "[d]uress always is a matter of line drawing about which reasonable minds can differ" (Dressler, *Exegesis of the Law of Duress: Justifying the Excuse and Searching for Its Proper Limits* (1989) 62 So. Cal. L. Rev. 1331). Indeed, the weight of scholarly commentary favors the Model Penal Code's definition of duress and its abolition of the common law murder exception to the duress defense.

I do not here suggest that the Legislature should adopt the Model Penal Code approach, under which duress is available as a defense to any crime, including capital murder. I suggest only that a construction of section 26 under which duress is a defense to noncapital murder, but not to capital murder, represents a moderate, middle-of-the road approach that a legislative body plausibly could have adopted to resolve a difficult and complex issue on which reasonable minds may differ.

The majority's discussion appears to assume that murder necessarily involves a *choice* to take an innocent life. Second degree murder, however, does not require an intent to kill. A person who engages in a provocative act (see *People v. Nieto Benitez* (1992) 4 Cal.4th 91) or who drives with great recklessness (see *People v. Watson* (1981) 30 Cal.3d 290) may be convicted of second degree murder under an implied malice theory. Yet, under the majority's construction, section 26 does not allow a duress defense even in situations of unintentional implied malice killings.

Imagine, for example, this scenario: Two armed robbers fleeing the scene of a store robbery force their way into a car that is leaving the parking lot. One robber holds a gun to the driver's head, while the other places a gun against the head of the driver's wife. They order the driver to take off at high speed and not to stop or slow down for stop signs or signal lights, threatening immediate death to the driver and his wife. If the driver complies, and an accident ensues resulting in the death of an innocent person, the driver could be prosecuted for second degree murder on an implied malice theory, and, under the majority's construction of section 26, the driver could not assert duress as a defense. I doubt that our Legislature intended to withhold the defense of duress under these or similar circumstances.

The majority expresses concern that if defendants can assert a duress defense to noncapital murder, the defense may be used to excuse killings by gang members. But most if not all gang-motivated killings are capital murder because it is a special circumstance that "the defendant intentionally killed the victim while the defendant was an active participant in a criminal street gang ... and the murder was carried out to further the activities of the criminal street gang." Moreover, the defense of duress is not available to a defendant who recklessly or intentionally placed himself in a situation where coercion to commit criminal acts could reasonably be anticipated. Because persons who join criminal street gangs or terrorist organizations can anticipate pressure to commit crimes, the defense would usually be unavailable to those individuals.

IV

Because, as I have concluded, duress is a defense to noncapital murder, a defendant charged with noncapital murder is entitled to a jury instruction on the defense if there is substantial evidence to support it. This means "evidence from which a jury composed of reasonable [people] could have concluded that there was [duress] sufficient to negate the requisite criminal intent." (*People v. Flannel* (1979) 25 Cal.3d 668.) Under section 26, the defense of duress is only available to defendants who present evidence of threats or menace sufficient to show a reasonable and actual belief that their life was presently and immediately endangered if participation was refused.

Here, defendant failed to present substantial evidence of duress. He testified that Ron Kiern told him, "Give me the rock or I'll beat the s___ out of you" and that he complied because he feared that Kiern, a stronger and bigger man, would beat him severely. Yet, Kiern did not threaten him with death, and there was no history of violence between the two men despite their long acquaintance. In addition, defendant voluntarily joined Kiern in the initial attack on the victim, thereby placing himself in the situation where he should have anticipated that Kiern would pressure him to commit further acts of violence. Throughout the day, defendant made no use of opportunities to leave Kiern and to obtain help for the victim.

Because defendant presented insufficient evidence of duress to warrant a jury instruction on that defense, I agree with the majority that the Court of Appeal properly affirmed defendant's conviction.

...

Notes and Problems

Scope of the Duress Defense. Although § 26, by its terms, applies only to threats to the life of the defendant, the courts have assumed that the defense could be asserted based on imminent and immediate threats to the life of a third party. See, *e.g.*, *People v. Coffman*, 34 Cal.4th 1, 100 (2004). Could a defendant assert a duress defense on the basis that he or she was threatened with serious, but non-lethal, harm? The statute would seem to rule out a duress defense in that situation; but the *Anderson* court, quoting LaFave, seems to hold that duress is a "choice of evils" defense, in which case, might the defendant have a defense to a minor crime even if the threat was less than one on his/her life? Justice Kennard, in her dissent, assumes that there is a limit on the defense not stated in § 26: "duress is not available to a defendant who recklessly or intentionally placed himself in a situation where coercion to commit criminal acts could reasonably be anticipated." Is this a reasonable interpretation of the statute?

The Model Penal Code and Duress. The Model Penal Code defines the defense as follows:

> **§ 2.09. Duress**
>
> (1) It is an affirmative defense that the actor engaged in the conduct charged to constitute an offense because he was coerced to do so by the use of, or a threat to use, unlawful force against his person or the person of another, which a person of reasonable firmness in his situation would have been unable to resist.
>
> (2) The defense provided by this Section is unavailable if the actor recklessly placed himself in a situation in which it was probable that he would be subjected to duress. The defense is also unavailable if he was negligent in placing himself in such a situation, whenever negligence suffices to establish culpability for the offense charged.

....

How does the California approach compare with that of the Model Penal Code?

Problem 81.

Defendant was one of thirty people in a bar when Killer shot and killed Victim, but he was the only one who was willing to testify against Killer before the grand jury. Subsequently, Defendant and his family received death threats from Killer's friends, and Defendant told the prosecutor he could not testify at Killer's trial. The prosecutor had Defendant arrested as a material witness and held in jail on high bail. Defendant then agreed to testify and was released from jail. At Killer's trial, Defendant first begged the judge not to make him testify and, when he was ordered to testify, he recanted his previous testimony and testified that he could not identify Killer as the murderer. Defendant has now been charged with perjury. (P.C. § 118.) What arguments should be made on his defense of duress?

Problem 82.

Defendant and Victim, prison inmates, were students in the prison metal shop class. While Victim was receiving instruction from the shop teacher, Defendant struck Victim on the back of the head with a hammer. Defendant is charged with assault with a deadly weapon by a prisoner serving a sentence less than life (P. C. § 4501), and he proposes to introduce the following evidence in support of his defenses of self-defense and duress: (1) Victim had previously threatened him with a hammer and later attacked him, (2) other inmates threatened to kill Defendant if he failed to "settle the problem with" Victim or if he sought protective custody, (3) Defendant had been warned that Victim planned to attack him with a "shank" concealed in the metal shop, and (4) Defendant reported to prison authorities that Victim had attacked him, but the authorities had failed to do anything about it. What arguments should be made as to whether Defendant should be permitted to present the defenses?

Chapter 12

Affirmative Defenses—Part II

The three otherwise very different affirmative defenses in this chapter have this in common: they all place the burden of proof on the defendant to prove the defense by a preponderance of the evidence. Section A addresses the necessity ("choice of evils") defense. Section B covers the defenses arising from the over-involvement of the police in generating the crime charged: the entrapment defense and the related due process claim of "outrageous police conduct." Section C explores the defense of insanity and its consequences.

A. Necessity

The defenses of necessity and duress [Chapter 11] are often confused, and, in fact, were confused by the court in the second case in this section. In *United States v. Bailey*, 444 U.S. 394, 409 (1980), the United States Supreme Court explained the difference between the two defenses:

> Common law historically distinguished between the defenses of duress and necessity. Duress was said to excuse criminal conduct where the actor was under an unlawful threat of imminent death or serious bodily injury, which threat caused the actor to engage in conduct violating the literal terms of the criminal law. While the defense of duress covered the situation where the coercion had its source in the actions of other human beings, the defense of necessity, or choice of evils, traditionally covered the situation where physical forces beyond the actor's control rendered illegal conduct the lesser of two evils. Thus, where A destroyed a dike because B threatened to kill him if he did not, A would argue that he acted under duress, whereas if A destroyed the dike in order to protect more valuable property from flooding, A could claim a defense of necessity.

See generally LaFave & Scott, Handbook on Criminal Law, 374–84 (1972). *People v. Lovercamp*, a prison escape case, is the first California case to recognize a necessity defense. *People v. Pena* considers a necessity defense to a drunk driving charge and sets out the standards for establishing the defense. In *People v. Heath*, the court explains the difference between necessity and duress.

People v. Lovercamp

43 Cal. App. 3d 823, 118 Cal. Rptr. 110 (1974)

GARDNER, P.J.

Defendant and her codefendant, Ms. Wynashe, were convicted by a jury of escape from the California Rehabilitation Center (Welf. & Inst. Code, § 3002).

Defendant and Ms. Wynashe were inmates of the California Rehabilitation Center. They departed from that institution and were promptly captured in a hayfield a few yards away. At trial, they made the following offer of proof:

They had been in the institution about two and one-half months and during that time they had been threatened continuously by a group of lesbian inmates who told them they were to perform lesbian acts—the exact expression was "f___ or fight." They complained to the authorities several times but nothing was done about their complaints. On the day of the escape, 10 or 15 of these lesbian inmates approached them and again offered them the alternative—"f___ or fight." This time there was a fight, the results of which were not outlined in the offer of proof. After the fight, Ms. Wynashe and defendant were told by this group of lesbians that they "would see the group again." At this point, both defendant and Ms. Wynashe feared for their lives. Ms. Wynashe was additionally motivated by a protective attitude toward defendant Lovercamp who had the intelligence of a 12-year-old. It was represented that a psychiatrist would testify as to defendant's mental capacity. On the basis of what had occurred, the threats made, the fact that officials had not done anything for their protection, Ms. Wynashe and defendant felt they had no choice but to leave the institution in order to save themselves.

As indicated, they did leave and were promptly captured.

Citing *People v. Richards* (1969) 269 Cal. App. 2d 768, and *People v. Whipple* (1929) 100 Cal. App. 261, the court rejected the offer of proof. The defendants then offered no evidence. The case was submitted to the jury and to the surprise of no one the jury found both defendants guilty.

While defendant makes several contentions on appeal, one is dispositive—the offer of proof. Other issues presented may or may not recur on retrial.

Some preliminary observations are in order.

When our culture abandoned such unpleasantries as torture, dismemberment, maiming and flogging as punishment for antisocial behavior and substituted in their place loss of liberty, certain problems immediately presented themselves. As a "civilized" people, we demanded that incarceration be under reasonably safe and humane conditions. On the other hand, we recognized that the institutional authorities must be afforded a certain firmness of program by which the malefactors be kept where sentenced for the allotted period of time. Realizing that a certain percentage of penal inmates are going to be uncooperative, disruptive and, in some cases, downright dangerous, we invested our institutional officials with disciplinary powers over inmates far above any such powers granted to governmental authorities outside prison walls.

It is hardly earth shattering to observe that prisons are not Brownie Camps and that within the inmate population are those who, if given the opportunity, will depart without due process of law. Therefore, as an aid to prison authorities and to discourage self-help release from incarceration, the offense of escape was born. Simply stated, if an inmate intentionally leaves lawful custody, he commits a new crime.

However, rather early in the legal history of the offense of escape, it became clear that all departures from lawful custody were not necessarily escapes or, to put it more accurately, there was a possible defense to an escape charge, to wit, necessity. In 1 Hale P.C. 611 (1736), it was written that if a prison caught fire and a prisoner departed to save his life, the necessity to save his life "excuseth the felony." So, too, we may assume that a prisoner with his back to the wall, facing a gang of fellow inmates approaching him with drawn knives, who are making it very clear that they intend to kill him, might be expected to go over the wall rather than remain and be a martyr to the principle of prison discipline.

However, the doctrine of necessity to "excuseth the felony" carried with it the seeds of mischief. It takes little imagination to conjure stories which could be used to indicate that to the subjective belief of the prisoner conditions in prison are such that escape becomes a necessity. Inevitably, severe limitations were affixed to this defense and the general rule evolved that intolerable living conditions in prison afforded no justification for escape. A reading of the cases invoking this rule presents a harsh commentary on prison life in these United States of America, revealing (with proper consideration of the sources of the complaints), prison life which is harsh, brutal, filthy, unwholesome and inhumane. A fair sampling of the authorities indicate that the defense has been rejected in cases involving unsanitary conditions in jail—"a filthy, unwholesome and loathsome place, full of vermin and uncleanliness"; fear of being shot; unmerited punishment at the hands of the custodian; or escape from solitary confinement when the cell was infested with bugs, worms and vermin and when the toilet was flushed the contents ran out on the floor; extremely bad food, guard brutality, inadequate medical treatment and inadequate recreational and educational programs. Under the above general rule, none of these situations excused the felony.

Traditionally, the courts have balanced the interests of society against the immediate problems of the escaping defendant. This has tended to focus attention away from the immediate choices available to the defendant and the propriety of his cause of action. Thus, reprehensible conditions have been found to be insufficient to justify the escape, the public interest outweighing the defendant's interest.

In a humane society some attention must be given to the individual dilemma. In doing so the court must use extreme caution lest the overriding interest of the public be overlooked. The question that must be resolved involves looking to all the choices available to the defendant and then determining whether the act of escape was the only viable and reasonable choice available. By doing so, both the public's interest and the individual's interest may adequately be protected. In our ultimate conclusion it will be seen that we have adopted a position which gives reasonable consideration to both interests. While we conclude that under certain circumstances a defense of necessity may be proven by the defendant, at the same time we place rigid limitations on the viability of the defense in order to insure that the rights and interests of society will not be impinged upon. We have not formulated a new rule of law but rather have applied rules long ago established in a manner which effects fundamental justice.

In California, the two leading authorities are *People v. Richards* and *People v. Whipple*.

Mr. Whipple escaped because he was the victim of "brutal treatment of extreme atrocity." The opinion was written at a time (1929) when writers, legal or otherwise, with a fine feeling for the delicacy of their readers left much to the imagination. Therefore, we are left to speculate as to the specific nature of the "brutal treatment of extreme atrocity" to which Mr. Whipple had been subjected. However, whatever treatment Mr. Whipple had received, it had occurred in a remote mountain camp where a complaint was useless.[1] He departed. His sole defense was that the conditions existing at the camp together with his brutal and inhumane treatment made his imprisonment intolerable and therefore justified the escape. The trial court instructed the jury that an escape founded on any alleged unsanitary condition or alleged harsh, brutal or inhumane treatment received by him at the hands of his custodian would constitute no defense to the charge.

On appeal, the court recognized that, generally speaking, "absolute necessity" would excuse the commission of a crime but insofar as an escape from jail was concerned, the authorities were in "practical accord" in holding that ordinary adverse circumstances did not afford such a defense. The court concluded that even if the conditions of imprisonment were so unwholesome as to seriously imperil the health and life of the prisoner or that prison guards might subject him to unjustifiable abuse or even serious physical injury, he escapes for those reasons "at his peril." Therefore, it was "with very great reluctance" that the judgment of conviction was affirmed.

Turning to the more specific problem of escape based on an alleged threat of forcible sexual attack, the reported cases reflect an attitude of the courts which might charitably be characterized as viewing it with alarm but with results varying from benign neglect to dynamic inertia.

In *Richards, supra*, an offer of proof was made that acts of sodomy had been inflicted on the defendant, that he complained but the guards would do nothing about it, that he had been threatened with death and that he had exhausted every possible remedy short of escape to avoid the threat of death. The trial court refused the offer of proof and refused an instruction on necessity.

Richards affirmed, rejecting the claim of necessity and observed that the principle of justification by necessity, if applicable, involved a determination that the harm or evil sought to be avoided by such conduct is greater than that sought to be prevented

1. The court observed that while he had made no complaint, the opportunity for effective complaint was to all intents and purposes nonexistent.

by the law defining the offense charged. So viewed, the court concluded that the crime of escape was a greater harm than the threat of sexual assault, and that the prisoner "... should be relegated to relief through established administrative channels, or, that failing, through the courts."

However, as the Attorney General concedes, there is oblique dicta in *Richards* which perhaps by negative implication suggests that if a prisoner were in immediate fear of his life or significant bodily injury and if no alternative course was availing, then perhaps the evidence might form a sufficient defense. Unfortunately for Mr. Richards, the court did not feel that the evidence was such that such a defense could be presented to the jury.

[The court discussed three out-of-state prison escape cases. In *State v. Green*, 470 S.W.2d 565 (Mo. 1971), the defendant had been a victim of a series of forceful acts of sodomy committed on him by numerous inmates. He had attempted to complain to the authorities who merely told him to "'fight it out, submit to the assaults, or go over the fence.'" On the day of escape, a group of four or five inmates told him that they would be at his cell that night and he would submit to their homosexual desires or they would kill or seriously harm him. The Missouri Supreme Court rejected the defendant's defense of necessity because, at the time of the escape, he was not "being closely pursued." In *People v. Noble*, 170 N.W.2d 916 (Mich. App. 1969), the Michigan Court of Appeal followed the same rationale in a case in which the defendant fled a prison work camp in desperation to avoid homosexual attacks by other prisoners. In *People v. Harmon*, 220 N.W.2d 212 (Mich. App. 1974), another panel of the Michigan Court of Appeal permitted the defendant to go to the jury on a defense of necessity on a showing that the defendant had been beaten and kicked by other inmates and was threatened with continued beatings if he did not give in to the inmates' sexual demands.]

We ... conclude that the defense of necessity to an escape charge is a viable defense. However, before Lovercamp becomes a household word in prison circles and we are exposed to the spectacle of hordes of prisoners leaping over the walls screaming "rape," we hasten to add that the defense of necessity to an escape charge is extremely limited in its application. This is because of the rule that upon attaining a position of safety from the immediate threat, the prisoner must promptly report to the proper authorities.

In *People v. Wester* (1965) 237 Cal. App. 2d 232, the court approved a jury instruction to the effect that even though a prisoner escapes to save his life, "'... a further, continued wilful and intentional departure from the limits of custody by him will constitute the crime of escape.'" The court held that such a prisoner escaping against his will would owe a duty to use reasonable efforts to render himself again to the custody of the law enforcement agency at the first available opportunity. Thus, the defense becomes meaningless to one who would use it as an excuse to depart from lawful custody and thereafter go his merry way relieved of any responsibility for his unseemingly departure. A prisoner cannot escape from a threat of death, homosexual attack or other significant bodily injury and live the rest of his life with an ironclad defense to an escape charge.

From all of the above, we hold that the proper rule is that a limited defense of necessity is available if the following conditions exist:

(1) The prisoner is faced with a specific threat of death, forcible sexual attack or substantial bodily injury in the immediate future;

(2) There is no time for a complaint to the authorities or there exists a history of futile complaints which make any result from such complaints illusory;

(3) There is no time or opportunity to resort to the courts;

(4) There is no evidence of force or violence used towards prison personnel or other "innocent" persons in the escape; and

(5) The prisoner immediately reports to the proper authorities when he has attained a position of safety from the immediate threat.

...

Whether any of the conditions requisite to this defense exist is a question of fact to be decided by the trier of fact after taking into consideration all the surrounding circumstances. The offer of proof in the instant case was sufficient to require the submission of this defense to the jury in an appropriate manner. The trial court erred in not submitting this matter to the jury.

...

Notes

The Necessity Defense Explained. The policy behind the necessity defense was described by the Ninth Circuit as follows:

> Necessity is, essentially, a utilitarian defense. It therefore justifies criminal acts taken to avert a greater harm, maximizing social welfare by allowing a crime to be committed where the social benefits of the crime outweigh the social costs of failing to commit the crime. Pursuant to the defense, prisoners could escape a burning prison; a person lost in the woods could steal food from a cabin to survive; an embargo could be violated because adverse weather conditions necessitated sale of the cargo at a foreign port; a crew could mutiny where their ship was thought to be unseaworthy; and property could be destroyed to prevent the spread of fire. [Citing a case for each example.]
>
> What all the traditional necessity cases have in common is that the commission of the "crime" averted the occurrence of an even greater "harm." In some sense, the necessity defense allows us to act as individual legislatures, amending a particular criminal provision or crafting a one-time exception to it, subject to court review, when a real legislature would formally do the same under those circumstances. For example, by allowing prisoners who escape a burning jail to claim the justification of necessity, we assume the lawmaker, confronting this problem, would have allowed for an exception to the law proscribing prison escapes.

Because the necessity doctrine is utilitarian, however, strict requirements contain its exercise so as to prevent nonbeneficial criminal conduct. For example, "[i]f the criminal act cannot abate the threatened harm, society receives no benefit from the criminal conduct." Note, *Applying the Necessity Defense to Civil Disobedience Cases*, 64 N.Y.U. L. Rev. 79, 102 (1989). Similarly, to forgive a crime taken to avert a lesser harm would fail to maximize social utility. The cost of the crime would outweigh the harm averted by its commission. Likewise, criminal acts cannot be condoned to thwart threats, yet to be imminent, or those for which there are legal alternatives to abate the harm.

United States v. Schoon, 939 F.2d 826, 828–29 (9th Cir. 1991).

The Model Penal Code and Necessity. The Model Penal Code defines the defense as follows:

§ 3.02. Justification Generally: Choice of Evils

(1) Conduct which the actor believes to be necessary to avoid a harm or evil to himself or to another is justifiable, provided that:

(a) the harm or evil sought to be avoided by such conduct is greater than that sought to be prevented by the law defining the offense charged; and

(b) neither the Code nor other law defining the offense provides exceptions or defenses dealing with the specific situation involved; and

(c) a legislative purpose to exclude the justification claimed does not otherwise plainly appear.

(2) When the actor was reckless or negligent in bringing about the situation requiring a choice of harms or evils or in appraising the necessity for his conduct, the justification afforded by this Section is unavailable in a prosecution for any offense for which recklessness or negligence, as the case may be, suffices to establish culpability.

People v. Pena

149 Cal. App. 3d Supp. 14, 197 Cal. Rptr. 264 (1983)

BERNSTEIN, J.

Appellant, Russell David Pena, appeals his conviction for violation of former Vehicle Code section 23102, subdivision (a), driving under the influence of intoxicating liquor. Appellant contends the trial court erred in refusing his proferred jury instruction regarding appellant's theory of his defense. That theory was predicated on the presumed availability of what is generally termed the defense of duress.[2] We hold that

2. In this opinion, "duress" is used interchangeably with terms such as "coercion," "compulsion," "necessity" or "justification." Although there are some distinctions, they are not material for purposes of this opinion. [As the Court of Appeal explains in the following case, *People v. Heath*, the terms are not interchangeable and the *Pena* court was in fact explaining and applying the necessity defense.

the defense was indeed available to appellant, and that the evidence adduced at trial mandated a jury instruction on the subject. Accordingly, we reverse the judgment of conviction.

...

The evidence presented at appellant's trial was essentially undisputed. Los Angeles County Sheriff's Deputy Frank Webb testified that he first encountered appellant at approximately 4 a.m. on November 1, 1981. Webb, on patrol in Pico Rivera, observed appellant and Sara Marrufo, appellant's girlfriend, asleep in a parked car. Webb stated that "due to the late hour," he decided to investigate the situation. He exited his patrol vehicle and approached the parked car, at which time he stated that he smelled alcohol. Webb then ordered the occupants, appellant and Sara, to exit their vehicle and demanded to see written identification. Both parties complied. Following this, Webb undertook a search of the "suspects" assertedly to ascertain if either of them were in possession of "weapons." Sara, at the time she was subjected to Deputy Webb's "weapons search," was dressed in a somewhat unusual manner. She was wearing a long fur coat and, according to the engrossed statement, "was semi-nude thereunder, wearing only a very brief see-through teddy nightgown" (Sara testified that she and appellant had attended a Halloween costume party earlier in the evening, and that her costume was supposed to be that of a "flasher"). Webb ordered Sara to open her coat, which she did very briefly. Webb thereupon ordered her to again open her coat and to keep it open. Deputy Webb then examined Sara's body with his flashlight. Following this examination, the deputy turned Sara around and pulled her coat up from the rear and continued his examination with the flashlight.

During his interrogation and search of appellant and Sara Marrufo, Deputy Webb ascertained the following:

1. The vehicle in which appellant and his girlfriend had been sleeping was registered to Sara's sister;
2. Appellant lived "about one block" from the location of the events above described;
3. Sara lived about three miles from the location;
4. Sara's identification showed her to be 20 years of age.

Deputy Webb concluded the encounter by ordering Sara to enter his vehicle inasmuch as the deputy had decided to take Sara home. Webb's only asserted reason for this action was that it was for Sara's "protection."[9] Webb drove from the scene with Sara in tow, leaving appellant in possession of Sara's sister's vehicle.

Appellant testified that he followed Webb and Sara in the sister's car. His reason for doing so was his fear for the physical safety of his girlfriend. Appellant had observed

---

Consequently, for the convenience of the reader, "necessity" will be substituted for the court's labeling of the defense throughout this opinion.—**Ed.**]

9. The record is devoid of any suggestion that Deputy Webb possessed the legal authority to take Sara home, or anywhere else, against her wishes.

Webb's earlier weapons search of Sara; it is at this point the only conflict in the evidence develops. Deputy Webb testified that he drove Sara directly home and only after this, while "exiting Sara Marrufo's doorway," did he observe "an unusual black shadow" which proved to be appellant. Appellant was sitting in the vehicle earlier described, with the motor running. Recalling the alcohol odor at the scene of his original encounter with appellant and Sara, Webb felt that appellant had driven to his current location while under the influence of alcohol. He ordered appellant out of the vehicle and, according to Webb, thereupon administered field sobriety tests which appellant failed. Webb then arrested appellant. Subsequently, appellant took an "intoxilyzer" (breath) test which showed appellant's blood alcohol level to be approximately .15.

However, according to Sara, Webb stopped his car "by some railroad tracks"; at that point, Webb observed appellant to be following them. Webb stated to Sara that appellant "would be made sorry" for following them. Webb then started his vehicle up again and drove to Sara's residence.

Appellant testified concerning his arrest by Webb as follows: After he was ordered out of the car in which he had followed Webb and Sara, appellant was immediately arrested and handcuffed by Webb. Appellant asserted that no field sobriety tests were administered to him by Webb, although he admitted to Webb that he had consumed several beers at the Halloween party he had earlier attended with Sara.

… [A]ppellant requested that the following instructions be given to the jury:

> "Evidence has been received to the effect that the reason defendant, Russell Pena, drove the car was because he believed that Sara Marrufo was in physical danger.
>
> "You are hereby instructed that if you find that it has been established by a preponderance of the evidence that the defendant had a good faith belief that Sara Marrufo might be in physical danger, and drove the car for her protection or to render possible aid, then you may acquit him based on this defense."

The trial court not only refused appellant's tendered instruction, but further instructed the jury, upon the panel's inquiry during its deliberations, that the defense of "justification" was in fact no defense to the charge.

The sole question on appeal is whether the trial court committed reversible error in refusing to instruct the jury, either by way of appellant's tendered instruction or a similar, court fashioned charge, regarding the applicability of the defense of [necessity].

Upon Proper Evidentiary Showing the Defense of [Necessity] Is Available to Any Criminal Charge Other Than a Capital Offense

…

Although California law regarding the "justification" defenses (i.e., "duress," "necessity," "compulsion," etc.) appears sparse in comparison to that of most American jurisdictions, there nonetheless exist several Court of Appeal decisions which provide some guidance as to the parameters of those defenses—most recently the court in *People v. Patrick* (1981) 126 Cal.App.3d 952, noted that:

> [Although] the exact confines of the necessity defense remain clouded, a well-established central element involves the emergency nature of the situation, i.e., the imminence of the greater harm which the illegal act seeks to prevent. The commission of a crime cannot be countenanced where there exists the possibility of some alternate means to alleviate the threatened greater harm.

In the leading California case regarding the applicability of the [necessity] defense to a charge of prison escape, *People v. Lovercamp* (1974) 43 Cal. App. 3d 823, the court fashioned a five part judicial test for determining the availability of the defense. In such cases, the *Lovercamp* court observed that it was not formulating a new rule of law, but rather was applying "rules long ago established in a manner which effects fundamental justice." ...

Two issues of apparent first impression in this jurisdiction must be addressed before disposition of the instant appeal can be effected:

(1) Is the [necessity] defense available to a defendant charged with misdemeanor driving under the influence?

(2) Is the [necessity] defense available to a defendant who commits an unlawful act in an effort to prevent imminent harm to a third party?

With respect to the first question, it appears settled that the [necessity] defense is available to a defendant charged with any crime except one which involves the taking of the life of an innocent person ...

Thus, we hold that the defense of [necessity], is available, presuming other requisites of such a defense are satisfied, where a defendant is charged with the violation of Vehicle Code section 23152, subdivision (a).

The [Necessity] Defense Is Applicable to Situations in Which the Threatened Harm Is to Persons Other Than the Defendant

It appears that no California case has directly addressed the question of whether the [necessity] defense is available in situations wherein the coercive circumstances arise from threatened harm not to the defendant personally, but to some party other than the accused. The classic example is that of a bank teller whose child has been kidnapped. The kidnapers order the teller to use his position of trust at the bank to embezzle money for the kidnapers. The teller is informed that his child will be killed if he does not comply with the demands. The teller himself is not threatened with bodily harm. Would an embezzlement under such circumstances constitute a crime?

It appears that virtually every jurisdiction in which the issue has been settled permits threats to third parties to satisfy the requisite coercive circumstance requirement so as to bring the [necessity] defense into play. Perhaps the best articulation of the rationale for permitting threats to persons other than the defendant to allow invocation of these defenses, appears in a Massachusetts case, *Commonwealth v. Martin* (Mass. 1976) 341 N.E.2d 885:

"Whatever the precise precedents, it is hardly conceivable that the law of the Commonwealth, or, indeed, of any jurisdiction, should mark as criminal those who intervene forcibly to protect others; for the law to do so would aggravate the fears which lead to the alienation of people from one another, an alienation symbolized for our time by the notorious Genovese incident.[a] To the fear of "involvement" and of injury to oneself if one answered a call for help would be added the fear of possible criminal prosecution."

...

In the case at bench, the People contend that Penal Code section 26[11] restricts the application of duress type defenses to cases in which the defendant's person is the object of coercive threats of bodily harm. The People's argument cannot withstand scrutiny. To begin, nothing in the language of section 26 can be construed as limiting the applicability of the duress-necessity defenses to the circumstances therein described. The section merely enumerates the classes of persons who, under the circumstances contemplated by the statute, are incapable of committing acts which constitute crimes. Nothing in the statute can be read to require the conclusion that a person not so enumerated, *i.e.*, a person who is capable of committing a crime, has in fact committed one by his action in a given case. Indeed, other sections of the Penal Code explicitly authorize, under certain circumstances, the commission of acts which ordinarily would constitute crimes. In particular, we refer to Penal Code sections 692–694:

"Lawful resistance to the commission of a public offense may be made:

1. By the party about to be injured;

2. By other parties." (Pen. Code, § 692.)

"Resistance sufficient to prevent the offense may be made by the party about to be injured:

1. To prevent an offense against his person, or his family, or some member thereof.

2. To prevent an illegal attempt by force to take or injure property in his lawful possession." (Pen. Code, § 693.)

---

a. The court is referring to the 1964 murder of Kitty Genovese, who was attacked on a residential street by a man wielding a hunting knife and, ten minutes later, was sexually assaulted and killed in the foyer of an apartment building where she had fled. A number of Genovese's neighbors, awakened by her screams, saw portions of the attacks, but no one intervened, and no one called the police until long after the assailant fled.

11. Penal Code section 26 provides:

"All persons are capable of committing crimes except those belonging to the following classes:

...

"Six—Persons (unless the crime be punishable with death) who committed the act or made the omission charged under threats or menaces sufficient to show that they had reasonable cause to and did believe their lives would be endangered if they refused."

"Any other person, in aid or defense of the person about to be injured, may make resistance sufficient to prevent the offense." (Pen. Code, §694.)

Case law construing the above quoted sections of the Penal Code uniformly holds that it is not necessary that the threatened harm be actual, only that it reasonably appear so: "Justification does not depend on the existence of actual danger but on appearance." *People v. Collins* (1961) 189 Cal.App.2d 575.

We hold that a defense of [necessity] may properly be predicated upon threats of harm to persons other than the accused.

Elements of the [Necessity] Defense

The following requirements have traditionally been held to be prerequisites to the establishment of the defense of [necessity]:

1. The act charged as criminal must have been done to prevent a significant evil;
2. There must have been no adequate alternative to the commission of the act;
3. The harm caused by the act must not be disproportionate to the harm avoided;
4. The accused must entertain a good-faith belief that his act was necessary to prevent the greater harm;
5. Such belief must be objectively reasonable under all the circumstances; and
6. The accused must not have substantially contributed to the creation of the emergency.

These determinations are for the trier of fact.

. . .

Appellant Was Entitled to an Instruction on the Defense of [Necessity].

We now evaluate the merits of the instant appeal in light of the foregoing legal principles. Appellant would be entitled to an acquittal of the charge against him, notwithstanding the fact of his operation of a motor vehicle while legally intoxicated, if he could convince the jury of the truth of the following:

(1) That he held a genuine belief that Sara Marrufo was in danger of assault by or through Deputy Webb;

(2) That appellant's good faith belief was objectively reasonable under the totality of the circumstances;

(3) That appellant operated his vehicle in obedience to his fear for Sara's safety and not for any other purpose;

(4) That appellant had no opportunity to engage alternative legal means of protecting Sara from the danger he believed she faced;

(5) That appellant was not substantially at fault in the creation of the emergency situation which he claims justifies his action in driving while intoxicated.

We observe that the requirement that appellant's fear be an objectively reasonable one does not require that appellant be in fact correct in his assessment of the situation.

Rather, as in any situation where a defendant claims as his defense that the charged acts were justified as having been undertaken in response to some emergency circumstance (i.e., self-defense), the defendant may rely on what he reasonably believes to be true. Whether appellant, in the instant case, had a reasonable belief that Sara was in danger from Deputy Webb is a question of fact. That Webb seemed clearly to be an on-duty police officer may be a factor to consider in assessing the reasonableness of defendant's fear, but it is certainly not the only such factor.[16] Other considerations which the jury could properly weigh include the credibility of Deputy Webb's asserted reason for taking Sara from the scene against her apparent wishes, the reasonableness or unreasonableness of Webb's detention and search of appellant and Sara and the character of his search of Sara in particular.

We note that in appellant's first trial the jury, during its deliberations, returned to the courtroom and requested from the court instructions on the "defense of justification." The court advised the jury that the defense of justification was not available as a defense to the charge. The first jury was unable to reach a verdict. At the second trial, we know from the docket, that the jury experienced considerable difficulty in dealing with the instructions. We also know that at both trials there was a request from the appellant for a specific instruction on the defense of [necessity] and that the instruction was refused. In view of the fact that [necessity] was appellant's only defense, it was error for the trial court to refuse to instruct the jury regarding the availability of this defense.

...

Problem

Problem 83.

Defendant, an ex-felon, picked up Friend to accompany him on a trip to visit his brother in the hospital. A week earlier he had encouraged Friend to buy and carry with her a gun to protect herself from her ex-husband. Friend had the gun with her, and she also had a six-pack of "strawberry daiquiris," which they began to consume. When they arrived at the hospital, Defendant informed Friend that she couldn't take the gun inside, and she put it in the glove compartment of the car. On their way out of the hospital 45 minutes later, Defendant noticed that Friend was stumbling and talking funny and giggling inappropriately. Defendant decided that he should not return the gun to her in her condition, so he put it in his pocket. A short time later, Defendant was pulled over for suspected drunk driving and subsequently arrested for possession of the gun. Defendant is now charged with being a felon in possession of a gun. (P.C. § 2900(a).) What are the arguments as to whether Defendant can defend on the basis of necessity?

---

16. Police officers, on duty or otherwise, have been known to commit crimes. Further, recent events demonstrate the possibility that police officers may be impersonated. Thus, we cannot hold that Deputy Webb's status as a law enforcement officer required, as a matter of law, that appellant be convinced of Webb's benign intention toward Sara.

People v. Heath

207 Cal.App.3d 892, 255 Cal. Rptr. 120 (1989)

Baxter, Associate Justice.

[Appellant was convicted of one count of burglary (P.C. § 459).]

STATEMENT OF FACTS

At 8 a.m. on February 10, 1987, Mr. and Mrs. Henry King left their Farmersville residence to drive into Fresno. At approximately 9:10 a.m., Tulare County Deputy Sheriff Mike Renteria responded to a silent alarm at the King residence, observed appellant leaving the house through a broken window, and apprehended him at the scene. Appellant was in possession of coins, jewelry, and a jewelry bag that were taken from the residence.

Appellant admitted committing the burglary to the investigating officers. Sergeant John Zapalac testified that appellant told him that he had acted alone but that Darryl Sodersten had dropped him off in front of the house and told him to break in. Appellant did not tell the officers that he was threatened or forced to commit the burglary.

The prosecutor introduced evidence that appellant, prior to perpetrating this burglary, removed a canvas covering a vehicle in the driveway and a sleeping bag that was kept in a storage shed so as to stake out the residence until its inhabitants left. Sergeant Zapalac testified that he believed appellant first broke into the storage shed, removed the sleeping bag, and spent the night near the house waiting for the Kings to leave. There were shoe tracks indicating that possibly three trips were made between the storage shed and the house. Sergeant Zapalac observed dirt on appellant's shoes and noted that his shoes were similar to the tracks near the sleeping bag.

...

DISCUSSION

I.

WAS IT REVERSIBLE ERROR TO INSTRUCT ON THE DEFENSES OF DURESS AND NECESSITY?

Appellant admitted at trial that he committed the burglary. His defense was that Darryl Sodersten threatened to kill him if he did not commit the burglary.

Appellant's testimony in support of his defense was as follows: He had purchased cocaine on credit from Darryl Sodersten and owed him approximately $400. The night before the burglary appellant paid him $30 and accompanied Sodersten and Mark Demeers in Sodersten's truck for a night of drinking and taking drugs. They drove around for nearly five hours until about 2 a.m. or 3 a.m. when Sodersten started talking about appellant committing a burglary to repay him. Sodersten drove to the King residence, pointed a loaded gun at appellant, and threatened to kill him and throw his body into a ditch if he refused to commit the burglary. Appellant walked toward the house, threw a metal planter through the window, noted that Sodersten and Demeers were watching him, and committed the burglary. He was in the house 10 to 15 minutes and was apprehended by Deputy Renteria shortly after exiting the broken window.

The trial court gave the standard duress instruction, CALJIC No. 4.40, to which there was no objection. It provides, as follows:

> "A person is not guilty of a crime when he engages in conduct, otherwise criminal, when acting under threats and menaces under the following circumstances:
>
> "1. Where the threats and menaces are such that they would cause a reasonable person to fear that his life would be in immediate danger if he did not engage in the conduct charged, and
>
> "2. If such person then believed that his life would be so endangered.
>
> "This rule does not apply to threats, menaces, and fear of future danger to his life."

Over appellant's objection, the court gave a special instruction requested by the prosecutor based on *People v. Pena* (1983) 149 Cal.App.3d Supp. 14. It provides as follows:

> "The following requirements have been held to be prerequisites to the establishment of the defense of justification or duress:
>
> "One, the act charged as criminal must have been done to prevent a significant evil;
>
> "Two, there must have been no adequate alternative to the commission of that act;
>
> "Three, the harm caused by the act must not be disproportionate to the harm avoided;
>
> "Four, the accused must entertain a good faith belief that his act was necessary to prevent the greater harm;
>
> "Five, such belief must be objectively reasonable under all of the circumstances; and,
>
> "Six, the accused must not have substantially contributed to the creation of the emergency."

Appellant contends that the special instruction referred to as "justification/duress" is actually a statement of the defense of necessity and misled the jury as to the correct elements of the proffered duress defense contained in CALJIC No. 4.40.

An analysis of appellant's contention requires three inquiries: (1) the basis of the special instruction; (2) the differences between the duress and necessity defenses; and (3) the possible effect of any instructional error.

A. *The Pena Instruction*

The special instruction requested by the prosecution was taken entirely from *People v. Pena, supra*, in which a defendant charged with misdemeanor drunk driving was denied an instruction that he drove the car in the good faith belief that his girlfriend might be in physical danger and he might need to protect her. The danger he perceived was from a police officer who searched her and drove her home. The circumstances of the search and transportation were sufficiently peculiar to warrant an instruction on the necessity defense.

[The court reviewed the *Pena* holding.]

An analysis of *Pena* clearly shows that its instruction is based on elements of the necessity rather than duress defense. The next question is whether there is any difference between duress and necessity and if such a difference has an effect on the instructions given in the instant case.

B. *Duress and Necessity*

. . .

California cases have clearly distinguished between the defenses of duress and necessity. The defense of duress is recognized by statute in Penal Code section 26, subdivision 6:

> "All persons are capable of committing crimes except those belonging to the following classes:
>
> "...
>
> "Six-Persons (unless the crime be punishable with death) who committed the act or made the omission charged under threats or menaces sufficient to show that they had reasonable cause to and did believe their lives would be endangered if they refused."

The defendant must show that the act was done under such threats or menaces that he had (1) an actual belief his life was threatened and (2) reasonable cause for such belief. A defendant claiming the defense of duress or coercion may properly rely on CALJIC No. 4.40.

Duress is an effective defense only when the actor responds to an immediate and imminent danger. "[A] fear of *future* harm to one's life does not relieve one of responsibility for the crimes he commits." (*People v. Lewis* (1963) 222 Cal.App.2d 136.) The person being threatened has no time to formulate what is a reasonable and viable course of conduct nor to formulate criminal intent. Thus, duress negates an element of the crime charged—the intent or capacity to commit the crime—the defendant need raise only a reasonable doubt that he acted in the exercise of his free will.

The defense of necessity, unlike duress, is not codified in this state. It was first judicially sanctioned as a defense to a nonviolent prison escape in *People v. Lovercamp* (1974) 43 Cal.App.3d 823 and has been recognized in prosecutions for kidnapping and false imprisonment. By definition, the necessity defense is founded upon public policy and provides a justification distinct from the elements required to prove the crime. The situation presented to the defendant must be of an emergency nature, threatening physical harm, and lacking an alternative, legal course of action. The defense involves a determination that the harm or evil sought to be avoided by such conduct is greater than that sought to be prevented by the law defining the offense charged. Necessity does not negate any element of the crime, but represents a public policy decision not to punish such an individual despite proof of the crime.

An important factor of the necessity defense involves the balancing of the harm to be avoided as opposed to the costs of the criminal conduct. Unlike duress, the threatened harm is in the immediate future, which contemplates the defendant having time to balance alternative courses of conduct. The defendant has the time, however limited, to form the general intent required for the crime, although under some outside pressure. Thus, the defense does not negate the intent element, and the defendant has the burden of proving the defense by a preponderance of the evidence.

The defenses of duress and necessity are clearly different. The duress defense, through its immediacy requirement, negates an element of the crime—the intent to commit the act. The defendant does not have the time to form criminal intent because of immediacy and imminency of the threatened harm and need only raise a reasonable doubt as to the existence or nonexistence of this fact. The necessity defense, in contrast, contemplates a threat in the immediate future. The defendant has the time, however limited, to consider alternative courses of conduct. The defendant has the burden of proving necessity by a preponderance of the evidence.

...

C. *Effect of the Pena Instruction*

It is clear after an analysis of *Pena* that the court erred in referring to the special instruction as "justification or duress" rather than "necessity." We conclude, however, that because the instructions correctly listed the elements of both defenses and the jurors had the benefit of both instructions, it is not reasonably probable that a different result would have occurred had the instruction not been mislabeled.

Appellant's own testimony presents sufficient justification to warrant instructions on both the duress and necessity defenses. He was first subject to an immediate and imminent threat to his life when Darryl Sodersten allegedly held a loaded gun to him in the vehicle. Such an imminent threat to his life clearly falls within the ambit of the duress defense. However, after he allegedly left the vehicle, walked to the King's residence, threw the planter through the window to secure entry and rummaged through the house, appellant was no longer subject to the same imminency of harm as when threatened in the vehicle. Once appellant was outside the immediate presence of Sodersten, the threat became one in the immediate future allowing appellant an opportunity, albeit brief, to balance his options, which is the very essence of the necessity defense. Appellant actually benefitted from both instructions because his own testimony negated the imminent harm element consistent with the duress defense.

The jury could have found from the evidence presented that appellant was threatened in the vehicle with death by Sodersten, but that the burglary was not committed by appellant until hours later. Under such circumstances, the necessity instruction would be of more value to appellant than the duress instruction.

It is clear that the jury was not confused by the defense instructions. It deliberated for only 25 minutes before returning a guilty verdict and never asked for further instructions.

In light of the overwhelming evidence against appellant, it is not reasonably probable that a different result would have occurred had the necessity instruction been correctly labeled.

...

B. Entrapment and Due Process

Entrapment is a defense which excuses the defendant's criminal conduct because of police conduct aimed at inducing the defendant to commit the crime. In *People v. Barraza*, the California Supreme Court adopts and explains the "objective" entrapment test (one focused on the police conduct) to be applied in California. In doing so, the Court refuses to follow the United States Supreme Court decisions, which adopted a "subjective" entrapment test (one focused on the predisposition of the defendant) for the federal courts. In *Hampton v. United States*, the defendant conceded he could not prove entrapment under the federal standard, but argued that the conduct of the federal officers was so outrageous as to violate due process.

People v. Barraza

23 Cal. 3d 675, 591 P.2d 947 (1979)

Mosk, J.

...

Count II charged a second sale of heroin on September 11, 1975; both the female agent and the defendant testified that the agent tried to contact defendant by telephoning the Golden State Mental Health Detoxification Center, where he worked as a patient care technician, several times during the three weeks between the dates of the two alleged heroin sale transactions. On September 11, the agent finally succeeded in speaking to defendant and asked him if he had "anything"; defendant asked her to come to the detoxification center. The two then met at the center and talked for some time—a few minutes according to the agent, more than an hour by the defendant's account.

The agent's version of this encounter described defendant as hesitant to deal because "he had done a lot of time in jail and he couldn't afford to go back to jail and ... he had to be careful about what he was doing." She further testified that after she convinced defendant she "wasn't a cop," he gave her a note, to present to a woman named Stella, which read: "Saw Cheryl [the agent]. Give her a pair of pants [argot for heroin]. [signed] Cal." The agent concluded her testimony by stating that she then left defendant, used the note to introduce herself to the dealer Stella, and purchased an orange balloon containing heroin.

Defendant described a somewhat different pattern of interaction with the agent at their September 11th meeting. He related that he had asked her to come and see him because he was "fed up with her" and wanted her to quit calling him at the hospital where he worked because he was afraid she would cause him to lose his job. He insisted he told her during their conversation that he did not have anything; that he had spent more than 23 years in prison but now he had held a job at the detoxification center for four years, was on methadone and was clean, and wanted the agent to stop "bugging" him. He testified that the agent persisted in her efforts to enlist his aid in purchasing heroin, and that finally—after more than an hour of conversation—when the agent asked for a note to introduce her to a source of heroin he agreed to give her a note to "get her off … [his] back." According to the defendant, he told the agent that he did not know if Stella had anything, and gave her a note which read: "Saw Cheryl. If you have a pair of pants, let her have them."

…

II

Defendant urges that his conviction on the second count must be reversed because the trial court erred in failing to instruct the jury *sua sponte* on the defense of entrapment. His contention requires that we reexamine the entrapment doctrine to determine the manner in which the defense must be raised.

Though long recognized by the courts of almost every United States jurisdiction,[1] the defense of entrapment has produced a deep schism concerning its proper theoretical basis and mode of application. The opposing views have been delineated in a series of United States Supreme Court decisions. The court first considered the entrapment defense in *Sorrells v. United States* (1932) 287 U.S. 435. The majority held that entrapment tended to establish innocence, reasoning that Congress in enacting the criminal statute there at issue could not have intended to punish persons otherwise innocent who were lured into committing the proscribed conduct by governmental instigation. This focus on whether persons were "otherwise innocent" led the majority to adopt what has become known as the subjective or origin-of-intent test under which entrapment is established only if (1) governmental instigation and inducement overstep the bounds of permissibility, and (2) the defendant did not harbor a preexisting criminal intent. Under the subjective test a finding that the defendant was predisposed to commit the offense would negate innocence and therefore defeat the

1. The defense appears to have first been asserted by Eve, who complained, when charged with eating fruit of the tree of knowledge of good and evil: "The serpent beguiled me, and I did eat." (Genesis 3:13.) Though Eve was unsuccessful in asserting the defense, it has been suggested that the defense was unavailable to her because the entrapping party was not an agent of the punishing authority.

defense. Finally, because entrapment was viewed as bearing on the guilt or innocence of the accused, the issue was deemed proper for submission to the jury.

Justice Roberts wrote an eloquent concurring opinion, joined by Justices Brandeis and Stone, in which he argued that the purpose of the entrapment defense is to deter police misconduct. He emphatically rejected the notion that the defendant's conduct or predisposition had any relevance: "The applicable principle is that courts must be closed to the trial of a crime instigated by the government's own agents. No other issue, no comparison of equities as between the guilty official and the guilty defendant, has any place in the enforcement of this overruling principle of public policy." Because he viewed deterrence of impermissible law enforcement activity as the proper rationale for the entrapment defense, Justice Roberts concluded that the defense was inappropriate for jury consideration: "It is the province of the court and of the court alone to protect itself and the government from such prostitution of the criminal law."

In *Sherman v. United States* (1958) 356 U.S. 369, the majority refused to adopt the "objective" theory of entrapment urged by Justice Roberts, choosing rather to continue recognizing as relevant the defendant's own conduct and predisposition. The court held that "a line must be drawn between the trap for the unwary innocent and the trap for the unwary criminal." Justice Frankfurter, writing for four members of the court in a concurring opinion, argued forcefully for Justice Roberts' objective theory: "The courts refuse to convict an entrapped defendant, not because his conduct falls outside the proscription of the statute, but because, even if his guilt be admitted, the methods employed on behalf of the Government to bring about conviction cannot be countenanced." He reasoned that "a test that looks to the character and predisposition of the defendant rather than the conduct of the police loses sight of the underlying reason for the defense of entrapment. No matter what the defendant's past record and present inclinations to criminality, or the depths to which he has sunk in the estimation of society, certain police conduct to ensnare him into further crime is not to be tolerated by an advanced society.... Permissible police activity does not vary according to the particular defendant concerned ..." "Human nature is weak enough," he wrote, "and sufficiently beset by temptations without government adding to them and generating crime." Justice Frankfurter concluded that guidance as to appropriate official conduct could only be provided if the court reviewed police conduct and decided the entrapment issue.

The United States Supreme Court recently reviewed the theoretical basis of the entrapment defense in *United States v. Russell* (1973) 411 U.S. 423, and once again the court split five votes to four in declining to overrule the subjective theory adopted in *Sorrells*.

The principle currently applied in California represents a hybrid position, fusing elements of both the subjective and objective theories of entrapment. In *People v. Benford* (1959) 53 Cal. 2d 1, this court unanimously embraced the public policy/deterrence rationale that Justices Roberts and Frankfurter had so persuasively urged. In doing so, we ruled inadmissible on the issue of entrapment the most prejudicial inquiries that are allowed under the subjective theory, i.e., evidence that the defendant "had previously committed similar crimes or had the reputation of being engaged in the commission of such crimes or was suspected by the police of criminal activities...."[2] In *Patty v. Board of Medical Examiners* (1973) 9 Cal. 3d 356, we reiterated the public policy basis for the defense, characterizing it as "crucial to the fair administration of justice." Despite the lessons of *Benford* and *Patty*, however, this court has continued to maintain that entrapment depends upon where the intent to commit the crime originated.

Chief Justice Traynor, dissenting in *People v. Moran* (1970) 1 Cal. 3d 755, in an opinion joined by two other justices of this court, recognized that in thus departing from the rationale adopted in *Benford*, we have seriously undermined the deterrent effect of the entrapment defense on impermissible police conduct. He reasoned that attempts to fix the origin of intent or determine the defendant's criminal predisposition divert the court's attention from the only proper subject of focus in the entrapment defense: the dubious police conduct which the court must deter. The success of an entrapment defense should not turn on differences among defendants; we are not concerned with who first conceived or who willingly, or reluctantly, acquiesced in a criminal project. What we do care about is how much and what manner of persuasion, pressure, and cajoling are brought to bear by law enforcement officials to induce persons to commit crimes. As Chief Justice Warren observed, the function of law enforcement manifestly "does not include the manufacturing of crime" (*Sherman v. United States*). Even though California courts do not permit introduction of the highly prejudicial evidence of subjective predisposition allowed in jurisdictions following the federal rule, our more limited focus on the character and intent of the accused is still misplaced and impairs our courts in their task of assuring the lawfulness of law enforcement activity.

Commentators on the subject have overwhelmingly favored judicial decision of the issue by application of a test which looks only to the nature and extent of police activity in the criminal enterprise. Professor Kamisar observed that only two law review articles in the past 25 years have favored the subjective test. (Kamisar, et al., Modern Criminal Procedure (4th ed. 1978 Supp.) p. 119.) The Model Penal Code has adopted an objective test (Model Pen. Code (Proposed Official Draft 1962) § 2.13(1)), and in recent years several state courts and legislatures have recognized that such a test is more consistent with and better promotes the underlying purpose of the entrapment defense. Such support for the position no doubt derives from a developing awareness that "entrapment is a facet of a broader problem. Along with illegal search and seizures, wire tapping, false arrest, illegal detention and the third degree, it is a type of lawless law enforcement. They all spring from common motivations. Each is a substitute for skillful and scientific investigation. Each is condoned by the sinister sophism that the end, when dealing with known criminals or the 'crim-

2. Justice Schauer, for the entire court in *Benford*, declared that "Entrapment is a defense not because the defendant is innocent but because, as stated by Justice Holmes, 'it is a less evil that some criminals should escape than that the Government should play an ignoble part.'"

inal classes,' justifies the employment of illegal means." (Donnelley, *Judicial Control of Informants, Stool Pigeons and Agent Provocateurs* (1951) 60 Yale L. Rev. 1091.)

For all the foregoing reasons we hold that the proper test of entrapment in California is the following: was the conduct of the law enforcement agent likely to induce a normally law-abiding person to commit the offense? For the purposes of this test, we presume that such a person would normally resist the temptation to commit a crime presented by the simple opportunity to act unlawfully. Official conduct that does no more than offer that opportunity to the suspect—for example, a decoy program—is therefore permissible; but it is impermissible for the police or their agents to pressure the suspect by overbearing conduct such as badgering, cajoling, importuning, or other affirmative acts likely to induce a normally law-abiding person to commit the crime.

Although the determination of what police conduct is impermissible must to some extent proceed on an ad hoc basis, guidance will generally be found in the application of one or both of two principles. First, if the actions of the law enforcement agent would generate in a normally law-abiding person a motive for the crime other than ordinary criminal intent, entrapment will be established. An example of such conduct would be an appeal by the police that would induce such a person to commit the act because of friendship or sympathy, instead of a desire for personal gain or other typical criminal purpose. Second, affirmative police conduct that would make commission of the crime unusually attractive to a normally law-abiding person will likewise constitute entrapment. Such conduct would include, for example, a guarantee that the act is not illegal or the offense will go undetected, an offer of exorbitant consideration, or any similar enticement.[4]

Finally, while the inquiry must focus primarily on the conduct of the law enforcement agent, that conduct is not to be viewed in a vacuum; it should also be judged by the effect it would have on a normally law-abiding person situated in the circumstances of the case at hand. Among the circumstances that may be relevant for this purpose, for example, are the transactions preceding the offense, the suspect's response to the inducements of the officer, the gravity of the crime, and the difficulty of detecting instances of its commission. We reiterate, however, that under this test such matters as the character of the suspect, his predisposition to commit the offense, and his subjective intent are irrelevant.

On the record of this case the trial court erred in failing to instruct the jury *sua sponte* on the defense of entrapment.[6]

. . .

---

4. There will be no entrapment, however, when the official conduct is found to have gone no further than necessary to assure the suspect that he is not being "set up." The police remain free to take reasonable, though restrained, steps to gain the confidence of suspects. A contrary rule would unduly hamper law enforcement; indeed, in the case of many of the so-called "victimless" crimes, it would tend to limit convictions to only the most gullible offenders.

6. In view of its potentially substantial effect on the issue of guilt, the defense of entrapment remains a jury question under the new test. However, for the reasons stated by Chief Justice Traynor in his dissenting opinion in *People v. Moran*, *supra*, three members of this court (Justices Mosk, To-

[Concurring and dissenting opinion of Richardson, J. omitted.]

Clark, J., dissenting.

The most significant question presented by this case is whether this court should adopt the "hypothetical-person" ("objective") test of entrapment.

The test now applied in California, in all but seven of the other states, and in the federal courts is the "origin-of-intent" ("subjective") standard. This test focuses, quite properly, upon the guilt of the particular defendant, asking whether he was predisposed to commit the crime charged. If he was ready and willing to commit the offense at any favorable opportunity, then the entrapment defense fails even if the police used an unduly persuasive inducement.

The guilt of the particular defendant is irrelevant under the hypothetical-person test. It focuses instead upon the conduct of the police. If the police use an inducement likely to cause a hypothetical person to commit the crime charged, then the fact that the particular defendant was ready and willing to commit it does not defeat the entrapment defense. The evil of the hypothetical-person test is apparent — it leads to acquittal of persons who are in fact guilty. By focusing on police conduct rather than the defendant's predisposition, it creates a risk of acquitting dangerous chronic offenders.

That risk is strikingly illustrated by the facts of this case. The evidence would support the conclusion that defendant is one of the most cynical manipulators of the criminal justice system imaginable, that he abused the trust placed in him as an employee of a drug detoxification program to sell heroin to the patients with whom he worked, nullifying the program's slight chances of success and wasting countless thousands of tax dollars, that he initially refused to sell heroin to the deputy solely because he suspected she was an undercover officer, and that, before finally agreeing to make the sale through his wife, he sought to immunize himself by "entrapping" the deputy into the conduct he now relies upon as the basis of his entrapment defense. If the factfinder takes this view of the evidence, but also concludes the officer's conduct would have induced a hypothetical person to commit the offense, defendant goes free.

The majority respond by quoting Justice Holmes' observation that "it is a less evil that some criminals should escape than that the Government should play an ignoble part." (quoting *Olmstead v. United States* (1928) 277 U.S. 438 (Holmes, J., dis.)) With deference to Justice Holmes, that is a false dichotomy. It is simply not true that society must choose between freeing criminals and tolerating official misconduct. Take the case in which an officer uses an unduly persuasive inducement but the defendant is ready and willing to commit the crime at any favorable opportunity. Society can and should insist upon both the criminal's being convicted and the officer's being disciplined. To assume that the officer will not be disciplined is but another instance of the majority's "curious cynicism concerning the rule of law in our society" which I have elsewhere decried.

---

briner, and Newman) are of the view that claims of entrapment should be exclusively for the trial courts to decide subject to appropriate appellate review.

The minority justices of the United States Supreme Court who have advocated the hypothetical-person test have argued that its adoption would increase public respect for the criminal justice system. (See, e.g., *Sherman v. United States* (1958) 356 U.S. 369 (Frankfurter, J., conc.)) However, the hypothetical-person approach is no way to achieve this respect. The public is, understandably, not offended by conviction of a defendant found—beyond a reasonable doubt and by unanimous vote of 12 citizens—to have been ready and willing to commit the crime charged. But the public will be offended by the adoption of an entrapment defense that ignores culpability and seeks to control police conduct by acquittal of professional criminals. As Justice Macklin Fleming has observed: "Each time the criminal process is thwarted by a technicality that does not bear on the innocence or guilt of the accused, we trumpet abroad the notion of injustice; and each time a patently guilty person is released, some damage is done to the general sense of justice." (Fleming, The Price of Perfect Justice: The Adverse Consequences of Current Legal Doctrine on the American Courtroom (1974) p. 9.)

Bernard E. Witkin, beyond question the foremost commentator on California law, expressed the same sentiment when he recently addressed himself to the historic contribution of the United States Supreme Court during the period when Earl Warren was Chief Justice. His subject was "'The Second Noble Experiment of the Century' conceived in altruism, and dedicated to the principle that technical forms of criminal procedure are more important than the substance of guilt or innocence of the accused." What Mr. Witkin has to say is always worthy of attention but his remarks on this occasion are particularly noteworthy because this court appears to see itself as keeper of the flame that might otherwise have died with the passing of the Warren era.

> "We begin with a simple and tragic admission: That there is a rising rate of crime and a falling rate of conviction and punishment for crime. And we are frequently told by bitter critics that the responsible agency is the judiciary; that the Courts have become increasingly concerned with barren technicalities of criminal procedure, and have lost sight of the primary objective of the criminal law.
>
> "Now none of us needs to be reminded that a system of criminal justice exists not just for the protection of the innocent but for the punishment of the guilty; and that only by consistent apprehension and conviction of the murderer, the burglar, the arsonist, the rapist, the drug-peddler, and other ... predators that infest our society, can the system justify itself in the eyes of our people. We are therefore in deep trouble if, as these critics would have us believe, the judges of our state and federal courts are frustrating law enforcement by placing burdensome restrictions on arrest, production of evidence, and trials."

After making it clear that he considers these criticisms justified with regard to the Warren court, Witkin concludes by saying: "The cases I have discussed, and many others, demonstrate the weird and wonderful solicitude of thin majorities of our highest court of the Warren era for the professional and nonprofessional criminal. Serenely confident, with a full head of steam, the court repeatedly found new and exciting grounds upon which to reverse the convictions for major crimes on records which overwhelmingly established guilt. And the nation's legal scholars and students writing in law school reviews, deluged us with extravagant praise for these decisions, referring to them—in what is surely the most preposterous misclassification ever made—as decisions establishing and protecting civil liberties." (Witkin, *The Second Noble Experiment of the Twentieth Century* (Sept.–Nov. 1977) Prosecutor's Brief 42–45.)

Whatever else one may say of the Warren Court, it refused to take the step the majority of this court take today. Indeed, in *Sherman v. United States*, Chief Justice Warren himself wrote the majority opinion in which the court declined to reconsider its adherence to the origin-of-intent test. With today's decision this court outdoes its mentor in rendering guilt irrelevant.

The judgment should be affirmed.

Problem

Problem 84.

Defendant is charged with transporting, selling or furnishing cocaine. (H & S Code § 11352(a).) Defendant does not dispute that he sold four ounces of rock cocaine to Informant (a civilian who was working with the police), but Defendant has testified that the circumstances of the sale were as follows. Defendant first contacted Informant in response to an advertisement she placed with a "976 date line" telephone service. The two had numerous telephone conversations during which Defendant expressed interest in going out with Informant, and Informant regularly asked him if he could get drugs for her. During the conversations, Informant indicated that she was willing to have sex with Defendant (including three-way sex with a woman friend of hers), and he understood that getting drugs was a condition of having sex. Defendant agreed to meet Informant and her friend at a fast food restaurant. Prior to the meeting, Defendant, acting on the understanding that Informant and her friend would have sex with him, arranged for Acquaintance to deliver cocaine to Informant at the restaurant. Acquaintance delivered the cocaine to Defendant, and when Defendant met with Informant and her "friend," and delivered the cocaine, he was arrested. What arguments should be made on Defendant's request that the jury be instructed on the defense of entrapment?

Hampton v. United States

425 U.S. 484, 96 S. Ct. 1646 (1976)

Mr. Justice Rehnquist announced the judgment of the Court in an opinion in which The Chief Justice and Mr. Justice White join.

→ Issue

This case presents the question of whether a defendant may be convicted for the sale of contraband which he procured from a Government informant or agent. The Court of Appeals for the Eighth Circuit held he could be, and we agree.

I

Petitioner was convicted of two counts of distributing heroin in violation of 21 U.S.C. § 841(a)(1) in the United States District Court for the Eastern District of Missouri and sentenced to concurrent terms of five years' imprisonment (suspended). The case arose from two sales of heroin by petitioner to agents of the Federal Drug Enforcement Administration (DEA) in St. Louis on February 25 and 26, 1974. The sales were arranged by one Hutton, who was a pool-playing acquaintance of petitioner at the Pud bar in St. Louis and also a DEA informant.

According to the Government's witnesses, in late February 1974, Hutton and petitioner were shooting pool at the Pud when petitioner, after observing "track" (needle) marks on Hutton's arms told Hutton that he needed money and knew where he could get some heroin. Hutton responded that he could find a buyer and petitioner suggested that he "get in touch with those people." Hutton then called DEA Agent Terry Sawyer and arranged a sale for 10 p.m. on February 25.

At the appointed time, Hutton and petitioner went to a prearranged meeting place and were met by Agent Sawyer and DEA Agent McDowell, posing as narcotics dealers. Petitioner produced a tinfoil packet from his cap and turned it over to the agents who tested it, pronounced it "okay," and negotiated a price of $145 which was paid to petitioner. Before they parted, petitioner told Sawyer that he could obtain larger quantities of heroin and gave Sawyer a phone number where he could be reached.

The next day Sawyer called petitioner and arranged for another "buy" that afternoon. Petitioner got Hutton to go along and they met the agents again near where they had been the previous night.

They all entered the agents' car, and petitioner again produced a tinfoil packet from his cap. The agents again field-tested it and pronounced it satisfactory. Petitioner then asked for $500 which Agent Sawyer said he would get from the trunk. Sawyer got out and opened the trunk which was a signal to other agents to move in and arrest petitioner, which they did.

Petitioner's version of events was quite different. According to him, in response to his statement that he was short of cash, Hutton said that he had a friend who was a pharmacist who could produce a non-narcotic counterfeit drug which would give the same reaction as heroin. Hutton proposed selling this drug to gullible acquaintances who would be led to believe they were buying heroin. Petitioner testified that they successfully duped one buyer with this fake drug and that the sales which led to the arrest were solicited by petitioner[3] in an effort to profit further from this ploy.

Petitioner contended that he neither intended to sell, nor knew that he was dealing in heroin and that all of the drugs he sold were supplied by Hutton. His account was at least partially disbelieved by the jury which was instructed that in order to convict

3. On appeal, petitioner's counsel, who was also his counsel at trial, conceded that petitioner was predisposed to commit this offense.

petitioner they had to find that the Government proved "that the defendant knowingly did an act which the law forbids, purposely intending to violate the law." Thus the guilty verdict necessarily implies that the jury rejected petitioner's claim that he did not know the substance was heroin, and petitioner himself admitted both soliciting and carrying out sales. The only relevance of his version of the facts, then, lies in his having requested an instruction embodying that version. He did not request a standard entrapment instruction but he did request the following:

> "The defendant asserts that he was the victim of entrapment as to the crimes charged in the indictment.
>
> "If you find that the defendant's sales of narcotics were sales of narcotics supplied to him by an informer in the employ of or acting on behalf of the government, then you must acquit the defendant because the law as a matter of policy forbids his conviction in such a case.
>
> "Furthermore, under this particular defense, you need not consider the predisposition of the defendant to commit the offense charged, because if the governmental involvement through its informer reached the point that I have just defined in your own minds, then the predisposition of the defendant would not matter."

The trial court refused the instruction and petitioner was found guilty. He appealed to the United States Court of Appeals for the Eighth Circuit, claiming that if the jury had believed that the drug was supplied by Hutton he should have been acquitted. The Court of Appeals rejected this argument and affirmed the conviction, relying on our opinion in *United States v. Russell*, 411 U.S. 423 (1973).

II

In *Russell* we held that the statutory defense of entrapment was not available where it was conceded that a Government agent supplied a necessary ingredient in the manufacture of an illicit drug. We reaffirmed the principle of *Sorrells v. United States*, 287 U.S. 435 (1932), and *Sherman v. United States*, 356 U.S. 369 (1958), that the entrapment defense "focus[es] on the intent or predisposition of the defendant to commit the crime," rather than upon the conduct of the Government's agents. We ruled out the possibility that the defense of entrapment could ever be based upon governmental misconduct in a case, such as this one, where the predisposition of the defendant to commit the crime was established.

In holding that "[i]t is only when the Government's deception actually implants the criminal design in the mind of the defendant that the defense of entrapment comes into play," we, of course, rejected the contrary view of the dissents in that case and the concurrences in *Sorrells* and *Sherman*. In view of these holdings, petitioner correctly recognizes that his case does not qualify as one involving "entrapment" at all. He instead relies on the language in *Russell* that "we may some day be presented with a situation in which the conduct of law enforcement agents is so outrageous that due process principles would absolutely bar the government from invoking judicial processes to obtain a conviction."

In urging that this case involves a violation of his due process rights, petitioner misapprehends the meaning of the quoted language in *Russell*. Admittedly petitioner's case is different from Russell's but the difference is one of degree, not of kind. In *Russell* the ingredient supplied by the Government agent was a legal drug which the defendants demonstrably could have obtained from other sources besides the Government. Here the drug which the Government informant allegedly supplied to petitioner both was illegal and constituted the corpus delicti for the sale of which the petitioner was convicted. The Government obviously played a more significant role in enabling petitioner to sell contraband in this case than it did in *Russell*.

But in each case the Government agents were acting in concert with the defendant, and in each case either the jury found or the defendant conceded that he was predisposed to commit the crime for which he was convicted. The remedy of the criminal defendant with respect to the acts of Government agents, which, far from being resisted, are encouraged by him, lies solely in the defense of entrapment. But, as noted, petitioner's conceded predisposition rendered this defense unavailable to him.

To sustain petitioner's contention here would run directly contrary to our statement in *Russell* that the defense of entrapment is not intended "to give the federal judiciary a 'chancellor's foot' veto over law enforcement practices of which it did not approve. The execution of the federal laws under our Constitution is confined primarily to the Executive Branch of the Government, subject to applicable constitutional and statutory limitations and to judicially fashioned rules to enforce those limitations."

The limitations of the Due Process Clause of the Fifth Amendment come into play only when the Government activity in question violates some protected right of the defendant. Here, as we have noted, the police, the Government informant, and the defendant acted in concert with one another. If the result of the governmental activity is to "implant in the mind of an innocent person the disposition to commit the alleged offense and induce its commission ...," *Sorrells*, the defendant is protected by the defense of entrapment. If the police engage in illegal activity in concert with a defendant beyond the scope of their duties the remedy lies, not in freeing the equally culpable defendant, but in prosecuting the police under the applicable provisions of state or federal law. But the police conduct here no more deprived defendant of any right secured to him by the United States Constitution than did the police conduct in Russell deprive Russell of any rights.

Mr. Justice Stevens took no part in the consideration or decision of this case.

Mr. Justice Powell, with whom Mr. Justice Blackmun joins, concurring in the judgment.

Petitioner, Charles Hampton, contends that the Government's supplying of contraband to one later prosecuted for trafficking in contraband constitutes a *per se* denial of due process. As I do not accept this proposition, I concur in the judgment of the Court and much of the plurality opinion directed specifically to Hampton's contention. I am not able to join the remainder of the plurality opinion, as it would unnecessarily reach and decide difficult questions not before us.

In *United States v. Russell*, 411 U.S. 423 (1973), we noted that significant "difficulties [attend] the notion that due process of law can be embodied in fixed rules." We also recognized that the practicalities of combating the narcotics traffic frequently require law enforcement officers legitimately to supply "some item of value that the drug ring requires." Accordingly, we held that due process does not necessarily foreclose reliance on such investigative techniques. Hampton would distinguish *Russell* on the ground that here contraband itself was supplied by the Government, while the phenyl-2-propanone supplied in *Russell* was not contraband. Given the characteristics of phenyl-2-propanone,[1] this is a distinction without a difference and *Russell* disposes of this case.

But the plurality opinion today does not stop there. In discussing Hampton's due process contention, it enunciates a *per se* rule:

> "[In *Russell*,] [w]e ruled out the possibility that the defense of entrapment could *ever* be based upon governmental misconduct in a case, such as this one, where the predisposition of the defendant to commit the crime was established." (Emphasis supplied.)
>
> "The remedy of the criminal defendant with respect to the acts of Government agents, which ... are encouraged by him, lies *solely* in the defense of entrapment." (Emphasis supplied.)

The plurality thus says that the concept of fundamental fairness inherent in the guarantee of due process would never prevent the conviction of a predisposed defendant, regardless of the outrageousness of police behavior in light of the surrounding circumstances.

I do not understand *Russell* or earlier cases delineating the predisposition-focused defense of entrapment to have gone so far, and there was no need for them to do so. In those cases the Court was confronted with specific claims of police "overinvolvement" in criminal activity involving contraband. Disposition of those claims did not require the Court to consider whether overinvolvement of Government agents in contraband offenses could ever reach such proportions as to bar conviction of a predisposed defendant as a matter of due process. Nor have we had occasion yet to confront Government overinvolvement in areas outside the realm of contraband offenses. In these circumstances, I am unwilling to conclude that an analysis other than one limited to predisposition would never be appropriate under due process principles.[4]

---

1. Although phenyl-2-propanone is not contraband, it is useful only in the manufacture of methamphetamine ("speed"), the contraband involved in *Russell*. Further, it is an essential ingredient in that manufacturing process and is very difficult to obtain.

4. Judge Friendly recently expressed the view:

> "[T]here is certainly a [constitutional] limit to allowing governmental involvement in crime. It would be unthinkable, for example, to permit government agents to instigate robberies and beatings merely to gather evidence to convict other members of a gang of hoodlums. Governmental 'investigation' involving participation in activities that result in injury to the rights of its citizens is a course that courts should be extremely reluctant to sanction." *United States v. Archer*, 486 F. 2d 670 (2nd Cir. 1973).

The plurality's use of the "chancellor's foot" passage from *Russell* may suggest that it also would foreclose reliance on our supervisory power to bar conviction of a predisposed defendant because of outrageous police conduct. Again, I do not understand *Russell* to have gone so far. There we indicated only that we should be extremely reluctant to invoke the supervisory power in cases of this kind because that power does not give the "federal judiciary a 'chancellor's foot' veto over law enforcement practices of which it [does] not approve."

I am not unmindful of the doctrinal[5] and practical[6] difficulties of delineating limits to police involvement in crime that do not focus on predisposition, as Government participation ordinarily will be fully justified in society's "war with the criminal classes." *Sorrells v. United States*, 287 U.S. 435 (1932) (opinion of Roberts, J.) This undoubtedly is the concern that prompts the plurality to embrace an absolute rule. But we left these questions open in *Russell*, and this case is controlled completely by *Russell*. I therefore am unwilling to join the plurality in concluding that, no matter what the circumstances, neither due process principles nor our supervisory power could support a bar to conviction in any case where the Government is able to prove predisposition.[7]

---

5. The plurality finds no source for a doctrine limiting police involvement in crime. While such a conclusion ultimately might be reached in an appropriate case, we should not disregard lightly Mr. Justice Frankfurter's view that there is a responsibility "necessarily in [the Court's] keeping ... to accommodate the dangers of overzealous law enforcement and civilized methods adequate to counter the ingenuity of modern criminals." *Sherman v. United States*, *supra* (concurring in result). In another context Mr. Justice Frankfurter warned that exclusive focus on predisposition creates the risk that the Court will "shirk" the responsibility that he perceived.

The discussion of predisposition, for example, often seems to overlook the fact that there may be widely varying degrees of criminal involvement. Taking the narcotics traffic as an example, those who distribute narcotics—the "pushers"—are the persons who, next to those who import or manufacture, merit most the full sanction of the criminal law. Yet, the criminal involvement of pushers varies widely. The hardcore professional, in the "business" on a large scale and for years, is to be contrasted with the high-school youth whose "pushing" is limited to a few of his classmates over a short span of time. Predisposition could be proved against both types of offenders, and under the flat rule enunciated today by the plurality the differences between the circumstances would be irrelevant despite the most outrageous conduct conceivable by Government agents relative to the circumstances. A fair system of justice normally should eschew unbending rules that foreclose, in their application, all judicial discretion.

6. I recognize that, if limitations on police involvement are appropriate in particular situations, defining such limits will be difficult. But these difficulties do not themselves justify the plurality's absolute rule. Due process in essence means fundamental fairness, and the Court's cases are replete with examples of judgments as to when such fairness has been denied an accused in light of all the circumstances. The fact that there is sometimes no sharply defined standard against which to make these judgments is not itself a sufficient reason to deny the federal judiciary's power to make them when warranted by the circumstances. Much the same is true of analysis under our supervisory power. Nor do I despair of our ability in an appropriate case to identify appropriate standards for police practices without relying on the "chancellor's" "fastidious squeamishness or private sentimentalism."

7. I emphasize that the cases, if any, in which proof of predisposition is not dispositive will be rare. Police over involvement in crime would have to reach a demonstrable level of outrageousness before it could bar conviction. This would be especially difficult to show with respect to contraband offenses, which are so difficult to detect in the absence of undercover Government involvement. One cannot easily exaggerate the problems confronted by law enforcement authorities in dealing effectively

. . .

[Dissenting opinion of BRENNAN, J., joined by STEWART, J. and MARSHALL, J., omitted.]

Problems

Problem 85.

Police received information that Defendant was engaged in drug trafficking and "ripping off" other drug dealers. Officer, acting undercover, approached Defendant about a plan to steal a shipment of cocaine, involving between 30 and 100 kg. from Officer's "boss," a supposed major drug dealer. Defendant agreed to undertake the theft and to pay Officer 50% of the cocaine if the amount taken was between 30 and 50 kg. and 60% if the amount was greater. Police then set up a sting operation using 85 kg. of cocaine in their possession. They placed the cocaine in a van, parked the van in the garage of a vacant house and left the key in the ignition, having rigged the ignition with a kill switch. Officer then advised Defendant of the shipment and its location, and, when Defendant and her henchmen arrived and attempted to drive the van away, the police activated the kill switch and arrested the thieves. Defendant is now charged with attempted grand theft (P.C. §§484, 487) and attempt to transport cocaine (H & S Code §11352) and, as to the latter charge, with a 25-year enhancement to sentence because the quantity of cocaine exceeded 80 kg. What arguments should be made as to whether the defendant has a complete or partial defense based on outrageous police conduct?

Problem 86.

Officer, working undercover, spent the evening with Defendant, Friend and two other men. Officer supplied cocaine and marijuana, and the group consumed the drugs and drank beer for several hours. (Officer later testified that he drank about three beers but only pretended to consume the drugs.) Officer, Defendant and Friend then went to a bar, where they drank more beer. Friend began talking about how he wanted to retaliate against Victim, who had "ripped him off." The three then drove to Victim's house, entered and found Victim. Friend confronted Victim and questioned him about the location of marijuana and money, and Defendant pointed a gun at Victim. Victim gave them marijuana, and Officer found Victim's wallet and took the money out. They also took Victim's gun. At some point Defendant and Victim became agitated with each other, and Officer stepped between them and punched Victim in the nose and then hit him in the back of the head. After the three left, they divided Victim's property.

Defendant is now charged with robbery (P.C. §211). What arguments should be made on Defendant's motion to dismiss on due process grounds?

---

with an expanding narcotics traffic, which is one of the major contributing causes of escalating crime in our cities. Enforcement officials therefore must be allowed flexibility adequate to counter effectively such criminal activity.

C. Insanity

In the criminal law, mental disease may be relevant at one or more of three different points of the criminal process—at the time of the offense, at the time of trial, and at the time of execution of sentence in a capital case. The materials in this chapter concern the first stage—the effect of mental disease or defect at the time the crime was committed. As noted in Chapter 3, a mental disease or defect may be used as evidence to show that the defendant did not form the mental state required by the crime ("diminished actuality"), or it may amount to "legal insanity" which will constitute an affirmative defense.[b]

The insanity defense has a long history. From the earliest days of the common law, the courts have recognized that some persons lack the mental capacity to conform to the strictures of the law. Thus, in 1582, William Lambart of Lincoln's Inn wrote that "If ... a mad man or a natural fool, or a lunatic in the time of his lunacy, or a child who apparently had no knowledge of good or evil, do kill a man, this is no felonious act ... for they cannot be said to have any understanding will." Lambart, Eirenarcha Cat. 21.218 (1582) (spelling modernized). Until the middle of the Nineteenth Century, the test of insanity in England was whether the defendant was "totally deprived of his understanding and memory, and doth not know what he is doing, no more than an infant, than a brute, or a wild beast ..." *Rex v. Arnold*, 16 Howell St. Tr. 695, 765 (1724).

The first modern insanity test was set out in *M'Naghten's Case*, 10 Clark & Fin. 200 (1843). There, the House of Lords said: "[To] establish a defence on the ground of insanity, it must be clearly proved that, at the time of the committing the act, the party accused was labouring under such a defect of reason, from disease of the mind, as not to know the nature and quality of the act he was doing; or, if he did know it, that he did not know he was doing what was wrong." The *M'Naghten* test was the earliest definition of insanity in California, and the one used in virtually all jurisdictions in the United States until the 1950s.

In time, as psychiatric knowledge grew and became more generally accepted, the *M'Naghten* test came to be criticized on two main grounds. The principal objection was that it was too narrow in scope, focusing only on the cognitive aspect of the personality, *i.e.*, the ability to know right from wrong, and excluding defendants who, because of mental illness, were unable to control their behavior. And the single track

---

b. With regard to a defendant's mental illness at the time of trial, if the illness is so severe that it prevents the defendant from understanding the nature of the proceedings against him/her and from assisting his/her attorney in the defense, he/she will be found to be incompetent to stand trial. See P.C. § 1367. With regard to a defendant's mental illness at the time set for execution, if a condemned person is insane, the Eighth Amendment's ban on cruel and unusual punishment prohibits a state from proceeding with the execution. *Ford v. Wainwright*, 477 U.S. 399 (1986).

emphasis on the cognitive aspect of the personality recognized no degrees of incapacity — either the defendant knew right from wrong or he did not and that was the only choice the jury was given. The other objection was that the *M'Naghten* test too tightly constrained expert psychiatric testimony, forcing the psychiatrist to testify in terms, "right" and "wrong," having little relationship to the psychiatrist's knowledge and experience. Edward de Grazia asked, "How [does one] translate 'psychosis' or 'psychopathy' or 'dementia praecox' or even 'sociopathy' or 'mental disorder' or 'neurotic character disorder' or 'mental illness' into a psychiatric judgment of whether the accused knew 'right' from 'wrong'?" de Grazia, *The Distinction of Being Mad*, 22 U. Chi. L. Rev. 339, 341 (1955). Justice Frankfurter, as a witness before the Royal Commission on Capital Punishment, declared: "I do not see why the rules of law should be arrested at the state of psychological knowledge of the time when they were formulated.... I think the *M'Naghten* Rules are in large measure shams. That is a very strong word, but I think the *M'Naghten* Rules are very difficult for conscientious people and not difficult enough for people who say, 'We'll just juggle them.'" (Report of the Royal Commission on Capital Punishment, 102 (1953).)

The first step in modifying *M'Naghten* came with the adoption, in some jurisdictions, of the "irresistible impulse" test as a supplement to *M'Naghten*. Under that test, a defendant who knew right from wrong might still be acquitted on grounds of insanity if the crime resulted from an impulse which the defendant was powerless to control. This test, too, came under criticism. Some psychiatrists questioned whether "irresistible impulses" actually exist; and it was also objected that the term "irresistible impulse" was still too narrow and carried the misleading implication that a crime impulsively committed must have been perpetrated in a sudden and explosive fit. Thus, the "irresistible impulse" test excluded the far more numerous instances of crimes committed after excessive brooding and melancholy by one unable to resist sustained psychic compulsion or to make any real attempt to control his or her conduct.

In 1954, in *Durham v. United States*, 214 F.2d 862 (D.C. Cir. 1954), the District of Columbia Circuit abandoned *M'Naghten* in favor of a new test: a defendant was not criminally responsible "if his unlawful act was the product of mental disease or mental defect." *Durham* addressed many of the criticisms leveled at *M'Naghten*. It eliminated *M'Naghten*'s exclusive "right-wrong" focus and, for the first time, removed the constraints on expert testimony, so that psychiatrists could provide all relevant medical information for the common sense application of the fact-finder. At the same time, *Durham* was criticized because determining whether a crime was the "product" of a mental disease or defect raised the same problems of causation encountered by the *M'Naghten* and irresistible impulse tests and because it failed to give the fact-finder any standard by which to measure the competency of the accused. As a result, psychiatrists when testifying that a defendant suffered from a "mental disease or defect" in effect usurped the jury's function.

The Model Penal Code, promulgated in 1962, attempted to meet the concerns with both *M'Naghten* and *Durham*. It provided: "A person is not responsible for criminal conduct if at the time of such conduct as a result of mental disease or defect he lacks substantial capacity either to appreciate the criminality [or wrongfulness] of his conduct or to conform his conduct to the requirements of law." MPC § 4.01. This definition of insanity was thought to improve on previous definitions in at least three respects: (1) it addressed both cognitive ("appreciate") and behavioral ("control") deficits; (2) with the use of the word "substantial," it recognized gradations of incapacity and neither required complete incapacity to establish insanity nor permitted a finding of insanity on evidence of *any* incapacity; and (3) it allowed for the use of meaningful psychiatric testimony. Over the next 20 years, a number of states (including California) adopted versions of the Model Penal Code test. In 1982, John Hinckley attempted to assassinate then-president Ronald Reagan. His subsequent acquittal on grounds of insanity sparked an abandonment of the Model Penal Code test and a return to the *M'Naghten* test by Congress and a number of states.

The history of the insanity defense in California is discussed in *People v. Skinner*, the first case in this section. In *Skinner*, the California Supreme Court analyzes the insanity test established by the voters in Proposition 8, the same proposition that eliminated the diminished capacity defense [see Chapter 3], and describes the present insanity defense in California as a return to the *M'Naghten* test. In *Jones v. United States*, the Supreme Court decides the constitutionality of committing defendants found not guilty by reason of insanity to psychiatric hospitals, possibly for life.

People v. Skinner

39 Cal. 3d 765, 704 P.2d 752 (1985)

Grodin, J.

For over a century prior to the decision in *People v. Drew* (1978) 22 Cal. 3d 333, California courts framed this state's definition of insanity, as a defense in criminal cases, upon the two-pronged test adopted by the House of Lords in *M'Naghten's Case* (1843) 10 Clark & Fin. 200: "[To] establish a defence on the ground of insanity, it must be clearly proved that, at the time of the committing the act, the party accused was labouring under such a defect of reason, from disease of the mind, as not to know the nature and quality of the act he was doing; *or*, if he did know it, that he did not know he was doing what was wrong." (Italics added; see *People v. Coffman* (1864) 24 Cal. 230.)

Over the years the *M'Naghten test* became subject to considerable criticism and was abandoned in a number of jurisdictions. In *Drew* this court followed suit, adopting the test for mental incapacity proposed by the American Law Institute: "A person is not responsible for criminal conduct if at the time of such conduct as a result of mental disease or defect he lacks substantial capacity either to appreciate the criminality [wrongfulness] of his conduct or to conform his conduct to the requirements of law."

In June 1982 the California electorate adopted an initiative measure, popularly known as Proposition 8, which (among other things) for the first time in this state established a statutory definition of insanity: "In any criminal proceeding ... in which a plea of not guilty by reason of insanity is entered, this defense shall be found by the trier of fact only when the accused person proves by a preponderance of the evidence that he or she was incapable of knowing or understanding the nature and quality of his or her act *and* of distinguishing right from wrong at the time of the commission of the offense." (Pen. Code, § 25, subd. (b) [hereafter section 25(b)], italics added.)

It is apparent from the language of section 25(b) that it was designed to eliminate the *Drew* test and to reinstate the prongs of the *M'Naghten* test. However, the section uses the conjunctive "and" instead of the disjunctive "or" to connect the two prongs. Read literally, therefore, section 25(b) would do more than reinstate the *M'Naghten* test. It would strip the insanity defense from an accused who, by reason of mental disease, is incapable of knowing that the act he was doing was wrong. That is, in fact, the interpretation adopted by the trial court in this case.

Defendant claims that the purpose of the electorate in adopting section 25(b) was to restore the *M'Naghten* test as it existed in California prior to this court's decision in *People v. Drew*. If read literally, he argues, section 25(b) would violate both the state and federal Constitutions by imposing criminal responsibility and sanctions on persons who lack the mens rea essential to criminal culpability.

The People do not dispute the proposition that the intent of the electorate was to reinstate the pre-*Drew* test of legal insanity. They argue, however, that section 25(b), "amplifies" and "clarifies" the *M'Naghten* test. Amicus curiae, the Criminal Justice Legal Foundation, agrees that the intent was not to adopt a stricter test than that applicable prior to *Drew*, but suggest that in fact there is no difference between the two prongs of the *M'Naghten* test—ability to distinguish between right and wrong, and knowledge of the nature and quality of the particular criminal act.

Mindful of the serious constitutional questions that might arise were we to accept a literal construction of the statutory language, and of our obligation wherever possible both to carry out the intent of the electorate and to construe statutes so as to preserve their constitutionality, we shall conclude that section 25(b) was intended to, and does, restore the *M'Naghten* test as it existed in this state before *Drew*. We shall also conclude that under that test there exist two distinct and independent bases upon which a verdict of not guilty by reason of insanity might be returned.

I

Defendant appeals from a judgment of conviction of second degree murder (§§ 187, 189) entered upon his pleas of nolo contendere and not guilty by reason of insanity, and a finding by the court, after a jury was waived, that he was sane at the time of the offense. (§ 1026, subd. (a).) In finding the defendant sane, the judge acknowledged that it was more likely than not that defendant suffered from a mental disease, paranoid schizophrenia, which played a significant part in the killing. The judge stated that under the *Drew* test of legal insanity defendant would qualify as insane, and also found that "under the right-wrong prong of section 25(b), the defendant would qualify as legally insane; but under the other prong, he clearly does not." Concluding that by the use of the conjunctive "and" in section 25(b), the electorate demonstrated an intent to establish a stricter test of legal insanity than the *M'Naghten* test, and to "virtually eliminate" insanity as a defense, the judge found that defendant had not established that he was legally insane.

Probation was denied and defendant was sentenced to a term of 15 years to life in the state prison.

Defendant strangled his wife while he was on a day pass from the Camarillo State Hospital at which he was a patient. Evidence offered at the trial on his plea of not guilty by reason of insanity included the opinion of a clinical and forensic psychologist that defendant suffered from either classical paranoic schizophrenia, or schizoaffective illness with significant paranoid features. A delusional product of this illness was a belief held by defendant that the marriage vow "till death do us part" bestows on a marital partner a God-given right to kill the other partner who has violated or was inclined to violate the marital vows, and that because the vows reflect the direct wishes of God, the killing is with complete moral and criminal impunity. The act is not wrongful because it is sanctified by the will and desire of God.

Although there was also evidence that would have supported a finding that defendant was sane, it was apparently the evidence summarized above upon which the trial judge based his finding that defendant met one, but not both, prongs of the *M'Naghten* test. Defendant knew the nature and quality of his act. He knew that his act was homicidal. He was unable to distinguish right and wrong, however, in that he did not know that this particular killing was wrongful or criminal.

In this context we must determine whether the trial court's conclusion that section 25(b), requires that a defendant meet both prongs of the *M'Naghten* test to establish legal insanity was correct, and if not, whether the court's finding that defendant met the "right-wrong" aspect of the test requires reversal with directions to enter a judgment of not guilty by reason of insanity.

II
The Insanity Defense in California

. . .

The test of legal insanity when the Penal Code of 1872 was adopted by the Legislature was the two-prong *M'Naghten* test recognized by this court in *People v. Coffman*: "The unsoundness of mind, or insanity, that will constitute a defense in a criminal action is well described by Tindal, C. J., in answer to questions propounded by the House of Lords to the Judges [citation]. He says, 'that to establish a defense on the ground of insanity, it must be clearly proved that, at the time of committing the act, the party accused was laboring under such a defect of reason, from disease of the mind, as not to know the *nature or quality of the act*, or if he did know it, that he did not know he was doing what was wrong.'" (Original italics.) *Coffman*'s exposition of the *M'Naghten* test was set out in the commissioners' note to section 1016, confirming the legislative understanding of the applicable definition of legal insanity.

For more than a century after *Coffman* recognized the *M'Naghten* test as applicable in this state it continued to be used, and although sometimes stated in the conjunctive, was in fact applied so as to permit a finding of insanity if either prong of the test was satisfied. We stated the test in the disjunctive in *Drew* and the instructions given by the trial court in that case did so also.

Because our statutes requiring mens rea, and our past formulation of the *M'Naghten* and ALI-*Drew* tests of insanity have afforded adequate defense to mentally ill persons who lack wrongful intent and might otherwise be subject to penal sanctions, we have not been called upon to consider the constitutional implications of the imposition of punishment on persons who act without that intent. Nor has the United States Supreme Court done so, although that court, too, has recognized repeatedly that except in regulatory offenses in which the sanctions are relatively light, the existence of wrongful intent is essential to criminal liability.

Because mens rea or wrongful intent is a fundamental aspect of criminal law, the suggestion that a defendant whose mental illness results in inability to appreciate that his act is wrongful could be punished by death or imprisonment raises serious questions of constitutional dimension under both the due process and cruel and unusual punishment provisions of the Constitution. In *Leland v. Oregon* (1952) 343 U.S. 790, the court upheld an Oregon law placing the burden of proving insanity beyond a reasonable doubt on the defendant and affirmed the right of the state to formulate the applicable test of legal insanity. In so doing, however, the court measured the law under due process standards, concluding that the irresistible impulse extension of the traditional insanity test was not "implicit in the concept of ordered liberty." The court thus seemingly accepted the proposition that the insanity defense, in some formulation, is required by due process (see also *Robinson v. California* (1962) 370 U.S. 660, suggesting that punishment for the status of being mentally ill would constitute cruel and unusual punishment). Scholars, too, suggest that abolition of the traditional insanity defense may be constitutionally impermissible if the result would be imposition of punishment on a mentally ill person for acts done without criminal intent.

This court suggested a similar view in *People v. Coleman* (1942) 20 Cal. 2d 399, where we observed: "Obviously an insane person accused of crime would be inhumanely dealt with if his insanity were considered merely to reduce the degree of his crime or the punishment therefor."

We need not face these difficult constitutional questions, however, if section 25(b) does no more than return to the pre-*Drew* California version of the *M'Naghten* test.

III
Post-Proposition 8—Return to M'Naghten

If the use of the conjunctive "and" in section 25(b) is not a draftsman's error, a defendant must now establish both that he "was incapable of knowing or understanding the nature and quality of his or her act and of distinguishing right from wrong." We recognize the basic principle of statutory and constitutional construction which mandates that courts, in construing a measure, not undertake to rewrite its unambiguous language. That rule is not applied, however, when it appears clear that a word has been erroneously used, and a judicial correction will best carry out the intent of the adopting body. The inadvertent use of "and" where the purpose or intent of a statute seems clearly to require "or" is a familiar example of a drafting error which may properly be rectified by judicial construction. Whether the use of "and" in section 25(b) is, in fact, a drafting error can only be determined by reference to the purpose of the section and the intent of the electorate in adopting it.

The ballot summaries and arguments are not helpful. The Attorney General's summary of Proposition 8 advises only that the measure included a provision "regarding ... proof of insanity." The analysis of the Legislative Analyst quotes the conjunctive language and states only that the provision "could increase the difficulty of proving that a person is not guilty by reason of insanity." No reference to the insanity provision appears in the arguments for or against Proposition 8. These omissions are not without significance, however. As we noted earlier, the insanity defense reflects a fundamental legal principle common to the jurisprudence of this country and to the common law of England[6] that criminal sanctions are imposed only on persons who act with wrongful intent in the commission of a *malum in se* offense. Since 1850 the disjunctive *M'Naghten* test of insanity has been accepted as the rule by which the minimum cognitive function which constitutes wrongful intent will be measured in this state. As such it is itself among the fundamental principles of our criminal law. Had it been the intent of the drafters of Proposition 8 or of the electorate which adopted it both to abrogate the more expansive ALI-*Drew* test and to abandon that prior fundamental principle of culpability for crime, we would anticipate that this intent would be expressed in some more obvious manner than the substitution of a single conjunctive in a lengthy initiative provision.

Applying section 25(b) as a conjunctive test of insanity would erase that fundamental principle. It would return the law to that which preceded *M'Naghten*, a test known variously as the "wild beast test" and as the "good and evil test" under which an accused could be found insane only if he was "totally deprived of his understanding and memory, and doth not know what he is doing, no more than an infant, than a brute, or a wild beast." (*Rex v. Arnold* (1724) 16 Howell St. Tr. 695.) We find nothing in the language of Proposition 8, or in any other source from which the intent of the electorate may be divined which indicates that such a fundamental, far-reaching change in the law of insanity as that was intended.

...

6. This concept of criminal responsibility is not one limited to the laws of this country and of England. In their article on the development of the insanity defense in California, Platt and Diamond trace the defense to Hebrew law, and also find the doctrine of criminal responsibility a recognized part of Greek and Roman philosophy. (Platt & Diamond, *The Origins of the "Right and Wrong" Test of Criminal Responsibility and Its Subsequent Development in the United States: An Historical Survey* (1966) 54 Cal. L. Rev. 1227.)

IV

Although the People agree that the purpose of section 25(b) was to return the test of legal insanity in California to the pre-ALI-*Drew* version of the *M'Naghten* test, they argue that reversal of this judgment is not required because both prongs of that test are actually the same. The findings of the trial judge in this case illustrate the fallacy inherent in this argument. It is true that a person who is unaware of the nature and quality of his act by definition cannot know that the act is wrong. In this circumstance the "nature and quality" prong subsumes the "right and wrong" prong.

The reverse does not necessarily follow, however. The expert testimony in this case supported the findings of the trial court that this defendant was aware of the nature and quality of his homicidal act. He knew that he was committing an act of strangulation that would, and was intended to, kill a human being. He was not able to comprehend that the act was wrong because his mental illness caused him to believe that the act was not only morally justified but was expected of him. He believed that the homicide was "right."

The People argue further that section 25(b) was intended to "clarify" the meaning of the right/wrong prong of the California *M'Naghten* test by establishing that the "wrong" which the defendant must comprehend is a legal, rather than a moral wrong. Under this formulation this defendant, who was able to recognize that his act was unlawful, would not escape criminal responsibility even though he believed his act was commanded by God. We fail to see the manner in which section 25(b) conveys this clarification of the *M'Naghten* test....

...

The concept of "wrong" was not limited to legal wrong in *People v. Wolff* (1964) 61 Cal. 2d 795. There this court explained that the California version of the *M'Naghten* test had been liberalized by holding that "knowing" in the sense of being able to verbalize the concepts of right and wrong was insufficient to establish legal sanity. Rather, the defendant must "know" in a broader sense—he must appreciate or understand these concepts.

...

Courts in a number of jurisdictions which have considered the question have come to the conclusion as we do, that a defendant who is incapable of understanding that his act is morally wrong is not criminally liable merely because he knows the act is unlawful. Justice Cardozo, in an opinion for the New York Court of Appeal, eloquently expressed the underlying philosophy: "In the light of all these precedents, it is impossible, we think, to say that there is any decisive adjudication which limits the word 'wrong' in the statutory definition to legal as opposed to moral wrong.... The interpretation placed upon the statute by the trial judge may be tested by its consequences. A mother kills her infant child to whom she has been devotedly attached. She knows the nature and quality of the act; she knows that the law condemns it; but she is inspired by an insane delusion that God has appeared to her and ordained the sacrifice. *It seems a mockery to say that, within the meaning of the statute, she knows that the act is wrong.* If the definition propounded by the trial judge is right, it would be the duty of a jury to hold her responsible for the crime. We find nothing either in the history of the rule, or in its reason or purpose, or in judicial exposition of its meaning, to justify a conclusion so abhorrent.... [¶] Knowledge that an act is forbidden by law will in most cases permit the inference of knowledge that, according to the accepted standards of mankind, it is also condemned as an offense against good morals. Obedience to the law is itself a moral duty. If, however, there is an insane delusion that God has appeared to the defendant and ordained the commission of a crime, we think it cannot be said of the offender that he knows the act to be wrong." (*People v. Schmidt* (N.Y. 1915) 110 N.E. 945, italics added.)[16]

The trial court found, on clearly sufficient evidence, that defendant could not distinguish right and wrong with regard to his act. No further hearing on the issue of sanity at the time of the act is required. The judgment is reversed and the superior court is directed to enter a judgment of not guilty by reason of insanity and to proceed thereafter pursuant to section 1026.[c]

Mosk, J., concurring.

...

Just as trial courts, prosecutors and defense counsel were achieving a reasonable detente with *People v. Drew* (1978) 22 Cal. 3d 333, the initiative measure known as Proposition 8 was prepared and submitted to the electorate. It contained the latent ambiguity discussed in the majority opinion. Therein lies one of the problems inherent in attempting to adopt rules of evidence and arcane principles of law by popular vote. It is somewhat comparable to the public deciding by popular vote the appropriate technique for surgeons to employ in brain surgery.

I am convinced that the use of "and" instead of "or" would have been discovered in the traditional legislative process. In an assembly committee, on the floor of the assembly, in a senate committee, on the floor of the senate, in the Governor's veto opportunity, such inadvertence would likely have been detected, or if the choice of

---

16. Justice Cardozo's opinion continued: "It is not enough, to relieve from criminal liability, that the prisoner is morally depraved. It is not enough that he has views of right and wrong at variance with those that find expression in the law. The variance must have its origin in some disease of the mind. The anarchist is not at liberty to break the law because he reasons that all government is wrong. The devotee of a religious cult that enjoins polygamy or human sacrifice as a duty is not thereby relieved from responsibility before the law. In such cases the belief, however false according to our own standards, is not the product of disease. Cases will doubtless arise where criminals will take shelter behind a professed belief that their crime was ordained by God, just as this defendant attempted to shelter himself behind that belief. We can safely leave such fabrications to the common sense of juries."

c. Section 1026, provides that when a defendant is found not guilty by reason of insanity, the defendant, unless he/she has recovered his sanity, shall be confined in a state hospital for the care and treatment of the mentally disordered or other appropriate facility until the defendant has recovered his/her sanity.

words was deliberate, such intent would have been clearly declared. In an initiative measure, however, no revision opportunity is possible and no legislative intent is available; the voter has only the choice of an enigmatic all or nothing.

In this instance the choice given voters was encumbered by at least 12 subjects subsumed within what was titled Proposition 8. The numerous subjects were itemized by the Attorney General in his prepared title for submission to the voters and he concluded with a catchall, "and other matters." I remain convinced that Proposition 8 was invalid as a clear violation of the constitutional prohibition against multiple subjects. For example, it would appear impossible to rationalize, as but one subject, a return to the *M'Naughton* rule of insanity and a guarantee of school safety. Regrettably, by a four-to-three majority, my colleagues expediently failed to invalidate the initiative. Had they done so, much of the subsequent uncertainties and incongruities in the criminal law would have been avoided.

Since I am bound by stare decisis to accept that untoward result, I must now join in undertaking the often thankless task of trying to inject some rational meaning into the numerous disparate subjects covered by Proposition 8. The clumsy effort to "return to *M'Naughton*" is but the latest controversy.

The analysis of the majority being as reasonable and pragmatic as the circumstances justify, I endorse their opinion.

Bird, C.J., dissenting.

In June of 1982, the voters adopted a ballot measure which radically altered the test for criminal insanity in this state. I cannot ignore the fact that they adopted language which unambiguously requires the accused to demonstrate that "he or she was incapable of knowing or understanding the nature and quality of his or her act *and* of distinguishing right from wrong at the time of the commission of the offense." (Italics added.) There is nothing in the statute, in Proposition 8 as a whole, or in the ballot arguments that implies that the electorate intended "and" to be "or." However unwise that choice, it is not within this court's power to ignore the expression of popular will and rewrite the statute.

Since appellant failed to establish his insanity under the test enunciated in Penal Code section 25, subdivision (b), I cannot join the decision of my brethren.

Note and Problem

The Constitution and the Insanity Defense. In *Skinner*, Justice Grodin based his analysis, in part, on the understanding that "the insanity defense, in some formulation, is required by due process" and that eliminating the *second* prong of the *M'Naghten* test might be unconstitutional as a violation of due process or the prohibition on cruel and unusual punishments. The Supreme Court has not addressed the former proposition, but, since the *Skinner* decision, four states—Idaho, Kansas, Montana and Utah—have eliminated the insanity defense. In *Clark v. Arizona*, 548 U.S. 735, 126 S. Ct. 2709 (2006), the Court considered the constitutionality of a state's definition of insanity. Arizona's definition of insanity eliminates the *first* prong of the *M'Naghten* test. The Court rejected the defendant's due process challenge to the definition. Does the *Clark* holding suggest that the Court would also uphold an insanity test which eliminated the *second* prong of the *M'Naghten* test?

Problem 87.

Defendant participated in a liquor store holdup, during which he shot and killed the store owner. As a result, he is charged with robbery (P.C. § 211) and first degree murder (P.C. §§ 187–189), and he has entered a plea of not guilty by reason of insanity. After Defendant's conviction at the guilt phase, defense and prosecution psychiatrists testified at the sanity phase. The defense psychiatrist testified to the effect that Defendant had "indications of a depressive condition" and anxiety, borderline mental retardation, and a "history of long-term addiction to alcohol and drugs." He also testified that Defendant's test results were "consistent with somebody who might have organic brain damage." In contrast, the prosecution psychiatrist testified that he saw no connection between any mental illness and Defendant's crimes and he thought Defendant was malingering. The prosecutor has requested that the jury be instructed in terms of P.C. § 29.8, which reads as follows:

> In any criminal proceeding in which a plea of not guilty by reason of insanity is entered, this defense shall not be found by the trier of fact solely on the basis of a personality or adjustment disorder, a seizure disorder, or an addiction to, or abuse of, intoxicating substances.

What arguments should be made regarding the prosecutor's request?

Jones v. United States

463 U.S. 354, 103 S. Ct. 3043 (1983)

Justice Powell delivered the opinion of the Court.

The question presented is whether petitioner, who was committed to a mental hospital upon being acquitted of a criminal offense by reason of insanity, must be released because he has been hospitalized for a period longer than he might have served in prison had he been convicted.

I

In the District of Columbia a criminal defendant may be acquitted by reason of insanity if his insanity is "affirmatively established by a preponderance of the evidence." D.C. Code § 24-301(j) (1981). If he successfully invokes the insanity defense, he is committed to a mental hospital. § 24-301(d)(1). The statute provides several ways of obtaining release. Within 50 days of commitment the acquittee is entitled to a judicial hearing to determine his eligibility for release, at which he has the burden of proving by a preponderance of the evidence that he is no longer mentally ill or dangerous. § 24-301(d)(2). If he fails to meet this burden at the 50-day hearing, the committed acquittee subsequently may be released, with court approval, upon certification of his recovery by the hospital chief of service. § 24-301(e). Alternatively, the acquittee is entitled to a judicial hearing every six months at which he may establish by a preponderance of the evidence that he is entitled to release. § 24-301(k).

Independent of its provision for the commitment of insanity acquittees, the District of Columbia also has adopted a civil-commitment procedure, under which an individual may be committed upon clear and convincing proof by the Government that he is mentally ill and likely to injure himself or others. § 21-545(b). The individual may demand a jury in the civil-commitment proceeding. § 21-544. Once committed, a patient may be released at any time upon certification of recovery by the hospital chief of service. §§ 21-546, 21-548. Alternatively, the patient is entitled after the first 90 days, and subsequently at 6-month intervals, to request a judicial hearing at which he may gain his release by proving by a preponderance of the evidence that he is no longer mentally ill or dangerous. § 21-546, 21-547.

II

On September 19, 1975, petitioner was arrested for attempting to steal a jacket from a department store. The next day he was arraigned in the District of Columbia Superior Court on a charge of attempted petit larceny, a misdemeanor punishable by a maximum prison sentence of one year. The court ordered petitioner committed to St. Elizabeths, a public hospital for the mentally ill, for a determination of his competency to stand trial. On March 2, 1976, a hospital psychologist submitted a report to the court stating that petitioner was competent to stand trial, that petitioner suffered from "Schizophrenia, paranoid type," and that petitioner's alleged offense was "the product of his mental disease." The court ruled that petitioner was competent to stand trial. Petitioner subsequently decided to plead not guilty by reason of insanity. The Government did not contest the plea, and it entered into a stipulation of facts with petitioner. On March 12, 1976, the Superior Court found petitioner not guilty by reason of insanity and committed him to St. Elizabeths pursuant to § 24-301(d)(1).

On May 25, 1976, the court held the 50-day hearing required by § 24-301(d)(2)(A). A psychologist from St. Elizabeths testified on behalf of the Government that, in the opinion of the staff, petitioner continued to suffer from paranoid schizophrenia and that "because his illness is still quite active, he is still a danger to himself and to others." Petitioner's counsel conducted a brief cross-examination, and presented no evidence. The court then found that "the defendant-patient is mentally ill and as a result of his mental illness, at this time, he constitutes a danger to himself or others." Petitioner was returned to St. Elizabeths. Petitioner obtained new counsel and, following some procedural confusion, a second release hearing was held on February 22, 1977. By that date petitioner had been hospitalized for more than one year, the maximum period he could have spent in prison if he had been convicted. On the basis he demanded that he be released unconditionally or recommitted pursuant to the civil-commitment standards in § 21-545(b), including a jury trial and proof by clear and convincing evidence of his mental illness and dangerousness. The Superior Court denied petitioner's request for a civil-commitment hearing, reaffirmed the findings made at the May 25, 1976, hearing, and continued petitioner's commitment to St. Elizabeths.

...

III

It is clear that "commitment for any purpose constitutes a significant deprivation of liberty that requires due process protection." *Addington v. Texas*, 441 U.S. 418 (1979). Therefore, a State must have "a constitutionally adequate purpose for the confinement." *O'Connor v. Donaldson*, 422 U.S. 563 (1975). Congress has determined that a criminal defendant found not guilty by reason of insanity in the District of Columbia should be committed indefinitely to a mental institution for treatment and the protection of society. Petitioner does not contest the Government's authority to commit a mentally ill and dangerous person indefinitely to a mental institution, but rather contends that "the petitioner's trial was not a constitutionally adequate hearing to justify an indefinite commitment."

Petitioner's argument rests principally on *Addington v. Texas*, in which the Court held that the Due Process Clause requires the Government in a civil-commitment proceeding to demonstrate by clear and convincing evidence that the individual is mentally ill and dangerous. Petitioner contends that these due process standards were not met in his case because the judgment of not guilty by reason of insanity did not constitute a finding of present mental illness and dangerousness and because it was established only by a preponderance of the evidence. Petitioner then concludes that the Government's only conceivably legitimate justification for automatic commitment is to ensure that insanity acquittees do not escape confinement entirely, and that this interest can justify commitment at most for a period equal to the maximum prison sentence the acquittee could have received if convicted. Because petitioner has been hospitalized for longer than the one year he might have served in prison, he asserts that he should be released unconditionally or recommitted under the District's civil-commitment procedures.

A

We turn first to the question whether the finding of insanity at the criminal trial is sufficiently probative of mental illness and dangerousness to justify commitment. A verdict of not guilty by reason of insanity establishes two facts: (i) the defendant committed an act that constitutes a criminal offense, and (ii) he committed the act because of mental illness. Congress has determined that these findings constitute an adequate basis for hospitalizing the acquittee as a dangerous and mentally ill person. We cannot say that it was unreasonable and therefore unconstitutional for Congress to make this determination.

The fact that a person has been found, beyond a reasonable doubt, to have committed a criminal act certainly indicates dangerousness. Indeed, this concrete evidence generally may be at least as persuasive as any predictions about dangerousness that might be made in a civil-commitment proceeding. We do not agree with petitioner's suggestion that the requisite dangerousness is not established by proof that a person committed a non-violent crime against property. This Court never has held that "violence," however that term might be defined, is a prerequisite for a constitutional commitment.

Nor can we say that it was unreasonable for Congress to determine that the insanity acquittal supports an inference of continuing mental illness. It comports with common sense to conclude that someone whose mental illness was sufficient to lead him to commit a criminal act is likely to remain ill and in need of treatment. The precise evidentiary force of the insanity acquittal, of course, may vary from case to case, but the Due Process Clause does not require Congress to make classifications that fit every individual with the same degree of relevance. Because a hearing is provided within 50 days of the commitment, there is assurance that every acquittee has prompt opportunity to obtain release if he has recovered.

Petitioner also argues that, whatever the evidentiary value of the insanity acquittal, the Government lacks a legitimate reason for committing insanity acquittees automatically because it can introduce the insanity acquittal as evidence in a subsequent civil proceeding. This argument fails to consider the Government's strong interest in avoiding the need to conduct a *de novo* commitment hearing following every insanity acquittal—a hearing at which a jury trial may be demanded, and at which the Government bears the burden of proof by clear and convincing evidence. Instead of focusing on the critical question whether the acquittee has recovered, the new proceeding likely would have to relitigate much of the criminal trial. These problems accent the Government's important interest in automatic commitment. We therefore conclude that a finding of not guilty by reason of insanity is a sufficient foundation for commitment of an insanity acquittee for the purposes of treatment and the protection of society.

B

Petitioner next contends that his indefinite commitment is unconstitutional because the proof of his insanity was based only on a preponderance of the evidence, as compared to *Addington*'s civil-commitment requirement of proof by clear and convincing evidence. In equating these situations, petitioner ignores important differences between the class of potential civil-commitment candidates and the class of insanity acquittees that justify differing standards of proof. The *Addington* Court expressed particular concern that members of the public could be confined on the basis of "some abnormal behavior which might be perceived by some as symptomatic of a mental or emotional disorder, but which is in fact within a range of conduct that is generally acceptable." In view of this concern, the Court deemed it inappropriate to ask the individual "to share equally with society the risk of error." But since automatic commitment under § 24-301(d)(1) follows only if the acquittee himself advances insanity as a defense and proves that his criminal act was a product of his mental illness, there is good reason for diminished concern as to the risk of error.[16]

---

16. That petitioner raised the insanity defense also diminishes the significance of the deprivation. The *Addington* Court noted that the social stigma of civil commitment "can have a very significant

More important, the proof that he committed a criminal act as a result of mental illness eliminates the risk that he is being committed for mere "idiosyncratic behavior." A criminal act by definition is not "within a range of conduct that is generally acceptable."

We therefore conclude that concerns critical to our decision in *Addington* are diminished or absent in the case of insanity acquittees. Accordingly, there is no reason for adopting the same standard of proof in both cases....[17]

C

The remaining question is whether petitioner nonetheless is entitled to his release because he has been hospitalized for a period longer than he could have been incarcerated if convicted. The Due Process Clause "requires that the nature and duration of commitment bear some reasonable relation to the purpose for which the individual is committed." *Jackson v. Indiana*, 406 U.S. 715 (1972). The purpose of commitment following an insanity acquittal, like that of civil commitment, is to treat the individual's mental illness and protect him and society from his potential dangerousness. The committed acquittee is entitled to release when he has recovered his sanity or is no longer dangerous. And because it is impossible to predict how long it will take for any given individual to recover—or indeed whether he ever will recover—Congress has chosen, as it has with respect to civil commitment, to leave the length of commitment indeterminate, subject to periodic review of the patient's suitability for release.

In light of the congressional purposes underlying commitment of insanity acquittees, we think petitioner clearly errs in contending that an acquittee's hypothetical maximum sentence provides the constitutional limit for his commitment. A particular sentence of incarceration is chosen to reflect society's view of the proper response to commission of a particular criminal offense, based on a variety of considerations such as retribution, deterrence, and rehabilitation. The State may punish a person convicted of a crime even if satisfied that he is unlikely to commit further crimes.

Different considerations underlie commitment of an insanity acquittee. As he was not convicted, he may not be punished. His confinement rests on his continuing illness and dangerousness. Thus, under the District of Columbia statute, no matter how serious the act committed by the acquittee, he may be released within 50 days of his acquittal if he has recovered. In contrast, one who committed a less serious act may be confined for a longer period if he remains ill and dangerous. There simply is no necessary correlation between severity of the offense and length of time necessary

---

impact on the individual." A criminal defendant who successfully raises the insanity defense necessarily is stigmatized by the verdict itself, and thus the commitment causes little additional harm in this respect.

17. A defendant could be required to prove his insanity by a higher standard than a preponderance of the evidence. See *Leland v. Oregon*, 343 U.S. 790 (1952). Such an additional requirement hardly would benefit a criminal defendant who wants to raise the insanity defense, yet imposition of a higher standard would be a likely legislative response to a holding that an insanity acquittal could support automatic commitment only if the verdict were supported by clear and convincing evidence.

for recovery. The length of the acquittee's hypothetical criminal sentence therefore is irrelevant to the purposes of his commitment.[19]

IV

We hold that when a criminal defendant establishes by a preponderance of the evidence that he is not guilty of a crime by reason of insanity, the Constitution permits the Government, on the basis of the insanity judgment, to confine him to a mental institution until such time as he has regained his sanity or is no longer a danger to himself or society....

[Dissenting opinion of Brennan, J., joined by Marshall and Blackmun, JJ. and dissenting opinion of Stevens, J. omitted.]

Note and Problem

The Effect of a Successful Insanity Defense. In California, the procedures to be taken after a successful insanity defense are set forth in Penal Code § 1026. In brief, unless it appears to the court that the defendant has fully recovered his or her sanity, the court is to order an evaluation of the defendant and then commit the defendant to the appropriate care facility or order the defendant placed on outpatient status. If the defendant is confined to an institution on an inpatient basis, the director makes semi-annual reports to the court on the defendant's progress. If, after the verdict, the court believes the defendant has fully recovered his or her sanity, the defendant is held in jail until civil commitment proceedings can be instituted. If the defendant is determined not to be a danger to the defendant or others, the defendant is released.

Problem 88.

In recent years, California (along with many other states) has enacted legislation permitting the civil commitment of convicted sex offenders after they have served their sentences. California's Sexually Violent Predator Act ("SVPA"), Wel. & Inst. Code § 6600, *et seq.*, went into effect on January 1, 1996. It defines a sexually violent predator as a person who has been "convicted of a sexually violent offense [rape, sodomy, lewd acts upon children under 14, oral copulation, sexual penetration by foreign object] against two or more victims for which he or she has received a determinate sentence and who has a diagnosed mental disorder that makes the person a

---

19. ... The inherent fallacy of relying on a criminal sanction to determine the length of a therapeutic confinement is manifested by petitioner's failure to suggest any clear guidelines for deciding when a patient must be released. For example, he does not suggest whether the Due Process Clause would require States to limit commitment of insanity acquittees to maximum sentences or minimum sentences. Nor does he explain what should be done in the case of indeterminate sentencing or suggest whether account would have to be taken of the availability of release time or the possibility of parole. And petitioner avoids entirely the important question how his theory would apply to those persons who committed especially serious criminal acts. Petitioner thus would leave the States to speculate how they may deal constitutionally with acquittees who might have received life imprisonment, life imprisonment without possibility of parole, or the death penalty.

danger to the health and safety of others in that it is likely that he or she will engage in sexually violent criminal behavior." A "diagnosed mental disorder" is defined in its entirety as "includ[ing] a congenital or acquired condition affecting the emotional or volitional capacity that predisposes the person to the commission of criminal sexual acts in a degree constituting the person a menace to the health and safety of others." Initially the Department of Corrections screens inmates six months before their release and refers suspected SVPs to the Department of Mental Health for full evaluation. If two evaluators agree that the inmate is an SVP, the Department requests the District Attorney in the county where the SVP was last convicted to file a commitment petition. If a petition is filed, the Superior Court holds a probable cause hearing, and, if probable cause is found, a jury trial is held. The District Attorney must prove beyond a reasonable doubt that the inmate is an SVP in order to win a commitment. If a commitment is ordered, the inmate receives treatment for his disorder, and either the inmate or the Department may petition the court for release of the inmate in the event that he or she is no longer an SVP.

During a 24-year period ending with his most recent conviction ten years ago, Inmate was convicted on five occasions for molesting children. The most recent conviction was for attempting to fondle two 13-year old boys. Inmate received no treatment while incarcerated, although pedophilia is concededly treatable. The District Attorney has now petitioned to have Inmate committed as an SVP. What arguments should be made as to whether committing Inmate would be unconstitutional?

Part IV

Vicarious Liability

The two chapters in this Part deal with the issue of who beside the principal—the person directly committing the acts constituting the crime—will be criminally responsible for the principal's conduct. As was noted in the discussion of conspiracy [see Chapter 9], participants in a conspiracy are vicariously liable for crimes committed by their co-conspirators. Participants in criminal ventures may also be vicariously liable as accomplices. Corporations may be vicariously liable for the criminal acts of their officers or agents who also may be liable for the crimes of the corporation. Chapter 13 considers the elements of accomplice liability and of corporate vicarious liability. Chapter 14 concerns the scope of vicarious liability in the situation where the principal commits crimes unintended by the vicariously liable parties.

Chapter 13

Accomplice and Corporate Vicarious Liability

Accomplice liability was well defined at the common law. Participants in felonies were classified as principals and accessories.

> According to the ancient analysis only the actual perpetrator of the felonious deed was a principal. Other guilty parties were called "accessories," and to distinguish among these with reference to time and place they were divided into three classes: (1) accessories before the fact, (2) accessories at the fact, and (3) accessories after the fact. At a relatively early time the party who was originally considered an accessory at the fact ceased to be classed in the accessorial group and was labeled a principal. To distinguish him from the actual perpetrator of the crime he was called a principal in the second degree. Thereafter, in felony cases there were two kinds of principals, first degree and second degree, and two kinds of accessories, before the fact and after the fact. (Perkins & Boyce, Criminal Law (3rd ed. 1982) Parties to Crime, ch. 6, § 8, p. 722.)

A principal in the first degree was one who perpetrated a crime "not only with his own hands, but 'through the agency of mechanical or chemical means, as by instruments, poison or powder, or by an animal, child, or other innocent agent' acting at his direction." (*Id.* at p. 736.) A principal in the second degree was one who "did not commit the crime with his own hands" but who "aided, counseled, commanded or encouraged the commission thereof in his presence, either actual or constructive." (*Id.*, at pp. 736, 738.) An accessory before the fact was one who "aided, counseled or encouraged the commission [of the crime], without having been present either actually or constructively at the moment of perpetration." (*Id.*, at p. 744.) An accessory after the fact was one who, after the commission of the crime, and with knowledge of the other's guilt, rendered assistance to hinder the detection, arrest, trial or punishment of a party to the crime (*Id.*, at pp. 748.) The cases in Section A discuss the current law of accomplice liability in California.

Corporate vicarious liability was unknown at the common law. At one time, it was thought that a corporation (or other collective entity) could not be guilty of crimes because it had no mind to satisfy a *mens rea* requirement and it had no body to be imprisoned. The movement away from this view began with public welfare offenses, where conviction could be had without proof of *mens rea* and where the punishment was a fine, which the corporation could be made to pay. The two cases in Section B set out the current law of corporate vicarious liability in California.

A. Accomplice Liability

In California, the distinction between principals in the first and second degree and between principals and accessories before the fact was eliminated in the 1872 Penal Code:

> All persons concerned in the commission of a crime, whether it be felony or misdemeanor, and whether they directly commit the act constituting the offense, or aid and abet in its commission, or, not being present, have advised and encouraged its commission, and all persons counseling, advising or encouraging children under the age of fourteen years, lunatics or idiots, to commit any crime, or who, by fraud, contrivance, or force, occasion the drunkenness of another for the purpose of causing him to commit any crime, or who, by threats, menaces, command or coercion, compel another to commit any crime, are principals in any crime so committed. (P. C. § 31.)

There remains a separate crime of accessory after the fact to a felony. See Penal Code § 32. Although defined in the Penal Code as principals for purposes of punishment (P.C. § 31), persons who aid and abet, advise or encourage criminal conduct are treated as accomplices for purposes of vicariously liability analysis. The first four cases define the elements of accomplice liability. In *People v. Collins*, the question is whether an accomplice can be guilty of a crime when the principal is working for the police. In *People v. McCoy*, the issue is whether an accomplice can be guilty of a greater crime than the principal. In *People v. Beeman*, the California Supreme Court addresses the mental state element of accomplice liability. The Court has to decide whether intent to further the principal's crime or mere knowledge that the crime is being furthered is the mental state the prosecution must prove. In *People v. Cooper*, the Court decides when a late-joiner to the criminal endeavor will be liable as an accomplice. The succeeding two cases raise the question of who is the principal in uncommon situations involving two actors. In *People v. Williams*, a murder prosecution, the actual shooter is acquitted, but the defendant who encouraged the shooting is convicted. *In re Joseph G.* involves a joint suicide attempt where one of the two participants survives. The Supreme Court has to determine whether the survivor is guilty of murder (as a principal) or only of the lesser crime of assisting a suicide.

People v. Collins

53 Cal. 185, 2 P.C.L.J. 62 (1878)

By The Court:

There was evidence tending strongly to show that the defendant requested Parnell to enter a certain building in the nighttime, and to steal therefrom a sum of money which he knew to be concealed there; and that the money, when stolen, should be divided between them. The evidence also tended to prove that instead of accepting and acting upon this proposal, Parnell immediately informed the Sheriff of it, who, after consultation with the District Attorney, advised Parnell to pretend to carry out the enterprise. It was therefore agreed between Parnell and the Sheriff, that when the money was taken it should be marked with acid, so that it could be identified; and that when the money was delivered to the defendant a signal should be given by Parnell, to enable the Sheriff to arrest the defendant with the money in his possession. The evidence tended to prove that this programme, as agreed upon by Parnell and the Sheriff was carried into effect; that Parnell entered the building, secured the money, marked it with acid, delivered a part of it to the defendant, gave the signal as agreed upon, and the Sheriff thereupon arrested the defendant with the money in his possession.

On this state of the evidence the Court instructed the jury that, if it was agreed between Parnell and the defendant that the former should enter the building and steal the money, to be divided between them, and if, in pursuance of the agreement, Parnell did enter the building and take the money and divide it with the defendant, the defendant was guilty of burglary, and the jury should so find, "without regard to the part taken in the offense by the witness Parnell, or as to the motives or intentions of said Parnell." This instruction was erroneous.

If Parnell entered the building and took the money with no intention of stealing it, but only in pursuance of a previously arranged plan between him and the Sheriff, intended solely to entrap the defendant into the apparent commission of a crime, it is clear that no burglary was committed, there being no felonious intent in entering the building, or taking the money. If the act of Parnell amounted to burglary, the Sheriff who counseled and advised it was privy to the offense; but no one would seriously contend, on the foregoing facts, that the Sheriff was guilty of burglary. The evidence for the prosecution showed that no burglary was committed by Parnell, for the want of a felonious intent, and the defendant could not have been privy to a burglary unless one was committed.

Judgement and order reversed, and cause remanded for a new trial.

Wallace, C.J., did not express an opinion in this case.

People v. McCoy

25 Cal.4th 1111, 24 P.3d 1210 (2001)

Chin, J.

We granted review to decide whether an aider and abettor may be guilty of greater homicide-related offenses than those the actual perpetrator committed. Because defenses or extenuating circumstances may exist that are personal to the actual perpetrator and do not apply to the aider and abettor, the answer, sometimes, is yes. We reverse the judgment of the Court of Appeal, which concluded otherwise.

I. Factual and Procedural History

Codefendants Ejaan Dupree McCoy and Derrick Lakey were tried together and convicted of crimes arising out of a drive-by shooting in Stockton in 1995. McCoy drove the car and Lakey was in the front passenger seat, with others in the back. The car approached four people standing on a street corner. McCoy leaned out of the window and shouted something. A flurry of shots was fired from the car toward the group. Witnesses saw both McCoy and Lakey shooting handguns. Two of the group were shot, one fatally. The other two escaped injury. Someone from outside the car returned fire, wounding Lakey. The evidence showed that McCoy fired the fatal bullets.

At trial, McCoy but not Lakey testified. McCoy admitted shooting but claimed he did so because he believed he would be shot himself. He said that earlier that day, he had driven by that same intersection, and someone fired shots in his direction. He decided to seek out a friend who might be able to help him determine who had fired at him. McCoy brought his gun for protection and picked up Lakey, who also had a gun. Across the street from his friend's house, McCoy saw three men standing near a tree. Thinking that one of them might be his friend, McCoy drove slowly toward the group, stopped, and called out to get their attention. McCoy then saw that the man was not his friend and that he held a "dark something" that appeared to be a gun. Believing that the man was going to shoot him, McCoy grabbed his own gun and fired until the gun was empty. Lakey also fired his gun out the car window.

A jury found McCoy and Lakey guilty of various crimes, including first degree murder and two counts of attempted murder. The Court of Appeal unanimously reversed McCoy's murder and attempted murder convictions, finding that the trial court prejudicially misinstructed the jury on McCoy's theory of unreasonable self-defense, a theory that, if the jury had accepted it, would have reduced the crimes to voluntary manslaughter and attempted voluntary manslaughter.

The Court of Appeal also reversed Lakey's murder and attempted murder convictions "for two independent reasons: (1) under California law, a defendant who is tried as an aider and abettor cannot be convicted of an offense greater than that of which the actual perpetrator is convicted, where the aider and abettor and the perpetrator are tried in the same trial upon the same evidence, and (2) on this record, we cannot conclude with reasonable certainty that any participant acted with malice in connection with [the murder and attempted murder counts], so we cannot say that the crimes of murder or attempted murder have been committed." Justice Hull dissented as to Lakey and would have affirmed his conviction.

We granted the Attorney General's petition for review limited to whether the Court of Appeal correctly reversed Lakey's murder and attempted murder convictions.

II. Discussion

...

Resolution of this question requires a close examination of the nature of aiding and abetting liability. "All persons concerned in the commission of a crime, ... whether they directly commit the act constituting the offense, or aid and abet in its commission, ... are principals in any crime so committed." (Pen.Code, § 31.) Thus, a person who aids and abets a crime is guilty of that crime even if someone else committed some or all of the criminal acts. Because aiders and abettors may be criminally liable for acts not their own, cases have described their liability as "vicarious." This description is accurate as far as it goes. But, as we explain, the aider and abettor's guilt for the intended crime is not entirely vicarious. Rather, that guilt is based on a combination of the direct perpetrator's acts and the aider and abettor's *own* acts and *own* mental state.

It is important to bear in mind that an aider and abettor's liability for criminal conduct is of two kinds. First, an aider and abettor with the necessary mental state is guilty of the intended crime. Second, under the natural and probable consequences doctrine, an aider and abettor is guilty not only of the intended crime, but also "for any other offense that was a 'natural and probable consequence' of the crime aided and abetted." (*People v. Prettyman* (1996) 14 Cal.4th 248.) Thus, for example, if a person aids and abets only an intended assault, but a murder results, that person may be guilty of that murder, even if unintended, if it is a natural and probable consequence of the intended assault. In this case, however, the trial court did not instruct the jury on the natural and probable consequences doctrine. It instructed only on an aider and abettor's guilt of the intended crimes. Accordingly, only an aider and abettor's guilt of the intended crime is relevant here. Nothing we say in this opinion necessarily applies to an aider and abettor's guilt of an unintended crime under the natural and probable consequences doctrine.

Except for strict liability offenses, every crime has two components: (1) an act or omission, sometimes called the actus reus; and (2) a necessary mental state, sometimes called the mens rea (Pen.Code, § 20). This principle applies to aiding and abetting liability as well as direct liability. An aider and abettor must do something *and* have a certain mental state.

We have described the mental state required of an aider and abettor as "different from the mental state necessary for conviction as the actual perpetrator." (*People v. Mendoza* (1998) 18 Cal.4th 1114.) The difference, however, does not mean that the mental state of an aider and abettor is less culpable than that of the actual perpetrator. On the contrary, outside of the natural and probable consequences doctrine, an aider and abettor's mental state must be at least that required of the direct perpetrator. "To prove that a defendant is an accomplice ... the prosecution must show that the defendant acted with knowledge of the criminal purpose of the perpetrator *and* with an intent or purpose either of committing, or of encouraging or facilitating commission of, the offense. When the offense charged is a specific intent crime, the accomplice must share the specific intent of the perpetrator; this occurs when the accomplice knows the full extent of the perpetrator's criminal purpose and gives aid or encouragement with the intent or purpose of facilitating the perpetrator's commission of the crime." (*People v. Prettyman.*) What this means here, when the charged offense and the intended offense—murder or attempted murder—are the same, i.e., when guilt does not depend on the natural and probable consequences doctrine, is that the aider and abettor must know and share the murderous intent of the actual perpetrator.

Aider and abettor liability is thus vicarious only in the sense that the aider and abettor is liable for another's actions as well as that person's own actions. When a person "chooses to become a part of the criminal activity of another, she says in essence, 'your acts are my acts.'" (Dressler, *Reassessing the Theoretical Underpinnings of Accomplice Liability: New Solutions to an Old Problem* (1985) 37 Hastings L.J. 91.) But that person's *own* acts are also her acts for which she is also liable. Moreover, that person's mental state is her own; she is liable for her mens rea, not the other person's.

As stated in another work by Professor Dressler, "many commentators have concluded that there is no conceptual obstacle to convicting a secondary party of a more serious offense than is proved against the primary party. As they reason, once it is proved that the principal has caused an *actus reus*, the liability of each of the secondary parties should be assessed according to his own *mens rea*. That is, although joint participants in a crime are tied to a single and common *actus reus*, the individual *mentes reae* or levels of guilt of the joint participants are permitted to float free and are not tied to each other in any way. If their *mentes reae* are different, their independent levels of guilt ... will necessarily be different as well." (Dressler, Understanding Criminal Law (2d ed. 1995) § 30.06[C].)

Professor Dressler explained how this concept operates with homicide. "An accomplice may be convicted of first-degree murder, even though the primary party is convicted of second-degree murder or of voluntary manslaughter. This outcome follows, for example, if the secondary party, premeditatedly, soberly and calmly, assists in a homicide, while the primary party kills unpremeditatedly, drunkenly, or in provocation. Likewise, it is possible for a primary party negligently to kill another (and, thus, be guilty of involuntary manslaughter), while the secondary party is guilty of murder, because he encouraged the primary actor's negligent conduct, with the intent that it result in the victim's death."

...

Moreover, the dividing line between the actual perpetrator and the aider and abettor is often blurred. It is often an oversimplification to describe one person as the actual perpetrator and the other as the aider and abettor. When two or more persons commit a crime together, both may act in part as the actual perpetrator *and* in part as the aider and abettor of the other, who also acts in part as an actual perpetrator. Although Lakey was liable for McCoy's actions, he was an actor too. He was in the car and shooting his own gun, although it so happened that McCoy fired the fatal shots. Moreover, Lakey's guilt for *attempted* murder might be based entirely on his own actions in shooting at the attempted murder victims. In another shooting case, one person might lure the victim into a trap while another fires the gun; in a stabbing case, one person might restrain the victim while the other does the stabbing. In either case, both participants would be direct perpetrators as well as aiders and abettors of the other. The aider and abettor doctrine merely makes aiders and abettors liable for their accomplices' actions as well as their own. It obviates the necessity to decide who was the aider and abettor and who the direct perpetrator or to what extent each played which role.

...

As another example, assume someone, let us call him Iago, falsely tells another person, whom we will call Othello, that Othello's wife, Desdemona, was having an affair, hoping that Othello would kill her in a fit of jealousy. Othello does so without Iago's further involvement. In that case, depending on the exact circumstances of the killing, Othello might be guilty of manslaughter, rather than murder, on a heat of passion theory. Othello's guilt of manslaughter, however, should not limit Iago's guilt if his own culpability were greater. Iago should be liable for his own acts as well as Othello's, which he induced and encouraged. But Iago's criminal liability, as Othello's, would be based on his own personal mens rea. If, as our hypothetical suggests, Iago acted with malice, he would be guilty of murder even if Othello, who did the actual killing, was not.

We thus conclude that when a person, with the mental state necessary for an aider and abettor, helps or induces another to kill, that person's guilt is determined by the combined acts of all the participants as well as that person's own mens rea. If that person's mens rea is more culpable than another's, that person's guilt may be greater even if the other might be deemed the actual perpetrator.[3]

As applied here, Lakey and McCoy were to some extent both actual perpetrators and aiders and abettors. Both fired their handguns, although McCoy's gun inflicted the fatal wounds. Once the jury found, as it clearly did, that Lakey acted with the necessary mental state of an aider and abettor, it could find him liable for both his and McCoy's acts, without having to distinguish between them. But Lakey's guilt was also based on his own mental state, not McCoy's. McCoy's unreasonable self-defense theory was personal to him. A jury could reasonably have found that Lakey did not act under unreasonable self-defense even if McCoy did. Thus, his conviction of murder and attempted murder can stand, notwithstanding that on retrial McCoy might be convicted of a lesser crime or even acquitted.

People v. Beeman

35 Cal. 3d 547, 674 P.2d 1318 (1984)

Reynoso, J.

Timothy Mark Beeman appeals from a judgment of conviction of robbery, burglary, false imprisonment, destruction of telephone equipment and assault with intent to commit a felony. (Pen. Code, §§ 211, 459, 236, 591, 221.) Appellant was not present

---

3. Because we cannot anticipate all possible nonhomicide crimes or circumstances, we express no view on whether or how these principles apply outside the homicide context.

during commission of the offenses. His conviction rested on the theory that he aided and abetted his acquaintances James Gray and Michael Burk.

...

James Gray and Michael Burk drove from Oakland to Redding for the purpose of robbing appellant's sister-in-law, Mrs. Marjorie Beeman, of valuable jewelry, including a 3.5 carat diamond ring. They telephoned the residence to determine that she was home. Soon thereafter Burk knocked at the door of the victim's house, presented himself as a poll taker, and asked to be let in. When Mrs. Beeman asked for identification, he forced her into the hallway and entered. Gray, disguised in a ski mask, followed. The two subdued the victim, placed tape over her mouth and eyes and tied her to a bathroom fixture. Then they ransacked the house, taking numerous pieces of jewelry and a set of silverware. The jewelry included a 3.5 carat, heart-shaped diamond ring and a blue sapphire ring. The total value of these two rings was over $100,000. In the course of the robbery, telephone wires inside the house were cut.

Appellant was arrested six days later in Emeryville. He had in his possession several of the less valuable of the stolen rings. He supplied the police with information that led to the arrests of Burk and Gray. With Gray's cooperation appellant assisted police in recovering most of the stolen property.

Burk, Gray and appellant were jointly charged. After the trial court severed the trials, Burk and Gray pled guilty to robbery. At appellant's trial they testified that he had been extensively involved in planning the crime.

[Burk and Gray testified that they had known Beeman for some time and both owed money to him. Two and one-half months before the robbery, Burk and Beeman began talking about robbing Beeman's relatives in Redding. Burk then approached Gray about participating in the robbery. About one week before the robbery, the discussions became more specific. Beeman gave Burk the address and discussed the ruse of posing as a poll taker. It was decided that Gray and Burk would go to Redding because Beeman wanted nothing to do with the actual robbery. Because Beeman was 6' 5" tall and 310 lbs., he feared being recognized. On the night before the robbery, Beeman drew a floor plan of the victim's house and told Burk where the diamond ring was likely to be found. Beeman agreed to sell the jewelry for 20 percent of the proceeds. After the robbery, Burk and Gray drove to Beeman's house with the "loot." Beeman then asked them to give him all of the stolen goods. Instead Burk and Gray gave Beeman only a watch and some rings which they believed he could sell. Sometime later Beeman asked for Gray's cooperation in recovering and returning the property.]

Appellant Beeman's testimony contradicted that of Burk and Gray as to nearly every material element of his own involvement. Appellant testified that he did not participate in the robbery or its planning. He confirmed that Burk had lived with him on several occasions, and that he had told Burk about Mrs. Beeman's jewelry, the valuable diamond ring, and the Beeman ranch, in the course of day-to-day conversations. He claimed that he had sketched a floor plan of the house some nine months prior to the robbery, only for the purpose of comparing it with the layout of a house belonging to another brother. He at first denied and then admitted describing the Beeman family cars, but insisted this never occurred in the context of planning a robbery.

Appellant stated that Burk first suggested that robbing Mrs. Beeman would be easy some five months before the incident. At that time, and on the five or six subsequent occasions when Burk raised the subject, appellant told Burk that his friends could do what they wanted but that he wanted no part of such a scheme.

Beeman admitted Burk had told him of the poll taker ruse within a week before the robbery, and that Burk told him they had bought a cap gun and handcuffs. He further admitted that he had allowed Burk to take some old clothes left at the apartment by a former roommate. At that time Beeman told Burk: "If you're going to do a robbery, you can't look like a bum." Nevertheless, appellant explained that he did not know Burk was then planning to commit this robbery. Further, although he knew there was a possibility Burk and Gray would try to rob Mrs. Beeman, appellant thought it very unlikely they would go through with it. He judged Burk capable of committing the crime but knew he had no car and no money to get to Redding. Appellant did not think Gray would cooperate.

Appellant agreed that he had talked with Gray on the phone two days before the robbery, and said he had then repeated he did not want to be involved. He claimed that Burk called him on the way back from Redding because he feared appellant would report him to the police, but knew appellant would want to protect Gray, who was his closer friend.

Appellant claimed he told the others to come to his house after the robbery and offered to sell the jewelry in order to buy time in which to figure out a way to collect and return the property. He took the most valuable piece to make sure it was not sold. Since Burk had a key to his apartment, appellant gave the diamond ring and a bracelet to a friend, Martinez, for safekeeping.[4] After Burk fled to Los Angeles, appellant showed some of the jewelry to mutual acquaintances in order to lull Burk into believing he was attempting to sell it. During this time Burk called him on the phone several times asking for money and, when appellant told him of plans to return the property, threatened to have him killed.

When confronted with his prior statement to the police that he had given one of the rings to someone in exchange for a $50 loan, appellant admitted making the statement but denied that it was true. He also claimed that his statement on direct examination that "his [Burk's] face was seen. He didn't wear a mask. Didn't do anything he was supposed to do ..." referred only to the reason Gray had given for wanting to return the victim's property.

Appellant requested that the jury be instructed in accord with *People v. Yarber* (1979) 90 Cal. App. 3d 895 that aiding and abetting liability requires proof of intent to aid. The request was denied.

4. Martinez corroborated that appellant had given him a diamond ring and other jewelry belonging to appellant's family for this purpose.

After three hours of deliberation, the jury submitted two written questions to the court: "We would like to hear again how one is determined to be an accessory and by what actions can he absolve himself"; and "Does inaction mean the party is guilty?" The jury was reinstructed in accord with the standard instructions, CALJIC Nos. 3.00 and 3.01.[a] The court denied appellant's renewed request that the instructions be modified as suggested in *Yarber*, explaining that giving another, slightly different instruction at this point would further complicate matters. The jury returned its verdicts of guilty on all counts two hours later.

...

II

There is no question that an aider and abettor must have criminal intent in order to be convicted of a criminal offense. (Pen. Code, § 20.) Decisions of this court dating back to 1898 hold that "the word 'abet' includes knowledge of the wrongful purpose of the perpetrator and counsel and encouragement in the crime" and that it is therefore error to instruct a jury that one may be found guilty as a principal if one aided or abetted. (*People v. Dole* (1898) 122 Cal. 486.) The act of encouraging or counseling itself implies a purpose or goal of furthering the encouraged result. "An aider and abettor's fundamental purpose, motive and intent is to aid and assist the perpetrator in the latter's commission of the crime." (*People v. Vasquez* (1972) 29 Cal. App. 3d 81.)

The essential conflict in current appellate opinions is between those cases which state that an aider and abettor must have an intent or purpose to commit or assist in the commission of the criminal offenses, and those finding it sufficient that the aider and abettor engage in the required acts with knowledge of the perpetrator's criminal purpose.[5]

The cases most often cited for the view that knowledge of the perpetrator's wrongful purpose is sufficient are *People v. Terry* (1970) 2 Cal. 3d 362, *People v. Ott* (1978) 84 Cal. App. 3d 118, *People v. Standifer* (1974) 38 Cal. App. 3d 733, and *People v. Ellhamer* (1962) 199 Cal. App. 2d 777. *Terry* and *Standifer* are said to have been catalysts for the transmutation of CALJIC No. 3.01 from its pre-1974 to its present form. As we shall explain, however, we believe this is a misconstruction of *Terry*. Neither that

---

a. Elsewhere the court describes the two instructions as follows:

CALJIC No. 3.00 defines principals to a crime to include "Those who, with knowledge of the unlawful purpose of the one who does directly and actively commit or attempt to commit the crime, aid and abet in its commission..., or ... Those who, whether present or not at the commission or attempted commission of the crime, advise and encourage its commission...." CALJIC No. 3.01 defines aiding and abetting as follows: "A person aids and abets the commission of a crime if, with knowledge of the unlawful purpose of the perpetrator of the crime, he aids, promotes, encourages or instigates by act or advice the commission of such crime."

5. Some cases which take the latter viewpoint intimate that the aider and abettor must also know that his acts will probably facilitate the perpetrator's commission of the offense.

opinion nor the weight of accepted authority supports the definition of aiding and abetting embodied in the current version of CALJIC No. 3.01.

In *Terry* this court held that an accomplice to robbery-murders need not have the intent to take the victims' property: "She was an aider or abettor if, with knowledge of Terry's criminal purpose, she encouraged, promoted, or assisted in the commission of the crimes. One who aids and abets does not necessarily have the intention of enjoying the fruits of the crime."

Relying on this language the Court of Appeal in *Standifer* rejected the defendant's contention that he must be found to have the same criminal intent as the perpetrator. The court held an instruction calling for a finding of "required" as opposed to "criminal" intent proper: "... we feel the test is 'did the defendant aid and abet the perpetrator with knowledge of the perpetrator's criminal intent.'"

The subsequent *Ellhamer* and *Ott* decisions explain the reasoning process behind the theory that knowledge is all that is required: "... the criminal intent of the aider and abettor is presumed from his actions with knowledge of the actor's wrongful purpose." In *Ott* the court specifically upheld the current version of CALJIC Nos. 3.00 and 3.01 against the argument that they omit the element of criminal intent.

The reasoning of *Ellhamer* and *Ott* has been forcefully and correctly criticized by a number of subsequent Court of Appeal opinions which find that the weight of authority requires an aider and abettor to have an intent or purpose to commit or assist in commission of the underlying offense. The leading case is People v. Yarber, *supra*, which explained that "[the] *Ellhamer/Ott* synthesis that intent is inferred from the knowledge by the aider and abettor of the perpetrator's purpose is sound, generally, as a matter of human experience, but we cannot extrapolate therefrom, as a matter of law, that the inference *must* be drawn. Intent is what must be proved; from a person's action with knowledge of the purpose of the perpetrator of a crime, his intent to aid the perpetrator can be inferred. In the absence of evidence to the contrary, the intent may be regarded as established. But where a contrary inference is reasonable—where there is room for doubt that a person intended to aid a perpetrator—his knowledge of the perpetrator's purpose will not suffice." (Original italics.)

...

We agree with the *Yarber* court that the facts from which a mental state may be inferred must not be confused with the mental state that the prosecution is required to prove. Direct evidence of the mental state of the accused is rarely available except through his or her testimony. The trier of fact is and must be free to disbelieve the testimony and to infer that the truth is otherwise when such an inference is supported by circumstantial evidence regarding the actions of the accused. Thus, an act which has the effect of giving aid and encouragement, and which is done with knowledge of the criminal purpose of the person aided, may indicate that the actor intended to assist in fulfillment of the known criminal purpose. However, as illustrated by *Hicks v. U.S.* (1893) 150 U.S. 442 (conviction reversed because jury not instructed that words of encouragement must have been used with the intention of encouraging and abetting crime in a case where ambiguous gesture and remark may have been acts of desperation) and *People v. Bolanger* (1886) 71 Cal. 17 (feigned accomplice not guilty because lacks common intent with the perpetrator to unite in the commission of the crime), the act may be done with some other purpose which precludes criminal liability.

...

Thus, we conclude that the weight of authority and sound law require proof that an aider and abettor act with knowledge of the criminal purpose of the perpetrator and with an intent or purpose either of committing, or of encouraging or facilitating commission of, the offense.

When the definition of the offense includes the intent to do some act or achieve some consequence beyond the *actus reus* of the crime (see *People v. Hood* (1969) 1 Cal. 3d 444), the aider and abettor must share the specific intent of the perpetrator. By "share" we mean neither that the aider and abettor must be prepared to commit the offense by his or her own act should the perpetrator fail to do so, nor that the aider and abettor must seek to share the fruits of the crime. Rather, an aider and abettor will "share" the perpetrator's specific intent when he or she knows the full extent of the perpetrator's criminal purpose and gives aid or encouragement with the intent or purpose of facilitating the perpetrator's commission of the crime. The liability of an aider and abettor extends also to the natural and reasonable consequences of the acts he knowingly and intentionally aids and encourages.

...

[Concurring and dissenting opinion of Richardson, J., omitted.]

Note and Problems

United States v. Hicks. In *United States v. Hicks*, 150 U.S. 442 (1893) (cited with approval in *Beeman*), the United States Supreme Court addressed both the act element and mental state element for accomplice liability. Hicks was convicted of the murder of Colvard under the following circumstances. Hicks and Rowe were Cherokee Indians, who were wanted for arrest by U.S. marshals and who were armed for purpose of resisting arrest. Colvard was a white man who traded with the Cherokees and was friendly with Hicks and Rowe. The night before the murder, all three attended a party, and there was a good deal of whiskey consumed. Early the next morning, Hicks and Colvard were riding together and encountered Rowe in the road. The witnesses testified to the following:

> As Colvard and Hicks approached the point where Stand Rowe was sitting on his horse, Stand Rowe rode out into the road and halted. Colvard then rode up to him in a lope or canter, leaving Hicks, the defendant, some 30 or 40 feet in his rear. The point where the three men were together on their horses was about 100 yards from where the four witnesses stood on the porch. The conversation between the three men on horseback was not fully heard by the four men on the porch, and all that was heard was not understood,

> because part of it was carried on in the Cherokee tongue; but some part of this conversation was distinctly heard and clearly understood by these witnesses; they saw Stand Rowe twice raise his rifle and aim it at Colvard, and twice he lowered it; they heard Colvard say, "I am a friend to both of you;" they saw and heard the defendant Hicks laugh aloud when Rowe directed his rifle toward Colvard; they saw Hicks take off his hat and hit his horse on the neck or shoulder with it; they heard Hicks say to Colvard, "Take off your hat and die like a man;" they saw Stand Rowe raise his rifle for the third time, point it at Colvard, fire it; they saw Colvard's horse wheel and ... saw Colvard fall from his horse; ... they saw Stand Rowe and John Hicks ride off together after the shooting.

Hicks denied that he had encouraged Rowe to shoot Colvard, saying that he had tried to persuade him not to shoot, and he testified that he only rode off with Rowe because he was afraid of him and that he separated from him a short while later.

Having determined that Hicks was not the actual murderer, the trial court instructed the jury on two possible bases for finding him liable as an accomplice:

> If the defendant was actually or constructively present at that time, and in any way aided or abetted by word or by advising or encouraging the shooting of Colvard by Stand Rowe, ... he is made a participant in the crime as thoroughly and completely as though he had with his own hand fired the shot which took the life of the man killed.
>
> [I]f he was actually present at that place at the time of the firing by Stand Rowe, and he was there for the purpose of either aiding, abetting, advising, or encouraging the shooting of Andrew J. Colvard by Stand Rowe, and that as a matter of fact he did not do it, but was present at the place for the purpose of aiding or abetting or advising or encouraging his shooting, but he did not do it because it was not necessary, ... the law says there is a ... condition where guilt is fastened to his act in that regard.

The Supreme Court held that the trial court erred in both of its instructions. As to the first, the Court found that it permitted conviction based on Rowe's reaction to the defendant's actions, without proof of the defendant's intent. As to the second, the Court found that it permitted conviction on the basis of the defendant's intent alone, without the defendant having provided any actual aid.

How should the court have instructed on the facts of this case?

Problem 89.

The following occurred in 1893. Victim seduced and had an affair with Maiden. Maiden's brothers learned of the seduction and went to the nearby town of Stevenson to find Victim and kill him. Victim's cousin, Helpful, learned of the danger and sent a warning telegram to Victim. However, Defendant, Maiden's brother-in-law, was present when Helpful's telegram was sent, and Defendant sent his own telegram to his friend, the Stevenson telegraph operator, telling him not to deliver Helpful's telegram. Helpful's telegram was not delivered, and the brothers caught up with Victim and killed him. What arguments can be made on whether Defendant is an accomplice to the killing? Would the result be different if the Stevenson telegraph operator had attempted to deliver Helpful's telegram but did not find Victim in time?

Problem 90.

Teenagers, Shooter, Aider and Abettor were charged with second-degree murder (P.C. §§ 187–189) and five counts of attempted murder (P.C. §§ 187, 664) on the following facts. On the night of the shootings, Aider, Abettor and Friend purchased and drank a case of beer. While driving around, they noticed a large party being held in a warehouse. They stopped and attempted to enter the party, but they were rebuffed, and an altercation ensued during which all three were hit and Friend was clubbed with a flashlight. The three left, threatening to come back with a gun. Aider and Abettor left Friend at a hospital for treatment and picked up Shooter, and, arming themselves with tire irons, they decided to return to the warehouse to get revenge. Arriving at the warehouse, they discovered that the warehouse was locked, and the partygoers refused to open the door. The three did some damage to the cars parked outside and then left. At the suggestion of Aider and Abettor, Shooter agreed to get his rifle. When the three returned to the warehouse, they were confronted by some of the partygoers, but Shooter pointed his rifle at them and they retreated. Shooter then fired a number of shots into the door of the warehouse, killing one person and wounding five. What arguments should be made as to whether Aider and Abettor can introduce evidence of their intoxication in defense of the charges?

People v. Cooper

53 Cal. 3d 1158, 811 P.2d 742 (1991)

Lucas, C.J.

We are called on to decide whether it is error to instruct a jury that the "getaway" driver in a robbery may be convicted of aiding and abetting the robbery, and therefore of being a principal rather than a mere accessory after the fact (Pen. Code, §§ 31, 32), even if the jury finds that the defendant did not form the requisite intent to facilitate or encourage commission of the robbery prior to the robbers' flight with the stolen property....

As our cases recognize, the prosecution must show an aider and abettor intended to facilitate or encourage the principal offense prior to or during its commission. The main issue here, therefore, is the duration of the commission of a robbery for purposes of determining whether a getaway driver is liable as an aider and abettor rather than an accessory.

We conclude that the commission of a robbery for purposes of determining aider and abettor liability continues until all acts constituting the robbery have ceased. The asportation, the final element of the offense of robbery, continues so long as the stolen property is being carried away to a place of temporary safety. Accordingly, in order to be held liable as an aider and abettor, the requisite intent to aid and abet must be formed *before or during such carrying away of the loot to a place of temporary safety*. Therefore, a getaway driver who has no prior knowledge of a robbery, but who forms the intent to aid in carrying away the loot during such asportation, may properly be found liable as an aider and abettor of the robbery.

...

I.
Background
A. Facts

Defendant drove his two codefendants to the parking lot of a shopping center. After he parked the car, the three alighted and conversed for several minutes. At one point, defendant walked over to a wall bordering a nearby school, peered over the top, and then returned to the car. Several minutes later, the codefendants ran across the parking lot and, without stopping, slammed into an 89-year-old shopper, stealing his wallet. Leaving the victim lying on the ground, the codefendants fled with the loot to defendant's car, which was moving with its two right-side doors open. After his co-defendants jumped inside, defendant hurriedly drove away.

B. Trial Court Proceedings

Defendant and his codefendants were charged with robbery. The charge against defendant was based on the theory that he aided and abetted the robbery by driving the getaway car, and therefore could be punished as a principal.[1] Defendant claimed that with respect to the robbery the evidence proved no more than he was an accessory after the fact.[2] Specifically, defendant contended the evidence did not show beyond reasonable doubt that he possessed prior knowledge of or intent to aid the robbery. Rather, he claimed the evidence might support the conclusion that he knew his companions were going to commit a theft and that he merely intended to assist them in the commission of that lesser crime. Defendant did not testify at his trial.

The court gave five instructions relevant to the issue presented in this case. First, it instructed that one who aids and abets the commission of a crime is guilty of all offenses that are the "actual and probable consequences" of that crime and that it is the jury's responsibility to decide whether the offense charged is such a consequence.[3]

---

1. Section 31 states: "All persons concerned in the commission of a crime, ... whether they directly commit the act constituting the offense, or aid and abet in its commission, ... are principals in any crime so committed."

2. Section 32 states: "Every person who, after a felony has been committed, harbors, conceals, or aids a principal in such felony, with the intent that such principal may avoid or escape from arrest, trial, conviction or punishment, having knowledge that said principal has committed such felony or has been charged with such felony or convicted thereof, is an accessory to such felony."

3. This instruction follows our reasoning in *People v. Croy* (1985) 41 Cal. 3d 1. However, because the trial court gave multiple instructions providing the jury with alternative bases for convicting defendant of robbery as an aider and abettor, it would be improper to rely on this proper instruction to affirm defendant's robbery conviction. We emphasize, however, the continued validity and vitality

Next, the court defined an aider and abettor as one who, with knowledge of the unlawful purpose of the perpetrators and with intent to commit, encourage, or facilitate commission of an offense, aids, promotes, or encourages commission of that offense.

Third, over defendant's objection, the court instructed: "The commission of the crime of robbery is not confined to a fixed place or a limited period of time. A robbery is still in progress after the original taking of physical possession of the stolen property while the perpetrator is in hot flight, that is, while in possession of the stolen property he is fleeing in an attempt to escape. Likewise, it is still in progress so long as he is still immediately being pursued in an attempt to capture him or regain the stolen property. A robbery is complete when the perpetrator has eluded his pursuers, if any; has reached a place of temporary safety and is in unchallenged possession of the stolen property after having effected an escape with such property."

Fourth, the court instructed that the "offense of being an accessory requires the specific intent that the perpetrator avoid or escape from arrest, trial, conviction, or punishment." (CALJIC No. 3.31.) Finally, the court defined an accessory after the fact as one who, "after a felony has been committed, harbors, conceals or aids a principal in such felony, with the intent that said principal may avoid or escape from arrest, trial, conviction or punishment, having knowledge that said principal has committed such felony...."

The jury convicted defendant and his codefendants of robbery....

...

II.
Discussion
A. Duration of "Commission" of Robbery

In *People v. Croy* (1985) 41 Cal. 3d 1, we expressly left open the question whether a person may properly be classified as an aider and abettor, where he had no knowledge of a robbery until the robber's entry into the getaway car but thereafter knowingly aided the robber in the getaway. To answer this question, we must first look to the elements of aiding and abetting liability. A person aids and abets the commission of a crime when he or she, (i) with knowledge of the unlawful purpose of the perpetrator, (ii) and with the intent or purpose of committing, facilitating or encouraging commission of the crime, (iii) by act or advice, aids, promotes, encourages or instigates the commission of the crime. (*People v. Beeman* (1984) 35 Cal. 3d 547.)

Beeman presupposes that, if a person in fact aids, promotes, encourages or instigates commission of a crime, the requisite intent to render such aid must be formed *prior to or during* "commission" of that offense. It is legally and logically impossible to both form the requisite intent and in fact aid, promote, encourage, or facilitate commission of a crime after the commission of that crime has ended.

---

of the *Croy* theory of aider and abettor liability for "any reasonably foreseeable offense committed" by the person[s] aided and abetted.

In the case before us, we must determine the duration of the commission of a robbery for purposes of assessing aider and abettor liability. We have held that once all elements of a robbery are satisfied, the offense has been initially committed and the principal may be found guilty of robbery, as distinct from a mere attempt. This threshold of guilt-establishment is a fixed point in time, but is not synonymous with "commission" of a crime for our purposes.

For purposes of determining aider and abettor liability, the commission of a robbery continues until all acts constituting the offense have ceased.[7] The taking element of robbery itself has two necessary elements, gaining possession of the victim's property and asporting or carrying away the loot. Thus, in determining the duration of a robbery's commission we must necessarily focus on the duration of the final element of the robbery, asportation.

Although for purposes of establishing guilt, the asportation requirement is initially satisfied by evidence of slight movement, asportation is not confined to a fixed point in time.[8] The asportation continues thereafter as long as the loot is being carried away to a place of temporary safety. Therefore, in order to fulfill the requirements of *Beeman* for conviction of the more serious offense of aiding and abetting a robbery, a getaway driver must form the intent to facilitate or encourage commission of the robbery *prior to or during the carrying away of the loot to a place of temporary safety.*

In determining the duration of the asportation, we reject the argument that commission of the robbery necessarily ends once the loot is removed from the "immediate presence" of the victim. Although the "immediate presence" language comes directly from section 211, this language does not pertain to the *duration* of robbery. Section

7. The logic of viewing "committed" as a fixed point in time for purposes of guilt-establishment and "commission" as a temporal continuum for purposes of determining accomplice liability can be seen from the perspectives of both the victim and the accomplice. The rape victim, for example, would not agree that the crime was completed once the crime was initially committed (i.e., at the point of initial penetration). Rather, the offense does not end until all of the acts that constitute the rape have ceased. Furthermore, the unknowing defendant who happens on the scene of a rape after the rape has been initially *committed* and aids the perpetrator in the continuing criminal acts is an accomplice under this concept of "commission," because he formed his intent to facilitate the commission of the rape *during its commission*. The dissent fails to recognize this important distinction. In the midst of its criticism of our analysis of the duration of a robbery's "commission" for purposes of aider and abettor liability, the dissent pauses to put forth in one conclusory sentence its preferred resolution of the issue. For purposes of determining "commission" in the aider and abettor context, the dissent adopts the inapposite rule of "slight asportation" used to distinguish mere attempts from successful robberies. Because the dissent embraces this rule without explanation or analysis, choosing instead to devote all but one sentence to a criticism of the rule we recognize today, we are unable to reciprocate with a similar lengthy criticism of the dissent's proposed rule.

8. This reasoning is consistent with a long line of Court of Appeal cases, left undisturbed by this court, holding that mere theft becomes robbery if the perpetrator, having gained possession of the property without use of force or fear, resorts to force or fear while carrying away the loot. In order to support a robbery conviction, the taking, either the gaining possession or the carrying away, must be accomplished by force or fear. Thus, these cases implicitly hold that the asportation component of the taking continues while the loot is carried away, and does not end on slight movement. The dissent's conclusion to the contrary is wholly without support and lacks logical foundation.

211 defines robbery as "the felonious taking of personal property in the possession of another, *from his person or immediate presence* ..." (Italics added.) Taking from the "person" and from the "immediate presence" are alternatives. These terms are spatially, rather than temporally, descriptive. They refer to the area *from which* the property is taken, not *how far* it is taken. Put another way, these limitations on the scope of the robbery statute relate to the "gaining possession" component of the taking as distinct from the "carrying away" component.

We also reject the argument for our purposes here that commission of the robbery continues through *the escape* to a place of temporary safety, regardless of whether or not the loot is being carried away simultaneously. In the context of certain statutes concerning ancillary consequences of robbery, robbery is said to continue through the escape to a place of temporary safety, whether or not the asportation of the loot coincides with the escape (hereafter, the escape rule).[10]

The escape rule originated in the context of the felony-murder doctrine in the landmark case of *People v. Boss* (1930) 210 Cal. 245. We have also applied the escape rule to several other ancillary consequences of robbery. (See, e.g., *People v. Laursen* (1972) 8 Cal. 3d 192 [kidnapping committed during escape from robbery is kidnapping "to commit robbery" within section 209]; *People v. Carroll* (1970) 1 Cal. 3d 581 [injury inflicted on robbery victim after property had been asported but before robber escaped to a place of temporary safety occurred "in the course of commission of the robbery" for purposes of bodily injury enhancement].)

Never, however, have we applied the escape rule in contexts other than the construction of statutes concerning certain ancillary consequences of robbery....

...

First, although we agree that the escape rule serves the legitimate public policy considerations of deterrence and culpability in the context of determining certain ancillary consequences of robbery, the rule does not similarly serve those considerations in the context of determining principal liability as an aider and abettor of a robbery. In *Laursen*, we recognized that the escape rule served public policy because the primary purpose of the kidnapping-to-commit-robbery statute is to impose harsher criminal sanctions to deter activity that substantially increases the risk of harm. Similarly, in *People v. Bigelow* (1984) 37 Cal. 3d 731, we pointed out that the escape rule is "used in felony-murder cases to determine when a killing is so closely related to an underlying felony as to justify an enhanced punishment for the killing." These considerations of deterrence and culpability are well served by application of

---

10. We note that the act of carrying away the loot to a place of temporary safety, and thereby the commission of the robbery for purposes of aider and abettor liability, may in many circumstances coincide with the escape to a place of temporary safety. However, the distinction drawn between the escape rule (applicable to certain ancillary consequences of robbery), and the rule adopted here for purposes of determining aider and abettor liability, is not a distinction without meaning. As we discuss below, it is a principled distinction. Moreover, we emphasize here that it is also an effective distinction. In certain circumstances, carrying away the loot will *not* coincide with the escape. For instance, the loot may either be abandoned in haste prior to the escape or be carried away by a second getaway car.

the escape rule to statutes concerning certain ancillary consequences of robbery. These same public policy considerations are not, however, equally applicable to the determination of aider and abettor liability.

A primary rationale for punishing aiders and abettors as principals to deter them from aiding or encouraging the commission of offenses is not served by imposing aider and abettor liability on a getaway driver in a robbery if that person was unaware of the robbery until after all of the acts constituting robbery, *including the asportation*, had ceased. Such a driver is powerless to either prevent the robbery, or end the acts constituting the robbery if such acts have already ceased. Although the law should also deter the getaway driver from helping the robbers escape from justice after commission of the crime has ended, this goal is appropriately served by the threat of liability as an accessory after the fact. Thus, in determining liability as an aider and abettor, the focus must be on the acts constituting the robbery, not the escape.

Furthermore, in our view, adopting the escape rule for purposes of determining aider and abettor liability would be inconsistent with reasonable concepts of culpability. As noted, in certain circumstances the asportation will not coincide with the escape. A getaway driver, whose intent to aid in the escape is formed after asportation has ceased, cannot facilitate or encourage commission of the robbery.[12] Rather, the effect of his or her actions is only to lessen the chance that the perpetrators will be captured and held accountable for their crimes. Thus the culpability of such a getaway driver is that of an accessory after the fact, rather than that of a principal. This distinction comports with the language of section 32, which expressly defines accessory liability as including a person who aids a principal with intent that the principal "avoid or escape from arrest."

Second, it would be illogical to adopt the escape rule for purposes of determining aider and abettor liability. Such a holding would eliminate the distinction between aider and abettor liability and accessory liability in the context of getaway drivers in a manner both contrary to statute, and out of step with reasonable concepts of culpability and practical considerations of deterrence, as discussed above. Moreover, the escape, not being an element of robbery, should not be used to define the duration of robbery for purposes of determining aider and abettor liability. Rather, in delineating a crime it is logical to look to the elements that constitute that crime.[13]

---

12. The intent of such a getaway driver is to be distinguished from one who agrees before (or during) commission of a robbery to be a getaway driver and thereby encourages and/or facilitates the commission of the robbery. In such circumstances, the driver could be liable as an aider and abettor of the robbery.

13. We note that asportation is not an element of burglary. Thus, the commission of the burglary and the escape will never coincide. For this reason, the distinction between commission for purposes of felony-murder liability and commission for purposes of aider and abettor liability is clearer in the burglary context than in robbery. Nonetheless, the fact that this distinction is also made in the burglary context supports our conclusion that the duration of an offense for purposes of aider and abettor liability must be determined with respect to the elements of the offense, rather than with respect to the escape.

...

Accordingly, we decline to adopt the escape rule, applicable in the context of certain ancillary consequences of robbery, for purposes of determining aider and abettor liability. For purposes of determining liability as an aider and abettor, the commission of robbery continues so long as the loot is being carried away to a place of temporary safety.

...

Kennard, J., dissenting.

I dissent.

For more than 100 years our law has recognized that a person who assists in the commission of an offense has a higher degree of moral culpability than a person who helps the perpetrator after the offense has been committed. This distinction has been acknowledged by the Legislature. (Pen. Code, §§ 31, 32, 33.) Nevertheless, choosing to ignore statutory law and established precedent, the majority now holds that a person who aids an escaping robber after the robbery has been completed may be held criminally liable as a principal to the robbery if the robber, at the time of the assistance, still has possession of the stolen property and the assistance is given before the robber has reached a place of "temporary safety."

The majority's "temporary safety" test finds no support in our previous decisions, draws a line that is inappropriate to the defendant's level of culpability, and is inconsistent with the general rule that one who aids a fleeing felon is not a principal in the commission of the felony. Whether a robber is carrying stolen property or has reached a place of "temporary safety" has no bearing on the type of offense committed by a person who aids in the robber's escape: a person who is not involved in a robbery until the property has already been forcibly taken and who then assists the robber's escape is, under established principles of law, only an accessory after the fact.

I

...

It has long been recognized that, assuming the other elements of the offense have been established, only slight asportation is necessary to make the crime of robbery complete. As the court in *People v. Beal* (1934) 3 Cal. App. 2d 251, observed more than 50 years ago: "The crime of robbery is complete when the robbers without lawful authority and by means of force or fear obtain possession of the personal property of another in the presence of its lawful custodian and reduce it to their manual possession. It is not necessary that, to complete the crime, they carry it out of the physical presence of the lawful possessor or make their escape with it." This is still the law. Accordingly, a "late joiner" (one who helps a robber to escape after the robber's asportation of stolen property) is criminally liable only as an accessory after the fact, irrespective of whether the robber has carried off the stolen property to a place of temporary safety. We addressed this question in *People v. Tewksbury* (1976) 15 Cal. 3d 953, where we stated that a person who aids only in the "escape" of one who has committed a robbery is an accessory after the fact, even if the robber is in possession of items taken in the commission of the crime.

In *Tewksbury*, the defendant's involvement in the robbery of a restaurant was established by the testimony of one Mary Pedraza. Pedraza testified that she was waiting for the defendant at a predetermined place near the restaurant and that shortly after the robbery the defendant told her something had gone wrong, a man had been killed, and they would have to leave quickly. They drove to Pedraza's house and divided the stolen money.

On appeal, the defendant argued that Pedraza was an accomplice to the robbery and therefore her testimony was insufficient to convict him without corroboration. (P.C. § 1111 [accomplice testimony must be corroborated].) We disagreed, concluding that although the jury could have found that Pedraza was an accomplice based on evidence that she might have participated in the planning of the robbery the evidence did not show that she was an accomplice as a matter of law. We also observed that Pedraza could not be an accomplice based solely on her participation in the escape after the robbery: "[I]t does not appear that accomplice status could be imputed to [Pedraza] on the ground that because the perpetrators of the crimes had not yet made their escape the crimes were still in progress when they met [Pedraza] at the rendezvous point. *Her conduct thereafter with knowledge of the crimes would, at most, constitute her being an accessory after the fact* (§ 32)." (*People v. Tewksbury*, italics added.) Thus, even though Pedraza helped the robber to escape *with the stolen property*, this court concluded that her liability was no more than that of an accessory after the fact.

The majority does not identify the source of its holding that in robbery the element of asportation continues until the robber has reached a place of temporary safety; it simply concludes, with no attempt to cite any supporting authority, that this is the case. This absence of authority is not surprising, for there appears to be no authority to support the majority's novel and unwarranted holding; certainly, this court has never held that in robbery asportation continues until the robber has reached a place of temporary safety.[3]

...

The most fundamental defect in the majority's unprecedented holding is that it leads to results that bear little or no relationship to the level of culpability of the accused, as these hypotheticals will illustrate:

1. A commits a murder. B, who had no prior knowledge of the crime, helps A to escape. Under established law, B is an accessory after the fact. If A robs the murder victim but is *not* in possession of property stolen from the victim when B assists A

3. The majority notes the existence of "a long line of Court of Appeal cases ... holding that mere theft becomes robbery if the perpetrator, having gained possession of the property without use of force or fear, resorts to force or fear while carrying away the loot." These cases, the majority asserts, "implicitly hold" that asportation continues for a period of time while the stolen property is being carried away. To the contrary, these cases merely establish that the offense of robbery is not committed until all of its elements have occurred.

in escaping, B is still an accessory after the fact. But under the majority rule, if A robs the murder victim and is in possession of the stolen property when B assists A in escaping, B is guilty of both robbery and, as a result of the felony-murder rule, first degree murder. (See § 189.)

2. A commits a robbery, and flees directly to the home of B. At the door, A tells B of the robbery and displays the stolen property. B allows A to hide in the house. Under the majority rule, B is guilty of robbery, because A has not reached a place of temporary safety at the time B lets him in the house. But if, during his flight, A had stopped briefly at a place of temporary safety before going to B's home, B would be an accessory, because the asportation of stolen property would have been complete at the moment A reached that place of temporary safety. In both instances, B's actions and knowledge of the facts of the robbery are the same; under the majority's holding, B's criminal liability turns on a fact of which he is unaware and which is totally unrelated to his degree of culpability.

3. B sees A push a woman to the ground, grab the woman's purse, and run, pursued by a police officer. B steps in front of the officer, impeding the pursuit of A, who drops the purse but manages to get away. Under the majority's holding, B would be guilty of robbery. But if B had interfered with the officer's pursuit only seconds later, after A had dropped the stolen purse, B would be merely an accessory after the fact because A, the robber, was no longer in possession of the stolen property when B helped A to escape.

If the purse had been stolen in a burglary rather than a robbery, under the majority's holding B would be an accessory regardless of when the burglar dropped the purse, for the simple reason that asportation is not an element of the offense of burglary.

4. A and B commit an armed robbery. As they flee, A has the gun while B carries the stolen property. Under the majority rule, if C helps A reach a place of temporary safety C is an accessory; but if C assists B, C is guilty of robbery because B was in possession of the stolen property when C facilitated B's escape.

These four examples highlight the anomalies that arise from the majority's attempt to carve out an exception to the general rule ... that a person who aids in the escape of a fleeing felon is an accessory after the fact. Whether a robber has reached a place of temporary safety or is carrying property stolen in the robbery at the time of the escape bears the most tenuous relationship to the degree of culpability of the person aiding in the escape. By using these circumstances to draw the line between a principal and an accessory, the majority has fashioned a rule that will dictate substantially different results for persons whose degree of culpability is essentially similar. Rather than creating illusory distinctions, we should apply to the crime of robbery the same rule that applies to other criminal offenses and treat "late joiners" who assist in the escape as accessories after the fact.

...

Mosk, J., and Broussard, J., concurred.

Problem

Problem 91.

Victim, a gas station cashier, was shot and killed during a robbery of the station. Defendant was subsequently arrested and charged with robbery (P.C. § 211) and first degree murder (P.C. §§ 187–189). At trial, there was substantial evidence that Defendant was the killer, but Defendant testified that Uncle had driven to the station with Defendant as a passenger and that he (Defendant) remained in the car while Uncle entered the store, presumably to get cigarettes. Defendant heard a gunshot and ran into the store to find that Uncle had shot Victim. Uncle grabbed the cash register, and the two ran out the door and drove away. While they were driving, Defendant pried open the cash register, took the money out and threw the cash register away. Assuming, *arguendo*, that the jury believes Defendant's testimony, what arguments should be made as to whether Defendant is guilty of the charges?

People v. Williams

75 Cal. App. 3d 731, 142 Cal.Rptr. 704 (1977)

SIMS, J.

Appellant has appealed from a judgment of imprisonment entered on jury verdicts which found her guilty of murder in the second degree ... The victim died from wounds inflicted by the appellant's sister. She shot him with her own weapon in response to an appeal that she do so from the appellant. At the time the appellant was engaged in a struggle with the victim over her own weapon, which was never fired. The sister was acquitted, and the appellant contends that the verdict finding her guilty must be set aside because it is inconsistent with the verdict acquitting her sister, who in fact fired the fatal shots. She also asserts that the finding that she used a gun in the commission of the offense cannot be sustained under the circumstances of this case.

We conclude, from our examination of the record, that the jury were justified in finding that the appellant, with malice, caused the victim's death by using her sister as an innocent agent to accomplish the intended death of the victim. The evidence supports the implied findings that the appellant was the aggressor in the mutual combat between herself and the victim; that her use of a deadly weapon supplied the necessary malice for murder; that, failing to decline any further struggle after the victim acted to protect himself, she was not entitled to justify his killing as in self-defense; and that through her entreaty, she was the effective cause of the discharge of the firearm in her sister's hand. The fact that the sister was acquitted is of no comfort to appellant, because each acted under different circumstances.

...

Appellant and her former boyfriend, Charles Brooks, had two children, aged six and seven, respectively, at the time of the events in question. They had been living separately, but recently she had spent a night with him at his house. The children were apparently in Brooks' custody but were actually kept by a friend of his.

On April 20, 1976, according to the appellant's prior statement to her uncle and subsequent statement to the police, Brooks telephoned appellant and asked her if she wanted to come over to his house to see the children. She drove over to the house where Charles Brooks lived with his brother Henry Brooks about 5 o'clock in the afternoon, and when she arrived she asked Brooks where the children were. The appellant told the police that Brooks told her they were upstairs. When, after they had both gone upstairs, appellant discovered the children were not there, she and Brooks began to argue. He told her to leave. A struggle ensued in which, according to her report to the officer, Brooks struck appellant with a hammer. She suffered a cut beneath her left eye. According to Brooks she struck her face against the door jam as he was attempting to pull her out of his room. He denied having invited her over, or having told her the children were there.

Appellant used the telephone at the house to call the police. On his arrival, Officer Churchill observed Brooks striking appellant and knocking her down in the front yard. The officer took Brooks into custody and then went in the house with appellant so the officer could continue his investigation of the incident. While they were in the house Brooks' brother-in-law, Tillman Washington, arrived with his wife and stepson. Brooks asked him to keep the house secure until he or his brother returned. The appellant refused to leave the house and insisted that she had some belongings upstairs that she wanted to get. Washington wanted her to leave and asked the officer to remain until she did so. The officer told her to go and to wait until Brooks was released from custody, and then the police would help her retrieve her belongings if necessary.

Appellant was angry and belligerent. With the officer's permission, she telephoned her sister Jo Ann and asked her to come over and pick her up. When Jo Ann, accompanied by their uncle, arrived she found the appellant bleeding and very upset. Jo Ann tried to calm her sister and get her to leave, but finally it was necessary for her and the uncle to physically escort appellant out of the house. As appellant was leaving she turned to the crowd which had gathered, and looking at Officer Churchill and Washington, who were standing together, shouted, "I'm going to kill both you mother f___" or words of similar import.

Appellant got into her uncle's pickup truck and drove off with him, followed by Jo Ann, driving the car in which appellant had driven to Brooks' residence. A short time later both vehicles stopped in the parking lot of a nearby store. Appellant, who had apparently calmed down, told Jo Ann she wanted to return to Brooks' house and get her belongings. Jo Ann tried to persuade her to go to a hospital instead, but was unsuccessful. She tried to calm her sister and told her not to argue with anyone at Brooks'. They returned directly together, according to Jo Ann, although they each gave statements to the police which indicated appellant returned home and secured a weapon.

During the foregoing events several people had assembled at the Brooks' house. In addition to Washington, the victim, his wife and stepson, the next door neighbors and their daughter and nephew were also in and out of the house. These witnesses all observed various aspects of the incidents which marked the defendant's two visits to the Brooks' house. From their testimony, although with some conflicts, the events which transpired may be pieced together as set forth herein.

On arrival at Brooks' house the two sisters approached the front door. Appellant knocked on the front door and entered while her sister waited outside. Once inside appellant asked permission to retrieve her belongings. Washington refused her request, and tried to calm her and convince her to leave. Meanwhile, Jo Ann had grown impatient and also asked appellant to leave. Appellant then walked toward the door followed by Washington. Jo Ann heard her say, "What you do that for?" As appellant and Washington reached the door, the appellant drew a weapon from her purse. A struggle broke out between them. Washington tried to grab her hands and remove the gun and the struggle continued.

Jo Ann approached and viewed the participants struggling over the gun. She did not know to whom the gun belonged or who had started the altercation. Jo Ann did observe that Washington had gained the upper hand, and that although appellant had a hand on the gun it was close to, and pointing at, the appellant's face. She thought Washington was going to kill her sister. Jo Ann produced a gun from her own clothing and yelled, "Drop my sister or I'll shoot!" or "Let my sister go or I'll shoot!" As the struggle continued appellant shouted, "Shoot him! Shoot him!" or "Kill him! Kill him!" Appellant at no time tried to retreat or end the struggle. Washington retained his grasp on the gun. Jo Ann then fired the gun three or four times and Washington died of the resulting gunshot wounds.

Appellant grabbed Jo Ann, who was in a trance-like state, and the two fled the scene in their car. They were spotted by an airborne patrol and were arrested a short time later. The gun Jo Ann threw out of the car was retrieved. An expended cartridge and two rounds of ammunition were also found near the gun.

The appellant did not testify in her own defense. Her sister's testimony supported her own defense that the homicide was justifiable as committed in defense of a third person. The court instructed the jury concerning the various degrees and forms of homicide, and the principles governing justification by reason of self-defense or defense of another. The jury acquitted Jo Ann but returned a verdict of second degree murder against the defendant.

I

When the facts are examined in the light of principles of law governing aiders and abettors, self-defense, defense of another, commission of a crime through the innocent agency of another, and criminal liability for acts reasonably resulting from the provocation of the use of deadly force, it is clear that any alleged inconsistency in the verdicts does not exist, and that the evidence sustains appellant's conviction of murder.

[The court concluded that the jury could have acquitted Jo Ann on the theory that she reasonably, albeit mistakenly, believed that Washington was the aggressor and she was acting in defense of a third party.]

D

"Under section 31 of the Penal Code, a person is a principal in a crime, although he does not directly commit the act constituting the offense, when he aids and abets in its commission, or, not being present, advises and encourages its commission." *People v. Koomer* (1961) 188 Cal.App.2d 676. In *People v. Smith* (1929) 96 Cal. App. 373, the defendant contended he could not be criminally responsible for the burglary committed by two men he had sent to retrieve materials, which he falsely represented were his, from the house of another. The court observed, "By their verdict the jury in the instant case found that the defendants Smith and Boreman were innocent agents of Peterson in the commission of the crime. There does not appear to be any cases directly in point in this state where an innocent party committed a criminal act at the instigation of another who alone possessed the criminal intent. However, in Russell on Crimes, volume 1, page 165, the author says: 'When an offense is committed through the medium of an innocent agent, the employer, though absent when the act is done, is answerable as a principal. Thus, if a child under years of discretion, a madman, or any other person of defective mind, is incited to commit a murder or other crime, the inciter is the principal *ex necessitate*, though he were absent when the thing was done.... And if a man give another a forged note that the other may utter it, if the latter be ignorant of the note being forged, the uttering by the latter is the uttering of the former, though the former were absent at the time of the actual uttering.' [¶] McClain in his work on Criminal Law, volume 1, section 187, says: 'The general maxim "*Qui facit per alium facit per se*" is applicable in criminal law to make one accountable for acts done for him by an agent under his instruction or by his consent. And in regard to the liability of the principal it is wholly immaterial whether the act is procured to be done through a guilty or an innocent agent. If the act is done through an innocent agent, the one who procures it to be done is guilty as principal, as though he had done the act himself. But if the agent or servant through whom the act is done is guilty, the principal or master is deemed an accessory before the fact only, unless present.' [¶] In Wharton's Criminal Law, volume 1, page 312, section 241, the author says: 'A party also who acts through the medium of an innocent or insane person, or a slave, is guilty, *though absent*, as principal in first degree.' (Italics ours.) [¶] Based upon such respectable authorities, the conclusion follows that Peterson, as the directing and procuring mind, was the principal in the burglary though absent in person and not actually participating in the commission of the crime. It makes no difference if he stood in the street outside the house and directed the actions of the agent or did so from his shop several miles away."

In the instant case the appellant maliciously and wilfully assaulted the victim with a deadly weapon. Finding her purpose frustrated by his resistance, she had no justifiable action other than to withdraw from the fray. There is nothing to give rise to the inference that Washington, if he had disarmed appellant, would have shot her.

Appellant, however, elected to continue the struggle. As we have seen, if she succeeded in wresting control of the weapon from Washington and killed him, she would be criminally responsible. We have no hesitancy in concluding that under those circumstances, her exhortation and command to her sister to shoot the victim render her liable for the same consequences.

In *People v. Ceballos* (1974) 12 Cal. 3d 470, the court noted: "In the United States, courts have concluded that a person may be held criminally liable under statutes proscribing homicides and shooting with intent to injure, or civilly liable, if he sets upon his premises a deadly mechanical device and that device kills or injures another." It applied the rule to sustain the conviction of the defendant of assault with a deadly weapon, because the use of such a device was not justifiable to prevent a burglary. So here the use of her sister's gun by appellant, when appellant herself was not justified in using such force, may subject appellant to criminal liability.

E

Our conclusions that the conviction must be upheld are strengthened by reference to the developing law of the liability of one participating in a felony involving force or violence for a homicide occurring during the course of such a crime.

...

In *People v. Gilbert* (1965) 63 Cal. 2d 690, the court analyzed the responsibility of the criminal for a killing committed by the victim or a police officer as follows: "When the defendant or his accomplice, with a conscious disregard for life, intentionally commits an act that is likely to cause death, and his victim or a police officer kills in reasonable response to such act, the defendant is guilty of murder. In such a case, the killing is attributable, not merely to the commission of a felony, but to the intentional act of the defendant or his accomplice committed with conscious disregard for life. [¶] Thus, the victim's self-defensive killing or the police officer's killing in the performance of his duty cannot be considered an independent intervening cause for which the defendant is not liable, for it is a reasonable response to the dilemma thrust upon the victim or the policeman by the intentional act of the defendant or his accomplice."

In *Taylor v. Superior Court* (1970) 3 Cal. 3d 578, the court recognized that it was not necessary for the accused to fire the first shot in order to make him responsible for a homicide committed by another in response to his actions. Malice was inferred from acts of provocation consisting of the robber's coercive conduct toward one of his victims, his repeated threats of "execution," and his confederate's intent and nervous apprehension as he held the victims at gunpoint. The court noted that it had been held that an accused's resistance to a command to put up his hands and his pointing his gun toward the officers and toward his kidnap-victim supplied the essential malice and provocation for the resulting gunplay, and that an accused's grasping the gun of an officer who was ordering him to leave a riot area was of similar import.

...

From the foregoing we conclude that as in *Gilbert*, [and] *Taylor I*, ... the appellant by her provocative conduct in assaulting Washington with a deadly weapon created a situation in which the dilemma was thrust not upon the victim or the policeman, but the potential rescuer. It was reasonably to be expected that the rescuer, be it of the victim or of the original aggressor, would reasonably respond by shooting at whomsoever appeared to be placing another in danger of great bodily injury, and such shooting should not be considered an independent intervening cause for which the appellant, who initiated the assault with a deadly weapon, is not liable.

...

In re Joseph G.

34 Cal. 3d 429, 667 P.2d 1176 (1983)

Mosk, J.

Joseph G., a minor, was charged in a juvenile court petition to declare him a ward of the court (Welf. & Inst. Code, § 602) with murder (Pen. Code, § 187) and aiding and abetting a suicide (Pen. Code, § 401). At the contested adjudication hearing, the court sustained the petition as to the murder count but dismissed the aiding and abetting charge as inapplicable; the court further found that the murder was in the first degree.

In the case before us a genuine suicide pact was partially fulfilled by driving a car over a cliff; the primary issue is whether the survivor, who drove the vehicle, is guilty of aiding and abetting the suicide rather than the murder of his deceased partner. We conclude that, under the unusual, inexplicable and tragic circumstances of this case, the minor's actions fall more properly within the statutory definition of the former (Pen. Code, § 401).

I.

The minor and his friend, Jeff W., both 16 years old, drove to the Fillmore library one evening and joined a number of their friends who had congregated there. During the course of the two hours they spent at the library talking, mention was made of a car turnout on a curve overlooking a 300- to 350-foot precipice on a country road known as "the cliff." Both the minor and Jeff declared that they intended to "fly off the cliff" and that they meant to kill themselves. The others were skeptical but the minor affirmed their seriousness, stating "You don't believe us that we are going to do it. We are going to do it. You can read it in the paper tomorrow." The minor gave one of the girls his baseball hat, saying firmly that this was the last time he would see her. Jeff repeatedly encouraged the minor by urging, "let's go, let's go" whenever the minor spoke. One other youth attempted to get in the car with Jeff and the minor but they refused to allow him to join them "because we don't want to be responsible for you." Jeff and the minor shook hands with their friends and departed.

The pair then drove to a gas station and put air in a front tire of the car, which had been damaged earlier in the evening; the fender and passenger door were dented and the tire was very low in air pressure, nearly flat. Two of their fellow students, Keith C. and Craig B., drove up and spoke with Jeff and the minor. The minor said, "Shake my hand and stay cool." Jeff urged, "Let's go," shook their hands and said, "Remember you shook my hand." The minor then drove off in the direction of the cliff with Jeff in the passenger seat; Keith and Craig surreptitiously followed them out of curiosity. The minor and Jeff proceeded up the hill past the cliff, turned around and drove down around the curve and over the steep cliff.

Two other vehicles were parked in the turnout, from which vantage point their occupants watched the minor's car plummeting down the hill at an estimated 50 miles per hour. The car veered off the road without swerving or changing course; the witnesses heard the car accelerate and then drive straight off the cliff. No one saw brakelights flash. The impact of the crash killed Jeff and caused severe injuries to the minor, resulting in the amputation of a foot.

Investigations following the incident revealed there were no defects in the steering or brake mechanisms. There were no skid marks at the scene, but a gouge in the pavement apparently caused by the frame of a motor vehicle coming into contact with the asphalt at high speed indicated that the car had gone straight over the cliff without swerving or skidding.

A few weeks after the crash, another friend of the minor discussed the incident with him. The minor declared he had "a quart" before driving over the cliff; the friend interpreted this to mean a quart of beer. The minor told his friend that he had "no reason" to drive off the cliff, that it was "stupid" but that he "did it on purpose." Just before the car went over the cliff, the minor told Jeff, "I guess this is it [Jeff]. Take it easy."

II.

The minor maintains that, under the peculiar circumstances presented here, he can be convicted only of aiding and abetting a suicide and not of murder. We begin by reviewing the development of the law relevant to suicide and related crimes.

At common law suicide was a felony, punished by forfeiture of property to the king and ignominious burial. Under American law, suicide has never been punished and the ancient English attitude has been expressly rejected. Rather than classifying suicide as criminal, suicide in the United States "has continued to be considered an expression of mental illness." (Hendin, Suicide in America (1982).) As one commentator has noted, "punishing suicide is contrary to modern penal and psychological theory." (Victoroff, The Suicidal Patient: Recognition, Intervention, Management (1982).)

Currently no state, including California, has a statute making a successful suicide a crime, nor does the Model Penal Code recognize suicide as a crime. Contemporary England, by abolishing its criminal penalties for suicide, has also adopted this more modern approach.

Attempted suicide was also a crime at common law. A few American jurisdictions have adopted this view, but most, including California, attach no criminal liability to one who makes a suicide attempt. The drafters of the Model Penal Code, adhering to the trend of decriminalizing suicide, rationalize that "The judgment underlying the Model Code position is that there is no form of criminal punishment that is acceptable for a completed suicide and that criminal punishment is singularly inefficacious to deter attempts to commit suicide.... It seems preposterous to argue that the visitation of criminal sanctions upon one who fails in the effort is likely to inhibit persons from undertaking a serious attempt to take their own lives. Moreover, it is clear that the intrusion of the criminal law into such tragedies is an abuse. There is a certain moral extravagance in imposing criminal punishment on a person who has sought his own self-destruction, who has not attempted direct injury to anyone else, and who more properly requires medical or psychiatric attention." Further, as one commentator has noted, "[the] current psychiatric view is that attempted suicide is a symptom of mental illness and, as such, it makes no more sense to affix criminal liability to it than to any other symptom of any other illness." (Note, *The Punishment of Suicide—A Need for Change* (1969) 14 Vill.L.Rev. 463.) Finally, it has been said that "all modern research points to one conclusion about the problem of suicide—the irrelevance of the criminal law to its solution." (*Id.*)

The law has, however, retained culpability for aiding, abetting and advising suicide. At common law, an aider and abettor was guilty of murder by construction of law because he was a principal in the second degree to the self-murder of the other. Most states provide, either by statute or case law, criminal sanctions for aiding suicide, but few adopt the extreme common law position that such conduct is murder. Some jurisdictions instead classify aiding suicide as a unique type of manslaughter. But the predominant statutory scheme, and the one adopted in California, is to create a sui generis crime of aiding and abetting suicide. "This latter structure ... reflects a fundamental shift in the understanding of the law. Since public morals are no longer imposed upon the would-be suicide, the traditional rationale that would support the proscription of assisting suicide as the assistance of a crime is accordingly eroded." (Englehardt & Malloy, *Suicide and Assisting Suicide: A Critique of Legal Sanctions* (1982) 36 Sw.L.J. 1003.) The modern trend reflected by this statutory scheme is therefore to mitigate the punishment for assisting a suicide by removing it from the harsh consequences of homicide law and giving it a separate criminal classification more carefully tailored to the actual culpability of the aider and abettor.

The California aiding statute, in effect since 1873, provides simply that "Every person who deliberately aids, or advises or encourages another to commit suicide, is guilty of a felony." This statute, although creating a felony, places California among the most lenient jurisdictions in its punishment for those who assist suicide. The sole California decision which even peripherally considers criminal liability for assisting suicide under this statute is *People v. Matlock* (1959) 51 Cal. 2d 682....

[In *Matlock*, the defendant, who was convicted of murder and robbery, had argued that he should have been convicted only of assisting a suicide because he killed the victim at the latter's behest. According to the defendant, the victim had only six months to live and sought a way to die but could not commit suicide without forfeiting the benefits of his insurance policy. The court, relying on an Oregon case, *People v. Bouse* (Ore. 1953) 264 P.2d 800, upheld the conviction. In *Bouse*, the defendant's wife drowned in the bathtub. The evidence was that she had told the defendant that she wanted to die, but the evidence was in conflict as to whether he merely ran the water and assisted his wife into the tub or whether he actually held his wife's head underwater while she struggled. The court explained that manslaughter under the assisting statute "contemplates some participation in the events leading up to the commission of the final overt act, such as furnishing the means for bringing about death—the gun, the knife, the poison, or providing the water, for the use of the person who himself commits the act of self-murder. But where a person actually performs, or actively assists in performing, the overt act resulting in death, such as shooting or stabbing the victim, administering the poison, or holding one under water until death takes place by drowning, his act constitutes murder, and it is wholly immaterial whether this act is committed pursuant to an agreement with the victim, such as a mutual suicide pact."]

Under *Matlock* and *Bouse*, the key to distinguishing between the crimes of murder and of assisting suicide is the active or passive role of the defendant in the suicide. If the defendant merely furnishes the means, he is guilty of aiding a suicide; if he actively participates in the death of the suicide victim, he is guilty of murder. If this literal formulation were to be applied mechanically to the facts in the case at hand, it would be difficult not to conclude that the minor, by driving the car, "actively participated" in the death of his friend Jeff. It must be remembered, however, that *Matlock* did not involve a suicide pact but instead dealt with the more straightforward situation in which a suicide victim is killed as a result of direct injury that the defendant inflicts on him, i.e., strangling. The reasoning which justified the application of the active/passive distinction in *Matlock* is therefore not wholly apposite to the peculiar facts shown here. The present case requires us instead to consider an entirely distinct situation to determine whether the minor's actions fall most appropriately within the conduct sought to be proscribed by Penal Code section 401.

It has been suggested that "[states] maintaining statutes prohibiting aiding ... suicide, attempt to do so to discourage the actions of those who might encourage a suicide in order to advance personal motives." (Note, *Criminal Aspects of Suicide in the United States* (1975) 7 N.C.Cent.L.J. 156.) A further rationale underlying statutes imposing criminal liability is that "the interests in the sanctity of life that are represented by the criminal homicide laws are threatened by one who expresses a willingness to participate in taking the life of another, even though the act may be accomplished with the consent, or at the request, of the suicide victim." (Model Pen. Code, § 210.5.)[5] Finally, "although the evidence indicates that one who attempts suicide is suffering

5. The Model Penal Code provisions on causing or aiding suicide are as follows: "(1) Causing Suicide as Criminal Homicide. A person may be convicted of criminal homicide for causing another to commit suicide only if he purposely causes such suicide by force, duress or deception. (2) Aiding or Soliciting Suicide as an Independent Offense. A person who purposely aids or solicits another to

from mental disease, there is not a hint of such evidence with respect to the aider and abettor.... [The] justifications for punishment apply to the aider and abettor, while they do not apply to the attempted suicide."

The mutual suicide pact situation, however, represents something of a hybrid between the attempted suicide and the aiding suicide scenarios. In essence, it is actually a double attempted suicide, and therefore the rationale for not punishing those who attempt suicide would seem to apply....

On the other hand, it cannot be denied that the individuals involved in the pact aid and abet each other in committing suicide: although such individuals are thus not totally lacking in blameworthiness, their criminal responsibility would appear to fall far short of the culpability of one who actively kills another at the request of the victim, such as the defendant in *Matlock*. We are thus faced with a dilemma: should one who attempts suicide by means of a mutual suicide pact be liable for first degree murder at one extreme, or at the other, only for aiding and abetting a suicide? The current law in California provides no options save these.

Traditionally under the common law the survivor of a suicide pact was held to be guilty of murder. "Whether the common law rules have been modified by the various state [aiding and abetting suicide] statutes is not entirely clear." (Note, *The Punishment of Suicide—A Need for a Change* (1969) 14 Vill. L. Rev. 463.) It has been suggested that "the reason for imposing criminal liability upon a surviving party to a suicide pact is the 'support' such a pact presents ... [¶] Besides the notion of 'support,'... [surviving] a suicide pact gives rise to a presumption ... that the participant may have entered into the pact in less than good faith. Survival, either because one party backed out at the last minute or because the poison, or other agent, did not have the desired effect, suggests that the pact may have been employed to induce the other person to take his own life." (Brenner, *Undue Influencing in the Criminal Law: A Proposed Analysis of the Criminal Offense of "Causing Suicide"* (1982) 47 Alb. L. Rev. 62.) The Model Penal Code, while recognizing that "when the pact is genuine all of the arguments against treating attempted suicide as criminal apply with equal force" to the case of a suicide pact survivor, is similarly concerned with the "danger of abuse in differentiating genuine from spurious agreements" to commit suicide. (Model Pen. Code, § 210.5.)

Under the facts presented here, these concerns are not particularly appropriate. First, the trial judge was satisfied there was a genuine suicide pact between Jeff and the minor. By "genuine," we mean simply that the pact was freely entered into and was not induced by force, duress or deception. There is no evidence in the present case that Jeff's participation in the pact was anything but fully voluntary and uncoerced. Second, because of the instrumentality used there was no danger of fraud: the potential consequences for the minor of driving the car off the cliff were identical to

---

commit suicide is guilty of a felony of the second degree if his conduct causes such suicide or an attempted suicide, and otherwise of a misdemeanor."

the potential consequences for Jeff, his passenger. Finally, the suicide and the attempted suicide were committed simultaneously by the same act.

These factors clearly distinguish the present case from the murder-suicide pact situation in which one party to the agreement actively kills the other (*e.g.*, by shooting, poison, etc.) and then is to kill himself. The active participant in that scenario has the opportunity to renege on the agreement after killing the other or to feign agreement only for the purpose of disposing of his companion and without any true intention to commit suicide himself. By contrast, in the case at hand the minor and Jeff, because of the instrumentality chosen, necessarily were to commit their suicidal acts simultaneously and were subject to identical risks of death.The potential for fraud is thus absent in a genuine suicide pact executed simultaneously by both parties by means of the same instrumentality. The traditional rationale for holding the survivor of the pact guilty of murder is thus not appropriate in this limited factual situation.

The anomaly of classifying the minor's actions herein as murder is further illustrated by consideration of Jeff's potential criminal liability had he survived. If Jeff, the passenger, had survived and the minor had been killed, Jeff would be guilty, at most, of a violation of Penal Code section 401. In order to commit suicide by this means, i.e., a car, only one of the parties to the pact, the driver, can be said to "control" the instrumentality. To make the distinction between criminal liability for first degree murder and merely aiding and abetting suicide turn on the fortuitous circumstance of which of the pair was actually driving serves no rational purpose. The illogic of such a distinction has been similarly recognized in the classic example of the parties to the pact agreeing to commit suicide by gassing themselves in a closed room. If the party who turns on the gas survives, he is guilty of murder; if on the other hand, the other person survives, that person's criminal liability is only that of an aider and abettor. "It would be discreditable if any actual consequences were made to hinge upon such distinctions." (Williams, The Sanctity of Life and the Criminal Law (1957).)

In light of the foregoing analysis we decline to ritualistically apply the active/passive distinction of *Matlock* to the genuine suicide pact situation in which the suicides are undertaken simultaneously by a single instrumentality. Given the inapplicability of *Matlock*, the actions of the minor constitute no more than a violation of Penal Code section 401.

The order declaring the minor a ward of the court is reversed and the cause is remanded to the trial court for further proceedings not inconsistent with this opinion.

Notes and Problem

Assisted Suicide and the Constitution. In *Washington v. Glucksberg*, 521 U.S. 702 (1997), the Supreme Court rejected a constitutional challenge to a state statute prohibiting aiding a person to commit suicide. The plaintiffs, gravely ill patients, doctors, and a non-profit organization that counsels people considering physician-assisted suicide, had argued that the Fourteenth Amendment's due process clause protected the fundamental liberty interest of a mentally competent, terminally ill adult to end his/her life in order to avoid further pointless suffering and anguish. In holding that there was no such liberty interest, the Court cited the long history of the prohibition against assisting suicide and the overwhelming rejection of such a right by the states today and found that the prohibition served the state's legitimate interests in preventing intentional killings, preserving life, preventing suicides by incompetent persons and others peculiarly vulnerable to pressure, protecting the medical profession's integrity and ethics and avoiding a possible slide towards voluntary and perhaps even involuntary euthanasia.

Limitations on Vicarious Liability. Just as it is not always the case that those who agree to the commission of a crime are guilty of conspiracy [see Chapter 9], it is not always the case that those who agree to the commission of a crime by another or who aid or encourage another in the commission of a crime are guilty of the other's substantive crime. In certain circumstances, courts have found a legislative intent not to punish the secondary party.

One such circumstance occurs where the legislature defines, as a substantive crime, the actions of only one of two necessary participants to the forbidden conduct. The classic case concerning this situation is *Queen v. Tyrell*, 1 Q.B. 710 (1893). In *Tyrell*, a girl under the age of consent was prosecuted for aiding and abetting a boy in the commission of statutory rape on her. The Court held that, since the statute was passed to protect young girls and was silent on the issue of punishing the girls, it would be assumed that Parliament intended that they go unpunished. A similar result was reached in California in the early case of *In re Cooper*, 162 Cal. 81 (1912). In *Cooper*, an unmarried woman who was living with a married man was charged with aiding and abetting his adultery. After first finding that the crime of adultery could only be committed by a married person, the court held:

> Where the idea of guilt on the part of an unmarried participant of such an offense as this is thus excluded by the terms of the statute defining the offense, we think it must be held to follow that such participant cannot be held punishable as being an aider and abettor in the offense, even though he or she be held to be an accomplice under the provisions of section 31 of the Penal Code. (*Id.* at 86.)

A second such circumstance is found where the legislature has enacted statutes providing different punishments for various necessary participants in a criminal endeavor. An illustrative case is *People v. Buffum*, 40 Cal. 2d 709 (1953). In *Buffum*, one of the issues for the court was whether a woman who had an illegal abortion could be prosecuted under Penal Code § 274 as an accomplice to the doctor who performed the abortions. However, in addition to § 274, the legislature had also enacted Penal Code § 275, which made it a crime for a woman to solicit an abortion. The court reasoned that, since the legislature had established a separate crime for the woman under § 275, it would defeat the legislative scheme to also permit the prosecution of the woman under § 274 for aiding and abetting the doctor. In a similar vein, in *People v. Pangelina*, 117 Cal. App. 3d 414 (1981), the court held that prostitutes working in a house of prostitution could not be prosecuted, under a conspiracy theory, for the felony of keeping a house of prostitution because the legislature had made it a misdemeanor to wilfully reside in a house of ill-fame, and permitting the felony prosecution would defeat the legislative scheme.

Problem 92.

Defendant, who was sixteen, and Boyfriend, who was twenty-one, broke into Owner's apartment while Owner was away and spent the night, engaging in sexual intercourse. Defendant is charged with burglary (P.C. § 459) based on her entry into the apartment with the intent to commit unlawful sexual intercourse (statutory rape) (P.C. § 261.5). What arguments should be made as to whether Defendant is guilty of burglary?

B. Corporate Vicarious Liability

The final two cases in this chapter concern the vicarious criminal liability of a corporation and its officers. In *Granite Construction Co. v. Superior Court,* the issue is whether a corporation can be prosecuted for a traditional *malum in se* crime, in this case, involuntary manslaughter, and the court addresses the corporation's statutory and constitutional challenges to the prosecution. If the corporation is guilty of a crime, what of the corporate officers? In *Sea Horse Ranch, Inc. v. Superior Court,* the court considers what evidence is sufficient to hold both the corporation and its president liable for involuntary manslaughter.

Granite Construction Co. v. Superior Court

149 Cal. App. 3d 465, 197 Cal.Rptr. 3 (1984)

WOOLPERT, ASSOCIATE JUSTICE.

In this petition, we are asked to exempt corporations from prosecution for manslaughter. We refuse, holding that corporations may be prosecuted for manslaughter under existing California law.

Petitioner, a corporation, is building a power plant known as the "Helms Pumped Storage Project." On January 23, 1981, seven construction workers were killed in an accident at that project. After evidence regarding this accident was presented to the Fresno County Grand Jury, petitioner was indicted for manslaughter.

The issue is whether the California Penal Code exempts corporations from prosecution for manslaughter under Penal Code section 192. This is a question of legislative intent.

The Penal Code applies to corporations. The code defines "person" to include a corporation as well as a natural person (Pen. Code, § 7). The Penal Code's sections on persons liable for crime, using unqualified language, make corporations proper defendants in any criminal case. Under section 26, any person is capable of committing crimes except children, idiots and those lacking *mens rea* through mistake of fact, *et cetera*. Under section 27, any person who commits a crime is liable for punishment. Thus the California Penal Code applies to corporations, and if they commit crimes, they are liable for punishment.

...

Petitioner claims surprise at the prosecution of a corporation for manslaughter, asserting that the indictment was "totally unforeseeable," and that a corporation may be charged with crimes against "property," but "not against the person." This attempt to distinguish crimes against property from crimes against the person relies on the corporation's nature as an economically motivated entity. While a corporation may directly benefit from a crime against property, crimes against persons are not as directly linked to the profit motive. This argument is unsuccessful. It overlooks the substantial indirect economic benefits that may accrue to the corporation through crimes against the person. To get these economic benefits, corporate management may shortcut expensive safety precautions, respond forcibly to strikes, or engage in criminal anticompetitive behavior. If any such risk-taking is a corporate action, the corporation becomes a proper criminal defendant.

Manslaughter is defined in Penal Code section 192: "Manslaughter is the unlawful killing of a human being, without malice. It is of three kinds: "1. Voluntary—upon a sudden quarrel or heat of passion. "2. Involuntary—in the commission of an unlawful act, not amounting to felony; or in the commission of a lawful act which might produce death, in an unlawful manner, or without due caution and circumspection...."

This statute does not rule out the prosecution of corporations. Unlike other states' definitions, it does not limit itself to natural persons by defining the act of manslaughter as the killing "of a human being ... by another."

Petitioner has argued that the absence of the word "person" in section 192 indicates that this statute was not intended to reach corporations. This argument is not convincing. Section 192 defines a crime. It does not define its own scope of application; this is unnecessary in light of sections 7 and 26. Though many sections of the Penal Code are in the form "any person who does X is guilty of Y," this would be an irrational statutory basis for distinction between crimes that can be committed by corporations from crimes that can only be committed by natural persons. If so, mayhem, kidnapping and assaults with intent to do great bodily harm could be committed by corporations, but murder and manslaughter could not. These results show that the use of "any person who" language does not provide a distinguishing factor that bars prosecution of corporations for manslaughter. When interpreting statutes, we prefer constructions that do not lead to absurd consequences.

Petitioner's underlying assumption is that the legislature did not consider making corporations responsible for crimes against persons when it enacted the Penal Code. Although the code's language expresses no such exception, we are asked to rewrite apparently clear language to conform to the unexpressed assumptions of the 1872 legislators. Because we find no contrary expression in the statute or in the California code commissioners' notes accompanying the 1872 codes, we find it more appropriate to follow the apparently clear language of these statutes. Although courts have assumed in dicta that there is some category of crime that "cannot" be committed by corporations, there is no provision in the Penal Code that makes this distinction. Under Penal Code section 31, principals chargeable with an offense need not directly commit the act constituting the offense. Traditional notions of fair play and substantial justice are not offended by applying the clear meaning of statutory terms, even when there is mistaken dictum to the contrary.

...

California Penal Code section 193 prescribes imprisonment as the ordinary punishment for manslaughter, but does not impose a fine. Petitioner argues that absence of an appropriate punishment for corporations at this juncture indicates that section 192 does not reach corporate defendants.

Section 672 provides appropriate punishment for corporate crimes.[1] This catchall fine section was enacted in 1872 along with the rest of the Penal Code and California's other general codes. These codes are to be construed as parts of the same statute. When construing a statute with several provisions, constructions that give effect to all are preferred.

...

[Although courts in other jurisdictions have held that] corporations ... may not be capable of forming "intent" or possess a "condition of the mind," California corporations can form intent, be reckless and commit acts through their agents. The criminal intent problem has not been squarely addressed, but corporations have been prosecuted for crimes of specific intent under the California Penal Code. (*W.T. Grant Co. v. Superior Court* (1972) 23 Cal. App. 3d 284 (corporation liable for grand theft); *People v. California Protective Corp.* (1926) 76 Cal. App. 354, 363 (corporation could "willfully" practice law and become liable for a fine for illegal practice of law); *People v. Palermo Land & Water Co.* (1907) 4 Cal. App. 717 (misdemeanor prosecution for refusing to sell water for irrigation).) The claim that corporations are not chargeable with specific intent crimes does not appear to have been raised in later cases....

...

Petitioner argues that the district attorney failed to seek an appropriate remedy against it, citing Labor Code section 6425.[8] We note that this section involves the

1. Penal Code section 672: "Upon a conviction for any crime punishable by imprisonment in any jail or prison, in relation to which no fine is herein prescribed, the court may impose a fine on the offender not exceeding five hundred dollars ($500) in cases of misdemeanors or five thousand dollars ($5,000) in cases of felonies, in addition to the imprisonment prescribed."

8. Labor Code section 6425: "Any employer, and every employee having direction, management, control, or custody of any employment, place of employment, or other employee, who willfully violates any occupational safety or health standard, order, or special order, or Section 25910 of the

"human" quality of willfulness, and expressly preserves a prosecutor's discretion to use Penal Code section 192 against employers.

Petitioner admits that Labor Code section 6425 applies to corporations, the word "employer" obviously including corporate employers. Although the section appears to have "only" misdemeanor significance, and allows for greater fines than here sought, nothing in the section implies a legislative intention to disallow other means of bringing corporations to the bar for homicide.

Furthermore, we must assume that when the Legislature used "person" in the last sentence of Labor Code section 6425, it knew the Penal Code definition included corporations. As a result, the preceding sentence: "Nothing in this section shall prohibit a prosecution [of an employer] under Section 192 of the Penal Code, rather than under this section, for the death of an employee," is evidence that prosecution of corporations for manslaughter was contemplated.

...

Note

The Model Penal Code and the Liability of Corporations. Under the Model Penal Code § 2.07(1), a corporation may be found criminally liable if:

> (a) the offense is a violation or the offense is defined by a statute other than the Code in which a legislative purpose to impose liability on corporations plainly appears and the conduct is performed by an agent of the corporation acting in behalf of the corporation within the scope of his office or employment, except that if the law defining the offense designates the agents for whose conduct the corporation is accountable or the circumstances under which it is accountable, such provisions shall apply; or
>
> (b) the offense consists of an omission to discharge a specific duty of affirmative performance imposed on corporations by law; or
>
> (c) the commission of the offense was authorized, requested, commanded, performed or recklessly tolerated by the board of directors or by a high managerial agent acting in behalf of the corporation within the scope of his office or employment.

Health and Safety Code, and that violation caused death to any employee, or caused permanent or prolonged impairment of the body of any employee, shall, upon conviction, be punished by a fine of not more than ten thousand dollars ($10,000), or by imprisonment for not more than six months, or by both; except that if the conviction is for a violation committed after a first conviction of such person, punishment shall be by a fine of not more than twenty thousand dollars ($20,000) or by imprisonment for not more than one year, or by both. Nothing in this section shall prohibit a prosecution under Section 192 of the Penal Code, rather than under this section, for the death of an employee. However, no person may be prosecuted under both this section and Section 192 of the Penal Code for the same act or omission."

Sea Horse Ranch, Inc. v. Superior Court

24 Cal. App. 4th 446, 30 Cal.Rptr.2d 681 (1994)

HANING, ASSOCIATE JUSTICE.

Petitioners Sea Horse Ranch, Inc. (the Ranch), and its president, Arbis "Al" Shipley, are charged by information with one count of involuntary manslaughter (Pen. Code, § 192, subd. (b)); ... The charges arise from an incident in which a horse escaped from the Ranch onto an adjacent state highway and collided with a car, killing the passenger. Petitioners moved to dismiss the information under section 995. The superior court denied the motion in substantial part, and petitioners seek writ review.

...

Facts

On March 23, 1992, well after 7:00 p.m., an automobile struck a horse that was running free on coastal Highway 1 in Half Moon Bay. The passenger in the car, 76-year-old Viola Scheutrum, was killed when the impact with the horse crushed the roof of the passenger compartment. The accident occurred directly in front of the main driveway of the Ranch. It was after dark, there were no streetlights and the highway was poorly lit.

An officer responding to the scene noticed no less than eight horses running free on the highway. They were not ambling, but running at a "trot[ ] to a gallop." The horses were dark brown, and were not picked up in the officer's headlights. The officer could not see the horses until he activated his red and blue strobe-light flashers.

The petition's assertion that "the prosecution presented no evidence suggesting that ... [petitioner] Shipley ... knew of the allegedly inadequate condition of the corral fence[,]" is misleading. Chuck Bunce, the Ranch's foreman, told the officer that all the horses on the highway belonged to the Ranch. The officer met with petitioner Shipley, who told the officer the horses had escaped through the corral fence on the west side. One Kevin Shipley, presumably related to petitioner Shipley, took the officer to an area of the corral fence on the western part of the Ranch, and identified it as the place where the horses got free.

The fenceposts were old, weather-worn, bug-infested and rotting. Several cross boards had been knocked off the posts where the wood was rotten, leaving a hole in the corral fence. The nails which had attached the cross boards were not in good condition. The boards were broken out from the inside, with no sign of vandalism. The fence was so dilapidated that when the officer leaned on a cross board, it fell off. The cross boards were mounted improperly on the outside of the fenceposts, making them more easily pushed out from animals on the inside. Contrary to common practice, there was no wire strung along the inside of the fence to keep horses away from the cross boards. Neither was there any electrical wire around the inside of the corral. The Ranch had not erected a fence along the front boundary with Highway 1 to keep the horses off the highway. The Ranch's border with the highway was not well-lit.

Although petitioners vigorously dispute the point, the Ranch has a history of escaping horses. An investigating officer, Detective Wendy Bear, testified that Bunce told her the horses had broken down the fence in the past and had escaped. Bear also testified that Mr. Jaycea Caudle, who lived on the Ranch premises, told her equine escapes were a "frequent occurrence." ...

The People also presented evidence suggesting that the Ranch's horses escaped onto Highway 1 on several previous occasions.... The evidence established that large groups of horses were running free on Highway 1 on four occasions in 1991 and early 1992, in the vicinity of the Ranch. On one of those occasions Bunce told the police he would take care of the horses; on another, petitioner Shipley told the police he "would need to look to see [sic] for the horses." On this latter occasion petitioner Shipley was cited by the Humane Society for having horses loose on the highway.

...

Discussion

...

II
Involuntary Manslaughter

[The court found that the extremely dilapidated condition of the fence, the improper construction of the fence, the failure to follow the common practice of installing some kind of wire to keep the horses away from the fence, the failure to have a "fall-back" measure of a perimeter fence on the border with the highway to keep horses off the road, and the fact that the horses were continually escaping near a busy highway with a 50 mph speed limit and without any street lighting were facts which could justify a finding of criminal negligence.]

B

Assuming there is a criminal negligence in this case, the next question is whether the Ranch, as a corporation, and its president, petitioner Shipley, are criminally liable. This issue comprises the bulk of the briefing. Under the facts of this case, at the probable-cause stage at which a reviewing court must draw every legitimate inference in favor of the information, that question must be answered in the affirmative. We emphasize that our discussion of criminal liability is only within the context of probable cause, and not the question of guilt or innocence to be determined at petitioners' trial.

It should be noted at the outset that petitioners concentrate on the criminal liability of petitioner Shipley. There is no separate discussion of the criminal liability of the corporation. The two are not coterminous. In California, a corporation may be criminally liable for the conduct of its officers or agents or employees. (*Granite Construction Co. v. Superior Court* (1983) 149 Cal. App. 3d 465.) "California corporations can form intent, be reckless and commit acts through their agents[;]" the criminal negligence of corporate officers or agents may be imputed to the corporation to support a charge of involuntary manslaughter. As we discuss below, the criminal negligence in this case is that of petitioner Shipley, the corporate president, presumably acting in the corporation's behalf; Shipley was not a casual or low-level employee with no decision-making authority. Thus, Shipley's negligence may be imputed to the corporation.

The liability of petitioner Shipley is a separate question. It is well settled that "[a]n officer of a corporation is not criminally answerable for any act of a corporation in which he [or she] is not personally a participant." (*Otis v. Superior Court* (1905) 148 Cal. 129.) In the context of negligent homicide such an officer would be said not to be liable unless he or she was personally aware of the omissions or other behavior that gives rise to the criminal negligence. The decisions involving criminal liability of corporate officers, either expressly or impliedly, focus either on the officer's direct participation in illegal conduct, or his or her knowledge and control of the illegal behavior. The mere fact of the officer's position at the apex of the corporate hierarchy does not automatically bestow liability.

Otis held that the president and vice-president of a newspaper corporation were not liable for publication of contumacious articles simply by virtue of their high office. The court stressed that the People had to show that the officers "personally caused, or, being in control, at least permitted, the publication of the articles in question."

Similarly, in *People v. International Steel Corp.* (1951) 102 Cal. App. 2d Supp. 935, a corporate officer was held criminally liable for violating an anti-pollution statute where he personally operated the facility which emitted the pollution (fumes from burning auto bodies), and by clear implication had knowledge of the violation. By contrast, the corporate secretary was found not liable; although he had knowledge of the burning operations, he had no control over them. "The secretary of a corporation, merely as such, is a ministerial officer, without authority to transact the business of the corporation upon his [or her] independent volition and judgment."

In *People v. Epstein* (1931) 118 Cal. App. 7, the general manager of a loan and investment corporation was liable for improper use of depositors' funds, where he signed checks and knew of the misappropriation of the funds. By contrast, in *People v. Lieber* (1956) 146 Cal. App. 2d Supp. 910, an officer of an incorporated pharmacy was not criminally liable for illegally dispensing a narcotic when there was no evidence he actively participated in the criminal conduct.

More current decisions are in accord with these older cases supporting the People's position. In *People v. Conway* (1974) 42 Cal. App. 3d 875, the defendant was found liable where he was aware of the false advertising of corporate sales employees, was in a position to control the employees' conduct, and tolerated, ratified or authorized their actions. In *People v. Regan* (1979) 95 Cal. App. 3d Supp. 1, the court refused to predicate criminal liability on the owner of a business for the conduct of an employee off the premises: "There is nothing in the record which gives any indication that appellant had knowledge of, or participated in, the illegal conduct." In *People v. Toomey* (1984) 157 Cal. App. 3d 1, liability was imposed on the basis of the knowing participation of the corporate officer.

Petitioners claim there is no evidence that petitioner Shipley had any knowledge of the negligence and thus had no direct participation in the offense of manslaughter.

They suggest the People seek to impose liability solely based on petitioner Shipley's status as president of the corporation, an impermissible theory of respondeat superior. The People respond that the record supports the reasonable inference that petitioner Shipley had the requisite knowledge and awareness. Extending to the information every legitimate inference, we must agree with the People.

Petitioner Shipley was present at the Ranch soon after the collision and it was he who informed the police that his horses had escaped through a hole in the fence. Petitioner Shipley had personal knowledge of prior escapes. Indeed, the transcript of the oral argument in municipal court ... reveals this conclusion of the magistrate: "It is the view of the court that—first of all, we took into account some evidence ... as to horses being loose on prior occasions and on some of those occasions Mr. Shipley being present at the scene of their capture or intended capture. [¶] Viewing all those incidences together, I think there are inferences that the court can legitimately draw as to his personal knowledge as to the [horses'] ability to escape to be a public nuisance, and, in effect, a threat to the public."

...

We thus conclude there is probable cause that petitioner Shipley had the requisite knowledge and awareness of the risks created by the Ranch's horses, and thus there is probable cause to suspect him of the criminal negligence necessary for the charge of involuntary manslaughter.[6]

...

Note

Corporate Officers and Strict Liability Crimes. *Sea Horse Ranch* held that a corporate officer may be held liable for a corporation's commission of a *malum in se* crime on proof of the officer's *mens rea.* May a corporate officer be held criminally liable for a corporation's commission of a strict liability crime? The Supreme Court has twice upheld such liability in the context of violations of the Federal Food, Drug and Cosmetic Act. See *United States v. Dotterweich,* 320 U.S. 277 (1943); *United States v. Park,* 421 U.S. 658 (1975). In *Dotterweich,* the Court held that liability could be imposed on any person having a "responsible share in the furtherance of the transaction which the statute outlaws" (320 U.S. at 284), and, in *Park,* the Court explained:

> The theory upon which responsible corporate agents are held criminally accountable for "causing" violations of the Act permits a claim that a defendant was "powerless" to prevent or correct the violation to "be raised defensively

6. The People also seem to argue that petitioner Shipley's position as corporate president supports criminal liability simply because, as president, he was in a position to control the Ranch's employees. The People extract unfortunately imprecise language from *Conway* out of context. In speaking in terms of a corporate officer being able to control unlawful employee conduct, *Conway* could be read to suggest that control without knowledge is sufficient to invoke criminal liability. This reading of *Conway* is too broad.

> at a trial on the merits." ... [T]he Government's ultimate burden [is to prove] beyond a reasonable doubt the defendant's guilt, including his power, in light of the duty imposed by the Act, to prevent or correct the prohibited condition.... The concept of a "reasonable relationship" to ... violation of the Act indeed imports some measure of blameworthiness.... [T]he Government establishes a prima facie case when it introduces evidence sufficient to warrant a finding ... that the defendant had, by reason of his position in the corporation, responsibility and authority either to prevent in the first instance, or promptly to correct, the violation complained of, and that he failed to do so ...

421 U.S. at 673–74. California has adopted the Supreme Court's approach. See *People v. Matthews*, 7 Cal. App. 4th 1052 (1992).

Chapter 14

Scope of Vicarious Liability

It is clear that a defendant who aids in the commission of a crime or conspires to commit it, will be guilty of the crime, if committed by the principal, just as if he/she were a principal. A person also will be guilty of any crime committed by the principal in furtherance of the original crime or as a natural and probable consequence of the original crime. Thus, the doctrine of vicarious liability holds the accomplice and co-conspirator strictly liable for certain crimes committed by the principal. The four cases in this chapter explore this concept, all in the context of a murder prosecution against an accomplice or co-conspirator who had joined with the principal to commit a lesser crime. *People v. Kauffman* is the seminal case on the scope of vicarious liability in California, and it describes and applies the natural and probable consequences doctrine. In *People v. Cavitt*, the defendants, who joined with a third person in the commission of a robbery, contend that the third party killed the robbery victim for reasons unrelated to the robbery and after the robbery had ended. In *People v. Medina*, a divided court must decide whether, in the context of a gang confrontation, defendants who joined in a fistfight with a member of a rival gang are guilty of the shooting murder of the rival by one of the combatants. In *People v. Chiu*, the court addresses the defendant's challenge to his conviction for first degree *premeditated* murder on the natural and probable consequences theory.

People v. Kauffman

152 Cal. 331, 92 P. 861 (1907)

Sloss, J.

William Kauffman, Frank Woods, William Henderson, John Courtney, William B. Kennedy, and Allan Goucher were by indictment jointly charged with the murder of one Eugene C. Robinson. Upon a separate trial Kauffman was convicted of murder in the second degree, and he now appeals from the order denying his motion for a new trial.

His principal contention is that the evidence was insufficient to justify the verdict of guilty. There was evidence tending to establish this state of facts: In January, 1902, the defendant, William Kauffman, rented rooms at 203 Turk street, in the city and county of San Francisco. These rooms were occupied by Kauffman, Henderson, and Goucher, who, together with Woods, Courtney, and Kennedy, devised a plan to rob the safe at Cypress Lawn Cemetery in San Mateo county. Having provided themselves with burglars' tools, nitroglycerin, and fuse for the purpose of breaking into the safe, they started on the night of the 20th of January, 1902, for Cypress Lawn. Before starting, each of the six, with the exception of Kauffman, had armed himself with a revolver. Kauffman had no revolver, but had on his person a small drill, and a bottle of nitroglycerin which he had made. In going to the cemetery the party divided into squads of three, for the purpose, it may reasonably be inferred, of lessening the danger of detection. Upon arriving at the cemetery they found an armed man upon the premises, and decided to return to San Francisco. They rode back on a street car until they reached the corner of Mission and Twenty-Ninth streets, where they found that the car went no further. Thence they started to walk into the city, proceeding along Valencia street, here again dividing into two parties of three each; Woods, Henderson, and Kauffman going ahead, and Kennedy, Goucher, and Courtney following at some little distance. After they had gone along in this way for some distance, Woods, Henderson, and Kauffman were called back by the others, who suggested the burglary of a coal yard. This proposition was objected to by the appellant and others, and was not carried out. Woods, Kauffman, and Henderson continued walking in advance of the others. Walking along Valencia street they had reached Seventeenth street, when they heard a call or yell, and saw Kennedy and Goucher running towards them. Kennedy turned and fired a shot back, and then climbed or jumped over a fence and disappeared. Goucher joined the three in advance, saying that he was not going to run, and added something about having a gun. The four had walked a short distance when Robinson, a police officer, came running up behind them and asked, "Who has got that gun?" Woods ordered him to throw up his hands. Two or three shots were exchanged, probably between Woods and Robinson, and then a fusilade of shots followed, in the course of which both Woods and Robinson were wounded. This encounter occurred at about 1 o'clock on the morning of January 21st, and Robinson died on the same day as the result of the wounds so received by him.... As has been said, the appellant was not armed, and during the shooting was standing still, his own testimony being to the effect that he held his hands up in the air. The theory of the people was that the killing of Robinson was an act committed in furtherance of a common design or conspiracy by the six defendants to commit an unlawful act, and that, therefore, Kauffman, as one of said conspirators, was criminally responsible for such killing, although he took no active part in the attack upon Robinson.

There is no dispute about the rules of law governing the criminal liability of each of several parties engaging in an unlawful conspiracy or combination. An apt statement of them, abundantly supported by authority is to be found in 8 Cyc. 641, in the following language: "The general rule is well settled that, where several parties conspire or combine together to commit any unlawful act, each is criminally responsible for the acts of his associates or confederates committed in furtherance of any prosecution of the common design for which they combine. In contemplation of law the act of one is the act of all. Each is responsible for everything done by his confederates, which follows incidentally in the execution of the common design as one of its probable and natural consequences, even though it was not intended as a part of the original design or common plan. Nevertheless the act must be the ordinary and probable effect of the wrongful act specifically agreed on, so that the connection between them may be reasonably apparent, and not a fresh and independent product of the mind of one of the confederates outside of, or foreign to, the common design. Even if the common design is unlawful, and if one member of the party depart from the original design as agreed upon by all of the members, and do an act which was not only not contemplated by those who entered into the common purpose, but was not in furtherance thereof, and not the natural or legitimate consequence of anything connected therewith, the person guilty of such act, if it was itself unlawful, would alone be responsible therefor."

The contention of the appellant is that the unlawful combination or conspiracy embraced only the proposed burglary at the cemetery, and that, when this project was abandoned by reason of the discovery of an armed guard on the premises, the conspiracy or common design was at an end, and that anything done thereafter was the individual act of the party doing it. If, as matter of law, it can be said that the criminal combination embraced no more than this contemplated burglary, and that the shooting of Robinson was not within the reasonable and probable consequences of the common unlawful design, it would follow that no case was made out against the appellant. But whether or not the act committed was the ordinary and probable effect of the common design or whether it was a fresh and independent product of the mind of one of the conspirators, outside of, or foreign to, the common design, is a question of fact for the jury. And, if there be any evidence to support the finding of the jury on this question, its determination is conclusive. In this case the people contended that the evidence justified the jury in finding that the common plan or design in which Kauffman and his codefendants had engaged included, not only the breaking into the safe, but also the protection of themselves and each other from arrest and detection while going to and coming from the scene of the proposed burglary, and that any act committed by any of them in the course of such going or coming for the purpose of resisting arrest and preventing consequent detection might be found to be within the scope of the common design or plan. Treating the extent of the conspiracy as a question of fact, the trial court submitted the question to the jury, giving them the following instruction: "If you find from the evidence in this case that the defendant and others entered into a conspiracy to commit a burglary, and that in connection with such a criminal purpose they had agreed to resist arrest and interference going to the scene of the proposed crime and returning therefrom, and that being confederated together for the felonious purpose of such burglary and resistance to the civil power of the state—even to the extent of taking human life—and that in furtherance of such a conspiracy one of the conspirators killed Officer Eugene C. Robinson, then it will be your duty to convict the defendant of the crime of murder because the law holds that all who entered into such a conspiracy assumed to themselves as a body the attribute of individuality, rendering whatever was done by one of the conspirators in furtherance of that design the act of all."

Was there evidence justifying the jury in finding that the conspiracy extended to the extent indicated in this instruction? ... The jury was certainly justified in believing that the division of the band into two parties of three was decided upon on the homeward, as on the outward journey, for the purpose of lessening suspicion, and that to all intents and purposes the six were going home together. Five of them were armed with deadly weapons, and several of them—Kauffman among others—had on their persons burglars' tools. For their own protection against the consequences of their felonious enterprise, it was necessary that these tools should not be discovered upon them by any officer of the law. Adding to this the consideration ... that pistols are used by burglars, not for breaking into safes, but for preventing interference with the criminal design or arrest by those who may discover its existence, and the further fact that there is evidence here to the effect that Kauffman himself had endeavored to secure a pistol before starting on the journey, we think it clear that there was ample evidence to justify the jury in finding that the common design or conspiracy embraced not only the actual burglary at Cypress Lawn Cemetery, but the protection of the party from arrest or interference on their way to and from the scene of the proposed crime.

...

Note

Withdrawal. Once there has been an agreement to commit a crime and an overt act by one of the parties toward commission of the crime, all of the parties are guilty of conspiracy irrespective of their subsequent actions or the success of the conspiracy. As is the case with regard to attempts [Chapter 9], once a crime is committed, subsequent actions of the defendant cannot "undo" the crime. However, a conspirator, or an accomplice who has contributed aid toward the commission of a crime, may avoid liability for any subsequent crime by his or her confederates by withdrawal from the conspiracy or aided crime prior to its commission. The California Supreme Court has never determined what constitutes a sufficient withdrawal, but the current standard jury instructions require that, for withdrawal as a conspirator, "there must be an affirmative and good faith rejection or repudiation of the conspiracy which must be communicated to the other conspirators of whom [the defendant] has knowledge" (CALJIC 6.20) and, for withdrawal as an accomplice, the defendant must do two things: "First, [the defendant] must notify the other principals known to [the defendant] of [the defendant's] intention to withdraw from the commission of [the crime]; second, [the defendant] must do everything in [the defendant's] power to prevent its commission" (CALJIC 3.03). Although the defendant has the burden of raising the issue of withdrawal, the prosecution bears the ultimate burden of proving beyond a reasonable doubt that the defendant did not withdraw prior to the commission of the crime. *People v. Fiu*, 165 Cal.App.4th 360 (2008).

Under the Model Penal Code, withdrawal from a conspiracy is accomplished by advising the other conspirators of the defendant's abandonment or informing law enforcement authorities of the existence of the conspiracy and defendant's participation. MPC § 5.03(7). Unlike the situation in California, the withdrawing defendant even may avoid conviction of conspiracy if the defendant "thwart[s] the success of the conspiracy, under circumstances manifesting a complete and voluntary renunciation of his criminal purpose." MPC 5.03(5). Is this a better rule?

People v. Cavitt

33 Cal.4th 187, 91 P.3d 222 (2004)

BAXTER, J.

Defendants James Cavitt and Robert Williams were convicted in separate trials of the felony murder of 58-year-old Betty McKnight, the stepmother of Cavitt's girlfriend, Mianta McKnight. Defendants admitted plotting with Mianta to enter the McKnight home, to catch Betty unawares and tie her up, and to steal Betty's jewelry and other property. On the evening of December 1, 1995, with Mianta's assistance, the plan went forward. Defendants entered the house, threw a sheet over Betty's head, bound this hooded sheet to her wrists and ankles with rope and duct tape, and escaped with guns, jewelry, and other valuables from the bedroom. Betty was beaten and left hog-tied, facedown on the bed. Her breathing was labored. Before leaving, defendants made it appear that Mianta was a victim by pretending to tie her up as well. By the time Mianta untied herself and called her father to report the burglary-robbery, Betty had died from asphyxiation.

The evidence at trial amply supported a finding that defendants were the direct perpetrators of the murder. However, there was also evidence that tended to support the defense theory—namely, that Mianta deliberately suffocated Betty, for reasons independent of the burglary-robbery, after defendants had escaped and reached a place of temporary safety. Defendants assert that the felony-murder rule would not apply to this scenario and that the trial court's instructions erroneously denied the jury the opportunity to consider their theory.

Because the jury could have convicted defendants without finding they were the direct perpetrators of the murder, we granted review to clarify a nonkiller's liability for a killing "committed in the perpetration" of an inherently dangerous felony under Penal Code section 189's felony-murder rule. We hold that, in such circumstances, the felony-murder rule requires both a *causal* relationship and a *temporal* relationship between the underlying felony and the act resulting in death. The causal relationship is established by proof of a logical nexus, beyond mere coincidence of time and place, between the homicidal act and the underlying felony the nonkiller committed or attempted to commit. The temporal relationship is established by proof the felony and the homicidal act were part of one continuous transaction. Applying these rules to the facts here, we affirm the judgments of the Court of Appeal.

BACKGROUND

Defendant James Cavitt started dating Mianta McKnight in January 1995. Mianta's father, Philip, and her stepmother, Betty, disapproved of the relationship. Concerned about Mianta's late-night dating and her high school truancy, Philip insisted that Mianta move from Oakland, where she had been living with Philip's niece, back to Brisbane to live with him and Betty. He hoped this would keep her away from Cavitt.

After moving back to Brisbane in November 1995, Mianta became upset that Philip and Betty did not allow her to go on dates with Cavitt. Her relationship with Betty in particular had been rocky for some time, and she often told her schoolmates that she hated Betty.

Around the end of November 1995, 17-year-old Mianta, 17-year-old Cavitt, and Cavitt's friend, 16-year-old defendant Robert Williams, developed a plan to burglarize the McKnight house, where Mianta was then living. The plan was to enter the house with Mianta's assistance, tie up Betty, and steal what they could find. The three scheduled the burglary-robbery for December 1. On that afternoon, Mianta purchased rope and packing tape on the way home from school. Later on, she placed a bed sheet outside the house and left the side door unlocked.

Around 6:30 p.m., Williams and Cavitt drove together to the McKnight house. They were wearing black clothes, gloves, and hockey masks and were carrying duct tape. Between 7:00 and 7:15 p.m., Mianta met them at the side door, gave them the rope she had just bought, and told them Betty was upstairs in bed. All three went upstairs. Cavitt and Williams threw the sheet over Betty's head. While Cavitt secured the sheet around Betty's head with duct tape, Williams fastened Betty's wrists together with plastic flex cuffs. Then they used the rope to bind her ankles and wrists together with the sheet, creating a kind of hood for Betty's head. During the process, Cavitt and Williams also punched Betty in the back with their fists to get her to be quiet. Betty sustained extensive bruising to her face, shoulders, arms, legs, ankles and wrists, consistent with blunt force trauma.

After Betty was immobilized, Cavitt, Williams, and Mianta ransacked the bedroom, removing cash, cameras, Rolex watches, jewelry, and two handguns. Before leaving, Cavitt and Williams pretended to bind Mianta and placed her on the bed next to Betty. Cavitt and Williams each claimed that Betty was still breathing, although with difficulty, when they left her, facedown on the bed.

After Mianta freed herself, she turned Betty over onto her back. Mianta claimed she removed duct tape from Betty's mouth. Betty did not move and did not appear to be breathing. Mianta called her father to tell him they had been robbed. She also told him Betty was unconscious. Philip immediately reported the incident to the Brisbane Police Department at 7:44 p.m. When the dispatcher called the McKnight house at 7:45 p.m., Mianta claimed that robbers had entered the house while she was downstairs watching television, had put a sheet over her head, and had knocked her unconscious; that she was eventually able to free herself; that she had called her father to report the crime; and that her stepmother was unconscious.

Brisbane police arrived at 7:52 p.m. Betty was on her back on the bed. She was not breathing and had no pulse. Her hands were bound behind her, and her wrists and ankles were tied together with a rope. Officers attempted cardiopulmonary resuscitation. Paramedics obtained a heartbeat at 8:11 p.m., but Betty had already suffered severe and irreversible brain injury. She was pronounced dead the next morning. The cause of death was insufficient oxygen, or anoxia, caused by asphyxiation. The injuries she sustained were a contributing cause.

During conversations with police and a neighbor, Mianta reiterated her claim that unidentified robbers had somehow entered the house, that they had wrapped her in a sheet and knocked her unconscious, and that she had been unable to untie herself until after the robbers left, at which point she discovered that her stepmother was unconscious. When police secured Philip's consent to conduct a polygraph of his daughter, however, Mianta eventually confessed to her involvement in the burglary-robbery. Cavitt and Williams were arrested on December 2 and also confessed. While being transported to juvenile hall, Cavitt said to Williams, "Man, we f___ up. We should have just shot her."

Police found the stolen jewelry, cameras, and handguns at Cavitt's home, as well as black clothing, gloves, and hockey masks.

Cavitt and Williams, who were tried separately, contended that Mianta must have killed Betty after they had left and for reasons unrelated to the burglary-robbery. To that end, they offered evidence tending to show that Mianta hated her stepmother, that Mianta had expressed to her schoolmates a desire to kill her stepmother, and that Betty could have been suffocated after Cavitt and Williams had returned to Cavitt's home with the loot.

Cavitt and Williams were convicted of first degree murder with the special circumstances of robbery murder and burglary murder, as well as certain lesser offenses....

DISCUSSION

This case involves the "complicity aspect" of the felony-murder rule. (*People v. Pulido* (1997) 15 Cal.4th 713.) As in *Pulido*, we are not concerned with that part of the felony-murder rule making a *killer* liable for first degree murder if the homicide is committed in the perpetration of a robbery or burglary. Rather, the question here involves "a *nonkiller's* liability for the felony murder committed by another."

Defendants contend that a nonkiller can be liable for the felony murder committed by another only if the act resulting in death facilitated the commission of the underlying felony. Since (in their view) the evidence here would have supported the inference that Mianta killed her stepmother out of a private animus, and not to advance the burglary-robbery, they claim that the trial court's failure to instruct the jury on the requirement that the killing facilitate the burglary-robbery mandates reversal of their felony-murder convictions. The Attorney General, on the other hand, asserts that no causal relationship need exist between the underlying felony and the killing. In his view, it is enough that the act resulting in death occurred at the same time as the burglary and robbery.

After reviewing our case law, we find that neither formulation satisfactorily describes the complicity aspect of California's felony-murder rule. We hold instead that the felony-murder rule does not apply to nonkillers where the act resulting in death is completely unrelated to the underlying felony other than occurring at the same time and place. Under California law, there must be a logical nexus—i.e., more than mere coincidence of time and place—between the felony and the act resulting in death before the felony-murder rule may be applied to a nonkiller. Evidence that the killing facilitated or aided the underlying felony is relevant but is not essential.

We also hold that the requisite temporal relationship between the felony and the homicidal act exists even if the nonkiller is not physically present at the time of the homicide, as long as the felony that the nonkiller committed or attempted to commit and the homicidal act are part of one continuous transaction.

A

...

1

Defendants contend that a nonkiller's liability for the felony murder committed by a cofelon depends on proof of a very specific causal relationship between the homicidal act and the underlying felony—namely, that the killer intended thereby to advance or facilitate the felony. Yet, defendants cite no case in which we have relieved a nonkiller of felony-murder liability because of insufficient proof that the killer actually intended to advance or facilitate the underlying felony. Indeed, the felony-murder rule is intended to eliminate the need to plumb the parties' peculiar intent with respect to a killing committed during the perpetration of the felony.[2] Defendants' formulation, which finds no support in the statutory text, would thwart that goal.

Moreover, defendants' formulation is at odds with a fundamental purpose of the felony-murder rule, which is "to deter felons from killing negligently or accidentally by holding them strictly responsible for killings they commit." (*People v. Billa* (2003) 31 Cal.4th 1064.) It is difficult to imagine how homicidal acts that are unintentional, negligent, or accidental could be said to have advanced or facilitated the underlying felony when those acts are, by their nature, unintended.

Defendants make little effort to grapple with the policies underlying the felony-murder rule and rely instead almost entirely on our oft-repeated observation in *People v. Vasquez* (1875) 49 Cal. 560 that "[i]f the homicide in question was committed by one of [the nonkiller's] associates engaged in the robbery, *in furtherance of their common purpose to rob*, he is as accountable as though his own hand had intentionally given the fatal blow, and is guilty of murder in the first degree." Relying on *Vasquez*, defendants claim the felony-murder rule requires proof that the homicidal act have advanced or facilitated the underlying felony. Defendants misread *Vasquez.*

In the century and a quarter since *Vasquez* was decided, we have never construed it to require a killing to advance or facilitate the felony, so long as some logical nexus existed between the two. To the contrary, in *People v. Olsen* (1889) 80 Cal. 122, we upheld an instruction that based a nonkiller's complicity on a killing that was committed merely "*in the prosecution of the common design*"—and, in *Pulido*, we observed

---

2. As we have previously explained, it is no defense to felony murder that the nonkiller did not intend to kill, forbade his associates to kill, or was himself unarmed.

that this instruction was "similar" to the *Vasquez* formulation. The similarity, of course, is that both require a logical nexus between the homicidal act and the underlying felony. Although evidence that the fatal act facilitated or promoted the felony is unquestionably relevant to establishing that nexus, California case law has not yet required that such evidence be presented in every case.

. . .

The Attorney General, on the other hand, contends that the requisite intent, combined with a killing by a cofelon that occurs while the felony is ongoing, is sufficient to establish the nonkiller's liability for felony murder. His formulation, in other words, would require only a temporal connection between the homicidal act and the underlying felony. This description of the relationship between the killing and the felony is incomplete. We have often required more than mere coincidence in time and place between the felony and the act resulting in death to establish a nonkiller's liability for felony murder. In *People v. Washington* (1965) 62 Cal.2d 777, for example, we reversed a conviction of felony murder where the accomplice was killed during the robbery by the *victim*. We held that Penal Code section 189 requires "that the felon or his accomplice commit the killing, for if he does not, the killing is not committed to perpetrate the felony." In *Pulido, supra*, we held that section 189 does not apply even where a cofelon committed the killing during a robbery, if the nonkiller did not join the felony until *after* the killing occurred.

The Attorney General correctly points out that we have approved instructions imposing felony-murder liability on a nonkiller "if a human being is killed by any one of several persons jointly engaged at the time of such killing in the perpetration of or an attempt to perpetrate the crime of robbery, whether such killing is intentional, or unintentional, or accidental." (*People v. Perry* (1925) 195 Cal. 623; *People v. Martin* (1938) 12 Cal.2d 466.) But this "well-settled" formulation does not suggest that *no* causal connection need exist between the felony and the act resulting in death. By its terms, the *Martin-Perry* formulation requires the parties to have been jointly engaged in the perpetration or the attempt to perpetrate the felony at the time of the act resulting in death. A confederate who performs a homicidal act that is completely unrelated to the felony for which the parties have combined cannot be said to have been "jointly engaged" in the perpetration or attempt to perpetrate the felony at the time of the killing. Otherwise, "if one of two burglars ransacking a home glances out of a window, sees his enemy for whom he has long been searching and shoots him, the unarmed accomplice, party only to the burglary, will be guilty of murder in the first degree." (Morris, *The Felon's Responsibility for the Lethal Acts of Others* (1956) 105 U. Pa. L. Rev. 50.)

California law thus has long required some logical connection between the felony and the act resulting in death, and rightly so. Yet the requisite connection has not depended on proof that the homicidal act furthered or facilitated the underlying felony. Instead, for a nonkiller to be responsible for a homicide committed by a cofelon under the felony-murder rule, there must be a logical nexus, beyond mere coincidence of time and place, between the felony the parties were committing or attempting to commit and the act resulting in death.

We therefore reject the assumption—shared by both parties—that the "in furtherance" and "jointly engaged" formulations articulate opposing standards of felony-murder liability. The latter does *not* mean—as the Attorney General suggests—that mere coincidence of time and place between the felony and the homicide is sufficient. And the former does *not* require—as defendants suggest—that the killer intend the homicidal act to aid or promote the felony. Rather, *Vasquez* and *Martin* have merely used different words to convey the same concept: to exclude homicidal acts that are completely unrelated to the felony for which the parties have combined, and to require instead a logical nexus between the felony and the homicide beyond a mere coincidence of time or place.

2

One of the most discussed cases in this area—*People v. Cabaltero* (1939) 31 Cal.App.2d 52 merits additional analysis.

In *Cabaltero*, six defendants were convicted of felony murder, based on the killing of an accomplice (Ancheta) during the perpetration of the robbery of a rural landowner (Nishida). The conspirators plotted to rob Nishida on payday by creating an altercation that would divert attention from the robbery. One of the conspirators was to create the distraction; two others were to rob Nishida; two more were to stand guard outside the building where the robbery was to take place; and Cabaltero was to drive the getaway car. The robbery proceeded as planned, and the loot was obtained at gunpoint without anyone firing a shot. Meanwhile, Ancheta, who was standing guard outside, fired shots at two people who had just driven up. Immediately after the shots were fired, one of the robbers emerged from the building, exclaimed, "Damn you, what did you shoot for," and shot Ancheta fatally.

Some courts and commentators have criticized *Cabaltero*, charging that it sustained felony-murder liability for nonkillers based merely on "the deliberate acts of one accomplice, outside the conspiracy, 'outside the risk' of the conspiracy, and serving only his personal animus." (Morris, *supra*.) As we have explained above, we agree that a nonkiller cannot be liable under the felony-murder rule where the killing has no relation to the felony other than mere coincidence of time and place. *Cabaltero* does not appear to be such a case, however. Viewing the situation objectively, it seems plain that Ancheta was shot as punishment for the greatly increased risk of detection caused by his decision to fire at two people who were approaching the building. To the extent the Ancheta shooting was intended to aid in the escape from the robbery, the homicide would satisfy even the strict causal connection demanded by defendants. Accordingly, a logical nexus between the homicide and the felony existed in that case.

3

Substantial evidence of a logical nexus between the burglary-robbery and the murder exists in this case as well. The record supports a finding that defendants and/or Mianta killed Betty to eliminate the sole witness to the burglary-robbery or that Betty died accidentally as a result of being bound and gagged during the burglary-robbery. Either theory is sufficient to support the judgment. Even if the jury believed that defendants did not want to kill Betty or that they conditioned their participation in the burglary-robbery on the understanding that Betty not get hurt, it would not be a defense to felony murder.

As defendants point out, however, the record might also have supported a finding that Mianta killed Betty out of a private animus and not to aid or promote the burglary-robbery. Defendants contend that the jury instructions, by omitting any requirement that the homicidal act be "in furtherance of" the burglary-robbery, failed to apprise the jury of this latter possibility and therefore mandate reversal of their convictions.

We disagree. Although we have used the "in furtherance" phrase with some frequency in our opinions, we also recognize that this wording has the potential to sow confusion if used in the instructions to the jury. Indeed, as we have explained above, the felony-murder rule does not require proof that the homicidal act furthered or facilitated the felony, only that a logical nexus exist between the two. We therefore do not find the jury instructions deficient merely because the "in furtherance" phrasing was omitted. We must instead measure the instructions against the applicable law as set forth in part A.1.

The instructions in Cavitt's case tracked CALJIC No. 8.27 and provided in relevant part: "If a human being is killed by one of several persons engaged in the commission of the crimes of robbery or burglary, all persons, who either directly and actively commit the act constituting that crime, or who with knowledge of the unlawful purpose of the perpetrator of the crime and with the intent or purpose of committing, encouraging or facilitating the commission of the offense, aid, promote, encourage or instigate by act or advice its commission, are guilty of murder in the first degree, whether the killing is intentional, unintentional or accidental." Williams's jury received a substantively similar instruction.

The instructions adequately apprised the jury of the need for a logical nexus between the felonies and the homicide in this case. To convict, the jury necessarily found that "the killing occurred *during* the commission or attempted commission of robbery or burglary" by "one of several persons *engaged in the commission* of those crimes." The first of these described a temporal connection between the crimes; the second described the logical nexus. A burglar who happens to spy a lifelong enemy through the window of the house and fires a fatal shot, as in Professor Morris's example, may have committed a killing while the robbery and burglary were taking place but cannot be said to have been "engaged in the commission" of those crimes at the time the shot was fired.

...

One would hardly be surprised to discover that targets of inherently dangerous felonies are selected precisely *because* one or more of the participants in the felony harbors a personal animus towards the victim. But it would be novel indeed if that commonplace fact could be used to exculpate the parties to a felonious enterprise of a murder committed in the perpetration of that felony, where a logical nexus between the felony and the murder exists. Defendants' focus on the killer's subjective motivation thus is not merely contrary to the felony-murder rule but would in practice swallow it up. Under the circumstances here, we reject the defense contention that the trial court erred in failing to give, sua sponte, a clarifying instruction to explain more fully the requisite connection between the felonies and the homicide.

B

Defendants challenge next the instructions concerning the temporal relationship between the homicide and the felonies. The defense theory was that Mianta killed Betty in the five or ten minutes after defendants had left the house and, along with the stolen property, had reached a place of temporary safety but before Mianta reported the crime. Thus, in their view, the burglary and robbery had ended before Betty was killed, relieving them of liability for felony murder.

The People contended that Betty was killed—or the acts resulting in her death were performed—while defendants were present or, at the least, before defendants reached a place of temporary safety. They also argued that defendants were guilty of felony murder, even if the homicide occurred after they had reached a place of temporary safety, as long as the felonies and the homicide constituted part of one continuous transaction. The trial court in both cases agreed, and instructed each jury that a killing "is committed in the commission of a felony if the killing and the felony are parts of one continuous transaction. There is no requirement that the homicide occur while committing or while engaged in the felony or that the killing be part of the felony, so long as the two acts are part of one continuous transaction."

We find no error. Our case law has consistently rejected a "strict construction of the temporal relationship between felony and killing as to both first degree murder and [the] felony-murder special circumstance." (*People v. Sakarias* (2000) 22 Cal.4th 596.) Instead, we have said that "a killing is committed in the perpetration of an enumerated felony if the killing and the felony are parts of one continuous transaction." (*People v. Hayes* (1990) 52 Cal.3d 577.) Indeed, we have invoked the continuous-transaction doctrine not only to aggravate a killer's culpability, but also to make complicit a nonkiller, where the felony and the homicide are parts of one continuous transaction.

Our reliance on the continuous-transaction doctrine is consistent with the purpose of the felony-murder statute, which "was adopted for the protection of the community and its residents, not for the benefit of the lawbreaker, and this court has viewed it as obviating the necessity for, rather than requiring, any technical inquiry concerning whether there has been a completion, abandonment, or desistence of the [felony] before the homicide was completed." (*People v. Chavez* (1951) 37 Cal.2d 656.) In particular, the rule "was not intended to relieve the wrongdoer from any probable consequence of his act by placing a limitation upon the *res gestae* which is unreasonable or unnatural. The homicide is committed in the perpetration of the felony if the killing and felony are parts of one continuous transaction" with the proviso "that felony-murder liability attaches only to those engaged in the felonious scheme before or during the killing." (*Pulido, supra.*)

This is not to say that Mianta, by remaining in the house with Betty, could have prolonged defendants' liability indefinitely. For example, if Mianta had untied Betty, revived her, and two weeks later poisoned her in retaliation for some perceived slight, the burglary-robbery and the murder would not be part of "one continuous transaction." Cavitt's fear that, because Mianta lived with the victim, the felonies "could be deemed to continue indefinitely" is therefore unfounded. Hence, no error appears in the Cavitt instructions.

. . .

. . . Moreover, the only "control" Mianta had over Betty was attributable to the fact that defendants had bound and gagged Betty during the burglary-robbery. Even if Mianta had decided to kill Betty for personal reasons, there was no evidence that she formed this private intent *after* defendants had left and reached a place of temporary safety. Inasmuch as concurrent intent to kill and to commit the target felonies "does not undermine the basis for a felony-murder conviction" (*People v. Gutierrez, supra*), a finding that Betty remained under Mianta's control at the time of the homicide was, in this particular situation, equivalent to a finding that the homicide was part of a continuous transaction with the burglary-robbery. . . .

. . .

[Concurring opinion of WERDEGER, J., joined by KENNARD, J., and concurring opinion of CHIN, J. omitted.]

Note and Problems

Problem 93.

Defendant and seven other young men, armed with guns, entered a tanning salon, beat and tied up Victim, the owner of the salon, and demanded money. While Defendant and others were ransacking the building looking for money and valuables, three of the gang stripped and sexually assaulted Victim. The gang then took money and jewelry and fled. In addition to being charged with robbery and assault with a deadly weapon, Defendant is charged with sexual assault (P.C. § 289). What arguments should be made as to whether he is guilty of the sexual assault? How would the arguments change if there were evidence that, while sexually assaulting Victim, the three men demanded that she tell them the location of her valuables?

Defining the Scope of a Conspiracy. The prosecutor, in his or her charging document, defines the scope and membership of the conspiracy which he or she will attempt to prove at trial. The prosecutor may have the option of defining a conspiracy narrowly, only encompassing the participants in a particular crime, or broadly, encompassing individuals or groups pursuing separate criminal activities which are linked by a common purpose. Obviously, the broader the conspiracy which is proved, the wider the liability of each of the members for substantive crimes committed by other members. The leading Supreme Court case on defining the scope of a conspiracy is *Kotteakos v. United States*, 328 U.S. 750 (1946). In *Kotteakos*, the Government charged nineteen persons with providing fraudulent information in order to secure loans from a federal agency. The Government proved that Brown was the key person in procuring the loans, and that he conspired with each of the other defendants to get loans for that defendant. Although Brown charged a commission to each of the defendants to secure the loans, none of the defendants except Brown shared in the proceeds obtained by other defendants. The Supreme Court held that, although each of the defendants had engaged in a conspiracy with Brown, the evidence was insufficient to prove the existence of a larger conspiracy among the various defendants.

The California Court of Appeal reached an opposite conclusion in the case of *Anderson v. Superior Court*, 78 Cal. App. 2d 22 (1947). There, seventeen defendants were jointly indicted with one Stern on allegations that they had conspired to commit, and were committing, illegal abortions. The evidence was that each of the other defendants, although they did not know each other, had referred one or more women to Stern for an abortion and had received a referral fee. After first noting that it was not necessary for each of the conspirators to "have seen the others, or have knowledge as to who all the members of the conspiracy are," the court found sufficient evidence of one general conspiracy, because the defendants "knew that Stern was engaged in the commission of abortions not casually but as a regular business and that others ... had conspired with him to further his operations."

The conspiracies in *Kotteakos* and *Anderson* have been described as "wheel" conspiracies, in contrast with other conspiracies described as "chain" conspiracies.

> ... In a wheel conspiracy, various defendants accused of individual criminal transactions are linked together by the fact that one defendant or one group of defendants participated in every transaction. For graphic purposes, the defendant or defendants implicated in every charge are described as the hub of the wheel and those charged with individual crimes as the spokes....
>
> ... As the name indicates a chain conspiracy involves the chain of distribution of some commodity, such as narcotics, from the initial manufacture or smuggling to the ultimate consumer. A chain conspiracy is similar to a wheel conspiracy in that the participants at opposite ends of the chain may not know or have any dealings with each other, but the two are different in that the participants in a chain conspiracy all deal with the same goods. A chain may, and frequently does, incorporate one or more subsidiary wheels.

P. Johnson, *The Unnecessary Crime of Conspiracy*, 61 Cal. L. Rev. 1137, 1168–71 (1973).

The courts have little trouble finding a general conspiracy in the case of a chain, but what is the rationale for finding a general conspiracy in the case of a wheel? In either case, what purpose is served by imposing liability on a defendant for crimes he or she did not specifically aid or encourage, done by people with whom the defendant never communicated?

Problem 94.

Kingpin was the head of a major drug gang in Oakland. Killer and Thug were experienced "hit" men for the gang. They had worked together on "missions" before, and Thug knew Killer to be "hardheaded." For some time, Kingpin had held a grudge against Chuckie, a drug dealer associated with another Oakland gang, and Kingpin had heard rumors that Chuckie was out to kill him. As a result, Kingpin ordered Killer and Thug to pick up automatic weapons, and kill Chuckie. The two drove to an area of Oakland Chuckie was thought to frequent and saw a young man, Victim, on the street. When Thug first saw Victim from the car, he said, "That's Chuckie." Killer said, "We're gonna get him." When they got close to Victim, Thug changed his mind and said, "That's not Chuckie," but Killer repeated, "We're gonna get him." They pulled around the corner, stopped the car and jumped out, carrying their weapons. As they walked back around the corner, they saw a police car. Thug said, "Police right there man. Don't do it. It ain't cool. That's not the dude, man. Come on." Killer said, "Man, f___ dat. We's gonna waste it up. We's gonna let dese n___ know we serious." Killer then fired several rounds, killing Victim.

Kingpin and Thug are charged (along with Killer) with first degree murder (P.C. §§ 187–189). What arguments should be made as to their guilt?

Problem 95.

Defendant was estranged from his wife, Wife, who was currently living with her boyfriend, Boyfriend. Defendant hated Boyfriend and suspected Wife and Boyfriend of having burglarized his house, and Boyfriend had threatened Defendant because Wife maintained a relationship with Defendant. Consequently, Defendant purchased a gun for protection against Boyfriend. Three days before the killing of Officer, Killer was arrested for possession of methamphetamine and brass knuckles. Killer's girlfriend, Tramp (who had also been Defendant's girlfriend), prevailed on Defendant to put up bail for Killer, and Killer was released from jail the day before the killing. Defendant, Killer and Tramp got high on methamphetamine, and Defendant told Killer he could pay back Defendant for posting bail by killing Boyfriend. Killer said he would need a gun, and Defendant gave Killer his gun and also $400 to purchase more methamphetamine. Killer stayed up all night smoking methamphetamine with a woman friend and then smoked more the next day. When Killer received a phone call from Tramp reporting that Defendant was angry because Killer had not returned with the methamphetamine, he decided to drive to Defendant's house with the gun handy in case he needed it to deal with Defendant. Killer was driving on a freeway when Officer pulled him over for a traffic violation. Afraid that he might be rearrested for driving under the influence and found in possession of methamphetamine and a gun, Killer shot and killed Officer. Defendant is now charged (along with Killer) with first degree murder (P.C. §§ 187–189). What are the arguments as to whether he is guilty?

People v. Medina

46 Cal.4th 913, 209 P.3d 105 (2009)

CHIN, J.

In this case, a verbal challenge by defendants (members of a street gang) resulted in a fistfight between defendants and the victim (a member of another street gang). After the fistfight ended, one of the defendants shot and killed the victim as he was driving away from the scene of the fight with his friend. The jury found the gunman guilty of murder and attempted murder of the friend, as the actual perpetrator, and two other participants in the fistfight guilty of those offenses as aiders and abettors. The Court of Appeal affirmed the gunman's convictions, but reversed the participants' convictions. It held there was insufficient evidence that the nontarget offenses of murder and attempted murder were a natural and probable consequence of the target offense of simple assault which they had aided and abetted.

Because a rational trier of fact could have concluded that the shooting death of the victim was a reasonably foreseeable consequence of the assault, on the facts of this case, we reverse the judgment of the Court of Appeal relating to the nonshooting defendants.

I. FACTS AND PROCEDURAL HISTORY

On the evening of January 2, 2004, Manuel Ordenes and his wife Amelia Rodriguez continued their New Year's celebration with a party at their home in Lake Los Angeles, California. Their neighbors Kirk and Abraham, a friend, Lisa, and Jason Falcon were present at their house. Jose Medina ("Tiny"), George Marron, and Raymond Vallejo, self-described members of the Lil Watts gang, were also present. Although Falcon was not identified as a gang member, he was always with Medina, Marron, and Vallejo. Ordenes had formerly been a member of the Lennox gang, a Lil Watts rival, although the two gangs were not rivals in the Lake Los Angeles area. Everyone was drinking alcohol and using methamphetamine.

Around 11:00 p.m., Ernie Barba drove to Ordenes's house with his friend, Krystal Varela, to pick up a CD. Barba went to the house, while Varela stayed at the car. When Ordenes or Rodriguez answered the door, Barba asked, "What's up?" On direct examination, Ordenes stated he heard aggressive voices inside the house saying, "Where are you from?" Later on cross-examination, he clarified that he heard Vallejo say, "Who is that?" and then ask Barba, "Where are you from?" From his experience as a former gang member, Ordenes knew that when a gang member asks another gang member "where are you from?" he means "what gang are you from?" a question which constitutes an "aggression step." He also knew that, if the inquiring gang member was an enemy, the question could lead to a fight or even death. If that gang member had a weapon, he would use it. Wanting to avoid problems in his house, and concerned that somebody was going to get killed, Ordenes ordered, "Take that into the streets, go outside, don't disrespect the house."

Medina, Marron, Vallejo, and Falcon left the house and joined Barba on the front porch. Once outside, Medina, Marron, and Vallejo approached Barba and continued to ask, "Where are you from?" Barba replied, "Sanfer," signifying a San Fernando Valley gang. Vallejo responded, "Lil Watts." Medina remarked, "What fool, you think you crazy?" Vallejo then punched Barba. Medina and Marron joined in the fight. According to Ordenes, Barba, even though outnumbered, defended himself well and held his own against the three attackers. All three "couldn't get [Barba] down." Krystal Varela confirmed that Barba was defending himself well.

Ordenes attempted to break up the fight and pull the attackers off Barba, but Falcon held him back. Eventually, Ordenes was able to pull Barba away and escort him to his car which was parked in front of the house. Barba got into the driver's seat, while Krystal Varela got into the passenger seat. At the car, Ordenes advised Barba to leave.

Varela heard someone in the yard say, "get the heat," which she understood to mean a "gun." Barba closed the driver's side door and drove off. As Ordenes was walking back to his house, he heard Lisa yell from the doorway, "Stop, Tiny. No, stop." Amelia Rodriguez then saw Medina walk into the middle of the street and shoot repeatedly at Barba's car as it drove away. Lisa, who was standing next to Rodriguez, yelled, "Tiny, you know you're stupid. Why you doing that? There's kids here. You f'd up." Barba died of a gunshot wound to the head.

The prosecution charged Medina, Marron, Vallejo, and Falcon with first degree murder (Pen. Code, § 187, subd. (a)) and with attempted willful, deliberate, premeditated murder (§§ 664, 187, subd. (a)). Under the prosecution's theory at trial, Medina was guilty as the actual perpetrator, while Marron, Vallejo, and Falcon were guilty as aiders and abettors.

At trial, Hawthorne Police Officer Christopher Port testified as the prosecution's gang expert. Officer Port was assigned to the gang intelligence unit and was familiar with the Lil Watts gang, a violent street gang from Hawthorne. He testified that Lil Watts gang members primarily committed narcotics offenses involving possession and sales, vandalism, and gun-related crimes, including assaults with firearms and semiautomatic firearms, drive-by shootings, and homicides. The police had identified defendants Medina and Vallejo as members of the Lil Watts gang, based on field contacts and their gang tattoos. The police considered Marron to be "affiliated" with the Lil Watts gang, having seen him with Lil Watts gang members, including Medina and Vallejo.

Officer Port testified that the Lake Los Angeles area where Ordenes lived is considered a "transient area for gangs." When a new gang member arrives there, he feels a need to establish himself by demanding respect, which is "the main pride" of a gang member. Officer Port testified that gang members view behavior that disrespects their gang as a challenge and a "slap in the face" which must be avenged. Gang members perceive that, if no retaliatory action is taken in the face of disrespectful behavior, the challenger and others will view the gang member and the gang itself as weak. According to Officer Port, violence is used as a response to disrespectful behavior and disagreements and as a means to gain respect.

Officer Port stated that, when a gang member asks another person, "where are you from?" he suspects that person is in a gang and wants to know what gang he claims as his. In response to hypothetical questions, Officer Port opined that when Barba responded "Sanfer," he was claiming membership in that gang, and that the Lil Watts gang members had viewed Barba's response as disrespectful and had started a fight to avenge themselves. Officer Port stated that a gang member who asks that question could be armed and probably would be prepared to use violence, ranging from a fistfight to homicide. He explained, "In the gang world problems or disagreements aren't handled like you and I would handle a disagreement.... When gangs have a disagreement, you can almost guarantee it's going to result in some form of violence, whether that be punching and kicking or ultimately having somebody shot and killed."

Ordenes testified that it is important for a gang to be respected and, above all, feared by other gangs. Once a gang is no longer feared, its members lose respect, are ridiculed, and become vulnerable and subject to attack by other gangs. He stated that death is sometimes an option exercised by gang members as a way to maintain respect. Ordenes further stated there are a lot of gang members occupying their "turfs" with guns.

The jury acquitted codefendant Falcon, but found defendants Medina, Marron, and Vallejo guilty as charged ...

The Court of Appeal affirmed Medina's conviction, but reversed the convictions of Marron and Vallejo on the ground there was insufficient evidence that the nontarget crimes of murder and attempted murder were a reasonably foreseeable consequence of simple assault, the target offense they had aided and abetted.

We granted the Attorney General's petition for review regarding the reversals of Marron's and Vallejo's judgments.

II. DISCUSSION

The Attorney General argues that, when the facts are viewed as a whole, there is substantial evidence to support the murder and attempted murder convictions of defendants Marron and Vallejo. We agree.

...

It is undisputed that Marron and Vallejo knowingly and intentionally participated in the fistfight that preceded the shooting, that Medina alone shot the victim, and that the jury convicted Marron and Vallejo of murder and attempted murder as aiders and abettors under the natural and probable consequences doctrine.

"A person who knowingly aids and abets criminal conduct is guilty of not only the intended crime [target offense] but also of any other crime the perpetrator actually commits [nontarget offense] that is a natural and probable consequence of the intended crime. The latter question is not whether the aider and abettor *actually* foresaw the additional crime, but whether, judged objectively, it was *reasonably* foreseeable." (*People v. Mendoza* (1998) 18 Cal.4th 1114.) Liability under the natural and probable consequences doctrine "is measured by whether a reasonable person in the defendant's position would have or should have known that the charged offense was a reasonably foreseeable consequence of the act aided and abetted." (*People v. Nguyen* (1993) 21 Cal.App.4th 518.)

"[A]lthough variations in phrasing are found in decisions addressing the doctrine—'probable and natural,' 'natural and reasonable,' and 'reasonably foreseeable'—the ultimate factual question is one of foreseeability." (*People v. Coffman and Marlow* (2004) 34 Cal.4th 1.) Thus, "[a] natural and probable consequence is a foreseeable consequence." (*Ibid.*) But "to be reasonably foreseeable [t]he consequence need not have been a strong probability; a possible consequence which might reasonably have been contemplated is enough." (*People v. Nguyen, supra.*) A reasonably foreseeable consequence is to be evaluated under all the factual circumstances of the individual case and is a factual issue to be resolved by the jury.

. . .

In examining the whole record in the light most favorable to the prosecution, we conclude that a rational trier of fact could have found that the shooting of the victim was a reasonably foreseeable consequence of the gang assault in this case. Medina, Marron, and Vallejo, members of the Lil Watts gang, repeatedly challenged Barba by asking, "Where are you from?" When Barba responded, "Sanfer," Vallejo declared he was a member of another gang, "Lil Watts." Medina remarked, "What fool, you think you crazy?" Apparently viewing Barba's response as disrespectful behavior, Medina, Marron, and Vallejo then attacked Barba.

The Court of Appeal emphasized there was no evidence that the assailants used weapons or were armed during the fistfight, or that the two gangs involved were in the midst of a "war" or had been involved in prior altercations. It further stressed that the shooting occurred after the fistfight had ended. However, the Court of Appeal's analysis ignores the testimony of the gang expert, Officer Port, and of Ordenes, and other evidence.

According to Ordenes, a gang member's query "where are you from?" means "what gang are you from?" and is a verbal challenge, which (depending on the response) could lead to a physical altercation and even death. Officer Port affirmed that a gang member who asks, "where are you from?" could be armed and probably would be prepared to respond with violence, ranging from a fistfight to homicide. As a former gang member, Ordenes foresaw precisely that result. He feared that somebody might get killed after Vallejo verbally challenged Barba, and, because of that fear, ordered defendants to "take that into the streets."

Once the fight ensued, the three men could not get Barba down. Despite being attacked and outnumbered by three aggressors, Barba defended himself well and held his own. Ordenes interrupted the fistfight while Barba was performing well and before the three attackers could vindicate themselves. Given the gang-related purpose of the initial assault and the fact that, despite being outnumbered, Barba exhibited strength against three aggressors who could not avenge themselves in response to what they considered disrespectful behavior by Barba, the jury could reasonably have found that a person in defendants' position (i.e., a gang member) would have or should have known that retaliation was likely to occur and that escalation of the confrontation to a deadly level was reasonably foreseeable as Barba was retreating from the scene.

The record supports that implicit finding by the jury. First, according to the testimony, gang members emphasize the need for respect, primarily in the form of fear. Officer Port testified that gang members view behavior that disrespects their gang as a challenge and "slap in the face" which must be avenged. Gang members perceive that, if no retaliatory action is taken in the face of disrespectful behavior, the challenger and other people will view the gang member and the gang itself as weak. Ordenes, a former gang member, confirmed that once a gang is no longer feared, its members lose respect, are ridiculed, and become vulnerable and subject to attack by other gangs. According to Officer Port, violence is used as a response to disrespectful behavior and disagreements, and as a means to gain respect. Ordenes confirmed that gang members consider death as a means to maintain respect in some circumstances.

Second, the record reveals that Lil Watts was a violent street gang that regularly committed gun offenses. Officer Port testified that Lil Watts members were involved "in all sorts of gun charges," including assaults with firearms, semiautomatic firearms, drive-by shootings, and homicides. Ordenes affirmed that many gang members occupied their turfs with guns. Regarding this specific incident, Ordenes ordered the Lil Watts gang members outside because he was concerned that somebody would be killed. Thus, because Lil Watts members had challenged a rival gang member, the jury could reasonably have inferred that, in backing up that challenge, a Lil Watts member either would have been armed or would have or should have known a fellow gang member was or might be armed.

Third, although there was no evidence the two gangs involved had an ongoing rivalry, Officer Port stated that the Lake Los Angeles area is considered a "transient area for gangs" where newly arrived gang members demand respect to establish themselves in that territory. Ordenes testified that members of Lil Watts, Sanfer, and Pacoima (another gang) live in the Lake Los Angeles area. Thus, escalating the violence with a gun was a foreseeable way for a Lil Watts gang member to exact revenge for Barba's initial disrespect and his later show of strength against the three aggressors, thereby establishing Lil Watts's turf domination in the neighborhood.

Fourth, although Vallejo argues that the fistfight and shooting were not one uninterrupted event, but rather two separate incidents, the evidence showed that Medina, Marron, and Vallejo did not consider the fight to be over and that the shooting resulted directly from that fight. Eyewitnesses testified that the events happened very quickly, in a matter of seconds, not minutes. After Ordenes had broken up the fight, someone yelled, "get the heat," just before the shooting....

...

Although there was no direct evidence of who specifically ordered, "get the heat," there was circumstantial evidence regarding the identity of the declarant. That evidence revealed that one of the gang participants actually knew that at least one fellow gang member had a gun. It was unlikely that Medina yelled "get the heat" to himself. Other evidence established that Rodriguez, like her husband, ordered the men to take their dispute outside because she was concerned for her children; Rodriguez yelled for the men to stop fighting; Ordenes successfully broke up the fistfight; Ordenes's neighbors Kirk and Abraham remained in the house during the fight; and Ordenes's friend, Lisa, tried to stop the shooting when she yelled from the doorway, "Stop, Tiny. No, stop." That evidence reflects that the people at the party other than defendants either wanted the fighting to end or were not present during the fighting, and had no reason to want Barba shot. In addition, Medina, Marron, Vallejo, and Falcon fled before the police arrived. The jury could reasonably have concluded that one of the Lil Watts members yelled, "get the heat," and that either Medina was asking his companions for a gun, or a companion was telling him to get out a gun.[2] The fact that at least two of the gang members knew a gun was available at the scene is further evidence that gun violence was foreseeable.

Thus, the evidence shows there was a close connection between the failed assault against Barba (in which Marron, Vallejo, and Medina directly participated) and the murder of Barba; Medina shot Barba because he disrespected Lil Watts; and the shooting and death were "not an unreasonable result to be expected from the [assault]." (*People v. Martinez* (1966) 239 Cal.App.2d 161.)

. . .

The dissenting opinion examines Ordenes's and Officer Port's testimony relating to the consequences of the challenge "Where are you from?" and concludes that, at most, they believed that a homicide was a possible, not probable, consequence of that challenge. The dissent emphasizes that Ordenes's actions in ordering the gang members out of his house and breaking up the fight further reflects that Ordenes did not foresee that the verbal challenge would *probably* result in a homicide.

Although the dissent (echoing the Court of Appeal) emphasizes that the shooting was not a *probable* consequence of the verbal challenge, the ultimate factual question is one of reasonable foreseeability, to be evaluated under *all* the factual circumstances of the case. The precise consequence need not have been foreseen. Even if Ordenes

2. The dissenting opinion argues that it was equally reasonable for the jury to have concluded that Medina himself shouted for a gun, his companions did not know what he was talking about, and when no one responded, he retrieved the gun himself. Nevertheless, the dissent does not dispute that, in view of all the evidence presented at trial, the jury could have reasonably concluded that one of the Lil Watts gang members yelled, "get the heat," and that either Medina was asking for and received a gun from a companion, or a companion was telling Medina to get out a gun. "[O]ur role on appeal is a limited one." (*People v. Ochoa* (1993) 6 Cal.4th 1199, 864 P.2d 103.) Under the substantial evidence rule, we must presume in support of the judgment the existence of every fact that the trier of fact could reasonably have deduced from the evidence. Thus, if the circumstances reasonably justify the trier of fact's findings, the opinion of the reviewing court that the circumstances might also reasonably be reconciled with a contrary finding does not warrant reversal of the judgment.

had not actually pinpointed, from the verbal challenge alone, the precise form of ensuing violence, he did foresee that the verbal confrontation by the Lil Watts gang members would likely escalate into some type of physical violence. Officer Port agreed that the challengers would be prepared to use physical violence.

Nor was it required that Vallejo and Marron "must have known Medina was armed." The issue is "whether, under all of the circumstances presented, a reasonable person in the defendant's position would have *or should have known* that the [shooting] was a reasonably foreseeable consequence of the act aided and abetted by the defendant." (*People v. Nguyen, supra.*)

Contrary to the dissent's suggestion, there was more here than just verbal challenges by gang members. There was evidence that Barba refused to succumb to the gang assault despite being substantially outnumbered and defendants were unable to avenge themselves because of Barba's show of strength; gang culture (in which defendants were involved) emphasizes respect, fear, and retaliatory violence in the face of disrespectful behavior; Lil Watts was a violent street gang that regularly committed gun offenses; and a Lil Watts gang member had ready access to a gun at the scene. Even if the three aggressors did not intend to shoot Barba when they verbally challenged him, or at the start of the fistfight, it was or should have been reasonably foreseeable to these gang members that the violence would escalate even further depending on Barba's response to their challenge. Thus, given the fact that defendants were unable to avenge themselves for the perceived multiple instances of disrespectful behavior by Barba, the jury could reasonably have found that defendants would have or should have known that retaliation was likely to occur and that escalation of the confrontation to a deadly level was reasonably foreseeable as Barba was retreating from the scene.

Accordingly, viewing the whole record in the light most favorable to the prosecution, we find there was sufficient evidence to support the murder and attempted murder convictions of defendants Marron and Vallejo.

...

Moreno, J., dissenting, joined by Kennard and Werdegar, JJ.

I dissent. In my view, the Court of Appeal reached the correct conclusion when it reversed the convictions of defendants Marron and Vallejo. I agree with the Court of Appeal that insufficient evidence supported those convictions based on the theory that the shooting of Barba by defendant Medina was a natural and probable consequence of the assault on Barba in which Marron and Vallejo participated. The Court of Appeal did not reach this conclusion lightly. The court applied the deferential substantial evidence standard of review to its inquiry. It also recognized the grim reality that disputes between gang members are in a different category from disputes between civilians. "As gang violence has become more prevalent and innocent bystanders have become victims of the violence in ever increasing numbers, our courts have recognized that a dispute between two neighbors and one between two gang members can lead to different consequences." Nonetheless, the Court of Appeal determined that even in the context of gang violence there was insufficient evidence to support the jury's verdict as to Vallejo and Marron.

...

What the Court of Appeal found was that the "only piece of evidence that might support an inference that someone other than Medina knew the shooting would take place was Varela's testimony that she heard someone say, 'Get the heat,' just prior to the sound of gunfire." To this, I would add the majority opinion's assertion—echoed by the Attorney General at argument—that both Ordenes and Port, the gang expert, testified, in effect, that a homicide is a reasonably foreseeable consequence of the challenge, "Where are you from?" I disagree with the majority's characterization of this evidence.

The majority opinion places enormous weight on the "Get the heat" testimony and goes to some lengths to establish, circumstantially, that the person who uttered this statement must have been either Vallejo or Marron. That analysis proceeds, however, from an ipse dixit assumption: "It was unlikely that Medina yelled 'get the heat' to himself." Medina was the one person in this episode who knew there was a gun somewhere because he used it to kill the victim. It is not unlikely, therefore, that Medina yelled out, "Get the heat." But this does not necessarily imply that his codefendants must have known Medina had a gun with him. It only establishes that Medina, who was evidently quite angry that the attack on Barba had been broken up, shouted for a gun, not that anyone knew what he was talking about. It is just as reasonable to conclude that he shouted this command and, when no one responded, he got the gun himself. Indeed, this conclusion is more consistent with the testimony of Rodriguez that, after everyone scattered, Medina stepped out into the street with the gun and fired it.

The other bit of evidence on which the majority relies is testimony regarding the consequences of the challenge, "Where are you from?" The majority asserts: "According to Ordenes, a gang member's query 'where are you from?' means 'what gang are you from?' and is a verbal challenge, which (depending on the response) could lead to a physical altercation and even death. Officer Port affirmed that a gang member who asks 'where are you from?' could be armed and probably would be prepared to respond with violence, ranging from a fistfight to homicide. As a former gang member, Ordenes foresaw precisely that result. He feared that somebody might get killed after Vallejo verbally challenged Barba and, because of that fear, ordered defendants to 'take that into the streets.'"

An examination of the reporter's transcript belies the majority's characterization of this evidence. What the transcript discloses is that both Ordenes and Port—and the former with considerable prodding from the prosecutor—were, at most, describing possible—not probable—consequences. For example, what Ordenes actually said, based on his experience as a gang member, was that the question, "Where are you from?" "would go on to a fight or whatever. [¶] [Q.] Or what? [¶] [A.] Or whatever else would happen. [¶] [Q.] What other things *could* happen from that? [¶] [A.] Well, death. [¶] [Q.] Death as by how? [¶] [A.] Whatever. Whatever you can use. [¶] [Q.] Okay. So if you have a weapon—[¶] [A.] You would use it." (Italics added.)

Thus, in my view, Ordenes's testimony describes a possible event, not a probable one, that might occur if weapons were present (but Ordenes did not testify that he knew or even suspected any of the defendants in this case were armed). The gang expert's testimony was equally attenuated. The expert testified that if the question "Where are you from?" was answered unsatisfactorily, "it's some form of misunderstanding that can go into some physical altercation. They *can* go from a fistfight to disrespecting each other ... verbally and all the way as far [as] homicide." (Italics added.)

Like Ordenes, then, the expert did no more than describe a range of possible results from a fistfight to verbal insults and, perhaps somewhere down the line, a killing, although how far down the line was not elucidated. Moreover, when the expert was asked, "when a gang member usually asks that question to someone else, in your experience are they usually armed?" the expert replied, "They *can* be. It's my opinion that if you're going to ask that question, that you're probably prepared to be in *some form of altercation* following the answer." (Italics added.) "Some form of altercation," of course, is exactly what happened in this case — a fistfight. It does not necessarily encompass a homicide.[2]

Nor do I agree that Ordenes's testimony about his concern when he told defendants and Barba to take their dispute outside the house was because he foresaw a probable homicide. It was the prosecutor who raised this specter: "[Q.] Okay. And when you heard somebody say, 'Where are you from,' did that start to concern you a little bit? [¶][A.] Yes, it did. [¶][Q.] Okay. And is that for the reasons you just stated right now, that you *knew* that somebody was going to get killed? [¶][A.] *For the reason that I didn't want no problems to my house* and also that reason too. [¶][Q.] Okay. So what happened after you heard the words, 'Where are you from?' [¶][A.] I said, 'Take that into the streets, go outside, *don't disrespect the house.*'" (Italics added.)

Again, despite the prosecutor's prodding, Ordenes's testimony is not evidence that he reasonably foresaw a homicide as a consequence of the challenge. Instead, his testimony evinced a concern that he did not want a fight — a fistfight or some other physical altercation — inside his house where there were women and children. That this domestic concern, rather than fear of a probable homicide, was behind his command for the men to leave his house is reflected in his wife's testimony. Rodriguez also told the men to leave the house because, as she testified, "they were kind of getting loud, so I told — they had my front door open and it was cold, so I told them to take that outside because my kids are in back asleep, and then I closed the door."

Moreover, Ordenes's conduct after ordering the men out is not consistent with the majority's interpretation of his testimony. Had he suspected a killing was in the

2. The majority highlights Port's general testimony that the "Lil Watts" gang participated in crimes involving firearms, and concludes: "[B]ecause Lil Watts members had challenged a rival gang member, the jury could reasonably infer that, in backing up that challenge, a Lil Watts member either would have been armed or would have or should have known a fellow gang member was or might be armed." I disagree with the conclusion that it can be reasonably inferred from Port's testimony that, because some gang members participated on some occasions in gun-related crimes, these particular defendants must have known Medina was armed in the specific circumstances of this case — where members from two gangs, who were *not* rivals, met at a party house in neutral territory.

offing, one would think he would have done something to protect himself from getting caught in the crossfire, but he did not. Rather, he followed the men outside, broke up their fight and walked Barba to his car, telling him, "Just get in the car, just leave, I'll take care of it." These are not the acts or the words of someone who is fearful that a killing is imminent. They are the acts and words of someone who is prepared for a low-level altercation that can be smoothed over eventually once the participants have been separated. Thus, I disagree with the majority's characterization of Ordenes's testimony as reflecting a fear "that somebody might get killed after Vallejo verbally challenged Barba ..."

Stripped to its essence, what the majority holds is that the challenge "Where are you from?" is so provocative in the context of gang culture that any response up to and including murder is a reasonably foreseeable consequence of that utterance, so as to justify a murder conviction not only of the actual perpetrator but also of any other gang members involved in the target offense, whatever the surrounding circumstances. I cannot subscribe to such an expansive interpretation of the natural and probable consequences doctrine even in the context of gang violence, which no one doubts is a plague upon some of our state's most vulnerable communities.

I must agree with the Court of Appeal: "Notwithstanding the violence which most gang confrontations spawn, on our facts, viewed objectively, we cannot conclude that an unplanned fight between unarmed combatants in front of a residence was reasonably likely to lead to a shooting resulting in death. In essence, the Attorney General is asking us to create a new theory of liability. An aider and abettor would be responsible for any crime that was a natural and *possible* consequence of the target crime. That, we cannot do."

Neither can I.

Problem

Problem 96.

D1, D2 and Killer ("Defendants") are members of a criminal street gang in City. V1, V2 and V3 ("Victims") are members of rival street gangs. Victims were sitting with other friends at an outdoor table of a fast food restaurant when Killer came out of a store across the street. He crossed the street and walked past the table, giving Victims a "disrespectful" stare. He then recrossed the street to confer briefly with D1 and D2 (who had come out of the store), and all three then approached Victims. Killer asked, "Where are you from?" After Victims identified their gang affiliations, Killer gave the name of his gang, while D1 and D2, standing behind Killer, made gang signs. Killer then pulled out a handgun and started shooting, and Victims scattered. V1 and V2 were shot and killed. D1 and D2 (along with Killer) were charged with two counts of first degree murder (P.C. §§ 187–189) and one count of attempted murder (P.C. §§ 187–189, 664). At trial, prosecution gang experts testified, *inter alia*, that: (1) in the majority of gang murders, the violence is preceded by the words

"Where are you from?"; (2) the challenge "Where are you from?" usually leads to some sort of violence or some sort of confrontation; (3) the police department does not keep statistics on how often gang members pose the challenge "Where are you from?" but it is probably 2,000 to 3,000 times a year in City; (4) last year there were 42 gang-related homicides in City. The defense gang expert testified: (1) "Where are you from?" challenges occur at least 10,000, maybe 20,000 times a year in City; (2) only a very low percentage of them result in murder; (3) when gang members fight, the use of a weapon is not likely. V3 testified, *inter alia*, that: (1) disrespectful staring and other gang challenges most likely lead to an argument or a fist fight; (2) he thought the confrontation with Defendants was going to lead to a fistfight; (3) he didn't expect a gun to be used; (4) D1 and D2 seemed startled and surprised when Killer pulled out a gun. D1 and D2 testified that they did not know Killer had a gun with him and were surprised when he pulled it out. Defendants were convicted at trial. What arguments should be made on appeal as to the sufficiency of the evidence?

People v. Chiu

59 Cal.4th 155, 325 P.3d 972 (2014)

Chin, J.

There are two distinct forms of culpability for aiders and abettors. "First, an aider and abettor with the necessary mental state is guilty of the intended crime. Second, under the natural and probable consequences doctrine, an aider and abettor is guilty not only of the intended crime, but also for any other offense that was a 'natural and probable consequence' of the crime aided and abetted." (*People v. McCoy* (2001) 25 Cal.4th 1111.) This case involves the second form of aider and abettor culpability. In this case, a jury found defendant, Bobby Chiu, guilty of first degree willful, deliberate and premeditated murder (premeditated murder), on the theory that either he directly aided and abetted the murder or he aided and abetted the "target offense" of assault or of disturbing the peace, the natural and probable consequence of which was murder. On the natural and probable consequences theory, the trial court instructed that the jury could find defendant guilty of first degree murder if it determined that *murder* was a natural and probable consequence of either target offense aided and abetted, and if in committing murder, the perpetrator acted willfully, deliberately, and with premeditation.

The Court of Appeal held that the trial court erred in failing to instruct that the jury must find first degree *premeditated* murder was the natural and probable consequence of either target offense. If the jury relied on the natural and probable consequences theory to return the first degree murder conviction, it "necessarily convicted defendant of first degree murder simply because that was the degree of murder the jury found the perpetrator committed." Being unable to find the error harmless, it reversed defendant's first degree murder conviction.

Like the Court of Appeal, we find instructional error, but for a different reason. We now hold that an aider and abettor may not be convicted of first degree *premeditated* murder under the natural and probable consequences doctrine. Rather, his or her liability for that crime must be based on direct aiding and abetting principles. Because the error here was prejudicial, we affirm the Court of Appeal's judgment reversing defendant's first degree murder conviction.

I. FACTS AND PROCEDURAL HISTORY

[A dispute between two high school students over girls was to be settled by a fight between them the following day at a pizzeria. One of the students declared that he was going to bring his "homies" with him, and the other student enlisted members of a criminal street gang on his side. Although one of the two protagonists never showed up at the pizzeria and the other left when he saw that a crowd had gathered there, various of their supporters began to fight, and a full-scale brawl ensued, involving as many as 25 people. Defendant was fighting with Gonzales when Che, one of defendant's friends, retrieved a gun from his car, pointed it at Gonzales (who ran) and subsequently shot and killed Treadway, a friend of Gonzales. The testimony was in conflict as to whether defendant called for Che to get the gun or encouraged him to shoot.]

The prosecution charged defendant with murder, with gang enhancement and firearm use allegations. At trial, the prosecution set forth two alternate theories of liability. First, defendant was guilty of murder because he directly aided and abetted Che in the shooting death of Treadway. Second, defendant was guilty of murder because he aided and abetted Che in the target offense of assault or of disturbing the peace, the natural and probable consequence of which was murder.

Regarding the natural and probable consequences theory, the trial court instructed that before it determined whether defendant was guilty of murder, the jury had to decide (1) whether he was guilty of the target offense (either assault or disturbing the peace); (2) whether a coparticipant committed a murder during the commission of the target offense; and (3) whether a reasonable person in defendant's position would have known that the commission of the *murder* was a natural and probable consequence of the commission of either target offense.

The trial court instructed that to find defendant guilty of murder, the People had to prove that the perpetrator committed an act that caused the death of another person, that the perpetrator acted with malice aforethought, and that he killed without lawful justification.

The trial court further instructed that if the jury found defendant guilty of murder as an aider and abettor, it had to determine whether the murder was in the first or second degree. It then instructed that to find defendant guilty of first degree murder, the People had to prove that the perpetrator acted willfully, deliberately, and with premeditation, and that all other murders were of the second degree.

The jury found defendant guilty of first degree murder ...

II. DISCUSSION

Penal Code section 31, which governs aider and abettor liability, provides in relevant part, "All persons concerned in the commission of a crime, whether it be felony or misdemeanor, and whether they directly commit the act constituting the offense, or aid and abet in its commission ... are principals in any crime so committed." An aider and abettor is one who acts "with knowledge of the criminal purpose of the perpetrator *and* with an intent or purpose either of committing, or of encouraging or facilitating commission of, the offense." (*People v. Beeman* (1984) 35 Cal.3d 547.)

"A person who knowingly aids and abets criminal conduct is guilty of not only the intended crime [target offense] but also of any other crime the perpetrator actually commits [nontarget offense] that is a natural and probable consequence of the intended crime." (*People v. Medina* (2009) 46 Cal.4th 913.) "Thus, for example, if a person aids and abets only an intended assault, but a murder results, that person may be guilty of that murder, even if unintended, if it is a natural and probable consequence of the intended assault." (*McCoy, supra.*)

A nontarget offense is a "natural and probable consequence" of the target offense if, judged objectively, the additional offense was reasonably foreseeable. (*Medina, supra.*) The inquiry does not depend on whether the aider and abettor actually foresaw the nontarget offense. Rather, liability "is measured by whether a reasonable person in the defendant's position would have or should have known that the charged offense was a reasonably foreseeable consequence of the act aided and abetted." Reasonable foreseeability "is a factual issue to be resolved by the jury."

We have not previously considered how to instruct the jury on aider and abettor liability for first degree premeditated murder under the natural and probable consequences doctrine. In *People v. Favor* (2012) 54 Cal.4th 868, we held that under the natural and probable consequences doctrine as applied to the premeditation allegation under section 664, subdivision (a), a trial court need only instruct that the jury find that attempted murder, not attempted *premeditated* murder, was a foreseeable consequence of the target offense. The premeditation finding—based on the direct perpetrator's mens rea—is determined after the jury decides that the nontarget offense of attempted murder was foreseeable.

[The court distinguished *Favor* on the grounds that: (1) unlike first degree murder and second degree murder, attempted murder and attempted premeditated murder are not separate crimes—rather, the finding of premeditation was only used to set the penalty; and (2) "the consequence of imposing liability for the penalty provision in *Favor* is considerably less severe than in imposing liability for first degree murder under the natural and probable consequences doctrine."]

Finding *Favor* not dispositive, we turn to the statutory and doctrinal bases of the natural and probable consequence doctrine to determine its application. The natural and probable consequences doctrine was recognized at common law and is firmly entrenched in California law as a theory of criminal liability.

...

In the context of murder, the natural and probable consequences doctrine serves the legitimate public policy concern of deterring aiders and abettors from aiding or encouraging the commission of offenses that would naturally, probably, and foreseeably result in an unlawful killing. A primary rationale for punishing such aiders and abettors—to deter them from aiding or encouraging the commission of offenses—is served by holding them culpable for the perpetrator's commission of the nontarget offense of second degree murder. It is also consistent with reasonable concepts of culpability. Aider and abettor liability under the natural and probable consequences doctrine does not require assistance with or actual knowledge and intent relating to the nontarget offense, nor subjective foreseeability of either that offense or the perpetrator's state of mind in committing it. It only requires that under all of the circumstances presented, a reasonable person in the defendant's position would have or should have known that the nontarget offense was a reasonably foreseeable consequence of the act aided and abetted by the defendant.

However, this same public policy concern loses its force in the context of a defendant's liability as an aider and abettor of a first degree premeditated murder. First degree murder, like second degree murder, is the unlawful killing of a human being with malice aforethought, but has the additional elements of willfulness, premeditation, and deliberation which trigger a heightened penalty. That mental state is uniquely subjective and personal. It requires more than a showing of intent to kill; the killer must act deliberately, carefully weighing the considerations for and against a choice to kill before he or she completes the acts that caused the death. Additionally, whether a direct perpetrator commits a nontarget offense of murder with or without premeditation and deliberation has no effect on the resultant harm. The victim has been killed regardless of the perpetrator's premeditative mental state. Although we have stated that an aider and abettor's "punishment need not be finely calibrated to the criminal's mens rea" (*Favor, supra*), the connection between the defendant's culpability and the perpetrator's premeditative state is too attenuated to impose aider and abettor liability for first degree murder under the natural and probable consequences doctrine, especially in light of the severe penalty involved and the above-stated public policy concern of deterrence.

Accordingly, we hold that punishment for second degree murder is commensurate with a defendant's culpability for aiding and abetting a target crime that would naturally, probably, and foreseeably result in a murder under the natural and probable consequences doctrine. We further hold that where the direct perpetrator is guilty of first degree premeditated murder, the legitimate public policy considerations of deterrence and culpability would not be served by allowing a defendant to be convicted of that greater offense under the natural and probable consequences doctrine. An aider and abettor's liability for murder under the natural and probable consequences doctrine operates independently of the felony-murder rule. Our holding in this case does not affect or limit an aider and abettor's liability for first degree felony murder under section 189.

Aiders and abettors may still be convicted of first degree premeditated murder based on direct aiding and abetting principles. Under those principles, the prosecution must show that the defendant aided or encouraged the commission of the murder with knowledge of the unlawful purpose of the perpetrator and with the intent or purpose of committing, encouraging, or facilitating its commission. Because the mental state component—consisting of intent and knowledge—extends to the entire crime, it preserves the distinction between assisting the predicate crime of second degree murder and assisting the greater offense of first degree premeditated murder. An aider and abettor who knowingly and intentionally assists a confederate to kill someone could be found to have acted willfully, deliberately, and with premeditation, having formed his own culpable intent. Such an aider and abettor, then, acts with the mens rea required for first degree murder.

[The court found that the instructional error was not harmless.]

[Justice Kennard, in an opinion joined by Chief Justice Cantil-Sakauye and Justice Liu, concurred in the reversal, but agreed with the holding of the Court of Appeal and therefore dissented from the majority's reasoning.]

Problem

Problem 97.

Defendant, V1 and V2 were a members of the Gateway gang. The Gateway gang were enemies of the Bishop gang, and there was a history of violence between them. Defendant's brother, Brother, was a member of the Bishop gang but wanted to leave the gang. When a gang member wants to leave a gang, he has to go through a beating by the gang before he is "jumped out" (allowed to leave). Defendant was concerned that, because of bad blood between himself and some members of the Bishop gang, the Bishops might be too hard on Brother, so he, V1 and V2 took Brother to the jump out. V1 had a gun, but the three agreed that V1 would not shoot unless shot at. The Gateway group met the Bishops at the jump out. Two members of the Bishops began to beat Brother, bloodying him and knocking him to the ground. Defendant intervened and attempted to pull Brother away. A Bishop gang member yelled at Defendant, and Defendant swung at him. Gunfire erupted, and V1 and V2 were shot and killed by a Bishop gang member. Defendant is charged with second degree murder (P.C. §§ 187–189) based on the theory that he committed the target offenses of disturbing the peace and assault or battery and that the killing was a natural and probable consequence of those crimes. What are the arguments regarding Defendant's guilt?

Part V
The Death Penalty

This final part of the book returns to the fundamental issues discussed in *Part I*, this time in the context of the death penalty, the most extreme penalty the state imposes for criminal conduct. The debate about the use of the death penalty again raises questions about the purposes of the criminal law, particularly about the efficacy of general deterrence and the role of retribution in setting penalties. The use of the death penalty in America also has challenged the three fundamental principles of American criminal law discussed in *Part I*. In various cases brought to the Supreme Court, it has been argued that the death penalty is arbitrarily imposed because of overbroad and vague standards, that it is disproportionate to the crimes for which it is authorized, and that it has been utilized in a racially discriminatory manner. While the death penalty is, in fact, employed relatively infrequently (it has been estimated that only 2–4% of all *murderers* are sentenced to death), it is perceived by persons on all sides of the death penalty debate as the central criminal law issue. The attention given to the death penalty by the courts, including the Supreme Court, the legislatures and the public means that death penalty law has come to define standards for criminal law generally.

California has had a death penalty since its admission as a state in 1850. From 1874 until 1972, juries were granted complete discretion to impose either life imprisonment or the death penalty on anyone convicted of first degree murder. It has been estimated that about 25% of convicted first degree murderers were sentenced to death during that period. In 1972, the California Supreme Court held the death penalty unconstitutional under the California Constitution's cruel or unusual punishment provision. *People v. Anderson*, 6 Cal. 3d 628 (1972). Six months later, the voters passed an initiative amending the constitution and restoring the death penalty. The current death penalty scheme was enacted by initiative in 1978. Since the restoration of the death penalty, more than 900 people have been sentenced to death in California, and California currently has over 700 people on death row, the largest death row in the country.

Chapter 15

The Death Penalty and the Constitution

As the Supreme Court Justices pointed out in *Ewing v. California* [Chapter 1], legislatures generally enjoy complete discretion in setting punishments for particular crimes or classes of crimes, and judges (and, in some cases, juries) enjoy a similar discretion, within the limits set out by the legislatures, in applying those punishments to particular defendants. And, in contrast with the substantial procedural protections afforded a defendant in the pre-trial and trial stages of the prosecution, at the sentencing stage, the defendant enjoys almost no procedural protections, except for the right to counsel. See *Williams v. New York*, 337 U.S. 241 (1948). As for the death penalty, although the Supreme Court had held that the Constitution afforded the defendant a right to counsel (see *Powell v. Alabama*, 287 U.S. 45 (1932)), as late as 1971, the Court emphatically rejected the claim that anything in the Constitution limited the states' discretion to impose the death penalty. See *McGautha v. California*, 402 U.S. 183 (1971).

A year and a half after *McGautha*, the Supreme Court dramatically reversed course in the landmark case of *Furman v. Georgia*, 408 U.S. 238 (1972). *Furman* was a 5–4 decision holding unconstitutional, under the Eighth Amendment, Georgia's death penalty scheme, and, by implication, those of the other states as well. Because each of the justices in the majority wrote his own opinion, the scope of, and rationale for, the decision were not determined by the case itself. However, all five justices focused on the infrequency with which the death penalty was imposed, and the positions of Justices Stewart and White—that the infrequency of its use created an unacceptable risk of arbitrariness—came to be accepted as the "holding" of *Furman*. Justice Stewart wrote that the death sentences at issue in *Furman* were "cruel and unusual in the same way that being struck by lightning is cruel and unusual" because, of the many persons convicted of capital crimes, only "a capriciously selected random handful" were sentenced to death. 408 U.S. at 309–10 (Stewart, J., concurring). Justice White wrote that, "the death penalty is exacted with great infrequency even for the most atrocious crimes and ... there is no meaningful basis for distinguishing the few cases in which it is imposed from the many cases in which it is not." 408 U.S. at 313 (White, J., concurring).

The five post-*Furman* cases in this chapter concern the Supreme Court's consideration of substantive limits imposed by the Eighth Amendment on the use of the death penalty.[a] *Gregg v. Georgia* was the Court's first case to consider the constitutionality of the state statutes enacted in the wake of *Furman*. In *Gregg*, the court has to decide whether the death penalty is in all cases a disproportionate punishment for murder and, if not, whether the Georgia scheme, on its face, satisfies the *Furman* concerns about the risk of arbitrariness. In *Lockett v. Ohio*, the issue is whether the Eighth Amendment requires that the defendant be permitted to present, and the sentencer be accorded discretion to consider, mitigation evidence. *Tison v. Arizona* and *Kennedy v. Louisiana* involve proportionality challenges to death sentences. In *Tison*, the defendant's contention is that the death penalty is a disproportionate punishment for an accomplice who neither killed, nor intended to kill. In *Kennedy*, the defendant contends that the death penalty is a disproportionate punishment for rape of a young child. The final case, *McCleskey v. Kemp*, involves an Eighth Amendment challenge based on an extensive empirical study indicating that race is a significant factor in determining who is sentenced to death.

Gregg v. Georgia

428 U.S. 153, 96 S. Ct. 2909 (1976)

Judgment of the Court, and opinion of Mr. Justice Stewart, Mr. Justice Powell, and Mr. Justice Stevens, announced by Mr. Justice Stewart.

The issue in this case is whether the imposition of the sentence of death for the crime of murder under the law of Georgia violates the Eighth and Fourteenth Amendments.

I

The petitioner, Troy Gregg, was charged with committing armed robbery and murder. In accordance with Georgia procedure in capital cases, the trial was in two stages, a guilt stage and a sentencing stage. [The evidence at the guilt trial established that Gregg and a traveling companion, Floyd Allen, while hitchhiking north in Florida, were picked up by the two victims. When the four stopped for a rest along the highway, Gregg shot and killed the victims and took their car and valuables. The jury found Gregg guilty of two counts of armed robbery and two counts of murder.]

At the penalty stage, which took place before the same jury, neither the prosecutor nor the petitioner's lawyer offered any additional evidence. Both counsel, however, made lengthy arguments dealing generally with the propriety of capital punishment under the circumstances and with the weight of the evidence of guilt. The trial judge

---

a. The chapter does not deal with the numerous procedural issues addressed by the Supreme Court in death penalty cases decided since *Furman*. For example, the Supreme Court has decided death penalty cases reviewing the competence of counsel (*e.g.*, *Strickland v. Washington*, 466 U.S. 668 (1984)), jury selection (*e.g.*, *Uttecht v. Brown*, 551 U.S. 1 (2007)), prosecutorial misconduct (*e.g.*, *Darden v. Wainwright*, 477 U.S. 168 (1986)), the use of victim impact evidence (*e.g.*, *Payne v. Tennessee*, 501 U.S. 808 (1991)) and the role of appellate review (*e.g.*, *Pulley v. Harris*, 465 U.S. 37 (1984)).

instructed the jury that it could recommend either a death sentence or a life prison sentence on each count. The judge further charged the jury that in determining what sentence was appropriate the jury was free to consider the facts and circumstances, if any, presented by the parties in mitigation or aggravation.

Finally, the judge instructed the jury that it "would not be authorized to consider [imposing] the penalty of death" unless it first found beyond a reasonable doubt one of these aggravating circumstances:

> "One—That the offense of murder was committed while the offender was engaged in the commission of two other capital felonies, to-wit the armed robbery of [the two victims].
>
> "Two—That the offender committed the offense of murder for the purpose of receiving money and the automobile described in the indictment.
>
> "Three—The offense of murder was outrageously and wantonly vile, horrible and inhuman, in that they [sic] involved the depravity of [the] mind of the defendant."

Finding the first and second of these circumstances, the jury returned verdicts of death on each count.

The Supreme Court of Georgia affirmed the convictions and the imposition of the death sentences for murder. After reviewing the trial transcript and the record, including the evidence, and comparing the evidence and sentence in similar cases in accordance with the requirements of Georgia law, the court concluded that, considering the nature of the crime and the defendant, the sentences of death had not resulted from prejudice or any other arbitrary factor and were not excessive or disproportionate to the penalty applied in similar cases. The death sentences imposed for armed robbery, however, were vacated on the grounds that the death penalty had rarely been imposed in Georgia for that offense and that the jury improperly considered the murders as aggravating circumstances for the robberies after having considered the armed robberies as aggravating circumstances for the murders.

We granted the petitioner's application for a writ of certiorari limited to his challenge to the imposition of the death sentences in this case as "cruel and unusual" punishment in violation of the Eighth and the Fourteenth Amendments.

II

Before considering the issues presented it is necessary to understand the Georgia statutory scheme for the imposition of the death penalty. The Georgia statute, as amended after our decision in *Furman v. Georgia*, 408 U.S. 238 (1972), retains the death penalty for six categories of crime: murder, kidnapping for ransom or where the victim is harmed, armed robbery, rape, treason, and aircraft hijacking. The capital defendant's guilt or innocence is determined in the traditional manner, either by a trial judge or a jury, in the first stage of a bifurcated trial.

If trial is by jury, the trial judge is required to charge lesser included offenses when they are supported by any view of the evidence. After a verdict, finding, or plea of guilty to a capital crime, a presentence hearing is conducted before whoever made the determination of guilt. The sentencing procedures are essentially the same in both bench and jury trials. At the hearing:

> "[T]he judge [or jury] shall hear additional evidence in extenuation, mitigation, and aggravation of punishment, including the record of any prior criminal convictions and pleas of guilty or pleas of nolo contendere of the defendant, or the absence of any prior conviction and pleas: Provided, however, that only such evidence in aggravation as the State has made known to the defendant prior to his trial shall be admissible. The judge [or jury] shall also hear argument by the defendant or his counsel and the prosecuting attorney ... regarding the punishment to be imposed."

The defendant is accorded substantial latitude as to the types of evidence that he may introduce. Evidence considered during the guilt stage may be considered during the sentencing stage without being resubmitted.

In the assessment of the appropriate sentence to be imposed the judge is also required to consider or to include in his instructions to the jury "any mitigating circumstances or aggravating circumstances otherwise authorized by law and any of [10] statutory aggravating circumstances which may be supported by the evidence...." The scope of the nonstatutory aggravating or mitigating circumstances is not delineated in the statute. Before a convicted defendant may be sentenced to death, however, except in cases of treason or aircraft hijacking, the jury, or the trial judge in cases tried without a jury, must find beyond a reasonable doubt one of the 10 aggravating circumstances specified in the statute. The sentence of death may be imposed only if the jury (or judge) finds one of the statutory aggravating circumstances and then elects to impose that sentence. If the verdict is death, the jury or judge must specify the aggravating circumstance(s) found. In jury cases, the trial judge is bound by the jury's recommended sentence.

In addition to the conventional appellate process available in all criminal cases, provision is made for special expedited direct review by the Supreme Court of Georgia of the appropriateness of imposing the sentence of death in the particular case. The court is directed to consider "the punishment as well as any errors enumerated by way of appeal," and to determine:

> "(1) Whether the sentence of death was imposed under the influence of passion, prejudice, or any other arbitrary factor, and
>
> "(2) Whether, in cases other than treason or aircraft hijacking, the evidence supports the jury's or judge's finding of a statutory aggravating circumstance..., and
>
> "(3) Whether the sentence of death is excessive or disproportionate to the penalty imposed in similar cases, considering both the crime and the defendant."

If the court affirms a death sentence, it is required to include in its decision reference to similar cases that it has taken into consideration.

A transcript and complete record of the trial, as well as a separate report by the trial judge, are transmitted to the court for its use in reviewing the sentence. The report is in the form of a 6 ½-page questionnaire, designed to elicit information about the defendant, the crime, and the circumstances of the trial. It requires the trial judge to characterize the trial in several ways designed to test for arbitrariness and disproportionality of sentence. Included in the report are responses to detailed questions concerning the quality of the defendant's representation, whether race played a role in the trial, and, whether, in the trial court's judgment, there was any doubt about the defendant's guilt or the appropriateness of the sentence. A copy of the report is served upon defense counsel. Under its special review authority, the court may either affirm the death sentence or remand the case for resentencing. In cases in which the death sentence is affirmed there remains the possibility of executive clemency.

III

We address initially the basic contention that the punishment of death for the crime of murder is, under all circumstances, "cruel and unusual" in violation of the Eighth and Fourteenth Amendments of the Constitution. In Part IV of this opinion, we will consider the sentence of death imposed under the Georgia statutes at issue in this case.

The Court on a number of occasions has both assumed and asserted the constitutionality of capital punishment. In several cases that assumption provided a necessary foundation for the decision, as the Court was asked to decide whether a particular method of carrying out a capital sentence would be allowed to stand under the Eighth Amendment. But until *Furman v. Georgia*, 408 U.S. 238 (1972), the Court never confronted squarely the fundamental claim that the punishment of death always, regardless of the enormity of the offense or the procedure followed in imposing the sentence, is cruel and unusual punishment in violation of the Constitution. Although this issue was presented and addressed in *Furman*, it was not resolved by the Court. Four Justices would have held that capital punishment is not unconstitutional *per se* [Chief Justice Burger and Justices Blackmun, Powell and Rehnquist]; two Justices would have reached the opposite conclusion [Justices Brennan and Marshall]; and three Justices, while agreeing that the statutes then before the Court were invalid as applied, left open the question whether such punishment may ever be imposed. [Justices Douglas, Stewart and White] We now hold that the punishment of death does not invariably violate the Constitution.

A

[Justice Stewart reviewed the history of the Eighth Amendment.]

It is clear from the foregoing precedents that the Eighth Amendment has not been regarded as a static concept. As Mr. Chief Justice Warren said, in an often-quoted phrase, "[t]he Amendment must draw its meaning from the evolving standards of decency that mark the progress of a maturing society." *Trop v. Dulles*, 356 U.S. 86 (1958). Thus, an assessment of contemporary values concerning the infliction of a challenged sanction is relevant to the application of the Eighth Amendment. As we develop below more fully, this assessment does not call for a subjective judgment. It requires, rather, that we look to objective indicia that reflect the public attitude toward a given sanction.

But our cases also make clear that public perceptions of standards of decency with respect to criminal sanctions are not conclusive. A penalty also must accord with "the dignity of man," which is the "basic concept underlying the Eighth Amendment." This means, at least, that the punishment not be "excessive." When a form of punishment in the abstract (in this case, whether capital punishment may ever be imposed as a sanction for murder) rather than in the particular (the propriety of death as a penalty to be applied to a specific defendant for a specific crime) is under consideration, the inquiry into "excessiveness" has two aspects. First, the punishment must not involve the unnecessary and wanton infliction of pain. Second, the punishment must not be grossly out of proportion to the severity of the crime.

B

Of course, the requirements of the Eighth Amendment must be applied with an awareness of the limited role to be played by the courts. This does not mean that judges have no role to play, for the Eighth Amendment is a restraint upon the exercise of legislative power....[19]

But, while we have an obligation to insure that constitutional bounds are not overreached, we may not act as judges as we might as legislators.

> "Courts are not representative bodies. They are not designed to be a good reflex of a democratic society. Their judgment is best informed, and therefore most dependable, within narrow limits. Their essential quality is detachment, founded on independence. History teaches that the independence of the judiciary is jeopardized when courts become embroiled in the passions of the day and assume primary responsibility in choosing between competing political, economic and social pressures." *Dennis v. United States*, 341 U.S. 494 (1951) (Frankfurter, J., concurring in affirmance of judgment).

Therefore, in assessing a punishment selected by a democratically elected legislature against the constitutional measure, we presume its validity. We may not require the legislature to select the least severe penalty possible so long as the penalty selected is

---

19. Although legislative measures adopted by the people's chosen representatives provide one important means of ascertaining contemporary values, it is evident that legislative judgments alone cannot be determinative of Eighth Amendment standards since that Amendment was intended to safeguard individuals from the abuse of legislative power. See *Weems v. United States*, 217 U.S. 349 (1910); *Furman v. Georgia* (BRENNAN, J., concurring). *Robinson v. California*, 370 U.S. 660 (1962), illustrates the proposition that penal laws enacted by state legislatures may violate the Eighth Amendment because "in the light of contemporary human knowledge" they "would doubtless be universally thought to be an infliction of cruel and unusual punishment." At the time of *Robinson* nine States in addition to California had criminal laws that punished addiction similar to the law declared unconstitutional in *Robinson*.

not cruelly inhumane or disproportionate to the crime involved. And a heavy burden rests on those who would attack the judgment of the representatives of the people.

This is true in part because the constitutional test is intertwined with an assessment of contemporary standards and the legislative judgment weighs heavily in ascertaining such standards. "[I]n a democratic society legislatures, not courts, are constituted to respond to the will and consequently the moral values of the people." *Furman v. Georgia* (Burger, C.J., dissenting). The deference we owe to the decisions of the state legislatures under our federal system (*Furman, supra*, Rehnquist, J., dissenting), is enhanced where the specification of punishments is concerned, for "these are peculiarly questions of legislative policy." *Gore v. United States*, 357 U.S. 386 (1958). Caution is necessary lest this Court become, "under the aegis of the Cruel and Unusual Punishment Clause, the ultimate arbiter of the standards of criminal responsibility ... throughout the country." *Powell v. Texas*, 392 U.S. 514 (1968) (plurality opinion). A decision that a given punishment is impermissible under the Eighth Amendment cannot be reversed short of a constitutional amendment. The ability of the people to express their preference through the normal democratic processes, as well as through ballot referenda, is shut off. Revisions cannot be made in the light of further experience.

C

In the discussion to this point we have sought to identify the principles and considerations that guide a court in addressing an Eighth Amendment claim. We now consider specifically whether the sentence of death for the crime of murder is a *per se* violation of the Eighth and Fourteenth Amendments to the Constitution. We note first that history and precedent strongly support a negative answer to this question.

The imposition of the death penalty for the crime of murder has a long history of acceptance both in the United States and in England. The common-law rule imposed a mandatory death sentence on all convicted murderers. And the penalty continued to be used into the 20th century by most American States, although the breadth of the common-law rule was diminished, initially by narrowing the class of murders to be punished by death and subsequently by widespread adoption of laws expressly granting juries the discretion to recommend mercy.

It is apparent from the text of the Constitution itself that the existence of capital punishment was accepted by the Framers. At the time the Eighth Amendment was ratified, capital punishment was a common sanction in every State. Indeed, the First Congress of the United States enacted legislation providing death as the penalty for specified crimes. The Fifth Amendment, adopted at the same time as the Eighth, contemplated the continued existence of the capital sanction by imposing certain limits on the prosecution of capital cases:

> No person shall be held to answer for a capital, or otherwise infamous crime, unless on a presentment or indictment of a Grand Jury ...; nor shall any person be subject for the same offense to be twice put in jeopardy of life or limb; ... nor be deprived of life, liberty, or property, without due process of law....

And the Fourteenth Amendment, adopted over three-quarters of a century later, similarly contemplates the existence of the capital sanction in providing that no State shall deprive any person of "life, liberty, or property" without due process of law.

For nearly two centuries, this Court, repeatedly and often expressly, has recognized that capital punishment is not invalid *per se*....

Four years ago, the petitioners in *Furman* and its companion cases predicated their argument primarily upon the asserted proposition that standards of decency had evolved to the point where capital punishment no longer could be tolerated. The petitioners in those cases said, in effect, that the evolutionary process had come to an end, and that standards of decency required that the Eighth Amendment be construed finally as prohibiting capital punishment for any crime regardless of its depravity and impact on society. This view was accepted by two Justices. Three other Justices were unwilling to go so far; focusing on the procedures by which convicted defendants were selected for the death penalty rather than on the actual punishment inflicted, they joined in the conclusion that the statutes before the Court were constitutionally invalid.

The petitioners in the capital cases before the Court today renew the "standards of decency" argument, but developments during the four years since *Furman* have undercut substantially the assumptions upon which their argument rested. Despite the continuing debate, dating back to the 19th century, over the morality and utility of capital punishment, it is now evident that a large proportion of American society continues to regard it as an appropriate and necessary criminal sanction.

The most marked indication of society's endorsement of the death penalty for murder is the legislative response to *Furman*. The legislatures of at least 35 States have enacted new statutes that provide for the death penalty for at least some crimes that result in the death of another person. And the Congress of the United States, in 1974, enacted a statute providing the death penalty for aircraft piracy that results in death. These recently adopted statutes have attempted to address the concerns expressed by the Court in *Furman* primarily (i) by specifying the factors to be weighed and the procedures to be followed in deciding when to impose a capital sentence, or (ii) by making the death penalty mandatory for specified crimes. But all of the post-*Furman* statutes make clear that capital punishment itself has not been rejected by the elected representatives of the people.

In the only statewide referendum occurring since *Furman* and brought to our attention, the people of California adopted a constitutional amendment that authorized capital punishment, in effect negating a prior ruling by the Supreme Court of California in *People v. Anderson*, 6 Cal. 3d 628 (1972), that the death penalty violated the California Constitution.

The jury also is a significant and reliable objective index of contemporary values because it is so directly involved. The Court has said that "one of the most important functions any jury can perform in making ... a selection [between life imprisonment and death for a defendant convicted in a capital case] is to maintain a link between contemporary community values and the penal system." *Witherspoon v. Illinois*, 391 U.S. 510 (1968). It may be true that evolving standards have influenced juries in recent decades to be more discriminating in imposing the sentence of death.[26] But the relative infrequency of jury verdicts imposing the death sentence does not indicate rejection of capital punishment *per se*. Rather, the reluctance of juries in many cases to impose the sentence may well reflect the humane feeling that this most irrevocable of sanctions should be reserved for a small number of extreme cases. Indeed, the actions of juries in many States since *Furman* are fully compatible with the legislative judgments, reflected in the new statutes, as to the continued utility and necessity of capital punishment in appropriate cases. At the close of 1974 at least 254 persons had been sentenced to death since *Furman*, and by the end of March 1976, more than 460 persons were subject to death sentences.

As we have seen, however, the Eighth Amendment demands more than that a challenged punishment be acceptable to contemporary society. The Court also must ask whether it comports with the basic concept of human dignity at the core of the Amendment. Although we cannot "invalidate a category of penalties because we deem less severe penalties adequate to serve the ends of penology," *Furman v. Georgia* (POWELL, J., dissenting), the sanction imposed cannot be so totally without penological justification that it results in the gratuitous infliction of suffering.

The death penalty is said to serve two principal social purposes: retribution and deterrence of capital crimes by prospective offenders.

In part, capital punishment is an expression of society's moral outrage at particularly offensive conduct. This function may be unappealing to many, but it is essential in an ordered society that asks its citizens to rely on legal processes rather than self-help to vindicate their wrongs.

> "The instinct for retribution is part of the nature of man, and channeling that instinct in the administration of criminal justice serves an important purpose in promoting the stability of a society governed by law. When people begin to believe that organized society is unwilling or unable to impose upon criminal offenders the punishment they 'deserve,' then there are sown the seeds of anarchy—of self-help, vigilante justice, and lynch law." *Furman v. Georgia* (STEWART, J., concurring).

"Retribution is no longer the dominant objective of the criminal law," *Williams v. New York*, 337 U.S. 241 (1949), but neither is it a forbidden objective nor one inconsistent with our respect for the dignity of men. Indeed, the decision that capital punishment may be the appropriate sanction in extreme cases is an expression of the

---

26. The number of prisoners who received death sentences in the years from 1961 to 1972 varied from a high of 140 in 1961 to a low of 75 in 1972, with wide fluctuations in the intervening years: 103 in 1962; 93 in 1963; 106 in 1964; 86 in 1965; 118 in 1966; 85 in 1967; 102 in 1968; 97 in 1969; 127 in 1970; and 104 in 1971. It has been estimated that before *Furman* less than 20% of those convicted of murder were sentenced to death in those states that authorized capital punishment.

community's belief that certain crimes are themselves so grievous an affront to humanity that the only adequate response may be the penalty of death.

Statistical attempts to evaluate the worth of the death penalty as a deterrent to crimes by potential offenders have occasioned a great deal of debate. The results simply have been inconclusive. As one opponent of capital punishment has said:

> "[A]fter all possible inquiry, including the probing of all possible methods of inquiry, we do not know, and for systematic and easily visible reasons cannot know, what the truth about this 'deterrent' effect may be....
>
> "The inescapable flaw is ... that social conditions in any state are not constant through time, and that social conditions are not the same in any two states. If an effect were observed (and the observed effects, one way or another, are not large) then one could not at all tell whether any of this effect is attributable to the presence or absence of capital punishment. A 'scientific'—that is to say, a soundly based—conclusion is simply impossible, and no methodological path out of this tangle suggests itself." Black, Capital Punishment: The Inevitability of Caprice and Mistake, 25–26 (1974).

Although some of the studies suggest that the death penalty may not function as a significantly greater deterrent than lesser penalties, there is no convincing empirical evidence either supporting or refuting this view. We may nevertheless assume safely that there are murderers, such as those who act in passion, for whom the threat of death has little or no deterrent effect. But for many others, the death penalty undoubtedly is a significant deterrent. There are carefully contemplated murders, such as murder for hire, where the possible penalty of death may well enter into the cold calculus that precedes the decision to act.[33] And there are some categories of murder, such as murder by a life prisoner, where other sanctions may not be adequate.

The value of capital punishment as a deterrent of crime is a complex factual issue the resolution of which properly rests with the legislatures, which can evaluate the results of statistical studies in terms of their own local conditions and with a flexibility of approach that is not available to the courts. Indeed, many of the post-*Furman* statutes reflect just such a responsible effort to define those crimes and those criminals for which capital punishment is most probably an effective deterrent.

In sum, we cannot say that the judgment of the Georgia Legislature that capital punishment may be necessary in some cases is clearly wrong. Considerations of federalism, as well as respect for the ability of a legislature to evaluate, in terms of its particular State, the moral consensus concerning the death penalty and its social utility as a sanction, require us to conclude, in the absence of more convincing evidence, that the infliction of death as a punishment for murder is not without justification and thus is not unconstitutionally severe.

---

33. Other types of calculated murders, apparently occurring with increasing frequency, include the use of bombs or other means of indiscriminate killings, the extortion murder of hostages or kidnap victims, and the execution-style killing of witnesses to a crime.

Finally, we must consider whether the punishment of death is disproportionate in relation to the crime for which it is imposed. There is no question that death as a punishment is unique in its severity and irrevocability. When a defendant's life is at stake, the Court has been particularly sensitive to insure that every safeguard is observed. *Powell v. Alabama*, 287 U.S. 45 (1932). But we are concerned here only with the imposition of capital punishment for the crime of murder, and when a life has been taken deliberately by the offender, we cannot say that the punishment is invariably disproportionate to the crime. It is an extreme sanction, suitable to the most extreme of crimes.

We hold that the death penalty is not a form of punishment that may never be imposed, regardless of the circumstances of the offense, regardless of the character of the offender, and regardless of the procedure followed in reaching the decision to impose it.

IV

We now consider whether Georgia may impose the death penalty on the petitioner in this case.

A

While *Furman* did not hold that the infliction of the death penalty *per se* violates the Constitution's ban on cruel and unusual punishments, it did recognize that the penalty of death is different in kind from any other punishment imposed under our system of criminal justice. Because of the uniqueness of the death penalty, *Furman* held that it could not be imposed under sentencing procedures that created a substantial risk that it would be inflicted in an arbitrary and capricious manner. Mr. Justice White concluded that "the death penalty is exacted with great infrequency even for the most atrocious crimes and ... there is no meaningful basis for distinguishing the few cases in which it is imposed from the many cases in which it is not." Indeed, the death sentences examined by the Court in *Furman* were "cruel and unusual in the same way that being struck by lightning is cruel and unusual. For, of all the people convicted of [capital crimes], many just as reprehensible as these, the petitioners [in *Furman* were] among a capriciously selected random handful upon whom the sentence of death has in fact been imposed.... [T]he Eighth and Fourteenth Amendments cannot tolerate the infliction of a sentence of death under legal systems that permit this unique penalty to be so wantonly and so freakishly imposed." (Stewart, J., concurring).[35]

Furman mandates that where discretion is afforded a sentencing body on a matter so grave as the determination of whether a human life should be taken or spared, that discretion must be suitably directed and limited so as to minimize the risk of wholly arbitrary and capricious action.

---

35. This view was expressed by other Members of the Court who concurred in the judgments. [Justices Douglas and Brennan] The dissenters viewed this concern as the basis for the *Furman* decision: "The decisive grievance of the opinions ... is that the present system of discretionary sentencing in capital cases has failed to produce evenhanded justice; ... that the selection process has followed no rational pattern." [Chief Justice Burger]

...

Jury sentencing has been considered desirable in capital cases in order "to maintain a link between contemporary community values and the penal system—a link without which the determination of punishment could hardly reflect 'the evolving standards of decency that mark the progress of a maturing society.' "[39] But it creates special problems. Much of the information that is relevant to the sentencing decision may have no relevance to the question of guilt, or may even be extremely prejudicial to a fair determination of that question. This problem, however, is scarcely insurmountable. Those who have studied the question suggest that a bifurcated procedure—one in which the question of sentence is not considered until the determination of guilt has been made—is the best answer. The drafters of the Model Penal Code concluded that if a unitary proceeding is used:

> "the determination of the punishment must be based on less than all the evidence that has a bearing on that issue, such for example as a previous criminal record of the accused, or evidence must be admitted on the ground that it is relevant to sentence, though it would be excluded as irrelevant or prejudicial with respect to guilt or innocence alone. Trial lawyers understandably have little confidence in a solution that admits the evidence and trusts to an instruction to the jury that it should be considered only in determining the penalty and disregarded in assessing guilt.
>
> "... The obvious solution ... is to bifurcate the proceeding, abiding strictly by the rules of evidence until and unless there is a conviction, but once guilt has been determined opening the record to the further information that is relevant to sentence. This is the analogue of the procedure in the ordinary case when capital punishment is not in issue; the court conducts a separate inquiry before imposing sentence."

When a human life is at stake and when the jury must have information prejudicial to the question of guilt but relevant to the question of penalty in order to impose a rational sentence, a bifurcated system is more likely to ensure elimination of the constitutional deficiencies identified in *Furman*.

But the provision of relevant information under fair procedural rules is not alone sufficient to guarantee that the information will be properly used in the imposition of punishment, especially if sentencing is performed by a jury. Since the members of a jury will have had little, if any, previous experience in sentencing, they are unlikely to be skilled in dealing with the information they are given. To the extent that this problem is inherent in jury sentencing, it may not be totally correctable. It seems clear, however, that the problem will be alleviated if the jury is given guidance regarding the factors about the crime and the defendant that the State, representing organized society, deems particularly relevant to the sentencing decision.

---

39. *Witherspoon v. Illinois*, 391 U.S. 510 (1968), quoting *Trop v. Dulles*, 356 U.S. 86 (1958) (plurality opinion).

The idea that a jury should be given guidance in its decisionmaking is also hardly a novel proposition. Juries are invariably given careful instructions on the law and how to apply it before they are authorized to decide the merits of a lawsuit. It would be virtually unthinkable to follow any other course in a legal system that has traditionally operated by following prior precedents and fixed rules of law. When erroneous instructions are given, retrial is often required. It is quite simply a hallmark of our legal system that juries be carefully and adequately guided in their deliberations.

While some have suggested that standards to guide a capital jury's sentencing deliberations are impossible to formulate, the fact is that such standards have been developed. When the drafters of the Model Penal Code faced this problem, they concluded "that it is within the realm of possibility to point to the main circumstances of aggravation and of mitigation that should be weighed *and weighed against each other* when they are presented in a concrete case." (Emphasis in original.)[44] While such standards are by necessity somewhat general, they do provide guidance to the sentencing authority and thereby reduce the likelihood that it will impose a sentence that fairly can be called capricious or arbitrary. Where the sentencing authority is required to specify the factors it relied upon in reaching its decision, the further safeguard

---

44. The Model Penal Code proposes the following standards:

(3) Aggravating Circumstances.

(a) The murder was committed by a convict under sentence of imprisonment.

(b) The defendant was previously convicted of another murder or of a felony involving the use or threat of violence to the person.

(c) At the time the murder was committed the defendant also committed another murder.

(d) The defendant knowingly created a great risk of death to many persons.

(e) The murder was committed while the defendant was engaged or was an accomplice in the commission of, or an attempt to commit, or flight after committing or attempting to commit robbery, rape or deviate sexual intercourse by force or threat of force, arson, burglary or kidnapping.

(f) The murder was committed for the purpose of avoiding or preventing a lawful arrest or effecting an escape from lawful custody.

(g) The murder was committed for pecuniary gain.

(h) The murder was especially heinous, atrocious or cruel, manifesting exceptional depravity.

(4) Mitigating Circumstances.

(a) The defendant has no significant history of prior criminal activity.

(b) The murder was committed while the defendant was under the influence of extreme mental or emotional disturbance.

(c) The victim was a participant in the defendant's homicidal conduct or consented to the homicidal act.

(d) The murder was committed under circumstances which the defendant believed to provide a moral justification or extenuation for his conduct.

(e) The defendant was an accomplice in a murder committed by another person and his participation in the homicidal act was relatively minor.

(f) The defendant acted under duress or under the domination of another person.

(g) At the time of the murder, the capacity of the defendant to appreciate the criminality [wrongfulness] of his conduct or to conform his conduct to the requirements of law was impaired as a result of mental disease or defect or intoxication.

(h) The youth of the defendant at the time of the crime.

ALI Model Penal Code § 210.6 (Proposed Official Draft 1962).

of meaningful appellate review is available to ensure that death sentences are not imposed capriciously or in a freakish manner.

In summary, the concerns expressed in *Furman* that the penalty of death not be imposed in an arbitrary or capricious manner can be met by a carefully drafted statute that ensures that the sentencing authority is given adequate information and guidance. As a general proposition these concerns are best met by a system that provides for a bifurcated proceeding at which the sentencing authority is apprised of the information relevant to the imposition of sentence and provided with standards to guide its use of the information.

We do not intend to suggest that only the above described procedures would be permissible under *Furman* or that any sentencing system constructed along these general lines would inevitably satisfy the concerns of *Furman*, for each distinct system must be examined on an individual basis. Rather, we have embarked upon this general exposition to make clear that it is possible to construct capital-sentencing systems capable of meeting *Furman*'s constitutional concerns.

B

We now turn to consideration of the constitutionality of Georgia's capital-sentencing procedures. In the wake of *Furman*, Georgia amended its capital punishment statute, but chose not to narrow the scope of its murder provisions. Thus, now as before Furman, in Georgia "[a] person commits murder when he unlawfully and with malice aforethought, either express or implied, causes the death of another human being." All persons convicted of murder "shall be punished by death or by imprisonment for life."

Georgia did act, however, to narrow the class of murderers subject to capital punishment by specifying 10 statutory aggravating circumstances, one of which must be found by the jury to exist beyond a reasonable doubt before a death sentence can ever be imposed. In addition, the jury is authorized to consider any other appropriate aggravating or mitigating circumstances. The jury is not required to find any mitigating circumstance in order to make a recommendation of mercy that is binding on the trial court, but it must find a statutory aggravating circumstance before recommending a sentence of death.

These procedures require the jury to consider the circumstances of the crime and the criminal before it recommends sentence. No longer can a Georgia jury do as Furman's jury did: reach a finding of the defendant's guilt and then, without guidance or direction, decide whether he should live or die. Instead, the jury's attention is directed to the specific circumstances of the crime: Was it committed in the course of another capital felony? Was it committed for money? Was it committed upon a peace officer or judicial officer? Was it committed in a particularly heinous way or in a manner that endangered the lives of many persons? In addition, the jury's attention is focused on the characteristics of the person who committed the crime: Does he have a record of prior convictions for capital offenses? Are there any special facts about this defendant that mitigate against imposing capital punishment (*e.g.*, his youth, the extent of his cooperation with the police, his emotional state at the time of the crime). As a result, while some jury discretion still exists, "the discretion to be exercised is controlled by clear and objective standards so as to produce non-discriminatory application." *Coley v. State*, 204 S.E.2d 612 (Ga. 1974).

As an important additional safeguard against arbitrariness and caprice, the Georgia statutory scheme provides for automatic appeal of all death sentences to the State's Supreme Court. That court is required by statute to review each sentence of death and determine whether it was imposed under the influence of passion or prejudice, whether the evidence supports the jury's finding of a statutory aggravating circumstance, and whether the sentence is disproportionate compared to those sentences imposed in similar cases.

In short, Georgia's new sentencing procedures require as a prerequisite to the imposition of the death penalty, specific jury findings as to the circumstances of the crime or the character of the defendant. Moreover, to guard further against a situation comparable to that presented in *Furman*, the Supreme Court of Georgia compares each death sentence with the sentences imposed on similarly situated defendants to ensure that the sentence of death in a particular case is not disproportionate. On their face these procedures seem to satisfy the concerns of *Furman*. No longer should there be "no meaningful basis for distinguishing the few cases in which [the death penalty] is imposed from the many cases in which it is not." (White, J., concurring).

...

V

The basic concern of *Furman* centered on those defendants who were being condemned to death capriciously and arbitrarily. Under the procedures before the Court in that case, sentencing authorities were not directed to give attention to the nature or circumstances of the crime committed or to the character or record of the defendant. Left unguided, juries imposed the death sentence in a way that could only be called freakish. The new Georgia sentencing procedures, by contrast, focus the jury's attention on the particularized nature of the crime and the particularized characteristics of the individual defendant. While the jury is permitted to consider any aggravating or mitigating circumstances, it must find and identify at least one statutory aggravating factor before it may impose a penalty of death. In this way the jury's discretion is channeled. No longer can a jury wantonly and freakishly impose the death sentence; it is always circumscribed by the legislative guidelines. In addition, the review function of the Supreme Court of Georgia affords additional assurance that the concerns that prompted our decision in *Furman* are not present to any significant degree in the Georgia procedure applied here.

For the reasons expressed in this opinion, we hold that the statutory system under which Gregg was sentenced to death does not violate the Constitution. Accordingly, the judgment of the Georgia Supreme Court is affirmed.

It is so ordered.

[Concurring opinion of White, J., joined by Burger, C.J. and Rehnquist, J., omitted. Concurring statement of Burger, C.J., joined by Rehnquist, J., omitted. Concurring

statement of BLACKMUN, J. omitted. Dissenting opinions of BRENNAN and MARSHALL, JJ. omitted.]

Notes

Justice Marshall's Dissent. In his dissent in *Gregg*, Justice Marshall argued that the death penalty could not be justified on the basis of either deterrence or retribution. With regard to deterrence, he quoted from a report of a United Nations Committee:

> "It is generally agreed between the retentionists and abolitionists, whatever their opinions about the validity of comparative studies of deterrence, that the data which now exist show no correlation between the existence of capital punishment and lower rates of capital crime."

428 U.S. at 233. With regard to retribution, Justice Marshall took issue with what he took to be the plurality's argument, *viz.*, "society's judgment that the murderer 'deserves' death must be respected not simply because the preservation of order requires it, but because it is appropriate that society make the judgment and carry it out." He argued:

> "The mere fact that the community demands the murderer's life in return for the evil he has done cannot sustain the death penalty, for as Justices Stewart, Powell, and Stevens remind us, 'the Eighth Amendment demands more than that a challenged punishment be acceptable to contemporary society.' To be sustained under the Eighth Amendment, the death penalty must 'compor[t] with the basic concept of human dignity at the core of the Amendment'; the objective in imposing it must be '[consistent] with our respect for the dignity of [other] men.' Under these standards, the taking of life 'because the wrongdoer deserves it' surely must fall, for such a punishment has as its very basis the total denial of the wrongdoer's dignity and worth."

Id. at 240–41. Who has the better of the argument?

The Companion Cases. The Court decided four other cases on the same day as *Gregg*. In *Proffitt v. Florida*, 428 U.S. 242 (1976), the Court upheld the Florida death penalty scheme, which, like the Georgia scheme, provided for a separate evidentiary hearing on aggravating and mitigating factors after a defendant was convicted of a capital offense and provided for automatic review in the state supreme court of any death sentence. The Florida scheme differed from the Georgia scheme in that, in Florida, the jury played only an advisory role and the judge actually determined the penalty, and the judge was not required to find any of the eight statutory aggravating circumstances beyond a reasonable doubt, but only to weigh them against the statutory mitigating circumstances. Nevertheless, the Court found the differences constitutionally insignificant.[b] In *Jurek v. Texas*, 428 U.S. 262 (1976), the Court upheld the Texas death

---

b. The Court subsequently held that the Florida scheme was unconstitutional because it permitted the trial judge, rather than the jury, to determine the existence of aggravating factors making the defendant death-eligible. See *Hurst v. Florida*, ___ U.S. ___, 136 S. Ct. 616 (2016).

penalty scheme, which differed in form from the Georgia scheme. If, at the guilt phase, the jury found the defendant guilty of one of five forms of aggravated murder, there would be a penalty phase at which the jury would be directed to answer three questions, which, if answered in the affirmative (beyond a reasonable doubt), would result in the imposition of a death sentence: (1) whether the conduct of the defendant causing the death was committed deliberately and with the reasonable expectation that the death would result; (2) whether it is probable that the defendant would commit criminal acts of violence constituting a continuing threat to society; and (3), if raised by the evidence, whether the defendant's conduct was an unreasonable response to the provocation, if any, by the deceased. The Court found that the guilt phase finding served the same purpose as the penalty phase finding of aggravating circumstances in Georgia and that the penalty phase questions sufficiently allowed for consideration of mitigating circumstances.[c] In *Woodson v. North Carolina*, 428 U.S. 280 (1976) and *(Stanislaus) Roberts v. Louisiana*, 428 U.S. 325 (1976), the Court held unconstitutional the death penalty schemes of North Carolina and Louisiana, respectively, because the death penalty was mandatory for conviction of specified offenses.

The "Statutory Narrowing" and "Meaningful Appellate Review" Requirements. In *Gregg*, the Supreme Court held that the Georgia scheme, on its face, satisfied the *Furman* concern about the risk of arbitrariness. Exactly what element or elements of the scheme were necessary to satisfy *Furman*, was made clear in later cases. In *Zant v. Stephens*, 462 U.S. 862 (1983), the Court explained that the *Gregg* holding was based on two features of the Georgia scheme: the legislative requirement that the jury find an "aggravating circumstance" in order to make the defendant death-eligible and the requirement that the Georgia Supreme Court review all death sentences for possible arbitrariness or disproportionality. See *Id.* at 876. Addressing the significance of the "aggravating circumstance" requirement, the Court said:

> To avoid this constitutional flaw [of arbitrary and capricious sentencing], an aggravating circumstance must genuinely narrow the class of persons eligible for the death penalty and must reasonably justify the imposition of a more severe sentence on the defendant compared to others found guilty of murder.... Our cases indicate, then, that statutory aggravating circumstances play a constitutionally necessary function at the stage of legislative definition: they circumscribe the class of persons eligible for the death penalty.

Id. at 877–78. As for the "meaningful appellate review" requirement, the Court has had little to say about its content, except to hold, in *Pulley v. Harris*, 465 U.S. 37 (1984), that comparative intercase proportionality review is not required.

THE CALIFORNIA DEATH PENALTY SCHEME

The present California death penalty scheme was established in 1978 by the enactment of Proposition 7, known as the Briggs Initiative. According to its author, the

---

c. The Court subsequently held the scheme unconstitutional because the three questions did not permit the jury to fully consider the defendant's mitigating evidence. See *Penry v. Lynaugh*, 492 U.S. 302 (1989).

initiative was intended to "give Californians the toughest death-penalty law in the country."

Penal Code §§ 190.1–190.5 govern the trial of capital cases. The trial of a capital case is in two phases. At the guilt phase, the fact-finder must determine whether the defendant is guilty of first degree murder, and, if so, whether the prosecution has proved one or more charged special circumstances true beyond a reasonable doubt. At present, there are 33 separately enumerated special circumstances which would make a first degree murderer death eligible (P.C. § 190.2(a)),[1] and they may be grouped as follows:

> 2 **"other murder" circumstances**: the defendant was convicted of more than one murder ((a)(3)) or was previously convicted of murder ((a)(2));
>
> 8 **"victim" circumstances**: the defendant intentionally killed a peace officer ((a)(7)), federal law enforcement officer or agent ((a)(8)), firefighter ((a)(9)), witness ((a)(10)), prosecutor or former prosecutor ((a)(11)), judge or former judge ((a)(12)), elected official or former elected official ((a)(13)) or juror ((a)(20));
>
> 6 **"manner" circumstances**: the murder was committed by a destructive device, bomb or explosive planted ((a)(4)) or mailed ((a)(6)) or was intentionally committed by lying in wait ((a)(15)), by the infliction of torture ((a)(18)), by poison ((a)(19)) or by shooting from a motor vehicle ((a)(21));
>
> 4 **"motive" circumstances**: the defendant committed the murder for financial gain ((a)(1)), to escape arrest ((a)(5)), because of the victim's race, color, religion, national origin or country of origin ((a)(16)) or to further the activities of a criminal street gang ((a)(22));
>
> 12 **felony circumstances**: the murder was committed while the defendant was engaged in, or an accomplice to robbery, kidnapping, rape, sodomy, child molestation, forcible oral copulation, burglary, arson, train wrecking, mayhem, rape by instrument or carjacking ((a)(17));
>
> 1 **"catchall" circumstance**: the murder was especially heinous, atrocious or cruel ((a)(14)).[2]

If the defendant is found guilty of first degree murder and a special circumstance is found true, the case proceeds to the penalty phase.[3] At the penalty phase, "evidence may be presented by both the people and the defendant as to any matter relevant to aggravation, mitigation and sentence." (P.C. § 190.3.) The trier of fact, in determining the penalty is instructed to take account of the following factors, if relevant:

---

1. There are two exceptions. If the defendant was not the actual killer and did not intend the killing, the defendant is only death-eligible if he or she acted with "reckless indifference to human life" and as a "major participant" in a special circumstances felony. (P.C. § 190.2(d)) If the defendant was under 18 at the time of the murder, he or she is not death-eligible. (P.C. § 190.5).

2. This circumstance was held unconstitutional on vagueness grounds. See *People v. Superior Court (Engert)*, 31 Cal. 3d 797.

3. If the defendant has entered a plea of not guilty by reason of insanity, the sanity issue will be tried before the penalty phase (P.C. § 190.1(c)).

> a) The circumstances of the crime of which the defendant was convicted in the present proceeding and the existence of any special circumstances found to be true ...
>
> (b) The presence or absence of criminal activity by the defendant which involved the use or attempted use of force or violence or the express or implied threat to use force or violence.
>
> (c) The presence or absence of any prior felony conviction.
>
> (d) Whether or not the offense was committed while the defendant was under the influence of extreme mental or emotional disturbance.
>
> (e) Whether or not the victim was a participant in the defendant's homicidal conduct or consented to the homicidal act.
>
> (f) Whether or not the offense was committed under circumstances which the defendant reasonably believed to be a moral justification or extenuation for his conduct.
>
> (g) Whether or not defendant acted under extreme duress or under the substantial domination of another person.
>
> (h) Whether or not at the time of the offense the capacity of the defendant to appreciate the criminality of his conduct or to conform his conduct to the requirements of law was impaired as a result of mental disease or defect, or the effects of intoxication.
>
> (i) The age of the defendant at the time of the crime.
>
> (j) Whether or not the defendant was an accomplice to the offense and his participation in the commission of the offense was relatively minor.
>
> (k) Any other circumstance which extenuates the gravity of the crime even though it is not a legal excuse for the crime.

The trier of fact is not required to make findings as to the aggravating and mitigating circumstances; rather, the test is whether the aggravating circumstances outweigh the mitigating circumstances. If a jury is the trier of fact, it is instructed:

> Each of you must decide for yourself whether aggravating or mitigating factors exist. You do not all need to agree whether such factors exist. If any juror individually concludes that a factor exists, that juror may give the factor whatever weight he or she believes is appropriate.
>
> Determine which penalty is appropriate and justified by considering all the evidence and the totality of any aggravating and mitigating circumstances. Even without mitigating circumstances, you may decide that the aggravating circumstances are not substantial enough to warrant death. To return a judgment of death, each of you must be persuaded that the aggravating circumstances both outweigh the mitigating circumstances and are also so substantial in comparison to the mitigating circumstances that a sentence of death is appropriate and justified.

CALCRIM 766.

In the event the defendant is sentenced to death by a jury, the trial judge must review the evidence and make a determination whether the jury's determination is contrary to law or the evidence, in which case the judge must modify the sentence. P.C. § 190.4. An appeal to the California Supreme Court is automatically taken from any death judgment. P.C. § 1239(b). In considering the appeal, the Supreme Court, unlike the Georgia Supreme Court, does not engage in comparative intercase proportionality review. *People v. Lang*, 49 Cal.3d 991, 1043 (1989).

Problem

Problem 98.

What are the arguments as to whether the California scheme meets the statutory narrowing requirement? What additional information might be relevant to the question?

Lockett v. Ohio

438 U.S. 586, 98 S. Ct. 2954 (1978)

Mr. Chief Justice Burger delivered the opinion of the Court with respect to the constitutionality of petitioner's conviction (Parts I and II), together with an opinion (Part III), in which Mr. Justice Stewart, Mr. Justice Powell, and Mr. Justice Stevens, joined, on the constitutionality of the statute under which petitioner was sentenced to death and announced the judgment of the Court.

We granted certiorari in this case to consider, among other questions, whether Ohio violated the Eighth and Fourteenth amendments by sentencing Sandra Lockett to death pursuant to a statute that narrowly limits the sentencer's discretion to consider the circumstances of the crime and the record and character of the offender as mitigating factors.

I

Lockett was charged with aggravated murder with the aggravating specifications (1) that the murder was "committed for the purpose of escaping detection, apprehension, trial, or punishment" for aggravated robbery, and (2) that the murder was "committed while ... committing, attempting to commit, or fleeing immediately after committing or attempting to commit ... aggravated robbery." That offense was punishable by death in Ohio. She was also charged with aggravated robbery. The State's case against her depended largely upon the testimony of a coparticipant, one Al Parker, who gave the following account of her participation in the robbery and murder.

Lockett became acquainted with Parker and Nathan Earl Dew while she and a friend, Joanne Baxter, were in New Jersey. Parker and Dew then accompanied Lockett, Baxter, and Lockett's brother back to Akron, Ohio, Lockett's home town. After they arrived in Akron, Parker and Dew needed money for the trip back to New Jersey. Dew suggested that he pawn his ring. Lockett overheard his suggestion, but felt that the ring was too beautiful to pawn, and suggested instead that they could get some money by robbing a grocery store and a furniture store in the area. She warned that the grocery store's operator was a "big guy" who carried a "45" and that they would have "to get him real quick." She also volunteered to get a gun from her father's basement to aid in carrying out the robberies, but by that time, the two stores had closed and it was too late to proceed with the plan to rob them.

Someone, apparently Lockett's brother, suggested a plan for robbing a pawnshop. He and Dew would enter the shop and pretend to pawn a ring. Next Parker, who had some bullets, would enter the shop, ask to see a gun, load it, and use it to rob the shop. No one planned to kill the pawnshop operator in the course of the robbery. Because she knew the owner, Lockett was not to be among those entering the pawnshop, though she did guide the others to the shop that night.

The next day Parker, Dew, Lockett, and her brother gathered at Baxter's apartment. Lockett's brother asked if they were "still going to do it," and everyone, including Lockett, agreed to proceed. The four then drove by the pawnshop several times and parked the car. Lockett's brother and Dew entered the shop. Parker then left the car and told Lockett to start it again in two minutes. The robbery proceeded according to plan until the pawnbroker grabbed the gun when Parker announced the "stickup." The gun went off with Parker's finger on the trigger firing a fatal shot into the pawnbroker.

Parker went back to the car where Lockett waited with the engine running. While driving away from the pawnshop, Parker told Lockett what had happened. She took the gun from the pawnshop and put it into her purse. Lockett and Parker drove to Lockett's aunt's house and called a taxicab. Shortly thereafter, while riding away in a taxicab, they were stopped by the police, but by this time Lockett had placed the gun under the front seat. Lockett told the police that Parker rented a room from her mother and lived with her family. After verifying this story with Lockett's parents, the police released Lockett and Parker. Lockett hid Dew and Parker in the attic when the police arrived at the Lockett household later that evening.

Parker was subsequently apprehended and charged with aggravated murder with specifications, an offense punishable by death, and aggravated robbery. Prior to trial, he pleaded guilty to the murder charge and agreed to testify against Lockett, her brother, and Dew. In return, the prosecutor dropped the aggravated robbery charge and the specifications to the murder charge, thereby eliminating the possibility that Parker could receive the death penalty.

Lockett's brother and Dew were later convicted of aggravated murder with specifications. Lockett's brother was sentenced to death, but Dew received a lesser penalty because it was determined that his offense was "primarily the product of mental deficiency," one of the three mitigating circumstances specified in the Ohio death penalty statute.

Two weeks before Lockett's separate trial, the prosecutor offered to permit her to plead guilty to voluntary manslaughter and aggravated robbery (offenses which each carried a maximum penalty of 25 years' imprisonment and a maximum fine of $10,000) ... if she would cooperate with the State, but she rejected the offer. Just prior to her trial, the prosecutor offered to permit her to plead guilty to aggravated murder without specifications, an offense carrying a mandatory life penalty, with the understanding that the aggravated robbery charge and an outstanding forgery charge would be dismissed. Again she rejected the offer.

[At trial, during the prosecution's case, the prosecutor again offered to allow Lockett to plead to a lesser charge, and Lockett again refused. Because Lockett decided not to testify, the defense presented no evidence.]

The jury found Lockett guilty as charged.

Once a verdict of aggravated murder with specifications had been returned, the Ohio death penalty statute required the trial judge to impose a death sentence unless, after "considering the nature and circumstances of the offense" and Lockett's "history, character, and condition," he found by a preponderance of the evidence that (1) the victim had induced or facilitated the offense, (2) it was unlikely that Lockett would have committed the offense but for the fact that she "was under duress, coercion, or strong provocation," or (3) the offense was "primarily the product of [Lockett's] psychosis or mental deficiency."

In accord with the Ohio statute, the trial judge requested a presentence report as well as psychiatric and psychological reports. The reports contained detailed information about Lockett's intelligence, character, and background. The psychiatric and psychological reports described her as a 21-year-old with low-average or average intelligence, and not suffering from a mental deficiency. One of the psychologists reported that "her prognosis for rehabilitation" if returned to society was favorable. The presentence report showed that Lockett had committed no major offenses although she had a record of several minor ones as a juvenile and two minor offenses as an adult. It also showed that she had once used heroin but was receiving treatment at a drug abuse clinic and seemed to be "on the road to success" as far as her drug problem was concerned. It concluded that Lockett suffered no psychosis and was not mentally deficient.

After considering the reports and hearing argument on the penalty issue, the trial judge concluded that the offense had not been primarily the product of psychosis or mental deficiency. Without specifically addressing the other two statutory mitigating factors, the judge said that he had "no alternative, whether [he] like[d] the law or not" but to impose the death penalty. He then sentenced Lockett to death.

...

III

Lockett challenges the constitutionality of Ohio's death penalty statute on a number of grounds. We find it necessary to consider only her contention that her death sentence is invalid because the statute under which it was imposed did not permit the sentencing judge to consider, as mitigating factors, her character, prior record, age, lack of specific intent to cause death, and her relatively minor part in the crime. To address her contention from the proper perspective, it is helpful to review the developments in our recent cases where we have applied the Eighth and Fourteenth Amendments to death penalty statutes. We do not write on a "clean slate."

A

Prior to *Furman v. Georgia*, 408 U.S. 238 (1972), every State that authorized capital punishment had abandoned mandatory death penalties, and instead permitted the jury unguided and unrestrained discretion regarding the imposition of the death penalty in a particular capital case. Mandatory death penalties had proved unsatisfactory, as the plurality noted in *Woodson v. North Carolina*, 428 U.S. 280 (1976), in part because juries, "with some regularity, disregarded their oaths and refused to convict defendants where a death sentence was the automatic consequence of a guilty verdict."

This Court had never intimated prior to *Furman* that discretion in sentencing offended the Constitution.... As recently as *McGautha v. California*, 402 U.S. 183 (1971), the Court had specifically rejected the contention that discretion in imposing the death penalty violated the fundamental standards of fairness embodied in Fourteenth Amendment due process and had asserted that States were entitled to assume that "jurors confronted with the truly awesome responsibility of decreeing death for a fellow human [would] act with due regard for the consequences of their decision."

The constitutional status of discretionary sentencing in capital cases changed abruptly, however, as a result of the separate opinions supporting the judgment in *Furman*....

Predictably, the variety of opinions supporting the judgment in *Furman* engendered confusion as to what was required in order to impose the death penalty in accord with the Eighth Amendment. Some States responded to what was thought to be the command of *Furman* by adopting mandatory death penalties for a limited category of specific crimes thus eliminating all discretion from the sentencing process in capital cases. Other States attempted to continue the practice of individually assessing the culpability of each individual defendant convicted of a capital offense and, at the same time, to comply with *Furman*, by providing standards to guide the sentencing decision.

Four years after *Furman*, we considered Eighth Amendment issues posed by five of the post-*Furman* death penalty statutes. Four Justices took the position that all five statutes complied with the Constitution; two Justices took the position that none of them complied. Hence, the disposition of each case varied according to the votes of three Justices who delivered a joint opinion in each of the five cases....

The joint opinion reasoned that, to comply with *Furman*, sentencing procedures should not create "a substantial risk that the death penalty [will] be inflicted in an arbitrary and capricious manner." *Gregg v. Georgia*, 428 U.S. 153 (1976). In the view of the three Justices, however, *Furman* did not require that all sentencing discretion be eliminated, but only that it be "directed and limited," so that the death penalty would be imposed in a more consistent and rational manner and so that there would be a "meaningful basis for distinguishing the ... cases in which it is imposed from ... the many cases in which it is not." The plurality concluded, in the course of invalidating North Carolina's mandatory death penalty statute, that the sentencing process must permit consideration of the "character and record of the individual offender and the circumstances of the particular offense as a constitutionally indispensable part of the process of inflicting the penalty of death," *Woodson v. North Carolina*, 428 U.S. 280 (1976), in order to ensure the reliability, under Eighth Amendment standards, of the determination that "death is the appropriate punishment in a specific case."

In the last decade, many of the States have been obliged to revise their death penalty statutes in response to the various opinions supporting the judgments in *Furman* and *Gregg* and its companion cases. The signals from this Court have not, however, always been easy to decipher. The States now deserve the clearest guidance that the Court can provide; we have an obligation to reconcile previously differing views in order to provide that guidance.

B

With that obligation in mind we turn to Lockett's attack on the Ohio statute. Essentially she contends that the Eighth and Fourteenth Amendments require that the sentencer be given a full opportunity to consider mitigating circumstances in capital cases and that the Ohio statute does not comply with that requirement....

We begin by recognizing that the concept of individualized sentencing in criminal cases generally, although not constitutionally required, has long been accepted in this country. See *Williams v. New York*, 337 U.S. 241 (1948). Consistent with that concept, sentencing judges traditionally have taken a wide range of factors into account. That States have authority to make aiders and abettors equally responsible, as a matter of law, with principals, or to enact felony-murder statutes is beyond constitutional challenge. But the definition of crimes generally has not been thought automatically to dictate what should be the proper penalty. And where sentencing discretion is granted, it generally has been agreed that the sentencing judge's "possession of the fullest information possible concerning the defendant's life and characteristics" is "[h]ighly relevant—*if not essential*—[to the] selection of an appropriate sentence ..." *Williams v. New York.* (Emphasis added.)

The opinions of this Court going back many years in dealing with sentencing in capital cases have noted the strength of the basis for individualized sentencing. For example, Mr. Justice Black, writing for the Court in *Williams v. New York*—a capital case—observed that the:

> "whole country has traveled far from the period in which the death sentence was an automatic and commonplace result of convictions—even for offenses today deemed trivial."

Ten years later, in *Williams v. Oklahoma*, 358 U.S. 576 (1959), another capital case, the Court echoed Mr. Justice Black, stating that "[i]n discharging his duty of imposing a proper sentence, the sentencing judge is authorized, *if not required*, to consider all of the mitigating and aggravating circumstances involved in the crime." (Emphasis added.) Most would agree that "the 19th century movement away from mandatory death sentences marked an enlightened introduction of flexibility into the sentencing process." *Furman v. Georgia* (BURGER, C. J., dissenting).

Although legislatures remain free to decide how much discretion in sentencing should be reposed in the judge or jury in noncapital cases, the plurality opinion in *Woodson*, after reviewing the historical repudiation of mandatory sentencing in capital cases, concluded that "in capital cases the fundamental respect for humanity underlying the Eighth Amendment ... requires consideration of the character and record of the individual offender and the circumstances of the particular offense as a constitutionally indispensable part of the process of inflicting the penalty of death." That declaration rested "on the predicate that the penalty of death is qualitatively different" from any other sentence. We are satisfied that this qualitative difference between death and other penalties calls for a greater degree of reliability when the death sentence is imposed. The mandatory death penalty statute in *Woodson* was held invalid because it permitted no consideration of "relevant facets of the character and record of the individual offender or the circumstances of the particular offense." The plurality did not attempt to indicate, however, which facets of an offender or his offense it deemed "relevant" in capital sentencing or what degree of consideration of "relevant facets" it would require.

We are now faced with those questions and we conclude that the Eighth and Fourteenth Amendments require that the sentencer, in all but the rarest kind of capital case,[11] not be precluded from considering, as a mitigating factor, any aspect of a defendant's character or record and any of the circumstances of the offense that the defendant proffers as a basis for a sentence less than death.[12] We recognize that, in noncapital cases, the established practice of individualized sentences rests not on constitutional commands, but on public policy enacted into statutes. The considerations that account for the wide acceptance of individualization of sentences in noncapital cases surely cannot be thought less important in capital cases. Given that the imposition of death by public authority is so profoundly different from all other penalties, we cannot avoid the conclusion that an individualized decision is essential in capital cases. The need for treating each defendant in a capital case with that degree of respect due the uniqueness of the individual is far more important than in noncapital cases. A variety of flexible techniques—probation, parole, work furloughs, to name a few—and various postconviction remedies may be available to modify an initial sentence of confinement in noncapital cases. The nonavailability of corrective

---

11. We express no opinion as to whether the need to deter certain kinds of homicide would justify a mandatory death sentence as, for example, when a prisoner—or escapee—under a life sentence is found guilty of murder. [The Court subsequently held, in *Sumner v. Shuman*, 483 U.S. 66 (1987), that a mandatory death sentence for murder by a prisoner serving a life sentence without possibility of parole was unconstitutional—**Ed.**]

12. Nothing in this opinion limits the traditional authority of a court to exclude, as irrelevant, evidence not bearing on the defendant's character, prior record, or the circumstances of his offense.

or modifying mechanisms with respect to an executed capital sentence underscores the need for individualized consideration as a constitutional requirement in imposing the death sentence.

There is no perfect procedure for deciding in which cases governmental authority should be used to impose death. But a statute that prevents the sentencer in all capital cases from giving independent mitigating weight to aspects of the defendant's character and record and to circumstances of the offense proffered in mitigation creates the risk that the death penalty will be imposed in spite of factors which may call for a less severe penalty. When the choice is between life and death, that risk is unacceptable and incompatible with the commands of the Eighth and Fourteenth Amendments.

C

The Ohio death penalty statute does not permit the type of individualized consideration of mitigating factors we now hold to be required by the Eighth and Fourteenth Amendments in capital cases....

...

[Under the Ohio statute,] once a defendant is found guilty of aggravated murder with at least one of seven specified aggravating circumstances, the death penalty must be imposed unless, considering "the nature and circumstances of the offense and the history, character, and condition of the offender," the sentencing judge determines that at least one of the following mitigating circumstances is established by a preponderance of the evidence:

> "(1) The victim of the offense induced or facilitated it.
>
> "(2) It is unlikely that the offense would have been committed, but for the fact that the offender was under duress, coercion, or strong provocation.
>
> "(3) The offense was primarily the product of the offender's psychosis or mental deficiency, though such condition is insufficient to establish the defense of insanity."

... We see, therefore, that once it is determined that the victim did not induce or facilitate the offense, that the defendant did not act under duress or coercion, and that the offense was not primarily the product of the defendant's mental deficiency, the Ohio statute mandates the sentence of death. The absence of direct proof that the defendant intended to cause the death of the victim is relevant for mitigating purposes only if it is determined that it sheds some light on one of the three statutory mitigating factors. Similarly, consideration of a defendant's comparatively minor role in the offense, or age, would generally not be permitted, as such, to affect the sentencing decision.

The limited range of mitigating circumstances which may be considered by the sentencer under the Ohio statute is incompatible with the Eighth and Fourteenth Amendments. To meet constitutional requirements, a death penalty statute must not preclude consideration of relevant mitigating factors.

Accordingly, the judgment under review is reversed to the extent that it sustains the imposition of the death penalty, and the case is remanded for further proceedings.

Mr. Justice Brennan took no part in the consideration or decision of this case.

[Concurring opinions of Blackmun, J. and Marshall, J. and opinions of White, J., dissenting in part and concurring, and Rehnquist, J., concurring in part and dissenting, omitted.]

Notes

The Relationship Between Furman and Lockett. Are the *Furman* and *Lockett* principles fundamentally incompatible? In *Walton v. Arizona*, 497 U.S. 639 (1990), Justice Scalia reached that conclusion and announced that he would no longer enforce *Lockett*. *Id.* at 656–57 (Scalia, J., concurring in part and concurring in the judgment). In his view, the *Furman* requirement "that States 'channel the sentencer's discretion by "clear and objective standards" that provide "specific and detailed guidance,"'" was altogether inconsistent with the *Lockett* requirement that the sentencer engage in "individualized sentencing" by considering virtually any mitigating evidence. In Justice Scalia's view, *Furman* was at least arguably grounded in the language of the Eighth Amendment, while *Lockett* was not. Justice Stevens disagreed, emphasizing that *Furman* and *Lockett* each apply to a different stage of the sentencing process:

> Justice Scalia ignores the difference between the base of the pyramid and its apex. A rule that forbids unguided discretion at the base is completely consistent with one that requires discretion at the apex. After narrowing the class of cases to those at the tip of the pyramid, it is then appropriate to allow the sentencer discretion to show mercy based on individual mitigating circumstances in the cases that remain.

497 U.S. at 718 (Stevens, J., dissenting). Subsequently, Justice Blackmun voiced a third opinion. Finding that "the constitutional goal of eliminating arbitrariness and discrimination from the administration of death can never be achieved without compromising an equally essential component of fundamental fairness—individualized sentencing," he concluded that the death penalty could not constitutionally be imposed. *Callins v. Collins*, 510 U.S. 1141, 1144 (Blackmun, J., dissenting from denial of cert.). Who is correct?

The Death Penalty for Rape. In *Coker v. Georgia*, 433 U.S. 584 (1977), the Supreme Court considered whether the death penalty was a constitutional punishment for the crime of rape of an adult woman. While serving sentences for murder, rape, kidnapping and aggravated assault, Coker escaped from prison. He entered a couple's house at night, tied up the man, raped the woman and kidnapped the woman in the couple's car. Rape was a capital crime, and after conviction of the various charges, Coker was sentenced to death. The Supreme Court held that imposition of the death penalty violated the Eighth Amendment. Applying the test for proportionality developed in *Gregg*, the plurality, over a forceful dissent by Chief Justice Burger for himself and

Justice Rehnquist, found the death penalty to be disproportionate because: (1) it did not comport with contemporary standards, since Georgia was the only state to impose the death penalty for rape of an adult woman and Georgia juries rarely imposed the death penalty on defendants convicted of rape (six times in 63 cases); and (2), even though rape was assumed to be second only to homicide as "the ultimate violation of self," the death penalty was excessive because rape did not compare with murder in terms of the depravity of the defendant and the injury to the victim and the public. Although the Justices made no mention of race, the decision was issued against a background of extreme racial discrimination in the use of the death penalty in rape cases. From 1930 until the decision in *Furman*, 455 persons were executed for rape in the United States, and almost 90% of them were black. The victims in all of the cases were white women. U.S. Law Enforcement Assistance Administration Reports (1930–1976).

Tison v. Arizona

481 U.S. 137, 107 S. Ct. 1676 (1987)

Justice O'Connor delivered the opinion of the Court.

The question presented is whether the petitioners' participation in the events leading up to and following the murder of four members of a family makes the sentences of death imposed by the Arizona courts constitutionally permissible although neither petitioner specifically intended to kill the victims and neither inflicted the fatal gunshot wounds. We hold that the Arizona Supreme Court applied an erroneous standard in making the findings required by *Enmund v. Florida*, 458 U.S. 782 (1982), and, therefore, vacate the judgments below and remand the case for further proceedings not inconsistent with this opinion.

I

Gary Tison was sentenced to life imprisonment as the result of a prison escape during the course of which he had killed a guard. After he had been in prison a number of years, Gary Tison's wife, their three sons Donald, Ricky, and Raymond, Gary's brother Joseph, and other relatives made plans to help Gary Tison escape again. The Tison family assembled a large arsenal of weapons for this purpose. Plans for escape were discussed with Gary Tison, who insisted that his cellmate, Randy Greenawalt, also a convicted murderer, be included in the prison break. The following facts are largely evidenced by petitioners' detailed confessions given as part of a plea bargain according to the terms of which the State agreed not to seek the death sentence. The Arizona courts interpreted the plea agreement to require that petitioners testify to the planning stages of the breakout. When they refused to do so, the bargain was rescinded and they were tried, convicted, and sentenced to death.

On July 30, 1978, the three Tison brothers entered the Arizona State Prison at Florence carrying a large ice chest filled with guns. The Tisons armed Greenawalt and their father, and the group, brandishing their weapons, locked the prison guards and visitors present in a storage closet. The five men fled the prison grounds in the Tisons' Ford Galaxy automobile. No shots were fired at the prison.

After leaving the prison, the men abandoned the Ford automobile and proceeded on to an isolated house in a white Lincoln automobile that the brothers had parked at a hospital near the prison. At the house, the Lincoln automobile had a flat tire; the only spare tire was pressed into service. After two nights at the house, the group drove toward Flagstaff. As the group traveled on back roads and secondary highways through the desert, another tire blew out. The group decided to flag down a passing motorist and steal a car. Raymond stood out in front of the Lincoln; the other four armed themselves and lay in wait by the side of the road. One car passed by without stopping, but a second car, a Mazda occupied by John Lyons, his wife Donnelda, his 2-year-old son Christopher, and his 15-year-old niece, Theresa Tyson, pulled over to render aid.

As Raymond showed John Lyons the flat tire on the Lincoln, the other Tisons and Greenawalt emerged. The Lyons family was forced into the backseat of the Lincoln. Raymond and Donald drove the Lincoln down a dirt road off the highway and then down a gas line service road farther into the desert; Gary Tison, Ricky Tison, and Randy Greenawalt followed in the Lyons' Mazda. The two cars were parked trunk to trunk and the Lyons family was ordered to stand in front of the Lincoln's headlights. The Tisons transferred their belongings from the Lincoln into the Mazda. They discovered guns and money in the Mazda which they kept, and they put the rest of the Lyons' possessions in the Lincoln.

Gary Tison then told Raymond to drive the Lincoln still farther into the desert. Raymond did so, and, while the others guarded the Lyons and Theresa Tyson, Gary fired his shotgun into the radiator, presumably to completely disable the vehicle. The Lyons and Theresa Tyson were then escorted to the Lincoln and again ordered to stand in its headlights. Ricky Tison reported that John Lyons begged, in comments "more or less directed at everybody," "Jesus, don't kill me." Gary Tison said he was "thinking about it." John Lyons asked the Tisons and Greenawalt to "give us some water ... just leave us out here, and you all go home." Gary Tison then told his sons to go back to the Mazda and get some water. Raymond later explained that his father "was like in conflict with himself ... What it was, I think it was the baby being there and all this, and he wasn't sure about what to do."

The petitioners' statements diverge to some extent, but it appears that both of them went back towards the Mazda, along with Donald, while Randy Greenawalt and Gary Tison stayed at the Lincoln guarding the victims. Raymond recalled being at the Mazda filling the water jug "when we started hearing the shots." Ricky said that the brothers gave the water jug to Gary Tison who then, with Randy Greenawalt went behind the Lincoln, where they spoke briefly, then raised the shotguns and started firing. In any event, petitioners agree they saw Greenawalt and their father brutally murder their four captives with repeated blasts from their shotguns. Neither made an effort to help the victims, though both later stated they were surprised by the shooting. The Tisons got into the Mazda and drove away, continuing their flight.

Physical evidence suggested that Theresa Tyson managed to crawl away from the bloodbath, severely injured. She died in the desert after the Tisons left.

Several days later the Tisons and Greenawalt were apprehended after a shootout at a police roadblock. Donald Tison was killed. Gary Tison escaped into the desert where he subsequently died of exposure. Raymond and Ricky Tison and Randy Greenawalt were captured and tried jointly for the crimes associated with the prison break itself and the shootout at the roadblock; each was convicted and sentenced.

The State then individually tried each of the petitioners for capital murder of the four victims as well as for the associated crimes of armed robbery, kidnapping, and car theft. The capital murder charges were based on Arizona felony-murder law providing that a killing occurring during the perpetration of robbery or kidnapping is capital murder and that each participant in the kidnapping or robbery is legally responsible for the acts of his accomplices. Each of the petitioners was convicted of the four murders under these accomplice liability and felony-murder statutes.

Arizona law also provided for a capital sentencing proceeding, to be conducted without a jury, to determine whether the crime was sufficiently aggravated to warrant the death sentence. The statute set out six aggravating and four mitigating factors. The judge found three statutory aggravating factors:

(1) the Tisons had created a grave risk of death to others (not the victims);

(2) the murders had been committed for pecuniary gain;

(3) the murders were especially heinous.

The judge found no statutory mitigating factor. Importantly, the judge specifically found that the crime was not mitigated by the fact that each of the petitioners' "participation was relatively minor." Rather, he found that the "participation of each [petitioner] in the crimes giving rise to the application of the felony murder rule in this case was very substantial." The trial judge also specifically found that each "could reasonably have foreseen that his conduct ... would cause or create a grave risk of ... death." He did find, however, three nonstatutory mitigating factors:

(1) the petitioners' youth—Ricky was 20 and Raymond was 19;

(2) neither had prior felony records;

(3) each had been convicted of the murders under the felony-murder rule.

Nevertheless, the judge sentenced both petitioners to death.

...

II

In *Enmund v. Florida*, this Court reversed the death sentence of a defendant convicted under Florida's felony-murder rule. Enmund was the driver of the "getaway" car in an armed robbery of a dwelling. The occupants of the house, an elderly couple, resisted and Enmund's accomplices killed them. The Florida Supreme Court found the inference that Enmund was the person in the car by the side of the road waiting to help his accomplices escape sufficient to support his sentence of death....

This Court, citing the weight of legislative and community opinion, found a broad societal consensus, with which it agreed, that the death penalty was disproportional to the crime of robbery-felony murder "in these circumstances." The Court noted that although 32 American jurisdictions permitted the imposition of the death penalty for felony murders under a variety of circumstances, Florida was 1 of only 8 jurisdictions that authorized the death penalty "solely for participation in a robbery in which another robber takes life." Enmund was, therefore, sentenced under a distinct minority regime, a regime that permitted the imposition of the death penalty for felony murder simpliciter. At the other end of the spectrum, eight States required a finding of intent to kill before death could be imposed in a felony-murder case and one State required actual participation in the killing. The remaining States authorizing capital punishment for felony murders fell into two somewhat overlapping middle categories: three authorized the death penalty when the defendant acted with recklessness or extreme indifference to human life, and nine others, including Arizona, required a finding of some aggravating factor beyond the fact that the killing had occurred during the course of a felony before a capital sentence might be imposed. Arizona fell into a subcategory of six States which made "minimal participation in a capital felony committed by another person a [statutory] mitigating circumstance." Two more jurisdictions required a finding that the defendant's participation in the felony was not "relatively minor" before authorizing a capital sentence.[3]

After surveying the States' felony-murder statutes, the *Enmund* Court next examined the behavior of juries in cases like Enmund's in its attempt to assess American attitudes toward capital punishment in felony-murder cases. Of 739 death row inmates, only 41 did not participate in the fatal assault. All but 16 of these were physically present at the scene of the murder and of these only 3, including Enmund, were sentenced to death in the absence of a finding that they had collaborated in a scheme designed to kill. The Court found the fact that only 3 of 739 death row inmates had been sentenced to death absent an intent to kill, physical presence, or direct participation in the fatal assault persuasive evidence that American juries considered the death sentence disproportional to felony murder simpliciter.

Against this background, the Court undertook its own proportionality analysis. Armed robbery is a serious offense, but one for which the penalty of death is plainly excessive; the imposition of the death penalty for robbery, therefore, violates the Eighth and Fourteenth Amendments' proscription "'against all punishments which by their excessive length or severity are greatly disproportioned to the offenses charged.'" *Weems v. United States*, 217 U.S. 349 (1910) (quoting *O'Neil v. Vermont*, 144 U.S. 323 (1892)); *cf. Coker v. Georgia*, 433 U.S. 584 (1977) (holding the death penalty disproportional to the crime of rape). Furthermore, the Court found that

3. Vermont fell into none of these categories. Vermont limited the death penalty to defendants who commit a second unrelated murder or murder a correctional officer.

Enmund's degree of participation in the murders was so tangential that it could not be said to justify a sentence of death. It found that neither the deterrent nor the retributive purposes of the death penalty were advanced by imposing the death penalty upon Enmund. The *Enmund* Court was unconvinced "that the threat that the death penalty will be imposed for murder will measurably deter one who does not kill and has no intention or purpose that life will be taken." In reaching this conclusion, the Court relied upon the fact that killing only rarely occurred during the course of robberies, and such killing as did occur even more rarely resulted in death sentences if the evidence did not support an inference that the defendant intended to kill. The Court acknowledged, however, that "it would be very different if the likelihood of a killing in the course of a robbery were so substantial that one should share the blame for the killing if he somehow participated in the felony."

That difference was also related to the second purpose of capital punishment, retribution. The heart of the retribution rationale is that a criminal sentence must be directly related to the personal culpability of the criminal offender. While the States generally have wide discretion in deciding how much retribution to exact in a given case, the death penalty, "unique in its severity and irrevocability," requires the State to inquire into the relevant facets of "the character and record of the individual offender." *Woodson v. North Carolina*, 428 U.S. 280 (1976). Thus, in Enmund's case, "the focus [had to] be on *his* culpability, not on that of those who committed the robbery and shot the victims, for we insist on 'individualized consideration as a constitutional requirement in imposing the death sentence.'" *Enmund v. Florida* (quoting *Lockett v. Ohio*, 438 U.S. 586 (1978)). (Emphasis in original.) Since Enmund's own participation in the felony murder was so attenuated and since there was no proof that Enmund had any culpable mental state, the death penalty was excessive retribution for his crimes.

...

... [I]t is ... clear that petitioners ... fall outside the category of felony murderers for whom *Enmund* explicitly held the death penalty disproportional: their degree of participation in the crimes was major rather than minor, and the record would support a finding of the culpable mental state of reckless indifference to human life. We take the facts as the Arizona Supreme Court has given them to us.

Raymond Tison brought an arsenal of lethal weapons into the Arizona State Prison which he then handed over to two convicted murderers, one of whom he knew had killed a prison guard in the course of a previous escape attempt. By his own admission he was prepared to kill in furtherance of the prison break. He performed the crucial role of flagging down a passing car occupied by an innocent family whose fate was then entrusted to the known killers he had previously armed. He robbed these people at their direction and then guarded the victims at gunpoint while they considered what next to do. He stood by and watched the killing, making no effort to assist the victims before, during, or after the shooting. Instead, he chose to assist the killers in their continuing criminal endeavors, ending in a gun battle with the police in the final showdown.

Ricky Tison's behavior differs in slight details only. Like Raymond, he intentionally brought the guns into the prison to arm the murderers. He could have foreseen that lethal force might be used, particularly since he knew that his father's previous escape attempt had resulted in murder. He, too, participated fully in the kidnapping and robbery and watched the killing after which he chose to aid those whom he had placed in the position to kill rather than their victims.

These facts not only indicate that the Tison brothers' participation in the crime was anything but minor; they also would clearly support a finding that they both subjectively appreciated that their acts were likely to result in the taking of innocent life. The issue raised by this case is whether the Eighth Amendment prohibits the death penalty in the intermediate case of the defendant whose participation is major and whose mental state is one of reckless indifference to the value of human life. *Enmund* does not specifically address this point. We now take up the task of determining whether the Eighth Amendment proportionality requirement bars the death penalty under these circumstances.

Like the *Enmund* Court, we find the state legislatures' judgment as to proportionality in these circumstances relevant to this constitutional inquiry. The largest number of States still fall into the two intermediate categories discussed in *Enmund*. Four States authorize the death penalty in felony-murder cases upon a showing of culpable mental state such as recklessness or extreme indifference to human life. Two jurisdictions require that the defendant's participation be substantial and the statutes of at least six more, including Arizona, take minor participation in the felony expressly into account in mitigation of the murder. These requirements significantly overlap both in this case and in general, for the greater the defendant's participation in the felony murder, the more likely that he acted with reckless indifference to human life. At a minimum, however, it can be said that all these jurisdictions, as well as six States which *Enmund* classified along with Florida as permitting capital punishment for felony murder simpliciter, and the three States which simply require some additional aggravation before imposing the death penalty upon a felony murderer, specifically authorize the death penalty in a felony-murder case where, though the defendant's mental state fell short of intent to kill, the defendant was a major actor in a felony in which he knew death was highly likely to occur. On the other hand, even after *Enmund*, only 11 States authorizing capital punishment forbid imposition of the death penalty even though the defendant's participation in the felony murder is major and the likelihood of killing is so substantial as to raise an inference of extreme recklessness. This substantial and recent legislative authorization of the death penalty for the crime of felony murder regardless of the absence of a finding of an intent to kill powerfully suggests that our society does not reject the death penalty as grossly excessive under these circumstances.

Moreover, a number of state courts have interpreted *Enmund* to permit the imposition of the death penalty in such aggravated felony murders. We do not approve or disapprove the judgments as to proportionality reached on the particular facts of these cases, but we note the apparent consensus that substantial participation in a violent felony under circumstances likely to result in the loss of innocent human life may justify the death penalty even absent an "intent to kill." ...

Against this backdrop, we now consider the proportionality of the death penalty in these midrange felony-murder cases for which the majority of American jurisdictions clearly authorize capital punishment and for which American courts have not been nearly so reluctant to impose death as they are in the case of felony murder simpliciter.

A critical facet of the individualized determination of culpability required in capital cases is the mental state with which the defendant commits the crime. Deeply ingrained in our legal tradition is the idea that the more purposeful is the criminal conduct, the more serious is the offense, and, therefore, the more severely it ought to be punished. The ancient concept of malice aforethought was an early attempt to focus on mental state in order to distinguish those who deserved death from those who through "Benefit of ... Clergy" would be spared. Over time, malice aforethought came to be inferred from the mere act of killing in a variety of circumstances; in reaction, Pennsylvania became the first American jurisdiction to distinguish between degrees of murder, reserving capital punishment to "wilful, deliberate and premeditated" killings and felony murders. 3 Pa. Laws 1794, ch. 1766 (1810). More recently, in *Lockett v. Ohio*, 438 U.S. 586 (1978), the plurality opinion made clear that the defendant's mental state was critical to weighing a defendant's culpability under a system of guided discretion, vacating a death sentence imposed under an Ohio statute that did not permit the sentencing authority to take into account "the absence of direct proof that the defendant intended to cause the death of the victim." In *Enmund v. Florida*, the Court recognized again the importance of mental state, explicitly permitting the death penalty in at least those cases where the felony murderer intended to kill and forbidding it in the case of a minor actor not shown to have had any culpable mental state.

A narrow focus on the question of whether or not a given defendant "intended to kill," however, is a highly unsatisfactory means of definitively distinguishing the most culpable and dangerous of murderers. Many who intend to, and do, kill are not criminally liable at all—those who act in self-defense or with other justification or excuse. Other intentional homicides, though criminal, are often felt undeserving of the death penalty—those that are the result of provocation. On the other hand, some nonintentional murderers may be among the most dangerous and inhumane of all—the person who tortures another not caring whether the victim lives or dies, or the robber who shoots someone in the course of the robbery, utterly indifferent to the fact that the desire to rob may have the unintended consequence of killing the victim as well as taking the victim's property. This reckless indifference to the value of human life may be every bit as shocking to the moral sense as an "intent to kill." Indeed it is for this very reason that the common law and modern criminal codes alike have classified behavior such as occurred in this case along with intentional murders. *Enmund* held that when "intent to kill" results in its logical though not inevitable consequence—the taking of human life—the Eighth Amendment permits the State to exact the death penalty after a careful weighing of the aggravating and mitigating circumstances.

Similarly, we hold that the reckless disregard for human life implicit in knowingly engaging in criminal activities known to carry a grave risk of death represents a highly culpable mental state, a mental state that may be taken into account in making a capital sentencing judgment when that conduct causes its natural, though also not inevitable, lethal result.

The petitioners' own personal involvement in the crimes was not minor, but rather, as specifically found by the trial court, "substantial." Far from merely sitting in a car away from the actual scene of the murders acting as the getaway driver to a robbery, each petitioner was actively involved in every element of the kidnapping-robbery and was physically present during the entire sequence of criminal activity culminating in the murder of the Lyons family and the subsequent flight. The Tisons' high level of participation in these crimes further implicates them in the resulting deaths. Accordingly, they fall well within the overlapping second intermediate position which focuses on the defendant's degree of participation in the felony.

Only a small minority of those jurisdictions imposing capital punishment for felony murder have rejected the possibility of a capital sentence absent an intent to kill, and we do not find this minority position constitutionally required. We will not attempt to precisely delineate the particular types of conduct and states of mind warranting imposition of the death penalty here. Rather, we simply hold that major participation in the felony committed, combined with reckless indifference to human life, is sufficient to satisfy the *Enmund* culpability requirement.[11] The Arizona courts have clearly found that the former exists; we now vacate the judgments below and remand for determination of the latter in further proceedings not inconsistent with this opinion.

It is so ordered.

Justice Brennan, with whom Justice Marshall joins, and with whom Justice Blackmun and Justice Stevens join as to Parts I through IV-A, dissenting.

[The dissenters argued that the facts were not sufficient to support the Court's conclusion that petitioners could be found to have acted with reckless indifference to human life. Petitioners were young, had no prior felony record and had no role in planning the escape. Their "presence at the scene of the murders, and their participation in flagging down the vehicle, and robbing and guarding the family, indicate nothing whatsoever about their subjective appreciation that their father and his friend would suddenly decide to kill the family." Petitioners were getting a jug of water for the victims when the shootings occurred, and they were surprised by the shootings because, as Raymond testified, "Well, I just think you should know when we first came into this we had an agreement with my dad that nobody would get hurt because we [the brothers] wanted no one hurt."]

---

11. Although we state these two requirements separately, they often overlap. For example, we do not doubt that there are some felonies as to which one could properly conclude that any major participant necessarily exhibits reckless indifference to the value of human life. Moreover, even in cases where the fact that the defendant was a major participant in a felony did not suffice to establish reckless indifference, that fact would still often provide significant support for such a finding.

III

Notwithstanding the Court's unwarranted observations on the applicability of its new standard to this case, the basic flaw in today's decision is the Court's failure to conduct the sort of proportionality analysis that the Constitution and past cases require. Creation of a new category of culpability is not enough to distinguish this case from *Enmund v. Florida*, 458 U.S. 782 (1982). The Court must also establish that death is a proportionate punishment for individuals in this category. In other words, the Court must demonstrate that major participation in a felony with a state of mind of reckless indifference to human life deserves the same punishment as intending to commit a murder or actually committing a murder. The Court does not attempt to conduct a proportionality review of the kind performed in past cases raising a proportionality question, but instead offers two reasons in support of its view.

A

One reason the Court offers for its conclusion that death is proportionate punishment for persons falling within its new category is that limiting the death penalty to those who intend to kill "is a highly unsatisfactory means of definitively distinguishing the most culpable and dangerous of murderers." To illustrate that intention cannot be dispositive, the Court offers as examples "the person who tortures another not caring whether the victim lives or dies, or the robber who shoots someone in the course of the robbery, utterly indifferent to the fact that the desire to rob may have the unintended consequence of killing the victim as well as taking the victim's property." Influential commentators and some States have approved the use of the death penalty for persons, like those given in the Court's examples, who kill others in circumstances manifesting an extreme indifference to the value of human life. Thus an exception to the requirement that only intentional murders be punished with death might be made for persons who actually commit an act of homicide; *Enmund*, by distinguishing from the accomplice case "those who kill," clearly reserved that question. But the constitutionality of the death penalty for those individuals is no more relevant to this case than it was to *Enmund*, because this case, like *Enmund*, involves accomplices who did not kill. Thus, although some of the "most culpable and dangerous of murderers" may be those who killed without specifically intending to kill, it is considerably more difficult to apply that rubric convincingly to those who not only did not intend to kill, but who also have not killed.

It is precisely in this context—where the defendant has not killed—that a finding that he or she nevertheless intended to kill seems indispensable to establishing capital culpability. It is important first to note that such a defendant has not committed an act for which he or she could be sentenced to death. The applicability of the death penalty therefore turns entirely on the defendant's mental state with regard to an act committed by another. Factors such as the defendant's major participation in the events surrounding the killing or the defendant's presence at the scene are relevant insofar as they illuminate the defendant's mental state with regard to the killings. They cannot serve, however, as independent grounds for imposing the death penalty.

Second, when evaluating such a defendant's mental state, a determination that the defendant acted with intent is qualitatively different from a determination that the defendant acted with reckless indifference to human life. The difference lies in the nature of the choice each has made. The reckless actor has not chosen to bring about the killing in the way the intentional actor has. The person who chooses to act recklessly and is indifferent to the possibility of fatal consequences often deserves serious punishment. But because that person has not chosen to kill, his or her moral and criminal culpability is of a different degree than that of one who killed or intended to kill.

...

In *Enmund*, the Court explained at length the reasons a finding of intent is a necessary prerequisite to the imposition of the death penalty. In any given case, the Court said, the death penalty must "measurably contribut[e]" to one or both of the two "social purposes"—deterrence and retribution—which this Court has accepted as justifications for the death penalty. *Enmund*, citing *Gregg v. Georgia*, 428 U.S. 153 (1976). If it does not so contribute, it "'is nothing more than the purposeless and needless imposition of pain and suffering' and hence an unconstitutional punishment." *Enmund*, quoting *Coker v. Georgia*, 433 U.S. 584 (1977). Enmund's lack of intent to commit the murder—rather than the lack of evidence as to his mental state—was the decisive factor in the Court's decision that the death penalty served neither of the two purposes. With regard to deterrence, the Court was:

> "quite unconvinced ... that the threat that the death penalty will be imposed for murder will measurably deter one who does not kill and has no intention or purpose that life will be taken. Instead, it seems likely that 'capital punishment can serve as a deterrent only when murder is the result of premeditation and deliberation' ..."[11]

As for retribution, the Court again found that Enmund's lack of intent, together with the fact that he did not kill the victims, was decisive. "American criminal law has long considered a defendant's intention—and therefore his moral guilt—to be critical to the degree of [his] criminal culpability." The Court concluded that "putting Enmund to death to avenge two killings that he did not commit and had no intention of committing or causing does not measurably contribute to the retributive end of ensuring that the criminal gets his just deserts." Thus, in *Enmund* the Court established that a finding of an intent to kill was a constitutional prerequisite for the imposition

---

11. The Court acknowledged that "it would be very different if the likelihood of a killing in the course of a robbery were so substantial that one should share the blame for the killing if he somehow participated in the felony." Nevertheless, the Court saw no reason to depart from its conclusion that the death penalty could not be justified as a deterrent in that case, because "competent observers have concluded that there is no basis in experience for the notion that death so frequently occurs in the course of a felony for which killing is not an essential ingredient that the death penalty should be considered as a justifiable deterrent to the felony itself." The trial court found that the killings in the case were not an essential ingredient of the felony. Thus the goal of deterrence is no more served in this case than it was in *Enmund*.

of the death penalty on an accomplice who did not kill. The Court has since reiterated that "*Enmund* ... imposes a categorical rule: a person who has not in fact killed, attempted to kill, or intended that a killing take place or that lethal force be used may not be sentenced to death." *Cabana v. Bullock*, 474 U.S. 376 (1986). The Court's decision today to approve the death penalty for accomplices who lack this mental state is inconsistent with *Enmund* and with the only justifications this Court has put forth for imposing the death penalty in any case.

B

The Court's second reason for abandoning the intent requirement is based on its survey of state statutes authorizing the death penalty for felony murder, and on a handful of state cases. On this basis, the Court concludes that only "a small minority *of those jurisdictions imposing capital punishment for felony murder* have rejected the possibility of a capital sentence absent an intent to kill, and we do not find this minority position constitutionally required." (Emphasis added.) The Court would thus have us believe that "the majority of American jurisdictions clearly authorize capital punishment" in cases such as this. This is not the case. First, the Court excludes from its survey those jurisdictions that have abolished the death penalty and those that have authorized it only in circumstances different from those presented here. When these jurisdictions are included, and are considered with those jurisdictions that require a finding of intent to kill in order to impose the death sentence for felony murder, one discovers that approximately three-fifths of American jurisdictions do not authorize the death penalty for a nontriggerman absent a finding that he intended to kill. Thus, contrary to the Court's implication that its view is consonant with that of "the majority of American jurisdictions," the Court's view is itself distinctly the minority position.

Second, it is critical to examine not simply those jurisdictions that authorize the death penalty in a given circumstance, but those that actually *impose* it. Evidence that a penalty is imposed only infrequently suggests not only that jurisdictions are reluctant to apply it but also that, when it is applied, its imposition is arbitrary and therefore unconstitutional. *Furman v. Georgia*, 408 U.S. 238 (1972). Thus, the Court in *Enmund* examined the relevant statistics on the imposition of the death penalty for accomplices in a felony murder. The Court found that of all executions between 1954 and 1982, there were "*only 6 cases out of 362 where a nontriggerman felony murderer was executed. All six executions took place in 1955.*" (Emphasis added.) This evidence obviously militates against imposing the death penalty on petitioners as powerfully as it did against imposing it on Enmund.

The Court in *Enmund* also looked at the imposition of the death penalty for felony murder within Florida, the State that had sentenced Enmund. Of the 45 murderers then on death row, 36 had been found to have "intended" to take life, and 8 of the 9 for which there was no finding of intent had been the triggerman. Thus in only one case—*Enmund*—had someone (such as the Tisons) who had neither killed nor intended to kill received the death sentence. Finally, the Court noted that in no Commonwealth or European country could Enmund have been executed, since all have either abolished or never employed a felony-murder doctrine.

The Court today neither reviews nor updates this evidence. Had it done so, it would have discovered that, even including the 65 executions since *Enmund*, "the fact remains that we are not aware of a single person convicted of felony murder over the past quarter century who did not kill or attempt to kill, and did not intend the death of the victim, who has been executed...." Of the 64 persons on death row in Arizona, all of those who have raised and lost an *Enmund* challenge in the Arizona Supreme Court have been found either to have killed or to have specifically intended to kill. Thus, like Enmund, the Tisons' sentence appears to be an aberration within Arizona itself as well as nationally and internationally. The Court's objective evidence that the statutes of roughly 20 States appear to authorize the death penalty for defendants in the Court's new category is therefore an inadequate substitute for a proper proportionality analysis, and is not persuasive evidence that the punishment that was unconstitutional for Enmund is constitutional for the Tisons.

...

Note and Problems

Problem 99.

Defendant and three others planned a liquor store robbery. According to the plan, Leader would enter the store with a gun and get the drop on the clerk. Defendant and Aider then would run into the store to assist in tying up the clerk and gathering the loot. Meanwhile, Driver would wait in the car. The four went to the liquor store, and Leader entered. Before Defendant and Aider could enter, shots were fired inside the store, and Leader came running out, having shot and killed the clerk. Defendant is charged with first degree murder (P.C. §§ 187–189), and the prosecution is seeking the death penalty. What are the arguments as to whether imposition of the death penalty on Defendant would be constitutional?

Problem 100.

Defendant was burglarizing Victim's house when he was surprised by Victim. Defendant attempted to escape and was backing away from the house with his gun drawn when he tripped on a wire causing the gun to go off. The bullet passed through the closed kitchen door and killed Victim. Defendant has been convicted of first degree murder (P.C. §§ 187–189), and the prosecutor is seeking the death penalty. What are the arguments as to whether imposition of the death penalty on Defendant would be constitutional?

Proportionality to the Offender. In *Coker* and *Tison*, the issue was whether the death penalty was proportional to the offense. The Supreme Court has also addressed whether, in two circumstances, the death penalty is proportional to a class of offenders. In *Atkins v. Virginia*, 536 U.S. 304 (2002), the Court overruled its earlier decision in *Penry v. Lynaugh*, 492 U.S. 302 (1989) and held that it would violate the Eighth Amendment to impose the death penalty on a defendant who was mentally retarded (since described by the Court as "intellectually disabled"). In *Roper v. Simmons*, 543 U.S. 551 (2005), the Court overruled its earlier decision in *Stanford v. Kentucky*, 492 U.S. 361 (1989) and held that it would violate the Eighth Amendment to impose the death penalty on a defendant who was under 18 years old at the time of the crime.

Kennedy v. Louisiana[d]

554 U.S. 407, 128 S. Ct. 2641 (2008)

Justice Kennedy delivered the opinion of the Court.

The National Government and, beyond it, the separate States are bound by the proscriptive mandates of the Eighth Amendment to the Constitution of the United States, and all persons within those respective jurisdictions may invoke its protection. Patrick Kennedy, the petitioner here, seeks to set aside his death sentence under the Eighth Amendment. He was charged by the respondent, the State of Louisiana, with the aggravated rape of his then-8-year-old stepdaughter. After a jury trial petitioner was convicted and sentenced to death under a state statute authorizing capital punishment for the rape of a child under 12 years of age. This case presents the question whether the Constitution bars respondent from imposing the death penalty for the rape of a child where the crime did not result, and was not intended to result, in death of the victim. We hold the Eighth Amendment prohibits the death penalty for this offense. The Louisiana statute is unconstitutional.

I

Petitioner's crime was one that cannot be recounted in these pages in a way sufficient to capture in full the hurt and horror inflicted on his victim or to convey the revulsion society, and the jury that represents it, sought to express by sentencing petitioner to death. At 9:18 a.m. on March 2, 1998, petitioner called 911 to report that his stepdaughter, referred to here as L. H., had been raped. He told the 911 operator that L.H. had been in the garage while he readied his son for school. Upon hearing loud screaming, petitioner said, he ran outside and found L.H. in the side yard. Two neighborhood boys, petitioner told the operator, had dragged L.H. from the garage to the yard, pushed her down, and raped her. Petitioner claimed he saw one of the boys riding away on a blue 10-speed bicycle.

[When police arrived, they found L.H. bleeding profusely from the vaginal area. She had been very seriously injured and required emergency surgery. In the weeks following the rape, both petitioner and L.H. reiterated the story petitioner had first told to the police. Nevertheless, eight days after the rape, on the basis of substantial evidence contradicting petitioner's story—including a call he made between 6:30

---

d. As amended on denial of rehearing. See 554 U.S. 945, 129 S. Ct. 1 (2008).

and 7:30 a.m. to ask a colleague how to get blood out of a white carpet because his daughter had "just become a young lady"—police arrested him. On June 22, 1998, L.H., for the first time, told her mother that petitioner had raped her.]

The State charged petitioner with aggravated rape of a child under La. Stat. Ann. § 14:42 and sought the death penalty. [The statute defined aggravated rape of a child as "anal or vaginal sexual intercourse" with a victim under the age of twelve years and, in combination with La. Code Crim. Proc. Art. 905.4 (aggravating circumstances), made one convicted of the crime death-eligible.]

The trial began in August 2003. L.H. was then 13 years old. She testified that she "woke up one morning and Patrick was on top of [her]." She remembered petitioner bringing her "[a] cup of orange juice and pills chopped up in it" after the rape and overhearing him on the telephone saying she had become a "young lady." L.H. acknowledged that she had accused two neighborhood boys but testified petitioner told her to say this and that it was untrue.

The jury having found petitioner guilty of aggravated rape, the penalty phase ensued. The State presented the testimony of S. L., who is the cousin and goddaughter of petitioner's ex-wife. S.L. testified that petitioner sexually abused her three times when she was eight years old and that the last time involved sexual intercourse. She did not tell anyone until two years later and did not pursue legal action.

The jury unanimously determined that petitioner should be sentenced to death. The Supreme Court of Louisiana [distinguishing *Coker v. Georgia*, 433 U.S. 584 (1977)] affirmed.

...

We granted certiorari.

II

The Eighth Amendment, applicable to the States through the Fourteenth Amendment, provides that "[e]xcessive bail shall not be required, nor excessive fines imposed, nor cruel and unusual punishments inflicted." The Amendment proscribes "all excessive punishments, as well as cruel and unusual punishments that may or may not be excessive." *Atkins v. Virginia*, 536 U.S. 304 (2002). The Court explained in *Atkins* and *Roper v. Simmons*, 543 U.S. 551 (2005), that the Eighth Amendment's protection against excessive or cruel and unusual punishments flows from the basic "precept of justice that punishment for [a] crime should be graduated and proportioned to [the] offense." *Weems v. United States*, 217 U.S. 349 (1910). Whether this requirement has been fulfilled is determined not by the standards that prevailed when the Eighth Amendment was adopted in 1791 but by the norms that "currently prevail." *Atkins*. The Amendment "draw[s] its meaning from the evolving standards of decency that mark the progress of a maturing society." *Trop v. Dulles*, 356 U.S. 86(1958) (plurality opinion). This is because "[t]he standard of extreme cruelty is not merely descriptive, but necessarily embodies a moral judgment. The standard itself remains the same, but its applicability must change as the basic mores of society change." *Furman v. Georgia*, 408 U.S. 238 (1972) (Burger, C. J., dissenting).

Evolving standards of decency must embrace and express respect for the dignity of the person, and the punishment of criminals must conform to that rule. As we shall discuss, punishment is justified under one or more of three principal rationales: rehabilitation, deterrence, and retribution. It is the last of these, retribution, that most often can contradict the law's own ends. This is of particular concern when the Court interprets the meaning of the Eighth Amendment in capital cases. When the law punishes by death, it risks its own sudden descent into brutality, transgressing the constitutional commitment to decency and restraint.

For these reasons we have explained that capital punishment must "be limited to those offenders who commit 'a narrow category of the most serious crimes' and whose extreme culpability makes them 'the most deserving of execution.'" *Roper* (quoting *Atkins*). Though the death penalty is not invariably unconstitutional, see *Gregg v. Georgia*, 428 U.S. 153 (1976), the Court insists upon confining the instances in which the punishment can be imposed.

Applying this principle, we held in *Roper* and *Atkins* that the execution of juveniles and mentally retarded persons are punishments violative of the Eighth Amendment because the offender had a diminished personal responsibility for the crime. The Court further has held that the death penalty can be disproportionate to the crime itself where the crime did not result, or was not intended to result, in death of the victim. In *Coker*, for instance, the Court held it would be unconstitutional to execute an offender who had raped an adult woman. And in *Enmund v. Florida*, 458 U.S. 782 (1982), the Court overturned the capital sentence of a defendant who aided and abetted a robbery during which a murder was committed but did not himself kill, attempt to kill, or intend that a killing would take place. On the other hand, in *Tison v. Arizona*, 481 U.S. 137 (1987), the Court allowed the defendants' death sentences to stand where they did not themselves kill the victims but their involvement in the events leading up to the murders was active, recklessly indifferent, and substantial.

In these cases the Court has been guided by "objective indicia of society's standards, as expressed in legislative enactments and state practice with respect to executions." *Roper*; see also *Coker* (plurality opinion) (finding that both legislatures and juries had firmly rejected the penalty of death for the rape of an adult woman); *Enmund* (looking to "historical development of the punishment at issue, legislative judgments, international opinion, and the sentencing decisions juries have made"). The inquiry does not end there, however. Consensus is not dispositive. Whether the death penalty is disproportionate to the crime committed depends as well upon the standards elaborated by controlling precedents and by the Court's own understanding and interpretation of the Eighth Amendment's text, history, meaning, and purpose.

Based both on consensus and our own independent judgment, our holding is that a death sentence for one who raped but did not kill a child, and who did not intend to assist another in killing the child, is unconstitutional under the Eighth and Fourteenth Amendments.

III

A

The existence of objective indicia of consensus against making a crime punishable by death was a relevant concern in *Roper, Atkins, Coker*, and *Enmund*, and we follow the approach of those cases here. The history of the death penalty for the crime of rape is an instructive beginning point.

In 1925, 18 States, the District of Columbia, and the Federal Government had statutes that authorized the death penalty for the rape of a child or an adult. Between 1930 and 1964, 455 people were executed for those crimes. To our knowledge the last individual executed for the rape of a child was Ronald Wolfe in 1964.

In 1972, *Furman* invalidated most of the state statutes authorizing the death penalty for the crime of rape; and in *Furman*'s aftermath only six States reenacted their capital rape provisions. Three States—Georgia, North Carolina, and Louisiana—did so with respect to all rape offenses. Three States—Florida, Mississippi, and Tennessee—did so with respect only to child rape. All six statutes were later invalidated under state or federal law.

Louisiana reintroduced the death penalty for rape of a child in 1995. Under the current statute, any anal, vaginal, or oral intercourse with a child under the age of 13 constitutes aggravated rape and is punishable by death. Mistake of age is not a defense, so the statute imposes strict liability in this regard. Five States have since followed Louisiana's lead: Georgia (1999); Montana (1997); Oklahoma (2006); South Carolina (2006); and Texas (2007). Four of these States' statutes [those of Montana, Oklahoma, South Carolina, Texas] are more narrow than Louisiana's in that only offenders with a previous rape conviction are death eligible. Georgia's statute makes child rape a capital offense only when aggravating circumstances are present, including but not limited to a prior conviction.

By contrast, 44 States have not made child rape a capital offense. As for federal law, Congress in the Federal Death Penalty Act of 1994 expanded the number of federal crimes for which the death penalty is a permissible sentence, including certain nonhomicide offenses; but it did not do the same for child rape or abuse....

[Whether Georgia should be included in the list of states authorizing the death penalty for rape of a child and whether Florida should be excluded from the list is subject to dispute.]

Definitive resolution of state-law issues is for the States' own courts, and there may be disagreement over the statistics. It is further true that some States, including States that have addressed the issue in just the last few years, have made child rape a capital offense. The summary recited here, however, does allow us to make certain comparisons with the data cited in the *Atkins, Roper*, and *Enmund* cases.

When *Atkins* was decided in 2002, 30 States, including 12 noncapital jurisdictions, prohibited the death penalty for mentally retarded offenders; 20 permitted it. When *Roper* was decided in 2005, the numbers disclosed a similar division among the States:

30 States prohibited the death penalty for juveniles, 18 of which permitted the death penalty for other offenders; and 20 States authorized it. Both in *Atkins* and in *Roper*, we noted that the practice of executing mentally retarded and juvenile offenders was infrequent. Only five States had executed an offender known to have an IQ below 70 between 1989 and 2002; and only three States had executed a juvenile offender between 1995 and 2005.

The statistics in *Enmund* bear an even greater similarity to the instant case. There eight jurisdictions had authorized imposition of the death penalty solely for participation in a robbery during which an accomplice committed murder, and six defendants between 1954 and 1982 had been sentenced to death for felony murder where the defendant did not personally commit the homicidal assault. These facts, the Court concluded, "weigh[ed] on the side of rejecting capital punishment for the crime."

The evidence of a national consensus with respect to the death penalty for child rapists, as with respect to juveniles, mentally retarded offenders, and vicarious felony murderers, shows divided opinion but, on balance, an opinion against it. Thirty-seven jurisdictions—36 States plus the Federal Government—have the death penalty. As mentioned above, only six of those jurisdictions authorize the death penalty for rape of a child. Though our review of national consensus is not confined to tallying the number of States with applicable death penalty legislation, it is of significance that, in 45 jurisdictions, petitioner could not be executed for child rape of any kind. That number surpasses the 30 States in *Atkins* and *Roper* and the 42 States in *Enmund* that prohibited the death penalty under the circumstances those cases considered.*

B

[Justice Kennedy rejected the argument that the failure of more states to make child rape a capital crime stemmed from the legislatures' misreading of *Coker* as barring the death penalty for all non-homicide crimes. He pointed out that the *Coker* plurality several times described the issue and the Court's holding as concerning only the constitutionality of the death penalty for rape of "an adult woman" or "adult female," and he argued that there was no evidence that state legislatures were confused by the holding and that, had the legislatures looked for guidance to the courts, they would have found that "[t]he state courts that have confronted the precise question before us have been uniform in concluding that *Coker* did not address the constitutionality of the death penalty for the crime of child rape."]

We conclude on the basis of this review that there is no clear indication that state legislatures have misinterpreted *Coker* to hold that the death penalty for child rape is unconstitutional. The small number of States that have enacted this penalty, then,

---

* When issued and announced on June 25, 2008, the Court's decision neither noted nor discussed the military penalty for rape under the Uniform Code of Military Justice. In a petition for rehearing respondent argues that the military penalty bears on our consideration of the question in this case. For the reasons set forth in the statement respecting the denial of rehearing, we find that the military penalty does not affect our reasoning or conclusions.

is relevant to determining whether there is a consensus against capital punishment for this crime.

C

Respondent insists that the six States where child rape is a capital offense, along with the States that have proposed but not yet enacted applicable death penalty legislation, reflect a consistent direction of change in support of the death penalty for child rape. Consistent change might counterbalance an otherwise weak demonstration of consensus. But whatever the significance of consistent change where it is cited to show emerging support for expanding the scope of the death penalty, no showing of consistent change has been made in this case.

Respondent and its *amici* identify five States where, in their view, legislation authorizing capital punishment for child rape is pending. It is not our practice, nor is it sound, to find contemporary norms based upon state legislation that has been proposed but not yet enacted. There are compelling reasons not to do so here. Since the briefs were submitted by the parties, legislation in two of the five States [Colorado and Mississippi] has failed. In Tennessee, the house bills were rejected almost a year ago, and the senate bills appear to have died in committee. In Alabama, the recent legislation is similar to a bill that failed in 2007. And in Missouri, the 2008 legislative session has ended, tabling the pending legislation.

Aside from pending legislation, it is true that in the last 13 years there has been change towards making child rape a capital offense. This is evidenced by six new death penalty statutes, three enacted in the last two years. But this showing is not as significant as the data in *Atkins*, where 18 States between 1986 and 2001 had enacted legislation prohibiting the execution of mentally retarded persons. Respondent argues the instant case is like *Roper* because, there, only five States had shifted their positions between 1989 and 2005, one less State than here. But in *Roper*, we emphasized that, though the pace of abolition was not as great as in *Atkins*, it was counterbalanced by the total number of States that had recognized the impropriety of executing juvenile offenders. When we decided *Stanford v. Kentucky*, 492 U.S. 361 (1989), 12 death penalty States already prohibited the execution of any juvenile under 18, and 15 prohibited the execution of any juvenile under 17. Here, the total number of States to have made child rape a capital offense after *Furman* is six. This is not an indication of a trend or change in direction comparable to the one supported by data in *Roper*. The evidence here bears a closer resemblance to the evidence of state activity in *Enmund*, where we found a national consensus against the death penalty for vicarious felony murder despite eight jurisdictions having authorized the practice.

D

There are measures of consensus other than legislation. Statistics about the number of executions may inform the consideration whether capital punishment for the crime of child rape is regarded as unacceptable in our society. These statistics confirm our determination from our review of state statutes that there is a social consensus against the death penalty for the crime of child rape.

Nine States—Florida, Georgia, Louisiana, Mississippi, Montana, Oklahoma, South Carolina, Tennessee, and Texas—have permitted capital punishment for adult or child rape for some length of time between the Court's 1972 decision in *Furman* and today. Yet no individual has been executed for the rape of an adult or child since 1964, and no execution for any other nonhomicide offense has been conducted since 1963.

Louisiana is the only State since 1964 that has sentenced an individual to death for the crime of child rape; and petitioner and Richard Davis, who was convicted and sentenced to death for the aggravated rape of a 5-year-old child by a Louisiana jury in December 2007, are the only two individuals now on death row in the United States for a nonhomicide offense.

After reviewing the authorities informed by contemporary norms, including the history of the death penalty for this and other nonhomicide crimes, current state statutes and new enactments, and the number of executions since 1964, we conclude there is a national consensus against capital punishment for the crime of child rape.

IV

A

As we have said in other Eighth Amendment cases, objective evidence of contemporary values as it relates to punishment for child rape is entitled to great weight, but it does not end our inquiry. "[T]he Constitution contemplates that in the end our own judgment will be brought to bear on the question of the acceptability of the death penalty under the Eighth Amendment." *Coker* (plurality opinion). We turn, then, to the resolution of the question before us, which is informed by our precedents and our own understanding of the Constitution and the rights it secures.

It must be acknowledged that there are moral grounds to question a rule barring capital punishment for a crime against an individual that did not result in death. These facts illustrate the point. Here the victim's fright, the sense of betrayal, and the nature of her injuries caused more prolonged physical and mental suffering than, say, a sudden killing by an unseen assassin. The attack was not just on her but on her childhood. For this reason, we should be most reluctant to rely upon the language of the plurality in *Coker*, which posited that, for the victim of rape, "life may not be nearly so happy as it was" but it is not beyond repair. We cannot dismiss the years of long anguish that must be endured by the victim of child rape.

It does not follow, though, that capital punishment is a proportionate penalty for the crime. The constitutional prohibition against excessive or cruel and unusual punishments mandates that the State's power to punish "be exercised within the limits of civilized standards." *Trop* (plurality opinion). Evolving standards of decency that mark the progress of a maturing society counsel us to be most hesitant before interpreting the Eighth Amendment to allow the extension of the death penalty, a hesitation that has special force where no life was taken in the commission of the crime. It is an established principle that decency, in its essence, presumes respect for the individual and thus moderation or restraint in the application of capital punishment.

To date the Court has sought to define and implement this principle, for the most part, in cases involving capital murder. One approach has been to insist upon general rules that ensure consistency in determining who receives a death sentence. See *California v. Brown*, 479 U.S. 538 (1987) ("[D]eath penalty statutes [must] be structured so as to prevent the penalty from being administered in an arbitrary and unpredictable fashion"). At the same time the Court has insisted, to ensure restraint and moderation in use of capital punishment, on judging the "character and record of the individual offender and the circumstances of the particular offense as a constitutionally indispensable part of the process of inflicting the penalty of death." *Woodson v. North Carolina*, 428 U.S. 280 (1976) (plurality opinion).

The tension between general rules and case-specific circumstances has produced results not all together satisfactory. See *Tuilaepa v. California*, 512 U.S. 967 (1994) ("The objectives of these two inquiries can be in some tension, at least when the inquiries occur at the same time"); *Walton v. Arizona*, 497 U.S. 639 (1990) (Scalia, J., concurring in part and concurring in judgment) ("The latter requirement quite obviously destroys whatever rationality and predictability the former requirement was designed to achieve"). This has led some Members of the Court to say we should cease efforts to resolve the tension and simply allow legislatures, prosecutors, courts, and juries greater latitude. See *id.* (advocating that the Court adhere to the *Furman* line of cases and abandon the *Woodson-Lockett* line of cases). For others the failure to limit these same imprecisions by stricter enforcement of narrowing rules has raised doubts concerning the constitutionality of capital punishment itself. See *Baze v. Rees*, 553 U.S. 35 (2008) (Stevens, J., concurring in judgment); *Furman*, (WHITE, J., concurring); *Callins v. Collins*, 510 U.S. 1141 (1994) (Blackmun, J., dissenting from denial of certiorari).

Our response to this case law, which is still in search of a unifying principle, has been to insist upon confining the instances in which capital punishment may be imposed. See *Gregg* (joint opinion of STEWART, POWELL, and STEVENS, JJ.) (because "death as a punishment is unique in its severity and irrevocability," capital punishment must be reserved for those crimes that are "so grievous an affront to humanity that the only adequate response may be the penalty of death" (citing in part *Furman* (BRENNAN, J., concurring); *id.* (Stewart, J., concurring)).

Our concern here is limited to crimes against individual persons. We do not address, for example, crimes defining and punishing treason, espionage, terrorism, and drug kingpin activity, which are offenses against the State. As it relates to crimes against individuals, though, the death penalty should not be expanded to instances where the victim's life was not taken. We said in *Coker* of adult rape:

> "We do not discount the seriousness of rape as a crime. It is highly reprehensible, both in a moral sense and in its almost total contempt for the personal integrity and autonomy of the female victim.... Short of homicide, it is the 'ultimate violation of self.' ... [But] [t]he murderer kills; the rapist, if no more than that, does not.... We have the abiding conviction that the death penalty, which 'is unique in its severity and irrevocability,' is an excessive penalty for the rapist who, as such, does not take human life." (plurality opinion).

The same distinction between homicide and other serious violent offenses against the individual informed the Court's analysis in *Enmund*, where the Court held that the death penalty for the crime of vicarious felony murder is disproportionate to the offense. The Court repeated there the fundamental, moral distinction between a "murderer" and a "robber," noting that while "robbery is a serious crime deserving serious punishment," it is not like death in its "severity and irrevocability."

Consistent with evolving standards of decency and the teachings of our precedents we conclude that, in determining whether the death penalty is excessive, there is a distinction between intentional first-degree murder on the one hand and nonhomicide crimes against individual persons, even including child rape, on the other. The latter crimes may be devastating in their harm, as here, but "in terms of moral depravity and of the injury to the person and to the public," *Coker*, they cannot be compared to murder in their "severity and irrevocability."

In reaching our conclusion we find significant the number of executions that would be allowed under respondent's approach. The crime of child rape, considering its reported incidents, occurs more often than first-degree murder. Approximately 5,702 incidents of vaginal, anal, or oral rape of a child under the age of 12 were reported nationwide in 2005; this is almost twice the total incidents of intentional murder for victims of all ages (3,405) reported during the same period. Although we have no reliable statistics on convictions for child rape, we can surmise that, each year, there are hundreds, or more, of these convictions just in jurisdictions that permit capital punishment. Cf. Brief for Louisiana Association of Criminal Defense Lawyers et al. as *Amici Curiae* 1–2, and n. 2 (noting that there are now at least 70 capital rape indictments pending in Louisiana and estimating the actual number to be over 100). As a result of existing rules, only 2.2% of convicted first-degree murderers are sentenced to death. But under respondent's approach, the 36 States that permit the death penalty could sentence to death all persons convicted of raping a child less than 12 years of age. This could not be reconciled with our evolving standards of decency and the necessity to constrain the use of the death penalty.

It might be said that narrowing aggravators could be used in this context, as with murder offenses, to ensure the death penalty's restrained application. We find it difficult to identify standards that would guide the decisionmaker so the penalty is reserved for the most severe cases of child rape and yet not imposed in an arbitrary way. Even were we to forbid, say, the execution of first-time child rapists, or require as an aggravating factor a finding that the perpetrator's instant rape offense involved multiple victims, the jury still must balance, in its discretion, those aggravating factors against mitigating circumstances. In this context, which involves a crime that in many cases will overwhelm a decent person's judgment, we have no confidence that the imposition of the death penalty would not be so arbitrary as to be "freakis[h]," *Furman* (Stewart, J., concurring). We cannot sanction this result when the harm to the victim, though grave, cannot be quantified in the same way as death of the victim.

It is not a solution simply to apply to this context the aggravating factors developed for capital murder. The Court has said that a State may carry out its obligation to ensure individualized sentencing in capital murder cases by adopting sentencing processes that rely upon the jury to exercise wide discretion so long as there are narrowing factors that have some "common-sense core of meaning ... that criminal juries should be capable of understanding." *Tuilaepa, supra.* The Court, accordingly, has upheld the constitutionality of aggravating factors ranging from whether the defendant was a "cold-blooded, pitiless slayer," *Arave v. Creech*, 507 U.S. 463 (1993), to whether the "perpetrator inflict[ed] mental anguish or physical abuse before the victim's death," *Walton*, to whether the defendant "would commit criminal acts of violence that would constitute a continuing threat to society," *Jurek v. Texas*, 428 U.S. 262 (1976) (joint opinion of Stewart, Powell, and Stevens, JJ.) All of these standards have the potential to result in some inconsistency of application.

As noted above, the resulting imprecision and the tension between evaluating the individual circumstances and consistency of treatment have been tolerated where the victim dies. It should not be introduced into our justice system, though, where death has not occurred.

Our concerns are all the more pronounced where, as here, the death penalty for this crime has been most infrequent. We have developed a foundational jurisprudence in the case of capital murder to guide the States and juries in imposing the death penalty. Starting with *Gregg*, we have spent more than 32 years articulating limiting factors that channel the jury's discretion to avoid the death penalty's arbitrary imposition in the case of capital murder. Though that practice remains sound, beginning the same process for crimes for which no one has been executed in more than 40 years would require experimentation in an area where a failed experiment would result in the execution of individuals undeserving of the death penalty. Evolving standards of decency are difficult to reconcile with a regime that seeks to expand the death penalty to an area where standards to confine its use are indefinite and obscure.

B

Our decision is consistent with the justifications offered for the death penalty. *Gregg* instructs that capital punishment is excessive when it is grossly out of proportion to the crime or it does not fulfill the two distinct social purposes served by the death penalty: retribution and deterrence of capital crimes.

As in *Coker*, here it cannot be said with any certainty that the death penalty for child rape serves no deterrent or retributive function. This argument does not overcome other objections, however. The incongruity between the crime of child rape and the harshness of the death penalty poses risks of overpunishment and counsels against a constitutional ruling that the death penalty can be expanded to include this offense.

The goal of retribution, which reflects society's and the victim's interests in seeing that the offender is repaid for the hurt he caused, does not justify the harshness of the death penalty here. In measuring retribution, as well as other objectives of criminal law, it is appropriate to distinguish between a particularly depraved murder that merits death as a form of retribution and the crime of child rape.

There is an additional reason for our conclusion that imposing the death penalty for child rape would not further retributive purposes. In considering whether retribution is served, among other factors we have looked to whether capital punishment "has the potential ... to allow the community as a whole, including the surviving family and friends of the victim, to affirm its own judgment that the culpability of the prisoner is so serious that the ultimate penalty must be sought and imposed." *Panetti v. Quarterman*, 551 U.S. 930 (2007). In considering the death penalty for nonhomicide offenses this inquiry necessarily also must include the question whether the death penalty balances the wrong to the victim.

It is not at all evident that the child rape victim's hurt is lessened when the law permits the death of the perpetrator. Capital cases require a long-term commitment by those who testify for the prosecution, especially when guilt and sentencing determinations are in multiple proceedings. In cases like this the key testimony is not just from the family but from the victim herself. During formative years of her adolescence, made all the more daunting for having to come to terms with the brutality of her experience, L.H. was required to discuss the case at length with law enforcement personnel. In a public trial she was required to recount once more all the details of the crime to a jury as the State pursued the death of her stepfather. And in the end the State made L.H. a central figure in its decision to seek the death penalty, telling the jury in closing statements: "[L. H.] is asking you, asking you to set up a time and place when he dies."

Society's desire to inflict the death penalty for child rape by enlisting the child victim to assist it over the course of years in asking for capital punishment forces a moral choice on the child, who is not of mature age to make that choice. The way the death penalty here involves the child victim in its enforcement can compromise a decent legal system; and this is but a subset of fundamental difficulties capital punishment can cause in the administration and enforcement of laws proscribing child rape.

There are, moreover, serious systemic concerns in prosecuting the crime of child rape that are relevant to the constitutionality of making it a capital offense. The problem of unreliable, induced, and even imagined child testimony means there is a "special risk of wrongful execution" in some child rape cases. *Atkins*. This undermines, at least to some degree, the meaningful contribution of the death penalty to legitimate goals of punishment. Studies conclude that children are highly susceptible to suggestive questioning techniques like repetition, guided imagery, and selective reinforcement.

Similar criticisms pertain to other cases involving child witnesses; but child rape cases present heightened concerns because the central narrative and account of the crime often comes from the child herself. She and the accused are, in most instances, the only ones present when the crime was committed. And the question in a capital case is not just the fact of the crime, including, say, proof of rape as distinct from abuse short of rape, but details bearing upon brutality in its commission. Although capital punishment does bring retribution, and the legislature here has chosen to use it for this end, its judgment must be weighed, in deciding the constitutional question, against the special risks of unreliable testimony with respect to this crime.

With respect to deterrence, if the death penalty adds to the risk of non-reporting, that, too, diminishes the penalty's objectives. Underreporting is a common problem with respect to child sexual abuse. [Citing studies showing that 88% of minor female rape victims did not report the rape to authorities] Although we know little about what differentiates those who report from those who do not report, one of the most commonly cited reasons for nondisclosure is fear of negative consequences for the perpetrator, a concern that has special force where the abuser is a family member. The experience of the *amici* who work with child victims indicates that, when the punishment is death, both the victim and the victim's family members may be more likely to shield the perpetrator from discovery, thus increasing underreporting. As a result, punishment by death may not result in more deterrence or more effective enforcement.

In addition, by in effect making the punishment for child rape and murder equivalent, a State that punishes child rape by death may remove a strong incentive for the rapist not to kill the victim. Assuming the offender behaves in a rational way, as one must to justify the penalty on grounds of deterrence, the penalty in some respects gives less protection, not more, to the victim, who is often the sole witness to the crime. It might be argued that, even if the death penalty results in a marginal increase in the incentive to kill, this is counterbalanced by a marginally increased deterrent to commit the crime at all. Whatever balance the legislature strikes, however, uncertainty on the point makes the argument for the penalty less compelling than for homicide crimes.

Each of these propositions, standing alone, might not establish the unconstitutionality of the death penalty for the crime of child rape. Taken in sum, however, they demonstrate the serious negative consequences of making child rape a capital offense. These considerations lead us to conclude, in our independent judgment, that the death penalty is not a proportional punishment for the rape of a child.

V

Our determination that there is a consensus against the death penalty for child rape raises the question whether the Court's own institutional position and its holding will have the effect of blocking further or later consensus in favor of the penalty from developing. The Court, it will be argued, by the act of addressing the constitutionality of the death penalty, intrudes upon the consensus-making process. By imposing a negative restraint, the argument runs, the Court makes it more difficult for consensus to change or emerge. The Court, according to the criticism, itself becomes enmeshed in the process, part judge and part the maker of that which it judges.

These concerns overlook the meaning and full substance of the established proposition that the Eighth Amendment is defined by "the evolving standards of decency that mark the progress of a maturing society." *Trop* (plurality opinion). Confirmed by repeated, consistent rulings of this Court, this principle requires that use of the death penalty be restrained. The rule of evolving standards of decency with specific marks on the way to full progress and mature judgment means that resort to the penalty must be reserved for the worst of crimes and limited in its instances of application. In most cases justice is not better served by terminating the life of the perpetrator rather than confining him and preserving the possibility that he and the system will find ways to allow him to understand the enormity of his offense. Difficulties in administering the penalty to ensure against its arbitrary and capricious application require adherence to a rule reserving its use, at this stage of evolving standards and in cases of crimes against individuals, for crimes that take the life of the victim.

The judgment of the Supreme Court of Louisiana upholding the capital sentence is reversed. This case is remanded for further proceedings not inconsistent with this opinion.

It is so ordered.

Justice ALITO, with whom THE CHIEF JUSTICE, Justice SCALIA, and Justice THOMAS join, dissenting.

The Court today holds that the Eighth Amendment categorically prohibits the imposition of the death penalty for the crime of raping a child. This is so, according to the Court, no matter how young the child, no matter how many times the child is raped, no matter how many children the perpetrator rapes, no matter how sadistic the crime, no matter how much physical or psychological trauma is inflicted, and no matter how heinous the perpetrator's prior criminal record may be. The Court provides two reasons for this sweeping conclusion: First, the Court claims to have identified "a national consensus" that the death penalty is never acceptable for the rape of a child; second, the Court concludes, based on its "independent judgment," that imposing the death penalty for child rape is inconsistent with "'the evolving standards of decency that mark the progress of a maturing society.'" Because neither of these justifications is sound, I respectfully dissent.

I

A

I turn first to the Court's claim that there is "a national consensus" that it is never acceptable to impose the death penalty for the rape of a child. The Eighth Amendment's requirements, the Court writes, are "determined not by the standards that prevailed" when the Amendment was adopted but "by the norms that 'currently prevail.'" (quoting *Atkins v. Virginia*, 536 U.S. 304 (2002)). In assessing current norms, the Court relies primarily on the fact that only 6 of the 50 States now have statutes that permit the death penalty for this offense. But this statistic is a highly unreliable indicator of the views of state lawmakers and their constituents. As I will explain, dicta in this Court's decision in *Coker v. Georgia*, 433 U.S. 584 (1977), has stunted legislative consideration of the question whether the death penalty for the targeted offense of raping a young child is consistent with prevailing standards of decency. The *Coker* dicta gave state legislators and others good reason to fear that any law permitting the imposition of the death penalty for this crime would meet precisely the fate that has now befallen the Louisiana statute that is currently before us, and this threat strongly discouraged state legislators—regardless of their own values and those of their constituents—from supporting the enactment of such legislation.

[Justice Alito argued that the *Coker* plurality's summary—"We have the abiding conviction that the death penalty ... is an excessive penalty for the rapist who, as such, does not take human life"—although dicta, implied that the death penalty for *any* rape would have been unconstitutional. He cited to state court opinions and commentators who, while recognizing the limits of the *Coker* holding, assumed that the logic of the decision would bar imposition of the death penalty for any non-homicide crime. He concluded that "the *Coker* dicta gave state legislators a strong incentive not to push for the enactment of new capital child-rape laws even though these legislators and their constituents may have believed that the laws would be appropriate and desirable," and, in support of that point, he cited to opponents' contentions that the recent Oklahoma and Texas child-rape bills were unconstitutional under *Coker*.]

C

Because of the effect of the *Coker* dicta, the Court is plainly wrong in comparing the situation here to that in *Atkins* or *Roper v. Simmons*, 543 U.S. 551 (2005). *Atkins* concerned the constitutionality of imposing the death penalty on a mentally retarded defendant. Thirteen years earlier, in *Penry v. Lynaugh*, 492 U.S. 302 (1989), the Court had held that this was permitted by the Eighth Amendment, and therefore, during the time between *Penry* and *Atkins*, state legislators had reason to believe that this Court would follow its prior precedent and uphold statutes allowing such punishment.

The situation in *Roper* was similar. *Roper* concerned a challenge to the constitutionality of imposing the death penalty on a defendant who had not reached the age of 18 at the time of the crime. Sixteen years earlier in *Stanford v. Kentucky*, 492 U.S. 361 (1989), the Court had rejected a similar challenge, and therefore state lawmakers had cause to believe that laws allowing such punishment would be sustained.

When state lawmakers believe that their decision will prevail on the question whether to permit the death penalty for a particular crime or class of offender, the legislators' resolution of the issue can be interpreted as an expression of their own judgment, informed by whatever weight they attach to the values of their constituents. But when state legislators think that the enactment of a new death penalty law is likely to be futile, inaction cannot reasonably be interpreted as an expression of their understanding of prevailing societal values. In that atmosphere, legislative inaction is more likely to evidence acquiescence.

D

If anything can be inferred from state legislative developments, the message is very different from the one that the Court perceives. In just the past few years, despite the shadow cast by the *Coker* dicta, five States have enacted targeted capital child-rape laws. If, as the Court seems to think, our society is "[e]volving" toward ever higher "standards of decency," these enactments might represent the beginning of a new evolutionary line.

Such a development would not be out of step with changes in our society's thinking since *Coker* was decided. During that time, reported instances of child abuse have increased dramatically;[2] and there are many indications of growing alarm about the sexual abuse of children. In 1994, Congress enacted the Jacob Wetterling Crimes Against Children and Sexually Violent Offender Registration Program, 42 U.S.C. § 14071, which requires States receiving certain federal funds to establish registration systems for convicted sex offenders and to notify the public about persons convicted of the sexual abuse of minors. All 50 States have now enacted such statutes. In addition, at least 21 States and the District of Columbia now have statutes permitting the involuntary commitment of sexual predators, and at least 12 States have enacted residency restrictions for sex offenders.

Seeking to counter the significance of the new capital child-rape laws enacted during the past two years, the Court points out that in recent months efforts to enact similar laws in five other States have stalled. These developments, however, all took place after our decision to grant certiorari in this case, which gave state legislators reason to delay the enactment of new legislation until the constitutionality of such laws was clarified. And there is no evidence of which I am aware that these legislative initiatives failed because the proposed laws were viewed as inconsistent with our society's standards of decency.

On the contrary, the available evidence suggests otherwise. For example, in Colorado, the Senate Appropriations Committee in April voted 6 to 4 against Senate Bill 195, reportedly because it "would have cost about $616,000 next year for trials, appeals, public defenders, and prison costs." Likewise, in Tennessee, the capital child-rape bill was withdrawn in committee "because of the high associated costs." ... Thus, the failure to enact capital child-rape laws cannot be viewed as evidence of a moral consensus against such punishment.

E

Aside from its misleading tally of current state laws, the Court points to two additional "objective indicia" of a "national consensus," but these arguments are patent makeweights. The Court notes that Congress has not enacted a law permitting the death penalty for the rape of a child, but due to the territorial limits of the relevant federal statutes, very few rape cases, not to mention child-rape cases, are prosecuted in federal court. Congress' failure to enact a death penalty statute for this tiny set of cases is hardly evidence of Congress' assessment of our society's values.

---

2. From 1976 to 1986, the number of reported cases of child sexual abuse grew from 6,000 to 132,000, an increase of 2,100%. By 1991, the number of cases totaled 432,000, an increase of another 227%. In 1995, local child protection services agencies identified 126,000 children who were victims of either substantiated or indicated sexual abuse. Nearly 30% of those child victims were between the age of four and seven. There were an estimated 90,000 substantiated cases of child sexual abuse in 2003.

Finally, the Court argues that statistics about the number of executions in rape cases support its perception of a "national consensus," but here too the statistics do not support the Court's position. The Court notes that the last execution for the rape of a child occurred in 1964, but the Court fails to mention that litigation regarding the constitutionality of the death penalty brought executions to a halt across the board in the late 1960's. In 1965 and 1966, there were a total of eight executions for all offenses, and from 1968 until 1977, the year when *Coker* was decided, there were no executions for any crimes. The Court also fails to mention that in Louisiana, since the state law was amended in 1995 to make child rape a capital offense, prosecutors have asked juries to return death verdicts in four cases. In two of those cases, Louisiana juries imposed the death penalty. This 50% record is hardly evidence that juries share the Court's view that the death penalty for the rape of a young child is unacceptable under even the most aggravated circumstances.[7]

F

In light of the points discussed above, I believe that the "objective indicia" of our society's "evolving standards of decency" can be fairly summarized as follows. Neither Congress nor juries have done anything that can plausibly be interpreted as evidencing the "national consensus" that the Court perceives. State legislatures, for more than 30 years, have operated under the ominous shadow of the *Coker* dicta and thus have not been free to express their own understanding of our society's standards of decency. And in the months following our grant of certiorari in this case, state legislatures have had an additional reason to pause. Yet despite the inhibiting legal atmosphere that has prevailed since 1977, six States have recently enacted new, targeted child-rape laws.

I do not suggest that six new state laws necessarily establish a "national consensus" or even that they are sure evidence of an ineluctable trend. In terms of the Court's metaphor of moral evolution, these enactments might have turned out to be an evolutionary dead end. But they might also have been the beginning of a strong new evolutionary line. We will never know, because the Court today snuffs out the line in its incipient stage.

II

A

The Court is willing to block the potential emergence of a national consensus in favor of permitting the death penalty for child rape because, in the end, what matters is the Court's "own judgment" regarding "the acceptability of the death penalty." Although the Court has much to say on this issue, most of the Court's discussion is not pertinent to the Eighth Amendment question at hand. And once all of the Court's irrelevant arguments are put aside, it is apparent that the Court has provided no coherent explanation for today's decision.

---

7. Of course, the other five capital child rape statutes are too recent for any individual to have been sentenced to death under them.

In the next section of this opinion, I will attempt to weed out the arguments that are not germane to the Eighth Amendment inquiry, and in the final section, I will address what remains.

B

A major theme of the Court's opinion is that permitting the death penalty in child-rape cases is not in the best interests of the victims of these crimes and society at large. In this vein, the Court suggests that it is more painful for child-rape victims to testify when the prosecution is seeking the death penalty. The Court also argues that "a State that punishes child rape by death may remove a strong incentive for the rapist not to kill the victim," and may discourage the reporting of child rape.

These policy arguments, whatever their merits, are simply not pertinent to the question whether the death penalty is "cruel and unusual" punishment. The Eighth Amendment protects the right of an accused. It does not authorize this Court to strike down federal or state criminal laws on the ground that they are not in the best interests of crime victims or the broader society. The Court's policy arguments concern matters that legislators should—and presumably do—take into account in deciding whether to enact a capital child-rape statute, but these arguments are irrelevant to the question that is before us in this case. Our cases have cautioned against using "'the aegis of the Cruel and Unusual Punishment Clause' to cut off the normal democratic processes," *Atkins* (Rehnquist, C. J., dissenting), in turn quoting *Gregg v. Georgia*, 428 U.S. 153 (1976), (joint opinion of Stewart, Powell, and Stevens, JJ.), but the Court forgets that warning here.

The Court also contends that laws permitting the death penalty for the rape of a child create serious procedural problems. Specifically, the Court maintains that it is not feasible to channel the exercise of sentencing discretion in child-rape cases, and that the unreliability of the testimony of child victims creates a danger that innocent defendants will be convicted and executed. Neither of these contentions provides a basis for striking down all capital child-rape laws no matter how carefully and narrowly they are crafted.

The Court's argument regarding the structuring of sentencing discretion is hard to comprehend. The Court finds it "difficult to identify standards that would guide the decisionmaker so the penalty is reserved for the most severe cases of child rape and yet not imposed in an arbitrary way." Even assuming that the age of a child is not alone a sufficient factor for limiting sentencing discretion, the Court need only examine the child-rape laws recently enacted in Texas, Oklahoma, Montana, and South Carolina, all of which use a concrete factor to limit quite drastically the number of cases in which the death penalty may be imposed. In those States, a defendant convicted of the rape of a child may be sentenced to death only if the defendant has a prior conviction for a specified felony sex offense.

Moreover, it takes little imagination to envision other limiting factors that a State could use to structure sentencing discretion in child rape cases. Some of these might be: whether the victim was kidnapped, whether the defendant inflicted severe physical injury on the victim, whether the victim was raped multiple times, whether the rapes occurred over a specified extended period, and whether there were multiple victims.

The Court refers to limiting standards that are "indefinite and obscure," but there is nothing indefinite or obscure about any of the above-listed aggravating factors. Indeed, they are far more definite and clear-cut than aggravating factors that we have found to be adequate in murder cases. See, *e.g.*, *Arave v. Creech*, 507 U.S. 463 (1993) (whether the defendant was a "cold-blooded, pitiless slayer"); *Walton v. Arizona*, 497 U.S. 639 (1990) (whether the "perpetrator inflict[ed] mental anguish or physical abuse before the victim's death"); *Jurek v. Texas*, 428 U.S. 262 (1976) (joint opinion of Stewart, Powell, and Stevens, JJ.) (whether the defendant "would commit criminal acts of violence that would constitute a continuing threat to society"). For these reasons, concerns about limiting sentencing discretion provide no support for the Court's blanket condemnation of all capital child-rape statutes.

That sweeping holding is also not justified by the Court's concerns about the reliability of the testimony of child victims. First, the Eighth Amendment provides a poor vehicle for addressing problems regarding the admissibility or reliability of evidence, and problems presented by the testimony of child victims are not unique to capital cases. Second, concerns about the reliability of the testimony of child witnesses are not present in every child-rape case. In the case before us, for example, there was undisputed medical evidence that the victim was brutally raped, as well as strong independent evidence that petitioner was the perpetrator. Third, if the Court's evidentiary concerns have Eighth Amendment relevance, they could be addressed by allowing the death penalty in only those child-rape cases in which the independent evidence is sufficient to prove all the elements needed for conviction and imposition of a death sentence. There is precedent for requiring special corroboration in certain criminal cases. For example, some jurisdictions do not allow a conviction based on the uncorroborated testimony of an accomplice. A State wishing to permit the death penalty in child-rape cases could impose an analogous corroboration requirement.

C

After all the arguments noted above are put aside, what is left? What remaining grounds does the Court provide to justify its independent judgment that the death penalty for child rape is categorically unacceptable? I see two.

1

The first is the proposition that we should be "most hesitant before interpreting the Eighth Amendment to allow the *extension* of the death penalty." (Emphasis added.) But holding that the Eighth Amendment does not categorically prohibit the death penalty for the rape of a young child would not "extend" or "expand" the death penalty. Laws enacted by the state legislatures are presumptively constitutional, and until today, this Court has not held that capital child rape laws are unconstitutional. Consequently, upholding the constitutionality of such a law would not "extend" or "expand" the death penalty; rather, it would confirm the status of presumptive constitutionality that such laws have enjoyed up to this point. And in any event, this

Court has previously made it clear that "[t]he Eighth Amendment is not a ratchet, whereby a temporary consensus on leniency for a particular crime fixes a permanent constitutional maximum, disabling States from giving effect to altered beliefs and responding to changed social conditions." *Harmelin v. Michigan*, 501 U.S. 957 (1991) (principal opinion).

2

The Court's final—and, it appears, principal—justification for its holding is that murder, the only crime for which defendants have been executed since this Court's 1976 death penalty decisions, is unique in its moral depravity and in the severity of the injury that it inflicts on the victim and the public. But the Court makes little attempt to defend these conclusions.

With respect to the question of moral depravity, is it really true that every person who is convicted of capital murder and sentenced to death is more morally depraved than every child rapist? Consider the following two cases. In the first, a defendant robs a convenience store and watches as his accomplice shoots the store owner. The defendant acts recklessly, but was not the triggerman and did not intend the killing. See, *e.g., Tison v. Arizona*, 481 U.S. 137 (1987). In the second case, a previously convicted child rapist kidnaps, repeatedly rapes, and tortures multiple child victims. Is it clear that the first defendant is more morally depraved than the second?

The Court's decision here stands in stark contrast to *Atkins* and *Roper*, in which the Court concluded that characteristics of the affected defendants—mental retardation in *Atkins* and youth in *Roper*—diminished their culpability. Nor is this case comparable to *Enmund v. Florida*, 458 U.S. 782 (1982), in which the Court held that the Eighth Amendment prohibits the death penalty where the defendant participated in a robbery during which a murder was committed but did not personally intend for lethal force to be used. I have no doubt that, under the prevailing standards of our society, robbery, the crime that the petitioner in *Enmund* intended to commit, does not evidence the same degree of moral depravity as the brutal rape of a young child. Indeed, I have little doubt that, in the eyes of ordinary Americans, the very worst child rapists—predators who seek out and inflict serious physical and emotional injury on defenseless young children—are the epitome of moral depravity.

With respect to the question of the harm caused by the rape of child in relation to the harm caused by murder, it is certainly true that the loss of human life represents a unique harm, but that does not explain why other grievous harms are insufficient to permit a death sentence. And the Court does not take the position that no harm other than the loss of life is sufficient. The Court takes pains to limit its holding to "crimes against individual persons" and to exclude "offenses against the State," a category that the Court stretches—without explanation—to include "drug kingpin activity." But the Court makes no effort to explain why the harm caused by such crimes is necessarily greater than the harm caused by the rape of young children. This is puzzling in light of the Court's acknowledgment that "[r]ape has a permanent psychological, emotional, and sometimes physical impact on the child." As the Court aptly recognizes, "[w]e cannot dismiss the years of long anguish that must be endured by the victim of child rape."

The rape of any victim inflicts great injury, and "[s]ome victims are so grievously injured physically or psychologically that life *is* beyond repair." *Coker* (opinion of Powell, J.) "The immaturity and vulnerability of a child, both physically and psychologically, adds a devastating dimension to rape that is not present when an adult is raped." Meister, *Murdering Innocence: The Constitutionality of Capital Child Rape Statutes*, 45 Ariz. L. Rev. 197 (2003). Long-term studies show that sexual abuse is "grossly intrusive in the lives of children and is harmful to their normal psychological, emotional and sexual development in ways which no just or humane society can tolerate." C. Bagley & K. King, Child Sexual Abuse: The Search for Healing (1990).

It has been estimated that as many as 40% of 7- to 13-year-old sexual assault victims are considered "seriously disturbed." A. Lurigio, M. Jones, & B. Smith, *Child Sexual Abuse: Its Causes, Consequences, and Implications for Probation Practice*, 59 Sep Fed. Probation 69 (1995). Psychological problems include sudden school failure, unprovoked crying, dissociation, depression, insomnia, sleep disturbances, nightmares, feelings of guilt and inferiority, and self-destructive behavior, including an increased incidence of suicide.

The deep problems that afflict child-rape victims often become society's problems as well. Commentators have noted correlations between childhood sexual abuse and later problems such as substance abuse, dangerous sexual behaviors or dysfunction, inability to relate to others on an interpersonal level, and psychiatric illness. Victims of child rape are nearly 5 times more likely than nonvictims to be arrested for sex crimes and nearly 30 times more likely to be arrested for prostitution.

The harm that is caused to the victims and to society at large by the worst child rapists is grave. It is the judgment of the Louisiana lawmakers and those in an increasing number of other States that these harms justify the death penalty. The Court provides no cogent explanation why this legislative judgment should be overridden. Conclusory references to "decency," "moderation," "restraint," "full progress," and "moral judgment" are not enough.

III

In summary, the Court holds that the Eighth Amendment categorically rules out the death penalty in even the most extreme cases of child rape even though: (1) This holding is not supported by the original meaning of the Eighth Amendment; (2) neither *Coker* nor any other prior precedent commands this result; (3) there are no reliable "objective indicia" of a "national consensus" in support of the Court's position; (4) sustaining the constitutionality of the state law before us would not "extend" or "expand" the death penalty; (5) this Court has previously rejected the proposition that the Eighth Amendment is a one-way ratchet that prohibits legislatures from adopting new capital punishment statutes to meet new problems; (6) the worst child rapists exhibit the epitome of moral depravity; and (7) child rape inflicts grievous injury on victims and on society in general.

The party attacking the constitutionality of a state statute bears the "heavy burden" of establishing that the law is unconstitutional. That burden has not been discharged here, and I would therefore affirm the decision of the Louisiana Supreme Court.

Note

The Federal Death Penalty. As a result of the enactment of the Federal Death Penalty Act of 1994 (see 18 U.S.C. §§ 3591–3598), federal law now authorizes the death penalty for a wide range of homicides, including a number of categories of unintentional killings. In addition, federal law authorizes the death penalty for four categories of non-homicidal crimes: treason (18 U.S.C. § 2381); espionage (18 U.S.C. § 794); drug trafficking in large amounts (18 U.S.C. § 3591(b)(1)); and attempted murder of a public officer, juror or witness by a major drug trafficker (18 U.S.C. § 3591(b)(2)). Would the death penalty be constitutional for any of these non-homicidal crimes?

Not only does the Act raise proportionality concerns, but it has been challenged on other constitutional grounds as well. In *United States v. Quinones*, 196 F.Supp.2d 416 (S.D.N.Y. 2002) and 205 F.Supp.2d 256 (S.D.N.Y. 2002), the district court held the Act unconstitutional on substantive and procedural process grounds:

> "In brief, the Court [finds] that the best available evidence indicates that, on the one hand, innocent people are sentenced to death with materially greater frequency than was previously supposed and that, on the other hand, convincing proof of their innocence often does not emerge until long after their convictions. It is therefore fully foreseeable that in enforcing the death penalty a meaningful number of innocent people will be executed who otherwise would eventually be able to prove their innocence. It follows that implementation of the Federal Death Penalty Act not only deprives innocent people of a significant opportunity to prove their innocence, and thereby violates procedural due process, but also creates an undue risk of executing innocent people, and thereby violates substantive due process."

205 F.Supp.2d at 257. The decision was reversed on appeal. *United States v. Quinones*, 313 F.3d 49 (2nd Cir. 2002). In *United States v. Fell*, 217 F. Supp. 2d 469 (D. Vt. 2002), the district court held the Act unconstitutional on procedural grounds because the relaxed evidentiary standards at the penalty phase, where the jury was required to make the death eligibility determination, violated defendants' confrontation and due process rights. That decision was vacated. *United States v. Fell*, 360 F.3d 135 (2nd Cir. 2004).

McCleskey v. Kemp

481 U.S. 279, 107 S. Ct. 1756 (1987)

Justice Powell delivered the opinion of the Court.

This case presents the question whether a complex statistical study that indicates a risk that racial considerations enter into capital sentencing determinations proves that petitioner McCleskey's capital sentence is unconstitutional under the Eighth or Fourteenth Amendment.

I

McCleskey, a black man, was convicted of two counts of armed robbery and one count of murder in the Superior Court of Fulton County, Georgia, on October 12, 1978. McCleskey's convictions arose out of the robbery of a furniture store and the killing of a white police officer during the course of the robbery. The evidence at trial indicated that McCleskey and three accomplices planned and carried out the robbery. All four were armed. McCleskey entered the front of the store while the other three entered the rear. McCleskey secured the front of the store by rounding up the customers and forcing them to lie face down on the floor. The other three rounded up the employees in the rear and tied them up with tape. The manager was forced at gunpoint to turn over the store receipts, his watch, and $6. During the course of the robbery, a police officer, answering a silent alarm, entered the store through the front door. As he was walking down the center aisle of the store, two shots were fired. Both struck the officer. One hit him in the face and killed him.

Several weeks later, McCleskey was arrested in connection with an unrelated offense. He confessed that he had participated in the furniture store robbery, but denied that he had shot the police officer. At trial, the State introduced evidence that at least one of the bullets that struck the officer was fired from a .38 caliber Rossi revolver. This description matched the description of the gun that McCleskey had carried during the robbery. The State also introduced the testimony of two witnesses who had heard McCleskey admit to the shooting.

The jury convicted McCleskey of murder. At the penalty hearing, the jury heard arguments as to the appropriate sentence. Under Georgia law, the jury could not consider imposing the death penalty unless it found beyond a reasonable doubt that the murder was accompanied by one of the statutory aggravating circumstances. The jury in this case found two aggravating circumstances to exist beyond a reasonable doubt: the murder was committed during the course of an armed robbery; and the murder was committed upon a peace officer engaged in the performance of his duties. In making its decision whether to impose the death sentence, the jury considered the mitigating and aggravating circumstances of McCleskey's conduct. McCleskey offered no mitigating evidence. The jury recommended that he be sentenced to death on the murder charge and to consecutive life sentences on the armed robbery charges. The court followed the jury's recommendation and sentenced McCleskey to death.

On appeal, the Supreme Court of Georgia affirmed the convictions and the sentences. This Court denied a petition for a writ of certiorari. The Superior Court of Fulton County denied McCleskey's extraordinary motion for a new trial. McCleskey then filed a petition for a writ of habeas corpus in the Superior Court of Butts County. After holding an evidentiary hearing, the Superior Court denied relief. The Supreme Court of Georgia denied McCleskey's application for a certificate of probable cause to appeal the Superior Court's denial of his petition, and this Court again denied certiorari.

McCleskey next filed a petition for a writ of habeas corpus in the Federal District Court for the Northern District of Georgia. His petition raised 18 claims, one of which was that the Georgia capital sentencing process is administered in a racially discriminatory manner in violation of the Eighth and Fourteenth Amendments to the United States Constitution. In support of his claim, McCleskey proffered a statistical study performed by Professors David C. Baldus, Charles Pulaski, and George Woodworth (the Baldus study) that purports to show a disparity in the imposition of the death sentence in Georgia based on the race of the murder victim and, to a lesser extent, the race of the defendant. The Baldus study is actually two sophisticated statistical studies that examine over 2,000 murder cases that occurred in Georgia during the 1970's. The raw numbers collected by Professor Baldus indicate that defendants charged with killing white persons received the death penalty in 11% of the cases, but defendants charged with killing blacks received the death penalty in only 1% of the cases. The raw numbers also indicate a reverse racial disparity according to the race of the defendant: 4% of the black defendants received the death penalty, as opposed to 7% of the white defendants.

Baldus also divided the cases according to the combination of the race of the defendant and the race of the victim. He found that the death penalty was assessed in 22% of the cases involving black defendants and white victims; 8% of the cases involving white defendants and white victims; 1% of the cases involving black defendants and black victims; and 3% of the cases involving white defendants and black victims. Similarly, Baldus found that prosecutors sought the death penalty in 70% of the cases involving black defendants and white victims; 32% of the cases involving white defendants and white victims; 15% of the cases involving black defendants and black victims; and 19% of the cases involving white defendants and black victims.

Baldus subjected his data to an extensive analysis, taking account of 230 variables that could have explained the disparities on nonracial grounds. One of his models concludes that, even after taking account of 39 nonracial variables, defendants charged with killing white victims were 4.3 times as likely to receive a death sentence as defendants charged with killing blacks. According to this model, black defendants were 1.1 times as likely to receive a death sentence as other defendants. Thus, the Baldus study indicates that black defendants, such as McCleskey, who kill white victims have the greatest likelihood of receiving the death penalty.[5]

5. Baldus' 230-variable model divided cases into eight different ranges, according to the estimated aggravation level of the offense. Baldus argued in his testimony to the District Court that the effects of racial bias were most striking in the midrange cases. "When the cases become tremendously aggravated so that everybody would agree that if we're going to have a death sentence, these are the cases that should get it, the race effects go away. It's only in the mid-range of cases where the decision-makers have a real choice as to what to do. If there's room for the exercise of discretion, then the [racial] factors begin to play a role." Under this model, Baldus found that 14.4% of the black-victim midrange cases received the death penalty, and 34.4% of the white-victim cases received the death penalty.

The District Court held an extensive evidentiary hearing on McCleskey's petition.... It concluded that McCleskey's "statistics do not demonstrate a prima facie case in support of the contention that the death penalty was imposed upon him because of his race, because of the race of the victim, or because of any Eighth Amendment concern." As to McCleskey's Fourteenth Amendment claim, the court found that the methodology of the Baldus study was flawed in several respects. Because of these defects, the court held that the Baldus study "fail[ed] to contribute anything of value" to McCleskey's claim. Accordingly, the court denied the petition insofar as it was based upon the Baldus study.

...

II

McCleskey's first claim is that the Georgia capital punishment statute violates the Equal Protection Clause of the Fourteenth Amendment.[7] He argues that race has infected the administration of Georgia's statute in two ways: persons who murder whites are more likely to be sentenced to death than persons who murder blacks, and black murderers are more likely to be sentenced to death than white murderers.[8] As a black defendant who killed a white victim, McCleskey claims that the Baldus study demonstrates that he was discriminated against because of his race and because of the race of his victim. In its broadest form, McCleskey's claim of discrimination extends to every actor in the Georgia capital sentencing process, from the prosecutor who sought the death penalty and the jury that imposed the sentence, to the State itself that enacted the capital punishment statute and allows it to remain in effect despite its allegedly discriminatory application.

[The Court rejected McCleskey's Equal Protection claim because his statistical showing failed to establish that either the jury, in deciding his case, or the legislature, in enacting or retaining the state's death penalty scheme, was acting with a "discriminatory purpose."]

---

7. Although the District Court rejected the findings of the Baldus study as flawed, the Court of Appeals assumed that the study is valid and reached the constitutional issues. Accordingly, those issues are before us. As did the Court of Appeals, we assume the study is valid statistically without reviewing the factual findings of the District Court. Our assumption that the Baldus study is statistically valid does not include the assumption that the study shows that racial considerations actually enter into any sentencing decisions in Georgia. Even a sophisticated multiple-regression analysis such as the Baldus study can only demonstrate a risk that the factor of race entered into some capital sentencing decisions and a necessarily lesser risk that race entered into any particular sentencing decision.

8. Although McCleskey has standing to claim that he suffers discrimination because of his own race, the State argues that he has no standing to contend that he was discriminated against on the basis of his victim's race. While it is true that we are reluctant to recognize "standing to assert the rights of third persons," this does not appear to be the nature of McCleskey's claim. He does not seek to assert some right of his victim, or the rights of black murder victims in general. Rather, McCleskey argues that application of the State's statute has created a classification that is "an irrational exercise of governmental power," because it is not "necessary to the accomplishment of some permissible state objective." It would violate the Equal Protection Clause for a State to base enforcement of its criminal laws on "an unjustifiable standard such as race, religion, or other arbitrary classification." Because McCleskey raises such a claim, he has standing.

III

McCleskey also argues that the Baldus study demonstrates that the Georgia capital sentencing system violates the Eighth Amendment.

...

B

Although our decision in *Gregg* as to the facial validity of the Georgia capital punishment statute appears to foreclose McCleskey's disproportionality argument, he further contends that the Georgia capital punishment system is arbitrary and capricious in application, and therefore his sentence is excessive, because racial considerations may influence capital sentencing decisions in Georgia. We now address this claim.

To evaluate McCleskey's challenge, we must examine exactly what the Baldus study may show. Even Professor Baldus does not contend that his statistics prove that race enters into any capital sentencing decisions or that race was a factor in McCleskey's particular case.[29] Statistics at most may show only a likelihood that a particular factor entered into some decisions. There is, of course, some risk of racial prejudice influencing a jury's decision in a criminal case. There are similar risks that other kinds of prejudice will influence other criminal trials. The question "is at what point that risk becomes constitutionally unacceptable," *Turner v. Murray*, 476 U.S. 28 (1986). McCleskey asks us to accept the likelihood allegedly shown by the Baldus study as the constitutional measure of an unacceptable risk of racial prejudice influencing capital sentencing decisions. This we decline to do.

Because of the risk that the factor of race may enter the criminal justice process, we have engaged in "unceasing efforts" to eradicate racial prejudice from our criminal justice system. *Batson v. Kentucky*, 476 U.S. 79 (1986).[30] Our efforts have been guided by our recognition that "the inestimable privilege of trial by jury ... is a vital principle, underlying the whole administration of criminal justice." *Ex parte Milligan*, 4 Wall. 2 (1866). Thus, it is the jury that is a criminal defendant's fundamental "protection of life and liberty against race or color prejudice." Specifically, a capital sentencing jury representative of a criminal defendant's community assures a "diffused impar-

---

29. According to Professor Baldus:

"McCleskey's case falls in [a] grey area where ... you would find the greatest likelihood that some inappropriate consideration may have come to bear on the decision.

"In an analysis of this type, obviously one cannot say that we can say to a moral certainty what it was that influenced the decision. We can't do that."

30. This Court has repeatedly stated that prosecutorial discretion cannot be exercised on the basis of race. Nor can a prosecutor exercise peremptory challenges on the basis of race. More generally, this Court has condemned state efforts to exclude blacks from grand and petit juries.

Other protections apply to the trial and jury deliberation process. Widespread bias in the community can make a change of venue constitutionally required. The Constitution prohibits racially biased prosecutorial arguments. If the circumstances of a particular case indicate a significant likelihood that racial bias may influence a jury, the Constitution requires questioning as to such bias. Finally, in a capital sentencing hearing, a defendant convicted of an interracial murder is entitled to such questioning without regard to the circumstances of the particular case.

tiality" in the jury's task of "express[ing] the conscience of the community on the ultimate question of life or death," *Witherspoon v. Illinois*, 391 U.S. 510 (1968).

Individual jurors bring to their deliberations "qualities of human nature and varieties of human experience, the range of which is unknown and perhaps unknowable." *Peters v. Kiff*, 407 U.S. 493 (1972). The capital sentencing decision requires the individual jurors to focus their collective judgment on the unique characteristics of a particular criminal defendant. It is not surprising that such collective judgments often are difficult to explain. But the inherent lack of predictability of jury decisions does not justify their condemnation. On the contrary, it is the jury's function to make the difficult and uniquely human judgments that defy codification and that "buil[d] discretion, equity, and flexibility into a legal system." H. Kalven & H. Zeisel, The American Jury 498 (1966).

McCleskey's argument that the Constitution condemns the discretion allowed decisionmakers in the Georgia capital sentencing system is antithetical to the fundamental role of discretion in our criminal justice system. Discretion in the criminal justice system offers substantial benefits to the criminal defendant. Not only can a jury decline to impose the death sentence, it can decline to convict or choose to convict of a lesser offense. Whereas decisions against a defendant's interest may be reversed by the trial judge or on appeal, these discretionary exercises of leniency are final and unreviewable. Similarly, the capacity of prosecutorial discretion to provide individualized justice is "firmly entrenched in American law." 2 W. LaFave & D. Israel, Criminal Procedure § 13.2(a). As we have noted, a prosecutor can decline to charge, offer a plea bargain, or decline to seek a death sentence in any particular case. Of course, "the power to be lenient [also] is the power to discriminate," K. Davis, Discretionary Justice, but a capital punishment system that did not allow for discretionary acts of leniency "would be totally alien to our notions of criminal justice." *Gregg.*

C

At most, the Baldus study indicates a discrepancy that appears to correlate with race. Apparent disparities in sentencing are an inevitable part of our criminal justice system. The discrepancy indicated by the Baldus study is "a far cry from the major systemic defects identified in *Furman*."[36] *Pulley v. Harris*, 465 U.S. 37 (1984). As this Court has recognized, any mode for determining guilt or punishment "has its weaknesses and the potential for misuse." Specifically, "there can be 'no perfect procedure for deciding in which cases governmental authority should be used to impose death.'" *Zant v. Stephens*, 462 U.S. 862 (1983) (quoting *Lockett v. Ohio* (plurality opinion of Burger, C. J.)). Despite these imperfections, our consistent rule has been that constitutional guarantees are met when "the mode [for determining guilt or punishment] itself has been surrounded with safeguards to make it as fair as possible." *Singer v.*

36. The Baldus study in fact confirms that the Georgia system results in a reasonable level of proportionality among the class of murderers eligible for the death penalty. As Professor Baldus confirmed, the system sorts out cases where the sentence of death is highly likely and highly unlikely, leaving a midrange of cases where the imposition of the death penalty in any particular case is less predictable.

United States, 380 U.S. 24 (1965). Where the discretion that is fundamental to our criminal process is involved, we decline to assume that what is unexplained is invidious. In light of the safeguards designed to minimize racial bias in the process, the fundamental value of jury trial in our criminal justice system, and the benefits that discretion provides to criminal defendants, we hold that the Baldus study does not demonstrate a constitutionally significant risk of racial bias affecting the Georgia capital sentencing process.[37]

V

Two additional concerns inform our decision in this case. First, McCleskey's claim, taken to its logical conclusion, throws into serious question the principles that underlie our entire criminal justice system. The Eighth Amendment is not limited in application to capital punishment, but applies to all penalties. Thus, if we accepted McCleskey's claim that racial bias has impermissibly tainted the capital sentencing decision, we could soon be faced with similar claims as to other types of penalty. Moreover, the claim that his sentence rests on the irrelevant factor of race easily could be extended to apply to claims based on unexplained discrepancies that correlate to membership in other minority groups, and even to gender. Similarly, since McCleskey's claim relates to the race of his victim, other claims could apply with equally logical force to statistical disparities that correlate with the race or sex of other actors in the criminal justice system, such as defense attorneys or judges. Also, there is no logical reason that such a claim need be limited to racial or sexual bias. If arbitrary and capricious punishment is the touchstone under the Eighth Amendment, such a claim could—at least in theory—be based upon any arbitrary variable, such as the defendant's facial characteristics, or the physical attractiveness of the defendant or the victim, that some statistical study indicates may be influential in jury decisionmaking. As these examples illustrate, there is no limiting principle to the type of challenge brought by McCleskey. The Constitution does not require that a State eliminate any demonstrable disparity that correlates with a potentially irrelevant factor in order to operate a criminal justice system that includes capital punishment. As we have stated specifically in the context of capital punishment, the Constitution does not "plac[e] totally unrealistic conditions on its use." *Gregg v. Georgia*.

---

37. ... The dissent repeatedly emphasizes the need for "a uniquely high degree of rationality in imposing the death penalty." Again, no suggestion is made as to how greater "rationality" could be achieved under any type of statute that authorizes capital punishment. The *Gregg*-type statute imposes unprecedented safeguards in the special context of capital punishment. These include: (i) a bifurcated sentencing proceeding; (ii) the threshold requirement of one or more aggravating circumstances; and (iii) mandatory State Supreme Court review. All of these are administered pursuant to this Court's decisions interpreting the limits of the Eighth Amendment on the imposition of the death penalty, and all are subject to ultimate review by this Court. These ensure a degree of care in the imposition of the sentence of death that can be described only as unique. Given these safeguards already inherent in the imposition and review of capital sentences, the dissent's call for greater rationality is no less than a claim that a capital punishment system cannot be administered in accord with the Constitution. As we reiterate, *infra*, the requirement of heightened rationality in the imposition of capital punishment does not "plac[e] totally unrealistic conditions on its use."

Second, McCleskey's arguments are best presented to the legislative bodies. It is not the responsibility—or indeed even the right—of this Court to determine the appropriate punishment for particular crimes. It is the legislatures, the elected representatives of the people, that are "constituted to respond to the will and consequently the moral values of the people." *Furman v. Georgia* (Burger, C. J., dissenting). Legislatures also are better qualified to weigh and "evaluate the results of statistical studies in terms of their own local conditions and with a flexibility of approach that is not available to the courts," *Gregg v. Georgia.* Capital punishment is now the law in more than two-thirds of our States. It is the ultimate duty of courts to determine on a case-by-case basis whether these laws are applied consistently with the Constitution. Despite McCleskey's wide-ranging arguments that basically challenge the validity of capital punishment in our multiracial society, the only question before us is whether in his case the law of Georgia was properly applied. We agree with the District Court and the Court of Appeals for the Eleventh Circuit that this was carefully and correctly done in this case.

VI

Accordingly, we affirm the judgment of the Court of Appeals for the Eleventh Circuit.

It is so ordered.

Justice Brennan, with whom Justice Marshall joins, and with whom Justice Blackmun and Justice Stevens join in all but Part I, dissenting.

...

II

At some point in this case, Warren McCleskey doubtless asked his lawyer whether a jury was likely to sentence him to die. A candid reply to this question would have been disturbing. First, counsel would have to tell McCleskey that few of the details of the crime or of McCleskey's past criminal conduct were more important than the fact that his victim was white. Furthermore, counsel would feel bound to tell McCleskey that defendants charged with killing white victims in Georgia are 4.3 times as likely to be sentenced to death as defendants charged with killing blacks. In addition, frankness would compel the disclosure that it was more likely than not that the race of McCleskey's victim would determine whether he received a death sentence: 6 of every 11 defendants convicted of killing a white person would not have received the death penalty if their victims had been black, while, among defendants with aggravating and mitigating factors comparable to McCleskey's, 20 of every 34 would not have been sentenced to die if their victims had been black. Finally, the assessment would not be complete without the information that cases involving black defendants and white victims are more likely to result in a death sentence than cases featuring any other racial combination of defendant and victim. The story could be told in a variety of ways, but McCleskey could not fail to grasp its essential narrative line: there was a significant chance that race would play a prominent role in determining if he lived or died.

The Court today holds that Warren McCleskey's sentence was constitutionally imposed. It finds no fault in a system in which lawyers must tell their clients that race casts a large shadow on the capital sentencing process. The Court arrives at this conclusion by stating that the Baldus study cannot "prove that race enters into any capital sentencing decisions or that race was a factor in McCleskey's particular case." Since, according to Professor Baldus, we cannot say "to a moral certainty" that race influenced a decision, we can identify only "a likelihood that a particular factor entered into some decisions," and "a discrepancy that appears to correlate with race." This "likelihood" and "discrepancy," holds the Court, is insufficient to establish a constitutional violation. The Court reaches this conclusion by placing four factors on the scales opposite McCleskey's evidence: the desire to encourage sentencing discretion, the existence of "statutory safeguards" in the Georgia scheme, the fear of encouraging widespread challenges to other sentencing decisions, and the limits of the judicial role. The Court's evaluation of the significance of petitioner's evidence is fundamentally at odds with our consistent concern for rationality in capital sentencing, and the considerations that the majority invokes to discount that evidence cannot justify ignoring its force.

III

A

It is important to emphasize at the outset that the Court's observation that McCleskey cannot prove the influence of race on any particular sentencing decision is irrelevant in evaluating his Eighth Amendment claim. Since *Furman v. Georgia*, 408 U.S. 238 (1972), the Court has been concerned with the risk of the imposition of an arbitrary sentence, rather than the proven fact of one. *Furman* held that the death penalty "may not be imposed under sentencing procedures that create a substantial risk that the punishment will be inflicted in an arbitrary and capricious manner." *Godfrey v. Georgia*, 446 U.S. 420 (1980). As Justice O'Connor observed in *Caldwell v. Mississippi*, 472 U.S. 320 (1985), a death sentence must be struck down when the circumstances under which it has been imposed "creat[e] an unacceptable *risk* that 'the death penalty [may have been] meted out arbitrarily or capriciously' or through 'whim or mistake.'" (Emphasis added.) This emphasis on risk acknowledges the difficulty of divining the jury's motivation in an individual case. In addition, it reflects the fact that concern for arbitrariness focuses on the rationality of the system as a whole, and that a system that features a significant probability that sentencing decisions are influenced by impermissible considerations cannot be regarded as rational. As we said in *Gregg v. Georgia*, 428 U.S. 153 (1976), "the petitioner looks to the sentencing system as a whole (as the Court did in *Furman* and we do today)": a constitutional violation is established if a plaintiff demonstrates a "*pattern* of arbitrary and capricious sentencing." (Emphasis added.) (joint opinion of Stewart, Powell, and Stevens, JJ.)

...

B

The Baldus study indicates that, after taking into account some 230 nonracial factors that might legitimately influence a sentencer, the jury more likely than not would have spared McCleskey's life had his victim been black. The study distinguishes between those cases in which (1) the jury exercises virtually no discretion because the strength or weakness of aggravating factors usually suggests that only one outcome is appropriate;[2] and (2) cases reflecting an "intermediate" level of aggravation, in which the jury has considerable discretion in choosing a sentence.[3] McCleskey's case falls into the intermediate range. In such cases, death is imposed in 34% of white-victim crimes and 14% of black-victim crimes, a difference of 139% in the rate of imposition of the death penalty. In other words, just under 59%—almost 6 in 10—defendants comparable to McCleskey would not have received the death penalty if their victims had been black.

Furthermore, even examination of the sentencing system as a whole, factoring in those cases in which the jury exercises little discretion, indicates the influence of race on capital sentencing. For the Georgia system as a whole, race accounts for a six percentage point difference in the rate at which capital punishment is imposed. Since death is imposed in 11% of all white-victim cases, the rate in comparably aggravated black-victim cases is 5%. The rate of capital sentencing in a white-victim case is thus 120% greater than the rate in a black-victim case. Put another way, over half—55%—of defendants in white-victim crimes in Georgia would not have been sentenced to die if their victims had been black. Of the more than 200 variables potentially relevant to a sentencing decision, race of the victim is a powerful explanation for variation in death sentence rates—as powerful as nonracial aggravating factors such as a prior murder conviction or acting as the principal planner of the homicide.

These adjusted figures are only the most conservative indication of the risk that race will influence the death sentences of defendants in Georgia. Data unadjusted for the mitigating or aggravating effect of other factors show an even more pronounced disparity by race. The capital sentencing rate for all white-victim cases was almost 11 times greater than the rate for black-victim cases. Furthermore, blacks who kill whites are sentenced to death at nearly 22 times the rate of blacks who kill blacks, and more than 7 times the rate of whites who kill blacks. In addition, prosecutors seek the death penalty for 70% of black defendants with white victims, but for only 15% of black defendants with black victims, and only 19% of white defendants with black victims. Since our decision upholding the Georgia capital sentencing system in *Gregg*, the State has executed seven persons. All of the seven were convicted of killing whites, and six of the seven executed were black. Such execution figures are especially striking in light of the fact that, during the period encompassed by the Baldus study, only 9.2% of Georgia homicides involved black defendants and white victims, while 60.7% involved black victims.

2. The first two and the last of the study's eight case categories represent those cases in which the jury typically sees little leeway in deciding on a sentence. Cases in the first two categories are those that feature aggravating factors so minimal that juries imposed no death sentences in the 88 cases with these factors during the period of the study. Cases in the eighth category feature aggravating factors so extreme that the jury imposed the death penalty in 88% of the 58 cases with these factors in the same period.

3. In the five categories characterized as intermediate, the rate at which the death penalty was imposed ranged from 8% to 41%. The overall rate for the 326 cases in these categories was 20%.

...

IV

The Court cites four reasons for shrinking from the implications of McCleskey's evidence: the desirability of discretion for actors in the criminal justice system, the existence of statutory safeguards against abuse of that discretion, the potential consequences for broader challenges to criminal sentencing, and an understanding of the contours of the judicial role. While these concerns underscore the need for sober deliberation, they do not justify rejecting evidence as convincing as McCleskey has presented.

The Court maintains that petitioner's claim "is antithetical to the fundamental role of discretion in our criminal justice system." It states that "where the discretion that is fundamental to our criminal process is involved, we decline to assume that what is unexplained is invidious." Reliance on race in imposing capital punishment, however, is antithetical to the very rationale for granting sentencing discretion. Discretion is a means, not an end. It is bestowed in order to permit the sentencer to "trea[t] each defendant in a capital case with that degree of respect due the uniqueness of the individual." *Lockett v. Ohio*, 438 U.S. 586 (1978). The decision to impose the punishment of death must be based on a "particularized consideration of relevant aspects of the character and record of each convicted defendant." *Woodson v. North Carolina*, 428 U.S. 280 (1976). Failure to conduct such an individualized moral inquiry "treats all persons convicted of a designated offense not as unique individual human beings, but as members of a faceless, undifferentiated mass to be subjected to the blind infliction of the penalty of death."

Considering the race of a defendant or victim in deciding if the death penalty should be imposed is completely at odds with this concern that an individual be evaluated as a unique human being. Decisions influenced by race rest in part on a categorical assessment of the worth of human beings according to color, insensitive to whatever qualities the individuals in question may possess. Enhanced willingness to impose the death sentence on black defendants, or diminished willingness to render such a sentence when blacks are victims, reflects a devaluation of the lives of black persons. When confronted with evidence that race more likely than not plays such a role in a capital sentencing system, it is plainly insufficient to say that the importance of discretion demands that the risk be higher before we will act—for in such a case the very end that discretion is designed to serve is being undermined.

Our desire for individualized moral judgments may lead us to accept some inconsistencies in sentencing outcomes. Since such decisions are not reducible to mathematical formulae, we are willing to assume that a certain degree of variation reflects the fact that no two defendants are completely alike. There is thus a presumption that actors in the criminal justice system exercise their discretion in responsible fashion, and we do not automatically infer that sentencing patterns that do not comport with ideal rationality are suspect.

As we made clear in *Batson v. Kentucky*, 476 U.S. 79 (1986), however, that presumption is rebuttable. *Batson* dealt with another arena in which considerable discretion traditionally has been afforded, the exercise of peremptory challenges. Those challenges are normally exercised without any indication whatsoever of the grounds for doing so. The rationale for this deference has been a belief that the unique characteristics of particular prospective jurors may raise concern on the part of the prosecution or defense, despite the fact that counsel may not be able to articulate that concern in a manner sufficient to support exclusion for cause. As with sentencing, therefore, peremptory challenges are justified as an occasion for particularized determinations related to specific individuals, and, as with sentencing, we presume that such challenges normally are not made on the basis of a factor such as race. As we said in *Batson*, however, such features do not justify imposing a "crippling burden of proof," in order to rebut that presumption. The Court in this case apparently seeks to do just that. On the basis of the need for individualized decisions, it rejects evidence, drawn from the most sophisticated capital sentencing analysis ever performed, that reveals that race more likely than not infects capital sentencing decisions. The Court's position converts a rebuttable presumption into a virtually conclusive one.

The Court also declines to find McCleskey's evidence sufficient in view of "the safeguards designed to minimize racial bias in the [capital sentencing] process." *Gregg v. Georgia* upheld the Georgia capital sentencing statute against a facial challenge which Justice White described in his concurring opinion as based on "simply an assertion of lack of faith" that the system could operate in a fair manner (opinion concurring in judgment). Justice White observed that the claim that prosecutors might act in an arbitrary fashion was "unsupported by any facts," and that prosecutors must be assumed to exercise their charging duties properly "absent facts to the contrary." It is clear that *Gregg* bestowed no permanent approval on the Georgia system. It simply held that the State's statutory safeguards were assumed sufficient to channel discretion without evidence otherwise.

It has now been over 13 years since Georgia adopted the provisions upheld in *Gregg*. Professor Baldus and his colleagues have compiled data on almost 2,500 homicides committed during the period 1973–1979. They have taken into account the influence of 230 nonracial variables, using a multitude of data from the State itself, and have produced striking evidence that the odds of being sentenced to death are significantly greater than average if a defendant is black or his or her victim is white. The challenge to the Georgia system is not speculative or theoretical; it is empirical. As a result, the Court cannot rely on the statutory safeguards in discounting McCleskey's evidence, for it is the very effectiveness of those safeguards that such evidence calls into question. While we may hope that a model of procedural fairness will curb the influence of race on sentencing, "we cannot simply assume that the model works as intended; we must critique its performance in terms of its results." Hubbard, *"Reasonable Levels of Arbitrariness" in Death Sentencing Patterns: A Tragic Perspective on Capital Punishment*, 18 U.C.D. L. Rev. 1113 (1985).

The Court next states that its unwillingness to regard petitioner's evidence as sufficient is based in part on the fear that recognition of McCleskey's claim would open the door to widespread challenges to all aspects of criminal sentencing. Taken on its face, such a statement seems to suggest a fear of too much justice. Yet surely the majority would acknowledge that if striking evidence indicated that other minority groups, or women, or even persons with blond hair, were disproportionately sentenced to death, such a state of affairs would be repugnant to deeply rooted conceptions of fairness. The prospect that there may be more widespread abuse than McCleskey documents may be dismaying, but it does not justify complete abdication of our judicial role. The Constitution was framed fundamentally as a bulwark against governmental power, and preventing the arbitrary administration of punishment is a basic ideal of any society that purports to be governed by the rule of law.

In fairness, the Court's fear that McCleskey's claim is an invitation to descend a slippery slope also rests on the realization that any humanly imposed system of penalties will exhibit some imperfection. Yet to reject McCleskey's powerful evidence on this basis is to ignore both the qualitatively different character of the death penalty and the particular repugnance of racial discrimination, considerations which may properly be taken into account in determining whether various punishments are "cruel and unusual." Furthermore, it fails to take account of the unprecedented refinement and strength of the Baldus study.

It hardly needs reiteration that this Court has consistently acknowledged the uniqueness of the punishment of death. "Death, in its finality, differs more from life imprisonment than a 100-year prison term differs from one of only a year or two. Because of that qualitative difference, there is a corresponding difference in the need for reliability in the determination that death is the appropriate punishment." *Woodson*. Furthermore, the relative interests of the state and the defendant differ dramatically in the death penalty context. The marginal benefits accruing to the state from obtaining the death penalty rather than life imprisonment are considerably less than the marginal difference to the defendant between death and life in prison. Such a disparity is an additional reason for tolerating scant arbitrariness in capital sentencing. Even those who believe that society can impose the death penalty in a manner sufficiently rational to justify its continuation must acknowledge that the level of rationality that is considered satisfactory must be uniquely high. As a result, the degree of arbitrariness that may be adequate to render the death penalty "cruel and unusual" punishment may not be adequate to invalidate lesser penalties. What these relative degrees of arbitrariness might be in other cases need not concern us here; the point is that the majority's fear of wholesale invalidation of criminal sentences is unfounded.

The Court also maintains that accepting McCleskey's claim would pose a threat to all sentencing because of the prospect that a correlation might be demonstrated between sentencing outcomes and other personal characteristics. Again, such a view is indifferent to the considerations that enter into a determination whether punishment is "cruel and unusual." Race is a consideration whose influence is expressly constitutionally proscribed. We have expressed a moral commitment, as embodied in our fundamental law, that this specific characteristic should not be the basis for allotting burdens and benefits. Three constitutional amendments, and numerous statutes, have been prompted specifically by the desire to address the effects of racism. "Over the years, this Court has consistently repudiated 'distinctions between citizens solely because of their ancestry' as being 'odious to a free people whose institutions are founded upon the doctrine of equality.'" *Loving v. Virginia*, 388 U.S. 1 (1967) (quoting *Hirabayashi v. United States*, 320 U.S. 81 (1943)). Furthermore, we have explicitly acknowledged the illegitimacy of race as a consideration in capital sentencing, *Zant v. Stephens*, 462 U.S. 862 (1983). That a decision to impose the death penalty could be influenced by race is thus a particularly repugnant prospect, and evidence that race may play even a modest role in levying a death sentence should be enough to characterize that sentence as "cruel and unusual."

...

Finally, the Court justifies its rejection of McCleskey's claim by cautioning against usurpation of the legislatures' role in devising and monitoring criminal punishment. The Court is, of course, correct to emphasize the gravity of constitutional intervention and the importance that it be sparingly employed. The fact that "capital punishment is now the law in more than two thirds of our States," however, does not diminish the fact that capital punishment is the most awesome act that a State can perform. The judiciary's role in this society counts for little if the use of governmental power to extinguish life does not elicit close scrutiny. It is true that society has a legitimate interest in punishment. Yet, as Alexander Bickel wrote:

> "It is a premise we deduce not merely from the fact of a written constitution but from the history of the race, and ultimately as a moral judgment of the good society, that government should serve not only what we conceive from time to time to be our immediate material needs but also certain enduring values. This in part is what is meant by government under law." The Least Dangerous Branch 24 (1962).

Our commitment to these values requires fidelity to them even when there is temptation to ignore them. Such temptation is especially apt to arise in criminal matters, for those granted constitutional protection in this context are those whom society finds most menacing and opprobrious. Even less sympathetic are those we consider for the sentence of death, for execution "is a way of saying, 'You are not fit for this world, take your chance elsewhere.'" *Furman*, quoting Stephen, Capital Punishments, 69 Fraser's Magazine 753 (1864).

For these reasons, "the methods we employ in the enforcement of our criminal law have aptly been called the measures by which the quality of our civilization may be judged." *Coppedge v. United States*, 369 U.S. 438 (1962). Those whom we would banish from society or from the human community itself often speak in too faint a voice to be heard above society's demand for punishment. It is the particular role of courts to hear these voices, for the Constitution declares that the majoritarian chorus may not alone dictate the conditions of social life. The Court thus fulfills, rather than disrupts, the scheme of separation of powers by closely scrutinizing the imposition of the death penalty, for no decision of a society is more deserving of "sober second thought." Stone, *The Common Law in the United States*, 50 Harv. L. Rev. 4 (1936).

V

At the time our Constitution was framed 200 years ago this year, blacks "had for more than a century before been regarded as beings of an inferior order, and altogether unfit to associate with the white race, either in social or political relations; and so far inferior, that they had no rights which the white man was bound to respect." *Dred Scott v. Sandford*, 19 How. 393 (1857). Only 130 years ago, this Court relied on these observations to deny American citizenship to blacks. A mere three generations ago, this Court sanctioned racial segregation, stating that "if one race be inferior to the other socially, the Constitution of the United States cannot put them upon the same plane." *Plessy v. Ferguson*, 163 U.S. 537 (1896).

In more recent times, we have sought to free ourselves from the burden of this history. Yet it has been scarcely a generation since this Court's first decision striking down racial segregation, and barely two decades since the legislative prohibition of racial discrimination in major domains of national life. These have been honorable steps, but we cannot pretend that in three decades we have completely escaped the grip of a historical legacy spanning centuries. Warren McCleskey's evidence confronts us with the subtle and persistent influence of the past. His message is a disturbing one to a society that has formally repudiated racism, and a frustrating one to a Nation accustomed to regarding its destiny as the product of its own will. Nonetheless, we ignore him at our peril, for we remain imprisoned by the past as long as we deny its influence in the present.

It is tempting to pretend that minorities on death row share a fate in no way connected to our own, that our treatment of them sounds no echoes beyond the chambers in which they die. Such an illusion is ultimately corrosive, for the reverberations of injustice are not so easily confined. "The destinies of the two races in this country are indissolubly linked together," *Plessy v. Ferguson*, 163 U.S. 537 (Harlan, J., dissenting), and the way in which we choose those who will die reveals the depth of moral commitment among the living.

The Court's decision today will not change what attorneys in Georgia tell other Warren McCleskeys about their chances of execution. Nothing will soften the harsh message they must convey, nor alter the prospect that race undoubtedly will continue to be a topic of discussion. McCleskey's evidence will not have obtained judicial acceptance, but that will not affect what is said on death row. However many criticisms of today's decision may be rendered, these painful conversations will serve as the most eloquent dissents of all.

...

[Dissenting opinion of Blackmun, J., joined by Marshall and Stevens, J.J. and, in part, by Brennan, J., and dissenting opinion of Stevens, J., joined by Blackmun, J., omitted.]

Notes

"Underprotection" of the Black Community. McCleskey's statistics established that, in the application of the death penalty in Georgia, although there was some "overenforcement" against Black defendants, there was far more "underprotection" of Black victims. Professor Randall Kennedy has argued that, historically, the consistent failure of criminal justice officials to treat crimes against Blacks as seriously as crimes against Whites has had more insidious consequences than the discriminatory treatment of Black suspects and defendants:

> Deliberately withholding protection against criminality (or conduct that should be deemed criminal) is one of the most destructive forms of oppression that has been visited upon African-Americans. The specter of the wrongly convicted black defendant rushed to punishment by a racially biased process is haunting ... even worse is racially selective underprotection. This form of discrimination is worse because it has directly and adversely affected more people than have episodic misjudgments of guilt. Racially selective underprotection is also worse in the sense that society is not as well equipped to combat it. Even before the abolition of slavery, officials everywhere acknowledged, at least in principle, that government is obliged to punish for crimes only duly convicted persons, regardless of race. Much more difficult to establish has been the idea that government is obliged to protect blacks from crime on the same terms as it protects whites.

R. Kennedy, Race Crime and the Law (1997), p. 29. Can the criminal justice system address this problem?

The "Inevitability" of Racial Disparities. The Court's suggestion that racial disparities in sentencing are "inevitable" has been challenged by the authors of the Georgia study. See D. Baldus, G. Woodworth & C. Pulaski, Jr., *Reflections on the "Inevitability" of Racial Discrimination in Capital Sentencing and the 'Impossibility' of its Prevention, Detection, and Correction*, 51 Wash. & Lee L. Rev. 357 (1994). They identify at least four possible approaches to dealing with racial discrimination in capital punishment: "(a) narrowing the class of death-eligible cases, (b) requiring standards to limit the exercise of prosecutorial discretion, (c) recognizing claims of racial discrimination in individual cases and evaluating those claims under burdens of proof comparable to those applied in other areas of the law, or (d) abolishing the death penalty." *Id.* at 362, n.7. They conclude that, "[w]hat some may describe as the inevitability of such sentences or the impossibility of preventing, detecting and correcting them reflects, in our judgment, only an unwillingness to make the effort." *Id.* at 419.

Reconsideration by Justice Powell. In 1991, after his retirement from the Court, Justice Powell, the author of *McCleskey v. Kemp*, was asked whether he would change his vote in any case:

> A. Yes, *McCleskey v. Kemp*.
>
> Q. Do you mean you would now accept the argument from statistics?
>
> A. No, I would vote the other way in any capital case.

Q. In *any* capital case?

A. Yes.

Q. Even in *Furman v. Georgia*?

A. Yes. I have come to think that capital punishment should be abolished.

J. Jefferies, Jr., JUSTICE LEWIS F. POWELL, JR. (1994), p. 451.

Reconsideration by Justice Blackmun. Shortly before his retirement from the Court, Justice Blackmun, who had voted to uphold the death penalty in earlier cases (including *Gregg v. Georgia*), also reached the conclusion that the death penalty was unconstitutional.

> From this day forward, I no longer shall tinker with the machinery of death. For more than 20 years I have endeavored—indeed, I have struggled—along with a majority of this Court, to develop procedural and substantive rules that would lend more than the mere appearance of fairness to the death penalty endeavor. Rather than continue to coddle the Court's delusion that the desired level of fairness has been achieved and the need for regulation eviscerated, I feel morally and intellectually obligated simply to concede that the death penalty experiment has failed. It is virtually self-evident to me now that no combination of procedural rules or substantive regulations ever can save the death penalty from its inherent constitutional deficiencies. The basic question—does the system accurately and consistently determine which defendants "deserve" to die?—cannot be answered in the affirmative.... The problem is that the inevitability of factual, legal, and moral error gives us a system that we know must wrongly kill some defendants, a system that fails to deliver the fair, consistent, and reliable sentences of death required by the Constitution.

Callins v. Collins, 510 U.S. 1141, 1145–46 (1994) (Blackmun, J., dissenting from denial of cert.)

The Death Penalty in the International Arena. The United States is among a minority of countries in the world which continue to employ the death penalty for ordinary crimes. (Some countries retain the death penalty only for extraordinary crimes, *i.e.*, treason, crimes during war-time or crimes against humanity.) None of the countries of Western Europe employs the death penalty for ordinary crimes. The overwhelming majority of Latin American countries (including the largest, Brazil and Argentina) do not have the death penalty for ordinary crimes. The death penalty has also been abolished for ordinary crimes in such countries as Australia, Canada, Israel and South Africa. Should the Supreme Court have considered the degree of international acceptance of the death penalty in evaluating "evolving standards of decency"?

Appendix

California Penal Code Provisions

Set forth below are the *current* versions of the substantive California Penal Code sections cited in the cases and problems. Some of the cases in the book concern the application of earlier versions of the sections. Note that, although the majority of crimes are contained in the Penal Code, a number of crimes, including crimes considered in this book, appear in other codes. For example, certain "white collar" crimes appear in the Business & Professions Code; narcotics crimes are defined in the Health & Safety Code; and vehicle-related crimes are set out in the Vehicle Code.

Preliminary Provisions

§7 Words used in this code in the present tense include the future as well as the present; words used in the masculine gender include the feminine and neuter; the singular number includes the plural, and the plural the singular; the word "person" includes a corporation as well as a natural person....

The following words have in this code the signification attached to them in this section, unless otherwise apparent from the context:

1. The word "willfully," when applied to the intent with which an act is done or omitted, implies simply a purpose or willingness to commit the act, or make the omission referred to. It does not require any intent to violate law, or to injure another, or to acquire any advantage.

2. The words "neglect," "negligence," "negligent," and "negligently" import a want of such attention to the nature or probable consequences of the act or omission as a prudent man ordinarily bestows in acting in his own concerns.

...

4. The words "malice" and "maliciously" import a wish to vex, annoy, or injure another person, or an intent to do a wrongful act, established either by proof or presumption of law.

5. The word "knowingly" imports only a knowledge that the facts exist which bring the act or omission with the provisions of this code. It does not require any knowledge of the unlawfulness of such act or omission.

...

10. The word "property" includes both real and personal property.

11. The words "real property" are coextensive with lands, tenements, and hereditaments.

12. The words "personal property" include money, goods, chattels, things in action, and evidences of debt.

. . .

§ 17 (a) A felony is a crime that is punishable with death, by imprisonment in the state prison, or notwithstanding any other provision of law, by imprisonment in a county jail under the provisions of subdivision (h) of Section 1170. Every other crime or public offense is a misdemeanor except those offenses that are classified as infractions.

(b) When a crime is punishable, in the discretion of the court, either by imprisonment in the state prison or imprisonment in the county jail under the provisions of subdivision (h) of Section 1170, or by fine or imprisonment in the county jail, it is a misdemeanor for all purposes under the following circumstances:

(1) After a judgment imposing a punishment other than imprisonment in the state prison or imprisonment in a county jail under the provisions of subdivision (h) of Section 1170.

(2) When the court, upon committing the defendant to the Division of Juvenile Justice, designates the offense to be a misdemeanor.

(3) When the court grants probation to a defendant without imposition of sentence and at the time of granting probation, or on application of the defendant or probation officer thereafter, the court declares the offense to be a misdemeanor.

(4) When the prosecuting attorney files in a court having jurisdiction over misdemeanor offenses a complaint specifying that the offense is a misdemeanor, unless the defendant at the time of his or her arraignment or plea objects to the offense being made a misdemeanor, in which event the complaint shall be amended to charge the felony and the case shall proceed on the felony complaint.

(5) When, at or before the preliminary examination . . . , the magistrate determines that the offense is a misdemeanor, in which event the case shall proceed as if the defendant had been arraigned on a misdemeanor complaint.

. . .

§ 20 In every crime or public offense there must exist a union, or joint operation of act and intent, or criminal negligence.

§ 21a An attempt to commit a crime consists of two elements: a specific intent to commit the crime, and a direct but ineffectual act done toward its commission.

Persons Liable to Punishment for Crime

§ 25 (a) The defense of diminished capacity is hereby abolished. In a criminal action, as well as any juvenile court proceeding, evidence concerning an accused person's intoxication, trauma, mental illness, disease, or defect shall not be admissible to show or negate capacity to form the particular purpose, intent, motive, malice aforethought, knowledge, or other mental state required for the commission of the crime charged.

(b) In any criminal proceeding, including any juvenile court proceeding, in which a plea of not guilty by reason of insanity is entered, this defense shall be found by the trier of fact only when the accused person proves by a preponderance of the evidence that he or she was incapable of knowing or understanding the nature and quality of his or her act and of distinguishing right from wrong at the time of the commission of the offense.

(c) Notwithstanding the foregoing, evidence of diminished capacity or of a mental disorder may be considered by the court only at the time of sentencing or other disposition or commitment.

§ 26 All persons are capable of committing crimes except those belonging to the following classes:

One—Children under the age of 14, in the absence of clear proof that at the time of committing the act charged against them, they knew its wrongfulness.

Two—Persons who are mentally incapacitated.

Three—Persons who committed the act or made the omission charged under an ignorance or mistake of fact, which disproves any criminal intent.

Four—Persons who committed the act charged without being conscious thereof.

Five—Persons who committed the act or made the omission charged through misfortune or by accident, when it appears that there was no evil design, intention, or culpable negligence.

Six—Persons (unless the crime be punishable with death) who committed the act or made the omission charged under threats or menaces sufficient to show that they had reasonable cause to and did believe their lives would be endangered if they refused.

§ 28 (a) Evidence of mental disease, mental defect, or mental disorder shall not be admitted to show or negate the capacity to form any mental state, including, but not limited to, purpose, intent, knowledge, premeditation, deliberation, or malice aforethought, with which the accused committed the act. Evidence of mental disease, mental defect, or mental disorder is admissible solely on the issue of whether or not the accused actually formed a required specific intent, premeditated, deliberated, or harbored malice aforethought, when a specific intent crime is charged.

(b) As a matter of public policy there shall be no defense of diminished capacity, diminished responsibility, or irresistible impulse in a criminal action or juvenile adjudication hearing.

(c) This section shall not be applicable to an insanity hearing ...

(d) Nothing in this section shall limit a court's discretion, pursuant to the Evidence Code, to exclude psychiatric or psychological evidence on whether the accused had a mental disease, mental defect, or mental disorder at the time of the alleged offense.

§ 29.2 (a) The intent or intention is manifested by the circumstances connected with the offense.

(b) In the guilt phase of a criminal action or a juvenile adjudication hearing, evidence that the accused lacked the capacity or ability to control his or her conduct for any reason shall not be admissible on the issue of whether the accused actually had any mental state with respect to the commission of any crime. This subdivision is not applicable to Section 26.

§ 29.4 (a) No act committed by a person while in a state of voluntary intoxication is less criminal by reason of his or her having been in that condition. Evidence of voluntary intoxication shall not be admitted to negate the capacity to form any mental states for the crimes charged, including, but not limited to, purpose, intent, knowledge, premeditation, deliberation, or malice aforethought, with which the accused committed the act.

(b) Evidence of voluntary intoxication is admissible solely on the issue of whether or not the defendant actually formed a required specific intent, or, when charged with murder, whether the defendant premeditated, deliberated, or harbored express malice aforethought.

(c) Voluntary intoxication includes the voluntary ingestion, injection, or taking by any other means of any intoxicating liquor, drug, or other substance.

§ 29.8 In any criminal proceeding in which a plea of not guilty by reason of insanity is entered, this defense shall not be found by the trier of fact solely on the basis of a personality or adjustment disorder, a seizure disorder, or an addiction to, or abuse of, intoxicating substances.

Parties to Crime

§ 30 The parties to crime are classified as:

1. Principals; and,
2. Accessories.

§ 31 All persons concerned in the commission of a crime, whether it be felony or misdemeanor, and whether they directly commit the act constituting the offense, or aid and abet in its commission, or, not being present, have advised and encouraged its commission, and all persons counseling, advising, or encouraging children under the age of fourteen years, or persons who are mentally incapacitated, to commit any crime, or who, by fraud, contrivance, or force, occasion the drunkenness of another for the purpose of causing him to commit any crime, or who, by threats, menaces, command, or coercion, compel another to commit any crime, are principals in any crime so committed.

§ 32 Every person who, after a felony has been committed, harbors, conceals or aids a principal in such felony, with the intent that said principal may avoid or escape from arrest, trial, conviction or punishment, having knowledge that said principal has committed such felony or has been charged with such felony or convicted thereof, is an accessory to such felony.

§ 33 Except in cases where a different punishment is prescribed, an accessory is punishable by a fine not exceeding five thousand dollars ($5,000), or by imprisonment pursuant to subdivision (h) of Section 1170, or in a county jail not exceeding one year, or by both such fine and imprisonment.

Crimes by and Against Executive Power of the State

§ 68 (a) Every executive or ministerial officer, employee or appointee of the State of California, a county or a city therein, or political subdivision thereof, who asks, receives, or agrees to receive, any bribe, upon any agreement or understanding that his or her vote, opinion, or action upon any matter then pending, or that may be brought before him or her in his or her official capacity, shall be influenced thereby, is punishable by imprisonment in the state prison for two, three, or four years and [a restitution fine], and, in addition thereto, forfeits his or her office, employment, or appointment, and is forever disqualified from holding any office, employment, or appointment, in this state.

§ 69 Every person who attempts, by means of any threat or violence, to deter or prevent an executive officer from performing any duty imposed upon such officer by law, or who knowingly resists, by the use of force or violence, such officer, in the performance of his duty, is punishable by a fine not exceeding ten thousand dollars ($10,000), or by imprisonment pursuant to subdivision (h) of Section 1170, or in a county jail not exceeding one year, or by both such fine and imprisonment.

Crimes Against Public Justice

§ 118 (a) Every person who, having taken an oath that he or she will testify, declare, depose, or certify truly before any competent tribunal, officer, or person, in any of the cases in which the oath may by law of the State of California be administered, willfully and contrary to the oath, states as true any material matter which he or she knows to be false, and every person who testifies, declares, deposes, or certifies under penalty of perjury in any of the cases in which the testimony, declarations, depositions, or certification is permitted by law of the State of California under penalty of perjury and willfully states as true any material matter which he or she knows to be false, is guilty of perjury.

...

§ 137 (a) Every person who gives or offers, or promises to give, to any witness, person about to be called as a witness, or person about to give material information pertaining to a crime to a law enforcement official, any bribe, upon any understanding or agreement that the testimony of such witness or information given by such person shall be thereby influenced is guilty of a felony.

(b) Every person who attempts by force or threat of force or by the use of fraud to induce any person to give false testimony or withhold true testimony or to give false material information pertaining to a crime to, or withhold true material information pertaining to a crime from, a law enforcement official is guilty of a felony ...

As used in this subdivision, "threat of force" means a credible threat of unlawful injury to any person or damage to the property of another which is communicated to a person for the purpose of inducing him to give false testimony or withhold true testimony or to give false material information pertaining to a crime to, or to withhold true material information pertaining to a crime from, a law enforcement official.

(c) Every person who knowingly induces another person to give false testimony or withhold true testimony not privileged by law or to give false material information pertaining to a crime to, or to withhold true material information pertaining to a crime from, a law enforcement official is guilty of a misdemeanor.

. . .

§ 138 (a) Every person who gives or offers or promises to give to any witness or person about to be called as a witness, any bribe upon any understanding or agreement that the person shall not attend upon any trial or other judicial proceeding, or every person who attempts by means of any offer of a bribe to dissuade any person from attending upon any trial or other judicial proceeding, is guilty of a felony.

(b) Every person who is a witness, or is about to be called as such, who receives, or offers to receive, any bribe, upon any understanding that his or her testimony shall be influenced thereby, or that he or she will absent himself or herself from the trial or proceeding upon which his or her testimony is required, is guilty of a felony.

§ 148 (a) (1) Every person who willfully resists, delays, or obstructs any public officer, peace officer, or an emergency medical technician,... in the discharge or attempt to discharge any duty of his or her office or employment, when no other punishment is prescribed, shall be punished by a fine not exceeding one thousand dollars ($1,000), or by imprisonment in a county jail not to exceed one year, or by both such fine and imprisonment.

. . .

§ 153 Every person who, having knowledge of the actual commission of a crime, takes money or property of another, or any gratuity or reward, or any engagement, or promise thereof, upon any agreement or understanding to compound or conceal such crime, or to abstain from any prosecution thereof, or to withhold any evidence thereof, except in the cases provided for by law, in which crimes may be compromised by leave of court, is punishable [according to the seriousness of the crime compounded].

§ 182 (a) If two or more persons conspire:

(1) To commit any crime.

(2) Falsely and maliciously to indict another for any crime, or to procure another to be charged or arrested for any crime.

(3) Falsely to move or maintain any suit, action, or proceeding.

(4) To cheat and defraud any person of any property, by any means which are in themselves criminal, or to obtain money or property by false pretenses or by false promises with fraudulent intent not to perform those promises.

(5) To commit any act injurious to the public health, to public morals, or to pervert or obstruct justice, or the due administration of the laws.

(6) To commit any crime against the person of the President or Vice President of the United States, the Governor of any state or territory, any United States justice or judge, or the secretary of any of the executive departments of the United States.

They are punishable as follows:

When they conspire to commit any crime against the person of any official specified in paragraph (6), they are guilty of a felony and are punishable by imprisonment pursuant to subdivision (h) of Section 1170 for five, seven, or nine years.

When they conspire to commit any other felony, they shall be punishable in the same manner and to the same extent as is provided for the punishment of that felony....

...

When they conspire to do any of the other acts described in this section, they shall be punishable by imprisonment in the county jail for not more than one year, or pursuant to subdivision (h) of Section 1170, or by a fine not exceeding ten thousand dollars ($10,000), or by both that imprisonment and fine....

...

§ 182.5 Notwithstanding subdivisions (a) or (b) of Section 182, any person who actively participates in any criminal street gang, as defined in subdivision (f) of Section 186.22, with knowledge that its members engage in or have engaged in a pattern of criminal gang activity, as defined in subdivision (e) of Section 186.22, and who willfully promotes, furthers, assists, or benefits from any felonious criminal conduct by members of that gang is guilty of conspiracy to commit that felony and may be punished as specified in subdivision (a) of Section 182.

§ 184 No agreement amounts to a conspiracy, unless some act, beside such agreement, be done within this state to effect the object thereof, by one or more of the parties to such agreement and the trial of cases of conspiracy may be had in any county in which any such act be done.

§ 186.22 (a) Any person who actively participates in any criminal street gang with knowledge that its members engage in or have engaged in a pattern of criminal gang activity, and who willfully promotes, furthers, or assists in any felonious criminal conduct by members of that gang, shall be punished by imprisonment in a county jail for a period not to exceed one year, or by imprisonment in the state prison for 16 months, or two or three years.

(b) (1) ... [A]ny person who is convicted of a felony committed for the benefit of, at the direction of, or in association with any criminal street gang, with the specific intent to promote, further, or assist in any criminal conduct by gang members, shall, upon conviction of that felony, in addition and consecutive to the punishment prescribed for the felony or attempted felony of which he or she has been convicted, be punished as follows:

(A) Except as provided in subparagraphs (B) and (C), the person shall be punished by an additional term of two, three, or four years at the court's discretion.

(B) If the felony is a serious felony, as defined in subdivision (c) of Section 1192.7, the person shall be punished by an additional term of five years.

(C) If the felony is a violent felony, as defined in subdivision (c) of Section 667.5, the person shall be punished by an additional term of 10 years.

...

Crimes Against the Person

§ 187 (a) Murder is the unlawful killing of a human being, or a fetus, with malice aforethought.

...

§ 188 Such malice may be express or implied. It is express when there is manifested a deliberate intention unlawfully to take away the life of a fellow creature. It is implied, when no considerable provocation appears, or when the circumstances attending the killing show an abandoned and malignant heart.

When it is shown that the killing resulted from the intentional doing of an act with express or implied malice as defined above, no other mental state need be shown to establish the mental state of malice aforethought. Neither an awareness of the obligation to act within the general body of laws regulating society nor acting despite such awareness is included within the definition of malice.

§ 189 All murder which is perpetrated by means of a destructive device or explosive, a weapon of mass destruction, knowing use of ammunition designed primarily to penetrate metal or armor, poison, lying in wait, torture, or by any other kind of willful, deliberate, and premeditated killing, or which is committed in the perpetration of, or attempt to perpetrate, arson, rape, carjacking, robbery, burglary, mayhem, kidnapping, train wrecking, or any act punishable under Section 206 [torture], 286 [sodomy accomplished with a minor or against the victim's will or in a state prison or jail], 288 [lewd act on child], 288a [oral copulation accomplished with a minor or against the victim's will or in a state prison or jail], or 289 [anal or genital penetration by foreign object for sexual purpose accomplished with a minor or against the victim's will], or any murder which is perpetrated by means of discharging a firearm from a motor vehicle, intentionally at another person outside of the vehicle with the intent to inflict death, is murder of the first degree. All other kinds of murders are of the second degree.

...

To prove the killing was "deliberate and premeditated," it shall not be necessary to prove the defendant maturely and meaningfully reflected upon the gravity of his or her act.

§ 190.2 (a) The penalty for a defendant who is found guilty of murder in the first degree is death or imprisonment in the state prison for life without the possibility of parole if one or more of the following special circumstances has been found ... to be true:

(1) The murder was intentional and carried out for financial gain.

(2) The defendant was convicted previously of murder in the first or second degree. For the purpose of this paragraph, an offense committed in another ju-

risdiction, which if committed in California would be punishable as first or second degree murder, shall be deemed murder in the first or second degree.

(3) The defendant, in this proceeding, has been convicted of more than one offense of murder in the first or second degree.

(4) The murder was committed by means of a destructive device, bomb, or explosive planted, hidden, or concealed in any place, area, dwelling, building, or structure, and the defendant knew, or reasonably should have known, that his or her act or acts would create a great risk of death to one or more human beings.

(5) The murder was committed for the purpose of avoiding or preventing a lawful arrest, or perfecting or attempting to perfect, an escape from lawful custody.

(6) The murder was committed by means of a destructive device, bomb, or explosive that the defendant mailed or delivered, attempted to mail or deliver, or caused to be mailed or delivered, and the defendant knew, or reasonably should have known, that his or her act or acts would create a great risk of death to one or more human beings.

(7) The victim was a peace officer ... who, while engaged in the course of the performance of his or her duties, was intentionally killed, and the defendant knew, or reasonably should have known, that the victim was a peace officer engaged in the performance of his or her duties; or the victim was a peace officer, as defined in the above-enumerated sections, or a former peace officer under any of those sections, and was intentionally killed in retaliation for the performance of his or her official duties.

(8) The victim was a federal law enforcement officer or agent who, while engaged in the course of the performance of his or her duties, was intentionally killed, and the defendant knew, or reasonably should have known, that the victim was a federal law enforcement officer or agent engaged in the performance of his or her duties; or the victim was a federal law enforcement officer or agent, and was intentionally killed in retaliation for the performance of his or her official duties.

(9) The victim was a firefighter ... who, while engaged in the course of the performance of his or her duties, was intentionally killed, and the defendant knew, or reasonably should have known, that the victim was a firefighter engaged in the performance of his or her duties.

(10) The victim was a witness to a crime who was intentionally killed for the purpose of preventing his or her testimony in any criminal or juvenile proceeding, and the killing was not committed during the commission or attempted commission, of the crime to which he or she was a witness; or the victim was a witness to a crime and was intentionally killed in retaliation for his or her testimony in any criminal or juvenile proceeding....

(11) The victim was a prosecutor or assistant prosecutor or a former prosecutor or assistant prosecutor of any local or state prosecutor's office in this or any other

state, or of a federal prosecutor's office, and the murder was intentionally carried out in retaliation for, or to prevent the performance of, the victim's official duties.

(12) The victim was a judge or former judge of any court of record in the local, state, or federal system in this or any other state, and the murder was intentionally carried out in retaliation for, or to prevent the performance of, the victim's official duties.

(13) The victim was an elected or appointed official or former official of the federal government, or of any local or state government of this or any other state, and the killing was intentionally carried out in retaliation for, or to prevent the performance of, the victim's official duties.

(14) The murder was especially heinous, atrocious, or cruel, manifesting exceptional depravity. As used in this section, the phrase "especially heinous, atrocious, or cruel, manifesting exceptional depravity" means a conscienceless or pitiless crime that is unnecessarily torturous to the victim.

(15) The defendant intentionally killed the victim by means of lying in wait.

(16) The victim was intentionally killed because of his or her race, color, religion, nationality, or country of origin.

(17) The murder was committed while the defendant was engaged in, or was an accomplice in, the commission of, attempted commission of, or the immediate flight after committing, or attempting to commit, the following felonies:

(A) Robbery in violation of Section 211 or 212.5.

(B) Kidnapping in violation of Section 207, 209, or 209.5.

(C) Rape in violation of Section 261.

(D) Sodomy in violation of Section 286 [by force, threats, etc. or with a minor].

(E) The performance of a lewd or lascivious act upon the person of a child under the age of 14 years in violation of Section 288.

(F) Oral copulation in violation of Section 288a [by force, threats, etc. or with a minor].

(G) Burglary in the first or second degree in violation of Section 460.

(H) Arson in violation of subdivision (b) of Section 451.

(I) Train wrecking in violation of Section 219.

(J) Mayhem in violation of Section 203.

(K) Rape by instrument in violation of Section 289.

(L) Carjacking, as defined in Section 215.

(M) To prove the special circumstances of kidnapping in subparagraph (B), or arson in subparagraph (H), if there is specific intent to kill, it is only required that there be proof of the elements of those felonies. If so established, those two special circumstances are proven even if the felony of kidnapping or arson is committed primarily or solely for the purpose of facilitating the murder.

(18) The murder was intentional and involved the infliction of torture.

(19) The defendant intentionally killed the victim by the administration of poison.

(20) The victim was a juror in any court of record in the local, state, or federal system in this or any other state, and the murder was intentionally carried out in retaliation for, or to prevent the performance of, the victim's official duties.

(21) The murder was intentional and perpetrated by means of discharging a firearm from a motor vehicle, intentionally at another person or persons outside the vehicle with the intent to inflict death....

(22) The defendant intentionally killed the victim while the defendant was an active participant in a criminal street gang..., and the murder was carried out to further the activities of the criminal street gang.

§ 191.5 (a) Gross vehicular manslaughter while intoxicated is the unlawful killing of a human being without malice aforethought, in the driving of a vehicle, where the driving was [under the influence of alcohol or drugs], and the killing was either the proximate result of the commission of an unlawful act, not amounting to a felony, and with gross negligence, or the proximate result of the commission of a lawful act that might produce death, in an unlawful manner, and with gross negligence.

(b) Vehicular manslaughter while intoxicated is the unlawful killing of a human being without malice aforethought, in the driving of a vehicle, where the driving was [under the influence of alcohol or drugs], and the killing was either the proximate result of the commission of an unlawful act, not amounting to a felony, but without gross negligence, or the proximate result of the commission of a lawful act that might produce death, in an unlawful manner, but without gross negligence.

(c) (1) Except as provided in subdivision (d) [increased sentence for prior convictions], gross vehicular manslaughter while intoxicated in violation of subdivision (a) is punishable by imprisonment in the state prison for 4, 6, or 10 years.

(2) Vehicular manslaughter while intoxicated in violation of subdivision (b) is punishable by imprisonment in a county jail for not more than one year or by imprisonment pursuant to subdivision (h) of Section 1170 for 16 months or 2 or 4 years.

...

(e) This section shall not be construed as prohibiting or precluding a charge of murder under Section 188 upon facts exhibiting wantonness and a conscious disregard for life to support a finding of implied malice, or upon facts showing malice consistent with the holding of the California Supreme Court in People v. Watson 30, Cal.3d 290.

. . .

§ 192 Manslaughter is the unlawful killing of a human being without malice. It is of three kinds:

(a) Voluntary—upon a sudden quarrel or heat of passion.

(b) Involuntary—in the commission of an unlawful act, not amounting to a felony; or in the commission of a lawful act which might produce death, in an unlawful manner, or without due caution and circumspection. This subdivision shall not apply to acts committed in the driving of a vehicle.

(c) Vehicular—

(1) Except as provided in subdivision (a) of Section 191.5, driving a vehicle in the commission of an unlawful act, not amounting to felony, and with gross negligence; or driving a vehicle in the commission of a lawful act which might produce death, in an unlawful manner, and with gross negligence.

(2) Driving a vehicle in the commission of an unlawful act, not amounting to felony, but without gross negligence; or driving a vehicle in the commission of a lawful act which might produce death, in an unlawful manner, but without gross negligence.

(3) Driving a vehicle in connection with a violation of [§ 550(a)(3), knowingly causing or participating in a collision or accident for the purpose of presenting a false claim] where the vehicular collision or vehicular accident was knowingly caused for financial gain and proximately resulted in the death of any person. This provision shall not be construed to prevent prosecution of a defendant for the crime of murder.

(d) This section shall not be construed as making any homicide in the driving of a vehicle punishable which is not a proximate result of the commission of an unlawful act, not amounting to felony, or of the commission of a lawful act which might produce death, in an unlawful manner.

(e) "Gross negligence," as used in this section, does not prohibit or preclude a charge of murder under Section 188 upon facts exhibiting wantonness and a conscious disregard for life to support a finding of implied malice, or upon facts showing malice, consistent with the holding of the California Supreme Court in People v. Watson (1981) 30 Cal.3d 290.

(f) (1) For purposes of determining sudden quarrel or heat of passion pursuant to subdivision (a), the provocation was not objectively reasonable if it resulted from the discovery of, knowledge about, or potential disclosure of the victim's actual or perceived gender, gender identity, gender expression, or sexual orientation, including under circumstances in which the victim made an unwanted nonforcible romantic or sexual advance towards the defendant, or if the defendant and victim dated or had a romantic or sexual relationship. Nothing in this section shall preclude the jury from considering all relevant facts to determine whether the defendant was in fact provoked for purposes of establishing subjective provocation.

(2) For purposes of this subdivision, "gender" includes a person's gender identity and gender-related appearance and behavior regardless of whether that appearance or behavior is associated with the person's gender as determined at birth.

§ 195 Homicide is excusable in the following cases:

1. When committed by accident and misfortune, or in doing any other lawful act by lawful means, with usual and ordinary caution and without any unlawful intent.

2. When committed by accident and misfortune, in the heat of passion, upon any sudden and sufficient provocation, or upon a sudden combat, when no undue advantage is taken, nor any dangerous weapon used, and when the killing is not done in a cruel or unusual manner.

§ 196 Homicide is justifiable when committed by public officers and those acting by their command in their aid and assistance, either—

1. In obedience to any judgment of a competent Court; or,

2. When necessarily committed in overcoming actual resistance to the execution of some legal process, or in the discharge of any other legal duty; or,

3. When necessarily committed in retaking felons who have been rescued or have escaped, or when necessarily committed in arresting persons charged with felony, and who are fleeing from justice or resisting such arrest.

§ 197 Homicide is also justifiable when committed by any person in any of the following cases:

1. When resisting any attempt to murder any person, or to commit a felony, or to do some great bodily injury upon any person; or,

2. When committed in defense of habitation, property, or person, against one who manifestly intends or endeavors, by violence or surprise, to commit a felony, or against one who manifestly intends and endeavors, in a violent, riotous or tumultuous manner, to enter the habitation of another for the purpose of offering violence to any person therein; or,

3. When committed in the lawful defense of such person, or wife or husband, parent, child, master, mistress, or servant of such person, when there is reasonable ground to apprehend a design to commit a felony or to do some great bodily injury, and imminent danger of such design being accomplished; but such person, or the person in whose behalf the defense was made, if he was the assailant or engaged in mutual combat, must really and in good faith have endeavored to decline any further struggle before the homicide was committed; or,

4. When necessarily committed in attempting, by lawful ways and means, to apprehend any person for any felony committed, or in lawfully suppressing any riot, or in lawfully keeping and preserving the peace.

§ 198 A bare fear of the commission of any of the offenses mentioned in subdivisions 2 and 3 of Section 197, to prevent which homicide may be lawfully committed, is not sufficient to justify it. But the circumstances must be sufficient to excite the fears of a reasonable person, and the party killing must have acted under the influence of such fears alone.

§ 198.5 Any person using force intended or likely to cause death or great bodily injury within his or her residence shall be presumed to have held a reasonable fear of imminent peril of death or great bodily injury to self, family, or a member of the household when that force is used against another person, not a member of the family or household, who unlawfully and forcibly enters or has unlawfully and forcibly entered the residence and the person using the force knew or had reason to believe that an unlawful and forcible entry occurred.

As used in this section, great bodily injury means a significant or substantial physical injury.

§ 199 The homicide appearing to be justifiable or excusable, the person indicted must, upon his trial, be fully acquitted and discharged.

§ 203 Every person who unlawfully and maliciously deprives a human being of a member of his body, or disables, disfigures, or renders it useless, or cuts or disables the tongue, or puts out an eye, or slits the nose, ear, or lip is guilty of mayhem.

§ 205 A person is guilty of aggravated mayhem when he or she unlawfully, under circumstances manifesting extreme indifference to the physical or psychological well-being of another person, intentionally causes permanent disability or disfigurement of another human being or deprives a human being of a limb, organ, or member of his or her body. For purposes of this section, it is not necessary to prove an intent to kill....

§ 207 (a) Every person who forcibly, or by any other means of instilling fear, steals or takes, or holds, detains, or arrests any person in this state, and carries the person into another country, state, or county, or into another part of the same county, is guilty of kidnapping.

...

(f) Subdivision[] (a) [does] not apply to any of the following:

(1) To any person who steals, takes, entices away, detains, conceals, or harbors any child under the age of 14 years, if that act is taken to protect the child from danger of imminent harm.

...

§ 211 Robbery is the felonious taking of personal property in the possession of another, from his person or immediate presence, and against his will, accomplished by means of force or fear.

§ 212 The fear mentioned in Section 211 may be either:

1. The fear of an unlawful injury to the person or property of the person robbed, or of any relative of his or member of his family; or,

2. The fear of an immediate and unlawful injury to the person or property of anyone in the company of the person robbed at the time of the robbery.

§ 220 (a)

(1) Except as provided in subdivision (b), any person who assaults another with intent to commit mayhem, rape, sodomy, oral copulation, or any violation of Section 264.1 [aiding a rape or violation of § 289], 288 [lewd act on child], or 289 [anal or genital penetration by foreign object for sexual purpose accomplished with a minor or against the victim's will] shall be punished by imprisonment in the state prison for two, four, or six years.

(2) Except as provided in subdivision (b), any person who assaults another person under 18 years of age with the intent to commit rape, sodomy, oral copulation, or any violation of Section 264.1 [aiding a rape or violation of § 289], 288 [lewd act on child], or 289 [anal or genital penetration by foreign object for sexual purpose accomplished with a minor or against the victim's will] shall be punished by imprisonment in the state prison for five, seven, or nine years

(b) Any person who, in the commission of a burglary of the first degree, as defined in subdivision (a) of Section 460, assaults another with intent to commit rape, sodomy, oral copulation, or any violation of Section 264.1 [aiding a rape or violation of § 289], 288 [lewd act on child], or 289 [anal or genital penetration by foreign object for sexual purpose accomplished with a minor or against the victim's will] shall be punished by imprisonment in the state prison for life with the possibility of parole.

§ 236 False imprisonment is the unlawful violation of the personal liberty of another.

§ 240 An assault is an unlawful attempt, coupled with a present ability, to commit a violent injury on the person of another.

§ 241 (a) An assault is punishable by fine not exceeding one thousand dollars ($1,000), or by imprisonment in the county jail not exceeding six months, or by both the fine and imprisonment.

...

(c) When an assault is committed against the person of a peace officer, firefighter, emergency medical technician, mobile intensive care paramedic, lifeguard, process server, traffic officer, code enforcement officer, animal control officer, or search and rescue member engaged in the performance of his or her duties, or a physician or nurse engaged in rendering emergency medical care outside a hospital, clinic, or other health care facility, and the person committing the offense knows or reasonably should know that the victim is a peace officer, firefighter, emergency medical technician, mobile intensive care paramedic, lifeguard, process server, traffic officer, code enforcement officer, animal control officer, or search and rescue member engaged in the performance of his or her duties, or a physician or nurse engaged in rendering emergency medical care, the assault is punishable by a fine not exceeding two thousand dollars ($2,000), or by imprisonment in the county jail not exceeding one year, or by both the fine and imprisonment.

...

§ 242 A battery is any willful and unlawful use of force or violence upon the person of another.

§ 243 (a) A battery is punishable by a fine not exceeding two thousand dollars ($2,000), or by imprisonment in a county jail not exceeding six months, or by both that fine and imprisonment.

(b) When a battery is committed against the person of a peace officer, custodial officer, firefighter, emergency medical technician, lifeguard, security officer, custody assistant, process server, traffic officer, code enforcement officer, animal control officer, or search and rescue member engaged in the performance of his or her duties, whether on or off duty, including when the peace officer is in a police uniform and is concurrently performing the duties required of him or her as a peace officer while also employed in a private capacity as a part-time or casual private security guard or patrolman, or a nonsworn employee of a probation department engaged in the performance of his or her duties, whether on or off duty, or a physician or nurse engaged in rendering emergency medical care outside a hospital, clinic, or other health care facility, and the person committing the offense knows or reasonably should know that the victim is a peace officer, custodial officer, firefighter, emergency medical technician, lifeguard, security officer, custody assistant, process server, traffic officer, code enforcement officer, animal control officer, or search and rescue member engaged in the performance of his or her duties, nonsworn employee of a probation department, or a physician or nurse engaged in rendering emergency medical care, the battery is punishable by a fine not exceeding two thousand dollars ($2,000), or by imprisonment in a county jail not exceeding one year, or by both that fine and imprisonment.

(c) (1) When a battery is committed against a custodial officer, firefighter, emergency medical technician, lifeguard, process server, traffic officer, or animal control officer engaged in the performance of his or her duties, whether on or off duty, or a nonsworn employee of a probation department engaged in the performance of his or her duties, whether on or off duty, or a physician or nurse engaged in rendering emergency medical care outside a hospital, clinic, or other health care facility, and the person committing the offense knows or reasonably should know that the victim is a nonsworn employee of a probation department, custodial officer, firefighter, emergency medical technician, lifeguard, process server, traffic officer, or animal control officer engaged in the performance of his or her duties, or a physician or nurse engaged in rendering emergency medical care, and an injury is inflicted on that victim, the battery is punishable by a fine of not more than two thousand dollars ($2,000), by imprisonment in a county jail not exceeding one year, or by both that fine and imprisonment, or by imprisonment pursuant to subdivision (h) of Section 1170 for 16 months, or two or three years.

(2) When the battery specified in paragraph (1) is committed against a peace officer engaged in the performance of his or her duties, whether on or off duty, including when the peace officer is in a police uniform and is concurrently performing the duties required of him or her as a peace officer while also employed in a private capacity as a part-time or casual private security guard or patrolman and the person

committing the offense knows or reasonably should know that the victim is a peace officer engaged in the performance of his or her duties, the battery is punishable by a fine of not more than ten thousand dollars ($10,000), or by imprisonment in a county jail not exceeding one year or pursuant to subdivision (h) of Section 1170 for 16 months, or two or three years, or by both that fine and imprisonment.

(d) When a battery is committed against any person and serious bodily injury is inflicted on the person, the battery is punishable by imprisonment in a county jail not exceeding one year or imprisonment pursuant to subdivision (h) of Section 1170 for two, three, or four years.

(e) (1) When a battery is committed against a spouse, a person with whom the defendant is cohabiting, a person who is the parent of the defendant's child, former spouse, fiancé, or fiancée, or a person with whom the defendant currently has, or has previously had, a dating or engagement relationship, the battery is punishable by a fine not exceeding two thousand dollars ($2,000), or by imprisonment in a county jail for a period of not more than one year, or by both that fine and imprisonment. If probation is granted, or the execution or imposition of the sentence is suspended, it shall be a condition thereof that the defendant participate in, for no less than one year, and successfully complete, a batterer's treatment program, ... or if none is available, another appropriate counseling program designated by the court....

...

§ 245 (a)

(1) Any person who commits an assault upon the person of another with a deadly weapon or instrument other than a firearm shall be punished by imprisonment in the state prison for two, three, or four years, or in a county jail for not exceeding one year, or by a fine not exceeding ten thousand dollars ($10,000), or by both the fine and imprisonment.

(2) Any person who commits an assault upon the person of another with a firearm shall be punished by imprisonment in the state prison for two, three, or four years, or in a county jail for not less than six months and not exceeding one year, or by both a fine not exceeding ten thousand dollars ($10,000) and imprisonment.

...

(c) Any person who commits an assault with a deadly weapon or instrument, other than a firearm, or by any means likely to produce great bodily injury upon the person of a peace officer or firefighter, and who knows or reasonably should know that the victim is a peace officer or firefighter engaged in the performance of his or her duties, when the peace officer or firefighter is engaged in the performance of his or her duties, shall be punished by imprisonment in the state prison for three, four, or five years.

(d) (1) Any person who commits an assault with a firearm upon the person of a peace officer or firefighter, and who knows or reasonably should know that the victim is a peace officer or firefighter engaged in the performance of his or her duties, when the peace officer or firefighter is engaged in the performance of his or her duties, shall be punished by imprisonment in the state prison for four, six, or eight years.

...

§ 246 Any person who shall maliciously and willfully discharge a firearm at an inhabited dwelling house, occupied building, occupied motor vehicle, occupied aircraft, inhabited housecar, ... or inhabited camper, ... is guilty of a felony, and upon conviction shall be punished by imprisonment in the state prison for three, five, or seven years, or by imprisonment in the county jail for a term of not less than six months and not exceeding one year.

As used in this section, "inhabited" means currently being used for dwelling purposes, whether occupied or not.

§ 246.3 (a) Except as otherwise authorized by law, any person who willfully discharges a firearm in a grossly negligent manner which could result in injury or death to a person is guilty of a public offense and shall be punished by imprisonment in a county jail not exceeding one year, or by imprisonment pursuant to subdivision (h) of Section 1170.

Crimes Against the Person Involving Sexual Assault, and Crimes Against Public Decency and Good Morals

§ 261 (a) Rape is an act of sexual intercourse accomplished with a person not the spouse of the perpetrator, under any of the following circumstances:

(1) Where a person is incapable, because of a mental disorder or developmental or physical disability, of giving legal consent, and this is known or reasonably should be known to the person committing the act....

(2) Where it is accomplished against a person's will by means of force, violence, duress, menace, or fear of immediate and unlawful bodily injury on the person or another.

(3) Where a person is prevented from resisting by any intoxicating or anesthetic substance, or any controlled substance, and this condition was known, or reasonably should have been known by the accused.

(4) Where a person is at the time unconscious of the nature of the act, and this is known to the accused. As used in this paragraph, "unconscious of the nature of the act" means incapable of resisting because the victim meets any one of the following conditions:

(A) Was unconscious or asleep.

(B) Was not aware, knowing, perceiving, or cognizant that the act occurred.

(C) Was not aware, knowing, perceiving, or cognizant of the essential characteristics of the act due to the perpetrator's fraud in fact.

(D) Was not aware, knowing, perceiving, or cognizant of the essential characteristics of the act due to the perpetrator's fraudulent representation that the sexual penetration served a professional purpose when it served no professional purpose.

(5) Where a person submits under the belief that the person committing the act is someone known to the victim other than the accused, and this belief is induced by any artifice, pretense, or concealment practiced by the accused, with intent to induce the belief.

(6) Where the act is accomplished against the victim's will by threatening to retaliate in the future against the victim or any other person, and there is a reasonable possibility that the perpetrator will execute the threat. As used in this paragraph, "threatening to retaliate" means a threat to kidnap or falsely imprison, or to inflict extreme pain, serious bodily injury, or death.

(7) Where the act is accomplished against the victim's will by threatening to use the authority of a public official to incarcerate, arrest, or deport the victim or another, and the victim has a reasonable belief that the perpetrator is a public official. As used in this paragraph, "public official" means a person employed by a governmental agency who has the authority, as part of that position, to incarcerate, arrest, or deport another. The perpetrator does not actually have to be a public official.

(b) As used in this section, "duress" means a direct or implied threat of force, violence, danger, or retribution sufficient to coerce a reasonable person of ordinary susceptibilities to perform an act which otherwise would not have been performed, or acquiesce in an act to which one otherwise would not have submitted. The total circumstances, including the age of the victim, and his or her relationship to the defendant, are factors to consider in appraising the existence of duress.

(c) As used in this section, "menace" means any threat, declaration, or act which shows an intention to inflict an injury upon another.

§ 261.5 (a) Unlawful sexual intercourse is an act of sexual intercourse accomplished with a person who is not the spouse of the perpetrator, if the person is a minor. For the purposes of this section, a "minor" is a person under the age of 18 years and an "adult" is a person who is at least 18 years of age.

(b) Any person who engages in an act of unlawful sexual intercourse with a minor who is not more than three years older or three years younger than the perpetrator, is guilty of a misdemeanor.

(c) Any person who engages in an act of unlawful sexual intercourse with a minor who is more than three years younger than the perpetrator is guilty of either a misdemeanor or a felony, and shall be punished by imprisonment in a county jail not exceeding one year, or by imprisonment pursuant to subdivision (h) of Section 1170.

(d) Any person 21 years of age or older who engages in an act of unlawful sexual intercourse with a minor who is under 16 years of age is guilty of either a misdemeanor or a felony, and shall be punished by imprisonment in a county jail not exceeding one year, or by imprisonment pursuant to subdivision (h) of Section 1170 for two, three, or four years.

...

§ 261.6 In prosecutions under Section 261, 262, 286, 288a, or 289, in which consent is at issue, "consent" shall be defined to mean positive cooperation in act or attitude pursuant to an exercise of free will. The person must act freely and voluntarily and have knowledge of the nature of the act or transaction involved.

A current or previous dating or marital relationship shall not be sufficient to constitute consent where consent is at issue in a prosecution under Section 261, 262, 286, 288a, or 289.

...

§ 262 (a) Rape of a person who is the spouse of the perpetrator is an act of sexual intercourse accomplished under any of the following circumstances:

(1) Where it is accomplished against a person's will by means of force, violence, duress, menace, or fear of immediate and unlawful bodily injury on the person or another.

(2) Where a person is prevented from resisting by any intoxicating or anesthetic substance, or any controlled substance, and this condition was known, or reasonably should have been known, by the accused.

(3) Where a person is at the time unconscious of the nature of the act, and this is known to the accused. As used in this paragraph, "unconscious of the nature of the act" means incapable of resisting because the victim meets one of the following conditions:

(A) Was unconscious or asleep.

(B) Was not aware, knowing, perceiving, or cognizant that the act occurred.

(C) Was not aware, knowing, perceiving, or cognizant of the essential characteristics of the act due to the perpetrator's fraud in fact.

(4) Where the act is accomplished against the victim's will by threatening to retaliate in the future against the victim or any other person, and there is a reasonable possibility that the perpetrator will execute the threat. As used in this paragraph, "threatening to retaliate" means a threat to kidnap or falsely imprison, or to inflict extreme pain, serious bodily injury, or death.

(5) Where the act is accomplished against the victim's will by threatening to use the authority of a public official to incarcerate, arrest, or deport the victim or another, and the victim has a reasonable belief that the perpetrator is a public official. As used in this paragraph, "public official" means a person employed by a governmental agency who has the authority, as part of that position, to incarcerate, arrest, or deport another. The perpetrator does not actually have to be a public official.

...

§ 270 If a parent of a minor child willfully omits, without lawful excuse, to furnish necessary clothing, food, shelter or medical attendance, or other remedial care for his or her child, he or she is guilty of a misdemeanor....

...

If a parent provides a minor with treatment by spiritual means through prayer alone in accordance with the tenets and practices of a recognized church or religious denomination, by a duly accredited practitioner thereof, such treatment shall constitute "other remedial care", as used in this section.

§ 273ab (a) Any person, having the care or custody of a child who is under eight years of age, who assaults the child by means of force that to a reasonable person would be likely to produce great bodily injury, resulting in the child's death, shall be punished by imprisonment in the state prison for 25 years to life.

§ 273.5 (a) Any person who willfully inflicts corporal injury resulting in a traumatic condition upon a victim described in subdivision (b) is guilty of a felony....

(b) Subdivision (a) shall apply if the victim is or was one or more of the following:

(1) The offender's spouse or former spouse.

(2) The offender's cohabitant or former cohabitant.

(3) The offender's fiancé or fiancée, or someone with whom the offender has, or previously had, an engagement or dating relationship....

(4) The mother or father of the offender's child.

(c) Holding oneself out to be the husband or wife of the person with whom one is cohabiting is not necessary to constitute cohabitation as the term is used in this section.

(d) As used in this section, "traumatic condition" means a condition of the body, such as a wound or external or internal injury, including, but not limited to, injury as a result of strangulation or suffocation, whether of a minor or serious nature, caused by a physical force.

...

§ 288. (a) ... [A]ny person who willfully and lewdly commits any lewd or lascivious act, ... upon or with the body, or any part or member thereof, of a child who is under the age of 14 years, with the intent of arousing, appealing to, or gratifying the lust, passions or sexual desires of that person or the child, is guilty of a felony....

...

(c) (1) Any person who commits an act described in subdivision (a) with the intent described in that subdivision, and the victim is a child of 14 or 15 years, and that person is at least 10 years older than the child, is guilty of a public offense and shall be punished by imprisonment in the state prison for one, two, or three years, or by imprisonment in a county jail for not more than one year. In determining whether the person is at least 10 years older than the child, the difference in age shall be measured from the birth date of the person to the birth date of the child.

(2) Any person who is a caretaker and commits an act described in subdivision (a) upon a dependent person, with the intent described in subdivision (a), is guilty of a public offense and shall be punished by imprisonment in the state prison for

one, two, or three years, or by imprisonment in a county jail for not more than one year.

. . .

§ 288a (a) Oral copulation is the act of copulating the mouth of one person with the sexual organ or anus of another person.

(b) (1) Except as provided in Section 288, any person who participates in an act of oral copulation with another person who is under 18 years of age shall be punished by imprisonment in the state prison, or in a county jail for a period of not more than one year.

(2) Except as provided in Section 288, any person over 21 years of age who participates in an act of oral copulation with another person who is under 16 years of age is guilty of a felony.

(c) (1) Any person who participates in an act of oral copulation with another person who is under 14 years of age and more than 10 years younger than he or she shall be punished by imprisonment in the state prison for three, six, or eight years.

(2) (A) Any person who commits an act of oral copulation when the act is accomplished against the victim's will by means of force, violence, duress, menace, or fear of immediate and unlawful bodily injury on the victim or another person shall be punished by imprisonment in the state prison for three, six, or eight years.

(B) Any person who commits an act of oral copulation upon a person who is under 14 years of age, when the act is accomplished against the victim's will by means of force, violence, duress, menace, or fear of immediate and unlawful bodily injury on the victim or another person, shall be punished by imprisonment in the state prison for 8, 10, or 12 years.

(C) Any person who commits an act of oral copulation upon a minor who is 14 years of age or older, when the act is accomplished against the victim's will by means of force, violence, duress, menace, or fear of immediate and unlawful bodily injury on the victim or another person, shall be punished by imprisonment in the state prison for 6, 8, or 10 years.

(3) Any person who commits an act of oral copulation where the act is accomplished against the victim's will by threatening to retaliate in the future against the victim or any other person, and there is a reasonable possibility that the perpetrator will execute the threat, shall be punished by imprisonment in the state prison for three, six, or eight years.

(d) [All of the above penalties are increased if the defendant acts in concert with another person.]

. . .

(f) Any person who commits an act of oral copulation, and the victim is at the time unconscious of the nature of the act and this is known to the person committing the act, shall be punished by imprisonment in the state prison for a period of three, six, or eight years. As used in this subdivision, "unconscious of the nature of the act" means incapable of resisting because the victim meets one of the following conditions:

(1) Was unconscious or asleep.

(2) Was not aware, knowing, perceiving, or cognizant that the act occurred.

(3) Was not aware, knowing, perceiving, or cognizant of the essential characteristics of the act due to the perpetrator's fraud in fact.

(4) Was not aware, knowing, perceiving, or cognizant of the essential characteristics of the act due to the perpetrator's fraudulent representation that the oral copulation served a professional purpose when it served no professional purpose.

(g) … [A]ny person who commits an act of oral copulation, and the victim is at the time incapable, because of a mental disorder or developmental or physical disability, of giving legal consent, and this is known or reasonably should be known to the person committing the act, shall be punished by imprisonment in the state prison, for three, six, or eight years.…

…

(i) Any person who commits an act of oral copulation, where the victim is prevented from resisting by any intoxicating or anesthetic substance, or any controlled substance, and this condition was known, or reasonably should have been known by the accused, shall be punished by imprisonment in the state prison for a period of three, six, or eight years.

(j) Any person who commits an act of oral copulation, where the victim submits under the belief that the person committing the act is someone known to the victim other than the accused, and this belief is induced by any artifice, pretense, or concealment practiced by the accused, with intent to induce the belief, shall be punished by imprisonment in the state prison for a period of three, six, or eight years.

(k) Any person who commits an act of oral copulation, where the act is accomplished against the victim's will by threatening to use the authority of a public official to incarcerate, arrest, or deport the victim or another, and the victim has a reasonable belief that the perpetrator is a public official, shall be punished by imprisonment in the state prison for a period of three, six, or eight years.

…

§290 …

(b) Every person [convicted of one of a list of sex crimes], for the rest of his or her life while residing in California, or while attending school or working in California, … shall be required to register with the chief of police of the city in which he or she is residing, or the sheriff of the county if he or she is residing in an unincorporated area or city that has no police department … within five working days of coming into, or changing his or her residence within, any city, county, or city and county…, and shall be required to register thereafter in accordance with the Act.

290.012 (a) Beginning on his or her first birthday following registration or change of address, the person shall be required to register annually, within five working days of his or her birthday, to update his or her registration with the entities described in 647subdivision (b) of Section 290.

§ 332 (a) Every person who by the game of "three card monte," so-called, or any other game, device, sleight of hand, pretensions to fortune telling, trick, or other means whatever, by use of cards or other implements or instruments, or while betting on sides or hands of any play or game, fraudulently obtains from another person money or property of any description, shall be punished as in the case of larceny of property of like value for the first offense, except that the fine may not exceed more than five thousand dollars ($5,000). A second offense of this section is punishable, as in the case of larceny, except that the fine shall not exceed ten thousand dollars ($10,000), or both imprisonment and fine.

(b) For the purposes of this section, "fraudulently obtains" includes, but is not limited to, cheating, including, for example, gaining an unfair advantage for any player in any game through a technique or device not sanctioned by the rules of the game.

(c) For the purposes of establishing the value of property under this section, poker chips, tokens, or markers have the monetary value assigned to them by the players in any game.

§ 368 (a) The Legislature finds and declares that crimes against elders and dependent adults are deserving of special consideration and protection, not unlike the special protections provided for minor children, because elders and dependent adults may be confused, on various medications, mentally or physically impaired, or incompetent, and therefore less able to protect themselves, to understand or report criminal conduct, or to testify in court proceedings on their own behalf.

(b) (1) Any person who knows or reasonably should know that a person is an elder or dependent adult and who, under circumstances or conditions likely to produce great bodily harm or death, willfully causes or permits any elder or dependent adult to suffer, or inflicts thereon unjustifiable physical pain or mental suffering, or having the care or custody of any elder or dependent adult, willfully causes or permits the person or health of the elder or dependent adult to be injured, or willfully causes or permits the elder or dependent adult to be placed in a situation in which his or her person or health is endangered, is punishable [either as a felon or misdemeanant].

...

(c) Any person who knows or reasonably should know that a person is an elder or dependent adult and who, under circumstances or conditions other than those likely to produce great bodily harm or death, willfully causes or permits any elder or dependent adult to suffer, or inflicts thereon unjustifiable physical pain or mental suffering, or having the care or custody of any elder or dependent adult, willfully causes or permits the person or health of the elder or dependent adult to be injured or willfully causes or permits the elder or dependent adult to be placed in a situation in which his or her person or health may be endangered, is guilty of a misdemeanor....

. . .

(g) As used in this section, "elder" means any person who is 65 years of age or older.

(h) As used in this section, "dependent adult" means any person who is between the ages of 18 and 64, who has physical or mental limitations which restrict his or her ability to carry out normal activities or to protect his or her rights, including, but not limited to, persons who have physical or developmental disabilities or whose physical or mental abilities have diminished because of age. . . .

(i) As used in this section, "caretaker" means any person who has the care, custody, or control of, or who stands in a position of trust with, an elder or a dependent adult.

. . .

Crimes Against the Public Health and Safety

§ 401 Every person who deliberately aids, or advises, or encourages another to commit suicide, is guilty of a felony.

Crimes Against the Public Peace

§ 415 Any of the following persons shall be punished by imprisonment in the county jail for a period of not more than 90 days, a fine of not more than four hundred dollars ($400), or both such imprisonment and fine:

(1) Any person who unlawfully fights in a public place or challenges another person in a public place to fight.

(2) Any person who maliciously and willfully disturbs another person by loud and unreasonable noise.

(3) Any person who uses offensive words in a public place which are inherently likely to provoke an immediate violent reaction.

§ 417 (a) (1) Every person who, except in self-defense, in the presence of any other person, draws or exhibits any deadly weapon whatsoever, other than a firearm, in a rude, angry, or threatening manner, or who in any manner, unlawfully uses a deadly weapon other than a firearm in any fight or quarrel is guilty of a misdemeanor, punishable by imprisonment in a county jail for not less than 30 days.

(2) Every person who, except in self-defense, in the presence of any other person, draws or exhibits any firearm, whether loaded or unloaded, in a rude, angry, or threatening manner, or who in any manner, unlawfully uses a firearm in any fight or quarrel is punishable as follows:

(A) If the violation occurs in a public place and the firearm is a pistol, revolver, or other firearm capable of being concealed upon the person, by imprisonment in a county jail for not less than three months and not more than one year, by a fine not to exceed one thousand dollars ($1,000), or by both that fine and imprisonment.

(B) In all cases other than that set forth in subparagraph (A), a misdemeanor, punishable by imprisonment in a county jail for not less than three months.

. . .

(c) Every person who, in the immediate presence of a peace officer, draws or exhibits any firearm, whether loaded or unloaded, in a rude, angry, or threatening manner, and who knows, or reasonably should know, by the officer's uniformed appearance or other action of identification by the officer, that he or she is a peace officer engaged in the performance of his or her duties, and that peace officer is engaged in the performance of his or her duties, shall be punished by imprisonment in a county jail for not less than nine months and not to exceed one year, or in the state prison for 16 months, or two to three years.

. . .

Criminal Threats

§ 422 (a) Any person who willfully threatens to commit a crime which will result in death or great bodily injury to another person, with the specific intent that the statement, made verbally, in writing, or by means of an electronic communication device, is to be taken as a threat, even if there is no intent of actually carrying it out, which, on its face and under the circumstances in which it is made, is so unequivocal, unconditional, immediate, and specific as to convey to the person threatened, a gravity of purpose and an immediate prospect of execution of the threat, and thereby causes that person reasonably to be in sustained fear for his or her own safety or for his or her immediate family's safety, shall be punished by imprisonment in the county jail not to exceed one year, or by imprisonment in the state prison.

(b) For the purposes of this section, "immediate family" means any spouse, whether by marriage or not, parent, child, any person related by consanguinity or affinity within the second degree, to any other person who regularly resides in the household, or who, within the prior six months, regularly resided in the household.

. . .

Crimes Against the Revenue and Property of the State

§ 424 (a) Each officer of this state, or of any county, city, town, or district of this state, and every other person charged with the receipt, safekeeping, transfer, or disbursement of public moneys, who either:

1. Without authority of law, appropriates the same, or any portion thereof, to his or her own use, or to the use of another; or,

. . .

Is punishable by imprisonment in the state prison for two, three, or four years, and is disqualified from holding any office in this state.

Crimes Against Property

§ 451 A person is guilty of arson when he or she willfully and maliciously sets fire to or burns or causes to be burned or who aids, counsels, or procures the burning of, any structure, forest land, or property.

(a) Arson that causes great bodily injury is a felony punishable by imprisonment in the state prison for five, seven, or nine years.

(b) Arson that causes an inhabited structure or inhabited property to burn is a felony punishable by imprisonment in the state prison for three, five, or eight years.

(c) Arson of a structure or forest land is a felony punishable by imprisonment in the state prison for two, four, or six years.

(d) Arson of property is a felony punishable by imprisonment in the state prison for 16 months, two, or three years. For purposes of this paragraph, arson of property does not include one burning or causing to be burned his or her own personal property unless there is an intent to defraud or there is injury to another person or another person's structure, forest land, or property.

...

§ 459 Every person who enters any house, room, apartment, tenement, shop, warehouse, store, mill, barn, stable, outhouse or other building, tent, vessel, ... floating home, ... railroad car, locked or sealed cargo container, whether or not mounted on a vehicle, trailer coach, ... any house car, ... inhabited camper, ... vehicle..., when the doors are locked, aircraft..., or mine or any underground portion thereof, with intent to commit grand or petit larceny or any felony is guilty of burglary....

§ 459.5 (a) Notwithstanding Section 459, shoplifting is defined as entering a commercial establishment with intent to commit larceny while that establishment is open during regular business hours, where the value of the property that is taken or intended to be taken does not exceed nine hundred fifty dollars ($950). Any other entry into a commercial establishment with intent to commit larceny is burglary. Shoplifting shall be punished as a misdemeanor [except if the defendant has previously been convicted of certain enumerated crimes].

(b) Any act of shoplifting as defined in subdivision (a) shall be charged as shoplifting. No person who is charged with shoplifting may also be charged with burglary or theft of the same property.

§ 460 (a) Every burglary of an inhabited dwelling house, vessel, ... which is inhabited and designed for habitation, floating home, or trailer coach, or the inhabited portion of any other building, is burglary of the first degree.

(b) All other kinds of burglary are of the second degree.

§ 470 (a) Every person who, with the intent to defraud, knowing that he or she has no authority to do so, signs the name of another person or of a fictitious person to any of the items listed in subdivision (d) is guilty of forgery.

(b) Every person who, with the intent to defraud, counterfeits or forges the seal or handwriting of another is guilty of forgery.

(c) Every person who, with the intent to defraud, alters, corrupts, or falsifies any record of any will, codicil, conveyance, or other instrument, the record of which is by law evidence, or any record of any judgment of a court or the return of any officer to any process of any court, is guilty of forgery.

(d) Every person who, with the intent to defraud, falsely makes, alters, forges, or counterfeits, utters, publishes, passes or attempts or offers to pass, as true and genuine, any of the following items, knowing the same to be false, altered, forged, or counterfeited, is guilty of forgery: any check, bond, bank bill, or note, cashier's check, traveler's check, money order, post note, draft, any controller's warrant for the payment of money at the treasury, county order or warrant, or request for the payment of money, receipt for money or goods, bill of exchange, promissory note, order, or any assignment of any bond, writing obligatory, or other contract for money or other property, contract, due bill for payment of money or property, receipt for money or property, passage ticket, lottery ticket or share purporting to be issued under the California State Lottery Act of 1984, trading stamp, power of attorney, certificate of ownership or other document evidencing ownership of a vehicle or undocumented vessel, or any certificate of any share, right, or interest in the stock of any corporation or association, or the delivery of goods or chattels of any kind, or for the delivery of any instrument of writing, or acquittance, release or discharge of any debt, account, suit, action, demand, or any other thing, real or personal, or any transfer or assurance of money, certificate of shares of stock, goods, chattels, or other property whatever, or any letter of attorney, or other power to receive money, or to receive or transfer certificates of shares of stock or annuities, or to let, lease, dispose of, alien, or convey any goods, chattels, lands, or tenements, or other estate, real or personal, or falsifies the acknowledgment of any notary public, or any notary public who issues an acknowledgment knowing it to be false; or any matter described in subdivision (b).

...

§484 (a) Every person who shall feloniously steal, take, carry, lead, or drive away the personal property of another, or who shall fraudulently appropriate property which has been entrusted to him or her, or who shall knowingly and designedly, by any false or fraudulent representation or pretense, defraud any other person of money, labor or real or personal property, or who causes or procures others to report falsely of his or her wealth or mercantile character and by thus imposing upon any person, obtains credit and thereby fraudulently gets or obtains possession of money, or property or obtains the labor or service of another, is guilty of theft. In determining the value of the property obtained, for the purposes of this section, the reasonable and fair market value shall be the test, and in determining the value of services received the contract price shall be the test. If there be no contract price, the reasonable and going wage for the service rendered shall govern. For the purposes of this section, any false or fraudulent representation or pretense made shall be treated as continuing, so as to cover any money, property or service received as a result thereof, and the complaint, information or indictment may charge that the crime was committed on any date during the particular period in question....

...

§485 One who finds lost property under circumstances which give him knowledge of or means of inquiry as to the true owner, and who appropriates such property to his own use, or to the use of another person not entitled thereto, without first making reasonable and just efforts to find the owner and to restore the property to him, is guilty of theft.

§ 486 Theft is divided into two degrees, the first of which is termed grand theft; the second, petty theft.

§ 487 Grand theft is theft committed in any of the following cases:

(a) When the money, labor or real or personal property taken is of a value exceeding nine hundred fifty dollars ($950), except as provided in subdivision (b).

(b) Notwithstanding subdivision (a), grand theft is committed in any of the following cases:

(1) (A) When domestic fowls, avocados, olives, citrus or deciduous fruits, other fruits, vegetables, nuts, artichokes, or other farm crops are taken of a value exceeding two hundred fifty dollars ($250).

(B) For the purposes of establishing that the value of domestic fowls, avocados, olives, citrus or deciduous fruits, other fruits, vegetables, nuts, artichokes, or other farm crops under this paragraph exceeds two hundred fifty dollars ($250), that value may be shown by the presentation of credible evidence which establishes that on the day of the theft domestic fowls, avocados, olives, citrus or deciduous fruits, other fruits, vegetables, nuts, artichokes, or other farm crops of the same variety and weight exceeded two hundred fifty dollars ($250) in wholesale value.

(2) When fish, shellfish, mollusks, crustaceans, kelp, algae, or other aquacultural products are taken from a commercial or research operation which is producing that product, of a value exceeding two hundred fifty dollars ($250).

(3) Where the money, labor, or real or personal property is taken by a servant, agent, or employee from his or her principal or employer and aggregates nine hundred fifty dollars ($950) or more in any 12 consecutive month period.

(c) When the property is taken from the person of another.

(d) When the property taken is any of the following:

(1) An automobile.

(2) A firearm.

§ 488 Theft in other cases is petty theft.

§ 496 (a) Every person who buys or receives any property that has been stolen or that has been obtained in any manner constituting theft or extortion, knowing the property to be so stolen or obtained, or who conceals, sells, withholds or aids in concealing, selling, or withholding any property from the owner, knowing the property to be so stolen or obtained, shall be punished by imprisonment in a county jail for not more than one year, or imprisonment pursuant to subdivision (h) of Section 1170. However, if the value of the property does not exceed nine hundred fifty dollars ($950), the offense shall be a misdemeanor, punishable only by imprisonment in the county jail not exceeding one year [except if the defendant has previously been convicted of certain enumerated crimes].

A principal in the actual theft of the property may be convicted pursuant to this section. However, no person may be convicted both pursuant to this section and of the theft of the same property.

. . .

§ 503 Embezzlement is the fraudulent appropriation of property by a person to whom it has been intrusted.

§ 511 Upon any indictment for embezzlement, it is a sufficient defense that the property was appropriated openly and avowedly, and under claim of title preferred in good faith, even though such claim is untenable. But this provision does not excuse the unlawful retention of the property of another to offset or pay demands held against him.

§ 518 Extortion is the obtaining of property from another, with his consent, or the obtaining of an official act of a public officer, induced by wrongful use of force or fear, or under color of official right.

§ 519 Fear, such as will constitute extortion, may be induced by a threat of any of the following:

1. To do an unlawful injury to the person or property of the individual threatened or of a third person.

2. To accuse the individual threatened, or any relative of his or her, or member of his or her family, of any crime.

3. To expose, or to impute to him, her, or them any deformity, disgrace or crime.

4. To expose any secret affecting him, her, or them.

5. To report his, her, or their immigration status or suspected immigration status.

§ 523 Every person who, with intent to extort any money or other property from another, sends or delivers to any person any letter or other writing, whether subscribed or not, expressing or implying, or adapted to imply, any threat such as is specified in Section 519, is punishable in the same manner as if such money or property were actually obtained by means of such threat.

§ 532 (a) Every person who knowingly and designedly, by any false or fraudulent representation or pretense, defrauds any other person of money, labor, or property, whether real or personal, or who causes or procures others to report falsely of his or her wealth or mercantile character, and by thus imposing upon any person obtains credit, and thereby fraudulently gets possession of money or property, or obtains the labor or service of another, is punishable in the same manner and to the same extent as for larceny of the money or property so obtained.

. . .

Malicious Mischief

§ 597.5 (a) Any person who does any of the following is guilty of a felony and is punishable by imprisonment pursuant to subdivision (h) of Section 1170 for 16 months, or two or three years, or by a fine not to exceed fifty thousand dollars ($50,000), or by both that fine and imprisonment:

(1) Owns, possesses, keeps, or trains any dog, with the intent that the dog shall be engaged in an exhibition of fighting with another dog.

(2) For amusement or gain, causes any dog to fight with another dog, or causes any dogs to injure each other.

(3) Permits any act in violation of paragraph (1) or (2) to be done on any premises under his or her charge or control, or aids or abets that act.

. . .

Miscellaneous Crimes

§ 645 (a) Any person guilty of a first conviction of [sexual assault of a minor], where the victim has not attained 13 years of age, may, upon parole, undergo medroxyprogesterone acetate treatment or its chemical equivalent, in addition to any other punishment prescribed for that offense or any other provision of law, at the discretion of the court.

(b) Any person guilty of a second conviction of [sexual assault of a minor] where the victim has not attained 13 years of age, shall, upon parole, undergo medroxyprogesterone acetate treatment or its chemical equivalent, in addition to any other punishment prescribed for that offense or any other provision of law.

§ 647 ... [E]very person who commits any of the following acts is guilty of disorderly conduct, a misdemeanor:

(a) Who solicits anyone to engage in or who engages in lewd or dissolute conduct in any public place or in any place open to the public or exposed to public view.

(b) Who solicits or who agrees to engage in or who engages in any act of prostitution. A person agrees to engage in an act of prostitution when, with specific intent to so engage, he or she manifests an acceptance of an offer or solicitation to so engage, regardless of whether the offer or solicitation was made by a person who also possessed the specific intent to engage in prostitution. No agreement to engage in an act of prostitution shall constitute a violation of this subdivision unless some act, in addition to the agreement, is done within this state in furtherance of the commission of an act of prostitution by the person agreeing to engage in that act. As used in this subdivision, "prostitution" includes any lewd act between persons for money or other consideration.

(c) Who accosts other persons in any public place or in any place open to the public for the purpose of begging or soliciting alms.

(d) Who loiters in or about any toilet open to the public for the purpose of engaging in or soliciting any lewd or lascivious or any unlawful act.

(e) Who lodges in any building, structure, vehicle, or place, whether public or private, without the permission of the owner or person entitled to the possession or in control of it.

(f) Who is found in any public place under the influence of intoxicating liquor, any drug, controlled substance, toluene, or any combination of any intoxicating liquor, drug, controlled substance, or toluene, in a condition that he or she is unable to exercise care for his or her own safety or the safety of others, or by reason of his or her being under the influence of intoxicating liquor, any drug, controlled substance, toluene, or any combination of intoxicating liquor, drug, or toluene, interferes with or obstructs or prevents the free use of any street, sidewalk, or other public way.

. . .

§ 653f (a) Every person who, with the intent that the crime be committed, solicits another to offer, or accept, or join in the offer or acceptance of a bribe, or to commit or join in the commission of carjacking, robbery, burglary, grand theft, receiving stolen property, extortion, perjury, subornation of perjury, forgery, kidnapping, arson or assault with a deadly weapon or instrument or by means of force likely to produce great bodily injury, or, by the use of force or a threat of force, to prevent or dissuade any person who is or may become a witness from attending upon, or testifying at, any trial, proceeding, or inquiry authorized by law, shall be punished by imprisonment in the county jail . . . or pursuant to subdivision (h) of Section 1170 . . .

(b) Every person who, with the intent that the crime be committed, solicits another to commit or join in the commission of murder shall be punished by imprisonment in the state prison for three, six, or nine years.

(c) Every person who, with the intent that the crime be committed, solicits another to commit rape by force or violence, sodomy by force or violence, oral copulation by force or violence, or any violation of Section 264.1, 288, or 289, shall be punished by imprisonment in the state prison for two, three, or four years.

(d) Every person who, with the intent that the crime be committed, solicits another to [manufacture, sell or transport controlled substances] shall be punished in a county jail not exceeding six months. Every person who, having been convicted of soliciting another to commit an offense specified in this subdivision, is subsequently convicted of the proscribed solicitation, shall be punished by imprisonment in a county jail not exceeding one year, or pursuant to subdivision (h) of Section 1170.

. . .

General Provisions

§ 664 Every person who attempts to commit any crime, but fails, or is prevented or intercepted in its perpetration, shall be punished, where no provision is made by law for the punishment of those attempts, as follows:

(a) If the crime attempted is punishable by imprisonment in the state prison, or by imprisonment pursuant to subdivision (h) of Section 1170, the person guilty of the attempt shall be punished by imprisonment in the state prison or in a county jail, respectively, for one-half the term of imprisonment prescribed upon a conviction of the offense attempted. However, if the crime attempted is willful, deliberate, and premeditated murder, as defined in Section 189, the person guilty of that attempt shall be punished by imprisonment in the state prison for life with the possibility of parole. If the crime attempted is any other one in which the maximum sentence is life imprisonment or death, the person guilty of the attempt shall be punished by imprisonment in the state prison for a term of five, seven, or nine years. The additional term provided in this section for attempted willful, deliberate, and premeditated murder shall not be imposed unless the fact that the attempted murder was willful, deliberate, and premeditated is charged in the accusatory pleading and admitted or found to be true by the trier of fact.

(b) If the crime attempted is punishable by imprisonment in a county jail, the person guilty of the attempt shall be punished by imprisonment in a county jail for a term not exceeding one-half the term of imprisonment prescribed upon a conviction of the offense attempted.

(c) If the offense so attempted is punishable by a fine, the offender convicted of that attempt shall be punished by a fine not exceeding one-half the largest fine which may be imposed upon a conviction of the offense attempted.

(d) If a crime is divided into degrees, an attempt to commit the crime may be of any of those degrees, and the punishment for the attempt shall be determined as provided by this section.

(e) Notwithstanding subdivision (a), if attempted murder is committed upon a peace officer or firefighter,...,[or any of various custodial officers], and the person who commits the offense knows or reasonably should know that the victim is such a peace officer, firefighter, [or any of various custodial officers] engaged in the performance of his or her duties, the person guilty of the attempt shall be punished by imprisonment in the state prison for life with the possibility of parole.

This subdivision shall apply if it is proven that a direct but ineffectual act was committed by one person toward killing another human being and the person committing the act harbored express malice aforethought, namely, a specific intent to unlawfully kill another human being. The Legislature finds and declares that this paragraph is declaratory of existing law.

...

§ **666** (a) Notwithstanding Section 490 [designating the punishment for petty theft], any person who, having been convicted of petty theft, grand theft, [joyriding]..., burglary, carjacking, robbery, or a felony violation of Section 496, and having served a term therefor in any penal institution or having been imprisoned therein as a condition of probation for that offense, and is subsequently convicted of petty theft, is punishable by imprisonment in the county jail not exceeding one year, or in the state prison.

(b) Subdivision (a) shall apply to any person who is required to register pursuant to the Sex Offender Registration Act, or who has a prior violent or serious felony conviction, as specified in clause (iv) of subparagraph (C) of paragraph (2) of subdivision (e) of Section 667, or has a conviction pursuant to subdivision (d) or (e) of Section 368.

...

§ **667** (a) (1)

In compliance with subdivision (b) of Section 1385, any person convicted of a serious felony who previously has been convicted of a serious felony in this state or of any offense committed in another jurisdiction which includes all of the elements of any serious felony, shall receive, in addition to the sentence imposed by the court for the present offense, a five-year enhancement for each such prior conviction on charges brought and tried separately. The terms of the present offense and each enhancement shall run consecutively.

...

(4) As used in this subdivision, "serious felony" means a serious felony listed in subdivision (c) of Section 1192.7. [The list of serious felonies includes virtually all crimes of violence to the person or crimes where another person is hurt by the defendant, serious property crimes (arson, burglary of an inhabited dwelling) and selling, furnishing, etc. drugs to a minor.]

...

(c) Notwithstanding any other law, if a defendant has been convicted of a felony and it has been pled and proved that the defendant has one or more prior serious and/or violent felony convictions as defined in subdivision (d), the court shall adhere to each of the following:

(1) There shall not be an aggregate term limitation for purposes of consecutive sentencing for any subsequent felony conviction.

(2) Probation for the current offense shall not be granted, nor shall execution or imposition of the sentence be suspended for any prior offense.

(3) The length of time between the prior serious and/or violent felony conviction and the current felony conviction shall not affect the imposition of sentence.

(4) There shall not be a commitment to any other facility other than the state prison. Diversion shall not be granted nor shall the defendant be eligible for commitment to the California Rehabilitation Center....

...

(d) Notwithstanding any other law and for the purposes of subdivisions (b) to (i), inclusive, a prior conviction of a serious and/or violent felony shall be defined as [(1) a violent or serious felony (as elsewhere defined), irrespective of the sentence imposed; (2) an out-of-state conviction for a crime that would have been a serious or violent felony if committed in California; (3) a juvenile adjudication based on a listed serious or violent felony, if the juvenile was 16 years of age or older at the time of the felony's commission].

(e) For purposes of subdivisions (b) to (i), inclusive, and in addition to any other enhancement or punishment provisions which may apply, the following shall apply where a defendant has one or more prior serious and/or violent felony convictions:

(1) If a defendant has one prior serious and/or violent felony conviction as defined in subdivision (d) that has been pled and proved, the determinate term or

minimum term for an indeterminate term shall be twice the term otherwise provided as punishment for the current felony conviction.

(2) (A) ... [I]f a defendant has two or more prior serious and/or violent felony convictions as defined in subdivision (d) that have been pled and proved, the term for the current felony conviction shall be an indeterminate term of life imprisonment with a minimum term of the indeterminate sentence calculated as the greater of:

(i) Three times the term otherwise provided as punishment for each current felony conviction subsequent to the two or more prior serious and/or violent felony convictions.

(ii) Imprisonment in the state prison for 25 years.

(iii) The term determined by the court [including the base term and any applicable enhancements].

(B) The indeterminate term described in subparagraph (A) shall be served consecutive to any other term of imprisonment for which a consecutive term may be imposed by law. Any other term imposed subsequent to any indeterminate term described in subparagraph (A) shall not be merged therein but shall commence at the time the person would otherwise have been released from prison.

...

The Prevention of Public Offenses

§ 692 Lawful resistance to the commission of a public offense may be made:

1. By the party about to be injured;
2. By other parties.

§ 693 Resistance sufficient to prevent the offense may be made by the party about to be injured:

1. To prevent an offense against his person, or his family, or some member thereof.
2. To prevent an illegal attempt by force to take or injure property in his lawful possession.

§ 694 Any other person, in aid or defense of the person about to be injured, may make resistance sufficient to prevent the offense.

Imprisonment and the Death Penalty

§ 1170 (h) (1) Except as provided in paragraph (3), a felony punishable pursuant to this subdivision where the term is not specified in the underlying offense shall be punishable by a term of imprisonment in a county jail for 16 months, or two or three years.

(2) Except as provided in paragraph (3), a felony punishable pursuant to this subdivision shall be punishable by imprisonment in a county jail for the term described in the underlying offense.

(3) Notwithstanding paragraphs (1) and (2), where the defendant (A) has a prior or current felony conviction for a serious felony ... or current conviction for a violent felony, (B) has a prior felony conviction in another jurisdiction for an offense that has all the elements of a serious felony or a violent felony, (C) is required to register as a sex offender pursuant, or (D) is convicted of a crime and as part of the sentence an enhancement [for multiple felonies involving fraud or embezzlement] is imposed, an executed sentence for a felony punishable pursuant to this subdivision shall be served in state prison.

§ 3003.5 (a) Notwithstanding any other provision of law, when a person is released on parole after having served a term of imprisonment in state prison for any offense for which registration is required pursuant to Section 290, that person may not, during the period of parole, reside in any single family dwelling with any other person also required to register pursuant to Section 290, unless those persons are legally related by blood, marriage, or adoption. For purposes of this section, "single family dwelling" shall not include a residential facility which serves six or fewer persons.

(b) Notwithstanding any other provision of law, it is unlawful for any person for whom registration is required pursuant to Section 290 to reside within 2000 feet of any public or private school, or park where children regularly gather.

(c) Nothing in this section shall prohibit municipal jurisdictions from enacting local ordinances that further restrict the residency of any person for whom registration is required pursuant to Section 290.

Offenses Relating to Prisons and Prisoners

§ 4501 (a) ... [E]very person confined in a state prison of this state who commits an assault upon the person of another with a deadly weapon or instrument shall be guilty of a felony and shall be imprisoned in the state prison for two, four, or six years to be served consecutively.

(b) ... [E]very person confined in a state prison of this state who commits an assault upon the person of another by any means of force likely to produce great bodily injury shall be guilty of a felony and shall be imprisoned in the state prison for two, four, or six years to be served consecutively.

§ 4573 (a) Except when otherwise authorized by law, or when authorized by the person in charge of the prison or other institution referred to in this section or by an officer of the institution empowered by the person in charge of the institution to give the authorization, any person, who knowingly brings or sends into, or knowingly assists in bringing into, or sending into, any state prison, prison road camp, prison forestry camp, or other prison camp or prison farm or any other place where prisoners of the state are located under the custody of prison officials, officers or employees, or into any county, city and county, or city jail, road camp, farm or other place where prisoners or inmates are located under custody of any sheriff, chief of police, peace officer, probation officer or employees, or within the grounds belonging to the institution, any controlled substance, the possession of which is prohibited by Division 10 (commencing with Section 11000) of the Health and Safety Code, any device, contrivance, instrument, or paraphernalia intended to be used for unlawfully injecting or consuming a controlled substance, is guilty of a felony punishable by imprisonment pursuant to subdivision (h) of Section 1170 for two, three, or four years.

(b) The prohibitions and sanctions addressed in this section shall be clearly and prominently posted outside of, and at the entrance to, the grounds of all detention facilities under the jurisdiction of, or operated by, the state or any city, county, or city and county.

Investigation and Control of Crimes and Criminals

§ 11411(d) Any person who burns or desecrates a cross or other religious symbol, knowing it to be a religious symbol, on the private property of another without authorization for the purpose of terrorizing the owner or occupant of that private property or in reckless disregard of the risk of terrorizing the owner or occupant of that private property ... [shall be punished by imprisonment as a felon under § 1170(h) for 16 months or two or three years or in the county jail for not more than one year and/or by a fine of not more than ten thousand dollars ($10,000)].

Control of Deadly Weapons

§ 18715 (a) Every person who recklessly or maliciously has in possession any destructive device or any explosive in any of the following places is guilty of a felony:

(1) On a public street or highway.

(2) In or near any theater, hall, school, college, church, hotel, or other public building.

(3) In or near any private habitation.

(4) In, on, or near any aircraft, railway passenger train, car, cable road, cable car, or vessel engaged in carrying passengers for hire.

(5) In, on, or near any other public place ordinarily passed by human beings.

(b) An offense under subdivision (a) is punishable by imprisonment pursuant to subdivision (h) of Section 1170 for a period of two, four, or six years.

§ 20200 A knife carried in a sheath that is worn openly suspended from the waist of the wearer is not concealed within the meaning of Section ... 21310.

§ 21310 ... [A]ny person in this state who carries concealed upon the person any dirk or dagger is punishable by imprisonment in a county jail not exceeding one year or imprisonment pursuant to subdivision (h) of Section 1170.

§ 25850 (a) A person is guilty of carrying a loaded firearm when the person carries a loaded firearm on the person or in a vehicle while in any public place or on any public street in an incorporated city or in any public place or on any public street in a prohibited area of unincorporated territory.

...

(c) Carrying a loaded firearm in violation of this section is punishable, as follows:

[as a felony or misdemeanor, (1)if the person has a prior felony conviction; (2) where the firearm is stolen; (3) where the person is an active participant in a criminal street gang; (4) where the firearm is not possessed lawfully; (5) where the person has been convicted of a crime against a person or property or a narcotics or dangerous drug violation; (6) where the person is not listed as a registered owner of the handgun; and in all other cases, as a misdemeanor.]

§ 29800 (a) (1) Any person who has been convicted of a felony under the laws of the United States, the State of California, or any other state, government, or country, or of an offense enumerated in … Section § 23515 [offenses involving violent use of a firearm], or who is addicted to the use of any narcotic drug, and who owns, purchases, receives, or has in possession or under custody or control any firearm is guilty of a felony.

…

§ 30605 (a) Any person who, within this state, possesses any assault weapon, except as provided in this chapter, shall be punished by imprisonment in a county jail for a period not exceeding one year, or by imprisonment pursuant to subdivision (h) of Section 1170.

§ 33215 Except as provided in Sections 33220 and 33225 and in Chapter 1 (commencing with Section 17700) of Division 2 of Title 2, any person in this state who manufactures or causes to be manufactured, imports into the state, keeps for sale, or offers or exposes for sale, or who gives, lends, or possesses any short-barreled rifle or short-barreled shotgun is punishable by imprisonment in a county jail not exceeding one year or imprisonment pursuant to subdivision (h) of Section 1170.

Index